The Rough

KU-146-186

South
America
ON A BUDGET

this edition written and researched by
Lucy Bryson, Robert Coates, Kiki Deere, Jen Foster, Anna
Kaminski, Ruth-Anne Lynch, Clemmy Manzo, Rachel Nolan,
Georgia Platman, Mani Ramaswamy, Ed Stocker, Ben Westwood,
Fran Yeoman

ROUGH
GUIDES

www.roughguides.com

Contents

◄◄ ZUMBAHUA MARKET, ECUADOR ◄ ANGEL FALLS, VENEZUELA

3

Introduction to
South America

Stretching from the warm tropical shores of the Caribbean to the wild and windswept archipelago of Tierra del Fuego, the South American continent is a dizzying treasure trove of landscapes that has long seduced independent travellers seeking an unforgettable experience. Spend a day trekking through humid jungle on the lookout for howler monkeys, and the next scaling a snow-capped volcano before taking a soothing hot-spring dip. Throw yourself into unbridled hedonism at colourful fiestas, explore ruins of ancient indigenous civilizations or just swing in a hammock on a white-sand beach.

BLUE-FOOTED BOOBY

The thirteen countries that comprise South America offer something for everyone: adventure junkie, birdwatcher, beach lover and aspiring archeologist alike. Although the continent shares a common history based on its original indigenous populations, European colonization, slavery and immigration, all of its countries are fascinating for the differences within their borders.

Portuguese-speaking **Brazil**, the largest, most populated country in South America, contains Rio de Janeiro, the vibrant colonial city of Salvador, the cultural hub of São Paulo, plus the largest rainforest in the world. While adventure tourists may not flock to **Uruguay**, its relaxed capital, Montevideo, is inviting and Punta del Este's beach resorts are worth checking out, if only briefly by budget-conscious day-trippers. Travellers seeking authenticity should look no further than landlocked **Paraguay**. While not on the average itinerary, the country's Jesuit ruins and national parks offer a glimpse of a South America untrammelled by the twenty-first century.

From sophisticated Buenos Aires to wild Patagonia, rainforest to glacier, and rolling grasslands to the mighty waterfalls of Iguazú, **Argentina** is one of South America's most enticing countries. No less beautiful is **Chile**, home to volcanoes, Patagonian icefields and the Atacama Desert. **Peru** has a dizzying range of scenery and archeological sites, including the ancient Inca capital Cusco and the must-see citadel of Machu Picchu. Naturalists should head straight for **Ecuador**'s Galápagos Islands, home to some of the continent's most astonishing wildlife. Neighbouring **Colombia** has much to offer, from the nightlife of Bogotá to the coffee-growing landscapes of the Zona Cafetera and well-preserved colonial towns of Cartagena and Popayán.

Bolivia is home to the world's biggest salt lake and most dangerous road as well as Isla del Sol, said to be the spiritual

REED BOAT ON LAKE TITICACA, BOLIVIA

centre of the Andean world. **Venezuela** boasts gorgeous national parks, spectacular beaches and the Amazon region of Guayana, which includes Angel Falls, the world's tallest waterfall. The **Guianas**, comprising the former British and Dutch colonies of Guyana and Suriname and the French overseas **département** of French Guiana, are often overlooked.

Wildlife

South America's stunning array of **wildlife** inhabits an extreme terrain of mountains, tropical rainforests, subtropical cloudforests, deserts and sprawling fertile grasslands. The continent's enormous geographic diversity provides endlessly varying and isolated habitats where new species are able to evolve. Complex ecosystems such as the rainforest canopy of the **Amazon basin** preserve a wealth of insects, birds, reptiles and mammals. Brazil's **Pantanal** region, the world's largest wetland, and the immense plains of **Los Llanos** in Venezuela are two of the continent's best spots for wildlife-watching, with plenty of opportunities to observe extraordinary concentrations of exotic birds and mammals. The wildlife of the **Galápagos Islands** played a crucial role in the development of Charles Darwin's theories on evolution and is unsurprisingly one of the continent's biggest attractions.

CAPOEIRA ON COPACABANA BEACH, RíO DE JANERIO

However, their three vibrant capital cities, Georgetown, Paramaribo and Cayenne respectively, are home to colonial wooden architecture in picturesque decay, Dutch bars, good Amazon hiking, deserted prison islands and French cuisine.

Backpackers will find an extensive range of accommodation on offer, with plenty of options for the tight budget. South America also boasts some of the best camping and hammock-slinging spots in the world. **Travel** within the continent requires a little patience, initiative and navigating of red tape and usually involves colourful bus journeys, budget flights and ferry crossings. See our **Ideas** section for more can't-miss destinations, events and activities throughout South

PARQUE NACIONAL LOS GLACIARES, ARGENTINA

Local food

Forget beans and rice. With more fruits than there are English names for, some of the best pasture-raised beef in the world and coastal cities with access to excellent fish, the hungry budget traveller will not starve for lack of tasty options. English, Dutch, French, Spanish and Portuguese colonialism translates to a wealth of culinary influences. In addition to this, prominent Italian (Brazil and Argentina), Chinese (Peru and Brazil) and Japanese (Brazil) communities have brought their palates and also left their mark. There is an overwhelming variety of inexpensive street food, and spicy peppers and sauces ensure that even the blandest offerings can pack an exciting punch. Try Bolivia's *salteñas* (street pasties), Venezuelan *arepas, ceviche* in Peru and roti in the Guianas. More adventurous eaters may find themselves up to the challenge of *cuy* (grilled guinea pig) in Ecuador, *hormigas culonas* (fried black ants) in Colombia, Guyana *pepperpot* (often made with cow's face) and piranha in the Amazon.

America, and check out our **Itineraries** to help chart the best adventures throughout the continent. Whether you follow these routes or set out on your own, our **Basics** section gives you all the practical information you will need about hostels, guesthouses, immunizations and border crossings. Each chapter within the **Guide** kicks off with a country profile covering key places not to miss, plus rough costs for food, accommodation and transport.

When to go

With about two-thirds of South America near the equator or the tropic of Capricorn, visitors to most destinations can expect a tropical or subtropical **climate** all year round. Temperatures rarely drop below 20°C, while rainforest regions average maximum temperatures of about 30°C. As you get further south (and don't forget the southern hemisphere reverses the seasons), you'll find stronger winters from June to August and milder summers from December to February, with the extreme south of the continent very cold between April and October. It's important to plan around the rainy season in each country, particularly when travelling in the Andes. Check the "When to go" information in the Basics section at the start of each country chapter for advice about region-specific weather.

Ideas Markets and festivals

INTI RAYMI, CUSCO, PERU Honour the sun god at Cusco's lavish and theatrical Inca festival. **See p.829**

WITCHES' MARKET, BOLIVIA Herbal remedies, curse-killers and good luck charms abound. **See p.188**

FERIA DE MATADEROS, ARGENTINA Mingle with gauchos, snack at *parrillas* and peruse local crafts at one of Buenos Aires's most fabulous events. **See p.65**

RIO CARNAVAL, BRAZIL Get ready for some serious partying at this legendary flesh-fest. **See p.264**

SEMANA SANTA, QUITO, ECUADOR Celebrate Holy Week at Quito's Good Friday parades. **See p.622**

OTAVALO CRAFTS MARKET, ECUADOR Shop for indigenous ceramics, musical instruments and loom-woven sweaters at this colourful market. **See p.635**

Ideas Ancient sites and lost cities

TIWANAKU, BOLIVIA This pre-Inca ruined city is considered by some to have been the cradle of Andean civilization.
See p.195

EASTER ISLAND, CHILE Explore this mysterious, remote island known for its enigmatic moai statues.
See p.521

SAN AGUSTÍN, COLOMBIA A dramatic landscape littered with hundreds of elaborately carved, gigantic, pre-Columbian monoliths.
See p.606

MACHU PICCHU, PERU Hike the ancient Inca Trail to this precipice-surrounded, awe-inspiring citadel. **See p.836**

CIUDAD PERDIDA, COLOMBIA Marvel at the ruins of this lost city of the Tayronas, only rediscovered in 1975. **See p.580**

NAZCA LINES, PERU These unforgettable shapes and figures are one of the continent's great mysteries. **See p.854**

13

Ideas Outdoor activities

CANOEING IN THE AMAZON BASIN Trek and canoe through the largest rainforest on the planet. **See p.342 & 898**

VOLCÁN COTOPAXI, ECUADOR Climb at midnight for a sunrise at the summit of this active Andean volcano. **See p.640**

WILDLIFE-SPOTTING, GALÁPAGOS ISLANDS The unique wildlife here inspired Darwin's theory of evolution. **See p.688**

RAFTING THE IGUAÇU FALLS, BRAZIL Get soaked marvelling at these cascading waterfalls. **See p.383**

PARQUE NACIONAL TORRES DEL PAINE, CHILE Ice-walk, fly-fish, kayak and mountaineer in this wild and beautiful national park. **See p.513**

BIRD-WATCHING, PARAGUAY Spot spectacular birdlife in the wilderness of the Chaco. **See p.781**

ITINERARIES

ITINERARIES

South America itineraries

You can't expect to fit everything South America has to offer into one trip – or two or three or four, to be fair – and we don't suggest you try. On the following pages a selection of itineraries will guide you through the different countries and regions, picking out a few of the best places and major attractions along the way. For those taking a big, extended trip around the continent you could join a few together, but remember that the distances you'll be covering can be vast. There is, of course, much to discover off the beaten track, so if you have the time it's worth exploring smaller towns, villages and wilderness areas further afield, finding your own perfect hill town, deserted beach or just a place you love to rest up and chill out.

SOUTHERN BRAZIL

1 RIO The beaches, the samba, the towering statue of Christ the Redeemer looming over it all – Rio has every base covered to kick off your trip in style. See p.263

2 COSTA VERDE Backed by forested mountain peaks, the coastline between Rio and São Paulo contains hidden gems like colonial Paraty and spectacular beaches at Ilha Grande. See p.283

3 MINAS GERAIS This state inland from Rio offers some of Brazil's most stunning historic towns – none more attractive than Ouro Preto. See p.293

4 BRASÍLIA Come see the vision of the future, circa 1960, courtesy of Oscar Niemeyer's modernist architecture. See p.345

5 THE PANTANAL If you're not going to make it out to the Galápagos during your travels, consider checking out the huge array of wildlife in this vast wetland. See p.355

6 ILHA DE SANTA CATARINA Some of the best beaches in the country can be found on the coast near Florianópolis. See p.384

7 SERRA GAÚCHA The mountain bases of Canela and Gramado serve two nearby parks with crashing falls and challenging climbs and hikes. See p.395

0   500 km

BRAZIL

Brasília
The Pantanal
Ouro Petro
Rio
Ilha de Santa Catarina
Serra Gaúcha

NORTHERN ARGENTINA AND URUGUAY

1 BUENOS AIRES The most cosmo-politan of all South American cities, worthy of a few days of anyone's time. See p.60

2 COLONIA DEL SACRAMENTO If you're just going to dip into Uruguay, you can't do better than the historic centre of this charming town. See p.929

3 ROSARIO The perfect spot to launch yourself into the Paraná Delta. See p.87

4 CÓRDOBA Wander from the colonial centre to Nuevo Córdoba, a neighbourhood chock-a-block with cool bars and restaurants in converted mansions. See p.78

5 MENDOZA Undoubtedly the best stop for wine-lovers, a sophisticated city with great restaurants and hundreds of nearby *bodegas*. See p.109

6 CERRO ACONCAGUA Whether you take two weeks to scale the summit or just see a bit on a day-hike, the tallest mountain in the western hemisphere will sear itself into your memory. See p.115

7 SALTA Its central plaza is a lovely place to begin an evening stroll. See p.98

8 PARQUE NACIONAL EL REY The lush cloudforests here hold colourful toucans, as well as other exotic flora and fauna. See p.103

9 IGUAZÚ FALLS Better to see the crashing waters from the trails and catwalks on the Argentina side. See p.96

CHILE AND ARGENTINA: THE LAKE DISTRICTS AND PATAGONIA

1 VOLCÁN VILLARICA Skiing, snowboarding, mountaineering – depending on the season, you may be able to experience the smouldering volcano up close. See p.473

2 LAGO LLANQUIHUE A sparkling blue lake lined with beaches and hemmed in by woods. See p.481

3 EASTERN CHILOE The less-developed side of the archipelago has no major tourist sights, just some low-key villages and some great coastal hiking. See p.492

4 SAN MARTÍN DE LOS ANDES A lower-key version of Bariloche: a hub for getting out to the nearby lakes and Parque Lanín. See p.126

5 PARQUE NACIONAL NAHUEL HUAPI Well-marked trails, plentiful campsites and huts, crystal-clear lakes and much more make this the most popular Patagonian park on the Argentine side. See p.135

6 PENINSULA VALDES Consider an eastern detour here to see abundant

winter and dream of Antarctica, 1000km away. See p.160

NORTHERN CHILE AND SOUTHERN BOLIVIA

① SANTIAGO Not the most dynamic capital city, but a nice enough place to arrive, get oriented and explore some interesting museums and neighbourhoods. See p.414

② VALPARAÍSO Ride the *ascensores* (funiculars) around the hilly streets by day, then eat, drink and carouse in the gritty port area at night. See p.427

③ PISCO ELQUI This charming village, with views over the Elqui valley, is the perfect place to sample a pisco sour. See p.442

④ PARQUE NACIONAL NEVADO DE TRES CRUCES Drive by arid salt flats, spot vicuñas and guanacos, and stay by a lake populated with colourful flamingos. See p.444

⑤ SAN PEDRO DE ATACAMA There aren't too many sights per se in this pre-Columbian settlement, but it's a perfect jumping off point for the *altiplano* wilderness. See p.448

⑥ SALAR DE UYUNI You'll have to go on a tour, but it's worth the trip to see the flat, white salt "lake", perfectly reflective in summer when covered with water. See p.218

⑦ POTOSÍ The colonial architecture and lively cafés are somewhat by the tragic legacy of the nearby silver mines at Cerro Rico. See p.212

⑧ SANTA CRUZ One of the rare places in Bolivia known for its excellent restaurant and club scene. See p.233

birdlife, a sea-lion colony and – if you time it right – whales on their migration route. See p.142

⑦ PERITO MORENO GLACIER The unquestioned highlight of Parque Nacional Los Glaciares, a calving glacier that provides theatrical drama for onlookers. See p.151

⑧ PARQUE NACIONAL TORRES DEL PAINE The most famous destination on the Chilean side of Patagonia – and perhaps the best trekking in the entire region. See p.513

⑨ USHUAIA If you've made it here you're practically at the end of the world – send a postcard, eat some seafood, ski in

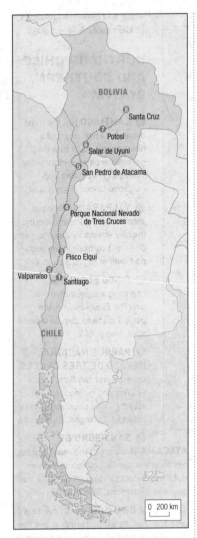

trekking in both the Cordillera Blanca and Cordillera Huayhuash. **See p.868**

③ INCA TRAIL TO MACHU PICCHU
You'll need to devote the better part of a week to acclimatizing and making the trek, but the lost Inca city at the end is a fantastic reward. **See p.834**

④ CUSCO As much of a hub as Lima and closer to many of the country's highlights – though its plazas, museums, restaurants and nightlife certainly stand on their own. **See p.818**

⑤ LAKE TITICACA Whether you visit the Uros islands on the Peru side or the sacred Isla del Sol in the Bolivian section, you're certain to be awed by the high-altitude lake. **See p.867 & p.200**

⑥ LA PAZ Now this is what an Andean capital city should be: delightfully situated high up in a canyon, full of interesting and inexpensive places to eat, drink and stay, and with an undeniable energy all its own. **See p.185**

⑦ COCHABAMBA Not the place to go for sightseeing, but a relaxed, unpretentious town good for soaking in the local café scene. **See p.229**

NORTHERN BRAZIL AND THE AMAZON

① MORRO DE SÃO PAULO The place to base yourself for the best beaches on Tinharé island: learn how to dive, catch some surf or just relax. **See p.314**

② SALVADOR For *candomblé,* capoiera or Carnaval, Bahia's capital is practically the country's capital. **See p.303**

③ OLINDA You won't find a prettier array of churches, plazas and houses anywhere in the north of the country. **See p.323**

④ FORTALEZA The central market is a sure bet to buy a hammock; take it with you to Jericoara, the best beach in the area. **See p.325**

PERU AND NORTHERN BOLIVIA

① LIMA Love it or hate it, you can nevertheless find plenty to occupy you in the capital, and the proximity to the sea makes it a great place to try out *ceviche.* **See p.803**

② HUARAZ This lively city, nestled in a valley, affords you an approach to

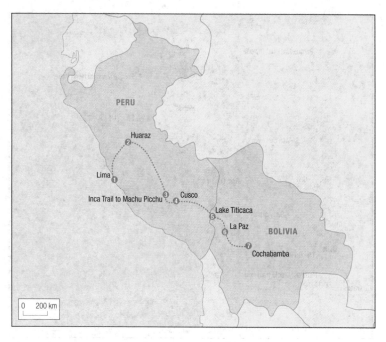

⑤ BELÉM There are some good restaurants and bars, but the main reason to come is its location at the mouth of the Amazon. **See p.332**

⑥ MANAUS After seeing the astounding Teatro Amazonas, grab some of the fine street food on offer and head to the lively port area. **See p.338**

⑦ AMAZON RIVER TRIP Float along the Rio Negro to a jungle lodge or even just a clearing where you can string up a hammock – or head along the Amazon all the way to Iquitos in Peru. **See p.342**

ECUADOR, COLOMBIA AND VENEZUELA

① GUAYAQUIL An alternative introduction to Ecuador than more traditional Quito; the Malecón and nearby beaches make it seem like a different land entirely. **See p.676**

② NARIZ DEL DIABLO TRAIN RIDE A five-hour journey starting in

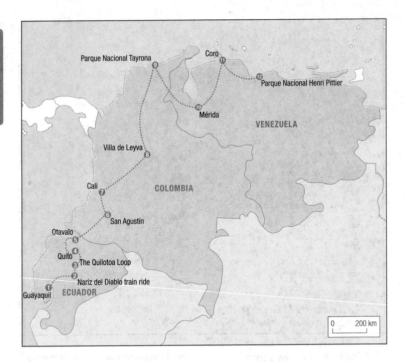

Riobamba and slicing its glorious way through the Andes. See p.651

③ THE QUILOTOA LOOP Hike for a few days around the peaceful waters of a volcanic crater lake. See p.643

④ QUITO Base yourself in the old town, where plaza after plaza provides a vantage point for historic churches and narrow walkways. See p.623

⑤ OTAVALO Few can resist the town's famous Saturday market, the ultimate place to purchase a hammock or woodcarving as a keepsake. See p.635

⑥ SAN AGUSTÍN A crazy array of monolithic statues, with a lovely mountain landscape serving as a backdrop. See p.606

⑦ CALI This might be Colombia's most fun and freewheeling city, with plenty of salsa clubs and streetlife to balance out the sober array of churches. See p.597

⑧ VILLA DE LEYVA A thoroughly unmodern and relaxed spot to be a centre for mountain tourism north of Bogotá. See p.558

⑨ PARQUE NACIONAL TAYRONA Beautiful beaches, lush flora and pre-Columbian ruins are the highlights of this pristine coastal park. See p.579

⑩ MÉRIDA Contemplate adventures to nearby mountains, a trip to wildlife-rich Los Llanos or just chill out in this laid-back city. See p.979

⑪ CORO The loveliest colonial town in Venezuela. See p.975

⑫ PARQUE NACIONAL HENRI PITTIER Another great mix of beaches, wildlife and walking trails – and it's relatively near Caracas, which makes your exit or travel connections easier. See p.968

BASICS

BASICS

Getting there

The easiest way to reach the northern parts of South America is by air via the US, usually through a hub such as Houston, Atlanta or Miami, while further south in the continent there are direct flights from some European cities to destinations in Brazil and Argentina. The national South American airlines, such as Aerolíneas Argentinas or LANChile, provide a reasonable choice of schedules and routes. Many immigration departments in South America insist that you have an onward or return ticket to enter the country, but the application of such rules is more strict in some countries than in others.

Airfares are seasonal, with the highest around July, August and mid-December to mid-January; you'll get the best prices during the dry winter (May, June and late Sept) and the wet summer (Feb–April, excluding Carnaval and Easter). Note also that flying on weekends is often more expensive. You can generally cut costs by going through a specialist flight agent, booking flights well in advance or taking advantage of web-only offers and airline frequent-flyer programmes. Another way to cut costs is to book with a tour operator that can put together a package deal including flights and accommodation, and perhaps tours as well.

FROM THE UK AND IRELAND

If you book your flight well in advance, flying to South America from the UK can be a bargain. Generally, returning within thirty days of your departure will enable you to find a cheaper fare than if you stay in South America for two or three months. British Airways operates direct flights to both Rio de Janeiro and São Paulo in Brazil and Buenos Aires in Argentina, but fares tend to be more expensive than those of their European and South American rivals. The best value-for-money airline depends on the country you are flying to, but generally a flight with a European airline such as Iberia, TAP or Air France, via their main airport in Madrid, Lisbon or Paris, is cheaper than flying via the US.

FROM THE US AND CANADA

Most South American airlines serving North America operate flights from New York or Miami. US airlines tend to fly out of their hubs: Delta from Atlanta and Continental from Houston. Flying through Miami affords you

---

ESTA CLEARANCE

Since 12 January 2009, the US government has required those travellers coming to or through the US on the Visa Waiver Program to apply for clearance via ESTA (Electronic System for Travel Authorization). This is not something to ignore – if you arrive at the airport without having done it, the airline won't allow you to check in. To apply for clearance visit Ⓦesta.cbp.dhs.gov/esta/. Make sure you do this at least 72 hours before travelling; you'll need your passport to hand and the admin fee at the time of publication is US$14. Once a traveller has received clearance, it remains valid for two years.

greater flexibility in travel planning and cheaper prices. There are flights to all major South American cities from at least one of the above. Direct flights from Canada are very limited; it's generally best to transfer at a US hub.

FROM AUSTRALIA AND NEW ZEALAND

The best deals to South America are offered by the major South American airlines Aerolíneas Argentinas and LANChile in conjunction with Qantas and Air New Zealand. Aerolíneas Argentinas flies from Sydney to Buenos Aires via Auckland, with connections across the continent; Qantas has code-shares with Varig and LANChile via Auckland to Santiago and beyond. There are also plenty of flights via the US, but most are not scheduled through to South America and therefore tend to take longer and cost more, as each sector has to be priced separately. Often airlines will charge more if you wish to stay in South America for longer than a month.

FROM CENTRAL AMERICA

Crossing overland from Panama into Colombia is not recommended as it entails traversing the Darién, a wild, lawless region occupied by guerrillas. The safest option is to fly – Bogotá and Caracas are the main points of entry – or take a boat from Panama to the Caribbean coast of Colombia. There are no ferry services, but boats can be chartered in Colón and San Blás in Panama to Cartagena, Colombia. The journey takes four to six days.

AIRLINES, AGENTS AND OPERATORS

Airlines

Aerolíneas Argentinas ⓦ www.aerolineas.com.ar
Air Canada ⓦ www.aircanada.ca
Air Europa ⓦ www.aireuropa.com
Air France ⓦ www.airfrance.com
Air New Zealand ⓦ www.airnz.com

SIX STEPS TO A BETTER KIND OF TRAVEL

At Rough Guides we are passionately committed to travel. We feel strongly that only through travelling do we truly come to understand the world we live in and the people we share it with – and tourism has brought a great deal of **benefit** to developing economies around the world over the last few decades. But the extraordinary growth in tourism has also damaged some places irreparably, and of course, **climate change** is exacerbated by most forms of transport, especially flying. This means that now more than ever it's important to **travel thoughtfully** and **responsibly**, with respect for the cultures you're visiting – not only to derive the most benefit from your trip but also to preserve the best bits of the planet for everyone to enjoy. At Rough Guides we feel there are six main areas in which you can make a difference:

- Consider what you're contributing to the **local economy**, and how much the services you use do the same, whether it's through employing local workers and guides or sourcing locally grown produce and local services.
- Consider the **environment** on holiday as well as at home. Water is scarce in many developing destinations, and the biodiversity of local flora and fauna can be adversely affected by tourism. Try to patronize businesses that take account of this.
- Travel with a purpose, not just to tick off experiences. Consider **spending longer** in a place, and getting to know it and its people.
- Give thought to how often you **fly**. Try to avoid short hops by air and more harmful night flights.
- Consider **alternatives to flying**, travelling instead by bus, train, boat and even by bike or on foot where possible.
- Make your trips "**climate neutral**" via a reputable carbon offset scheme. All Rough Guide flights are offset, and every year we donate money to a variety of charities devoted to combating the effects of climate change.

AIR PASSES AND ROUND-THE-WORLD TICKETS

If you're visiting South America as part of a world trip, a round-the-world (RTW) ticket offers the greatest flexibility – and if your starting point is Australia or New Zealand, it may even be cheaper. Many international airlines are now aligned with one of two globe-spanning networks: "Star Alliance" (@www.staralliance.com), which has 28 members including Air Canada, Air New Zealand, bmi, Continental, Lufthansa, SAS, Singapore Airlines, Thai, TAP and United; or "One World", which combines routes via eleven airlines including American, British Airways, Cathay Pacific, Iberia, LANChile, Mexicana and Qantas. Fares depend on month, point of origin and the number of continents or the distance travelled, and in general the more expensive options include South America, but they are worth exploring.

If you plan to do a fair amount of travelling within South America consider buying an airpass with your main ticket. These passes offer substantial savings, but can be bought only outside South America when buying an international ticket. See p.32 for more information.

See p.32 for more information.

Alitalia @www.alitalia.com
American Airlines @www.aa.com
Avianca @www.avianca.com
British Airways @www.ba.com
Caribbean Airlines @www.caribbean-airlines.com
Continental Airlines @www.continental.com
Delta Airlines @www.delta.com
Iberia Airlines @www.iberia.com
KLM @www.klm.com
LANChile @www.lanchile.com
Lloyd Aéreo Boliviano @www.labairlines.com.bo
Northwest @www.nwa.com
Qantas @www.qantas.com.au
TAM @www.tam.com.br
TAP Air Portugal @www.flytap.com
United Airlines @www.united.com
Varig @www.varig.com

Agents and operators

Adventure Center US ☎1-800/228-8747, @www.adventurecenter.com. Hiking and "soft adventure" specialists with trips deep into most South American countries.

Austral Tours Australia ☎1800/620833, @www.australtours.com. Central and South American specialist covering the region from Ecuador to Easter Island and Tierra del Fuego, with special tours to Machu Picchu and the Amazon.

Australian Andean Adventures Australia ☎02/9299 9973, @www.andeanadventures.com.au. Trekking in Argentina, Peru, Bolivia and Chile.

Backroads US ☎1-800/462-2848, @www.backroads.com. Cycling, hiking and multi-sport tours to Argentina, Ecuador, Galápagos, Chile and Peru.

Cheapflights @www.cheapflights.com. No direct booking, but lists flights and offers from dozens of operators, with web links to most.

Dragoman UK ☎01728/861133, @www.dragoman.co.uk. A range of South American overland trips, including a new line with all accommodation in hotels rather than in tents.

Expedia @www.expedia.com. Discount airfares, all-airline search engine and daily deals.

Hotwire US @www.hotwire.com. Bookings from the US only. Last-minute savings of up to forty percent on regular published fares. Travellers must be at least 18 and there are no refunds, transfers or changes allowed. Log-in required.

Journey Latin America UK ☎020/8747 8315, @www.journeylatinamerica.co.uk. Knowledgeable and helpful staff, good at sorting out stopovers and open-jaw flights. Also does package tours.

Last Frontiers UK ☎01296/653000, @www.lastfrontiers.com. Very knowledgeable Latin America specialists with a wide range of tailor-made tours.

Lastminute.com @www.lastminute.com. Package holiday and flight-only deals available at short notice.

Priceline.com @www.priceline.com. Name-your-own-price auction website that has deals at around forty percent off standard fares, as well as a regular flight-finder. Be sure to check the terms before bidding.

REI Adventures US ☎1-800/622-2236, @www.rei.com/travel. Climbing, cycling, hiking, cruising, paddling and multi-sport tours to many countries in the continent.

Skyauction @www.skyauction.com. Auction tickets and travel packages using a "second bid" scheme. The best strategy is to bid the maximum you're willing to pay, since if you win you'll pay just enough to beat the runner-up regardless of your maximum bid.

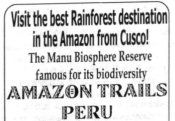

STA Travel UK ☎ 020/8998 2931, ☯ www
.statravel.co.uk. Low-cost flights and tours for
students and under-26s, though other customers
welcome.

Trailfinders UK ☯ www.trailfinders.com. One
of the best-informed and most efficient agents for
independent travellers.

Travelocity ☯ www.travelocity.com. Destination
guides, hot web fares and deals for car rental,
accommodation and lodging.

Travel Cuts Canada ☎ 1-800/667-2887, US
☎ 1-866/246-9762; ☯ www.travelcuts.com.
Canadian student-travel organization.

Wilderness Travel US ☎ 1-800/368-2794,
☯ www.wildernesstravel.com. Adventure travel and
wildlife tours throughout South America.

W&O UK ☎ 0845/277 3366, ☯ www.wandotravel
.com. Discounted flights agent and tours, plus "soft
landing package", which includes accommodation
and airport transfer.

Getting around

**Most South Americans travel by bus, and there is almost
nowhere that you can't reach in this way. The major routes are
comfortable and reliable and always cost-effective. Moreover,
you will see more, and meet more people, if you travel by bus.
Remember, though, that distances between towns can be
huge, and that in more remote areas such as Patagonia there
are few bus and no train services. If you have a little spare
cash and limited time, you may want to fly occasionally, or rent
a car to explore at leisure. There are frequent flights within
and between South American countries; the former are generally much cheaper. Check out the airpasses detailed on p.32,
which can offer great value for money if used to the full.**

BY BUS

This is by far the cheapest way to see the
continent. While you can, technically, travel
all the way from the tropical north to Tierra
del Fuego by bus, there are few direct
international services and you usually have
to disembark at the border, cross it, then
get on another bus to a large city in the
new country, from where you can travel
pretty much anywhere within that country.
The process is repeated at most border
crossings.

Terminals are often situated on the
outskirts of towns – follow the signs to the
terminal (in Spanish-speaking countries) or
the *rodoviária* (in Brazil). Levels of comfort
vary, so a quick visual check in the terminal
will give you an idea of which company

to go for. With better bus companies on
long-distance routes, the **seating options**
usually include normal seats, seats that partly
recline and "cama" seats that recline fully to
become beds. They are priced according to
the level of comfort. Some of the cheapest
companies only have one level of comfort
and that can mean anything from wooden
seats to standing in an aisle.

BY CAR

South American **roads**, especially outside the
major cities, are notorious for their bumpy,
potholed and generally poor conditions. Most
car rental companies in South America do
not allow their vehicles to be driven across
borders, making independent exploration of
the continent by car difficult.

If you are determined to go it alone and drive around South America, you will find car rental companies at all airports and in most major cities. Hotels can advise you of better-value local places, but often it's better to book in advance online. Costs are high due to skyrocketing insurance rates, but the independence of a car may be worth it. Check your **insurance** carefully for exclusions, as car theft, vandalism and general security are renowned problems in many parts of South America, especially Argentina and Brazil, and you may not be covered for these. Damage to tyres or the underside of the car may also be excluded.

Rental charges vary from country to country and depend on the model of car. You will be required to present a credit card and usually an International Driving Licence. Driving standards are poor, so beware, especially at night. Honk your horn before going round any corner – the locals do this with great gusto, so no one will find you rude. South Americans drive on the right except in Suriname and Guyana.

BY AIR

If you plan to do a lot of of travelling around Latin America, consider one of the reasonable **airpasses**. These are a godsend if you want to see as much as possible in a limited time.

The **All America Airpass** (ⓦwww .allairpass.com) is valid for one year from the first departure date and offers special fares throughout the Americas on seventeen airlines. It comprises individual segment passes that combine to make a multi-sector trip from US$400 to US$1800. The passes are only available to travellers with a scheduled international return ticket and must be bought in the traveller's country of origin. After you have used the first sector on your pass the ticket is non-refundable. Remember that many Latin American countries charge a departure tax when leaving their airports on international flights – this tax is payable locally in cash and not included in the airpass price.

The **Mercosur Airpass** covers travel in Argentina, Brazil, Chile, Paraguay and Uruguay. Prices are calculated on a miles-flown basis. There is a maximum of two stopovers and four flight coupons for each country, and the pass is valid for seven to thirty days. The pass is available directly from the participating airlines (Varig, Aerolíneas Argentinas, Aerolineas del Sur and Pluna). You can rebook to change dates (but not reroute); for more information see ⓦwww .latinamerica.co.uk/mercosur_airpass.htm. Both LAN Chile (ⓦwww.lan.com) and TAM (ⓦwww.tam.com.br) also offer their own, slightly cheaper airpasses for routes they fly.

BY TRAIN

Trains are much less frequent and efficient than South American buses, but if you have a little time to spare they provide a wonderful way to see the countryside and wildlife, as they tend to travel more exotic routes. Typically they are less expensive than buses, but services in popular tourist areas can be pricey. Two of the most famous routes are from Cusco to the start of the Inca Trail in Peru (see p.828) and the Serra Verde Express between Curitiba and the coast in Brazil (see p.378). There are several types of train, including the fast and efficient *ferrotren*, stopping at major stations only; the average *tren rápido*; the slower *expreso*, which stops at most stations; and the super-slow and amazingly cheap *mixto*, which stops for everyone – and their livestock too.

BY BOAT

There are several ferry and catamaran services on South America's **lakes**, especially in Chile, Argentina, Peru and Bolivia, providing unforgettable views. Those relevant to a single country are explored in the country chapter but there are two cross-border crossings that are recommended: the Southern Lakes Crossing (see p.133) between Argentina and Chile, and the Lake Titicaca Crossing (p.203) between Bolivia and Peru.

One of the finest ways to soak up the slow pace of South American life is to travel some of the continent's **rivers** by boat. Unfortunately, the riverboat industry is in decline, especially on the Amazon, with more passengers flying and cargo-only replacing many travel boats. However, several riverboat services survive, recom-

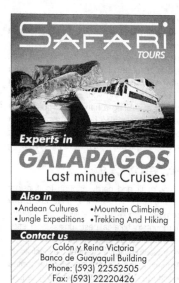

mended for anyone with time and patience, particularly on the narrower, less-frequented rivers. Shop around, as boats vary hugely in quality. Your ticket will include hammock space and basic food, but drinks are extra and will probably be expensive on board – it's best to bring your own supplies. You should also bring a hammock, rope, insect repellent, a sleeping bag and aim to be on board well before departure to ensure that you don't get put right next to the toilets.

BY BICYCLE

If you're fit and hardy enough to consider cycling in South America, there are a few common-sense rules. Given the terrain, a mountain bike is best, unless you stick to paved roads and well-travelled routes. In adventure travel centres, especially in Argentina and Chile, bikes can be rented for short periods, but if you're doing serious cycling, bring your own. Bikes and bike parts tend to be of a lower quality in South America than in other parts of the world, so give your bike a thorough check before you go. Carry a basic repair kit and check the

bike daily when you arrive. Weather can be a problem, especially in Patagonia, where winds can reach 80kmph, and be aware that bicycle theft – particularly in larger towns – is common; bring a good bike lock. Finally, remember that South American drivers can be a hazard, so try to avoid major roads and motorways if at all possible.

HITCHHIKING

Hitchhiking is still fairly common in rural South America, and it isn't hard to get a lift if you're on the road early. Be aware, though, that many drivers now expect to be paid – it's only in the Southern Cone that hitchhiking seems to be understood to be free. Prices are usually around that of a bus fare, but if you head to the local truck park or refuelling station (most towns have one), ask around for the going rate. Hitch-hiking in South America, like anywhere in the world, is a potentially perilous enter-prise – travellers should be aware that they do so at their own risk. Couples and groups are safest; women should never hitchhike alone.

Accommodation

The range of accommodation available in South America – and the variety of price and quality that goes with it – is enormous and, should you be leaving on a multi-country tour, you'll find that the US$10 that buys you a night's rest in Ecuador won't even stretch to breakfast in the Southern Cone or French Guiana.

Most local tourist offices will provide a list of available accommodation but bear in mind that establishments often pay to be included on these lists and that they may include little outside the main tourist hotspots. Generally, tourist boards will not recommend specific accommodation, nor book it.

Usually there is no shortage of places to stay, but use common sense if you plan to

be somewhere at the time of a local festival, such as in Rio for Carnaval. Obviously, accommodation fills up quickly at these times, prices skyrocket and it's best to book well in advance. While the types of lodging described below offer an overview of your options in Latin America, names, classifications and prices vary from country to country. For information regarding the nomenclature in a specific country, check the "Accommodation" section of the relevant chapter.

HOSPEDAJES, RESIDENCIAS, ALBERGUES AND PENSIONES

These categories of accommodation are all used throughout South America and are interchangeable terms, although **pensiones** (known as *pensoes* in Portuguese) and **residenciales** are officially the most basic forms of accommodation. Generally, the Andean countries are the least expensive, and you should be able to find a decent room in a *residencial* or *pensión* for under US$10 (US$5 for dorms). For this price you should expect a bed, shared bathroom and intermittent hot water. In Brazil, the room cost will usually include breakfast but most other places are room only. In the south of Argentina and Chile, you can expect to spend around US$40 a night – check out the quality of the local *casas familiares* (family houses where you stay with a local family in a room in their house), which can be the best value for money in these areas.

HOSTALES, HOSTERÍAS AND HACIENDAS

Hostales tend to fill the gap between the totally basic *pensión* and hotels, and come in many shapes, sizes and forms. Usually they include private bathrooms and hot water, clean towels and maybe a television, and cost from US$5 to US$20 per night. In the southern countries, though, *hostales* may be youth hostels.

Hosterías and **haciendas** are often old, sprawling estates converted into hotels, and are perhaps the grandest places to stay in the continent. They are often furnished in period style and offer excellent home-cooked meals, fires, hot water and maybe a swimming pool. Be aware that *hostería* can also refer to a family-style hotel complex

out of town, so check which kind of *hostería* you're getting first.

CAMPING

Camping is most popular in the southern region of Latin America, particularly in the Cone areas of Argentina and Chile. It is wise to stick to official sites that are usually well equipped, with hot, running water, toilets, firepits and maybe even a self-service laundry. Camping is not really a popular or viable option in the northern countries unless as part of an organized tour, and is practically non-existent in Colombia, French Guiana and Paraguay.

YOUTH HOSTELS

Youth hostels are not always the most viable option in South America, but in the more expensive southern countries like Argentina and Chile, they are a more attractive option: competition means that many have great facilities and offer extras, from free internet to party nights. Prices average US$8–15 per night and most are open all year, although some only open in January and February for the South American summer. If you are planning on using hostels extensively, consider getting an official **HI card** which will quickly pay for itself in discounted rates.

Hostelling organizations

Argentina Hostelling International Argentina/Red Argentina de Alojamiento para Jóvenes (RAAJ), Florida 835, piso 3, Buenos Aires ☎011/4511-8723, ⊛www.hostels.org.ar.
Brazil Federação Brasileira dos Albergues de Juventude (FBAJ) Río de Janeiro R da Assambleia 10, room 1211 ☎21/2531-1085, ⊛www.hostel.org.br.
Chile Asociación Chilena de Albergues Turísticos Juveniles, Hernando de Aguirre 201, Providencia, Santiago ☎02/233-3220, ⊛www.hostelling.cl.
Hostelling International ⊛www.hihostels.com. Membership cards and worldwide hostel booking.
Peru Asociación Peruana de Albergues Turísticos Juveniles Av. Casimiro Ulloa 328, Miraflores, Lima ☎014/446-5488, ⊛www.limahostell.com.pe.

Health

The potential health risks in South America read like a textbook of tropical diseases and the possibilities could easily deter nervous travellers before they even set out. But if you prepare for your trip carefully and take sensible precautions while travelling, you will probably face nothing worse than a mild case of "Montezuma's revenge" as your system gets used to foreign germs and unhygienic conditions.

It is important to get the best health advice before you travel – prevention is always better than cure. The Centre for Disease Control (🌐 www.cdc.gov) offers comprehensive and up-to-date advice on health for travellers and is worth consulting on each of the countries you wish to visit. About ten weeks before you travel, **vaccinations** can be arranged with your doctor or a specialized tropical diseases clinic. Bring your vaccination record when you travel. If you are taking any prescription drugs your doctor can prescribe enough for the time you are away, and you should also take a list with you and a covering letter in case of emergencies. Good **medical insurance** is essential (see p.42). It is important to declare any pre-existing conditions, and also to ensure that you have sufficient cover for all the extra activities you may undertake (particularly diving and extreme sports).

GENERAL PRECAUTIONS

Common illnesses such as traveller's **diarrhoea** can be largely avoided by steps such as washing your hands before eating and drinking bottled water. Unpasteurized dairy products and all un-refrigerated food should be avoided and fruit and vegetables should be washed and peeled. Take care with shellfish, lettuce and ice. If you do fall ill, rest and replace the fluids you have lost by drinking plenty of water and an oral re-hydration solution. A home-made option is 1tsp salt and 8tsp of sugar in 1 litre of water. An anti-diarrhoeal tablet can usually alleviate symptoms.

Two other common afflictions are **heat stroke** and **altitude sickness**. Seek immediate treatment for the former; gentle acclimatization is advised to avoid the latter. Avoid dehydration by drinking bottled water and staying off alcohol.

Pharmacies abound in every town but bringing a basic first-aid kit is sensible. Essentials in remote areas include insect repellent, bandages, painkillers, anti-diarrhoeal tablets and antiseptic cream.

BITES AND STINGS

The general advice is to use an **insect repellent** containing 35 percent DEET, especially in rural areas or where malaria is endemic, and to wear light clothes that cover as much of your body's surface as possible. It is wise to use a mosquito net or a mosquito coil containing permethrin at night, especially in the cheaper hotels.

Venomous **spiders and snakes** exist throughout the continent and bites from these, while rare, merit seeking medical advice as soon as possible. Most responsible tour companies carry anti-venom but in the absence of this, prompt medical attention is the only answer. A photo or description of the offending species may be useful but never attempt to catch or kill it as this can provoke further bites, and don't listen to so-called local knowledge involving tourniquets, sucking venom or anything else – go to hospital.

A much more likely nuisance when visiting wilder areas are the itchy **bites** given by tiny black sand flies or painful bites of ants and ticks. Hairy caterpillars are also capable of giving nasty stings similar to burns.

MOSQUITO-BORNE DISEASES

Malaria prevention is two-fold; in addition to avoiding mosquito bites as detailed above, travellers should be sure to take a prescription anti-malarial drug, typically malarone (usually the best option), chloroquine or doxycycline – consult with a doctor before taking any. These should generally be started several weeks before you travel, and the full course must be completed. Symptoms can occur any time up to a year after travel, so it's important to inform your doctor about your travel history.

Yellow fever is a serious disease carried by mosquitoes which, like malaria, can be avoided by vaccination and taking sensible precautions against insect bites. It is present in most of South America except the far south. Vaccination is theoretically required for entry into some countries, particularly Bolivia and French Guiana.

Dengue fever is also mosquito-borne and there is no vaccine. The mosquitoes carrying the virus tend to live near stagnant water so it's more of a problem in poor areas. It has become a serious health issue in Brazil, Bolivia, Paraguay and Argentina, but is present in most countries in South America. Symptoms include high fever and aching limbs. Drink fluids, take paracetamol and seek medical attention immediately.

INTESTINAL PROBLEMS

Other than the traveller's diarrhoea that usually lasts no more than a few days there are a number of more serious problems that you can encounter on your travels. **Cholera**, for example, is an acute infection with watery diarrhoea and vomiting; **dysentery** has similar symptoms but includes bleeding. If your diarrhoea persists for a week and your symptoms includes a chill or fever or bleeding, or if you are too ill to drink, seek medical help.

To avoid problems, always use bottled water, even for cleaning your teeth. Avoid buying food from street vendors unless the food is piping hot and think carefully about swimming in lakes and rivers. If bottled water isn't available, there are various methods of

treating water: boiling water for a minimum of five minutes is the most effective method. Filtering alongside chemical sterilization is the next best option. Pregnant women or people with thyroid problems should consult their doctors about chemical sterilization formulae.

Medical resources for travellers

Before travelling to South America travellers should seek health advice. Useful websites and major organizations are listed below:

UK and Ireland
Fit for Travel ⓦ www.fitfortravel.scot.nhs.uk. NHS website with information about travel-related diseases and how to avoid them.
MASTA (Medical Advisory Service for Travellers Abroad) ⓦ www.masta-travel-health .com. Comprehensive website for medical advisory services for travel abroad. See website or call ☏ 020/7731-8080 for the nearest clinic.
Tropical Medical Bureau Republic of Ireland ☏ 1850/487-674, ⓦ www.tmb.ie.

US and Canada
Canadian Society for International Health 1 Nicholas St, Suite 1105, Ottawa, ON K1N 7B7 ☏ 613/241-5785, ⓦ www.csih.org. Distributes a free pamphlet, "Health Information for Canadian Travellers", containing an extensive list of travel health centres in Canada.
Center for Disease Control 1600 Clifton Rd NE, Atlanta, GA 30333 ☏ 1-800/311-3435, ⓦ www .cdc.gov/travel. US Department of Health and Human Services travel health and disease control department. Publishes outbreak warnings, suggested inoculations, precautions and other background information for travellers.
International Society for Travel Medicine ⓦ www.istm.org. Has a full list of clinics specializing in international travel health.
Travel Health Online ⓦ www.tripprep.com. Travel Health Online provides an online comprehensive database of necessary vaccinations for most countries, as well as destination and medical service provider information.

Australia and New Zealand
Travellers' Medical and Vaccination Centres ⓦ www.tmvc.com.au. Contains a list of all Travellers Medical and Vaccination Centres throughout Australia, New Zealand and Southeast Asia, plus general information on travel health.

Culture and etiquette

South America is a vast continent and it's difficult to generalize about how to dress or behave; ultimately, you should try to behave unobtrusively and dress modestly if not at the beach.

CULTURAL HINTS

People generally shake hands upon introduction and women generally kiss acquaintances on both cheeks, although you can defer to a handshake if you prefer. It is common to wish people you meet on the street "Buenos días" ("bom dia" in Brazil) or "buenas tardes" ("boa tarde" in Brazil). Politeness is a way of life in South America, and pleasantries are always exchanged before getting to any kind of business. You should also be polite to street vendors, no matter how annoyed you get with their peddling of their wares. Remember that this is their livelihood and smile, saying "no, gracias" or "não, obrigado", but if you decide to buy something, be firm – ask the price and confirm it before offering cash. Dress with respect in official or religious buildings.

Remember that in most Latin American countries, locals have a lax attitude to time, so expect people to arrive late in social situations and don't get annoyed if they do.

CRAFTS AND MARKETS

Shops and markets in South America tend to offer a wide range of beautifully crafted goods and antiques for the visitor. Prices are usually reasonable; you can bargain in markets and outside the tourist drags, but only do so if you really think the item is worth less than its asking price. Check that you are not purchasing objects plundered from the jungle or made from endangered species.

As a rule of thumb, native crafts are usually of the best quality and cheapest when bought close to the source. Buying such items, rather than mass-produced alternatives, is a good way to help local *artesania* and give something back to the communities you're visiting.

PUBLIC HOLIDAYS AND FESTIVALS

Travelling through South America entails negotiating a variety of public holidays that differ from country to country. The essential ones are listed in the "Opening hours and public holidays" section of each chapter, but bear in mind that, particularly in more remote areas, some towns and villages celebrate saints' days and other local holidays that shut down businesses and make travel difficult. Check with local tourist information offices (where they exist) for more details. South Americans are not known for passing up an excuse to celebrate, and we have included the finer festivals in the relevant chapters.

Every country in Latin America has **Carnival** (known in Spanish and Portuguese as *Carnaval*); the exact time varies, but official celebrations usually take place on the days before Ash Wednesday and Lent. There are national variations, of course: in Ecuador, for instance, the festivities are most visibly represented by the water fights throughout the country. There are a couple of locations where Carnaval has become famous internationally such as Oruro in Bolivia and Encarnación in Paraguay. The most famous Carnaval of all, however, is in Rio de Janeiro, Brazil. This variegated event lasts for weeks before and after the "official" Carnaval time and is an extravagant mix of dance, sweat, drink, laughter and colour.

Work and study

Opportunities for volunteer and non-profit work abound, but be prepared to pay something towards your upkeep. Paid opportunities are few and far between, and some are likely to be illegal.

TEACHING ENGLISH

Qualified English teachers with a CELTA, TEFL or TESUL should be able to find work, but you are strongly advised to arrange your work placement before you travel. Qualified schoolteachers from English-speaking countries can also find work and if you have a Master's degree, you can teach at university. However, turning up and looking for work is likely to leave you frustrated and/or violating local laws – officially you will require a work permit. The British Council (ⓦwww.britishcouncil.org) and the TEFL website (ⓦwww.tefl.com) each has a list of English-teaching vacancies. Most jobs are in the larger cities.

LANGUAGE STUDY

Latin America has long been a hugely popular destination for people wishing to brush up on their Spanish: Cusco, Peru; Buenos Aires, Argentina; Sucre, Bolivia; and Quito, Ecuador are the most popular destinations and a huge variety of courses and levels are available. In Brazil, most of the large cities are great locations for learning Portuguese. You can also learn indigenous languages such as Quechua in Bolivia or Guaraní in Paraguay. Typically, three types of course are on offer: a classroom-based course, a more active learning course through activities and excursions, or the live-in option with a host family.

Language schools

Academia Latinoamericana de Español ☎1-801/268-2468 (US), ⓦwww.latinoschools .com. Spanish classes in Ecuador, Peru and Bolivia.
Amerispan PO Box 58129, Philadelphia, PA 19102 ☎1-800/879-6640 (US), ⓦwww.amerispan.com. Spanish courses and volunteer opportunities.

Apple Languages ☎1-703/835-9762 (US), ☎01509/211612 (UK), ⓦwww.applelanguages .com. High-quality Spanish schools throughout Latin America.
Bridge Linguatec ☎1-800/724-4210 (US), ⓦwww.bridgelinguatec.com. Spanish and Portuguese classes in Argentina, Chile and Brazil.
Don Quijote ⓦwww.donquijote.org. High-quality, internationally recognized courses offered in Argentina, Bolivia, Chile, Ecuador and Peru.
Escuela Runawasi ☎00591/4424-8923, ⓦwww .runawasi.org. Quechua and Spanish-language and literature lessons in Cochabamba, Bolivia.
Simón Bolívar Spanish School ☎005937/283-9959, ⓦwww.bolivar2.com. Based in Cuenca, Ecuador with courses based on a study of the country.
Spanish Study Holidays ☎01509/211612 (UK), ⓦwww.spanishstudyholidays.com. Courses from one week to nine months.

VOLUNTEERING

Volunteer opportunities are available in social, developmental, environmental and conservation work in many South American countries, though you will be expected to pay for the privilege. Working alongside local people on a worthwhile project that captures your interest can be an unforgettable experience.

Volunteer organizations

While many positions are organized prior to arrival, it's also possible to pick something up on the ground through word of mouth. Noticeboards in the more popular backpacker hostels are always good sources of information.
Earthwatch Institute ☎1-800/776-0188 (US), ⓦwww.earthwatch.org. Long-established research company offering environmental and social volunteer programmes throughout the continent.
Global Vision International ☎01727/250250 (UK), ⓦwww.gvi.co.uk. Conservation projects in the Amazon.

Global Volunteer Network ☏ 0800/032-5035 (UK), Ⓦ www.globalvolunteernetwork.org. Volunteer opportunities in community projects in several South American countries.

Projects Abroad ☏ 01903/708300 (UK), Ⓦ www .projects-abroad.co.uk. Teaching, conservation and community projects throughout Latin America.

Travel essentials

COSTS

South America is not as cheap as it used to be but, if approached in the right way, you can still travel for less here than you would on other continents. French Guiana, Argentina, Chile and Brazil are the most expensive countries, with prices often comparable to North America, Europe and Australia. Bolivia, Peru and Ecuador still remain budget destinations but the highlights such as the Galápagos Islands, the Amazon jungle and mountain-climbing can add a lot of expense to the trip.

CRIME AND PERSONAL SAFETY

South America is a continent by poverty and attendant crime levels which, while much magnified by tales in the foreign news media, certainly do exist. In general, cities are more dangerous than rural areas, although the very deserted mountain plains can harbour bandits. Many of the working-class *barrios* of big cities are "no-go" areas for tourists, as are the marginal areas near them. One of the biggest problems in urban areas is **theft**, and bag snatching, handbag slitting and even armed robbery are problems in cities such as Buenos Aires, Lima, Rio, Salvador, Recife, George-town, Quito and Cusco. Take particular care on the street, in taxis and in restau-rants. Any unsolicited approach from a stranger should be treated with the utmost suspicion, no matter how well dressed or trustworthy they may look.

Preventative measures

There are obvious preventative measures you can take to avoid being mugged: avoid isolated and poorly lit areas, especially at night; never walk along a beach alone at night, or even in a pair if female. Keep a particular eye out in busy areas and watch out on public transport and at bus stations, where pickpocketing is rife. If you need to hail a taxi, get someone at your hotel to recommend one, or hail a moving one – never get into a "taxi" that just happens to be parked at the kerbside or which has two drivers. Avoid wearing expensive jewellery and watches, dress down, and keep cameras out of sight.

Car-jackings can also be a problem, particularly in certain areas of Brazil. When driving in the city, keep doors locked and windows closed, particularly at night, and be especially vigilant at traffic lights.

Drugs

Just say no! In South America drug trafficking is a huge, ugly and complicated enterprise, and large-scale dealers love to prey on lost-looking foreigners. Don't let anyone else touch your luggage, be sure to pack it yourself and don't carry anything – no matter how innocuous it may seem – for anyone else. You will find that drugs, particularly marijuana and cocaine, are fairly ubiquitous in the region, but you should be aware that they are illegal and that punishments are severe. Tourists

PRICES

At the beginning of each country chapter you'll find a guide to "**rough costs**", including food, accommodation and travel. These costs are quoted in US$ to make comparison easy; within the chapter itself prices are quoted in local currency. Note that prices and exchange rates change all the time, which may affect the accuracy of those figures we have quoted.

are likely to come off much worse than locals at the hands of the South American police, something of which the dealers and pushers are very aware. If you happen to visit a region famed for drug trafficking, stay well away from anything that looks (or smells) like trouble.

The only **legal drugs** on sale in South America are the leaves of coca, which are available in Bolivia and Peru. They are usually used to make *mate de coca*, a hugely popular tea in the Andes, and one that's claimed to cure altitude sickness (among other things). Some people chew the leaves as this is meant to produce a mildly intoxicating state, but the taste and texture may well convince you that you can do without the alleged high. If you want to try *mate de coca* or chewing on coca leaves, be aware that there is a possibility that you could test positive for cocaine use in the weeks following your trip.

Reporting crime

In case you are mugged or robbed, you should make sure that you have a photocopy of your passport and plane tickets in a safe place. Call the local police immediately and tell them what happened. It's likely that they won't do much more than take a statement, but you'll need it for insurance purposes. In some South American countries there is a special "tourist police" force, used to dealing with foreigners and, hopefully, able to speak English.

ELECTRICITY

The standard electrical current in most South American countries is 220V, 50Hz. The main exceptions are Colombia, Ecuador and Venezuela, where a 110V, 50Hz current is used and Suriname, where 127V is standard. Some major tourist cities also use a 110V, 50Hz current, at odds with the rest of their country, including La Paz and Potosí in Bolivia and Rio de Janeiro and São Paulo in Brazil. There is no standard plug shape in most countries and plugs in use may vary greatly. For the most part they are flat two-pin (as in the US), but three-pin plug sockets are sometimes found and you may even see sockets with flattened or angled pins.

The South American attitude to safety may be a little more lax than you are used to, and it is not unusual to see plugs that obviously don't fit, forcibly pushed into sockets. Take particular care with electrical showers, common in the poorer countries.

GAY AND LESBIAN TRAVELLERS

Rural, Catholic South America is not overly welcoming towards homosexuality. Homosexual acts are technically illegal in some countries, although this usually means simply that local gay couples tend to keep themselves to themselves and avoid flaunting their orientation. Gay and lesbian travellers would probably be safest following their example – public displays of affection between two men or two women could invite trouble in much of the continent.

Things are generally easier in the big cities, though, and there are a couple of major destinations where anything goes. Brazil boasts most of them – Rio de Janeiro, Salvador and São Paulo provide safe and welcoming havens for any sexual orientation, as do Buenos Aires and Santiago. If you are looking for thumping night life and a very "out" scene, then these cities are the best in the continent.

INSURANCE

A typical **travel insurance policy** provides cover for the loss of baggage, tickets and – up to a certain limit – cash, as well as cancellation or curtailment of your journey. Most of them exclude so-called dangerous sports unless an extra premium is paid: this category can include scuba-diving, white-water rafting, windsurfing and trekking, though probably not kayaking or jeep safaris. Many policies can be changed to exclude coverage you don't need – for example, sickness and accident benefits can often be excluded or included at will. If you take medical coverage, ascertain whether benefits will be paid as treatment proceeds or only after your return home, and whether there is a 24hr medical emergency number. When securing baggage cover, make sure that the per-article limit will cover your most valuable possession. If you need to make a claim, you should keep receipts for medicines and medical treatment and, in the event you have anything stolen, you must obtain an official statement from the police.

INTERNET

Internet access is now almost ubiquitous in cities and towns across South America (though it is more restricted in the Guianas) and only in rural areas is it difficult to come by. Connection speeds and costs vary from country to country, and in some cases from area to area. The website ⓦwww.kropla .com gives details of how to plug your laptop in when abroad, phone country codes around the world, and has information about electrical systems in different countries.

MAIL

Post offices in cities and major towns offer a wide range of services; those in villages are much more basic, with shorter opening hours and slow service. Hotels in capital cities may sell stamps and have a post box – if you are staying in one, this can be the most convenient way to send a letter home. Expect airmail to take from a week to a month to Western Europe and the USA.

MAPS

Excellent maps of the continent of South America, covering the region at a scale of 1:5,000,000, are produced by Canada's International Travel Maps and Books (ⓦwww.itmb.com). They also publish individual country and regional maps. Once in South America good maps can be hard to find, and often the only source of accurate maps is the military – check at the local tourist offices on where to purchase them. If you'd rather be safe than sorry, buy maps at home and bring them with you.

MONEY

ATMs are widely available in most large cities, but in smaller towns and rural areas don't expect to rely solely on using international debit cards to access funds. Traveller's cheques are much less widely accepted than they once were: pre-paid **currency cards** are an excellent alternative, though these, too, require access to an ATM. There is still nothing as easy to use as cash, preferably US dollars, and it makes sense always to carry at least a few small-denomination notes for when all else fails.

Credit card fraud is a problem in the continent, particularly in Brazil and Venezuela; be sure to keep an eye on your card and to retain your copy of the transaction slip. In many countries credit cards will only be accepted in the biggest hotels and shops, and banks will sometimes refuse to offer cash advances against them. Payments in plastic may also incur high surcharges when compared to cash payments.

When **exchanging money**, you should use only authorized bureaux de change, such as banks, cambios and tourist facilities, rather than deal with moneychangers on the streets. For details on each country, consult the "Money and banks" section at the beginning of each chapter. In remote and rural areas, and for shopping in local markets and stalls, **cash** is a necessity – preferably in small denominations of local currency.

PHONES

The mobile phone is causing **public phone boxes** to disappear in many South American countries. Where phone boxes exist, they usually operate with cards, available from newspaper kiosks. There are, however, plenty of *cabinas telefónicas*, stores originally dedicated to telephone communications, most of which have now branched out into internet access as well. You can make direct-dial international calls from most Latin American phones, apart from remote areas, where calls must be

---

CALLING FROM ABROAD

To phone abroad, you must first dial the international access code of the country you are calling from, then the country code of the country you are calling to, then the area code (usually without the first zero) and then the phone number. In some South American countries there may be different international access codes for different providers. See below for details.

International access codes when dialling from:

Argentina ☏00	**French Guiana** ☏00
Australia ☏0011	**Guyana** ☏001
Bolivia ☏0010 (Entel) ☏0011 (AES) ☏0012 (Teledata) ☏0013 (Boliviatel)	**Ireland** ☏00
	New Zealand ☏00
Brazil ☏0014 (Brasil Telecom) ☏0015 (Telefónica) ☏0021 (Embratel) ☏0023 (Intelig) ☏0031 (Telemar)	**Paraguay** ☏002
	Peru ☏00
	Suriname ☏002
Canada ☏011	**UK** ☏00
Chile ☏00	**Uruguay** ☏00
Colombia ☏009 (Telecom) ☏007 (ETB/Mundo) ☏005 (Orbitel)	**US** ☏011
	Venezuela ☏00
Ecuador ☏00	

Country codes when dialling to:

Argentina ☏54	**Ireland** ☏353
Australia ☏61	**New Zealand** ☏64
Bolivia ☏591	**Paraguay** ☏595
Brazil ☏55	**Peru** ☏51
Canada ☏1	**Suriname** ☏597
Chile ☏56	**UK** ☏44
Colombia ☏57	**Uruguay** ☏598
Ecuador ☏593	**US** ☏1
French Guiana ☏594	**Venezuela** ☏58
Guyana ☏592	

made through an operator. International phone calls are, in general, expensive from South America. Calls are usually cheaper between 7pm and 5am and at weekends, although cheap rates vary in some countries.

Avoid calling long distance from hotels unless you have a cheap long-distance **phone card** with a free or local access number; even then check to see if the establishment charges for such calls. Generally, the cheapest way to call is using **Skype** or a similar service over the internet; many internet cafés throughout the continent offer this service.

Mobile phones

If you want to use your **mobile phone** in South America, you'll need to check with your phone provider whether it will work abroad, and what the call charges are. Generally speaking, UK, Australian and New Zealand mobiles should work fine in South America. However, with US mobiles only tri-band models are likely to work outside the States.

You are likely to be charged extra for incoming calls when abroad, as the people calling you will be paying the usual rate. If you're in the country for a while, and assuming your phone is unlocked (most contract phones are locked so that they can only be used on one network – your provider can usually unlock it for a fee), you can buy a **SIM card** from a local telephone company and use it in your phone. These are usually pretty cheap and your calls will be charged at a local rate. If you don't have a mobile phone and are staying a few months in one country, consider buying a local phone, easily done for less than US$50.

TOURIST INFORMATION

The quantity and quality of tourist information varies from country to country, but in general, don't expect too much. While almost every city in Brazil and Argentina will have at least one well-equipped tourist office, they are much thinner on the ground in countries like Paraguay and the Guianas.

You should make the most of any operational office you find there. Fortunately, there is a lot of information about South America on the internet that will help you plan your trip and answer questions about history, language and current events. We've listed websites wherever pertinent throughout the guide; the following is a general list of places to begin your research.

South America on the internet

ⓦ **www.buenosairesherald.com** English-language newspaper, updated weekly.

ⓦ **www.clarin.com** The largest Spanish-language daily newspaper in the world, printed in Buenos Aires.

ⓦ **www.cotal.org.ar** Confederation of Latin American Tourist Organizations.

ⓦ **www.lapress.org** Non-profit news organization based in Lima, producing independent news and analysis.

ⓦ **www.latinnews.com** Real-time news feed with major stories from all over South America in English.

ⓦ **www.zonalatina.com/Zlmusic** Excellent directory of regional music links and information, covering everything from Mariachi and Sertaneja to Shakira.

ⓦ **www.planeta.com/south.html** Excellent selection of online ecotravel and ecotourism resources for South America.

ⓦ **www.roughguides.com** Travel articles, apps and guides covering the whole of South America.

ⓦ **www.saexplorers.org** The website of the South American Explorers Club, a non-profit organization with the latest research, travel and adventure information.

TIME ZONES

Most of South America is spread across only two times zones, with the outlying islands spread across five:

GMT-6: Galapagos Islands and Easter Island

GMT-5: Colombia, Ecuador and most of Peru

GMT-4.5: Venezuela (a new time zone created by President Chavez in 2007)

GMT-4: Chile, Bolivia, Guyana, Paraguay, western Brazil and the Falklands

GMT-3: Argentina, Uruguay, French Guiana, Suriname and most of Brazil

GMT-2: Fernando de Noronha (Brazil) and South Georgia

YOUTH AND STUDENT DISCOUNTS

Various official and quasi-official youth/student ID cards are available and are worth the effort to obtain: they soon pay for themselves in savings. Full-time students are eligible for the International Student ID Card (ISIC; ⓦ www.isiccard.com), which entitles the bearer to special air, rail and bus fares and discounts at museums, theatres and other attractions. For Americans, there's also a health benefit, providing up to US$3000 in emergency medical coverage and US$100 a day for sixty days in the hospital, plus a 24hr hotline to call in the event of a medical, legal or financial emergency.

You have to be 26 or younger to qualify for the International Youth Travel Card, which carries the same benefits. Teachers qualify for the International Teacher Card, offering similar discounts. All these cards are available from student travel specialists including STA (see p.31).

TRAVELLERS WITH DISABILITIES

South America is not the friendliest of destinations for travellers with disabilities and many places are downright inaccessible. The more modern the society, the more likely you are to find services for physically challenged travellers – this means that while Bolivia and Paraguay are pretty impenetrable, much of inhabitable Chile and Argentina, as well as several cities in Brazil, are more accessible. Unfortunately, though, you may need to compromise over destination – big hotels in major cities that are very much on the tourist trail are much more likely to have facilities to cater to your needs than idyllic cabañas in the middle of nowhere. You might be limited as regards mobility, too, as local buses will probably prove difficult and you might need to settle for taxi services or internal flights. In any case, check with one of the agencies below before planning anything.

UK

Access Travel 6 The Hillock, Astley, Lancashire M29 7GW ⓣ 01942/888-844, ⓦ www .access-travel.co.uk. Small tour operator that can arrange flights, transfers and accommodation. Personally checks out places before recommendation and can guarantee accommodation standards in many countries – for places they do not cover, they can arrange flight-only deals.

US and Canada

Directions Unlimited 123 Green Lane, Bedford Hills, NY 10507 ⓣ 1-800/533-5343. Tour operator specializing in custom tours for people with disabilities.

Australia

Australian Council for Rehabilitation of the Disabled PO Box 60, Curtin, ACT 2605 ⓣ 02/6282 4333; 24 Cabarita Rd, Cabarita, NSW 2137 ⓣ 02/9743 2699. ACROD furnishes lists of travel agencies and tour operators for people with disabilities.

WOMEN TRAVELLERS

Though violent attacks against women travellers are not very common, many women find that the barrage of hisses, hoots and comments in parts of South America comes close to spoiling their trip. It's unlikely that a woman travelling alone will leave the continent without harassment, some of which can be threatening, most of which is just *pesado* (annoying). Latin American men are not renowned for their forward-thinking attitudes towards women's emancipation, and genuinely see nothing wrong with the heady sense of machismo that rules much of the continent. You may find that attitudes are less polarized in country areas.

There are measures you can take to avoid being hassled. Don't go to bars or nightclubs alone – this is an activity only undertaken by prostitutes in the region, and you will be considered fair game. Don't be sarcastic or scream if approached, as the man in question may feel that you are showing him up in front of his friends and get more aggressive. However, don't be afraid to seem rude; even the mildest polite response will be considered an indication of interest. Watch how the local women behave and where they go, and never be afraid to ask for help if you feel lost or threatened.

Solo women travellers should also avoid going to remote locations alone, and if you go as part of an organized visit, check the credentials of the tour company. Your safety may be in their hands, so asking around is a good idea. There are emergency numbers given in individual chapters of this book. However, if you are attacked, you should contact the tourist police and your country's embassy as well as getting medical attention and going to the regular police.

Argentina

HIGHLIGHTS

IGUAZÚ FALLS:
the world's largest waterfalls
are framed by lush, subtropical jungle

MENDOZA:
wineries and lofty peaks
lie just outside this
sophisticated metropolis

BUENOS AIRES:
tango and football
rule in this European-
style capital

BARILOCHE:
an outdoor adventure hub
with stunning mountain vistas

GLACIAR PERITO MORENO:
a frozen landscape
that splinters and creaks

USHUAIA:
the end of the Earth
and just 1000km from Antarctica

ROUGH COSTS

DAILY BUDGET Basic US$35/
occasional treat US$60

DRINK Beer (1ltr bottle)
US$1–1.50 (shop) US$3–5
(bar/restaurant)

FOOD *Asado* beef US$9

**CAMPING/HOSTEL/BUDGET
HOTEL** US$8/12/36

TRAVEL Bus/air fare from
Buenos Aires to Córdoba
US$40/120

FACT FILE

POPULATION 39.8 million

AREA 2,766,890 sq km

OFFICIAL LANGUAGE Spanish

CURRENCY Argentine peso (AR$)

CAPITAL Buenos Aires (Greater
Buenos Aires population,
13 million)

INTERNATIONAL PHONE CODE
☎54

TIME ZONE GMT -3 (clocks
currently don't change in summer
and winter)

Introduction

Even without the titanic wedge of Antarctica that cartographers include in its national territory, Argentina ranks as the world's eighth largest country. Stretching from the Tropic of Capricorn to the most southerly reaches of the planet's landmass, it encompasses a staggering diversity of climates and landscapes: hot and humid jungles in the northeast; bone-dry highland steppes in the northwest; through endless grasslands to windswept Patagonia and the end-of-the-world archipelago of Tierra del Fuego.

Argentina offers a variety of attractions, many of them influenced by generations of immigration from Europe. Above all, though, the extent and diversity of the country's natural scenery is staggering. Due north of the capital, Buenos Aires, stretches **El Litoral**, a region of subtropical riverine landscapes featuring the awe-inspiring **Iguazú** waterfalls. Tucked away in the northwest are the spectacular, polychrome **Quebrada de Humahuaca** gorge and the **Valles Calchaquíes**, stunningly beautiful valleys where high-altitude vineyards produce the delightfully flowery *torrontés* wine.

West and immediately south of Buenos Aires are the seemingly endless grassy plains of the **Pampas**. This is where you'll still glimpse traces of traditional **gaucho** culture, most famously celebrated in **San Antonio de Areco**. Here, too, you'll find some of the country's best *estancias*. As you move west, the **Central Sierras** loom on the horizon: within reach of **Córdoba**, the country's vibrant second city, are some of the oldest resorts on the continent. The regional capital of **Mendoza** is the country's wine capital and from here the scenic Alta Montaña route climbs steeply to the Chilean border, passing **Cerro Aconcagua**, Argentina's highest mountain and a dream challenge for mountaineers from around the world.

In the far south, San Juan and La Rioja provinces are relatively uncharted

territory but their star attractions are **Parque Nacional Talampaya**, with its giant red cliffs, and the nearby **Parque Provincial Ischigualasto**, usually known as Valle de la Luna on account of its intriguing, moon-like landscapes.

Argentina claims the lion's share of the wild, sparsely populated expanses of **Patagonia** and the archipelago of **Tierra del Fuego**. An almost unbroken chain of national parks here make for some of the best trekking anywhere on the planet – certainly include the savage granite peaks of the **Parque Nacional Los Glaciares** in your itinerary. For wildlife enthusiasts the **Peninsula Valdés** is also essential viewing, famous above all else as a breeding ground for Southern Right whales.

CHRONOLOGY

1516 The first Europeans reach the Río de la Plata and clash with Querandí natives.

1535 Pedro de Mendoza founds Buenos Aires.

1609 First missions to the Guaraní people established in the upper Paraná.

1806 The British storm Buenos Aires only to be expelled within a few months.

1810 The first elected junta sworn in to replace Spanish leaders.

1816 Independence is declared in the city of Tucumán.

1854 First railways built.

1912 Introduction of universal male suffrage.

1920s Towards the end of the decade, Argentina is the seventh richest country in the world.

1930 Hipólito Yrigoyen overthrown in a military coup.

1943 Military coup led by Juan Domingo Perón results in ousting of constitutional government.
1946 Juan Domingo Perón elected president.
1952 Perón's wife Evita dies at the age of 33.
1955 Perón overthrown in a military coup and exiled.
1973 Perón returns and is re-elected.
1974 Perón dies and power defaults to his third wife Isabelita.
1976 Videla leads military coup against Isabel Perón, marking the beginning of the "Dirty War".
1978 Argentina hosts, and wins, the World Cup in the middle of a military dictatorship.
1982 The military invades the Falkland Islands (Islas Malvinas) and is defeated by the British.
1983 Democracy is restored and radical Raúl Alfonsín is elected.
1995 Peronist Menem stands for a second term.
2001 President De la Rúa resigns in the midst of economic collapse and rioting.
2003 Néstor Kirchner is elected.
2008 His wife Cristina Fernández de Kirchner is inaugurated as the country's first elected female president.

Basics

ARRIVAL

The vast majority of visitors to Argentina arrive at Buenos Aires' **Ezeiza International Airport**, although other major cities also have flight connections to countries within South America. There are no direct international **rail** links, but a plethora of **international bus routes** link Argentina with its neighbours: Chile, Brazil, Bolivia, Uruguay and Paraguay.

From Bolivia

There are three entry points into Argentina from Bolivia: Villazón, Bermejo and Yacuiba. You'll need to complete the requisite formalities at Bolivia's migration and customs office on the border and then register on the Argentina side.

WHEN TO VISIT

Buenos Aires is probably at its best during spring, when purple jacaranda trees are in bloom all over the city and the weather is typically sunny and warm. For spectacular autumnal colours, visit **Mendoza** between April and May, or else in early March to witness its international harvest festival. Unless heading to **Bariloche** to ski, Patagonia is best avoided in the depths of winter. Instead, plan a visit between October and April, but if heading to **Peninsula Valdés**, be sure not to miss the whale season, at its peak in November.

From Brazil

Most people crossing from Brazil to Argentina do so at Foz do Iguaçu. If you're just going for the day you only need to get your passport stamped on the Argentine side, but if going for longer you must pass through both controls. The bus that takes you across the border stops at the Brazilian and Argentine passport controls and waits for passengers to get their passports stamped.

From Chile

Travellers coming from the high Andes should note that the crossings there are seasonal. In the north, advance booking is recommended for the San Pedro de Atacama–Jujuy and Salta bus crossing. The most popular border crossing from Chile to Argentina is the Santiago–Mendoza route via the Los Libertadores tunnel. If you're coming from the south, routes in the Lake District include Osorno–Bariloche, and Temuco–San Martín de Los Andes. Further south still are the Puerto Natales–El Calafate and Punta Arenas–Río Gallegos crossings. Those heading to the world's southernmost city should cross by boat from Puerto Williams to Ushuaia (weather dependent).

From Paraguay

Visitors can cross the Paraguayan border into Posadas (Argentina) from Encarnación (Paraguay). Travellers crossing here will have to go through migration control at both sides of the border, which are open 24 hours. Another popular option is the Puerto Falcón (Paraguay) to Clorinda (Argentina) crossing, but you can also cross into the Argentinian cities of Formosa, Pocitos, Corrientes, Barranqueras and Iguazú.

From Uruguay

From Colonia del Sacramento, the crossing is easy and quick with the Buquebus ferry service (⌨www .buquebus.com), with a fast service taking an hour and the slower but cheaper service three hours. Otherwise opt for the more scenic route with Cacciola Viajes (⌨www .cacciolaviajes.com) from Carmelo to Tigre. If travelling by car, you can cross the border in Fray Bentos further north.

VISAS

Citizens of the EU, US, Canada, South Africa, Australia and New Zealand do not require **visas**, though in 2010 Argentina introduced reciprocal entry fees for countries that charge Argentine citizens to enter: the US (US$131), Canada (US$150) and Australia (US$100) are subject to **one-off arrival fees**, valid for five years. Tourists are routinely granted 90-day entry permits – the easiest way to renew your tourist visa is to cross the border into one of the neighbouring countries. Tourists who overstay the 90-day limit must pay an AR$300 fine when leaving the country.

GETTING AROUND

Argentina is a huge country and you are likely to spend a considerable proportion of your budget on travel. Air travel is relatively expensive – and tourists also get charged a much higher rate than local residents – so most people travel by bus. Car rental is useful in places, but too expensive for most budget travellers, unless they can share the cost. Extra fees are charged for drivers under 25.

By air

Argentina's most important domestic airport by far is Buenos Aires' **Aeroparque Jorge Newbery**. There are connections (with Aerolíneas Argentinas, LAN and LADE) to most provincial capitals and major tourist centres; Andes serves Puerto Madryn and Salta among other destinations. Some cut-price deals booked in advance can work out to be not much more than the bus. One of the best deals is the "Visit Argentina" **airpass** sold by Aerolíneas Argentinas and valid for domestic flights on Aerolíneas and its subsidiary, Austral, covering more than thirty destinations. This pass must be bought abroad; it is not sold in Argentina.

Many smaller airports are not served by public transport, though some airline companies run shuttle services to connect with flights; otherwise, you're stuck with taxis.

By bus

There are hundreds of private **bus** companies, most of which concentrate on one particular region, although a few, such as TAC, operate pretty much nationwide. Most buses are modern, plush models designed for long-distance travel, and your biggest worry will be what video the driver or conductor has chosen. On longer journeys, snacks and even hot meals are served (included in the ticket price), although these vary considerably in quality. The more luxurious services are usually worth the extra money for long night-rides; some even have waiters. *Coche cama* services have wide, reclinable seats, and *semi-cama* services are not far behind in terms of comfort. Most companies also offer *cama suite* or *cama ejecutivo* services, which have completely reclinable seats and often include an on-board meal.

Buying **tickets** is normally a simple on-the-spot matter, but you must plan in advance if travelling in peak summer season (mid-Dec to Feb), especially if you're taking a long-distance bus from Buenos Aires or any other major city to a particularly popular holiday destination. If in Buenos Aires look for kiosks advertising *venta de pasajes* – these are authorized ticket sellers and will save you having to visit the cavernous Retiro terminal before you leave.

By car

You are unlikely to want or need a car for your whole stay in Argentina, but you'll find one pretty indispensable if you hope to explore some of the more isolated areas of Patagonia, Tierra del Fuego, the Northwest, and Mendoza and San Juan provinces.

To **rent a car**, you need to be over 21 (25 with some agencies); most foreign licences are accepted for tourists. Bring your passport as well as a credit card for the deposit. Before you drive off, check that you've been given insurance, tax and ownership papers. Check too for dents and paintwork damage, and get hold of a 24-hour emergency telephone number. Also, pay close attention to the small print, most notably what you're liable for in the event of an accident: excess normally doesn't cover you for the first AR$5000 or so, and you may not be covered for windscreens, headlights, tyres and more – all vulnerable on unsurfaced roads. Look for unlimited mileage deals, as the per-kilometre charge can

otherwise exceed your daily rental cost many times over given the vast distance you're likely to be covering.

By train

Argentina's **rail** network, developed with British investment from the late nineteenth century, collapsed in the 1990s with the withdrawal of government subsidies. Certain long-distance services were maintained by provincial governments, but these tend to be slower and less reliable than buses. Though you may not want to use Argentine trains as a method of getting around, the country's famous **tourist trains**, where the aim is simply to travel for the sheer fun of it, are a major attraction. There are two principal stars: *La Trochita*, the Old Patagonian Express from Esquel; and the *Tren a los Nubes* (April–Nov only), one of the highest railways in the world, which climbs through the mountains from Salta towards the Chilean border.

ACCOMMODATION

You can often tell by a hotel's **name** what kind of place to expect: the use of the term *posada* for example usually suggests a slightly rustic feel, but generally comfortable or even luxurious. In a similar vein, *hostería* is often used for smallish, high-end hotels – oriented towards the tourist rather than the business person. *Hostal* is sometimes used too – but doesn't refer reliably to anything – there are youth hostels called *hostales* as well as high-rise modern hotels.

Residenciales and *hospedajes* are basically simple hotel-style accommodation. Most are reasonably clean and comfortable and a few of them stand out as some of Argentina's best budget accommodation.

A very different experience from staying in a hotel is provided by Argentina's *estancias*, as the country's large ranches are called. **Estancia** accommodation is generally luxurious, and with a lot more character than hotels of a similar price; for between US$100 and US$200 per person a day you are provided with all meals, invariably including a traditional *asado* or barbecue. At working *estancias* you will have the chance to observe or join in ranch activities such as cattle herding and branding, while almost all of them include activities such as horse-riding and swimming in the price. To book *estancia* accommodation, either approach individual establishments directly (they're recommended throughout the text) or try one of the two specialist agencies in Buenos Aires: Comarcas, Laprida 1380 (☎011/4821-1876, ⊛www.comarcas.com.ar) and Estancias Argentinas, Diagonal Roque Sáenz Peña 616, 9th Floor (☎011/4343-2366 ⊛www.estanciasargentinas.com).

Hostels and campsites

Youth hostels are known as *albergues juveniles*, *albergues de la juventud* or simply *hosteles* in Argentina. Accommodation is generally in dormitories, though most places also have one or two double rooms, which are often excellent value. Facilities vary from next to nothing to internet access, washing machines, cable TV and patios with barbecue facilities.

There are plenty of **campsites** (*campings*) – most towns and villages having their own municipal site – but standards vary wildly. At the major resorts, there are usually plenty of privately owned, well-organized sites, with facilities ranging from provisions stores to volleyball courts and TV rooms. In less touristy towns, municipal sites can be rather desolate and not particularly secure: it's a good idea to check with locals before pitching your tent.

FOOD

Traditionally, Argentine food could be summed up in a single word: **beef**. Not just any beef, but succulent, cherry-red, healthy meat raised on some of the greenest, most extensive pastures known to cattle. The **barbecue** or *asado* remains a national institution, but it's not the whole story.

An *asado* is prepared on a **parrilla** (grill), and this national dish is served everywhere, at restaurants also known as *parrillas*. Usually there's a set menu, but the establishments themselves vary enormously. Traditionally, you start off by eating the offal before moving on to the choicer cuts, but you can choose to head straight for the steaks and fillets. The lightly salted meat is usually served with nothing on it, other than the traditional condiments of *chimichurri* – olive oil with salt, garlic, chilli pepper, vinegar and bayleaf – and *salsa criolla*, similar but with onion and tomato and red pepper added.

Alongside the *parrilla*, pizza and pasta are the mainstays of Argentine cuisine, a reflection of the country's important Italian heritage. Those staying in Argentina for a while may get frustrated by the lack of menu choices, especially in rustic areas, although the **variety** of restaurants in the cities, especially Buenos Aires, reflects a mosaic of different communities who have migrated to Argentina over the decades: not just Italian and Spanish but Chinese, Middle Eastern, German, Welsh, Japanese and Peruvian. **Vegetarians** will find that there are few options on most menus, but staples such as basic salads, *provoleta* (delicious melted cheese) and *tartas* (a kind of quiche) are almost always available, as well as pastas with meat-free sauces. In larger towns vegetarian restaurants are growing in popularity.

There are plenty of *minutas* or **snacks** to choose from. The *choripán*, a large sausage in a bap, is a national favourite, as is the ubiquitous *milanesa*, a breaded veal escalope. Excellent local-style fast food is also available in the form of *empanadas*, pasties that come with an array of fillings, from the traditional beef or mozzarella cheese to salami, roquefort and chard. *Humitas* are made of steamed creamed sweetcorn, served in neat parcels made from the outer husk of corn cobs. *Tamales* are maize-flour balls, stuffed with minced beef and onion, wrapped in maize leaves and simmered. The typical main dish, *locro*, is a warming, substantial Andean stew based on maize, with onions, beans and meat thrown in.

Where to eat

Argentines love **dining out**, and in Buenos Aires especially, places stay open all day and till very late: in the evening hardly any restaurant starts serving dinner before 8.30pm, and in the hotter months – and all year round in Buenos Aires – very few people turn up before 10pm. By South American standards the quality of restaurants is high. You can keep costs down by taking advantage of restaurants' *menú del día* or *menú ejecutivo* – good-value set meals for as little as AR$15 served primarily, but not exclusively, at lunchtime. In the evening *tenedor libre* restaurants are just the place if your budget's tight. Here, you can eat as much as you like, they're usually self-service (cold and hot buffets plus grills) and the food is fresh and well prepared, if a little dull.

Cheaper hotels and more modest accommodation often skimp on **breakfast**: you'll be lucky to be given more than tea or coffee, and some bread, jam and butter, though *medialunas* (small, sticky croissants) are sometimes also served. The sacred national delicacy *dulce de leche* (a type of caramel) is often provided for spreading on toast or bread, as is top-notch honey.

DRINK

Fizzy drinks (*gaseosas*) are popular with people of all ages and are often drunk to accompany a meal. Although few beans are grown in the country, good, if expensive, **coffee** is easy to come by in Argentina. In the cafés of most towns and cities you can find a decent espresso, or delicious *café con leche* (milky coffee) for breakfast. *Mate*, the bitter national drink, prepared in a special gourd and drunk through a metal straw known as a *bombilla*, is a whole world unto itself, with special rules of etiquette and ritual involved. It is almost exclusively drunk at home.

Argentina's **beer** is more thirst-quenching than alcoholic and mostly comes as fairly bland lager. The Quilmes brewery dominates the market with lagers such as Cristal; in Mendoza, the Andes brand crops up all over the place; while Salta's own brand is also good. Most breweries also produce a *cerveza negra*, a kind of stout. Patagonia produces some excellent artisanal ales, most only available within the region. If you want draught beer you must ask for a *chopp*.

Argentine **wine** is excellent and reasonably priced – try the Malbec grape

---

ARGENTINE WINE

Argentina is the world's fifth-largest producer of wine, and more than three-quarters of the stuff flows out of Mendoza. Enjoying around three hundred days of sunshine a year and a prime position at the foothills of the Andes, Mendoza's high-altitude vineyards are now producing premium vintages on a par with Chile's. The idyllic desert climate (cool nights, little rain and low humidity) works especially well for reds: Malbec – brought over from Bordeaux – is Argentina's star grape, producing rich fruity flavours that go down superbly well with the ubiquitous steak.

variety. The locally distilled *aguardientes* or firewaters are often deliciously grapey. There is no national alcoholic drink or cocktail, but a number of Italian vermouths and digestifs are made in Argentina. Fernet Branca is the most popular, a demonic-looking brew the colour of molasses with a rather bitter, medicinal taste, invariably combined with cola, whose colour it matches, and consumed in huge quantities by students and young people.

CULTURE AND ETIQUETTE

Argentines are generally friendly, outgoing and incredibly welcoming to foreigners. In all but the most formal contexts, Argentines greet with one kiss on the cheek (men included), even on first meeting.

Table manners follow the Western norm and, in general, visitors are unlikely to find any huge culture shock in Argentine etiquette. Service in shops or restaurants is generally very courteous (however the latter often painfully slow compared to Western standards) and conversations should be started with a "buen día" or "buenas tardes".

SPORTS AND OUTDOOR ACTIVITIES

Argentina is a highly exciting destination for outdoors enthusiasts, whether you're keen to tackle radical rock faces or prefer to appreciate the vast open spaces at a more gentle pace, hiking or on horseback. World-class fly-fishing, horseriding, trekking and rock climbing options abound, as do opportunities for white-water rafting, skiing, ice climbing, and even – for those with sufficient stamina and preparation – expeditions onto the Southern Patagonian Icecap. The Patagonian Andes provide the focus for most of these activities – particularly the area of the central Lake District around Bariloche and El Calafate/El Chaltén, but Mendoza and the far northwest of the country, around Salta and Jujuy, are also worth considering for their rugged mountain terrain. If you're keen on any of the above activities (bar angling, of course), ensure you have taken out appropriate insurance cover before leaving home.

Hiking and climbing

Argentina offers some truly marvellous **hiking** possibilities, and it is still possible to find areas where you can trek for days without seeing a soul. Most of the best treks are found in the national parks – especially the ones in Patagonia – but you can also find less-known but equally superb options in the lands bordering the parks. Most people head for the savage granite spires of the Fitz Roy region around El Chaltén, an area whose fame has spread so rapidly over the last ten years that it now holds a similar status to Chile's renowned Torres del Paine, not far away, and is packed in the high season (late Dec to Feb). The other principal trekking

---

NATIONAL PARK INFORMATION

The National Park Headquarters at Santa Fe 690 in Buenos Aires (Mon–Fri 8am–2pm; ☎011/4311-0303, ⊛www.parquesnacionales.gov.ar) has an information office with introductory leaflets on the nation's parks. A wider range of free leaflets is available at each individual park, but these are of variable quality and limited funding means that many parks give you only ones with a basic map and a brief park description. Contact the headquarters well in advance if you are interested in voluntary or scientific projects.

destination is the mountainous area of Nahuel Huapi National Park which lies to the south of Bariloche, centring on the Cerro Catedral massif and Cerro Tronador.

For **climbers**, the Andes offer incredible variety – from volcanoes to shale summits, from the continent's loftiest giants to some of its fiercest technical walls. You do not have to be a technical expert to reach the summit of some of these and, though you must always take preparations seriously, you can often arrange your climb close to the date through local agencies – though it's best to bring as much high-quality gear with you as you can. The climbing season is fairly short – generally November to March, though December to February is the best time. The best-known, if not the most technical, challenge is South America's highest peak, **Aconcagua** (6962m), accessed from the city of Mendoza. In the far south are the Fitz Roy massif and Cerro Torre, which have few equals on the planet in terms of sheer technical difficulty and grandeur of scenery. On all of these climbs, but especially those over 4000m, you must acclimatize thoroughly, and be fully aware of the dangers of altitude sickness.

Skiing

The main **skiing** months are July and August (late July is peak season), although in some resorts it is possible to ski from late May to early October. Snow conditions vary wildly from year to year, but you can often find excellent powder. The most prestigious resort for downhill skiing is modern Las Leñas, which offers the most challenging slopes and once hosted the World Cup; followed by the Bariloche resorts of Cerro Catedral and Cerro Otto. These are the longest-established in the country and are still perhaps the classic Patagonian ski centres, with their wonderful panoramas of the Nahuel Huapi region. Ski gear is widely available to rent. For updates on conditions and resorts, check out the Andesweb website (Ⓦ www.andesweb.com).

COMMUNICATIONS

There are Correo Argentino **post offices** throughout the country, and you may also come across *locutorios* offering postal services. International post is relatively expensive and not always reliable; use registered post if possible and try to avoid sending items of value.

Making **local phone calls** in Argentina is cheap and easy. In cities and towns, you are never far from a call centre (known as a *locutorio*). It's worth asking about phone cards offering cheap minutes if you are planning to make a number of **national calls**. **Mobile calls** are expensive (which is why Argentines tend to send text messages whenever possible) but mildly cheaper if calling

---

ARGENTINA ON THE WEB

Ⓦ www.turismo.gov.ar The official tourist website for Argentina.

Ⓦ www.welcomeargentina.com Well-presented website about Argentina, containing information about accommodation and activities, and detailed transport advice.

Ⓦ www.buenosaires.gov.ar City government site for Buenos Aires, with up-to-date details on cultural events.

Ⓦ www.livinginargentina.com Online magazine with articles in English about Argentine culture and travel.

Ⓦ www.buenosairesherald.com Buenos Aires' English-language newspaper, with national and international news updated daily.

someone with the same phone company. The main ones are Claro, Personal and Movistar. If you're in Argentina for more than a couple of weeks, you may want to buy a pay-as-you-go SIM card (called a chip) to avoid extortionate roaming fees on your mobile.

Cheap **internet** cafés are everywhere in Argentina and, in all but the most remote areas, the connections are fairly fast. If you have your own laptop, note that many cafés and restaurants – especially in Buenos Aires – have free wi-fi.

CRIME AND SAFETY

Argentina is one of the continent's safest countries and, as long as you take a few basic precautions, you are unlikely to encounter any problems during your stay. Indeed, you'll find many of the more rural parts of the country pretty much risk-free: people leave doors unlocked, windows open and bikes unchained. More care should be taken in large cities and some of the border towns, particularly the northeastern ones, where poverty and easily available arms and drugs make opportunistic crime a more common occurrence. Some potential pitfalls are outlined here, not to induce paranoia but on the principle that to be forewarned is to be forearmed.

By Argentine standards, **Buenos Aires** is currently suffering something of a crime wave, and incidents of violence and armed robbery are definitely on the increase. It's sometimes difficult to know how much local anxiety is due to a genuine increase in crime and how much to middle-class paranoia, a lot of it provoked by sensationalist news channels. But, in general, serious crime tends to affect locals more than tourists. Nevertheless, you should not take unmarked taxis and you're advised to be wary when taking a taxi from areas where serious money circulates. Avoid walking around the

quieter neighbourhoods after dark, and be especially wary in Once and Constitución. Stick to the touristy areas of La Boca like the Caminito (the non-touristy part is to be avoided and is considered dangerous). In the rare event of being held up at gunpoint, don't play the hero. Locals warn that this is especially the case if your mugger is a child, since they know that, as minors, they can't be jailed even if they shoot someone.

Theft from hotels is rare but, as anywhere else in the world, do not leave valuables lying round the room. Some hostels have lockers; it's worth having a padlock of your own.

Drugs are frowned upon in general. They attract far more stigma here than in most European countries, for example, and Argentine society at large draws very little in the way of a line between "acceptable" soft drugs and "unacceptable" hard drugs. You're very much advised to steer clear of buying or partaking yourself – the penalties are stiff if you get caught.

HEALTH

If you're planning to travel in rural areas within Salta, Jujuy or Misiones provinces, **malaria** tablets are recommended. Vaccinations against **yellow fever** should be taken before visiting forested areas in the north of Argentina, including Iguazú Falls. All travellers over one year of age should be given the **hepatitis A** vaccination at least two weeks before arrival. If you're heading off the beaten track, vaccinations against typhoid and rabies are also recommended.

INFORMATION AND MAPS

Argentina's main **National Tourist Office** is at Santa Fe 883 in Buenos Aires (Mon–Fri 9am–5pm; ☎011/4312-2232, ⓦwww.turismo.gov.ar) and offers maps of the country and general information about getting around. Every province maintains a *Casa de Provincia* in Buenos Aires too, where you can pick up information about what there is to see or do, prior to travelling. The standard of information you'll glean from them varies wildly, often reflecting the comparative wealth of a given province.

The clearest and most accurate **map** of the whole country is the one you can get free from the national tourist office; it's called Rutas de la Argentina and has small but clear inset maps of twenty towns and cities as well as a 1:2,500,000 national map, the ideal scale for most travellers. Another useful resource for route planning is the website ⓦwww .ruta0.com. The ACA (Automóvil Club, ⓦwww.aca.org.ar) produces individual maps for each province, which vary enormously in detail and accuracy; the regional maps or route planners the club publishes may be enough for most travellers.

MONEY AND BANKS

The **Argentine peso** is divided into one hundred centavos. In Argentina, it's represented by the dollar sign ($) but to avoid confusion we have used the symbol AR$ throughout this section. Notes come in 2, 5, 10, 20, 50 and 100 peso denominations, and 1 peso and 5, 10, 25 and 50 centavo coins are also in circulation. Guard your loose change in Buenos Aires as you will need it for the buses. Try to cash large notes in hotels and supermarkets – never in taxis – and look out for counterfeit money. Check your notes for a watermark, and that the number is printed in shiny green.

Argentina still has a relatively healthy **economy**, by South American standards, even since the crisis in

early 2002, when the peso was sharply devalued. It has since settled at around 4 to the US dollar. Although the cost of basic products rocketed following the devaluation, the price of most services has remained relatively low, turning Argentina into an economical country to visit, although locals increasingly complain about the country's high inflation. It may still seem expensive if you arrive from Peru or Bolivia. If you are paying **cash**, it's always worth trying for a discount, especially at hotels.

ATMs (*cajeros automáticos*) are plentiful in Argentina, though you can sometimes be caught out in very remote places, especially in the northwest. Note that withdrawals are usually limited to AR$1000 a day although, at the time of going to press, there were plans to increase the limit. **Traveller's cheques** are not really a viable option as fewer and fewer banks seem to accept them.

Hotels and other types of commerce, especially at the luxury end of the market, may charge foreigners in US dollars, rather than Argentine pesos, as it's historically the more stable currency and has the added effect of making prices seem smaller than their peso equivalent. This practice is mostly found, of course, in more touristy locations, such as Buenos Aires, Ushuaia and Bariloche.

OPENING HOURS AND HOLIDAYS

Most **shops and services** are open Monday to Friday from 9am to 7pm,

PUBLIC HOLIDAYS

Jan 1 New Year's Day (*Año Nuevo*)
March 24 Day of Truth and Justice
April 2 Malvinas Remembrance Day
Easter (varies) Easter Friday is a public holiday (Easter Thursday is optional)
May 1 Labour Day (*Día del Trabajo*)
May 25 May Revolution Day
June 20 Flag Day (*Día de la Bandera*)
July 9 Day of Independence (*Día de la Independencia*)
Aug 17 Remembrance of General San Martín's death (*Día del Paso a la Inmortalidad del General José de San Martín*)
Oct 12 Columbus Day (*Día de la Raza*)
Dec 8 Day of the Immaculate Virgin Mary
Dec 25 Christmas (*Navidad*)
Note that for some holidays the exact date may vary slightly from year to year.

and Saturday till 2pm, although later in large towns, including Buenos Aires. In smaller towns they may close at some point during the day for between one and five hours – sometimes offset by later closing times in the evening, especially in the summer. Supermarkets seldom close during the day and are generally open much later, often until 8 or 10pm, and on Saturday afternoons. Large shopping malls don't close before 10pm and their food and drink sections (*patios de comida*) may stay open as late as midnight. Most of them open on Sundays, too. **Banks** mostly open on weekdays only, from 10am to 5pm, while casas de cambio more or less follow shop hours. In the northeast, bank opening hours may be more like 7am to noon, to avoid the hot, steamy afternoons.

In addition to the national **holidays** listed above, some local anniversaries or saints' days are also public holidays when everything in a given city may close down. Festivals of all kinds, both religious and profane, celebrating local patrons such as Santa Catalina or the Virgin Mary, or showing off produce such as handicrafts, olives, goats or wine, are good excuses for much partying and pomp.

Buenos Aires

With a huge variety of high-class restaurants, hotels and boutiques, as well as an eclectic mix of French, English and modern architecture, **BUENOS AIRES** is deservedly known as the "Paris of South America". The influence of immigrants from all over the world, Italian and Spanish above all, can be seen in its street names, restaurants, architecture and language. Sip a coffee in the famous *Café Tortoni*, visit a dark and romantic tango hall to watch the nation's famous sultry dance, or simply walk the streets of Recoleta and watch the heavily made-up ladies in their fur-coats walking tiny dogs on Chanel leads. If you grow weary of the people, noise and buses of the capital you can head out of the city to the waterways of the Paraná Delta, the quiet streets of La Plata or San Antonio de Areco, home of Argentina's gauchos.

What to see and do

The city's museums and sights are well distributed between the central areas of Recoleta, Retiro, Palermo and San Telmo, and the *microcentro*, which covers the stretch around Avenida Corrientes, south of Avenida de Julio. The historic *barrio* (neighbourhood) of San Telmo is one of the most interesting for visitors, on account of its atmospheric streets, surviving (if often faded) nineteenth-century architecture, and its Sunday antiques market. The *microcentro* has the greatest concentration of shops and commerce, but Palermo Viejo should also be on every visitor's itinerary for its leafy streets lined with design and fashion shops, and hip bars and restaurants.

Plaza de Mayo

The **Plaza de Mayo** has been at the heart of the best and worst moments of

Argentina's history – host to founding presidents, devastating military coups, the fanaticism of Evita, the dark days of the "Dirty War", and desperate crowds after the economic crisis. It has been bombed by its own military, filled to the brink with patriots, and left deserted, guarded by the federal police, in times of uncertainty, and even now it is still the spiritual home of the **Madres de la Plaza de Mayo**. These women, whose grown-up children "disappeared" during the Military Dictatorship (1976–1983), have marched in the plaza every Thursday (3.30–4pm) for over thirty years demanding information about their children's whereabouts. The huge pink building at the river end of the plaza is the **Casa Rosada** (free tours Sat & Sun 10am–8pm; ☎011/4344-3804, ⊛www.casarosada.gov.ar), home to the offices of the president and the executive branch of government. On the south side of the building is the **Museo de la Casa Rosada** (⊛www.museo.gov.ar) which has interesting displays on Argentina's previous presidents and the events surrounding their term in office, but is closed for refurbishment until late 2011.

At the opposite end of the plaza is the **Cabildo** which, though much altered, is one of the only examples of colonial architecture left in this part of the city. During the week there is a small crafts market and a lovely café here, as well as a **museum** of historical artefacts (Tues–Fri 10.30am–5pm, Sat & Sun 11.30am–6pm; AR$4; guided tours daily 12.30pm, 2pm (free) & 3.30pm; AR$6; ☎011/4334-1782). The **Catedral Metropolitana** (Mon–Fri 8am–7pm, Sat & Sun 9am–7.30pm; free guided tours, Spanish only; ☎011/4331-2845), close by, is a largely unattractive building, but is worth a look for its imposing columns.

Avenida de Mayo

Heading west behind the Cabildo, **Avenida de Mayo** is one of the city's

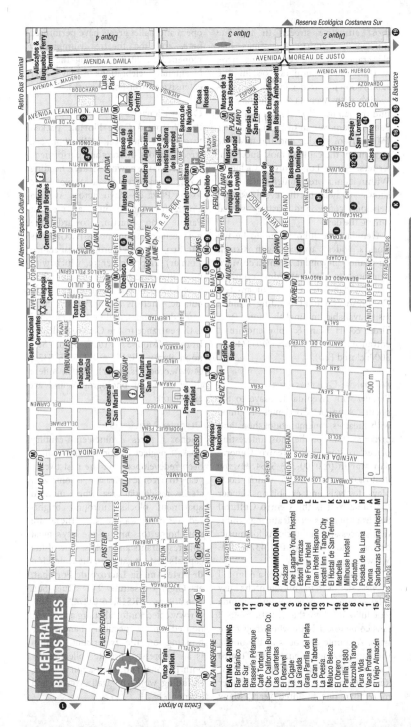

CENTRAL BUENOS AIRES

Reserva Ecológica Costanera Sur

ARGENTINA BUENOS AIRES

EATING & DRINKING

Bar Británico	18
Bar Sur	17
Brasserie Pétanque	11
Café Tortoni	9
Cbc California Burrito Co.	4
Las Cuartetas	6
El Desnivel	14
La Cigale	3
La Girada	5
Gran Parrilla del Plata	12
La Gran Taberna	10
La Poesía	13
Maluco Beleza	7
El Obrero	19
Parrilla 1880	16
Piazzolla Tango	8
Pura Vida	2
Vaca Profana	1
El Viejo Almacén	15

ACCOMMODATION

Alcázar	D
Che Lagarto Youth Hostel	G
Estoril Terrazas	B
The Four Seasons	L
Gran Hotel Hispano	F
Hostel Inn - Tango City	K
El Hostal de San Telmo	C
Marbella	E
Milhouse Hostel	J
Ostinatto	H
Posada de la Luna	A
Roma	I
Sandanzas Cultural Hostel	M

most attractive streets. In the late nineteenth century, Argentina's first skyscrapers were erected along here, and an underground rail system (the *subte*) soon followed. Close to the intersection with Avenida 9 de Julio, you'll find the famous *Café Tortoni* (Mon–Sat 8am–3.30am, Sun until 1am), with over 150 years of service and the favourite of many of the capital's most successful writers, Jorge Luis Borges included. Within its mirrored golden walls, tango shows are held in the evenings, and delicious coffee and pastries served during the day.

Avenida 9 de Julio claims to be the world's widest avenue (with sixteen busy lanes): beyond it, Avenida de Mayo continues to the **Plaza de Congreso**, and the fabulous Greco-Roman-style **Congreso Nacional** building (guided visits available in English Mon, Tues, Thurs & Fri 11am & 4pm; enquire at entrance on south side; ☎011/4010-3000; closed Feb).

Avenida Corrientes

Parallel with Avenida de Mayo to the north, Avenida Corrientes is lined with theatres, cinemas, bookshops and pizzerias. One of the most interesting places to stop is the **Teatro General San Martín** (☎0800-333-5254, ⓦwww.teatrosanmartin.com.ar) which hosts plays, festivals and exhibitions. Under the same roof is the **Centro Cultural San Martín** arts space, featuring exhibition spaces and auditoriums for music, drama and film (☎011/4374-1251, ⓦwww.ccgsm.gov.ar).

The much-loved **Obelisco**, a 67m-tall obelisk, stands in the middle of the busy intersection of Corrientes and Avenida 9 de Julio. It is here that ecstatic football fans come to celebrate when their team wins. A couple of blocks to the north, the huge French Renaissance **Teatro Colón** (☎011/4378-7100, ⓦwww.teatrocolon.org.ar) still stands tall after more than one hundred years. Many opera and ballet greats have performed here, and the theatre triumphantly reopened in 2010 – during the city's bicentenary celebrations in May – after extensive refurbishment works.

Calle Florida

Pedestrianized **Calle Florida**, packed throughout the week with shoppers, street vendors, buskers and performers, runs across the downtown area, heading north from Avenida de Mayo, close to the Plaza de Mayo, across Avenida Corrientes and ending at pleasant Parque San Martín. Towards the northern end is the impressive **Galerías Pacífico** (ⓦwww.progaleriaspacifico.com.ar) shopping centre, which with its vaulted and frescoed ceiling, offers a welcome respite from the crowds outside. There is an inexpensive food court downstairs, and on the first floor is the entrance to the **Centro Cultural Borges** (Mon–Sat 10am–9pm, Sun noon–9pm; AR$15; ☎011/5555-5359, ⓦwww.ccborges.org.ar), which offers three floors of photography and art exhibitions.

Puerto Madero

Buenos Aires' nineteenth-century docks, neglected for decades, have been redeveloped over the past twenty years to become a pleasant, if somewhat sterile, residential area, where modern apartment blocks surround bright-red restored warehouses. These are now home to some of the city's most chic restaurants and hotels. One of the capital's best art galleries, the **Colección de Arte Amalia Lacroze de Fortabat**, at Olga Cossettini 141 (Tues–Sun noon–9pm, AR$15; ☎011/4310-6600, ⓦwww.coleccionfortabat.org.ar), is housed in a peculiar hangar-style building on the waterfront. Within is an impressive private collection by both national and international artists, including works by Dali, Warhol and Turner.

Nearby along the river's edge is the **Reserva Ecológica Costanera Sur** (entrance at Av. Tristán Achával Rodríguez 1550; Tues–Sun 8am–6pm; free; ☎011/4315-1320), a large expanse of reclaimed and regenerated land. It makes a delightful afternoon stroll, and they hold full-moon tours once a month. In front of the entrance, a small craft market is held on weekends.

Montserrat

Along with neighbouring San Telmo, cobble-stoned **Montserrat** is the oldest suburb of the city, and the most popular until a yellow fever outbreak in the nineteenth century forced wealthier families to move to the areas around Palermo. The *barrio*'s principal street is Calle Defensa, named after residents who, trying to force back British invaders in the early 1800s, poured boiling oil from their balconies onto the attacking soldiers.

The neo-Baroque **Iglesia de San Francisco** (Mon–Fri 7am–7pm, Sat 5.30am–7.30pm, Sun 10–11am & 5.30–7.30pm; ☎011/4331-0625), at the corner of Alsina and Defensa, has an intricately decorated interior that can just about be made out through the atmospheric gloom. Nearby is the small **Museo de la Ciudad**, Alsina 412 (Mon–Fri 11am–7pm, Sat & Sun till 8pm; AR$1, ☎011/4331-9855), which houses informative and well-presented changing exhibitions about the city. One block west of Defensa is the collection of buildings known as the **Manzana de las Luces** (guided visits daily at 3pm, Sat & Sun also 4.30pm & 6pm, Spanish only; AR$7; info at Perú 272; ☎011/4342-9930, ⓦwww.manzanadelasluces.gov.ar), which dates back to 1686. Originally housing a Jesuit community, it has also been home to numerous official institutions throughout its history, and today it accommodates both the **Colegio Nacional**, an elite high school, as well as Buenos Aires' oldest church, **San Ignacio** (daily 8am–8pm; ☎011/4331-2458), begun in 1675.

San Telmo

San Telmo begins further south along Defensa, on the far side of Avenida Belgrano. With its myriad of antique stores and junk shops, as well as a range of busy, late-opening restaurants and bars (especially around the intersection of Chile and Defensa), it's a great place to wander. For fresh food and a variety of eclectic antiques head to the **San Telmo Food Market** (daily 8am–1pm & 3–7pm). The market takes up an entire city block, with an entrance on each side, including one on Defensa near the corner of Estados Unidos.

A few blocks further, **Plaza Dorrego** is a great place to pause for a coffee under the leafy trees, at least on weekdays when it's quieter. On Sundays the area is completely taken over by the **Feria de San Pedro Telmo** (10am–5pm; buses #9, #10, #24, #28 or #86 easily picked up downtown). Vintage watches, posters, antique clothes and jewellery are all on display at this huge open-air antiques market, enlivened by street performers and live tango acts. Another great place for antique-spotting is the **Pasaje de la Defensa**, Defensa 1179, a converted mansion filled with hidden shops, cafés and workshops.

Calle Defensa continues, across the busy, ugly avenues of San Juan and Juan de Garay, to **Parque Lezama**, whose green acres are home to the **Museo Histórico Nacional** Defensa 1600 (Wed–Sun 11am–6pm; free; ☎011/4307-1182). Small and delightful, this museum was recently renovated and has an interesting permanent exhibition on Argentina's history. The **Museo de Arte Moderno de Buenos Aires (MAMBA)**, at Av. San Juan 350, (Mon–Fri noon–7pm, Sat & Sun 11am–8pm; AR$1, Tues free; ☎011/4342-3001, ⓦwww.museodeartemoderno.buenosaires.gov.ar) reopened its doors at the end of

2010. Its collection focuses mainly on Argentine art from the 1920s until the present day, and includes pieces by Xul Solar and Antonio Berni.

La Boca

Easily accessible from Parque Lezama, the suburb of **La Boca** is known for the Caminito and as home to one of Argentina's leading football clubs, **Boca Juniors**, arch-rivals of the River Plate team on the other side of town.

The **Caminito** is a small area of brightly coloured buildings along the river, created in the 1950s by the neighbourhood's most famous artist, **Benito Quinquela Martín**. These days the Caminito is a serious tourist trap, though it has an interesting open-air **arts and crafts fair** (daily 10.30am–6pm), street performers, and restaurants and cafés charging tourist prices.

A visit to the Boca Juniors' stadium, **La Bombonera** (Brandsen 805, three blocks west of Avenida Almirante Brown; ☎011/4362-2050), is definitely worthwhile, even if you can't score tickets to a game. The starting point is the fascinating **Museo de la Pasión Boquense** (daily 10am–6pm; AR$28; ☎011/4362-1100, ⓌЖwww.museoboquense.com), a must for football fans; guided tours of the stadium start from here (daily 11am–5pm hourly; AR$12 extra).

La Boca can be reached by **bus** #29 from Corrientes or Plaza de Mayo, #86 from Plaza de Mayo or #53 from Constitución. Note that La Boca has a bad reputation for **robberies**, so leave your valuables at home and do not stray from the touristy area around Caminito.

Recoleta

Immediately north of the city centre, the wide streets of upper-class Recoleta are most famously home to the **Recoleta Cemetery** at Avenida Quintana and Junín (daily 7am–5.45pm; free), surrounded by café-lined streets and their designer-clad denizens. Immensely popular, it is the resting place of some of Argentina's leading celebrities, including Evita herself, buried under her maiden name of Duarte. A map is available at the entrance to guide you around the great monuments of dark granite, white marble and gleaming bronze.

Next door are the white walls of the **Basílica de Nuestra Señora del Pilar** (daily 7.30am–9.30pm; free; ☎011/4803-6793). The eighteenth-century Jesuit building has been beautifully restored, and is much in demand for fashionable weddings: inside, the magnificent Baroque silver altarpiece, embellished with an Inca sun and other pre-Hispanic details, was made by craftsmen from the north of Argentina. Adjacent, the **Centro Cultural de Recoleta** (Tues–Fri 2–9pm, Sat & Sun 10am–9pm; free; ☎011/4803-1040, Ⓦwww.centroculturalrecoleta.org), at Junín 1930, is a fabulous art space with interesting temporary exhibitions.

If by now you're in need of a coffee or a shopping fix, note that **Buenos Aires Design**, a shopping centre focusing on chic Argentine design products and homeware, adjoins the cultural centre. The large terrace upstairs overlooks a park, and is a great place for an afternoon drink.

Visible from the terrace of Buenos Aires Design, the **Museo Nacional de Bellas Artes** (Tues–Fri 12.30–8.30pm, Sat & Sun 9.30am–8.30pm; free; ☎011/4803-0802, Ⓦwww.mnba .org.ar) is at Avenida del Libertador 1473. Within the imposing, columned building is a traditional art gallery, primarily displaying European paintings but also with a small but valuable collection of colonial and modern Argentine work. For more local artworks, go to the **Museo Xul Solar** (Tues–Fri noon–7.30pm, Sat noon–7pm; AR$10; ☎011/4824-3302, Ⓦwww.xulsolar.org .ar), further to the southwest at Laprida 1212, near the corner of Calle Mansilla, which focuses on the bright and colourful Cubist paintings of twentieth-century Argentine artist Alejandro Xul Solar.

Palermo

Expansive, middle-class **Palermo** stretches around Avenida del Libertador as it heads north from Recoleta, taking in the high-rise apartments near the north of Avenida Santa Fe, the chic cafés and hotels of Palermo Viejo, and the leafy streets and late-night bars of Palermo Hollywood. On or near tree-lined Libertador are three unmissable museums. The **Museo de Arte Decorativo**, Libertador 1902 (Tues–Sun 2–7pm; AR$5; ☎011/4801-8248, ⊛www.mnad.org.ar), is housed in Palacio Errázuriz, one of the city's most original private mansions, with a lovely café in its patio. The collection is of mainly European sculpture, art and furnishings, all beautifully displayed.

At Libertador 2373 you'll find the small and inviting **Museo de Arte Popular Hernández** (Wed–Fri 1–7pm; Sat & Sun 10am–8pm; AR$1, free Sun; ☎011/4801-9019, ⊛www.museohernandez.org.ar) whose displays focus on local silverwork and textiles. A few blocks away, in a striking modern building at Av. Figueroa Alcorta 3415, stands **Malba**, the **Museo de Arte Latinamericano de Buenos Aires** (Thurs–Mon noon–8pm, Wed till 9pm; AR$20, on Wed free for students and AR$8 for adults; ☎011/4808-6500 ⊛www.malba.org.ar). The permanent display of modern Latin American art from the early twentieth century on is a refreshing break from stuffier museums. The art bookshop downstairs is one of the city's best, and the light and modern café (Sun–Wed 9am–9pm, Thurs–Sat until 1am) is recommended. In the foyer there is an excellent cinema showing Argentine and international films (Thurs–Sun 2pm–late; AR$17, students and pensioners AR$8).

The heart of trendy **Palermo Viejo** is Plaza Serrano, officially named **Plaza Cortázar** after the Argentine novelist Julio Cortázar, surrounded by cafés, bars and restaurants. Every Saturday and Sunday (2–8pm) the plaza is host to markets full of locally designed clothes, and craft. Stroll along the connecting streets for fashion boutiques, bookstores and music shops. **Palermo Hollywood** is across the train tracks to the north. Here Calle Humboldt and Calle Fitzroy are home to excellent restaurants and bars, while along Calle Niceto Vega a variety of late-night bars abound.

Mataderos

Over an hour by bus from the centre, **Mataderos** in the southwestern corner of the city, has a bloody past as home to the city's slaughterhouses (big business in the world's beef capital). Today, it is worth a visit for the **Feria de Mataderos**, held on Sunday for most of the year but on Saturday evenings in summer (Jan–March Sat 6pm–midnight, April–Dec Sun 11am–8pm; buses #36, #92 & #126; Mon–Fri ☎011/4323-9400 ext 2830, weekends 011/4687-5602, ⊛www .feriademataderos.com.ar). A celebration of all things gaucho, the Feria has stalls selling leatherwork, *mate*, gourds and silver, as well as folk music and displays of horseriding, plus some of the best *empanadas* in the city.

Arrival

Air All international flights arrive at Ezeiza International Airport (☎011/5480-6111, ⊛www .aa2000.com.ar), 35km (45min) west of the city centre. Manuel Tienda Léon run tourist buses (every 30min; 6am–9pm, less frequent outside these times; AR$45 one-way; ☎011/4315-5115, ⊛www.tiendaleon.com), which drop you at Av. E Madero 1299 (at San Martín) in the Retiro area – for an extra AR$5 per person you get a transfer from the terminal to a specific address in town. A taxi or *remise* (radio cab) will cost around AR$120. Buenos Aires' domestic airport is Aeroparque Jorge Newbery (☎011/5480-6111) on the Costanera Norte, around 6km north of the city centre. Local bus #33 (AR$1.20) runs along the Costanera past the airport and will take you to

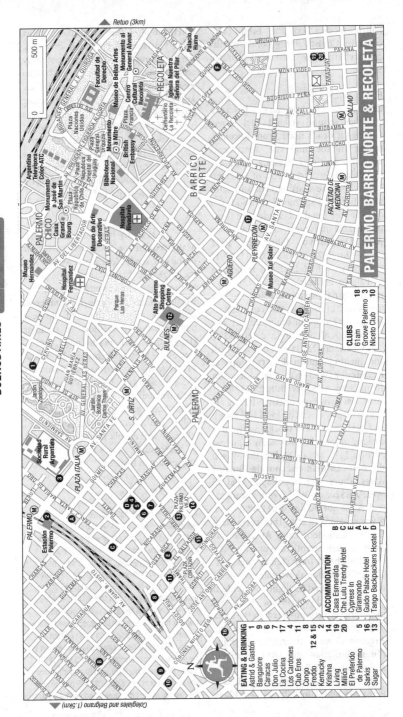

PALERMO, BARRIO NORTE & RECOLETA

▲ Retuo (3km)

0 — 500 m

▲ Colegiales and Belgrano (1.5km)

CLUBS

61am	18
Groove Palermo	3
Niceto Club	10

ACCOMMODATION

Casa Esmeralda	B
Che Lulu Trendy Hotel	C
Cypress In	E
Giramondo	A
Guido Palace Hotel	F
Tango Backpackers Hostel	D

EATING & DRINKING

Astrid & Gastón	1
Bangalore	9
Caracas	6
Don Julio	7
La Cocina	17
Los Cardones	4
Club Eros	11
Congo	8
Freddo	12 & 15
Kentucky	2
Krishna	14
Living	19
Milión	20
El Preferido de Palermo	5
Sarkis	16
Sugar	13

Paseo Colón, on the fringe of the *microcentro*. Note also that Manuel Tienda Léon (see p.65; AR$17) runs a minibus service for not much less than a taxi would cost.

Bus All domestic and international services arrive at Retiro bus terminal, at Avenida Antártida and Ramos Mejía. Taxis are plentiful and the Retiro *subte* (metro) station is just a block away, outside the adjoining train station. A variety of buses (around AR$1.25) leave from outside, including #5 and #50, to Congreso, and #106 to Palermo Viejo. Take extra care around this area, as pickpockets are known to operate.

Ferry Ferry services from Uruguay (see p.925) arrive at Terminal Dársena Norte (often just known as the Terminal Buquebús) at Víamonte y Costanera Sur, just a few blocks from the *microcentro*.

Train The main stations are Retiro, Constitución and Once (W www.tbanet.com.ar). See p.73.

Information

Tourist information There are a number of *centros de informes* around the city run by the Secretaria de Turismo, including one at Av. Alicia Moreau de Justo 200 in Puerto Madero (Mon–Sun 9am–6pm; T 011/4313-0187, W www .bue.gov.ar). Probably the best is at Florida 100 and Av. Diagonal Roque Sáenz Peña (Mon–Sun 9am–6pm). You can also pick up local (and national) information from the well-organized National Tourist Office at Santa Fe 883 (Mon–Fri 9am–5pm; T 011/4312-2232, W www.turismo .gov.ar), which has details of the provincial tourist offices within the capital.

Travel agents and tours Say Hueque, Viamonte 749, 6th Floor (T 011/5199-2517, W www .sayhueque.com) is a professional tour operator covering all of Argentina (and parts of Chile). Agreste, Viamonte 1636 (T 011/4373-4442) offers adventurous trips across the country to destinations such as the Saltos de Moconá, Jujuy and the Valle de la Luna. Buenos Aires Tur, Lavalle 1444, Office 16 (T 011/4371-2304, W www.buenosairestur.com), offers city tours of Buenos Aires, including tango shows, and visits to Tigre and nearby *estancias*. ASATEJ, Florida 835, 3rd Floor (T 011/4114-7528, W www.asatej.com) is a young and dynamic travel agency, offering some of the cheapest flight deals in the city as well as international packages; student discounts available.

City transport

Bus Buses (W www.loscolectivos.com.ar) are one of the most useful (and cheap) ways of getting

round the city – and indeed the only way of reaching many of the outlying districts. Invest in a combined street and bus-route booklet, such as the Guía "T" (AR$10), widely available from street kiosks, to work out the routes. One-way tickets (AR$1.10–1.40) are acquired from a machine on the bus, which gives change for coins (no notes). Many services run all night.

Remise These are radio cabs or minicabs, plain cars booked through an office (and therefore preferred by some wary locals). Not particularly economical for short journeys, they're cheaper than taxis for getting to the airport, and for early morning starts you may prefer to book one; try *Remises Uno* (T 011/4638-8318). It's safest to call a radio taxi at night. Ask your hostel for their preferred company or try Taxi Alo (T 011/4855-5555).

Subte The easiest part of the public transport system to get to grips with is the underground railway or *subte*, which serves the city centre and the north of the city from 5am until 10.30pm (Mon–Sat) and from 8am to 10pm (Sun and public holidays). There are six lines, plus a "premetro" system serving the far southwestern corner of the city, linking up with the *subte* at the Plaza de los Virreyes, at the end of line E. Lines A, B, D and E run from the city centre outwards, while lines C and H (still under construction) run between Retiro and Constitución, connecting them all. Tickets cost AR$1.10 one-way and are bought from the booths at each station. If you are going to travel a lot buy a card of 10 tickets – you can share them, and it saves queuing up, or you can buy a pre-pay swipe card.

Taxis The city's black-and-yellow taxis are spectacularly plentiful. The meter starts at AR$5.20 (charges increase at night), and you should calculate on a ride costing around AR$12 per twenty blocks.

Accommodation

Finding accommodation in Buenos Aires shouldn't be a problem but advance planning is advised, especially for high season. Discounts can sometimes be negotiated, particularly if you are staying for more than a few days.

Hostels

Most hostels have communal kitchens and offer free or cheap internet, breakfast and laundry.
Casa Esmeralda Honduras 5765, at Bonpland T 011/4772-2446. Small, friendly hostel with a shady back garden, hammocks and a large living area. Slightly tired look but a good location to kick back and meet people. Dorms AR$50, rooms AR$150.

Che Lagarto Youth Hostel Venezuela 857, at Piedras ☎011/4343-4845, ⓦwww.chelagarto .com. Rooms are standard but the sociable atmosphere, cool bar/restaurant (meals AR$20–40) and lovely tree-shaded back garden make *Che* a top traveller hangout. Dorms AR$40, rooms AR$180.

Estoril Terrazas A.v de Mayo 1385 (1st & 6th Floors) at Uruguay ☎011/4372 5494, ⓦwww.hostelestoril.com.ar. Directly opposite the Palacio Barolo, one of Buenos Aires' most stunning buildings, *Estoril* has to be among the top hostels in the world. Extremely comfortable and always impeccably clean, it offers all amenities and has a roof terrace with perfect views of Av. de Mayo and Congreso. Ask for the roof-top dorm. Dorms AR$50, rooms AR$180.

Giramondo Guemes 4802 ☎011/4772-6740, ⓦwww.hostelgiramondo.com. Spacious Palermo hostel in an early twentieth century townhouse. Has a vast, lower-ground floor bar area – a great place for partying and meeting fellow travellers. More upmarket "suites" (from AR$155) are down the road at Oro 2472. Dorms AR$40, rooms from AR$105; discounts for long stays.

El Hostal de San Telmo Carlos Calvo 614 and Peru ☎011/4300-6899, ⓦwww.elhostalde santelmo.com. Located in one of the prettiest parts of San Telmo, Buenos Aires' original hostel is cheaper than most, friendly and well kept. Dorms AR$35, rooms AR$110–120.

Hostel Inn – Tango City Piedras 680, at Chile ☎011/4300-5776, ⓦwww.hitangocity.com. Large, fun hostel popular with party animals (there's a themed party every Friday). A plethora of activities is organized, including *asado* nights, Spanish lessons, free walking tours and tango excursions. There's another hostel at Humberto Primo 820. Dorms AR$50, rooms AR$155.

Milhouse Hostel Hipólito Yrigoyen 959 and Bdo de Irigoyen ☎011/4345-9604, ⓦwww.milhousehostel .com. A large, lively hostel in a colonial-style building with a huge range of activities on offer. *Milhouse* opened a new outpost at Av. de Mayo 1245 in 2008. One of the city's most popular, so book well in advance. Full English breakfast AR$20. Dorms AR$48.

Ostinatto Chile 680 and Perú ☎011/4362-9639, ⓦwww.ostinatto.com. Falls squarely in the category of "hip" hostel, with cool minimalist design, spacious dorms and extremely friendly staff. Hosts tango shows and film viewings and there's a decent happy hour in the bar from 6–11pm. More expensive than some other hostels, but well worth it. If you feel like treating yourself there are two self-contained apartments, the loft (AR$330) and penthouse (AR$370). Dorms AR$46, rooms AR$220.

Sandanzas Cultural Hostel Balcarce 1351 and Cochabamba ☎011/4300-7375, ⓦwww .sandanzas.com.ar. One of Buenos Aires' smallest hostels, set slightly off the beaten track. The cosy common room is the setting for a variety of cultural events. Dorms AR$45, rooms AR$160.

Tango Backpackers Hostel Paraguay 4601, at Thames, Palermo Viejo ☎011/4776-6871, ⓦwww .tangobp.com. This party hostel, located next to Plaza Italia (ideal for transport links), is made up of several grand old properties with high ceilings and a lovely library space. There's a large rooftop terrace next to the kitchen. Dorms AR$49, rooms AR$170.

Hotels and B&Bs

Alcázar Av. de Mayo 935 ☎011/4345-0926. This old hotel with a lovely central staircase features basic rooms, all with heating, a fan and private bathroom. AR$170.

Che Lulu Trendy Hotel Pasaje Emilio Zola 5185, at Godoy Cruz, Palermo Viejo ☎011/4772-0289, ⓦwww.chelulu.com. On a colourful *pasaje* in Palermo, *Che Lulu* offers a down-to-earth and homely experience. AR$180.

Cypress In Costa Rica 4828 and Borges ☎011/4833-5834, ⓦwww.cypressin.com. Sleek B&B, with designer features and a neat location in the heart of Palermo's "Soho" area. AR$400 (20 percent discount for cash).

The Four Hotel Carlos Calvo 535 and Bolívar ☎011/4362-1729, ⓦwww.thefourhotel.com. This B&B in a traditional San Telmo house has stylish but affordable rooms, personalized service and a gorgeous terrace. AR$195.

Gran Hotel Hispano Av. de Mayo 861, at Tacuari ☎011/4345-2020, ⓦwww.hhispano.com.ar. Metres from the famous *Café Tortoni*, this family-run classic retains its original Spanish-style architecture. Most rooms are centred on a beautiful old courtyard, while some have balconies looking onto the street below. AR$220.

Guido Palace Hotel Guido 1780 and Callao ☎011/4812-0674, ⓦwww.guidopalace.com.ar. This 60-room hotel is an affordable, no-frills option in upmarket Recoleta, near the cemetery. Triples and quadruple rooms are also available. AR$260.

Marbella Av. de Mayo 1261 ☎011/4383-8566, ⓦwww.hotelmarbella.com.ar. Calm, good-value lodgings in a central location. Rooms are modern with cable TV and decent-sized bathrooms, and there is also an economical restaurant. AR$230 (discounts for cash).

Posada de la Luna Perú 565 and México ☎011/4343-0911, ⓦwww.posadaluna.com. Attractively decorated B&B set in a colonial townhouse between San Telmo and the Centro. Home-made bread and jam is served with breakfast and there's a jacuzzi and sun deck. No hotel sign outside the door means it's still a relatively well-kept secret. AR$280.

Roma Av. de Mayo 1413 and Uruguay ☎011/4381-4921. Low prices and a central location are the draw at the *Roma*. Slightly noisy rooms, some with balconies looking onto Av. de Mayo. Doubles AR$150.

Eating

Buenos Aires has a busy, increasingly diverse, restaurant scene. Many restaurants offer a good-value *menu del día* (lunchtime set menu) on weekdays, usually including a drink; this is an excellent way to sample the best of BA's restaurants at much lower prices. It is wise to book at the more popular places.

Downtown

Cbc – California Burrito Co. Lavalle 441, Centre ☎011/4328-3056, ⊛www.californiaburritoco .com. Busy central burrito joint, ideally placed for lunch on the go. White-flour tortillas are packed with seemingly endless combinations of fresh ingredients; portions are enormous. Three burrito and drink special from AR$20. Open Mon–Fri noon–11pm, Sat & Sun noon–7pm.

Las Cuartetas Av. Corrientes 838, Centre ☎011/4326-0171. Big, brightly lit Corrientes pizzeria, opposite the Gran Rex theatre. Large pizzas from AR$40. Open Mon–Sat lunch and dinner, Sun dinner only.

Freddo Around town, including Alto Palermo Shopping and Armenia 1618 ⊛www.freddo .com.ar. Buenos Aires' best ice-cream chain. *Dulce de leche* fans will be in heaven, and the passionfruit mousse flavour (*maracuyá mousse*) is superb. Branches throughout the city. Prices from AR$14.

La Giralda Corrientes 1453. ☎011/4371-3846. Brightly lit and austerely decorated Corrientes café, famous for its *chocolate espeso con churros* (AR$24). A perennial hangout for students and intellectuals, and a good place to observe the *porteño* passion for conversation. Open Mon–Sat 7am–2am.

La Gran Taberna Combate de los Pozos 95, Montserrat ☎011/4951-7586. A popular, bustling and down-to-earth restaurant a block from the Congreso. The vast, reasonably priced menu offers a mixture of Spanish dishes, including a good selection of seafood, *porteño* staples and a sprinkling of more exotic dishes such as *ranas a la provenzal* (frogs' legs with parsley and garlic, AR$95). Many dishes are large enough to share. Mains AR$30–50. Open daily noon–4pm & 8pm–2am.

Pura Vida Reconquista 516, Centre ☎011/4393-0093. American-style juice and health food bar serving a mainly business clientele looking for an alternative to beef. Lunch specials include soup and half a wrap (AR$24). Juices from AR$10.50 and salads AR$20. Open Mon–Fri 9am–7pm & Sat 10.30am–5pm.

San Telmo and La Boca

Brasserie Pétanque Defensa 596, San Telmo ☎011/4342-7930, ⊛www.brasseriepetanque.com. Authentic and chic French-owned brasserie, serving French classics (onion soup, steak tartare, crème brûlée and even snails). Weekday lunch deal AR$35 (main course and drink). Closed Monday evening.

El Desnivel Defensa 855, San Telmo ☎011/4300-9081, ⊛www.parrillael desnivel.com.ar. Classic San Telmo *parrilla* with accessible prices, great meat and a friendly, slightly rowdy atmosphere; popular with tourists. *Lomo* steak AR$42. Closed Monday lunch.

Gran Parrilla del Plata Chile 594, San Telmo ☎011/4300-8588, ⊛www.parrilladelplata.com. Excellent-value steakhouse whose *medallón de lomo* (AR$47) has to be one of the tenderest cuts in town. Open daily for lunch and dinner (closed Sun lunch).

El Obrero Caffarena 64, La Boca ☎011/4362-9912, ⊛www.bodegonelobrero.com.ar. With Boca Juniors souvenirs on the walls and tango musicians moving from table to table at weekends, the atmosphere at the hugely popular and moderately priced *El Obrero* is as much a part of the fun as the simple homely food (*lomo* steak AR$26, pasta dishes AR$19). Very popular, so prepare to line up at weekends. Get a taxi there as the local area can be unsafe. Closed Sun.

Parrilla 1880 Defensa 1665, San Telmo ☎011/4307-2746. Extremely good *parrilla* joint, right opposite Parque Lezama. Its walls are lined with photos and drawings from the restaurant's famous and mostly bohemian clients, and the very friendly owner makes sure everyone is happy. Mains AR$30–50. Closed Sun night and all day Mon.

Palermo and around

Club Eros Uriarte 1609, Palermo Viejo ☎011/4832-1313. Fun, noisy cantina at a neighbourhood sports and social club, offering Argentine standards at bargain prices. Half a *bife de chorizo* costs AR$20, pasta dishes are from AR$14 and a bottle of Argentina's favourite tipple, Vasco Viejo, is only AR$16. Open daily noon–3.30pm and 8.30pm–midnight.

La Cocina Pueyrredón 1508, Recoleta
☎011/4825-3171. Tiny place serving *locro* (a filling
corn stew from the northeast of Argentina; AR$18)
and a selection of delicious Catamarca-style
empanadas (AR$5 each). Closed Sun.

Don Julio Guatemala 4699, Palermo Viejo
☎011/4831-9564. Excellent *parrilla* with
choice cuts of meat, a good wine list and smart,
efficient service. *Lomo*, fries, salad and wine will
set you back AR$70–80. Open daily noon–4.30pm
& 7.30pm–1am.

Kentucky Santa Fe 4602, Palermo Viejo
☎011/4773-7869. A Buenos Aires institution that's
been around since 1942, serving excellent pizzas and
empanadas. Expect old-school waiters in white shirts
and bow-ties, and a grungy clientele. The *empanadas*
are large and worth the higher than normal price of
AR$5, while promo deals include two slices of mozza-
rella pizza, one *faina* and a glass of beer or wine for
AR$13. Open daily until late (open 24hr on Fri & Sat).
There's also a sister restaurant at Santa Fe 4202.

Krishna Malabia 1833, Palermo Viejo ☎011/4833-
4618. Tiny bohemian spot on Plaza Palermo
Viejo run by the International Society for Krishna
Consciousness and serving tasty vegetarian Indian
food. Go for the mixed *thali* (AR$35) with a ginger
lemonade (AR$8). Closed Mon. Open lunch only on
Tues and Wed–Sun lunch and dinner.

El Preferido de Palermo Borges y Guatemala,
Palermo Viejo ☎011/4774-6585. Fun, *pulpería*-
style diner with bottles and cans packing the
shelves and hams hanging from the ceiling. Menu
choices include a lentil and bacon stew (AR$30)
and *milanesa* (breaded escalope) with potatoes
(AR$25). Open Mon–Sat 10.30am–11.30pm.

Sarkis Thames 1101, Villa Crespo ☎011/4772-
4911. Excellent tabbouleh (AR$13), *keppe crudo*

(raw meat with onion – much better than it sounds;
AR$22) and falafel (AR$25) at this popular restaurant serving a fusion of Armenian, Arab and Turkish
cuisine. Close to Palermo Viejo, and great value for
money (very popular so expect of large queues).
Open daily for lunch and dinner.

Drinking and nightlife

You'll find that Buenos Aires offers a lively nightlife
every day of the week. The only exception is
perhaps on Monday, when some venues, especially
in the centre, tend to close. Wednesday is known
as "After Office", and you'll find the city's bars and
clubs packed from 6pm. Keep in mind that Buenos
Aires starts – and finishes – late, so clubs don't
fill up until the early hours. Check out What's Up
Buenos Aires (Ⓦwww.whatsupbuenosaires.com)
for up-to-date information and articles on the city's
cultural and nightlife happenings, or Wipe (Ⓦwww
.wipe.com.ar; Spanish only).

Bars and pubs

Bangalore Humboldt 1416, Palermo Viejo
☎011/4779-2621. Fine traditional pub in Palermo
"Hollywood", popular with locals, expats and
tourists. Happy hour until 10pm; pints and curries
served. Open daily.

Bar Británico Corner of Defensa and Brasil, San
Telmo ☎011/4361-2107. Old men, bohemians
and night owls while away the small hours in this
traditional wood-panelled bar overlooking Parque
Lezama. Open 24hr.

Los Cardones Jorge Luis Borges 2180
☎011/4777-1112, Ⓦwww.cardones.com.ar. One of
the best *peñas* in town – a bar where traditional folk
musicians play. Does two for one on litres of Brahma
on Wed and Thurs. Open Wed–Sat from 9pm.

La Cigale 25 de Mayo 597, Centro ☎011/4312-
8275. One of Buenos Aires' most happening bars,
attracting an up-for-it crowd. Regularly hosts live
music and DJs. Open Mon–Fri from 6pm & Sat from
8pm. Closed Sun.

Caracas Guatemala 4802, Palermo ☎011/4776-
8704, Ⓦwww.caracasbar.com. Trendy Palermo
Viejo venue attracting a cool crowd. Has a lovely
roof terrace and serves Venezuelan food. Decent
happy hour – including artisan beer – every evening
6pm–midnight. Open Mon–Sat 7pm–5am.

Congo Honduras 5329, Palermo ☎011/4833-5857.
Sleek interiors and atmospheric lighting at this
popular hang-out. Particularly heaving in summer
thanks to a stunning outside area. Closed Mon.

Milión Paraná 1048 ☎011/4815-9925, Ⓦwww
.milion.com.ar. Grand bar housed in a turn-of-the-
century townhouse. Overrun with gringos these

days, but a decent place to start the night and another venue with a great garden. Open from noon daily, except Sat & Sun (eve only).

La Poesía Chile 502 ☎011/4300-7340. Old-fashioned establishment that feels a bit like a Spanish tapas bar. From the owners of the equally excellent *El Federal* (Carlos Calvo 599), *La Poesía* serves three types of artisan beer (AR$9–10) and does a wide range of *picada* tasting platters (AR$29–52). Open daily until 2am.

Sugar Costa Rica 4619 ☎011/4831-3276, ⓦwww.sugarbuenosaires.com. Not the place to come if you're looking for an authentic *porteño* night out. This American-run bar feels more US frat party than BA boozer. But if you fancy a decent hamburger and a ridiculously cheap happy hour (7pm–midnight), with pints of beer for AR$8, then *Sugar* is your bar. Open daily noon–5am.

Vaca Profana Lavalle 3683, Abasto ☎011/4867-0934, ⓦwww.vacaprofana.com.ar. Pint-sized venue with excellent programme of music (check the website for the schedule). Tapas served. Closed Jan.

Nightclubs

Amerika Gascón 1040, Villa Crespo ☎011/4865-4416, ⓦwww.ameri-k.com.ar. The city's biggest gay club, with three dancefloors playing mainly electro. Open Thurs–Sun.

Crobar Marcelo Freyres s/n, Paseo de la Infanta ☎011/4778-1500, ⓦwww.crobar.com.ar. Glitzy club near the Hipódromo Argentino that plays commercial dance music and regularly welcomes international DJs like the Godskitchen collective. Open Fri & Sat from 11.30pm.

Glam Cabrera 3046, Barrio Norte ☎011/4963-2521, ⓦwww.glambsas.com.ar. One of the city's hottest gay bar-discos. Several lounge areas and and dancefloors play everything from Latino beats to 1980s classics. Thurs & Sat from 1am.

Groove Palermo Av. Santa Fe 4389 ⓦwww.palermogroove.com. Club specializing in live music, often rock and international bands. Also one of the host venues of legendary alternative rock/reggae nights Fiesta Clandestina. Open Sat night for club nights and for live music during the week (see website for listings).

Living M T de Alvear 1540, Centro ☎011/4811-4730, ⓦwww.living.com.ar. Laidback club in a rambling old building with two bars, a coffee stand and a long, narrow dancefloor that gets very packed. Plays a fun, danceable mix of funk, disco and rock music. Open from 7pm Thurs and from 10pm Fri & Sat.

Maluco Beleza Sarmiento 1728, Centre ☎011/4372-1737, ⓦwww.malucobeleza.com.ar.

Long-running Brazilian club, playing a mix of *lambada*, afro-samba and reggae to a lively crowd of Brazilians and Brazilophiles. Wed & Fri–Sun.

Niceto Club Niceto Vega 5510, Palermo Viejo ☎011/4779-9396, ⓦwww.nicetoclub.com. One of BA's best clubs, *Niceto* has a roster of mainly reggae and electronic music at weekends, regularly hosting Zizek nights (electro *cumbia* meets reggae, hip-hop and reggaeton). Live gigs before 1.30am most nights.

Entertainment

Cultural centres

Buenos Aires has a number of excellent and popular cultural centres promoting culture and the arts. Entry is free, although special temporary exhibitions occasionally charge a fee.

Centro Cultural Borges Viamonte 525 ☎011/5555-5358, ⓦwww.ccborges.org.ar. Named after Argentina's most famous writer; there's a permanent area dedicated to him, as well as exhibitions, a cinema and workshops. Open Mon–Sat 10am–9pm and Sun 12pm–9pm.

Centro Cultural Recoleta Junín 1930 ☎011/4803-1040, ⓦwww.centroculturalrecoleta.org. Located next to the famous cemetery, this is an excellent centre with a particular focus on visual arts. Open Mon–Fri 2pm–9pm and Sat & Sun 10am–9pm.

Ciudad Cultural Konex Sarmiento 3131 ☎011/4864-3200, ⓦwww.ciudadculturalkonex.org. Atmospheric cultural centre in converted warehouse, located in the Once part of town. Hosts film and theatre productions as well as live music. Also the spiritual home of legendary drumming outfit La Bomba de Tiempo. Open daily.

ND Ateneo Espacio Cultural Paraguay 918 ☎011/4328-2888, ⓦwww.ndateneo.com.ar. Cultural space and theatre with an emphasis on live music. Has shows from 9pm most evenings and there are also regular evening debates.

Tango shows

Tango shows are expensive (expect to pay upwards of AR$150; more with dinner), but they are the best way to see a series of top tango dancers in one evening, and most are well worth the splurge. All the following have nightly shows, and most include dinner. Prices range from around AR$80 (without food) to VIP treatment with haute cuisine for as much as AR$900.

Bar Sur Estados Unidos 299, at Balcarce, San Telmo ☎011/4362-6086, ⓦwww.bar-sur.com.ar. This cosy little joint puts on fancy shows and encourages audience participation.

MILONGAS

Milongas – regular dance clubs, usually starting with lessons (beginners welcome) – are popular with tango dancers young and old. They are a great way to try the moves for yourself and to get a feel for the scene for a fraction of the price of a dinner show (entrance usually costs AR$5–15). Among the city's best *milongas* are *La Viruta* (Armenia 1366, Palermo ℡011/4774-6357), *Salón Canning* (Scalabrini Ortiz 1331, Palermo ℡011/4832-6753), *La Catedral* (Sarmiento 4006, Almagro ℡011/15-5325-1630) and *Centro Cultural Torquato Tasso* (Defensa 1575, San Telmo ℡011/4307-6506). *Confitería Ideal* (Suipacha 380–384, San Nicolas ℡011/5265-8069), a beautiful if crumbling relic of a dancehall, also holds afternoon classes.

Café Tortoni Av. de Mayo 829, Centre ℡011/4342-4328, ⓦwww.cafetortoni.com.ar. Buenos Aires' most famous café offers an affordable and rather theatrical tango show downstairs at AR$80–100.

Esquina Carlos Gardel Carlos Gardel 3200, Abasto ℡011/4867-6363 ⓦwww.esquinacarlos gardel.com.ar. Although very touristy, this smart venue, named after the king of tango, remains a classic. Shows from AR$295 (without food).

Piazzolla Tango Florida 165, Microcentro ℡011/4344-8200 ⓦwww.piazzollatangoshow .com. Housed in a grand old theatre in the centre, the show here is made up of two singers, an orchestra and a set of tango dancers, with prices starting at US$78.

El Viejo Almacén Av. Independencia 300, at Balcarce, San Telmo ℡011/4307-6689. Dinner and show from 8pm or show only from 10pm.

Shopping

Buenos Aires offers some of the best shopping in South America, from high-end designer stores and air-conditioned malls to weekend markets and cutting-edge boutiques. Best buys include leather goods (handbags, belts, shoes), wine, home design and handicrafts (particularly handmade jewellery). Top shopping areas include Avenida Santa Fe, Palermo Viejo and San Telmo. Downtown Calle Florida is a famous shopping street from yesteryear but is a bit of a tourist trap today.

Malls The city's malls house Argentina's most successful brands, as well as big international names; they open every day of the week until 10pm. Try Alto Palermo (Santa Fé and Coronel Díaz, Palermo, ⓦwww.altopalermo.com.ar), Galerías Pacífico (Florida and Córdoba, Centre, ⓦwww .progaleriaspacifico.com.ar) or Paseo Alcorta (Salguero 3172 and Figueroa Alcorta, Palermo Chico, ⓦwww.paseoalcorta.com.ar); the last named has a large Carrefour hypermarket downstairs. The largest of all is Unicenter

(ⓦwww.unicenter.com.ar), north of the city in the outer suburbs, full of designer shops, a cinema, and with an IMAX close by. You can get there on the #60 bus from the centre, or by taxi.

Markets The city's *ferias* usually take place on weekends and are an excellent place to pick up inexpensive local handicrafts. The most extensive are: the Feria "Hippy" next to Recoleta cemetery (Sat & Sun); Plaza Dorrego in San Telmo, spreading half a dozen blocks along Defensa (Sun); and the Feria de Mataderos (p.65; Sat or Sun depending on time of year). For locally made and designed clothes head to Plaza Serrano in Palermo, weekends from 3pm onwards, when the cafés surrounding the plaza are converted into indoor markets filled to the brim with affordable clothes and jewellery.

Palermo Viejo After the economic crash of the early noughties, this low-rise area became a hotbed of creative and design talent, and the streets have since filled to bursting with tiny, beautifully presented boutiques. The area is perfect for browsing but choice boutiques include: Condimentos (Honduras 4874) for comely local jewellery designs, 28 Sport (Gurruchaga 1481) for top-quality shoes for men and women, and SoldBA (Costa Rica 4656), cool T-shirt heaven.

Directory

Banks and exchange The centre has a host of casas de cambio for foreign exchange or traveller's cheques; shop around for the best rate. Banks will also change to or from dollars.

Embassies and consulates Australia, Villanueva 1400 ℡011/4779 3500; Bolivia, Av. Corrientes 545, 2nd Floor ℡011/4394-1463; Brazil, Cerrito 1350 ℡011/4515 2400; Canada, Tagle 2828 ℡011/4808-1000; Chile, Peña 547℡011/4331-6228; Ireland, Av. del Libertador 1060, 6th Floor ℡011/5787-0801; New Zealand, Carlos Pellegrini 1427, 5th Floor ℡011/4328-0747; UK, Dr Luis Agote 2412 ℡011/4808-2200; United States,

Av. Colombia 4300 ☎011/5777-4533; Uruguay, Av. Las Heras 1907 ☎011/4807-3040.

Hospitals Private hospitals: Hospital Británico (Pedriel 74 ☎011/4309-6400) has English-speaking doctors and 24hr emergency care; for non-emergency visits there is also a more central location at Marcelo T de Alvear 1573 (☎011/4812-0040). Hospital Alemán (Av. Pueyrredón 1640, between Beruti and Juncal ☎011/4827-7000), emergency (enter on Beruti) and non-emergency care; English spoken. Public hospital: Hospital Juan A Fernández (Cerviño 3356, at Bulnes, ☎011/4808-2600).

Internet Internet cafés are everywhere in Buenos Aires, and many *locutorios* (phone shops) also have internet; rates are inexpensive and they tend to open late.

Laundry Laundries are plentiful and inexpensive (though not usually self-service). Expect to pay around AR$8–15 for a wash and dry.

Left luggage Retiro bus station and both the domestic and international airports have left luggage services. Your hostel may be prepared to look after your luggage if you have a return booking. The services of South American Explorers (☎011/430-79625, ⓦwww.saexplorers.org) include luggage storage. Visit their clubhouse in San Telmo (Estados Unidos 577) for details.

Pharmacies Pharmacies are plentiful. Farmacity (ⓦwww.farmacity.com.ar) has branches throughout the city, many open 24hr (for example, at Florida 474, between Corrientes and Lavalle, Centre, ☎011/4322-6559).

Police In an emergency call 101. Tourist Police, Comisaría del Turista, Av. Corrientes 436, ☎011/4346-5748 or 4346-7000 ext 1801/5748 or 0800-999-5000 (24hr), English spoken.

Post office Correo Argentina has branches all over town (ⓦwww.correoargentino.com.ar).

Moving on

Air Aerolíneas Argentinas and LAN Argentina both fly to all major cities in Argentina, usually with several services daily. Andes flies to Salta (daily Sun–Fri) and Puerto Madryn (Mon, Wed & Fri), while LADE (Perú 714 ☎0810-810-5233), the former army airline, also has cheap but infrequent flights around the country.

Bus All services arrive and depart from Retiro bus station (Terminal de Omnibus). Domestic services to: Bariloche (19–25hr), Córdoba (9–11hr), Mendoza (14–16hr), Neuquén (14–19hr), Puerto Iguazú (17–18hr), Puerto Madryn (18–20hr), Rosario (4hr), Salta (20–22hr). International services to: La Paz (48hr), Montevideo (8–9hr), Santiago de Chile (19hr), São Paulo (34hr), Rio de Janeiro (40hr).

Ferry The most efficient and cheapest way to get to Uruguay is by ferry. The two main companies are Colonia Express (Pedro de Mendoza 330, Dársena Sur; ☎011/4313-5100, ⓦwww.coloniaexpress .com) and Buquebus (Av. Antartida Argentina 821; ☎011/4316-6500, ⓦwww.buquebus.com). Prices from around AR$85 one-way to Colonia, AR$150 to Montevideo. Depending on which boat you board it can take between 30min–3hr to reach Uruguay. Unless you are going on a weekend or public holiday you can buy your tickets an hour before the boat leaves but it's worth booking in advance online for the best rates.

Train These days, the railway is little used in Argentina as a means of long-distance travel, with the exception of services from Retiro station (Av. Ramos Mejía, just to the east of Plaza San Martín) to Córdoba (Mon & Fri; 15–16hr; AR$30–90; Ferrocentral ☎011/4108-8800), Tucumán (Mon & Fri; 25hr; AR$45–130; Ferrocentral), Rosario (twice daily; 7–8hr; AR$40; ☎0800-333-3822) and the provinces of Buenos Aires and La Pampa. Retiro is also the departure point for trains to Tigre (except the *Tren de la Costa*, see p.74) and the northern suburbs. Trains to the Atlantic Coast and La Plata leave from Constitución; those to Mercedes and Lobos in the province of Buenos Aires and Santa Rosa from Once.

Around Buenos Aires

Argentina's most spectacular scenery can feel frustratingly far from the capital, but, thankfully, Buenos Aires province offers several rewarding – and easily accessible – destinations for a day-trip or more. **Tigre**, just north of Buenos Aires, is the gateway to the watery recreation of the Paraná Delta. A trip to the provincial capital, **La Plata**, is essential for natural history enthusiasts; the city's Museo de la Plata is home to an extraordinary array of megafauna skeletons. And a slice of gaucho life is the draw at **San Antonio de Areco**, where late nineteenth-century houses and cobbled streets combine with gaucho culture to charming effect. Taking the ferry across the Río de la Plata to **Colonia**, in Uruguay (see p.929), also makes a great day out. Wandering around the old town's cobbled streets – a UNESCO World Heritage Site – and eating in the sunny main plaza is a welcome relief from busy Buenos Aires.

TIGRE AND THE DELTA

A short train ride north of the city centre, the river port of **TIGRE** distributes the timber and fruit produced in the delta of the **Paraná River**. Originally a remote system of rivers dotted with inaccessible islands, the Delta is now crowded with weekend homes and riverside restaurants.

What to see and do

The river itself is the principal attraction. To experience it, head for Tigre's **Estación Fluvial** from where inexpensive local wooden ferries leave every twenty minutes or so. Take one of these to "Tres Bocas" (AR$19.50) where there are two or three good restaurants and cafés with riverfront verandas, or simply enjoy a cruise. A tourist office at the Estación Fluvial can give you a map of the islands and details of the numerous boat companies serving them (among them Río Tur ☎011/4731-0280, ⒲www .rioturcatamaranes.com.ar, leaving from the Los Mimbreros dock, and Sturla ☎011/4731-1300, ⒲www.sturlaviajes .com.ar, from the Estación Fluvial). The town of Tigre is often forgotten by tourists plying the river, but it too has some interesting places to visit. About four blocks from the Estación Fluvial is the colourful **Puerto de Frutos** (daily 10am–6pm) where hundreds of baskets made from Delta plants, spices, wooden furniture, and handicrafts are on sale. Across the bridge you'll find the ageing but well thought-out **Museo Naval**, at Paseo Victorica 602 (Mon–Fri 8.30am–5.30pm, Sat & Sun 10.30am–6.30pm; AR$3) and if you keep walking up the

river the spectacular **Tigre Club**, now the **Museo de Arte Tigre** (Wed–Fri 10am–7pm, Sat & Sun noon–7pm, AR$5), will come into view. The carefully restored early twentieth-century building gives an idea of how the other half lived, and there are great views from the terrace.

Arrival

Train To get to Tigre you can either take a direct train from Retiro (Mitre line, every 10min; 1hr; AR$1.35) or take the train to Bartolomé Mitre (every 15min), walk across the bridge to Maipú station, and jump on the more scenic *Tren de la Costa* (every 20min; AR$12 one-way). This train runs through the older suburbs and stations to the north of the city.

Accommodation

Delta Hostel Coronel Morales 1418, Tigre ☎011/5245-9776, ⒲www.tigredeltahostel.com. ar. This friendly hostel offers free massages and organizes a host of activities such as boat trips and kayaking on the Delta, as well as typical Argentine *asados*. Dorms AR$50, rooms AR$220.

Eating and drinking

There are numerous cheap and cheerful *parrillas* on the mainland. A more romantic option, however, is to stop off by boat at one of the secluded riverside restaurants.
Beixa Flor Arroyo Abra Vieja 148, ☎011/4728-2397, ⒲www.beixaflor.com.ar. This quiet and colourful restaurant serves up delicious home-made food (ranging from river fish to *bife de chorizo*) out in its peaceful garden or by its private beach. If you can't bear to tear yourself away, book yourself into one of their rooms for the night. Three-course meal around AR$100. Open all day every day.

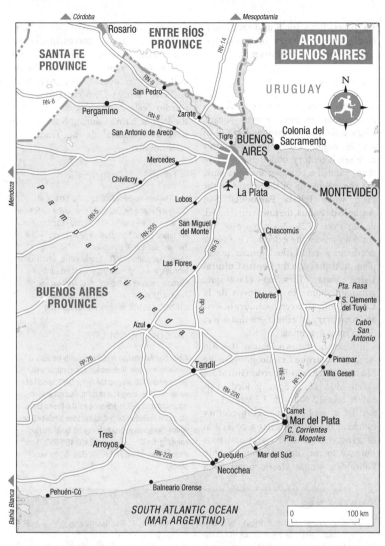

AROUND BUENOS AIRES

Córdoba Mesopotamia

N

ENTRE RÍOS PROVINCE

RN-14

SANTA FE PROVINCE

URUGUAY

Rosario

RN-9

San Pedro

RN-8

Pergamino Zarate

RN-8

San Antonio de Areco Tigre **BUENOS AIRES**

Colonia del Sacramento

Mercedes

Chivilcoy La Plata **MONTEVIDEO**

Mendoza

P
a
m
p
a

RN-5

Lobos

RN-205

San Miguel del Monte Chascomús

RN-3

Las Flores

H
ú
m
e
d
a

BUENOS AIRES PROVINCE

Dolores Pta. Rasa
S. Clemente del Tuyú

Cabo San Antonio

RP-30

Azul

RP-76 Pinamar

RN-11 Villa Gesell

Tandil

RN-226 RN-2

Camet
Mar del Plata
C. Corrientes
Pta. Mogotes

Tres Arroyos

RN-228 Quequén Mar del Sud

Necochea

Pehuén-Có Balneario Orense

Bahía Blanca

SOUTH ATLANTIC OCEAN (MAR ARGENTINO)

0   100 km

El Gato Blanco Rio Capitán 80, ☎011/4728-0390, ⓦwww.gato-blanco.com. A family favourite, *El Gato Blanco* has an attractive deck area and flower-filled garden, as well as a mini playground. Inside is an elegant tea room. Three-course meal around AR$100. Open daily for lunch.

SAN ANTONIO DE ARECO

The refined pampas town of **SAN ANTONIO DE ARECO**, set on the meandering Río Areco 110km northwest of Buenos Aires, is the spiritual home of the gaucho or Argentine cowboy. A robust tourist industry has grown around the gaucho tradition: silver and leather handi-craft workers peddle their wares in the town's shops, historic **estancias** (ranches) accommodate visitors in the surrounding countryside and an annual **gaucho festival** draws massive crowds every November. While bicycles rule the streets here, you'll also spot beret-clad *estancia* workers on horseback, trotting about the cobblestones.

What to see and do

The leafy town centre is laid out in a grid fashion around the main square, **Plaza Ruiz de Arellano**, and is full of genteel, slightly decaying, single-storey nineteenth-century buildings, many of them painted a blushing shade of pink. On the south side of the square, is the plain white **Iglesia Parroquial San Antonio de Padua**, the town's first chapel, dating from 1728. A sculpture of San Antonio graces the exterior. One block north, in a refurbished former power plant at Alsina 66, is the **Centro Cultural Usina Vieja** (Tues–Sun 11am–5pm; AR$1.50), home to the **Museo de la Ciudad**, with nineteenth-century objects and temporary art exhibitions that depict life in rural Argentina.

Just north of town, across the Río Areco, lies **Parque Criollo**, home to the **Museo Gauchesco Ricardo Güiraldes** (Wed–Mon 11am–5pm; guided visits Sat & Sun 12.30pm & 3.30pm; A$4). Set in a replica nineteenth-century *estancia*, the museum has a collection of gaucho art and artefacts and pays homage to the life of author Ricardo Güiraldes, whose classic novel, *Don Segundo Sombra* (1926) – set in San Antonio de Areco – served to elevate the *mate*-sucking, horse-breaking, cow-herding gaucho from rebellious outlaw to respected and romantic national icon. Demonstrations of gaucho feats are held every year in the Parque Criollo during November's week-long **Fiesta de la Tradición** celebrations.

Arrival and information

Bus The bus station (☎02326/453-904) is at General Paz and Av. Dr Smith, a six-block walk from the town centre along Calle Segundo Sombra. There are buses to and from Buenos Aires (every 1–2hr; 2hr) and Rosario (6 daily; 4hr).

Tourist information The tourist office, which loans bicycles, is a short walk from the main square towards the river at the corner of Arellano and Zerboni (Mon–Fri 8am–7pm; Sat & Sun till 8pm ☎02326/453165, ⓦwww.visiteareco.com).

Accommodation

While San Antonio de Areco can easily be visited on a day-trip from Buenos Aires, you might well be charmed into staying the night. Book ahead at weekends (the town is a popular destination for *porteños*) and well in advance for the Fiesta de la Tradición in November, or contact the tourist office, which can arrange homestays with families. For camping, try *Club River* (☎02326/453-590), 1km west of town along Zerboni, AR$50–60 for two people.

ESTANCIAS

Reflecting Argentina's changing economic climate, many of the country's estancias – vast cattle and horse estates once lorded over by wealthy European settlers – are staying afloat by moving into the tourism market and converting into luxury accommodation. For anyone with latent aristocratic or cowboy aspirations, *estancias* offer the chance to milk cows, ride horses, go fly-fishing, play polo or simply tuck into a juicy slab of steak plucked straight off the *asado* while swanning poolside with a glass of Malbec.

Running the gamut from simple family farmhouses to Pampas dude ranches and ostentatious Italianate mansions, *estancias* are a character-filled throwback to the Argentina of yesteryear. For a list of *estancias* offering accommodation in and around San Antonio de Areco, see ⓦwww.visiteareco.com or sanantoniodeareco.com. For more information on *estancias* in other parts of Argentina, visit ⓦwww.estanciasargentinas.com, www.estanciastravel.com, www.estanciasenargentina.com or www.ranchweb.com.

Hostal de Areco Zapiola 25 ☏ 02326/456-118, ⓦ www.hostaldeareco.com.ar. Centrally-located in a pink colonial building, this B&B has a nice sunny garden and offers decent doubles with private bathrooms. AR$150.

Hostel Gaucho Zerboni 308 ☏ 02326/453-625, ⓦ www.hostelgaucho.com.ar. Decent, centrally located option with friendly staff and free access to the all-important barbecue equipment. Dorms AR$65, rooms AR$170.

Eating and drinking

Many of San Antonio de Areco's restaurants and bars have been given Old World-style makeovers, and their continued patronage by weathered *estancia* workers gives them an air of authenticity.

Almacén de Ramos Generales Zapiola 143 ☏ 02326/456376, ⓦ www.ramosgeneralesareco.com.ar. Old bottles and gaucho paraphernalia line the walls of this delightful *parrilla;* the rabbit and trout specials and waist-softening desserts ensure a steady stream of regulars. Mains around AR$50. Open all day every day.

La Esquina de Merti Arellano 149 ☏ 02326/456705, ⓦ www.esquinademerti.com.ar. Dolled up like a traditional corner store, this spacious and atmospheric plaza-side restaurant excels in fast and friendly service. *Parrilla* for two AR$70; pastas around AR$25. Open daily until 1am.

La Olla de Cobre Matheu 433 ☏ 02326/453105, ⓦ www.laolladecobre.com.ar. A small chocolate factory and sweet shop selling superb house-made *alfajores*. Sample before buying. Closed Tues.

LA PLATA

La Plata became the capital of the province of Buenos Aires in 1880, when the city of Buenos Aires was made the Federal Capital. Close enough to make an easy day-trip, it has a relaxed, small city feel. The geometric design, by French architect Pedro Benoît, and grid-numbered streets, were designed to make navigating the city easy but at times do exactly the opposite.

What to see and do

The most famous attractions can be found north of the city centre, next to the zoo, and in the middle of the pleasant **Paseo del Bosque**, a lush parkland. The **Museo de la Plata** (Tues–Sun 10am–6pm; AR$6) was the first museum built in Latin America and has a wonderful collection of skeletons, stuffed animals and fossils, set in a crumbling building in the midst of the university. Though desperately in need of refurbishment, the museum is well worth visiting to see the vast whale bones and the models of prehistoric animals.

From the Paseo del Bosque (Av. Iraola), avenidas 51 and 53 lead down through the historic centre to the **Plaza Moreno**. On its far side stands the colossal, neo-Gothic brick **Catedral**, with an impressive marble interior of thick columns and high vaulted ceilings. Roughly halfway between the two is **Plaza San Martín**, the lively heart of the city. On the western side, the **Centro Cultural Pasaje Dardo Rocha** (daily 9am–10pm; free) occupies the city's former train station, taking up an entire block between avenidas 49 and 50, 6 and 7. Behind the elegant, French- and Italian-influenced facade are housed a cinema and various exhibition spaces, including the excellent **Museo de Arte Contemporáneo Latinoamericano** (summer Tues–Fri 10am–8pm, Sat & Sun 4pm–10pm; winter Tues–Fri 10am–8pm, Sat & Sun 2–9pm; free).

Arrival and information

Bus Buses for La Plata leave from Retiro bus station every 30min (1hr 10min; AR$7 one-way).
Train The train journey from Constitución station is much slower than travelling by bus. Trains leave approximately every 30min (1hr 30 min; AR$2.10).
Tourist information There's a tourist office inside the Pasaje Dardo Rocha cultural centre (daily 9am–5.30pm, ☏ 0221/427-1535). Many of the best places to eat and drink are just south of here, around the junction of avenidas 10 & 47.

Eating and drinking

Cerveceria Modelo Diagonal 54, 496 ☏ 0221/421-1321. Old-school classic restaurant and café housed in a century-old building with legs

MAR DEL PLATA

Argentina's beaches are somewhat overshadowed by neighbouring Uruguay's golden sands (in particular glamorous Punta del Este; see p.935). Still, a seaside outing in summer is a quintessential Argentine experience – and Mar del Plata, boasting some 50km of beach 400km south of Buenos Aires, is the country's number one resort. In the summer season (mid-December to March), millions of city-dwellers descend on the place generating vibrant eating, drinking and entertainment scenes (or overcrowding and overpricing, depending on your point of view).

Though Mar del Plata may have lost some of the lustre of yesteryear, glimpses of glamour still abound in the city's restored early twentieth-century mansions (check out French-style Villa Ortiz Basualdo, now the Museo Municipal de Arte, at Av. Colón 1189, and the Centro Cultural Victoria Ocampo, Matheu 1851). The renowned International Film Festival is held in Mar del Plata in November, showing new Argentine and international films.

Nearby Cariló and Mar de los Pampas are both eco-resorts which provide a more laidback seaside experience, set within beautiful pine forests. Rent a house or stay in a luxury hotel and chill out for a few days – but be warned, these are boutique resorts for Argentina's rich and famous, so you won't find anything nearing a mid-range or budget accommodation option.

There are numerous daily buses from Buenos Aires to Mar del Plata (5–6hr), or you can make the journey less comfortably by train, from Constitución station (AR\$55–90), or fly across in less than an hour.

of ham hanging from the ceiling. Serves excellent draft beer; paella and home-made pan dulce (sweet buns) are the house speciality. Open daily for lunch and dinner.

Vitaminas Diagonal 74, 1640 ☏0221/482-1106. Colourful vegetarian café serving up healthy meals and snacks including exotic salads and freshly squeezed juices. Open Mon–Sat lunch and dinner.

Moving on

Bus Mar del Plata (12 daily; 5hr); Puerto Madryn (4 daily; 18hr).

Córdoba Province

CÓRDOBA PROVINCE, 700km northwest of Buenos Aires, marks Argentina's geographical bull's-eye. Serene towns dot its undulating **Central Sierras**, the second highest mountain range in Argentina after the Andes. The province is one of the country's more affordable travel destinations – except perhaps in high season when many city-dwellers flock to its cool heights – and a relaxed place to **learn Spanish**, go **skydiving** or just hang out for a few weeks sipping *mate* with the super-friendly locals.

Most of the action takes place in and around **Córdoba city**, which has the country's highest concentration of bars and clubs outside Buenos Aires. South of Córdoba city in the verdant **Calamuchita Valley**, towns such as **Alta Gracia** and Germanic, beer-brewing **Villa General Belgrano** have historically served as getaways for Argentina's elite. Northwest of the capital in the **Punilla Valley**, laidback towns such as **Capilla del Monte** are growing in popularity among bohemian *porteños* looking for a clean, green break from city life.

CÓRDOBA

Argentina's second largest city, unpretentious **CÓRDOBA** boasts beautifully restored colonial architecture, plentiful restaurants and a legendary nightlife

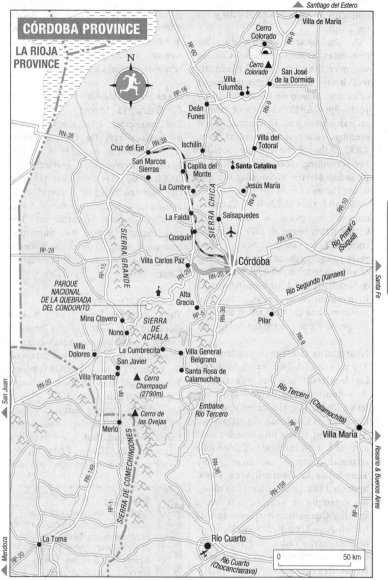

(best experienced when the university is in session). It is a great base for exploring the province: indeed, especially during the city's stiflingly hot summers, you'll soon be lured west to the Sierras' cooler elevations.

Plaza San Martín and around

Once the bloody stage for bullfights, executions and military parades, **Plaza San Martín** was converted into a civilized public square, replete with fountains and semi-tropical foliage, in the 1870s.

On the square's western side, the two-storey, sixteenth-century **Cabildo** was once the city's colonial headquarters. It now accommodates the tourist office and **Museo de la Ciudad** (daily 10am–8pm; AR$2) and hosts concerts, art exhibitions and, in summer, tango evenings (*Patio de Tango*: Fri 9pm; AR$7), although the dates are sporadic. For something more reliable, head to Plaza San Martín on Saturday at 10pm where there's a free tango get-together.

Alongside the Cabildo is the **Catedral**, one of the oldest in the country. Construction began in 1577 but wasn't completed for another two hundred years, rendering the cathedral something of an architectural mongrel, with a mix of Neoclassical and Baroque styles and a Romanesque dome thrown in for good measure. Note the trumpeting angels in indigenous dress gracing the bell towers.

Manzana de los Jesuitas

The seventeenth-century **Manzana de los Jesuitas** (Tues–Sun 10am–noon & 5–8pm; AR$10 guided visit), or Jesuit Block, two blocks southwest of the plaza, is Córdoba's top attraction. A testament to the missionaries who arrived hot on the heels of Córdoba's sixteenth-century colonizers, the **Templo de la Compañía de Jesús**, built in 1640, is the oldest surviving Jesuit temple in Argentina. It has a striking Cusqueño altarpiece, and its barrel-shaped vaulted roof is made of Paraguayan cedar. The block also houses a private chapel, **Capilla Doméstica** (guided visits on request).

Monasterio de Santa Teresa

Southwest of Plaza San Martín at Independencia 146 is the **Iglesia Santa Teresa**, part of a working convent that contains the **Museo de Arte Religioso Juan de Tejeda**, Independencia 122

(Wed–Sat 9.30am–12.30pm; AR$8; ℡0351/570-2545). It has perhaps the finest collection of sacred art in the country, including Jesuit artefacts and religious paintings from Cusco.

Museo de Bellas Artes Dr Genaro Pérez

The municipal art gallery, **Museo de Bellas Artes Dr Genaro Pérez**, at Av. General Paz 33 (Tues–Sun 10am–8pm; voluntary payment of AR$4; ℡0351/434-1646), housed in a late nineteenth-century French-style mansion, features nineteenth and twentieth-century Argentine art. The permanent collection has numerous landscape paintings from the **Escuela Cordobesa**, a movement led by master Genaro Pérez.

Nueva Córdoba

The neighbourhood of **Nueva Córdoba**, just south of the historic centre, is full of late nineteenth-century mansions converted into hip bars and restaurants. Diagonal Avenida Hipólito Yrigoyen cuts through the neighbourhood, which extends from Plaza Vélez Sarsfield to Parque Sarmiento (see p.82). Just over halfway down is the **Paseo del Buen Pastor**, Av. Hipólito Yrigoyen 325 (Daily 10am–10pm), a former women's prison recently

---

TREAT YOURSELF

Skydiving

Córdoba is the most affordable place in Argentina to jump out of an aeroplane. Tumbling out of the door at 2500m, you get a bird's-eye view, after twenty seconds of face-flattening freefall, of city sprawl, a patchwork of green fields and the Central Sierras. The guys at CEPAC (℡0351/15-687-8471, ⊛www.cepac.com.ar) have 35 years' skydiving experience, charging AR$695 for a tandem jump with extras like the filming included.

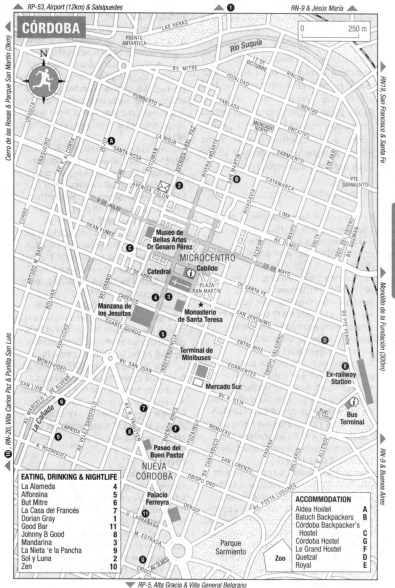

RP-53, Airport (12km) & Salsipuedes | ① | RN-9 & Jesús María

CÓRDOBA

0 — 250 m

Río Suquía

MICROCENTRO

Museo de Bellas Artes Dr Genaro Pérez

Catedral | Cabildo | PLAZA SAN MARTÍN

Manzana de los Jesuitas

Monasterio de Santa Teresa

Terminal de Minibuses

Mercado Sur

Ex-railway Station

Bus Terminal

Paseo del Buen Pastor

NUEVA CÓRDOBA

Palacio Ferreyra

Parque Sarmiento

Zoo

Cerro de las Rosas & Parque San Martín (3km)

RN-20, Villa Carlos Paz & Punilla San Luis

RN19, San Francisco & Santa Fe

Monolito de la Fundación (300m)

RN-9 & Buenos Aires

EATING, DRINKING & NIGHTLIFE	
La Alameda	4
Alfonsina	5
But Mitre	6
La Casa del Francés	7
Dorian Gray	1
Good Bar	11
Johnny B Good	8
Mandarina	3
La Nieta 'e la Pancha	9
Sol y Luna	2
Zen	10

ACCOMMODATION	
Aldea Hostel	A
Baluch Backpackers	B
Córdoba Backpacker's Hostel	C
Córdoba Hostel	G
Le Grand Hostel	F
Quetzal	D
Royal	E

RP-5, Alta Gracia & Villa General Belgrano

converted into a culinary and cultural precinct featuring art exhibitions and free concerts. Flanked by fountains and landscaped grassy knolls, it is one of the city's most popular spaces for chilling out in the summer.

Museo Superior de Bellas Artes Palacio Ferreyra

An exemplary art museum, the **Museo Superior de Bellas Artes Palacio Ferreyra**, Av. Hipólito Irigoyen 511 (Tues–Sun 10am–8pm; AR$3), features four floors of works in an opulent 1916 palace built in the French classical style. The top floor has rolling contemporary art exhibitions, while the basement level is devoted to photography. In between, some three hundred artists are represented, including Pablo Picasso and Argentinian artists Fernando Fader and Lino Enea Spilimbergo. A little further south is the hilltop **Parque Sarmiento**, one of the city's most popular green spaces.

Arrival and information

Air Córdoba's Aeropuerto Internacional Taravella is 12km north of downtown at Pajas Blancas. A bus runs frequently between the airport and city centre (AR$2). Taxis to the centre cost around AR$70.

Bus The frenetic long-distance bus station (T0351/428-4141) is several blocks east of the centre at Blvd Perón 380. Public buses run downtown; a taxi costs AR$10. Local buses for some provincial destinations leave from the Terminal de Minibuses behind the Mercado Sur market on Boulevard Arturo Illia.

Tourist information The principal tourist office is in the Cabildo (daily 8am–8pm; T0351/434-1200, Wwww.cordobaturismo.gov.ar) on Plaza San Martín. Far more helpful is the tourist office in the bus station (daily 8am–8pm; T0351/433-1987), whose friendly staff can assist with finding accommodation and provide city and provincial maps. There is also a tourist office in the airport (daily 8am–8pm; T0351/434-8390).

Tours Downtown walking tours (2hr) leave from Deán Funes 75 (daily summer 9.30am & 4.30pm; winter 10am & 4pm, in English upon request; T0351/15-663-6884). The cost is AR$70 for one person or AR$50 if two or more. Double-decker bus tours (1hr 30min) are run by City Tour (Mon 2.30pm & 4.30pm, Tues & Thurs 4.30pm, Fri 11am, 2.30pm & 4.30pm, Sat & Sun 11am & 4.30pm; AR$35; T0351/424-6605) and depart from Plaza San Martín near the cathedral.

Accommodation

Córdoba has some of the best-value hostels and hotels in the country, although many of the latter are quite old-fashioned. There is a fully serviced campsite (T0351/433-8409; AR$7–10 per person) at Miguel Lillo s/n (behind the Complejo Feriar).

Hostels

All hostels listed here offer tour-booking services and include internet, breakfast and use of kitchen.

Aldea Hostel Santa Rosa 447 T0351/426-1312, Wwww.aldeahostel.com. This bright, ambitious hostel, opened a few years ago, has space for a hundred people and is bursting with extras: two games rooms, a TV lounge, leafy patio, study room and roof terrace. Discounts for longer stays. Dorms AR$40, rooms AR$110.

Baluch Backpackers San Martín 338 T0351/422-3977, Wwww.baluchbackpackers.com. Clean and bright, this hostel has a cosy lounge area, helpful staff and hosts weekly barbecues on its roof terrace. Some rooms have a/c. Late risers might be put off by the ambient street noise. Dorms AR$40, rooms AR$120.

Córdoba Backpacker's Hostel Deán Funes 285 T0351/422-0593, Wwww.cordobabackpackers.com.ar. A climbing wall, bar, pool table, tour desk and roof terrace with dead-on cathedral views are just some of the perks of this bustling, central hostel. Dorm AR$35, rooms AR$95.

Córdoba Hostel Ituzaingó 1070 T0351/468-7359, Wwww.cordobahostel.com.ar. In the heart of trendy Nueva Córdoba, this four-floor HI hostel can also organize activities like horseriding and skydiving for you. Dorms AR$30, rooms AR$95

Le Grand Hostel Buenos Aires 547 T0351/422-7115, Wwww.legrandhostel.com. The largest hostel on the scene and located in Nueva Córdoba, an area popular with students. There's a chill-out room with huge flat-screen TV, an excellently equipped kitchen and decent outside area. Dorms AR$45, rooms AR$140.

Hotels

Quetzal San Jerónimo 579 T0351/422-9106, Wwww.hotelquetzal.com.ar. Despite the off-putting exterior, offers cheerful rooms with en-suite bathrooms. Steer clear of the noisy bedrooms facing the street. AR$180.

Royal Blvd Juan Domingo Perón 180 T0351/421-5000, Wwww.hotelmontecarlo.com.ar. Spartan but comfortable, this is an appealing option if you want to be close to the bus station. Breakfast included. AR$160.

Eating

Córdoba is a real delight for winers and diners. There are restaurants for refined taste buds, boisterous drinking holes serving pub grub, and plenty of eat-on-the-run *empanada* joints for lining your stomach before a night out on the Fernet and cola (Córdoba's potent signature tipple). The pick of the fashionable restaurants are in Nueva Córdoba.

La Alameda Obispo Trejo 170. Savour inexpensive Argentine staples like *empanadas* and *humitas* for a few pesos, while sitting outside on wooden benches, or indoors where customers' poetry and art adorns the walls. Closed Sun.

Alfonsina Duarte Quiros 66 ☎0351/ 427-2847. Antique typewriters, exposed brickwork and a jolly crowd are the hallmarks of this wildly popular restaurant that offers a taste of Argentina's northwest. Good *locro* (maize-based stew) and *empanadas*. Mains AR$25–35. Open daily; Sun eve only. There's another branch at Belgrano 763.

La Casa del Francés Independencia 512 ☎0351/425-4258. Extremely popular restaurant in the style of a French bistrot, serving excellent-value meat off the *parrilla*, with steaks around AR$35. Open daily 12.30pm–3pm & 8.30pm–midnight (closed Sun eve and Mon lunchtime).

Mandarina Obispo Trejo 171 ☎0351/ 426-4909. This spacious, chilled-out crowd-pleaser has plenty of vegetarian options. Mediterranean and Asian mains are prepared with gourmet flair. The two-course set lunch is good value at AR$34. Open daily 8am–2am.

La Nieta 'e la Pancha Belgrano 783 ☎0351/ 15-679-2749. Locally sourced ingredients are imaginatively prepared at this elegant restaurant, which does flavourful chicken, goat, trout and pasta dishes at reasonable prices (mains AR$35–50). Leave room for the ice cream with *peperina* (a locally grown herb; AR$25). Mon–Fri eve only, Sat & Sun open from 11.30am. Closed Tues.

Sol y Luna Av. Gral Paz 278 & Montevideo 66 ☎0351/425-1189, 🌐www.solylunaonline.com.ar. Load your plate with a variety of hot and cold dishes at this vegetarian buffet (AR$59 per kilo) with bright, hip decor. Set lunches AR$19.25. Open Mon–Sat 12pm–3.30pm.

Drinking and nightlife

Córdoba is no wallflower when it comes to partying, with Nueva Córdoba the late-night hotspot for the young, mainstream masses. Hipsters gravitate to the revived warehouse district of El Abasto, just north of the centre, for its edgy bars and nightclubs. Further afield, in the Chateau Carreras neighbourhood, the chic discos *Carreras, Club F* and *Cruz* cater for an energized crowd that grooves to *cuarteto* music – a Córdoba speciality.

But Mitre Marcelo T de Alvear 635 ☎0351/15-425-4999, 🌐www.butmitre.com. Córdoba's largest disco attracts a mixed crowd of students, posers and foreigners to three floors of hedonism and electro mayhem. Open Thurs–Sat.

Dorian Gray Blvd Las Heras & Roque Sáenz Peña. Bizarre decor and an alternative ambience draw an eclectic crowd who throw shapes well into the small hours to mostly electro music. Open Fri & Sat.

Good Bar Buenos Aires & Larrañaga. The surfboard out the front and white leather lounges might inspire you to slip into Hawaiian-style boardshorts or a white string bikini. You'll certainly wish you had at 2am when you're sweating buckets on the basement dancefloor. Open Sun–Wed 7pm–3am & Thurs–Sat till 5am.

Johnny B Good Av. Hipólito Yrigoyen 320, Nueva Córdoba and Av. Rafael Núñez 4791, Cerro de las Rosas ☎0351/424-3960, 🌐www.jbgood.com. Both branches of this resto-bar are much-loved local landmarks. Attend to hunger pangs with nachos (AR$36.90) and a beer (AR$9.90), or on weekends, swig cocktails to live rock music at the Cerro de la Rosas location. Open daily until late.

Zen Av. Julio A Roca 730 ☎0351/15-513-9595, 🌐www.zendisco.com.ar. This gay-friendly club has two throbbing dancefloors and hosts kooky live shows. Fri & Sat 11pm–5am.

Shopping

Bookshops Librería Blackpool, Deán Funes 395 (☎0351/423-7172). Sells novels and travel guides in English.

Markets On weekend evenings (5–9.30pm) there is an arts and crafts market at the Paseo de las Artes on the western edge of Nueva Córdoba in the bohemian Güemes neighbourhood, around Belgrano and Archaval Rodriguez streets.

Shopping centre Nuevocentro Shopping, Duarte Quirós 1400 (☎0351/482-8193, 🌐www.nuevocentro.com.ar; Sun–Thurs 10am–11pm, Fri & Sat till 1am).

Directory

Hospital Hospital Sanatorio Allende, at Av. Hipólito Yrigoyen 384 (☎0351/426-9200, 🌐www.sanatorioallende.com).

Laundry Laveraps at Los Granaderos 308, Chacabuco 313 and Belgrano 76.

Police Colón 1200.

Post office Av. General Paz 201.

Spanish school Caseros Spanish School, Caseros 873 (☎0351/593-8106, 🌐www.cordoba-spanish.com.ar), has Spanish classes arranged in six different skills levels, from US$145 for 20 weeks.

Moving on

Air Internal to: Buenos Aires (12 daily; 1hr 15min); Mendoza (2 daily; 1hr 20min); Rosario (2 daily; 1hr). International to: destinations in Brazil, Chile, Panama and Uruguay.

Bus Alta Gracia (every 15min, 1hr); Buenos Aires (hourly; 11hr); Capilla del Monte (hourly; 1hr 30min); Mendoza (7 daily; 10hr); San Juan (5 daily; 8hr); Rosario (6 daily; 5hr); Salta (4 daily; 12–14hr); Villa General Belgrano (every 30min; 2hr 30min).

ALTA GRACIA

The pleasant colonial town of **ALTA GRACIA**, 38km south of Córdoba at the entrance of the Calamuchita Valley, was once a genteel summer refuge for the *porteño* bourgeoisie. Alta Gracia continues to bask in the reflected glory of its former residents: Jesuit missionaries, the Spanish composer Manuel de Falla and the Guevara family have all left their mark here.

What to see and do

Easily walkable on foot, the centre of town is dominated by its impressive Jesuit *estancia*, one of the finest examples in Argentina. But it's also a great springboard for walking in the nearby countryside or, for the more adventurous, skydiving.

Plaza Manuel Solares and around

Alta Gracia came into its own after 1643 when it was chosen as the site of a Jesuit *estancia*. When the Jesuits were expelled in 1767, the *estancia* was left to the elements, only briefly re-inhabited in 1810 by Viceroy Liniers. The *estancia* buildings have been well preserved and overlook the town's main square, **Plaza Manuel Solares**. The **Iglesia Parroquial Nuestra Señora de la Merced**, dating from 1762, stands alongside the Jesuits' original living quarters, which have been converted into the UNESCO World Heritage-listed **Museo de la Estancia Jesuitica de Alta Gracia** –

Casa del Virrey Liniers (summer: Tues–Fri 9am–8pm, Sat & Sun 9.30am–8pm; winter: Tues–Fri 9am–1pm & 3–7pm, Sat & Sun 9.30am–12.30pm & 3.30–6.30pm; AR$5, free on Wed; guided tours in English; ☎03547/421-303). Here, a dramatic Baroque doorway leads to a cloistered courtyard and a motley collection of furniture and religious paintings.

Ernesto "Che" Guevara house and museum

A twenty-minute walk uphill from the plaza brings you to the leafy residential neighbourhood of **Villa Carlos Pellegrini**, whose crumbling mansions once served as holiday homes and residences for moneyed socialites. The Guevara family moved within these circles after relocating from Rosario to Alta Gracia in the 1930s in the hope that the fresh mountain air would alleviate the asthma plaguing their four-year-old son, **Ernesto "Che" Guevara**. The family's former home, Villa Beatriz, at Avellaneda 501, has been converted into the **Museo Casa de Ernesto "Che" Guevara** (summer: daily 9am–8pm; winter: Mon 2pm–7pm & Tues–Sun 9am–7pm; ☎03547/428-579; AR$5), showcasing Che's personal effects as well as photographs charting his progression from carefree kid to swarthy teenager, to sideburn-sporting revolutionary. Among the museum's highlights are video interviews with Che's childhood companions, a handwritten resignation letter to Fidel Castro and photos from a visit Castro and Hugo Chávez made to the house in 2006.

Arrival and information

Bus Regular buses from Córdoba (every 30min; 1hr) stop at the bus terminal on Calle P. Butori and Avenida Presidente Perón, around eight blocks west of Lake Tajamar (although minibuses stop nearer the centre on Calle Lucas V Córdoba).

Tourist information The tourist office is in the clock tower alongside the Tajamar reservoir at the corner of Av. del Tajamar and Calle del Molino

(Dec–Feb daily 8am–11pm; March–Nov Mon–Thurs 8am–8pm & Fri–Sun till 9pm; ☎03547/428-128, ⓦwww.altagracia.gov.ar).

Accommodation and eating

If you're after some peace and quiet, Alta Gracia is just the place to spend the night. At the eastern edge of town, the *Hosteria Country El Biguá*, Ruta C45 Km2 (☎03547/15-526-160; AR$20 per person) offers camping and cabañas in the grounds of a former *estancia*.

Alta Gracia Hostel Paraguay 218 ☎03547/428-810, ⓦwww.altagraciahostel.com.ar. A homely hostel five blocks from the main square. Dorms AR$35.

Morena Sarmiento 413 ☎03547/426-365, ⓦwww.morena-ag.com.ar. Set in a white, neocolonial house, this restaurant's menu runs the gamut from prawn ravioli to paella and veal in mushroom sauce. The pizzas and fish dishes are also pretty good. Mains AR$40–50. Closed Mon, Tues–Thurs dinner only.

Moving on

Bus Villa General Belgrano (every 30min; 1hr).

VILLA GENERAL BELGRANO

The twee resort town of **VILLA GENERAL BELGRANO**, 50km south of Alta Gracia, unabashedly exploits its Germanic heritage with all kinds of kitsch. Founded by the surviving seamen of the *Graf Spee*, which sank off the coast of Uruguay in 1939, the town's main street, **Avenida Julio Roca**, comes over like an alpine theme park, with folksy German beer houses and eateries resembling Swiss chalets. You'll either love it or hate it.

What to see and do

The best (and some might argue the only) reason to visit Villa General Belgrano is to sink steins of locally brewed beer at the annual **Oktoberfest**. Held during the first two weeks of October in Plaza José Hernández, it is considered the continent's best celebration of this drunken German tradition.

The most popular day-trip from Villa General Belgrano is 30km west to the alpine-flavoured village of **La Cumbrecita** (eight buses daily), where there are good opportunities for hiking, abseiling and cooling off in the Río Almbach.

Arrival and information

Bus The bus terminal is on Av. Vélez Sarsfield, a 10-min walk northwest of the main street, although all buses make drop-offs and pick-ups in the town centre.

Mountain bike rental Cerro Negro, Av. Julio Roca 625 ☎03546/462-785.

Tourist information The tourist office is at Av. Julio Roca 168 (daily 8.30am–8.30pm; ☎03546/461-215, ⓦwww.vgb.gov.ar).

Accommodation

Hotels in town are overpriced; cabañas make a good alternative for groups of four or five. The *El Arroya* campsite (☎03546/463-855, AR$30 per person) is five blocks south of the town centre at Nicaragua 571, and the shady *La Florida* campground (☎03546/461-298, Ⓔlaflorida @calamuchitanet.com.ar, AR$30 per person), along the RP5 east of the town centre, has lovely grounds with a swimming pool and bungalows.

Albergue El Rincón Alexander Fleming s/n, 15min walk northwest of the bus station ☎03546/461-323, ⓦwww.calamuchitanet.com.ar /elrincon. Set on a farm, this stellar, relaxed hostel has dorms (AR$30–40) and plenty of grass for pitching your tent (AR$20–30 per person). Breakfasts with home-made cereal, bread and jam are AR$10. AR$140.

El Viejo Nogal 25 de Mayo 149 ☎03546/463-174, ⓦwww.elviejonogal.viajesdelsur.com. Charming, fully-equipped cabañas with high wooden ceilings and cable TV, set around a cute pool. Massive low-season discounts. Cabins AR$220 (5-day minimum stay in high season).

Posada Düsseldorf Av. Julio A Roca 224 ☎03546/461-372, ⓦwww.dusseldorf.com.ar. Located on one of the town's thoroughfares, this posada has decent-sized rooms, a swimming pool and an adjoining travel agency. Breakfast included. AR$240.

Eating and drinking

The town's numerous cafés and restaurants dish up Germanic food of varying quality.

Café Rissen Av. Julio Roca 36 ☎03546/464-100. Situated on the main strip, this twee café is probably the most popular in town. Excellent cakes and sandwiches of the Germanic variety are on the menu. The Black Forest gateau comes highly recommended (AR$18). Open daily 8am–midnight.

El Ciervo Rojo Av. Julio Roca 210 ☎03546/461-345. Good for goulash (AR$45), *salchicha* (sausage; AR$35) and house-brewed beer. Open daily from 8.30am.

Los Pinos Av. Julio Roca 73 ☎03546/461-832. The extensive menu swerves from wurst to pizza (mains around AR$30), but the beer (AR$12 a glass) is what you're really here for, brewed out the back in a factory with a 24,000-litre capacity. Guided brewery tours on weekends (AR$15). Open all day, every day.

Viejo Munich Av. San Martín 362 ☎03546/463-122, ⓦwww.cervezaartesanal.com. The trout, goulash and venison mains aren't too bad, but the beer – brewed on-site and in nine different varieties – is the real star of the show. Free brewery tours Mon, Tues, Fri & Sat 10.45am & 11.45am. Closed all day Wed and Thurs lunchtime.

Moving on

Bus Alta Gracia (every 30min; 1hr); Córdoba (every 30min; 2hr).

CAPILLA DEL MONTE

CAPILLA DEL MONTE attracts more alternative lifestyle-types in summer than you can shake an incense stick at. Situated 102km north of Córdoba city, the idyllic mountain town lies at the base of **Cerro Uriturco**, which, at 1979m, is the Sierra Chica's highest peak and is claimed by many locals to possess an inexplicable magnetic pull.

Set at the confluence of two (often dry) rivers on the northern edge of the Punilla Valley, Capilla del Monte's former glory can be glimpsed in its slowly decaying nineteenth-century mansions. Perhaps drawn here by Uriturco's magnetism, artisans and New Age healers have since become the town's more conspicuous residents, and their businesses can be easily visited using the maps and listings provided by the tourist office.

What to see and do

Capilla del Monte makes a good base for outdoor adventure sports, including **horseriding** in the surrounding countryside, **rock climbing** the strange sandstone formations around the hamlet of **Ongamira**, **hiking** to the summit of Cerro Uriturco (about 4hr to the top; $20; register at the base of the mountain), strolling through the multicoloured rock formations of **Los Terrones** (9am–dusk; AR$19; transfers organized with additional cost; ⓦwww.losterrones.com) or **paragliding** in the Sierras.

Arrival and information

Bus The bus station is near the centre at the corner of Corrientes and Rivadavia. Empresa Sarmiento runs buses to and from Córdoba every hour (2hr 30min).

Tourist information Pick up a map and area information at the tourist office in the old railway station on Av. Pueyrredón s/n (daily 8am–9pm; ☎03548/481-903, ⓦwww.capilladelmonte.gov.ar).

THE TRUTH IS OUT THERE

Capilla del Monte hosts an international UFO convention every November, organized by local "research" group Centro de Informes OVNI, Juan Cabus 297 (☎03548/482-485, ⓦwww.ciouritorco.org) – OVNI is Spanish for UFO). Mystical tourism is gaining in popularity, with local tour operators jumping on the extraterrestrial bandwagon by offering guided tours to sites of supposed UFO landings as well as night excursions to observe celestial happenings on remote mountaintops. You'll be in good hands with Viajes Ángel (☎03548/15-634-532), Diagonal Buenos Aires 183, which does a convincing range of otherworldly tours (AR$65 per person for around 4hr).

Accommodation and eating

Campers are spoilt for choice in Capilla del Monte; the closest campsite to town is the riverside *Calabalumba* (☎ 03548/489-601), at the end of General Paz, with a range of facilities. Tent pitches AR$12 per person per day; cabañas sleep up to six for AR$140.

Los 3 Gómez 25 de Mayo 452 ☎ 03548/482-647, ⊛ www.hostelencapilladelmonte.com. Newly opened, laidback hostel with a decent outdoor area. Discounts for HI members. Dorms AR$45, rooms AR$150.

El Duende Azul Chubut 75 & Aristóbulo del Valle ☎ 03548/15-569-667, ⊛ www .cordobaserrana.com.ar/elduendeazul.htm. A guesthouse in tune with the town's hippy vibe. Frolic in the big garden or hang out in the common area overrun by pixie and elf figurines. The simple but pretty rooms have en-suites and the lovely owners arrange detox programmes.

Maracaibo Buenos Aires 182 ☎ 03548/482-741. This unpretentious restaurant is a good all-rounder, serving fish, pasta and chicken mains (AR$22–32), as well as lots of vegetarian options; the vegetable and corn lasagne (AR$33 for two) is filling and tasty. Fri–Wed 11am–4pm & 7pm–12am, closed Thurs.

The Northeast

Sticky summers, *mate* tea and *chamamé* folk music characterize the sultry northeastern provinces of Entre Ríos, Corrientes, Misiones and Santa Fe, an area known as **El Litoral**. Most of the region is wedged between two awesome rivers, the Paraná and the Uruguay, which converge near Buenos Aires as the Río de la Plata. Eclipsing every other attraction in the region are the **Iguazú Falls**, the world's most spectacular waterfalls, framed by lush subtropical forest. Located in the northeastern corner of Misiones Province, the falls straddle the border with Brazil. South of **Iguazú**, the well-preserved Jesuit Mission ruins at **San Ignacio Miní** make for the region's second-biggest draw.

Further afield, in Corrientes Province, the sprawling wetlands of **Esteros del Iberá** offer prime wildlife-spotting opportunities. The river-hugging, siesta-loving city of **Corrientes** is increasingly opening itself up to tourism, while Argentina's third-largest city (and the birthplace of Che Guevara), **Rosario**, in Santa Fe Province, has some handsome historic buildings, arresting monuments and a lively weekend party atmosphere. The star of Entre Ríos Province is the **Parque Nacional El Palmar**, with its forest of towering *yatay* palms, an easy day-trip from the resort town of **Colón**.

If you have a problem with heat and humidity, steer clear of this region between December and March, when temperatures in the far north often creep above 40°C.

ROSARIO

Super-stylish **ROSARIO** is a cleaner, greener, less daunting version of Buenos Aires. The city where Che Guevara learned to crawl is home to a handsome, academic and culturally inclined population of just over one million.

Sprawled on the banks of the **Río Paraná**, Rosario's assets are its riverside beaches, parks, restaurants, bars and museums. For an enjoyable day-trip, the sandy beaches of the subtropical **delta islands** lie just a short boat or kayak ride away. There is stylish shopping to be found in Rosario's pedestrianized centre, and free public wi-fi access throughout the city. *Extranjeros* are still very much a novelty here, and whether you're in town to chill or to party, you'll be warmly received by the friendly locals.

What to see and do

The leafy parks, historic buildings and excellent shopping opportunties make central Rosario a pleasant place to wander around at any time of year, while the riverfront and beaches are extremely appealing during the summer months.

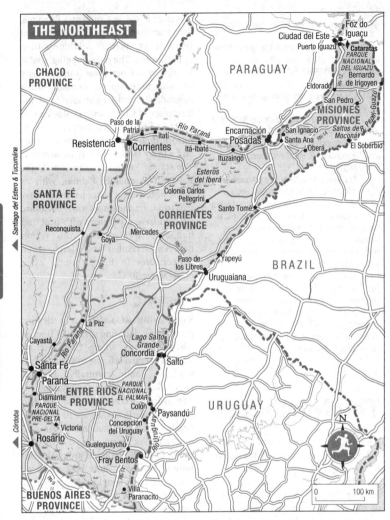

Start your stroll at the Plaza 25 de Mayo and be sure to check out the nearby Catedral de Rosario and Monumento a la Bandera, both postcard images of the city, before hitting the shops or settling down for a spot of sunbathing.

Plaza 25 de Mayo and around

The tree-lined **Plaza 25 de Mayo** lies three blocks west of the river. Here, at the heart of the city, you'll find some of the city's grandest buildings, including the late nineteenth-century **Catedral de Rosario** (daily 8am–noon & 4–9pm; free), with its striking Italianate marble altar. On the southern side, the **Museo Municipal de Arte Decorativo Firma y Odilio Estévez** (Wed–Fri 3–8pm, Sat & Sun 10am–8pm; AR$2; ✆0341/480-2547) houses the lavish art collection of the Estévez family, Galician immigrants who struck it big cultivating *mate*. Pieces include a Goya painting, a Flemish tapestry and Greek sculptures.

Monumento a la Bandera

Rising just east of the plaza, the **Monumento a la Bandera** (Monument to the Flag) is Rosario's most eye-catching landmark. A stark piece of nationalistic architecture, it marks the place where, in 1812, General Belgrano first raised the Argentinian flag. Take the **lift** up its 70m tower for panoramic city views (Mon 1–7pm, Tues–Sun 9am–6pm; AR$4).

Costanera

Rosario's **Costanera** (riverfront) extends for around 20km from north to south, providing plenty of green space to sunbathe or sip *mate*, as well as waterfront restaurants, bars and museums. The central **Parque Nacional de la Bandera** – a narrow strip of parkland – is the main setting for regular markets and festivals. As you stroll north, the park merges with **Parque de España** and the large brick **Centro Cultural Parque de España** (Tues–Sun 3–7pm; AR$2; ☎0341/426-0941, ⓦwww.ccpe.org.ar), which hosts changing modern art exhibitions. Half a kilometre north, is the **Museo de Arte Contemporáneo de Rosario** (Thurs–Tues 2–8pm winter, 3–9pm summer; AR$4; ☎0341/480-4981, ⓦwww.macromuseo.org.ar), a kitsch temple to modern Argentine art housed inside a converted grain silo, its facade painted in pastel shades. The building – as well as the views from the top floor – outshines the displays, while the gallery's riverfront café, *Davis*, serves good food.

Most of the summer beach action happens 8km north of the centre at

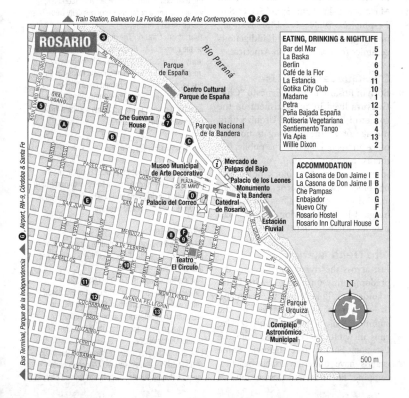

the **Balneario La Florida** (Dec–April 8am–9pm; AR$4; bus #153). Just south of here is the Rambla Catalunya (with a free beach) and Avenida Carrasco, an upmarket restaurant, bar and club strip that is the hub of Rosario's vibrant summer nightlife.

Parque de la Independencia

The **Parque de la Independencia**, 3km southwest of Plaza 25 de Mayo, is one of Argentina's largest urban green spaces. Within its extensive grounds are a football stadium, a racetrack, a theme park, a rose garden and two museums. The **Museo Municipal de Bellas Artes Juan B Castagnino** (Wed–Mon 1–7pm; suggested donation AR$5; ☎0341/480-2542), at Av. Pellegrini 2202, has an important collection of European and Argentine fine art. West of the lake, the **Museo Histórico Provincial Dr Julio Marc** (Tues–Fri 9am–5pm, Sat & Sun 3–7pm; free; ☎0341/472-1457) is strong on religious artefacts and indigenous ceramics from across Latin America.

Che Guevara's house

Born in Rosario in 1928, **Ernesto "Che" Guevara** lived in an apartment on the corner of Entre Ríos and Urquiza until the age of 2. The building is now an office and is not open to the public, but there's nothing to stop you gawking from the street. One block north and one block east, at the corner of Tucumán and Mitre, a mural of Che's intense and haggard-looking face dominates a small neighbourhood square.

Alto Delta islands

Just across the river from Rosario, the predominantly uninhabited **Alto Delta islands** are linked to the mainland by regular passenger ferries in the summer, while a weekend-only service runs in winter. **Ferries** leave from the Estación Fluvial (see below). Some islands have underdeveloped beaches, camping facilities and restaurants. A

good way to explore the delta is by taking a **kayak excursion** (AR$120 for 7hr) with the multilingual guides at Bike Rosario (☎0341/155-713812, ⊛www.bikerosario.com.ar); the package includes a cycling tour of Rosario.

Arrival and information

Air Rosario's airport (☎0341/451-1226) is 10km northwest of the centre. There are no buses into town; a taxi ride is around AR$25 or take a taxi to the Fisherton neighbourhood, from where buses #115, #116 and #160 run to the bus terminal.

Bus The Terminal de Omnibus Mariano Moreno is twenty blocks west of the centre, at Santa Fe and Cafferata (☎0341/437-3030). Buses #141 and #146 go to the centre. Bus fares must be paid in exact change or using pre-paid passes. Passes, which can be bought from newsagents and grocery stores, offer savings on multiple journeys.

Ferry The Estación Fluvial (☎0341/448-3737), in Parque Nacional de la Bandera, has ferries to the Delta islands. There are services year-round on weekends and a number of services daily Dec–March (AR$11 return).

Tourist information The riverside tourist office is on the corner of Av. Belgrano and C Buenos Aires (daily 9am–6pm; ☎0341/480-2230, ⊛www .rosarioturismo.com). An information kiosk in the bus terminal has city maps and hotel listings.

Train The train station (☎0800/333-3822) is 3km northwest of the centre, with slow services three times weekly to Buenos Aires.

Accommodation

Rosario has experienced a hostel boom in recent years and at weekends many fill up with party-hard *porteños*. The only time you need to book ahead is on weekends and public holidays.

Hostels

All hostels listed here have double rooms as well as dorms, kitchen facilities, and offer free internet and breakfast.

Che Pampas Rioja 812 ☎0341/424-5202, ⊛www.chepampas.com. Why can't every hostel come with a giant mirrorball, Che Guevara pop art, neon chandeliers and a red PVC throne? In the summer, you'll appreciate the a/c in the dorm rooms. Dorms AR$35.

La Casona de Don Jaime I Presidente Roca 1051 ☎0341/527-9964, ⊛www.youthhostelrosario .com.ar. Hugely popular party hostel whose lively bar, *Roots*, offers late-night reggae music and tasty pizzas. The quieter sister hostel, *La Casona de Don Jaime II*, at San Lorenzo 1530 (☎0341/530-2020) must be one of the only hostels in Argentina to boast its own climbing wall. Staff at both hostels can arrange boating, kayaking and cycling excursions. Dorms AR$45, rooms AR$140.

Rosario Inn Cultural House Sargento Cabral 54 ☎0341/421-0358, ⊛www .rosarioinnhostel.com.ar. With a fantastic location near the river, this light-drenched hostel has two patios to hang out in and bikes for rent. Tango and theatre classes offered. Dorms AR$40 with buffet breakfast.

Hotels

Embajador Santa Fe 3554 ☎0341/438-6367, ⊛www.hotelembajadorrosario.com. The best of several decent options right in front of the bus station, this spick-and span-hotel offers rooms with cable TV, wireless internet and a/c. Breakfast included. AR$175.

Nuevo City San Juan 867 ☎0341/447-1655, ⊛www.hotelnuevocity.com.ar. All rooms at this humble hotel have TV, a/c and private bathroom. Request one of the few rooms with external windows. Breakfast included. AR$180.

Eating

The bulk of Rosario's restaurants are clustered along Avenida Pellegrini, although in summer you'll want to take advantage of the waterfront aspect and pull up an outdoor chair at one of the many popular restaurants along the Costanera. Many of these riverfront restaurants open until the small hours during the summer months, although most are closed by around 10pm (later at weekends) during winter.

La Baska Tucumán 1118 ☎0341/411-1110. The *empanadas* here are piping hot and come with a huge range of heavenly fillings including prawns, tuna, mushrooms and Roquefort cheese. (AR$2).

La Estancia Av. Pellegrini at Paraguay ☎0341/440-7373. Rosario's most popular restaurant is an old-fashioned place with a vast menu. The emphasis is on – you guessed it – beef, and it's fun to watch the impeccably suited waiters rush around with exotic cuts of sizzling cow. Mains around AR$35. Open daily 8.30am–1am.

Peña Bajada España Av. Italia at España ☎0341/426-1168. Fish restaurant with a tranquil wooden terrace overlooking the river. Access is by elevator. Barbecued fish feasts from AR$30.

Petra Av. Pelligrini 1428 ☎0341/449-8369. For a fixed price of AR$35, diners can help themselves from the heaving salad bar before loading up on pizza, seafood and grilled meats at this bustling dinner spot. Customers are free to fill their plates as many times as they like, and even desserts are included in the price. Open daily noon–3pm & 6–11pm.

Rotiseria Vegetariana Mendoza 937 ☎0341/447-7533. A staggering array of meat-free dishes is served at this inexpensive (AR$22 per kilo) Asian buffet, and the sushi, stir fries and soya burgers make a welcome change from barbecued meat. Open Mon–Sat 11.30am–3pm & 6–10pm.

Via Apia Av. Pellegrini 961 ☎0341/481-3174. It's easy to miss this small Italian restaurant among the vast neon-lit food palaces of Avenida Pellegrini, but the crisp stone-baked pizzas (AR$30) are arguably the best in the city. Open Mon–Sat 6–11pm.

Drinking and nightlife

Rosario's good-looking locals and party spirit all combine to make it a great place in which to go out. In summer, the clubs and bars in the riverfront Estación Fluvial attract a modish crowd. Summer fun also transfers to Rambla Catalunya, a waterfront avenue in the city's north. Note that nightlife in Rosario doesn't really get going until well after midnight, with some clubs not opening until after 2am.

Bar del Mar Balcarce and Tucumán. A restaurant-bar with an aquatic theme and colourful mosaics; good for people-watching before painting the town red. Beers AR$12.

Berlin Pje Zabala 1128, between the 300 block of Mitre and Sarmiento ⊛www.elberlin.com.ar. Regular events and a steady flow of German beer (AR$12) keep locals coming back to this trendy bar. Open Thurs–Sat 11pm until late.

Café de la Flor Mendoza 862 ⊛www.cafe delaflor.com.ar. Live music, DJs and pizza fuel the boisterous alternative crowd at this cavernous joint. Open Thurs–Sun; shows start around 8pm.

Gotika City Club Mitre 1539 ⊛www.gotika cityclub.com.ar. Spacious, gay-friendly club in a converted church; come here when you have some serious energy to burn. Hosts regular shows. Entry AR$20. Open Fri–Sun; gets going around 1am.

Madame Brown 3126. This is *the* club for party animals – a mainstream disco with three dance-floors blaring *cumbia*, reggaeton, electronica and rock. Over-21s only. Entry AR$20. Open Fri–Sat 2am until late.

Sentiemento Tango Calle Corrientes 152. This cavernous bar and dance hall has an old-worldy vibe and is an ideal place to take your first tango steps. A range of ages share the dancefloor; tango classes daily from 8.30pm (AR$10).

Willie Dixon Suipacha and Guemes. Rock out at this live music venue that hosts quality Argentinian acts: a disco follows the band. Entry AR$15 for disco only. Open Thurs–Sat; shows start around 9am.

Shopping

Bookshops Ameghino Bookshops, Corrientes 868 (☎0341/447-1147) stocks English-language books.
Clothes The pedestrianized Av. Córdoba is a busy shopping street flanked with handsome historic buildings, many of which now function as chic boutiques and department stores. Falabella, at Cordoba and Sarmiento, is a vast department store with good bargains to be found during end-of-season sales.
Markets The Mercado de Pulgas del Bajo flea market is on every weekend afternoon in the Parque Nacional de la Bandera, near Av. Belgrano 500. Handmade crafts, used books and antiques are on sale.

Directory

Banks and Exchange Banco de la Nación Argentina at Córdoba 1026; Branches of HSBC at Santa Fe 1064, San Martin 902 and Córdoba 1770/72. Rosario Transatlantica Casa de Cambio generally offers decent exchange rates and has branches at Rioja 1198 and Cordoba 1463.
Internet Chat & Play, at Corrientes 1621, has high-speed internet. Open Mon–Sat 9.30am–3am. Note that there's free wi-fi access at many parks and public spaces.
Laundry Lavandería VIP, at Maipú 654.
Post office Buenos Aires and Córdoba on Plaza 25 de Mayo.

Spanish school Punto Spanish, Level 5, San Luis 1486 (☎0341/424-0035, ⊛www.puntospanish.com). Group and one-on-one Spanish classes for reasonable rates.

Moving on

Air Buenos Aires (3 daily; 55min); Córdoba (2 daily; 1hr); Mendoza (2 daily; 3hr); Montevideo in Uruguay (daily; 1hr 20min); Santa Fe (3 daily; 1 hr).
Bus Buenos Aires (every 30min; 4hr); Córdoba (every 30min; 6hr 30min); Corrientes (7 daily; 10–12hr); Montevideo in Uruguay (1 daily; 9hr); Puerto Iguazú (3 daily; 19hr); Salta (6 daily; 16hr).
Train Buenos Aires (2 weekly; 7hr).

PARQUE NACIONAL EL PALMAR

Only after ranching, farming and forestry had pushed the graceful *yatay* palm to the brink of extinction did it find salvation in the **PARQUE NACIONAL EL PALMAR**. The 85-square-kilometre park, on the banks of the Río Uruguay, lies 50km north of Colón at Km199 on the RN14, and is a stark reminder of how large chunks of Entre Ríos Province, Uruguay and southern Brazil once looked. Many of the **palms**, which can grow up to 18m high, are over 300 years old. Trails wind through the park, past palm savannas, streams and riverside beaches. Sunset is the perfect time to pull out the camera, when the palms look stunning silhouetted against a technicolour sky. El Palmar's creation in 1966 also did wonders for the habitat

---

CROSSING FROM COLÓN INTO URUGUAY

Colón, on the Río Uruguay 320km north of Buenos Aires, makes an inviting base for visiting the Parque Nacional El Palmar (see above), 50km to the north. Colón is also a prime gateway to Uruguay, and is linked to the city of Paysandú, 16km southeast, by the Puente Internacional General Artigas. It is 8km from Colón to the Uruguayan border (immigration office open 24hr a day) and a further 8km to Paysandú: approximately four buses daily make the journey. Colón's bus terminal is on the corner of Paysandú and 9 de Julio. There are frequent services to Concordia (9 daily; 2hr 15min), passing Parque Nacional El Palmar, and plenty of connections to Buenos Aires (14 daily; 5hr 30min). Colón's helpful tourist office is in the port area on the corner of Avenida Costanera and Gouchón (Mon–Fri 6am–8pm, Sat & Sun 8am–8pm; ☎03447/421-233, ⊛www.colon.gov.ar).

of local subtropical **wildlife**, including capybaras, vizcachas, monitor lizards, raccoons and the venomous *yarará* pit viper. Parakeets, egrets, *ñandúes* (a large, flightless bird similar to an ostrich) and storks are some of the bird species that can be spotted here.

To **get to the park**, catch any Concordia-bound bus from Colón (9 daily; 30min) along the RN14 to the entrance (where you pay AR$12 entry). From here it's a 10-km walk, drive or hitchhike to the visitor centre and adjacent **Los Loros campground** (℡03447/423-378; AR$4 per tent, plus AR$6 per person), with showers and a basic store. To **stay in Colón**, try the *Amarello Hotel* at Calle Urquiza 865 (℡03447/424063, ⓦwww .colonentrerios.com.ar/amarello; AR$120 with breakfast included); it has plain en-suite rooms in a range of sizes.

CORRIENTES

Subtropical **CORRIENTES** is one of the northeast's oldest cities (it was founded in 1588) but doesn't offer much in the way of conventional attractions. That said, its compact historic centre, elegantly crumbling buildings and shady riverside area make it an ideal place for a leg stretch between long bus rides. Party people will be at home here during the heat of summer – Corrientes has been dubbed Argentina's "Capital of Carnaval", and each January and February the city explodes in a riot of colourful costumes and thumping drums.

What to see and do

Corrientes' historic core fans out in grid fashion from the shady main square, **Plaza 25 de Mayo**. The square is framed by some of the city's most important nineteenth-century buildings, including the pink Italianate **Casa de Gobierno** and the plain **Iglesia de Nuestra Señora de la Merced** (daily 8am–noon & 5–8pm; free). On the plaza's northeast corner, the **Museo de Artesanía** (daily 8am–1pm & 3–9pm; free) showcases regional basketwork, leather and ceramics within a whitewashed colonial residence.

One block south of the main square is Corrientes' 2.5-km riverside avenue, the **Avenida Costanera General San Martín**, flanked by pretty jacaranda and native *lapacho* trees. It is the favoured haunt of fishermen, *mate-* and *tereré-* sippers, joggers, mosquitoes, daydreamers and courting couples. Locals flock to its promenades on summer evenings after emerging refreshed from siestas. There are a few small riverside **beaches** here, but swimming is not recommended as the river's currents are notoriously strong.

Arrival and information

Air Corrientes' airport (℡03783/458-340) is 10km northeast of the city centre. Free shuttle services can take you from the airport to the centre.
Bus The bus terminal (℡03783/449-435) is 4km southeast of the city centre. Local buses run

---

FEELING HOT, HOT, HOT!

Despite the oppressive heat that strikes in summer, the city manages to muster up heroic levels of energy for the annual, Brazilian-style Carnaval Correntino (ⓦwww .carnavalescorrentinos.com), which takes place throughout January and February in the open-air Corsódromo at Avenida Centenario 2800. Raucous street parties, which frequently include bucketloads of iced water being thown over the sweaty hordes, take place each weekend throughout Carnaval season. Alternatively, if you're in town over the second weekend in December, check out the Festival del Chamamé (ⓦwww.corrienteschamame.com), a celebration of regional folk dancing and music.

frequently between the terminal and the centre; a taxi will set you back around AR$9. There are direct bus services to Buenos Aires (6 daily; 12hr); Posadas (9 daily; 5hr; change here for more regular services to Puerto Iguazú); Puerto Iguazú (1 daily; 10hr); Rosario (3 daily; 10hr).

Tourist information The provincial tourist office (Mon–Fri 7am–1pm & 3–9pm; ☏03783/427-200, ⓦwww.turismocorrientes.com.ar) is at 25 de Mayo 1330, and there is also a municipal tourist office where the Costanera meets Pellegrini (daily 7am–9pm; ☏03783/474-702).

Moving on

Air Aerolineas Argentinas (☏03783/458-339) flies to Buenos Aires (2 daily) and Asunción in Paraguay (4 weekly).
Bus There are direct bus services to Buenos Aires (6 daily; 12hr); Posadas (9 daily; 5hr; change here for more regular services to Puerto Iguazú); Puerto Iguazú (1 daily; 10hr); Rosario (3 daily; 10hr).

ESTEROS DEL IBERÁ

A vast area of marshy swampland, the Esteros del Iberá comprises a series of lagoons, rivers, marshes and floating islands, much of which is protected in the **RESERVA NATURAL DEL IBERÁ**. The islands are created by a build-up of soil on top of a mat of intertwined water lilies and other plants; these in turn choke the flow of water, creating what is in effect a vast, slow-flowing river, draining eventually into the Río Paraná. The wetlands make up nearly fifteen percent of Corrientes province – spreading annually in the rainy season and gradually contracting until the rains come again. With the protection of the natural reserve, the area's **wildlife** is thriving, and there's an extraordinary variety: some three hundred species of birds, many brilliantly coloured; forty species of mammals, including capybara, marsh and pampas deer, otters and howler monkeys; and many fish, amphibians and reptiles, including caimans. Take a trip out onto the water, and you can enjoy remarkably close encounters with many of them. For more information on the reserve visit ⓦwww.esterosdelibera.com.

What to see and do

Access to the reserve is from the tranquil village of **Colonia Carlos Pellegrini**, on the banks of the Laguna del Iberá. At the approach to the village, immediately before the rickety wooden bridge that is the only way in, former poachers staff the Centro de Interpretación, the reserve's **visitor centre**, which has useful information as well as a fascinating photo display. A nearby forest trail is a good place to spot (and hear) howler monkeys. The **Laguna del Iberá** itself is covered in water lilies, especially the yellow-and-purple *aguapé*, and its floating islands teem with a rich microcosm of bird and aquatic life. Birds include storks, cormorants, egrets, ducks and other waterfowl, while around the edges of the lake lives the *chajá* (horned screamer), a large grey bird with a startling patch of red around the eyes, as well as snakes (including the alarming yellow anaconda) and caimans. The capybara, the world's largest rodent, makes an unlikely swimmer, but in fact spends most of its time in the water – listen out for the splash as it enters.

Tours to the wetlands can be arranged in the village, and are highly recommended – without a guide it is hard to get your bearings, and you'll miss much of the wildlife. A variety of trips are on offer, by boat (you'll be poled through the marshier sections, where a motor is useless), on foot or on horseback; there are also moonlit night-time tours to see the nocturnal species.

Arrival and information

There's very little to Colonia Carlos Pellegrini, a grid of sandy streets around the Plaza San Martín, and very few facilities – bring enough cash to cover your entire stay. It lies 120km from the village of Mercedes (3hr approx; departures

Mon–Sat at noon; AR$30 one-way). Mercedes has a helpful tourist office (daily 8am–noon & 4–8pm; ☏03773/420-100) and you can also arrange private 4x4 transfers from here, through your accommodation in Colonia Carlos. Ten buses run daily from Corrientes to Mercedes (3hr). Access to Colonia Carlos is also possible from Posadas, to the northwest, but this is still slower, and frequently impassable in the wet (3 buses weekly with Nordestur, 5–6hr; AR$90 one-way; ☏03722/445-588).

Accommodation

The best accommodation in the village is provided by a handful of gorgeous posadas: they also provide food (often on a full-board basis) and organize tours.

Don Justino Hostel ☏03773/499-415, ✉ibertatours@hotmail.com. Good-quality budget accommodation with both private rooms and dorms. Rooms have a/c and prices include breakfast and towels. Dorms AR$45, rooms AR$130.

Posada Ypa Sapukai ☏03773/420-155, ⊛www .iberaturismo.com.ar. The most affordable of the posadas, this charming lakeside place has a small pool, lookout tower, impeccable rooms and beautiful garden. AR$100 per person per day full-board, excursions AR$60.

SAN IGNACIO

The riverside town of **SAN IGNACIO** is home to one of the major sights of northern Argentina – the dramatic remains of the Jesuit Missions at San Ignacio Miní. There's little clue of that in the centre, though, where this is just another hot, sleepy town. If you time the buses right you can visit the Jesuit missions at **San Ignacio Miní** and move on the same day, but there are a couple of other attractions worth visiting should you be staying longer.

The main street south will lead you past the **Casa de Horacio Quiroga** (daily 8am–6.30pm; AR$5; ☏03752/470-124), a museum to the Uruguayan-born Argentine writer of Gothic short stories, who made his home here in the early twentieth century. The same road continues to **Puerto Nuevo** on the Río Parana, a couple of kilometres away, where a

sandy beach offers wo[...] across the river to Paraguay. [...] more time you could also hea[...] **Parque Provincial Teyú Cuaré**, [...] 10km south of the village on a goo[...] unpaved road. Here there are camping facilities and you can seek out the **Peñón Reina Victoria**, a rock face said to resemble Queen Victoria's profile.

San Ignacio Miní

SAN IGNACIO MINÍ (daily 7am–7pm; AR$18; ticket valid for 15 days) was one of many Jesuit missions set up throughout Spanish America to convert the native population to Christianity. Originally established further north in what is now Brazil, the missionaries gradually moved south to avoid attack from Portuguese *bandeirantes* (piratical slave traders), eventually settling here in 1696. The mission became a thriving small town, inhabited by the local Guaraní, but, following the suppression of the Jesuits, was abandoned in the early nineteenth century. Rediscovered around a hundred years ago, the ruins are now among the best-preserved of their kind in Latin America, a UNESCO World Heritage Site with some spectacular Baroque architecture.

At the entrance, at the northeastern end of the village, an excellent **Centro de Interpretación Regional** looks at the life of the mission and its Guaraní inhabitants. Rows of simple *viviendas* (stone-built, single-storey living quarters which once housed Guaraní families) lead down to a grassy Plaza de Armas, overlooked by the **church** that dominates the site. The roof and most of the interior have long since crumbled away, but much of the magnificent facade, designed by the Italian architect Brazanelli, still stands and many fine details can be made out. Twin columns rise either side of the doorway, and the walls are decorated with exuberant bas-relief sculpture executed by Guaraní craftsmen.

such in San Ignacio,
off at the western
ento. Posadas
urly; 4–5hr).
entro de Informes
v. Sarmiento and
Ask here, or at the
d light shows, held
most evenings at San Ignacio Miní.

Accommodation and eating

There's not a great deal of quality when it comes to food, but for budget eats, try one of the pizzerias and snack bars near the ruins. There is a decent supermarket on San Martín, between Avenida Sarmiento and Belgrano.

Hospedaje El Descanso Pellegrini 270, towards the outskirts of the village around ten blocks south of the bus terminal ☎03752/470-207. Smart little bungalows with private bathrooms but no a/c; breakfast AR$3. AR$80.

Residencial Doka Alberdi 518 ☎03752/470-131, ✉recidoka@yahoo.com.ar. Rooms with a/c, TV, en-suite bathrooms and small kitchens, right next to the ruins. AR$100.

Residencial San Ignacio San Martín 823, corner Sarmiento ☎03752/470-047. The largest hotel in town is located right in the centre. Comfortable and modern rooms with TV and a/c. Internet on site. Great value and within walking distance to ruins. AR$130.

IGUAZÚ FALLS

Around 275 individual cascades, the highest with a drop of over 80m, make up the stunning **IGUAZÚ FALLS** (*Cataratas de Iguazú*, or simply *Las Cataratas*). Strung out along the rim of a horseshoe-shaped cliff 2.7km long, their thunderous roaring can be heard from miles away, while the mist thrown up rises 30m high in a series of dazzling rainbows. In the Guaraní language Iguazú means "great water", but clearly the Guaraní are not given to overstatement, for there's little doubt that these are the most spectacular falls in the world: only the Victoria Falls in Africa can compare in terms of size, but here the shape of the natural fault that created the falls means that you can stand with the water crashing almost all around you.

This section of the Río Iguazú makes up the border between Brazil and Argentina and the subtropical forests that surround the falls are protected on both sides: by the **Parque Nacional Iguazú** in Argentina, and the **Parque Nacional do Iguaçu** over the border (see p.383). These parks are packed with exotic wildlife, and even on the busy catwalks and paths that skirt the edges of the falls you've a good chance of seeing much of it. Orchids and serpentine creepers adorn the trees, among which flit vast, bright butterflies. You may also see toucans overhead and – if you're lucky – shy capuchin monkeys. Look out too for the swallow-like *vencejo*, a remarkable small bird, endemic to the area, which makes its nest behind the curtains of water.

The Parque Nacional Iguazú

Thanks to an extensive system of trails and catwalks that lead around, above and below the falls, the Argentine side offers better close-up views of Iguazú, while the Brazilian side has sweeping panoramic views. Everything lies within the **Parque Nacional Iguazú** (daily Oct–Feb 9am–7pm, March–Sept 9am–6pm; AR$85; ⓦwww.iguazuargentina.com), whose entrance lies 18km southeast of Puerto Iguazú along RN12. The visitor centre here can provide a map of the park and various handy leaflets. It's also the departure point of the **Tren de la Selva**, a natural-gas-fuelled train. This leaves every 30 minutes from 8.30am (last at 4pm, 4.30pm in summer) for Cataratas Station, which gives access to the walking trails and the Garganta del Diablo walkway.

Several well-signposted trails (most wheelchair-accessible) take you along a series of catwalks and paths to the park's highlights. The **Paseo Superior**, a short trail that takes you along the top of the first few waterfalls, makes a good introduction. For more drama, and a much wetter experience, the **Paseo Inferior** winds down through the forest before taking you to within metres of some of the smaller falls. At the bottom of this trail, a regular free boat service leaves for **Isla San Martín**, a rocky island in the middle of the river. Note that the boat doesn't run when water levels are high afer heavy rains. The same jetty is also the departure point for more thrills-oriented boat rides, such as those offered by Iguazú Jungle Explorer (☎03757/421-600, ⓦwww .iguazujunglexplorer.com; from AR$50 for a gentle nature ride to AR$220 for white-water fun).

At the heart of the falls is the truly unforgettable **Garganta del Diablo** (The Devil's Throat), a powerhouse display of natural forces in which 1800 cubic metres of water per second hurtles over a semicircle of rock into the misty river canyon below. The 1-km catwalk takes you to a small viewing platform within just a few metres of the staggering, sheer drop of water. Often shrouded in mist during winter mornings and early afternoons, the Garganta del Diablo is best visited later in the day, when the views tend to be clearer.

PUERTO IGUAZÚ

PUERTO IGUAZÚ is an inevitable stop if you're visiting the falls on a budget – it's a perfectly pleasant town with all the facilities you need, if a little dull. On the western edge of town, the **Hito Tres Fronteras** is an obelisk overlooking the rivers Iguazú and Parana at the point where they meet and form the three-way border between Argentina, Brazil and Paraguay. From here, "El Práctico" buses to the National Park run every half-hour (7am–7.15pm; AR$5 each way); you can also pick them up at intervals all the way along the main street, Avenida Victoria Aguirre.

Arrival and information

Air The airport is 25km southeast of Puerto Iguazú (☎03757/422-013). Buses meet flights and run to the bus terminal (☎03757/422-962; AR$8 one-way).

Bus All national and international bus services arrive at and leave from the bus terminal on Av. Córdoba, at Av. Misiones. There are a number of private information booths and travel agents to be found here.

National Park office Av. Victoria Aguirre 66 (Tues–Sun 8am–5pm winter, 8am–6pm summer; ☎03757/420-722).

Tourist information Av. Victoria Aguirre 311 (Mon–Fri 7am–9pm, Sat & Sun 8am–noon & 4–8pm; ☎03757/420-800).

Accommodation

There are a number of big resort hotels near the falls, but budget travellers head for Puerto Iguazú, where there are plenty of good hostels and inexpensive guesthouses. In high season, July and around Easter, reservations are recommended.
Lilian Fray Luis Beltrán 183 ☎03757/420-968, ⓔhotellilian@yahoo.com.ar. One of the slickest of

---

CROSSING INTO BRAZIL

To make your trip to Iguazú complete you should really visit the Brazilian side (see p.383), where the view is more panoramic, and the photography opportunities are excellent. There are no direct buses from Puerto Iguazú to the falls on the Brazilian side – you will need to take one of the regular international buses marked "Brasil" from the main street or bus station (AR$5), which will drop you at the border for immigration formalities. From the border pick up another bus towards Foz, changing to yet another for the falls themselves. If time is short, it's well worth considering sharing a taxi (approximately AR$100 return). Change some Brazilian cash before you go, for bus fares and the like, and bear in mind that, from October to March, Brazil is one hour ahead of Argentina.

the budget options, offering spotless modern rooms with good bathrooms. AR$205.

Marcopolo Inn ☎0375/421-823, ⓦwww .hostel-inn.com. Recently refurbished HI hostel with six-bed dorms and double rooms. There's a pool, free Iinternet and wi-fi, large kitchen, and friendly ambience. Dorms AR$60, rooms AR$220.

Noelia Residencial Fray Luis Beltrán 119, between Moreno and Belgrano ☎03757/420-729, ⓔresidenciafamiliarnoelia@yahoo.com.ar. Excellent value, family-run hotel not far from the bus station, with a/c, private baths and a lovely patio where breakfast is served. AR$160.

Viejo Americano RN12, 5km from town towards the national park ☎03757/420-190, ⓦwww.viejoamericano.com.ar. Excellent hotel/ campsite out of town with beautiful verdant grounds and a large pool. Camping AR$32 per person, rooms AR$270.

Eating and drinking

With a few exceptions, restaurants in Iguazú serve bland and touristy fare. At the falls there are several food cafés, but the food is expensive and uninspiring, so consider packing a picnic.

Las Canitas Av. Victoria Aguirre y Pombero. This lively local *peña* is a little off the main restaurant strip, but worth the walk for the warm welcome, live music and tasty grilled meats. Non-carnivores can tuck into vegetable kebabs and some interesting salads. Mains AR$20–35. Open daily 6pm until late.

Gallo Negro Av. Victoria Aguirre at Curupi. Probably the best in town; a good-looking ranch-style *parrilla* on the main street, with outdoor seating on a veranda. Cover charge of AR$8 per person includes unlimited access to the inviting salad bar. Mains AR$25–50. Open daily 11.30am–late.

Gustos del Literal Av. Misiones 209; no phone. This pocket-sized restaurant and bar serves lip-smackingly good dishes from neighbouring Paraguay. Try the *Chipa Guazu* – a warm, crumbly combination of fresh corn and white cheese, that here comes covered In tangy tomato sauce. Good cocktails too. Mains AR$20–25. Daily 8.30am–midnight.

La Rueda Córdoba 28 ☎03757/422-531. Pleasant restaurant where fish is a speciality, with outdoor seating. Mains AR$20–50. Mon–Tues 8pm–midnight, Wed–Sun noon–midnight.

Moving on

Air Aerolineas Argentinas (ⓦwww.aerolineas argentinas.com) has several daily flights to Buenos Aires (1hr 45min) from Puerto Iguazú airport. For international destinations, TAM (ⓦwww.tam.com .br) flies from the larger airport at Foz do Iguacu on the Brazilian side of the border. Taxi drivers will take you from your hotel to the airport at Foz, allowing time for completing visa formalities, for around AR$100.

Bus National and international bus services leave from the terminal on Av. Córdoba, at Av. Misiones. Travellers heading for destinations in Brazil will find that buses departing from Argentina are cheaper and more comfortable than those departing from across the border in Brazil, although it is often necessary to book well in advance. Crucero del Norte (ⓦwww.crucerodelnorte.com.ar) has regular departures to destinations across Argentina as well as to Sao Paulo and Rio de Janeiro in Brazil, Asunción in Paraguay, Santiago In Chile and Santa Cruz in Bolivia.

The northwest

Argentina's northwest is an area of deserts, red earth and whitewashed colonial churches, punctuated with pockets of cloudforest and lush green jungle. The pretty and inviting city of **Salta** is known for its well-preserved colonial architecture and makes a great base for visiting the wonderful natural formations of the **Quebrada del Toro** and **Quebrada de Cafayate**, as well as the stylish wine-producing villages of the **Valles Calchaquíes**, such as **Cafayate**. To the north of Salta loom three jungle-clad **cloudforests** – El Rey above all is worth a visit – along with the busy market town of **San Salvador de Jujuy**, with its palm trees and wild Andean feel. As you head further north the seven-coloured **Quebrada de Humahuaca** ravine can be seen from the small mud-brick towns of **Tilcara** and **Humahuaca**.

SALTA

SALTA is one of Argentina's most elegant provincial capitals, with leafy plazas, well-preserved colonial architecture and, thanks to the altitude,

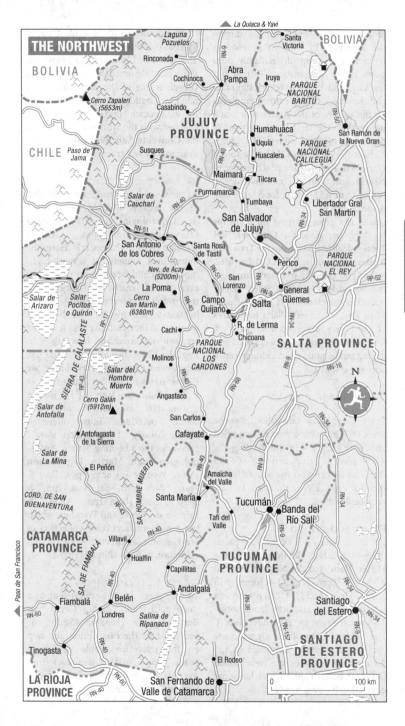

THE NORTHWEST

BOLIVIA

La Quiaca & Yavi

Laguna Pozuelos

Santa Victoria

BOLIVIA

Rinconada

Cochinoca

Abra Pampa

Iruya

PARQUE NACIONAL BARITÚ

San Ramón de la Nueva Oran

Cerro Zapaleri (5653m)

Casabindo

JUJUY PROVINCE

Humahuaca

CHILE

Paso de Jama

Susques

Uquía

Huacalera

PARQUE NACIONAL CALILEGUA

Maimará

Tilcara

Salar de Cauchari

RN-40

Purmamarca

Tumbaya

Libertador Gral San Martín

RN-51

San Salvador de Jujuy

San Antonio de los Cobres

Santa Rosa de Tastil

Perico

PARQUE NACIONAL EL REY

RP-52

Nev. de Acay (5200m)

San Lorenzo

Salar de Arizaro

Salar Pocitos o Quirón

La Poma

Cerro San Martín (6380m)

Campo Quijano

Salta

General Güemes

SIERRA DE CALALASTE

Cachi

R. de Lerma

Chicoana

SALTA PROVINCE

PARQUE NACIONAL LOS CARDONES

RP-43

Molinos

RN-16

Salar del Hombre Muerto

Angastaco

RN-68

N

Cerro Galán (5912m)

San Carlos

Salar de Antofalla

Cafayate

Antofagasta de la Sierra

Salar de La Mina

Amaicha del Valle

El Peñón

CORD. DE SAN BUENAVENTURA

SA. HOMBRE MUERTO

Santa María

Tucumán

Banda del Río Salí

RP-43

Tafí del Valle

CATAMARCA PROVINCE

Villavil

TUCUMÁN PROVINCE

Hualfin

Capillitas

RN-40

Andalgalá

RN-38

Fiambalá

Belén

Santiago del Estero

Paso de San Francisco

Londres

Salina de Ripanaco

RN-60

RN-157

Tinogasta

SANTIAGO DEL ESTERO PROVINCE

El Rodeo

LA RIOJA PROVINCE

San Fernando de Valle de Catamarca

0   100 km

ARGENTINA

THE NORTHWEST

a pleasantly balmy climate during the summer. In the winter months temperatures drop dramatically, and snow is not uncommon. Throughout the city, and in its hotels, restaurants and museums, there's a strong emphasis on the culture of the Andes, and you'll notice that the food is spicier than in the south of the country. Attractions include the cable-car ride to the top of **Cerro San Bernardo**, a peach-coloured Neoclassical church, and wonderful *peñas* that mix spicy food and live Andean music.

Salta is a great jumping-off point for the high passes of the **Quebrada del Toro** – ideally viewed from the **Tren a las Nubes** – and for the **Valles Calchaquíes**, where you can stay overnight amongst the vineyards of **Cafayate**. A less-visited option is the cloudforest national park of **El Rey**, to the east. Salta has scores of good backpacker hostels, but these tend to fill up quickly at weekends and during public holidays, making advance booking essential.

What to see and do

The verdant **Plaza 9 de Julio** lies at the heart of Salta, with scenic cafés nestled under its arches – in the evening the whole place is lit up, and half of Salta seems to descend on the square for an evening stroll. This is the place to start your exploration.

Plaza 9 de Julio
On the southern side of the leafy plaza, the whitewashed **Cabildo** houses the **Museo Histórico del Norte** (Tues–Sat 9.30am–1.30pm & 3.30–8.30pm, Sun 9.30am–1pm; AR$5), which displays an eclectic array of artefacts, from horse-drawn carriages to everyday objects. The balcony here offers a great view over the goings-on in the square. Facing the museum is the ornate Neoclassical **Catedral**, built in 1882, which has some interesting frescoes inside.

Just east of the plaza, Calle Caseros leads to two more interesting churches. The blood-red **Iglesia y Convento San Francisco**, designed by architect Luigi Giorgi, is one of the most impressive religious buildings in the country. Its exuberance makes a fascinating contrast with the whitewashed walls of the **Convento San Bernardo**, a lesson in simplicity and tranquillity in design.

Museums
A new and controversial addition to the area is MAAM, the **Museo de Arqueología de Alta Montaña** (Tues–Sun 11am–7pm; AR$30; Ⓦmaam.culturasalta.gov.ar). Here the mummified remains of several high-mountain child sacrifices are on display, even though many locals argue that the perfectly preserved remains should be laid to rest instead. The beautiful exhibits of Inca clothing and jewellery are well organized and have labels in English. Close by, at La Florida 20, the **Museo Casa de Arías Rengel de Bellas Artes** (Tues–Sat 9am–1pm & 5–9pm, Sun 9am–1pm; AR$5) houses a wonderful collection of nineteenth-century paintings. Those interested in the history of the region should check out the adjoining **Museo Antropológico Juan Martín Leguizamón** (Mon, Wed & Fri 8am–7pm, Tues & Thurs 8am–9pm, Sat 9am–1pm & 3–7pm; Sun 10am–1pm; AR$5), at Ejército del Norte and Polo Sur, which has a modern, accessible collection of pre-Hispanic arteifacts, as well as an exhibition of high-altitude burials.

Cerro San Bernardo
To the east of the microcentro a steep path leads you up **Cerro San Bernardo** hill (1458m; 45min), or you can take the easy option and hop on the **teleférico** (cable car; daily 10am–7.45pm; AR$12 one-way) from Avenida Hipólito Yrigoyen, between Urquiza and Avenida San Martín, at

the eastern end of Parque San Martín. At the top are lush, well-manicured gardens complete with waterfalls, and a small café with sweeping views over Salta and out to the Lerma valley and Andes mountains beyond.

Arrival

Air Salta's airport (℡0387/424-2904) is 10km southwest of the city centre. Airbus (℡0387/1568-32897; AR$12) runs between the airport and central Salta; a taxi should cost no more than AR$40.

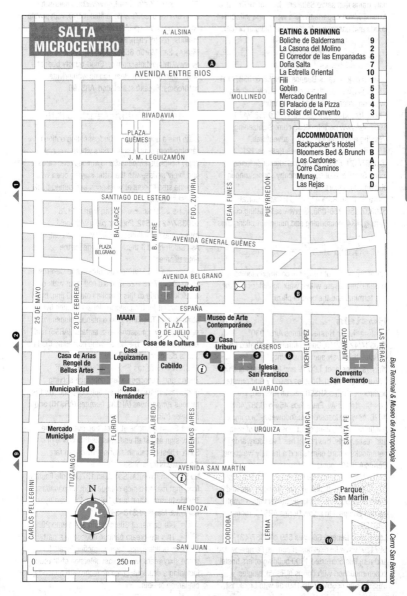

SALTA MICROCENTRO

EATING & DRINKING
Boliche de Balderrama   9
La Casona del Molino   2
El Corredor de las Empanadas   6
Doña Salta   7
La Estrella Oriental   10
Fili   1
Goblin   5
Mercado Central   8
El Palacio de la Pizza   4
El Solar del Convento   3

ACCOMMODATION
Backpacker's Hostel   E
Bloomers Bed & Brunch   B
Los Cardones   A
Corre Caminos   F
Munay   C
Las Rejas   D

A. ALSINA
AVENIDA ENTRE RIOS
MOLLINEDO
RIVADAVIA
PLAZA GUEMES
J. M. LEGUIZAMÓN
SANTIAGO DEL ESTERO
BALCARCE
B. MITRE
FDO. ZUVIRIA
DEAN FUNES
PUEYRREDÓN
PLAZA BELGRANO
AVENIDA GENERAL GUÉMES
AVENIDA BELGRANO
Catedral
ESPAÑA
MAAM
PLAZA 9 DE JULIO
Museo de Arte Contemporáneo
Casa Uriburu
CASEROS
VICENTE LOPEZ
JURAMENTO
LAS HERAS
Casa de la Cultura
Casa Leguizamón
Casa de Arias Rengel de Bellas Artes
Cabildo
Iglesia San Francisco
Convento San Bernardo
Municipalidad
Casa Hernández
ALVARADO
25 DE MAYO
20 DE FEBRERO
Mercado Municipal
FLORIDA
JUAN B. ALBERDI
BUENOS AIRES
URQUIZA
CATAMARCA
SANTA FE
ITUZAINGÓ
AVENIDA SAN MARTÍN
CARLOS PELLEGRINI
MENDOZA
Parque San Martín
CORDOBA
LERMA
SAN JUAN
N
0   250 m

ARGENTINA

THE NORTHWEST

Bus Terminal & Museo de Antropología

Cerro San Bernardo

Bus All buses arrive at the bus terminal
(☎0387/401-1143) eight blocks east of the
main plaza along Parque San Martín. It has luggage
storage, cafés, chemists and bakeries but
no internet.

Train Bus #5 links the bus terminal with the train
station, at Ameghino 690, via Plaza 9 de Julio. The
only trains that serve Salta are the tourist *Tren a las
Nubes,* which departs twice a week, and infrequent
goods and passenger trains to the Chilean border.

Tour operators

MoviTrack Safaris Buenos Aires 68 ☎0387/431-
6749, ⊛www.movitrack.com.ar. Lively 1–2 day
overland safaris and sightseeing tours.

Norte Trekking Los Juncos 173 ☎0387/439-
6957, ⊛www.nortetrekking.com. Sightseeing,
trekking and mountaineering adventures.

Ricardo Clark Expediciones Caseros 121
☎0387/421-5390, ⊛www.clarkexpediciones
.com. Small ecotourism company specializing in
birdwatching tours.

Salta Rafting Ruta 47, Km 34, Cabra Corral
☎0387/156-856-085, ⊛www.saltarafting.com.
Rafting, 4X4, horseriding and mountain-biking trips.

Accommodation

There are plenty of budget accommodation options
in Salta, and all are within walking distance of the
bus terminal and the central plaza.

Hostels

Backpacker's Hostel Buenos Aires 930
☎0387/423-5910. One of three HI-affiliated hostels
in Salta, this lively spot wins points for its free
dinners, large pool, LCD TV and fun events such as
five-a-side football. Doubles have TV and private
bathroom. Dorms AR$50, rooms AR$160.

Los Cardones Av. Entre Rios 454 ☎0387/431-
4026, ⊛www.loscardones.todowebsalta.com.ar.
A little out of the centre but close to lots of bars
and restaurants, this hostel has five courtyards,
hammocks, board games and a friendly welcome.
Dorms AR$40, rooms AR$110.

Corre Caminos Vicente Lopéz 353 ☎0387/422-
0731, ⊛www.saltahostel.com. Basic rooms and
clean bathrooms in this lively hostel with a small
garden and pool to enjoy. Dorms AR$45, rooms
AR$120.

Las Rejas General Güemes 569 ☎0387/421-
5971, ⊛www.lasrejashostel.com.ar. Family-owned
and run, this converted 1900 building offers hostel
accommodation with dorms (AR$55), singles
(AR$95) and doubles (AR$150) all with breakfast,

as well as more luxurious accommodation at the
adjoining B&B, where rooms start at AR$250. Inside
the B&B there's also a well-equipped four-person
apartment, with kitchen, for AR$440.

Hotels

Bloomers Bed & Brunch Vicente Lopéz 129
☎0387/422-7449, ⊛www.bloomers-salta
.com.ar. Five beautifully decorated rooms, with private
bathrooms and a spectacular breakfast (there's an
in-house pastry chef), which changes daily. AR$320.

Munay San Martín 656 ☎0387/422-4936,
⊛www.munayhotel.com.ar. Good-quality budget
hotel, with basic but clean rooms with private
bathrooms. Breakfast included. AR$190.

Eating, drinking and nightlife

Salta has a good range of budget eating options,
ranging from simple snack bars where you can
enjoy delicious *empanadas* to atmospheric cafés
and lively *peñas*, with the latter staying open well
into the small hours at weekends and during peak
tourist seasons.

Boliche de Balderrama San Martín 1126
☎0387/421-1542. Popular *peña* with local
music, and sometimes dancing while you eat.
Ask beforehand if there is a charge for the
entertainment.

La Casona del Molino Luis Burela and Caseros
2500 ☎0387/434-2835. It's a half-hour walk or
a quick taxi ride to this rambling old building, but
well worth it for the delicious local food and lively
atmosphere. The fairly priced menu includes *empanadas, locro, guaschalocro, tamales* (AR$5) and
humitas (AR$10). The house wine comes by the litre
and is dangerously drinkable.

El Corredor de las Empanadas Corner of
Zuriria and Necochea. Pleasant place serving
northwestern treats, with an outdoor patio. Try the
famous *empanadas* (AR$3), *humitas* (AR$10) and
tamales (AR$5).

Doña Salta Córdoba 46. Don't be put off by the
tacky sign and staff uniforms, as this is one of
Salta's best restaurants for northwestern fare.
Empanadas from AR$3.

La Estrella Oriental San Juan 137. Middle Eastern
food that makes a nice change from *empanadas*.
Try the hummus and lamb kebabs, followed by
baklawa. Mains AR$18–24.

Fili Corner of Güemes and Sarmiento 29.
This ice-cream parlour, housed in a natty
Art Deco building, has been attracting locals for
some sixty years with its vast selection of flavours,
including a delicious *dulce de leche* with almonds,
cinnamon or both.

Goblin Caseros 445. Every city has to have an Irish pub, and Salta's is not a bad option for pub grub and draught beer. Mains start at around AR$20.

Mercado Central La Florida and San Martín. Good for lunch, with a range of inexpensive food stalls offering everything from hot dogs and fries to *locro* and *humitas*, with prices starting around AR$3.

El Solar del Convento Caseros 444 ☎0387/421-5124. Stylish decor, attentive service and thoughtfully prepared traditional dishes combine to make this restaurant a standout on Salta's dining scene. The wine list is extensive, and local "champagne" is served on the house. Mains AR$35–60.

Directory

Banks and exchange There are several banks with ATMS at Plaza 9 de Julho, and Av. Espana is lined with banks including HSBC, Banco Francés, Santander and Citibank. There are further cashpoints and exchange services at the corner of Espana and Mitre.

Car rental Rent a Truck, Buenos Aires 1 (☎0387/431-0740).

Internet Salta Internet, Florida 55.

Post office Deán Funes 170.

Moving on

Air Buenos Aires (2–3 daily; 2hr 30min); Córdoba (2–3 daily; 1hr 30min); Tucumán (2–3 daily; 40min).

Bus There are regular direct departures from Salta to Buenos Aires (around 20hr) as well as to Rosario, Puerto Iguazú, Córdoba, Tucumán, La Quica and Mendoza.

LA QUEBRADA DEL TORO

There are several ways to experience the dramatic, ever-changing scenery of the **Quebrada del Toro** gorge and its surrounding towns; you can rent a car, take an organized tour or hop on the **Tren a los Nubes** – a fabulous if expensive experience (Thurs & Sat Feb–Oct only; US$140 approx). Leaving early from Salta and the Lerma valley, you start to ascend the multicoloured gorge of the Río El Toro, usually tranquil but sometimes torrential in spring. The rail tracks acend to a dizzying 4200m above sea level, allowing you to experience this exceptional engineering achievement (there are 21 tunnels and more than 13 viaducts, the highlight of them the 64m-high, 224m-long **Polvorilla Viaduct**, almost at the top of the line). Along the way there are various stops and photo opportunities, usually including the town of **Santa Rosa de Tastil**, the pre-Incan site of **Tastil**, and the small mining town of **San Antonio de los Cobres**, where local artists sell their jewellery, clothing and toys by the train station.

PARQUE NACIONAL EL REY

The spectacular cloudforests of the **PARQUE NACIONAL EL REY** (9am–dusk; free) lie just under 200km from Salta. Set in a natural, half-moon-shaped amphitheatre, locked in by the curving **Crestón del Gallo** ridge to the northwest, and the higher crest of the **Serranía del Piquete** (1700m) to the east, El Rey features an upland enclave covered in lush green vegetation, with high year-round humidity and precipitation but with very distinct seasons – very wet in summer, dry (or at least not so wet) in winter. The park is frequently covered in a low-lying mist, the signature feature of cloudforests, protecting the plants and animals beneath it. El Rey is particularly good for **birdwatching**: the giant toucan is the park's symbol, and is easily spotted, while at least 150 other bird species also live here, as well as jaguar and howler monkeys.

There is just one access road to the park (the RP20), and if visiting independently it is advisable that you check in with the **guardaparques** at the park entrance before you set off. They can advise you on the status of the rivers you'll need to cross to access the park. The only options for an overnight stay at the park are to pitch tent at one of the two official **camping** spots, basic but with toilets and showers – one of which is close to the Popayán River and the other is near to the park authorities. Again, check with the *guardaparques* at the entrance for directions and prices.

The easiest way to discover the park is on an **organized trip** from Salta (see p.102).

VALLES CALCHAQUÍES

To the south of Salta lie the stunning **VALLES CALCHAQUÍES**, the valleys of the Río Calchaquí, fed by snowmelt from the Andes. Here you'll find some of the highest vineyards in the world. You can rent your own car from Salta to explore the area, which would give you the opportunity to hike through some of the wonderful cactus forests of the **Cuesta del Obispo** in the **Parque Nacional Los Cardones**; and you can visit the little towns of **Cachi** and **Cafayate** which are easily accessible by bus. There are also tours from both Cafayate and Salta.

CACHI

CACHI lies around 160km southwest of Salta, along an incredibly scenic route with mountainous views across lush valleys. Cachi is small and still quite undiscovered, but what it lacks in services, it makes up for in scenery and location. The permanently snow-covered **Nevado del Cachi** (6380m), 15km to the west, looms over the town.

What to see and do

Truth is, there's not a great deal to detain you in Cachi other than the tranquil and picturesque nature of the place itself. A small **Plaza Mayor**, shaded by palms and orange trees, marks the centre of town and on the north side you'll find the well-restored **Iglesia San José**. Its bright white exterior gives way to an interior made almost entirely, from pews to confessional, of porous cactus wood. Not far away, the **Museo Arqueológico Pío Pablo Díaz** (Mon–Sat 8.30am–6.30pm,

Sun 10am–1pm; AR$2) displays local archeological finds in an attractive building with a wonderful patio. For the more energetic, a hiking track to the west of the village will lead you to **Cachi Adentro** (6km), where you'll have wonderful views of the surrounding landscape and may see the endless fields of drying paprika which line the route from March to May.

Arrival

Bus Buses from Salta (and local buses from nearby villages) drop passengers off at the main square. From there all services are within walking distance.

Accommodation

There are relatively few places to stay in Cachi itself, and most budget travellers looking for a bed head on to Cafayate.

Hostería ACA Sol del Valle J.M. Castilla (at the top of the hill) ☎03868/491-105, ✆www.soldelvalle.com.ar. A lovely, if pricey, option, whose modern rooms offer views over the valley. There's an inviting pool, and the spotless rooms have cable TV and wi-fi. AR$380.

Municipal Camping Av. Automóvil Club Argentina (at the end) ☎03868/491-053. Basic clean campsite, with cabins on offer. Pool and shaded areas. AR$4 per person.

Nevado de Cachi Ruiz de los Llanos ☎03868/491-004. Right next to the bus stop on the plaza, this small family-run hotel has been recently refurbished and now offers spick-and-span rooms centred on a leafy courtyard. There's a good grilled meat restaurant too, open to non-guests. AR$160.

Eating

ACA Sol del Valle J.M. Castilla. The hotel restaurant serves local food, including hearty soups and stews, as well as cakes, sandwiches and pastries at the adjoining café-bar. The setting is wonderful and the staff friendly. Mains AR$20–28.

El Jagüel Av. General Güemes. Delicious locally made *locro* (AR$4) and *empanadas* (AR$2).

Moving on

Bus There are frequent onward services to Cafayate (2hr 30min), Salta (2hr) and local destinations.

AROUND CACHI

The 157-km drive from Cachi to Cafayate takes you through some of the region's most spectacular scenery and some delightful little towns. A short stop in **Molinos** (60km from Cachi) is recommended to view the local crafts, see the picturesque adobe houses and check out a fabulous church, the eighteenth-century **Iglesia de San Pedro Nolasco**. Beyond the town of Angastaco, the red sandstone **Quebrada de las Flechas** gorge is filled with dangerous-looking arrow-head formations. Shortly afterwards the road passes through **El Ventisquero**, the "wind-tunnel", and the natural stone walls of **El Cañón**, over 20m high.

CAFAYATE

The largest town in the region, and the main tourist base, is **CAFAYATE**. Set amid apparently endless vineyards, it makes a perfect place to hole up for a few days while exploring the surrounding area on horseback or sipping the local wines at nearby *bodegas*. The town is lively, filled with inviting plazas and popular restaurants.

What to see and do

Cafayate is another town where there's really not a great deal to do – the pleasure lies in getting out into the countryside and exploring the vineyards. A couple of museums will fill a few hours, however. The **Museo Arqueológico** (daily 11am–8pm; donation admission; ☏03868/421-054), at the corner of Colón and Calchaquí, is the private collection of late collector Rodolfo Bravo. On display alongside archeological relics are local ceramics, and everyday items from the colonial period. The **Museo de la Vid y el Vino** on Av. General Güemes (Mon–Fri 10am–1pm & 5–8pm; AR$2; ☏03868/21125) is an interesting introduction to wine-making in the area and shows, through old machinery, the improvements and developments made to local viticulture in recent times.

Arrival and information

Bus Buses from Salta and nearby villages use the small terminal on Belgrano, east of the plaza, though some will drop you off at your destination as you pass through town. Ask the driver. Buses from Tucumán arrive at the terminal on Güemes Norte and Alvarado.

Tourist information A kiosk on the plaza (Mon–Fri 9am–8pm, Sat & Sun 7am–1pm & 3–9pm) dispenses information about where to stay, what to do and where to rent bikes or hire horses. Look for the helpful hand-drawn map of the wineries.

Tour operators Puna Turismo, at San Martín 82 (☏03868/421-808), can arrange horse rides, trekking, 4x4 tours, winery tours and mountain-bike adventures. Turismo Cordillerano, at Camila Quintana de Niño 59 (☏03868/422-137), offers trekking, and excursions to the Valle Calchaquí.

Accommodation

The recent boom in tourism has generated a range of options in budget accommodation. All are within walking distance of the plaza, and can advise on winery visits.

Hostal de Valle San Martín 243 ☏03868/421-039, ⊛www.nortevirtual .com. Large, light spacious rooms, set around a luscious patio. Ask for a room upstairs. AR$215.

WINERY VISITS

There are some world-class wineries around Cafayate and most offer tours in English and Spanish with a tasting afterwards. Taking a tour is a great way to see which wines you prefer, and to appreciate the whole process. Two of the most popular are Bodega Etchart on RN40 (daily 9am–5pm; ☏03868/421-529, ⊛www.bodegasetchart.com) and Bodega La Rosa on RN68 (Mon–Fri 8am–12.30pm & 1.30–7pm; ☏03868/421-201). Both are within walking or cycling distance, and offer free tours. Ask at the information centre on the small plaza in Cafayate for a winery map of the area.

Hostel Ruta 40 Güermes Sur 178 ☎03868/421-689, ⓦwww.hostel-ruta40.com. The newest and most lively hostel in town, with clean dorms (AR$50) and small doubles (AR$220). HI discount.

Rusty K Hostal Rivadavia 281 ☎03868/422-031, ⓦwww.rustykhostal.com.ar. Central, friendly hostel with a pleasant garden to relax in. Dorms AR$50, rooms AR$160.

Eating and drinking

Restaurants and cafés surround the main plaza, where in summer you can join crowds of locals strolling through the city at dusk with an ice cream.

Baco Güermes Norte and Rivadavia. Simple decor and friendly staff make this corner restaurant popular, as do its pizzas (AR$24), trout (AR$30) and local wines.

Carreta de Don Olegario Güermes Sur 20 and Quintana de Niño on the east side of the plaza. Popular for its reasonably priced local dishes, this well-located restaurant features live traditional music as well as hearty goat and meat stews, veggie-friendly tortillas and pasta dishes, and delicious cheeses (mains AR$25–40). There's a good selection of wines from local *bodegas* too. Open daily noon–3pm and 7–11pm.

Las Dos Marias San Martin 27. This simple restaurant on the plaza serves traditional local dishes and is a great place for a mid-morning coffee or a relaxed evening meal with wine. The *humitas* (AR$6) are excellent. Daily 8am–2pm and 5–11pm.

Heladería Miranda Av. Güermes, half a block north of the plaza. Gourmet ice creams in exotic flavours; try the famous wine sorbets.

Moving on

Bus Salta (3–4 daily; 5hr); Tucumán (3 daily; 6–8hr).

SAN SALVADOR DE JUJUY

Generally playing second fiddle to its prettier cousin Salta, **SAN SALVADOR DE JUJUY** (known as Jujuy) lies 90km to the north. Although it is the highest provincial capital in the country, at 1260m above sea level, Jujuy is set in a lush pocket of humidity and greenery. It's a busy place, with a frantic, market feel, where crumbling colonial buildings are juxtaposed with neon signs. Most travellers pass through for just one night on their way to the surrounding attractions, and they're probably right to do so – there are few real sights here. The real lure is out of town, above all to the north in the spectacular colours of the **Quebrada de Humahuaca** and the small towns of **Tilcara** and **Humahuaca**.

What to see and do

If you have time to kill in Jujuy, head to the lively **Plaza General Belgrano**, east of the city centre. This large, green open space is generally crowded with young locals, checking out the craftsmen and market sellers who set up stalls here. Across town, the late eighteenth-century **Catedral** (Mon–Fri 7.30am–1pm & 5–9pm, Sat & Sun 8am–noon & 5–9pm) makes up for a plain facade with a wonderfully decorative interior, above all a spectacular pulpit decorated by local artists over two centuries ago. This has a rival in the intricate pulpit of the nearby **Iglesia San Francisco**, whose tiny human figures, columns and scenes are thought to have been carved in Bolivia.

Arrival and information

Air Jujuy's airport (☎0388/491-1102), 30km southeast of the city, is serviced by TEA Turismo,

> **TREAT YOURSELF**
>
> Just 19km west of Jujuy are the thermal hot springs of the Termas de Reyes and the Hotel Termas de Reyes (☎0388/392-2522, ⓦwww.termasdereyes.com; AR$490). Sinking into a hot mineral spa bath, or relaxing with a mineral mud mask, is just the way to shake off a long bus ride. There are fourteen private thermal baths for three people, with stunning panoramic views, as well as two saunas. The #14 public bus runs to Termas from the main bus terminal (4 daily; 20min).

which runs a shuttle service to and from the city centre (AR$8; ☏0388/423-6270). A taxi will cost around AR$30.

Bus The ugly bus terminal (☏0388/422-6299), at Iguazú and Av. Dorrego, just south of the centre across the Río Chico, serves all local, regional and national destinations, and also offers services to Chile and Bolivia.

Tourist Information Dirección Provincial de Turismo, Belgrano and Gorriti (Mon–Fri 7am–9pm, Sat & Sun 8am–9pm; ☏0388/422-1325, ⓦwww .turismo.jujuy.gov.ar).

Tour operators Noroeste, at San Martín 155 (☏0388/423-7565, ⓦwww.noroestevirtual.com .ar) is a youth travel agency attached to *Club Hostel*; Tour Andino, at S Perez 355 (☏0388/424-2303, ⓦwww.tourandino.com.ar) offers adventure breaks including sandboarding, parasailing and trekking among others.

Accommodation

Club Hostel San Martín 155 ☏0388/423-7565, ⓦwww.hihostels.com. Busy, lively hostel with a small pool, within walking distance of the bus terminal and the centre. Dorms AR$35.

🚶 **Hostal Casa de Barro** Otero 294 ☏0388/422-9578, ⓦwww.casadebarro .com.ar. Wonderful and welcoming, with clean spacious dorms and private rooms, an excellent on-site restaurant and a pleasant common area. Dorms AR$35, rooms AR$90.

Munay Tierra de Colores Alvear 1230 ☏0388/422-8435, ⓦwww.munayhotel.com.ar. Just north of the centre, this friendly small hostel has clean, rather dark rooms with private bathrooms. AR$190.

🚶 **Yok Wahi** La Madrid 168 ☏0388/422-9608, ⓦwww.yokwahi.com. Friendly, central and basic with great breakfast. Dorms AR$45, rooms AR$110.

Eating and drinking

The open-air market, next to the bus station, is a great place to fill up on *empanadas*, grilled meat sandwiches, coffee, hot chocolate and the like for just a few pesos.

Cacao Sarmiento 330 ☏0388/423-2037. Sophisticated formal dining, good tapas and an extensive list of local wines. Mains from AR$35. Daily 8.30am–12.30pm.

La Candelaria Alvear 1346. West of the city, this *parrilla* is a local institution, and a must for any meat-lover. Large steak AR$32.

Madre Tierra Belgrano 619. Fresh salads (AR$12), juices and vegetarian food. Closed Sun.

Zorba Belgrano 802. Large, two-storey restaurant serving Greek food, as well as local favourites. Mains AR$30. Open for breakfast, lunch and dinner.

Directory

Banks and exchange Alvear is lined with banks that accept foreign cards, including HSBC at Alvear 970.

Car rental Sudamerics, Belgrano 601 (☏0388/422-9034, ⓦwww.sudamerics.com).

Post office La Madrid and Independencia.

Moving on

Bus Buenos Aires (3 daily; 20hr); Cordoba (3 daily; 12–13hr); Tucumán (6 daily; 5hr); Jujuy (hourly; 2hr); Cafayate (4 daily, 4hr).

QUEBRADA DE HUMAHUACA

The scintillating, multicoloured **QUEBRADA DE HUMAHUACA** gorge stretches 125km north of Jujuy, past the exclusive resort of **Purmamarca** and the town of **Tilcara**, with its pre-Columbian archeological site, all the way to the busy village of **Humahuaca**. From there you can carry on to reach the border crossing with Bolivia at **La Quaica**, nearly 2000m higher and 150km further on. The region is popular with Argentine holidaymakers, who come to stay in the many swish spas and resorts, to hike and take in the extraordinary mountain scenery.

Purmamarca

As you head north, the first substantial settlement you reach along RN9 is **PURMAMARCA** at Km 61. This small town sits at the foot of the stunning **Cerro de los Siete Colores** (Hill of Seven Colours) and is an ideal base for horseriding and hiking excursions. Purmarmarca is popular with Argentine tourists, and home to scores of luxury hotels as well as more budget-friendly options. Despite this tourist influx it retains plenty of rustic Andean charm, thanks to its traditional adobe buildings and colourfully dressed locals. The village has a fantastic seventeenth-century church, the **Iglesia Santa Rosa de Lima**, at its heart – faithfully maintained and still in use today.

Tilcara

The busy tourist town of **TILCARA** is a favourite with Argentine holidaymakers for its fantastic restaurants, affordable hotels and above all the pre-Incan **pukará** or fortress (daily 9am–6pm; AR$5, free Tues). Discovered in 1903 and heavily reconstructed in the 1950s, the site enjoys a wonderful, commanding location, covered in giant cacti. To get here, follow the signposted trail from the centre of town over the bridge across the Río Huasamayo. Keep your entrance ticket for admission to the **Museo Arqueológico** (daily 9am–7pm; AR$2, free Tues), on the south side of the square in a beautiful colonial house. The well-presented collection includes a mummy from San Pedro de Atacama.

Humahuaca

HUMAHUACA is the main tourist town in the Quebrada; a small, attractive place, originally founded in 1591. Numerous shops, restaurants and craft stalls stand all around the leafy plaza. On the east side, the tiny **Iglesia de la Candelaria**, constructed in 1631 and rebuilt in the nineteenth century, has some interesting artworks. The cool, high-ceilinged interior offers a refreshing break from the dry heat outside. Beside the church, steps lead up to the base of the **Monumento a la Independencia**, a masculine and dramatic sculpture. There are awesome views from here, pocked by human-size cacti.

Arrival and information

Bus Buses leave every hour from Jujuy and run up the Quebrada to Purmamarca (1hr), Tilcara (1hr 30min–2hr) and Humahuaca (3hr), dropping off locals at farms and houses along the way. Only certain companies go all the way to La Quiaca –

look for El Quiaqueño, Panamericano and Balut. Both Tilcara and Humahuaca have a central bus terminal that offers luggage storage; at other towns you will be dropped off at the main plaza.

Tourist information The region's best tourist office is in Ticara, at Belgrano 590 (daily 8am–noon and 1–9pm; ☎0388/495-5720). It has lists of accommodation throughout the region and free maps. Otherwise there is a small tourist office in Humahuaca (Mon–Fri 9–6pm), in the white colonial *cabildo* building on the plaza. A small donation is required for maps.

Tour operators Tilcara Tours, at Bustamente 159 in Jujuy (☎0388/422-6113), organizes good guided tours into the Quebrada de Humahuaca.

Accommodation

The best budget accommodation is found in Tilcara and Humahuaca, although campgrounds can be found in nearly every town in the valley.

Tilcara

Malka San Martín (at the top of the hill) ☎0388/495-5197, ⊛www.malkahostel.com.ar. It's a strenuous uphill walk to this hostel which has comfortable cabañas for up to six people – great value if travelling in a group – as well as dorms and private rooms. HI discounts. Dorms AR$65, rooms AR$230.

Tilcara Hostel Bolívar 166 ☎0388/495-5105, ⊛www.tilcarahostel.com. A 10-min walk from the bus station, this new hostel has clean dorms (AR$40) and excellent value doubles complete with kitchen and private bathroom (AR$150). There are also fully equipped eight-person cabañas (AR$350).

Humahuaca

Hostal Humahuaca Buenos Aires 447 ☎03887/421-064, ⊛www.humahuacahostal.com.ar. Located just off the main plaza, this small hostel has slightly dark but cool dorm rooms set around a bright patio. Dorms AR$40, rooms AR$140.

Posada el Sol Barrio Medalla Milagrosa (across the river) ☎0388/421-1466, ⊛www.posadaelsol.com.ar. Follow the signs from the bus station to this small rustic house on the outskirts of town. Small, comfortable dorms (AR$36) and doubles (AR$105) in peaceful surroundings. HI discounts.

Eating and drinking

Tilcara

El Nuevo Progreso Lavelle 351. This intimate, candle-lit spot serves delicious Andean cuisine in hearty portions. The llama steaks are good, and there's a decent wine list sourced from local *bodegas*. Live music some evenings. Mains from AR$25. Daily 6–11pm.

Pucará Padilla (at the top of the hill). This restaurant on the way to the ruins offers new ways of preparing traditional food. Desserts are particularly good. Mains AR$22–34. Open for lunch and dinner.

Humahuaca

La Casa Vieja corner of Buenos Aires and Salta. More regional dishes, including a very substantial *locro*. Good lunch spot. Mains from AR$25. Daily from 7pm.

El Portillo Tucumán 69. This hotel restaurant serves traditional food including llama meat, quinoa and Andean potatoes in a rustic environment. Mains AR$20. Daily 7pm–midnight.

Mendoza and San Juan

The vast midwestern provinces of **Mendoza** and **San Juan** are sparsely populated, sun-fried playgrounds for lovers of mountains and vineyards. The highest peaks outside the Himalayas rise to the west, capped by the formidable **Cerro Aconcagua**, whose icy volcanic summit punctures the sky at nearly 7000m, an irresistible magnet for experienced climbers. Further south down the Andean cordillera is the see-and-be-seen resort of **Las Leñas**, whose powdery slopes deliver some of the best skiing in South America. Come summer, snowmelt rushes down the mountains, swelling rivers and creating ideal **white-water rafting** conditions, especially along the Cañon de Atuel near the small city of **San Rafael**.

At the foothills of the mountains, the same sunshine that pummels the region's inhospitable, parched desertscapes also feeds its celebrated grapevines. Wine enthusiasts will feel right at home in the eminently liveable city of **Mendoza**, the region's urban hub,

which offers easy access to Argentina's best *bodegas*. North of here, the provincial capital of **San Juan** and the village of **Valle Fértil** act as good bases for two of the country's most striking UNESCO World Heritage-listed parks: the bizarrely shaped rock formations of **Ischigualasto** (also known as Valle de la Luna), and, just over the border in the province of La Rioja, the wide-bottomed canyon, pre-Columbian petroglyphs and rich wildlife of **Talampaya**.

For more arresting scenery, make for the tumbleweed town of **Malargüe** which is within easy reach of the cave network of **Caverna de las Brujas** and **La Payunia**, where guanacos roam across lava-strewn pampas.

MENDOZA

The sophisticated metropolis of **MENDOZA**, with a population of around a million, has the country's best wineries on its doorstep. Set in a valley less than 100km east of the Andes' loftiest snow-covered mountains, downtown is characterized by elegant, fountain-filled plazas and wide, sycamore-lined avenues. An earthquake in 1861 laid waste to Mendoza's former colonial glories, but the modern, low-rise city that rose in its wake is certainly no eyesore. *Mendocinos* know how to enjoy the good life, and, along with taking their siestas seriously (many businesses close between 1pm and 4pm), they enjoy dining at the city's many fine restaurants and al fresco drinking along the spacious sidewalks.

Mendoza makes an ideal base for exploring some of Argentina's undisputed highlights. Hundreds of *bodegas*, offering wine-tasting tours, lie within easy reach of downtown. **Tour operators** run a range of white-water rafting, horseriding, paragliding and skydiving excursions, and those looming peaks offer skiing in winter and world-class mountain climbing in summer.

What to see and do

At the junction of the city's two principal thoroughfares – Avenida Sarmiento and Avenida Mitre – the spacious **Plaza Independencia** is the physical and cultural heart of Mendoza. Fountains and sycamore trees create an ideal space for chilling out or, over summer, taking in one of the regular outdoor concerts. One block east and south of here, **Plaza España** trumps Independencia in the beauty stakes, thanks to the Andalucian tilework gracing its stone benches, tree-lined paths, pretty fountains and monument to Spain's discovery of South America.

Museo del Pasado Cuyano

The **Museo del Pasado Cuyano** (Mon–Fri 9am–12.30pm; donation), at Montevideo 544, is the city's history museum, housed in a mansion dating from 1873. The collection includes an exhibition on General San Martín along with religious art, weaponry and period furniture.

Parque General San Martín

A four-square-kilometre green space you could easily spend a day exploring, the forested **Parque General San Martín**, one kilometre west of Plaza Independencia, is one of the most impressive urban parks in the country. Whether you're navigating it by foot, bike, horse or public bus, be sure to grab a map at the **information centre** (daily June–Aug 8am–6pm, rest of year 8am–7pm; ☏0261/420-5052, ext 221) just inside the park's grand gated main entrance.

Within lie some fifty thousand trees, a rose garden, tennis courts, an observatory, swimming pool, lake, zoo, football stadium, amphitheatre and, in the southeastern corner, the **Museo de Ciencias Naturales y Antropológicas Juan Cornelio Moyano** (Tues–Fri 8am–1pm & 2–7pm, Sat & Sun 3–7pm; ☏0261/428-7666, AR$2). This contains an intriguing collection of pre-Columbian mummies, fossils and stuffed animals. Sweeping city views are to be had from the top of **Cerro de la Gloria** (Glory Hill), crowned by a bronze monument to San Martín's liberating army.

Arrival and information

Air The airport (☏0261/441-0900, ext 521) is 7km north of downtown. A taxi or *remise* to the city centre costs AR$20.

VISITING WINERIES

Barrel-loads of wineries offer free tours and tastings (some also have restaurants offering gourmet lunches), with the majority in the satellite towns of Maipú (15km southeast), Luján de Cuyo (7km south) and the eastern suburb of Guaymallén, all accessible by public transport from the city centre. Many Mendoza-based tour companies offer half-or full-day winery excursions, but if there are four or more of you, it can be more fun and cheaper to rent a taxi and hit the *bodegas* of your choice independently (call ahead for appointments; also note that most close on Sun). Or if you want to exercise between swills, rent a bike in Maipú from Bikes and Wines (☏0261/410-6686, ⓦwww.bikesandwines.com, AR$35 per day), arm yourself with their winery map, and cycle a 40km circuit, stopping at vineyards along the way. To reach Maipú from downtown Mendoza, catch *colectivos* #171, #172 or #173 from Rioja (between Catamarca and Garibaldi) and ask to be let off at Plazoleta Rutini (45min).

If time only allows for one winery, walk around the corner to Bodega La Rural (Mon–Fri 9.30am–5pm, Sat & Sun 10am–1pm, ☏0261/497-2013) at Montecaseros 2625, which has an informative on-site wine museum. For expert advice on which wineries to visit, pick up a free copy of *Wine Republic* magazine from the tourist office or speak to the helpful staff at *Vines of Mendoza* (see p.114).

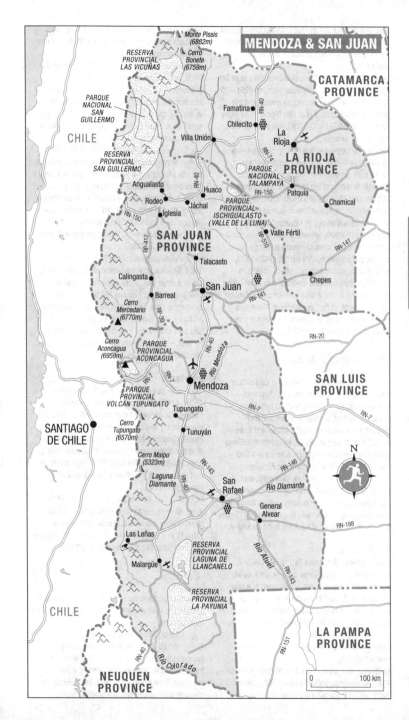

MENDOZA & SAN JUAN

Bus The bus station (☎0261/431-5000) lies just east of the centre at Av. Gobernador Videla and Av. Acceso Este (RN7); a taxi to the centre costs AR$5.

Tourist information The city tourist office is at San Martín and Garibaldi (daily 9am–9pm; ☎0261/420-1333, ⊛www.turismo.mendoza.gov.ar) and the provincial tourist office is at San Martín 1143 (daily 8am–9pm; ☎0261/420-2800). Ask staff for a list and map of wineries.

Tour operators Argentina Rafting, at Potrerillos (☎02624/482-037, ⊛www.argentinarafting .com), runs white-water rafting trips down the Class III–IV rapids of the Mendoza River; Aymara, at 9 de Julio 1023 (☎0261/420-2064, ⊛www .aymara.com.ar), specializes in guided Aconcagua treks; Bikes and Wines, at Urquiza 1601, Maipu (☎0261/410-6686, ⊛www.bikesandwines.com), organizes bicycle tours to wineries. Campo Base, at Peatonal Sarmiento 229 (☎0261/425-5511, ⊛www.campobase.com.ar), offers adventure excursions that combine trekking, mountain biking and abseiling in one action-packed day; El Rincón de los Oscuros, at Av. Los Cóndores, Potrerillos (☎02624/48-3030, ⊛www.rincondelososcuros .com) are horseriding specialists.

Accommodation

Mendoza has dozens of outstanding backpacker hostels, the best of which have gardens and swimming pools and fill up fast; all listed here include breakfast, kitchen, internet and tour-booking services. Book well in advance if travelling in early March, as the city packs out for the *Fiesta de la Vendimia* wine festival. Campers will find a shady spot to pitch their tents at *El Suizo* on Av. Champagnat in El Challao, 6km northwest of Mendoza (☎0261/444-1991, ⊛www.camping suizo.com.ar; AR$15 per person), with a swimming pool, restaurant and outdoor cinema. Bus #115 runs there from the corner of Av. Alem and San Martín.

Hostels

Hostel Alamo Necochea 740 ☎0261/429-5565, ⊛www.hostelalamo.com.ar. On a quiet residential street, this yellow mansion is a real godsend for those looking for a sociable but well-mannered backpackers' retreat. The massive supermarket opposite will delight self-caterers, as will the hostel's glassed-in dining area looking onto a Zen-like garden. Dorms AR$50, rooms AR$130.

Hostel Campo Base Mitre 946 ☎0261/429-0707, ⊛www.campobase.com.ar. Although the dorms (AR$45) are a bit cramped, this well-located hostel is a hit with party people and Aconcagua climbers (treks are organized through the affiliated tour company).

Hostel Independencia Mitre 1237 ☎0261/423-1806, ⊛www.hostelindependencia.com.ar. Boisterous party hostel in a gorgeous mansion. The location and common areas are among the best in the city; the bathrooms, sadly, are not. If you're sensitive to noise or alcohol, go elsewhere. Dorms AR$48, rooms AR$100.

Hostel Lao Rioja 771 ☎0261/438-0454, ⊛www.laohostel.com. The most inviting of the city's hostels, this English-run place is often full. Chilled-out but buzzing, it has plenty of common space, travel photography graces its walls, there's a large garden with a pool and hammocks, a roof terrace, wi-fi and very clean dorm rooms. Wine flows when the owner is feeling generous. Dorms AR$55, rooms AR$160.

Winca's Hostel Sarmiento 717 ☎0261/425-3804, ⊛www.wincashostel.com.ar. This hostel, set in a large peach-coloured house, has a chef's-quality kitchen and big backyard with swimming pool. The dorms, however, are small and dark. The owners have another hostel at San Lorenzo 19 and fully furnished apartments for rent – a good option for couples or long-term stayers. Dorms AR$35.

Hotels

Confluencia Hostal Av. España 1512 ☎0261/429-0430, ⊛www.hostal confluencia.com.ar. Perfect for couples who want more privacy and sophistication than a hostel, this modern boutique hotel offers spacious doubles (and quadruples) with wooden floorboards and private bathrooms. There's a TV lounge and large roof terrace with mountain views. Breakfast included. AR$140.

Quinta Rufino Rufino Ortega 142 ☎0261/420-4696, ⊛www.quintarufinohostel.com.ar. A B&B offering large rooms with private bathroom and cable TV in a converted villa. It's a short stroll to the city's bar strip. Breakfast included. AR$160.

Eating

Mendoza has some exceptional restaurants, many specializing in local produce, Pacific seafood and regional wine.

Anna Bistro Juan B Justo 161 ☎0261/425-1818. Cocktail-sipping diners lounge outside on white leather couches amid fragrant foliage and romantic lighting at this top-notch French-run restaurant. The eclectic menu features standouts like seafood pasta

(AR$24). Set lunches are good value. Tues–Sun
noon–3pm & 8–11pm.

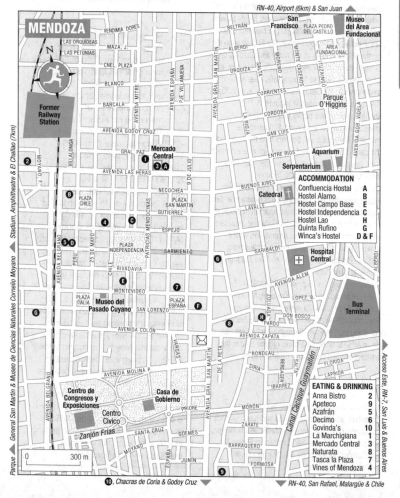

Govinda's San Martín 453, bus ride or
taxi from centre ☏0261/424-3799. Simply
the best vegetarian restaurant in the city; load up
your plate with lovingly prepared dishes from the
gigantic buffet (AR$21 per kilo). No alcohol served.
Open Mon–Sat for lunch (noon–2.30pm) and dinner
(6–10pm); lunch only on Sun.

La Marchigiana Patricias Mendocinas 1550
☏0261/423-0751. This airy, family affair is
widely considered to be the city's best Italian
restaurant amd scores extra points for its very fair
prices (mains start at under AR$25). Sun–Thurs
noon–3pm and 8pm–midnight (Fri until 12.30am,
Sat until 1am).

Mercado Central Las Heras between España &
Patricias Mendocinas. This bustling indoor market is
full of inexpensive cafés offering local dishes such
as *humitas* and *empanadas,* and is a great place to
try goodies such as Andean goat's cheeses. Most
snacks AR$2–3.

Naturata Don Bosco 73 ☏0261/420-3087.
Wholesome vegetarian buffet in light and airy
surroundings on a leafy residential street (AR$20
all-you-can-eat or AR$2.80 per kilo). Closed Sun.

Tasca la Plaza Montevideo 117
☏0261/420-0603. Flickering candles set off
the wooden floorboards, bright-red walls and funky
Mendocino art at the city's coolest tapas bar and
restaurant where you can swill a mojito (AR$15)
with your grilled king prawns (AR$25).

ACCOMMODATION

Confluencia Hostal	A
Hostel Alamo	B
Hostel Campo Base	E
Hostel Independencia	C
Hostel Lao	H
Quinta Rufino	G
Winca's Hostel	D & F

EATING & DRINKING

Anna Bistro	2
Apeteco	9
Azafrán	5
Decimo	6
Govinda's	10
La Marchigiana	1
Mercado Central	3
Naturata	8
Tasca la Plaza	7
Vines of Mendoza	4

Azafrán Sarmiento 765 ℡0261/429-4200. From venison ravioli to Patagonian deer, the dining experience at this lauded restaurant is pure gourmet. The sommelier will guide diners on a rummage in the wine cellar, where more than 450 vintages from 80 different vineyards are stocked. Mains around AR$40. Mon–Sat 12.30–4pm and 8pm–1am.

Drinking and nightlife

Mendoza's bar scene is concentrated along trendy Aristides Villanueva, where pavement tables fill with drinkers on summer evenings. The best nightclubs are in outlying neighbourhoods like El Challao to the northwest, Las Heras to the north and Chacras de Coria to the south. Women generally get in free, and while *Mendocinos* like to party late, keep in mind that a city law stipulates that last entry is at 2.30am.

Apeteco San Juan and Barraquero, A sophisticated crowd packs into this sleek, cavernous club on weekends. Following the midnight live music set, punters lose their cool on the dancefloor to a mixed soundtrack of electronica, rock, reggaeton and salsa. Open Wed–Sat. Free entry until 11pm, then AR$20 for men.

Decimo Garibaldi 7, 10th floor of Edificio Gómez. Yuppie wine bar and restaurant par excellence. Set on the top floor of a downtown apartment block, it offers a winning combination of city and mountain views along with a hundred Argentinian wines to wrap your palate around (small bottles from AR$15). Put on your glad rags and live the high life. Mon–Sat 6pm–3am.

Vines of Mendoza Espejo 567 ℡0261/438-1031, ⓦwww.vinesofmendoza.com. A swanky wine-tasting room with more than sixty wines from regional boutique *bodegas*. Let the English-speaking staff talk you through a tasting session (from AR$45) or nurse a glass of *vino tinto* in the wisteria-shaded courtyard. Daily 3–10pm.

Directory

Banks and exchange Banco de la Nación Argentina accepts foreign cards and has branches across the city, including San Martín and Gutierrez, and España 1275. Cambio Express, at Espejo 58 and Cambio Santiago, Av. San Martín 119, will exchange foreign cash.

Car rental Alamo Nacional Rent, Pvo de la Reta 928 (℡0261/429-3111); Avis, Pvo de la Reta 914 (℡0261/429-6403); Hertz, Espejo 415 (℡0261/423-0225); Via Rent a Car, San Juan 931 (℡0261/429-0876).

Internet The WH Internet & Games chain (℡0261/423-3398) has cybercafés at San Martín 1178, Las Heras 61 and Peatonal Sarmiento 219. Only the San Martín branch opens Sundays.

Laundry Lavandería Necochea, 25 de Mayo 1357.

Post office San Martín and Colón.

Shopping There is a handicraft market on Plaza Independencia every weekend. The upscale Mendoza Plaza shopping mall (ⓦwww.mendozaplaza shopping.com), at Av. Acceso Este 3280 in Guaymallén, to the east of the city centre, has around 200 shops and restaurants, plus a cinema.

Winery lunches

Try to make time (and room in the budget) for a trip out of town for a gourmet lunch among the vineyards at a nearby **bodega**: ask at the tourist office or pick up the *Vines of Mendoza* magazine for further listings. The restaurant at *Ruca Malen* (Ruta Nacional 7km 1059, Luján de Cuyo; take a bus to Luján and then a taxi for $AR20; ℡0261/410-6214, ⓦwww .bodegarucamalen.com; lunch daily) looks out on to vineyards and mountains, and lunch is a belly-busting five-course degustation (AR$110), with each delectable plate – from roasted aubergine in plum sauce to *dulce de leche* mousse – perfectly paired with *bodega* wine. *La Bourgogne* (Roque Sáenz Peña 3531, Vistalba, Luján de Cuyo, taxi from Luján AR$15; ℡0261/498-9400, ⓦwww.carlospulentawines.com; closed Sun & Mon) is attached to the Vistalba winery (producing since 2002) and prepares French cuisine using regional and seasonal produce. Dishes like veal in mushroom sauce (AR$66) and quince tart with lavender ice cream (AR$25) go down a treat with a bottle of *vino* (AR$50 upwards). Reserve in advance and ask for a table by the window with cordillera and vineyard views.

Spanish school Intercultural, at Rep de Siria 241 (☎0261/429-0269, ⓦ www.spanishcourses.com. ar), offers one-week courses.

Moving on

Air Buenos Aires (4 daily; 1hr 50min); Córdoba (2 daily; 1hr 20min); Santiago de Chile (2 daily; 40min). Bus Bariloche (2 daily; 18hr); Buenos Aires (every 30min; 17hr); Córdoba (hourly; 10hr); Salta (9 daily; 19hr); San Juan (hourly; 2hr 30min); San Rafael (hourly; 3hr 15min); Santiago de Chile (12 daily, 7hr).

ALTA MONTAÑA

The cathedral-like peaks of the Parque Provincial Aconcagua lie just three hours west of Mendoza, easily visited on a popular day-trip dubbed the **ALTA MONTAÑA ROUTE**. Leaving behind verdant vineyards and climbing into barren hills, this scenic excursion follows the RN7 (the highway to Santiago de Chile), following the former Trans-Andean railway and the Río Mendoza into the spectacular Uspallata Valley, where *Seven Years in Tibet* was filmed. From the crossroads village of Uspallata (105km west of Mendoza), it's a further 65km to **Los Penitentes**, a winter ski resort with 28 pistes (☎0261/428-3601, ⓦwww.penitentes.com), and in summer, a base for Aconcagua climbers (see below). Some 6km west of Los Penitentes lies one of the area's most photographed landmarks, the **Puente del Inca**, a natural stone bridge traversing the Río de las Cuevas at 2700m. Beneath it, thermal waters seep among the ruins of an abandoned 1940s spa resort. The route passes Parque Provincial Aconcagua and ends at the Chilean border where a statue of **Cristo Redentor** (Christ the Redeemer) commemorates the 1902 peace pact between historic enemies.

Parque Provincial Aconcagua

At 6959m, **CERRO ACONCAGUA** – "the roof of the Americas" – lords it over the 710-square-kilometre Parque Provincial Aconcagua. The highest mountain in both the western and the southern hemispheres, Aconcagua's faces are ringed by five glistening glaciers. In 1985, the discovery of an **Inca mummy** at 5300m on Aconcagua's southwest face lent further weight to the theory that the Incas worshipped the mountain and offered it human sacrifices.

Nowadays, Inca worshippers have been replaced by ardent mountain climbers, who ascend in droves throughout summer. Only the most experienced attempt the **climb** without a professional guide. Taking into account acclimatization time, it should take at least thirteen days to reach the summit. There are three possible routes – south, west or east – with the least difficult being the western route leaving from the Plaza de Mulas (4230m). For **route details** and advice on what to take, see ⓦwww.aconcagua.mendoza .gov.ar. Easier **day hikes** are also possible in the park as well as multi-day treks to base camps and mountain *refugios*.

Arrival and information

Bus Expresso Uspallata operates four buses daily from Mendoza to the base camps at Los Horcones and Punta de Vacas.

Tourist information and permits To trek or climb in the Parque Provincial Aconcagua between mid-Nov and mid-March, you need to obtain a permit (bring your passport) from the Dirección de Recursos Naturales Renovables (Mon–Fri 8am–6pm, Sun & Sun 9am–1pm; ☎0261/425-8751), at San Martín 1143, 2nd floor, in Mendoza. Foreign trekkers pay AR$150–330 to hike in the park (price depends on number of days in park and time of year). From Feb 21–March 15 & Nov 15–Nov 30 the fee to climb the mountain is AR$500; this rises to AR$1000 Dec 1–Dec 14 & Feb 1–Feb 20; and AR$1500 Dec 15–Jan 31. The rest of the year snow cover makes the climb extremely dangerous; the fee at this time is AR$1500–2000 and climbers must apply for a special permit.

Tour operators Due to the mountain's unpredict-able weather (storms claim lives every year), climbers are advised to go on organized trips with experienced local guides. Mendoza-based operators that specialize in Aconcagua trips include

Aconcagua Trek, at Barcala 484 (☎0261/429-5007, ✆www.aconcaguatrek.com); Aymara, at 9 de Julio 1023 (☎0261/420-2064, ✆www.aymara.com.ar); Campo Base, at Peatonal Sarmiento 229 (☎0261/425-5511, ✆www.campobase.com.ar); Fernando Grajales Expeditions (☎0261/428-3157, ✆www.grajales.net); and Inka Expediciones, at Juan B Justo 242 (☎0261/425-0871, ✆www.aconcagua.org.ar). Fernando Grajales Expeditions and Aconcagua Trek can make the arrangements for mule hire.

Accommodation

For accommodation at or near the base camps, there are options at Puente del Inca (where many people spend a couple of days acclimatizing), Las Cuevas and Los Penitentes. On the mountain trail, it is possible to overnight on day two at the *Refugio Plaza de Mulas* (☎0261/421-4330, ✆www.refugioplazademulas.com.ar; dorms AR$75, rooms AR$250), where there are hot showers and cooked meals (included in price).

Hostel Campo Base Penitentes Los Penitentes ☎0261/425-5511, ✆www.penitentes.com.ar. This lively, 28-bed hostel, with well-equipped kitchen, is a jumping-off point for organized ski trips in the winter and Aconcagua climbs in the summer. Dorms AR$75 including breakfast and dinner; prices halve Oct–May.

La Vieja Estación Puente del Inca ☎0261/452-1103. A hostel with large dorm rooms and communal bathrooms. The restaurant and bar will warm the cockles, and a variety of excursions are offered. Dorms AR$35.

Eating and drinking

Make the most of hostel kitchens, and bring plenty of food supplies, as refuelling opportunities are few and far between once inside the park itself. During ski season, the resort hotels of Penitentes offer decent, if unspectacular, food, while snacks and hot drinks can be found at Puente del Inca's outdoor market.

SAN RAFAEL AND AROUND

In the heart of wine country, the laid-back city of **SAN RAFAEL,** 230km south of the provincial capital, likes to think of itself as a smaller, friendlier version of Mendoza; its wide, flat streets are filled with cyclists and its leafy plazas are squeaky clean. The city itself offers few distractions, and boredom will probably set in once you've become acquainted with the main square, **Plaza San Martín**, and visited the **Museo de Historia Natural** (daily 8am–1pm & 2.30–7pm; AR$1), on Isla Diamante, 6km south of the centre, where the pre-Columbian displays include ceramics from Ecuador and a mummified child dating from 40 AD.

There are, however, worthwhile sights just beyond the city itself in the San Rafael department, including six hundred square kilometres of vineyards and around eighty **bodegas.** Most of the wineries are small, family-run affairs; the tourist office has a list of those open to the public. For **white-water rafting** enthusiasts, the **Cañon del Atuel**, a short journey to the southwest, is one of the top destinations in the country for riding the rapids. For adventurous types, San Rafael-based tour operator Risco Viajes (Av. Hipólito Yrigoyen 284; ☎02627/436-439, ✆www.riscoviajes.com), offers everything from one-day wine tasting trips (AR$290) and three-day excursions to hot spas (AR$700 including accommodation) to mountain-biking and climbing adventures in the surrounding peaks.

Arrival and information

Air San Rafael's airport is 5km west of downtown, with daily flights to and from Buenos Aires. There are buses to the centre (AR$2); a taxi costs around AR$15.

Bus The centrally located bus terminal is at Coronel Suárez, between calles Almafuerte and Avellaneda. There are connections to Buenos Aires (4 daily; 13hr); Las Leñas (June–Sept 1 daily, Dec–Feb 3 weekly on Tues, Thurs & Sat; 2hr 40min); Malargüe (3 daily; 2hr 30min); Mendoza (hourly 3hr 15min).

Tourist information The friendly tourist office is on the corner of avenidas Hipólito Yrigoyen and Balloffet (daily 8am–9pm; ☎02627/424-217, ✆www.sanrafaelturismo.gov.ar).

Accommodation

San Rafael's accommodation options lack the range and quality found in Mendoza. If you're camping, make for the shady *Camping El Parador* on Isla Río Diamante, 6km south of downtown (AR$6 per tent).

Rex Hipólito Yrigoyen 56 ☎02627/422-177, ⓦwww.rexhotel.com.ar. This bright, modern hotel on the main drag has spotless rooms arranged around a quiet courtyard. Cable TV, breakfast and parking included. AR$180.

Tierrasoles Hostel Alsina 245 ☎02627/433-449, ⓦwww.tierrasoles.com.ar. A family-run HI hostel offering modest dorms, a simple breakfast and cheap internet. You have to be a contortionist to use the toilets though. Dorms AR$58, rooms AR$164.

Trotamundos Hostel Barcala 300 ☎02627/432-795, ⓦwww.trotamundoshostel.com.ar. A new, funky hostel in a converted historical building with a large open-plan kitchen and plenty of activities laid on for guests. Includes breakfast and wi-fi access. Dorms AR$50, rooms AR$120.

Eating and drinking

San Rafael springs to life post-siesta, when locals pack the restaurants, bars, nightclubs and ice-cream parlours along Hipólito Yrigoyen.

La Fusta Hipólito Yrigoyen 538. The best *parrilla* in the city, where you can tuck into a juicy steak (AR$30) and quaff local wine without breaking the bank. Open daily noon–3.30pm and 8.30pm–midnight.

Jockey Club Belgrano 330 ☎02627/487-007. Upscale and with an Old-World feel, this much-loved restaurant serves well-prepared, filling mains including good pasta, fish and chicken dishes. Set lunch AR$45. Daily noon–3pm and 7–11pm.

Lorenzo Hipólito Irigoyen 1850. The dancefloor at this popular bar is often shaking, thanks to a mixed soundtrack of rock, retro and electronica. On steamy nights, the drinking spills into the garden. Occasional live music. Open Thurs–Sat until late.

Tienda del Sol Hipólito Yrigoyen 1663. A hip, modern restaurant with outdoor tables, serving imaginative beef, chicken and fish mains (around AR$25), along with a wide range of regional wines. Open daily 8pm–midnight.

LAS LEÑAS

Some 180km southwest of San Rafael and 445km south of Mendoza, the exclusive ski resort of **LAS LEÑAS** is to winter what Uruguay's Punta del Este is to summer – a chic party playground for *porteño* socialites. Between June and September (snow permitting), they flock here on week-long packages. Beyond après-ski glamour, the setting of Las Leñas is exquisite. The resort, which sits at 2240m, has the dramatic Cerro Las Leñas (4351m) towering over its 29 runs and thirteen lifts. Pistes range in difficulty from nursery slopes to hair-raising black runs, with night-time and cross-country skiing also possible.

In summer, Las Leñas transforms into an outdoor action hub, offering horseriding, white-water rafting, trekking, climbing, abseiling, 4x4 tours, mountain biking, summer skiing and even scuba-diving in high-altitude lakes.

Arrival and information

Bus During the ski season there are daily buses from Mendoza (7hr), Malargüe (1hr 30min) and San Rafael (2hr 40min). Regular direct buses also run from Buenos Aires (14hr; book through the central tourist office).

Lift ticket office Mid-June to late Sept 7.30am–5pm (☎02627/471-100, ⓦwww.laslenas.com). Daily lift ticket prices range seasonally from AR$99 to $AR152.

Tourist information The resort's office for booking ski packages and accommodation is in Buenos Aires at Bartolomé Mitre 401, 4th floor (Mon–Fri 9am–6pm; ☎011/4819-6000, ⓦwww.laslenas.com).

Accommodation

Las Leñas accommodation needs to be booked through the resort's central Buenos Aires office (see above). Low-priced lodging is non-existent. If you are in a group, the most affordable places are the self-catering apartments known as "dormy houses": *Laquir, Lihuén, Milla* and *Payén* cost around AR$500–600 per night and accommodate up to five people.

José Hostel ☎02627/1560-0962, ⓔjosehostel @yahoo.com. The closest hostel to Las Leñas, 18km away in Los Molles. The owner, a ski-patroller, runs a tight ship, with two large dorm rooms, a kitchen, wine bar, fireplace, TV lounge, book exchange and wi-fi. Dorms from AR$95 including transport to and from Las Leñas; from AR$55 without the transfer.

Eating and drinking

Innsbruck A log cabin *confitería* in the ski village where you can buy expensive fast food (a steak is AR$35) to enjoy over a beer from a terrace with piste views. Open for breakfast, lunch and dinner, as well as cocktails until the small hours.

El Refugio In the central Pirámide building ☎02627/471-100 ext 1134. Dip into cheese fondue (AR$80) at this pricey French restaurant. Reservations necessary.

UFO Point The appetizing pizzas served here have earned this restaurant a devoted following, but at around AR$60 (serves 2), they're not cheap. The restaurant is open for breakfast, lunch and dinner; at night it turns into a club with electronic music.

MALARGÜE

Set at the arid base of the Andes, 186km southwest of San Rafael, **MALARGÜE** is a small, nondescript town that's a jumping-off point for some of Argentina's most remarkable scenery. In winter its *raison d'être* is as an affordable base for **skiing** at the resort of Las Leñas (see p.117), while in summer the surrounding landscape offers ample opportunities for hiking, horseriding, fishing and white-water rafting. Worthwhile day-trips from town are to the underground limestone caves of **Caverna de las Brujas** (73km southwest), the volcanic wonderland of **La Payunia** (208km south), and to **Laguna de Llancanelo** (65km southeast), a high-altitude lagoon speckled pink with flamingos.

What to see and do

Malargüe's flat, compact centre is easy to get your head around: the wide main drag is the RN40, known in town as **Avenida San Martín**. Here you'll find the tourist office, shops and the main square, **Plaza General San Martín**. Just south of the tourist office is the landscaped greenery of **Parque del Ayer** ("Park of Yesteryear"), filled with sculptures and native trees. Opposite, you can take a free guided tour at the

Observatorio Pierre Auger(Mon–Fri 5–6pm; ☎02627/471-562, ⓦwww.auger.org.ar), an astrophysics centre that studies cosmic rays.

Laguna de Llancanelo

Some 65km east of Malargüe lies the nature reserve of **Laguna de Llancanelo**, a vast lakeland area famous for its abundant birdlife. Alongside the flamingos that flock here in their thousands, herons and black neck swans can be easily spotted. Also look out for the *coipo*, a rodent similar in appearance to the capybara but a little smaller in size. The best way to visit the reserve is with a guided tour, such as those offered by Karen Travel (Av. San Martin 54, Malargue; ☎02627 470-342, ⓦwww.karentravel.com.ar).

Arrival and information

Bus Malargüe's bus terminal (☎02627/470-690) is at Esquibel Aldao and Fray Luis Beltrán, four blocks south and two west of Plaza San Martín.

Tourist information The tourist office (daily 8am–10pm; ☎02627/471-659, ⓦwww.malargue .gov.ar) is on the RN40 four blocks north of the plaza.

Tour operators Many local companies run tours to La Payunia, Laguna de Llancanelo and Caverna de las Brujas, as well as horseriding and other adventure activities. Check out Karen Travel at San Martín 1056 (☎02627/470-342, ⓦwww .karentravel.com.ar), where you can also hire 4x4s.

Accommodation

Malargüe has plenty of affordable places to stay, including a handful of well-run hostels. Prices rise significantly during the winter, when Malargüe becomes a popular base for skiing at Las Leñas. Some Malargüe hotels offer fifty percent discounts on Las Leñas ski-lift tickets if you stay in town. The campsite *Camping Polideportivo* (summer only) is conveniently located at Capdeval and Esquibal Aldao (☎02627/470-691; AR$18).

Cabañas Newen Mapu Av. Roca and Villa del Milagro ☎02627/472-318, ⓦwww.newenmapu .com. Buy yourself some space with a two-storey cabaña (sleeps 6, AR$480) complete with cable TV, full kitchen, fireplace and mountain views. Prices halve in the low season.

Ecohostel Colonia Pehuenche I, Finca N. 65, 5km south of town (free transfer from the Choique Turismo Alternativo office at San Martín and Rodríguez) ☎02627/1540-2439, ⊛www .hostelmalargue.com. There's some serious stargazing and R&R to be had at this rustic HI hostel set on an organic farm. Home-made meals and horseriding excursions offered. Dorms AR$51, rooms AR$151.

Hostel La Caverna Cte Rodríguez 445 ☎02627/472-569, ⊛www.lacavernahostel.com.ar. This hostel has a spacious common area and plenty of dorm beds. The self-catering apartment out back is ideal for groups. Free laundry and internet. Dorms AR$40, rooms AR$160.

Eating and drinking

El Bodegon de Maria Rufino Ortega at General Villegas. Trout and pizza get all the attention at this welcoming rustic-style restaurant. Set lunch AR$25. Daily noon–2.30pm and 7–11pm.

Cuyam-Co 8km west of Malargüe in El Dique. Catch your own meal and have it cooked to perfection at this trout farm. AR$35 for full menu and AR$15 to fish for your dish and then have it cooked. **Río Grande** RN40 Norte ☎02627/471-589. The restaurant in this upmarket hotel serves decent steaks (AR$20), pastas (AR$15–30) and trout ($AR25). Open daily for breakfast, lunch and dinner.

Moving on

Bus Mendoza (3 daily; 5hr); San Rafael (3 daily; 2hr 30min); Las Leñas (1 daily during ski season; 1hr 30min).

AROUND MALARGÜE

The **CAVERNA DE LAS BRUJAS** ("Witches' Cave") is an otherworldly limestone cave filled with incredible rock formations, including **stalactites and stalagmites** with rather suggestive names (eg "Virgin's Chamber"). The cave, located 73km southwest of Malargüe and 8km along a dirt road off the RN40, is within a provincial park and is staffed by *guardaparques*. Guided visits (AR$20) are the only way to see the cave and numbers are restricted to nine at a time. The **temperature** inside the grotto can be 20°C lower than outside, so be sure to wrap up.

Continuing along the RN40, you'll reach the entrance to **LA PAYUNIA** at El Zampal. This expansive, wildlife-rich reserve spans 4500 square kilometres. Flaxen grasslands, black lava flows and eight hundred threatening-looking volcanoes (the highest concentration of volcanic cones in the world) provide a starkly wild backdrop for the guanaco, puma and condor that call it home.

The best way to see La Payunia is on a day-trip from Malargüe that takes in the Caverna de las Brujas along the way (for tour operators, see p.118). If you want to visit the cave independently, you must first make an appointment and **register** with Malargüe's tourist office.

SAN JUAN

SAN JUAN is a modern, low-rise provincial capital. In 1944, one of South America's most powerful earthquakes (8.5 on the Richter scale) razed the city, killing more than ten thousand people. Essentially a poorer, smaller and less attractive version of its southerly neighbour Mendoza, San Juan is unlikely to capture your imagination. It does, however, make a convenient base for sampling the fruits of nearby wineries as well as for excursions to some of Argentina's most iconic natural wonders – the sculptural desert landscapes of **Parque Provincial Ischigualasto** and the surreal rock formations of **Parque Nacional Talampaya**.

Try to avoid visiting in the summer, when *Sanjuaninos* cope with the midday heat by taking long, sluggish siestas.

What to see and do

The leafy Plaza 25 de Mayo, flanked by a couple of inviting cafés, marks the city centre. On its northwestern side, the modern cathedral's 50-m brick campanile is a nod to St Mark's in Venice. If the mood takes, climb the **bell tower** (daily 9am–1pm & 5–8pm; AR$3) for great city and countryside vistas. Not far away at Sarmiento 21 Sur, opposite the tourist office, is the whitewashed childhood home of former Argentine president **Domingo Faustino Sarmiento** (1811–88), now a museum (Tues–Fri 9am–1.30pm & 5–9.30pm, Mon & Sat 8.30am–1.30pm; AR$3; guided tours every 30min). Although damaged in the 1944 earthquake, the house has been lovingly restored and displays belongings and paraphernalia from Sarmiento's eventful life.

More ancient history is represented at the **Museo de Ciencias Naturales** (daily 9am–1pm; AR$3; ☎0264/421-6774), in the former train station at Av. España and Av. Maipú, the final resting place of the skeleton of the carnivorous **dinosaur**, Herrerasaurus, excavated in the Parque Provincial Ischigualasto (see p.122). And finally, if all that has left your mouth dry, drop into the historic **Bodega Graffigna** (Tues–Fri 9am–1pm, Sat 9am–8pm, Sun 10am–2pm; free; ☎0264/421-4227), at Colón 1342 Norte, which houses the Museo de Vino Santiago Graffigna, and perhaps more importantly, a wine bar where you can quench your thirst and sample provincial vintages.

Arrival and information

Air Las Chacritas airport (☎0264/425-4133) is 12km east of the city centre. A taxi downtown costs around AR$15.

Bus The bus station (☎0264/422-1604), at Estados Unidos 492 Sur, is eight blocks east of Plaza 25 de Mayo.

Tourist information The tourist office at Sarmiento 24 Sur has good city and provincial information (Mon–Fri 7.30am–8.30pm , Sat & Sun 9am–8.30pm; ☎0264/421-0004; ⓦwww.turismo .sanjuan.gov.ar).

Tour operators Companies offering Ischigualasto and Talampaya excursions include Algarrobo, at Sarmiento 62 Sur (☎0264/427-2487, ⓦwww .algarroboturismo.com.ar); and Triassic Tour, at Hipólito Yrigoyen 294 Sur (☎0264/421-9528, ⓦwww.grupohuaco.com.ar).

Accommodation

Economical accommodation is of a reasonable standard in San Juan. A convenient campsite is *Camping Don Bosco* (☎0264/425-3663, AR$5 per person), 3km east on RN20, with hot showers and a swimming pool. Catch bus #19 from the centre.

Colpa Hostel-Apart 25 de Mayo 554 Este ☎0264/422-5704, ⓦwww.colpahostel sanjuan.com.ar. The spotless rooms in this stylish hostel-cum-apartment complex have first-rate beds and – hallelujah – a/c. It's AR$50 per person, whether you're sharing or alone. Includes breakfast, two kitchens, swimming pool and TV room.

Jardín Petit 25 de Mayo 345 Este ☎0264/421-1825. A welcoming hotel with cosy, simple rooms and an inviting patio and pool. Breakfast included. AR$200, though discounts can sometimes be arranged.

San Juan Hostel Av. Cordoba 317 Este ☎0264/4201-835, ⓦwww.sanjuanhostel.com. Helpful staff, a central location and a comfortable common area make up for the depressing dorms and basic bathrooms at this backpackers' pad. Includes breakfast and internet. Dorms AR$35, rooms AR$110.

Zonda Hostel C Caseros 486 Sur ☎0264/420-1009 ⓦwww.zondahostel.com.ar. Conveniently located four blocks from the bus station, this 35-bed HI hostel has a TV room, patio, kitchen, free internet and breakfast. Dorms AR$30.

Eating and drinking

Antonio Gómez Supermercado, General Acha and Córdoba. The heaving paellas (AR$25) draw the lunchtime crowd at this Spanish-centric market stall. Lunch only.

De Sanchez Rivadavia 55 Oeste. The city's classiest restaurant serves beautifully prepared salmon (AR$45) and beef (AR$35) with a fine selection of local wines by the glass and bottle. After the meal, browse the adjoining book and music shop. Mon–Sat 12.30–3pm and 9pm–midnight.

Remolacha Ignacio and Sarmiento ⓦwww .parrillaremolacha.com.ar. Traditional and hugely popular *parrilla* with a vast range of meaty treats to be enjoyed indoors or al fresco. Vegetarians won't starve either, thanks to some decent meat-free pasta dishes, mixed vegetable grills and interesting salads. Set meals from AR$40 Daily 11am–3pm and 9pm–2am.

El Ricón de Nápoli Rivadavia 175 Oeste. Noisy and cheerful fast-service restaurant whipping up pizza, pasta, burgers and plenty of grilled meat (mains AR$10–20).

🏃 **Soychú** Av. José Ignacio de la Roza 223 Oeste. Slip into something elasticated before gorging yourself on one of the continent's best vegetarian all-you-can-eat-buffets (AR$20). Don't pass up the offer of a freshly squeezed juice. Open for lunch and dinner Mon–Sat, lunch only Sun.

Directory

Banks and exchange Several banks on General Acha accept foreign cards, including Banco Macro at Gral Acha 41, HSBC at Gral Acha Sur 320 and Banco de la Nación Argentina at Avenida Rioja Sur 218.
Car rental Renta Auto, San Martín 1593 Oeste (℡0264/423-3620).
Internet You're never too far from an internet booth in San Juan. Late opening and good connections at Cyber le Red, Tucuman Norte 910; Cyber 51 at Av. Libertador General San Martín Oeste 51; and Upe at Mendoza Sur 21.
Laundry Laverap, Rivadavia 498 Oeste.
Post office Av. José Ignacio de la Roza 259 Este.

Moving on

Air Buenos Aires (daily; 1hr 50min).
Bus Buenos Aires (10 daily; 16hr); Córdoba (5 daily; 8hr); Mendoza (hourly; 2hr 30min); San Rafael (2 daily; 5hr 30min); Valle Fértil (3 daily; 4hr). Most long-distance buses, including two daily services to Santiago de Chile, require a change in Mendoza.

DAY-TRIPS FROM SAN JUAN

The neighbouring UNESCO World Heritage-listed parks of **Ischigualasto** (better known as Valle de la Luna) and **Talampaya** lie in the provinces of San Juan and La Rioja respectively. The former is known for its otherworldly rock formations, the latter its red sandstone cliffs. Both can be visited on day-trips from San Juan, but the sleepy village of **San Agustín de Valle Fértil**, 250km northeast, is a much closer base. Some **tour operators** pack both parks into one day-long excursion, stopping off at Talampaya in the morning when the wind is low and the light best illuminates the red in the sandstone,

before taking in Ischigualasto in the mid-to-late afternoon.

San Agustín de Valle Fértil
Set in a valley carved out by the Río San Juan and surrounded by olive groves and sheep pasture, **SAN AGUSTÍN DE VALLE FÉRTIL** is something of a verdant oasis in an otherwise desert province. Valle Fértil is also ideally located for visiting both Talampaya and Ischigualasto. Head here with plenty of ready cash, as the one and only cashpoint regularly runs out of banknotes and cards are rarely accepted as means of payment.

Arrival and information

Bus The bus terminal is at Mitre and Entre Rios; there are three daily services from San Juan (4hr) and three weekly from La Rioja (4hr).
Tourist information The super-friendly tourist office (daily 7am–1pm & 2–10pm, ℡02646/420-104, ✉ischigualasto@sanjuan.gov.ar) is at Plaza San Agustín and can advise on tours and transport to the parks, as well as bicycle and horseriding excursions to view pre-Hispanic petroglyphs in the nearby mountains.

Accommodation

Camping Valle Fértil Rivadavia s/n ℡02646/420-015. Well-established campsite with plenty of shade (AR$10 per tent for up to four people, supplement of AR$2 per person extra).
Campo Base Valle de la Luna Tucamán between San Luis and Libertador ℡02646/420-063, ⓦwww.hostelvalledelaluna.com.ar. This modest but welcoming hostel has a kitchen, TV lounge, free breakfast and tour advice. Dorms AR$32 (discount for HI members).
Eco Hostel Mendoza 42 ℡02644/226-733. A cooling swimming pool and nightly tango lessons make this basic hostel popular with backpackers. Two blocks from the bus station. Dorms AR$35, rooms AR$70.

🏃 **Hostería Valle Fértil** Rivadavia 5400 ℡02646/420-015, ⓦwww.alkazarhotel .com.ar. The village's most inviting accommodation, thanks to its setting on a breezy hillside overlooking the Dique San Agustín reservoir. Some of the small, modern rooms have lake views. There's a restaurant, and guests can use the swimming pool in the *hosteria*'s cabaña complex down the hill. AR$250.

Pension Doña Zoila Mendoza between Rivadavia & Laprida ☎ 02646/420-308. This budget pension has bare-bones rooms and shared bathrooms set around a peaceful, grapevine-shaded courtyard. AR$120.

Eating

There are no bars as such in Valle Fértil, just a couple of shops with games machines and plastic tables and chairs.

La Cocina de Zulma North side of the plaza. Tuck into pesto pasta served with steak for a bargain AR$15.

La Florida South side of the plaza. Above-average Argentinian fare (mains AR$20–40) and very attentive service. Open for lunch and dinner.

Hosteria Valle Fertil The restaurant here is open to non-guests and serves unpretentious dishes such as omelettes, salads and soups (mains from AR$25). It's the only restaurant in the town to accept credit and debit cards – useful when the cashpoint runs out of banknotes.

Parque Provincial -Ischigualasto

Sculpted by more than two million years of erosion, wind and water, the **PARQUE PROVINCIAL ISCHIGUALASTO**, otherwise known as the Valle de la Luna (Moon Valley), is San Juan's most visited attraction. Set in a desert valley between two mountain ranges some 80km north of Valle Fértil, it is considered one of the most significant **dinosaur graveyards** on the planet. Skeletons dating from the Triassic era around two hundred million years ago have been unearthed here.

Given its size (150 sq km), you need a **car** to explore the park properly; rangers accompany visitors in convoy on a bumpy 45-km circuit of the park's highlights (2–3hr), imparting explanations of its paleontological history, photogenic moonscapes and precarious sandstone rock formations. The southern section of the circuit resembles the arid lunar landscapes of Cappadocia in Turkey, with surreally shaped rock formations dubbed El Submarino (the submarine), El Esfinge

(the sphinx) and Cancha de Bolas (bowling alley); while further north on the circuit lie stark white fields strewn with petrified tree trunks. If you're lucky, you might catch a glimpse of some of the park's inhabitants, which include hares, red foxes, armadillos, lizards, guanacos, snakes and condors.

Arrival and information

Bus The easiest way to visit the park is on an organized tour. Turismo Vesa, at Mitre (no number), Valle Fértil (☎ 02646/420-143) offers daily trips from Valle Fértil. For those coming independently, note that Empresa Vallecito buses from San Juan to La Rioja run on Mon, Wed & Fri and pass the Los Baldecitos checkpoint, a 5-km walk to the park entrance, where the park authorities hire out vehicles.

Park information The park entrance, where there's a helpful *guardaparque* post, is along a signposted road off the RP510 at Los Baldecitos. Entrance (daily April–Sept 9am–4pm, Oct–March 8am–5pm) is AR$70 per person and includes a guided tour. An extra AR$255 buys you a range of special tours, including 2-hr guided bicycle excursions, full-moon night tours and 3-hr treks to the top of Cerro Morado (1748m), with tremendous views of the park. Make use of the toilet facilties and cafés at the entrance, as there are none within the park itself.

Accommodation

Campers can pitch their tents for AR$5 next to the park visitors' centre, where there is also a bathroom and small café. Most people spend the night in nearby Valle Fértil (see p.121) and get a transfer to the park with one of the village's tour operators.

Parque Nacional Talampaya

Familiar from regular appearances on posters promoting Argentinian tourism, the smooth sandstone cliffs and surreal rock formations of **PARQUE NACIONAL TALAMPAYA** are far more eye-boggling in reality. The centrepiece of the park is a 220-million-year-old **canyon**, with 180m-high rust-red sandstone cliffs rising on either side, rendering everything in between puny and insignificant. At the centre of the canyon, armadillos and grey foxes scurry among groves of cacti and native trees in a lush **botanical garden**. Elsewhere, erosion has carved out towering columns and gravity-defying **rock formations** where condors and eagles have found nesting sites.

Other park highlights include a series of pre-Hispanic **petroglyphs and pictographs** etched onto gigantic rock faces. Thought to be around a thousand years old, the etchings depict llamas, pumas, hunters, stepped pyramids and phallic symbols.

Arrival and information

Talampaya lies 93km northeast of Ischigualasto and around 190km from Valle Fértil, but the closest urban centre to the park is actually Villa Unión, an entirely forgettable town in La Rioja Province, 55km away along the RP26.

Bus Organized tours from San Juan, Valle Fértil, La Rioja or Villa Unión are the easiest ways to visit the park. Otherwise, buses from Villa Unión to La Rioja and Valle Fértil can drop you off on the main road.

Park information The *guardería* (daily April–Sept 9am–4pm, Oct–March 8am–5pm; AR$20; ✆03825/470-397) is staffed year-round. Private vehicle are not allowed inside; official guides with their own trucks offer excursions (2hr 30min AR$45 per person; 4hr 30min AR$60 per person).

Accommodation and eating

There is a basic, windswept campsite next to the *guardería*; it can get brutally cold at night. A small shop here sells snacks and simple meals.

Lake District

The Argentine **LAKE DISTRICT** in northern Patagonia is an unspoiled region of azure glacial lakes, pristine rivers, snow-clad mountains, extinct volcanoes and verdant alpine forests. Dominated until the late nineteenth century by the indigenous Mapuche people, the Lake District is now Argentina's top year-round vacation destination – the place to go for

hiking, camping, fishing, watersports, biking, climbing and skiing.

A series of spectacular national parks runs down the region's serrated Andean spine, providing easy access to wilderness. The northernmost of Patagonia's national parks is **Parque Nacional Lanín** in Neuquén Province, accessible from both the sleepy fishing town of **Junín de los Andes** or its dressier neighbour **San Martín de los Andes**. As you head south, the dazzling 110km route between San Martín de los Andes and the upmarket village of **Villa La Angostura** afford roadside vistas of snowcapped peaks reflected in picture-perfect lakes as well as the first glimpse of the gigantic **Parque Nacional Nahuel Huapi**.

The route continues south to the lakeside party town of **Bariloche**, the region's transport hub and base for hiking in **Nahuel Huapi** in summer, skiing in winter and gorging on chocolate and locally brewed beer all year round. Further south, in the province of Chubut, the dusty town of **Esquel** is within day-trip distance of the **Parque Nacional Los Alerces**, a dramatic wilderness area of lakes, rivers, glaciers and thousand-year-old alerce trees; it also boasts one of the world's most famous trains, the **Old Patagonian Express**.

PARQUE NACIONAL LANÍN

The dramatic snow-clad cone of extinct Volcán Lanín rises 3776m at the centre of its namesake **PARQUE NACIONAL LANÍN** (entrance AR$12). Lanín sits on the Chilean border, spanning 4120 square kilometres of varied Andean terrain. Fishing enthusiasts flock to its glacial lakes and trout-filled rivers, campers pitch their homes lakeside at free or Mapuche-run campgrounds, while trekkers take advantage of the park's hiking trails. Forests of monkey-puzzle trees (also known as araucaria or *pehuén*) are the trademark of the northern section of the park. Volcano views are best from **Lago Huechulafquen**, 22km northwest of Junín de los Andes.

Lanín's southern sector is best explored from **San Martín de los Andes** (p.126), set on the eastern shores of the park's **Lago Lácar**, or on the first part of the Seven Lakes Route (see box, p.129). Optimal visiting months are from October to mid-May, when there are organized excursions and municipal buses three times daily from Junín.

JUNÍN DE LOS ANDES

The trout are everywhere in pint-sized **JUNÍN DE LOS ANDES**, from decorating the street signs to populating the Río Chimehuín. Junín is well-positioned for tours to the **Parque Nacional Lanín** (see p.123), in particular the area around Puerto Canoa on **Lago Huechulafquen**, 22km northwest of town along a rough road. A favourite fishing spot is the **Boca del Chimehuín**, halfway to Puerto Canoa along the same road (ask your bus driver to stop).

For something to do in town, take a stroll around the **Vía Christi** sculpture walkway, which starts at the base of Cerro de la Cruz, a 15-min walk west of Plaza San Martín at the end of Avenida Antártida Argentina. A path winds through a pine-forested hillside dotted with sculptures and mosaics depicting the Stations of the Cross, which fuse Catholic and Mapuche symbolism. In bad weather, check out the **Paseo Artesanal** behind the tourism office on the main square; various cabins here (daily 10am–5pm) sell Mapuche crafts alongside woollen knits and handmade wooden crockery.

Arrival and information

Air Chapelco airport (☎02972/428-388), which Junín shares with San Martín de los Andes, is 19km south of town. A taxi to the centre costs around AR$60.

Bus The bus station is three blocks from the main square at Olavarría and F.S. Martín.
Tourist information The tourist office is opposite Plaza San Martín at Padre Milanesio and Coronel Suárez (open 8am–9pm; ☎02972/491-160, ⓦwww.junindelosandes.gov.ar). Fishing licences can be purchased here (AR$75 a day or AR$250 a week). Next door is the helpful Parque Nacional Lanín information office (Dec–March daily 8am–10pm, rest of year Mon–Fri 8am–5pm; ☎02972/492-748, ⓔpnljunin@fronteradigital.net.ar).

Accommodation

Hotel prices hit Andean peaks in the summer, when advance bookings are recommended. The pretty *La Isla* campsite (☎02972/492-029, AR$10 per person) is within easy reach of the main plaza, on an island at the eastern end of Gines Ponte, and has hot showers and a shady, riverside setting.
Albergue Tromen Lonquimay 195 ☎02972/491-498, ⓔtromen@fronteradigital.net.ar. A character-less but serviceable budget option with a variety of dorm rooms and doubles scattered around a large house. The bottom floor has a TV room and kitchen. Dorms AR$35, rooms AR$100.
La Casa de Aldo y Marita 25 de Mayo 371 ☎02972/491-042, ⓔcasademaritayaldo@hotmail .com. A cosy stone cottage half a block from the river with two five-bed dorms and a well-equipped kitchen. The house out back with rickety floor-boards and drooping beds is not half as nice. The owners rent out large rubber dinghies (AR$40 for 2hr) for leisurely river floats. Dorms AR$35.
Hostería Chimehuín Coronel Suárez and 25 de Mayo ☎02972/491132, ⓦwww.interpatagonia .com/hosteriachimehuin. The rooms in this good-value B&B have windows that look out onto a landscaped garden with porch furniture. Wi-fi and breakfast included. AR$200.

Eating and drinking

Aside from the following options, there are just a few mediocre pizza joints and rotisseries, so Junín de los Andes might be just the place to stock up on fresh produce and go wild in the kitchen. The supermarket is on 9 de Julio and Panil.
Panadería La Ideal Gral Lamadrid and O'Higgins. Seemingly the whole town gathers here each morning for coffee, newspapers and fantastic sweets and sandwiches. Nothing over AR$15. Open 8am–1pm & 4–9pm.
Ruca Hueney Padre Milanesio and Coronel Suárez. The only proper restaurant in town serves, you

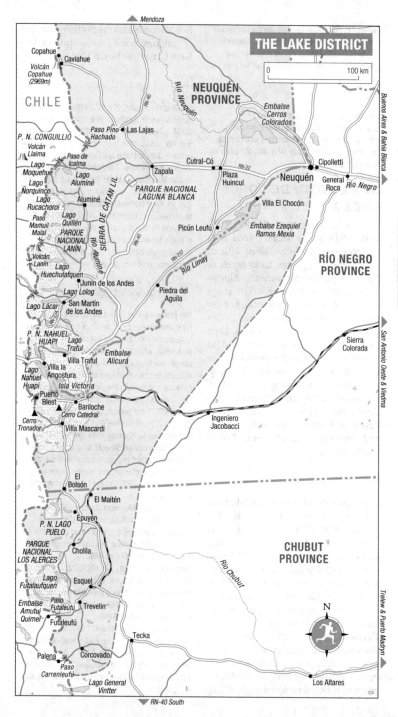

THE LAKE DISTRICT

0   100 km

CHILE

NEUQUÉN PROVINCE

RÍO NEGRO PROVINCE

CHUBUT PROVINCE

ARGENTINA

LAKE DISTRICT

Mendoza

Copahue
Caviahue
Volcán Copahue (2969m)

P. N. CONGUILLIÓ
Volcán Llaima
Lago Moquehue
Lago Ñorquinco
Lago Rucachoroi
Paso Mamuil Malal
PARQUE NACIONAL LANÍN
Volcán Lanín
Lago Huechulafquen
Lago Lolog
Lago Lácar
P. N. NAHUEL HUAPI
Lago Traful
Lago Nahuel Huapi
Isla Victoria
Puerto Blest
Cerro Tronador
Villa Mascardi

Paso Pino Hachado
Las Lajas
Paso de Icalma
Lago Aluminé
Aluminé
Lago Quillén
Junín de los Andes
San Martín de los Andes
Villa Traful
Villa la Angostura
Bariloche
Cerro Catedral

SIERRA DE CATAN LIL

PARQUE NACIONAL LAGUNA BLANCA

Zapala
Cutral-Có
Plaza Huincul
Picún Leufú
Piedra del Aguila

Embalse Alicurá

Embalse Cerros Colorados

Cipolletti
Neuquén
General Roca
Río Negro
Villa El Chocón
Embalse Ezequiel Ramos Mexía

Río Neuquén
RN-22

Río Limay
RN-237

Sierra Colorada

Ingeniero Jacobacci

El Bolsón
El Maitén
Epuyén
P. N. LAGO PUELO
PARQUE NACIONAL LOS ALERCES
Lago Futalaufquen
Embalse Amutui Quimei
Paso Futaleufú
Futaleufú
Cholila
Esquel
Trevelin
Tecka
Palena
Paso Carrenleufú
Corcovado
Lago General Vintter

Río Chubut

Los Altares

N

RN-40 South

guessed it, trout (AR$48) alongside the traditional *parrilla* choices. They also have a less expected variety of Middle Eastern dishes from hummus (AR$12) to tabbouleh (AR$20) and baklava (AR$15).

Moving on

Bus The bus company Castelli goes to Lago Huechulafquen in Parque Nacional Lanín (Jan to mid-March 3 daily; 1hr 30min); Neuquén (3 daily; 6hr); Pucón in Chile (1 daily; 4hr); San Martín de los Andes (12 daily; 1hr).

SAN MARTÍN DE LOS ANDES

Pleasant but pricey, **SAN MARTÍN DE LOS ANDES** is a smaller version of neighbouring Bariloche, albeit without the gobsmacking vistas, tacky hotels or packs of party-hard students. Alpine-style chalets, boutique chocolate shops and upscale restaurants line the holiday town's impeccably clean streets. San Martín is set on the shores of **Lago Lácar**, in a peaceful valley wedged between two forested mountains. The lake offers great summer splashing, while hiking and biking trails lead off to lakeside viewpoints. Pleasure boats depart from the pier for excursions to Paso Hua-Hum near the Chilean border and to the bay of Quila Quina on Lácar's southern shore.

What to see and do

The **Museo de los Primeros Pobladores** (Mon–Fri 10am–7pm, Sat & Sun 4–7pm; ☎02972/428-676; AR$1), set in a 1930s wooden house on the main plaza, puts the area in a historical context and displays Mapuche art and pre-Columbian artefacts. If you're here in winter (June–Oct) and wondering where all the people are, your answer may lie 19km south on the slopes of **Cerro Chapelco** (☎02972/427-845, ⓦwww.cerrochapelco.com; one-day ski pass AR$230), where there are 29 ski runs, excellent options for beginners and a snowboard park and night skiing.

San Martín is also the northern starting or finishing point for the **Ruta de Los Siete Lagos** (see box, p.129).

Arrival and information

Air Chapelco Airport (☎02972/428-388) is 25km from town, with minibus connections to the centre (AR$40). Taxis to the centre cost AR$70.
Bus The bus terminal is on General Villegas between Juez del Valle and Coronel Diaz.
Tourist information The helpful tourist office is on San Martín and J.M. de Rosas (open 8am–9pm; ☎02972/427-347, ⓦwww.sanmartindelosandes .gov.ar). For trekking and camping maps as well as general park information, head to the Intendencia del Parque Nacional Lanín, on the corner of Perito Moreno and Eduardo Elordi (Mon–Fri 8am–3pm; ☎02972/427-233, ⓦwww .parquenacionallanin.gov.ar).

Accommodation

San Martín's prices reflect its popularity with Argentina's upper crust. Advance reservations are necessary during the height of summer and in the ski season, when prices can double. Backpackers can choose from a handful of good hostels, although prices are somewhat inflated. There are three campsites, with the pick of the pitches the Curruhuinca Mapuche community-run *Camping Lolen* (AR$15 per person), beautifully positioned on the lake at Playa Catritre, 4km southwest of town.
La Colorada Av. Koessler 1614 ☎02972/411-041, ⓦwww.lacoloradahostel.com.ar. This hostel, housed in a bright-red cabin, has a fireplace, big backyard and well-equipped kitchen. Some of the dorm rooms (AR$65) have private bathrooms. Breakfast included.
Hostería Laura Misionero Mascardi 632 ☎02972/427-271, ⓔhosterialaura@smandes .com.ar. There's plenty of charm and comfort to the simple little rooms in this unassuming wooden house. Breakfast included. AR$210.
Puma Hostel Fosberry 535 ☎02972/422-443, ⓦwww.pumahostel.com.ar. A serviceable enough hostel with plenty of party potential, three double rooms, dorm beds (AR$60), kitchen and laundry. Breakfast included. AR$180.
Secuoya Hostel Rivadavia 411 ☎02972/424-485. The welcoming staff, tranquil vibe, spotless kitchen and wooden floorboards make this superb little hostel feel more like a guesthouse. The doubles are a bit pokey, but the three-bed dorm rooms (AR$60) are a treat.

SAN MARTÍN DE LOS ANDES
0
250 m
N
CARLOS WEBER
TRES DE CABALLERIA
ASUNCION FOSBERY
JOSE CALDERON
RUDECINDO ROCA
PERITO MORENO
GENERAL ROCA
AV. SAN MARTIN
GENERAL VILLEGAS
GABRIEL OBEID
ALMIRANTE BROWN
ANTU-HUE
TTE CNEL PEREZ
MARIANO MORENO
CAPITAN DRURY
BELGRANO
EDUARDO ELORDI
SARMIENTO
MISIONERO MASCARDI
TENIENTE RAMAYON
CACIQUE CURRUHUINCA
JUEZ DEL VALLE
CORONEL DIAZ
CORONEL ROHDE
RIVADAVIA
Intendencia of Parque Nacional Lanín
Museo de los Primeros Pobladores
PLAZA SAN MARTÍN
PLAZA SARMIENTO
Bus Terminal
Laco Lácar
Mirador Bandurrias
Mirador Arrayán
Bariloche, Cerro Chapelco & RN- 234
D, Junín & Chapelco Airport (25km)
ACCOMMODATION
La Colorada D
Hostería Laura C
Puma Hostel A
Secuoya Hostel B
EATING & DRINKING
Cervecería El Regional 6
Dama Juana 2
Darmas 5
Downtown Matias 1
La Fondue de Betty 3
El Tenedor 4

Eating and drinking

Dining out is an expensive pastime in San Martín, but generally worth every peso. Restaurants are open noon–4pm and 8pm–midnight unless otherwise noted.

Cervecería El Regional Villegas 965 ⓣ02972/411-941. This brewery is the local favourite for its familial atmosphere, home-made pilsner on tap (AR$16) and massive *tablas* (antipasti platters) of pâtés, smoked trout, boar sausage and other local delicacies (AR$98 for two). The deer ravioli with wild mushroom sauce (AR$38) is to die for. You won't get warmer service anywhere else in town.

Dama Juana Coronel Pérez 860 ⓣ02972/411-941. This neighbourhood bistro is named after the large jugs of wine (AR$25) on offer here. The vibe is less formal than other spots in town, but the pastas (AR$20–35) are every bit as good.

Darmas Misionero Mascardi 892 ⓣ02972/412-888. The newest restaurant on the block has a more casual atmosphere and a wider menu than most, with Mediterranean dishes like *gambas al ajillo* and white fish in tomato and caper sauce. The space is a whimsically decorated living room of a large house with wood fireplace. Mains AR$25–50.

Downtown Matias Calderón and Coronel Díaz ⓦwww.downtownmatias.com. So this is where all the nocturnal action is – a cool, two-storey Irish pub and restaurant that shakes its drunken groove well into the small hours. Aside from a dancefloor the complex has a smoking room, darts and backgammon. It's up a long, bumpy driveway, so take a cab if you're wearing heels. Guinness AR$12. Open Jan & Feb Tues–Sun, rest of year Wed–Sat; 8pm to late.

La Fondue de Betty Villegas 586 ⓣ02972/422-522. Warm your hands on a fondue pot at this European-style, intimate restaurant. Cheese, meat and chocolate fondue are served up by the owners themselves alongside French favourites like beef bourguignon. Mains AR$30–60.

El Tenedor Villegas 745 ☎02972/427-597. The cheapest place to fill up on grilled meat. For AR$52 go nuts with endless refills on *parrilla* and unlimited sides of french fries, salads and *milanesas*. For AR$59 get access to all the *empanadas*, goulash and other appetizers you can stomach plus a main course of trout or deer. Drinks and desserts not included.

Moving on

Air Buenos Aires (daily during ski season; 2hr).
Bus Bariloche (2 daily; 3hr 30min); Junín de los Andes (12 daily; 1hr); Villa La Angostura (2–4 daily; 2hr 30min).

VILLA LA ANGOSTURA

A hit with well-heeled Argentines, **VILLA LA ANGOSTURA** is a lovely little wooden village spread loosely along the northern shores of Lago Nahuel Huapi. It makes a tranquil alternative to Bariloche and is the obvious place to overnight before taking a stroll in the unique woodlands of **Parque Nacional Los Arrayanes**. Most of the village's shops and restaurants are in the commercial area known as **El Cruce**, spread along the RN231 (Av. Arrayanes as it passes through town), a squeaky-clean main street with twee log-cabin buildings. The pretty lakeside handful of tea houses known as **La Villa** is an easy 3-km downhill walk from here along Boulevard Nahuel Huapi, where you'll find the two ports and entrance to Parque Nacional Los Arrayanes.

Ten kilometres northeast of town is **Cerro Bayo** (☎02944/494-189, ⓦwww.cerrobayoweb.com), a lovely small ski resort in winter, catering for hiking and mountain biking in the summer. Villa La Angostura is also the southern start (or end) point for the scenic Ruta de Los Siete Lagos (see p.129), which heads north to San Martín de los Andes.

Parque Nacional Los Arrayanes

A mini-park nestled within the mammoth Parque Nacional Nahuel Huapi (see p.135), **PARQUE NACIONAL LOS ARRAYANES** (daylight hours, last entry 2pm; AR$40) lies at the tip of Península Quetrihué, which dips into **Lago Nahuel Huapi** from Villa La Angostura. The diminutive park (just over seventeen square kilometres) shelters the **Bosque de los Arrayanes**, the world's last stand of rare *arrayán* myrtle woodland. Some of the trees here are more than 650 years old. The myrtle's corkscrew-like trunks, terracotta-coloured bark and white flowers are a stunning contrast to a blue sky or shimmering lake.

To **reach the Bosque**, you can either hike, bike in or take a boat. To hike, follow the undulating trail (12km one-way) from the park entrance to the end of the peninsula; allow for a 5 to 6-hour round trip. Cycling is allowed on the trail and bikes can be rented in El Cruce for around AR$30 per hour. A shortcut to the Bosque is to take a 3-hour round-trip boat ride and walk from either the jetty at **Bahía Mansa** or **Bahía Brava**, which are right across from each other in La Villa. The cheapest tour (AR$130 per person) is led by Captain Jorge Rovella (☎02944/1551-2460, ⓦwww.vela-aventura.com.ar) on his small boat every day at 3.30pm. Larger, more expensive catamarans also run out of the two jettys, while organized boat tours operate from Bariloche.

Arrival and information

Bus The bus station is at Av. Siete Lagos 35, just uphill from the main avenue (☎02944/494-961).
Tourist information Pick up a map or organize accommodation at the tourist office (Dec–Feb daily 8am–10pm, rest of year 8.30am–8.30pm; ☎02944/494-124, ⓦwww.villalaangostura.gov.ar), across the road from the bus terminal at Av. Siete Lagos 90.

RUTA DE LOS SIETE LAGOS

The **Ruta de los Siete Lagos** (Seven Lakes Route) is one of South America's most picturesque drives. It winds for 110km between San Martín de Los Andes and Villa La Angostura along the RN234, traversing the dense alpine forests, snow-capped Andean peaks, brilliant blue lakes, trout-stuffed rivers and plunging waterfalls of two magnificent Patagonian national parks – **Lanín** and **Nahuel Huapi**. In summer the road is lined by purple and yellow wild flowers, and the dramatic snow-covered mountains make the view in winter.

Seven principal photogenic **alpine lakes** are visible or accessible from the roadside. From north to south they are: Machónico, Falkner, Villarino, Escondido, Correntoso, Espejo and Nahuel Huapi. You can spend the night en route at numerous free and serviced lakeside campsites as well as at *refugios* and lodges. The first half of the road is paved, while the final stretch, between Lago Villarino and Lago Espejo, is a bumpy dirt track, with vehicles spewing up walls of blinding dust in their wake. After rainfall, the road becomes a muddy mess. Despite obvious hazards from rip-roaring cars and buses, the route is also extremely popular with cyclists. You can rent a bike in Bariloche for this trip. Check in with the tourism office before setting out in winter as parts of the road can be closed due to snow.

Accommodation

Built solely to accommodate tourists, Villa La Angostura is luxury central, with the most exclusive hotels hugging the lakeshore. But there are two good hostel options. The closest campsite to downtown is the very lovely *Camping Unquehué* (℡02944/494-103, ⊛www.campingunquehue .com.ar; pitches AR$33, rooms AR$200), half a kilometre west of the bus station on Av. Siete Lagos. **Hostel La Angostura** Barbagelata 157 ℡02944/494-834, ⊛www.hostellaangostura.com .ar. It's a short uphill walk west of Plaza San Martín to this enormous green house fronted by wind chimes. The comfortable dorms (AR$60) are en suite and the front room is a huge chill-out space, with pool table, TV lounge and kitchen. Breakfast and wi-fi is included and there are bikes for rent. AR$190.

🏃 **Italian Hostel** Los Maquis 215 ℡02944/494-376, ⊛www.italianhostel.com. Two blocks south of the main street, this lovely hostel has spacious dorms (AR$50) as well as doubles and triples set in a large wooden-beamed house with plenty of smaller communal nooks to have a chat. Extras include wi-fi, breakfast, bike rental, backyard hammocks, herb garden and well-equipped kitchen with a recycling system. Closed April–Oct. AR$150. **Verenas Haus** Los Taiques 268 ℡02944/494-467, ⊛www.verenashaus.com.ar. The town's most affordable B&B-style option offers six impeccable if dark private rooms (ask for discounts in low season). Board games, wi-fi and a good breakfast are on offer in the living room. AR$210.

Eating

Most restaurants in town are of the upmarket variety, although many of the tea houses serve inexpensive sandwiches. That said, it's not impossible to eat full meals on the cheap. All are open approximately noon–4pm and 8pm–midnight. **La Caballeriza** Av. Los Arrayanes 44. ℡02944/494-248. A good-value restaurant that locals will direct you towards for the best beef. Hard-to-find vegetable *parrilla* with pumpkin, courgettes, peppers and more is big enough to share. Mains AR$32–60. **La Encantada** Belvedere 69 ℡02944/495-436. Skip the usual dinners; the draw here is the woodfire pizza (AR$24–55). The locally smoked trout or salmon make the perfect topping. Closed Sun night and Mon. **Gran Nevada** Av. Los Arrayanes 102. This bare-bones eatery is always full because of the gigantic portions of dirt-cheap food. Full *parrilla* with sides AR$22.

Moving on

Bus Bariloche (hourly; 1hr); San Martín de los Andes (2–4 daily; 2hr 30min).

BARILOCHE

Set on the southeastern shores of sparkling Lago Nahuel Huapi and framed by dramatic snowcapped

Andean peaks, **BARILOCHE** has its breathtaking setting to thank for its status as one of Argentina's top holiday destinations. Argentines will tell you that it is the country's most European or Swiss-tinged city, but Bariloche itself is a rather ugly hotchpotch of high-rise hotels, garish souvenir stores and faux chalets. That said, the lake and surrounding landscape are stunning – snowy evergreens in winter and covered with purple and yellow wild flowers in summer. The lake is at its best when the sun is reflecting off a placid, cobalt-blue surface, but it can rapidly transform into a tempestuous sea, lashing icy wind through the streets, sending every warm-blooded being indoors to huddle around a pot of cheese fondue or a round of hot chocolate.

Aside from lake views, Bariloche's forte is as an **outdoor adventure** hub. The town's proximity to the lakes, mountains, forests and rivers of Parque Nacional Nahuel Huapi makes it one of the top spots in the country for white-water rafting, zip-lines through the forest canopy, kayaking, paragliding, mountain biking, trekking and climbing. Come winter, the fun shifts to the nearby pistes of Cerro Catedral (see p.134). To avoid the crowds, come in **spring** or **autumn**.

What to see and do

Bariloche's heart is its **Centro Cívico**, a spacious plaza dominated by an equestrian statue of a defeated-looking General Roca. Forming a horseshoe around the square are a set of attractive, mid-twentieth-century public buildings constructed of local timber and green-grey stone, a collaboration between Ernesto de Estrada and famed Argentinian architect Alejandro Bustillo, who also built the **cathedral** a few blocks away. Within these buildings is the **Museo de la Patagonia** (Mon–Fri 10am–12.30pm & 2–7pm, Sat 10am–5pm, closed Sun; AR$3), which does an exemplary job of tracing the area's Mapuche and European history. Bariloche's main drag, **Calle Mitre**, runs east of the plaza.

In the height of summer, you might be tempted to dip a toe beneath the lake's frosty surface; the most popular **beach** is rocky Playa Bonita, 8km west of town (buses #10, #20, #21 or #22), or, for a warmer and more secluded dip, head 13km southeast to Villa Los Coihues on Lago Gutiérrez (buses #41 or #50). Pick up a map and schedule for the useful network of municipal buses at the tourism office.

For the most camera-battery-depleting 360-degree **views** in the region, catch a local bus (#10, #11 #20 or #22) west of Bariloche to Avenida Bustillo Km 18 and take the chairlift (AR$20) or poorly marked trail (a 30-min steep walk) to the lookout at **Cerro Campanario**.

Arrival

Air The airport (ⓣ02944/426-162) lies 14km east of the centre. Local bus #72 runs into town every couple of hours; a taxi or *remise* will set you back around AR$40.

Bus and train The bus terminal (ⓣ02944/432-860) and train station (ⓣ02944/423-172) lie next to each other, a couple of kilometres east of the centre. Local buses #10, #20 and #21 run into town along C Moreno; a taxi to the Centro Cívico costs around AR$11. Many intercity buses also drop at

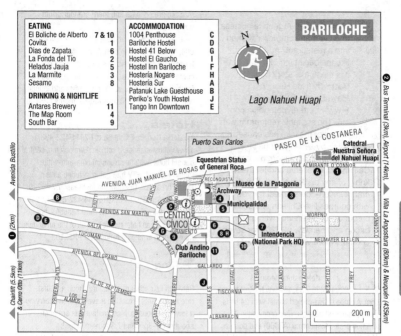

EATING	
El Boliche de Alberto	7 & 10
Covita	1
Dias de Zapata	6
La Fonda del Tío	2
Helados Jauja	5
La Marmite	3
Sesamo	8

DRINKING & NIGHTLIFE	
Antares Brewery	11
The Map Room	4
South Bar	9

ACCOMMODATION	
1004 Penthouse	C
Bariloche Hostel	D
Hostel 41 Below	G
Hostel El Gaucho	I
Hostel Inn Bariloche	F
Hostería Nogare	H
Hostería Sur	A
Patanuk Lake Guesthouse	B
Periko's Youth Hostel	J
Tango Inn Downtown	E

BARILOCHE

Lago Nahuel Huapi

the C Moreno stop in the city centre, so check with your driver.

Information

Club Andino Bariloche 20 de Febrero 30 ☎02944/527-966, ✉info@activepatagonia.com.ar. Sells maps, can register hikers and has information on hikes and *refugios* in Parque Nacional Nahuel Huapi. Also arranges minibus transfers to Pampa Linda, the trailhead for the hike to Refugio Otto Meiling and Ventisquero Negro (Black Glacier). Open Dec–Feb 9am–9pm, rest of year 9am–1pm & 4.30–8.30pm.

Intendencia del Parque Nacional Nahuel Huapi Av. San Martín 24 ☎02944/423-111, ⊕www.nahuelhuapi.gov.ar. Pick up official national park pamphlets here. Open Mon–Fri 9am–3pm, Sat & Sun 9am–6pm.

Tourist information The busy tourist office (daily 8am–9pm; ☎02944/429-850, ⊕www.barilochepatagonia.info) is in the Centro Cívico.

Accommodation

Bariloche's accommodation is among the most expensive in Argentina. Bookings are essential in the high season (mid-Dec to Feb and July–Aug). Many of the cabins and hotels that lie west of town along Avenida Bustillo offer great lake views and are a quieter alternative to staying in town. A large number of excellent backpacker hostels have kitchens, internet and tour-booking services. The closest campground to town is the forested *La Selva Negra*, at Av. Bustillo Km 2.95 (☎02944/441013, ⊕www.campinglaselvanegra.alojar.com.ar; AR$25 per person), with good facilities.

Hostels

1004 Penthouse San Martín 127 ☎02944/432-228, ⊕www.penthouse1004.com.ar. Swan around this hostel and take in the panoramic mountain and lake vistas from the tenth floor of an apartment block. Travellers hang out in the mellow living room, or watch the sunset – *vino* in hand – from the balcony. The dorms are not as stylish as the common area. Dorms AR$45, rooms AR$130.

Bariloche Hostel Salta 528 ☎02944/425-460, ⊕www.barilochehostel.com.ar. With great lake views, polished wooden floorboards and slick modern bathrooms, this intimate hostel is a real gem. Dorm beds are AR$40 or treat yourself to one of their luxurious double rooms (AR$220). Price includes breakfast.

"An Irish chef, Argentine hostess and German sommelier walked into a restaurant" may sound like the beginning of a joke but it is the actual story behind **Butterfly** (Hua Huan 7831 Playa Bonita ☏02944/461-441, ⓦwww.butterflypatagonia.com.ar). The six-table restaurant with a view of the lake has caused quite a stir by serving Michelin-worthy meals at a reasonable price. Call ahead to reserve and let them know of any dislikes and they will craft a seven-course meal for you with courses like Chilean sea bass carpaccio or pea ravioli with fried bacon and parsley. AR$200 for seven courses, more with wine pairings.

🏃 **Hostel 41 Below** Juramento 94 ☏02944/436-433, ⓦwww.hostel41below.com. A chilled, Kiwi-owned hostel with 24 beds, friendly staff and quality music grooving in its common area. Most dorms (AR$60) and doubles (AR$190) have partial lake views, as the hostel has a completely glass front.

Hostel El Gaucho Belgrano 209 ☏02944/522-464, ⓦwww.hostelelgaucho.com. A friendly German/Argentine couple run this spick-and-span operation right downtown. Hanging carpets liven up the rather bare dorms (AR$50) and nicer doubles (AR$195).

Hostel Inn Bariloche Salta 308 ☏02944/552-782. This HI hostel, smack in the middle of town, offers both breakfast and dinner included in the price. While the atmosphere is a little antiseptic, one benefit is a number of smaller common areas including a DVD player. Dorms AR$75, rooms AR$300.

🏃 **Patanuk Lake Guesthouse** Juan Manuel de Rosas 585 ☏02944/434-991, ⓦwww.patanuk.com. Right on the lake with its own private pebble beach, this guesthouse-cum-hostel wins hands down in the atmosphere category. The spacious six-bed dorms (AR$70) enjoy gorgeous views and the doubles (AR$240) have private bathrooms. From the lobby with fireplace you'll feel like you are floating on the lake. Breakfast included and bicycles for rent.

Periko's Youth Hostel Morales 555 ☏02944/522-326, ⓦwww.perikos.com. Recharge at this rustic cabin with a big backyard swinging with hammocks. The four- and six-bed dorms

(AR$50) are en suite and there are four bright doubles (AR$160).

Tango Inn Downtown Salta 514 ☏02944/400-004, ⓦwww.tangoinn.com. A four-storey mega-hostel with stupendous lake views. A good place to come to make friends, as it has a Jacuzzi plus table football and pool tables. Big breakfasts and lounge with wide screen TV. Dorms AR$65, rooms AR$100.

Hotels

Hostería Nogare Elflein 58 ☏02944/422-438, ⓦwww.hosterianogare.com.ar. A welcoming, central budget hotel, with five pleasant blue-and-white rooms with cable TV. Internet is included as is a hearty breakfast. Discounts in low season. AR$220.

Hostería Sur Beschtedt ☏02944/422-677. This two-star hotel may not be the most beautiful, but it does offer clean hotel rooms with all of the amenities, from wi-fi to arranging excursions. AR$210.

Eating

Between its decadent chocolate shops and first-rate restaurants, expect to leave Bariloche carrying a few extra pounds. Most restaurants are open about noon–3pm and 7.30pm–midnight.

El Boliche de Alberto Elflein 158 (☏02944/434-568), Villegas 347 (☏02944/431-433) and Bustillo 8800 (☏02944/462-285); ⓦwww.elbolichedealberto.com. Make a glutton of yourself at this popular local *parrilla* that serves massive portions. An outrageously large *bife de chorizo* is AR$30. The second location on Villegas focuses on home-made pasta.

Covita Vicealmirante O'Connor 511 ☏02944/421-708, ⓦwww.covitacocinanatural.com.ar. This tiny restaurant does gourmet but affordable takes on dishes like aubergine quiche with borscht, sweet and sour tofu, or Asian curries. Tons of vegetarian and vegan options. Mains AR$30–40. Closed Sun.

Dias de Zapata Morales 362 ☏02944/423-128. This colourful Mexican-owned restaurant serves mains like quesadillas and tacos (AR$25–30), as delicious as they are generous. Noon menu includes main, ice cream and a drink (one choice is lemon margarita) for AR$40. Arrive before 9pm for cheap cocktails and to skip the queues.

La Fonda del Tío Mitre 1330 ☏02944/435-011. Packed to the fluorescent-lit rafters with ravenous locals, this unpretentious, economical diner does outstanding versions of Argentinian staples (beef, *milanesas* and pastas). The set meal is a steal at AR$30 for beef, sides, drink and dessert.

Helados Jauja Moreno 18. In a country known for its ice cream, *Jauja* is recognized as the best. Try a scoop of white chocolate, *dulce de leche* with chocolate chips, or blackcurrant for AR$5. Open late.

La Marmite Mitre 329 ☏02944/423-685. This old-fashioned joint hung with antlers is a bit of a wallet-sapper. So stick to the traditional afternoon tea or cheese fondue (AR$95 for two). Closed Sun lunch.

Sesamo Elfein 56 ☏02944/464-567. Follow the Hebrew lettering on the wall to this wonderful Middle Eastern spot. The best deals are the vegetarian platter, heaped with stuffed grape leaves, hummus, baba ghanoush, squash quiche and salads for AR$44, or the meat platter with different kinds of *shawarma* for AR$49. *Shakshuka*, a delicious dish of eggs in spicy tomato sauce, is AR$28. They also have a nice selection of wine. Open Mon–Sat noon–3pm and 7pm–midnight; Sun 6pm–midnight.

Drinking and nightlife

Exhaustion after a day on the slopes/rapids/trails leaves many travellers tucked in bed by 10pm, but those with more energy can enjoy any number of bars and after-midnight action in the four similar lakeside discos: *Cerebro* (Av. Juan Manuel de Rosas 406), *Genux* (Av. Juan Manuel de Rocas 412), *Roket* (Av. Juan Manuel de Rosas 424) and *Pacha* (España 415). These days most are filled with young Brazilian ski bunnies.

Antares Brewery Elfein 47 ⓦwww.cervezaantares .com. Sip the Antares microbrew at a comfortable pub right at the source. Decent pub snacks and barley wine if beer is not your thing. Happy hour 6–8pm. Pint of artisanal beer AR$17. Open 6pm to late.

The Map Room Urquiza 248. Adorned with maps from around the world, this dimly lit gastropub does a great steak sandwich. Only place in town for an American-style breakfast before hitting the slopes. Closed Sun.

South Bar Juramento 30. Locals and tourists meet at this no-frills Irish bar to share cheap pints and mixed drinks (gin and tonic AR$15). Stay out late until the tables are pushed aside and the dancing commences.

Shopping

Books Cultura Librería, Elfein 74, stocks some English-language books and travel guides.
Chocolate C Mitre has numerous chocolate shops (some the size of supermarkets) selling row upon mouth-watering row of gourmet chocolate. The local favourite is Mamuschka, at Mitre 216 (ⓦwww .mamuschka.com), though Abuela Goye, at Mitre 258 (ⓦwww.abuelagoye.com.ar) is cosier and has shorter queues.
Markets The bustling Feria Municipal (known colloquially as Mercado de Artensanias) is held daily behind the Centro Cívico on Urquiza between Mitre and Moreno, and sells locally made crafts.

Directory

Car rental Avis, at San Martín 162 (☏02944/431-648, ⓦwww.andesrentacar.com.ar); Budget, at Mitre 717 (☏02944/422-482, ⓦwww.budget bariloche.com.ar).
Hospital Moreno 601 (☏02944/426-100).
Police Centro Cívico (☏02944/422-772).
Post office Moreno 175 and numerous smaller branches.
Spanish school ECELA, at Pasaje Gutiérrez 843 (☏02944/428-935, ⓦwww.ecela.com), offers private and group classes (max 6 people).
Tour operators Aguas Blancas, Morales 564 (☏02944/432-799, ⓦwww.aguasblancas.com .ar), runs rafting excursions; Bike Cordillera at Av. Bustillo Km 18.6 (☏02944/524-828) rents bicycles; Overland Patagonia (☏02944/456-327, ⓦwww.overlandpatagonia.com) offers a range of backpacker-friendly excursions, including a four-day Ruta 40 trip to El Calafate in summer; Pura Vida (☏02944/400-327) offers kayaking trips on the lake; Turisur, at Mitre 219 (☏02944/426-109, ⓦwww.bariloche.com/turisur) specializes in boat trips.

Moving on

Air Buenos Aires (6–8 daily; 2hr); El Calafate (daily; 1hr 45min); Esquel (2–3 weekly; 30min); Mar de Plata (1 weekly; 35min). There are also seasonal flights to Córdoba, Mendoza, Puerto Madryn and Trelew, as well as direct international flights to a number of cities in Brazil and Chile.
Boat Catedral Turismo, at Palacios 263 (☏02944/425-444, ⓦwww.crucedelagos.com), organizes boat crossings from Bariloche to Puerto Montt in Chile (see p.484; Sept–April; 12hr; US$170). The scenic journey, known as the Cruce Internacional de los Lagos (Three Lakes Crossing) cruises lakes Huapi, Frieas and Todos Los Santos, with the overland segments traversed by bus. Optional overnight stops at Puerto Blest and Peulla.
Bus El Bolsón (11 daily; 1hr 30min); Buenos Aires (6 daily; 21hr); El Calafate (4 weekly; 34hr); Esquel (15 daily; 4hr 30min); Mendoza (2 daily, 18hr);

Puerto Madryn (2 daily; 12hr); Puerto Montt in Chile (2 daily; 6hr); San Martín de Los Andes (5 daily; 3hr 30min); Villa La Angostura (hourly; 1hr 30min). **Train** The Tren Patagónico (☎02944/422-450, ⓦwww.trenpatagonico-sa.com.ar) runs once weekly on Sunday from Bariloche to Viedma (18hr).

DAY-TRIPS FROM BARILOCHE

Most day-trips from Bariloche, as Argentina's outdoor adventure capital involve conquering – or at least ogling – the mountains, rivers and lakes on its doorstep. Outside the winter months, when **skiing at Cerro Catedral** reigns supreme, the most popular excursions are cycling or driving the scenic **Circuito Chico** route (see below), **white-water rafting** on the class III-IV Río Manson some 80km southwest of Bariloche, and hiking in **Parque Nacional Nahuel Huapi** (see p.135). Local tour operators also offer kayaking, kitesurfing, windsurfing, scuba-diving, horseriding, canyoning, rock climbing, mountain-biking, parapenting, scenic flights, bus tours on the Ruta de Los Siete Lagos (see box, p.129) and boating trips.

Shopaholics and beer-lovers will find their spiritual home 123km south of Bariloche in the hippy-ish town of **El Bolsón**, where the outstanding **fería artesanal** (every Tues, Thurs and Sat from 10am to 3pm), sells locally crafted wares and food. Afterwards, sample a pint of the local brew at *Cervecería El Bolsón*, at RN258 Km 124 (ⓦwww .cervezaselbolson.com), have a hearty meal at local favourite *A Punto*, at Av. Sarmiento 2434 (☎02944/483-780; closed Mon) or stay on in the valley for exemplary hiking in the surrounding mountains.

Circuito Chico
The **CIRCUITO CHICO**, a 65km road circuit heading west of Bariloche along the shores of Lago Nahuel Huapi, is an essential day excursion. It can be explored by bike (5–7hr), rental car,

minibus tour (4hr) or by catching a public bus and jumping on and off wherever you fancy. The first photo stop en route is the luxurious, mountain-framed **Llao Llao Hotel and Spa** at Km 25 along Avenida Bustillo (☎02944/448-530, ⓦwww.llaollao.com), an alpine-style creation by architect Alejandro Bustillo. Non-guests can feast on pastries at the hotel's decadent afternoon tea (4–7pm; AR$75).

Just after the turn-off for the *Llao Llao* is **Puerto Pañuelo**, where boats leave for leisure trips to Puerto Blest, Isla Victoria and the Parque Nacional Los Arrayanes (see p.128). Beyond here the traffic dissipates and the circuit follows an undulating road flanked by thick forest. The scenery is superb, with worthwhile stops at **Villa Tacul**, **Lago Escondido**, **Bahia López** and **Punto Panorámico**, the last of these offering the most recognized postcard shot of the region. For a detour, the pretty Swiss village of **Colonia Suiza** offers an enjoyable opportunity for a lunch or afternoon tea break.

Cycling the circuit allows the flexibility to leave the main road and ride along forested trails to hidden beaches and lakes. As traffic is heavy along the first 20km stretch west of Bariloche, it's best to take a bus (#10, #11 #20 or #22) from downtown to Av. Bustillo Km 18.6, where Bike Cordillera (☎02944/524-828) rents bicycles for AR$45 a day. To see the circuit by **public bus**, take #20 along the lakeshore for *Llao Llao* and Puerto Pañuelo or #10 inland for Colonia Suiza. In summer, #11 does the entire circuit.

Cerro Catedral
Named for a summit (2405m) that resembles the spires of a Gothic cathedral, **CERRO CATEDRAL** (☎02944/409-000, ⓦwww.catedral altapatagonia.com; mid-June to Oct; pass AR$250) is one of South America's top ski resorts, offering bedazzling lake

and cordillera views, more than fifty runs, forty lifts and descents up to 9km long. The village of **Villa Catedral**, just 20km south of Bariloche, lies at the base of the mountain and has hotels, restaurants and ski-hire shops. When the snow melts, Cerro Catedral stays open for trekking; a cable car and chairlift provide access to *Refugio Lynch* (1870m; dorms AR$40), from where trails lead to *Refugio San Martín* or *Refugio Frey*. Mountain biking, abseiling and horseriding are other popular summertime activities on the mountain. Buses marked "Catedral" leave from Moreno 470 in Bariloche.

PARQUE NACIONAL NAHUEL HUAPI

Spanning a whopping 7050 square kilometres, the magnificent **PARQUE NACIONAL NAHUEL HUAPI** (@www .nahuelhuapi.gov.ar) is deservedly one of Argentina's most visited national parks. It incorporates **Lago Nahuel Huapi**, a sapphire-blue glacial lake flanked by forest-quilted slopes. In the park's wild heart lie forests of cypress and beech trees, crystal-clear rivers, cascading waterfalls, lupin-filled meadows, ancient craggy glaciers and formidable snow-capped summits. Nahuel Huapi's crown is **Cerro Tronador**, an extinct volcano whose three icy peaks (around 3500m) straddle the borders of Argentina and Chile. Wildlife includes Patagonian hares, guanacos and condors, although in the height of summer, humans rule the roost.

What to see and do

Nahuel Huapi has three distinct **zones** – northern, central and southern – and helpful *guardaparques* are stationed at key points to advise on trekking, fishing and camping.

The northern zone

The park's **northern zone**, which lies just south of the town of San Martín de los Andes (see p.126), adjoins Parque Nacional Lanín (see p.123). This zone is defined by sky-blue **Lago Traful**, accessible from a turn-off on the Ruta de los Siete Lagos (see p.129). Also here is the **Paso Cardenal Samoré**, a popular overland pass into Chile (Argentinian immigration open 8am–8pm; Chilean side open 8am–7pm).

The central and southern zones

The **central zone**, which incorporates the pretty Parque Nacional Los Arrayanes (see p.128) and Isla Victoria, has **Lago Nahuel Huapi** as its centre-piece. In summer, this zone buzzes with tourists on boating, kayaking, cycling and hiking excursions. The southern zone has the best trails and facilities for hikers, and is focused around **Lago Mascardi**, ideal for swimming and diving in summer.

ESQUEL

Cowboys and urban sophisti-cates should feel equally at home in **ESQUEL**, the main town in northern Chubut province. Some 340km south of Bariloche, Esquel means "bog" in the Mapuche language, a name that says nothing of the town's arresting mountainous backdrop. Although Esquel is often relegated to a pit stop en route to Bariloche or Chile, the town makes a perfect base to explore the lush **Parque Nacional Los Alerces** and for riding the historic **Old Patagonian Express** steam train on a touristic loop (see box, p.138). Other local draws include the tea-house-filled Welsh settlement of **Trevelin**, 23km south, and in winter, the ski resort of **La Hoya** (℡02945/453-018, @www.skilahoya .com), 12km northeast, where there are 22km of runs, plenty of off-piste skiing and a season that often extends into early October.

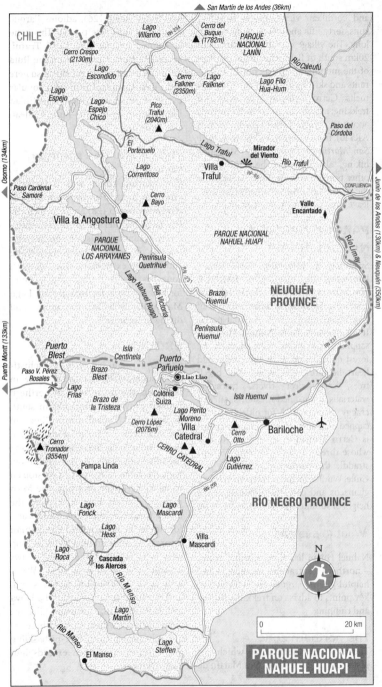

San Martín de los Andes (36km)

CHILE

Lago Villarino

Cerro del Buque (1782m)

PARQUE NACIONAL LANÍN

Río Caleufú

Cerro Crespo (2130m)

Lago Escondido

Cerro Falkner (2350m)

Lago Falkner

Lago Filo Hua-Hum

Lago Espejo

Lago Espejo Chico

Pico Traful (2040m)

Osorno (134km)

Paso del Córdoba

El Portezuelo

Lago Traful

Mirador del Viento

Río Traful

Lago Correntoso

Villa Traful

RP-65

CONFLUENCIA

Paso Cardenal Samoré

Cerro Bayo

Valle Encantado

Junín de los Andes (130km) & Neuquén (350km)

Villa la Angostura

PARQUE NACIONAL NAHUEL HUAPI

PARQUE NACIONAL LOS ARRAYANES

Península Quetrihué

RN-231

Río Limay

Lago Nahuel Huapi

Isla Victoria

Brazo Huemul

NEUQUÉN PROVINCE

Península Huemul

RN-237

Puerto Blest

Isla Centinela

Puerto Pañuelo

Puerto Montt (133km)

Paso V. Pérez Rosales

Brazo Blest

Llao Llao

Isla Huemul

Lago Frías

Brazo de la Tristeza

Colonia Suiza

Lago Perito Moreno

Cerro López (2076m)

Villa Catedral

Cerro Otto

Bariloche

Cerro Tronador (3554m)

CERRO CATEDRAL

Lago Gutiérrez

Pampa Linda

RN-258

RÍO NEGRO PROVINCE

Lago Fonck

Lago Mascardi

Lago Hess

Villa Mascardi

Lago Roca

Cascada los Alerces

N

Río Manso

Lago Martín

0   20 km

Río Manso

El Manso

Lago Steffen

PARQUE NACIONAL NAHUEL HUAPI

El Bolsón (55km) & Esquel (222km)

Arrival and information

Air Esquel's airport is 21km east of town; Urielito offers airport minibus transfers (☎02945/155-0830; AR$12).

Bus The bus terminal (☎02945/451-584) lies eight blocks from the town centre on the corner of A.P. Justo and Av. Alvear, the main street.

Tourist information The tourist office is at Av. Alvear and Sarmiento (Jan & Feb 7am–11pm, March–Dec 8am–10pm; ☎02945/451-927, ⓦwww.esquel.gov.ar).

Train The train station (see box, p.138), from which *La Trochita* departs, is at Roggero and Brun.

Accommodation

El Hogar del Mochilero Roca 1028 ☎02945/452-166, ⓦwww.cpatagonia.com/esq /hogar. Locate this camper's paradise by the white statue of a backpacker out front. The best option is year-round camping (AR$3 per person) in the tree-filled garden at the back. There are also bunk beds in a rustic dormitory (AR$15). Has a kitchen and common area.

Hostel Sol Azul Rivadavia 2869 ☎02945/455-193, ⓦwww.hostelsolazul.com.ar. The cosiest hostel in town boasts a wood-burning stove, heated floors and an all-stone bar. The dorms (AR$50) are small with bunk beds for four and lockers. Winter specials get as low as AR$30.

Lago Verde Volta 1081 ☎02945/452-251. Small but impeccable rooms set behind a quiet family home with a cute rose-filled garden. AR$90.

Planeta Hostel Av. Alvear 2833 ☎02945/456-846, ⓦwww.planetahostel.com. A hostel with delightful owners, wacky artistic touches, an indoor climbing wall and a bright little kitchen. The dorm beds (AR$55) are just what the chiropractor ordered and there's one tiny double room. Internet, wi-fi and breakfast included. Book ahead as there are only four rooms in total. AR$130.

Eating and drinking

La Barra Sarmiento 638 ☎02945/454-321. This *parrilla* serves big juicy slabs of tenderloin

---

TREKKING IN NAHUEL HUAPI

Parque Nacional Nahuel Huapi has an outstanding network of well-marked trails as well as numerous campsites and eight *refugios* (basic staffed mountain huts, AR$25–40) to overnight in. The **hiking season** runs Dec–March, although snow at high altitudes sometimes cuts off trails. January and February are the warmest and busiest hiking months, although this is also prime time for *tábanos* – intensely annoying biting horseflies that infest the lower altitudes. Spring in the park can be quite windy, while in autumn the leaves of the *ñire* and *lenga* trees turn a brilliant shade of red.

Before heading for the hills, trekkers should visit **Club Andino Bariloche**, at 20 de Febrero 30 in Bariloche (see p.131). Here, knowledgeable staff give out trekking maps and can answer questions about the status of trails, campsites and *refugios* as well as transport to trailheads. They also register solo hikers for safety reasons. Club Andino offers daily bus transfers to **Pampa Linda** (AR$60 return), 90km southwest, for the unforgettable hike to *Refugio Otto Meiling*, which cowers dramatically beneath Cerro Tronador, nestled between the Castaño Overa and Alerce glaciers.

All of the park's **refugios** are spectacularly sited in the park's southern zone and have bathrooms with cold water and dorms (bring a sleeping bag, all supplies and a torch). River water is safe to drink untreated, as is the water from *refugio* taps. Fully equipped kitchens can be used for a small fee. Staff also prepare hot meals, sell snacks and stock an impressive selection of alcohol, although prices reflect the fact that everything has been lugged up the mountain on their backs. Trails link many of the *refugios*, allowing hikers to embark on multi-day treks or return to Bariloche every couple of days for a hit of civilization.

There are authorized **campsites** at all major park locations, each of which costs AR$25 per person, including *Lago Roca* near Cascada Los Alerces, *Los Rápidos* (☎02944/461-861) and *La Querencia* (☎011/1561-6300) at Lago Mascardi, and *Pampa Linda*. **Hosterías** within the park are expensive; *Hostería Pampa Linda*, at the base of Cerro Tronador (☎02944/490-517, ⓦwww.hosteriapampalinda.com.ar) is the most affordable at AR$240 and also has an adjacent basic *refugio* (AR$55).

accompanied with home-made mayonnaise on lacy tablecloths. Massive mixed grill for one person AR$55. Open daily 12.10–14.30pm & 20.30–23.30pm although as they note "we open when we are ready."

Empanadería Molinari 633 ☎02945/454-687. The delightful owner serves the best deal in town: a dozen fried *empanadas* with beef, vegetable, corn or chicken fillings for AR$35.

Fitzroya Pizza Rivadavia 1048 ☎02945/450-512. Cheesy pizzas loaded with creative toppings such as broccoli, salmon and trout (starting at AR$20) are delivered piping hot. Open noon–3pm & 7.30pm–midnight.

Moe Bar Rivadavia 873. Cocktails and classic rock are the orders of the night at this dark and rowdy drinking hole with half a yellow car protruding from its entrance. Tend to your hunger pangs with one of their tasty pizzas (AR$25). Open late.

Moving on

Air Bariloche (2–3 weekly; 30min); Buenos Aires (1 daily Mon–Sat, 2 weekly in winter; 3hr); and occasional services to Puerto Madryn.
Bus Bariloche (15 daily; 4hr 30min); El Bolsón (15 daily; 2hr 30min); El Calafate (1 daily; 29hr); El Chaltén (1 daily; 26hr); Comodoro Rivadavia (5 daily; 9hr); Futaleufú in Chile (Jan & Feb 2 daily 3 times a week; rest of year 2 daily twice a week; 2hr); Mendoza (1 daily; 24hr).

PARQUE NACIONAL LOS ALERCES

PARQUE NACIONAL LOS ALERCES, 40km west of Esquel, encompasses 2630 square kilometres of gorgeous, glacier-carved Andean landscape. Although far less visited than Parque Nacional Nahuel Huapi to the north, its network of richly coloured lakes and pristine rivers makes it a prime destination for anglers, while countless hiking trails through verdant forests attract summer walkers and campers. It's easily navigable on a day-trip from Esquel via the very popular lake tour (see p.129).

The *alerce* (or Patagonian cypress) that grows here is one of the oldest living species on the planet, with some examples surviving as long as 3000 years. In size, they're almost comparable to the grand sequoias of California, growing to 70m tall and 4m wide.

THE OLD PATAGONIAN EXPRESS

Puffing and chugging its way across the arid Andean foothills at around 25kph, the **Old Patagonian Express** is both a museum on wheels and a classic South American train journey. Affectionately known as "*La Trochita*" ("little narrow gauge" in Spanish), the locomotive's tracks are a mere 75cm wide. Built in 1922 to connect sheep farmers in isolated, windswept communities with faraway markets for their goods, the train only stopped running in 1993. Immortalized in Paul Theroux's 1979 train-travel narrative, the express is today mostly involved in short, round-trip tourist jaunts. Passengers pile into antique wooden coaches, complete with wood-burning furnaces and dining cars, to puff from Esquel to a Mapuche community plus museum called **Nahuel Pan** and back (44km return; 3hr). Peering out the window, you might spot guanacos, rheas and hares – and you will certainly see cows.

Trains leave each Saturday at 10am in winter and every day at 10am in summer. Based on demand, extra trips are made in winter and 2pm trips are added in summer (Jan to mid-Feb Mon–Sat 10am & 2pm; rest of Feb Mon–Sat 10am; March & April Tues & Fri 10am; further information on ☎02945/451-403, ⊛www.latrochita.org.ar).

As a much less frequent **alternative route**, *La Trochita* also chuffs the 38km between El Maitén and Norquinco (based on demand; call ahead on ☎02945/495-190), lurching past the *Estancia Leleque*, owned by Italian clothing mogul Benetton. El Maitén is 130km northeast of Esquel and can be reached three times weekly by a bus.

Occasionally, the train makes the 165-km journey all the way from Esquel to El Maitén, where there is a museum and railway repair shops.

What to see and do

Though the *alerce* gives the park its name, the flora is wildly varied: **Valdivian temperate rainforest** thrives in its luxuriant western zone near the Chilean border, which is deluged by around 3000mm of annual rainfall. Elsewhere, incense cedar, bamboo-like *caña colihue, arrayán, coihue, lenga* and southern beech thrive. Most visitors gravitate towards the park's user-friendly and photogenic **northeast sector** where there is a network of four dazzling lakes – **Rivadavia**, **Verde**, **Menéndez** and **Futalaufquen**. The emerald-hued Lago Verde is often the first port of call for day-trekkers and campers. Spilling over from Lago Verde is the **Río Arrayanes**, crossed by a suspension bridge that marks the start of an easy hour-long interpretive loop walk.

One main dusty, bumpy road (the RP71) runs through Los Alerces. Public transport is scarce outside peak season, so a vehicle is recommended; otherwise, hikers need to walk along the road between trails, enduring clouds of body-coating dust from passing cars and trucks. Some hikes, including the trek to the summit of **Cerro Alto El Dedal** (1916m), require registration with the national park office first. The most popular day excursion is the **boat trip** leaving from either Puerto Limonao (3km north of the ranger's office, 9.30am departure) or Puerto Chucao (halfway around the Lago Verde/Río Arrayanes loop trail, 11.30am departure). The boats cross Lago Menéndez to visit **El Abuelo** (The Grandfather), a 57m-high *alerce* estimated to be more than 2600 years old. Tours with English-speaking guides can be booked through tour operators in Esquel (see p.137) and leave every day according to demand.

Arrival

Bus The RP71 is the main road through the park and is usually accessible year-round, although occasionally blocked by snow in winter. Peak season is Jan–Feb, when Transportes Esquel (☎02945/453-529, ✆www.transportesesquel .com.ar) runs buses to the park three times daily; it takes three bumpy hours to reach Lago Verde. There is no public transport March–Dec.

Information

Tourist information The ranger's office (open daily 8am–1pm; ☎02945/471-020) is at Villa Futalaufquen, a village with a smattering of shops, public telephones, eateries and accommodation options (which close in winter). A museum and visitors' centre here (daily Jan–Easter 8am–9pm, Easter–Nov 9am–4pm; ☎02945/471-015) can provide information on camping, park accommodation, hiking and fishing (and sells fishing permits). Park entrance is AR$20.

Accommodation

A number of cabañas, *hosterías* and campsites lie within the park, including pricey lodges that cater for anglers. There are a dozen free campsites with no facilities at all, five basic campsites with cold-water bathrooms (AR$10) and five organized campsites (AR$15–30) with hot water, gas and electricity. The closest campsite to Villa Futalaufquen is *Los Maitenes* (☎02945/471-006; AR$16), 400m from the *Intendencia*. Other organized campsites are at Lago Futalaufquen, Bahía Rosales, Lago Verde and Lago Rivadavia.

ARGENTINA LAKE DISTRICT

CROSSING INTO CHILE

Esquel is well placed for crossing into Chilean Patagonia, with several buses weekly making the 2-hr trip to the settlement of Futaleufú, where there is excellent white-water rafting on its namesake river. A bus leaves Esquel (travelling south via Trevelin) twice daily three times a week in January and February, and twice daily two times a week the rest of the year. At the Chilean border (immigration open Jan & Feb 8am–9pm, rest of year 8am–8pm), passengers transfer to a minibus for the final 10km leg to Futaleufú.

Patagonia

Lonely, windswept and studded with glaciers, **PATAGONIA** conjures up an undeniable mystique, a place where pioneers, outlaws, writers and naturalists have long come in search of open space and wild adventure. And while Argentina's southernmost chunk is now an established destination for the summer tourist hordes, you'll hardly care. Whether standing on a beach watching orcas feast on baby elephant seals or strapped into crampons on the Southern Patagonian Ice Cap, you'll find Patagonia still has its mojo.

For those short on time, domestic flights offer a way to hop between Patagonia's key attractions, but to truly appreciate the region's vastness, it is best to travel overland – by bus, 4x4 or bike. After hundreds of kilometres of desolate steppe, nothing quite bedazzles like the sight of serrated Andean peaks rising up on the horizon like a Gothic mirage.

Two main arteries traverse Patagonia. The recently paved RN40 runs parallel to the Andes and links some of Patagonia's major sights: the 10,000-year-old rock art of the **Cueva de las Manos Pintadas**; the Fitz Roy sector of **Parque Nacional Los Glaciares** around the village of El Chaltén; and the **Perito Moreno** and **Upsala** glaciers in the park's southern sector, both easy day-trips from El Calafate. To the east, the RN3 loosely traces the Atlantic seaboard, passing the town of **Puerto Madryn**, a launching pad for the marine wildlife-rich shores of **Península Valdés**, before heading south to the Welsh heartland of **Trelew**, a short jump to the continent's largest penguin colony at **Punto Tombo**.

December to February are the warmest months to visit Patagonia, but to avoid the crowds, inflated prices and high winds, March and April are better. Tourism all but grinds to a halt come winter, despite the fact that there is less

> ### ESTANCIAS IN PATAGONIA
>
> Patagonia's empty steppe is speckled with isolated *estancias*, many of which open their doors to visitors. While most cater for high-end tourists, others are more modest and allow camping in their grounds. Good examples include *Estancia Telken* (see p.148), near Perito Moreno, and *Estancia Menelik* (p.148). Contact Estancias de Santa Cruz in Buenos Aires (Viamonte 920, 5th floor, office H; ☏011/5237-4043, ⓦwww.estanciasdesantacruz.com) for bookings and a comprehensive list of *estancias* in Patagonia.

difference between winter and summer temperatures than you might think.

PUERTO MADRYN AND PENÍNSULA VALDÉS

Having spent hours travelling through the barren bleakness of the Pampas, you may wonder why you bothered when you first hit **PUERTO MADRYN**. A windy, sprawling, seaside city clinging to the barren coast of northern Patagonia, it has no obvious tourist attractions. However, its proximity to one of the world's most prolific nature reserves – the **Reserva Faunística Península Valdés**, 17km to the north – makes it an essential stop. More than a million Magellanic penguins make their summer home in the Península Valdés, along with a permanent population of 75 colonies of seals and sea lions, and more than two thousand dolphins. Topping even that is a breeding colony of more than two thousand southern right whales that can be observed directly from the beach of **Puerto Pirámides**, the only town on the peninsula, in winter. From October to April you can spot groups of orca (killer whales) on the hunt for baby sea lions.

Puerto Madryn may be a bit bleak, but it's easy to get around on foot, and has

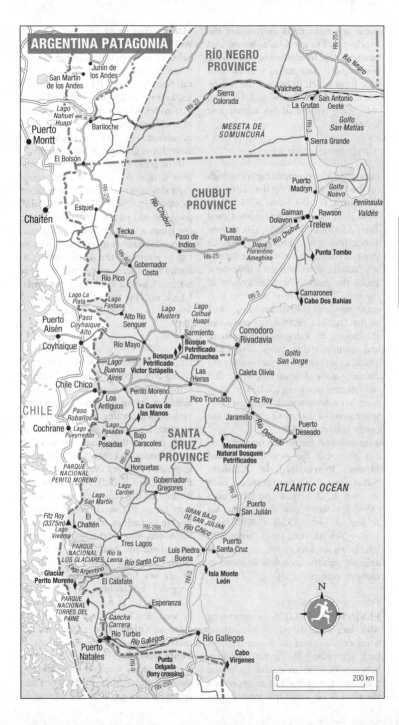

ARGENTINA PATAGONIA

RÍO NEGRO PROVINCE

San Martín de los Andes
Junin de los Andes
Puerto Montt
Lago Nahuel Huapi
Bariloche
El Bolsón
Esquel
Chaitén
Sierra Colorada
Valcheta
La Grutas
San Antonio Oeste
MESETA DE SOMUNCURÁ
Golfo San Matías
Sierra Grande
RN-23

CHUBUT PROVINCE

Río Chubut
Puerto Madryn
Golfo Nuevo
Península Valdés
Gaiman
Dolavon
Rawson
Trelew
Tecka
Paso de Indios
Las Plumas
Dique Florentino Ameghino
RN-25
Punta Tombo
Gobernador Costa
Río Pico
Lago La Plata
Lago Fontana
Alto Río Senguer
Lago Musters
Lago Colhué Huapi
Sarmiento
Bosque Petrificado J.Ormachea
Comodoro Rivadavia
Camarones
Cabo Dos Bahías
RN-3
Puerto Aisén
Paso Coyhaique Alto
Coyhaique
Río Mayo
Bosque Petrificado Víctor Szlápelis
Las Heras
Caleta Olivia
Golfo San Jorge
Lago Buenos Aires
Chile Chico
Perito Moreno
Pico Truncado
Fitz Roy
CHILE
Los Antiguos
La Cueva de las Manos
Jaramillo
Puerto Deseado
Paso Roballos
Cochrane
Lago Pueyrredón
Lago Posadas
Bajo Caracoles
Posadas
Las Horquetas
SANTA CRUZ PROVINCE
Monumento Natural Bosques Petrificados
Río Deseado
PARQUE NACIONAL PERITO MORENO
Lago San Martín
Lago Cardiel
Gobernador Gregores
RN-40
ATLANTIC OCEAN
Fitz Roy (3375m)
Lago Viedma
El Chaltén
GRAN BAJO DE SAN JULIÁN
Río Chico
Puerto San Julián
RN-288
PARQUE NACIONAL LOS GLACIARES
Río la Leona
Tres Lagos
Luis Piedra Buena
Puerto Santa Cruz
Lago Argentino
Río Santa Cruz
Glaciar Perito Moreno
El Calafate
Isla Monte León
RN-3
PARQUE NACIONAL TORRES DEL PAINE
Esperanza
Cancha Carrera
Río Turbio
Río Gallegos
Puerto Natales
Punta Delgada (ferry crossing)
Cabo Vírgenes
RN-9
RN-255

N

0   200 km

ARGENTINA

PATAGONIA

some fine restaurants overlooking the beach as well as good-value hostels and budget hotels. In addition to tours to the peninsula, it also makes a convenient base from which to explore the nearby Welsh towns of Trelew and Gaiman, with their traditional tea houses and leafy plazas.

What to see and do

Located in a lovely rambling house high on the cliffs overlooking the ocean, the **Ecocentro**, at Julio Verne 3784 (Wed–Mon 3–7pm; April–June also closed Tues; AR$38; ☎02965/457-470, ⓦwww.ecocentro.org.ar), promotes research into and conservation of marine life and is a fantastic place to learn a little more about the animals and geography of the area. The three-level building, with stunning views from the reading room at the top, has permanent interactive exhibitions on Patagonian ecosystems and southern right whales, as well as a changing art exhibition. Just outside the entrance is the skeleton of a whale that was beached nearby in 2001. To get here it's either a 40-min walk along the coast to the south of the city or a taxi from the centre of town (AR$15).

For more on the local ecosystem, you can also visit the newly remodelled **Museo Provincial de Ciencias Naturales Y Oceanográfico**, back in town at D. Garcia and Menéndez (Mon–Fri 9am–1pm & 3–7pm, Sat & Sun 3–7pm; AR$8; ☎02965/451-139), which has nine small rooms with interesting displays including preserved animals, and the complete skeletons of many marine mammals.

Península Valdés

PENÍNSULA VALDÉS is brimming with life: birds hover in the strong wind, dolphins surf the waves, sea lions bark aggressively. With vast distances between viewing areas and no public transport, the easiest way to appreciate the place is on a day-trip from Puerto Madryn. You could also rent a car to visit independently, which can be good value if you are travelling in a group, but note that all the roads are dirt tracks and can be a challenge if it has been raining. Either way you'll want to stop in **Puerto Pirámides**, where you can board a boat to visit the nearby sea-lion colony and, in season, see frolicking whales up close. It's an unforgettable experience.

If you get to Puerto Pirámides via your own vehicle, you could stop for lunch right downtown at a rustic lodge called *El Refugio* (☎02965/495-031), which has good fish and pizzas. A local bus runs a few times a week from the bus station in Puerto Madryn to Puerto Pirámides (3hr), returning the same afternoon; handy if you want to stay out here, but not much use for visiting the peninsula. Check with the tourist office in Puerto Madryn for up-to-date timetables.

Tours

Organized minibus **tours** (10–12hr round-trip from Puerto Madryn, bring lunch and warm clothes) all have much the same itinerary, with minor variations according to the season and weather. First stop, a short drive out of town, is to pay the entrance fee and visit the **information centre**, followed by an impressive look out over the **Isla de los Pájaros** (Bird Island). Next, across the isthmus on the peninsula proper, you'll stop off in the small resort town of **Puerto Pirámides**, where sea-lion- and whale-watching boat trips are offered. From here you head north to **Punto Norte**, at the far tip of the peninsula, to see sea lions, elephant seals and penguins sun-bathing on the beach; sometimes orcas make an appearance as well. You'll also see penguins up close at **Caleta Valdés**, followed by more elephant seals and dolphins at **Punta Delgada**. Marine life is present throughout the year but some viewing stations close from Easter to June; optimal viewing is between September and February, but whales can be seen from June to December.

Tours leave Puerto Madryn early in the morning and cost around AR$200 not including the optional boat trip (AR$80) nor the park entrance (AR$40). Most tours include lunch. Recommended **tour operators** include: Tito Bottazzi, at Mitre 80 (☎02965/474-110); and Alora Viaggio, at Roca 27 (☎02965/455-106, ⓦwww.aloraviaggio .com). For scuba-diving and snorkelling in the area consult Scuba Duba, at Brown 893 (☎02965/452-699) or Lobo Larsen, at Roca 885 (☎02965/470-277, ⓦwww.lobolarsen.com).

Arrival and information

Air Puerto Madryn's airport, Aeropuerto El Tehuelche (☎02965/451-909) is 5km west of town. Tour agency Flamenco Tour (☎02965/455-505 will run you into town for AR$15 or take a taxi

to the centre for AR$20. You can also fly into nearby Trelew Airport (☎02965/428-021), an hour away, which has more scheduled flights. A taxi from there is around AR$120.

Bus The bus terminal is on avenidas Avila and Independencia, four blocks from the centre of town and close to most accommodation.

Tourist information The large tourist office is on Av. Roca 223, along the coastal boulevard (daily 8am–10pm; ☎02965/456-067, ⓦwww.madryn .gov.ar/turismo).

Accommodation

Most accommodation is close to the centre of town and within walking distance of the bus terminal. It's much cheaper to stay in Puerto Madryn than within the nature reserve at Puerto Pirámides, but if you prefer the latter, consider one of two good options: *Cabañas del Mar*, at Av. de las Ballenas (☎02965/495-049, ⓦwww .piramides.net; AR$350), or *La Nube del Angel*, at Segunda Baja (☎02965/495-070; AR$350). For camping, the best option is the municipal camping site behind the beach in Puerto Pirámides

PUERTO MADRYN

Muelle Cmte Luis Piedra Buena

Museo Oceanográfico

Bus Terminal

Plaza San Martín

Monumento al Indio Tehuelche (4km), Ecocentro & Punta Loma (19km)

Playa Doradilla (17km) & Península Valdés (100km)

EATING, DRINKING & NIGHTLIFE	
Ambigú	3
Los Colonos	4
De Miga	5
Disco La Frontera	6
Margarita	3
La Oveja Negra	7
Quemehuencho Churrería	8
Vernardino	2
Vesta Patagonia	1

ACCOMMODATION	
Bahia Nueva	B
Chepatagonia Hostel	A
El Gaulicho	G
J & S	D
El Muelle Viejo	C
Posada del Catalejo	E
El Retorno	F
Sentir Patagonia Hostel	I
La Tosca	H

0   200 m

Trelew (65km)

Like the idea of waking up to the sight of whales at play from your luxury king-size bed? An ocean-facing room at **Las Restingas**, at Primera Baja al Mar (☎02965/495-101, ⓦwww.lasrestingas.com), on the beach at Puerto Pirámides, could be just the thing. Quadruple rooms offer a cheaper option for groups, and the hotel also has an attractive beachfront restaurant (open to non-guests) serving delicious seafood, with mains starting at AR$28, as well as a heated pool and gym, all with stunning beach views. Ask for a room downstairs to get a private terrace with access to the sea.

(☎02965/495-084), or *Camping El Golfito*, at Camino a Loberia Punta Loma, not far out of Puerto Madryn (☎02965/454-544; from AR$15 per person).

Hostels

All hostels listed here include breakfast, internet and use of kitchen. Hotels tend to be a cheaper bet for doubles than hostels, unless you are bent on cooking. Prices drop greatly outside the January to March high season.

Chepatagonia Hostel A Storni 16, ☎02965/455-783, ⓦwww.chepatagoniahostel.com.ar. Right on the waterfront, the dorms are not worth writing home about for style but the mattresses are wonderful. Wi-fi and breakfast included. Dorms AR$48, rooms AR$150.

El Gualicho Marcos A Zar 480 ☎02965/454-163, ⓦwww.elgualicho hostel.com.ar. The best hostel in town. Warm, cosy six-bed dorms with private bathrooms, plus a lively common area with bean bags, wi-fi and a pleasant garden and grill area. Excursions organized. Call ahead for free pick-up from the bus station. Dorms AR$55, rooms AR$220.

Posada del Catalejo Mitre 446 ☎02965/475-224, ⓦwww.posadadelcatalejo.com.ar. Popular B&B-type hostel close to the beach and the town centre. Large brightly painted rooms with crisp white sheets, and a lovely homely feel; wi-fi too. Dorms AR$45, rooms AR$160.

El Retorno Bartolomé Mitre 798 ☎02965/450-6044, ⓦwww.elretornohostel.com.ar. A welcoming hostel with somewhat dated decor. Small dorms

with 4–8 beds (AR$45–50), as well as en-suite doubles (AR$130) with TV and comfy mattresses. Free pick-up from bus terminal if prearranged.

Sentir Patagonia Hostel Sarmiento 437 ☎02965/471-050, ⓦwww.sentir-patagonia.com .ar. Recently renovated and reopened, this hostel has modern facilities and English-speaking staff. Three blocks from the bus station, the brick building may look grim from the outside but it is less institutional inside. Dorms AR$50, rooms AR$130.

La Tosca Sarmiento 437 ☎02965/456-133, ⓦwww.latoscahostel.com. Located four blocks from the bus station, this hostel may not be the prettiest, but it's friendly, close to the beach and has a nice garden out back. The helpful staff will pick you up from the bus station on request. Dorms AR$45.

Hotels

Bahia Nueva Av. Roca 67 ☎02965/451-677, ⓦwww.bahianueva.com.ar. Overlooking the boulevard and the beach, this is a reliable central choice. The rooms are large and bright, and the buffet breakfast is well presented and delicious. AR$320.

J & S 9 de Julio 57 ☎02965/476-074. Budget hotel with basic but clean doubles, one block from the beach. Good choice if you want something somewhat modern, with private bathroom, but don't want to spend too much. Discounts for longer stays. AR$210.

El Muelle Viejo Av. Hipólito Yrigoyen 38 ☎02965/471-1284, ⓦwww.muelleviejo.com. Pleasant, modern, wood-floored rooms with a deck with views of the ocean. Common areas and reception are a little old-fashioned but the staff are welcoming. There's parking out back. AR$300.

Eating and drinking

Unless otherwise noted restaurants are open noon–4pm and 8pm–midnight.

Ambigú Roca and Roque Sáenz Peña ☎02965/472-541. Looks like an exclusive restaurant from the outside but has a chummy caféteria-esque interior. Try the yummy pizzas (AR$23) or home-made pastas (AR$37). Open late.

Los Colonos Roca and A. Storni ☎02965/458-486, ⓦwww.loscolonosmadryn.com.ar. Located in the hull of a large wooden ship on the main street, this place is just plain fun. Their speciality is seafood; oven-baked fish goes for around AR$40.

De Miga 9 de Julio 160 ☎02965/475-620. Inexpensive café serving their namesake overstuffed sandwiches (AR$15) and large pizzas (AR$19). Popular with locals.

Quemehuencho Churreria Roque
Sáenz Peña 212 ☏ 02965/1540-4016.
Churros stuffed with every imaginable filling from
the usual *dulce de leche* to home-made fruit
preserves. This is also a great place for the *mate*
novice, as the waiters will explain the different
varieties and help you brew the bitter drink. And
then you can chase it with more *churros*. Open
noon–9pm.

Vernardino Blvd Brown 860 ☏ 02965/474-289.
Wonderful beach views from this modern restaurant
set right off the boulevard. Best at lunch: try the
fresh salads (AR$15) or the salted calamari (AR$22).

Vesta Patagonia Punta Cuervas ☏ 02965/470-
766. Although this restaurant is also open for dinner
(from 9pm), the best time to come here is at sunset,
as the restaurant is located at the end of the beach
near the Ecocentro, a 35-min walk from the centre.
Sipping drinks on their terrace watching the sun
sink is just perfect. Try any of their fish dishes
(starting at AR$25).

Nightlife

Disco La Frontera 9 de Julio 254. Electronica
music and visiting DJs. It's only open on the
weekends, and don't even think about going
before 2am.

Margarita Roque Sáenz Peña 15 ☏ 02965/470-
885. Come here after 11pm to enjoy some good
music and rub shoulders with the locals. Also
serves expensive but good-quality bar meals.

La Oveja Negra Hipólito Yrigoyen 144. Relaxed pub
with a studenty atmosphere, live music and snack
food. Open very late.

Directory

Banks and Exchange Banco Galicia, at Mitre 25
(☏ 02965/452-323; Mon–Fri 9am–3pm) changes
money and has an ATM. Thaler, on corner of Av.
Roca and Sarmiento (☏ 02965/455-858; daily
10am–6pm) is a friendly casa de cambio.
Internet Cyber Internet Arnet, at Marcos A Zar 125.
Post Office Gobernador Maíz 293.

Moving on

Air Flights from Puerto Madryn to: Buenos Aires
(2–3 weekly; 2hr); Comodoro Rivadavia (2–3 weekly;
1hr); Viedma (2–3 weekly; 45min). Trelew Airport, an
hour away, is served by more frequent flights.
Bus Buenos Aires (1 daily; 18hr); Bariloche
(2 weekly; 14–15hr); Comodoro Rivadavia
(2–4 daily; 8hr); Rio Gallegos (1 daily; 16hr); Trelew
(8 daily; 1hr); Viedma (2 daily; 5–6hr).

DAY-TRIPS FROM PUERTO MADRYN

Puerto Madryn was originally founded
and settled in 1865 by 153 Welsh families
who bravely battled the frigid weather
and arid land. Despite all odds, the town
survived and more settlers arrived,
enabling the fledging community to
expand to the southeast, founding
Trelew (pronounced trey-le-oo) and
Gaiman. Both are easily reached by
local bus from Puerto Madryn, making
them an interesting combined day-trip.
A little further afield, the penguin
colony at **Punto Tumbo** provides an
interesting counterpoint to the sea life
at Península Valdés.

Trelew and Gaimain

TRELEW doesn't offer a huge amount
in the way of sights, but a visit to one of
its two great museums is well worth it.
The **Museo Regional Pueblo de Lewis**
(Mon–Fri 8am–8pm, Sat & Sun 5–8pm;
AR$3), at the corner of Lewis Jones 9100
and Fontana, has fascinating displays on
Welsh settlement in the area. Nearby,
the highly acclaimed **Museo Paleontológico Egidio Feruglio** (Mon–Fri
10am–6pm, Sat & Sun 10am–8pm;
AR$15; ✆ www.mef.org.ar), at Fontana
140, houses one of the country's most
important paleontological collections;
excellent guided tours in English,
German and Italian (free on request)
can lead you through the exhibits.

From Trelew it is a twelve-minute
bus ride to **GAIMAN**. Much smaller
and prettier than its busy neighbour,
Gaiman's claim to fame is its **Welsh
Teas**, so renowned that even Princess
Diana came to enjoy one in 1995. Served
at around 3pm every day in decidedly
lovely cottage gardens and restaurants
with floral tablecloths, they consist
of freshly brewed tea, home-made
cakes and jams, scones, toast and the
famous *Torta Negra* (traditional Welsh
fruitcake). For around AR$35, you
won't go hungry.

Arrival and information

Air Trelew Airport (☏02965/428-021) is only 15min from the centre of town. A taxi to the centre will cost AR$10, or AR$15 to Gaiman.
Bus Buses from Puerto Madryn to Trelew (Línea 28 de Julio) leave every 15–20min and take an hour. The bus from Trelew to Gaiman leaves every 15min; it will drop you off at the edge of the main plaza.
Tourist information Mitre 387, Trelew (☏02965/431-519, ⊛www.trelewpatagonia.gov.ar).

Accommodation

Agora Hostel Edwin Roberts 33, Trelew ☏02965/426-899, ⊛hostelagora.com.ar. The cheapest beds in town are the dorms (AR$48) at this hostel, which also sports a clean kitchen and rather depressing common area.
Plas y Coed: Casa de Té Main square, Gaiman ☏02965/491-133. Serves a wonderful afternoon tea with home-made cakes, tarts, fresh tea and scones. They also offer rooms with private bathrooms (AR$150) and a lovely living area. Tea AR$35 per person. Only open for tea weekends and holidays.
Ty Gwyn 9 de Julio 147, Gaiman ☏02965/491-009, ℮tygwyn@cpsarg .com. Has a cottage-style dining area serving large portions of freshly baked bread, locally made jams and wonderful cakes. If you can't pull yourself away, stay the night in one of their simple but comfortable rooms (AR$140). Open daily 2–7.30pm.
Yr Hen Ffordd Michael Jones 342, Trelew ☏02965/491-394, ⊛www.yrhenffordd.com.ar. Sparely but charmingly decorated in the best Welsh fashion, this B&B will make you feel you are at high tea all day. Warm owners preside over this historic brick building. AR$180.

Eating and drinking

Ty Cymraeg Matthews 74, Gaiman ☏02965/491-010, ⊛www.casagalesadete.com.ar. This adorable riverside cottage will do the normal tea but also offers a good breakfast.
Los Tres Chinos San Martín 188, Trelew. By now you know the drill: no charm, just bottomless plates of meat and sides for AR$38. The twist here is the few Asian options.
El Viejo Molino C Gales 250, Trelew ☏02965/428-019. This former wheat mill was converted into the most atmospheric restaurant in town. Now its wood-burning oven fires up steaks that are accompanied by pastas. Mains AR$25–55.

Punto Tumbo

Just short of three hours south of Puerto Madryn, the **Reserva Provincial Punta Tumbo** (Aug–April; AR$30 park entrance), home to the largest penguin nesting site on the continent, makes a perfect spot to get up close to the creatures. Aside from the million or so Magellanic penguins wandering the area – so curious and numerous you may have to step around them on the path – you'll be treated to a vast variety of birds from rock cormorants to kelp gulls flying overhead. The reserve can be visited independently by car or on a long day's tour from Puerto Madryn, arranged by local tour agencies (often arranged through your hostel). These usually include stops in Trelew and Gaiman on the way home for around AR$200.

RUTA 40

RN 40 runs from the top to the bottom of Argentina, following the line of the Andes all the way to the far south from the border with Bolivia in the north. It covers 5000km and eleven provinces, crosses eighteen important rivers on 236 bridges, and connects thirteen great lakes and salt flats, twenty national parks and hundreds of communities. In recent years the section between **El Calafate** and **Bariloche** has become increasingly popular with backpackers, and buses depart once per day along this route. If you don't travel between them via Ruta 40, you'll need to catch a bus all the way to the coast to Caleta Olivia, and then back inland. This is classic Patagonian landscape: miles of flat grassland, with hundreds of cattle roaming freely, interrupted by only the occasional village or *estancia*.

There's little to see along the way apart from the stunning deserted grassland landscape itself. However, the ancient **cave paintings** near the unattractive town of Perito Moreno almost justify the journey on their own, while the leafy oasis of nearby **Los Antiguos** makes a great place to break the trip. With transport of your own, you can also visit the wonderful and isolated **Parque Nacional Perito Moreno**, just off the road along route 37.

LOS ANTIGUOS

A 16-hr bus ride from El Calafate brings you to the small, oasis-like town of **LOS ANTIGUOS**, a little under halfway to Bariloche. Set on the banks of deep blue **Lago Buenos Aires** (after Lake Titicaca in Bolivia, the second-biggest in South America) and sheltering from the winds in the lee of the Andes, Los Antiguos comes as a welcome break from the endless grassy plains and is a great base from which to visit the **Cueva de las Manos Pintadas**. The wealth of luxuriant vegetation and the wonderful riverfront adds to the attraction. The town sports the title of "National Cherry Capital" and gets booked out in January for the **Fiesta Nacional de la Cereza** (the National Cherry Festival).

A worthwhile afternoon can be spent visiting the nearby cherry farms: ask at the tourist office for details.

Arrival and information

Bus There is no bus terminal in Los Antiguos – buses stop along the main street.

Tourist information Av. 11 de Julio 446 (⊕02963/491-261, @losantiguos.tur.ar). Can recommend tour operators and local guides for the trip to Cueva de las Manos Pintadas.

Tour operators Patagonia Emotions, at Cruz del Sur 137 (⊕011/15628-42177) can arrange tours to the caves, as can the helpful Turismo Toscas Bayas, at 11 de Julio 797 (⊕02963/491-016). Chalten Travel is at Lago Buenos Aires 537 (⊕0297/1541-31836, @www.chaltentravel.com).

Accommodation

Albergue Padilla San Martín 44 ⊕02963/491-140. One of the least expensive options in town, with large dorm rooms and space for camping. Dorms AR$40, camping AR$8 per person.

Albergue y Bungalows Sol de Mayo 11 de Julio 133a ⊕02963/491-232. Central and friendly, this hostel offers basic dorms with clean bathroom and a bungalow. Dorms A$40, room AR$200.

Argentino 11 de Julio 850 ☏ 02963/491-132. Central hotel with comfortable en-suite rooms, all with TV. Can also arrange local tours such as fishing, and visits to the Cueva de las Manos Pintadas. AR$120.

Camping Municipal Two kilometres from the centre ☏ 02963/491-265. Lovely campsite with hot showers and cabañas for up to four people. Camping from AR$8, cabañas AR$100.

Eating and drinking

Along the main street of Los Antiguos, Avenida 11 de Julio, you'll find many food options, bakeries and takeaway food stores.

El Negro 'B' Parrilla 11 de Julio 571. This is a popular *parrilla*, also serving fish and pasta. Mains from AR$20.

Pizza Uno 11 de Julio 895. Offers delicious pizzas and *empanadas*, plus a delivery service. A large pizza costs AR$15.

CUEVA DE LAS MANOS PINTADAS

The **CUEVA DE LAS MANOS PINTADAS** is an astounding cave displaying 9000-year-old cave paintings depicting guanacos, abstract figures and hundreds upon hundreds of hand stencils made by ancient local inhabitants. The cave is easily accessible from **Perito Moreno**, but Los Antiguos makes a far more pleasant base from which to take one of the organized day tours. Expect to pay around AR$200 for a 6–8hr tour including entrance fees.

Accommodation

Estancia Telken RN 40 ☏ 02963/432-079, ⓦ www.estanciasdesantacruz.com. Located on the road to the cave, this working sheep ranch provides nicely decorated doubles, with home-cooked meals included. Also camping (AR$20). Open Oct–April. AR$260.

Estancia Los Toldos RN40 ☏ 02963/432-730, ⓦ www.estanciasdesantacruz.com. The caves are actually located inside this *estancia*'s perimeters. There are dorm rooms available (AR$60) as well as comfortable doubles (AR$300). Open Nov–April.

PARQUE NACIONAL PERITO MORENO

Created in 1937, the **PARQUE NACIONAL PERITO MORENO** covers over 11,500 square kilometres of windy Patagonian steppe and stunning high-mountain landscapes. Not to be confused with the eponymous famous glacier, accessible from Calafate, the national park is located just off Ruta 40 towards the town of Gobernador Gregores. The park is hard to get to unless you have your own transport, and you may find yourself alone among the abundant wildlife, which includes guanacos, flamingos and condors. There are several enjoyable short hikes (self-guided), which are not too challenging. You'll need to register with the park officials at the park entrance (daily 8am–10pm; ⓦ www.parquesnacionales .gov.ar) before you set off.

Accommodation

There are four basic camping grounds within the park but there are no services and no fires permitted. Otherwise the two *estancias* which border the park provide comfortable accommodation.

Estancia Menelik RN37 ☏ 011/ 4836-3502, ⓦ www.cielospatagonicos.com. Located just outside the park, and offering pleasant doubles in a 1920s homestead, with all meals included in the rate. The old shearing shed has been renovated and offers dorm accommodation (AR$100). Activities include horseriding excursions into the park. Open Nov–April. AR$500.

La Oriental ☏ 02962/452-235, ⓦ www .estanciasdesantacruz.com. Only 1km from the tranquil Lago Belgrano, this *estancia* offers simple doubles (all meals included) as well as camping (AR$20), and organizes many activities within the park such as horseriding and birdwatching. Open Nov–March. (Doubles AR$350)

EL CHALTÉN

Argentina's self-proclaimed "national trekking capital", the rapidly growing village of **EL CHALTÉN** lies within the boundaries of the Parque Nacional

Los Glaciares, 217km northwest of El Calafate. It is set at the confluence of two pristine rivers, with the granite spires of Monte Fitz Roy (3405m) and Cerro Torre (3102m) protruding like jagged teeth on the horizon. El Chaltén means "smoking mountain", a name given to Monte Fitz Roy by the Tehuelche, who probably mistook the wisps of cloud around its summit for volcanic activity.

El Chaltén is Argentina's youngest village, created in 1985 as an outpost against Chilean encroachment. Since then it has experienced a tourist boom, with campers, hikers and climbers descending in droves every summer. The town just built its first ATM and still doesn't get mobile phone reception.

High season is January and February. In spring the winds are fierce; March is the best month to visit, with fewer tourists and less wind. Most businesses close between Easter and mid-October.

Hikes from El Chaltén

The sky-puncturing peaks of Fitz Roy and Torre offer some of the planet's most challenging technical climbing, but there are plenty of paths for beginners. In contrast to Chile's Torres del Paine (see p.513), those short on time can enjoy a number of day-hikes in the national park with trailheads that start right in town.

The trail most travelled is the relatively flat hike to **Laguna Torre** (11km; 6hr round-trip), which follows the Río Fitz Roy to a silty lake resplendent with floating icebergs, overlooked by Cerro Torre. A more strenuous hike is to **Laguna de los Tres** (12.5km; 8hr), which ascends sharply to a glacial lake with in-your-face views of Fitz Roy. This is impassable in winter.

For the best panoramic views in the area – of both Fitz Roy and Torre as well as Lago Viedma – hike uphill to 1490m-high **Lomo del Pliegue Tumbado**

(12km; 8hr). Shorter walks include those to the **Chorrillo del Salto** waterfall (4km; 2hr) and uphill to the **Los Condores** viewpoint (1km; 1hr 30min) overlooking the town. A classic multi-day hike is the **Monte Fitz Roy/Cerro Torre loop** (3 days, 2 nights), which leaves either from El Chaltén or just beyond the park's boundaries at *Hostería El Pilar* (15km north of town, frequent bus transfers; ☎02962/493-002, ⊛www.hosteriaelpilar .com.ar). There are four free **campsites** (with latrines only) along the route.

Weather in the park is predictably unpredictable, and cloud often obscures the peaks of Fitz Roy and Torre. The park office produces an excellent **free trekking map**, but for something more detailed, the 1:50,000 Monte Fitz Roy & Cerro Torre map published by Zagier and Urruty can be purchased in El Chaltén.

Arrival and information

Bus Buses arrive and depart from individual offices in the town centre. There are services to Bariloche (1–2 daily, none in winter; 30hr); El Calafate (8 daily, 1 in winter; 3hr 30min); and Perito Moreno (1–2 daily, none in winter; 13hr).

Parque Nacional Los Glaciares office The excellent park office is in a wooden house at the entrance to town (Oct–March daily 9am–6pm, April 9am–5pm, May–Sept 9am–4pm; ☎02862/493-004, ⓔseccionallagoviedma@apn.gov.ar), with free maps, wildlife exhibits, video screenings and advice on leave-no-trace camping. All buses that arrive in El Chaltén stop here for an English- or Spanish-language introduction to the rules of the park. Climbers and those using the *Laguna Toro* campsite must register here first.

Tourist information The tourist office is next door to the post office at Güemes 21 (Oct–March daily 8am–9pm, rest of year Mon–Fri 9am–6pm; ☎02962/493-270, ⊛www.elchalten.com).

Tour operators Fitz Roy Expediciones, at San Martín 56 (☎02962/493-017, ⊛www.fitzroyexpediciones .com.ar), organize trekking on Glaciar Torre, teach ice climbing and lead expeditions on the continental ice cap. In the same office is Patagonia Aventura (☎02962/493-110, ⊛www.patagonia-aventura .com), which offers daily transfers to Lago Viedma (18km south), boat excursions across the lake to

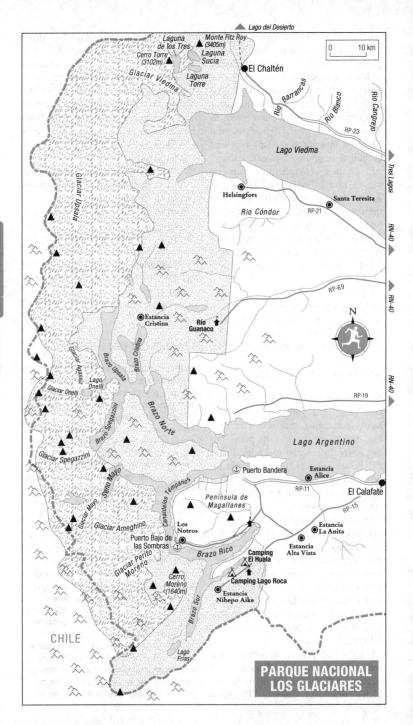

PARQUE NACIONAL LOS GLACIARES

The Parque Nacional Los Glaciares hugs the eastern slopes of the Andes, extending for 170km along the border with Chile. A UNESCO World Heritage Site, nearly half of the park's six thousand square kilometres consist of virtually inaccessible continental ice fields. Elsewhere, thirteen glaciers sweep down from craggy mountains into two parallel turquoise lakes – Argentino and Viedma – while dry Patagonian steppe and sub-Antarctic forests of ñire (Antarctic Beech) and lenga (Lenga Beech) trees provide exceptional trekking country and a home for endangered huemul deer, red fox and puma. The park's northern section can be reached from the village of El Chaltén, where the jagged jaws of the Fitz Roy Mountain Range dominate a skyline as dramatic as anything in Torres del Paine in Chile. Tremendous glaciers, including the show-stopping Glaciar Perito Moreno, are the stars of the park's southern sector, within easy reach of the resort town of El Calafate. For details on the park offices and where to stay and eat in the area, check out the listings for nearby bases El Chaltén (see p.149) and El Calafate (see p.154).

the snout of Glaciar Viedma and ice climbing on the glacier. They also run twice-daily boat trips across Lago del Desierto (37km north), from where there are spectacular views of Fitz Roy. All tour agencies except Chalten Travel (@ www.chaltentravel.com), which runs the bus to El Calafate, shut down in winter.

Accommodation

Reserve a bed in advance if you are coming in January or February. A number of backpacker hostels cater to the young hiking crowd: most offer kitchen facilities, dorms and costly double rooms – couples will find better value at B&Bs. Most shut down at irregular times in the winter so call ahead. There are two free campsites with latrines in town; the least exposed is Camping Madsen, north of the centre at the end of San Martín. Most hostels in town let campers use their showers for AR$5. El Chaltén has three private campsites, including the forested, riverside El Refugio, at Calle 3 (@ 02962/493-321; AR$15), with hot showers and an adjacent basic hostel (AR$30) for when the wind blows your tent away.

Hostels

Albergue Aylen-Aike Trevisan 125 @ 02962/493-317, @ www.elchalten.com/aylenaike. A bright, riverside hostel with four-to-ten-bed dorms (AR$70), superb views from the kitchen and a relaxed living room with TV and stereo. Closed April–Oct.

Albergue Patagonia San Martín 493 @ 02962/493-019, @ www.elchalten .com/patagonia. This cosy, friendly HI hostel set in a wooden house has attentive staff, inviting communal spaces, mountain bikes for rent, a

well-equipped kitchen and hand-washing facilities. Downsides are lockers located outside the simple four-person dorms (AR$60) and cramped communal bathrooms. Simple doubles in the main building or more upmarket, tastefully decorated doubles (from AR$180), with tiled floors and private bathrooms, next door. Closed June–Sept.
Complejo Hem-Herhu Las Loicas 600 @ 02962/493-224. An intimate if slightly shambolic hostel on the edge of town, with spacious dorm rooms (AR$50) and shared kitchen. The owners also run a cute sushi restaurant next door in an A-frame cabin, with romantic lighting and red-and-black decor.
Condor de los Andes Av. Río de las Vueltas and Halvorsen @ 02962/493-101, @ www .condordelosandes.com. A well-run hostel with a respectful vibe, lots of light in the front room, clean four- and six-bed dorms with en suites (AR$90 and AR$70 respectively), a basic kitchen and staff who organize excursions and lunch boxes. Closed mid-April to Sept. AR$280.
Rancho Grande San Martín 520 @ 02962/493-005, @ www.ranchograndehostel.com. This less-than-ideal hostel will probably be your only option if you come in June or July. The indifferent owners shut down the main building and house visitors in dorms (AR$70) in the small cabin next door, which has the benefit of some rustic charm. Breakfast is not included, but use of a tiny kitchen is. AR$270.

Hotels

Hostería Koonek Lionel Terray 415 @ 02962/493-304, @ www.hosteriakoonek.com.ar. Kind owners run this small B&B with four simple rooms with satellite TV and wi-fi. Breakfast included. AR$230.

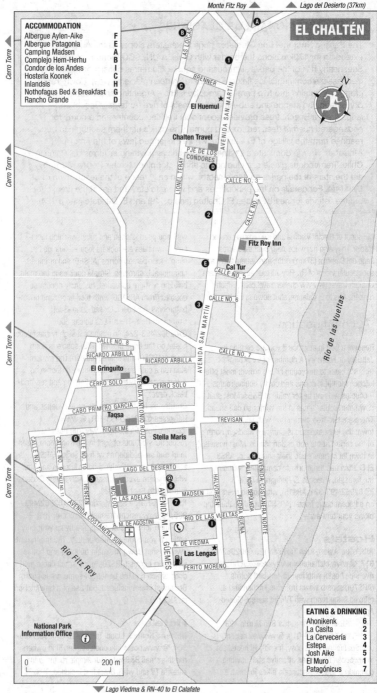

Monte Fitz Roy ▲   ▲ Lago del Desierto (37km)

EL CHALTÉN

Cerro Torre ◀
Cerro Torre ◀
Cerro Torre ◀
Cerro Torre ◀

ACCOMMODATION
Albergue Aylen-Aike   F
Albergue Patagonia   E
Camping Madsen   A
Complejo Hem-Herhu   B
Condor de los Andes   I
Hostería Koonek   C
Inlandsis   H
Nothofagus Bed & Breakfast G
Rancho Grande   D

LAS LOICAS
BRENNER
LIONEL TERAY
AVENIDA SAN MARTIN

Ⓐ
Ⓑ ❶
Ⓒ
El Huemul ★
Chalten Travel
PJE DE LOS CONDORES
Ⓓ
CALLE NO. 3
❷
CALLE NO. 4
Fitz Roy Inn
Ⓔ **Cal Tur**
CALLE NO. 5
CALLE NO. 6
❸
CALLE NO. 7

Río de las Vueltas

CALLE NO. 8
RICARDO ARBILLA   RICARDO ARBILLA
El Gringuito
CERRO SOLO   CERRO SOLO
AVENIDA ANTONIO ROJO
CABO PRIMERO GARCIA
Taqsa   RIQUELME
TREVISAN
Stella Maris   Ⓕ
AVENIDA SAN MARTIN
Ⓖ
Ⓗ
CALLE NO. 12
CALLE NO. 9
CALLE NO. 10
CALLE NO. 11
AVENIDA COSTANERA SUR
HENSEN
MCLEOD
LAS ADELAS
LAGO DEL DESIERTO
Ⓗ❺
❹
Ⓘ ❻
MADSEN
❼
A. M. DE AGOSTINI
RIO DE LAS VUELTAS
AVENIDA M. M. GÜEMES
HALVORSEN
PIEDRA BUENA
CALLE ROSA SEPULVEDA
AVENIDA COSTANERA NORTE
A. DE VIEDMA
★ **Las Lengas**
PERITO MORENO

Río Fitz Roy

Ⓘ **National Park Information Office**

0 _____ 200 m

▼ Lago Viedma & RN-40 to El Calafate

EATING & DRINKING
Ahonikenk   6
La Casita   2
La Cervecería   3
Estepa   4
Josh Aike   5
El Muro   1
Patagónicus   7

Inlandsis Lago del Desierto 480
⊤ 02962/493-276, ⊛ www.inlandsis.com
.ar. This boutique B&B near the river has eight small but stylish en-suite doubles with exposed brickwork and mountain views. Breakfast and internet included, and the conscientious owners make a delicious lunchbox (AR$22). Closed April–Oct. AR$360 but check in for frequent specials.

Nothofagus Bed & Breakfast Hensen and Riquelme ⊤ 02962/493-101, ⊛ www.nothofagus BB.com.ar. A bright and homely B&B with wooden furnishing and a rustic country feel; three rooms are en suite, while the other four share a bathroom. Some rooms have great mountain views. Closed May–Sept. AR$180.

Eating and drinking

Ahonikenk Güemes 23 ⊤ 02962/493-070. An unassuming diner that does huge portions of *milanesas*, pizza and home-made pasta. The lasagne (AR$22) is a meat-and-cheese mountain.

La Casita San Martín 430 ⊤ 02962/493-042. For a post-hike pick-me-up, go straight for the stick-to-your-bones *locro* (AR$30) a local stew made with lamb, bacon, vegetables and "everything else", according to the proprietress. Pool tables provide some amusement in the cheery red house. Often the only place open in winter. Open noon–midnight.

La Cervecería San Martín 564. ⊤ 02962/493-109. At the end of a hard day's hiking, you have to fight for a seat in this snug, driftwood-adorned microbrewery. They'll bring over popcorn and breadsticks even if you're just sampling the excellent pilsner. As well as beer and hard liquor, the menu includes vegetable soup (AR$20), pizza (starting at AR$30) and other pub grub. Outdoor bench seating under the firs is for the hardy. Closed April–Sept.

Estepa Cerro Solo and Antonio Rojo. Among the upscale restaurants in town, this is the best deal, with Fitz Roy views thrown in. Go gourmet with dishes like roasted Patagonian lamb or your choice of pizzas or calzones with lots of vegetarian fillings. Mains start at AR$30. Closed mid-April to Sept.

Josh Aike Lago Desierto 104. A convivial *chocolatería* set in a rickety two-storey timber cabin, where you can sip bittersweet hot chocolate while taking in great views of the mountains. Closed Easter–Oct.

El Muro San Martín 948 ⊤ 02962/493-248. Grilled pizza, steak with peppers and bacon, sweet and sour lamb ribs and salmon *sorrentinos* are just some of the tempting creations dished up at this country-style restaurant (mains around AR$30). There's a climbing wall out back to help you work up an appetite. Closed April–Oct.

Patagónicus Güemes and Madsen. The best pizza in town (starting at AR$20) is served to hungry diners at big wooden tables. Closed April–Sept.

La Tapera San Martín 249 ⊤ 02962/493-138. When the menu is recited in person by the chef, you know you're in for food prepared with passion. House staples include tapas plates, lamb and lentil stew and vegetable crêpes, and the decor features a wood-burning stove. Mains start at AR$40. For a good deal come at lunch. Closed mid-April to Oct.

HIKE, BIKE AND SAIL INTO CHILE

From El Chaltén, it's possible to cross to Villa O'Higgins in Chile (see p.502) by undertaking an adventurous two-day trip by boat and foot (or bicycle) in the summer. Start by catching a bus from El Chaltén and heading 37km north to the southern end of Lago del Desierto. The lake's northern shore can be reached either by scenic boat ride or by hiking (5hr) along its eastern shore to a free campsite. After overnighting at the campsite (⊛ www.villaohiggins.com), get up early the next morning, grab an exit stamp from the Argentine police and hike or cycle (be prepared to carry your bike part of the way along a muddy single-track forest trail) over the pass into Chile (approx 16km; allow for a full day and bring plenty of supplies). Horses can be hired from Lago del Desierto to help with the luggage burden (AR$60).

The trail ends at Lago O'Higgins, where you go through the Chilean passport-stamping ritual. It's possible to camp and buy meals here at the lakeside hamlet and *estancia* of *Candelario Mancilla*. A boat crosses the lake to the hamlet of Villa O'Higgins (summer only, Wed & Sat 5.30pm; 5hr), the final settlement on Chile's stunning 1000km-plus Carretera Austral. Ask at El Chaltén's tourist office for boat times and general information on this increasingly popular route. Note the border crossing is only open November to March.

EL CALAFATE

If global warming were suddenly to lay waste to the Perito Moreno glacier, **EL CALAFATE** would promptly fizzle out in its wake. The brazen tourist town, whose population has exploded from six thousand permanent residents in 2001 to more than 22,000 in 2010, exists primarily to absorb the huge number of visitors who come to gawk and walk on one of the world's natural wonders. Luckily, Perito Moreno is the only glacier in the nearby Parque Nacional Los Glaciares to show no signs of receding.

Beyond El Calafate's main drag, Avenida Libertador, heaving with tourism outfits, restaurants and supermarkets, the roads leaving the city centre become more and more authentic, leading to wooden farmhouses and pastures where horses graze. But new hotels are going up all the time, vying for views of snow-clad Andean peaks and the milky-blue 1600-square-kilometre **Lago Argentino**. Visitor season reaches its crowded peak in January and February.

What to see and do

There are few attractions in El Calafate itself, although the **Centro de Interpretación Histórica**, at Av. Brown and Bonarelli (daily 10am–8pm; AR$17; ☎02902/492-799), does a dramatic job of recounting the area's natural and cultural history in Spanish and English, complete with recreations of Patagonian megafauna. A bird reserve lies just north of town (head along Calle Ezequel Bustillo) at **Laguna Nimez** (9am–9pm; AR$2), where there are exotic waterfowl such as Chilean flamingos and black-necked swans.

Finally, although not as well-preserved as the rock art at Cueva de las Manos Pintadas (see p.148), the 4000-to-7000-year-old cave and cliff paintings at **Punta Walichu** (daily guided tours summer at 9am & 3pm, winter at 2pm; AR$49;

☎02902/497-003), 7km east of town on the shores of Lago Argentino, are worth visiting. They depict animals, people and human hands. Morresi Viajes, at Av. Libertador 1341, runs excursions with bilingual guides (fantastic value at AR$65, including transfer and entrance; ☎02902/492-276). Or if you have your own car you can drive there and pay the AR$50 fee to enter.

Arrival and information

Air El Calafate's airport (☎02902/491-220) is 23km east of downtown. The bus to the airport, called Ves Patagonia (☎02902/494-355) runs into town and if booked ahead of time will pick you up at your hotel. A taxi to the centre costs AR$50.

Bus The bus terminal is at Av. Julio A Roca, one block up the staircase from Av. Libertador, the main street.

Parque Nacional Los Glaciares office The national park office, in a historic wooden cabin on Av. Libertador 1302, has maps, sells fishing licences and has updated information on park campsites (Mon–Fri 8am–4pm, Sat & Sun rangers available by telephone; ☎02902/491-005).

Tourist information The tourist office is on Coronel Rosales just after the bridge (daily 8am–8pm; ☎02902/491-90, ⊛www.elcalafate .gov.ar). There's also a branch in the bus terminal (daily: April–Sept 8am–9pm, Oct–March 8am–10pm).

Accommodation

Reserve in advance for January and February. Outside high season (Nov–Easter) the town's inflated prices come down a notch. For **camping** in the centre, try the well-serviced, riverside *El Arroyo* at José Pantín s/n (☎02902/492-233; AR$14). Inside the park, 50km from town, the tranquil *Lago Roca* (☎02902/499-500, ⊛www.losglaciares.com /campinglagoroca; AR$16), beside the lake of the same name, has showers, a restaurant, bike hire and telephones.

Hostels

There are many backpacker hostels in town, although their double rooms tend to be pricey for what you get. All hostels listed here include breakfast, internet and use of kitchen.

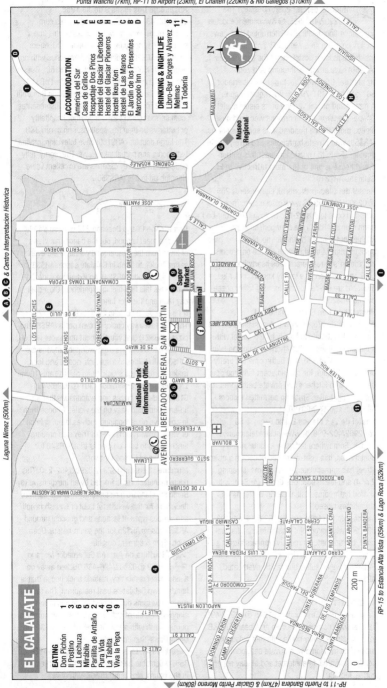

Punta Walichu (7km), RP-11 to Airport (23km), El Chaltén (220km) & Río Gallegos (310km)

EL CALAFATE

EATING
Don Pichón	1
Il Postino	3
La Lechuza	6
Mirábile	5
Parillita de Antaño	2
Pura Vida	4
La Tablita	8
Viva la Pepa	9

ACCOMMODATION
America del Sur	F
Casa de Grillos	A
Hospedaje Dos Pinos	E
Hostel del Glaciar Libertador	G
Hostel del Glaciar Pioneros	H
Hostel Ikeu Ken	I
Hostel de Las Manos	C
El Jardín de los Presentes	B
Marcopolo Inn	D

DRINKING & NIGHTLIFE
Libro-Bar Borges y Alvarez	8
Melmac	11
La Tolderia	7

Museo Regional

Laguna Nimez (500m)

▲ A, B, C & Centro Interpretación Histórica

National Park Information Office

Super Market

Bus Terminal

RP-15 to Estancia Alta Vista (35km) & Lago Roca (52km)

RP-11 to Puerto Bandera (47km) & Glaciar Perito Moreno (80km)

200 m

ARGENTINA

PATAGONIA

155

America del Sur Puerto Deseado 153
☎ 02902/493-525, ⓦ www.americahostel
.com.ar. In-floor heating, uninterrupted lake views, an airy common area without TV and cool staff make this modern hostel one of the best. Dorms (AR$50) have private bathrooms. AR$260.

Hostel del Glaciar Libertador Av. Libertador 587 ☎ 02902/491-792, ⓦ www.glaciar.com. A newer and pricier version of its sister hostel *Glaciar Pioneros*, this enormous wooden house sleeps more than a hundred, has spotless dorms (AR$50) with private bathrooms and lovely bright doubles. From the outside at least this gingerbread house is one of the most attractive in El Calafate. AR$310.

Hostel del Glaciar Pioneros Los Pioneros 255 ☎ 02902/491-243, ⓦ www.glaciar.com. There are pros and cons to this 92-bed HI hostel. The four-bed dorm rooms (AR$50) are cramped, as is the kitchen, but some of the newer double rooms have been tastefully furnished with private bathrooms and the on-site restaurant does hearty home-style cooking, overseen by a locally known chef. Also available are six-bed dorms for very tall or obese people. AR$200.

Hostel Ikeu Ken FM Pontoriero 171
☎ 02902/495-175, ⓦ www.patagoniaikeuken
.com.ar. An intimate but lively hilltop hostel with a balcony that enjoys the afternoon sun and lake vistas. Dorms (AR$50) and bathrooms are pretty ordinary, although the two adjacent fully equipped cabañas, with kitchens and private bathrooms, are highly sought after. Smoking permitted indoors. Minimum age 14. AR$180.

Hostel de Las Manos Egidio Feruglio 59
☎ 02902/492-996, ⓦ www.hosteldelasmanos.
com.ar. Somewhere between a hostel and a guesthouse, this light-drenched house on a quiet street has immaculate private rooms (sleeping 2 or 4) and less salubrious dorms (AR$40) with shared bathrooms. Call ahead in winter as it is sometimes closed.

Marcopolo Inn Calle 405, No. 82 ☎ 02902/493-899, ⓦ www.marcopoloinncalafate.com. Its pool table, bar area and inexpensive dinners attract a young, raucous crowd. The clean, modern dorms (AR$60) have en suites but can be overheated. AR$290.

Hotels

Casa de Grillos Los Condores 1215 ☎ 02902/491-160, ⓦ www.casadegrillos.com.ar. A peaceful B&B in a two-storey family home with four colourful, themed rooms (some with private bathroom), a comfy living area, free internet and all-day tea and coffee. AR$330.

Hospedaje Dos Pinos 9 de Julio 358
☎ 02902/491-271, ⓦ www.losglaciares.com
/losdospinos. Popular with tour buses, this impersonal holiday complex, which sleeps 200, offers camping (AR$20), rudimentary dormitories with no bedding (AR$50) or basic doubles (AR$150). Guests can use the communal kitchen. Breakfast AR$12.

El Jardin de los Presentes Guido Bonarelli 72 ☎ 02902/491-518, ⓦ www.lospresentes
.com.ar. You couldn't ask for warmer hospitality or better value than this spotless, family-run B&B. The large doubles (AR$180) have television, private bathrooms and partial lake views. The roomy, fully equipped two-storey cabañas are excellent value, sleeping up to five (AR$350).

Eating

Don Pichón Puerto Deseado 242 ☎ 02902/492-577. The meat is good, but the panoramic views of town from the wraparound windows are even better. Tuck into lamb in Calafate sauce (AR$38) or mushroom risotto (AR$24). An extensive wine list completes this fine-dining experience. Closed all day Mon and Tues for lunch.

Il Postino Av. 9 de Julio 29 ☎ 02902/493-777. This tiny takeaway cooks its own pasta (AR$8) and pizzas (AR$21) that you can heat up at your hostel. No place to sit but the oven-warmed *empanadas* (AR$3) with fillings like spinach, ricotta and leek, make a great to-go snack. Open daily 11am–10pm.

La Lechuza Av. Libertador 1301 ☎ 02902/491-610. Wood-fired pizzas and *empanadas* that are lip-smacking and easy on the wallet. Choose from imaginative pizza toppings such as lamb, salmon or venison. Mains AR$20–60. They also prepare lunch boxes to take on glacier trips (AR$40 for *empanadas* and salad for two).

Mirábile Libertador 1329 ☎ 02902/492-230. This pasta manufacturer is fronted by an inexpensive (by Bariloche standards) restaurant. Argentine families flock here for the wonderful trout or squash ravioli and various types of lasagne and gnocchi (around AR$35). *Locro* AR$25 for the pasta-haters. Open noon–3pm & 8pm–midnight.

Parillita de Antaño Gobernador Moyano 1089 ☎ 02902/496-486. Tucked away on a side street is this tiny, historic brick house that is hands down Calafate's best restaurant. The family-run *parrilla* turns out the best tenderloin in town alongside excellent grilled vegetables and pumpkin puree. Finish with a fruit flambé. Mains AR$30–60. Open Thurs–Sun 8pm until late.

Pura Vida Av. Libertador 1876 ☎ 02902/493-356. Delectable baked pumpkin stew served in the gourd, plus lamb ravioli with olive cream sauce, are just some of the hearty post-glacier warmers that accompany an upbeat Latin soundtrack. The service is first-rate and cushions and wooden furnishings create a cosy, hippyish ambience. Mains AR$30–68. Open 7.30–11.30pm; closed Wed.

La Tablita Colonel Rosales 28 ☎02902/491-065. *Muy buena carne* (from AR$40) – many say the best in town – is plucked straight off the fiery *asador*. The setting is rather quiet and lacks charm, but the food makes up for it. Open noon–3.30pm & 7pm–midnight.

🏃 **Viva la Pepa** Emilio Amado 833 ☎02902/491-880. A delightful owner presents Patagonian favourites like lamb and trout in imaginative combinations as savoury crêpes and sandwiches (AR$30–60). Ask for a half portion to leave room for a dessert crêpe with the city's namesake *calafate* berry. The best lunch option in town. Open daily 10am–midnight.

Drinking and nightlife

Libro-Bar Borges y Alvarez Av. Libertador 1015 ☎02902/491-464. This bar-cum-café provides shelves of English- and Spanish-language books to accompany their coffees or Scotch whiskies (up to AR$120 a shot). Walk past the twee chocolate stops – this laidback spot has the best hot chocolate (AR$18) in town. Open daily 10–2am.
Melmac Walter Roil 50 ☎02902/494-393. A new bar kitted out with gaucho-esque decor. Good live music packs the house, and mixed drinks and

board games fill in the gaps earlier in the day. Open 6pm to "last man standing".
La Toldería Av. Libertador 1177. Those with energy to burn and the opposite sex on their mind flock here for live music and a let-it-all-hang-out dance-floor that on weekends throbs until sunrise with electronica, rock and pop. Earlier in the evening they serve an expanded menu including an excellent steak with French fries (AR$30). Open summer noon–6am and winter 8pm–6am; closed Mon.

Directory

Banks and exchange There are pleny of banks along Av. Libertador.
Car rental Localiza Rent a Car, at Av. Libertador 687 (☎02902/491-398, ☻www.localiza.com); On Rent a Car, at Av. Libertador 1831 (☎02902/493-788, ☻www.onrentacar.com.ar); Servi Car 4WD, at Av. Libertador 820 (☎02902/492-801, ☻www .servicar4x4.com.ar).
Internet Av. Libertador has a variety of internet cafés.
Laundry El Lavadero, 25 de Mayo 43 (☎02902/492-182).
Police Av. Libertador 835 (☎02902/491-824).
Post office Av. Libertador 1133.
Tour operators Hielo & Aventura, at Av. Libertador 935 (☎02902/492-205, ☻www.hieloyaventura .com) offers ice-trekking trips and boat excursions to see Glaciar Perito Moreno; Fernandez Campbell, at Av. Libertador 867 (☎02902/491-155, ☻www .fernandezcampbell.com) runs Upsala and Perito

VISITING PERITO MORENO

The **entrance fee** for the Perito Moreno section of the park is AR$75 (payable at the entrance, 30km before the glacier), although some people avoid the charge by sneaking in outside the park's opening hours (8am–8pm).

Most tour operators in El Calafate (see above) offer all-inclusive **day excursions** to the glacier starting from AR$205; all include a catamaran cruise, and around three hours to roam the boardwalks. A typical schedule is to leave El Calafate at 9am and return at 5pm. To visit independently, take one of the **buses** that leave from El Calafate's terminal three times daily (AR$60 return; 1hr; for an extra AR$20 they will pick you up from your hostel at 8am but not drop you back). You could also rent a taxi (AR$300 including a 3-hr wait at the glacier) or a car (roughly AR$200 per day), taking either the less-travelled gravel RP15 past historic *estancias*, or the less scenic but paved RP11.

One-hour **catamaran excursions** to see Perito Moreno's southern face leave from Puerto Bajo de las Sombras, 6km from the boardwalks with Hielo & Aventura (minibus shuttle from boardwalk; hourly 10.30am–3.30pm; AR$50); to see the northern face, catamarans leave from Canal de los Témpanos, just 1km from the boardwalks with Fernandez Campbell (hourly 10.30am–4.30pm; AR$50). For a close-up view of Perito Moreno's crevasses and lagoons, Hielo & Aventura offers ice-trekking trips (wearing crampons) on its surface from AR.

Moreno boat excursions; *Hostel del Glaciar Los Pioneros* (see p.156) offers recommended day tours to the glacier that are popular with backpackers.

Moving on

Air Bariloche (daily; 1hr 45min); Buenos Aires (daily; 3hr); Trelew (daily; 1hr 30min); Ushuaia (daily; 1hr 10min); also sporadic services to Comodoro Rivadavia, Puerto Madryn, Río Gallegos and Río Grande.
Bus Bariloche (1–2 daily; 34hr); El Chaltén (8 daily, 2 in winter; 3hr 30min); Perito Moreno (daily in summer; 13hr); Río Gallegos (4 daily; 4hr).

UPSALA AND OTHER GLACIERS

Although receding fast, **GLACIAR UPSALA** remains the longest glacier in the park and indeed in South America. The same height as Perito Moreno, Upsala is twice as long, 7km wide and known for carving huge translucent, blue-tinged icebergs that bob around Lago Argentino like surreal art sculptures. Located 45km west of El Calafate, Upsala is accessible by **catamaran excursion** along Lago Argentino's northern arm (boats leave from Puerto Bandera). All-day tours, usually called "All Glaciers" or "Other Glaciers", which also take in the Spegazzini, Onelli, Bolados and Agassiz glaciers, are run by Fernandez Campbell (AR$290, plus AR$40 park entrance).

Since 2009 the access to Upsala has been limited by the fact that it is calving so rapidly: the boats can't navigate through the icebergs. So after viewing Upsala from far away, the boat motors onward for a grand finale at Perito Moreno. Ask if conditions have changed and if not, if this tour ("All Glaciars") is still available. Boats are generally packed, but this excursion is well worthwhile: the closest thing to experiencing Antarctica without actually going there.

RÍO GALLEGOS

Grim and windy **RÍO GALLEGOS** is an inevitable stop for travellers heading south to Ushuaia, north towards Puerto Madryn or west to El Calafate or Chile. The capital of Santa Cruz province, the city lies on the banks of the estuary of the Río Gallegos, a river whose giant, sea-going brown trout lure **fly-fishing** enthusiasts from around the world.

What to see and do

Río Gallegos' city centre has a couple of worthwhile free museums and some nicely restored historical wooden buildings. Housed in an early settler home dating from 1890, on Albedí at Elcano, the **Museo de los Pioneros** (daily 10am–7.30pm; free; ☎02966/437-763) is decked out with period furniture and old photographs. They also have periodic exhibitions of coins or letters from the turn of the century. Better still, the **Complejo Cultural Santa Cruz**, the huge pink building at Ramón y Cajal 51 (Mon–Fri 10am–7pm, Sat & Sun 11am–7pm; free; ☎02966/426-427), offers rolling contemporary art exhibitions, a motley collection of stuffed regional fauna, dinosaur models and artefacts from the indigenous Tehuelche. They sometimes screen free movies at 8pm. If live animals interest you more, consider a tour with a local operator to the **penguin colony** at Cabo Vírgenes, a nesting site for around 180,000 Magellanic penguins, 140km southeast of the city; trips are on offer between October and March.

Arrival and information

Air Río Gallegos' airport is 6km west of downtown. There are no buses to the centre; taxis cost AR$40.
Bus The bus station (☎02966/442-585) is 2km west of town at the corner of Av. Eva Perón and the RN3. A taxi to the centre costs AR$18; bus #A runs downtown.

Tourist information There is a provincial tourist office that can give you information on all of Santa Cruz (summer Mon–Fri 9am–9pm, winter 9am–4pm; ⓣ 02966/438-725, ⓦ www. riogallegos.gov.ar) at Av. San Martín 791 and a municipal office with Information just on Rio Gallegos (Mon–Fri 8am–4pm; ⓣ 02966/436-920, ⓦ www.turismo.mrg.gov.ar) at Av. Roca 1587. There is also an office at the bus station (open Mon–Fri 8am–8pm; ⓣ 02966/442-159).

Accommodation

Accommodation is generally expensive, of poor quality and fills up quickly in summer. The closest campsite is *ATSA*, half a kilometre southwest of the bus terminal at Asturias and Yugoslavia (ⓣ 02966/156-7758; AR$10, electricity an additional AR$10).

Colonial Urquiza 212 and Rivadavia ⓣ 02966/422-329, ⓔ ines_frey@hotmail.com. A warm and chatty *dueña* runs this rambling old house, in which lurk a hotchpotch of basic rooms with lumpy pillows and shared bathrooms. AR$80.

Hospedaje Elcira Pje Zuccarino 431 ⓣ 02966/429-856. Handy for the bus station, this neat guesthouse is popular with Argentines and has dorm rooms (AR$40), one double and a big kitchen and TV area. Looks like grandma's house, and has the only kitchen open for guests to use in town. AR$80.

Sehuén Rawson 160 ⓣ 02966/425-683, ⓦ www .hotelsehuen.com. Boasts 34 tidy, spacious rooms (some triples and quadruples) all en-suite and with TV. Breakfast included. AR$198.

Eating and drinking

British Club Roca 935 ⓣ 02966/432-668, ⓦ www.britishclub.com.ar. If you ask nicely the waiters will let you in for a look at the (technically) members-only part of this stronghold of British immigrants and their descendants, immortalized in Bruce Chatwin's book. There are still some to be found propping up the bar each night. The adjoining restaurant serves a hearty range of beef, lamb, fish and pasta dishes (mains around AR$50), but the atmosphere rather than the food is the highlight. English tea and accompaniments served at 5pm. Open lunch until late.

Café Central Roca 923. No matter what time your bus gets in (and the schedules can be erratic) this unpretentious wooden bar/café is always open for a snack and some free wi-fi. Skip the underwhelming pizza in favour of the *menu ejecutivo*, a starter, main and dessert with soft drink for AR$40. The coffee (AR$7) is outstanding, or head straight for a *caipirinha* (AR$25) or pisco sour (AR$25) – nods to neighbouring Brazil and Chile. Open 24hr.

Laguanacazul Gob Lista and Sarmiento ⓣ 02966/444-144. This art-filled waterfront restaurant is the best in the city by a mile. Genial young chef Mirko Ionfrida uses locally sourced ingredients (think guanaco and rhea) to cook up memorable haute cuisine. Lamb is his signature dish. Mains AR$40–75. Open daily 10.30am–3pm & 7pm–2am.

La Vieja Esquina Velez Sarsfield, 97 ☎02966/438-400. Locals say skip the pizzerias on Roca and San Martín, citing grease, and instead make for this no-frills eatery. All pizzas are under AR$50. Open lunch until late.

Directory

Banks and exchange Thaler, San Martín 484 (☎0296/436-052).
Internet @, at Av. Roca 1426; otherwise, numerous *locutorios* in town offer internet services.
Post office San Martín at Av. Roca.
Tours Maca Tobiano, at Roca 988 (☎02966/422-466, ⊛www.macatobiano.com), runs day-trips to Cabo Vírgenes from AR$150.

Moving on

Air Buenos Aires (daily; 3hr); El Calafate (daily; 50min); Comodoro Ridavavia (daily; 1hr 15min); Río Grande (2 weekly; 1hr 15min); Ushuaia (daily; 55min).
Bus El Calafate (4–5 daily; 4hr); Comodoro Rivadavia (12 daily; 10–12hr); Puerto Madryn (7 daily; 18–19hr); Río Grande (3 daily; 9–10hr); Ushuaia (2 daily, both In the morning; 12hr) and in Chile Punta Arenas (2 daily; 3hr 30min); Puerto Natales (2 weekly; 4hr).

Tierra del Fuego

A rugged and isolated archipelago at the extreme southern tip of the continent, **TIERRA DEL FUEGO** ("Land of Fire") marks the finish line for South America. Here the Andes range marches into the chilly southern oceans, deciduous forests and Ice Age glaciers lie a stone's throw from a wildlife-rich shoreline, penguins and sea lions huddle on rocky islets, salmon and trout thrash about in the rivers and sheep and guanacos graze on arid windswept plains.

The archipelago is shared, with historic hostility, by Argentina and Chile, and only about a third of Isla Grande (Tierra del Fuego's main island and the largest in South America) belongs to Argentina. This includes **Ushuaia**, however, the region's top destination. As locals will proudly point out, it is the planet's southernmost inhabited city. It's a jumping-off point for the lakes and mountains of **Parque Nacional Tierra del Fuego**, as well as historic **estancias**, boat trips on the **Beagle Channel**, downhill and cross-country skiing in the winter, and cruises to **Antarctica** in summer.

To the north, a stop in the unattractive town of **Río Grande** may be a necessary evil if you are travelling to or from the Argentinian mainland; though it's a destination in its own right for fly-fishermen in hot pursuit of brown trout.

High season is from December to February, when days are longest and warmest. Spring (Oct to mid-Nov) is beautiful and lush, but even windier than normal. Autumn (late March to April) is, arguably, the best time to visit, when the countryside is lit up in warm shades of red and orange. But Ushuaia's growing status as a winter-sports playground ensures the "uttermost part of the earth" is now a year-round destination.

USHUAIA

USHUAIA is the end of the world as we know it. But aside from some conspicuous casinos and strip joints, there's nothing fire and brimstone here. Quite the contrary: the world's southernmost city is cold, damp and disarmingly pretty, set on a bay on the wildlife-rich shores of the **Beagle Channel** with a backdrop of jagged mountains and glaciers.

Ushuaia lies 3500km south of Buenos Aires and just 1000km north of frosty **Antarctica**, a fact you'll have no problem detecting. Even in summer

EATING, DRINKING & NIGHTLIFE

137 Restaurante	8
Bambu	1
Bodegón Fueguino	5
Chocolates Ushuaia	6
Dreamland	2
Dublín	4
Invisible Pub	9
La Rueda	7
El Turco	10
Un Lugar…en el Fin del Mundo	3
Volver	11

ACCOMMODATION

Antarctica Hostel	E
Cruz del Sur	F
Freestyle	D
Galeazzi-Basily B&B	A
Hostería Rosa de los Vientos	B
La Posta Albergue	H
Torre al Sur	C
Yakush	G

you need to bundle up, or follow the lead of the original inhabitants who got around just fine naked and slathered in seal grease. Another thing you'll need plenty of here is money because, as the gateway to Antarctica, Ushuaia is relatively expensive. Looking back at the town from a boat bobbing in the Beagle Channel, though, with a view of colourful houses stacked on sloping streets, framed by arresting snow-clad peaks, you'll probably think it's worth it.

What to see and do

A former penal colony, Ushuaia is not the best-planned town, but it makes a pleasant place to relax, gorge on seafood and take in some history in the museums and nearby *Estancia* *Harberton*. Most of the tourist and commercial action is centred on **San Martín** and **Maipú** streets, while boats leave from the Muelle Turístico down by the pier. List-tickers can have their passports stamped in the post office to prove they've made it to the globe's end. For **active pursuits**, there's good hiking in Parque Nacional Tierra del Fuego, ice climbing or trekking on nearby glaciers, horseriding in nature reserves, scuba-diving in the chilly harbour, boating to penguin and sea-lion colonies, and in winter dog-sledding or skiing through pristine white valleys.

Museo del Fin del Mundo

The **Museo del Fin del Mundo**, at Maipú 173 and Rivadavia (Oct–March daily 9am–8pm, rest of year Mon–Sat

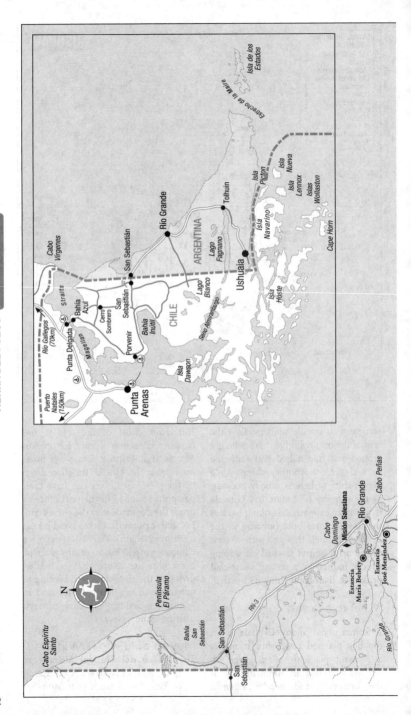

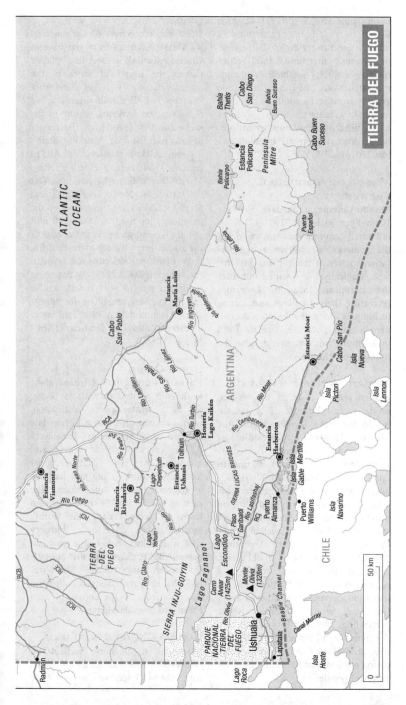

ARGENTINA

TIERRA DEL FUEGO

noon–7pm; AR$15; ☎02901/421-863, ⓦwww.tierradelfuego.org.ar/museo), offers a good overview of the region's indigenous, maritime and settler history. Exhibits include a quaint reconstruction of an old-style grocery store and a room with stuffed regional creatures. Some exhibits have spilled over into another historic house down the street at Maipú 465 (☎02901/422-551).

Museo de Maquetas Yámana

Mundo Yámana, at Rivadavia 56 (daily 10am–8pm; AR$10; ☎02901/422-874), is a small gem of a museum exploring the remarkable lifestyle and egalitarian society of the Yámana Indians, who, tragically, were wiped out after the European invasion. Dioramas recreating their dwellings and fishing techniques along the Beagle Channel demonstrate how the Yámana lived in harmony with nature despite the inhospitable climate.

Museo Marítimo y Presidio

Known around town as the "museo de la carcel" because it is housed inside the city's former prison, the **Museo Marítimo y Presidio**, at Yaganes and Gobernador Paz (daily 10am–8pm, regular tours in English 2pm daily; AR$50; ☎02901/437-481, ⓦwww.museomaritimo.com), is both a maritime history and a prison museum. There are models of the ships that first explored the Magellan Straits, the Beagle Channel and Argentina's Antarctic expeditions. Grim old prison cells contain life-size models and recount the lives of former convicts, including deranged child serial killer Cayetano Santos Godino, whose protruding, oversized ears earned him the moniker "El Petiso Orejudo" (The Big-Eared Short Guy). A wing of the prison has been left bare and makes for poignant wandering.

Glaciar Martial

There are lofty views of Ushuaia and the Beagle Channel from the base of **Glaciar Martial**, a receding glacier that is the source of much of the town's water supply. To get there, walk 7km up Luis Fernando Martial road or take a taxi (AR$16), or one of the minibuses that leave from the corner of Juan Fadúl and Av. Maipú (9.30am–5.30pm; AR$10 one-way or AR$15 return). From here, a chairlift (Nov–March daily 9.30am–4.45pm, June–Oct daily 10am–4.45pm, closed April and May; AR$25) whisks passengers up the mountain; it's then a further 90-min uphill hike and scramble to the base of the glacier. From the top of the chairlift, three municipal **ski runs** are open in the winter (pass AR$45). A charming mountain *refugio* sells snacks, coffee and mulled wine, and offers dormitory-style accommodation with cold-water bathrooms and no electricity (Nov–March; AR$60).

Cerro Castor

Far from turning into a frozen ghost town over winter, Ushuaia is taking off as a **winter-sports** destination, with a ski season that runs from late May to early September. The Sierra Alvear ranges, northeast of town and accessible from the RN3, are great for cross-country skiing and harbour a growing number of resorts. The pick of the bunch, 26km away from town, is **Cerro Castor**, the world's most southerly ski resort, a blustery spot with 22km of downhill runs (ski passes AR$110 a day; ☎02901/499-301, ⓦwww.cerrocastor.com). Minibuses (AR$20 one-way) leave frequently from the waterfront at the corner of Juan Fadul and Avenida Maipú.

Beagle Channel boat trips

A scenic boat ride along the **BEAGLE CHANNEL** (the passage heading east from Ushuaia) lets you get up close and personal with the region's marine wildlife, including sea lions, penguins, whales, steamer ducks, cormorants and albatross. Excursions are between 2 hours 30 minutes and eight hours (AR$150–245), in vessels that range from small fishing boats to large catamarans. The more popular shorter trips take in the sea-lion colony at **Isla de los Lobos**, the sea-bird-nesting site at **Isla de los Pájaros** and then sail past **Faro Les Eclaireurs**, often incorrectly dubbed "the Lighthouse at the End of the World". Longer trips take in the penguin colony at **Isla Martillo** (Oct–May only) or head west into the national park or east to *Estancia Harberton*. Boats leave from the Muelle Turístico, where a number of agencies offer tours.

Estancia Harberton

Tierra del Fuego's oldest farmstead, **Estancia Harberton** (mid-Oct to mid-April daily 10am–7pm; guided tours AR$40; ☎02901/422-742; ⊛www .estanciaharberton.com), perches on a secluded peninsula in a sheltered bay overlooking the Beagle Channel. Built in 1886, this working sheep station lies 85km east of Ushuaia along a scenic road. The land was a government donation to the English missionary Reverend Thomas Bridges in recognition of his work with the local indigenous population and for rescuing shipwreck victims from the channels. His descendants now run the farm, offering guided tours, sugar hits in the tea room, overnight stays in basic cottages and free camping on the property (ask permission first).

There is also a **marine wildlife museum** on the property (mid-Oct to mid-April daily 10am–7pm; AR$20; ⊛www.acatushun.org), featuring an amazing assortment of skeletons of Tierra del Fuego's sea mammals and birds. Minibuses for the *Estancia* leave Ushuaia from Juan Fadúl and Avenida Maipú several times daily (AR$150

return). Some day-long Beagle Channel boat excursions stop here too.

Arrival and information

Air Ushuaia's airport is 4km southwest of the centre. A taxi downtown costs AR$15.

Bus Buses leave from the tour agency that represents them; see "Moving on" (p.167) or ask at the tourist office where to buy tickets for your destination.

Fishing licences To purchase a fishing licence, head to the Club Caza y Pesca at the corner of Maipú and 9 de Julio (Mon–Fri 9am–5pm, ☎02901/423-168). Licences are also available at the National Park office.

Parque Nacional Tierra del Fuego office Av. San Martín 1395 (Mon–Fri 9am–4pm; ☎02901/421-315, ⊛www.parquesnacionales.gov.ar).

Tourist information The tourist office is at Av. San Martín 674 (Mon–Fri 8am–6pm; Sat & Sun 9am–6pm; ☎02901/432-001, ⊛www .turismoushuaia.com). Register here if you plan to go hiking anywhere but the main route through Parque Nacional Tierra del Fuego, as many area trails are poorly marked. There are also tourist offices at the Muelle Turístico (Mon–Fri 8am–10pm, Sat & Sun 9am–8pm; ☎02901/437-666) and at the airport, open to coincide with flight arrivals (☎02901/423-970).

Accommodation

In summer, book accommodation in advance and be prepared for high prices. Some hostels have winter specials, usually offering a dorm for three nights at a slight discount. The closest campsite to town is *Camping Pista del Andino*, 3km uphill at Alem 2873 (☎02901/435-890, ⊛www.lapi stadelandino.com.ar; AR$28 per person), with bay views and good facilities, including a kitchen and bike rental. They offer free pick-up from town.

Hostels

For the budget traveller, a number of excellent hostels offer good services and plenty of *buena onda* (good vibes). All have kitchens, free breakfast and internet.

Antarctica Hostel Calle Antartida Argentina 270 ☎02901/435-774, ⊛www.antarcticahostel.com. This sociable hostel has a light-drenched lounge area, spotless loft kitchen, coin-operated laundry machines and a downstairs bar that takes things up a notch at night. The plain upstairs dorms (AR$55) are a bit of a hike from the downstairs bathrooms. AR$150.

Cruz del Sur Deloqui 242 ☏ 02901/434-099, ⓦ www.xdelsur.com.ar. Based in a new building down the road from their former location, the same helpful Canadian-Italian owners are at it again. Bright colours are reminiscent of school, but there's plenty of hot water. Dorms AR$55.

Freestyle Gobernador Paz 866 ☏ 02901/432-874, ⓦ www.ushuaiafreestyle.com. Promoting itself as a "five-star hostel", this backpacker's favourite certainly looks more like a hotel, attached as it is to *Hotel Austral* and with the rare distinction of having a pool. Only the young party crowd and top-floor communal lounge with pool table and pumping stereo suggest otherwise. Dorms (AR$55) are clean and spacious, while private doubles (AR$160) have bathtubs.

🏃 **La Posta Albergue** Perón Sur 864 ☏ 02901/444-650, ⓦ www.laposta-ush .com.ar. Too bad it's so far from town (20-min walk) because this sparkling hostel ticks every other box: two kitchens, free laundry, free local calls, well-scrubbed dorms (AR$55) and staff who will bend over backwards to help you.

Torre al Sur Gobernador Paz 1437 ☏ 02901/430-745, ⓦ www.torrealsur.com.ar. A rickety wooden blue-and-white mansion that's not the most salubrious hostel you'll ever clap eyes on, but the dorms are the cheapest in the centre (AR$65) and provide 360-degree mountain, harbour and city views.

Yakush Piedrabuena 118 ☏ 02901/435-807, ⓦ www.hostelyakush.com.ar. Spacious and modern yet move-right-in-cosy, this central hostel, which overlooks the main drag, has a piano and owners who know their stuff. The dorms (AR$60) are roomy enough to spread out in, and one of the doubles is en suite. AR$150.

Hotels

All hotels listed here include breakfast and internet.

🏃 **Galeazzi-Basily B&B** Gobernador Valedéz 323 ☏ 02901/423-213, ⓦ www.avesdelsur .com.ar. Run by hospitable English- and French-speaking owners, this large family house on a quiet residential street a few blocks from the centre has small, simple rooms with shared bathroom, use of kitchen, and hot drinks and persistent cake offers all day. The two self-contained cabañas in the backyard offer more privacy and sleep up to four. AR$180.

Eating

Cheap restaurants are thin on the ground in Ushuaia. Seafood is king here, especially the tasty *centolla* (king crab); *cordero* (lamb), a speciality of Patagonia, is well-represented.

137 Restaurante San Martín 137 ☏ 02901/435-005. The crowds speak for themselves at this busy restaurant. If you're not excited by pizza (from AR$35) or pasta (from AR$20), you'll warm to the king crab *empanadas* (AR$7). Open 11am–1am.

Bambu Piedrabueno 276. You don't often see "vegetarian", "cheap" and "Ushuaia" in the same sentence, but this Asian takeaway buffet fits the bill (large portions under AR$10). Open Mon–Fri 11am–5pm.

🏃 **Bodegón Fueguino** San Martín 895 ☏ 02901/431-972. Park yourself down on a sheepskin-draped wooden bench in this historic wooden house (built 1896) and order what this restaurant does best – succulent roast lamb, served in a choice of twelve different sauces (AR$29–45). Closed Mon. Open 12.30–3pm and 8pm–midnight.

🏃 **Chocolates Ushuaia** San Martín 783 ☏ 02901/476-3250. Sometimes you have to travel to the end of the earth for the world's best hot chocolate. Open noon–8pm.

La Rueda San Martín and Rivadavia ☏ 02901/436-540. If you have endless hunger and are attracted to various slow-roasting animals (lamb, chicken, beef) turning on the spit over a fire pit in the display window, this is your place. All-you-can-eat *parrilla* including salads, a soft drink and dessert for AR$65. Open noon–11pm.

El Turco San Martín 1410. Typical Argentine fare, with the emphasis on pizza at reasonable prices (around AR$40). Open Mon–Sat noon–3pm and 8pm–midnight.

Un Lugar...en el Fin del Mundo Roca 258 ☏ 02901/434-441. This humble restaurant offers good value (for Ushuaia) as well as warm service and hearty fare. Everything – down to the heart-shaped mashed potatoes – is served with love. Mains range from pepper steak (AR$32) to paella ($69 for two). Open noon–3pm and 8pm–midnight.

Volver Av. Maipú 37 ☏ 02901/423-977. For everything fishy and one heck of a realistic Che Guevara statue, take your appetite to this harbourfront institution. While waiting for your food (mains AR$40–120) greet the king crab in the fish tank or get an eyeful of the eclectic knick-knacks tacked to the wall. Sea bass with king crab sauce is a favourite. Open Tues–Sun noon–3pm, 7.30pm–midnight. Nov–Easter closed Sun lunch.

Drinking and nightlife

Dreamland 9 de Julio and Deoqui. This funky bar, with white couches, a disco ball and mood lighting, pulses to electronic music when it's not hosting live music or tango nights. Beers (AR$10) and cocktails (AR$15) are served until late.

Dublin 9 de Julio 168. The best of the Ushuaia Irish bars that battle it out for the dubious crown of "world's most southerly Irish pub". Wooden furnishings and a musty smell provide the perfect backdrop for sinking a bottle of Guinness (AR$15) with a plate of *picadas*. If you are a cocktail hound check out the daily happy hour special. Open 2pm until late.

Invisible Pub San Martín 19. Rock on night or day at this cavernous pub, which screens music DVDs and stages live bands. Beer (AR$10) and burgers (AR$18) are the nutritional staples. Open daily 8am–4am.

Directory

Car rental Crossing Patagonia, at Maipú 857 (℡02901/435-475, ⊕www.crossingpatagonia .com).

Banks and exchange Thaler, at Av. San Martín 299.

Post office Gob. Godoy 118.

Spanish school Finis Terrae Spanish School, at Rosas 475 (℡02901/433-871, ⊕www.spanish patagonia.com).

Tour operators All Patagonia, at Juan Fadul 60 (℡02901/433-622, ⊕www.allpatagonia .com) runs Antarctic expeditions, scenic flights and nature and sailing excursions; Patagonia Adventure Explorers, at Maipú, Laserre (also ℡02901/433-622) runs Beagle Channel boat trips in a smaller boat to get closer to the islands to see wildlife; Rumbo Sur, at San Martín 350 (℡02901/422-275, ⊕www.rumbosur.com.ar) organizes Antarctica cruises, Beagle Channel boat trips and a range of excursions in and around Ushuaia; Ushuaia Divers (℡02901/444-701, ⊕www.ushuaiadivers.com.ar) operates diving trips in the Beagle Channel to see shipwrecks, sea lions and king crabs.

Moving on

Air Buenos Aires (8 daily; 3hr 45min); El Calafate (8 daily; 1hr 10min); Río Gallegos (daily; 55min); sporadic services to Puerto Madryn (2hr) and Trelew (2hr), plus international connections to Punta Arenas and Santiago de Chile.

Bus The following companies operate from Ushuaia: Lider, at Gob Paz 921 (℡02901/436-421) to Río Grande; Marga y Taqsa, at Godoy 41 (℡02901/435-453) to Río Gallegos and Río Grande; Montiel, at Deloqui 110 (℡02901/421-366) to Río Grande; Pacheco, at San Martín 1267 (℡02901/437-073) for connections from Río

Grande to Punta Arenas; Tecni Austral, at Roca 157 (℡02901/431-408) for Comodoro Rivadavia, El Calafate, Puerto Natales, Punta Arenas, Río Gallegos and Río Grande.

El Calafate (Mon–Sat once daily; 18hr); Puerto Natales (4 weekly; 16hr); Punta Arenas (daily except Tues; 12hr); Río Gallegos (2–3 daily; 13hr); Río Grande (12–16 daily; 4hr).

PARQUE NACIONAL TIERRA DEL FUEGO

Wet and wild **PARQUE NACIONAL TIERRA DEL FUEGO**, 12km west of Ushuaia, stretches from the Beagle Channel in the south to the border with Chile in the west. Encompassing 630 square kilometres of mountains, waterfalls, glaciers, lakes, rivers, valleys, sub-Antarctic forest and peat bog, most of the park is closed to the public, with less than 30km of accessible trails. With a couple of days up your sleeve, you could tackle all the short treks in the park. The most popular is the **Costera Trail** (11km return; 3hr 30min), which follows the shoreline through coastal forest of deciduous beech trees, affording spectacular views of the Beagle Channel, passing grass-covered mounds that were former campsites of the indigenous Yámana and offering birdwatchers prime opportunities for spotting Magellanic woodpeckers, cormorants, gulls and oystercatchers.

For the park's best views, trudge to the top of 970m-high **Cerro Guanaco Trail** (8km return; 8hr). Another popular trail, **Hito XXIV Trail** (5km return; 3hr), is a level path tracing the shores of Lago Roca and ending at a small obelisk that marks the border with Chile (it is illegal to continue beyond here). Guanacos, Patagonian grey foxes, Fuegian foxes, Southern river otters and some ninety bird species are among the park's fauna; introduced Canadian beavers and European rabbits also run amok, wreaking environmental havoc. The **entry fee** for the park is AR$30, to be paid at the office at the park entrance in summer. It's free in winter.

PARQUE NACIONAL TIERRA DEL FUEGO

Beagle Channel

0   2 km

Arrival and information

Bus The easiest way to reach the park without your own transport is with the buses that leave Ushuaia from the corner of Juan Fadul and Av. Maipú (AR$70 return). If your hotel calls ahead the bus can arrange to pick you up between 9am and 1pm. They pick up and drop off in the park at the Alakush Visitors Centre (☎020901/1546-7148). Last pick-up 5pm.
Train El Tren del Fin del Mundo (AR$130 return or AR$110 one-way; ☎02901/431-600, ⓦwww .trendelfindelmundo.com.ar) runs to the park on the world's most southerly (and possibly slowest) steam train, along tracks originally laid by prisoners for transporting wood. Trains leave three times daily in the summer, once daily in winter from the Fin del Mundo station, 8km west of Ushuaia.

Accommodation

There are four rudimentary free **campsites** plus one serviced campground at Lago Roca. This has hot showers, a restaurant and a lakeside setting (☎02901/433-313; AR$18). Alongside the Lago Roca campground is a *refugio* with dormitory-style accommodation plus a new complex with twenty beds (AR$40).

RÍO GRANDE

Trout fishing aside, the only reason to be in dreary, gusty **RÍO GRANDE** is to change buses or to use the airport if all flights servicing Ushuaia, 230km southwest, are booked. Built on its namesake river, Río Grande consists of grid after grid of flat urban sprawl, its colourful houses and the "promenade of lovers" along the main street the city's only aesthetic saving grace. Sheep and oil are the economic staples, while the **Monumento a la Trucha** – a giant trout statue on the RN3 – explains why high-rolling anglers are drawn to the nearby rivers.

What to see and do

The **Museo Municipal Virginia Choquintel**, at Alberdi 555 (Mon–Fri 9am–5pm, Sat 3–7pm; free; ☎02964/ 430-647), has exhibits on the region's indigenous and pioneering history. A 20-min ride out of town is the more

TREAT YOURSELF

It used to be that the best meal in Ushuaia was a fussy presentation in one of the huge restaurants overlooking the harbour. No more, now that *Kalma Restó* (Antartida Argentina 57; ☎02901/425-786, ⓦwww.kalmaresto.com .ar) has appeared on the scene. The chef himself comes out to explain the dishes which are adorned with edible flowers and delicate sauces, as you dine in his intimate restaurant (make a reservation, as there are only eight tables). With dishes like lamb cooked three ways at AR$90 and a "Fuegian" paella for two featuring shrimp and king crab at $120, the best meal in Ushuaia is not even that much more expensive than a so-so meal at the average tourist restaurant. You won't miss the view once you get a load of the food. Open Tues–Sun noon–2.30pm & 8pm–midnight.

interesting museum at the **Misión Salesiana**, at RN3 Km 2980 (daily 10am–7pm; AR$5; ☎02964/421-642), a mission founded in 1899 to catechize the Selkam people. The preserved chapel is a charming national historic monument and other buildings house an excellent museum of history, anthropology and natural science, detailing the decline of the indians in the face of massacres and disease. From town, take bus line "D" from any of the bus stops along San Martín.

Arrival and information

Air Río Grande's airport (☎02964/431-340) lies 5km west of town and is serviced by Aerolíneas Argentinas and LADE flights. A taxi to the centre costs AR$15.

Bus The newly built bus terminal is at Finocchio 1149, a 10-min walk from San Martín, the city's main drag.

Fishing licences Pick up a fishing licence at the Asociación de Pesca con Mosca, at Montilla

1040 (Mon–Fri 10.30am–1.30pm & 4–8pm, Sat 10.30am–2pm; ☎02964/1545-8048).

Tourist information The friendly tourist office is at Plaza Almirante Brown, Rosales 350 (Mon–Fri 9am–5pm; ☎02964/431-324, ⓦwww.riogrande .gov.ar).

Accommodation

Most hotels are fishing for wealthy anglers, leaving budget travellers low on options. If you want to brave the relentless wind, try the wooded riverside campsite about ten blocks from downtown at O'Higgins and Montilla (☎02964/420-536, ⓔnauticorg@speedy.com.ar; AR$10).

Albergue Hotel Argentino San Martín 64 ☎02964/422-546. The only hostel in town, housed in a historic clapboard house with wood-burning stoves, recently underwent a facelift. The low-lying leather tables and comfy couches make a good place to enjoy free wi-fi and the friendly chatter of the owner. The basic dorms (AR$70) are in a converted wood shed out the back.

Hospedaje Noal Obligado 557 ☎02964/427-516. Offering great value, this wood-panelled hotel has plain, spotless rooms with comfortable beds and TV. Some singles, and some with private bathrooms. AR$120.

Eating and drinking

Epa!!! Bar-Café Rosales 445. With leather booths dolled up in 1950s-style shades of purple and yellow, this diner offers fruit juices, cocktails, various pizzas and, during the day, a set menu (chicken and rice, drink and dessert) for AR$20. A beer is AR$12. Open weekdays 9am–3am, weekends until 5am.

Narcizo Grill Coffee Bar Espora 624 ☎02964/430-137. The perfect place to have a gourmet coffee or glass of local wine (try the Malbec "del fin del mundo") without breaking the bank. It also has good-value main courses including the local trout served with spinach and cherry tomatoes (AR$48) or a mouth-watering steak sandwich (AR$32). Open Mon–Thurs 7am–2am, Fri–Sat 7am–4pm.

Moving on

Bus Punta Arenas in Chile (3 weekly; 8hr); Río Gallegos (3 daily, all In the morning; 9–10hr); Ushuaia (every 30min; 3–4hr).

Bolivia

ROUGH COSTS

DAILY BUDGET Basic US$18/with
the occasional treat US$28

DRINK Small beer US$11.50

FOOD Fixed three-course lunch
menu US$12

HOSTEL/BUDGET HOTEL US$4–6/
US$8–10

TRAVEL Bus: La Paz–Copacabana
(155km) US$2

FACT FILE

POPULATION 9.1 million

AREA 1,098,581 sq km

LANGUAGE Spanish (also more than
thirty indigenous languages)

CURRENCY Boliviano, aka Peso

CAPITAL La Paz

INTERNATIONAL PHONE CODE
☏591

TIME ZONE GMT -4hr

Introduction

Surrounded by Brazil, Paraguay, Argentina, Chile and Peru, Bolivia lies at the heart of South America. Stretching from the majestic icebound peaks and bleak high-altitude deserts of the Andes to the exuberant rainforests and vast savannas of the Amazon basin, it embraces an astonishing range of landscapes and climates, and encompasses everything outsiders find most exotic and mysterious about the continent.

Three centuries of Spanish colonial rule have certainly left their mark, most obviously in some of the finest colonial architecture on the continent. Yet the European influence is essentially a thin veneer overlying indigenous cultural traditions that stretch back long before the Conquest: while Spanish is the language of business and government, more than thirty indigenous languages are still spoken.

Bolivia is dominated by the mighty **Andes**, which march through the west of the country along two parallel chains. In the north and east, they give way to the tropical rainforests and grasslands of the **Amazon and eastern lowlands**, in the southeast to the dry thornbrush and scrub of the **Chaco**. Yet, despite its extraordinary biodiversity and myriad attractions, Bolivia remains one of South America's least-visited countries.

Most visitors spend a few days in the fascinating city of **La Paz**, which combines a dizzying high-altitude setting with an intermingling of traditional indigenous and modern urban cultures. Close by is the magical **Lake Titicaca**, and the towns of **Coroico and Sorata** which serve as a good base for trekking, climbing or mountain biking in the **Cordillera Real**, a range of high Andean peaks which, plunge precipitously down into the Amazon basin through the dramatic, deep valleys of the **Yungas**. The best base for visiting the Bolivian Amazon further north is **Rurrenabaque**, the jumping-off point for exploring the diversity of flora and fauna in the **Madidi National Park**.

South of La Paz, the southern **Altiplano** – the bleak, high plateau that stretches between the Andes – has historically been home to most of Bolivia's population. In **Potosí** you can experience underground life in the mines of **Cerro Rico**, while to the southwest, Uyuni is the gateway to the astonishing landscape of the **Salar de Uyuni** and the **Reserva de Fauna Andina Eduardo Avaroa**. Also well worth visiting are the towns of **Sucre**,

WHEN TO VISIT

Climate varies much more as a result of altitude and topography than it does between different seasons. Winter (May–Oct), is the dry season, and in many ways the best time to visit Bolivia, with sunny, trek-friendly highland days and slightly lower temperatures in the generally hot and humid lowlands. While highland temperatures hover in the mid-teens most of the year (albeit with chilly winter nights), the summer rainy season (Dec–March), can see lowland temperatures reach 31°C. Rain affects the condition of roads throughout the country, especially in the Amazon, where river transport takes over from often impassable overland routes. The parched Altiplano and mountainsides nevertheless briefly transform into lush grassland, as wild flowers proliferate and the earth comes to life.

with its fine colonial architecture, and **Santa Cruz**, a brash, modern and lively tropical metropolis – and a good base for exploring the rainforests of the **Parque Nacional Amboró** and the immaculately restored Jesuit missions of **Chiquitos**.

CHRONOLOGY

1000 BC Founding of Tiwanaku on the shores of Lake Titicaca, centre of a colonial empire comprising much of modern Bolivia, southern Peru, northeast Argentina and northern Chile.

c.1000 AD Tiwanaku dramatically collapses, most likely as a result of a prolonged drought.

Eleventh to fifteenth centuries The Aymara take control of the Altiplano, maintaining a more localized culture and religion.

Mid-fifteenth century The Aymara are incorporated into the Inca Empire, albeit with a limited degree of autonomy.

1532 Francisco Pizarro leads his Spanish conquistadors to a swift and unlikely defeat of the Inca army in Cajamarca, (Bajo) Peru.

1538 Pizarro sends Spanish troops south to aid the Aymaran Colla as they battle both the remnants of an Inca rebellion and their Aymara rivals the Lupaca. Spanish control of the territory known as Alto Peru is established.

1545 The continent's richest deposit of silver, Cerro Rico, is discovered, giving birth to the mining city of Potosí.

1691 San Javier is founded as the first of the Chiquitos Jesuit missions.

1767 The Spanish crown expels the Jesuit order from the Americas.

1780–82 The last major indigenous uprising, the Great Rebellion, is led by a combined Inca-Aymara army of Túpact Amaru and pac Katari.

1809 La Paz becomes the first capital in the Americas to declare independence from Spain.

1824 The last Spanish army is destroyed at the battle of Ayacucho in (Bajo) Peru.

1825 The newly liberated Alto Peru rejects a union with either (Bajo) Peru or Argentina, and adopts a declaration of independence, and Bolivia is born.

1879 Chile begins the War of the Pacific by occupying the entire Bolivian coastline and invading Peru.

1899 The Federal Revolution consolidates power of the new tin-mining barons and creates a new administrative capital in La Paz.

1904 Bolivia finally cedes its coastline to Chile, in addition to losing the Acre to Brazil.

1932–35 The Chaco War with Paraguay ends in stalemate and huge loss of life.

1952 The National Revolution sees armed civilians defeat the army in La Paz and the ascension to power of the MNR (Revolutionary Nationalist Movement).

1964 A resurgent army led by General René Barrientos seizes power, beginning eighteen years of military dictatorship.

1967 Che Guevara is captured and executed in the hamlet of La Higuera.

1970s General Hugo Banzer heads a brutal military regime, coinciding with an unprecedented period of economic growth.

1980–81 The most brutal and corrupt regime in modern Bolivian history is led by General Luis García Meza.

1985 Bolivia plunges into a recession as the bottom falls out of the tin market, and the economic vacuum is filled by the production and export of cocaine.

Late 1990s US-backed coca eradication policies provoke widespread resistance, led by indigenous activist Evo Morales.

2005 Evo Morales is elected as Bolivia's first indigenous president with an absolute majority and a programme of nationalization and agrarian reform.

2008 Morales suspends US Drug Enforcement programme, accusing agents of espionage. In retaliation, the US adds Bolivia to its drugs blacklist and suspends trade preferences.

2009 New constitution agreed, giving greater rights to indigenous people. Morales is elected for a second term.

Basics

ARRIVAL

Bolivia isn't the easiest country to fly to. The only direct services are from **Miami** in the US and from neighbouring South American countries, the most frequent connections being from **São Paulo** in Brazil, **Buenos Aires** in Argentina and **Lima** in Peru. In Bolivia itself there are only two international airports: **El Alto** in La Paz (see p.190) and **Viru Viru** in Santa Cruz (see p.234); the former boasts the highest airport location in the world. Once you're in Bolivia,

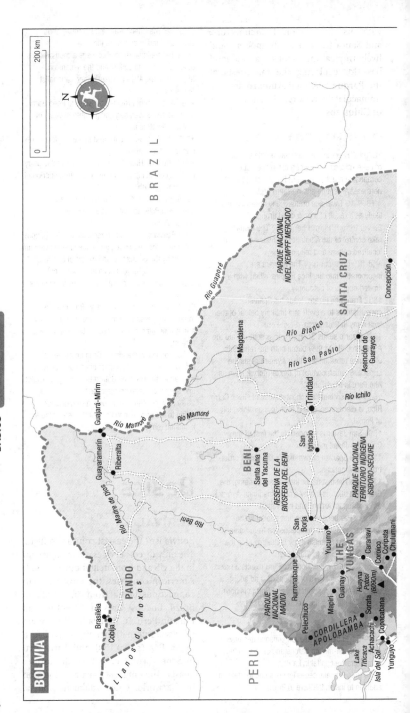

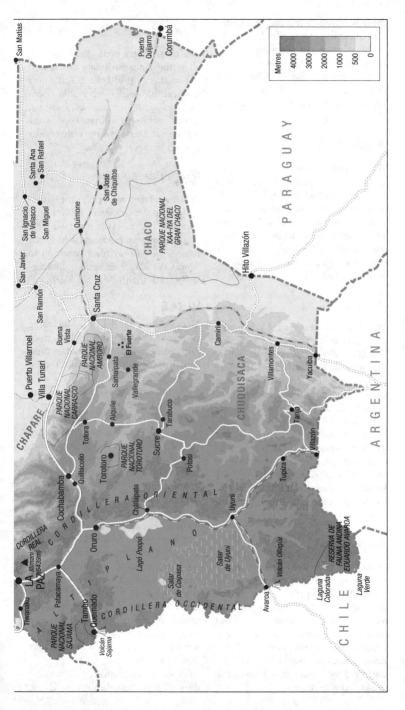

flying is actually a relatively cheap and convenient way to get around, especially in the rainy season when many roads are impassable. Bolivia has land borders with Argentina, Brazil, Chile, Peru and Paraguay; full details of the main border crossings are given in accounts of relevant departure points.

From Argentina

The principal border crossing is from La Quiaca in Argentina to Villazón in the southern Altiplano (see box, p.219), with regular bus and train connections to the desert town of Tupiza. There's also a crossing between Pocitos in Argentina and Yacuiba in the Chaco (see p.241), from where it's possible to travel by bus or train to Santa Cruz.

From Brazil

The busiest crossing is the rail border at Quijarro (see p.241), near the Brazilian city of Corumbá, where the Bolivian Pantanal meets its more famous Brazilian counterpart. From Quijarro, it's a full day's train journey to Santa Cruz. There are also a couple of borders in Amazonia, from Guajará-Mirim (transit point Porto Velho) by boat across the Rio Mamoré to Guayaramerín, from where there are regular onward flights; and from Brasiléia (transit point Rio Branco), to Cobija, the capital of Pando province (see p.248).

From Chile

There are two trans-Andean routes which cross from Chile, the most popular being the road up from Arica on the coast to Tambo Quemado (see p.209), and on to La Paz. A more adventurous option is the remote border crossing of Laguna Verde, at the southern edge of Reserva Eduardo Avaroa, accessible via organized tours from the Chilean town of San Pedro de Atacama.

From Peru

The most widely used land border of all is the Yunguyo-Kasani crossing at the southern tip of Lake Titicaca near Copacabana, easily accessible from Puno in southern Peru. Less busy but just as easy to get to from Puno is the crossing at Desaguadero, with regular onward transport to La Paz.

From Paraguay

For the adventurous only, the trans-Chaco border between Bolivia and Paraguay (see p.241) is navigable only in the dry season, during which the route – all the way from Asunción to Santa Cruz – is served by an endurance-testing two- to three-day bus journey.

VISAS

Many visitors to Bolivia – including citizens of the **United Kingdom**, most European countries, **Canada**, **New Zealand** and **Australia** – don't need a visa. Citizens of South Africa need a visa but can purchase one on arrival for about US$50 per person. However, citizens of the **United States** are required to obtain a visa before they travel, at a cost of US$135 per person; they're valid for five years and allow visitors to enter Bolivia three times a year, with a maximum of ninety days per year spent in the country. US citizens will also need a passport valid for the next six months, with at least one blank page, as well as proof that they have the necessary funds to leave the country (such as a photocopy of your credit card). A passport photo is also required, as is proof of onward travel (a copy of a hotel reservation will usually do the trick). You can obtain an application form for the visa at the airport or border, or download one from ⓦ www.bolivia-usa.org.

For other nationalities, the situation does change periodically, so always check with your local embassy or consulate a month or two before travelling. On arrival, you'll be issued with a **tourist card** (*tarjeta de turismo*) valid for thirty or ninety days, depending on your nationality. Before entry, check the number of days you're allowed to stay and make sure the border officials give you the stamp with the maximum number of days your nationality allows you; if they give you less than the maximum, you can request it on the spot (though there's no guarantee you'll get it) or go to the immigration office in La Paz or the nearest city to your border crossing and receive another stamp. The annual limit, at the time of writing, was restricted to ninety days, and, officially at least, you cannot just cross the border and get another ninety-day card.

GETTING AROUND

Bolivia's topography, size and lack of basic infrastructure mean that getting around is often a challenge, especially in the rainy season. However, buses are very cheap and numerous, and even flying within the country is very affordable.

By plane

La Paz, Santa Cruz, Sucre and Cochabamba are all connected by **daily flights** (B$550–900), and there are also frequent services to Tarija, Trinidad, Rurrenabaque and a number of remote towns in the Amazon and the eastern lowlands. There is currently one main commercial carrier, AeroSur (Ⓦwww .aerosur.com), as well as a smaller internal lowland operator, Amaszonas (Ⓦwww.amaszonas.com). The new, state-run Boliviana de Aviacion (Ⓦboa .bo) was introduced with the aim of bringing air travel to the masses, and offers low fares on domestic flights to all major cities, as well as three flights per week to Buenos Aires. The **Bolivian air force** also operates passenger services

under its commercial arm Transportes Aereo Militar (TAM; ☎02/212-1582, Ⓦwww.tam.bo), particularly to the further-flung corners of the country. Busier routes should be booked at least several days in advance. Note that flights are often cancelled or delayed, especially in the Amazon, where the weather can cause disruption.

By bus

Bolivia's **buses** are run by a variety of private companies and ply all the main routes in the country. Due to poor road conditions, journey times are unpredictable, and you should always be prepared for major delays, especially in the rainy season. When travelling in the highlands, always bring warm clothing and a blanket or sleeping bag, as journeys can get bitterly cold. A government programme to pave the country's road network is being rolled out slowly – and a new road from Santa Cruz to the Brazilian border is nearing completion.

By train

The sole Andean operator, FCA (Empresa Ferroviaria Andina; Ⓦwww .fca.com.bo), runs two passenger lines – *Expreso del Sur* and *Wara Wara del Sur* – from Oruro south across the Altiplano via Uyuni and Tupiza to Villazón on the Argentine border. A separate company, Ferroviaria Oriental (☎03/338-7230, Ⓦwww.ferroviariaoriental.com), runs two lines in the lowlands: one from Santa Cruz east to the Brazilian border at Quijarro (a service known as the "death train" – a reference to its speed and not its safety record); the other from Santa Cruz south to Yacuiba in the Chaco, on the Argentine border.

By boat

Although Bolivia is a landlocked country, there are still several regions – particularly Lake Titicaca and the

Amazon – where water is still the best way of getting around. There are two main forms of **river transport** in the Bolivian Amazon: dugout canoes, powered by outboard motors, are used to visit protected areas such as the Parque Nacional Madidi; alternatively, more economic but less comfortable cargo boats ply the Río Mamoré, between Trinidad and Guayaramerín on the Brazilian frontier, and the Río Ichilo, between Trinidad and Puerto Villaroel in the Chapare.

By car

If you're short on time or want to get to some really out-of-the-way destinations, **renting a car** is an option, though it's often easier and not much more expensive to hire a taxi or *camioneta* to drive you around for a day or longer.

Outside towns, most roads are unpaved and in very poor condition, so **four-wheel drive** (4x4) is essential. Petrol stations are few and far between and breakdown services even scarcer. Generally, you'll pay a flat fee of B$220–350 per day, plus about B$2–3 extra for each kilometre you drive; 4x4s cost about double. Recommended companies with offices in La Paz and Santa Cruz are Barbol Rent a Car (☎02/282-0675, ⓦwww .barbolsrl.com) and Avis (☎02/211-1870, ⓦwww.avis.com.bo). You'll need to be over 25, and to leave a major credit card or large cash deposit as security; most rental companies will include insurance cover with the hire price but it is worth checking.

ACCOMMODATION

While **accommodation** in Bolivia is generally good value, the standard is not particularly high, especially in smaller towns. Room rates vary according to season, rising during the high tourist season (May–Sept) and on weekends in popular resort towns, and doubling or tripling during major fiestas.

Budget travellers will almost always be able to find a double room, often with a private bathroom, in a clean and reasonably comfortable hotel for around **B$50–70**. There are also usually at least one or two places offering **dorm beds** at a low price. Even in the coldest highland cities, heating is usually non-existent; in the lowlands, heat, rather than cold, is often a problem, though all but the cheapest rooms are equipped with a fan. Whatever climactic zone you're in, all but the cheapest places usually have **hot water**, although the reliability and effectiveness of water-heating systems varies considerably. Most common are the individual electric heaters that you'll find attached to the tops of showers; don't touch the apparatus while the water is running, as you might get an electric shock. Remember, the less water, the warmer it will be – it requires a delicate balance to get right.

Camping

With few designated campsites and an abundance of inexpensive accommodation, few travellers **camp** in Bolivia unless exploring the country's wilderness areas. Beyond the cities and towns, you can camp almost everywhere, usually for free; make sure you ask for permission from the nearest house first; local villages may ask for a small fee of a few bolivianos. In some **national parks** you'll also find shelters where you can stay for a minimal charge.

FOOD AND DRINK

The style of eating and drinking varies considerably between Bolivia's three main geographical regions – the Altiplano, the highland valleys and the tropical lowlands – differences that reflect the produce commonly available in each region and the different cultural traditions of their inhabitants. Each region has *comidas típicas* (traditional dishes).

All larger towns in Bolivia have a fair selection of **restaurants**; almost all offer enormously filling good-value set lunches, or *almuerzos*, usually costing between B$8 and B$20, while many offer a set dinner, or *cena*, in the evening and also have a range of à la carte main dishes (*platos extras*), rarely costing more than B$15–30. For B$30–40 you should expect a very good meal in more upmarket restaurants, while about B$40–60 will get you most dishes even in the best restaurants in La Paz or Santa Cruz.

Food

While Altiplano cuisine is dominated by the humble **potato**, often served in hearty soups (llama and mutton are also common), the valley regions cook with **corn**, often used as the basis for thick soups known as *laguas,* or boiled on the cob and served with fresh white cheese – a classic combination known as *choclo con queso*. Meat and chicken are often cooked in spicy sauces known as *picantes*: a valley mainstay is *pique a lo macho*, a massive plate of chopped beef and sausage fried together with potatoes, onions, tomatoes and chillies. In the tropical lowlands, **plantains** and **yucca** take the place of potatoes; beef is also plentiful – the lowlands are cattle-ranching regions, so beef is of good quality and relatively cheap.

Although Bolivia is obviously not the place to come for seafood, fish features regularly on menus, especially the succulent *trucha* (trout) and *pejerrey* (kingfish) around Lake Titicaca, and the juicy white river fish known as *surubí* and *pucú* in the lowlands. Ordinary restaurants rarely offer much in the way of vegetarian food, although you can almost always find eggs and potatoes of some description (usually fried), as well as the ubiquitous potato soup, often cooked without meat. The situation changes a great deal in cities and in popular travellers' haunts, where a cosmopolitan selection of vegetarian dishes, salads and pancakes is widely available, and wholly vegetarian restaurants are becoming increasingly common.

The most popular snack throughout Bolivia is the **salteña**, a pasty filled with a spicy, juicy stew of meat or chicken with chopped vegetables, olives and hard-boiled egg. It's usually sold from street stalls and eaten in the mid-morning accompanied by a cold drink and a spoonful or two of chilli sauce if desired.

Drink

Mineral water is fairly widely available in large plastic bottles – a good thing, as it's best not to drink tap water. The delicious variety of tropical fruits grown in Bolivia are available as juices from market stalls throughout the country, and freshly squeezed orange and grapefruit **juice** is also sold on the streets from handcarts for about B$2 a glass. **Tea and coffee** are available almost everywhere, as well as *mates*, or herbal teas – *mate de coca* is the best known and a good remedy for altitude sickness, but many others are usually available.

Locally produced alcoholic drinks are widely available in Bolivia, and drinking is a serious pastime. Beer is available almost everywhere – Paceña (half litre B$6–10), produced in La Paz, is the most popular and widely available, followed by Huari, made by the same company but with a slightly saltier taste. Although not widely consumed, Bolivia also produces a growing variety of exceptional high-altitude – and highly underrated – **wines** (*vinos*), mostly from the Tarija Valley; the best labels are Campos de Solana, Concepción and Kohlberg. A glass of red wine (*vino tinto*) will cost B$8–12. While production is still a fraction of what neighbouring Argentina and Chile achieve,

Bolivia's wines deserve – and may yet attract – an equally high profile.

One of the problems the industry has faced is that much cultivation is dedicated to muscat grapes, which, rather than being used for fine **wines**, are used to a produce a white grape brandy called *singani*, the beverage most Bolivians turn to when they really want to get drunk. It's usually mixed with Sprite or 7 Up, which creates a fast-acting combination known as *chuflay*. Finally, no visit to the Cochabamba is complete without a taste of *chicha cochabambina*, a thick, mildly alcoholic yeasty-flavoured beer made of fermented maize and considered sacred by the Incas.

CULTURE AND ETIQUETTE

There isn't really such a thing as an all-encompassing Bolivian culture, as traditions vary widely according to different regions and climates, as well as according to social class and ethnic background; the country has more then different ethnic groups. That said, there is a distinction made between the "'camba'" (people from the lowlands) and "'colla'" (those from the highlands). In recent years, tension between the two regions has heightened as a result of sweeping reform on land distribution and nationalization introduced by President Morales.

Spanish is the official language in Bolivia, and it's a great place to brush up on your language skills as Bolivians speak slowly and clearly compared with their Chilean or Argentine neighbours. Indigenous languages including Aymara, Quechua and Gurani are also widely spoken. Catholicism is the predominant religion though you may find that some festivals and celebrations involve a mishmash of Catholic and native beliefs with offerings made to both the Virgin Mary and Pachamama (mother earth).

Generally speaking, Bolivians are friendly folk and will go out of their way to help you. It is polite and common practice to pepper any requests with "por favor" and "gracias", and greet people with "buenos días" or "buenas tardes" before starting a conversation. There is little concept of personal space in Bolivia and people will typically stand very close when speaking to you.

Chewing coca leaf is seen as an integral part of daily life for many Bolivians. The controversial leaf is commonly chewed into a round ball, and kept in hamster-like fashion in the side of the cheek, or used to make herbal tea. It is said to combat tiredness and altitude sickness, and quell hunger, and is also used in ritual ceremonies.

When eating out at a restaurant, or taking part in a guided tour, a ten percent tip is appreciated, and increasingly expected. Many museums and historical landmarks do charge higher fees to foreigners and many tourists find this frustrating. If you are not sure of what you are being asked to pay, it is best to ask around to establish the going rate before assuming you are being ripped off. In markets, you will need to haggle.

SPORTS AND OUTDOOR ACTIVITIES

Dominated by the dramatic high mountain scenery of the Andes, Bolivia is ideal for **trekking, mountain biking** and **climbing**; whether you want to stroll for half a day, take a hardcore hike for two weeks over high passes down into remote Amazonian valleys, or climb one of the hundred peaks over 5000 metres, it's all possible. The best season for outdoor activity is between May and September, while the most pleasant and reliable weather is between June and August.

The easiest way to go trekking or climbing is with a tour operator. There are dozens of these in La Paz (see box, below) and in several other cities, with treks costing between B$200–350 per person per day, depending on what's included and how many people are in the group.

The activity rated by many travellers as one of the highlights of South America is a bike ride down the road from La Paz to Coroico in the Yungas, a thrilling 3500 metre descent along what was once dubbed the **world's most dangerous road**. Over the last decade, a number of tour companies have set up trips down the road, and it is easy to organize as a day-trip from La Paz. You don't need any previous experience but bear in mind that several bikers have been killed on this route in the past, and though the most dangerous stretch was bypassed in 2007, some vehicles still use it. Attempting the trip in the rainy season (Nov–March) is not recommended.

COMMUNICATIONS

Airmail (*por avión*) to Europe and North America tends to take between one and two weeks to arrive; mail to the rest of the world outside the Americas and Europe takes longer. Letters cost about B$8 to Europe, a little less to the US and Canada, and about B$10 to Australia and New Zealand. For a small extra charge, you can send letters certified (*certificado*), which is more reliable, but even then it's not a good idea to send anything you can't afford to lose.

There are **ENTEL** phone centres in all cities and most towns, where you can make local, national and international

ORGANIZED TOURS

Tours to the salt flats, the jungle and Bolivia's national parks are offered by most operators and agencies across the country. Some agencies are less reputable and responsible than others, and it is always worth shopping around before booking a tour (see also individual cities and regions). The following come recommended:

Amboro Tours (based in Santa Cruz but can organize tours by phone or email) C Pari 81, Santa Cruz ☎03/339-0600, ⓦwww.amboro tours.com. Recommended agency specializing in trips to national parks within the Amazon, including Jesuit Mission tours and the Ché Guevara route. They also organize excursions from La Paz to Lake Titicaca.

America Tours Ground-floor office 9, Edificio Avenida, Av. 16 de Julio 1490, La Paz ☎02/237-4204, ⓦwww.america-ecotours .com. Efficient and reliable travel agency. They're the main booking agent for Chalalán Ecolodge in Parque Nacional Madidi, and a good resource for booking internal flights, as well as trips to the Pampas del Yacuma and the Salar de Uyuni.

Bolivian Journeys Sagárnaga 363, La Paz ☎02/235-7848, ⓦwww.bolivianjourneys .org. Highly regarded mountaineering specialists, offering well-organized and professionally equipped expeditions into the Cordillera Real.

Crillon Tours Av. Camacho 1223, La Paz ☎02/233-7533, ⓦwww.titicaca.com. Eco-friendly agency who work alongside local communities to provide cultural immersion experiences. They offer a variety of tours throughout Bolivia, including pricey hydrofoil cruises on Lake Titicaca and tours of Tiwanaku.

Fremen Av. 6 de Agosto, Edificio V Centenario, La Paz ☎02/240-8200, ⓦwww.andes -amazonia.com. La Paz branch of the excellent and highly respected Cochabamba-based agency offering a wide range of tailor-made tours throughout Bolivia, including river trips on the Río Mamoré on their own luxury floating hotel, the *Reina de Enín*.

Kanoo Tours Calle Illampu 832, Zona Rosario, La Paz ☎02/246-0003, ⓦwww.kanootours.com. Englishman Phil is fast becoming La Paz's leading source of information for the budget traveller, with quality tours and bookings arranged across the country. Also has branches in the *Loki Hostel* and the *Adventure Brew Hostel*.

Ruta Verde Tours Calle 21 de Mayo 318, Santa Cruz ☎03/339-6470, ⓦwww.rutaverdebolivia .com. Pricey but excellent Dutch/Bolivian-run tour operator offering trips to the salt flats and jungle, with sustainability as a priority.

calls. While there are a few coin-operated **telephone booths** in the street, most use **prepaid cards**. These are widely available at street stalls, which are often sited next to booths, and come in denominations of 10, 20 and 50 bolivianos. If you're dialling long-distance within Bolivia, you'll need the respective area code, which for La Paz, Oruro and Potosí is ℡02; for Beni, Pando and Santa Cruz ℡03; and for Cochabamba, Chuquisaca and Tarija ℡04.

Calling internationally, the cheapest option is via an internet phone or Skype service, which will cost no more than the standard surfing rate. **Internet cafés** themselves are ubiquitous in all but the most remote corners of Bolivia. The speed of machines and servers isn't usually very fast, but with a little patience you'll get a connection eventually. Expect to pay about B$3–8 per hour.

CRIME AND SAFETY

In recent years, Bolivia's crime levels have risen partly in response to the country's worsening economic situation. If you apply **common sense precautions**, however, there's no need to be paranoid: the vast majority of crime against tourists is opportunistic theft, and **violence is rare**. An increasingly common method of theft is through the use of **fake police officers** and fake taxi drivers. Fake policemen may approach you on the street and ask to search you or see your documents (before making off with them) or may ask you to go with them in a taxi to the "police station". Be aware that real policeman would never do this, so on no account hand over your documents or valuables and never accompany a stranger in a taxi.

Another trick is for **fake taxi drivers** or even minibus drivers to pick up unsuspecting passengers before either stopping in a deserted part of town where they and/or their associates rob the victims, or, in even worse scenarios, kidnap and seriously assault the victims

to force them to reveal their PINS. Always check the ID of any taxi you take and only ever use official ones; better still, whenever possible ask your hotel to order one for you.

Another common means of theft is the "spitting" or "mustard" trick. You may be spat on or have a substance such as mustard spilt on you; a "helpful passer-by" will stop you, point out the offending substance and attempt to clean it off you (while their partner in crime quickly relieves you of your valuables). If this happens to you, don't stop and walk on as quickly as possible before stopping to clean yourself up.

Political upheaval is pretty much a regular feature of everyday life in Bolivia, both in terms of **street protests** and **road blockades**. While traditionally these have been focused on the Altiplano and organized by radical Aymara, in recent years there has been an upsurge in protests and attacks by right-wing pro-autonomists in the Amazon and eastern lowlands. At the time of writing, the situation was much calmer but it is always worth keeping an eye on the news and asking around before you travel.

HEALTH

Though levels of hygiene and sanitation are generally poor in Bolivia, you can reduce the risk of getting ill. Avoid drinking tap water and watch out for ice in drinks, as well as uncooked or unpeeled fruit and vegetables. Appreciate the risks of buying food from street vendors and always check that food has been properly cooked.

Altitude sickness is a common complaint in La Paz, Potosí and on the salt-flats tour. Mild symptoms include dizziness, headaches and breathlessness. Bolivians swear by coca tea (*mate de coca*) but resting and drinking plenty of non-alcoholic fluids should also help. Anyone with more severe symptoms should get immediate medical help.

It is advisable to get vaccinated against yellow fever before you travel to Bolivia; bring a doctor's certificate with you. Use mosquito repellent with a high DEET content and wear long sleeves and trousers to avoid insect-borne diseases such as malaria and dengue fever.

Bolivia is home to a wide range of venomous snakes and spiders. Watch where you step and seek medical advice if you are bitten or stung.

When looking for healthcare, it is always best to opt for private clincs (*clínica*) rather than state-run hospitals, which are often over-crowded and poorly equipped.

INFORMATION AND MAPS

Most major cities have a regional **tourist office**, either run by the city municipality or by the departmental prefecture. Local Bolivian tour operators are generally a good source of information, and many are happy to answer queries, often in English, though obviously their main aim is to sell you one of their tours.

It's worth buying a good map of the country to take with you, as these are rarely available in Bolivia itself. The best general map is the *Travel Map of Bolivia* (1:2,200,000), produced by O'Brien Cartographics; it can be purchased online from ⓦwww.saexplorers.org or www.boliviaweb.com.

MONEY AND BANKS

The Bolivian currency is the **boliviano**, sometimes referred to as the peso. It's usually written "B$" or "Bs" and is subdivided into 100 centavos. Notes come in denominations of 10, 20, 50, 100 and 200 bolivianos; coins in denominations of 1, 2 and 5 bolivianos, and of 5, 10, 20 and 50 centavos. At the time of writing, the **exchange rate** was roughly B$6.97 = US$1. US dollars can be changed at banks, **withdrawn at ATMs**, hotels or shops and by street moneychangers almost everywhere in the country, and are a good way of carrying emergency backup funds. Most day-to-day costs will be charged in B$ though tourist-based activities – especially the more upmarket kind – will often be quoted in US$. The easiest way to access funds in cities and larger towns is by using plastic; Visa and MasterCard are most widely accepted. Banks in all major cities and larger towns are connected to the nation-wide Enlace network of **ATMs**. In rural areas and smaller towns it's important to carry plenty of cash, as plastic and traveller's cheques are fairly useless.

OPENING HOURS AND HOLIDAYS

Public offices in Bolivia have adopted a new system, *horario continuo*, whereby they work Monday to Friday straight

PUBLIC HOLIDAYS

Jan 1 New Year's Day (*Año Nuevo*)

February/March Carnaval, celebrated throughout the country in the week before Lent. The Oruro Carnaval (see p.209) is the most famous, but Santa Cruz, Sucre and Tarija also stage massive fiestas.

Easter Semana Santa is celebrated with religious processions throughout Bolivia. Good Friday is a public holiday.

May 1 Labour Day.

May/June Corpus Christi. La Paz stages the Señor del Gran Poder, its biggest and most colourful folkloric dance parade.

June 21 Aymara New Year (*Año Nuevo* or *Inti Raymi*). Crowds flock to the Tiwanaku ruins for a colourful ceremony of thanks to the sun and Pachamama (mother earth).

July 16 Virgen del Carmen. Processions and dances in honour of the Virgen del Carmen, the patron saint of many towns and villages across Bolivia.

August 6 Independence Day (*Día de la Patria*). Parades and parties throughout the country, notably in Copacabana.

November 1–2 All Saints (*Día de Todos Santos*) and Day of the Dead (*Día de los Muertos*).

December 25 Christmas Day (*Navidad*).

through from 8.30am to 4pm without closing for lunch.

Bank opening hours are generally Monday to Friday from 8.30am to noon and 2.30pm to 6pm; some branches are also open on Saturdays from 9am until noon. ENTEL **telephone** offices usually open daily from around 8am to 8pm, sometimes later.

Bolivians welcome any excuse for a party, and the country enjoys a huge number of national, regional and local **fiestas**, often involving lengthy preparation and substantial expense.

La Paz

Few cities have a setting as spectacular as **LA PAZ**, founded in 1548 as La Ciudad de Nuestra Señora de la Paz – the City of Our Lady of Peace – and now the political and commercial hub of Bolivia. Home to more than a million people, and sited at over 3500m above sea level, the sprawling city lies in a narrow, bowl-like canyon, its centre cradling a cluster of church spires and office blocks themselves dwarfed by the magnificent icebound peak of **Mount Illimani** rising imperiously to the southeast. On either side, the steep slopes of the valley are covered by the ramshackle homes of the city's poorer inhabitants, which cling precariously to even the harshest gradients. From the lip of the canyon, the satellite city of **El Alto** sprawls in all directions across the Altiplano, a dirt-poor yet dynamic locus of urban Aymara culture and protest. The fact that its grid-locked main streets control access to La Paz below has often been exploited by the Aymara in recent years, with roadblocks used for political leverage.

What to see and do

There are still some fine colonial palaces and churches in the centre, with one of the main plazas, **San Francisco**, bisected by the frantic thoroughfare of Av. Mariscal Santa Cruz and its continuation, Av. 16 de Julio, collectively known as **El Prado**. While tiny, congested pavements and nose-to-tail traffic often present a challenge just to stay on your feet, most visitors are nevertheless enthralled by the energy of La Paz's **street life** and the blazing colour of its indigenous population; once you're used to it, it's easier to explore what is really a very compact city. Though in general the architecture is rather drab and functional, and most

of the surviving colonial buildings are in a poor state of repair, their crumbling facades and dilapidated balconies obscured by tangled phone lines and electric cables, there's at least one street, **Calle Jaén**, where you can get a sense of how La Paz used to look. Many of the city's museums are also conveniently situated here. To the west of the Prado, lung-busting lanes sweep up to the travellers' enclave of **Calle Sagárnaga** and the Aymara bustle of **Mercado Buenos Aires** beyond. To the south lies the wealthy suburb of **Sopocachi**, the preserve of the city's nightlife and eating scenes. Whatever direction you head in, the far horizon is ever dominated by the majestic, snow-covered, 6439-metre peak of Illimani.

Plaza Murillo

Though it remains the epicentre of Bolivia's political life, the Plaza Murillo – the main square of the colonial city centre – has an endearingly provincial feel, busy with people feeding pigeons and eating ice cream in the shade.

On the south side of the plaza stand two great symbols of political and spiritual power in Bolivia, the **Catedral** (daylight hours; free) – which, with its rather plain facade and relatively unadorned interior is fairly unremarkable – and the **Palacio Presidencial** (Presidential Palace; closed to public), with its yellow facade, thin, elegant columns and ceremonial guards in red nineteenth-century uniforms. On the east side of the plaza is the **Palacio Legislativo**, the seat of the Bolivian parliament, built in a similar Neoclassical style in the early twentieth century.

On the southwest corner of the plaza on Calle Socabaya, the Palacio de Los Condes de Arana, one of La Paz's finest surviving colonial palaces, houses the **Museo Nacional de Arte** (Tues–Sat 9.30am–12.30pm & 3–7pm, Sun 9.30am–12.30pm; B$10). The palace itself is a magnificent example of Baroque architecture, with a grand portico opening onto a central patio overlooked by three floors of arched walkways, all elaborately carved from pink granite in a rococo style with stylized shells, flowers and feathers. The museum's art collection, meanwhile, is centred firmly on colonial religious art, featuring several works by the great master of Andean colonial painting, Melchor Pérez de Holguín, as well as by contemporary Bolivian artists.

Calle Ingavi

A block northeast from Plaza Murillo along Calle Ingavi on the corner with Yanacocha, the **Iglesia Santo Domingo** (daylight hours; free) has a richly detailed eighteenth-century facade carved from soft white stone in Mestizo-Baroque style, exemplifying the combination of Spanish and indigenous symbolism characteristic of Andean colonial architecture.

A little further down Calle Ingavi is the small but rewarding **Museo de Etnografía y Folklore** (Mon–Sat 9am–noon & 3–7pm, Sun 9am–12.30; B$15), housed in an elegant seventeenth-century mansion, with a variety of costumes and artefacts representing three of Bolivia's most distinctive indigenous cultures: the **Aymara** culture, formed of thirty ethnic groups in the Cordillera Oriental; the **Uru-Chipayas**, who subsist in the Altiplano around Oruro; and the Quechua-speaking **Tarabuqueños** from the highlands east of Sucre.

Calle Jaén and its museums

A short walk uphill from Calle Ingavi on Calle Gerardo Sanjinez and then left along Calle Indaburo brings you to the foot of Calle Jaén, the best preserved colonial street in La Paz and home to no fewer than four municipal museums (all Tues–Fri 9.30am–12.30pm & 3–7pm, Sat & Sun 9am–1pm) all accessed on a single B$4 ticket, sold at the **Museo Costumbrista Juan de Vargas** at the top of the street (the entrance is just around the corner on Calle Sucre). Set inside a renovated colonial mansion, this museum gives a good introduction to the folkloric customs of the Altiplano and history of La Paz. Housed in the same building but accessed from Calle Jaén, the **Museo Litoral** (closed for renovation at the time of writing) is dedicated to one of Bolivia's national obsessions: the loss of its coastline to Chile during the nineteenth-century War of the Pacific (see p.173). Next door, the **Museo de Metales Preciosos**, also known as the Museo del Oro, has a small but impressive hoard of Inca and Tiwanaku gold ornaments, housed in a steel vault, and informative displays explaining the techniques used by pre-Columbian goldsmiths. On the other side of the road, inside the sumptuous mansion which was once the home of the venerated independence martyr after whom it's now named, the **Museo Casa Murillo** houses an eclectic collection, ranging from colonial religious art and portraits of former presidents to artefacts used in Kallawaya herbal medicine.

Set around yet another pretty colonial courtyard a little further down Calle Jaén, the delightful, independently owned **Museo de Instrumentos Musicales** (daily 9.30am–1pm & 2.30–6.30pm; B$5) features an astonishing variety of handmade musical instruments from all over Bolivia, including the indigenous *charangos*, some of which you can pick up and play.

Plaza San Francisco

Though the frenetic traffic running alongside detracts from its charm, the **Plaza San Francisco** is the focal point for the city's Aymara population. It is one of the liveliest plazas in La Paz, busy with people enjoying snacks and juices or crowding around the many

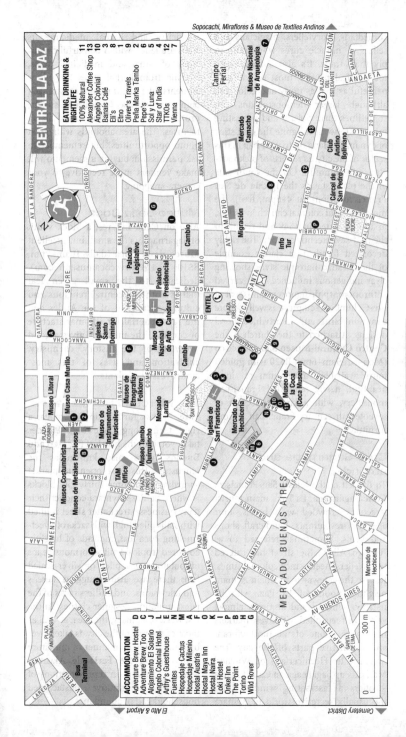

CENTRAL LA PAZ

EATING, DRINKING & NIGHTLIFE
100% Natural 11
Alexander Coffee Shop 13
Angelo Colonial 10
Banais Café 3
Eli's 8
Etno 1
Oliver's Travels 9
Peña Marka Tambo 2
Pepe's 6
Sol y Luna 5
Star of India 4
TTKOs 12
Vienna 7

ACCOMMODATION
Adventure Brew Hostel D
Adventure Brew Too C
Alojamiento El Solario J
Angelo Colonial Hotel L
Arthy's Guesthouse E
Fuentes M
Hospedaje Cactus A
Hospedaje Milenio F
Hostal Austria O
Hostal Maya Inn K
Hostal Naira I
Loki Hostel P
Onkel Inn B
The Point H
Torino G
Wild Rover

Mercado de Hechicería

300 m

comedians, storytellers, magicians and sellers of miracle cures who come to ply their trade. It's also a focal point for political protest, most of which is peaceful as well as noisy and colourful, although larger demonstrations can sometimes turn violent, and protesting miners are wont to ignite the odd stick of dynamite. Hang on to your bag in this sector of the city, as reports of pickpocketing are common. On the south side of the plaza stands the **Iglesia de San Francisco** (Mon–Sat 4–6pm; free), the most beautiful colonial church in La Paz, first constructed in 1549 and rebuilt in the mid-seventeenth century. The richly decorated facade is a classic example of the Mestizo-Baroque style, showing clear indigenous influence, with carved anthropomorphic figures reminiscent of pre-Columbian sculpture as well as more common birds and intertwined floral designs. Attached to the church is the **Centro Cultural-Museo San Francisco** (Mon–Sat 9am–6pm; B$20 with guided tours available), a museum set in a beautiful, newly renovated Franciscan monastery, with a large collection of seventeenth-century Franciscan art and furniture.

Calle Sagárnaga and around

To the left of the Iglesia San Francisco, **Calle Sagárnaga**, La Paz's main tourist street, is crowded with hotels, tour agencies, restaurants, handicraft shops and stalls. Sometimes referred to as "Gringo Alley", the street has catered to travellers' needs since colonial times. It's also the gateway to the main Aymara neighbourhoods of La Paz, with its narrow, winding and at times almost vertical streets filled with lively markets that make it one of the most vibrant and distinctive parts of the city. The Mercado de Hechicería – or Witches' Market – up Sagárnaga on Calle Linares – offers a fascinating window onto the usually secretive world of Aymara

mysticism and herbal medicine. Its stalls are laden with a colourful cornucopia of ritual and medicinal items, ranging from herbal cures for minor ailments like rheumatism or stomach pain to incense, coloured sweets, protective talismans and dried llama foetuses. The area abounds with great photo opportunities, but remember to ask permission; buying a memento will make vendors more receptive to your camera-snapping.

Museo de la Coca

Also on Calle Linares, a block south of Sagárnaga, is the small but excellent **Museo de la Coca** (daily 10am–7pm; B$10; ⓦwww.cocamuseum.com), dedicated to the small green leaf that is both the central religious and cultural sacrament of the Andes and the raw material for the manufacture of cocaine. The museum gives a good overview of the history, chemistry, cultivation and uses of this most controversial of plants.

The Mercado Buenos Aires

Three blocks further up Sagárnaga, a right turn along Calle Max Paredes takes you into the heart of the **Mercado Buenos Aires**, also known as the Huyustus. This vast open-air market sprawling over some thirty city blocks is where La Paz's Aymara conduct their daily business; street after street is lined with stalls piled high with sacks of sweet-smelling coca leaf, mounds of brightly coloured tropical fruit, enormous heaps of potatoes and piles of silver-scaled fish; there are also smuggled stereos and televisions, and endless racks of the latest imitation designer clothes. In the last week of January, the area, as well as most of the rest of the city, is taken over by stalls selling all manner of miniature items during the **Feria de Alasitas**, which is centred on representations of Ekeko, the diminutive mustachioed household god of abundance.

Museo Tambo Quirquincho

Just northwest of Plaza San Francisco, **Plaza Alonso de Mendoza** is a pleasant square named after La Paz's founder, whose statue stands at its centre. On the southern side of the square on Calle Evaristo Valle, the **Museo Tambo Quirquincho** (Tues–Fri 9.30am–12.30pm & 3–7pm, Sat & Sun 10am–1pm; B$5) is one of the most varied and interesting in La Paz, its collection focusing on the city's culture and history, with exhibits including an extensive collection of grotesque yet beautiful folkloric masks, several rooms full of quaint old photos of La Paz, and a room dedicated to the city's quintessential icon, the **chola**. This is the vernacular term for the ubiquitous Aymara women dressed in voluminous skirts and bowler hats who dominate much of the day-to-day business in the city's endless markets.

Plaza Sucre and the San Pedro Prison

Two blocks southwest of the Prado along Calle Colombia, **Plaza Sucre** lies at the centre of San Pedro, one of the city's oldest suburbs. Also known as the **Plaza San Pedro**, the square's tranquil and well-tended gardens surround a statue of Bolivia's first president, and are popular with portrait photographers with ancient box cameras. On the southeast side of the square rises the formidable bulk of the **Cárcel de San Pedro**, one of La Paz's most infamous attractions. A prison with no guards, San Pedro is essentially controlled by the prisoners, who work to pay for cells: those with money can live quite well in luxurious accommodation complete with mobile phones and satellite television, while those without any income sleep in the corridors and struggle to survive on the meagre official rations.

CYCLING THE DEATH ROAD

One of the most popular trips in Bolivia, and some travellers' sole reason for crossing the border, is a chance to hurtle down the infamous Death Road. This exhilarating 3500 metre descent along the old road from La Paz to Coroico, in the north Yungas, attracts thousands of adrenalin junkies each year, and is easy to organize as a day-trip from La Paz. Though a bypass means that this rough, narrow track chiselled out of near-vertical mountainsides is not as dangerous as it once was, be under no illusions: cyclists have been killed or seriously injured on this route in the recent past, and you should choose a tour operator with care. As well as this option, there are many other excellent (and quieter) mountain-biking alternatives if you want to get off the beaten track. Recommended La Paz operators are:

Downhill Madness Sagárnaga 339 ☎02/239-1810; also Av. 16 de Julio 1490 ☎02/231-8375, ⓦwww.madness-bolivia.com. A recommended agency for cycling the "world's most dangerous road", with top-of-the-range Rocky Mountain bikes, a good safety record and English-speaking guides.

Gravity Assisted Mountain Biking Ground-floor office 10, Edificio Avenida, Av. 16 de Julio 1490 ☎02/231-3849, ⓦwww.gravitybolivia.com. The original and possibly still the best downhill mountain-biking operator, offering daily trips to Coroico or the Zongo Valley with excellent US-made bikes and experienced,

enthusiastic English-speaking guides. Also offers a range of single-track options for more experienced bikers.

Zzip – The Flying Fox ☎02/231-3849, ⓦwww.ziplinebolivia.com. If the road itself wasn't terrifying enough, anyone wanting to add an extra challenge to their Death Road trip might consider an additional leap of faith onto 1555 metres of zip lines where you can reach speeds of up to 85kmph as you fly over coca fields in the valley below. Reservations can be made online, or with any of the operators listed on the website including Gravity Assisted Mountain Biking and Kanoo Tours.

The interior is like a microcosm of Bolivian society – there are shops, restaurants, billiard halls and even crèches, as the prisoners' families often live with them. Although San Pedro is officially closed to tourists, it is not usually difficult to enter by asking around at the plaza outside. People offering tours of the prison charge about B$400 (with a percentage being given to the prisoners), but be aware that it is illegal and potentially very dangerous to go inside.

Sopocachi, Miraflores and around

South of Plaza San Francisco, the busy, tree-lined Prado ends at the Plaza del Estudiante, to the south of which lies the relatively wealthy suburb of **Sopocachi**, home to some of the city's best restaurants and a lively nightlife centred around the parallel Avenidas 6 de Agosto and 20 de Octubre. Shortly before the Prado ends at Plaza del Estudiante, a left turn down the steps and two blocks along Calle Tiahuanaco brings you to the **Museo Nacional de Arqueología** (Mon–Fri 9.30am–12.30pm & 3–6pm, Sat 10am–noon, Sun 10am–1pm; B$20; Ⓦ www.bolivian.com/arqueologia), also known as Museo Tiahuanaco. Set inside a bizarre neo-Tiwanaku building, it houses a reasonable collection of textiles, ceramics and stone sculptures from the Inca and Tiwanaku cultures, though the exhibits are poorly explained and in Spanish only.

The **Museo de Textiles Andinos**, Plaza Benito Juarez 488 (Mon–Sat 9.30am–noon & 3–6.30pm, Sun 10am–12.30pm; B$15) in the student suburb of Miraflores, northeast of the Prado, is a must-see for textile lovers. Set in a beautifully kept house, the museum has an interesting display of textiles from all over the Bolivian Andes. The museum's gift shop sells products made by Quechuan women, who receive ninety percent of the profits.

Arrival

Air International and domestic flights arrive at the small El Alto airport (flight information on ☎ 02/281-0240), on the rim of the Altiplano about 11km from La Paz and at over 4000m above sea level. The easiest way into town from here is by taxi; they wait right outside the terminal and the half-hour ride should cost about B$50. Also, Cotranstur run shuttle minibuses (*micros*) down into the city and the length of the Prado to Plaza Isabella La Católica (B$1–2 per person; every 10min). Internal flights with the military airline TAM arrive at the military airport (☎ 02/284-1884), alongside the commercial airport on Av. Juan Pablo II in El Alto. Taxis wait here for passengers, but there's no shuttle bus; to get down to La Paz by public transport you'll need to catch any *micro* heading west along Av. Juan Pablo II to La Ceja, the district on the edge of the Altiplano above La Paz, and change there.

Bus Buses from southern and eastern Bolivia and international buses arrive at the Terminal Terrestre on Plaza Antofagasta, about 1km northeast of Plaza San Francisco. From here, it's a short taxi ride or a twenty-minute walk down Av. Montes to the main accommodation areas in the city centre. Buses from Copacabana, Tiwanaku, Sorata and Charazani arrive in the cemetery district, high up on the west side of the city. Plenty of *micros* head down to the city centre from here, but it's a pretty chaotic part of town, so it's a good idea to take a taxi – be careful to choose an official one. Buses from Coroico and Chulumani in the Yungas, and from Rurrenabaque and the Beni, arrive in the Villa Fátima district, in the far northeast of the city. The different companies all have offices around the intersection of Av. de las Américas and Calle Yanacachi. Again, plenty of *micros* head down to the city centre from here, but a taxi is quicker and easier.

Information

Tourist information There's a small office (Mon–Fri 8.30am–noon & 2.30–7pm; Sat & Sun 9.30am–1pm ☎ 02/237-1044) on Plaza del Estudiante at the end of the Prado, which has plenty of information on La Paz and the surrounding area. The helpful staff usually includes one English speaker, and they sell good city and regional maps and offer flyers for most of the main tour agencies, which are the best places to go for information on the rest of the country. An InfoTur office, Av. Mariscal Santa Cruz with Columbia (Mon–Fri 8.30am–6pm, Sat & Sun 9am–1.30pm; ☎ 02/265-1778) also has limited information and basic maps.

City transport

Bus, micro and trufi There are two main forms of public transport in La Paz: city buses and privately owned minibuses, known as *micros*. Though quicker and more numerous than the big buses, *micros* can be incredibly cramped and their routes very confusing. The names of the *micros'* destinations are written on signs inside the windscreen and bellowed incessantly by the driver's assistants so it's usually enough to wait by any major intersection until you hear the name of your destination shouted out. Your third option is a *trufi* – basically a car operating as a *micro* with a maximum of four passengers and following fixed routes. *Trufis* charge a flat rate of about B$3 in the city centre, *micros* about B$1.30 and buses B$1.20–1.30.

Taxi Unlicensed taxis charge about B$4 per passenger for journeys anywhere in the centre of town – there are sometimes meters but it's best to agree on the fare at the beginning of the journey. The more reliable marked radio taxis charge about B$10–15 for anywhere in the city centre regardless of the number of passengers.

Accommodation

There's plenty of budget accommodation in La Paz, though things get busier and pricier in the peak tourist season from June to August. Most places to stay are in the city centre within a few blocks of Plaza San Francisco, close to or in the midst of the colourful market district and within walking distance of most of the city's main attractions.

Near the bus station

Adventure Brew Hostel Av. Montes 533 ☎02/246-1614, ⓦwww.theadventurebrewhostel.com. Housed in a refurbished five-storey building within walking distance of the bus station, this place has both dorms and private rooms; guests in both receive a free breakfast (pancakes and coffee) and internet access. The hostel is so popular, they've opened an annexe down the road, *Adventure Brew Too.* Advanced booking recommended. Dorms B$50–65, rooms B$174.

Arthy's Guesthouse Av. Montes 693 ☎02/228-1439, ⓦarthyshouse.tripod.com. Very pleasant hostel situated halfway between the bus station and Plaza San Francisco, and suitable for those looking for peace, quiet and comfort. Rooms are simple but decent, and there's a lovely lounge with cable TV, games and a fire for when it's particularly cold. No breakfast, but guests have use of a kitchen. Dorms B$140.

The Point Alto de la Alianza Street 693 ☎02/228-0679, ⓦwww.thepointhostels.com. Comfy beds, free breakfast, hammocks and a jacuzzi make for good value for money, but it's a shame the chill-out room is right above the bar, which can get noisy. Dorms B$35–50, rooms B$110–120.

Plaza Murillo and east of the Prado

Hospedaje Milenio Yanacocha 860 ☎02/228-1263, ⓔhospedajemilenio@hotmail.com. It's a bit of a climb to this hostel – it's three steep blocks up from Plaza Murillo – but for those looking for pleasant, quiet and excellent-value accommodation, it's worth the effort. Staff are friendly, rooms are comfortable and there's a communal area with cable TV and book exchange. Breakfast available (B$13). B$60.

Hostal Austria Yanacocha 531 ☎02/240-8540. Walk up the dark stairs from the street, and the hotel is on your left. It's a cosy place with clean but occasionally dark rooms, a kitchen, internet facilities and a comfortable communal area with sofas and cable TV. B$70–90.

Loki Hostel Loayza 420 ☎02/211-9042, ⓦwww.lokihostel.com. Housed in a huge colonial mansion, facilities at this place are good – decent mattresses, free breakfast, atmospheric bar and a roof terrace. It's a great place to meet other travellers, and it organizes wild party nights. Online booking available. Dorms B$40–55, rooms B$130–150.

Torino Socabaya 457 ☎02/240-6003. This hotel's simple rooms are often empty, but it's cheap and central (just off Plaza Murillo), showers are hot and rooms are set around an elegant colonial courtyard (the restaurant in the courtyard can get rather noisy, however). The reception area has cable TV, a chess game or two and a small book exchange. B$140.

Wild Rover Comercio 1476 ☎02/211-6903, ⓦwww.wildroverhostel.com. A very popular backpacker option, this place is an established party hostel – but with quieter corners. It has a comfy TV room and a decent bar with pool tables, serving food for the homesick all day, including shepherd's pie and fry-ups at about B$30. Staff speak English and there's free internet and breakfast. Dorms B$40–56, rooms B$140–150.

Calle Sagárnaga and west of the Prado

Alojamiento El Solario Murillo 776 ☎02/236-7963, ⓔelsolariohotel@yahoo.com. Popular budget option, close to Plaza San Francisco, with welcoming staff and a friendly atmosphere.

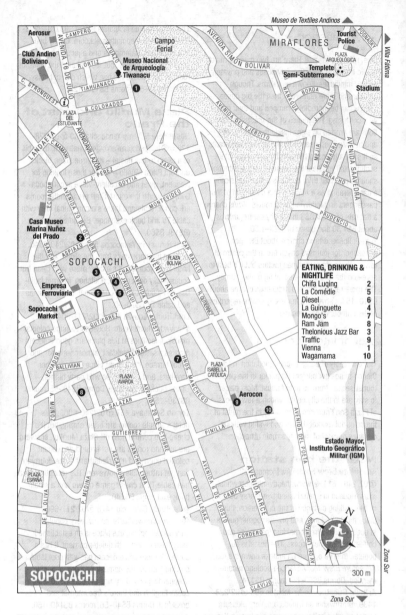

Aerosur
CAMPERO
Campo
Ferial
MIRAFLORES

AVENIDA SIMON BOLIVAR

Tourist
Police

POSNASKY

Villa Fátima ▶

Club Andino
Boliviano

R. ORTIZ

PZ.PUERTO

AVENIDA 16 DE JULIO

Museo Nacional
de Arqueología
Tiwanacu

TIHUANACO

PLAZA
ARQUEOLÓGICA

Templete
Semi-Subterraneo

BORDA

NANAUA

Stadium

C. STRONGUES

B. COLORADOS

❶

AVENIDA DEL EJERCITO

J. M. LOZA

PLAZA
DEL
ESTUDIANTE

LANDAETA

C. MAMANI

AVENIDA VILLAZON

ECUADOR

ZAPATA

J. J. PEREZ

GOYTIA

MEJIA

SARACHO

GAMARRA

AVENIDA SAAVEDRA

AVENIDA 20 DE OCTUBRE

MONTEVIDEO

Casa Museo
Marina Nuñez
del Prado

ASPIAZU

❷

PRUDENCIO

SANCHEZ LIMA

SOPOCACHI

PLAZA
BOLIVIA

CAP. RAVELO

Empresa
Ferroviaria

❸

GUACHALLA

❹

JAUREGUI

AVENIDA ARCE

AVENIDA 6 DE AGOSTO

❺

❻

F. GUTIERREZ

Sopocachi
Market

QUITO

ECUADOR

R. GUTIERREZ

ZUAZO Y

BALLIVIAN

PLAZA
AVAROA

B. SALINAS

❼

PLAZA
ISABEL LA
CATÓLICA

HNOS. MANCHEGO

❽

P. SALAZAR

Aerocon

❾

❿

AVENIDA DEL POETA

GUTIERREZ

PINILLA

ASCARRUNZ

SANCHEZ LIMA

AVENIDA 6 DE OCTUBRE

Estado Mayor,
Instituto Geográfico
Militar (IGM)

PLAZA
ESPAÑA

DE LA OLIVA

P. MEDINA

C. DE VILLEGAS

C. DE CAMPOS

AVENIDA ARCE

CORDERO

N

CLAVIJO

SOPOCACHI

0   300 m

Zona Sur ▶

EATING, DRINKING & NIGHTLIFE

Chifa Luqing	2
La Comédie	5
Diesel	6
La Guinguette	4
Mongo's	7
Ram Jam	8
Thelonious Jazz Bar	3
Traffic	9
Vienna	1
Wagamama	10

There's a kitchen, communal area and free internet available. It's basic but clean and comfortable. Dorms B$20–25, rooms B$60.

Angelo Colonial Hotel Av. Mariscal Santa Cruz 1058 ☎02/212-5067, ✉turismoangelo@yahoo .com. Good, very central option, with friendly staff and clean rooms, each with shared bath and

kitchen facilities. Rooms at the front are lighter and have balconies, but overlook the noisy Prado. Internet access available. Rooms B$170.

Fuentes Linares 988 ☎02/233-4145, ⊛www .hotelfuentesbolivia.com. Unlike so many hotels, *Fuentes* delivers on the promise its plush exterior. For the price (24hr hot water, free internet and continental breakfast are included), you'll struggle to find as neat, bright and comfortable a stack of rooms anywhere in La Paz. B$170.

Hospedaje Cactus Jiminez 818 ☎02/245-1421, ©hostal_cactus@hotmail.com. Popular with backpackers, this hostel is a basic but friendly and good-value place, with a good location on a quiet road just off the main tourist street. Guests can make use of a kitchen, small terrace, book exchange and internet (not included). B$56–60.

Hostal Maya Inn Sagárnaga 339 ☎02/231-1970, ©mayahost_in@hotmail.com. Large, very central place with decent, clean rooms (some are dark; ask for one with an outside window). Continental breakfast is included. Rooms with private bath come with cable TV. There's also internet (not included) and laundry facilities. B$105.

Onkel Inn Calle Columbia 257 ☎02/249-0456, 🌐www.onkel-inn-highlanders.com. This HI-affiliated hostel is in an excellent location with TV room, jacuzzi and free internet – though guests have reported that showers are not always hot. Basic breakfast included. Dorms B$60, rooms B$250.

Eating

La Paz has an excellent range of restaurants, cafés and street stalls to suit pretty much all tastes and budgets – from traditional eateries that dish up local meat-based delicacies to the more exotic ethnic restaurants and tourist-orientated spots with international menus. For those whose stomachs have adjusted to basic local food, the cheapest places to eat are the city's markets, where you can get entire meals for less than B$10. Street food is another good low-cost option: the ubiquitous *salteñas* and *tucumanes* (B$2–3) – delicious pastries filled with meat or chicken with vegetables – make excellent mid-morning snacks, especially if

washed down by the freshly squeezed orange and grapefruit juice which is sold from wheeled stalls all over the city.

Cafés

100% Natural Sagárnaga 345. Largely vegetarian health-food joint, big on fruit juices, soya and the like. Juices B$7–8. Daily from 8am.

Alexander Coffee Shop Av. 16 de Julio 1832, C Potosí 1091, C Montenegro in Zona Sur and El Alto airport. Very fashionable but expensive chain café where you can rub shoulders with the Bolivian elite; several locations in the city, serving extremely good coffee and fantastic cakes. Iced coffee B$21. Daily 9am–1am.

Banais Café Sagárnaga 161. Adjacent to *Hostal Naira* (see above), this pleasant café lacks something in atmosphere but has heavenly breakfasts, with huge bowls of muesli, cereal and fruit, as well as decent crêpes, salads and sandwiches. Smoothie B$12. Daily 7am–10pm.

Pepe's Jimenez 894, just off Linares between Sagárnaga and Santa Cruz. Friendly little place with colourful decor and a winning menu of sandwiches, omelettes, crêpes and great organic coffee. Box lunches also available. Burger B$22. Often closed Sun.

Restaurants

Angelo Colonial Linares 922, just off Sagárnaga. Popular, characterful hangout set around a colonial courtyard and imaginatively decorated with all manner of antiques. Food can be hit and miss, but it's a lovely place to have a meal, especially in the evenings when there's a cosy, romantic feel. Llama steak B$43.

Chifa Luqing 20 de Octubre with Aspiazu. Excellent Chinese food in a wonderful colonial setting. Free delivery service Mon–Sat (☎02/242-4188).

La Comédie Pasaje Medinacelli 2234 ☎02/242-3561. Beautifully decorated French restaurant with excellent dishes, including steaks, carpaccio and pasta. Highly recommended. Grilled trout B$48. Mon–Fri from noon, Sat & Sun from 7pm.

Eli's Av. 16 de Julio with Bueno. Cosy, 1950s-style film-themed corner bistro in business since 1942, with a great selection of cakes and pastries and an extensive good-value menu of delicious American staples such as burgers and Philly cheese steaks. Cheeseburger B$16.50.

Oliver's Travels Murillo 1014. Uncharismatic gringo pub often filled with beered-up expats, with saving graces of sofas, big-screen TVs, and comfort food (think bangers and mash, pies and pints of tea). Service can be slow. Big fry-up B$40. Daily 10am till late.

La Guinguette Fernando Guachalla with 20 de Octubre, Sopocachi. This charming Parisian-style bistro offers excellent cuisine and professional service, and is the perfect place to while away an evening or afternoon if you're yearning for a touch of sophisticated dining that doesn't completely blow the budget. Mains B$35–50. Mon–Sat 10am until late, closed Sun.

Star of India Calle Cochabamba 170 ☏ 02/211-4409. Frequently recommended as a good curry spot, with excellent curry-based *almuerzos* (B$30). Delivery service available. Mon–Sat from 9am, Sun from 4pm.

Vienna Zuazo 1905 ☏ 02/244-1660. Impressive restaurant boasting exquisite Austrian cuisine and immaculate service, but still surprisingly good value with simpler dishes from B$16. Lemon chicken B$36. Closed Sat.

Wagamama Pasaje Pinilla 2557, just off Av. Arce ☏ 02/243-4911. Upmarket and authentic Japanese restaurant with a varied menu including sublime sushi and sashimi; it's not particularly cheap, however. Mains B$35–50. Closed Mon.

Drinking, nightlife and entertainment

La Paz is generally fairly quiet on weekday evenings, but explodes into life on Friday nights when much of the city's male population goes out drinking. In the city centre – and above all in the market district along Max Paredes and Av. Buenos Aires – there are countless rough and ready *whiskerías* and karaoke bars. Going out to one of these bars is certainly a very authentic Bolivian experience, but is best avoided for women unless part of a mixed group.

With one or two exceptions, the more cosmopolitan nightspots are concentrated in the suburb of Sopocachi, running the gamut from live jazz to raucous travellers' hangouts. And although La Paz's club scene isn't what it was, you can still find a busy dancefloor heaving to just about any kind of music. For more traditional entertainment, head to one of the folk music venues known as *peñas*, where – with varying degrees of authenticity – you can witness age-old Andean music and dance.

Bars and nightclubs

Diesel Av. 20 de Octubre with Rosendo Gutiérrez. Industrial-chic bar with an extraordinary post-apocalyptic design, complete with aircraft engines hanging from the ceiling and bathrooms straight out of a science-fiction movie. Mon–Sat from 7pm.

Etno Jaén 722. Arty bar/café tucked away in La Paz's most charming street, with dimly lit wooden tables, good coffee and a relaxed vibe. Mojito B$20. Mon–Sat 10am till late.

Mongo's Hermanos Manchego 2444. The original gringo rendezvous, and some still say the best, where televised sports and decent food give way to serious drinking, live music and raucous dancing as the evening wears on. Packed out on weekends. Daily 7pm till the wee hours.

Ram Jam Calle Presbitero Medina 2421. Spacious and hugely popular bar/club with a discreet layout and an anything-goes music policy. Also serves good food, including some of La Paz's best curries. Daily 6.30pm until late.

Sol y Luna Cochabamba with Murillo. Snug bar-café serving strong coffee and cold beer in a mellow, candlelit atmosphere. There's live music at night, pool tables, a book exchange and typical Dutch dishes. Daily 9am–1am.

Thelonious Jazz Bar Av. 20 de Octubre 2172. The best jazz bar in town, with an intimate basement atmosphere and live music Tues–Sat. B$25 cover charge. Closed Sun and Mon.

Traffic Av. Arce 2549. Long-established crowd-puller with international DJs and live music, as well as the usual range of cocktails and beers.

TTKOs Calle Mexico 1555. One of the better bars nearer the centre, this basement is an unpretentious hangout for foreigners and locals alike. Often hosts live music. Entry B$10.

Cinemas and peñas

Cine Center Zona Sur Av. Rafael Pabón ☏ 900/770 077, ⊛ www.cinecenter.com.bo. A smart 18-screen complex with shops, restaurants and a bowling alley. Tickets from B$25.

Cine Monje Campero Corner of Av. 16 de Julio and Calle Bueno ☏ 02/233-3332. The most comfortable big-screen cinema in central La Paz, with afternoon and evening showings.

Cine Municipal 6 de Agosto Av. 6 de Agosto 2284 ☏ 02/244-2629. Wonderful old Art Deco cinema bypassing Hollywood for a more engaging programme of Latin American and European film.

Peña Marka Tambo Jaén 710 ☏ 02/228-0041. Hosts perhaps the most authentic traditional music and dance show in La Paz from an ideal setting in an old colonial mansion. Has one of the best-value cover charges in town at B$30. The food, however, is mediocre. Shows start at 10pm.

Directory

Banks and exchange There are plenty of banks with ATMs in the centre of town, especially on Av. Camacho, and a growing number of freestanding ATMs with withdrawals in US$ and B$. The best places to change cash and traveller's cheques include Money Exchange International, Mercado 990 with Yanacocha (Mon–Fri 8.30am–12.30pm & 2.30–7pm, Sat 9am–12.30pm) and Casa de Cambios, Colon 330 between Mercado and Potosí (Mon–Fri 9.30am–noon & 2.30–4.30pm).

Car rental American, Av. Camacho 1574 ℡02/220-2933; Barbol Rent a Car, Héroes de Km 7777, opposite El Alto airport ℡02/282-0675, ⓦwww.barbolsrl.com); Localiza, at *Hotel Radisson*, Av. Arce 2177, ℡02/244-1111.

Embassies and consulates Argentina, Aspiazu 497 ℡02/241-7737; Australia, Aspiazu 416 ℡02/211-5655; Brazil, Edificio Multicentro, Av. Arce ℡02/244-0202; Canada, Plaza España with Sanjinez ℡02/241-5021; Colombia, Calle 9, Calacoto 7835 ℡02/278-4491; Chile, Calle 14, Calacoto 8024 ℡02/279-7331; Ecuador, Edificio Hermann, Av. 16 de Julio 1440 ℡02/231-9739; Paraguay, Edificio Illimani, Av. 6 de Agosto ℡02/243-3176; Peru, Edificio Alianza, Av. 6 de Agosto 2190 ℡02/244-0631; UK, Av. Arce 2732 ℡02/243-3424; USA, Av. Arce 2780 ℡02/216-8222; Venezuela, Av. Arce 2678 ℡02/243-2023.

Immigration The *migración* office is on Av. Camacho 1468, ℡02/211-0960 (Mon–Fri 8.30am–4pm), for tourist visa extensions and information.

Internet access There are internet cafés all over the city; most charge about B$2–4 an hour. Try Punto Entel, Potosí 1110 (Mon–Sat 8am–9.30pm); MicroNet, Av. Mariscal Santa Cruz 1088, Ed. Sagrados (Mon–Fri 9am–9pm); *Banaís Café*, Sagárnaga 161 (daily 7am–10pm).

Outdoor equipment There are a number of shops around Sagárnaga selling clothing and equipment for trekking and climbing. The best option is Tatoo at Calle Illampu 828, ℡02/245-1265.

Police Edificio Olimpio, Plaza Tejada Sorzano, opposite the stadium in Miraflores (daily 24hr; ℡02/222-5016). This is the place to report thefts for insurance claims.

Post office Correo Central, Av. Mariscal Santa Cruz with Oruro (Mon–Fri 8am–8pm, Sat 8am–6pm, Sun 9am–noon).

Shopping With its many markets, La Paz is a great place for shopping, with a wide range of *artesanía* (handicrafts) on sale from all over the country. You'll find dozens of shops and stalls along Calle Sagárnaga and the surrounding streets selling traditional textiles, leather items, silver jewellery and talismans. Beware that most fossils sold on this street are fake.

Telephone centres The main ENTEL office is at Ayacucho 267, just below Mercado (daily 7am–midnight). There are phone booths all over the city which accept cards; these can be bought at any kiosk or small store. The cheapest option is always an internet call – and many internet cafés in central La Paz will have Skype.

Moving on

Air International and domestic flights depart from the small El Alto airport (℡02/281-0122), up on the Altiplano, 11km or so from the centre of town. Taxis should cost around B$50, depending on how bad the traffic is. Alternatively, take one of the *micros* – marked "aeropuerto" – that run up and down the Prado. TAM flights leave from the nearby military airport (℡02/284-1884). Between them, TAM, Aerosur (ⓦwww.aerosur.com) and Amaszonas (ⓦwww.amaszonas.com) cover most destinations with at least one or two flights daily.

Bus Most long-distance buses depart from the Terminal Terrestre on Plaza Antofogasta, about 1km northwest of Plaza San Francisco (℡02/228-5858), while buses and *micros* for the Lake Titicaca region and the north leave from the Cemetery District high up on the northwest slopes of the city. *Micros* race up here constantly from Plaza San Francisco; look for those marked "Cementerio". Buses for the Yungas and northern Amazon region leave from the Villa Fátima district high up on the northeast side of the city; regular *micros* marked "Villa Fátima" ply Av. 6 de Agosto. Terminal Terrestre to: Cochabamba (hourly; 7hr 30min); Oruro (every 30min, with connections to Uyuni; 3hr 30min); Potosí (every evening, with connections to Sucre, Tarija & Tupiza; 11hr). There are also daily departures to international destinations – Arica (8hr); Buenos Aires (50hr); Cusco (12hr) and Lima (27hr). Cemetery District to: Copacabana (regular services throughout the day; 3hr 30min); Sorata (every 30min; 4hr). Villa Fátima to: Chulumani (hourly; 3hr 30min); Coroico (every 30min; 3hr); Rurrenabaque (daily; 18–25hr). Also weekly services to Cobija, Guayaramerín and Riberalta in the dry season.

TIWANAKU

The most worthwhile attraction within a few hours of La Paz is the mysterious ruined city of **TIWANAKU** (also spelled Tiahuanaco), set on the Altiplano 71km to the west. It's Bolivia's most impressive archeological site, and was declared a cultural patrimony site by UNESCO in 2000.

Founded some three millennia ago, Tiwanaku became the capital of a massive empire that lasted almost a thousand years, developing into a sophisticated urban-ceremonial complex that, at its peak, was home to some fifty thousand people. Tiwanaku remains a place of exceptional symbolic meaning for the Aymara of the Altiplano, who come here to make ceremonial offerings to the *achachilas*, the gods of the mountains. The most spectacular of these, the **Aymara New Year**, takes place each June 21 (the winter solstice), when hundreds of *yatiris* (traditional priests) congregate to watch the sun rise and celebrate with music, dancing, elaborate rituals and copious quantities of coca and alcohol.

Though the city of Tiwanaku originally covered several square kilometres, only a fraction of the site has been excavated, and the main ruins (daily 9am–4.30pm; B$80) occupy a fairly small area that can easily be visited in half a day. Two museums by the entrance house many of the smaller archeological finds, as well as several large stone monoliths. The main ruins cover the area that was once the ceremonial centre of the city, a jumble of tumbled pyramids and ruined palaces and temples made from megalithic stone blocks, many weighing over a hundred tons. It requires a leap of the imagination to visualize Tiwanaku as it was at its peak: a thriving city whose great pyramids and opulent palaces were painted in bright colours and inlaid with gold, surrounded by extensive residential areas built largely from mud brick (of which little now remains) and set amid lush green fields, rather than the harsh, arid landscape you see today.

Minibuses to Tiwanaku depart from the corner of Aliaga and Eyzaguirre in the cemetery district in La Paz (every 30min; 1hr 30min; B$20 return ticket); on the way back they leave from the square in Tiwanaku town. You can hire a guide outside the museum to show you around the ruins for a small fee, but if you want a guided tour – especially one in English – then you're far better off coming with an agency from La Paz (see box, p.181); most run one-day tours to the site for about B$70–90 (plus entrance fee) per person.

Lake Titicaca, Cordillera Real and the Yungas

The region immediately around La Paz is sometimes known as "Little Bolivia", because the variety of landscapes it encompasses can seem like a microcosm of the entire country. To the northwest lies the vast, high-altitude Lake Titicaca, with its idyllic islands, Isla del Sol and Isla de la Luna, and lakeside pilgrimage town of Copacabana. East of here is the Cordillera Real, the highest and most spectacular section of the Bolivian Andes, easily explored from La Paz, or else from the magical outpost of Sorata. Sweeping down from the Cordillera Real, the Yungas is a rugged region of forest-covered mountains, rushing rivers and fertile valleys, with the humid languor of Coroico at its heart.

LAKE TITICACA

Some 75km northwest of La Paz, **Lake Titicaca**, an immense, sapphire-blue lake, easily the largest high-altitude body of water in the world, sits astride the border with Peru at the northern end of the Altiplano. The area around the lake is the heartland of the Aymara, whose distinct language and culture

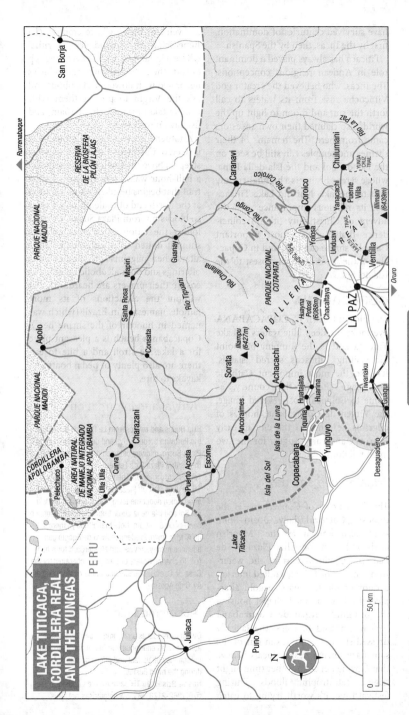

LAKE TITICACA, CORDILLERA REAL AND THE YUNGAS

San Borja

Rurrenabaque

RESERVA DE LA BIOSFERA PILÓN LAJAS

PARQUE NACIONAL MADIDI

Apolo

PARQUE NACIONAL MADIDI

CORDILLERA APOLOBAMBA

ÁREA NATURAL DE MANEJO INTEGRADO NACIONAL APOLOBAMBA

Pelechuco

Ulla Ulla

Cunva

Charazani

Puerto Acosta

Escoma

Caranavi

Río Coroico

Mapiri

Santa Rosa

Río Tipuani

Consata

Guanay

Río Challana

Coroico

Yanacachi

Puente Villa

Yolosa

Unduavi

YUNGA CRUZ TRAIL

Chulumani

Río Zongo

Illimani (6439m)

Ventilla

TAKESI TRAIL

CHORO TRAIL

PARQUE NACIONAL COTAPATA

Sorata

Illampu (6427m)

CORDILLERA REAL

Achacachi

Huayna Potosí (6088m)

Chacaltaya

LA PAZ

Ancoraimes

Huatajata

Huarina

Tiwanaku

Tiquina

Guaqui

Isla de la Luna

Yunguyo

Copacabana

Isla del Sol

Desaguadero

Oruro

Río La Paz

PERU

Lake Titicaca

Juliaca

Puno

N

0   50 km

have survived centuries of domination, first by the Incas, then by the Spanish.

Titicaca has always played a dominant role in Andean religious conceptions. The Incas, who believed the creator god Viracocha rose from its waters to call forth the sun and moon to light up the world, also claimed their own ancestors came from here. The remains of their shrines and temples can still be seen on the Isla del Sol and the Isla de la Luna, whose serene beauty is a highlight of any visit to the lake. Nor did Lake Titicaca lose its religious importance with the advent of Christianity: it's no coincidence that Bolivia's most important Catholic shrine can be found in Copacabana, the lakeside town closest to the Isla del Sol.

COPACABANA

The pleasant town of **COPACABANA** overlooks the deep blue waters of Lake Titicaca and is the jumping-off point for visiting Titicaca's sacred islands. It's also the most important Catholic pilgrimage site in the country, as home to Bolivia's most revered image, the Virgen de Copacabana; hordes of pilgrims descend on the city in early February and early August for the two main religious fiestas.

What to see and do

The focal point of Copacabana is the imposing **Catedral** (daily 7.30am–8pm; free), also known as the "Moorish Cathedral", set on the Plaza 2 de Febrero six blocks east of the waterfront. Inside the bright, vaulted interior, a door beside the massive gold altarpiece leads to a small chapel housing the beautiful **Virgen de Copacabana** herself. Encased in glass, the lavishly dressed statue is only taken out of the sanctuary during fiestas: locals believe that moving her at any other time might trigger catastrophic floods. During festival time, it's worth trying to catch

a "vehicle blessing" ceremony (La Benedición de Movilidades), a ritual where car and truck owners line up outside the cathedral with their vehicles decorated with flowers and ribbons and ask the Virgin to protect them. This usually takes place at about 10am, and usually on weekends.

Another interesting religious site is **Cerro Calvario**, the hill that rises steeply above the town to the north. It's a half-hour walk up to the top along a trail that begins beside the small church at the north end of Calle Bolívar, five or so blocks up from Plaza Sucre. The trail follows the stations of the cross up to the summit dotted with ramshackle stone altars where pilgrims light candles, burn offerings and pour alcoholic libations to ensure their prayers are heard. Though without the attractions of its more famous namesake in Brazil (which was named in honour of the shrine here), Copacabana's **beach** is a pleasant place for a lakeside stroll and a bite to eat; there are also plenty of pedal boats and kayaks to hire.

Arrival and information

Bus Buses and *micros* from La Paz and Kasani at the Peruvian border arrive and depart from just off Plaza Sucre, midway between the lakeshore and the central Plaza 2 de Febrero.

Tourist information The tourist office is on Av. 16 de Julio, just off Plaza Sucre. Helpful staff have information about the town and accessing the Isla del Sol and Isla de la Luna. English spoken. Mon–Fri 8am–noon & 2–6pm. Note that although there's no ATM in town, Prodem on Av. 6 de Agosto can advance money on Visa and MasterCard for a hefty fee. To change dollars or traveller's cheques, try the Casa de Cambio Copacabana at the eastern end of Av. 6 de Agosto.

Accommodation

Owing to its role as a pilgrimage centre, Copacabana has an enormous number of places to stay, though they fill up fast and prices double or triple during the main fiestas.

Hostal Brisas de Titicaca Av. 6 de Agosto ☎02/862-2178, ⓦ www.hotelbrisas.net. This

COPACABANA

ACCOMMODATION
La Cúpula	B
Hostal Brisas de Titicaca	D
Hostal Copacabana	F
Hostal Emperador	G
Hostal Las Olas	A
Hostal Leyenda	E
Hostal Sonia	H
Utama Hotel	C

EATING & DRINKING
La Cúpula	B
La Orilla	1
Pueblo El Viejo	2
Puerta del Sol	4
Restaurant Colonial	3
Restaurant Fawny	5

Kasani & Peru   Horca del Inca

HI hostel is right on the shore, and has internet, laundry facilities and good views of the lake. Some English spoken. B$80–100.

Hostal Copacabana Busch, near 16 de Julio, ☏02/862-2022. Clean, simple rooms around a charming courtyard with breakfast available (B$9). B$40–50.

Hostal Emperador Murillo 235 ☏02/862-2083. Good budget option, popular with backpackers, with clean, simple rooms (with or without bath) set around a bright courtyard. Staff are friendly and full of great tourist tips. There are kitchen and laundry facilities and breakfast is available. B$30–40.

Hostal Leyenda Av. Costanera with Busch ☏07/350-8898. The faux-Inca-ruin facade of the building is slightly absurd but the quirkily decorated rooms are pleasant, with quaint balconies overlooking the lake. Bathrooms are in need of some TLC. Basic breakfast included. B$140.

Hostal Sonia Murillo 256 ☏07/196-8441. Run by the same owners as the *Emperador*, this place is an equally good option, and as well as kitchen facilities there is a rooftop terrace with lovely views. B$50.

TREAT YOURSELF

La Cúpula Michel Pérez 1–3 ☏02/862-2029, ⓦwww .hotelcupula.com. Delightful hotel (and the nicest place to stay in Copacabana), built in neo-Moorish style on a hillside overlooking the town and lake. It offers light and airy rooms as well as spectacular lake views, a nice garden with hammocks, kitchen, laundry and a superb restaurant with dishes made to order. Breakfast is included and reservations are recommended. B$167–195.

Hostal Las Olas ☏02/862-2112, ⓦwww.hostallasolas.com. Or, a little further along Michel Pérez, opt instead for one of these lovingly decorated appartments with breathtaking views, kitchenettes and tranquil outdoor spaces. B$265.

Utama Hotel Michel Pérez with San Antonio
☎02/862-2013. Set around a brightly coloured
inner courtyard, this 25-bed hotel is very inviting,
and the owner is accommodating, offering a
constant supply of tea and fruit. Rooms have
private bathrooms and cable TV, and breakfast is
included. B$139.

Eating and drinking

There's no shortage of restaurants in Copacabana,
most catering to travellers and pilgrims, and some
doubling as bars and evening hangouts. There are
also a number of stalls along the waterfront selling
decent and cheap local *almuerzos*.

La Cúpula Inside the hotel of the same name on
Michel Pérez. Cosy restaurant overlooking the lake
and serving good breakfasts, fruits and salads
as well as tasty, veggie-friendly main courses
(B$25–40), served up in a bright room with views
over the lake; great packed lunches for island trips.
Closed Tues am.

La Orilla Av. 6 de Agosto. Mix of good fish dishes
and international cuisine, from Hershey pancakes
to imaginative *trucha* dishes. Daily 10.30am–2pm
& 5–9pm. Stuffed trout with spinach, bacon and
ginger B$30.

Pueblo El Viejo Av. 6 de Agosto. Dark, cosy café
with good coffee; a nice place to relax, and the
most popular gringo hangout in town. Mains
B$30–40. Open till late.

Puerta del Sol Av. 6 de Agosto and Bolívar. Good-
value local place with Bolivian and international
dishes. Also does boxed lunches. Closed Mon.

Restaurant Colonial Off Av. 6 de Agosto, near
corner with Av. 16 de Julio. Good range of *trucha*
dishes as well as Mexican and standard Bolivian
fare. Service can be painstakingly slow, but sat
in the pleasant courtyard, or airy restaurant, you
probably won't mind. Trout *a la diabla* B$35.

Restaurant Fawny Av. Busch, between 16 de Julio
and Bolívar. Go along a short alleyway to reach a
typical Bolivian eatery serving good, filling grub. Set
lunch menu B$8.

Moving on

Bus There are regular departures from Plaza Sucre
to both La Paz (3hr 30min) and Puno (4hr) as well
as daily departures to Cusco, generally via Puno
(10hr), Arequipa (9hr) and Lima (18hr). Note that
between Copacabana and La Paz, you will be asked
to get off the bus and pay a small fee to cross the
lake in a boat, while your bus is transported across
on a larger raft.

ISLA DEL SOL

Just off the northern tip of the Copacabana Peninsula about 12km northwest
of Copacabana, the **Isla del Sol** (Island
of the Sun) has been attracting pilgrims
and visitors for many hundreds of years.
Now a quiet backwater, the island was
one of the most important religious
sites in the Andean world in the
sixteenth century, revered as the place
where the sun and moon were created
and where the Inca dynasty was born.
Scattered with **enigmatic ancient ruins**
and populated by traditional Aymara
communities, Isla del Sol is an excellent
place to spend some time hiking and
contemplating the magnificent scenery.
Measuring 9.5km long and 6.5km across
at its widest point, the Isla del Sol is the
largest of the forty or so islands in Lake
Titicaca, with three main settlements –
Yumani, Ch'alla and Ch'allapampa. You
can visit the island (along with nearby
Isla de la Luna, see p.201) on a day- or
even half-day trip from Copacabana,
but it's really worth spending at least
one night on the island to fully appreciate its serene beauty.

What to see and do

The best way to see the Isla del Sol is
to walk the length of the island from
Yumani in the south to Ch'allapampa
in the north, or the other way round –
a four-hour hike. When you land, you
may be asked to pay a charge of B$5
to the island community. From the
lakeshore at **Yumani**, where most boats
dock, a functional Inca stairway, the
Escalera del Inca, runs steeply up to
the village through a natural amphitheatre covered by some of the finest Inca
agricultural terracing on the island,
irrigated by bubbling stone canals fed
by a natural spring believed to have
magic powers.

Two parallel paths – an inland
ridge-top one that provides great views
and another that runs along the island's

east coast – head from Yumani in the south to Cha'llapampa at the other end of the island. About an hour and a half north of Yumani on the coastal path you reach the quiet village of Ch'alla, which sits above a calm bay, and from where the path drops to **Playa Ch'alla**, a picturesque stretch of sand. About an hour's walk from Ch'alla is the island's northernmost settlement, **Ch'allapampa**, a pleasant and peaceful village founded by the Incas as a centre for the nearby ceremonial complexes. From here it's a forty-minute walk northwest along an easy-to-follow path to the **Chincana** (8am–6pm; small fee), the ruined Inca complex of rambling interlinked rooms, plazas and passageways built around the sacred rock where the creator god Viracocha is believed to have created the sun and moon.

Arrival and information

Boat Full- and half-day boat tours to the Isla del Sol leave every morning from the beach at the end of Av. 6 de Agosto in Copacabana – boats usually depart at around 8am for a full day (B$25 return ticket). Half-day tours to the south (B$15) will only give you a few hours on the island, and are only recommended if you are very pushed for time.

Accommodation

Yumani is home to the majority of the island's accommodation, most of which offers sporadic (and usually cold) water, and pretty basic conditions. There are also a couple of simple but friendly places to stay in Ch'allapampa. Hostel owners will be waiting to greet you when you get off the boat. Most places charge between B$20–30 per person per night for private rooms.

Hostal Arco Iris About 10min along the main path on the right, Yumani. Simple rooms, with comfortable beds in a homely setting. B$20–40.

Hostal Inca Pacha About 1km up the winding path, Yumani ☎07/198-0468. This HI-affiliated hostel is well organissed and offers a choice of private (B$70 with breakfast included) and shared bathrooms, plus a kitchen. B$50.

Hostal Inca Uta Near the northern landing jetty at Ch'allapampa ☎07/353-4990, ⓦwww .hostalincauta.web.bo. Large yellow building with basic rooms, friendly owners and limited electricity. B$25–30 per person.

Hostal Inti Wayra Near the church, Yumani ☎07/249-3508, ⓦwww.intiwayra.web.bo. A good choice, with excellent views and friendly owners. B$60.

Wiki Wata One of the first hostels on the path up from the beach, Yumani ☎07/127-4158, Ⓔwilkawata@hotmail.com. One of the nicest hostels on the south of the island with a charming patio looking out to the lake. Breakfast B$15–20. B$60.

Eating

Most of the hostels have basic restaurants serving pizza, pasta and freshly caught Titicaca trout upon request. There's also usually al fresco dockside catering to meet the incoming boats. However, prices across the board tend to be higher than on the mainland due to transport costs and the lack of running water.

ISLA DE LA LUNA

About 8km east of the Isla del Sol, the far smaller **Isla de la Luna** (Island of the Moon) was another important pre-Columbian religious site. For much

---

TOURS

There are numerous private boats and tour companies making the trip to the islands, including a number of upmarket packages from La Paz-based agencies. The below come recommended:

Crillon Tours Av. Camacho 1223, La Paz ☎02/233-7533 ⓦwww.titicaca.com. La Paz agency that runs a variety of pricey one- and two-day tours, with accommodation at their exclusive ecolodge on the Isla del Sol.

Transturin Av. Arce 2678, La Paz ☎02/242-2222, ⓦwww.transturin.com. Luxurious one- and two-day catamaran cruises to the Isla del Sol, including a night in the agency's hotel at Chúa on the southern end of the lake.

of the twentieth century, the island was used as a prison for political detainees, yet for the Incas it was a place of great spiritual importance. Known as Coati ("Queen Island"), it was associated with the moon, considered the female counterpart of the sun, and a powerful deity in her own right. The main site on the island – and one of the best-preserved Inca complexes in Bolivia – is a temple on the east coast known as **Iñak Uyu** (daily 8am–7pm; B$5), the "Court of Women", probably dedicated to the moon and staffed entirely by women. From the beach a series of broad Inca agricultural terraces lead up to the temple complex, a series of stone buildings with facades containing eleven massive external niches still covered in mud stucco, all around a broad central plaza.

It takes about an hour by boat from the Isla del Sol to reach the island, and some agencies will include a brief visit to Isla de la Luna with the Isla del Sol tour. If you want to stay longer, you can hire a private sail boat (for about B$80) or private motor boat (B$150), both including hire of a driver, from Isla del Sol to take you to the island and back. It's possible to camp on the island, but ask permission and bring your own food and drinking water; another alternative is the basic *hostal* next to the ruins which can put you up for approximately B$15 a night.

Moving on

Bus Regular buses leave Copacabana for La Paz from Plaza Sucre, while crossing into Peru from Copacabana is just as easy. *Micros* to the border at Kasani, fifteen minutes away, leave from Plaza Sucre every half an hour or so when full. At Kasani you can get your exit stamp at passport control (8am–9pm) then walk across to Peru, where *micros* and taxis wait for passengers to take them to Yunguyo, which has regular departures for Puno and on to Cusco. Alternatively you can catch one of the tourist *micros* which travel direct from Copacabana to Puno several times a day; these are run by all the companies with offices around Plaza Sucre and, at around B$30, cost just a little more than the public *micros*.

TREKKING AND CLIMBING IN THE CORDILLERA REAL

The easiest base from which to explore the Cordillera Real is La Paz. Many of the best and most popular treks start close to the city, including the three so-called "Inca trails" which cross the Cordillera, connecting the Altiplano with the warm, forested valleys of the Yungas. Two of these ancient paved routes – the Choro Trail and the Takesi Trail – are relatively easy to follow without a guide; the third, the Yunga Cruz Trail, is more difficult. You can do all three of these treks, as well as many other more challenging routes, with any of the adventure tour agencies based in La Paz (see box, p.181).

The other major starting point for trekking is the small town of Sorata. From here, numerous trekking routes take you high up among the glacial peaks, while others plunge down into the remote forested valleys of the Yungas. The Sorata Guides and Porters Association (see p.203) provides trekking guides, mules and porters. Further afield, the remote and beautiful Cordillera Apolobamba, a separate range of the Cordillera Oriental, north of Lake Titicaca and with almost no tourist infrastructure, offers excellent trekking possibilities for the more adventurous traveller. However, due to unpredictable weather conditions and the region's remoteness, it's unadvisable to attempt these treks without a guide.

With so many high peaks, the Cordillera Real is also obviously an excellent place for mountain climbing, for both serious and inexperienced climbers. Huayna Potosí (6090m), near La Paz, is one of the few peaks over 6000m in South America which can be ascended by climbers without mountaineering experience (albeit with the help of a specialist agency – you should check carefully that the guide they provide is qualified and experienced, and the equipment adequate).

Boat It is also possible to reach Peru by crossing the lake. The best way to do this is by the bus and catamaran tours from La Paz to Puno – or vice versa – with Transturin (see p.201).

THE CORDILLERA REAL

Stretching for about 160km along the northeastern edge of the Altiplano, the **Cordillera Real** – the "Royal Range" – is the loftiest and most dramatic section of the Cordillera Oriental in Bolivia, with six peaks over 6000m high and many more over 5000m forming a jagged wall of soaring, icebound peaks separating the Altiplano from the tropical lowlands of the Amazon Basin. Easily accessible from La Paz, the mountains are perfect for climbing and trekking (see box, p.202) – indeed, walking here is the only way to really appreciate the overwhelming splendour of the Andean landscape. Populated by isolated **Aymara communities** that cultivate the lower slopes and valleys and raise llamas and alpacas on the high pastures, the cordillera is a largely pristine natural environment. Here, the mighty **Andean condor** is still a common sight, pumas, though rarely seen, still prowl the upper reaches, and the elusive Andean spectacled bear roams the high cloud-forest that fringes the mountains' upper eastern slopes.

SORATA

Set at an altitude of 2695m, **SORATA** is a placid and enchanting little town, and is the most popular base for trekking and climbing in the Cordillera Real. Hemmed in on all sides by steep mountain slopes, often shrouded in clouds and with a significantly warmer climate than La Paz, it was compared by Spanish explorers to the Garden of Eden. There's not a lot to do in Sorata itself except hang out and relax while preparing for (or recovering from) some hard trekking or climbing, or less strenuous walks in the surrounding countryside.

Arrival and information

Bus Buses from La Paz pull up every hour from 5am until 4pm in front of the bus company, Transportes Unificada, on the Plaza Enrique Peñaranda. The road is mainly paved but very steep in places, and can be hair-raising.

Tourist information For information and advice on trekking in the surrounding mountains, try the Sorata Guides and Porters Association, whose office lies opposite the *Residencial Sorata*, just off the plaza on Calle Sucre (☎07/327-2763). They can arrange guides for all the main trekking routes around Sorata; they also organize mule hire and have a limited amount of camping equipment available for rent, though don't count on what you need being available. Guides charge about B$175 per day. Andean Epics, at *Lagunas Café* just off the main plaza (☎07/127-6685, ⌨www.andeanepics .com), is an excellent option for mountain biking, and trekking, and their five-day bike, jeep and canoe trips to Rurrenabaque are highly recommended. The tour usually leaves on Tuesdays.

Accommodation

There's a good choice of inexpensive places to stay in Sorata, as well as a couple of mid-range options with creature comforts, whose appeal grows the longer you've spent climbing or trekking in the surrounding mountains.

Altai Oasis ☎07/151-9856. Follow the path past the *Hostal El Mirador*, take the first right down the hill, then the next right-hand turning to drop steeply down towards the hostel. Alternatively, take a taxi for about B$15. Set by the river, this is an exquisite place to stay, with lush, sprawling grounds, swinging hammocks and a peaceful feel. Dorms B$50, rooms B$120, camping B$30 per person.

Hostal Jordán III Calle Murillo with Bolívar, ☎07/328-8144, ⌨www.soratajordan.com. With terraces looking out over the square, this is an excellent place to watch the world go by. Facilities include a kitchen and a comfy DVD room. Continental breakfast available (B$10). B$70.

Hostal El Mirador Muñecas 400 ☎07/350-5453. A good-value, very popular option, a 5min walk from the plaza. Rooms are basic but there's a lovely terrace with beautiful views, hot showers and a laidback feel. B$40–60.

Hostal Panchita On the plaza, next to the church ☎02/213-4242. A welcoming, simple place with a sunny courtyard and clean rooms (though the "hot" shower doesn't quite live up to its name). B$50.

Las Piedras Villa Elisa 2 ☎ 07/191-6341. A bit
further out of town, *Las Piedras* is a serene place
with characterful rooms, balconies with deckchairs
and an inviting communal area with games and
plenty of cushions to relax on. Breakfast with
home-made yoghurt and wholemeal bread is
available and the German owner will make you feel
at home. B$60–100.

Residencial Sorata Corner of the main plaza
☎ 02/213-6672. Set in the delightful, rambling
nineteenth-century Casa Gunther, this *residencial*
makes you feel you've stepped back in time by
at least eighty years. There are lovely gardens,
attractive simple rooms and a huge, wonderfully
decorated drawing room. B$50–70.

Eating and drinking

While there's not a huge range of culinary choice
in town, the setting more than makes up for it. As
well as the usual gringo and Bolivian standbys, you
can sample some great home-made baking, and
even a curry.

Altai Oasis (see p.203). It is worth the walk, or taxi
from town, to get to the on-site bar and restaurant
at this hostel. You'll find hearty home-cooking,
excellent breakfasts and a bar with beautiful
wooden furnishings.

Café Illampu Fifteen to twenty minutes' walk
across the valley on the road leading to the Gruta
de San Pedro. Worth a visit for its delicious breakfasts, milkshakes, bread and pastries, served in a
wonderfully relaxing setting. Closed Tues.

Casa Reggae One block west of *Hostal El Mirador*. A
basic outdoor bar with drinks and sandwiches in the
evening and a chilled out, hippyish feel. Eve only.

Pizzeria Italia There are numerous pizza restaurants on the plaza; the best of an uninspiring bunch
is the pizzeria attached to *Hostal Panchita*, with
fairly decent and quickly turned-out pizza.

Restaurante Jalisco Plaza Enrique Peñaranda. This
simple restaurant boasts a rather varied menu of
Mexican and Italian food, as well as more traditional
dishes. The enchiladas are surprisingly tasty (B$20).

Moving on

Bus From both sides of Plaza Enrique Peñaranda,
rival bus companies run services every half hour to
La Paz (4hr) until 5pm.

THE YUNGAS

East of La Paz, the Cordillera Real drops
precipitously into the Amazon lowlands,
plunging down through a region of

COCA IN THE YUNGAS

The Yungas is one of Bolivia's major
coca-producing regions, a role it
has played since the colonial era.
Considered sweeter and better
for chewing than that produced in
the Chapare region, Yungas coca
still dominates the Andean market,
and remains legal for traditional
use. It's worth checking on the
coca-eradication situation before
travelling anywhere off the beaten
track in the Yungas; if an eradication
campaign starts up before you
arrive, strange gringos wandering
around the backcountry might easily
be misidentified as undercover US
drug-enforcement agents. With
president Morales's attempts to have
the coca leaf taken off the official
narcotics list, however, the situation
may become more relaxed in the
near future.

rugged, forest-covered mountains and
deep subtropical valleys known as **The
Yungas**, abundant with crops of coffee,
tropical fruit and coca. Three of the
well-built stone roads that linked the
agricultural outposts of the Yungas to
the main population centres before the
Spanish conquest, the so-called "Inca"
trails – the **Takesi**, **Choro** and **Yunga
Cruz** – are still in good condition, and
make excellent three- to four-day hikes
from La Paz. The most frequently visited
Yungas town is the idyllic resort of
Coroico, set amid spectacular scenery
and tropical vegetation. From Coroico,
the road continues north towards
Rurrenabaque and the Bolivian Amazon
(see p.244). Alternatively, you can avoid
Coroico and head to **Chulumani**, a less-
touristed Yungas market town that's the
centre of the equally scenic but less-
visited **South Yungas**.

COROICO

Rightly considered one of the most
beautiful spots in the Yungas, the

peaceful little town of **COROICO** is perched on a steep mountain slope with panoramic views across the forest-covered Andean foothills to the icy peaks of the Cordillera Real beyond. It enjoys a warm and pleasantly humid climate, and this, combined with the dramatic scenery and good facilities, makes it an excellent place to relax and recuperate – especially if you've spent the day cycling the '"Death Road"' (see box, p.189).

What to see and do

Most visitors to Coroico spend much of their time relaxing on the peaceful **Plaza Principal**, lounging by a swimming pool, sipping a cold drink and enjoying the fantastic views. For those with a bit more energy, though, there are some pleasant walks through the surrounding countryside, with forested mountain slopes covered in a lush patchwork of coffee and coca plantations, and banana and orange groves. If you're feeling adventurous, consider a canyoning trip – where anyone looking for their adrenalin fix can clamber and climb their way along a series of river gorges and waterfalls – with community ecotourism agency, El Vagante (℡02/241-3065, ⓦwww .elvagante.com; ask at the office on the corner of the main square).

Arrival and information

Bus Buses and *micros* from La Paz arrive in the newly built bus station on the southwest side of town, opposite the football pitch. If you're coming to Coroico from anywhere else, you'll have to catch a pick-up truck for the fifteen-minute ride up from the main road at Yolosa – these drop passengers off outside the Mercado Municipal, on Sagárnaga.
Tourist information The office at the bus station has maps and information on activities and walks around the town. For trekking information, the office on the main square (daily 8am–8pm; ℡07/306-9888) offers a wealth of local information with guides available for trips to nearby Afro-Boliviano communities, the Camino del Inca and waterfall

hikes. Another good source of information is ⓦwww.vivecoroico.com.

Accommodation

For a small town Coroico has a good range of places to stay, aimed primarily at visitors from La Paz. At weekends and on public holidays everywhere gets very full and prices go up, so it's worth booking in advance. Conversely, things are pretty quiet midweek, when prices are much more reasonable.

El Cafetal Beside the hospital, about a 10-min walk southeast of the town centre ℡07/195-4991, ⓔdanycafetal@hotmail.com. A gorgeous retreat far from the lazy bustle of town, *El Cafetal* has clean, pleasant rooms, a pool, terraces and sweeping grounds. Rooms with private bath open onto balconies with exhilarating views, and there's also a restaurant with excellent and homely food (see p.206). B\$120.

Hostal Kory Linares 3501 ℡02/243-1234. Long-standing backpacker favourite, with plenty of small but clean rooms (with or without bath) around a series of terraces and a large, sparklingly clean swimming pool. The views across the valley are stunning. There's also a reasonable restaurant, a kitchen for guest use and laundry facilities. B\$60–70.

Hostal Sol y Luna Just under 1km outside town, uphill on Julio Zuazo Cuenca, beyond the *Hotel Esmeralda* ℡07/156-1626, ⓦwww.solyluna -bolivia.com. Tranquil hideaway with cooking facilities, spread out on a beautiful hillside garden, with hammocks, fire pits, a hot bath and plunge pools. There are also several basic rooms with shared bath (doubles B\$80–140 per person) in the main

TREAT YOURSELF

La Senda Verde Situated 20min outside of Coroico (a taxi will usually charge about B\$30) and set next to the river in a beautiful valley, this is the kind of gorgeous hideaway you won't ever want to leave. There are sprawling, lush grounds to wander around, a swimming pool, pretty views and an outdoor restaurant serving up tasty meals. Accommodation is in two- to four-person cabins, which are dotted around the grounds. ℡07/153-2703 or 02/213-996; B\$280 for two people, including breakfast.

building, and camping space is available for B$20 per person.

Residencial Pando Calle Pando with Calle 10 de Abril ☎ 07/010-7642. This is pretty basic, but rooms are set around a sweet courtyard and it's one of the cheapest places in town. Pay B$5 extra for hot water. B$50.

Eating and drinking

There's lots of variety on offer when it comes to places to eat, from pizza and Mexican food, to quality French cuisine, German pastries and even Swiss fondue, as well as plenty of places serving inexpensive standard Bolivian cuisine. Nightlife tends to involve drinking beer in the town's bar-restaurants, or poolside in the better hotels.

Back-Stube Linares, off the main plaza. German café/restaurant serving snacks, sandwiches and deliciously decadent home-made cakes. The terrace has wonderful views of the valleys below. *Filete a la pimienta* B$45. Closed Mon and Tues.

Café Arco Iris On main square. Small friendly café with excellent cakes and breakfasts from B$15. Also sells local craftwork and jewellery. Daily 8am–9pm.

El Cafetal See p.205. Small French-run restaurant with panoramic views and a delicious menu of crêpes, soufflés, and fish and meat dishes, as well as great coffee. Closed Tues.

La Casa Calle Julio Cuenca. German/Bolivian-run restaurant where walls are adorned with an eclectic range of trinkets and completed jigsaw puzzles. Specializes in fondues at B$40. Daily 6pm till late.

El Club Panchecho. Second-floor social club for gringos and locals alike, good for a quiet beer or a coffee over a game of pool or ping pong. Beer B$10–12. From 2pm.

Villa Bonita Calle Héroes del Chaco. *Villa Bonita* has delicious home-made ice cream and good Italian dishes. Daily noon–6pm.

Moving on

Bus and micro Services to La Paz depart from the bus station in Coroico every half an hour until 6pm.

CHULUMANI

From Unduavi on the road from La Paz to the Yungas, a side road heads east off the main highway towards the provincial capital of **CHULUMANI**, a very tranquil little town set on a steep hillside overlooking a broad river valley. Life here is taken at an easy pace. With its palm-shaded plaza and steep, narrow cobbled streets lined with neat houses with red-tiled roofs, the main attractions of Chulumani are the surrounding hamlets, splendid scenery and exuberant tropical vegetation of the countryside.

Arrival and information

Bus Buses leave from Villa Fátima in La Paz more or less every 30min (4hr) and arrive outside the bus offices on Plaza Libertad.

Tourist information There's no reliable tourist centre in Chulumani; however, English-speaking Javier Sarabia, owner of the *Hostal Country House* (see below), is a mine of information on hikes from Chulumani. He also runs guided excursions and camping trips on foot or by jeep, and can arrange bicycle and motorbike rental. There's no ATM, but the Prodem bank, a few blocks southwest of the main plaza, can change US dollars and give cash advances on Visa and MasterCard (for a 5 percent fee).

Accommodation

Hostal Country House 1km southeast of town, beyond the *mirador* (no phone). By far the best option in Chulumani, this quirky little guesthouse extends a welcoming, homely feel, with comfortable rooms (private bath and breakfast included) around a lovely garden with a small swimming pool. The owners are very friendly and informative, and the food is delicious. Rooms B$70 per person.

Hostal Dion Alianza, just off the plaza ☎ 02/213-6070. A good budget choice with clean rooms with or without private bath. B$50.

Eating and drinking

The selection of places to eat in Chulumani is disappointing, and the better places are usually open only at weekends. If your budget is really tight, try one of the places grouped around the plaza serving cheap *almuerzos*, although none look too salubrious.

Cafetería Dely's Located underneath *Hostal Dion*, and run by the same people, this is an oasis offering burgers, fruit juices and the like, in a cool, fresh interior.

Panorama Inside the hotel of the same name, a block or so north of the plaza on Murillo. The most reliable restaurant in town, serving decent set *almuerzos* and standard main courses including fresh trout.

Moving on

Bus Services leave for La Paz from outside the bus offices on Plaza Libertad once the bus is full (daily 8am until 5pm). If you're looking to go from Chulumani to Coroico, or vice versa, it's generally easier (and quicker) to go back to La Paz and take a direct bus.

The Southern Altiplano

South of La Paz, the **Southern Altiplano** stretches 800km to the Chilean and Argentine borders. Set at an average altitude of around 3700m, this starkly beautiful landscape is the image most frequently associated with Bolivia: a barren and treeless expanse whose arid steppes stretch to the horizon, where snowcapped mountains shimmer under deep-blue skies.

The unavoidable transport nexus of the Altiplano is the tin-mining city of **Oruro**, 230km south of La Paz, a grim monument to industrial decline that comes alive once a year during the **Carnaval**. Some 310km further southeast of Oruro is the legendary silver-mining city of **Potosí**, a city of sublime colonial architecture, marooned at 4100m above sea level and filled with monuments to a glorious but tragic past.

The Altiplano grows more desolate still as it stretches south towards the Argentine border. From the forlorn railway town of **Uyuni**, 323km due south of Oruro by road and rail, you can venture into the dazzling white **Salar de Uyuni**, the **world's largest salt lake**. Beyond the Salar in the far southwestern corner of the country is the **Reserva de Fauna Andina Eduardo Avaroa**, a bleak-looking nature reserve of lunar landscapes, home to a surprising array of wildlife.

Southeast of Uyuni, the Altiplano changes character. The pleasant little mining town of **Tupiza** is surrounded by arid red mountains and cactus-strewn badlands eroded into deep gullies and rock pinnacles. In the far south of the country lies the provincial capital of **Tarija**, a remote yet welcoming city set in a deep and fertile valley that enjoys a much warmer climate than the Altiplano.

PARQUE NACIONAL SAJAMA

Southwest of La Paz, the road to Chile passes through a desert plain from the middle of which rises the perfect snowcapped cone of Volcán Sajama. At 6542m, Sajama is the tallest mountain in Bolivia and the centre of the country's oldest national park, the **Parque Nacional Sajama**. The park encompasses the entire mountain, the slopes of which support the highest forest in the world, as well as much of the surrounding desert, where pumas, rare Andean deer and the rarely seen, flightless, ostrich-like rheas. Mountain climbers are drawn by the peak's relative ease of ascension – only permitted between April and October, when the ice is sufficiently frozen – and the mountain's lower slopes, containing bubbling geysers and hot springs, which make for excellent hiking.

The administrative centre of the park, where you can register to climb the mountain and arrange guides, mules and porters, is the village of **SAJAMA**. There are two ways to reach Sajama by public transport from La Paz. The first is to take any Oruro-bound bus as far as the crossroads town of **Patacamaya**, from where a *micro* goes directly to Sajama every day at about 1pm, returning to Patacamaya at 7am the next day. The other way of

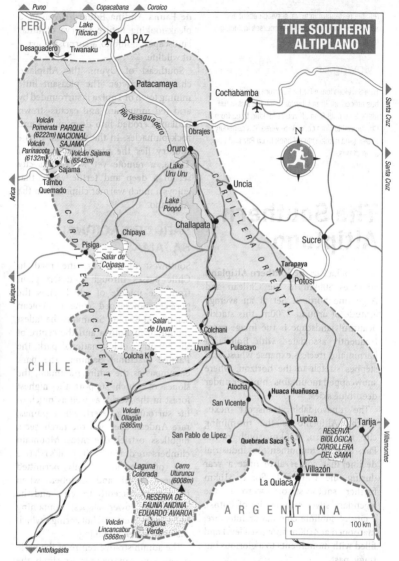

THE SOUTHERN ALTIPLANO

reaching the park is to get on a bus from La Paz (several daily; 3hr 30min–4hr) headed for Arica in Chile and alight at the turn-off to Sajama on the main road. Jeeps from the village usually wait there to collect passengers arriving from La Paz; it's a 12-km drive back to the village.

For pre-trip information, contact **SERNAP** at Av. Mariscal Santa Cruz, Edificio Litoral no. 150 in La Paz (☎02/211-1360, ⓦwww.sernap.gov.bo). On arrival in Sajama village you must register at the park office (daily 8am–noon & 2.30–7pm) and pay a small entrance fee. There is very basic **accommodation** in the village as well as various places serving simple and inexpensive **food**.

ORURO

Huddled on the bleak Altiplano some 230km south of La Paz, the grim mining city of **ORURO** was the economic powerhouse of Bolivia for much of the twentieth century, due to enormous mineral wealth in the surrounding mountains and tin mines established here in the late nineteenth century. Since the fall of world tin prices in 1985, however, Oruro's fortunes have plummeted and more than two decades of economic decline have made it a shadow of its former self.

What to see and do

Oruro is a cold and rather sombre place, with the melancholic air of a city forever looking back on a golden age. There's not much reason to stop in Oruro – outside of Carnaval time – but it is a pleasant enough city with some worthwhile museums.

Plaza 10 de Febrero, Casa de Cultura and Museo Minero

The town's main plaza, Plaza 10 de Febrero, is a pleasant square shaded by cypress trees. Two blocks east of the plaza, at Av. Galvarro, the fascinating **Casa de Cultura** (Mon–Sat 9am–6pm; B$10 including guided tour) is a former home of the "King of Tin" Simón I. Patiño, who was one of the world's wealthiest men when he died in 1947. With the original imported furniture, decadent chandeliers and children's toys all still intact, the museum is an intriguing insight into the luxurious life of one of the few Bolivians who got rich from the country's huge mineral wealth. Five blocks west of the plaza stands the **Santuario del Socavón** (Sanctuary of the Mineshaft), home to the image of the Virgin del Socavón, the patron saint of miners, in whose honour the Carnaval celebrations are staged. The abandoned mineshaft beneath the church is now home to the **Museo Minero** (daily 9am–1pm & 3–6pm; B$10), which has an interesting display of equipment explaining the history of mining, as well as two fearsome-looking statues of El Tío, the devil-like figure worshipped by Bolivian miners as the king of the underworld and owner of all minerals.

Museo Antropológico

In the south of the city, at Av. España and Urquidi, the **Museo Antropológico Eduardo López Rivas** (Mon–Fri 8am–noon & 2–6pm, Sat & Sun 10am–6pm; B$5) is home to an extensive archeo-

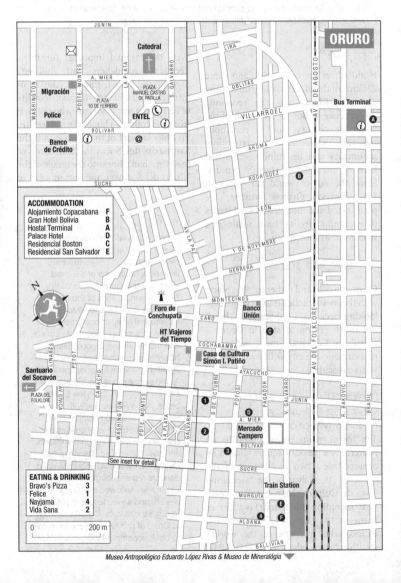

ORURO

ACCOMMODATION
Alojamiento Copacabana   F
Gran Hotel Bolivia   B
Hostal Terminal   A
Palace Hotel   D
Residencial Boston   C
Residencial San Salvador E

EATING & DRINKING
Bravo's Pizza   3
Felice   1
Nayjama   4
Vida Sana   2

0   200 m

logical and ethnographic collection from the Oruro region with displays featuring arrowheads, stone tools, jewellery and a wonderful collection of traditional masks.

Arrival and information

Bus Almost all long-distance buses pull in at the Terminal Terrestre, ten blocks northeast of the city centre on Av. Rajka Bakovic. A taxi into town from here should cost B$8 per person, the flat rate for journeys within the city; alternatively, take any *micro* heading south along Av. 6 de Agosto.

Tourist information The office (Mon–Fri 8am–noon & 2.30–6.30pm; ☎02/525-0144) is on the south side of Plaza 10 de Febrero, though it is rarely open outside of Carnaval. There is also a fairly useless kiosk at the bus terminal manned by the tourist police, where you might get a map if you're lucky.

Train The train station (☎02/527-4605) is a short walk southeast of the city centre on Av. Galvarro (note that the ticket office is closed all day Sat). Only first-class tickets are sold in advance; the rest can be bought the day before travel at the earliest.

Accommodation

There's a fairly good range of places to stay in Oruro – though a lack of good budget choice; during Carnaval prices go up by as much as five times, and most places will only rent rooms for the entire weekend. There are several places to stay near the train station, which is handy for those catching an early morning or late-night train.

Alojamiento Copacabana Av. Galvarro 6352 ☎02/525-4184. A handy option very close to the train station; rooms are well-kept, and the staff are friendly. B$50.

Gran Hotel Bolivia Calle Rodriguez 131, between 6 de Agosto and Velasco Galvarro ☎02/524-1047, ✉granhotelbolivia@hotmail.com. Two blocks from the bus station, this hotel is one of the more reasonably priced in Oruro with clean, basic rooms, with or without private bathroom. Breakfast is available. B$80–120.

Hostal Terminal Av. 21 de Enero ☎02/527-3431. Conveniently situated next to the bus station, this *hostal* has decent rooms, with or without private bath and all with cable. B$80.

Palace Hotel Mier 392, just along from the main square ☎02/525-5132. Slightly run-down hotel just two blocks from the plaza, with cosy rooms and

cable TV. Disappointing breakfast but served in room with an excellent panorama of the city. B$180.

Residencial Boston Pegador 1159 ☎02/527-4708. Pleasant hostel whose good-value rooms come with or without private bath. Staff can be less than friendly, however. B$80.

Residencial San Salvador Av. Galvarro 6325 ☎02/527-6771. Near the train station, and basic but clean. Rooms have private bath and cable TV. B$20.

Eating and drinking

Oruro has a fairly diverse selection of places to eat, though most don't open until mid-morning. There are plenty of cheap roast-chicken restaurants and snack bars on Av. 6 de Octubre, where late on Friday and Saturday night stalls serve the local speciality *rostro asado*, roasted sheep's head, from which the face is peeled off and served along with the eyeballs.

Bravo's Pizza Corner of Bolívar and Potosí. Serves up decent pizza in a cheerful second-floor restaurant overlooking the plaza; there's also a salad bar. Pizza from B$19, breakfast B$20–22.

Felice Junin, between 6 de Octubre and S Galvarro. Excellent set lunch deals with three courses (B$16) in a smart-looking dining area with a relaxed atmosphere. Lunchtimes only, closed Sun.

Nayjama Corner of Pagador and Aldana. By far the best restaurant in town – and very popular with locals – serving huge portions of delicious local food, with specialities including sublime roast lamb and *criadillas* (bull testicles). Not for the faint-hearted.

Vida Sana Av. 6 de Octubre, between Mier and Bolívar. A good veggie option with a simple salad bar. Some dishes can be a bit hit and miss, but the huge portions make up for it. Lunch menu B$12. Also serves evening meals from 5.30pm.

Moving on

Bus All buses leave from the Terminal Terrestre, with regular connections to La Paz (every 30min; 3hr 30min) and Cochabamba (every half-hour; 4hr). Departures for Potosí (8hr) and Sucre (10hr) leave in the evening between 6 and 9pm, and several companies run overnight buses to Uyuni (8hr). There are also twice-daily departures for Iquique in Chile (at 1pm and 2am; 8hr).

Train Note that it's best to try to buy your ticket in advance, and you'll need your passport to purchase one. Expreso del Sur trains run to Uyuni, Atocha, Tupiza and Villazón every Tuesday and Friday, leaving at 3.30pm; Wara Wara del Sur trains leave for the same destinations on Wednesday and Sunday evenings at 7pm.

POTOSÍ

Set on a desolate, windswept plain amid barren mountains at almost 4100m above sea level, **POTOSÍ** is the highest city in the world, and at once the most fascinating and tragic place in Bolivia. Given its remote and inhospitable location, it's difficult to see at first glance why it was ever built here at all. The answer lies in **Cerro Rico** ("Rich Mountain"), the conical peak that rises imperiously above the city to the south and that was, quite simply, the richest source of silver the world had ever seen.

The **silver rush** of Cerro Rico was triggered in 1545 by a llama herder who was caught out after dark on the mountain's slopes. He started a fire to keep warm, and was amazed to see a trickle of molten silver run out from the blaze. News of this discovery soon reached the Spaniards, and the rush was soon underway. Over the next twenty years the new city of Potosí became the richest single source of silver in the world, and its population mushroomed to more than one hundred thousand, making it easily the largest metropolis in the Americas.

By the beginning of the seventeenth century Potosí was home to more than 160,000 people and boasted dozens of magnificent churches, as well as theatres, gambling houses, brothels and dance halls. For the **indigenous workers and African slaves** who produced this wealth, however, the working conditions were appalling and the consequences catastrophic. Estimates of the total number who died over three centuries of colonial mining in Potosí run as high as nine million, making the mines of Potosí a central factor in the demographic collapse that swept the Andes under Spanish rule.

What to see and do

Potosí's legacy reflects both the magnificence and the horror of its colonial past. The city is a treasure-trove of colonial art and architecture, with hundreds of well-preserved buildings, including some of the finest churches in Bolivia.

Plaza 10 de Noviembre

The centre of the city is the **Plaza 10 de Noviembre**, a pleasant tree-shaded square with a small replica of the Statue of Liberty, erected in 1926 to commemorate Bolivian independence. On the north side of the square, the site of the original church (which collapsed in 1807) is now occupied by the twin-towered **Catedral**, completed in Neoclassical style in 1836. To the east of the square lies the **Plaza 6 de Agosto**, at the centre of which is a column commemorating the Battle of Ayacucho in 1824, which secured Bolivian independence early the following year.

Casa Real de la Moneda

West of the Plaza 10 de Noviembre on Calle Ayacucho stands the unmissable **Casa Real de la Moneda**, or Royal Mint (Tues–Sat 9–10.30am & 2.30–5.30pm, Sun 9–10.30am; B$20 includes tours in Spanish or English; Ⓦwww.bolivian.com/cnm). One of the most outstanding examples of colonial civil architecture in all South America, it is now home to one of the best museums in Bolivia. The vast and eclectic collection includes the original machinery used in the various stages of the minting process, some of Bolivia's finest colonial religious art, militaria, archeological artefacts and a display of coins and banknotes.

Built between 1759 and 1773, La Moneda is a truly formidable construction, built as part of a concerted effort by the Spanish crown to reform the economic and financial machinery of the empire to increase revenues. Covering 7500 square metres, La Moneda is enclosed by stout stone walls over a metre thick with only a few barred windows looking out, giving it the appearance of a fortress. Inside, the rambling two-storey complex of about **two hundred rooms** is set around five internal courtyards, all finely built with cut stone blocks and neat brickwork. In addition to housing the heavy machinery and equipment needed to produce coins – much of which is well preserved and on display – La Moneda also housed troops, workers, African slaves and the senior royal officials responsible for overseeing operations. A vital nerve centre of Spanish imperial power in the Andes, it also served as a prison, treasury and near-impregnable stronghold in times of disorder.

La Torre de la Compañia de Jesus

Also on Calle Ayacucho stands **La Torre de la Compañia de Jesus** (Mon–Fri 8am–noon & 2–6pm, Sat & Sun 8.30am–12.30pm & 2.30–6.30pm; B$10), a bell tower which is all that now remains of a Jesuit church originally founded in 1581. Completed in 1707 and recently restored, the grandiose tower is one of the finest eighteenth-century religious monuments in Bolivia and a sublime example of the Mestizo-Baroque style. You can climb to the top of the tower, from where there are excellent views of the city and Cerro Rico.

Convento and Museo Santa Teresa

The **Convento-Museo Santa Teresa** (Calle Ayacucho; Mon & Wed–Sat 9–11am & 2.30–5pm, Tues and Sun 3–5pm; B$21) is a beautiful colonial church and convent worth visiting both for its fine collection of colonial religious painting and sculpture, and for a somewhat disturbing insight into the bizarre lifestyle of nuns in the colonial era. Visits are by guided tour only, so you need to get here at least an hour before closing.

Arrival and information

Bus All buses (except those from Uyuni) arrive at the Terminal de Buses on Av. Universitaria. Buses from Uyuni pull in at the various bus company offices on the corner of Av. Universitaria and Sevilla. From the terminal, a taxi into the city centre costs about B$5–8 per person, or you can catch *micro* A heading up Av. Universitaria, which will take you to Plaza 10 de Noviembre, the central square.

Tourist information The best place for information is the Oficina de Turismo Municipal (Mon–Fri 8am–noon & 2–6pm, Sat 8am–noon; ☏ 02/622-6408), accessible through the arch of Torre de la Compañia on Calle Ayacucho, a block west of Plaza 10 de Noviembre.

Accommodation

With night-time temperatures often falling below zero, the main consideration when choosing where

CERRO RICO

Immediately south of Potosí the near-perfect cone of Cerro Rico rises above the city, pockmarked with the entrances to the thousands of mines that lead deep into its entrails. The tour operators listed below run regular tours of the mines. Be warned, though, that this is an unpleasant and highly dangerous environment, where safety precautions are largely left to fate; anyone suffering from claustrophobia, heart or breathing problems is advised against entering. Some question the ethics of making a tourist attraction of a workplace where conditions are so appalling; however, most visitors find the experience one of the most unforgettable in Bolivia.

Tours of the mines begin with a visit to the miners' market on and around Plaza El Calvario, where you can buy coca leaves, dynamite, black-tobacco cigarettes, pure cane alcohol and fizzy soft drinks – you should take a selection of these as gifts for the miners you'll be visiting. Two established operators offering mine tours are: Koala Tours and Sin Fronteras (for details see p.214).

POTOSÍ TOURS

A number of tour operators offer half-day trips to the mines of Cerro Rico, purportedly fixed at B$70–80 per person. One of the best is Koala Tours at Ayacucho 5 (☎02/622-2092, @k_tours_potosi@hotmail.com), with trips run by experienced (some ex-miner) multilingual guides. For trips to the Salar de Uyuni, try Andean Salt Expeditions, on the corner of Padilles and Linares (☎02/622-5175, @turismo_potosi@hotmail.com), or Sin Fronteras, Bustillos 1092 (☎02/622-4058).

to stay in Potosí is warmth. A couple of places have central heating, but otherwise try to find a room that gets some sun during the day.

La Casona Chuquisasa 460 ☎02/623-0523, @www.hotelpotosi.com. A relaxed, backpacker-friendly place set around a pleasant, brightly painted courtyard. Showers are often cold. Basic breakfast is included. Dorms B$35.

Hostal Colonial Calle Hoyos 8 ☎02/622-4265, @www.hostalcolonial-bo.com. Spacious rooms with heating, grand-looking communal spaces, accommodating staff and internet included. Probably one of the best hotels in Potosí but overpriced for what it is – if you feel in need of comfort, this is perhaps the closest you will get. B$315.

Hostal Compañía de Jesús Chuquisaca 445 ☎02/622-3173. Delightful converted colonial building in the centre of town with clean, snug and good-value rooms, toasty hot showers and a welcoming family atmosphere. Simple breakfast included. B$100–110.

Hostal María Victoria Chuquisaca 148 ☎02/622-2132. Tucked away in a pretty street, this restful old colonial house is run by friendly staff. There are warm showers, plus an on-site travel agency and pleasant terrace. Dorms B$35, rooms B$120.

Koala Den Junín 56 ☎02/622-6467, @ktourspotosi@hotmail.com. A travellers' favourite, this charming, amicable hostel owned and run by Koala Tours features decent dorms and very inviting private rooms. Heating in all rooms means you won't feel the frost, and there are great showers, a lovely communal area, a kitchen and a large DVD collection. Internet access and breakfast are included. Dorms B$35, rooms B$150.

Eating and drinking

Potosí's popularity with travellers is reflected in the city's growing variety of places to eat, with more and more cafés and restaurants offering vegetarian food and travellers' favourites like pizza and pasta. The Mercado Central – on Bolívar, between Bustillos and Oruro – is your best bet for large portions of cheap local food.

4060 Calle Ayachucho 4. Named after Potosí's altitude, this popular café/pub has a varied menu and is a good place for a drink. Eve only. Steak B$40.

Café Kaypichu Millares 14. Follow the stairs to the first floor for this sweet, simple café with healthy, tasty vegetarian food, as well as meat options, including llama steaks and delicious sandwiches (B$80). Closed Mon.

La Candelaria Ayacucho 5. Mellow, first-floor travellers' café serving up a combination of traditional Bolivian recipes and international favourites. It also has a book exchange, tourist information, internet access (B$3–4 per hour) and a cosy covered terrace on the second floor. Breakfast B$25. Daily 9am til late.

La Casona Pub Frías 38. The liveliest nightspot in town, housed in an eighteenth-century mansion whose inside walls are decorated with contemporary graffiti. The atmosphere is friendly, and there's ice-cold beer and live music, as well as heating for the cold nights. Eve only.

El Fogón Frías 58. Smart restaurant popular with locals, who come for the roaring fires and obliging service, as well as the healthy portions of steak, fish, local specialities, salads and sandwiches. Open daily for lunch and dinner.

Potocchi Millares 13. Small café-restaurant serving reasonable traditional Bolivian and international food – it's worth visiting for the live folkloric music shows it hosts several nights a week, when there's a small cover charge.

Sumaj Orcko Quijarro 46. Inexpensive locals' favourite serving large portions of hearty regional cuisine and good-value set almuerzos (B$15). Closed Sun eve.

Directory

Banks and exchange The Banco Nacional de Bolivia on Junín changes cash and travellers cheques, and several shops along Bolívar change US dollars. There are several ATMs where you can withdraw cash on Visa or MasterCard, including the Banco Mercantil, on Padilla and Hoyos, and Banco de Crédito, on Bolívar and Sucre.

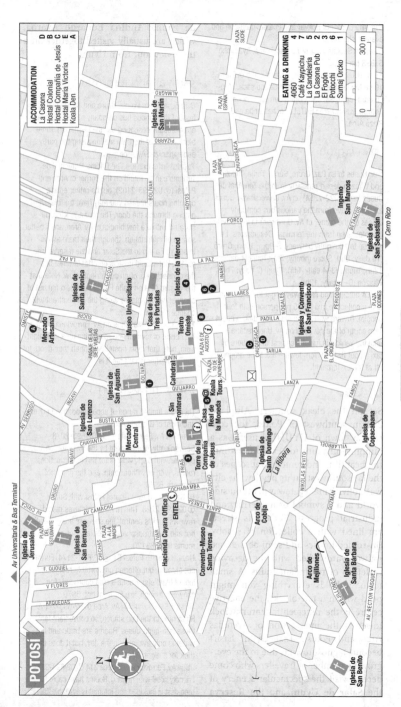

POTOSÍ

ACCOMMODATION
La Casona — D
Hostal Colonial — B
Hostal Compañía de Jesús — C
Hostal María Victoria — E
Koala Den — A

EATING & DRINKING
4060 — 4
Café Kaypichu — 7
La Candelaria — 5
La Casona Pub — 2
El Fogón — 3
Potocchi — 6
Suma Orcko — 1

0   300 m

Iglesia de San Martín
Plaza Sucre
Plaza España
Plaza Alonzo
Iglesia de Santa Monica
Museo Universitario
Casa de las Tres Portadas
Iglesia de la Merced
Teatro Omiste
Mercado Artesanal
Iglesia de San Agustín
Catedral
Sin Fronteras
Casa Real de la Moneda
Koala Tours
Iglesia de San Lorenzo
Mercado Central
Torre de la Compañía de Jesús
Iglesia de Santo Domingo
La Ribera
Iglesia de Copacabana
Iglesia y Convento de San Francisco
Iglesia de San Sebastián
Ingenio San Marcos
Cerro Rico

Plaza Arnada
Chiquisaca
Plaza El Croue
Plaza Dodone
Periodista
Nogales
Padilla
Millares
La Paz
Linares
Betanzos
Porco
Hoyos
Bolívar
Pizarro
Almagro

S. Chacon
Sucre
Pasaje de las Siete Vueltas
Junín
Bolívar
Bustillos
Chayanta
Oruro
Ingavi
Av Serrudo
Quijarro
Lanza
Tarija
Cobija
La Ribera
Nikolas Bevito
Guzman
Villarroel
Fanola

Plaza 6 de Agosto
Plaza 10 de Noviembre

Iglesia de Jerusalén
Plaza del Estudiante
Av Cívica
Plaza a la Madre
Iglesia de San Bernardo
Chichas
F. Ququiel
V Flores
Arquedas
Convento-Museo Santa Teresa
Hacienda Cayara Office
ENTEL
Santa Teresa
Cochabamba
Ayacucho
Av Camacho
Bolívar
Frias
Arco de Cobija
Arco de Mejillones
Mejillones
Iglesia de Santa Bárbara
Av Rector Vasquez
Iglesia de San Benito

Av Universitaria & Bus Terminal

N

BOLIVIA

THE SOUTHERN ALTIPLANO

215

Cinema Corner of Bolívar and Potosí. Afternoon and evening showings.

Internet Second floor of *La Candelaria*, Ayacucho 5. B$3 per hour.

Post office Correo Central, a block south of Plaza 10 de Noviembre on Lanza and Chuquisaca. Mon–Fri 8am–8pm, Sat 8am–6pm, Sun 9am–noon.

Telephone centres ENTEL, Cochabamba and Plaza Arce.

Moving on

Bus Buses to La Paz, Oruro, Sucre, Tarija, Tupiza and Villazón depart regularly from the Terminal de Buses (☎02/622-7354) on Av. Universitaria. Buses for Uyuni leave from the various bus company offices on the corner of Av. Universitaria and Sevilla, two blocks up from the terminal. Destinations: La Paz (up to 10 nightly between 7–9pm; 10hr); Oruro (10 daily; 8hr); Sucre (hourly; 3hr); Tarija (1 daily; 12hr); Tupiza (3–4 daily; 9hr); Uyuni (2 daily; 7hr); Villazón (6–7 daily; 12hr).

Taxi A quicker and nicer way to get to Sucre is to take a collective taxi (B$35 per person with four people). Drivers wait at the old bus station – about 1km south of the new one on Av. Universitaria – until the vehicle is full. It's easiest to get there by taxi (about B$6–8) from town – ask to be dropped off at the ex-terminal.

UYUNI

Set on the bleak southern Altiplano 212km southwest of Potosí, the cold railway town of **UYUNI** is useful as a jumping-off point for expeditions into the beautiful and remote landscapes of the far southwest. In its heyday, the city was Bolivia's main gateway to the outside world and a symbol of modernity and industrial progress. Today, its streets are lined with a collection of shabby, tin-roofed houses and semi-abandoned railway yards filled with the decaying skeletons of redundant trains. A small town, it holds everything you might need within a few blocks; the effective centre is the nineteenth-century clock tower at the intersection of Avenidas Arce and Potosí. That Uyuni hasn't become a ghost town is due to the ever-growing number of travellers who come here to visit the spectacular scenery of the **Salar de Uyuni** and the **Reserva**

de **Fauna Andina Eduardo Avaroa**, which are usually visited together on a three-day tour from Uyuni.

Arrival and information

Bus Buses from Potosí, Oruro and Tupiza pull up in front of the various bus company offices (an area optimistically described as "the terminal"), three blocks north of the train station along the partly pedestrianized Av. Arce.

Tourist information The Oficina Municipal de Turismo can be found on the corner of Arce and Potosí (☎02/693-2102), but its rather erratic opening hours means you may have trouble even getting through the door. The tour agencies, all situated within a few blocks of Av. Arce, are a better source of information, though their main aim is to sell you a trip to the Salar and the reserve (see p.218). Hotels and hostels do offer internet but the connection is often agonizingly slow. Note that there is an ATM on Calle Potosí but it is often out of service; various places along the same street will change money.

Train The train station is on Av. Ferroviaria, right in the centre of town. If you're arriving on a late-night train, note that most hostels will open their doors to you, no matter what time it is.

Accommodation

There's a limited range of accommodation in Uyuni, and most of it is fairly basic.

Avenida Av. Ferroviaria 11 ☎02/693-2078. Conveniently located right by the train station, and popular with backpackers for its clean functional rooms, with or without bath, and the good hot showers. B$60.

HI Salar de Uyuni Hostel Potosí with Sucre ☎02/693-2228. This HI hostel receives mixed reviews but it's central, the showers are generally hot and the atmosphere is relaxed. Dorms B$45, rooms from B$120.

Hostal Marith Potosí 61 ☎02/693-2174. Further out of town, but offering comfortable rooms (and lots of blankets) around a nice courtyard. The showers, though, are far from hot. B$70.

Hostal San Salvador Av. Arce ☎02/693-2407. Right next to the bus station, so convenient for those late-night buses. Rooms are basic and hot water is only available in the day, but it does the trick for a night. B$60–70.

Julia Av. Ferroviaria with Arce 314 ☎02/693-2134. Friendly hotel with heating. Rooms have cable TV, breakfast is included and internet is available. B$120.

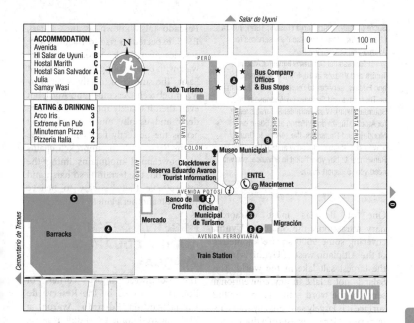

ACCOMMODATION
Avenida   F
Hl Salar de Uyuni   B
Hostal Marith   C
Hostal San Salvador   A
Julia   E
Samay Wasi   D

EATING & DRINKING
Arco Iris   3
Extreme Fun Pub   1
Minuteman Pizza   4
Pizzeria Italia   2

Salar de Uyuni

PERÚ
Todo Turismo
Bus Company Offices & Bus Stops
COLÓN
Museo Municipal
Clocktower & Reserva Eduardo Avaroa Tourist Information
ENTEL
@ Macinternet
AVENIDA POTOSÍ
Banco de Credito
Oficina Municipal de Turismo
Mercado
Migración
AVENIDA FERROVIARIA
Barracks
Train Station
Cementerio de Trenes
BOLIVAR
AVAROA
AVENIDA ARCE
SUCRE
CAMACHO
SANTA CRUZ

0   100 m

UYUNI

Samay Wasi Potosí 965 ☎02/693-3956. Good-value, decent rooms and the possibility of heating and cable TV for a small amount extra each. B$160.

Eating and drinking

As with accommodation, the range of places to eat in Uyuni is pretty limited. The food market on Potosí and Avaroa has cheap and decent local dishes, while there are a fair few restaurants concentrated around the pedestrianized Plaza Arce, offering generally overpriced and gringo-oriented food.
Arco Iris Plaza Arce. Popular with travellers, with a cosy atmosphere in which to pass a chilly night with all the usual backpacker favourites on offer. Daily eve only.
Extreme Fun Pub Av. Potosí 9. A good place to let off some steam with the friends you've made on a salt-flat tour. It has an entertaining cocktail list, a friendly vibe and a party atmosphere. Daily till late.
Minuteman Pizza In the *Toñito Hotel*, Av. Ferroviaria. The best place to eat in town, with a warm, secluded ambience, great decor and arguably the best pizza in Bolivia (they're thin, crispy, and loaded with top quality ingredients). Also serves pasta dishes, creative salads and delicious muffins and pancakes. Pizza service starts at 5pm daily, but it's open for breakfast too.
Pizzeria Italia Plaza Arce. Invariably packed with tourists, this place trades more on its gregarious

vibe than its food; while the pizza is tasty enough, the pasta dishes are best avoided. Mains including pizza B$25–35.

Moving on

Bus Buses leave from the handful of offices on Av. Arce. Todo Turismo (Santa Cruz 155; ☎02/693-3337) buses to La Paz are supposedly the most comfortable option but at B$180 are by far the most expensive. Service (with heating and toilet) leaves daily at 8pm. Advance booking recommended. Destinations: La Paz (1 daily; 11hr); Oruro (2–3 daily; 8hr); Potosí (4 daily; 7–8hr);

CROSSING INTO CHILE FROM UYUNI

Passenger trains no longer run from Uyuni to Calama in Chile so to cross the border you will need to go via Laguna Verde in the far south of the Reserva Eduardo Avaroa, which can be arranged through one of the tour agencies in Uyuni; most agencies have daily departures. The officials at this border post have been known to charge small unauthorized fees for letting you cross.

Sucre (4 daily; 10hr); Tarija (1 daily; 18hr); Tupiza (1 daily; 7hr). There are also daily services to Avaroa and Calama in Chile.

Train Expreso del Sur trains leave for Atocha, Tupiza and Villazón at 10.40pm on Tuesdays and Fridays; services to Oruro leave at 12.05am on Thursdays and Sundays (ie Wednesday and Saturday night). Wara Wara del Sur trains leave for Atocha, Tupiza and Villazón at 2.50am on Mondays and Thursdays; the service to Oruro leaves at 1.45am on Tuesday and Friday mornings. Remember to buy your ticket in advance; you will need your passport as ID.

SALAR DE UYUNI

One of Bolivia's most extraordinary attractions, the **Salar de Uyuni**, covering some 9000 square kilometres of the Altiplano west of Uyuni, is by far the largest salt lake in the world. The Salar is not a lake in any conventional sense of the word – though below the surface it is largely saturated by water, its uppermost layer consists of a thick, hard crust of salt, easily capable of supporting the weight of a car. Tours will take you to the striking cactus-covered **Isla del Pescado** (also known as Inca Huasi, B$15, expected to rise to B$30), where a series of paths lead you on a short walk with breathtaking vistas of the vast Salar. The surface is mostly covered by water between December and April, but even then it's rarely more than a metre deep, and usually much less. Driving across the perfectly flat white expanse of the Salar, with the unbroken chains of snowcapped mountains lining the far horizon, the terrain is so harsh and inhospitable that it's easy to believe you're on another planet.

RESERVA DE FAUNA ANDINA EDUARDO AVAROA

The southwesternmost corner of Bolivia is covered by the **Reserva de Fauna Andina Eduardo Avaroa**, a 7147-square-kilometre wildlife reserve, ranging between 4000m and 6000m in altitude and encompassing some of the most startling scenery in Bolivia.

VISITING THE SALAR AND THE RESERVE

Pretty much the only way to visit the Salar de Uyuni and Reserva De Fauna Andina Eduardo Avaroa is on an organized tour, which can be easily arranged from Uyuni. The standard trip (usually between B$700–800, including food, accommodation, transport and Spanish-speaking guide) is a three-day tour by 4x4 around a circuit comprising the Salar de Uyuni and Lagunas Colorada and Verde in the reserve; four-day and longer trips are also available, if you find enough people who are interested in doing the trip as a group. Note that wind-chill temperatures can drop to anything from -25°C to -40°C and that you should bring sun block and sunglasses to counter the very real possibility of snow blindness, as well as a good sleeping bag and plenty of warm clothing (your agency should be able to rent you a sleeping bag).

Bear in mind that issues such as late departures, inadequate accommodation and vehicle breakdowns are problems that may occur no matter which agency you choose, but it's definitely worth paying a little more to ensure good safety conditions and good food. The cheaper agencies tend to have older cars, bad (and often cold) food and dangerous (and often drunk) drivers. The best method of choosing an agency is to talk to travellers just returned from a tour and to request a written contract detailing exactly what you are paying for; however, the following agencies have been repeatedly recommended by travellers: Cordillera Traveller Tours Av. Ferroviaria ☏02/693-3304, ⓦwww.cordilleratraveller.com; Andes Salt Expeditions Av. Arce, main square ☏02/693-2116 and Oasis Tours Av. Arce ☏02/693-2308, ⓦwww.oasistours-bo.com. Oasis also offers three-day tours with a slightly different, and therefore less crowded, route).

Like the Salar de Uyuni, the desolate landscapes of this remote region possess an otherworldly beauty, with glacial salt lakes whose icy waters are stained bright red or emerald green, snowcapped volcanic peaks, high-altitude deserts and a wide range of rare **Andean wildlife** including the world's largest population of the **James flamingo**, the elusive **Andean fox** and herds of **graceful vicuñas**. There is an entrance fee (B$150) into the reserve, which is usually not included in the tour price and paid at a rangers' office at the point of entry.

TUPIZA

Some 200km southeast of Uyuni, the isolated mining town of **Tupiza** nestles in a narrow, fertile valley that cuts through the harsh desert landscape with its cactus-strewn badlands, deep canyons and strangely shaped rock formations and pinnacles. The town draws visitors largely because of its **dramatic surrounding desert landscape**, ideal for hiking, horseriding or just touring by jeep. All these activities are easily arranged in this friendly town, which features a rapidly growing but well-organized tourist industry.

In the late nineteenth and early twentieth centuries, Tupiza was the home of one of Bolivia's biggest mining barons, Carlos Aramayo. His mines were rich enough to attract the attention of the infamous North American gunslingers **Butch Cassidy and the**

Sundance Kid, who are believed to have died in a shoot-out in the town of **San Vicente**, some 100km to the northwest.

Arrival and information

Bus The bus terminal is on Av. Arraya, three blocks south and two blocks east of the main square, Plaza Independencia.

Tourist information There is no formal tourist office in the town, but the main tour operators (see box, p.220) will be able to tell you all you need to know. There are no ATMs in town, but you can access money through cash advances on Visa or MasterCard credit cards at Prodem (Mon–Fri 8.30am–12.30pm & 2.30–6pm, Sat 9am–noon) and Banco de Crédito (9.30am–12.30pm & 2–5pm), both on the main plaza, for a fee. Several cambios east of the plaza on Calle Avaroa will change traveller's cheques, as well as US dollars, Argentine pesos and sometimes Peruvian soles.

Train The train station is three blocks east of the main plaza on Plazuela Adolfo Torres del Carpio, just off Av. Serrudo.

Accommodation

There is a small range of accommodation in Tupiza, all of it inexpensive and relatively simple, and aimed specifically at backpackers on limited budgets. If arriving late, it is best to call ahead.

Hostal Valle Hermoso Av. Pedro Arraya 478 ☎02/694-2592, ✆hostalvh@hotmail.com. A welcoming, HI-affiliated hostel with a cosy rooftop terrace and comfortable common room. The clean, sunny dorms and private rooms (with or without bath) are set around a small patio shaded by a giant fig tree. They have also opened an annexe at Pedro Arraya 505. Dorms B$35, rooms B$80.

Mitru Av. Chicas 187 ☎02/694-3001, ✆mitru @hotmail.com. A particularly pleasant place to stay is this popular hotel, mainly because of its sunny central courtyard complete with swimming pool. Rooms are clean, there's a games room and breakfast is included. B$110–120. Run by the same owners are *Anexo Mitru*, Avaroa s/n, and *Refugio del Turista*, Av. Santa Cruz 244, which has dorms (B$30) and doubles (B$70), with use of a kitchen.

Residencial El Rancho Av. Pedro Arraya 86 ✆02/694-3116. The most decent of the real cheapies, with basic but clean and spacious rooms (with or without bath) set around a patio; rooms upstairs are far nicer and lighter. There's also use of a simple kitchen. B$40.

La Torre Av. Chichas 220 ✆02/694-2633, ✉latorrehotel@yahoo.es. A friendly, family-run place with good rooms (with or without private bath and cable TV), a small sunny roof terrace and a communal lounge with cable TV. Good continental breakfast is included. B$45.

Eating and drinking

There's a limited choice of places to eat and drink in Tupiza. As usual, the cheapest place for food is the market, on the first floor of the corner of Calles Chichas and Florida. Local specialities include *asado de cordero* (roast lamb), usually served on weekends, and *tamales* stuffed with dehydrated llama meat – the best are to be found outside the Mercado Negro on Av. Chichas.

Alamo Avaroa 203. A bizarre US-diner-style bar/restaurant with walls covered in celebrity pictures.

The food is cheap, and served in large portions. Beer B$10. Daily from 5pm.

Bella Napoli Calle Florida. There are numerous, similar pizza restaurants on Florida serving breakfasts, pizza and pasta dishes to gringos at gringo prices, but this is the best of the bunch, with tasty thin-crust pizzas served in an inviting atmosphere.

California Plaza Independencia. A local favourite, with cheap, filling fare, serving breakfasts, hamburgers, pizzas and a particularly appetizing lasagne.

Los Helechos Avaroa. A bit more expensive but a good bet for reliable local dishes, served up in huge portions. Lunch menu B$15. Opens early for breakfast.

Moving on

Bus Buses depart from the terminal on Av. Arraya. Cochabamba (daily at 6pm); La Paz (2 daily; 16hr); Potosí (2 daily; 8hr); Tarija (several departures between 7pm & 8pm; 8hr); Uyuni (1 daily; 6hr); Villazón (4.30am, 10.30am and at hourly intervals in the afternoon; 3hr).

Train Expreso del Sur trains leave for Villazón at 4.10am Wednesday and Saturday mornings; services to Atocha, Uyuni and Oruro leave at 6.25pm on Wednesday and Saturday evenings. Wara Wara del Sur trains leave for Villazón at 9.05am on Monday and Thursday mornings, and to Atocha, Uyuni and Oruro at 7.05pm on Monday and Thursday evenings. Be sure to buy your ticket in advance.

ORGANIZED TOURS FROM TUPIZA

Tupiza's tour agencies all offer broadly similar guided excursions into the desert landscapes around the town in 4x4s or on horseback, as well as longer but not terribly rewarding trips to San Vicente, where Butch Cassidy and the Sundance Kid are thought to have died. The agencies can also organize trips to the Reserva de Fauna Andina Eduardo Avaroa and the Salar de Uyuni, a four-day circuit that should cost about B$1200–1300 per person (plus reserve entrance fees) in a jeep with at least four passengers. There are certainly advantages to doing the trip from Tupiza, as this way round accommodation tends to improve over the course of the three nights, and you hit the salt flat highlight on the last day. Recommended agencies in Tupiza are:

La Torre Tours *Hotel La Torre* ✆02/694-2633, ✉latorrehotel@hotmail.com. Established tour company offering a variety of different takes on the salt-flats tour, as well as horseriding and Butch Cassidy tours.

Tupiza Tours Av. Chichas 187, inside the *Hotel Mitru* ✆02/694-3003, ✇www.tupizatours.com. Experienced tour outlet with standard tours to

the Salar as well as the option of tailor-made trips to suit different times and budgets.

Valle Hermoso Tours Av. Pedro Arraya 478, inside the *Hostal Valle Hermoso* ✆02/694-2370, ✇www.bolivia.freehosting.net. Offers trekking, horseriding and jeep tours around Tupiza, and recommended tours to the Salar.

TARIJA

In the far south of the country, the isolated city of **TARIJA** is in many ways a world apart from the rest of Bolivia. Set in a broad, fertile valley at an altitude of 1924m, Tarija is famous for its **wine** production, and the valley's rich soils and mild climate have historically attracted large numbers of Andalucian farmers. The surrounding countryside is beautiful, particularly in the spring (Jan–April), when the vineyards come to fruit and the whole valley blooms.

What to see and do

Tarija's tree-lined avenues and temperate climate give the city a laidback ambience. The two main squares, Plaza Luis de Fuentes and Plaza Sucre, are lined with excellent restaurants and cafés – perfect for a glass of the region's increasingly well-known wine. At nightfall, the streets around the Mercado Central, at the corner of Sucre and Bolívar, transform into a bustling street market, and are perfect for picking up bargain food and clothes prior to a trip to the salt flats.

Plazas Luis de Fuentes and Sucre

The centre of town is the tranquil, palm-lined **Plaza Luis de Fuentes**, named after the city's founder, whose statue stands in the middle. It's a pleasant place to sit in the sun and watch the world go by. The small, charming **Plaza Sucre**, two blocks southeast of the main plaza, is surrounded by restaurants and coffee bars, and is the centre for much of the town's nightlife.

Museo Paleontológico

A block south of the plaza on the corner of Virginio Lema and Trigo, the **Museo Paleontológico** (Mon–Fri 8am–noon & 3–6pm, Sat 9am–noon & 3–6pm; free) offers a fantastic collection of fossils and skeletons from the Tarija Valley. Most of the specimens on display are of mammals from the Pleistocene era, between a million and 250,000 years ago, many of them from species similar to ones that still exist today, such as horses, bears and llamas.

Casa Dorada

Also worth visiting is the **Casa Dorada** (Mon–Fri 8.30am–noon & 2.30–6pm; B$5), also known as Casa de la Cultura, on the corner of Ingavi and Trigo. Built in the nineteenth century in the Art Nouveau style by a wealthy merchant, the house has been restored and declared a national monument. You can wander through its rooms with photo displays depicting the history of Tarija, or check out one of the many cultural events hosted here, including concerts and dance performances.

Arrival and information

Air The airport (☎ 04/664-3135) is on the outskirts of town a few kilometres further east along Av. Las Américas. A taxi into the town centre from here should cost about B$20, and there are also frequent *micros* into the centre (B$10).

Bus The bus terminal is ten blocks or so southeast of the city centre on Av. Las Américas; it's about twenty minutes into the city centre on foot from here, or a short taxi ride (B$6–8). Alternatively, catch one of the frequent *micros* that run along Av. Las Américas from the stop opposite the terminal. Note that after midnight until about 7am, all taxis charge a minimum of B$10.

Tourist information There are two tourist information offices in Tarija: the Oficina Departamental de Turismo (Mon–Fri 8am–noon & 2.30–6.30pm; ☎ 04/663-1000) on the Plaza Luis de Fuentes tends to be rather unfriendly and not very helpful; the Oficina Municipal de Turismo (Mon–Fri 8am–noon & 2.30–6.30pm, Sat 8am–noon; ☎ 04/663-3581) on the corner of Bolívar and Sucre is a much better bet; friendly staff offer a wealth of information, maps and leaflets.

Accommodation

Tarija has a good range of accommodation, almost all in the very centre of town – the exceptions are around the bus terminal, though there's no point staying down there unless you're just passing the night before continuing your journey.

Hostal Bolívar Bolívar 256 ✆04/664-2741. Quiet, clean option set around a pretty courtyard, with reasonable rooms (all have private bath, but those with cable TV are newer and much nicer) and a communal living room. Breakfast included. B$140.

Hostal Miraflores Sucre 920 ✆04/664-3355 or 04/664-4976. Converted colonial house with a sunny central courtyard and helpful and efficient staff. Choose between comfortable (and significantly more expensive) rooms with cable TV, private bath and breakfast, or small, spartan and much cheaper rooms without. B$150.

Hostal Segovia Angel Calabi, right by the bus terminal ✆04/663-2965. Friendly hostel with clean rooms, with or without bath and all with cable TV, conveniently located right by the bus terminal. B$100.

Hosteria España Alejandro Corrado 546 ✆04/664-1790, ✉guimediaz@yahoo.com.ar. A relaxed place popular with backpackers on a budget. It's very simple and the bathrooms could do with a clean, but there's an amiable atmosphere and a kitchen. Rooms with private bath also come with cable TV. Dorms B$40, rooms B$140.

Residencial El Rosario Ingavi 777 ✆04/664-3942. Friendly, sparkling clean and quiet hostel featuring small but decent rooms with comfortable beds. The showers are reliably hot. B$80.

Eating and drinking

Nowhere is Tarija's strong Argentine influence more evident than in its restaurants. Good-quality grilled beef features strongly, ideally accompanied by a glass of local wine, while *Tarijeños* are also justly proud of their distinctive traditional cuisine of meat dishes cooked in delicious spicy sauces – try *ranga-ranga*, *saice* or *chancao de pollo*.

Bufalo Plaza Luis de Fuentes. Has a good range of international and Bolivian dishes, and is a pleasant place to people-watch. The lasagne comes recommended. Main dishes B$30–50.

Chingos Plaza Sucre. Local favourite, serving very tasty steaks served with a heap of chips and salad. They also do takeaways (✆02/663-2222).

Taverna Gattopardo Plaza Luis de Fuentes. It may have gringo prices, but it's worth treating yourself to the delicious food (try the steak) – and great service – served in a lovely, atmospheric restaurant with seating outside on the plaza.

Thai Kaffe Plaza Sucre. Bar attracting young locals with coffee, hamburgers and oriental cuisine. It transforms into a popular watering hole in the evenings.

El Tropero Lema and Daniel Campos. Authentic Argentine steakhouse with outdoor seating, serving excellent grilled beef and chicken as well as a filling *almuerzo*.

Directory

Banks and exchange The Banco Nacional de Bolivia, opposite the *Hotel Gran Tarija* on Sucre, changes cash and traveller's cheques and has an ATM that takes Visa and MasterCard. There are several other ATMs in town, including one at the Banco de Santa Cruz on Trigo and Lema.

Cinema Virgina Lema 126 (corner of Plaza Sucre).

Immigration Ingavi 789 (on corner of Ballivián). Mon–Fri 8.30am–12.30pm & 2.30–6.30pm.

Internet access There are plenty of places to surf the web in the city centre; try Consultel on Plaza Sucre (B$3 per hour).

Post office The Correo Central is on Lema, between Sucre and Trigo.

Taxi 4 de Julio ✆04/664-6555.

Telephone centres The ENTEL office is on Lema and Daniel Campos.

WINE IN THE TARIJA VALLEY

There are some worthwhile excursions close to Tarija in the warm and fertile Tarija valley, which is notable as Bolivia's prime wine-producing region. A visit to one of the nearby bodegas (wineries) to see how the wines are produced (and sample a few glasses at source) makes an excellent half-day excursion from the city. Generally, you can only visit the closest bodegas on an organized trip with a Tarija-based agency, but this can cost between B$100–200 per person depending on the size of the party (see "Directory" above). However, you can independently visit the lovely Casa Vieja bodega, about 35km from Tarija. *Micros* marked "v" leave from the corner of Campero and Corrado every half-hour or so (B$5) and will drop you off in the village of Concepción, from where it's a ten-minute walk from the plaza to the bodega – ask the driver or anyone in the village for directions. You can taste the wine, wander around the pretty vineyards and eat lunch in the restaurant.

Tour operators VTB Turismo Receptivo inside the *Hostal Carmen*, at Ingavi 784 (☎04/664-4342), and Viva Tours, 15 De Abril with Delgadillo (☎04/663-8325, ✉vivatour@cosett.com.bo), both run one-day tours of the city and around the vineyards and bodegas of the Tarija Valley with experienced English-speaking guides. Sur Bike, on the corner of Ballivián and Ingavi (☎07/619-4200), organizes cycling tours and rents bikes and equipment.

Moving on

Air There are regular flights to Cochabamba, La Paz and Santa Cruz, with tickets available from AeroSur, 15 de Abril 143, between Daniel Campos & Colón ☎04/663-0893, and TAM, Madrid and Trigo ☎04/664-2734.

Bus La Paz (1–2 daily between 7–8am; 24hr); Oruro (nightly; 20hr); Potosí (3–4 daily; 12hr); Tupiza (2 nightly; 10hr); Villazón (nightly; 10hr). There are also daily services to destinations in Argentina and Chile; the closest border crossing into Argentina is at Bermejo (10 daily; 7hr).

The central valleys

East of the Altiplano, the Andes march gradually down towards the eastern lowlands in a series of rugged mountain ranges, scarred with long, narrow valleys and blessed with rich alluvial soils. Both in climate and altitude, the **Central Valleys** are midway between the cold of the Altiplano and the tropical heat of the lowlands.

The administrative and political centre of Bolivia during Spanish rule, and still officially the capital of the republic, **Sucre** is a masterpiece of immaculately preserved colonial architecture, filled with elegant churches and mansions, and some of Bolivia's finest museums. The charms of **Cochabamba**, on the other hand, are more prosaic. Although lacking in conventional tourist attractions, it's a pleasant and interesting city – and not only due to the lack of

tourists. It is also the jumping-off point for an adventurous journey south into the **Parque Nacional Torotoro**, Bolivia's smallest national park, boasting labyrinthine limestone caves, deep canyons and waterfalls, dinosaur footprints and ancient ruins.

East of Cochabamba, the main road to Santa Cruz passes through the **Chapare**, a beautiful region of rushing rivers and dense tropical forests, where the last foothills of the Andes plunge down into the Amazon basin. The area has become notorious in recent decades as the source of most of Bolivia's coca crop, and, with Evo Morales continuing to fight for the international community to distinguish between the coca leaf in its traditional natural form and the leaves which are processed into cocaine, it seems that one of the great dramas of contemporary Bolivia has some way to run. It isn't wise to stray too far off the beaten track, though the area is generally perceived to be much safer than in recent years.

SUCRE

Set in a broad highland valley on the eastern edge of the Altiplano, **SUCRE**, declared a UNESCO World Heritage Site in 1991, is widely considered the most sophisticated and beautiful city in Bolivia, with some of the finest Spanish colonial architecture in South America and a pleasant, spring-like climate all year round. Neon signs are banned, and a municipal regulation requires all buildings to be whitewashed once a year, maintaining the characteristic that earned Sucre another of its many grandiose titles: "La Ciudad Blanca de Las Américas" – the White City of the Americas. It is also the administrative and market centre for a mountainous rural hinterland inhabited by the Quechua-speaking indigenous communities, particularly renowned for their beautiful weavings. These can be seen – and bought – in the city itself or on a day-trip to **Tarabuco**, a rural town about 60km southeast of Sucre that hosts a colourful Sunday market.

Founded some time between 1538 and 1540 and initially named Chuquisaca, Sucre's official title subsequently changed to Villa de la Plata (City of Silver). After independence, it was made the capital of the new **Republic of Bolivia** and renamed **Sucre**, but the city's economic importance declined. When the seat of both congress and the presidency was moved to La Paz after the civil war between the two cities in 1899, the transfer merely confirmed long-established realities. Sucre remained the seat of the supreme court and was allowed to retain the title of official or constitutional capital, an honorary position it still holds today.

What to see and do

The extravagance of Sucre's silver mine-funded past is immediately evident in the beautifully preserved architecture of the city's churches, palaces and administrative buildings. Most visitors enjoy a few hours wandering the streets and admiring the grandeur of the city centre; the attractive Plaza de 25 de Mayo is the best place to start. The Casa de la Libertad offers an excellent insight into the significance of the city in Bolivia's history. Within easy walking distance of the plaza, you'll find a plethora of lavishly decorated churches, as well as excellent restaurants and some lively bars. When you're ready to explore beyond the city centre, consider a visit to the dinosaur footprints at Cal Orko.

Plaza 25 de Mayo

The centre of Sucre is the spacious **Plaza 25 de Mayo**, shaded by tall palms and dotted with benches where people of all social classes pass the time of day. It's a great place to watch the world go by while having your shoes shined or enjoying a hot *salteña* (arguably Bolivia's

best) and a cool glass of the orange juice sold from handcarts by ever-present street vendors.

Casa de la Libertad

On the northwest side of the Plaza 25 de Mayo stands the simple but well-preserved colonial facade of the original seventeenth-century Jesuit University. Now known as the **Casa de La Libertad** (Tues–Sat 9am–noon & 2.30pm–6.30pm, Sun 9am–noon; B$15 including guided tours in Spanish, English and French), this was where the **Bolivian act of independence** was signed on August 6, 1825, and it now houses a small but very interesting museum dedicated to the birth of the republic. Inside, a copy of the document proclaiming a sovereign and independent state is on display in the assembly room (with the original displayed every August 6), as well as a gallery of portraits of almost all of Bolivia's presidents.

The Catedral and Iglesia de San Miguel

Sucre's sixteenth-century Catedral is also to be found on Plaza 25 de Mayo and is open on Sundays only; next door is the **Museo de la Catedral** (Calle Nicolás Ortiz 61; Mon–Fri 10am–noon & 3–5pm, Sat 10am–noon), which has a wonderful collection of important religious relics.

Half a block northwest of Plaza 25 de Mayo along Calle Arenales, the modest whitewashed Baroque facade of the **Iglesia de San Miguel** (sporadic opening hours; best to visit during Sunday mass between 6.30pm and 8pm), completed in 1621, conceals one of the most lavish church interiors in Sucre, with glorious carved Baroque altarpieces covered in gold leaf and an exquisite panelled Mudéjar ceiling of intricate interlocking geometric shapes.

Museo de Arte Indígena

Housed in an elegant colonial building on the corner of Calles San Alberto and Potosí, the fascinating **Museo de**

Arte Indígena (Mon–Fri 8am–noon & 2.30–6pm; B$16; ⊛www.bolivianet .com/asur/museosp.htm) is dedicated to the distinctive weavings of two local Quechua-speaking indigenous groups, the Jalq'a and the Tarabuqueños, and provides an excellent insight into a distinctly Andean artistic expression.

Museo Universitario Charcas

On the corner with Bolívar and Dalence is the rambling but worthwhile **Museo Universitario Charcas** (Mon–Fri 8.30am–noon & 2.30–6pm, Sat 9am–noon & 3–6pm; B$15), housed in a delightful seventeenth-century mansion. It is really four museums in one, combining the university's archeological, anthropological, colonial and modern art collections. Visits are by guided tour only, mostly in Spanish, and last at least an hour.

Convento-Museo La Recoleta

On the southeast side of Plaza Pedro de Anzures stands the **Convento-Museo La Recoleta** (Mon–Fri 9–11.30am & 2.30–5.30pm, Sat 3–5pm; B$10), a tranquil Franciscan monastery that now houses an interesting little museum of colonial religious art and materials related to the missionary work of the Franciscan order in Bolivia. Visits are by guided tour in Spanish only.

The footprints at Cal Orko

Five kilometres outside Sucre on the road to Cochabamba, the low mountain of **Cal Orko** is home to the world's largest collection of **dinosaur footprints**, discovered in 1994 by workers at a local cement works and limestone quarry. The site has been declared a national monument, and has become a major tourist attraction for its five thousand or so prints from at least 150 different types of dinosaur that cover an area of around 30,000 square metres of near-vertical rock face; it requires a good guide and some imagination to appreciate the footprints, as they're not easy to spot at first sight. The prints are on quite unstable rock, and some are at risk of crumbling away, so to protect the rock face visitors are not allowed to get too close. To see the footprints, head to **Parque Cretacio** (Mon–Fri 9am–5pm, Sat & Sun 10am–5pm; tours B$30; guides available at 10am, 12.30pm & 3pm). *Micros* A and 3 take you to outside the site, however the easiest way to visit the park is to take the Dino Truck, a colourful painted pick-up which leaves Mon–Sat at 9.30am, 12.30pm and 2.30pm from outside the cathedral. For an alternative experience, go to the university tourist office and ask to see another set of footprints, not officially studied as yet, but which you can get much closer to. You will require sturdy shoes, and the guided tour will cost around B$80, depending on the group size.

Arrival and information

Air The airport (☎04/645-4445) is about 8km northwest of the city; *micros* I and F run from there into the centre of town along Av. Siles (30min); alternatively, a taxi should cost about B$15–20.

Bus All long-distance buses arrive and depart from the bus terminal, about 3km northwest of the town centre on Ostria Gutiérrez. From here it's a B$6 taxi ride into the centre of town, or you can catch *micro* A, which runs down to the Mercado Central, a block north of the main Plaza 25 de Mayo. Collective taxis arriving from Potosí will drop you off outside your hotel or anywhere else in the centre of town.

Tourist information There is a wealth of information on offer in Sucre. The main municipal tourist office (Mon–Fri 8.30am–noon & 2–6pm; ☎04/645-1083 or 04/642-7102) is on the first floor of the Casa de Cultura, a block southeast of Plaza 25 de Mayo on Calle Argentina; there's also an Oficina Universitaria de Turismo (Mon–Fri 9am–noon & 3–6pm) on Calle Estudiantes, just off the Plaza 25 de Mayo, run by enthusiastic student guides who sometimes volunteer to show you around for free, although a tip is always welcome. A newer InfoTur office has also opened up at Dalence with Argentina (Mon–Fri 8am–noon & 2–6pm, weekends 9am–noon & 3–6pm). Tourist police ☎04/648-0467.

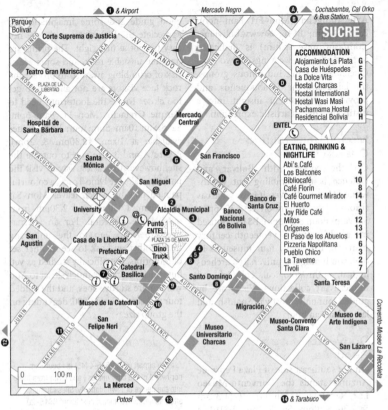

Accommodation

Sucre has a pretty good range of accommodation, almost all of it conveniently located in the heart of the old city centre.

Alojamiento La Plata Ravelo 32 ☎04/645-2102. Popular budget option offering small, basic but clean rooms with shared bath around an attractive courtyard, as well as recently added (and more comfortable) rooms in the back. There's also a terrace, and the location – opposite the market – is noisy but very central. B$50–80.

Casa de Huéspedes San Marco Ancieto Arce 233 ☎04/646-2087. A peaceful and friendly place to stay, with simple rooms (B$40 per person) as well as longer-stay apartments. Don't miss the terraces with views across the city. B$80.

La Dolce Vita Calle Urcullo 342 ☎04/691-2014. Central guesthouse with friendly staff, good views from a relaxed terrace and nicely decorated rooms. Books up fast so call ahead. B$95.

Hostal Charcas Ravelo 62 ☎04/645-3972. Modern, central establishment, with helpful, welcoming staff, abundant hot water and the obligatory sunny rooftop terrace. Rooms are scrupulously clean, if rather cramped, and those with private bathrooms lack ventilation. There's also a communal living room with cable TV, and breakfast is available (B$8). B$80–140.

Hostal International Guillermo Loayza 119 ☎04/644-0471, ✉hisucre@yahoo.com. It may be a 15-min walk to town, but the friendly backpackers, sociable feel and great facilities at this hostel make up for it. It has a good kitchen and huge garden, and is just minutes from the bus station. The dorm rooms are spacious and comfortable. Breakfast and internet are available but not included. Dorms B$39, rooms B$100.

Hostal Wasi Masi Calle Urcullo 233 ☎04/645-3951, ⊛www.wasi-masi.com. This is a sociable option with an excellent book exchange and basic rooms set around a leafy outdoor space. Minimum stay two nights. B$120.

Pachamama Hostal Ancieto Arce 450 ☎04/645-3673, ✉Hostal_Pachamama@hotmail.com. Centrally located hostel with good views of the surrounding city and simple rooms with hot showers. Kitchen use available. B$90–110.

Residencial Bolivia San Alberto 45 ☎04/645-4346. Friendly and good-value *residencial*, with spacious, airy rooms (with or without bathroom) set around a bright courtyard with plenty of plants. A meagre breakfast is included. B$50–70.

Eating

Sucre is home to a good variety of restaurants where you can get everything from the spicy local cuisine to authentic French, Italian and vegetarian food at reasonable prices. The markets are great places to find cheap, filling lunches (usually about B$12–15 for a two-course meal with a drink) : try the second floor of Mercado Central on Calle Zabelo and the food hall in Mercado Negro on Calle Junín. Make sure not to miss the huge fresh fruit salads in Mercado Central.

Abi's Café Plaza 25 de Mayo 32. Very friendly café on the square with excellent milkshakes (B$8), good snacks and a selection of cakes and ice creams, such as *Copa Vienesa* (B$17), that make for a perfect afternoon sit-down.

Los Balcones Plaza 25 de Mayo. Upstairs overlooking the plaza, this smart restaurant is a lovely place to watch the world go by while enjoying steaks, sandwiches and the huge salad bar.

Café Gourmet Mirador Plaza de la Recoleta. A fantastic place to sit in the sun, admire the gorgeous views and feel like you're somewhere in the Mediterranean. The menu includes reasonably authentic crêpes, tapas and pasta dishes, and the hot chocolate is delicious.

El Huerto Ladislao Cabrera 86. Ask a local for the best restaurant in town, and chances are they'll direct you here. The menu features excellent meat and fish dishes cooked to both traditional Bolivian and sophisticated international recipes, served outdoors in a beautiful garden. It's some distance from the city centre, but well worth the taxi fare. Lunchtimes only.

El Paso de los Abuelos Bustillo 216. The best *salteñas* in town but go before lunchtime as they sell out fast. Closed Sun.

Pizzeria Napolitana Plaza 25 de Mayo 30. Sucre's longest-established Italian restaurant, serving tasty pizza and pasta, home-made ice cream, strong coffee and a daily choice of different set lunches (B$25).

Pueblo Chico Plaza 25 de Mayo. Coffee is the speciality in this charming bar-café set just off the plaza in a pretty courtyard, with a selection of "celebrity coffees" – try a Jim Carey or a Janis Joplin. Also offers a range of snacks and juices,

and serves as a lively bar in the evenings. Coffees B$12–15.

La Taverne Ancieto Arce 35. Authentic French restaurant serving classic dishes like *coq au vin*, *boeuf bourguignon* and rabbit for about B$40, as well as excellent home-made pâté and delicious chocolate gateaux. Reservations recommended (☎04/645-5719). Eve only, closed Sun.

Tivoli Corner of Argentina and Olaneta. Charming restaurant serving probably the best and most authentic pizza in town.

Drinking and nightlife

A high student population and a stream of party-loving backpackers means Sucre has a good range of bars and clubs, and is a great place to either enjoy a quiet beer or really let your hair down.

Bibliocafé N. Ortíz 50. Bohemian bar-café attracting a good mix of locals and travellers from early evening until late with its mellow live music and intimate atmosphere. Snacks and light meals are also available.

Café Florín Calle Bolívar 567, one block from the plaza. Dutch-run establishment with an excellent range of beers and cocktails with a happy hour from 9.30–10.30pm. Also serves up exceptionally tasty curries, and Bolivian specialities.

Joy Ride Café N. Ortíz 14. Trendy, Dutch-run bar-café and the most popular gringo spot in town for food and night-time drinking, serving tasty breakfasts, meals and snacks as well as excellent coffee, cocktails and cold beer; there's a small, charming patio upstairs. From 7.30am on weekdays and 9am on weekends, until late; particularly busy on Friday and Saturday nights.

Mitos Francisco Cerro. Basement disco attracting locals and tourists alike to dance the night away to a mix of latin and western beats. Weekends only. Entry B$5–10.

Orígenes Azurduy 473 ☎02/645-7091. Venue staging a folkoric show with traditional dances from across Bolivia. Not just for gringos, and worth a night out if you're missing out on carnival, but still feels a bit artificial, and the food is overpriced. Shows on Tues, Fri, Sat and Sun at 9pm.

Directory

Banks and exchange Casa de Cambios Ambar, San Alberto 7, and El Arca, España 134, both change traveller's cheques and cash dollars at reasonable rates. There are also plenty of ATMs around town where you can withdraw cash on Visa or MasterCard, including at Banco de Santa Cruz and Banco Nacional de Bolivia, opposite each other at San Alberto with España.

Car rental Auto Cambio Chuquisaca, Av. Jaime Mendoza 1106 ☎04/646-0984; Imbex, Serrano 165 ☎04/646-1222.

Cinema Cine Universal, Plaza 25 de Mayo. Shows subtitled new releases.

Internet access There are internet cafés all over the city, most of which charge about B$3–4 an hour: try Cyber-Station on the east side of the plaza or Café Internet Maya on Arenales 5.

Post office Correo Central, Junín with Ayacucho. Mon–Fri 8am–8pm, Sat 8am–6pm.

Telephone centres The main ENTEL office is at España 271 with Camargo, and there are smaller Punto ENTEL offices on the northeast side of Plaza 25 de Mayo and on the corner of Ravelo with Junín, plus numerous card-operated phone booths on Plaza 25 de Mayo and at major intersections around the city.

Moving on

Air Daily flights to La Paz and Santa Cruz. AeroSur, Arenales 31 ☎04/646-2141; TAM, at the airport ☎04/645-1310.

Bus Services run from the bus terminal in the northwest of the city on Ostria Gutiérrez to: Cochabamba (several daily; 12hr); La Paz (4 daily; 12hr); Oruro (2 daily; 10hr); Potosí (hourly; 3hr); Tarabuco (4 daily; 1hr); Santa Cruz (5–6 daily; 15hr).

Taxi Collective taxis for Potosí cost B$35 per person with 4 people (2hr 30min); drivers wait just outside the bus station (by the clock) until full.

TARABUCO

By far the most popular excursion from Sucre is to the small rural town of **Tarabuco**, set amid undulating

mountains about 65km southeast of the city. The town itself is an unremarkable collection of red-tiled adobe houses and cobbled streets, but its real claim to fame is the Sunday market. This is the focus for the indigenous communities of the surrounding mountains, the Tarabuqueños, who come to sell the beautiful weavings for which they're famous throughout Bolivia. The market is actually a bit of a tourist trap, but the stalls selling weavings and other handicrafts to tourists are still far outnumbered by those selling basic supplies such as dried foodstuffs, agricultural tools, sandals made from tyres, big

SUCRE TOUR OPERATORS

Most agencies in Sucre will offer a Sunday tour to the Tarabuco market as well as city tours and trips to the salt flats and mines of Potosí. Some offer more adventurous biking and hiking excursions in the surrounding countryside.

Bolivia Specialist N. Ortíz 30 ☎04/643-7389, ⓦwww.boliviaspecialist.com. Hiking, biking and a tour to just about anywhere in Bolivia can be booked from this central office.

Candelaria Tours J Perez 301 in Plazuela Cochabamba ☎04/644-0340, ⓦwww.candelaria tours.com. Reliable company specializing in

cultural and historical tours around Sucre and Potosí as well as variations on the salt-flat tours.

Joy Ride Bolivia Next door to the *Joy Ride Café* at Ortíz 14 ☎04/642-5544, ⓦwww.joyridebol .com. Popular operator offering adventurous mountain biking, paragliding and horseriding trips.

bundles of coca and pure alcohol in great steel drums.

Buses and trucks to Tarabuco from Sucre (1hr; about B$10) leave most mornings from Av. de las Américas returning in the afternoon; however, it's much more convenient to go in one of the **tourist buses** (they usually charge around B$25–50 for the return trip) organized by hotels and tour agencies in Sucre. Every Sucre tour operator will offer a trip to Tarabuco, some with guided tours in English (see Sucre tour operators on p.228).

COCHABAMBA

Set at the geographical centre of Bolivia, midway between the Altiplano and the eastern lowlands, **COCHABAMBA** is one of the country's most vibrant and youthful cities and the commercial hub of the country's richest agricultural region, the Cochabamba Valley, known as the breadbasket of Bolivia. It's a friendly and unpretentious city, also known as the "City of Eternal Spring" for its year-round sunny climate matched by the warmth and openness of its population, and is perfect for relaxing in one of the many cafés and hideaways around Calle España.

What to see and do

Though Cochabamba isn't the place for colonial architecture, there are at least a couple of historic sights. Shopaholics will love the huge outdoor market of La Cancha, and there are also opportunities for exploring the understated attractions of the surrounding valleys.

Plaza 14 de Septiembre and around

The centre of Cochabamba is **Plaza 14 de Septiembre**, a placid and pleasant square with flower-filled ornamental gardens and plenty of benches where *Cochabambinos* sit under the shade of tall palm trees. A block south of the plaza on the corner of Calles Aguirre and Jordán stands the extensive **Museo Archeológico** (Mon–Fri 8am–6pm, Sat 8.30am–noon; B$20), which explains the evolution of pre-Hispanic culture in the Cochabamba region.

Convento de Santa Teresa

The lovely **Convento de Santa Teresa** (Mon–Fri 8.30am–11.30am & 2–5pm; B$20) on Ecuador and Baptista (the entrance is on Baptista, through the small café) is worth visiting. As well as the convent, this beautiful building houses a church built within a church (the original church was destroyed in the 1700s). The nuns still live on the site, though they are now housed in the complex next door.

La Cancha

The commercial heart of this market city is in the south, with its massive rambling street markets. An entire block between Calles Tarata and Pulucayo is occupied by the massive covered street market known as **La Cancha** (Quechua for "walled enclosure"), where *campesinos* and merchants come to buy and sell their produce. Wandering through the market's sprawling labyrinth of stalls is the best way to get a feel for the vibrant commercial culture of the city and the surrounding region.

Palacio Portales

About 1km north of the city centre, with its entrance off Av. Posí, the **Palacio Portales** (visits by guided tour only; Mon–Fri 3.30–6pm, Sat 10–11.30am, Sun 11–11.30am; B$10) is the luxurious house built for the Cochabamba-born "King of Tin", Simón Patiño – though he never actually lived here. Built between 1915 and 1922 in a bizarre mix of architectural styles, including French Neoclassical and Mudéjar, the palace's interior is decorated with astonishing opulence. If anything, though, it's the lush, magnificent gardens (same hours; admission included with Palace entrance, or free if visiting the **gardens** only) that really impress, laid out in perfect proportion by Japanese specialists and featuring a beautiful and rare ginkgo tree.

Cristo de la Concordia

About 1.5km east of the city is the Cristo de la Concordia – a statue of Christ modelled on the one in Rio but just slightly taller. To reach the summit, you can walk up the steep steps (though be warned, there have been reports of muggings), or take the five-minute cable-car ride (Tues–Sat 10am–6pm, Sun 9am–6pm; B$8 return) for excellent views of the city.

Arrival and information

Air Cochabamba's extremely modern but underused Jorge Wilsterman Airport is a few kilometres outside town; a taxi into the city centre should cost about B$20; alternatively, take *micro* B, which goes up Av. Ayacucho to Plaza 14 de Septiembre.

Bus The bus terminal is on Av. Ayacucho just south of Av. Aroma, from where many of the city's hotels are within easy walking distance; otherwise, a taxi to anywhere in the city centre should cost about B$7 per person. Buses from the Chapare region east of Cochabamba arrive around the junction of Av. Oquendo and Av. 9 de Abril to the southeast of the city centre.

Tourist information The tourist office (Mon–Fri 8am–noon & 2.30–6.30pm, Sat 8.30am–noon; T04/451-0023) is on Plaza 14 de Septiembre, and distributes free maps and leaflets on tours to the surrounding attractions.

Tour operators Fremen, at Tumulsa N-0245 T04/425-9392, Wwww.andes-amazonia.com; Bolivia Cultura, at Ecuador 342 T04/452-6028, Wwww.boliviacultura.com. Bolivia Cultura also run Spanish lessons with host family options, and offer worthwhile volunteering opportunities, with a minimum of three months for placements (Wwww .volunteeringbolivia.org).

Accommodation

Accommodation in Cochabamba is functional and reasonably priced, but mostly unexceptional and generally not aimed at tourists (the city sees few).

The only time accommodation is difficult to find is in mid-August during the Fiesta de la Virgen de Urkupiña in nearby Quillacollo; it's best to book in advance during this period.

Hostal Colonial Junín N-0134 T04/422-1791. Friendly and good-value family-run place offering clean but simple rooms on two floors. Overlooks a charming garden with lush tropical vegetation. B$60.

Hostal Elisa Lopéz S-0834 T04/425-4406. Helpful and friendly little place just a block away from the bus terminal. It's much nicer than it appears from outside, with small but clean rooms (with or without bath and cable TV) around a pleasant central garden with outdoor seating. Internet access and breakfast are available. B$80.

Hostal Florida 25 de Mayo S-0583 T04/425-7911, Efloridahostel@elatinmail.com. Justly popular backpackers' favourite halfway between the bus terminal and the city centre. The simple but clean rooms (with or without bath) are set around a sunny courtyard. Breakfast is extra. Doubles B$80.

Residencial Familiar Sucre 552 (between Lanza & San Martin) T04/422-7988. Set in a lovely building with rooms around a pretty courtyard, this hostel is spotless, with decent rooms and plenty of character. The location is very central. B$70.

Eating and drinking

The best places to eat if you're on a tight budget are Cochabamba's many markets, and the choice of restaurants in the city is broad, with some very good meals available at relatively low prices. Boulevar Recolta, a modern pedestrianized strip on the right-hand turning from the roundabout before Av. Pando, is a popular night-time place for a meal and a drink; there's an abundance of modern restaurants, bars and a few karaoke joints too.

Café Kausay 25 de Mayo with Ecuador. Sweet little café serving pancakes, waffles, breakfasts and aromatic coffee; you can also buy coffee from the Yungas here. Latte B$5. Mon–Sat 8.30am–10pm.

La Cantonata Corner of España and Mayor Rocha. Smart Italian restaurant with great service, serving up filling pasta dishes.

Casablanca 25 de Mayo 344. Trendy Hollywood-themed bar serving cold beer, fruity cocktails and the usual fare of pizzas, pasta, breakfasts and sandwiches. There's a pile of magazines to browse through and the restaurant also hosts jazz gigs and art exhibits. Mains B$26–45. Closed Sun afternoon.

Espresso Café Bar Esteban Arce 340, on the corner of Plaza Principal. A bustling, characterful café, very popular with locals who come for the delicious coffee and variety of cakes. Large coffee B$9. Closed Sun.

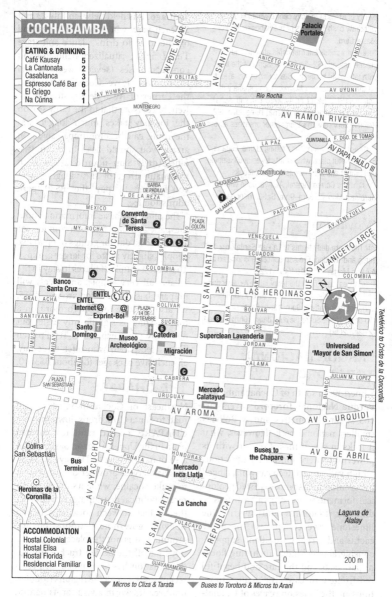

COCHABAMBA

EATING & DRINKING
Café Kausay	5
La Cantonata	2
Casablanca	3
Espresso Café Bar	6
El Griego	4
Na Cúnna	1

ACCOMMODATION
Hostal Colonial	A
Hostal Elisa	D
Hostal Florida	C
Residencial Familiar	B

Teleférico to Cristo de la Concordia

▼ *Micros to Cliza & Tarata*   ▼ *Buses to Torotoro & Micros to Arani*

El Griego España con Ecuador. Atmospheric Greek restaurant with excellent *pastizio*, and ideal for a cosy late-night drink. Mon–Sat 4.30pm–1am.

Na Cúnna Av. Salamanca 580. If you're craving a taste of Guinness (no pints though, sadly), this popular Irish café-bar is the place to come.

Directory

Banks and exchange Casa de Cambio Exprinter, on the west side of Plaza 14 de Septiembre, changes cash dollars and traveller's cheques, and there are street moneychangers at all the major intersections in the centre of town. There are also plenty of ATMs in the city centre where you can withdraw cash in dollars or bolivianos on Visa or MasterCard.

Internet access Internet cafés abound and most charge around B$2–3 per hour. Some of the best with late-night hours are *Black Cat*, on Achá, just off the main square, *Cliksmania*, on España with Colombia, and *ENTEL* on Av. Ayacucho with Achá.

Laundry Superclean Lavandería, 16 de Julio 392. Reliable service with several other branches across town.

Outdoor equipment The Spitting Llama, España 615. A useful place which rents bikes and camping equipment and sells novels and guidebooks.

Post office Correo Central, Av. Ayacucho with Av. Heroínas. Mon–Fri 8am–9pm, Sat 8am–noon.

Moving on

Air There are daily flights to La Paz, Santa Cruz, Tarija and Trinidad. The Aerosur office is located at Av. San Martín 150 (⊕04/451-1727).

Bus Buses leave from the terminal on Av. Ayacuco. La Paz (every 30min; 7hr); Oruro (every 30min; 4hr); Potosí (nightly at 8pm; 10hr); Santa Cruz (10 daily; 12hr); Sucre (several daily; 10hr); Trinidad (2 daily; 20hr).

PARQUE NACIONAL TOROTORO

Some 139km south of Cochabamba, the **Parque Nacional Torotoro** covers just 165 square kilometres and is Bolivia's smallest national park. However, what it lacks in size it makes up for with its powerful scenery and varied attractions – high valleys and deep canyons, ringed by low mountains whose twisted geological formations are strewn with fossils, dinosaur footprints and labyrinthine limestone cave complexes. The park's cactus and scrubby woodland supports considerable wildlife – including flocks of parakeets and the rare and beautiful red-fronted macaw. The main attractions are the limestone caves of **Umajalanta**, the beautiful, waterfall-filled **Torotoro Canyon**, and hiking expeditions to the pre-Inca ruined fortress of **Llama Chaqui**.

The small town of Torotoro's main annual celebration is the **Fiesta de Tata Santiago**. It is held between July 23 and 25 each year, when the *ayllus* descend on the town to drink, dance and stage Tinku fights, ritualized hand-to-hand combats. Buses (several weekly; 7hr) to Torotoro leave Cochabamba from the corner of Av. 6 de Agosto and Av. Republica. Note that in the rainy season the journey takes much longer and the route can become impassable. On arrival you should head to the tourist office (daily 8am–noon & 2–5pm), on the main street of the village, where you'll need to pay the B$30 park admission fee.

The office has basic information about the park and can find you a guide for about B$80 a day for groups of up to five people (slightly more for larger groups). There are a couple of places to stay in the village, all very simple, and locals will prepare basic meals for around B$15. It's also possible to visit Torotoro on a tour – which is significantly easier but obviously more expensive. Try Fremen Tours (see p.230) who offer three-day, all-inclusive packages for about B$3000.

THE CHAPARE

Northeast of Cochabamba, the main road to Santa Cruz drops down into the **CHAPARE**, a broad, rainforest-covered plain in the Upper Amazon Basin and an area of natural beauty. However, it's also Bolivia's largest provider of coca grown to make cocaine; while it's unclear how recent political developments will affect the conflict between coca farmers and Bolivian government troops on the ground, this is not the place for expeditions far off the beaten track – though the situation has been much calmer in recent years. For all the region's troubles, however, it's worth a visit for its natural beauty and the peaceful towns along the main Cochabamba to Santa Cruz road, which are perfectly safe to visit, unless you go during one of the sporadic road blockades by protesting *cocaleros*; these are usually announced in advance, so make sure to look through the local newspapers before your trip.

The small laidback town of **Villa Tunari** is a good place to break a journey between Cochabamba and Santa Cruz and also to get a brief introduction to the Amazon lowlands. In Cochabamba, regular minibuses leave from the corner of Av. Oquendo and Av. 9 de Abril (5hr); alternatively you can take a bus heading to Santa Cruz and inform the driver you want to get off just after the Espíritu Santo Bridge. The best place to stay is *Hotel Villa Tunari*, with clean, decent rooms and hot showers (rooms B$40). The best restaurant in town is in the *Hotel Las Palmas*, on the main plaza; there are also a number of passable food stalls in the market. There is an ATM in Villa Tunari, but it is frequently out of order so it's best to bring sufficient cash.

A few kilometres south of Villa Tunari, some 6226 square kilometres of the forested northern slopes of the Andes are protected by the **Parque Nacional Carrasco** to the east. Plunging steeply down from high mountain peaks, the park encompasses a variety of ecosystems from high Andean grasslands and cloudforest to dense tropical rainforest and also supports a great range of wildlife, including all the major Amazonian mammals and more than seven hundred species of bird.

The eastern lowlands

Stretching from the last foothills of the Andes east to Brazil and south to Paraguay and Argentina, Bolivia's **eastern lowlands** were until recently among the least-known and least-developed regions in the country; however, the area has undergone astonishingly rapid development, while its economy has grown to become the most important in the country, fuelled by oil and gas, cattle-ranching and massive agricultural development. At the centre of this economic boom is the regional capital of **Santa Cruz**, a young, lively city and the ideal base for exploring the many attractions of the surrounding area. A 90-minute drive west of the city are the pristine rainforests protected by the **Parque Nacional Amboró**; the beautiful cloudforest that covers the upper regions of the park can be visited from the idyllic resort town of **Samaipata**. From Samaipata, you can also head further southwest to the town of **Vallegrande** and the nearby hamlet of **La Higuera**, where the iconic Argentine revolutionary, Ernesto "Che" Guevara, was killed in 1967. East of Santa Cruz, the railway to Brazil passes through the broad forested plains of **Chiquitos**, whose beautiful **Jesuit mission churches** bear witness to one of the most extraordinary episodes in Spanish colonial history, when a handful of priests established a semi-autonomous theocratic state in the midst of the wilderness. Finally, south of Santa Cruz, the vast and inhospitable **Chaco**, an arid wilderness of dense thorn and scrub, stretches south to Argentina and Paraguay.

SANTA CRUZ

Set among the steamy, tropical lowlands just beyond the last Andean foothills, **SANTA CRUZ** has emerged in recent decades as the economic powerhouse of Bolivia. An isolated frontier town until the middle of the twentieth century, the city has grown in the last fifty years to become the second biggest in the country, as well as the locus of Bolivia's wealthy right wing. The election of Evo Morales and his plans for constitutional reform have met with increasingly violent opposition here, culminating in the late 2008 expulsion of the US ambassador, whom Morales accused of fomenting political agitation, and a march on the city by Morales's Aymaran supporters. While you're unlikely to encounter any trouble, the situation remains unstable and it's worth keeping an eye on the media for new developments. The city layout consists of a series of rings – called *anillos* – with the colonial city centre inside the Primer Anillo, and almost everything you need within the first two or three.

What to see and do

Largely because most of it is so new, Santa Cruz has little to match the colonial charm of highland cities like Sucre and Potosí, and few conventional tourist sights beyond several mediocre museums and an architecturally unexciting cathedral. While some travellers find its unapologetic modernity, commercialism and pseudo-Americanism unappealing, others enjoy its blend of dynamism and tropical insouciance. Be careful walking around the city centre at night as there have been several reports of muggings.

Plaza 24 de Septiembre

At the centre of Santa Cruz is **Plaza 24 de Septiembre**, a spacious, lively square with well-tended gardens shaded by tall trees. On the south side of the plaza stands the salmon-pink **Catedral** (Tues–Sun 8.30am–6pm; free), or **Basílica Mayor de San Lorenzo**, a hulking brick structure with twin bell towers built between 1845 and 1915 on the site of an original church dating back to 1605. The cool, vaulted interior has some fine silverwork around the altar, but the best religious art is tucked away in the adjacent **Museo de Arte Sacro** (Mon & Tues 10am–noon & 4–6pm, Sun 10am–noon & 6–8pm; B$10); the entrance is just to the right as you face the altar. To the west of the cathedral on Independencia is **Manzano Uno** (Tues–Sat 10am–12.30pm and 4–9pm, Sunday 4–9pm; free), a small exhibition space showcasing some excellent displays of national and international sculpture, photography and painting.

Museo Etno-folklórico

Four blocks north and a block east of Plaza 24 de Septiembre inside the Parque Arenal fa little park with an artificial lake), the **Museo Etno-folklórico** (Mon–Fri 9.30am–noon & 2.30–5.30pm) houses a small but varied collection of artefacts that provides a good introduction to the different indigenous ethnic groups of the eastern lowlands. Exhibits include photographs, samples of traditional dress including feather headdresses worn by dancers at religious festivals, and wooden animal masks. At the time of writing, the museum was closed for refurbishment but expected to reopen by early 2011.

Biocentro Güembé and Jardín Zoológico

About a 30-minute taxi ride from the city centre, at Km 7 Camino a Porongo, Zona Los Batos (entry B$90; ☎03/370-0700, ⓦwww.biocentroguembe.com), **Biocentro Güembé** is a tranquil park retreat with more than enough to keep anyone entertained for a day or two. There are ten swimming pools, as well as opportunities for mountain biking, kayaking and beach volleyball. There is also a large butterfly house, orchid display and meditation centre (daily 8.30am–6pm; B$80). Camping costs B$180 per person with park access included. The **Jardín Zoológico** (daily 9am–6pm; B$10) is on the Third Anillo, and houses an intriguing collection of tropical birds and reptiles as well as deers, llamas and bears.

Arrival and information

Air Santa Cruz's main airport is the modern Aero puerto Viru-Viru (☎03/385-2400) 17km north of the city centre, from where it's a B$20 flat-fare taxi ride into the centre of town; alternatively, you can

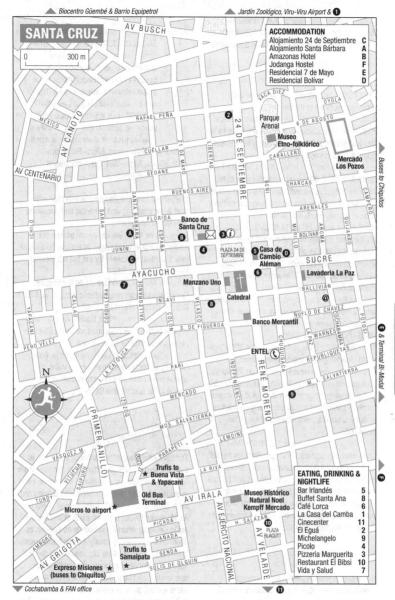

SANTA CRUZ

0   300 m

AV BUSCH

ACCOMMODATION

Alojamiento 24 de Septiembre	C
Alojamiento Santa Bárbara	A
Amazonas Hotel	B
Jodanga Hostel	F
Residencial 7 de Mayo	E
Residencial Bolívar	D

Parque Arenal

Museo Etno-folklórico

Mercado Los Pozos

Buses to Chiquitos

Banco de Santa Cruz

Casa de Cambio Alemán

Lavadería La Paz

Manzano Uno

Catedral

Banco Mercantil

ENTEL

E & Terminal Bi-Modal

BOLIVIA

THE EASTERN LOWLANDS

N

Trufis to Buena Vista & Yapacani

Old Bus Terminal

Micros to airport

Museo Histórico Natural Noel Kempff Mercado

Trufis to Samaipata

Expreso Misiones (buses to Chiquitos)

EATING, DRINKING & NIGHTLIFE

Bar Irlandés	5
Buffet Santa Ana	8
Café Lorca	6
La Casa del Camba	1
Cinecenter	11
El Eguá	2
Michelangelo	9
Picolo	4
Pizzería Marguerita	3
Restaurant El Bibsi	10
Vida y Salud	7

catch a *micro* (every 15min; B$1–3) to the corner of Avenidas Irala and Cañoto, outside the old bus terminal. The city's second airport, the smaller Aeropuerto El Trompillo is used by both the military airline, TAM, and Amazon specialist, Amaszonas. **Bus** Long-distance buses and all trains arrive and depart from the recently completed Terminal Bi-Modal de Transporte, the combined bus and train terminal about 2km east of the city centre just Secondside the Anillo at the end of Av. Brasil. There are always plenty of taxis outside; alternatively, you can reach the city centre by catching any *micro* heading east along Av. Brasil and marked "Plaza 24 de Septiembre".

Tourist information Santa Cruz's Unidad de Turismo (Mon–Fri 8am–4pm; ☎03/336-9595 ext 17) is on the west side of Plaza 24 de Septiembre.

Accommodation

Most budget accommodation is conveniently located in or close to the old city centre.

Alojamiento 24 de Septiembre Santa Bárbara 79 ☎03/332-1992. Centrally located with basic facilities and shared showers in a clean, if not especially appealing, courtyard. B$50.

Alojamiento Santa Bárbara Santa Bárbara 151 ☎03/332-1817, ✉alojstabarbara@yahoo.com. No-frills budget option with basic but clean rooms with cool tiled floors and shared bath (but no fans) around a small courtyard. B$50.

Amazonas Hotel Junín 214 ☎03/333-4583. Just off the main square, this hotel offers good-value rooms with cable TV and private bathrooms. B$150.

Jodanga Hostel El Fuerte 1380 (near Parque Urbano) ☎03/339-6542, ⊛www.jodanga.com. Purpose-built backpackers' hostel. Excellent facilities include kitchen, free internet, free breakfast and TV room, as well as a swimming pool. The atmosphere, however, can seem sterile. Dorms B$65–75, rooms from B$80.

Residencial 7 de Mayo Av. Interradial ☎03/348-9634. Sparkling new establishment directly opposite the new Terminal Bi-Modal de Transporte, thus convenient if you're arriving late, leaving early or just passing through. The clean, modern rooms come in a variety of prices depending on whether or not you want a private bath and a/c or fan. B$50–60.

Residencial Bolívar Sucre 131 ☎03/334-2500. Long-standing backpackers' favourite with helpful staff and small but immaculately clean dorms (B$60 per person) and rooms (with fan and private or shared bath) around a cool, leafy patio with hammocks and a resident toucan. Worth phoning in advance to reserve a room if you're arriving late. Breakfast available. B$180.

Eating

Santa Cruz's relative wealth and cosmopolitanism are reflected in the city's wide variety of restaurants.

Buffet Santa Ana Ingavi 164. Good-value buffet (B$20–25), popular with both meat-eaters and vegetarians. Closed Sun.

La Casa del Camba Av. Cristóbal de Mendoza 539. The best of the many traditional *Cruceño* restaurants on this stretch of the Second Anillo, and a great place to enjoy moderately priced *parillada*

(barbecued meat), *majao de charque* (rice with beef jerky, fried egg and bananas) and *pacumutu* (massive shish kebab).

Picolo 21 de Mayo 90. Ice-cream parlour set among a lurid array of bright tables and fake waterfalls. Excellent ice cream for the hot afternoons. Ice-cream sundae B$22.

Pizzeria Marguerita Plaza 24 de Septiembre. Cosy restaurant serving fantastic pizza as well as Bolivian dishes. Mains B$25–40.

Restaurant El Bibsi Plaza Blacutt. An extremely popular buffet-style restaurant, charging B$25 per person. Very popular at weekends.

Vida y Salud Ayacucho with Vallegrande. Great little veggie restaurant serving good-value *almuerzos* as well as à la carte options in the evening. Set lunch menu B$15–20.

Drinking, nightlife and entertainment

The Equipetrol area, to the northwest of the city, is the main area for nightlife: after 10pm, the streets are lined with revellers and cars blaring loud music. Head to clubs on Av. San Martín for hedonistic dancing and drink deals, or for a slightly calmer scene, check out Av. Monseñor Rivero, between the First and Second Anillo. Dress up smart if you want to go to clubs, as doormen will turn away scruffy-looking backpackers.

Bar Irlandés Plaza 24 de Septiembre. On the first floor of the Bolívar shopping centre, with tables overlooking the plaza, this upmarket Irish-themed bar is a great place to enjoy a beer, cocktail or coffee while watching the world go by outside. Gets very lively with locals and travellers in the evenings, especially on weekends.

Café Lorca Sucre 8. Popular café with excellent but expensive food. A good place for a drink in the evenings, and they hold regular art exhibitions, events and live music. Mon–Thurs 9am–11.30pm, Fri & Sat 9.30am–3am and Sun 5–11.30pm.

Cinecenter 2nd Anillo, Av. El Trompillo between Monseñor Santiesteban and René Moreno. Big multiscreen complex with fast-food joints and coffee bars, as well as a range of international films (usually subtitled but worth checking individual films).

El Eguá Av. 24 de Septiembre with Rafael Peña. Central cuban salsa club where the dancefloor gets packed on weekends. Salsa classes during the week. Entry B$10.

Directory

Banks and exchange You can change US dollars and traveller's cheques at the Casa de Cambio Alemán (Mon–Fri 8.30am–noon & 2.30–6pm, Sat 8.30am–noon) on the east side of Plaza 24 de Septiembre, and there are plenty of banks with ATMs where you can make cash withdrawals on Visa or MasterCard – try Banco Ganadero on Bolívar with Beni.
Internet There are numerous internet cafés around the city centre, especially along Calle Murillo between Ballivián and Parque Arenal; most charge around B$6–8 per hour. Try Light-Soft Internet on Junín 333, Web Boli on Ballivián 267, between La Paz and Cochabamba, or the small shop inside the Bolívar shopping complex on the main plaza.
Laundry Hostels are the best bet for laundry but Lavanderia Sofia on Calle Santa Bárbara 118c is also reliable.

Moving on

Air As well as several daily flights to Cochabamba, La Paz and Sucre, operated by Aerosur, Av. Irala 616 (☎03/336-4446), there are less frequent flights to further-flung lowland destinations serviced by Amaszonas (☎03/357-8988) and TAM (☎03/337-1999), both of whom operate out of Aeropuerto El Trompillo (see p.235).
Bus Buses depart from the Terminal Bi-Modal de Transporte. Cochabamba (2 daily; 12hr; connections to La Paz, Oruro & Uyuni); Potosí (2–3 daily; 18hr); Sucre (4–5 daily; 15hr); Trinidad (4–5 daily; 12hr). There are also daily departures to Argentine destinations, including Buenos Aires.
Train Trains to Quijarro, on the Brazilian border, leave at 5pm on Mondays, Wednesdays and Fridays, and at 7.30pm on Tuesdays, Thursdays and Saturdays. There's also a daily service (Mon–Sat) at 12pm; be aware though that these are run by the cheaper – and less comfortable – Ferroviaria Oriental company. Trains can be chilly, so be sure to wrap up. From the station in Quijarro, it's a five-minute taxi ride to the border town of Corumbá (B$5 per person).

PARQUE NACIONAL AMBORÓ

Forty kilometres west of Santa Cruz, the **Parque Nacional Amboró** covers some 4300 square kilometres of a great forest-covered spur of the Andes jutting out into the eastern plains. Amboró's steep, densely forested slopes support an astonishing biodiversity, including more than 830 different types of bird and pretty much the full range of rainforest

---

TOUR OPERATORS IN THE LOWLANDS

If you plan to head to Amboró National Park, it is cheaper to organize a tour from Samaipata, and you'll get more time in the rainforest for your money. However, the following companies in Santa Cruz are all well established and have good reputations:

Amboró Tours Calle Libertad 417, 2nd Floor ☎03/339-0600, ☻www.amborotours.com. A long-established Bolivian firm offering standard trips to the Jesuit Missions, multi-day trips into the Amboró National Park (two days, one night camping with a minimum of four people; B$617), as well as cultural tours.
Fremen Tours Beni 79, Edificio Libertador ☎03/333-8535, ☻www.andes-amazonia.com. Specializes in river tours in Trinidad but can also help with Jesuit Mission trips and other all-inclusive tours in Bolivia and Peru.

Rosario Tours Arenales 196 ☎03/336-9977, ☻www.rosariotours.com. Standard tours as well as trips to the Bolivian Pantanal.
Ruta Verde Tours Calle 21 de Mayo 318 ☎03/339-6470, ☻www.rutaverdebolivia.com. Highly recommended Dutch/Bolivian-run tour operator with excellent local knowledge, who organize tours to national parks like Amboró and Noel Kempff Mercado National Park, as well as trips further afield.

mammals, including jaguars, giant anteaters, tapirs and several species of monkey, while its enormous range of plant and insect species is still largely unexplored.

The northern gateway to the park is the picturesque and peaceful town of **Buena Vista**, some 100km northwest of Santa Cruz along the main road to Cochabamba. There are two ways to visit the park from Buena Vista. The easiest is to go on an organized trip with one of the tour operators in town. For about B$500 per person (two person minimum) they offer two-day excursions, camping overnight or staying in one of the refuges in the park, with all meals, a Spanish-speaking guide, camping equipment and transport included. They can also arrange longer trips and treks deeper into the park. For the most recommended tours to the park, contact Amboró Tours or Ruta Verde in Santa Cruz (see the box on Tour Operators p.237), or Roadrunners in Samaipata (see below).

SAMAIPATA

Some 120km west of Santa Cruz, the tranquil little town of **SAMAIPATA** is enjoying growing popularity as a tourist destination among Bolivians and foreign travellers alike. Nestled in an idyllic valley surrounded by rugged, forest-covered mountains, it's the kind of place where many travellers plan to stay a couple of days and end up staying for a week or longer. Just 9km outside town stands one of Bolivia's most intriguing archeological sites – the mysterious, ruined pre-Hispanic ceremonial complex known as El Fuerte (see box, p.239).

What to see and do

At the centre of town lies the small **Plaza Principal**, the core of the grid of tranquil streets lined with white-washed houses under red-tiled roofs. A few blocks north on Bolívar, the small **Museo Archeológico** (Mon–Sun 9am–noon & 2–6pm; B$50, including entrance to El Fuerte) shows a short film explaining the significance of El Fuerte, and houses a small collection of archeological finds from all over Bolivia, including beautiful Inca-carved ceremonial *chicha*-drinking cups, Inca stone axes and mace heads, and a range of pottery. Innumerable walking trails run through the surrounding countryside, the beautiful cloudforests of the Parque Nacional Amboró are within easy reach, and most tour companies also offer day-trips to nearby valleys where you might spot condors overhead, climb mountainous ridges for breathtaking vistas, or enjoy an afternoon splashing around in some of the area's spectacular waterfalls. One-day tours into the park usually cost about B$250 based on a minimum of two people; the park is also a wonderfully serene place to camp out.

Arrival and information

Micro *Micros* leave Av. Grigota in Santa Cruz for Samaipata daily at 4pm (3hr) and arrive in Samaipata in the Plaza Principal.

Taxi From Santa Cruz, shared taxis depart from the corner of Chávez Ortiz and Solis de Olguin (B$25–35 per person, with four people in a taxi; 2hr 30min).

Tourist information For information on Samaipata and the surrounding area, the best place to go is the helpful and enthusiastic English, German and Spanish-speaking Roadrunners (℡03/944-6294, ⓦwww.the-roadrunners.info), next to *Café Latina* on Calle Bolívar. Ben Verhoef Tours (Campero 217; ℡03/944-6365, ⓦwww.benverhoeftours.com) is also a good source of information and can organize a variety of tours and activities, including the Ché Guevara route, Jesuit Missions tours, camping and 4x4 trips. There is a small tourist office inside the museum on Bolívar but it is not very well stocked.

Accommodation

There's a good range of budget accommodation in Samaipata, including a couple of tranquil out-of-town options. Note that it fills up (and prices go up) at weekends and public holidays, particularly between October and April.

Guesthouse La Vispera ℡03/944-6082, ⓦwww.lavispera.org. You can camp in this secluded paradise, which features comfortable lodgings, idyllic location amid orchards and terraced herb, vegetable and flower gardens, and friendly owners who will happily share their immense knowledge and love of the region with you. B$30 per person for camping, or B$40 if you need to hire one of their tents. Cabins B$100–190 per person.

Hostal Andorina Calle Campero ☎03/944-6333, ⓦwww.andorinasamaipata.com. A tranquil, meditative place to stay, with sunny patios and hammock-strewn balconies, characterful rooms and dorms, and a homely TV room where films are shown every night. Free internet and a good breakfast is included and there's a library and book exchange. Dorms B$40, rooms B$90.

El Jardín Calle Arenales final ☎07/311-9461, ⓦwww.eljardinsamaipata.blogspot.com. Tranquil place to relax, a 10min walk from town with comfortable cabins, kitchen, laundry service and a spacious garden with a wonderfully relaxed vibe. Camping B$15, cabins B$30 per person.

Paola Hotel Main plaza ☎03/944-6093, ⓔpaolahotel_samaipata@hotmail.com. A good-value central hotel with clean rooms, hot showers, a kitchen and a large terrace with exhilarating views. Breakfast included. Rooms B$30 per person.

Eating and drinking

Samaipata's status as a resort town and its significant international community ensure a varied range of restaurants and cafés.

La Chakana Plaza Principal. A small European-run café with delicious food, including fresh salads and sticky cakes and cookies. There's also a book exchange and detailed tourist information.

Nomads Calle Bolívar 77, one block from the plaza. You might think you've walked into someone's house party at this friendly, rustic bar, which offers cheap, strong cocktails, and good drinks deals with a happy hour from 8–9pm.

La Oveja Negra Campero. A good bet for an evening drink, with fragrant coffee, vegetarian food and a dart board. Closed Tues.

Tierra Libre Just off the plaza on Sucre. This newly opened place boasts some wonderful local and international dishes – try the lasagne. Closed Wed.

La Vaca Loca Plaza Principal. Serves up luxurious ice cream, to be devoured in the balmy garden.

Directory

Internet Expensive internet access (B$5–7 per hour) can be found next to *La Vaca Loca* café (see above)

Money There are no banks or ATMs in Samaipata, but La Cooperativa La Merced on Calle Sucre, a block east of the plaza, will change dollars.

Telephone office The ENTEL office is on the main plaza.

Moving on

Bus Buses to Santa Cruz leave Samaipata's main plaza at about 4am Mon–Fri, with other services on Sunday from noon–4pm. Buses to Sucre and Vallegrande pass by the highway, between 6.30pm and 7.30pm for Sucre, and 11.30am–12.30pm and 3.30pm–4.30pm for Vallegrande. Catch the bus from outside *Restaurant El Turista* on the main Sucre–Santa Cruz highway.

Taxi The easiest option for returning to Santa Cruz is to take one of the shared taxis leaving from the petrol station on the main highway (10min from the main plaza). You may have difficulties finding one after 6pm.

VALLEGRANDE AND LA HIGUERA

West of Samaipata on the old road from Santa Cruz to Cochabamba, a side road leads to the market town of **VALLE-**

EL FUERTE

Located 10km east of Samaipata, **El Fuerte** (daily 9am–5pm; B$50) is a striking and enigmatic ancient site with a great sandstone rock at its centre, carved with a fantastic variety of abstract and figurative designs and surrounded by the remains of more than fifty **Inca buildings**. The easiest way to reach El Fuerte is by taxi from Samaipata (about B$25–30 one way, or B$70 return with two hours' waiting time), or to join a guided tour with one of the tour agencies in town. While it's possible to walk to the ruins in about two to three hours – just follow the road out of town toward Santa Cruz for a few kilometres, then turn right up the marked side road that climbs to the site – it's a tiring, very hot walk, and it's advisable to take a taxi to the site and just walk back, otherwise you'll probably end up too exhausted to fully appreciate the ruins.

> ## REVOLUTION CHE
>
> Probably the most famous revolutionary of the twentieth century, Ernesto "'Che'"
> Guevara was executed in the hamlet of La Higuera about 50km south of Vallegrande
> on October 9, 1967. Visitors to the area may be surprised to learn that this iconic hero
> spent his final days hiding out in a remote ravine with only a few bedraggled followers.
> An Argentine-born doctor, Che became a close ally of Fidel Castro during the Cuban
> Revolution and then turned his sights to Bolivia, which he hoped would prove to be
> the kick-off point for a continent-wide revolution. With a small band of rebel followers,
> Che tried to drum up support for change but CIA-backed Bolivian troops were
> determined to quell any kind of revolution, and he was soon forced into hiding.
>
> When Che was eventually captured, his last words were: "Shoot, coward, you
> are only going to kill a man". His body was flown to Vallegrande and put on display
> for the world's press in the town hospital. Today Che's grave and the hamlet of
> La Higuera attract a steady trickle of pilgrims, and many locals in Samaipata and
> Vallegrande are happy to share their thoughts and stories about Che.

GRANDE. Vallegrande leapt briefly to the world's attention in 1967, when it witnessed the end game of a doomed guerrilla campaign led by Cuban revolutionary hero, **Ernesto "Che" Guevara** (see box above). There is a small **museum** (Mon–Fri 10am–noon, 3–5pm & 7–9pm, Sat 10am–noon; B$10) in the municipal **Casa de Cultura** on the central Plaza 26 de Enero, which houses an unexciting collection of local archeological finds and photographs of Che.

The most comfortable place to stay is the friendly *Hostal Juanita* (☏03/942-2231; B$80–100 for room with private bathroom), and the best restaurant is probably the German-run *El Mirador* (eves only; closed Mon), which offers a daily selection of tasty beef, pork, chicken and trout dishes.

La Higuera, the hamlet where Che Guevara met his end, lies about 50km south of Vallegrande and can be reached by taxi or lorry in 2 to 3 hours, or by getting buses to Pucará from Vallegrande and getting local transport from there. It's a miserable collection of simple adobe houses with tiled roofs and a one-room **Museo Histórico del Che** (Thurs & Sun, opening hours timed with tours; B$10), with the atmosphere of a shrine, complete with relics including Che's machete, bullets and ammo clips.

Both Vallegrande and La Higuera can also be visited on a tour; try agencies in Samaipata (p.238) or Santa Cruz (p.237). Daily buses run to Vallegrande.

CHIQUITOS: THE JESUIT MISSIONS

East of Santa Cruz stretches a vast, sparsely populated plain which gradually gives way to swamp as it approaches the border with Brazil. Named **CHIQUITOS** by the Spanish, this region was the scene of one of the most extraordinary episodes in Spanish colonial history. In the eighteenth century, a handful of Jesuit priests established a series of flourishing mission towns, where previously hostile indigenous Chiquitanos converted to Catholicism, adopting European agricultural techniques and building some of the most **magnificent colonial churches** in South America. This theocratic, socialist utopia ended in 1767, when the Spanish crown expelled the Jesuits from the Americas. Six of the ten Jesuit mission churches have since been restored and are recognized as UNESCO World Heritage Sites. Their incongruous splendour in the midst of the wilderness is one of the most remarkable sights in Bolivia.

The six missions can be visited in a five- to seven-day loop by road and rail from Santa Cruz. A rough road runs northeast to **San Javier** and **Concepción**, then continues to **San Ignacio** (from where the churches of **San Miguel**, **San Rafael** and **Santa Ana** can all be visited by taxi in a day). From San Ignacio, the road heads south to **San José**. Buses connect all these mission towns as far as San José, from where you can get the train back to Santa Cruz or continue east to the Brazilian border. Alternatively, many agenices organize tours to the missions; see the list of Santa Cruz's agencies on p.237.

THE CHACO

South of the Santa Cruz–Quijarro railway line, the tropical dry forest gradually gives way to **the Chaco**, a vast and arid landscape that stretches beyond the **Paraguayan border**. The Chaco is one of the last great wildernesses of South America and supports plenty of wildlife, including jaguars, peccaries and deer – much of it now protected by the **Parque Nacional Kaa-Iya del Gran Chaco**, the largest protected area in all South America. The park covers over 34,000 square kilometres southeast of Santa Cruz adjacent to the Paraguayan border. There are no organized tourist facilities in the Chaco, so unless you have your own 4x4 and are prepared to organize a wilderness adventure, your view of the region will be limited to what you can see from the window of a bus or train.

There are two routes through the Bolivian Chaco, both starting from Santa Cruz. The first and less taxing is the route by road or railway down the region's western edge to the towns of **Villamontes**, the biggest settlement in the Bolivian Chaco, and **Yacuiba** on the Argentine border. The second and more strenuous is along the rough **trans-Chaco road**, which splits off from the road and rail route to Yacuiba at Boyuibe, heading east to the Paraguayan border at **Hito Villazón**, from where it runs across the heart of this great wilderness to Asunción. This arduous and adventurous journey (served by daily buses from Santa Cruz) takes 24 hours in the May to September dry season, when conditions are good, and much longer after rain, when the road turns to mud.

The Amazon basin

About a third of Bolivia lies within the **Amazon Basin**, a vast, sparsely populated and largely untamed lowland region of swamp, savanna and tropical rainforest, which supports a bewildering diversity of plant and animal life. Roads are poor in the best of conditions, and in the rainy season between November and April are often completely impassable; even in the dry season sudden downpours can quickly turn roads to quagmires.

Linked by road to Santa Cruz, the capital of the Beni – the northeastern lowlands region – is **Trinidad**, the starting point for slow boat journeys down the **Río Mamoré** to the Brazilian border or south into the **Chapare**. From Trinidad, a long and rough road heads east across the Llanos de Moxos, passing through the **Reserva del Biosfera del Beni** – an excellent place to get close to the wildlife of the savanna – before joining the main road down into the region from La Paz at Yucumo.

Just north of Yucumo, the small town of **Rurrenabaque**, on the banks of the Río Beni, is the obvious destination for anyone wanting a taste of the Amazon, given its proximity to the pristine forests of the **Parque Nacional Madidi**, one of Bolivia's most stunning protected areas. From Rurrenabaque, the road continues north to the city of **Riberalta**, a centre for rubber and Brazil nut collection, and on to the Brazilian border and the remote, forest-covered department of **Pando**.

TRINIDAD

Close to the Río Mamoré, some 500km northwest of Santa Cruz, the city of **TRINIDAD** is the capital of the Beni and a modern commercial city dominated by a vigorous cattle-ranching culture and economy. Hot and humid, with few real attractions, Trinidad doesn't really merit a visit in its own right. It is, however, the jumping-off point for adventurous trips to the rainforest and savanna that surround it.

What to see and do

Though most of its buildings are modern, Trinidad maintains the classic layout of a Spanish colonial town, its streets set out in a neat grid around a central square, the **Plaza Ballivián**. Shaded by tall trees hiding three-toed sloths, and with well-maintained gardens, the plaza is the most popular hangout in town. A popular place to

go for the afternoon is the river port of **Puerto Varador**, about 13km out of town, where a number of simple restaurants serve up fresh fish. Take a *mototaxi* to the Mercado Campesino on Av. Oscar Paz Hurtado, where *micros* leave regularly for the port; it's about a half-hour journey.

Arrival and information

Air The airport is located to the northeast of town; a *mototaxi* into the centre should cost B$5–6.
Boat If you are arriving by boat from Guayaramerín to the north, or Puerto Villarroel in the Chapare to the south, you will dock at Puerto Varador, Trinidad's river port, about 13km west. *Mototaxis* ply the 30-min route back into town.
Bus Buses from Santa Cruz, Guayaramerín and Rurrenabaque arrive at the Terminal Terrestre on Av. Romulo Mendoza between Calles Viador Pinto Saucedo and Beni. Buses from San Borja arrive just behind the terminal on Av. Beni.
Tourist information There's a well-stocked and helpful tourist office on Av. 6 de Agosto, next to the *Campanario Hotel* (Mon–Fri 8am–12.30pm & 2.30–6pm). There are a number of ATMs in town; remember to get cash here if you're heading further into the Amazon (including ATM-less Rurrenabaque).

Accommodation

Hostal Copacabana Villaviencio 627 ☎03/462-2811. Pretty basic and a bit further from the main plaza, but the upstairs rooms with private bath and balcony are spacious and pleasant, and all rooms come with cable TV. Rooms with air conditioning are also available, but cost quite a bit extra. B$40–90.
Hostal Palmas La Paz 365 ☎03/462-6979. The rooms downstairs are dark and rather dire, while those upstairs are airier and cooler. All come with fans, and there's a choice of shared or private bath with cable TV. B$40.
Residencial 18 de Noviembre Av. 6 de Agosto with Santa Cruz, two blocks west of the plaza ☎03/462-1272. Basic, good-value place, with a pleasant, hammock-strewn garden and rooms with private or shared bath. B$30–40.

Eating

There are some pretty good restaurants on and around Plaza Ballivián. The beef in Trinidad is

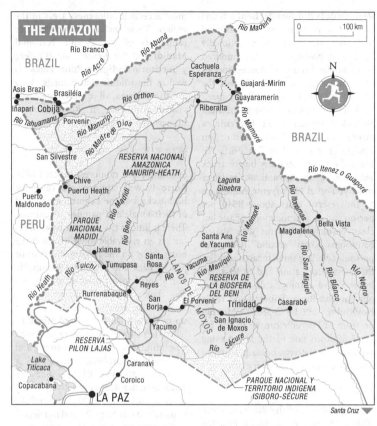

THE AMAZON

Río Branco

BRAZIL

Río Abuná

Río Madeira

Cachuela Esperanza

Guajará-Mirim

Asis Brazil   Brasiléia

Río Acre

Río Orthon

Guayaramerín

Iñapari Cobija

Río Tahuamanu   Porvenir

Riberalta

Río Manuripi

Río Mamoré

BRAZIL

San Silvestre

Río Madre de Dios

RESERVA NACIONAL AMAZONICA MANURIPI-HEATH

Río Itenez o Guaporé

Chive   Puerto Heath

Laguna Ginebra

Río Itonamas

Puerto Maldonado

Río Madidi

Bella Vista

PERU

PARQUE NACIONAL MADIDI

Río Beni

Santa Ana de Yacuma

Río Mamoré

Magdalena

Río San Miguel

Río Blanco

Río Negro

Ixiamas

Río Tuichi   Tumupasa   Santa Rosa

Río Yacuma

Río Maniquí

LLANOS DE MOXOS

Río Heath

Reyes

Rurrenabaque   San Borja

El Porvenir

RESERVA DE LA BIOSFERA DEL BENI

Trinidad   Casarabé

Yacumo

San Ignacio de Moxos

RESERVA PILON LAJAS

Río Sécure

Lake Titicaca   Caranavi

Copacabana   Coroico

LA PAZ

PARQUE NACIONAL Y TERRITORIO INDIGENA ISIBORO-SÉCURE

0   100 km

N

Santa Cruz ▼

excellent and very good-value, while the local speciality is *pacumutu*, great chunks of meat marinated and grilled on a skewer.

La Casona Plaza Ballivián. Lively and popular place with a great atmosphere and good *almuerzos* as well as steak, hamburgers and fried river fish. Mains B$25–50.

Club Social 18 de Noviembre Plaza Ballivián. A vast, elegant dining hall with a rather old-fashioned feel, serving up good-value, filling *almuerzos* and standard Bolivian dishes like *milanesa* (fried meat coated with breadcrumbs) and *pique macho* (a heaped plate of sausage, beef, onions and fries). Fixed lunch menu B$15. Daily lunchtimes only.

Don Pedrito Calle Manuel Maraza. Out of the centre, but worth a taxi ride for its great variety of local river fish, served on a narrow patio underneath mango trees; try the *pacu* or *surubí*.

Heladería Kivon Plaza Ballivián. Ice-cream parlour right on the plaza serving cakes, sandwiches and main meals. Single ice-cream scoop B$5.

Moving on

Air Between them, Amaszonas, 18 de Noviembre 267 ☎03/462-2426 and TAM, corner of Bolívar & Santa Cruz ☎03/462-2363, cover most destinations. **Bus** From the Terminal Terrestre, Av. Romulo Mendoza to: Santa Cruz (4–5 daily; 10hr). Services to Guayaramerín, San Borja and Rurrenabaque supposedly leave daily in the dry season; be aware that these services will usually arrive in their respective destinations hours after the predicted time, and you may be squashed into a tiny minibus for the duration of the journey.

RESERVA DE LA BIOSFERA DEL BENI

Covering some 1350 square kilometres of savanna and rainforest to the east of the mission town of San Borja, the

Reserva de la Biosfera del Beni was one of the first protected areas established in Bolivia. The reserve is exceptionally biodiverse, hosting some five hundred species of bird and one hundred species of mammal. Unusually for Bolivia, the reserve also has very well-organized facilities for visitors, based at the Beni Biological Station at **El Porvenir**, a former ranch about 100km west of San Ignacio on the road to San Borja. To reach the station take any bus or truck west from San Ignacio and ask the driver to let you off at El Porvenir. Admission to the reserve costs about B$40 per person and accommodation in basic but clean barrack-like rooms with shared bathrooms costs around B$60 per person, including three meals a day. For the latest information and to let them know you're coming, call the reserve office in San Borja, Trinidad and 18 de Noviembre (☏03/895-3895). **Moving on** from El Porvenir can be tricky: try flagging down one of the few passing vehicles; alternatively, buses heading to Trinidad usually pass by every morning.

RURRENABAQUE

Set on the banks of the Río Beni about 400km by road north of La Paz, the small town of **RURRENABAQUE** has recently emerged as the most popular ecotourism destination in the Bolivian Amazon. Rurrenabaque, or "Rurre," is close to some of the best-preserved and most accessible wilderness areas in the region. These include the spectacular rainforests of the **Parque Nacional Madidi** and the **Reserva de Biosfera y Territorio Indígena Pilón Lajas**, as well as the wildlife-rich pampas along the **Río Yacuma**, all of which are easily visited with one of Rurrenabaque's numerous tour agencies.

What to see and do

Surrounded by rainforest-covered hills, Rurre is well equipped to cater for backpackers at the beginning and end of their jungle and pampas adventures. There is little in the way of formal sights but it's an enjoyable town to watch the boats go by on the mighty Río Beni or just lie back and relax in a hammock. For a small town, there is an impressive choice of hostels and restaurants. If you've an afternoon to spare, head up to **Oscar's Butterfly Pool Mirador**, which has a lovely swimming pool with a beautiful view, bar and restaurant, and a friendly atmosphere. You can ask a *mototaxi* to take you (B$10) and pay the B$25 entrance fee; alternatively many of the agencies (see p.247) can organize trips, which can be easier and not necessarily more expensive.

Arrival and information

Air Due to often impassable roads, many people choose to fly to Rurrenabaque – the alternative

---

RURRENABAQUE

ACCOMMODATION

El Curichal	A
Hostal Beni	C
Hostal Santa Ana	D
Los Tucanes de Rurre	B

EATING & DRINKING

Bar Moskkito	5
La Cabaña	1
La Casa del Campo	4
Monkey's Bar	3
Narguila	2
La Perla de Rurre	6

0   500 m

is a nightmarish bus journey of at least 18hr (and sometimes a lot more). Both Amaszonas and TAM have daily flights to Rurrenabaque from La Paz; make sure you book ahead. Note that flights are frequently delayed or cancelled due to bad weather conditions, even in the dry season. All flights arrive at the airstrip – which was finally paved in July 2010 – a short distance north of the town, and are met by free hotel minibuses for those with reservations, and airline shuttle buses for those without, which charge a small fee for transport to their offices in the centre of town.
Bus Buses arrive at the Terminal Terrestre, a few blocks away from the centre of town on the corner of Calles Guachalla and 18 de Noviembre; you can get a motorbike taxi into the centre for about B$5.
Tourist information There is a small office at Vaca Diez and Avaroa (8am–noon & 2.30–6pm) with flyers, maps and enthusiastic staff. Note that there are no ATMs in Rurrenabaque. Some tour agencies accept payment with traveller's cheques and credit cards, and there are a couple of places where you may change cheques or get advance cash on credit cards, though only for a large commission: try the

Prodem bank on Comercio (9am–6pm) – they will do cash advances with a 5 percent fee.

Accommodation

For a small town, Rurre has an impressive number of places to stay though rooms can still be difficult to find in high season (May–Aug) – book ahead.
El Curichal Comercio and Beni ☎03/892-2647, ✉elcurichal@hotmail.com. Located further out of town, *El Curichal* is very quiet and has numerous hammocks in a pretty garden in which to relax and enjoy the silence. B$60–70.
Hostal Beni Comercio and Ancieto Arce ☎03/892-2408. Clean and modern rooms set around a peaceful patio. Rooms with air conditioning are available but they're double the price. B$70–160.
Hostal Santa Ana Calle Avaroa ☎03/892-2399. Simple, clean rooms, plus ample chill-out spaces and hammocks. B$60–70.
Los Tucanes de Rurre Corner of Ancieto Arce and Bolívar ☎03/892-2039, ✉tucanesderurre @hotmail.com. A very popular and spacious hostel

with hammocks hung around the grounds, a huge roof terrace, pool table, bar and free breakfast. B$70–120.

Eating and drinking

A large number of restaurants have sprung up in Rurrenabaque to cater to the ecotourism boom. Many bars have adopted a jungle theme – expect fake vines and plastic trees galore.

Bar Moskkito Vaca Diez. A favourite drinking haunt with pool tables, cocktails and the obligatory happy hour.

La Cabaña Bottom of Av. Santa Cruz. Try this place for large meat and fish dishes and filling *almuerzos*, as well as great views of the river at sunset.

La Casa del Campo Vaca Diez with Avaroa. If you've eaten so much bland backpacker fare that you've forgotten what real food tastes like, reawaken your taste buds at this delightful restaurant, where heavenly, healthy food is served up along with excellent coffee. Main dishes B$30–48.

Monkey's Bar Avaroa, between Vaca Diez and Santa Cruz. A travellers' favourite that serves tasty pizzas and strong cocktails; backpackers flock here in the evening for the 7–9pm happy hour, busy atmosphere and pool tables.

Narguila Corner of Santa Cruz and Avaroa. Offers good Israeli food as well as local dishes (served in huge portions) and delicious juices.

TREAT YOURSELF

A five-hour boat ride from Rurrenabaque will bring you to the spectacular Chalalán ecolodge in the heart of the Madidi National Park. The Chalalán project is run entirely by the rainforest community of San José de Uchupiamonas and is hailed as one of the world's greatest conservation success stories. Trips to the lodge don't come cheap, with a four-day and three-night programme from La Paz (one night in Rurrenabaque, two in the lodge) costing about B$2200 per person, but it is well worth the splurge. Go to ⓦ www.chalalan.com for a full list of booking agents. Or book direct at the Chalalán office in Rurrenabaque (Comercio; ☎03/892-2419), or their office in La Paz (Sagárnaga 189, 2nd floor; ☎02/231-1451). Advance booking essential.

La Perla de Rurre Corner of Bolívar and Vaca Diez. This moderately priced place dishes up mouth watering lowland river fish specialities, including the delicious *surubí a la plancha* in the house sauce, in a plant-filled patio shaded by tall mango trees.

Moving on

Air Between them, Amaszonas, Comercio between Santa Cruz and Vaca Diez (☎03/892-2472), and TAM, corner of Santa Cruz and Avaroa (☎03/892-2398), cover La Paz, Santa Cruz and most lowland destinations with regular departures.

Boat When the road is closed in the rainy season, motorized canoes occasionally carry passengers between Rurrenabaque and Guanay, a small town about 230km northwest of La Paz (6–8hr) and Riberalta (8–10 days), though you'll have to book in advance with one of the tour agencies.

Bus In the dry season, there are daily departures for La Paz (minimum of 18hr) and Trinidad (10–20hr), and, when possible, departures to Guayamerín and Riberalta.

THE NORTHERN AMAZON FRONTIER

From Rurrenabaque a dirt road continues north across a wide savanna-covered plain towards the remote backwater of the **Northern Amazon Frontier**, more than 500km away. As the road draws near to **Riberalta**, the largest city in the region, the savanna gives way to dense Amazonian rainforest. East of Riberalta, the road continues 100km to **Guayaramerín**, on the banks of the Río Mamoré, which is the main border crossing point if you're heading north into Brazil.

RIBERALTA

Set on a bluff above a great sweep of the Río Madre de Dios, sleepy, sun-baked **RIBERALTA** is the second biggest town in the Amazon lowlands, with a population of about 40,000, largely employed in the processing and export of Brazil nuts. At least twelve hours by road from Rurrenabaque when conditions are good in the dry season, there's no great reason to stop unless you're heading for Cobija (see p.248) and want to break your journey.

Arrival

Air The airport is a 10-min walk along Av. Ochoa from the town centre.

Bus Buses arrive and depart from the offices of various transport companies in the centre of town around República de Brasil.

Accommodation

Hotel Lazo Calle Nicolas Salvatierra ☎03/852-2352 or 03/852-8326. Basic but clean place a couple of blocks from the plaza. B$70–80.

Residencial Los Reyes ☎03/852-8018. Pleasant hotel near the airport. B$60.

Eating and drinking

Cabaña Tom Southeast corner of the plaza. *Tom's Cabin* does decent *almuerzos* as well as the two Beni stalwarts: beef steaks and river fish.

Club Social Nautico Parque Costanera, on the riverfront. Good Bolivian food and cheap *almuerzos*; you can also cool off in the swimming pool for B$10.

Moving on

Air Between them, Amaszonas (☎03/852-3933), and TAM (☎03/852-2646) cover La Paz, Santa Cruz and most lowland destinations with regular departures.

Bus There are 4–5 daily services to Guayaramerín (3hr) and, when possible, services to Rurrenabaque, Trinidad and Cobija, leaving from their respective company offices.

GUAYARAMERÍN

On the banks of the Río Mamoré some 86km east of Riberalta, **GUAYARA-MERÍN** is the main crossing point on Bolivia's northern border, a modern and prosperous frontier town with a distinctly Brazilian flavour and a thriving economy based on duty-free sales. Most people only come here to cross into Brazil (see "Crossing into Brazil", p.248).

TOUR AGENCIES IN RURRENABAQUE

A growing number of tour agencies offer trips to the rainforest and the pampas lowlands, generally lasting three nights. Most guides speak only Spanish, but agencies can usually arrange an English-speaking interpreter for larger groups. Prices for all-inclusive two-night trips to both the pampas and the jungle start at about B$500 (not including park entrance fees; B$150 for Santa Rosa reserve on the Pampas Tour, and B$125 for the Madidi National Park) – though expect to pay much more if you want anything more than the most basic accommodation. Repeatedly recommended options include:

Bala Tours Av. Santa Cruz with Comercio ☎03/892-2527, ⊛www.balatours.com. Specializes in longer five- to eight-day camping tours into Parque Nacional Madidi, as well as standard selva (jungle) and pampas programmes. They're more expensive, but the jungle tours in particular are very highly recommended, and they own their own camps.

Flecha Avaroa with Santa Cruz ☎07/112-2080, ⊛flecha-tours.com. Popular, friendly agency offering three- to four-day tours of the pampas and rainforest, as well as longer trips into the Parque Nacional Madidi.

Madidi Travel Comercio between Santa Cruz and Vaca Diez ☎03/892-2153, ⊛www.madidi-travel.com. Environmentally conscious agency offering tailor-made tours. Profits go towards conservation and community work.

Mapajo Ecoturismo Indígena Comercio with Vaca Diez ☎03/892-2317. Indigenous community-run agency specializing in five-, four- and three-night lodge-based trips into the Reserva de la Biosfera y Territorio Indígena Pilón Lajas; the lodge is fully operated and owned by the Río Quiquibey communities.

San Miguel del Bala Comercio between Vaca Diez and Santa Cruz ☎03/892-2394, ⊛www.sanmigueldelbala. Not the best option for spotting animals but excellent for a cultural experience of a Tacana community, and near enough to Rurre for a day-trip if you're in a rush (two days, one night at B$840 per person).

Villa Alcira Comercio s/n ☎07/409-2054, ✉ziplinecanopy.bolivia@gmail.com. A chance to fly through the tree canopy on a series of high-speed zip-lines. Trips depart daily at 8am and 2pm.

Arrival and information

Air The airport is four blocks east of the plaza along Calle 25 de Mayo.

Bus Buses from Riberalta and beyond arrive at the Terminal de Buses, about 3km from the centre of town along Calle Beni; a motorbike taxi from here should cost about B$5.

Tourist information The post office is on Calle Oruro, three blocks south of the plaza. The ENTEL office is on Calle Mamoré, two blocks north of the plaza. The *Hotel San Carlos*, a block north and east from the Plaza on Av. 6 de Agosto, changes traveller's cheques – the only place in town that does – and also changes dollars and Brazilian reais. There are no ATMs in town but there is a Prodem on the main square.

Accommodation and eating

There is a reasonable choice of budget hotels and guesthouses in town though very few tourists choose to stay much more than a night here. The best places to eat are on and around the plaza; the two *heladerías* are good for ice cream, coffee, juices and snacks.

Hotel Santa Ana 25 de Mayo and 16 de Julio ☎03/855-3900. If you get stuck before your border crossing, try this reasonable hotel with an inviting garden, located just east of the plaza on Av. 25 de Mayo. B$70–100.

Moving on

Air Amaszonas, Av. 25 de Mayo and 16 de Julio (☎03/855-3731), and TAM (☎03/855-3924), cover most destinations.

Bus Buses to Riberalta leave throughout the day (3hr) from the terminal on Calle Beni; in the dry season, services attempt the long journeys to Trinidad, Rurrenabaque and Cobija – the length of the journeys vary widely due to road conditions.

COBIJA AND THE PANDO

The northwesternmost tip of Bolivia is covered by the department of **the Pando**, a remote and sparsely populated rainforest region that until recently was accessible only by boat along the Madre de Dios, Tahuamanu and Orthon rivers, which flow into the region from Peru; today, a rough road cuts through the rainforest running from just south of Riberalta to Cobija.

With a population of just fifteen thousand, **COBIJA** is the smallest departmental capital in Bolivia, an isolated border town with a distinctly Brazilian flavour. The town's busiest area is around the central plaza, close to the Río Acre, which forms the border with Brazil. The Bolivian **immigration office** is on the main border crossing, the international bridge over the Río Acre at the end of Av. Internacional. A taxi ride from the town centre to the federal police office (where you'll need to clear immigration) in the Brazilian town of **Brasiléia** will cost a steep B$70–80; otherwise it's a twenty-minute walk or you can take a cheaper motorcycle taxi or a canoe. Be aware that you need an international **yellow-fever vaccination certificate** to enter Brazil here. If you need a visa go to the Brazilian Consulate (Mon–Fri 8.30am–1.30pm), just off the plaza on Calle Ayacucho. From Brasiléia, there are regular buses to **Río Branco**, where you can get further onward connections.

Brazil

HIGHLIGHTS

THE AMAZON:
take in lush jungle scenery and native settlements on the world's largest river

SALVADOR:
watch Afro-Brazilian martial art at one of Salvador's capoeira schools

THE PANTANAL:
a vast wetland full of wildlife

CIDADES HISTÓRICAS:
great food and beautiful architecture

IGUAÇU FALLS:
straddling Argentina and Brazil, this is one of the planet's most impressive waterfalls

RIO DE JANEIRO:
sunbathing and somba in one of the world's most beautiful cities

ROUGH COSTS

DAILY BUDGET Basic US$55/ occasional treat US$65

DRINK Skol beer (600ml bottle) US$2

FOOD *Prato comercial/prato feito* (basic set meal) US$5–7.50

HOSTEL/BUDGET HOTEL US$20/ US$70

TRAVEL Bus: Rio–São Paulo (352km) US$45.

FACT FILE

POPULATION 191 million

AREA 8,511,965 sq km

LANGUAGE Portuguese

CURRENCY Real (R$)

CAPITAL Brasília (population 2.5 million)

INTERNATIONAL PHONE CODE ☏55

TIME ZONE GMT -3/-4hr

Introduction

Brazil has an energy like no other nation on earth. Despite massive variations across its regions and a glaring gap between rich and poor, Brazilians across the country are extremely friendly, beautiful, football and beach-crazed – and they certainly know how to party. It's a huge country (larger than the United States excluding Alaska) with all the diverse scenic and cultural variety you'd expect, from Bahian beaches to Amazonian jungles. But Brazil is cosmopolitan too – you could as easily find yourself dancing samba until sunrise as you could eating sashimi amid a crowd of Japanese Brazilians. Rio and São Paulo are two of the world's great metropolises and eleven other cities each have more than a million inhabitants.

Brazilians are one of the most **ethnically diverse** peoples in the world: in the extreme south, German and Italian immigration has left distinctive European features; São Paulo has the world's largest Japanese community outside Japan; there's a large black population concentrated in Rio and Salvador; and Indian influence is pervasive in Amazônia and the northeastern interior. The country has enormous natural resources, and rapid postwar industrialization made it one of the world's ten largest economies. But **economic contradictions** mean that this hasn't improved the lives of many of its citizens: there is a vast (and growing) middle class, but cities are still dotted with **favelas** and other slums.

Nowhere, however, do people know how to enjoy themselves more – most famously in the orgiastic annual four-day celebrations of **Carnaval**, but also reflected in the lively year-round nightlife you'll find almost everywhere. Brazil has the most relaxed and tolerant attitude to **sexuality**, straight and gay, of anywhere in South America. And the country's hedonism also manifests itself in a highly developed **beach culture**, superb music and dancing, and rich regional cuisines.

CHRONOLOGY

1500 Off course, en route to India on behalf of Portugal, Pedro Álvares Cabral lands in Bahia.

1502 Amerigo Vespucci enters Guanabara Bay and calls it Rio de Janeiro.

1549 King João unifies 15 hereditary captaincies under governor-general Tomé de Sousa, who founds Salvador, the first capital. Portuguese settlers begin to flow in.

WHEN TO VISIT

If Carnival is the main thing on your mind, then try to arrive in Rio, Salvador or Recife before the action – dates change each year from February to early March. This is also the main tourist season and warmest part of the year for most of Brazil (Jan–March), with higher accommodation prices and crowded beaches and hostels. The other big draw is Reveillon (New Year), when beds in Rio are especially hard to find. As you go further south it gets noticeably cooler, so it's best to visit places like Foz do Iguaçu, Florianópolis and São Paulo between November and April. In the Amazon the less rainy and humid months are between May and October, while the Northeast has pretty good weather all year round.

1555 French take possession of Rio and are finally expelled by the Portuguese in 1567.

1574 Jesuits given control of converted Indians.

1630 Dutch West India Company fleet captures Pernambuco.

1654 Brazilians, without Portuguese aid, defeat and expel the Dutch.

1695 *Bandeirantes* discover gold in Minas Gerais.

1759 Jesuits expelled by prime minister Marquis de Pombal, who grants legal rights to Indians and helps centralize Brazilian government.

1763 Capital shifted from Salvador to Rio.

1789 First rebellion against Portuguese ends in defeat when José Joaquim da Silva Xavier, known as Tiradentes, is executed.

1807 Napoleon I invades Portugal. Portuguese prince regent Dom João evacuates to Brazil.

1808 Dom João declares Rio temporary capital of the empire, opens harbours to commerce and abolishes restrictions on Brazilian trade and manufacturing.

1823 With Dom João (King João IV) in Portugal, his son, Dom Pedro, declares Brazil independent and crowns himself emperor.

1825 Portugal recognizes independent Brazil.

1854 Slave trade abolished, slavery continues.

1864–70 War of the Triple Alliance pits landlocked Paraguay against Argentina, Uruguay and Brazil.

1888 Princess Isabel, acting as regent, signs the "Golden Law" abolishing slavery.

1907 Brazil and Japan sign a treaty allowing Japanese immigration to Brazil.

1930 Great Depression leads to revolution. Getúlio Vargas rises to power.

1937 Vargas declares himself dictator, creates the "New State," the Estado Novo.

1944 Brazil accepts US aid in return for bases, joins Allies in World War II, and sends Expeditionary Force to fight in Italy.

1956 Juscelino Kubitschek elected president with an ambitious economic programme. Construction of Brasília begins.

1960 Brasília declared capital of Brazil.

1964 Massive population growth, disparity in wealth, economic inflation and fears of a rising proletariat lead to a military coup.

1969 General Emilio Garrastazú Médici assumes presidency. Censorship and torture are routine and thousands are driven into exile.

1983–84 Mass campaign in Rio and São Paulo for direct elections.

1985 Tancredo Neves wins electoral college vote – military rule ends.

1994 Inflation peaks. President Cardoso introduces real as new currency along with new economic plan.

2002 Liberal Luiz Inácio Lula da Silva elected on promises to curb hunger and create jobs.

2006 Lula re-elected; raises minimum wage by 13 percent and announces new economic plan.

2010 Lula succeeded by Dilma Rousseff, Brazil's first female president, on the promise of continuity.

Basics

ARRIVAL

There are direct **flights** to Rio and São Paulo from Europe, North America, Asia, South Africa, and from most major Latin American cities, while easy connections are available from Australia and New Zealand via Argentina or Chile. Brazil also has a well-developed network of domestic flights. **Overland crossings** are possible from every South American country except Chile, Ecuador and Suriname. The first two have no land borders with Brazil, and Suriname, while adjacent, has no official crossing. Colombia and Peru can be accessed **by boat** (see p.611 & p.345). Flights from Santiago, Quito and Paramaribo, however, depart for major Brazilian cities. If you enter Brazil overland, remember that it's a vast place and that crossing points can be very remote.

From Argentina

Most people crossing between Argentina and Brazil do so at the frontier at **Foz do Iguaçu** (see p.97). Another handy crossing further south is at the Argentine city of Paso de los Libres, across the border from **Uruguaiana**, 694km west of Porto Alegre. There are daily **flights** from Buenos Aires to Brazil's main southern and central cities.

From Bolivia

You can reach Bolivia's southeastern border by train from the station a few

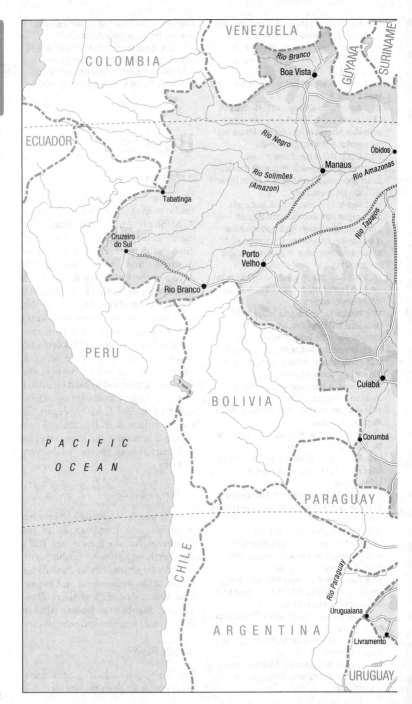

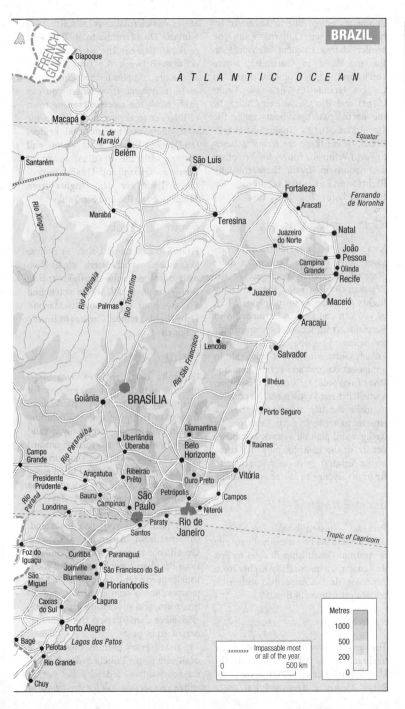

BRAZIL

ATLANTIC OCEAN

Equator

Tropic of Capricorn

FRENCH GUIANA

Oiapoque

Macapá

Santarém

I. de Marajó

Belém

São Luis

Fortaleza

Fernando de Noronha

Aracati

Rio Xingu

Marabá

Teresina

Natal

Juazeiro do Norte

João Pessoa

Campina Grande

Olinda

Recife

Rio Araguaia

Rio Tocantins

Palmas

Juazeiro

Maceió

Aracaju

Rio São Francisco

Lencóis

Salvador

Goiânia

BRASÍLIA

Ilhéus

Porto Seguro

Diamantina

Rio Paranaíba

Uberlândia

Uberaba

Belo Horizonte

Itaúnas

Campo Grande

Araçatuba

Ribeirao Prêto

Ouro Preto

Vitória

Presidente Prudente

Bauru

Petrópolis

Campos

Rio Paraná

Londrina

Campinas

São Paulo

Niterói

Paraty

Rio de Janeiro

Santos

Foz do Iguaçu

Curitiba

Paranaguá

São Miguel

Joinville

Blumenau

São Francisco do Sul

Florianópolis

Caxias do Sul

Laguna

Bagé

Porto Alegre

Lagos dos Patos

Pelotas

Rio Grande

Chuy

Metres

1000

500

200

0

Impassable most or all of the year

0   500 km

kilometres out of Puerto Suárez or by hourly bus from Quijarro. From the border there's frequent transport to the *rodoviária* in **Corumbá**, where you'll find regular onward buses to Campo Grande (5–7hr), São Paulo (21hr) and Rio de Janeiro (26hr). In the north, passenger boats make the 10-min crossing to **Guajará-Mirim** in Brazil, where there are frequent buses to Porto Velho, for connections to other destinations in Brazil. There are daily **flights** from La Paz to Rio, Salvador, São Paulo and other Brazilian cities.

From the Guianas

It's a bumpy 8-hr bus ride from George-town in Guyana to **Lethem**, a quiet place about 130km northeast of the Brazilian city Boa Vista. There are daily **flights** from Georgetown to Boa Vista, or you can connect via **Paramaribo** in Suriname, from where there are flights to Belém. Crossing to Brazil from French Guiana involves a brief ride in a dugout taxi-boat across the Oiapoque River from Saint Georges to **Oiapoque**, a small dirt-road settlement. It's possible to make the trip at any time but it's smarter to arrive in gritty Oiapoque by daylight and plan on a quick exit; buses depart for the 12-hr journey to Macapá on the Amazon, twice daily. You can also **fly** from Cayenne to Macapá and Belém.

From Paraguay

Paraguay's busiest border crossing is from Ciudad del Este over the Puente de la Amistad (Friendship Bridge) to **Foz do Iguaçu**. There are daily **flights** from Asunción to São Paulo, Rio and other major destinations in Brazil.

From Uruguay

The most travelled overland route to Brazil is via **Chuí** (Chuy on the Uruguayan side), 527km south of Porto Alegre. A less-used but more atmospheric crossing is from Rivera to **Santana Do Livramento**, 497km west of Porto Alegre in the heart of Gaúcho country. Between the two, there are also more complicated crossings from Melo to Aceguá, from where you can easily reach the more interesting town of **Bagé**, or to **Jaguarão**. Finally, in the west, there are international bridges (and buses) linking Bella Unión and Artigas with the Brazilian towns of **Barra do Quarai** and **Quarai** respectively. There are daily **flights** from Montevideo to Rio and São Paulo.

From Venezuela

From Santa Elena de Uairén in Bolívar (Venezuela's southeastern state) two daily buses make the four-hour trip to **Boa Vista** in Brazil, where you'll find a twelve-hour connection to Manaus. Daily **flights** connect Caracas to Brazil's major cities.

VISAS

Generally, Brazil requires **visas** based on the principle of reciprocity of treatment given to its citizens. Visitors from most European nations, including Britain and Ireland, need only a valid passport and either a return or onward ticket or evidence of funds to purchase one, to enter Brazil. You fill in an entry form on arrival and get a tourist visa allowing you to stay for ninety days. Try not to lose the receipt of this entry form; you'll need it if you plan to extend. Citizens from **Australia**, **USA** and **Canada** need visas in advance, available from Brazilian consulates abroad; you'll usually need a return or onward ticket, a passport photo, completed visa application form, and processing fee (Aus$49, US$130 or Can$91 respectively; more if organized by post).

In Brazil, entry permits and visas are dealt with by the **Polícia Federal**. Every state capital has a federal police station with a visa section: ask for the *delagacia* *federal.* You can extend tourist permits for another ninety days if you apply at least fifteen days before expiry; if you want to stay longer again you'll have to leave Brazil and re-enter. A R$76 charge is made on tourist permit and visa extensions. If you stay past the visa date without having extended it you will be charged R$9 per day before you leave the country.

GETTING AROUND

Travel in Brazil is usually straightforward: it's generally by bus or plane, though there are a few passenger trains, too, and given the long distances involved it's usually good value. Hitchhiking over any distance is not recommended. In the **Amazon**, travel is by boat, a slow yet fascinating river experience (see p.331 for more details).

By air

Brazil relies heavily on air travel. **TAM** (🌐www.tam.com.br), **GOL** (🌐www.voegol.com.br) and **Trip** (🌐www.voetrip.com.br) serve most domestic destinations, while **Webjet** (🌐www.webjet.com.br), **Avianca** (🌐www.avianca.com.br) and **Azul** (🌐www.voeazul.com.br) all offer competitive fares to popular cities. A useful flight comparison website is 🌐www.submarinoviagens.com.br, though you'll almost always get a better deal purchasing on the relevant airline's site (if they don't allow foreign card transactions, however, you may have to use a travel agent). If you plan on flying within Brazil at least four times in thirty days, and don't mind sticking to an itinerary, it makes sense to buy an **airpass** with TAM or Gol. These need to be purchased from an agent before you travel (you can't buy them in Brazil); each costs somewhere between US$500 and US$1200 for between five and nine flights.

The US$36 **departure tax** is usually, but not always, included in the price of your international ticket.

By bus

Hundreds of bus companies offer services that criss-cross Brazil. **Bus travel** prices range from 25 to 75 percent of the cost of air travel, and is usually the best-value option for journeys of under eight hours – although in more remote areas buses tend to be packed and the roads in poor condition. Intercity buses leave from the **rodoviária**, a bus station usually built on city outskirts. **Prices** are standardized even when more than one firm plies the same route, and there are often two levels of bus service: the perfectly comfortable *convencional* and marginally more expensive *executivo*; on the latter you're usually supplied with a blanket, newspaper and snack. **Leitos** are luxury buses that do nocturnal runs between major cities, with fully reclining seats in curtained partitions. All long-distance buses are comfortable enough to sleep in, however, and have on-board toilets. Bring water and a sweater or jacket for the often-cool air conditioning.

For most journeys it's best to buy your ticket at least a day in advance, from the *rodoviária* or some travel agents. An exception is the Rio–São Paulo route, with services every 15 to 30 minutes. If you cross a state line you'll get a small form asking for your passport number (*identidade*); give it to the driver before you get on board.

By car

Brazil has one of the highest rates of driving accidents in the world. Cities are well signposted but, outside urban areas, many roads are death traps: poorly lit at night, in bad condition and lightly policed. In addition, few road rules are obeyed. Worth avoiding at night are the **Via Dutra**, linking Rio and São Paulo, because of the huge numbers of trucks and the treacherous ascent and descent of the Serra do Mar, and the **Belém–Brasília highway**, whose potholes and uneven asphalt make it difficult enough to drive even in daylight. Avoid driving after dark in Mato Grosso and the Amazon too – armed roadside robberies do happen. Service stations don't always accept international credit cards, so bring cash. **Renting a car** is easy – Hertz, Avis and other international companies operate, alongside local alternatives like Interlocadora, Nobre, Localiza and Unidas – rental offices (*locadoras*) are at every airport and in most towns.

An **international driving licence** is recommended: foreign licences are accepted for visits of up to six months but you may find it tough convincing a police officer of this. The police can be intimidating, pointing to trumped-up contraventions when they're probably angling for a bribe. If such an on-the-spot *multa*, or fine, is suggested it's your choice whether to stand your ground or pay up. Whatever you do, stay calm and bend over backwards to appear polite. If your passport is confiscated, demand to be permitted to call your consulate – there should always be a duty officer available.

By taxi

Metered **taxis** are easy to flag down and relatively inexpensive, though base fares vary from place to place. An alternative is the radiotaxi, a metered cab you can call to pick you up – generally cheaper on airport trips and the like.

ACCOMMODATION

The best-value options are usually **hostels** (*albergues*), which in most cases offer dorms (*dormitórios*) and private rooms. There's an extensive network of Hostel International-affiliated hostels, so it's worth taking out an HI membership (🌐www.hihostels.com). In most bigger cities and resorts you'll find numerous **private hostels** for R$30–45 a night per person. Slightly higher in price are the small, family-run hotels, called **pensão** (*pensões* in the plural) or *hotel familiar*. *Pensões* are often better in small towns than in large cities. You'll also find **pousadas**, which can be just like a *pensão*, or a small, luxurious or offbeat hotel. In the Amazon and the Pantanal, pousadas tend to be purpose-built **fazenda** lodges geared towards upscale ecotourism. Website 🌐www.hiddenpousadasbrazil .com promotes a range of reliable options right across the country.

Hotels proper run the gamut from cheap dives to ultra-luxe. The Brazilian star system (one to five) depends on bureaucratic requirements more than on standards – many perfectly good hotels don't have stars. A **quarto** is a room without a bathroom; an **apartamento** or suite is en suite (with private shower); an **apartamento de luxo** is an *apartamento* with a fridge/mini-bar. A **casal** is a double room, a **solteiro** a single. *Apartamentos* normally come with telephone, air conditioning (*ar condicionado*), TV and fan (*ventilador*). Room **rates** vary tremendously by region and season. Generally, for R$80–150 a night you can stay in a reasonable mid-range hotel, with private bathroom and air conditioning. During the off-season hotels in tourist areas offer hefty discounts of around 25 to 35 percent – and even in high season at hotels and pousadas it's always worth asking "*tem desconta?*" ("is there a discount?").

Brazilian **campsites** are usually found on the coast near larger beaches. These have basic facilities – running water and toilets, a simple restaurant – and are popular with young Argentines and Brazilians.

FOOD AND DRINK

Brazil has four main **regional cuisines**: **comida mineira**, from Minas Gerais, is based mainly on pork with imaginative use of vegetables and thick bean sauces; **comida baiana** (see p.311), from Bahia, has a rich seafood base and an abundance of West African ingredients; **comida do sertão**, from the interior of the Northeast, relies on rehydrated, dried or salted meat and regional fruits, beans and tubers; and **comida gaúcha** from Rio Grande do Sul, the world's most carnivorous diet, revolves around *churrasco* – charcoal-grilling every meat imaginable. **Feijoada** is the closest Brazil comes to a national dish: a stew of pork, sausage and smoked meat cooked with black beans and garlic, garnished with slices of orange. Eating it is a national ritual at weekends, when restaurants serve *feijoada* all day.

Alongside regional restaurants, there are **standard meals** available everywhere for about R$8–12: **prato comercial** and **prato feito** (literally, pre-made dish) are two very budget-friendly phrases you'll see on many (usually lunchtime) menus, consisting of *arroz e feijão* (rice and beans), a choice of steak (*bife*), chicken (*frango*) or fish *peixe*, and often served with salad, fries and *farinha*, dried manioc (cassava) flour that you sprinkle over everything. *Farofa* is toasted *farinha*, and usually comes with onions and bits of bacon mixed in. The **prato do dia** (plate of the day) or set-menu **prato executivo** are similarly cheap and usually very filling (R$10–20). Also economical are **lanchonetes**, ubiquitous Brazilian snack bars where you eat at the counter. These serve a range of *salgados* (savoury snacks) like *pão de queijo* (cheese profiteroles), *pastel* (fried pastry with meat or cheese filling) and *coxinha* (shredded chicken in corn

dough, battered and fried), or cheap meals like a *bauru* – a basic filling steak meal with fries and salad.

Restaurantes a kilo are the lunch choices of most Brazilian office workers, where you choose from (sometimes vast) buffets and pay by weight (*por kilo*); they cost anything from R$10–25 for a big plateful. **Rodizio** restaurants can be fantastic deals – specialized restaurants (such as pizza or sushi), where you pay a set fee and eat as much as you want of the endless supply of food waiters bring around. The *churras-caria*, the classic Brazilian **steakhouse**, operates similarly, with a constant supply of charcoal-grilled meat on huge spits brought to your table.

There are more **fruits** than there are English words for them. Some of the fruit is familiar – *manga* (mango), *maracujá* (passion fruit), *limão* (lime) – but most of it has only Brazilian names: *jaboticaba, fruta do conde, sapoti* and *jaca*. The most exotic fruits are Amazonian: try *bacuri, cupuaçu* and *açaí*. The last-named is often served *na tigela* with *guaraná*, crushed ice, sliced bananas and granola – a ubiquitous filling smoothie – from any *lanchonete*.

Drink

Brazil is famous for **coffee** and you'll find decent espresso in many cafes, but in lots of local places the coffee comes ready loaded with copious amounts of sugar (Brazilians add it to *everything* and you'll draw looks if you don't follow suit). **Tea** (*cha*) is

---

RESSACA (HUNGOVER)? TRY ENGOV

Caipirinhas go down easily and don't strike at once, which makes getting *bêbado* (drunk) easy. If you know you're going to overdo it, do what the locals do; stop into a local *farmácia* and buy some gold packets of Engov tablets, a cheap, over-the-counter hangover preventative and "cure" whose ingredients, aluminium hydroxide, caffeine, acetylsalicylic acid and pyrilamine maleate can be found in antacids, aspirin, and antihistamines. You're meant to take one before your first drink and another after the last; but it helps the next day too, trust us.

surprisingly good: try **cha mate**, a strong green tea with a caffeine hit, or one of the wide variety of herbal teas, most notably that made from *guaraná*. Fruit in Brazil is put to excellent use in **sucos**: fruit is popped into a liquidizer with sugar and crushed ice to make deliciously refreshing drinks (ask for *sem açucar* if you don't want sugar). Made with milk rather than water it becomes a **vitamina**.

Beer (*cerveja*) is mainly of the lager/pilsner type. Brazilians drink it ice-cold, mostly from 600ml bottles. Draught beer is *chopp*. The regional beers of Pará and Maranhão, *Cerma* and *Cerpa*, are generally acknowledged as the best; of the nationally available brands *Skol*, *Brahma*, *Antarctica* and *Bohemia* are all popular. Despite the undoubted improvement in the quality of Brazilian **wines**, those imported from Chile and Argentina remain more reliable.

As for spirits, stick to what Brazilians drink – **cachaça**, sugar-cane liquor. The best way to drink it is in a **caipirinha** – *cachaça* mixed with fresh lime, sugar and crushed ice – which along with football and music is one of Brazil's great gifts to the world. One thing to remember when enjoying Brazil's beverages: most clubs and some bars will give you an **individual card** when you enter upon which your drinks are tabulated. Don't lose it. Even if you have paid, unless you have the receipt at the door, you will have difficulty leaving and may even have to pay again.

CULTURE AND ETIQUETTE

The most widely spoken language in Brazil is **Portuguese**. Educated Brazilians often speak a little English, and there are plenty of Spanish-speakers, but knowing Spanish is of limited help in interpreting spoken Portuguese. You will do yourself a huge favour and likely make several new friends if you learn some Portuguese – even a little effort goes a long way.

On the whole, Brazilians are very friendly, open people (you'll be guided to your stop by passengers on public transport if you ask for help). The pace differs depending on the region. In major cities things operate fairly quickly and on a schedule. Things work in the Northeast too, but in their own special way – you're better off slowing to their pace.

Though attitudes vary regionally, in general it is true that Brazilians are remarkably open with their **sexuality**. Brazil's reputation as a sex destination is not completely without merit – prostitution is legal and you'll see love motels (hourly rates) everywhere. Also be aware that while Brazilians are very accepting of gays and lesbians during Carnaval, Latin machismo still applies here and Brazilians can be as bigoted as anybody. Whatever you do, use protection (a condom is a *camisinha*).

SPORTS AND OUTDOOR ACTIVITIES

Brazilian **football** (*futebol*) is globally revered and a privilege to watch, at its best reminding you why it's known as "the beautiful game". In fact, you won't really have experienced Brazil until you've attended a match. Stadiums are

---

JEITINHO

To make things happen for you in Brazil you first need to understand the concept of *jeitinho*. Literally it means, "a knack", a "fix" or "twist", but in a larger sense it means "a way" and it's how Brazil works. Can't get tickets to the football game two minutes before the match? Go to the head of the line and get creative. Bouncer giving you trouble getting into the club? Smile, joke, and get persuasive. In other words start blagging. In Brazil, there's always a way to get what at first glance seems impossible.

spectacular sights, games enthralling and crowds are wildly enthusiastic. The finest stadiums (*estadios*) are the temples of Brazilian football, such as **Maracanã** in Rio and the Art Deco **Pacaembu** in São Paulo. **Tickets** are not expensive, ranging from R$15 to R$150 depending on whether you stand on the terraces (*geral*) or opt for stand seats (*arquibancada*) – major championship and international matches may cost more. You can usually pay at the turnstile, though there are long last-minute queues. Regional rivalries are strong; fans are seated separately and given different exit routes to prevent fighting. In Rio, **Flamengo** and **Fluminense** have long had an intense rivalry and dominated the city's football; in São Paulo there is a similar rivalry between **São Paulo** and **Corinthians**.

The other major national sport is **volleyball** (*volei*), mostly played on the beach, though the hard-court game is also popular and sand is imported inland for beach volleyball championships elsewhere. In Rio especially, beach **foot-volleyball** (*futevolei*) has also gained significant popularity. The full range of **outdoor activities** is available across the country, with regional highlights like hang-gliding in Rio, hiking in the Serra do Mar, and river-based pursuits in the Amazon and Pantanal.

COMMUNICATIONS

There are **internet cafés** everywhere in Brazil – even obscure jungle towns have air-conditioned places with web connections – and **wi-fi** has made significant headway in major cities, particularly in hotels and cafés in tourist areas. Prices vary from R$2 to R$6 per hour. Most have headphones and Skype **available**.

You may wish to buy a **SIM card** to insert in your mobile phone – most telephone company offices sell these (R$10–25), though some have laborious bureaucratic requirements; TIM is often the least problematic. Bear in mind that rates will apply only to calls within the same state – calling to and "roaming" within other states is charged at a hefty premium.

Public phones are operated by phone-cards (*cartão telefônico*), available at newspaper stands, and are significantly cheaper for local landline calls than from cellphones. Different phone companies compete within different areas of Brazil, and pay phones display which company code should be used. This doesn't affect **local calls** – just dial the seven- or eight-digit number – but for **long-distance or international calls** (charged at around R$6.50 per minute), you must first select a phone company (Embratel, code 021, is reliable). Dial this code first, then the area or country code. To call Rio from anywhere else in Brazil, for example, dial 021+21 (phone company code + city code) followed by the seven-digit number. For international calls, add an extra zero before the company

---

BRAZIL ON THE NET

Ⓦ www.brasil.gov.br Government site with information on Brazilian culture, environment and current affairs in English.

Ⓦ www.braziltour.com Official site of the Brazilian Ministério do Turismo.

Ⓦ www.brazilmax.com Self-described *Hip Guide to Brazil* covering travel, arts and politics across the country.

Ⓦ www.virtually-brazil.com Virtual panoramic tours of attractions and hotels.

Ⓦ www.gringoes.com Brazilian culture, arts, sports and travel in English.

Ⓦ www.riotimesonline.com Focused on news and entertainment in Rio, but with information for travellers across Brazil.

code. International calls can also be made from booths in a *posto telefônico* – you're billed at the end. A reverse-charge call is a *chamada a cobrar*.

Post offices – *correios* – are identified by their bright yellow postbox signs. International stamps cost R$1.60 for up to ten grams. Airmail letters to Europe and North America take around two weeks, and though generally reliable, it's better not to send valuables.

CRIME AND SAFETY

Brazil's reputation as a rather dangerous place is not entirely undeserved, but it is often overblown, and many visitors arrive with an exaggerated idea of the perils lying in wait. **Street crime** can be a problem, especially in the evenings and late at night (the targeting of tourists is worst in Rio, Salvador and Recife), but the key is to be sensible and not let fear grip you. Criminals are also getting more sophisticated – there has been a reported increase in the **cloning of ATM cards**, so you should check your online account often.

Personal safety

Being a gringo attracts unwelcome attention but it also provides a measure of protection. The Brazilian police can be extremely violent to criminals, and law enforcement tends to take the form of periodic crackdowns. Therefore criminals know that injuries to foreign tourists mean a heavy clampdown, which in turn means slim pickings for a while. If you are unlucky enough to be the victim of an **assalto** (a mugging), remember, it's your possessions that are the targets. Don't resist: your money and anything you're carrying will be snatched, your watch yanked off, but within seconds it will all be over. Most *assaltos* happen at night, in back streets and desolate areas of cities, so stick to

busy, well-lit streets, and where possible take taxis; city buses generally run late too, and are safe for the most part (though mind your belongings when it's crowded).

Buses, beaches and hotels

Long-distance **buses** are pretty secure, but it pays to keep an eye on your things. Get a **baggage check** on your luggage from the person loading it and keep an eye on your possessions until they are loaded. Overhead racks are less safe, especially during night journeys.

On city **beaches**, never leave things unattended; any beachside bar will stow things for you. Shared **rooms** in pousadas and hostels usually have lockers (bring a padlock) and even many cheap hotels have **safes** (*caixas*).

Police and drugs

If you are robbed or held up, it's not necessarily a good idea to go to the **police**. Except with something like a theft from a hotel room, they're unlikely to be able to do much, and reporting something will likely take hours even without the language barrier. You may have to do it for insurance purposes, when you'll need a local police report; this could take a full and very frustrating day so consider how badly you want to be reimbursed. If your passport is stolen in a city where there is a consulate, get in touch with the consulate first and take their lead.

Both **marijuana** (*maconha*) and **cocaine** (*cocaína*) are fairly common but be warned: if the police find either on you, you will be in serious trouble. The following cannot be overstated: under no circumstances do you want to spend any time in a Brazilian jail.

HEALTH

Public healthcare in Brazil varies tremendously from poor to sometimes quite good, but private medical and dental treatment is generally more reliable; costs are significantly less than in North America. Check directories at the end of each section for hospital information and refer to advice from your country's embassy or consulate. Standard drugs are available in *farmácias* (pharmacies) without prescriptions.

INFORMATION AND MAPS

Popular destinations in Brazil have friendly and helpful **tourist offices**, as do most state capitals, many of which distribute free city maps and booklets. Generally the airport information offices have the best English-speakers and are usually open the longest. They also have decent free **maps** but little else in English. EMBRATUR is the national tourist organization and has a useful website (⊕www.embratur.gov.br).

FESTIVALS AND CELEBRATIONS

Reveillon New Year's Eve. Major cities along the coast try to outdo each other with fireworks. Rio's is nearly always the biggest.

Lavagem do Bonfim Second Thursday of January. Hundreds of women in traditional Bahian garb clean the steps of Salvador's beloved church with perfumed water (food and music follow).

Celebration of Yemanjá February 2. Devotees make offerings on beaches along the coast to celebrate the goddess of the sea. Salvador's Praia Vermelha hosts one of the largest.

São Paulo Bienal Biennial in March (next in 2012). The largest arts event in Latin America.

The Passion Play Ten days leading up to Easter. Latin America's largest passion plays are enacted in Nova Jerusalem, outside Recife.

Bumba-meu-boi June 13–29. The people of São Luis re-enact the folk tale of a farmer who, having killed another farmer's ox, must resurrect it or face his own death. Costumes, dancing, *capoeira*, heckling and hilarity ensue.

São João June 13–24. Celebrations of Saint John happen in all Brazil, but Salvador, Pernambuco and cities in the Northeast have the most raucous celebrations with *forró*, drinking and eating.

Paraty International Literary Festival (FLIP) Early August. Some of Brazil's and the world's best authors converge on Paraty, with events and talks in Portuguese and English, and performances by top Brazilian musicians. ⊕www.paraty.com.br/flip.

Rio International Film Festival Early October. The country's biggest film festival, showcasing 200 mainstream and independent releases.

Cirio de Nazaré Second Sunday in October. An effigy of the Virgin of Nazaré is carried across the water from Vila de Icoaraci to the port of Belém.

Oktoberfest October 10–27. German-settled Blumenau has all the beer-swilling, German food and traditional garb you'd expect. ⊕www.oktoberfestblumenau.com.br.

Grand Prix November. Brazil's Interlagos circuit near São Paulo is one of the most atmospheric Grand Prix venues. ⊕www.gpbrasil.com.

MONEY AND BANKS

The Brazilian currency is the real (pronounced "hey-al") and is made up of one hundred centavos. Notes are for 2, 5, 10, 20, 50 and 100 reais; coins are 1, 5, 10, 25 and 50 centavos, and 1 real. At the time of writing, US$1 = R$1.60, £1 = R$2.60 and €1 = R$2.30. **ATMs** are available all over Brazil, though not all accept foreign cards and many non-airport ATMs are inactive after 8pm or 10pm. The major credit cards are widely accepted.

OPENING HOURS AND PUBLIC HOLIDAYS

Basic **opening hours** for shops and businesses are weekdays from 9am until 6pm and Saturday 9am to 1pm. Shopping centres are usually open 10am to 10pm and are closed Sundays. Museums and historic monuments generally cost just a few reais and follow regular business hours, though many are closed on Mondays. In addition to the public holidays listed, there are plenty of local and state holidays when you'll also find everything closed.

Carnaval is by far the most important festival in Brazil and when it comes, the country comes to a halt as it gets down to some of the most serious partying in the world. The most familiar and most spectacular celebration is in **Rio** (see p.264), one of the world's great sights, televised live to the whole country. **Salvador**'s Carnaval (see p.305) is now almost as commercialized, with big headline performers, and has a reputation as being even wilder than Rio's. **Olinda** and its winding colonial hilltop streets next to Recife make for a fun and perhaps less frenzied experience, while **Fortaleza** also has a good reputation.

PUBLIC HOLIDAYS

January 1 New Year's Day
February/March (varies) Carnaval. Takes place on the five days leading up to Ash Wednesday
March/April (varies) Good Friday
April 21 Remembrance of *Tiradentes*
May 1 Labour Day
June 11 Corpus Christi
September 7 Independence Day
October 12 Nossa Senhora Aparecida
November 2 Dia dos Finados (Day of the Dead)
November 15 Proclamation of the Republic
December 25 Christmas Day

Rio de Janeiro

The citizens of **RIO DE JANEIRO** call it the *cidade marvilhosa* – and there can't be much argument about that. It's a huge city with a stunning setting, extending along 40km of sandy coast, sandwiched between an azure sea and jungle-clad mountains. The city's unusual name has a curious history: Portuguese explorers arriving at the mouth of Guanabara Bay on 1 January, 1502 thought they had discovered the mouth of an enormous river which they named the January River or Rio de Janeiro. By the time the first settlement was established and the error was realized, the name had already stuck.

Although riven by inequality, Rio has great style. Its international renown is bolstered by a series of symbols that rank as some of the greatest landmarks in the world: the **Corcovado** mountain supporting the great statue of Christ the Redeemer; the rounded incline of the **Sugarloaf mountain** standing at the entrance to the bay; the **Maracanã stadium**, a huge draw for football fans; and the sweeps of **Copacabana** and **Ipanema beaches**, probably the most famous lengths of sand on the planet. It's a setting enhanced by a frenetic nightlife scene and the annual sensuality of **Carnaval**, an explosive celebration which – for many people – sums up Rio and her citizens, the **cariocas**.

What to see and do

Getting around this vast metropolis is easier than you might think, and the city can easily be split into three major sectors. **Centro** contains the last vestiges of the metropolis's colonial past, and its major sites are easily walkable in one day. The most obvious place to start is the **Praça XV de Novembro**, while south of here are the lively *bairros* of **Lapa**, capital of Brazil's samba scene, and the unmissable bohemian *bairro* of **Santa Teresa** on the hills above. It's the **Zona Sul**, or southern sector, however, where

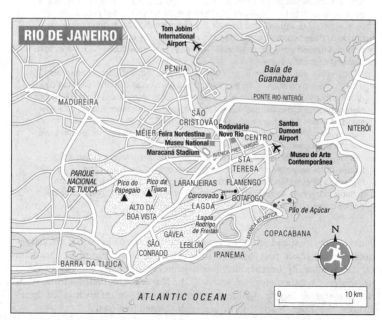

CARNAVAL

Carnaval is celebrated in all of Brazil's cities, but Rio's is the biggest and most famous of all. From the Friday before Ash Wednesday to the following Thursday, the city shuts up shop and throws itself into the world's most famous manifestation of unbridled hedonism. Rio's carnival ranks as the most important celebration on the Brazilian calendar, easily outstripping either Christmas or Easter. In a poverty-stricken city, it represents a moment of release, when *cariocas* can express their aspirations in music and song.

The action

Rio's street celebrations happen all over town, though the biggest processions (known as *blocos* or *bandas*) happen day and night on Avenida Rio Branco (Metrô Carioca). The processions include loudspeaker-laden floats blasting out frenetic samba and thousands of hyped-up revellers. Most neighbourhoods also have their own samba school, competing in three leagues, each allowing promotion and relegation. It's a year-round occupation, with schools mobilizing thousands of supporters, choosing a theme, writing the music and learning the dances choreographed by the carnavelesco – the school's director. By December, rehearsals have begun and the sambas are released to record stores. From September to February a visit to a samba school is a must (see p.280), and all year you can also check out the *Cidade do Samba* (Rua Rivadávia Correa, Gamboa, Centro ⊛www.cidadedosambarj.com.br), a huge centre where carnival floats are constructed and tourist samba spectacles take place.

The main procession of *Grupo Especial* schools – known as the Desfile – takes place on the Sunday and Monday nights in the purpose-built Sambódromo at Rua Marques de Sapucaí (Metrô Praza Onze/Central do Brasil), a concrete structure 1700m long that can accommodate ninety thousand spectators. Some schools may have thirty thousand participants; they compete for points awarded by judges according to the presentation of their song, story, dress, dance and rhythm. Each school must parade for between 85 and 95 minutes, with the bateria, or percussion section, sustaining the cadence that drives the school's song and dance. The carros alegóricos (decorated floats) carry prominent figures, and the porta-bandeira ("flag bearer") carries the school's symbol. The bulk of the procession behind is formed by the alas – hundreds of costumed individuals, each linked to a part of the school's theme.

The parade at the Sambódromo starts at 7.30pm, with eight schools (see also p.280) parading on each of the two nights, and goes on till 8am the following day. *Arquibancada* (high stand) 9 is usually reserved for foreign visitors (from R\$500 per night) while stand 3 is the best value for a reasonable view (from R\$220). Cheaper stands 4, 6 and 13 all have restricted views (from R\$100). Tickets, available from Riotur (see p.275), Banco do Brasil and numerous agents and hotels around town, need to be booked well in advance.

Finally, carnival balls (*bailes de Carnaval*) and other live shows are also a big feature of festivities before and during the main event. Check out Lapa's *Fundição Progresso* (⊛www.fundicaoprogresso.com.br) for appearances by top samba schools in the run-up, and Leblon's *Scala* (⊛www.scalario.com.br) for no-holds-barred affairs each night.

you're likely to spend most of your time, in no small part because of the 16km of sandy **beaches** that line its shores. Despite being somewhat run-down and largely ignored by visitors, the **Zona Norte** (north and west of Centro) has a few attractions that merit a visit: fans of the "beautiful game" should make the pilgrimage to the **Maracanã football stadium**, while for the more culturally minded there's the **Museu Nacional**.

Praça XV de Novembro

"Praça Quinze" (Metrô Uruguaiana/Carioca) was once the hub of Rio's social and political life, taking its name from the day in 1889 when Marechal Deodoro de Fonseca proclaimed the Republic of Brazil. On the south side of the square is the imposing **Paço Imperial** (Tues–Sun noon–6pm; free), which now serves as an exhibition space. It was here in 1808 that the Portuguese monarch, Dom João VI, established his court in Brazil, and the building continued to be used for royal receptions and special occasions: on May 13, 1888, Princess Isabel proclaimed the end of slavery here. Just south is the bold, Neoclassical **Palácio Tiradentes**, the Rio state parliament, while to the north is the **Arco de Teles,** constructed on the site of the old *pelourinho* (pillory) in around 1755 and now leading to an area of lively after-work bars.

On the Rua I de Março side of Praça Quinze, the **Igreja de Nossa Senhora do Carmo da Antigá Sé** (Mon–Fri 9am–5pm) served until 1980 as Rio's cathedral. Inside, the high altar is detailed in silver and boasts a beautiful work by the painter Antônio Parreires. Below, in the **crypt**, rest the supposed remains of Pedro Alvares Cabral, Portuguese discoverer of Brazil – though his final resting place is more likely to be Santarém in Portugal.

North to São Bento

Heading up **Rua 1 de Março** from the *praça*, you'll pass the church of **Santa Cruz dos Militares** (Mon–Fri 10am–3pm), dating from 1628 and rebuilt in granite and marble by the army in 1780; a display of ecclesiastical and military oddments is to be found inside. The grand interior of the **Centro Cultural Banco do Brasil** (Tues–Sun 10am–9pm; ⓦwww.bb.com.br /cultura), Rio's most dynamic arts centre, is just north of here and worth a look around. Just beyond, the enormous

Candelária church (Mon–Fri 7.30am–4pm, Sat–Sun 9am–noon) looms into view, luxuriously decorated inside in marble and bronze. The northward continuation of Rua 1 de Março, the Ladeira de São Bento, leads to the hilltop **Igreja e Mosteiro de São Bento** (daily 7am–6pm, Sun mass at 9am), founded by Benedictine monks in 1633. The facade is pleasingly simple with twin pyramid-shaped spires, while the interior is richly adorned in gold designs and statues of saints, popes and bishops executed by the deft hand of Mestre Valentim.

Museu Histórico Nacional

The **Museu Histórico Nacional** (Tues–Fri 10am–5.30pm, Sat & Sun 2–6pm; R$6; ⓦwww.museuhistoriconacional .com.br) is uncomfortably located in the shadow of the Av. Presidente Kubitschek flyover, which runs south along the waterfront from Praça XV de Novembro. The large collection contains some pieces of great interest, from furniture, firearms and locomotives to displays on indigenous societies and the sugar, gold, coffee and beef trades – though disproportionate weight is given to the monarchy and slavery is barely touched upon. Nevertheless, the varied collection makes this one of Brazil's most important museums.

Carioca, Saara and Campo de Santana

The bustling square **Largo da Carioca** (Metrô Carioca) is dominated from above by the cloistered **Igreja e Convento de Santo Antônio** (Mon–Fri 8am–7pm, Sat & Sun 9–11am), though the square's other historical buildings were, sadly, lost to ugly new high-rises. This, Rio's oldest church, built between 1608 and 1620, is a tranquil refuge decorated in marble and Portuguese tiling. Adjoining it, the striking **Igreja de São Francisco da Penitência** (Tues–Fri 1–4pm) contains extensive

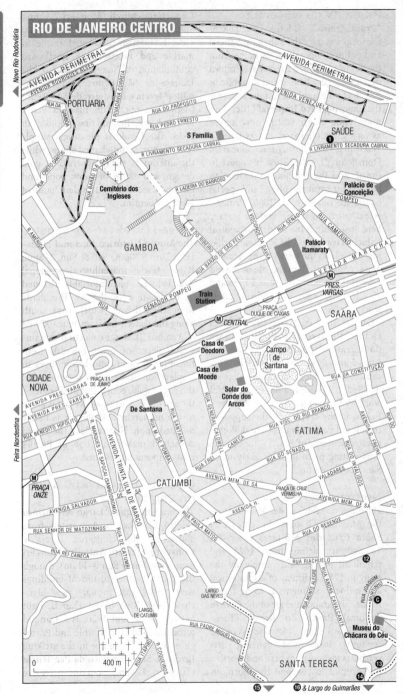

RIO DE JANEIRO CENTRO

Novo Rio Rodoviária ▲

AVENIDA PERIMETRAL

AVENIDA RODRIGUES ALVES

AVENIDA PERIMETRAL

RUA DA GAMBOA

PORTUARIA

RUA RIVADAVIA CORREIA

RUA DO PROPÓSITO

AVENIDA VENEZUELA

RUA DA GAMBOA

RUA CRISTO SANTOS

RUA PEDRO ERNESTO

S Família

SAÚDE ❶

R LIVRAMENTO SECADURA CABRAL

R LIVRAMENTO SECADURA CABRAL

RUA BARÃO DA GAMBOA

Cemitério dos Ingleses

R LADEIRA DO BARROSO

Palácio de Conceição

POMPEU

R AMÉRICA

GAMBOA

R 20 RIBEIRO

RUA BARÃO DE SÃO FÉLIX

R VISCONDE DA RAVEA

RUA SENADOR

RUA CAMERINO

Palácio Itamaraty

AVENIDA MARECHAL

RUA

SENADOR POMPEU

Train Station

Ⓜ CENTRAL

Ⓜ PRES. VARGAS

PRAÇA DUQUE DE CAXIAS

SAARA

Casa de Deodoro

Campo de Santana

RUA DA CONSTITUÇÃO

CIDADE NOVA

PRAÇA 11 DE JUNHO

Casa de Moede

Solar do Conde dos Arcos

AVENIDA PRES. VARGAS

AVENIDA PRES. VARGAS

De Santana

RUA SANTANA

RUA GENERAL CALDWELL

CANECA

RUA VISC. DO RIO BRANCO

FATIMA

AVENIDA G. FREIRE

RUA DO INVALIDOS

RUA DO

RUA BENEDITO HIPÓLITO

RUA M. DE POMBAL

RUA FREI

RUA DO SENADO

VALADARES

Ⓜ PRAÇA ONZE

AVENIDA TRINTA UM DE MARÇO

AVENIDA MEM. DE SÁ

PRAÇA DE CRUZ VERMELHA

AVENIDA MEM. DE SÁ

RUA MARQUÊS DE SAPUCAÍ (SAMBODROMO)

CATUMBI

AVENIDA SALVADOR

SÁ

AVENIDA H.

RUA SENHOR DE MATOZINHOS

RUA DE CATUMBI

RUA PAULA MATOS

RUA DO RESENDE

RUA REI CANECA

RUA RIACHUELO

❶❷

RUA MONTE ALEGRE

RUA ANDRÉ CAVALCANTE

RUA JOAQUIM MURTINHO

Ⓒ

LARGO DAS NEVES

LARGO DE CATUMBI

RUA PADRE MIGUELINHO

Museu do Chácara do Céu

RUA TTAPIRU

RUA COQUEIROS

DO ORIENTE

SANTA TERESA

❶❸

0 ————— 400 m

❶❹

Feira Nordestina ▲

❶❺ ▼   ❶❻ & Largo do Guimarães ▼

Baía de Guanabara

Ilha das Cobras

Ilha Fiscal

N

▶ Niterói & Paquetá

NIGHTLIFE	
Carioca da Gema	9
Cine Ideal	5
Club Six	8
Democráticos	12
Semente	10
The Week	1

EATING & DRINKING	
Bar do Arnaudo	14
Bar do Gomez	15
Bar Luiz	4
Beduino	7
Café do Theatro	6
Confeitaria Colombo	3
Cosmopolita	11
Manaíta	2
Pilão de Pedra	4
Simplesmente	16
Sobrenatural	13

PRAÇA MAUÁ

Igreja e Mosteiro de São Bento
R D. GERARDO

CENTRO

Espaço Cultural da Marinha

Igreja de Sta. Rita

PRAÇA PIO X

Centro Cultural Banco do Brasil

ⓘ N. S. da Candelária

Igreja Santa Cruz dos Militares

Museu Naval e Oceanográfico

ALFÂNDEGA

Ⓜ URUGUAIANA

Arco de Teles
❷

Antigá Sé

PR. XV DE NOVEMBRO

Ferry Terminal

Paço Imperial

Palácio Tiradentes

Santissimo Sacramento
IGREJA DE SÃO FRANCISCO DE PAOLA

Real Gabinete de Leitura

Menezes Cortes Rodoviária

Museu do Imagem e Som

Museu Histórico Nacional

PRAÇA TIRADENTES

Ⓜ CARIOCA

Santa Casa de Misericórdia

Convento de S. Antônio

LARGO DE CARIOCA

Museu Nacional das Belas Artes

Santa Luzia

Santos Dumont Airport

Theatro Municipal
❻

Petrobrás

Tram Terminal

Biblioteca Nacional

PRAÇA FLORIANO

Ⓜ

PRAÇA TALIA

PRAÇA QUATRO DE JULHA

PRAÇA SENADORS. FILHO

Grande Oriente do Brasil

Catedral

Fundição Progresso

❽ CINELANDIA

LAPA

Passeio Público

Museu Instrumental

Museu de Arte Moderna

❾

Arcos da Lapa

❿ ⓫

Escadaria Selarón Ⓐ

Capela do Menino Deus

Convento e Igreja de Santa Teresa

Ⓑ

Parque das Ruinas

Ⓓ

GLÓRIA

Enseada da Glória

Monumento dos Mortos na II Guerra Mundial

Parque do Flamengo

GLÓRIA Ⓜ

▼ Ⓔ, Ⓕ & Ⓖ

ACCOMMODATION	
Art Hostel	F
Baron Garden	E
Casa Mango Mango	C
Marajó	A
Maze Inn	G
Rio Hostel	D
Villa Rica	B

gold and silver ornamentation. Lively shopping street Rua Uruguaiana heads north from here towards the Candelária, while heading westwards along ruas Alfândega and Passos takes you through Rio's best (and cheapest) market area, known as **Saara**. It was originally peopled by Jewish and Arab merchants, who moved into the area after a ban prohibiting their residence within the city limits was lifted in the eighteenth century.

A block south of Saara's, the **Igreja de São Francisco de Paula** (Mon–Fri 9am–1pm), the site of the Mass to "swear-in" the Brazilian Constitution in 1831, which contains meticulous decoration by Mestre Valentim. Rio's most ornate interior is to be found two blocks west, however, at the **Real Gabinete Português de Leitura** (Mon-Fri 9am–6pm), probably Rio's most ornate building, dating from 1887 and containing a library with 350,000 leather-bound volumes. At Saara's western end you come upon a surprisingly peaceful park, the **Campo de Santana**, where Emperor Dom Pedro I proclaimed Brazil's independence from Portugal in 1822 – now complete with ponds, strutting peacocks and scuttling agoutis; avoid this area outside of working hours, as it's not safe.

Nova Catedral

To the southwest of the Largo da Carioca, the unmistakeable form of the **Nova Catedral** Metropolitana (daily 7.30am–6pm) rises up like some futuristic teepee. Built between 1964 and 1976, it's an impressive piece of modern architecture, resembling the blunt-topped Mayan pyramids of Mexico. The cathedral is 75m high and has a capacity of 20,000. Inside, it feels vast, its remarkable sense of space enhanced by the absence of supporting columns. The most striking features are the four huge stained-glass windows, each measuring 20m by 60m. Over the road is the ugly Cubist-style

headquarters of Petrobrás, the state oil company, and to its rear the station for trams up to Santa Teresa, which traverse the **Arcos da Lapa**.

Cinelândia: Praça Floriano

At the southern end of Av. Rio Branco, the dead-straight boulevard that cuts through the centre from north to south, you reach the area known as **Cinelândia** (Metrô Cinelândia), named for long-gone 1930s movie houses. At the centre of impressive square **Praça Floriano** is a bust of **Getúlio Vargas**, still anonymously decorated with flowers on the anniversary of the former-dictator's birthday, March 19. At the northern end is the **Theatro Municipal** (Mon–Fri 1–4pm), modelled on the Paris Opera Garnier – all granite, marble and bronze, with a foyer decorated in Louis XV-style white and gold with green onyx handrails.

Across the road is the **Museu Nacional das Belas Artes** (Tues–Fri 10am–6pm, Sat & Sun noon–5pm; R$5, Sun free), a grandiose construction imitating the Louvre in Paris. The European collection includes Eugéne Boudin, Nicolas Antoine Taunay and Frans Post, but the more modern Brazilian collection is of most interest, containing paintings and sculpture by most of the Brazilian masters. The neighbouring **Biblioteca Nacional** (Mon–Fri 9am–8pm, Sat 9am–3pm) is also of note; its stairway is decorated by important artistic figures like Eliseu Visconti, Rodolfo Amoedo and Henrique Bernadelli, and with reading rooms feature Art Nouveau ceilings. A short walk to the southeast, at the edge of the Parque do Flamengo, is the **Museu de Arte Moderna** (Tues–Sun noon–6pm; R$5) which contains a range of twentieth-century modern Brazilian art – start upstairs with pieces from the 1920s.

Lapa

Immediately southwest of Cinelândia is *bairro* **Lapa**, a gracefully decaying neighbourhood and the beating heart of Rio's **samba scene** (see p.279). Its **Passeio Público** park (daily 7.30am–9pm) was opened in 1783 and is now a little past its best, but this green oasis still charms – with busts of famous figures from the city's history by Mestre Valentim de Fonseca, one of Brazil's most important sculptors. Lapa's most recognizable feature is the eighteenth-century aqueduct known as the **Arcos da Lapa**. Built to a Roman design and consisting of 42 wide arches, in its heyday it carried water from the Rio Carioca to the thirsty citizens of the city, though today it carries *bondes* (trams) up into *bairro* Santa Teresa. The **Escadaria Selarón**, steps leading upwards from Rua Joaquim Silva into the latter district, are a remarkable feat of art and obsession, an ascending tiled mosaic by ever-present Chilean Selarón.

Santa Teresa

Further southwest, is **Santa Teresa**, a leafy *bairro* of labyrinthine, cobbled streets and steps (*ladeiras*), clinging to a hillside with stupendous views of the city and bay. Atmospheric but slightly dishevelled early nineteenth-century mansions and walled gardens line the streets; the resident community here enjoys something of a bohemian reputation. Santa Teresa is Rio's main artistic neighbourhood: in July or August around a hundred artists open their studios, offering the public an opportunity to look (as well as to enjoy an enormous street party) – though on any weekend the *bairro* is buzzing with visitors.

The most picturesque way to get to Santa Teresa is by taking the *bonde* (pronounced "bonji": one of Rio's last remaining **electric trams**; every 30min 7am–9pm; R$0.60), which climbs from near Largo da Carioca, across the eighteenth-century Aqueduto da Carioca, and continues along two lines up and across the neighbourhood,

affording glorious panoramic views. On the way back down, alight at the *bairro*'s tiny centre square, **Largo do Guimarães**, for a drink or meal at any number of lively bar/restaurants: the *Bar do Arnaudo* (see p.278) is the classic traditional meeting-place. From there, it's an enjoyable 10-min walk downhill to art gallery **Museu Chácara do Céu** at Rua Murtinho Nobre 93 (Wed–Mon noon–5pm; ⓦwww.museuscastromaya .com.br; R$2;), in a modernist building surrounded by gardens. It holds a good, eclectic collection of twentieth-century art, though its best works by Matisse, Picasso, Dali and Monet were stolen in a daring raid during Carnaval 2006 and have never been recovered.

A pathway links the museum to the **Parque das Ruínas** (Wed–Sun 10am–5pm), an attractive public garden containing the ruins of a mansion that was once home to a Brazilian heiress. Following her death the mansion fell into disrepair, but reopened as a cultural and exhibition centre in the 1990s.

Glória and Catete

Heading into the Zona Sul from Centro, the *bairro* of **Glória** has one major attraction well worth making the effort to visit. Atop the Morro da Glória, opposite the Glória metro station, is the eighteenth-century **Igreja de Nossa Senhora da Glória do Outeiro** (Tues–Fri 9am–5pm, Sat & Sun 9am–noon). Notable for its innovative octagonal ground plan and domed roof, the latter decked with striking seventeenth-century blue-and-white *azulejos* and nineteenth-century marble masonry, this architectural gem is arguably the prettiest church in the city.

At Rua do Catete 153, adjacent to the **Catete** metro station, the Palácio do Catete houses the **Museu da República** (Tues–Fri noon–5pm, Sat & Sun 2–6pm; R$6, Sun free; ⓦwww.museuda republica.org.br). The displays begin with the period of the establishment of the first Republic in 1888 and end with Presidente Vargas's 1954 suicide, though it's the palace's spectacular Moorish Hall and opulent marble and stained glass that make a visit so worthwhile. Behind the palace is the Parque do Catete, a pleasing tranquil spot, and at the park's southern end is the **Museu de Folclore Edison Carneiro** (Tues–Fri 11am–6pm, Sat & Sun 3–6pm; R$4) a fascinating diversion, holding a folkloric collection of leatherwork, musical instruments, ceramics, toys and Afro-Brazilian cult paraphernalia from all over Brazil.

Flamengo

Busy during the day, the tree-lined streets of **Flamengo** are also lively after dark with residents eating in the local restaurants; it's tranquil enough to sit out on the pavements around large square **Largo do Machado**. The closest **beach** to the city centre is here (Metrô Largo do Machado/Catete), a superb place for walking, people-watching, volleyball and admiring the view across the bay to Niterói – though the sea here is not thought to be especially clean.

Skirting the beach as far as Botafogo Bay is the **Parque do Flamengo** (known locally as "Aterro"), the biggest land reclamation project in Brazil, designed by the great landscape architect Roberto Burle Marx and completed in 1960. The park comprises 1.2 square kilometres of prime seafront, and is extremely popular for sports – there are countless football pitches that operate 24hr. Take a look at the quirky **Museu Carmen Miranda** (Tues–Fri 10am–5pm, Sat 2–5pm; free), in front of Av. Rui Barbosa 560, at the southern end of the park. Carmen was born in Portugal, raised in Lapa, and made it big in Hollywood in the 1940s. She became the patron saint of Rio's Carnaval transvestites, and the museum contains a wonderful collection of kitsch memorabilia from the period, as well as some of the star's costumes and personal possessions.

Botafogo

Botafogo (Metrô Botafogo) curves around the bay between Flamengo and the Sugarloaf, a *bairro* known as much for its lively arts scene, restaurants and hostels as its uncomfortably heavy traffic. The bay is dominated by yachts moored near Rio's yacht club, while seven blocks inland the district's top attraction is the **Museu do Índio** (Tues–Fri 9am–5.30pm, Sat & Sun 1–5pm; R$5; ⊛www.museudoindio .org.br) at Rua das Palmeiras 55. Housed in an old colonial building, the museum has a broad and imaginative collection, containing utensils, musical instruments, tribal costumes and ritual devices from many of Brazil's dwindling populations of indigenous peoples, as well as an extensive library and multi-sensory displays.

Directly south of here at the foot of Rua São João Batista is the **Cemitério São João Batista**, the Zona Sul's largest resting place, with extravagant tombs for the Rio elite – Carmen Miranda and Bossa Nova master Tom Jobim are both to be found in its central area. Most of Botafogo's best bars and restaurants lie westwards around Rua Visconde de Caravelas. The **Cobal de Humaitá**, a partially covered complex of some twenty eateries, lies nearby on Rua Voluntários da Pátria.

Urca and the Sugarloaf

The small, wealthy *bairro* of **Urca** stands on a promontory formed by a land reclamation project and flanked by golden beaches. Facing Flamengo, the **Praia da Urca**, only 100m long, is frequented almost exclusively by the *bairro*'s inhabitants, while in front of the cable-car station (see p.271), is **Praia Vermelha**, a gorgeous cove sheltered from the Atlantic and popular with swimmers.

The beaches aren't the main draw, however: a cable-car ride up the **Pão de Açúcar** is not to be missed. Rising where Guanabara Bay meets the

Atlantic Ocean, Mountani **Sugarloaf**, is so named because of its supposed resemblance to the ceramic or metal mould used during the refining of sugar cane (though it actually looks more like a giant termite mound). The **cable-car** station (daily 8am–10pm; every 30min; R$44; ⓦwww.bondinho.com.br) is located at Praça Gen. Tibúrcio (bus "Urca" or "Praia Vermelha" from Centro or #511 and #512 from Zona Sul). The 1325-m journey is made in two stages, first to the summit of **Morro da Urca** (220m), then onwards to Pão de Açúcar itself (396m). You can also hike the first section along a clearly marked trail from Praia Vermelha and purchase a cheaper cable-car ticket (R$30) for the second stage. Aim to arrive well before sunset on a clear day and you'll find views as glorious as you could imagine right over the city.

Copacabana and Leme

Leme and **Copacabana** are different stretches of the same 4km beach. At the northeastern end of the Praia do Leme, the Morro do Leme rises up to the ruined Forte do Leme, a 30-min cobblestone walk from the army's sports club (8am–5pm daily; R$4), great for more wonderful views of the Zona Sul and Guanabara Bay. Leme morphs into Copacabana at Av. Princesa Isabel, at night a fairly seedy red-light district. The **Praia de Copacabana** runs a further

3km to the military-owned **Forte de Copacabana** (Tues–Sun 10am–5pm; R$4), certainly worth a wander around and a drink at its branch of *Confeitaria Colombo*. Immortalized in song by Barry Manilow, the beach is amazing, right down to its over-the-top mosaic pavements, designed by Burle Marx to mimic rolling waves. The seafront is backed by a line of high-rise hotels and apartments that have sprung up since the 1940s, while a steady stream of noisy traffic clogs the two-lane **Avenida Atlântica**. A strong undercurrent at Copacabana means that it is dangerous even for strong swimmers – don't do anything the locals don't do. Another problem is theft: take only the money and clothes that you will need.

Arpoador, Ipanema and Leblon

On the other side of the point from Forte de Copacabana, the lively waters off **Arpoador** are popular with families and the elderly, as the ocean here is calmer than its neighbours – and the "Arpoador rock" often draws crowds to applaud the sunset. From here, as far as the unkempt and balding greenery of the **Jardim de Alah**, 3km away, you're in **Ipanema**; thereafter lies **Leblon**. The beaches here are stupendous and packed at weekends. Stalls sell fresh coconuts, while for bars and restaurants you'll need to walk a couple of blocks inland.

THE GIRL FROM IPANEMA

It was at a bar called Veloso in 1962 that master composer-musicians Tom Jobim and Vinicius de Moraes sat down and penned *Garota de Ipanema* – The Girl from Ipanema – which put both bossa nova and Ipanema on the global arts map. The song was inspired by 15-year-old local girl Heloisa Paez Pinto, who would pass each morning on her way to the beach. These days the bar has been renamed *A Garota de Ipanema*, and is located at Rua Vinicius de Moraes 49 – changed from Rua Montenegro in honour of the lyricist – while the song has been kept alive through numerous cover versions by the likes of Frank Sinatra and Shirley Bassey. Heloisa posed as a *Playboy* playmate in 1987 and 2003 – the latter at the age of 58 – and now runs a chain of fashion stores (one next door to the bar, at Rua Vinicius de Moraes 53). No prizes for guessing the name.

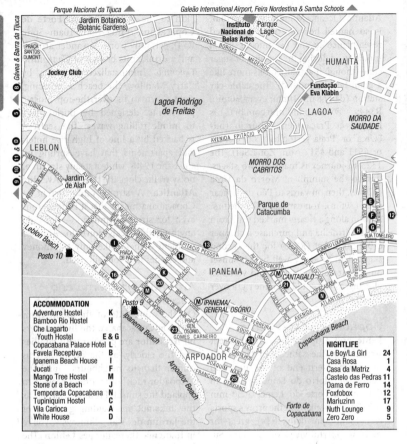

ACCOMMODATION

Adventure Hostel	K
Bamboo Rio Hostel	H
Che Lagarto Youth Hostel	E & G
Copacabana Palace Hotel	L
Favela Receptiva	B
Ipanema Beach House	I
Jucati	F
Mango Tree Hostel	M
Stone of a Beach	J
Temporada Copacabana	N
Tupiniquim Hostel	C
Vila Carioca	A
White House	D

NIGHTLIFE

Le Boy/La Girl	24
Casa Rosa	1
Casa da Matriz	4
Castelo das Pedras	11
Dama de Ferro	14
Foxfobox	12
Mariuzinn	17
Nuth Lounge	9
Zero Zero	5

As with Copacabana, Ipanema's beach is unofficially divided according to the particular interests of beach users; the "rainbow beach" between Rua Farme de Amoedo and Rua Teixeira de Melo is where gay men are concentrated, while posto 9 beyond is firmly for the party crowd; posto 10 is a little more low-key. On Sunday, the seafront road is closed to traffic, and given over to strollers, skateboarders and rollerbladers.

Since the 1960s, Ipanema and Leblon have developed a reputation as a fashion centre, and are now seen as amongst the most chic *bairros* in all of Brazil. Try to visit on a Friday for the **food and flower market** on the Praça de Paz, or on Sunday for the **Feira Hippie** bric-a-brac market at Praça General Osório. Bars and restaurants are scattered throughout the two *bairros*, though many of Rio's best restaurants are located around Leblon's Rua Dias Ferreira.

Lagoa, Gávea and Jardim Botânico

Inland from Ipanema's plush beaches is the Lagoa Rodrigo de Freitas, always referred to simply as **Lagoa**. A lagoon linked to the ocean by a narrow canal that passes through Ipanema's Jardim de Alah, Lagoa is fringed by wealthy apartment buildings. On Sundays, its 8-km perimeter pathway comes alive with strollers, rollerbladers, joggers and cyclists. Summer evenings are

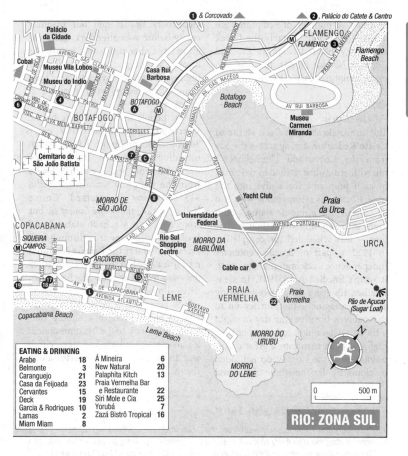

EATING & DRINKING			
Arabe	18	Á Mineira	6
Belmonte	3	New Natural	20
Caranguejo	21	Palaphita Kitch	13
Casa de Feijoada	23	Praia Vermelha Bar	
Cervantes	15	e Restaurante	22
Deck	19	Siri Mole e Cia	25
Garcia & Rodrigues	10	Yorubá	7
Lamas	2	Zazá Bistrô Tropical	16
Miam Miam	8		

RIO: ZONA SUL

0   500 m

especially popular, with food stalls and live music at parks on the southeastern and western shores of the lagoon.

North of Leblon, heading west from Lagoa's shores, is **Gávea**, home of the **Jockey Club**. Races take place four times a week throughout the year (Mon 6.30–11.30pm, Fri 4–9.30pm, Sat & Sun 2–8pm; shorts not allowed). Any bus marked "via Jóquei" will get you here; get off at Praça Santos Dumont at the end of Rua Jardim Botânico. About 3km northwest of the Jockey Club, at Rua Marquês de São Vicente 476, is the **Instituto Moreira Salles** (Tues–Sun 1–8pm; free; ☎21/3284-7400, Wims.uol.com.br), one of Rio's most beautiful cultural centres. Completed in 1951, the

house is one of the finest examples of modernist architecture in Brazil – and the gardens, landscaped by Roberto Burle Marx, are attractive too.

To the northwest of Lagoa lies the **Jardim Botânico** *bairro*, whose **Parque Lage** (daily 8am–5pm), designed by the English landscape gardener John Tyndale in the early 1840s, consists of primary forest with a labyrinthine network of paths and ponds, and the artsy *Café do Lage*. A little further west is the **Jardim Botânico** itself (daily 8am–5pm; R$5; ⓦwww.jbrj.gov.br), half of it natural jungle, the other half laid out in impressive avenues lined with immense imperial palms that date from the garden's inauguration in 1808. A number of sculptures are dotted throughout, notably the Greek mythology-inspired *Ninfa do Eco* and *Caçador Narciso* (1783), the first two metal sculptures cast in Brazil.

Corcovado and Christ the Redeemer

The unmistakeable Art Deco **statue of Cristo Redentor**, gazing across the bay from the **Corcovado** ("hunchback") hill with arms outstretched in welcome, or as if preparing for a dive into the waters below, is synonymous with Rio de Janeiro. The immense statue – 30m high and weighing over 1000 metric tons – was scheduled for completion in 1922 as part of Brazil's centenary independence celebrations. In fact, it wasn't finished until 1931. In clear weather, it's every bit as awe-inspiring as you'd imagine – the journey up to the statue is breathtaking day or night – though what ought to be one of Rio's highlights can turn into a great disappointment if the Corcovado is hidden by cloud. By day the whole of Rio and Guanabara Bay is laid out magnificently before you; after dark, the flickering city lights of this vast metropolis create a stunning visual effect far more impressive than any artificial light show, enhanced by your position at Jesus's feet.

Most people reach the statue by the **Corcovado cog train** (daily every 30min 8.30am–6pm; R$45 return including entrance fee; ⓦwww .corcovado.com.br), which leaves from the station at Rua Cosme Velho 513 (take any bus marked "Cosme Velho" or take the *Metrô Superfície* bus from Largo do Machado station) and proceeds slowly upwards through lush forest as it enters the **Parque Nacional da Tijuca** (see box, below). Taxis (R$25 one-way from Largo do Machado) can drive almost to the mountaintop, at which point you pay the entrance fee (R$20) and switch to a shuttle bus. Walking is not to be recommended: it's an extremely long and steep climb and there have been robberies along the trail.

PARQUE NACIONAL DA TIJUCA

The mountains running southwest from the Corcovado are covered with forest, representing the periphery of the Parque Nacional da Tijuca (daily 8am–6pm; free). The park offers sixteen walking trails and some excellent views of Rio, and makes an appealing retreat from the city for a few hours. The trails are steep and not for the unfit, but if you have the energy for an all-day climb, you can trek all the way to the coastal Pedra da Gávea (842m) or Pico da Tijuca (1021m) in the far north of the forest, above the popular picnic spot known as Bom Retiro. Public transport to the park is not especially convenient, so it's most easily visited by car, taxi or on a tour. Alternatively, take the metro to Saens Peña at the end of Linha 1 and catch bus #221 or #233 towards "Barra da Tijuca", asking to be let off at Alta de Boa Vista right by the park entrance.

Excellent small-group hiking tours are run by Rio Hiking (☏21/9721-0594, ⓦwww .riohiking.com.br; from R$160 per person) – a guide is essential for the challenging hike to Pedra da Gávea. For a bird's-eye view take a tandem hang-glider flight from the Pedra Bonita ramp above São Conrado west of Leblon; an experienced and reliable operator is Go Up Brasil (☏21/9177-9234; ⓦwww.goup.com.br; R$240), with daily flights when weather permits; price includes pick-up and drop-off.

If you want to cycle, enter the park in the Zona Sul at Rua Pacheco Leão, which runs up the side of the Jardim Botânico to the Entrada dos Macacos and on to the Vista Chinesa, from where there's a marvellous view of Guanabara Bay and the Zona Sul.

Maracanã Stadium

Football fans will not want to miss a visit to the **Maracanã** (Metrô Maracanã; Linha 2) – arguably the world's most famous football stadium and steeped in soccer history. With a capacity of 100,000, this monumental arena hosted the World Cup final in 1950 when, much to the disappointment of the hosts, the home nation were defeated 2–1 by Uruguay. Few fans realize that the real name of the stadium is actually **Estadio Mario Filho,** and that *Maracanã* is a nickname derived from the Brazilian word for a macaw and given to a nearby river. But it's not just football that earns the stadium its place in the record books. In 1991 former Beatle Paul McCartney played to a crowd of 180,000 people here, the highest ever concert attendance. It's certainly worth coming to a game here (see tours, below) but if your visit doesn't coincide with a match, you can tour the stadium and the one-room **Museu dos Esportes** (daily 9am–5pm; R$30) – the entrance is the nearest to the metro.

Quinta da Boa Vista

The area covered by the **Quinta da Boa Vista** (daily 9am–6pm; Metrô São Cristóvão) was once incorporated in a *sesmaria* – colonial plot of land – held by the Society of Jesus in the seventeenth century, before becoming the country seat of the Portuguese royal family in 1808. The park, with its wide expanses of greenery, tree-lined avenues, lakes and games areas, is an excellent place for a stroll, though it can get crowded at weekends. Looking out from a hilltop in the centre of the park is the imposing Neoclassical **Museu Nacional** (Tues–Sun 10am–4pm; R$3; @ www.museunacional .ufrj.br). Its archeological section deals with the human history of Latin America; in the Brazilian room, exhibits of Tupi-Guarani and Marajó ceramics lead on to the indigenous ethnographical section, uniting pieces collected from the numerous tribes that once populated Brazil and with displays on Brazilian folklore and Afro-Brazilian cults. The surprisingly spacious **Rio Zoo** (daily 9am–4.30pm; R$6) is located next door.

Arrival

Air Santos Dumont Airport (@ 21/3814-7070), southeast of Centro, handles regional flights. Tom Jobim International Airport, known as Galeão (@ 21/3398-5050), is located 15km north of the centre; frequent buses link the airports with the *rodoviária*, city centre and Zona Sul beaches (R$10) – there's no need to take an over-priced taxi (R$85 from Galeão to the Zona Sul).

Bus Buses arrive at the *Rodoviária Novo Rio* (@ 21/3213-1800), 3km northwest of the centre at Av. Francisco Bicalho. Late at night, take a taxi (from R$30 to Copacabana/Ipanema), otherwise take the *Metrô Integração* bus to the Largo do Machado metro station (one payment for bus and train).

Information and tour operators

Tourist information Riotur's most helpful office is Av. Princesa Isabel 183, Copacabana (Mon–Fri 9am–6pm; @ 21/2544-7992). Alô Rio is an English telephone information service (daily 8am–8pm; @ 0800/285-0555).

Tour operators Favela Tour runs responsible, community-approved trips to Rocinha by minibus (@ 21/3322-2727, @ www.favelatour.com .br; R$70) and Architectur has astute walking tours through Rocinha run by favela residents (@ 21/8115-3703, @ www.favelaarchitectour .com; R$70). Heli Rio arranges helicopter trips over the city (@ 21/2437-9064, @ www.helirio.com.br). Rio Hiking offers a variety of trips around the city and state, as well as nightlife tours and adventure sports (@ 21/9721-0594, @ www.riohiking.com .br). All operators speak English; book tours personally rather than going through commission-hungry hostels/hotels.

City transport

Bus Buses are frequent and many run 24hr; numbers and destinations are clearly marked on the front. Get on at the front and pay the seated conductor; guard your valuables closely. Bus routes/numbers are available on the *Guia de Itinerários* at @ www.rioonibus.com.

Ferry Frequent crossings from the terminal at Praça XV de Novembro to Niterói (see p.281) cost R$2.60 and take 20min.

Metro Rio's two-line metro runs Mon–Sat 5am–midnight, Sun 7am–11pm. Tickets are sold as singles (*ida*; R$2.60) and no discount is given on multi-journey tickets. Combined metro and bus tickets (*superfície* or *integração*) are available for various popular routes.

Taxi Rio's taxis come in two varieties: yellow with a blue stripe or white with a red-and-yellow stripe; the latter are more comfortable radio cabs, which you order by phone. Both have meters and you should insist that they are activated (except from the *rodoviária*; pick up a ticket at the booth). Try ☎21/2252-0054 for Catete/Santa Teresa/Centro or ☎21/2560-2022 for Copacabana/Ipanema.

Tram See Santa Teresa, p.269.

Accommodation

Rio is by no means cheap, and during Carnaval (when you should book well in advance) you can expect to pay way over the odds. That said, there are numerous youth hostels, catering to a massive crowd of budget travellers. Accommodation is cheapest in Botafogo, Catete and Santa Teresa, with Copacabana a little more and Ipanema the most expensive. Most options include breakfast; check before you book. For a more authentic *carioca* experience, get in touch with *Cama e Café* (Mon–Sun 9am–4pm; ☎21/9638-4850, ❀www.camaecafe.com), who arrange rooms with local families in Santa Teresa for most budgets.

Lapa and Santa Teresa

Casa Mango Mango Rua Joaquim Murtinho 587, Santa Teresa ☎21/2508-6440, ❀www.casa-mangomango.com. A wide range of bright and airy rooms in a large historical house, complete with pool, lounge with wi-fi and guest kitchen. Dorms R$40, rooms R$140.

Marajó Rua São Joaquim da Silva 99, Lapa ☎21/2224-4134. Excellent choice for budget travellers not keen on the hostel scene. Modern facilities, clean, spacious rooms and friendly service in the heart of vibrant Lapa – though it can be a little noisy at night. R$80.

Rio Hostel Rua Joaquim Murtinho 361, Santa Teresa ☎21/3852-0827, ❀www.riohostel.com. A cool backpacker hangout for bohemian types, with a small pool and a great bar serving *caipirinhas* until dawn. For every seven nights, you get one night free. Dorms R$40, rooms R$130.

Villa Rica Rua Conde de Lages 2, Lapa ☎21/2232-2983, ❀www.hotelvillarica.com.br. Good value, more upmarket Lapa option, and though its location is good, with Glória Metrô and a superb Sunday market right outside, it is seedy at night. Well-equipped rooms and free wi-fi. Ask for a discount, which should bring the price down to around R$150 from the quoted R$200.

Catete, Flamengo and Botafogo

Art Hostel Rua Silveira Martins 135, Catete ☎21/2205-1983, ❀www.arthostelrio.com. In a nineteen-century building near the metro, this is an artsy place with bags of atmosphere. Ask to see several dorms before choosing one. Café with wi-fi at front, roof terrace and video room. Dorms R$30, rooms R$105.

Baron Garden Rua Barão de Guaratiba, Morro da Glória; no phone, ❀www.barongarden.com. A colonial house with grand views, pool and garden, a short walk from Flamengo beach and Catete Metrô. A real find, aimed more at the 30-plus budget traveller. Dorms R$50, rooms R$100.

Tupiniquim Hostel Rua Sao Manuel 19, Botafogo ☎21/3826-0522, ❀www.tupiniquimhostel.com.br. Billed as an alternative hostel, there's no denying the facilities on offer: fast internet, pool table, climbing wall, bar and BBQ terrace. Great value, but fills fast. Dorms R$30, rooms R$80.

Vila Carioca Rua Estacio Coimbra 84, Botafogo ☎21/2535-3224, ❀www.vilacarioca.com.br. Small and friendly hostel near the metro, with neat, balconied dorm rooms, patio and chill-out area. Has internet access and a/c. Dorms R$32, rooms $110.

Copacabana

Bamboo Rio Hostel Rua Lacerda Coutinho 45 ☎21/2236-1117, ❀www.bamboorio.com. Three blocks from the beach in a quiet, leafy suburb, *Bamboo Rio* is a new hostel with refreshingly colourful, a/c rooms, a good pool (though not exactly the spa they like to call it) and a pleasant garden with wild monkeys. Great value, considering the facilities. Dorms R$32, rooms $130.

Che Lagarto Youth Hostel Rua Anita Garibaldi 87 ☎21/2256-2778 & Rua Santa Clara 305 ☎21/2257-3133, ❀www.chelagarto.com. Two branches of the most established chain of hostels in Rio, with decent facilities including a bar with samba nights. Dorms R$36.

Jucati Rua Tenente Marones de Gusmão 85 ☎21/2547-5422, ❀www.edificiojucati.com.br. On an attractive residential square, this is

STAY IN A FAVELA

Contrary to what the media would have you believe, Rio does have safe *favelas*, and staying in one can be an enjoyable, enlightening experience.

Favela Receptiva Estrada das Canoas 610, São Conrado ☏ 21/9848-6737, @www.favelareceptiva.com. A well-organized network of clean and comfortable host homes within small, friendly community Vila Canoas. Good breakfasts included; cultural tours and dance classes available. R$55 per person.

The Maze Inn Rua Tavares Bastos 414 Casa 66, Catete ☏ 21/2558-5547, @www.jazzrio .com. An eccentric, inspiring option with a staggering view across Guanabara Bay. Gaudí-esque in design and with a variety of rooms, the British-Brazilian owners do a big breakfast, and also run a popular monthly jazz night. Dorms R$50, rooms R$100.

Copa's best bargain if you're travelling in a group. All apartments have a double and two bunks, TV, kitchenette and wi-fi. R$150.

Stone of a Beach Rua Barata Ribeiro 111 ☏ 21/3209-0348, @www.stoneofabeach.com. If big hostels are your thing you won't regret staying here: spacious, clean and with numerous facilities (a/c, kitchen, bar, jacuzzi), it's also friendly and unpretentious. Dorms R$33.

Temporada Copacabana Edificio Av. Atlantica 3196 ☏ 21/2255-0681, @www.temporada copacabana.com.br. It won't win awards, but if you always dreamed of staying on the seafront and can't afford the *Copacabana Palace*, this is your place. No breakfast. R$150.

Ipanema and Leblon

Adventure Hostel Rua Vinicius de Moraes 174 ☏ 21/3813-2726, @www.adventurehostel.com .br. Don't let the name put you off: this is a well-maintained HI hostel and while they don't have many beds, the rooms are spacious. Dorms R$40.

Ipanema Beach House Rua Barão da Torre 485 ☏ 21/3202-2693, @www.ipanemahouse .com. Actually three blocks from the seafront, but a welcoming, laidback hostel nonetheless, with hippy-chic rooms and great socializing at the outdoor pool and bar. Dorms R$45, doubles R$140.

Mango Tree Hostel Rua Prudencio de Moraes 594 ☏ 21/2287-9255, @www .mangotreehostel.com. A block from posto 9 on the beach, this is easily Ipanema's best cheap option. Spacious dorms, grand bathrooms and an overgrown garden with hammocks. Dorms R$35, rooms R$140.

The White House Estrada do Vidigal ☏ 21/2249-4421, @www.riowhitehouse.com. A seafront guesthouse/hostel beyond Leblon with an everyone-is-family atmosphere and long-stayers enjoying the large veranda and spectacular view. Dorms R$40, rooms R$90.

Eating and drinking

As you might expect, Rio offers a huge variety of cuisines to discerning diners. In general, *cariocas* eat well at lunch, so you'll find most restaurants in Centro and other office districts only open during the day. At night eating and drinking are always done together, whether in an informal bar with shared *petiscos* (tapas plates) or more pricey fine dining – especially in Santa Teresa, Botafogo, Copacabana, Ipanema and Leblon.

Centro and Lapa

Bar Luiz Rua Carioca 39, Centro. This manic, but essentially run-of-the-mill, restaurant and bar, serving German-style food and ice-cold *chopp*, was founded in 1887 and is quite an institution. Still a popular meeting place for intellectuals, the food is a little overpriced; try the *bolinhos de bacalao* (R$25). Closed Sun.

Beduino Av. Presidente Wilson 123, Centro. Popular and inexpensive Arabic restaurant which, unlike its rivals, offers a decent meze and falafel meal – great option for vegetarians and carnivores alike. Closed Sun.

Café do Theatro Praça Floriano, Centro. Founded in 1894 within Rio's most grandiose Neoclassical/Art Nouveau building, and richly adorned with Assyrian-inspired mosaics. The menu of Brazilian *petiscos* is expensive, but the atmospheric setting inside the Theatro Municipal makes it a great place to take a break from sightseeing. Mon–Fri 11am–4pm.

Confeitaria Colombo Rua Gonçalves Dias 32, Centro. Great for a huge buffet breakfast/lunch, afternoon tea and cakes, or even a good-quality budget lunch (R$20) at its adjoining *Salão Bilac*. Closed Sun.

Cosmopolita Travessa do Mosqueira 4, Lapa. An excellent Portuguese restaurant established in 1926 with a loyal and bohemian clientele. Fish dishes are the firm favourites; try the *lula* (squid; R$34 for two). Closed Sun.

Manaita Rua de Ouvidor 45, Centro. Japanese *rodizio*, with expensive sushi buffet (R$45) or more reasonable noodle dishes – in faux-Japanese surroundings. Closed Sun.

Pilão de Pedra Rua Carioca 53, Centro. Just up from *Bar Luiz*, this place is hugely popular with office workers who take advantage of the extensive buffet of eighty different dishes for cheap eats. R$15 for a good plateful. Closed Sun.

Santa Teresa

Bar do Arnaudo Rua Almirante Alexandrino 316. An excellent mid-priced place to sample traditional food from Brazil's northeast, such as *carne do sol* (sun-dried meat), *macaxeira* (sweet cassava) and *pirão de bode* (goat meat soup). Closed Mon all day and Sat & Sun from 8pm.

Bar do Gomez Corner of Rua Áurea and Rua Monte Alegre. Santa Teresa's best bar and Portuguese grocery, doing a roaring trade in red wine, *chopp* and *petiscos* (try the succulent *bolinhos de bacalhau*, R$8) to a friendly crowd of locals and visitors. On the Paulo Mattos tram line.

Simplesmente Rua Paschoal Carlos Magno 115. Santa Teresa's best bet for an evening drink, with excellent live music and *petiscos* including superb *caldos* (R$6). The friendly Bohemian vibe spills out onto the road. Tues–Fri 7pm–3am, Sat–Sun 2pm–3am.

Sobrenatural Rua Almirante Alexandrino 432. Quite a pricey fish restaurant (*moquecas* and Amazonian fish dishes are the highlights; R$80 for two), but nearly always has great live music. Deliberately rustic decor and an inviting place for a leisurely meal. Closed Mon.

Flamengo, Botafogo and Urca

Belmonte Praia do Flamengo 300. The first *Belmonte* bar, this is a Rio institution, open all night and spilling out into the road. Good beer and excellent *petiscos* too.

Lamas Rua Marquês de Abrantes 18, Flamengo. This 130-year-old restaurant serves well-prepared Brazilian food (the *Oswaldo Aranha* steak, pan-fried with lots of garlic, is popular) until 4am each night. Always busy and vibrant, a good example of middle-class *carioca* tradition.

Á Mineira Rua Visconde da Silva 152, Humaitá, Botafogo ☎21/2535-2835. A superb value unlimited buffet (R$24) introducing the food of Minas Gerais, with soups, grilled meats, vegetarian dishes and desserts. Phone for free pick-up from your hotel/hostel.

Miam Miam Rua General Góes Monteiro 34, Botafogo. Splashing out here is well worthwhile, with creative international fusion dishes (R$40) like duck gnocchi or hot-pepper-encrusted tuna, plus superb cocktails served up in friendly, bohemian surroundings.

Praia Vermelha Bar e Restaurante Círculo Militar, Praça General Tibúrcio, Urca. Some of the best thin-crust pizza in Rio (from 6pm; R$25) served up in unbeatable surroundings overlooking the beach and Sugarloaf.

Yorubá Rua Arnaldo Quintela 94, Botafogo ☎21/2541-9387. Friendly restaurant serving moderately priced Bahian cooking with strong African influences. Service is slow, but the *bobó* and *moquecas* are well worth the wait. Sat–Sun lunch only, closed Mon & Tues.

Copacabana

Arabe Av. Atlântica 1936. One of very few good restaurants on Av. Atlântica, this is a reasonably priced Lebanese spot with an excellent-value *por kilo* lunch – heavy on meat though vegetarians won't go hungry. At night have a cold beer and snack on the terrace.

Caranguejo Rua Barata Ribeiro 771, corner of Rua Xavier da Silveira. Excellent, mid-priced seafood – especially the *caranguejo* (crab, from R$30) – served in an utterly unpretentious environment packed with locals and tourists. Closed Mon.

Cervantes Av. Prado do Júnior 335 (restaurant) and Rua Barata Ribeiro 7 (bar). Doing a roaring trade day and night (until 5am), this restaurant/bar linked at the rear serves speciality thick-wedge meat sandwiches with a slice of pineapple (the garlic chicken one – R$20 – is sublime), plus full meals from R$35 for two.

Deck Av. Atlântica 2316, corner of Siqueira Campos. This busy place is probably the cheapest of the seafront options, with an *executivo* set lunch for R$12 and an unlimited evening pizza and pasta *rodizio* for R$15 until 11pm.

Siri Mole e Cia Rua Francisco Otaviano 50 ☎21/2267-0894. A rarity in Rio: an excellent Bahian restaurant, serving beautifully presented dishes (many spicy) in an upmarket yet comfortable setting. There are a few tables outside where you can munch on *acarajé* and other Bahian snacks. Mains from R$35.

Ipanema and Leblon

Casa da Feijoada Rua Prudente de Morais 10, Ipanema. *Feijoada*, traditionally served only on Saturday, is available seven days a week here, along with other classic, moderately priced and extremely filling Brazilian dishes, from R$20.

Garcia & Rodrigues Av. Ataulfo de Paiva 1251, Leblon. A bit pricey but a foodie's paradise nonetheless: an excellent bistro, wine shop, ice-cream parlour, bakery and deli – good for fresh bread, take-away salads and prepared meals (from R$30).

New Natural Rua Barão de Torre 167, Ipanema. Excellent vegetarian *por kilo* lunch place that always has a couple of meat choices as well. Expect numerous salads, soya dishes and fresh juices. Closed Sun.

Palaphita Kitch Quiosque 20, Parque do Cantagalo, Av. Epitácio Pessoa, Lagoa ☎ 21/2227-0837. On the Ipanema side of Lagoa, this is a supremely romantic spot by the water, where you can kick off your shoes by candlelight and enjoy a drink plus great carpaccio and other antipastis (from R$20). At weekends phone for a reservation. Tues–Sun 5pm–late.

Zazá Bistrô Tropical Rua Joana Angelica 40, Ipanema ☎ 21/2247-9102. Unique, kitsch, South Asian bistro where there's always something different going on. Downstairs is more traditional, upstairs is all cushions, rugs and low Moroccan tables. Inventive cocktails and tropical fruit juices too. Try the phenomenal Argentine picanha steak, the Thai shrimp, or the namorado fish with plantain puree (from R$35) – plus inventive cocktails and tropical fruit juices.

Nightlife

Live music

Lapa is Rio's nightlife heart and the undisputed capital of samba: every Friday night around Avenida Mem de Sá and Rua do Lavradio one of the world's biggest street parties takes place, with numerous bars offering the real deal – those below are some of the best. Despite Lapa's obvious appeal, be careful walking around after dark; if in doubt take a taxi. During rehearsals for Carnaval (Sept–Jan), don't miss a trip to an Escola do Samba (Samba School; see box p.280).

Carioca da Gema Av. Mem de Sá 79, Lapa. Samba bar-cum-pizzeria, this is a more upmarket but very fun place with especially lively nights Monday and Friday. Mon–Sat from 6pm.

Casa Rosa Rua Alice 550, Laranjeiras. Sunday evening here (from 6pm) is one of Rio's best treats, with live samba followed by hip-hop/*baile funk* in one room and live rock/reggae/*forró* in the other, for a flirty 20s/30s crowd. A good *feijoada* dinner is thrown in for just R$3 extra (regular entry R$22).

Democráticos Rua do Riachuelo 93, Lapa. Never short on atmosphere, this traditional *gafieira* (dance hall) has been going since 1867, with popular live *forró* (Wed) and usually samba Thurs–Sat. Check the programme on ❀ www .clubedosdemocraticos.com.br.

Feira Nordestina São Cristovão. A 48-hr non-stop party in a stadium every weekend might sound far-fetched, but exactly that has been hosted here for decades. *Forró*, funk and reggae for the Zona Norte and Northeastern Brazilian masses, with foods and crafts stalls.

Semente Rua Joaquim Silva 138, Lapa. A small bohemian bar, but also one of Rio's hottest music spots, where some of the biggest names in samba have cut their teeth. Sun–Thurs only from 8pm.

Nightclubs

Rio's vibrant club scene offers a music mix from pop and rock to hip-hop and *funk carioca* (or *baile funk*), as well as superb Brazilian electronica, samba and MPB (*Música Popular Brasileira*). Most places don't get going until midnight; entry fees R$20–60.

Casa da Matriz Rua Henrique Novaes 107, Botafogo ❀ beta.matrizonline.com.br. Stylish club with different music each night, from rock to reggae and samba to drum 'n' bass.

Castelo das Pedras Favela Rio das Pedras, Jacarepaguá ❀ www.castelodaspedras.com .br. Rio's most popular *funk carioca* venue, with 3000-strong crowds of sweating, gyrating bodies. An hour from the Zona Sul; go on a Sunday night tour with ❀ www.bealocal.com or if you're confident take a van (around 11pm) from ruas Bartolomeu Mitre and Conde Bernadotte in Leblon.

Club Six Rua das Marrecas 38, Lapa ❀ www .clubsix.com.br. A rustic townhouse club on three floors, with entrance (R$30) including unlimited beer. Hip-hop and *baile funk* is the norm; there's techno on Saturdays.

Mariuzinn Av. N.S. Copacabana 435, Copacabana ❀ www.mariuzinn.com.br. Copacabana's oldest existing disco, and still as hot as ever. A casual, mainstream affair with single *cariocas* looking to end their night as a couple. Weekend nights charge R$40 with all drinks included.

Nuth Lounge Av. Armando Lombardi 999, Barra da Tijuca ❀ www.nuth.com.br. One of Rio's most popular clubs; get their early as queues are huge and it's packed throughout the week; Sunday has a post-beach crowd. Mondays are for over-40s; the rest of the week it's taken over by the beach crowd.

Zero Zero Av. Padre Leonel Franca 240, Gávea. A trendy club frequented by a wealthy but music-loving crowd. Some of Brazil's top

SAMBA SCHOOLS

From September to February the ultimate highlight of Rio's nightlife is a visit to a samba school, when the emphasis is as much on raising funds for their extravagant Carnaval parade (see p.264) as it is on perfecting routines. Expect drummers and dancers en masse, and thousands of hyped-up revellers. There are many schools, of which a few are listed here; each has its own weekly programme. Check the websites and keep your ear to the ground.

Beija-Flor Rua Pracinha Wallace Paes Leme 1652, Nilopolis ☏21/2253-2860, ⓦwww.beija-flor.com.br. Carnaval champions 2008.

Mangueira Rua Visconde de Niterói 1072, Mangueira ☏21/2567-4637, ⓦwww .mangueira.com.br. Probably the most famous and largest school; weekend events attract many tour groups.

Portela Rua Clara Nunes 81, Madureira ☏21/3390-0471. Thought of as a highly traditional school, with monthly Sunday *feijoadas* with samba a city highlight.

Salgueiro Rua Silva Telles 104, Tijuca ☏21/2238-5564, ⓦwww.salgueiro.com.br. Carnaval champions 2009. A great night out.

Unidos da Tijuca Clube dos Portuários, Av. Francisco Bicalho 47, São Cristovão ⓦwww.unidosdatijuca.com.br. Carnaval champions 2010; popular with a mixed gay and straight crowd.

DJs play an eclectic mix. Over-25s only; Sunday draws a gay crowd.

Gay and lesbian nightlife

Rio has one of the world's liveliest gay nightlife scenes, though you may be surprised that many venues are "GLS" ("gay, lesbian and sympathizers") with clubbers of all persuasions hanging out. Much action takes place around Rua Farme de Amoedo in Ipanema – ask at gay bar *Bofetada* about circuit parties held all over the city. For up-to-date information check out ⓦwww.riogaylife.com.

Le Boy/La Girl Rua Raul Pompéia 102, Copacabana ⓦwww.leboy.com.br or www.lagirl .com.br. Separate gay and lesbian clubs for which the partitions are removed late at night. A vast interior with drag shows, podiums and dark rooms. Lively Sun, closed Mon.

Cine Ideal Rua Carioca 64, Centro ⓦwww .cineideal.com.br. This young and often-wild GLS club in a former cinema is usually only open Fri/Sat. Open-air terrace and mezzanine, as well as an open bar, and a crowd eager for *beijos* (kisses).

Dama de Ferro Rua Vinicius de Moraes 288, Ipanema. On two floors, with a gallery, lounge and nightclub forming an unlikely ensemble. Closed Mon & Tues.

Foxfobox Rua Siqueira Campos 143, Copacabana. A small, trendy, basement club playing underground techno and alternative music to an animated GLS crowd. Closed Mon–Wed.

The Week Rua Sacadura Cabral 154, Centro ⓦwww.theweek.com.br. Rio's biggest club, full stop, famous for great house music. GLS crowd on Fridays and almost exclusively gay men Saturdays. Swimming pool and two DJ rooms.

Moving on

Air Some domestic departures leave from Aeroporto Santos Dumont in Centro, while international flights go from Galeão (or Aeroporto António Carlos Jobim) to the north; an executive bus service to both (every 20min; R$8) plies the beaches from Leblon to Copacabana, Botafogo and Flamengo. Belo Horizonte (10 daily; 1hr); Foz de Iguassu (5 daily; 4hr); Salvador (6 daily; 3hr); São Paulo (every 30 min; 1hr).

Bus Local buses #127 and #128 link Copacabana, Centro and Ipanema with the *rodoviária*, while #172 connects it with Botafogo, Glória and Flamengo; a metro-bus connection is also available from Largo do Machado. Book intercity services a couple of days in advance; tickets are on sale at the "Condo" mall on the southern side of Largo do Machado. Tour company Cruz the Coast (☏21/8264-9836, ⓦwww .cruzthecoast.blogspot.com) operates a hop-on, hop-off guided minibus service north to Bahia, with a 12-day suggested itinerary including hostel pick-ups (R$650, not including accommodation).

Belo Horizonte (hourly; 8hr); Foz do Iguassu (3 daily; 22hr); Salvador (3 daily; 18hr); São Paulo (every 15min; 6hr).

Directory

Banks and exchange Banks are located throughout the city, and especially along Av. Rio Branco in Centro. Bradesco is best for foreign cards.

Car rental Most agents are located along Av. Princesa Isabel in Copacabana. Avis ☎21/2542-3392; Hertz ☎21/2275-3245; Localiza-National ☎800/99-2000. Prices start at $40 per day.

Consulates Argentina, Praia de Botafogo 228 ☎21/2553-1646; Australia, Av. Presidente Wilson 231, Centro ☎21/3824-4624; Canada, Av. Atlantica 1130, Copacabana ☎21/2543-3004; UK, Praia do Flamengo 284, Flamengo ☎21/2555-9600; US, Av. Presidente Wilson 147, Centro ☎21/3823-2000.

Hospitals Try a private clinic such as Sorocaba Clinic, Rua Sorocaba 464, Botafogo (☎21/2286-0022) or Centro Médico Ipanema, Rua Anibal Mendonça 135, Ipanema (☎21/2239-4647). For non-emergencies, Rio Health Collective has a phone-in service (☎21/3325-9300, ext 44) with details of doctors who speak foreign languages.

Police Emergency number ☎190. The beach areas have police posts at regular intervals. The efficient, English-speaking Tourist Police are at Av. Afrânio de Melo Franco (opposite the Teatro Casa Grande), Leblon (☎21/3399-7170).

Post office Central branch on Rua 1 de Março (Mon–Fri 8am–noon & 2pm–6pm and Sat 8am–1pm).

Shopping Rio is replete with high-class shopping malls and designer stores. Budget shoppers however should head to Saara (see p.268), where quality goods are available at reasonable prices, or the Hippie Fair market held every Sun at Praça General Osório in Ipanema, with souvenirs, street shows and typical foods. For handicrafts check out Brasil & Cia, at Rua Maria Quitéria in Ipanema.

Visas The Polícia Federal handles tourist permit and visa extensions at its office in Terminal A at Galeão airport (Mon–Fri 8am–4pm; ☎21/2203-4000, ⊛www.dpf.gov.br).

Rio de Janeiro state

Though many travellers dash through the state in order to reach its glorious capital city, there are enough regional attractions to more than reward visitors. Either side of Rio lie two idyllic sections of coast. To the east beyond Rio's neighbouring city **Niterói** is the **Costa do Sol**, an area of gorgeous white beaches peppered with a string of low-key resort towns and three large **lakes** – Maricá, Saquarema and Araruama. The trendy and commercial resort town of **Búzios** is popular with the affluent but less of a draw for budget travellers. To the south of Rio is one of Brazil's most magnificent landscapes, the **Costa Verde**, dotted with charming resort towns and blessed with dreamy stretches of deserted beach. The colonial town of **Paraty** is one of the region's highlights, while **Ilha Grande**'s verdant forests create a stunning unspoilt setting. The mountainous wooded landscape and relatively cool climate of the state's interior make a refreshing change from the coastal heat. Immediately to the north of Rio, high in mist-cloaked mountains, lies the imperial city of **Petrópolis**, with the magnificent **Parque Nacional Serra dos Orgãos** nearby. In the far west lies another breathtaking protected area, the **Parque Nacional Itatiaia**.

NITERÓI

Cariocas have a tendency to sneer at **NITERÓI**, typically commenting that the best thing about the city is the view back across Guanabara Bay to Rio. The vistas are undeniably gorgeous, but there are a few things to see too – without the need to stay overnight.

What to see and do

The Oscar Niemeyer-designed **Museu de Arte Contemporânea** (Tues–Sun 10am–6pm; R$4; ⊛www.macniteroi .com.br) is Niterói's biggest draw. Opened in 1996 and located just south of the centre on a promontory, the spaceship-like building offers breathtaking 360-degree views of the bay and a worthy, though hardly exciting, permanent display of Brazilian art from the 1950s to the 1990s, plus temporary exhibitions. But the real work of art is the building itself: trademark Niemeyer curves which even his most hardened critics find difficult to dismiss. Beautiful **Praia de Icaraí** lies near the city's centre, but as the water in the bay is none too clean, take a bus to **Camboinhas** or **Itacoatiara**, long stretches of sand every bit as good as Rio's Zona Sul.

Arrival and information

Bus Services from N.S. de Copacabana and Largo do Machado, via the 14km Rio–Niterói bridge, take you into the centre of Niterói; MAC and Icaraí neighbourhood are a further bus journey (numerous services; look on front of bus) or a 30-min walk.

Ferry The best way to get to Niterói is via ferry (see p.276). MAC is just 1.5km from the ferry terminal, but consider taking a taxi as there have been reports of robberies.

Tourist office Estrada Leopoldo Fróes 773, São Francisco (ⓦwww.neltur.com.br, ☎0800/282-7755).

Eating

A wide selection of eateries are to be found along the seafront in São Francisco *bairro*, beyond Icaraí.

Da Carmine Rua Mariz e Barros, 305, Icaraí. Has the city's best pizzas by far, and, though not cheap, it won't break the bank.

Mercado de Peixe São Pedro Av. Visconde do Rio Branco, 55. Be sure to visit this small market complex, five minutes' walk north from the ferry terminal, with a superb group of low-key seafood restaurants and stalls. Tues–Sun, lunchtime only.

BÚZIOS

The most famous resort on this stretch, "discovered" by Bridget Bardot in 1964 and nicknamed "Brazil's St Tropez", is Armação dos Búzios, or **BÚZIOS** as it's commonly known. A former whaling town, it's now cashing in on the upscale tourist market. Bardot described the sea here as "foaming like blue champagne" and the seafront promenade, the **Orla Bardot**, now bears a statue of her in homage. From December to February the population swells from 20,000 to 150,000, and boats now take

pleasure-seekers island-hopping and scuba-diving along the very beautiful coastline. If a crowded 24hr resort full of high-spending beautiful people and buzzing nightclubs is your thing then you're sure to fall for Búzios; if not, give it a miss – at least in high season.

Arrival and information

Bus Direct buses from Rio run at least five times a day, arriving at the *rodoviária* on Estrada da Usina Velha.

Tourist information The helpful tourist office is on Praça Santos Dumont (☎22/2623-2099, ⓦwww .buzios.com.br).

Accommodation

Búzios Central Hostel Av. José Bento Ribeiro Dantas 1475 ☎22/2623-9232 ⓦwww .buzioscentral.com.br. An HI-affiliated hostel with attractive gardens and a plunge pool. Dorms are a little cramped but reasonable, and small doubles the cheapest you'll get in town. Dorms R$40, rooms R$114.

Meu Sonho Av. José Bento Ribeiro Dantas 1289, Ossos ☎22/2623-0902, ⓦwww.meusonhobuzios .com.br. The best "budget" pousada in town and just a block from the beach, with clean, basic rooms and a plunge pool. R$150.

Eating, drinking and nightlife

Restaurants in Búzios are, predictably, expensive; cheaper options include the grilled fish stalls on the beaches and numerous pizza places in outlying parts of town.

Bananaland Rua Manoel Turíbio de Farias 50. On a street parallel to Rua das Pedras, this is the best *por kilo* restaurant in Búzios, and one of the cheapest for a good meal (R$25). Outstanding buffet of salads and hot dishes.

Chez Michou Crêperie Rua das Pedras 90. Belgian-owned, this has long been the town's most popular hangout, thanks to its open-air bar, cheap drinks and authentic crêpes. Open until dawn for post-*Pacha* or *Privilége* clubbers.

Pacha Búzios Av. José Bento Ribeiro Dantas, 151 ☎ 22/2292-9606, ⊛ www.pachabuzios.com. The venue of choice for trendy clubbers, Ibiza-based *Pacha* has helped bring Balearic glitz and top-name DJs to Búzios. Fri–Sat from 11pm; entry from R$40.

Privilège Av. José Bento Ribeiro Dantas, 550. 22 ☎ 22/2620-8585, ⊛ www.privilegenet.com.br. Despite *Pacha*'s rise as venue of choice in the last few years, *Privilège* is still the town's biggest club, has a great party atmosphere, and at half the price of its rival, is much better value. Fri–Sat from 11pm; entry from R$20.

Sawasdee Av. José Bento Ribeiro Dantas 422 ⊛ www.sawasdee.com.br. Excellent, spicy Thai food, with great vegetarian choices, seafood and meat options (meals from R$30).

ILHA GRANDE

ILHA GRANDE comprises 193 square kilometres of mountainous jungle, historic ruins and beautiful beaches; it's excellent for some scenic tropical rambling. The entire island, lying about 150km southwest of Rio, is a state park with limits on building development and a ban on motor vehicles.

What to see and do

Ilha Grande offers lots of beautiful **walks** along well-maintained and fairly well-signposted trails. As you approach the low-lying, whitewashed colonial port of **Vila do Abraão**, the mountains rise dramatically from the sea, and in the distance there's the curiously shaped summit of **Bico do Papagaio** ("Parrot's Beak"), which ascends to a height of 980m. There's little to see in Abraão itself, but it's a pleasant base from which to explore the island. A half-hour walk along the coast west are the ruins of the **Antigo Presídio**, a former prison for political prisoners that was dynamited

in the early 1960s. Among the ruins, you'll find the *cafofo*, the containment centre where prisoners who had failed in escape attempts were immersed in freezing water. Just fifteen minutes inland from Abraão, overgrown with vegetation, stands the **Antigo Aqueduto**, which used to channel the island's water supply. There's a fine view of the aqueduct from the **Pedra Mirante**, a hill near the centre of the island and, close by, a waterfall provides the opportunity to cool off.

For the most part the **beaches** – **Aventureiro**, **Lopes Mendes**, **Canto**, **Júlia** and **Morcegoare**, to name a few – are wild, unspoilt and most easily reached by boat, though most have some form of basic accommodation or camp ground. Araçatiba is home to a sizeable village, accessed by boat direct from Angra dos Reis.

Arrival and information

Bus From Rio's *rodoviária* to the ferry posts, five buses per day depart for Mangaratiba, while there's an hourly service to Angra dos Reis.

Ferry Boats (⊛ www.barcas-sa.com.br) run from Mangaratiba, leaving at 8am and returning at 5.30pm, and from Angra dos Reis, at 3.15pm Mon–Fri and 1.30pm at weekends, returning at 10am every day. Tickets cost R$6.50 (R$14 at weekends) for the one-hour journey.

Tourist information There is a tourist office in Angra dos Reis at Av. Ayrton Senna (☎ 24/3365-5186), but no office on the island itself. Online try ⊛ www.ilhagrande.org.

Accommodation

Great pousadas are to be found all over Ilha Grande, though Abraão has the largest choice, generally mid-priced. Reservations are essential in the high season, especially at weekends, but prices may be halved off-season. *Camping Peixoto* (⊛ www .campingdopeixoto.com.br; R$18 per person) is the best of the island's campsites.

Che Lagarto Praia do Canto, Abraão ☎ 21/3361-9669 ⊛ www.chelagarto.com. Much like the members of the same chain in Rio (see p.276), this is a well-organized hostel with breakfast served on a glorious wooden sun deck overlooking the sea. Dorms R$45, rooms R$140.

PARQUE NACIONAL DO ITATIAIA

On the border with Minais Gerais, 167km west of Rio, the Parque Nacional do Itatiaia takes its unusual name from an Indian word meaning "rocks with sharp edges". Holding the distinction of being Brazil's first national park (1937) it's incredibly varied, from dense Atlantic forest in the foothills, through to treeless, grassy summits. The park's loftiest peak, Agulhas-Negras, is the second-highest in Brazil, at 2789m.

There's no shortage of walking trails here, as well as a couple of two-day walks for serious hikers. The better, but more difficult, of the two is the Jeep Trail, which scales the valley and ultimately reaches the peak of Agulhas-Negras. The second is the Tres Picos Trail – easier, but care should still be taken as the path becomes narrow and slippery as it rises. A guide is recommended for both trails (available from hotels within the park) and essential for the Jeep Trail, for which you should seek prior permission from the IBAMA office at the park entrance. Itatiaia is also a popular birdwatching destination, thanks to its varied terrain and flora: highland species present in the park include the Itatiaia Spinetail – a small, brownish, skulking bird that occurs only in this range of mountains.

Practicalities

Access to the park is via the town of Itatiaia – buses between Rio and São Paulo stop here. Local buses (30min) run from the footbridge in Itatiaia, a short walk from the *rodoviária*, to the park visitors' centre. Staying in the town of Itatiaia is the cheapest way to visit, despite the 30-min bus ride.

Simon Rodavia Br-485 km12, PN Itatiaia ☎24/3352-1122. A huge hotel within the park boundaries, this is the most convenient place to stay if you are thinking of hiking the park's trails: the Tres Picos trail begins just behind the hotel. Comfortable; some rooms have attractive views over the valleys. R$160.

Pousada Isa About 500m from the *rodoviária*, Itatiaia; no phone. Turn right out of the bus station and look for the "pousada" sign. Best option for budget travellers, as it's basic and not especially attractive, but clean and reliable nevertheless and includes a half-decent breakfast. R$35.

Holandês Rua do Assembléia, Abraão ☎24/3361-5034. Always popular, this trendy youth hostel is behind the beach next to the Assembléia de Deus. Accommodation in dorms or lovely chalets (which sleep up to 3) in lush gardens. Dorms R$40, rooms R$110.

Lagamar Praia Grande de Araçatiba ☎24/9221-8180; ⊛www.pousadalagamar .com.br. Superb value pousada surrounded by lush jungle in a quiet fishing hamlet at the island's western end. Generous seafood dinners and large breakfast are included. Boat available direct from Angra. R$140.

Oásis Praia do Canto, Abraão ☎24/3361-5549. Cosy, friendly and one of the nicest pousadas on the island. Rooms are unpretentious and simply furnished. It's located at the far end of the beach, a 10-min walk from the jetty. R$160.

Eating

Most pousadas serve decent meals, and some gourmet cooking, while there are also independent restaurants where fish and seafood figure heavily. *Rei do Moqueca* at Rua da Praia in Abraão serves reasonably priced meals, while *Rei dos Caldos* offers wonderful fish soups. *Tropicana* at Rua da Praia28 serves an interesting menu of French dishes with a Brazilian twist (from R$30), in a verdant garden.

Directory

Banks and exchange Bring plenty of cash: there's no ATM, nowhere to change money or travellers' cheques and few places accept credit cards.
Scuba-diving The Elite Dive Center (☎24/3361-5501; ⊛www.elitedivecenter.com.br) is the only PADI-registered dive centre on the island.

PARATY AND AROUND

PARATY, 236km from Rio along the BR-101, is the Costa Verde's main attraction, and rightly so. Inhabited since 1650, Paraty remains much as it was in its heyday as a staging post for the eighteenth-century trade in Brazilian gold. Today, UNESCO considers the city one of the world's most important examples of Portuguese colonial architecture, and it has been named a national monument. Besides the town's charmingly relaxed atmosphere, the main draws are its **churches** and nearby **beaches**.

What to see and do

One of Brazil's first planned urban projects, Paraty's centre is a warren of narrow, pedestrianized cobbled streets bordered by houses built around quaint courtyards. The cobbles of the streets are arranged in channels to drain off storm water and allow the sea to enter and wash the streets at high tides and full moon.

Churches

Paraty's **churches** traditionally each served a different sector of the population. **Nossa Senhora dos Remédios** (daily 9am–5pm), on the Praça da Matriz, is the town's most imposing building. Although the original church was built on the site in 1668, the current construction dates from 1873 (with building having begun 84 years earlier). Along Rua do Comércio is the smallest church, the **Igreja do Rosário** (Mon–Fri 9am–5pm), once used by the slaves, while at the southern edge of the town, the Portuguese Baroque **Igreja de Santa Rita** (Wed–Sun 10am–noon & 2–5pm) served the freed *mulattos* and dates from 1722. The oldest and most architecturally significant of the town's churches, it now houses the **Museu de Arte Sacra de Paraty**, with religious artefacts from all of the town's churches.

Beaches and islands

From the **Praia do Pontal**, across the Perequé-Açu river from town, and from the port quay, boats leave for the **beaches** of Parati-Mirim, Iriríguaçu

– known for its waterfalls – Lula and Conceição. In fact, there are 65 islands and about two hundred beaches to choose from – ask around for the current favourites. Hotels and travel agents sell tickets for trips out to the islands, typically for around R$30 per person, leaving Paraty at noon, stopping at three or four islands, giving time for a swim, and returning at 6pm. For an hour's **hike**, walk the trail to perfect **Praia do Sono**, 12km southwest of town. A little way beyond (21km from Paraty) and reached by a steep winding road is the village of **Trindade** (7 daily buses; 45min). Sandwiched between the ocean and Serra do Mar, it's crammed with tourists in peak season. Famed for its **beaches**, the best are across the rocky outcrops to **Praia Brava** and **Praia do Meio**, some of the most attractive mainland beaches on this stretch of coast, and completely unspoilt.

Arrival and information

Bus The *rodoviária* is about half a kilometre from the old town on Rua Jango de Padúa; turn right out of the bus station and walk straight ahead.

Tourist information On the corner of Av. Roberto Silveira and Praça Chafariz (daily 8am–7pm; ☏24/3371-1897).

Accommodation

Casa do Rio Hostel Rua Antonio Vidal 120 ☏24/3371-2223, ⊛www.paratyhostel.com. A smart HI hostel with a large communal area, though the dorms are somewhat cramped. Helpful staff and tours on offer. Dorms R$28, rooms R$90.

Pousada Guaraná Rua Cinco, no. 13, Portal de Paraty ☏24/3371-6362, ⊛www .pousadaguarana.com.br. A smart yet artistic, spacious and very good value pousada ten minutes from the Centro Historico. A pool, plant-filled gardens, soft music and great attention to detail all make this a very relaxing choice. R$130.

Solar dos Gerânios Praça da Matriz ☏24/3371-1550. Beautiful Swiss/Brazilian owned place filled with rustic furniture and curios. Rooms are spartan but impeccable; most have a balcony and all are en suite. Superb value. Reservations advised – request a room overlooking the *praça*. R$100.

Eating and drinking

Banana da Terra Rua Dr Samuel Costa 198
☎24/3371-1725. Paraty's most interesting
restaurant, where the food is based on local
ingredients. The grilled fish with garlic-herb
butter and banana is delicious (R$35), as are the
wonderful desserts. Evenings only except Fri–Sun,
when lunch is also served; closed Tues.

Beija Flor Rua Dr Pereira. A Lebanese-
Portuguese café in a quiet corner of the historic
centre – a good place for a cold beer or
caipirinha and some savoury snacks. Open from
4pm; closed Wed.

Sabor da Terra Av. Roberto Silveira 180. The
inexpensive *Sabor da Terra* is Paraty's best *por kilo*
(R$15 per kilo) restaurant, offering a wide variety
of hot and cold dishes, including excellent seafood.
The restaurant even has its own fishing boats,
guaranteeing a fresh meal.

PETRÓPOLIS

Some 66km to the north of Rio, high in
the mountains, stands the imperial city

PARQUE NACIONAL SERRA DOS ORGÃOS

The **Parque Nacional Serra dos Orgãos** is breathtakingly beautiful and refreshingly
easy to visit from Petrópolis's less attractive neighbour, **Teresópolis**. Dominated
in its lower reaches by lush Atlantic forest, the bare mountain peaks that emerge
from the trees create a stunning effect against the backdrop of a clear blue sky. It is
these peaks that give the park its name, the rocks reminding the early Portuguese
explorers of the pipes of cathedral organs.

There are a number of **walking trails** in the park, most of them short, easily
accessible and suitable for people who like their hiking easy, though all have
uphill stretches. Many of the park's most recognizable landmarks are visible
on the horizon from Teresópolis. The most famous of all is the **Dedo de Deus**
(Finger of God) – a bare, rocky pinnacle that points skyward – while arguably
more picturesque is the **Cachoeira Véu da Noiva** waterfall. The longest and most
challenging trail is the **Pedra do Sino** (Stone Bell), starting some distance from the
park entrance, passing the bell-shaped rock formation (at 2263m the park's highest
point) and emerging some 30km further on close to the town of Petrópolis – a guide
is strongly recommended.

Practicalities

Buses to Teresópolis run hourly from Rio and every 90min from Petrópolis, arriving
at the *rodoviária* on Rua 1 de Maio. **Tourist information** is at Av. Rotariana (daily
8am–7pm; ☎21/2642-1737, ⓦwww.teresopolis.rj.gov.br). Teresópolis is located
right at the edge of the park, the entrance being just to the south of town (head
towards the Dedo de Deus). The **park office** at the entrance (daily 8am–5pm)
rents out camping equipment and can provide information on local **guides**. There
is a R$3 entrance charge, increasing to R$8 if you wish to walk the Pedra do Sino
trail. If you're not camping or walking straight on to Petrópolis, you'll probably
want to base yourself in Teresópolis, where there are a couple of reasonable
accommodation options.

Pousada Villa Tiroleza Rua da Mariana 144 ☎21/2742-7337, ⓦwww
.pousadatiroleza.com.br. A handsome chalet-style building with a rustic wooden
interior and a sauna. Excellent value. R$130.

Recanto do Lord Rua Luiza Pereira Soares ☎21/2742-5586, ⓦwww
.teresopolishostel.com.br. An HI hostel, some distance from the centre of town
but well worth the trek for the savings you'll make. Great service, with dorms and
double rooms, and a glorious view over town. Dorms R$25, rooms R$130.

For **eating**, there's plenty of *por kilo* lunch places for cheap eats, but if you're
looking for something a little different, try *Cheiro do Mato* at Rua Delfim Moreira
(☎21/ 2742-1899). This reasonably priced vegetarian restaurant has a diverse menu
that will satisfy even the staunchest of carnivores.

of **PETRÓPOLIS**, so named because in the nineteenth century Emperor Dom Pedro II had a summer palace built here, rapidly making the place a popular retreat for Brazilian aristocracy. En route the scenery is dramatic, climbing among forested slopes that suddenly give way to ravines and gullies, while clouds shroud the surrounding peaks. You can easily tour Petrópolis in a day – its cultural attractions and stunning setting make it well worth the trip.

What to see and do

The **Palácio Imperial** on Rua da Imperatriz (Tues–Sun 11am–5.30pm; R$8; Ⓦwww.museuimperial.gov.br) is a fine structure, set in beautifully maintained gardens. Upon entry, you're given felt overshoes with which to slide around the polished floors of this royal residence, and inside there's everything from Dom Pedro II's crown to the regal commode. The cathedral of **São Pedro de Alcântara** (Tues–Sun 8am–6pm) blends with the surrounding architecture, but is much more recent than its neo-Gothic style suggests – it was finished in 1939. Inside lie the tombs of Dom Pedro himself and several royal personages.

Perhaps the town's most recognizable building is the **Palácio de Cristal** (Tues–Sun 9am–6pm) on Rua Alfredo Pachá, essentially a greenhouse erected for the local horticultural society in 1879, though competing for the honour is the alpine chalet **Casa Santos Dumont** (Tues–Sun 9.30am–5pm), which is well worth visiting for the collection of the personal oddments of the famous aviator.

Arrival and information

Bus Buses leave Rio for Petrópolis every 15min (sit on the left side of the bus for best views), arriving at the *rodoviária* on Rua Dr Porciúncula, from where it's a further 10km by local bus into town.
Tourist information Helpful branches are found around town, at Praça da Liberdade and at the *rodoviária* (both daily 9am–6pm; Ⓣ800/241-516).

Accommodation

There are a few reasonable options in town, though most are very classy former colonial mansions.
Albergue Quitandinha Rua Uruguai, 570 Ⓣ24/2247-9165, Ⓦwww.alberguequitandinha .com.br. Ten rooms and a dorm within wooden cabins, a bus ride from the *Centro Historico*. Dorms R$40, rooms R$120.
Comércio Rua Dr Porciúncula 55. One of the cheapest options in town, though by no means a bargain. Rooms without bathroom are cheapest. R$100.
Pousada 14 Bis Rua Santos Dumont 196 Ⓣ24/2231-0946, Ⓦwww.pousada14bis.com.br. A themed pousada based on the life of aviator Santos Dumont. Rooms are nothing flashy, but decorated in attractive colonial style. R$140.

Eating

Restaurants are surprisingly lacklustre in Petrópolis, most of the best being some distance from town.
Armazem Rua Visconde de Itaboraí 646. Welcoming bar-restaurant with live music most nights and a varied menu of meat and fish that will suit most tastes. Try *camarão com catupiry* (R$19.90).
Arte Temporada Rua Ipiranga 716 Ⓣ24/2237-2133. Based in the converted stable of a beautiful mansion. Offerings include Brazilian local specialities, such as trout and fine salads (from R$30). Wed–Sun lunchtime, Fri & Sat also dinner.
Braganca Rua Raul de Leon 109. In the hotel of the same name, this mid-priced Portuguese restaurant has various lunch options for two people (from R$35).
Rink Marowil Praca da Liberdade 27. Cheap *por kilo* lunch restaurant right on the square. The food is nothing to write home about, but you'll struggle to find better value for money.

Minas Gerais

Explorers flocked to **Minas Gerais** (literally "general mines") following the discovery of gold in 1693, and with the unearthing of diamonds and other gemstones the state has been exploited for these abundant natural resources ever since. For a hundred years the region was by far the wealthiest in Brazil, but as the gold reserves became

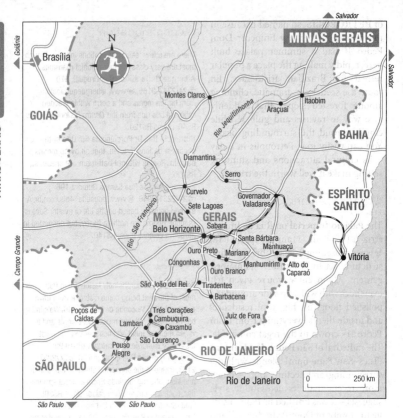

Brasília

Montes Claros

Itaobim

Araçuaí

GOIÁS

Rio Jequitinhonha

BAHIA

Diamantina

Serro

Curvelo

ESPÍRITO
SANTO

Governador
Valadares

Sete Lagoas

MINAS GERAIS

Belo Horizonte

Sabará

Santa Bárbara

Manhuaçú

Ouro Preto

Mariana

Vitória

Congonhas

Manhumirim

Alto do
Caparaó

Ouro Branco

São João del Rei

Tiradentes

Barbacena

Poços de
Caldas

Trés Corações
Cambuquira

Juiz de Fora

Lambari

Caxambú

Pouso
Alegre

São Lourenço

RIO DE JANEIRO

SÃO PAULO

Rio de Janeiro

0   250 km

Rio São Francisco

São Paulo   São Paulo

exhausted so Minas Gerais declined, and by the mid-nineteenth century it was a backwater. Today extraction of workaday minerals like iron-ore sustains much of the region, while visitors flock in to visit a series of startlingly beautiful towns left behind by the boom. They're filled with glorious churches encrusted in gold, built in the over-the-top local version of Baroque architecture – *Barroco Mineiro* – while many also have magnificent decoration by local artists. And all of this is set in an area of stunning natural beauty, with a few towns connected by historic steam trains.

BELO HORIZONTE

Founded at the beginning of the eighteenth century by *bandeirantes* in search of gold and gemstones, **BELO HORIZONTE**, capital of Minas Gerais, nestles between the beautiful hills of the Serra do Curral. The third-largest city in Brazil may at first appear daunting and uninspired, but what this cosmopolitan metropolis lacks in aesthetics it makes up for in traditional Minas hospitality, and hidden treasures like eclectic architecture and beautiful European-style parks will soon have you enchanted. Thanks to its proximity to the *Cidades Históricas*, Belo Horizonte also serves as a good base to explore the region.

What to see and do

For all its size, the centre of Belo Horizonte is fairly easy to explore on foot. Heading south from the *rodoviária*, walk to Praça Raul Soares and then take

Rua dos Guajajaras for the bustling **Mercado Central** (Mon–Sat 7am–6pm, Sun 7am–1pm), which has more than four hundred stalls and restaurants selling anything from cheeses to bamboo artefacts and bric-a-brac. Heading east you reach Av. Afonso Pena, home to the beautiful **Parque Municipal** (Tues–Sun 6am–6pm). Inspired by the Parisian belle époque parks like the beautiful gardens of the Palace of Versailles, its pleasant shaded walkways, lakes and greenery – including two thousand species of tree – are especially busy on Sunday afternoons.

If you are in town on a Sunday morning, don't miss the **Arts and Crafts Fair** on Av. Afonso Pena, the largest open-air fair in Latin America, with three thousand stalls. More modern artwork can be viewed nearby at the galleries of the **Palácio das Artes**, housed in a fine modern building at Av. Afonso Pena 1537. Further south you'll reach the **Praça da Liberdade** with its famous **Niemeyer building,** designed by renowned Brazilian modern architect Oscar Niemeyer, before reaching the Neoclassical **Palácio da Liberdade**. Finish your day around **Praça Savassi**, where you can sip a *caipirinha* in one of many trendy bars in the area.

Museu Histórico Abílio Barreto

Just to the south of the centre at Av. Prudente de Morais 202 in Cidade Jardim, the **Museu Histórico Abílio Barreto** (Tues–Sun 10am–5pm; free) is set within a beautiful colonial mansion, the sole remnant of the small village of Curral del Rey. It is home to some interesting photographs, furniture, sculptures and documents of the time.

Mangabeiras

In the Mangabeiras neighbourhood, southeast of the centre, the **Praça do Papa** has commanding views of the entire city. The monument in the square pays homage to Pope John Paul II, who held a mass here in 1980. Bus #4103 (or #2001-C) from Av. Afonso Pena between Av. Amazonas and Rua Tamóios will get you up here. Stay on the same bus to continue to the mountainous edge of the city, where the vast **Parque das Mangabeiras** (Tues–Sun 8am–6pm), a pleasant spot for a relaxing walk, supports capuchin monkeys and other wildlife in the trees overhead.

Pampulha

Set around an artificial lake, the smart, modernist neighbourhood of Pampulha, north of the city centre (an hour's journey on bus #2215A, B or C from Av. Paraná between Rua Tamoios and Rua Carijós) contains some architectural gems, the work of great modern Brazilian designers Oscar Niemeyer and Roberto Burle Marx. The **Museu de Arte de Pampulha** (MAP; Tues–Sun 9am–7pm; R$6), on a peninsula in the lake, is one of the finest; a work of art in itself (though also housing a small collection inside), originally designed to be a casino before becoming a museum in 1957. Also in Pampulha is the compelling **Igreja de São Francisco de Assis** (Tues–Sat 9am–5pm, Sun 9am–1pm; R$2) among the finest works of Niemeyer, Burle Marx and Candido Portinari, who created the beautiful *azulejo* tile facade. Nearby is Belo Horizonte's largest stadium, the **Mineirão**, with a capacity of 90,000; it's the home ground of football team Atlético Mineiro. A Sunday home derby here against Cruzeiro is unmissable.

Arrival and information

Air Confins Airport (☎ 31/3689-2700), officially called Tancredo Neves, is 38km north of the centre; take the inexpensive a/c bus (1hr) to the central *rodoviária* (a pricier though no better *executivo* bus also operates to central BH). For taxis (R$90), get a fixed rate voucher inside the terminal. Some domestic flights use Pampulha airport (☎ 31/3490-2001), 9km from downtown; take city bus #1202 to the *rodoviária*.

Bus *Rodoviária* (☎ 31/3271-3000), Praça Rio Branco, at the northern end of the city centre.

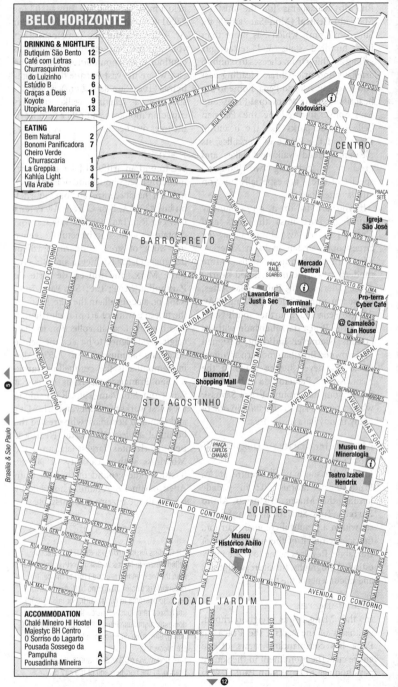

BELO HORIZONTE

DRINKING & NIGHTLIFE

Butiquim São Bento	12
Café com Letras	10
Churrasquinhos do Luizinho	5
Estúdio B	6
Graças a Deus	11
Koyote	9
Utopica Marcenaria	13

EATING

Bem Natural	2
Bonomi Panificadora	7
Cheiro Verde Churrascaria	1
La Greppia	3
Kahlúa Light	4
Vila Árabe	8

ACCOMMODATION

Chalé Mineiro HI Hostel	D
Majestyc BH Centro	B
O Sorriso do Lagarto	E
Pousada Sossego da Pampulha	A
Pousadinha Mineira	C

A, Airports & Pampulha

Rodoviária

CENTRO

Igreja São José

Mercado Central

Pro-terra Cyber Café

@ Camaleão Lan House

BARRO PRETO

Lavanderia Just a Sec

Terminal Turístico JK

Diamond Shopping Mall

STO. AGOSTINHO

Museu de Mineralogia

Teatro Izabel Hendrix

LOURDES

Museu Histórico Abílio Barreto

CIDADE JARDIM

Brasília & São Paulo

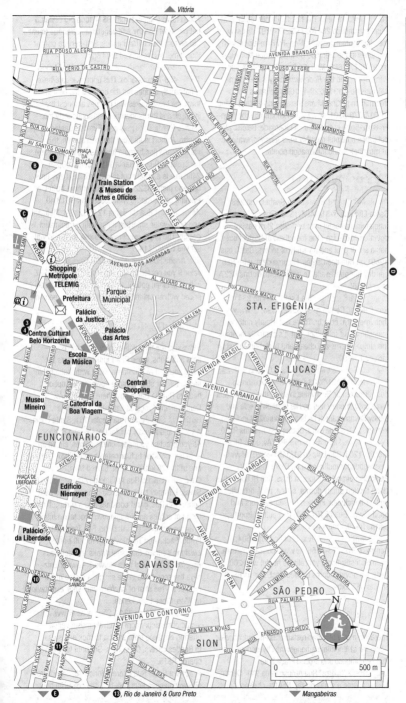

▲ Vitória

RUA POUSO ALEGRE

RUA CERIO DE CASTRO

AVENIDA BRANDÃO

RUA POUSO ALEGRE

RUA MATIAS BARBOSA
AV. L. DOS SANTOS
RUA BUENÓPOLIS
RUA ESMALTINA
RUA G. MASCI

RUA ANHANGUERA
RUA PROF. GALBA VELOSO

RUA RIO DE JANEIRO
RUA GUAICURUS

RUA ITAJUBÁ

AVENIDA DO CONTORNO

RUA BUENO BRANDÃO

RUA SALINAS

RUA MÁRMORE

RUA EURITA

AV SANTOS DUMONT

PRAÇA DA ESTAÇÃO

AVENIDA FRANCISCO SALES

RUA ASSIS CHATEAUBRIAND

RUA AQUILES LOBO

RUA CRISTAL

Train Station & Museu de Artes e Ofícios

RUA ESPIRITO SANTO
AVENIDA

AVENIDA DOS ANDRADAS

RUA DOMINGOS VIEIRA

Shopping Metrópole
TELEMIG

AL. ÁLVARO CELSO

RUA ALVARES MACIEL

STA. EFIGÊNIA

Prefeitura

Parque Municipal

AVENIDA DO CONTORNO

Palácio da Justiça

Centro Cultural Belo Horizonte

AFONSO PENA

Palácio das Artes

AVENIDA PROF. ALFREDO BALENA

RUA GRÃO PARÁ

RUA MANAUS

Escola da Música

RUA DA BAHIA
RUA JOÃO PINHEIRO
RUA SERGIPE
RUA AL. ÁGUAS
RUA PERNAMBUCO

PARAÍBA

AVENIDA BRASIL

RUA DOS OTONI

S. LUCAS

RUA PADRE ROLIM

AVENIDA FRANCISCO SALES

Museu Mineiro

Central Shopping

RUA RIO GRANDE DO NORTE

AVENIDA BERNARDO MONTEIRO

AVENIDA CARANDAÍ

RUA CEARÁ

RUA PIAUÍ

RUA MARANHÃO

RUA GRÃO PARÁ

RUA DANTE

Catedral da Boa Viagem

FUNCIONÁRIOS

AVENIDA BRASIL

RUA GONÇALVES DIAS

PRAÇA DE LIBERDADE

Edifício Niemeyer

RUA CLAUDIO MANOEL

AVENIDA GETULIO VARGAS

RUA POUSO ALTO

RUA STA. RITA DURÃO

AV CRISTÓVÃO COLOMBO

RUA DOS INCONFIDENTES

Palácio da Liberdade

RUA PERNAMBUCO

RUA RIO GRANDE DO NORTE

SAVASSI

AVENIDA AFONSO PENA

AVENIDA DO CONTORNO

RUA MONTE ALEGRE

RUA PROF. ESTEVÃO PINTO

RUA CÍCERO FERREIRA

ALBUQUERQUE

RUA SERGIPE
RUA AL. ÁGUAS

PRAÇA SAVASSI

RUA TOMÉ DE SOUZA

SÃO PEDRO

RUA LUZ

RUA ALUMÍNIO

RUA PALMIRA

N

RUA VIÇOSA
RUA RAUL POMPEI
RUA PADRE ODORICO
RUA LAVRAS

AVENIDA DO CONTORNO

RUA MINAS NOVAS

RUA PIAU

RUA GRÃO MOGOL

RUA CALDAS

SION

ERNARDO FIGEIREDO

RUA FINO

0   500 m

▼   ▼ ⑬, Rio de Janeiro & Ouro Preto   ▼ Mangabeiras

Tourist Information The helpful Belotur office is at Rua Pernambuco 284 (☎31/3277-9797, ⊛www .belohorizonte.mg.gov.br; Mon–Fri 8am–6pm), with branches at the Mercado Central, Parque Municipal (☎31/3277-7666; Mon–Fri 8am–7pm, Sat & Sun 8am–3pm), and the *Rodoviária* (daily 8am–10pm). Alô Turismo (☎31/3220-1310) is Belotur's information hotline. Minas's state tourist office Setur (☎31/3270-8501; ⊛www.turismo.mg.gov.br; Mon–Fri 8am–5pm) is on Praça da Liberdade. Belotur also publishes a helpful monthly *Guia Turístico*, available at most hotels and information points.

Accommodation

Chalé Mineiro HI Hostel Rua Santa Luzia 288, Santa Efigênia ☎31/3467-1576, ⊛www .chalemineirohostel.com.br. Some 2km east of downtown, this isn't the friendliest of hostels but it has a small pool and a variety of rooms. Catch bus #9801 on Rua dos Caetés. No breakfast; wi-fi R$6 per day but only available until 10pm. Dorms R$27, rooms R$65.

Majestyc BH Centro Rua Espírito Santo 284 (cnr Rua Caetés), Centro ☎31/3222-3390, ⊛www .hotelmajestyc.com.br. There is certainly nothing majestic about this place, but it's centrally located, the simple rooms are cheap and buffet breakfast is included. R$50.

O Sorriso do Lagarto Calle Cristina 791, São Pedro ☎31/3283-9325, ⊛www.osorriso dolagarto.com.br. Best value in town, this small hostel has a cosy, friendly feel and its location in safe and trendy Savassi cannot be beaten. Breakfast included, kitchen, wi-fi a little extra. Dorms R$30, rooms R$80.

Pousada Sossego da Pampulha Av. José Dias Bicalho 1258, São Luiz ☎31/3491-8020, ⊛www .sossegodapampulha.com.br. Close to the Pampulha airport and tourist sites, this HI hostel has clean though pricey dorms, sauna, pool, breakfast and wi-fi included, kitchen for self-caterers and good views. Bus #5401 from Pampulha airport. Dorms R$49, rooms R$100.

Pousadinha Mineira Rua Espírito Santo 604, Centro ☎31/3273-8156, ⊛www.pousadamineira .com.br. Institutional yet reliable hostel with 200 beds. No private rooms or breakfast. Dorms R$20, sheets R$5 extra.

Eating

There are plenty of cheap restaurants and *lanchonetes* – popular at lunchtime amongst the city workers – on Rua Pernambuco and around Praça Sete.

Bem Natural Rua Afonso Pena 941, Centro (inside a small plaza). Not the cheapest *por kilo* in town (expect to pay R$17 for a big plateful) but plenty of healthy and vegetarian offerings (meat dishes too) plus natural juices. Self-service only at lunchtime; soups served until 6pm.

Bonomi Panificadora Rua Cláudio Manoel 488, Funcionários. This upmarket café/bakery is not strictly budget, but the coffee is the best in town, the bread, cakes and pastries amongst the best in Brazil, and the sandwiches and soups tasty too.

Cheiro Verde Churrascaria Rua dos Caetés 236, Centro. A short walk from the train station, this *churrascaria* has bargain lunches (R$10 per plate).

La Greppia Rua da Bahia 1196, Centro. Open 24hr, this is a great spot to grab a bite at any time day and night. R$22 unlimited lunchtime buffet, or evening pasta *rodizio* with dessert for R$13.40.

Kahlúa Light Rua da Bahia 1216, Centro. Pleasant and good-value smartish place with a minimalist design. The *prato executivo* changes daily and will set you back R$14.

Vila Árabe Rua Pernambuco 781, Savassi. Good value if you opt for the sizeable meze for two (R$37, with vegetarian option), though otherwise moderately priced with an unlimited buffet for R$40 per person.

Drinking and nightlife

Savassi is teeming with trendy – if expensive – bars and clubs, while Rua Pium-í continues the trend south of Av. Contorno, lined with fashionable hangouts. For slightly more downmarket options, head to Rua da Bahia anywhere between Av. Carandaí and Praça da Estação.

Butiquim São Bento Rua Kepler 131, Santa Lúcia. A young and friendly bar for unashamed flirting. As you practise your best chat-up lines, sip on an excellent cocktail to lubricate your chat box. Or try one of the 28 kinds of beer. Closed Mon.

Café com Letras Rua Antônio de Albuquerque 781, Savassi. Trendy bar/bookshop open until the early hours with DJs, great cocktails and a scrumptious menu of crêpes and imaginative vegetarian bites.

Churrasquinhos do Luizinho Rua Turquesa 327, Prado. Packed on Thurs with up to 500 people, *Luizinho's* serves the usual drinks and delicious *espetos* (grilled beef on a skewer) – owner Luiz says the secret lies in the sauce, a recipe of his mother's. Free shot of *cachaça* with your *espetinho* on Mon. Closed weekends.

Estúdio B Contorno 3849, São Lucas ⊛www .estudiobmusicbar.com.br. Lively music venue offering anything from samba to rock and salsa to Beatles covers. Open Tues–Sat until late. Cover charge R$15.

Graças a Deus Rua Padre Odorico 68, São Pedro ⊛www.gracasadeus.com.br. Little colourful house from the outside but darker lighting inside, with wooden tables and chilled beats setting the mood. Mean *caipívodkas*.

Koyote Rua Tomé de Souza 912, Savassi. Young crowd, fun atmosphere and a pleasant spot for an evening drink in the Savassi district, with tables spilling out onto the street. Closed Mon.

Utopica Marcenaria Av. Raja Gabáglia, 4700, Santa Lúcia ✆ www.utopica.com.br. Current king of BH's live music scene, located a few kilometres south of Centro. Samba on Thurs, rock/MPB on Fri, funk/soul on Sat and *forró* on Sun. Cover R$12.

Directory

Banks and exchange There are plenty of banks downtown on Av. João Pinheiro between Rua dos Timbiras and Av. Afonso Pena.

Car rental Numerous options at the airports; Hertz at Av. Prof. Magalhães Penido 101, Pampulha ☎31/3492-1919; Alpina Serviços Automotivos at Rua dos Timbiras 2229 ☎31/3291-6111; Localiza at Av. Bernardo Monteiro 1567 ☎31/3247-7956; Locaralpha at Av. Santa Rosa 100 ☎31/3491-3833.

Consulates Argentina, Rua Ceará 1566, 6th floor, Funcionários ☎31/3047-5490; Paraguay, Rua Guandaus 60, apt. 102, Santa Lúcia ☎31/3344-6349; UK, Rua Cláudio Manoel 26, Funcionários ☎31/3225-0950; Uruguay, Av. do Contorno 6777, Santo Antônio, ☎31/3296-7527.

Medical Ambulance ☎192. Pronto Socorro do Hospital João XXIII, Av. Alfredo Balena 400, Santa Efigênia (☎31/3239-9200).

Internet Camaleão Lan House, at Rua São Paulo 1409; *Pro-Terra Cyber Café*, at Av. Augusto de Lima 134; near the *rodoviária*, try the top floor of the neighbouring shopping mall.

Laundry Lavanderia Just a Sec, at Rua dos Guajajaras 1268, Centro (Mon–Fri 8am–6pm, Sat 8am–1pm).

Police ☎190. For visa extensions go to the Polícia Federal at Rua Nascimento Gurgel 30, Gutierrez (☎31/3330-5200).

Post office Central *Correio*, Av. Afonso Pena 1270 (Mon–Fri 8am–5pm).

Taxis Coomotaxi ☎31/3419-2020 or ☎0800/39-2020; Coopertáxi/BH ☎31/3421-2424 or ☎0800/97-92424.

Moving on

Air Domestic flights depart from Pampulha and Confins, with international flights from Confins only. Regular a/c airport buses leave from the *rodoviária* for Pampulha (first bus daily 4.15am, last bus around 11pm) and Confins (first bus daily 4.30am, last bus around 10pm). Brasília (12 daily; 2hr); Rio de Janeiro (10 daily; 1hr); Salvador (4 daily; 3hr); São Paulo (20 daily; 1hr 30min).

Bus Brasília (4 daily; 13 hr); Diamantina (4 daily; 5hr); Ouro Preto (hourly; 2hr 30min); Rio de Janeiro (hourly; 8hr); São João del Rei (6 daily; 4hr); São Paulo (hourly; 9hr).

Train The train station (☎31/3273-5976) at Praça da Estação serves just one route, to Vitória on the coast, with a daily 7.30am departure (14hr) following the valley of the Rio Doce through Minas's industrial heartland.

CIDADES HISTÓRICAS

Minas Gerais's **CIDADES HISTÓRICAS** started life as mining camps, as rough and basic as imagination can make them. But the wealth of the surrounding mountains transformed them, and today they are considered to be among the most beautiful cities in the Americas, with cobbled streets and alleyways, gilded Baroque churches and beautifully preserved colonial buildings surrounded by rugged landscapes. **Ouro Preto** and **Diamantina** are both UNESCO World Heritage Sites and are the best places for budget travellers to base themselves; **Tiradentes** is pricier though barely less impressive, easily accessed from attractive and affordable **São João del Rei**.

OURO PRETO

Founded at the end of the seventeenth century, **OURO PRETO**, or "Black Gold", could well be the prettiest town in Brazil. Built on a hill in the Serra do Espinhaço, the former capital of Minas Gerais is home to some of the finest Baroque architecture in the country and was the birthplace of renowned sculptor **Aleijadinho**. The town was also the focal point of the **Inconfidência Mineira**, a failed attempt in 1789 to break from the colony and form a Brazilian republic. People flock to Ouro Preto from all over Brazil for **Semana Santa**, with its grand

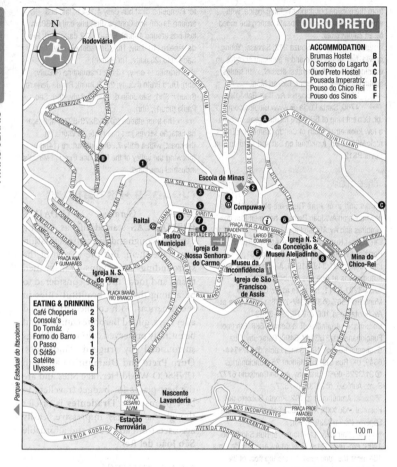

ACCOMMODATION

Brumas Hostel	B
O Sorriso do Lagarto	A
Ouro Preto Hostel	C
Pousada Imperatriz	D
Pouso do Chico Rei	E
Pouso dos Sinos	F

EATING & DRINKING

Café Chopperia	2
Consola's	8
Do Tomáz	3
Forno do Barro	4
O Passo	1
O Sótão	5
Satélite	7
Ulysses	6

0   100 m

processions Passion plays in open-air theatres, while **Carnaval** also attracts large crowds; book in advance at both these times. Other enjoyable festivals in this lively university town include the **Festival do Cinema Brasileiro** in mid-June, **Festival do Jazz** in September and **Festival das Letras**, a literary event, in November.

What to see and do

The town is best explored on foot, taking in the cobbled passageways between its handful of stunning churches, two excellent museums, and numerous shopping and eating options – but be prepared for lots of uphill climbing.

Praça Tiradentes

Praça Tiradentes lies at the heart of Ouro Preto, with several sights right on the square. The **Museu da Inconfidência** (Tues–Sun noon–6pm; R$6, students R$3) inside the Paço Municipal describes the town's fascinating local history, and includes the tomb of Tiradentes, leader of the failed *Inconfidência Mineira* rebellion. Numerous documents, torture instruments, Indo-Portuguese images and statuettes – notably nine exquisite figures by Aleijadinho – and other interesting

Parque Estadual do Itacolomi

ALEIJADINHO

The most important sculptor in colonial Brazil, Antônio Francisco Lisboa (1738–1814) was born in Ouro Preto to a slave mother and a Portuguese architect father, Manoel Lisboa. Self-taught, Aleijadinho was exceptionally prolific, turning out scores of profoundly original works, an achievement made all the more remarkable by the fact that from his mid-thirties he suffered from a degenerative disease (presumably leprosy) which led to loss of movement in his legs and hands, eventually forcing him to sculpt using chisels strapped to his wrists while apprentices moved him around on a trolley (the name Aleijadinho translates literally as "little cripple"). His extraordinary works reflect his Christian spirituality and abound in many of the *cidades históricas*, particularly Ouro Preto, where the Museu Aleijadinho offers further insights. His most famous works of all, however, sculpted towards the end of his life, are the 76 life-size figures at the Basílica do Senhor Bom Jesus de Matosinhos in the otherwise utterly unremarkable town of Congonhas, a convenient stopping-off point between Ouro Preto (or Belo Horizonte) and São João del Rei – the works were credited with introducing greater realism into Baroque art. To visit them, leave baggage at the Congonhas *rodoviária*, from where you'll need about four hours for local bus connections and to make the most of the site.

everyday objects bring the eighteenth-century to life. On the opposite side of the square, inside the vast **Escola de Minas**, the **Museu de Ciência e Técnica da Escola de Minas** (Tues–Sun noon–5pm; R$3) houses a large geological and mineralogical collection, including gemstones from all over the world. There is also an **astronomical observatory** (Sat 8–10pm).

Two churches and Aleijadinho

Arguably the most beautiful church in Ouro Preto, the **Igreja de São Francisco de Assis** (Tues–Sun 8.30am–noon & 12.30–5pm; R$6, students R$3, including entry to the Museu Aleijadinho), east of Praça Tiradentes, is one of the most important works of Aleijadinho (see above). The exterior was entirely sculpted by the great master himself and the ceilings decorated by his partner Athayde. The **Museu Aleijadinho** (Tues–Sat 8.30am–noon & 1.30–5pm, Sun 12–5pm), containing many more beautiful works, is located in the **Igreja Matriz de N.S. da Conceição**. The church designed by his father, also houses Aleijadinho's simple tomb.

Mina do Chico-Rei

Close to the **Igreja Matriz de N.S. da Conceição**, at Rua Dom Silvério 108, is the **Mina do Chico-Rei** (daily 8am–5pm; R$10/R$5 students). The abandoned mine has claustrophobic tunnels to explore, and gives a good sense of the scale of the local mining operations (this was only a small mine). It's also an interesting place to learn more about Chico-Rei ("Little King") himself, a legendary figure said to have been an enslaved African king who bought himself and his people out of slavery and became fabulously wealthy.

Teatro Municipal and Igreja Matriz N.S. do Pilar

A little further west of Praça Tiradentes, is the beautiful and still-functioning **Teatro Municipal** (Mon–Fri 9am–5.30pm, Sat & Sun 10am–5pm; R$2), which is worth a look for its simple wooden interior. According to the Guinness Book of Records, this is the oldest opera house in the Americas, inaugurated on June 6, 1770; people used to bring their own chairs to performances.

If you continue downhill to the foot of **Rua Brigador Mosqueira**, you'll

Pouso do Chico Rei Rua Brigadeiro Musqueira 90, Centro ☎31/3551-1274, ⊛www.pousodochicorei .com.br. Definitely worth paying the extra to stay at this friendly, historic family pousada, previously graced by pre-eminent Brazilian singers Vinicius de Moraes and Dori Caymmi. Wooden floorboards provide a rustic touch and an upstairs living room with grandfather clock adds to a homely feel. All rooms are individually furnished and some have commanding views of the Carmo church. A large breakfast is served in the dining room (a room with antiques and cosy fireplace); while complementary tea and cake is available at any time, as is wi-fi access. Doubles from R$175.

come to the early eighteenth-century **Igreja Matriz N.S. do Pilar** (Tues–Sun 9–10.45am & noon–4.45pm; R$4), the most opulent church in Minas Gerais, as well as one of the oldest. Over-the-top even by Baroque standards, it's said to be the second-richest in Brazil, with 434kg of gold and silver used in its decoration.

Parque Estadual do Itacolomi

A 20-min bus journey outside of town (numerous local buses pass), the **Parque Estadual do Itacolomi** (☎31/8433-2266; Tues–Sun 8am–5pm, last entry 3.30pm; R$7) is a great place to spend a day immersed in nature, with well-organized trails ranging in length from 1.5km to 16km. **Camping** is usually permitted here if you're feeling adventurous (around R$15; phone to confirm).

Arrival and information

Bus The *rodoviária* (☎31/3559-3225) is on Rua Padre Rolim 661, a 10-min walk northwest of the city centre. Buses from Mariana stop right by Praça Tiradentes – get off here for most accommodation options.

Tourist information The helpful Centro Cultural Turístico is at Praça Tiradentes 4 (daily 8.15am–7pm).
Train The train station (☎31/3551-7705) is south of town on Praça Cesário Alvim 102.

Accommodation

Make sure that you book in advance in high season and at weekends. Expect substantial discounts midweek and off-season.
Brumas Hostel Ladeira de São Francisco de Paula 68 ☎31/3551-2944, ⊛www.brumashostel .com.br. This clean and pleasant HI hostel offers a pleasant communal area with couches, books and a good breakfast. Guest kitchen and laundry service. Dorms R$35, rooms R$90.
O Sorriso do Lagarto Rua Conseheiro Quintiliano 271 ☎31/3551-4811, ⊛www.osorrisodolagarto .com.br. A 10-min walk from Praça Tiradentes, this hostel has big clean dorms with a good breakfast included, brightly decorated rooms and a guest kitchen. Dorms R$35.
Ouro Preto Hostel Travessa das Lajes 32, Antônio Dias ☎31/3551-6011, ⊛www.ouropretohostel .com. Grand views and a relaxed feel at this new HI hostel a short walk from the Igreja da Conceição. Attractive communal areas (breakfast buffet included) and private rooms. Dorms R$30, rooms R$80.
Pousada Imperatriz Rua Direita 179 ☎31/3551-5435. Great value, these simple but (mostly) spacious double rooms have a TV and in some cases a private bathroom. Prime location by the bars below Praça Tiradentes. R$60.
Pouso dos Sinos Rua Costa Senna 30 ☎31/3551-1138, ⊛www.pousodossinos.com.br. This rambling antique-filled building in an ideal location next to the Igreja de São Francisco contains a variety of large attractive rooms with up to five beds – some have private bath. No internet or breakfast. Dorms R$40, doubles R$110.

Eating and drinking

Good cheap eateries are scattered throughout Ouro Preto. Night-time action is centred on Rua Direita (aka Rua Conde de Bobadella) where students spill out of bars to chat on the street, while there are a couple of options along Rua Barão de Carmargos and weekly late parties are held at school and university halls elsewhere (look out for flyers).
Café Choperia Real Rua Barão de Camargo 8. A few psychedelic paintings decorate this popular joint with tables on the cobbled street in front,

perfect for a *chopp* on a warm evening. Live bossa nova or MPB most nights from 8pm, plus a decent *prato executivo* for R$12.

Consola's Rua da Conceiçao 18, behind the Matriz N.S. da Conceiçao. You can't argue with the value of this place, serving reasonable pizza for R$11, plus the usual steak dinners and excellent (huge) *comida mineira* at R$25 for two. Closed Tues.

Do Tomáz Rua Senado Rocha Lagoa 75. Very simple place with paint wearing off the walls, but the lunch dishes change daily, it's super-friendly and the price hits the spot at R$7.

Forno do Barro Praça Tiradentes 54. Excellent (if a little salty) range of *mineira* specialities kept warm on the stove; lunch & dinner buffet R$15 plus pizzas and bar vibe at night.

O Passo Rua São José 56 ☎31/3552-3716. Upmarket dining with excellent large pizzas (R$26) and pastas, buzzing most weekend evenings for a pre- or post-dinner drink on the terrace, often with live jazz. Call for pizza delivery.

O Sótão Rua Direita 124. Fun, colourful paintings decorate this smarter student-friendly place with straw lights. Nice cocktails and light bites such as filled pancakes. Live chilled bossa nova sets the mood from 8pm. Closed Mon.

Satélite Rua Direita 97. Good place to grab a snack (try the *batatas recheadas* for R$9); gets really lively late at night, with locals sipping on beer and cheap *caipirinhas*.

Ulysses Rua Bernardo Vasconcelos 25. Family-run place with the cheapest lunches in town (11am–2pm) served on a little terrace for an incredible R$6. You can see the eponymous owner at work in the little kitchen at the back. Closed Mon.

Directory

Banks and exchange All the major banks with ATMs are located along Rua São José; HSBC at no. 201 changes travellers' cheques.

Internet Compuway, Praça Tiradentes 52 (Mon–Fri 8am–9pm, Sat until 6pm); Raitai, Rua Paraná 100 (daily 9am–9pm).

Laundry Ask at your hotel/hostel as there are no laundries in downtown. Nacente Lavanderia, at Rua dos Inconfidentes 5 (Mon–Fri 8am–5pm, Sat 8am–noon) picks up and drops off washing.

Shopping The *Feria do Artesanato* on Praça Largo do Coimbra sells a variety of local artefacts made from soapstone.

Moving on

Bus Belo Horizonte (10 daily; 2hr); Brasilia (daily at 7.30pm; 11hr 30min); Mariana (every 30min; 30min); Rio (daily at 10pm; 7hr); São João del Rei (4 daily; 4hr).

Train The historic *Trem da Vale* steam train runs between Ouro Preto and Mariana on Fri, Sat & Sun, leaving at 11am and returning at 2pm (1hr; R$18 single, R$30 return).

MARIANA

A half-hour bus ride from Ouro Preto, lovely **MARIANA**, founded in 1696 and named after King Dom João V's wife Maria Ana de Austria, is home to two of Minas's most elegant town squares and a beautifully preserved colonial centre. The town can be visited as a day-trip from Ouro Preto, but it's also a great place to stay should you wish to escape the hordes of tourists elsewhere.

What to see and do

Once more important than Ouro Preto and home to the first governors of the state, Mariana today is no more than a small town. Head first to the impressive, elaborate **Catedral de N.S. da Assunção** (Tues–Sun 7am–6pm) on Praça Cláudio Manoel. The church was designed by Aleijadinho's father and contains many carvings by the man himself; in addition, the *tapa o vento* door, painted by Athayde, is considered by many to be the most beautiful in South America. Further riches include 365kg of gold and a beautiful German organ with 1039 flutes and a keyboard made of elephants' teeth. **Organ concerts** are held on Friday at 11am and Sunday at midday.

Not far away, at Rua Frei Durão 49, the former bishop's palace now houses the **Museu Arquidiocesano de Arte Sacra** (Mon–Fri 8.30am–noon & 1.30–5pm, Sat & Sun 8.30am–2pm; R$5), a lovely building holding religious treasures, more paintings by Athayde and sculptures by Aleijadinho. Two stunning Baroque churches stand on the **Praça Minas Gerais**: the **Igreja de São Francisco de Assis** (daily 8am–5pm), with more Aleijadinho carving, is the final resting place of Athayde; the relative restraint of the **Igreja do Carmo** (daily 9am–4pm) makes an interesting contrast.

Mina da Passagem

On the outskirts of town in the direction of Ouro Preto, **Mina da Passagem** (Mon & Tues 9am–5pm, Wed–Sun 9am–5.30pm; R$26; ⊛www.minasdapassagem.com .br) is one of the oldest and richest deep-shaft gold mines in the region. From the beginning of the eighteenth century to the mine's closure in 1985, 35 tons of gold were extracted from here. Today it is worth visiting for the roller-coaster journey down into the tunnels alone, in a rickety cart that wobbles along the irregular tracks, taking you 120m below ground. En route you pass caverns where as many as three thousand slaves daily sweated blood and tears at the rock face. You continue on foot, with the option of taking a refreshing dip in a spectacularly clear lagoon. Any bus going between Ouro Preto and Mariana will drop you at the mine.

Arrival and information

Bus Most Transcotta buses from Ouro Preto will drop you off at Praça Tancredo Neves at the heart of town. The *rodoviária* (☎31/3557-1215) is a couple of kilometres west of the centre – local buses ply the route to town every few minutes.
Tourist Information The excellent Terminal Turístico (daily 8am–5pm; ☎31/3557-1158) is on Praça Tancredo Neves.
Train The station for the steam train from Ouro Preto is right by the *rodoviária*.

Accommodation

Central Rua Frei Durão 8 ☎31/3557-1630. Set within a beautiful colonial building, this very basic sixty-room hotel has a slightly strange, soulless feel, though it's reliable enough, cheap, and in the perfect location. R$70.
Faisca Rua Antônio Olinto 48 ☎31/3557-1206, ⊛www.hotelfaisca.com.br. Thirty-five smart spotless rooms in the centre of town; excellent value with breakfast and wi-fi included. Doubles R$90.

Mariana Hostel Rua Mestre Vicente 41 ☎31/3557-1435, ⊛www.marianahostel.com.br. HI hostel five-minutes' walk from the centre, with sparkling rooms and bathrooms, a communal area, breakfast and wi-fi included. Dorms R$38, rooms R$90.

Eating

Cozinha Real Rua Antônio Olinto 34. Next door to the *Hotel Faisca*, this place offers a good range of *mineira* food (buffet lunch R$18), with friendly staff and live music Fri & Sat nights. Closed Sun.
Pizzaria Dom Silveiro Praça Gomes Freire 242. Top-notch wood-fired pizza in atmospheric surroundings (from 6.30pm; R$27 for two), while a decent-sized *prato feito mineira* is served at lunchtime (R$7).
Rancho Praça Gomes Freire 108. Excellent local cuisine kept warm on a wooden stove. Lunchtime buffet (R$16), soups (R$5) and *petiscos* (from R$9) at night. Closed Mon.

Moving on

Bus There are regular Transcotta buses to Ouro Preto (30min), leaving from Praça Tancredo Neves and the *rodoviária*.
Train The *Trem da Vale* connects Mariana with Ouro Preto (see p.296).

SÃO JOÃO DEL REI

Named in honour of Dom João V, king of Portugal, **SÃO JOÃO DEL REI** was one of the first settlements in the region, dating back to the end of the seventeenth century. Today the modern city has a historic centre with imposing Baroque churches surrounded by a less-than-attractive surfeit of postwar apartment blocks; it's one of the few gold towns to have found a thriving place in the modern world. Though its neighbour Tiradentes is clearly the prettier town, staying here is certainly a more economical alternative; on Fridays, weekends and public holidays you can ride between the two on the *Maria Fumaça* **steam train**.

What to see and do

Colonial buildings catch you unawares as you wander through the town: ruas

Santo Antônio and Getulio Vargas are particularly well preserved. Right on the town's wide central artery, with a stream running through the middle, the beautiful, classical **Teatro Municipal** on Rua Hemilio Alves (Mon–Fri 8–11am and 1–5pm; R$10) is worth seeing – or catch one of the regular performances or concerts here; the tourist office has details of current shows. A couple of buildings away is the **Brazilian Expeditionary Force Museum** (Museu FEB; daily 8am–4pm; R$1), which tells the story of the country's involvement in World War II, including combat garbs, radios, photographs, weapons, banknotes and fascinating news clippings from the period. The **Railway Museum**, at the station four blocks east (Tues–Sun 9–11am and 1–5pm; R$1, free with a train ticket), has interesting facts on the origins of the *Maria Fumaça*, and also houses the first engine to run on the track here.

On Rua Getulio Vargas, visit the stunning 1721 Baroque **Catedral de Nossa Senhora de Pilar** (daily 8am–8pm, closed at lunchtime; free), which has extensive gold gilding over the altar and attractive tiling. Close by, the **Museu Regional** (Tues–Fri noon–5.30pm; Sat & Sun 8am–1pm; R$1), on Largo Tamandaré, has a rich collection of historical and artistic objects from furniture to paintings, housed in a beautifully restored mansion.

Igreja de São Francisco de Assis

The most impressive and important of the city's churches, the 1774 Baroque **Igreja de São Francisco de Assis** (daily 8am–5.30pm, Sun until 4pm; R$2), gives onto the beautiful Praça Frei Orlando, lined with towering palms. A deceivingly large place with carvings by Aleijadinho and his pupils, it also has a graveyard to the rear where President Tancredo Neves is buried. One of Brazil's most revered politicians, he is credited with masterminding the return to democracy in the 1980s.

Arrival and information

Bus The *rodoviária* (☎32/3373-4700) is 2km northeast of town; take a local bus from in front of the Drogaria Americana outside and get off at Av. Tancredo Neves. Taxis (☎32/3371-2028) charge R$15.

Tourist information The tourist office (Mon–Fri 8am–6pm ☎32/3372-7388) is located right in the centre by the stream on Av. Tancredo Neves.

Accommodation

Brasil Av. Tancredo Neves 395 ☎32/3371-2804. Facing the river, the biggest hotel in town gives a whole new meaning to faded grandeur, with fifty very simple but clean rooms that probably haven't changed much since the hotel opened in 1881. R$80.

HI Hostel Vila Av. Oito de Decembro ☎32/3371-9263, ⊛www.vilahostel.com. Best value in town, with well-kept small dorms and singles. Breakfast included and tranquil communal areas and garden. A 10-min uphill walk from the train station. Dorms R$35.

Pousada Estação do Trem Rua Maria Tereza 45 ☎32/3372-1985, ⊛www.pousadaestacaodotrem .com.br. With attractive wooden furnishings, rugs and soft lighting, this historic house is good value, right by the weekend train service to Tiradentes. Wi-fi and breakfast included. R$130.

Eating and drinking

Cabana do Zotti Av. Tiradentes 805. Drinking spot with snacks and a pleasant atmosphere within a stone, brick and wood setting; busy at weekends.

Del Rei Cafe Av. Tiradentes 553. Open until late, this restaurant-cum-*chopperia* serves reasonable pizza, lunchtime *pratos feitos* and tasty filled crêpes.

Pantanal Rua Getúlio Vargas. A popular joint to have an evening drink close to the Igreja do N.S. do Carmo.

Pelourinho Rua Hermilio Alves 276. A decent and cheap self-service *por kilo* place with a great variety of *mineira* food, right in the centre of town by the stream.

Villeiros Rua Padre José Maria Xavier 132. A homely, comfy *por kilo* restaurant at lunchtime with a good range of typical *mineira* food. At night there's a more expensive à la carte menu from R$40 for two. Close to São Francisco church.

Directory

Banks and exchange All banks and ATMs are on Av. Tancredo Neves.

Internet World Game Internet, at Rua Ministro Gabriel Passos 281 (daily 9am–10pm). The mall adjoining *Del Rei Café* offers free wi-fi.

Post office Av. Tiradentes 500 (Mon–Fri 9am–5pm, Sat 9am–noon).

Shopping The *Feria do Artesanato*, held every Sun on Av. Presidente Tancredo Neves, sells local crafts.

Moving on

Bus Belo Horizonte (8 daily; 3hr 30min); Ouro Preto (daily 3am and 6pm; 4hr); Rio (Mon–Fri 8am, 2pm & midnight, Sat 6am & 2pm, Sun 10am, 4pm and midnight; 5hr 30min); São Paulo (8 daily; 7hr 30min); Tiradentes (every 30min; 30min).

Train The *Maria Fumaça* leaves São João for Tiradentes on Fri, Sat, Sun and public holidays at 10am and 3pm, returning at 1pm and 5pm (R$18 single, R$30 return).

TIRADENTES

With its quaint historic houses, cobblestone streets and horse-drawn carriages, **TIRADENTES** at first appears like something out of a movie set. Surrounded by mountains, the charming town is better appreciated during the week, as Brazilian tourists swarm in at weekends for a romantic break or to shop at the many little boutiques around town. Costs here are the most expensive in Minas, but even despite this it's worth staying a night or two to fully appreciate the rich atmosphere, explore the town's cobbled alleyways – and, if you like the outdoors – go walking for an hour or two in the surrounding countryside.

What to see and do

Despite being described as a *cidade histórico*, modern Tiradentes is little more than a village, which at least ensures that everything is easily found. The chief landmark, pretty much at the highest point in town, is the **Igreja Matriz de Santo Antônio** (daily 9am–5pm; R$4). Among the largest and most gold-laden of Minas Gerais' Baroque churches, it also features some of Aleijadinho's last works, and the classic view from the church steps is the most photographed in the state. Nearby, at Rua Padre Toledo 190, in the former home of one of the heroes of the *Inconfidência Mineira*, the **Museu Padre Toledo** (Tues–Sun 9am–5pm; R$3) has period furnishings and art, documents dating back to the eighteenth century, and a preserved slave quarters. The slaves themselves built and worshipped at the small, dignified and supremely attractive **Igreja da N.S. do Rosário dos Pretos** (Tues–Sun 10am–5pm; R$2), down the hill, which also contains three sculptures of black saints.

Arrival and information

Bus The *rodoviária* is in the centre of town off Rua Gabriel Passos.

Tourist information The Secretária de Turismo is on the main square at Rua Resende Costa 71 (daily 9am–5pm; ☎32/3355-1212).

Train The train station for services from São João del Rei is 1km southeast of the main square.

Accommodation

Tiradentes caters primarily for the well-to-do and there's a distinct lack of budget options. Try visiting midweek when many pousadas offer discounts.

Pousada Arco-Iris Rua Frederico Ozanan 340 ☎32/3355-1167, ⊛www.arcoiristiradentesmg .com.br. Next to the *Pousada da Bia*, this place has clean spacious rooms with private bath, a big back garden and a little pool. Free internet. R$120.

Pousada da Bia Rua Frederico Ozanan 330 ☎32/3355-1173, ⊛www.pousadadabia .com.br. Set in a beautiful plot of land with a little herb garden and pool, and offering a variety of comfortable and homely rooms. Small charge for wi-fi. R$120.

Eating and drinking

Most restaurants and bars are centred on Largo das Forras, often featuring throngs of affluent Brazilian visitors eating in Tiradentes is consequently expensive; your best bet if in a small group is to share a *comida mineira*, usually large enough for two or three people.

Confidências Mineiras Rua Ministro Gabriel Passos 26. Warm candlelit place with an infinite range of *cachaças* to choose from.

Divino Sabor Rua Gabriel Passos 300. Popular place with some tables outside. Buffet for R$18 or reasonable price *por kilo*. Closed Mon.

Libertas Espaco Cultural Rua Israel Pinheiro 106 ⊛www.libertasespacocultural .com.br. A short uphill walk from the railway station (20min from the main square), this is the town's most happening outdoor space for live music and festivals of anything, from fashion to *cachaça*. Two bars and a nightclub keep things lively most weekends; ask around town to see what's on.

Mandalun Largo das Forras 88. Although the menu may at first seem expensive, there are some cheap international options among the selection of Lebanese food, such as hamburgers (R$6), sandwiches (R$12) and pizzas (R$16).

Panela de Minas Rua Gabriel Passos 23. Typical *mineira* food served *por kilo* at the town's most popular lunch spot, plus decent pizzas at night.

Viradas do Largo Rua do Moinho 11. On a back street a 5-min walk behind the *rodoviária*, this is considered the best value in town for good food. While not cheap, the huge meals (R$40–70) serve up to three.

Directory

Banks and exchange All banks with ATMs are located off Rua Gabriel Passos, close to Largo das Forras.

Internet Game Mania Lan House, Rua dos Incôfidentes (daily 9am–10.30pm).

Post office Rua Resende Costa 73 (Mon–Fri 9am–5pm).

Moving on

Bus Buses leave regularly for São João del Rei (30min), from where you can connect to other destinations.

Train The *Maria Fumaça* departs for São João on Fri, Sat, Sun and public holidays at 1pm and 5pm.

DIAMANTINA

Beautiful **DIAMANTINA**, six hours by bus from Belo Horizonte, is the most isolated of the historic towns yet well worth the trip. Nestled in the heart of

the Serra do Espinhaço, it is surrounded by a breathtakingly wild and desolate landscape. Named after abundant diamond reserves first exploited in 1729, the town is rich in history and was designated a UNESCO World Heritage Site in 1999, though it also manages to retain a lively, friendly atmosphere. It's the home town of visionary 1950s president **Juscelino Kubitschek**, who founded Brasília; a statue is dedicated to him on Rua Macau Meio.

What to see and do

Diamantina's narrow streets are set on two exceptionally steep hills. Fortunately, almost everything of interest is tightly packed into the central area close to the main cathedral square, the Praça Conselheiro Mota. The **Museu do Diamante** (Tues–Sat noon–5pm, Sun 9am–noon; R$2) is right on the square at Rua Direita 14, bringing the colonial period vividly to life through an extraordinary variety of exhibits. They include real gold, real and fake diamonds, mining paraphernalia and reproductions of paintings depicting slaves at work. There are also a number of swords, pistols, guns and torture instruments that were used on slaves.

Mercado Velho and Casa da Glória

The **Mercado Velho** on Praça Barão de Guaicuí, just below the cathedral square, is an exceptional structure, worth visiting for the building alone; the market itself is held only on weekends. The wooden arches inspired Niemeyer's design for the exterior of the Presidential Palace in Brasilia. Also more worthwhile for the building than its contents is the eighteenth-century **Casa da Glória**, which is uphill from the tourist office at Rua da Glória 298 (Tues–Sun 8am–6pm); it was inspired by Venetian structures. This former residence of diamond supervisors, see of the first bishops of Diamantina and subsequently a school, is now part of the Centre of Geology and contains a collection of maps, gemstones and minerals.

Two churches

The **Igreja de N.S. Senhora do Carmo** on Rua do Carmo (open sporadically Tues–Sun; not lunchtimes), built between 1760 and 1765, is probably the most interesting of Diamantina's churches, with an exceptionally rich interior including an organ built in 1782 on which Lobo de Mesquita, considered the best composer of religious music of the Americas, performed many of his own works. Just downhill from here, the **Igreja de Nossa Senhora do Rosário dos Pretos** (same opening hours) was built in 1728 to serve local slaves and features an intricately painted ceiling.

Arrival and information

Air Trip (🌐www.voetrip.com.br) flies to Diamantina from Belo Horizonte from R$160.

Bus The *rodoviária* is on a steep hill, about a 10-min walk above the centre of town (20min if walking uphill); a taxi costs around R$10.

Tourist information Centro de Atendimento ao Turista, Praça JK 23 (Mon–Sat 9am–6pm, Sun 9am–2pm; ☎38/3531-8060, ✉catdiamantinaturismo@yahoo.com.br).

Accommodation

Diamantina Hostel Rua do Bicame 988 ☎38/3531-5021, 🌐www.diamantinahostel.com.br. This HI hostel is spotless and has a great view, yet the rooms are dark and not especially inviting. A 15-min (uphill) walk from town and 10min from the *rodoviária*. Dorms R$28 with card, R$35 without.

JK Largo Dom João 135 ☎38/3531-8715, ✉hotel_jk@yahoo.com.br. Set in an ugly 1960s building opposite the *rodoviária*, this could be Minas's biggest bargain, with basic but serviceable rooms, friendly staff and breakfast included. Two more basic-ish options lie on the same street. Dorms R$20, doubles R$40.

Pousada dos Cristais Rua Jogo da Bola 53 ☎38/3531-2897, 🌐www.pousadadoscristais.com.br. Lovely pousada with well-decorated spacious rooms, a pleasant patio and pool, with commanding views of the surrounding landscape. Good breakfast included. R$90.

Eating and drinking

There's a decent variety of budget options around the town centre, most serving *comida mineira*. Bars around Rua da Quintanda such as *Café A Baiúca* have tables spilling onto the square – perfect to watch life go by as you sip a *chopp*.

Apocalypse Praça Barão do Guaicuí 78. A popular and slightly upmarket *por kilo* restaurant across from the market, worth a visit as much for the hilarious English translation of the menu (baked namorado fish comes out as "boyfriend to the oven"), as for the genuinely good food: *comida mineira* and Italian food, plus sublime desserts (expect to pay R$18).

Grupiara Rua Campos Carvalho. As you walk through the lovely old doors that conjure up images of the town at its height, the garish green, white and orange painted walls come as a bit of a surprise. Good cheap food, though, *por kilo* for lunch, and pastas at night.

HS Alimentacão Rua da Quitanda 57. The cheapest place in town for reasonably tasty *por kilo* food.

Livraria Espaço B Beco da Tecla 31. Just off the cathedral square, this is the place for good coffee and cakes late into the evening, in sophisticated bookshop surroundings.

CONCEIÇÃO DO MATO DENTRO

If you're making the journey from Belo Horizonte to Diamantina, consider turning the trip into a 5 to 6 day circuit returning via the historic church at Conceição do Mato Dentro and one of the tallest waterfalls in Brazil, the Cachoeiro do Tabuleiro, together some 90km southeast of Diamantina and served by a daily bus. The *Tabuleiro Eco Hostel* (☎31/3231-7065, 🌐www.tabuleiroecohostel.com.br) is the ideal place to stay and enjoy the beautiful countryside, with great facilities (camping R$12, rooms R$25).

Listings

Banks and exchange All banks with international ATMs are located around the central squares.
Internet *Padaria Central*, Rua Joaquim Costa 34 (Mon–Sat 6am–9pm and Sun 6am–1pm) is a cyber-bakery behind the *Mercado Central*.
Post office Praça Monsenhor Neves 59A.

Moving on

Bus Buses for Belo Horizonte leave at midnight, 6am, 10.45am, 3.30pm and 6pm daily (6hr). There is no service from Diamantina to Brasília.

The Northeast

THE NORTHEAST (Nordeste) of Brazil covers an immense area and features a variety of climates and scenery, from dense equatorial forests to palm fringed beaches. It comprises all or part of the nine states of Maranhão, Piauí, Ceará, Rio Grande do Norte, Paraíba, Pernambuco, Alagoas, Sergipe and Bahia, which altogether form roughly a fifth of Brazil's land area and have a combined population of 36 million.

Notorious for its poverty within Brazil, the region has been described as the largest concentration of poor people in the Americas. Yet it's also one of the most rewarding areas of Brazil to visit, with a special identity and culture nurtured by fierce regional loyalties. The Northeast has the largest concentration of Brazilians of African descent, most of whom live on or near the coast, mainly around Salvador and Recife, where the syncretism of African and Brazilian culture is reflected in all aspects of daily life – especially in its food, music and religion. In the *sertão* (the semi-arid region inland), though, Portuguese and Indian influences predominate in popular culture and racial ancestry. The region also offers more than two thousand kilometres of practically unbroken tropical beaches with white sands, blue sea and palm trees.

As for the climate, the **rains** come to Maranhão in February, in Piauí and Ceará in March, and points east in April, lasting about three months. That said, Maranhão can be wet even in the dry season, and Salvador's skies are liable to give you a soaking any time of year.

SALVADOR

Dramatically set at the mouth of the enormous bay of Todos os Santos, its old city atop a cliff, peninsular **SALVADOR** has an extraordinary energy. Its foundation in 1549 marked the beginning of Brazil's permanent occupation by the Portuguese. It wasn't an easy birth: the Caeté Indians killed and ate both the first governor and bishop before they were eventually subdued. Then, in 1624, the Dutch destroyed the Portuguese fleet in the bay and took the town by storm, only to be forced out within a year by a joint Spanish and Portuguese fleet.

These days, there's a strange feeling to the old town – the number of tourist shops makes it feel a little like a Brazilian colonial Disneyland. This is Brazil, however, so the crowds of tourists also attract traders, anglers and hustlers who are bound to ensure your stay, however long, is interesting and eventful.

If you tire of the city, go down to the pier and grab a boat for the choppy ride over to **Morro de São Paulo**, an island with beautiful beaches that's just two hours away. Here, with a beachside room in a pousada, you'll lie in your hammock and wonder why you'd ever go home.

What to see and do

Salvador is built around the craggy, fifty-metre-high bluff that dominates the eastern side of the bay, and splits

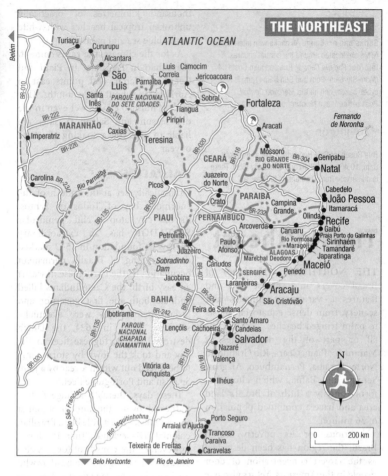

THE NORTHEAST

ATLANTIC OCEAN

Turiaçu
Cururupu
Alcantara
São Luis
Parnaíba
Luis Correia
Camocim
Jericoacoara
Santa Inês
PARQUE NACIONAL DO SETE CIDADES
Tianguá
Sobral
Fortaleza
Fernando de Noronha
BR-010
BR-222
MARANHÃO
BR-316
Piripiri
Aracati
Imperatriz
BR-226
Caxias
Teresina
BR-020
CEARÁ
BR-116
Mossoró
RIO GRANDE DO NORTE
BR-304
Genipabu
Natal
Carolina
BR-230
Rio Parnaíba
Picos
Juazeiro do Norte
Cabedelo
João Pessoa
Itamaracá
BR-135
BR-020
PIAUÍ
Crato
PARAÍBA
Campina Grande
BR-232
Olinda
Recife
PERNAMBUCO
Arcoverda
Caruaru
Gaibú
Praia Porto do Galinhas
Petrolina
Paulo Afonso
Rio Formoso
Sirinhaém
Tamandaré
Maragoji
Japaratinga
Juazeiro
Sobradinho Dam
Canudos
ALAGOAS
Marechal Deodoro
Maceió
Jacobina
BR-407
SERGIPE
Penedo
Laranjeiras
Aracaju
BAHIA
BR-324
São Cristóvão
Ibotirama
Feira de Santana
BR-242
PARQUE NACIONAL CHAPADA DIAMANTINA
Lençóis
Cachoeira
Santo Amaro
Candeias
BR-135
Nazaré
Salvador
BR-020
Vitória da Conquista
BR-101
Valença
Ilhéus
Rio São Francisco
Rio Jequitinhonha
Porto Seguro
Arraial d'Ajuda
Trancoso
Caraíva
Teixeira de Freitas
Caravelas

N

0   200 km

Belém

Belo Horizonte   Rio de Janeiro

the central area into upper and lower sections. The heart of the old city, **Cidade Alta** (upper city, or simply Centro), is strung along its top – this is the administrative, cultural and heavily touristed centre of the city where you'll find most of the bars, restaurants, hostels and pousadas. This cliff-top area is linked to the more earthy financial and commercial district, **Cidade Baixa** (lower city), by precipitous streets, a funicular railway and the towering Art Deco liftshaft of the **Carlos Lacerda elevator** (daily 24hr; R$0.15), the city's largest landmark. Stretching down the cliff and along the coast are beaches, forts and expensive hotels: **Barra** is a quieter neighbourhood where you will find more restaurants and pousadas.

Praça Municipal

Praça Municipal, Cidade Alta's main square overlooking Cidade Baixa, is the place to begin exploring. Dominating the *praça* is the **Palácio do Rio Branco** (Mon–Fri 9am–6pm; free), the old governor's palace, burnt down and rebuilt during the Dutch wars. Regal plaster eagles were added by nineteenth-century restorers, who turned a plain colonial mansion into an imposing palace. The fine interior is a blend of Rococo plasterwork, polished wooden floors, painted walls and ceilings. Inside is a museum, the **Memorial dos Governadores** (same hours; free), with colonial pieces, though it's less interesting than the building itself. Also facing the square is the **Câmara Municipal**, the seventeenth-century city hall.

Rua da Misericórdia

In the northeastern corner of the square you'll find the **Museu da Misericórdia** where you can learn more about the history of medicine in Brazil (Mon–Sat 10am–5pm, Sun 1–5.30pm; R$5; includes tour in Portuguese only). The main room of this seventeenth-century former hospital, the Salão Nobre, has 170 square metres of painted wood ceilings and walls covered with pretty Portuguese tiles. The museum has wonderfully photogenic views of the Baía de Todos os Santos, too.

Praça da Sé

Rua da Misericórdia leads into the **Praça da Sé**, the heart of Cidade Alta, where the *executivo* buses terminate.

The square lies at the southern end of **Pelourinho** or **Pelô**, the historic district, home to some of the city's finest colonial mansions, though less than twenty years ago it was decaying and run-down. To the north is a wide plaza known as **Terreiro de Jesus**, the very heart of Pelô, and home to the **Catedral Basílica** (Mon–Sat 8.30–11.30am & 1.30–5.30pm), which was once the chapel of the largest Jesuit seminary outside Rome. It's considered one of the most important Baroque monuments in Salvador, and its interior is one of the city's most beautiful, particularly the panelled ceiling of carved and gilded wood. To the left of the altar is the tomb of **Mem de Sá**, third governor general of Brazil (1557–72), remembered for successfully bringing peace and economic prosperity to what was at the time a turbulent and unstable colony. You're likely to see some capoeira in full swing as you exit the church, as groups often perform on the Cathedral's front steps.

Museu Afro-Brasileiro

Those keen to learn more about the black contribution to Brazilian culture,

---

IMPORTANT DATES IN SALVADOR

Lavagem do Bonfim (second Thurs in Jan). The washing of the church steps by *baianas* (local Bahian women) in traditional dress is followed by food, music and dancing.

Yemanjá (Feb 2). A celebration of *candomblé*, a popular Afro-Brazilian religious cult, with a procession and offerings to the sound of Afro-Brazilian music.

Carnaval (week preceding Lent). The largest street party in the world takes place in Salvador. There's an accepting atmosphere but it's worth bearing in mind that all-black *blocos* (street bands and groups) may be black culture groups who won't appreciate being joined by non-black Brazilians, let alone gringos; be sensitive or ask before leaping in.

Festa de Santo Antônio (June 13). The main celebration of the patron saint of matrimony is held at Largo de Santo Antônio.

Dia de São João (June 24). The biggest holiday in Bahia outside Carnaval celebrates Saint John with *forró* (Northeastern Brazilian folk dance), straw hats and traditional food.

Independência da Bahia (July 2). Celebrating the expulsion of the Portuguese and the province's independence since the year 1823.

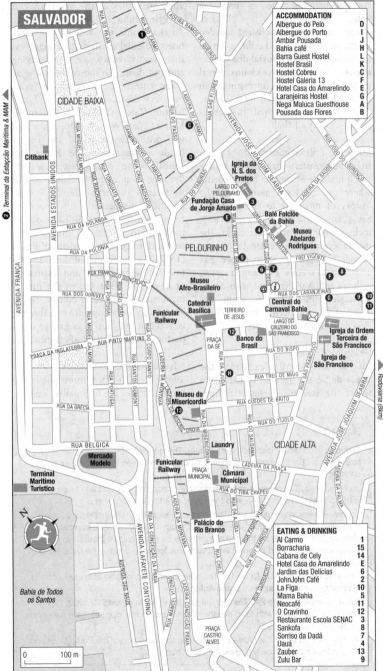

Convento do Carmo & Forte da Capoeira ▲   ▲ Ⓐ, Ⓑ, Comércio and Igreja do Bonfim & Santo Antônio

SALVADOR

Ⓐ, Terminal da Estação Marítima & MAM ▲

ACCOMMODATION

Albergue do Pelo	D
Albergue do Porto	I
Ambar Pousada	J
Bahia café	H
Barra Guest Hostel	L
Hostel Brasil	K
Hostel Cobreu	C
Hostel Galeria 13	F
Hotel Casa do Amarelindo	E
Laranjeiras Hostel	G
Nega Maluca Guesthouse	A
Pousada das Flores	B

CIDADE BAIXA

Citibank

RUA DO PILAR
RUA DO CARMO
LADEIRA RAMOS DE QUEIROZ
LADEIRA DO CARMO
RUA DAS FLORES
RUA DO PASSO
CAMINHO NOVO DO TABOÃO
RUA DO TABOÃO
RUA JOGO DO LOURENÇO
LADEIRA DA SAÚDE
AVENIDA JOSÉ JOAQUIM SEABRA

Ⓒ
Ⓓ

Igreja da N. S. dos Pretos
LARGO DO PELOURINHO
Ⓔ

Fundação Casa de Jorge Amado

Balé Folclôe da Bahia

Museu Abelardo Rodrigues

Ⓕ

PELOURINHO

RUA MIGUEL CALMON
AVENIDA ESTADOS UNIDOS
RUA CRUZ MACHADO
RUA TORQUATO BAHIA
RUA RIACHUELO
RUA DA HOLANDA
RUA DA POLONIA
RUA FRANCISCO GONÇALVES
RUA DOS OURIVES
RUA PORTUGAL
RUA SÃO JOÃO
RUA PINTO MARTINS

AVENIDA FRANÇA

PRAÇA DA INGLATERRA

RUA MIGUEL CALMON

RUA DA GRECIA

RUA BELGICA

Museu Afro-Brasileiro

Funicular Railway

Catedral Basilica

TERREIRO DE JESUS

Central do Carnaval Bahia

RUA DOS LARANJEIRAS

Ⓖ

Praça da Sé

⑫ **Banco do Brasil**

LARGO DO CRUZEIRO DO SÃO FRANCISCO

Igreja da Ordem Terceira de São Francisco

Igreja de São Francisco

RUA DO BISPO
RUA TRES DE MAIO
RUA SÃO FRANCISCO

Ⓗ

RUA DA AJUDA

Museu da Misericordia ⑬

RUA CUEDES DE BRITO

RUA DO TIJOLO

RUA DA MISERICORDIA
RUA DO SALDANHA

CIDADE ALTA

Laundry

AVENIDA JOSÉ JOAQUIM SEABRA

LADEIRA DA PALMA

Mercado Modelo

Funicular Railway

PRAÇA MUNICIPAL

Câmara Municipal

RUA DO TIRA CHAPEU

Terminal Marítimo Turístico

Palácio do Rio Branco

RUA FADRE VIEIRA
RUA RUY BARBOSA
RUA CHILE

AVENIDA DA CONCEIÇÃO DA PRAIA
AVENIDA LAFAYETE CONTORNO
RUA DA MONTANHA
LADEIRA DA CONCEIÇÃO PRAIA

N

Bahia de Todos os Santos

PRAÇA CASTRO ALVES

0   100 m

EATING & DRINKING

Al Carmo	1
Borracharia	15
Cabana de Cely	14
Hotel Casa do Amarelindo	E
Jardim das Delicias	6
JohnJohn Café	2
La Figa	10
Mama Bahia	5
Neocafé	11
O Cravinho	12
Restaurante Escola SENAC	3
Sankofa	8
Sorriso da Dadá	7
Uauá	4
Zauber	13
Zulu Bar	9

▲ Rodoviária (8km)

⑭, ⑮, Ⓘ, Ⓙ, Ⓚ, Ⓛ, Barra, Beaches, Forts ▼ & Airport   ▼ Museu da Arts Sacra will enjoy the excellent **Museu Afro-Brasileiro** (Mon–Fri 9am–6pm, Sat 10am–5pm; R$6) by the Cathedral which houses different collections of artefacts of ancient African civilizations, from jewellery and musical instruments to masks and sculptures of *orixás* (African gods). The basement contains the **Museu Arqueológico e Etnológico**, which is largely given over to ceramics, basket-ware, textiles and wooden and bone objects.

São Francisco

Behind the **Terreiro de Jesus**, on nearby Largo do Cruzeiro de São Francisco, are the superb carved stone facades of two ornate Baroque buildings in a single, large complex dedicated to St Francis: the **Igreja de São Francisco** and the **Igreja da Ordem Terceira de São Francisco** (daily 8am–5pm). The latter was erected at the beginning of the eighteenth century, primarily as a display of the wealth and power of the ruling colonizers who were keen to demonstrate to the world that they were the most powerful empire in the Americas. Over one hundred kilograms of gold were transported here and used to decorate the Baroque interior; the walls are decorated with imperious paintings as well as *azulejos* (glazed coloured tiles).

Largo do Pelourinho

The beautiful, cobbled **Largo do Pelourinho**, down narrow Rua Alfredo de Brito has changed little since the eighteenth century. Lined with solid colonial mansions, it's topped by the Asian-looking towers of the **Igreja da Nossa Senhora dos Pretos** (closed for renovation at the time of research), built by and for slaves and still with a largely black congregation. Across from here is the **Fundação Casa de Jorge Amado** (Mon–Fri 9am–6pm, Sat 10am–5pm; free), a museum given over to the life and work of the hugely popular novelist; you can have fun spotting his rich and famous friends in the collection of photographs.

Mercado Modelo

Cidade Baixa has few sights, but it is well worth the effort to get to the **Mercado Modelo** (Mon–Sat 9am–7pm; Sun 9am–4pm), which is full of Bahian handicrafts, trinkets and beachwear – great for gifts and souvenirs. You'll find it across the street from the bottom of the Lacerda elevator, behind a row of outdoor handicraft stalls.

GET YOUR FITA ON

You'll see coloured ribbons reading *Lembrança do Senhor do Bonfim da Bahia* everywhere in Salvador, often with someone trying to give them to you as a "gift." They're called *fitas* (ribbons) and the phrase roughly means "Remembrance of Our Lord of a Good End." Originating in the early nineteenth century, these *fitas* were originally worn around the neck after miraculous cures. Traditionally they were silk and 47cm long (the length of the right arm of an altar statue of Jesus); nowadays they're made of nylon and act as talismans rather than giving thanks for past cures. Superstitions surrounding *fitas* are many and varied. Everyone agrees, though, that you're not meant to buy your own (hence the "gift" pitch; you get one for yourself free, plus ten for your friends and family that you pay for) and that someone else is meant to tie it in three knots on your left wrist. Each knot gets you one wish. The catch? The wishes only come true when the *fita* breaks – naturally. If you purposefully break it, not only will your wishes go ungranted but you'll also have bad luck. Usually they break after three months or so, but they can last up to a year. Some say *fitas* identify you as a tourist, but you're just as likely to be identified without the bracelet, and having bought one once at least you can fend off all the other vendors.

Colonial Forts

Above Pelourinho in Santo Antônio is the **Forte Santo Antônio Além do Carmo** (free), which is now the home to several capoeira schools that have rechristened it **Forte da Capoeira**. There are terrific views of the city from inside the fort.

Another fort worth visiting is the **Forte de Santo Antônio da Barra**, past the beach at **Praia do Porto da Barra**, at the end of the peninsula. The site of South America's first lighthouse, it now houses the **Museu Náutico da Bahia** (Tues–Sun 8.30am–7pm, open daily in July; R$5). The sea views and the room of 25 ships-in-bottles by Manecha Brandão are worth the entrance fee alone, but you'll also find recovered archeological treasures from coastal shipwrecks here.

Igreja do Bonfim

The **Igreja do Bonfim** (Tues–Sun 7am–6pm; free), located at the top of the peninsula of Itapagipe, is worshipped at by both Candomblistas (followers of *candomblé*, a religion based on African beliefs) and Catholics alike. The annual Lavagem do Bonfim procession ends here, when *candomblé* priestesses wash the church's steps. The church houses the **Museu dos Ex-Votos do Senhor do Bonfim** (Tues–Sat 8am–noon & 1–5pm; free), lined with heart-wrenching photos of supplicants, written pleas for divine aid and thanks for wishes fulfilled. Hanging from the ceiling are a hundred body parts made of plastic and wood, offerings from the hopeful and the thankful. The church is a 30-minute bus ride from the centre (take "Bonfim" from the bottom of the Lacerda elevator in Praça da Sé), or take a taxi.

Arrival

Air Aeroporto Internacional Dep. Luís Eduardo Magalhães (℡71/3204-1010) is 23km northeast of the city, connected to the centre by an hourly shuttle express bus service to Praça da Sé (45min–1hr 30min depending on traffic, last bus at 10pm; R$3) via the beach districts and Campo Grande. A taxi to the centre will set you back around R$80.

Bus The *rodoviária* (℡71/3616-8300) is 8km east of the centre. To get to the Cidade Alta take a taxi (about R$25) or catch the *executivo* bus from the

---

SALVADOR'S BEACHES

All of the beaches listed below can be reached by bus (heading to either "Vilas do Atlântico" or "Praias do Flamengo") from Praça da Sé.

Aldeia Hippie In Arembepe, about 50km from Salvador. Aldeia Hippie Beach was made famous by Mick Jagger and friends in the 1960s.

Jardim de Alah Perfect for long walks thanks to the large and spacious sandy beach; also good for surfing.

Praia da Onda This beach in Ondina is good for surfing (although watch the rocks) and even fishing.

Praia de Aleuluia The perfect spot to grab some lunch at one of the many bars or restaurants along the beach. Good waves for surfing too.

Praia de Itapoã One of the most scenic beaches, mainly because of its tall, lilting palm trees.

Praia de Jaguanibe Strong winds make this a perfect spot to surf, windsurf and kite-surf.

Praia de Stella Maris Good for long walks as well as surfing.

Praia do Farol da Barra Windswept palms and thatched huts punctuate this small, rocky beach near the lighthouse.

Praia do Porto da Barra The closest swimming beach to historic Salvador is calm and narrow, and just a short bus ride away.

CRIME AND SAFETY

Salvador has more problems with robberies and muggings than anywhere else in the Northeast save Recife. The buildings in tourist-heavy Pelourinho have video cameras perched on them and the area is heavily policed until late at night. It's safe, but you'll definitely feel you're being observed by shady characters, so it's worth taking a few precautions. Don't wander down poorly lit side streets at night unless you are within sight of a policeman and don't use the Lacerda elevator after early evening. Avoid walking up and down the winding connecting roads between the Cidade Alta and Cidade Baixa, and be careful about using city buses on Sundays when few people are around; the *executivo* bus is a safer option. Give the Avenida do Contorno – the seafront road that runs north from the harbour – a miss too; it's dangerous even in daylight when robberies are not uncommon. Also, do not walk up Rua das Flores on the way to Santo Antônio at night or during the day, nor be enticed by the reggae beats coming from Praça do Reggae in Largo de Pelourinho as you're highly likely to get robbed at any time of day. Avoid Baixa Sapateiro in Pelouinho after 7pm as there are quite a few drug addicts and thieves. Lastly, the area between Praça da Sé and Praça Campo Grande (in particular Av. 7 de Setembro and Av. Carlos Gomez), while busy by day, is ominous at night. If you're in Pelourinho late at night and need to get back to a hostel in Barra, take a taxi.

Iguatemi shopping centre across the busy road. The bus costs R$3 and makes a stately progress through the beach districts of Pituba and Rio Vermelho before dropping you off at the Praça da Sé.

Information

Tourist information The main office of the state tourist agency, Bahiatursa (Ⓦ www.bahiatursa.ba.gov.br), is in Pelourinho, at Rua João de Deus 1, corner of Rua das Laranjeiras (daily 8am–9pm; ☎71/3321-2133). There are also branches at the airport (daily 7.30am–11pm; ☎71/3204-1444) and at the *rodoviária* (daily 7.30am–10pm; ☎71/3450-3871). Another source of information is the tourist hotline, "Disque Turismo" – call ☎71/3103-3103 and you should find an English-speaker at the other end.
Tour operators Internet Café.com, Rua João de Deus 02, corner of Terreiro de Jesus, 1st Floor, Pelourinho (☎71/3321-2147) are helpful for travel arrangements; Salvador Bus (☎71/3356-6425, Ⓦ www.salvadorbus.com.br) operate double-decker buses for various city-tours, with tickets available at hotels and travel agencies; Visão Turismo, Aeroporto Internacional Dep. Luís Eduardo Magalhães (☎71/3204-1300, Ⓦ www.visaotur.com.br) and at Rua dos Algibebes 6, Comércio (☎71/3319-0834) can help you book budget flights.

City transport

Bus The bus system is efficient, cheap (R$2.50) and easy to use, running till 11pm on weekdays and 10pm on weekends. To reach the centre, any bus with "Sé", "C. Grande" or "Lapa" on the route card will do. Buses with route card "Flamengo" leave from Praça da Sé passing Barra, and stopping off at all the beaches to the north – the last stop is Ipitanga.
Frescão (a/c buses) run most of the same routes and usually cost R$5, although they are not as regular as the standard buses, with departures approximately every 30min.
Ladeira Elevator This elevator in Praça da takes you down to the Cidade Baixa.
Taxi Taxis are metered and plentiful and are recommended at night, even for short distances within the Cidade Alta. An average trip between Pelô and Barra will cost R$30. Chame-Taxi ☎71/3241-2266 and Elitte Taxi ☎71/3460-4040 are recommended taxi companies.

Accommodation

Salvador is the second most popular tourist destination in Brazil and consequently full of hotels. Unless you want to stay near a beach (in which case you'll want to choose Barra over expensive and distant Ondina), the best area to head for is Cidade Alta, not least because of the spectacular view across the island-studded bay. While pousada prices generally stay within reason be aware that during Carnaval rates can double or even triple, while out of season good discounts may be on offer.

Pelourinho

Pelourinho lies in the heart of the city, and is the perfect spot to base yourself if you want to be at the very centre of the action.

Albergue do Pelo Rua do Passo 5 ☎71/3242-8061, ⓦwww.alberguedopelo.com.br. Poky, spartan dorms and doubles but management is friendly and the price is pretty reasonable given the central location. Dorms R$25, rooms R$60.

🏃 **Bahia Café** Praça da Sé 20 ☎71/3322-1266, ⓦwww.bahiacafehotel.com. Rustic doors open onto pleasantly colourful rooms, all of which are en suite. The wooden interiors and side lamps made by local artist Marta give the place a warm and homely touch. Room 8, with views onto the Praça, is the best. R$160.

Hostel Galeria 13 Rua da Ordem Terceira 23 ☎71/3266-5609, ⓦwww.hostelgaleria13.com. Have an afternoon dip in the pool or unwind in the dimly lit Moroccan chill-out room before heading out on the town at this English-owned hostel with comfy bunks all made of local wood. The two dogs, Spartan and Zulu, pad around the premises keeping you company, and owner Paul is always more than happy to point you in the right direction in town. Breakfast is served till noon. Dorms R$25.

Laranjeiras Hostel Rua da Ordem Terceira 13 ☎71/3321-1366, ⓦwww.laranjeirashostel.com.br. HI hostel with long thin dorm rooms that have unbelievably high top bunks, a crêperie in the lobby and a mezzanine chill-out area that's good for mingling with other travellers. The long windows, which look out over the colourful cobbled streets, are perfect for people-watching. HI discounts offered. Dorms R$35, rooms R$110.

Santo Antônio

Only 10 minutes' walk from Pelourinho, this quiet residential neighbourhood offers a bit of tranquillity and respite from Pelo's hustle and bustle.

Hostel Cobreu Ladeira do Carmo 22 ☎71/3117-1401 ⓦwww.hostelcobreu.com. A steep staircase leads you up to colourful dorms with polished parquet floors. The corridors are decorated with vibrant graffiti by a renowned local artist, as is the little communal chill-out area, which has nice views over town. Dorms R$26, rooms R$65.

🏃 **Nega Maluca Guesthouse** Rua dos Marchantes 15, Santo Antônio ☎71/3242-9249, ⓦwww.negamaluca.com. The windy, narrow corridors of this Israeli-owned hostel easily get clogged up with satisfied travellers. Dorms all have deposit boxes for valuables, as well as electrical sockets and lamps above each bed. There's a rooftop terrace with hammocks overlooking the upper part of Salvador, as well as a chill-out area at the back. Dorms R$26, rooms R$70.

🏃 **Pousada das Flores** Rua Direita de Santo Antônio 442 ☎71/3243-1836, ⓦwww.pflores.com.br Set in a stunning four-storey colonial mansion dating from 1740, this more upmarket pousada has palatial rooms, some with excellent views of the Santo Antônio Church. *Berimbãos* (percussion instruments) decorate the walls on the ground floor while upstairs local wooden furniture gives the place a warm, cosy touch. Good discounts in low season. R$200.

Barra and the beaches

If you want a bit of respite from the hustle and bustle of central Salvador, Barra is the area to stay in, and there are some nice beaches just a few steps away.

Albergue do Porto Rua Barão de Sergy 197, Barra ☎71/3264-6600, ⓦwww.alberguedoporto.com.br. Comfy hostel with a relaxed vibe, good-sized dorms and hammocks slung in between the rooms. There's also a pool table, PlayStation, big TV and a good selection of films in the living room, as well as a kitchen and a supermarket just next door. Free internet. Dorms R$35, rooms R$150.

Ambar Pousada Rua Afonso Celso 485, Barra ☎71/3264-6956, ⓦwww.ambarpousada.com.br. The breakfast room has slightly dreary tablecloths and a grandma-esque feel but the rooms are clean and some open onto the inner courtyard. Staff are helpful and Barra beach is just a ten-minute walk away. Dorms R$36, rooms R$130.

Barra Guest Hostel Rua Recife 234 ☎71/8774-6667, ⓦwww.barraguesthostel.com. Set in a colonial house, this comfy hostel has clean dorms with lockers and personal reading lamps. There's

also cheap European grub, a free *caiprinha* every night at 7pm, as well as weekly BBQ nights and surfboard hire. Free wi-fi. Dorms R$40, rooms R$60.
Hostel Brasil Rua Recife 4 ⊕71/3254-9637, ⓦwww.hostelbrasil.com.br. Fun and welcoming hostel, ten minutes from Barra Beach. The spacious dorms all have individual lockers and there's a chill-out area with colourful beanbags that are perfect to sink into after a long day's surfing. Laundry and internet facilities available, and they can also help with travel arrangements. Dorms R$36, rooms R$76.

Eating

Eating out is a pleasure in Salvador. There's a huge range of restaurants and the local cuisine (*comida baiana*; see below) is deservedly famous all over Brazil. Street food is fabulous too and readily available all over town, with plenty of vendors

---

COMIDA BAIANA

The secret to Bahian cooking is twofold: a rich seafood base, and traditional West African **ingredients** such as palm oil, nuts, coconut and hot peppers. Many ingredients and dishes have African names: most famous of all is *vatapá*, a bright yellow porridge of palm oil, coconut, shrimp and garlic, which looks vaguely unappetizing but is delicious. Other dishes to look out for are *moqueca*, seafood cooked in the inevitable palm-oil based sauce; *caruru*, with many of the same ingredients as *vatapá* but with the addition of loads of okra; and *acarajé*, a deep-fried bean cake stuffed with *vatapá*, salad and (optional) hot pepper. Bahian cuisine also has good **desserts**, which are less stickily sweet than elsewhere: *quindim* is a delicious coconut cake, flavoured with vanilla, often with a prune in the centre.

Street *baianas*, women in traditional white dress, serve *quindim*, *vatapá*, slabs of maize pudding wrapped in banana leaves, fried bananas dusted with icing sugar, and fried sticks of sweet batter covered with sugar and cinnamon – all gorgeous.

---

selling all sorts of local delicacies. While Pelourinho has a growing number of stylish, expensive places, it's still relatively easy to eat well for less than R$25.

Restaurants

Cabana de Cely Av. Marquês de Leão, corner of Rua D. Marcos Teixeira, Barra ⊕71/3264-0250. One block from the beach, this is a hugely popular seafood restaurant, especially on Sundays when lunches drag on all day, and the *cachaça* and Skol come out to play. Try the *caranguejo* (crab) starter (R$4.10); there are also a few meat dishes on offer such as *picanha acebolad*a (steak with onions; R$38 for two). Open Tues–Sat 11am–midnight, Sun 11am–6pm.
Jardim das Delícias Rua João de Deus 12, Pelourinho ⊕71/3321-1449. Set in a courtyard away from the hustle and bustle, this place is like entering a little hidden magical world within the walls of Pelourinho. Fresh high-quality ingredients mean prices are higher than other places around town, but it's definitely worth splashing out a bit more to seriously please your taste buds. Try the *badejo Jardim das Delícias* (white fish marinated with herbs and served with plantain) for R$45. Open daily 11am–11pm.
La Figa Rua das Laranjeiras 17, Pelourinho ⊕71/3322-0066. Named after a Brazilian good-luck charm, this Italian-owned trattoria with red and white tablecloths and a few tables lining the cobbled street serves delicious *spaghetti all'aragosta* (spaghetti with lobster; R$30). Its sister pizzeria (closed Mon) at the end of the block is renowned for its *pizza alla pescatore* (pizza with fish; R$32). Daily 11am–midnight; closed Sun dinner and Mon lunch.
Mama Bahia Rua das Portas do Carmo 21, Pelourinho ⊕71/3322-4397. An enjoyable corner restaurant that's good for a bottle of cheap wine and some Bahian standards; choose your dishes carefully and you'll get a feast for just R$30. Tagliatelle with seafood for two will set you back R$65. Daily 11am–10pm.
Neocafé Rua Santa Isabel 9A, Pelourinho ⊕71/3321-0849. A funky place with a good vibe serving good-value dishes such as *ostras gratinadas* (oysters au gratin; R$15) and pork chop with mango chutney (R$18). North African lamps decorate the rooms, along with local photography that is available for purchase. Every weekend there's a different set menu (R$30) that includes tasty dishes from a variety of cuisines, from Indian to Italian. Tues–Sun noon–late.
Restaurante Escola SENAC Praça José de Alencar 13/19, Largo de Pelourinho, Pelourinho ⊕71/3324-4553. The municipal restaurant school, set in a

restored mansion, may look expensive from outside, but it's actually good value, offering a set-price buffet (R$32) of forty labelled Bahian dishes and more than twelve desserts. Mon–Sat 11.30am–3.30pm & 6.30–10pm; Sun 11.30am–3.30pm.

Sorriso da Dadá Rua Frei Vicente 5, Pelourinho ☎71/3321-9642. You certainly won't get much of a *sorriso* (smile) here, but locals still rave about the Bahian cuisine, even though you get less for your money than a few years ago, Meat dishes for two will set you back R$52.80. Daily 11.30am–midnight.

Uauá Rua Gregório de Matos 36, Pelourinho ☎71/3321-3089. A smarter option with interior decor evocative of the mud huts of northern Brazil. There are plenty of seafood dishes (stewed shrimp and fish in coconut and palm oil R$48 for two) on the menu, alongside meat dishes (*carne de sol*; R$38). Mon–Sat 11am–11pm.

Zulu Bar Rua das Laranjeiras 15, Pelourinho ☎71/8784-3172. This is the place to come if you're craving some cheap comfort food, and there are plenty of veggie dishes on offer, as well as curries and fish and chips. It's lively in the evenings and the high wooden chairs are the perfect spot to enjoy a drink while looking out onto the street – try the bar's unique take on the fruity *zumorangi caipirinha* (R$7.50). Daily 11am–2am.

Cafés

Al Carmo ☎71/3242-0283. Entering this tranquil place, it's easy to imagine a Portuguese colonialist puffing at his cigar here a few centuries ago. It's the perfect spot for a coffee (R$3), away from the heat and bustle of Salvador's streets. There's also an italian restaurant with a terrace out back. Daily 11.30am–1.30am.

Bahia Café Praça da Sé 20, Pelourinho ☎71/3322-1266. A selection of sandwiches (R$10), soups (R$6), salads (R$16) and superb coffees (R$3) to choose from, as well as reasonably priced *caipirinhas* for R$5, at this hotel with a chilled-out internet café bang in the centre of town. Mon–Sat 10am–10pm, Sun 11am–10pm.

JohnJohn Café Av. Estados Unidos 397, Comércio ☎71/3327-0102 ⊛www.johnjohncafe.com.br. Bright café with mouth-watering cakes on display, perfect for a snack as you head to the nearby Mercado Modelo. There's a variety of dishes on offer, including mini lamb burgers for R$15.90 and quiche for R$5.50. Mon–Fri 8am–8pm.

Drinking and nightlife

Make sure you're in town on a Tuesday night as it's Salvador's biggest party night, with bands playing Afro-Brazilian music around town as locals and tourists alike dance away on the streets.

Borracharia Rua Conselheiro Pedro Luís 101-A, Rio Vermelho. Make your way through scattered piles of tyres as you enter this club-cum-tyre workshop in Salvador's bohemian district. The music changes depending on the night, but rock 'n' roll and hip-hop tend to be the musical flavours of choice. Fri & Sat 10pm–late (R$20).

Casa do Amarelindo Rua das Portas do Carmo 6, Pelourinho. Smart, intimate bar with a leafy indoor area serving superb *maracujá caipirinhas* (R$10). Wind your way up the spiral staircase to the first-floor terrace where there's a small pool and lovely views across the bay. Daily 4pm–11.30pm.

O Cravinho Terreiro de Jesus 5, Pelourinho ☎71/3322-6759. *The* place to kick the night off with a few drinks before heading to *Fundo do Cravinho* at the back to try some frenetic salsa (cover R$3). The speciality here is *cravinhos*, flavoured *cachaça* shots with root infusions (R$2). Daily 11am–11pm.

🏃 **Sankofa** Rua Frei Vicente 7, Pelourinho ☎71/3321-7236. The hippest African bar and club in town and a true local hangout. Spread over two storeys; the ground floor has live bands as well as DJs, while a more chilled-out area with a tiny smoking terrace awaits upstairs. Entry R$10.

Zauber Multicultura Ladeira da Misericordia 11, Comércio ☎71/3326-2964. Tricky to find but worth it once you get there, this club attracts an alternative crowd. As you cross the small (and very high) bridge, you enter a large dance floor where you can dance to reggae and dub sounds, before heading upstairs to the chill-out loft. Thurs only 10pm–late. R$10; free entry for women before 11pm. Take a taxi as the area's a bit dodgy.

Shopping

Instituto de Artesanato Visconde de Mauá Rua Gregório de Matos 27, Pelourinho ⊛www.maua.ba.gov.br. This place was founded by the government to promote regional artists. You'll find carving, ceramics and hammocks at fixed prices, among other handicrafts, here. Mon–Fri 10am–6pm.

Mercado Modelo Praça Visconde de Cayru 250. Handicraft market in Cidade Baixa. Mon–Sat 6am–1pm.

Shopping Barra Av. Centenário 2992. Large mall that's handy for the Barra beaches. Mon–Sat 9am–10pm, Sun food hall only noon–9pm.

Entertainment

You cannot miss the **Balé Folclórico da Bahia** at Rua Gregório de Matos 29, Pelourinho

(☎71/33221962 ⓦwww.balefolcloricodabahia
.com.br), with frantic drumming as radiant dancers
in colourful dresses spin around tapping their feet
and moving their bodies to Afro-Brazilian music.
Performances are on Mon, Wed, Thurs, Fri, Sat at
8pm. Make sure you buy tickets in advance from
the box office. Another event worth heading to is
the weekly jazz concert at MAM, Av. Contorno
(Museum of Modern Art; ☎71/3117-6139;
Saturdays 6pm–10pm, entry before 9pm; R$5),
near the marina in the Cidade Baixa.

Directory

Banks and exchange Banks with ATMs are found
throughout the city. There's the Confidence Câmbio
and Banco do Brasil at the international airport; in
town, there is a Citibank on Av. Estados Unidos 558,
Comércio. There is a Banco do Brasil on the Terreiro
de Jesus square in Pelourinho.
Embassies and Consulates UK, Av. Estados
Unidos 18B, 8th Floor, Comercio ☎71/3243-7399;
US, Av. Tancredo Neves 1632, Room 1401, Salvador
Trade Center, Torre Sul, Caminho das Árvores,
☎71/3113-2090.
Hospitals Hospital Aliança, Av. Juracy Magalhães
Jr. 2096, Rio Vermelho (☎71/2108-5600); Hospital
São Rafael, Av. São Rafael 2152, São Marcos
(☎71/3281-6111).

Internet Bahia Café, Praça da Sé 20 (R$3/hr);
Internet Café.com (R$3/hr) on Rua João de Deus
02, corner of Terrero de Jesus, 1st Floor, Pelourinho,
has Skype; Internet do F@rol, Av. Sete de Setembro
42, Barra (R$3/hr).
Laundries O Casal at Av. Sete de Setembro 3564,
Barra (☎71/3264-9320); Wash & Dry, Ladeira da
Praça 4, Pelourinho (☎71/3321-0821).
Left luggage Malubag at the airport (☎71/3204-
1150; 24hr) has small/large lockers for R$8/10
per day.
Pharmacies Farmácia Sant'ana, Largo Porto da
Barra, Barra (☎71/3267-8970); Drogaleve, Praça
da Sé 6, Pelourinho (☎71/3322-6921).
Police The tourist police, DELTUR, are at Praça
José de Anchieta 14, Cruzeiro de São Francisco,
Pelourinho ☎71/3116-6817 or 3116-6512.
Post office Largo do Cruzeiro de São Francisco 20,
Pelourinho (Mon–Fri 9am–5pm, Sat 8am–12pm).

Moving on

Air The usual suspects, GOL and TAM, have daily
flights to Fortaleza, Rio, São Paulo and Recife, and
several a day to other destinations throughout
Brazil. TAM and other international carriers have
direct flights to Miami, Buenos Aires and Lima.
During the week the public "Aeroporto" bus
leaves Praça da Sé every 15min between 5am

CAPOEIRA

Capoeira began in Angola as a ritual fight to gain the nuptial rights of women
when they reached puberty. It has evolved into a graceful, semi-balletic art form
somewhere between fighting and dancing. It's usually accompanied by the
characteristic rhythmic twang of the berimbau (single-string percussion instrument),
and takes the form of a pair of dancers/fighters leaping and whirling in stylized
"combat" – which, with younger capoeiristas, occasionally slips into a genuine fight
when blows land accidentally and tempers fly. There are regular displays on Terreiro
de Jesus and near the entrances to the Mercado Modelo in Cidade Baixa, largely for
the benefit of tourists and their financial contributions, but still interesting. The best
capoeira, though, can be found in the academias de capoeira, organized schools
with classes you can watch for free. If you want a really cool capoeira experience,
get out of Pelourinho and up to the Forte Santo Antônio, just a short walk up the hill.
Inside the renovated white fort are several schools of capoeira where the setting may
contribute to making you feel more like a Jedi knight or Shaolin monk in training.

Academia de João Pequeno de Pastinha
Largo Santo Antônio, Forte Santo Antônio
☎71/3323-0708, ⓦwww.joao-pequeno.com.
You can watch, or if you want to join in, there
are two-to three-hour classes (Mon, Wed, & Fri,
9am, 7.30pm).
Associação de Capoeira Mestre Bimba Rua
das Laranjeiras 1, Pelourinho ☎71/3322-0639

ⓦwww.capoeiramestrebimba.com.br. Probably
the most famous academia, it sometimes has
classes open to tourists.
Forte de Santo Antônio Praça Barão do
Triunfo, Largo de Santo Antônio (☎71/3117-
1488, ⓔfortesantoantonio@gmail.com). Classes
open to tourists.

& 10.10pm (weekends every 30min, 5.40am–9.10am; R$3).

Boat Boats to Tinharé depart daily from the Terminal Turistico Maritimo, the blue building at the water's edge behind the Mercado Modelo. Buy tickets (R$75 one-way) a half-hour in advance. Lancha Ilha Bela (℡71/9195-6744) departs 8.30am, returns 3pm; Catamará Farol do Morro (℡71/3319-4570) departs 1pm, returns 9am (Mon–Sat); Catamará Biônica de Tinharé (℡71/3326-7674) departs 9am, 12pm & 2pm, returns 8am, 11.30am and 3pm.

Bus Buses leave for all parts of the country from Terminal Rodoviária Armando Viana de Castro, Av. ACM 4362, Pituba (℡71/3616-8300). Useful bus companies are Águia Branca (℡71/4004-1010); Linha Verde (℡71/3450-0321); Real Expresso (℡71/3450-9310). Destinations include Rio (27hr), Sao Paulo (33hr), Recife (12hr), Belo Horizonte (24hr) and Fortaleza (21hr).

MORRO DE SÃO PAULO

For a respite from Salvador's hustle and bustle, head to the village of **MORRO DE SÃO PAULO** on the island of **Tinharé**, about 75km southwest of Salvador. Morro has a great atmosphere, with plenty of surfing and diving as well as reggae bars and beach parties that last till the early hours of the morning. It's popular among locals and tourists alike who want to catch some rays on the pristine beaches and swim the island's clear waters. With no roads on the island (people use wheelbarrows to transport things along the sandy paths), it's still relatively peaceful and undeveloped, though at the weekends, especially between December and March, vast crowds descend.

What to see and do

There are four main beaches in Morro (known simply as **First**, **Second**, **Third** and **Fourth beaches**), with the first being the closest (and therefore most popular) to the village centre and the fourth being the furthest away (and thus quietest). Accommodation and restaurant prices increase the further you move towards the Fourth Beach. A good

> **ISLAND ACTIVITIES**
>
> You can enjoy all sorts of activities in Morro, from water-skiing and wake-boarding to capoeira and yoga lessons.
>
> **Diving** enthusiasts or anyone wishing to learn scuba can contact Companhia do Mergulho on First Beach (℡75/3652-1200). They operate day and night dives in fast boats to clear-water areas around the island. **Horseback rides** along the beach can be organized by calling ℡75/3652-1070 or 1056. **Surfing** instruction is offered by Morro Surf School (℡75/8836-4042).

idea is to settle for the Second Beach, given its close location to the town centre and its fun party atmosphere.

On arrival at the dock you will have to pay a R$10 **Taxa de Turismo** – expect to be quickly besieged by tenacious locals offering to be your "guide". You can shake them off relatively easily by heading straight to the Tirolesa Zipline (daily 10am–5.30pm), a 70-m high and 350-m long zip-wire that will whiz you down to the First Beach in no time. The 25-second ride from the top of the hill is a great way to check out Morro's beaches from above as well as have a little adrenaline kick before relaxing into Morro's laidback vibe. To get to the zip-line, head along the coastal path up the hill, past the pousadas and the health clinic and make your way to the back of the lighthouse by the fort. Of course, you can just as easily, if less dramatically, walk to the beach in five minutes from the pier.

Arrival and information

You can reach Tinharé by air or sea. It's obviously much quicker to fly, but it's also far more expensive. **Air** Aero Star flies daily to and from the island from Salvador (R$231 one-way; ℡71/3377-4406, ⊛www.aerostar.com.br). Adey Táxi Aéreo also has three flights there and back daily (R$225 one-way; ℡71/3204-1993).

Boat Boats to the island depart daily from Salvador's Terminal Turístico Marítimo; tickets cost R$75 each way. See p.314 for more details.

Tourist information The tourist information office, SIT (☎ 75/3652-1083, ⓦ www.morrosp.com.br), is close to the dock, at the very start of the main path that leads to the First Beach. Staff here are friendly, speak some English and can give excellent advice about food and lodging. A good website for the history of the island and information about pousadas, restaurants and nightlife is ⓦ www.morrodesaopaulo.com.br.

Accommodation

There is plenty of affordable accommodation on First and Second beaches – for R$40 to R$60 you can find a room on the seafront, with a hammock where you can listen to the waves crash all night.

Hostel Morro de São Paulo Rua da Fonte Grande, a 5-min walk from the pier and First Beach ☎ 75/3652-1521 or 9962-1287, ⓦ www.hosteldomorro.com.br. Simple but clean dorms and doubles in a leafy verdant setting. There's a communal kitchen and laundry facilities. HI discounts available. Dorms R$48, rooms R$120.

Pousada Aradhia Third beach ☎ 75/3652-1341 or 8139-6257 ⓦ www.pousadaaradhia.net. Quiet rooms giving onto a small tropical garden, all with a little veranda with hammocks. The pool's the place to mingle with other travellers. R$150.

Pousada Estrela do Mar Second beach ☎ 75/3652-1784 or 8805-8554. Spotless, albeit slightly poky, rooms (with a/c and en suite) at this relaxed pousada with a communal terrace with hammocks overlooking Second Beach. You may well catch a glimpse of semi-resident monkey Chico who tends to swing around the premises. R$60.

Eating

There are plenty of cheap restaurants lining First and Second beaches – you'll find everything from crêpes and sushi to pizza, fruit, sandwiches and Bahian specialities.

Chez Max Third beach ☎ 75/3652-1754. This welcoming Italian restaurant has plenty of daily specials to tickle your taste buds, as well as wood-oven pizzas (from R$20) for those wanting a quick European fix.

Jamaica Second beach ☎ 75/3652-1669. Bob Marley murals cover the walls of this Bahian *churrascaria* (steak house; R$25), which serves some good quality meat grilled right before your eyes.

Mar dos Corais Praça Aureliano Lima 100, town centre, a 10-min walk from First Beach. ☎ 75/3652-1091. The perfect place at any time of day, but particularly for breakfast: coffees, fresh juices, as well as all sorts of delectable sweetmeats (R$4.80–15) and fruit salads (R$2.50). Daily noon–11pm.

Drinking and nightlife

Clubs, bars, beach and full moon parties - there's always something going on in Morro. Second Beach is the place to start (and often end) the evening, with dozens of *caipirinha* vendors and bars playing beats catering to all sorts of musical tastes, with dancing on the beach going on till the wee hours. To get to the clubs listed below, follow the path through the town centre and head up the hill.

Pulsar Disco Caminho do Forte. This jungly three-storey club located on the side of a hill hosts themed nights, from foam parties to "back to the 80s" nights. Tues & Sat only (Sat only in April, May and June). R$30.

Toca do Morcego Caminho do Farol. Friday night's the night at this club that's five minutes' walk up the hill from the centre of town. Soak in the sea view as you sip on unbelievably potent *caipirinhas* and groove to dance tunes until the early hours. Cover R$35.

RECIFE

RECIFE, the Northeast's second-largest city, appears rather dull at first, but it's lent a colonial grace and elegance by **Olinda** (see p.323), 6km to the north and considered part of the same conurbation. Recife's colonial centre, known as Recife Antigo, is surprisingly pleasant, with a few quiet squares where an inordinate number of impressive churches lie cheek by jowl with the less appealing urban sprawl of the past thirty years. North of the centre are some pleasant leafy suburbs, dotted with museums and parks, and to the south is the modern beachside district of **Boa Viagem**.

What to see and do

Modern Recife sprawls over the mainland, but the heart of the city

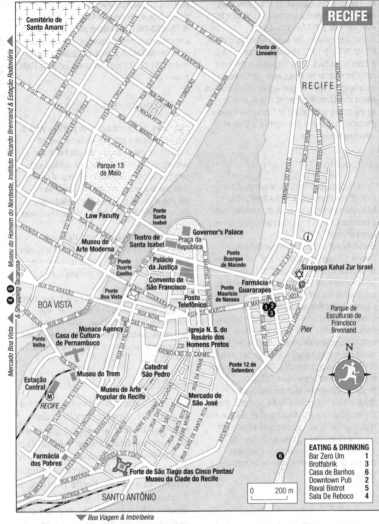

▲ Shopping Tacaruna (800m) & Olinda

RECIFE

Cemitério de Santo Amaro

RUA PEDRO AFONSO LEITE
RUA 2 DE JULHO
AVENIDA NORTE

Ponte de Limoeiro

RECIFE

RUA ARARIPINA

AV. VISC. DE SUASSUNA
RUA DO SOSSEGO
RUA BPO. CARDOSO AYRES
RUA MARQUES DO POMBAL
RUA CEL. LUIZ

RUA COF. MEIRA LINS
RUA JORN. MARIO MELO
RUA JOÃO LIRA

Parque 13 de Maio

RUA DO PRÍNCIPE
RUA DO RIACHUELO
RUA PRINCESA ISABEL
RUA DA UNIÃO
RUA DA SAUDADE

Law Faculty

Ponte Santa Isabel

Museu de Arte Moderna

Teatro de Santa Isabel

Praça da República

Governor's Palace

AVENIDA CONDE DA BOA VISTA

Ponte Santa Isabel

Palácio da Justiça

Ponte Buarque de Macedo

Sinagoga Kahal Zur Israel

RUA DO ARAGÃO

Ponte Duarte Coelho

Convento de São Francisco

Farmácia Guararapes

BOA VISTA

Ponte Boa Vista

Posto Telefônico

Ponte Mauricio de Nassau

Parque de Esculturas de Francisco Brennand

RUA VELHA
RUA DR. JOSÉ MARIANO
RUA DAS FLORES
RUA NOVA
RUA DE MARÇO

Pier

N

Monaco Agency
Casa de Cultura de Pernambuco

Igreja N. S. do Rosário dos Homens Pretos

Ponte Velha

RUA DA PALMA

AVENIDA NS. DO CARMO

Ponte 12 de Setembro

Catedral São Pedro

Estação Central

Museu do Trem

RECIFE

Museu de Arte Popular de Recife

Mercado de São José

RUA FLORIANO PEIXOTO

Farmácia dos Pobres

Forte de São Tiago das Cinco Pontas/ Museu da Ciade do Recife

0   200 m

SANTO ANTÔNIO

▼ Boa Viagem & Imbiribeira

EATING & DRINKING	
Bar Zero Um	1
Brotfabrik	3
Casa de Banhos	6
Downtown Pub	2
Raval Bistrot	5
Sala De Reboco	4

is actually three small islands, **Santo Antônio**, **Boa Vista** and **Recife** proper, connected with each other and the mainland by more than two dozen bridges over the rivers Beberibe and Capibaribe. From south to north you have the Boa Viagem district, then Santo Antônio situated between Recife (to the northeast) and Boa Vista (to the west). Where Boa Vista stretches north leaving Santo Antônio Centro behind, is Olinda.

Recife Island

There's not that much to see on Recife island proper but this once run-down part of the city now has some bars and restaurants and is a pleasant place during the day to walk around. One of the few sites is the **Sinagoga Kahal Zur Israel**, Rua do Bom Jesus 197 (Tues–Fri 9am–4.30pm, Sun 2–5.30pm; R$4; ☎81/3224-2128), built in 1637 and said to be the first synagogue in the whole of the Americas. At the pier south of the synagogue you can hire a rowing boat (R$4 one-way) to take you across the water to a little reef housing the curious **Parque de Esculturas de Francisco Brennand**, where you can see a series of rather phallic statues by renowned local artist Brennard. From here you can walk along the reef all the way to Boa Viagem, although it's quite a walk (45min–1hr).

RECIFE AND OLINDA ONLINE

ⓦ www.olindaarteemtodaparte. com.br Official site with pictures and listings of everything Olinda.
ⓦ www.recife.info An excellent, thorough site with information on everything from shopping to Carnaval.

Praça da República

The broad **Avenida Dantas Barreto** forms the spine of the central island of **Santo Antônio**, and ends in the fine **Praça da República**, lined with majestic palms and home to the governor's palace as well as Recife's most ornate theatre. The centre's narrow, crowded streets make a pleasant contrast to some of the financial district's towering skyscrapers.

Santo Antônio do Convento de São Francisco

Perhaps the most enticing of the central buildings on Santo Antônio is the seventeenth-century Franciscan complex known as the **Santo Antônio do Convento de São Francisco**, on Rua do Imperador (Mon–Fri 8–11.30am & 2–5pm, Sat 8–11.30am; R$2), a combination of church, convent and museum. Built around a beautiful, small cloister, the museum has some strange but delicately painted statues of saints and other artwork rescued from demolished or crumbling local churches. The highlight is the **Capela Dourada** (Golden Chapel), a rather vulgar demonstration of colonial prosperity. Finished in 1697, the Rococo chapel has the usual wall-to-ceiling-to-wall ornamentation, except that everything is covered with gold leaf.

Pátio de São Pedro and around

Just off the Avenida Dantas Barreto, the impressive **Catedral de São Pedro** (Mon–Fri 8–12am & 2–5pm) stands on the graceful Pátio de São Pedro. Inside there's some exquisite woodcarving and a *trompe l'oeil* ceiling. The Pátio is also home to the **Museu de Arte Popular de Recife** (Mon–Fri 9am–5pm; free), which has some interesting exhibits from Northeast Brazil, including pottery and wooden sculpture. The colonial buildings that line the square have been beautifully preserved, and in the evenings you can

CRIME AND SAFETY

Recife and Olinda have a bad reputation throughout Brazil. Everyone has a story about how they were followed, harassed, mugged or intimidated. It's enough to send even seasoned travellers rushing back to their hostels at sundown for fear of turning into flak-jacket-wearing Cinderellas.

While it's true that crime rates are high, if you take the usual precautions you should stay safe: be discreet, don't wear fancy watches and jewellery, know where you're going, travel with a friend, take taxis or public transport at night, stick to populated, well-lit areas and be wary of open, free drinks. When withdrawing money, it's best (and safest) to use an ATM in a shopping centre. CIA-Tur, the Tourist Police, patrol areas of the city that tourists normally visit, like Olinda, and are on emergency call should you need them (☎190, ⓦ www.ciatur.pe.gov.br).

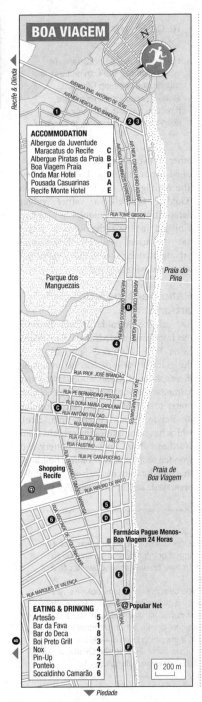

Recife & Olinda

BOA VIAGEM

N

AVENIDA ENG. ANTONIO DE GÓIS

AVENIDA HERCULANO BANDEIRA

ACCOMMODATION
Albergue da Juventude
   Maracatus do Recife   C
Albergue Piratas da Praia   B
Boa Viagem Praia   F
Onda Mar Hotel   D
Pousada Casuarinas   A
Recife Monte Hotel   E

AVENIDA CONSELHEIRO AGUIAR

AVENIDA DOMINGOS FERREIRA

RUA TOMÉ GIBSON

A

Parque dos
Manguezais

*Praia do
Pina*

AVENIDA CONSELHEIRO AGUIAR

AVENIDA DOMINGOS FERREIRA

RUA PROF. JOSÉ BRANDÃO

RUA PE BERNARDINO PESSOA

RUA DONA MARIA CAROLINA

RUA ANTÔNIO FALCÃO

RUA MAMAGUAPA

RUA FÉLIX DE BRITO MELO

RUA FAUSTINO

RUA PE CARAPUCEIRO

RUA DOS NAVEGANTES

C

Shopping
Recife

RUA RIBEIRO DE BRITO

RUA SUMARÉ BARBOSA

*Praia de
Boa Viagem*

5

D

**Farmácia Pague Menos-
Boa Viagem 24 Horas**

RUA VISCONDE DE JEQUITINHONHA

E

7

RUA MARQUÊS DE VALENÇA

@ Popular Net

RUA SETUBAL

EATING & DRINKING
Artesão   5
Bar da Fava   1
Bar do Deca   8
Boi Preto Grill   3
Nox   4
Pin-Up   2
Ponteio   7
Socadinho Camarão   6

F

0   200 m

▼ Piedade

---

soak up the view over a beer at one of the many bars that set up tables outside.

Recife is probably the best big Brazilian city in which to find **artesanato** (crafts), and the area around São Pedro is the place to look for it. Browse the stalls lining the square's adjacent winding streets, or head east to the **Mercado de São José**, an excellent place for local crafts.

Once you've stocked up on souvenirs, head to the **Forte das Cinco Pontas**, off the western end of Avenida Dantas Barreto. Built in 1630 by the Dutch, the fort was the last place they surrendered upon expulsion in 1654, and is worth visiting for its splendid views over the sea.

Museu do Homem do Nordeste

Though it's a fair distance from Boa Vista, it's worth making the trip to the fascinating **Museu do Homem do Nordeste** in Casa Forte at Av. 17 de Agosto 2187 (Tues–Fri 8am–5pm, Sat & Sun 1–5pm; R$4). The museum depicts everyday life and folk culture with more than twelve thousand exhibits ranging from carriages used by seventeenth-century sugar barons to present day northeastern carnival costumes. To get here, take the "Via Barbosa" bus from the post office or from Parque 13 de Maio, at the bottom of Rua do Hospício, a pleasant half-hour drive through leafy northern suburbs. The museum is on the left, but hard to spot, so ask the driver or conductor where to get off.

Instituto Ricardo Brennand

One of Recife's most impressive attractions is the **Instituto Ricardo Brennand** (Tues–Sun 1pm–5pm, R$5), which belonged to one of the sons of the city's renowned Brennard family. The Instituto is impressive right from the entrance, a long road colonnaded on either side with palm trees, and is home to Brennand's impressive collection of art, including Greco-Roman mythological figures, suits of armour and a collection of Swiss-army knives with more functions than you can count. To get here, catch bus "EDU Caxangá" on Avenida Domingos Ferreira and take it to the end of the line. Continue on foot to the end of the road, turn right onto Rua Isaac Buril. The institute is at the end of this road on the left.

Boa Viagem

Regular buses make it easy to get down to the district of **BOA VIAGEM** and the beach, an enormous skyscraper-lined arc of sand that constitutes the longest stretch of urbanized seafront in Brazil. Recife, too, was once studded with beaches, but they were swallowed up by industrial development, leaving only Boa Viagem within the city's limits.

The narrow **beach** is packed at weekends and deserted during the week, with warm natural rock pools to wallow in just offshore when the tide is out. Pavilions punctuate the pavement along the noisy road, selling all sorts of refreshing drinks from coconut water to pre-mixed *batidas* (rum cocktails). There have been a small number of shark attacks over the years, but they usually involve surfers far offshore.

Arrival and information

Air Recife's Aeroporto Internacional dos Guararapes (☎81/3322-4353) is only 11km from the city centre, at the far end of Boa Viagem. You can buy a voucher for an airport taxi from the COOPSETA desk at arrivals (☎81/3462-1584; ten percent discount for ISIC members). Taxis to Boa Viagem cost about R$20, to Santo Antônio about R$35, to Olinda, R$59. Bus #043 from right outside goes to Shopping Tacaruna, west of the city centre (R$1.85).
Bus The *rodoviária* (☎81/3452-2824) is about 14km from the centre. From here the Metrô (R$1.30; ☎81/2102-8500, ⓦ www.metrorec.com.br), an overground rail link, whisks you through various *favelas* to the old train station in the centre, Estação Central ("Recife"). From here, to get to your hotel in Olinda catch the Rio Doce/Princesa Isabel bus; there are no direct buses to Boa Viagem so it's best to take a taxi.

Tourist information The state tourist office, EMPETUR (ⓦ www.setur.pe.gov.br), runs several information posts, some of which have good English-speakers – most have helpful, free maps and event calendars: the office at the airport (24hr; ☎81/3182-8299) is best. There are also branches at the *rodoviária* (daily 8am–8.30pm; ☎81/3182-8298) and Recife Island (Rua da Guia and Travessa do Bom Jesus; daily 8am–8.30pm; ☎81/3355-3402). Make sure to pick up the monthly cultural pamphlet (*What's On – Acontece Em Recife e Olinda*) as well as the free maps of the greater Recife area.
Tour operators Martur, Recife Palace Hotel, Av. Boa Viagem, 4070, Loja 04, Boa Viagem (☎81/3465-7778, ⓦ www.martur.com.br) organize flights, cruises and trips to Fernando de Noronha.

City transport

Bus Most city buses originate and terminate on the central island of Santo Antônio, on Av. Dantas Barreto, either side of the Pracinha do Diário (aka Praça da Independência). They range in price from R$1.60 to R$3. To get from the city centre to Boa Viagem, take buses marked "Aeroporto", "Boa Viagem", "Setúbal/Principe", "Setúbal/Conde de Boa Vista" or "Candeios", or catch the more comfortable air-conditioned mini-van marked "Aeroporto" (R$2.30), from outside the offices of the *Diário de Pernambuco*, on the Pracinha do Diário; it goes every 20min and costs R$2.50.
Taxi The bus system is so thorough and comparatively cheap that it rarely makes sense to take a taxi. They're metered and straightforward to use, though the cost can add up.

Accommodation

Although the run-down town centre is the cheapest place to stay, we don't really recommend it. Boa Viagem is a good option, where the beach compensates for the steep prices, even if you'll most likely end up in a high-rise over the beach. Otherwise, consider staying in Olinda (see p.324). As ever, if you want to visit during Carnaval, you'll need to book months in advance.

Boa Viagem

Albergue da Juventude Maracatus do Recife Rua Maria Carolina 185 ☎81/3326-1221. Bare but functional dorm rooms in a safe setting, with a swimming pool and free breakfast. Dorms R$30.

Albergue Piratas da Praia Av. Cons Aguiar 2034/307, corner with Rua Prf. Osias Ribeiro ☎81/3326-1281, ⊛www.piratasdapraia.com. One of Boa Viagem's few hostels, with perfectly comfortable dorms in a colourful setting. Lockers available. Discount for HI members. Dorms R$38.

Boa Viagem Praia Av. Boa Viagem 5576 ☎81/3462-6454, ⊛www.boaviagempraia.com .br. Located on the southern beachfront, this place feels a bit like an airport hotel, with formulaic decor and anodyne appearance, although the front rooms open onto Boa Viagem's beach and all have a/c, cable TV, fridge & wi-fi. R$164.

Onda Mar Hotel Rua Ernesto de Paula Santos 284 ☎81/2128-4848, ⊛www.ondamar.com.br. The hotel staff can be a bit surly, but there are great views from the pool area, the rooms are pretty spacious and it's only a few minutes' walk to Boa Viagem's beach. R$165.

Pousada Casuarinas Rua Antônio Pedro Figueiredo 151 ☎81/3325-4708, ⊛www.pousadacasuarinas .com.br. Grab a book and put your feet up in one of the hammocks in the leafy outdoor area or have a dip in the refreshing pool. Rooms have tiled floors and wooden motifs, and some have an outdoor

veranda. Laundry and wireless internet available. Single rates are available. R$139.

Eating

If you're in Recife Antigo at lunchtime, head to Mercado Boa Vista, always full of locals tucking into some seriously delicious food at the food stalls.

Boa Viagem

Artesão Rua Pedro Bérgamo 36 ☎81/3326-7989. Paper lanterns line the front of this welcoming restaurant serving tasty local por kilo (R$29.90) grub at lunchtime; for those craving a taste of European food, gorge on the pizza buffet for a bargain R$10.90 in the evenings. Por kilo at lunchtime (R$29.90), pizza buffet for a bargain R$10.90 in the evenings. Daily 11.30am–1am.

Bar da Fava Rua Padre Oliveira Rolin 37A, Jardim Beira Rio, Pina ☎81/3463-8998, ⊛www .bardafava.com.br. Renowned for its exquisitely prepared *favas* (broad beans) that accompany virtually every meal, this simple place with tables lining the pavement is one of the most popular joints in Recife and an absolute must for *fava* fans. Tues–Sat 11am–midnight.

Boi Preto Grill Av. Boa Viagem 97, Pina ☎81/3466-6334, ⊛www.churrascariaboipreto .com.br. Long-established restaurant with a splendid buffet that includes mussels and sushi along with all-you-can-eat quality *churrascaria* for R$25.90. Pricier on the weekends (R$32.90). Mon–Thurs noon–4pm & 6.30–11pm, Fri–Sun noon–midnight.

Pin-Up Av. Herculano Bandeiro 204, Pina ☎81/3466-0001, ⊛www.pinupburgueria.com.br. American-style diner with excellent-value and tasty burgers for R$11.40 and milkshakes for R$8.50. There's also a sister restaurant in the Shopping Recife (see opposite). Mon 5.30pm–midnight, Tues–Thurs 5.30pm–1am, Fri & Sat 5.30pm–5am, Sun 5pm–midnight.

Ponteio Av. Boa Viagem 4824 ☎81/3326-2386, ⊛www.ponteiorecife.com.br. One of the few beachside restaurants, this busy *churrascaria* is popular for quality *rodizio* (all you can eat) and its sushi buffet. Mon–Thurs R$21.90, Fri & Sat R$26.90, Sundays R$32. Mon–Thurs 12–4pm, Fri–Sun 12–11pm.

Recife Antigo

Brotfabrik Rua da Moeda 87 ☎81/3424-2250, ⊛www.brotfabrik.com.br. Bakery selling excellent coffee, *salgados* (R$2), pastries and sandwiches (R$2.50), as the constant queue attests. The perfect spot to grab a quick bite as you tour the city. Mon–Fri 7am–7pm.

Casa de Banhos By the Brennand sculptures ☎81/3075/8776. Set in a former bathhouse, this restaurant serving regional dishes is the perfect stopover if you're heading to Boa Viagem after visiting the Brennand sculptures, and has with fantastic views of the old town and the port. Try the *muqueca de peixe* (fish stew; R$41 for three people). Wed & Thurs 11am–4pm, Fri–Sun 11am–6pm.

Drinking and nightlife

A great place to start the evening is around Rua do Bom Jesus in Recife Antigo, home to plenty of bars and restaurants with tables spilling onto the pedestrian streets. There's also some action in Boa Viagem, where bars open and close with bewildering speed. The liveliest area here is around Praça de Boa Viagem, quite a long way down the beach from the city centre, near the junction of Avenida Boa Viagem and Rua Bavão de Souza Leão. The variety of music and dance is enormous, and Recife has its own frenetic carnival music, the *frevo*, as well as the *forró* you'll find all over the Northeast. Make sure you use taxis at night.

Boa Viagem
Rua do Bom Jesus is where all the action takes place so head here and you'll find dozens of bars in which to indulge in some potent *caipirinhas*.
Bar do Deca Rua José Maria de Miranda 140 ☎81/3465-9656. This restaurant-cum-bar with tables overflowing onto the street remains a local favourite; astound your taste buds with some top-notch *carne guizada*, washed down with a tasty *caipirinha* or two. Thurs and Fri are the busiest nights. Mon–Sat noon–3am.
Nox Av. Engenheiro Domingos Ferreira 2422 ☎81/3325-5809, ⊛www.clubnox.com.br. This is where Recife's cool kids hang out – in one of Brazil's most modern clubbing settings with a state of the art sound system pumping out electronica, complemented by luminous blue and purple decor and a chill-out lounge on the roof. Thurs–Sat 10pm–6am. Entrance R$15.
Socaldinho Camarão Av. Visconde de Jequitinhonha 106 ☎81/3462-9500, ⊛www.socaldinho camarao.com.br. If you fancy some footie action, head here and join the locals for a beer (R$3.70) over a gripping game of Brazilian *futebol* as you munch on some shrimp flambéd with *cachaça* (R$22.95 for three people). Daily 11.30am–late.

Recife Antigo
Bar Zero Um Rua Vigário Tenório 199 ☎81/3224-4405. Enjoy a carafe of beer – the bar's staple drink – on the pedestrianized street just outside

before heading back in to shake your groove on the dancefloor to some live pop and samba-rock music on Fri and Sat. Mon–Sat 6pm–late.
Downtown Pub Rua Vigário Tenório 105 ☎81/3424-6317, ⊛www.downtownpub.com.br. Mosh away to some rock or sway to some reggae or reggaeton at this popular joint – more of a club than its name suggests – which attracts its fair share of tourists. Wed–Sat 10pm–late. Cover charge varies; usually R$25. Women free on Wed till midnight.
Sala De Reboco Rua Gregório Júnior 264 ☎81/3228-7052, ⊛www.saladereboco.com.br. If you're really keen to pick up some authentic *forró pé-de-serra nordestino* (Northeastern Brazilian folk dance) skills, head to one of the country's best *casas de forró*, drawing a loyal and passionate crowd as well as some of Brazil's best *forrozeiros*. Thurs–Sat 10pm–late.

Entertainment

If you want to get a real feel for some regional music it's worth checking out an *espaço cultural* or two. The *Espaço Nodaloshi*, at Estrada dos Remédios 1891 in Madalena (☎81/3228-3511), frequently brings together large numbers of musicians from all over Pernambuco, generally starting the shows around 10pm or later. The *Espaço Cultural Alberto Cunha Melo*, at Rua Leila Félix Karan 15 in Bongi (☎81/3228-6846), runs similar live music shows.
Parque Carvalheira Rua Manoel Didier 53, Imbiribeira ☎81/3471-6111, ⊛www.carvalheira .com.br (Mon–Fri 9am–5pm). It's the *cachaça* (sugar-cane spirit) tasting at the *cachaça* museums here that makes visiting them so much fun.

Shopping

Mercado São José Rua São José, Santo Antônio. Stock up on some local crafts, or simply peruse the stacks of curious herbal medicines and everyday items as locals go about their daily shopping. Mon–Fri 6am–6pm, Sun 6am–noon.
Shopping Paço Alfândega Rua Alfândega 35, Recife Island ⊛www.pacoalfandega.com.br. Chic, refurbished former customs building on Recife Island. Mon–Sat 10am–10pm, Sun noon–9pm.
Shopping Recife Rua Pe. Carapuceiro 777, Boa Viagem ⊛www.shoppingrecife.com.br. Large, suburban shopping mall with multiplex (Mon–Sat 10am–10pm, Sun noon–9pm).

Directory

Banks and exchange There are plenty of banks with ATMs in Boa Viagem and Recife including

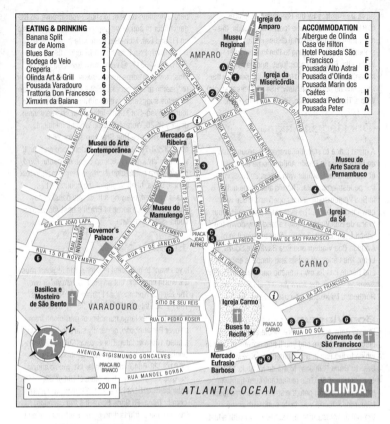

EATING & DRINKING
Banana Split	8
Bar de Aloma	2
Blues Bar	7
Bodega de Veio	1
Creperia	5
Olinda Art & Grill	4
Pousada Varadouro	6
Trattoria Don Francesco	3
Ximxim da Baiana	9

ACCOMMODATION
Albergue de Olinda	G
Casa de Hilton	E
Hotel Pousada São Francisco	F
Pousada Alto Astral	B
Pousada d'Olinda	C
Pousada Marin dos Caétes	H
Pousada Pedro	D
Pousada Peter	A

Igreja do Amparo
Museu Regional
AMPARO
Igreja da Misericôrdia
Museu do Arte Contemporânea
Mercado da Ribeira
Museu de Arte Sacra de Pernambuco
Igreja da Sé
Museu do Mamulengo
Governor's Palace
PRACA JOAO ALFREDO
CARMO
Basilica e Mosteiro de São Bento
VARADOURO
SITIO DE SEU REIS
RUA D. PEDRO ROSER
Igreja Carmo
Buses to Recife ★
PRACA DO CARMO
Convento de São Francisco
AVENIDA SIGISMUNDO GONCALVES
PRACA RIO BRANCO
RUA MANOEL BORBA
Mercado Eufrasio Barbosa
0   200 m
ATLANTIC OCEAN
OLINDA

HSBC. It's best to use Banco 24 in Shopping Tacaruna, Av. Gov. Agamenon Magalhaes 153, Santo Amaro (Mon–Sat 9am–10pm, Sat noon–8pm).
Embassies and consulates UK, Av. Conselheiro Aguiar 2941, 3rd floor (☎81/2127-0230); US, Rua Gonçalves Maia 163, Boa Vista (☎81/3416-3050).
Hospital Real Hospital Português de Beneficência, Av. Agamenon Magalhaes 4760, Boa Vista (☎81/3416-1122).
Internet Caravela, Rua do Bom Jesus 183, Recife Antigo (☎81/3424-1952); Popular Net, Rua Barão de Souza Leão 75, Boa Viagem (☎81/3341-9704).
Laundries Cinco a Sec, Rua Boa Padre Carapuceiro 800, Boa Viagem (☎81/3466-5335); Vivaz Lavanderia, Av. Cons Aguiar 2775, Boa Viagem (☎81/3466-3755).
Pharmacies Farmácia dos Pobres, Av. Dantas Barreto 498, Santo Antônio (☎81/3301-8173); Farmácia Pague Menos, Av. Cons Aguiar 4635, Boa Viagem, 24hrs (☎81/3301-4209).
Police CIATUR, Rua Bernardo Vieira de Mêlo 102, Piedade ☎81/3439-9696 or 3181-1717.

Post office Av. Guararapes 61, Santo Antônio, ☎81/3425-3644.

Moving on

Air TAM and Gol connect Recife with the rest of the country.
Bus Buses depart from the *rodoviária* 13km out of town, Rodovia 232, Km15, Jabotão dos Guararapes (☎81/3452-1103). For current prices and routes check Penha (⊛nspenha.locaweb.com.b); Progresso (⊛www.autoviacaoprogresso.com.br), Guanabara (⊛www.expressoguanabara.com.br), and São Geraldo (⊛www.saogeraldo.com.br). To get to Olinda, catch the "Pau Amarelo", "Jardim Atlântico", or "Rio Doce/Princesa Isabel" bus from Rua do Sol to Praça do Carmo, just by Olinda's main post office. Alternatively, take a taxi from central Recife to Olinda, which should cost around R$25 and will take about 15min.

Fortaleza (3 daily; 12hr); João Pessoa (11 daily; 2hr); Maceió (8 daily; 4hr); Natal (10 daily; 4hr

30min); Salvador (daily; 12hr); among other destinations, several times daily.

OLINDA

Designated a UNESCO World Heritage Site, **OLINDA** is, quite simply, one of Brazil's most impressive examples of colonial architecture: a maze of cobbled streets, hills crowned with brilliant white churches, pastel-coloured houses, Baroque fountains and graceful squares. The city is most renowned for its **Carnaval**, which attracts visitors from all over the country, as well as sizeable contingents from Europe. Founded in 1535, the old city is spread across several small hills looking back towards Recife. Despite its size, Olinda can effectively be considered a neighbourhood of Recife: a high proportion of its residents commute to the city so **transport links** are good, with buses leaving every few minutes.

What to see and do

Olinda's colonial highlights include more churches than you could wish to see in an afternoon, and a curious puppet museum. Much of the appeal lies in wandering through the picturesque streets.

Alto da Sé

Olinda's hills are steep, so don't try to do too much too quickly. A good spot to have a drink and plan your attack is the **Alto da Sé**, the highest square in town, not least because of the stunning view of Recife's skyscrapers shimmering in the distance, framed in the foreground by Olinda's church towers, gardens and palm trees. There's always an arts and crafts **market** here during the day, which is busiest in the late afternoon; though there's plenty of good stuff, there's little here you can't get cheaper in Recife or the interior.

The **Igreja da Sé** (Mon–Sat 8am–noon & 2–5pm; free), on the *praça*, is bland and austere inside – more of a museum than a living church – but is worth a look if only to see the eighteenth-century sedan chair and large wooden sculptures in the small room at the northeast wing. It's also notable for being at the highest point in the region's landscape, making it visible from all the other churches for miles around. The viewing patio at the back right-hand side of the church offers a particularly beautiful view of the city.

Convento de São Francisco

Olinda is home to eighteen **churches** seemingly tucked away around every corner. The Dutch burned most of them down in the seventeenth century, and left the Portuguese to restore them during the following centuries. If you only have time to visit one, head to the impressive Convento de São Francisco (Rua São Francisco; Mon–Fri 9am–noon & 2–5pm, Sat 9am–noon; R$3), the country's oldest Franciscan convent. It was built in 1585 and is comprised of a chapel, church, cloister and sacristy. Particular highlights are the tiled cloister depicting the lives of Jesus and St Francis of Assisi, and the sacristy's beautiful Baroque furniture carved from jacaranda wood. Behind the convent there's a patio with grand panoramas across the ocean.

Museu do Mamulengo

The fascinating **Museu do Mamulengo**, Rua de São Bento 344 (Tues–Fri 9am–5pm, Sat & Sun 10am–6pm; free), houses an excellent collection of more than one thousand traditional puppets, some dating as far back as the eighteenth century. Folk puppets, with diverse outfits and exaggerated faces, played – and still play – an important role in religious festivities and street gatherings, including the famed Carnaval.

Arrival and information

Bus From Recife, catch the "Pau Amarelo", "Jardim Atlântico", or "Rio Doce/Princesa Isabel" bus (the latter also from Recife's *rodoviária*) from Rua do Sol to Praça do Carmo, just by Olinda's main post office and a two-minute walk up into the old city. Buses #973, #983 or #992 also depart from Tacaruna Derby Shopping in Recife and will drop you off at Praça do Carmo.

Tourist information The state tourist office, EMPETUR (ⓦwww.setur.pe.gov.br), runs an office at Rua Prudente de Morais 472 (Mon–Fri 9am–5pm, Sat & Sun 9am–7pm).

Tour operators Victor Tur, Av. Sigismundo Gonçalves 732, Carmo, Olinda(ⓣ81/3429-1532, ⓦwww.pousadamarindoscaetes.com.br) is an agency run out of the *Pousada Marin dos Caétes* that arranges bus and air tickets and car rentals, as well as city and beach tours.

Accommodation

Albergue de Olinda Rua do Sol 233, Carmo ⓣ81/3429-1592, ⓦwww.alberguedeolinda .com.br. Located on a main road by the seafront, this HI hostel has a good-sized outdoor area with hammocks and a pool, ideal for mingling with other travellers. Rooms are a bit on the plain side with just the bare necessities, but they're clean enough and the place itself has a friendly vibe. Free wi-fi. HI discount available. Dorms R$35, rooms R$80.

Casa de Hilton Rua do Sol 77 ⓣ81/3494/2379, ⓔcasadehilton@bol.com.br. The eponymous Hilton rents out a few rooms in this bright yellow house at an unbeatable price; the tatty furniture has seen better days but the rooms are adequately comfortable for a few nights, and there's also a communal kitchen for those wanting to self-cater. Dorms R$20, rooms R$60.

Pousada Alto Astral Rua 13 de Maio 305 ⓣ81/3439-3453, ⓦwww.pousadaaltoastral .com. Funky pousada decorated with some imposing Carneval mannequins. The staff are incredibly friendly and the breakfast area is perfect for mingling with other travellers. Rooms are warm, colourful and superb value, plus there's a pool. If there are four of you ask for room eight – spacious and with incredible views over the city. R$70.

Pousada d'Olinda Praça Conselheiro João Alfredo 178 ⓣ81/3493-6011, ⓦwww.pousadadolinda .com.br. The rooms here are set around a courtyard and pool area, and there's one massive but pleasant dorm that sleeps fourteen, with hard beds and a mezzanine. There's a lovely garden at the back with lounge chairs perfect for catching some rays, as well as an old swing to catch a bit of a breeze. Dorms R$30, rooms R$95.

Pousada Marin dos Caétes Av. Sigismundo Gonçalves 732, Carmo ⓣ81/3493-1556,

ⓦwww.pousadamarindoscaetes.com.br. The tiny rooms here look like something out of a doll's house or a young girl's room, with sunny colours and flowery bedspreads. The bathrooms are also pretty poky, but clean nonetheless. R$75.

Pousada Pedro Rua 27 de Janeiro 95 ⓣ81/3439-9546, ⓦwww.pousadapedro .com.br. A spiral staircase leads up to the more expensive rooms in the main house of this charming *pousada*, while the cheaper rooms are around the pool area at the back. Rooms are attractive and spacious with plenty of sunlight, and the bathrooms spic-and-span. All have air conditioning. R$140.

Pousada São Francisco Rua do Sol 127 ⓣ81/3429-2109, ⓦwww.pousadasaofrancisco .com.br. Definitely more of a hotel than a pousada, this place has a good-sized pool, a pool table and 45 bright, comfortable rooms, with wooden parquet floors and Afro-Brazilian local art decorating the walls. All have a/c, fridge, cable tv and wi-fi. R$132.

Eating

If you want to eat for less than R$20 in Olinda, try the *comida por kilo* places along the seafront and in Novo Olinda. For a bit more, you can eat far better in the old town. Best and least expensive of all, though, is to join the crowds drinking and eating serious street food at the Alto da Sé. These charcoal-fired delights can't be recommended too highly; try *acarajé*, made from women sitting next to sizzling wok-like pots – bean-curd cakes, fried in palm oil, slit, and filled with salad, dried shrimps and *vatapá*.

Banana Split Praça do Carmo 5 ⓣ81/4104-0445. Plenty of tasty snacks to choose from at this German-owned place, including a ricotta and sun-dried tomato sandwich (R$7), soups (R$5) and tasty fresh fruit juices (R$2–5). There's also iced coffee (R$6.50) and frappuccinos (R$5), perfect for cooling off. Daily 8am–10pm.

Blues Bar Rua do Bonfim 66 ⓣ81/3429-8272, ⓦwww.bluespizzaria.com.br. The blues may only only happen sporadically but there are plenty of pizzas to choose from (R$18.90–37), including sweet ones. Tues–Sun 6pm–midnight.

Creperia Praça João Alfredo 168 ⓣ81/3429-2935. This agreeable crêperie is decorated with knick-knacks, local art and exposed brickwork, and has an open-air patio. Wash down the scrumptious crêpes (from R$10.90) with one of their tasty fresh juices (R$3.30). Daily 11am–11pm.

Olinda Art & Grill Rua Bispo Coutinho 35 ⓣ71/3429-9406. Perched on the side of the hill with fantastic views over Recife and the coast, this popular place kitted out with wooden furniture, a sprinkle of brickwork, and lanterns seemingly pinched from a Victorian street will make you feel like you're sitting in a tree-house, even more so after a few unbelievably potent *caipirinhas* (R$2.50 on Wed & Thurs, otherwise R$4.20). The food here is excellent value – a *picanha suína* (pork steak) will set four people back R$39.90. Live music every day 9–10.30pm. Tues–Sat 12am–11pm, Sun noon–7pm.

Pousada Varadouro Rua 15 de Novembro 98 ☎81/3439-1163. Tasty local grub at this small cheap restaurant set on the ground floor of *Pousada Varadouro* and serving por kilo food (R$18). Locals swarm in here on their lunch break so get here early; if you'd rather not sit indoors, head to the back and eat by the pool. Mon–Fri 11.40am–3pm.

Trattoria Don Francesco Rua Prudente de Morais 358 ☎81/3429-3852. Olinda's most popular Italian serves delicious handmade pasta (lasagna R$26.50, *tagliatelle ai funghi* R$29.80), and the chequered tablecloths and jars of home-made tomato sauce lining the wall add a touch of authenticity. Mon–Fri 12–3pm & 6.30–11pm, Sat 6.30pm–midnight.

Drinking and nightlife

Bar de Aloma Rua do Amparo ☎81/3439-0576. High Gothic windows and comfy seating at this low-key bar in the centre of town make it the perfect spot to while away an evening. Locals flock here on Tuesdays to push on with the beers once *Bodega de Veio* (just up the road) closes shop. Tues–Sat 7pm–2am.

Bodega de Veio Rua do Amparo 212 ☎81/3429-0185. A little shop selling everything from brooms to packets of beans transforms on Tuesday nights: locals bring in their vinyl discs which are played on a first-come-first-basis served as the young pour out onto the streets and enjoy cheap beers and *caipirinhas* (R$5). The action usually kicks off around 7pm and goes on until 11pm.

Ximxim da Baiana Avenida Sigismundo Gonçalves 742 ☎81/3439-8447. The place to head to for some good old *forró* on Wednesday nights – virtually all the town is here so it's best to practise your moves beforehand. They also serve good food (*carne de sol* R$12). Tues–Sun 6pm–2am.

Directory

Banks and exchange There are no ATMs in Olinda's historical centre – it's best to head to Banco 24 in Shopping Tacaruna in Recife (see p.322).

Pharmacies Farmácia Bicentenária, Rua S Miguel 277, Novo Olinda (☎81/3429-2148).

Post office Av. Dr Joaquim Nabuco 2445 ☎81/3439-7740

Shopping Crafts aplenty are available at the Mercado da Ribeira, Rua Bernardo Vieira de Melo (daily 9am–6.30pm).

FERNANDO DE NORONHA

Recife is one of the main launch points for this beautiful archipelago 545km off the coast of Pernambuco. It has pristine beaches and is environmentally protected so it's absolutely terrific for scuba-diving. The water is clear for more than 30m in many places, with turtles, dolphins and a wide range of fish species to observe. Since 1988 much of the archipelago has been protected as a marine national park to maintain its ecological wonders (it's also the breeding territory for many tropical Atlantic birds). The main island, **ILHA DE FERNANDO DE NORONHA**, has plenty of gorgeous beaches. While you can no longer swim with the dolphins, you're likely to see quite a few should you visit, though you'll have to wake up early – they enter the bay every day between 5am and 6am.

It's not cheap to get here (from R$900, two daily flights from Recife with Gol and TRIP), and you're also charged the **TPA tax** (Taxa de Preservaçao; daily R$38.24), which goes towards protecting the archipelago, but it can be quite an experience. For more information, including restaurants and places to stay, check the government-run website, Ⓦ www.noronha.pe.gov.br.

FORTALEZA

FORTALEZA, the capital city of the State of Ceará, is home to some of the nicest urban beaches in the country, although it's the wild beaches to the north that remain its most popular attraction; crystal-clear waters and palm-fringed beaches are just one selling point – this is any kite-or windsurfer's paradise.

Since the nineteenth century, the city has been the commercial centre of the northern half of the Northeast, and is today Brazil's fifth largest metropolitan area. Given Fortaleza's lack of any intrinsic appeal, it remains more suited to breaking your journey on your way up the coast, and is a good base for day-trips to the celebrated **beaches**: Cumbuco, Jericoacoara, Canoa Quebrada, Morro Branco and Lagoinha.

What to see and do

You can do Fortaleza in a day, and, culturally, much of what there is to see can be done before noon. The nerve centre of the city is its largest square, **Praça José de Alencar**, four blocks inland from the train station. Fortaleza's downtown streets are crowded with shops, with hawkers colonizing pavements and plazas, so much of the centre seems like one giant market. To the east is Praia de Iracema, home to the bulk of Fortaleza's nightlife, while further south is Praia do Futuro, the city's best beach. Downtown is fine to hang out in during the day, but it's deserted and unnerving at night. Wandering around the area on a Sunday by yourself is also best avoided.

Museu de Arte e Cultura Popular

Situated in a former nineteenth-century prison, the **Museu de Arte e Cultura Popular** (Mon–Fri 8am–4.30pm, Sat 8am–noon; free), located just above the tourist office, houses, a noteworthy collection of folk art, from Cearense *artesanato* (crafts) to paintings and sculptures produced by Ceará's artists.

Igreja da Sé and Mercado Central

Fortaleza's cathedral, the **Igreja da Sé**, is an unmistakeable landmark in the centre of town. Its dark, neo-Gothic architectural style is almost shocking at first, and striking rather than beautiful. Megalithic flying buttresses

lift the weird building from the ground, all black and grey with age and city grime. Next to it, on Rua Conde d'Eu, the **Mercado Central** dominates the skyline: a huge complex resembling a parking garage crowded with hundreds of small stores. The market, and the nearby shops diagonally across from the cathedral, are the best places in the city to buy a **hammock**.

Centro Dragão do Mar

The **Centro Dragão do Mar de Arte e Cultura** (Tues–Fri 8.30am–9.30pm, ☏85/3488-8600, ⊛www.dragaodomar .org.br; Sat & Sun 2.30–9.30pm), a couple of blocks east of the market, makes a strident modernist landmark in the city; its steel and glass curves blend surprisingly well with the brightly coloured, attractive old terraced buildings over and around which it is built. Within the complex, there's a small, shiny-domed planetarium, cinemas, an auditorium and a couple of museums. There's also a bookshop, toilets and, in the tower that supports the covered walkway between the two main sections of the Centro, a small but very good, perpetually packed coffee bar, the *Torre do Café*. At night the square below is Fortaleza's most vibrant nightlife spot although it does draw brazen panhandlers.

Beaches in town

The main city beaches begin steps away from downtown with **Praia de Iracema**, although this is a pretty dull stretch during the day; further south you will find **Praia do Meireles** and **Praia do Mucuripe**. Sadly, the water off all these beaches is badly **polluted**, and you are advised not to go in. For **swimming**, head over to the city's best beach, **Praia do Futuro**. Getting there will involve taking a bus marked either "Praia do Futuro" or "Caça e Pesca" from Avenida da Abolição, a taxi or a minim forty-five minute walk along

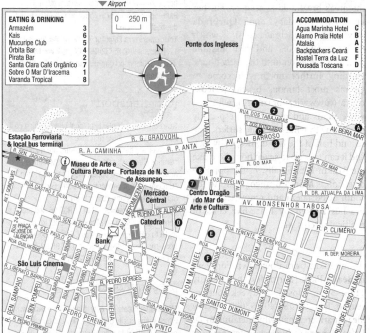

FORTALEZA (upper map)

0 500 m

A. B Praia do Futuro
2 3, 4 5, 6 & 7
Beach Park

Ponte dos Ingleses

Praia de Iracema

Praia do Mucuripe

Estação Ferroviária

CENTRO

See map below for detail

RUA DOS TABAJARAS
AV. ALMIRANTE BARROSO
AV. MONSENHOR TABOSA
RUA TENENTE BENÉVOLO

Buses to Caucaia

Praia do Meireles

Cyber Café **1**

@ AV. ABOLIÇÃO

AV. BEIRA MAR

C

@ Evolution Video Cyber Café **8**

MEIRELES

RUA PEREIRA VALENTE

VARJOTA

9

Monte Klinikum Hospital

Droga Nunes

AVENIDA SANTOS DUMONT

PRAÇA CORAÇÃO DE JESUS

AVENIDA HERACLITO GRAÇA

Buses to Aquiraz

AV. JOÃO CORDEIRO

R. VISCONDE RIO BRANCO

10

AV. PADRE ANTÔNIO TOMAS

RUA ANTÔNIO SALES

RUA BARÃO DE STUDART

AVENIDA DESEMBARGADOR MOREIRA

AV. SENADOR VIRGÍLIO TÁVORA

AVENIDA COLOMBO SOUSA

Shopping Del Paseo

5à Sec

ALDEOTA

FATIMA

Estação Rodoviária

RÍO COCÓ

RUA ENG. SANTANA JÚNIOR

Shopping Iguatemi

EATING & DRINKING

ΔTLΔ∏T⏀DZ	2
Assis, O Rei da Pichanha	9
Chico do Caranguejo	3
Colher de Pau	8
Croco Beach	4
Neide do Camarão	5
Ponto do Guaraná	1
Real Sucos	10
Sorveteria 50 sabores	6
Tia Nair	7

ACCOMMODATION

Atalaia	A
Hotel Pousada Arara	B
Mundo Latino	C
Pousada 0031	D

▼ Airport

(lower map)

EATING & DRINKING

Armazém	3
Kais	6
Mucuripe Club	5
Órbita Bar	4
Pirata Bar	2
Santa Clara Café Orgânico	7
Sobre O Mar D'Iracema	1
Varanda Tropical	8

0 250 m

Ponte dos Ingleses

ACCOMMODATION

Agua Marinha Hotel	C
Alamo Praia Hotel	B
Atalaia	A
Backpackers Ceará	E
Hostel Terra da Luz	F
Pousada Toscana	D

Estação Ferroviária & local bus terminal

RUA DOS TABAJARAS

R. DOS POTIGUARAS

B

AV. BEIRA MAR **A**

R. G. GRADVÖHL

AV. A. TAMANDARE

AV. ALM. BARROSO

3

R. A. CAMINHA

R. P. ANTA

R. DO MAR

RUA GUANACÉS

R. DO MAR

1 Museu de Arte e Cultura Popular

5 Fortaleza de N. S. de Assunçao

Mercado Central

RUA JOSÉ AVELINO

Centro Dragão do Mar de Arte e Cultura

6

7

AV. MONSENHOR TABOSA

8

R. DR. ATUALPA DA LIMA

R. P. CLIMÉRIO

Catedral

D

E

F

RUA TENENTE BENÉVOLO

R. DEP. MOREIRA

Bank

São Luis Cinema

RUA SEN. ALENCAR

PRAÇA JOSÉ DE ALENCAR

RUA GUILHERME ROCHA

RUA LIBERATO BARROSO

R. PEDRO BORGES

RUA PINTO

AV. SANTOS DUMONT

the seafront through an industrial and *favela* neighbourhood. Here the beaches are lined with restaurants and bars, and seem to stretch as far as you can see. In term of safety, by day the beaches are fine (though you should look out for **shark warnings**) but the area between Praia Meireles and Praia do Futuro is unsafe at any time and should not be walked by night.

Beaches out of town

The state of Ceará has plenty of incredible beaches on offer if you are prepared to travel a bit further. All can be reached on tours or by regular buses from the *rodoviária*. Felix Tur (☎85/3242-7200, ⓦ www.felixtur.com.br) has transport to those listed below.

With its emerald-green waters, **Cumbuco**, only 35km north of Fortaleza, is by far Brazil's best beach for kite-surfing. *Pousada 0031* can organize lessons (☎85/8617-9119). Make sure you go on a **dune-buggy ride** to check out the area's breathtaking scenery. Further up is the popular **Canoa Quebrada** (ⓦ www.canoa-quebrada.com) which has dramatic cliffs and fun nightlife which that goes on until the early hours. Heading further north you come to Ceará's most famous beach, **Jericoacoara** (ⓦ www.jeri-brazil.org), with fine white sands and high dunes, especially popular with wind- and kite surfers. The second half of the trip up here is by 4x4, and it can take up to seven hours to make the 312km trip. Finally, in the opposite direction is **Morro Branco**, 80km to the south of Fortaleza and renowned for its beaches backed by maze-like cliffs of multicoloured sand.

Beach Park

About 16km from downtown Fortaleza is **Beach Park** (Porto das Dunas; daily 11am–5pm, closed midweek out of season; R$110; ☎85/4012-3000, ⓦ www.beachpark.com.br), which claims to be Latin America's biggest water park. It

certainly has some hair-rising rides and makes for a fun day-trip from Fortaleza. You can get here on organized tours (contact Felix Tur: ☎85/3242-7200, ⓦ www.felixtur.com.br; R$25) or by taxi (approx 20min; R$60).

Arrival and information

Air Fortaleza's Aeroporto Internacional Pinto Martins (☎85/3392-1030) is about 8km from downtown. To get into town, first take the "404 Aeroporto bem Fica" (R$1.80) bus to the corner of Av. de Maio and Av. dos Expedicionários. Then transfer to bus "011 Circular 1" (R$1.60). Or take a taxi which will take 15min and cost about R$33.

Bus The bus station, Rodoviária João Thomé (☎85/3230-1111), is about 10km from Av. Beira Mar on Av. Borges de Melo 1630. To get to the centre of town, take the bus with route card "Aguanambi Centro".

Tourist information At the time of writing there were three tourist information booths, one at the airport (☎85/3392-1667; daily 6am–midnight), SETFOR in the Mercado Central (☎85/3105-1475; Mon–Fri 9am–5pm, Sat 8am–noon) and the best, run by FORTUR, the municipal tourist organization, downtown at Praça do Ferreira (Mon–Fri 9am–5pm; ☎85/8879-7580), which also stocks the best city maps.

Tour operators Felix Tur, Av. Beira Mar 3958, loja 17, Mucuripe (☎85/3242-7200, ⓦ www.felixtur .com.br), has good day-trips to beaches and other attractions.

City transport

Bus Fortaleza has plenty of local buses, which cost R$1.80. Useful routes that take you to the main beaches and back to the city centre are marked "Grande Circular", "Caça e Pesca", "Mucuripe" and "P. Futuro". Two buses, the "Circular 1" and "Circular 2", run services that cover Fortaleza's outskirts and centre respectively.

Taxi Taxis are metered, start at R$2.96 and are parked along Praia do Meireles. Expect to pay over R$18 to get anywhere in town. For pre-booked taxis, try Cooperativa Radio Táxi (☎85/3254-5744) or Disque Táxi (☎85/3287-7222).

Accommodation

The budget hotels, as ever, tend to be downtown, which hums busily during the day but empties at night – it's best to stay elsewhere. Close by is Praia de Iracema, with a decent enough range of accommodation, while Praia Meireles further south is home to more upmarket hotels.

Praia de Iracema

Agua Marinha Hotel Av. Almirante Barroso 701 ☎85/3453-2000 🌐www.aguamarinhahotel.com .br. Clean well-equipped rooms (all with cable tv, a/c and fridge) with tiled floors and the odd piece of locally made wicker furniture. There are great sea views from the inviting pool out back. R$165.

Alamo Praia Hotel Av. Almirante Barroso 885 ☎85/3219-7979, 🌐www.alamohotel.com.br. A little stuffy inside, with no-frills rooms that are on the small side, but the place is pretty clean and handy for the beach and the nightlife. R$100.

Atalaia Av. Beira Mar 814 ☎85/3219-0658. Basic but perfectly functional rooms in a little pink house that's a stone's throw away from the beach. There's also a 24/7 cyber-café within the premises. R$140.

Backpackers Ceará Av. Dom Manoel 89 ☎85/3091-8997, 🌐www.pousadabackpackers .hpg.ig.com.br. Somewhat camouflaged until you notice the animated wall painting, this place buzzes with travellers, though it can feel a little impenetrable, with its barbed wire, CCTV and coded locks. Rooms are comfortable, but be ready to battle against the worn-out fans. R$40.

The city centre

Hostel Terra da Luz Rua Rodrigues Junior 278 ☎85/3082-2260, 🌐www.hostelterradaluz .com. This hostel has a cosy atmosphere and scribbled guests' notes coat the upstairs walls. The dorms are clean and colourful and there's also a communal kitchen and free internet. Dorms R$30, rooms R$75.

Pousada Toscana Rua Rufino de Alencar 272 ☎85/3088-4011, 🌐www.pousadatoscana.com .br. A pleasant pousada with a bright-blue exterior and imitation columns in the entrance, as well as a patio-cum-garden at the back. Rooms are simple but rather nondescript. R$55

Praia Meireles & Praia do Mucuripe

Mundo Latino Rua Ana Bilhar 507 ☎85/3242-8778, 🌐www.mundolatino.com.br. The breakfast room and communal area are not exactly alluring with their PVC-covered sofas, but staff are helpful and the a/c rooms are spacious. Internet facilities available, plus free wi-fi. R$100.

Pousada Arara Av. Aboliçao 3806, Mucuripe ☎85/3263-2277, 🌐www.hotelarara.com.br. A

friendly hotel in a safe setting, although it's on a main road so not too quiet. Rooms are clean and comfortable although the owners have a penchant for adorning their walls with tropical sunset prints. There's a nice enough pool at the back, as well as a little barbecue area. R$120.

Eating

Downtown, Praça do Ferreira offers a few por kilo *lanchonetes* (self-service cafeterias), and Iracema has a few good restaurants, while the Centro Dragão do Mar has at least seven pavement cafés overflowing with people having fun. The beaches all have a smattering of good restaurants as well as beach huts offering some of the best deals on seafood; the Centro Dragão do Mar is also a popular spot, particularly in the evenings, with plenty of pavement cafes full of youngsters having a good time.

Aldeota

Real Sucos Heráclito Graça 1709 ☎85/3244-3923; also at Shopping Aldeota ☎85/3458-1104 and Shopping Benfica ☎85/3281-4029. Chain serving excellent juices (R$4.50) and *açaí* with lots of sandwich options (R$8); the *cajú* juice is especially good.

Iracema

Santa Clara Café Orgânico Rua Dragão do Mar 81, Centro Dragão do Mar ☎85/3219-6900. Try the popular espresso (R$1.50) or sip on a frozen cappuccino (R$4) at Fortaleza's best coffee joint. Tues–Sun 3–10pm.

Sobre O Mar d'Iracema Rua dos Tremenbés 02, Praia de Iracema ☎85/3219-6999. This two-storey restaurant overlooking the Ponte dos Ingleses is a great place for a sunset seafood meal. Try the *peixada cearense* (fish stew cooked with vegetables; R$46 for two). Daily 9am–2am.

Tia Nair Rua Ildefonso Albano 68, Praia de Iracema ☎85/3219-1461, ⓦwww.saboresedelicias.com.br. Despite the menu's unappetizing photos, this seafront place has good food at great prices. A *mariscada* (seafood platter) for R$65 will feed three hungry bellies. Daily 11am–midnight, Fri & Sat until 1am.

Varanda Tropical Av. Monsenhor Tabosa 714, Praia de Iracema ☎85/3219-5195. Open-fronted restaurant on the main road where office workers swarm in on their lunch break for its good per kilo grub (R$18.90). Mon–Sat 11am–midnight, Sun 11am–4pm.

Meireles

Ponto do Guaraná Av. Beira Mar 3127-A, Meireles ☎85/3086-5650. *Guaraná* addicts should head here – there's plenty of flavours to choose from including lemon (R$2.50), *acerola* (R$2.90) and *açaí* (R$3.50). Sandwiches are also available (R$6). Daily 6.15am–9.45pm.

Mucuripe

Neide do Camarão Av. da Abolição 4772, ☎85/3248-2680. You buy your shrimp at the door (R$20 per kg), choose how you want it prepared, hand it to the waiter, then eat the crispy shrimp, shell and all, washed down with ice-cold beer. Local, authentic, and awesome. Mon–Fri 4–11.30pm, Sat & Sun 11am–11.30pm.

Sorveteria 50 sabores Av. Beira Mar 4690, Mucuripe ☎85/3263-1714. The fifty flavours of ice cream here change with the seasons, even if it feels like the weather never does. Try the plum or *maracujá* (R$8 for two huge scoops).

Varjota

Assis, O Rei da Picanha Rua Frederico Borges 505 ☎85/3267-4759. Relaxed local restaurant on a street corner which hums at lunchtime with peckish beachgoers. A *moqueca* (stew) will set you back R$11.99 while a fish dish costs R$17.99. Daily 11am–1am.

Colher de Pau Rua Frederico Borges 204 ☎85/3267-3773. A popular, family-run restaurant serving up local Cearense cuisine at reasonable prices, with plates you can share with a friend. Daily 11am–midnight.

Praia do Futuro

ΔTLΔⱯTDZ Av. Zezé Diogo 5581 ☎85/3249-4606. This polished tiki bar with the inexplicable pseudo-Greek motif has plenty of delicious fish options (R$34.99 for two), plus meat dishes to share (R$54.90) and pasta for those craving some comfort food (R$27.90). Daily 8am–6pm, until late on Thursdays.

Chico do Caranguejo Av. Zezé Diogo 4930 ☎85/3262-0108 ⓦwww.chicodocaranguejo .com.br. A chilled-out crab-house that sells the eponymous *caranguejo* for just R$3.49 per crab, as well as other good-value dishes (filet R$32.90 for two). There's live music on Saturdays and Sundays, as well as *forró* nights on Thursdays. Daily 8am–5pm, Thursdays until 1am.

Croco Beach Av. Zezé Diogo 3125 ☎85/3521-9600 ⓦwww.cocobeach.com.br. Probably Futuro's most popular beach restaurant, serving a bargain stingray stew to share (R$27.90) as well as plenty of meat dishes (R$48.90 for two). You can even get a massage as your food's being cooked. Daily 9am–5pm, Tues & Thurs until midnight, Sun until 7.30pm.

Drinking and nightlife

Fortaleza is justly famous for its *forró*. There's no better way to see what Cearenses do to have fun than to spend a night in a *dancetaria*. One of the busiest nightlife areas is the streets around the Ponte dos Ingleses. Most *dancetarias* open at 10pm, but they don't really get going until about midnight. Other nightlife is mainly out by the beaches: Meireles appeals to a broad cross-section of the local and tourist populations, whereas Iracema is slightly younger.

Armazém Av. Almirante Barroso 444, Praia de Iracema ☎85/3219-4322. This *forró* and house nightclub near the Centro Dragão complex draws a crowd who dress to impress. Inside, the lights flash, music pumps and the dancing goes on until late. Best on Wed for *forró*, house on Fri & Sat 10pm–4am. Entry R$15.

Kais Rua Dragão do Mar 92 ☎85/3219-7821. Bar-cum-restaurant right in the centre of Dragão's nightlife with plenty on offer for *cachaça*-lovers: ten premium beverages to pick from ranging R$22.50–48.50. There are salads (R$19.50), meat dishes (R$32,50) and pizzas (R$23.50) available to soak up the hard stuff. Open daily 7pm–3.30am.

Mucuripe Club Travessa Maranguape 108, Centro ☎85/3254-3020 ⓦwww.mucuripe .br. This large clubbing complex hosts some of the country's best DJs and is home to five different areas catering to all musical tastes, from samba to electronica. Fridays are best. Entry R$25. No flip-flops or shorts.

Órbita Bar Rua Dragão do Mar 207 ☎85/3453-1421, ⓦwww.orbitabar.com.br. Live Brazilian and international rock music followed by electronica beats at this studenty bar. Thurs–Sun from 9pm. Entry R$20.

Pirata Bar Rua dos Tabajaras 325 ☏ 85/4011-6161, ⓦ www.pirata.com.br. It's become a bit of a tourist trap – a Brazilian mag has even rated it as one of the 1001 places to see in the country before you die – but it promises to have "the craziest Monday in the world", with young locals dancing away to the beats of live bands. There's even a free *sopão da madrugada* ("dawn soup") served at 3am to re-energize the party until it ends in the wee hours. Entry R$30.

Directory

Banks and exchange There are a fair number of ATMs near the beaches and hotels with several HSBC locations: Rua Major Facundo 302, Centro; Av. Monsenhor Tabosa 1200, Praia da Iracema; Av. Santos Dumont 3581, Aldeota.

Embassies and consulates UK, British Honorary Consulate, Rua Leonardo Mota 501, Meireles (☏ 85/242-0888); US, Torre Santos Dumont, Avenida Santos Dumont 2828, Suite 708, Aldeota (☏ 85/486-1306).

Hospital Monte Klinikum Hospital, Rua República do Libano 747 (☏ 85/4012-0012, ⓦ www.monteklinikum.com.br).

Internet *Cyber Café*, in *Pousada Atalaia* (24/7; R$3 per hr); *Evolution Vídeo Cyber Café*, Av. da Abolição 3230, Meireles (R$4 per hr); *Cyber Café*, Av. da Abolição 2655, Meireles (R$4 per hr).

Laundry 5 à Sec, Rua Cel Jucá 470, Aldeota (☏ 85/3267-5034).

Pharmacies Farmácia Santa Branca, Av. da Universidade 3089, Benefica (☏ 85/3223-0000); Droga Nunes, Av. Sen Virgílio Távora 597, Meireles (☏ 85/3433-1818).

Police The tourist police are open 24/7 and can be found at Av. Almirante Barroso 805, Praia da Iracema (☏ 85/3101-2488).

Post office Av. Mons Tabosa 1561, Meireles (☏ 85/3248-1544; Mon–Fri 8am–5pm, Sat 8am–noon).

Moving on

Air TAM and Gol both fly several times a day to São Paulo, Rio, Brasília, Belem and Recife.

Bus To get to the *rodoviária*, catch bus with route card "Aeroporto" from Rua Gen. Sampaio by Praça José de Alencar. There are regular departures from the *rodoviária* to almost all parts of the Northeast, including Canoa Quebrada, Jericoacoara, João Pessoa, Natal, Recife, Salvador, as well as Rio and São Paulo.

Guanabara Express (ⓦ www.expressoguanabara.com.br) operates routes to several Northeast states; Viação Nordeste, (ⓦ www.viacaonordeste.com.br) go to Natal and João Pessoa; Redencão (ⓦ www.redencaoonline.com.br) to Brasilia. For Rio and São Paulo try São Geraldo (ⓦ www.saogeraldo.com.br), Itapemirim (ⓦ www.itapemirim.com.br) or Nossa Senhora da Penha (ⓦ www.nspenha.com.br).

The Amazon

The Amazon is a vast forest – the largest on the planet – and a giant river system, covering over half of Brazil and a large portion of South America. The forest extends into Venezuela, Colombia, Peru and Bolivia, where the river itself begins life among thousands of different headwaters. In Brazil only the stretch below Manaus, where the waters of the **Rio Solimões** and the **Rio Negro** meet, is actually known as the **Rio Amazonas**. The daily flow of the river is said to be enough to supply a city the size of New York with water for nearly ten years, and its power is such that the muddy

---

TRAVELLING BY BOAT IN THE AMAZON

The range of boat transport in the Amazon runs from luxury tourist vessels and large three-level riverboats to smaller one- or two-level boats and covered launches operated by tour companies. Prices are generally calculated per day, and include food: as a rule local boats are less expensive than tourist boats and launches. On longer journeys there are different classes; avoid *cabine*, sweltering cabins, and choose instead *primeiro* (first class), sleeping in a hammock on deck. *Segundo* (second class) is often hammock space in the lower deck or engine room. Bring provisions, and prepare to practise your Portuguese. The popular four- to six-day Belém–Manaus trip costs about R$240 (for *primeiro* hammock space).

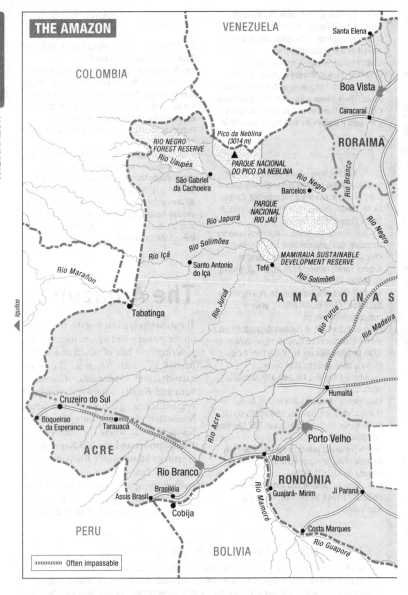

THE AMAZON

VENEZUELA

Santa Elena

COLOMBIA

Boa Vista

Caracaraí

RORAIMA

RIO NEGRO
FOREST RESERVE

Pico da Neblina
(3014 m)

Rio Uaupés

PARQUE NACIONAL
DO PICO DA NEBLINA

Rio Negro

Rio Branco

São Gabriel
da Cachoeira

Barcelos

Rio Negro

Rio Japurá

PARQUE
NACIONAL
RIO JAÚ

Rio Içá

Rio Solimões

MAMIRAUA SUSTAINABLE
DEVELOPMENT RESERVE

Rio Marañon

Santo Antonio
do Içá

Tefé

Rio Solimões

AMAZONAS

Iquitos

Rio Juruá

Rio Purus

Rio Madeira

Tabatinga

Humaitá

Cruzeiro do Sul

Boqueirao
da Esperanca

Tarauacá

Rio Acre

Porto Velho

ACRE

Abunã

RONDÔNIA

Rio Branco

Brasiléia

Guajará-Mirim

Ji Paraná

Assis Brasil

Cobija

Rio Mamoré

PERU

BOLIVIA

Costa Marques

Rio Guaporé

xxxxxxx Often impassable

Amazon waters stain the Atlantic a silty brown for over 200km out to sea.

BELÉM

Strategically placed on the Amazon River estuary, **BELÉM** was founded by the Portuguese in 1616 as the City of Our Lady of Bethlehem (Belém). Its original role was to protect the river mouth and establish the Portuguese claim to the region, but it rapidly became established as an Indian slaving

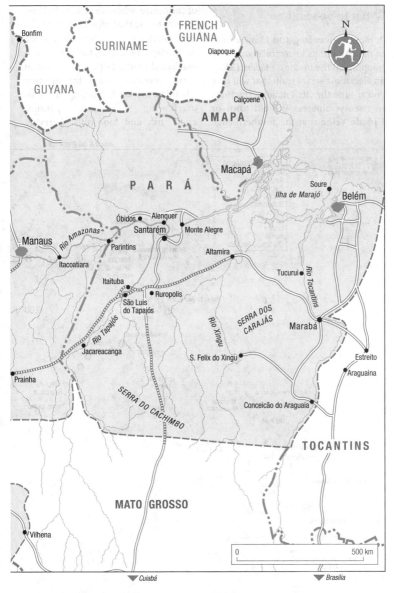

port and a source of cacao and spices from the Amazon. Belém prospered following the rubber boom at the end of the nineteenth century but suffered a disastrous decline after the crash of 1914 – it kept afloat, just about, on the back of Brazil nuts and the lumber industry. Nowadays, it remains the economic centre of northern Brazil, and the chief port for the Amazon. It is also a remarkably attractive place, with a fine colonial centre.

What to see and do

A pleasant way to get to know a little of the city and its historical sights is by hopping on the *Bonde do Belém* (R$1), an electronic steam train that will take you around the city's major attractions in twenty minutes. The old town or **Cidade Velha** is at the southern edge of the centre, where the Cathedral and fort sit around the Praça da Sé. Immediately north on the waterfront lies one of the city's highlights, the **Ver-o-Peso market**, the largest open-air market in Latin America – visit in the morning when the market is bustling, its stalls overflowing with spices, potions, crafts, fish and foodstuffs. Carrying

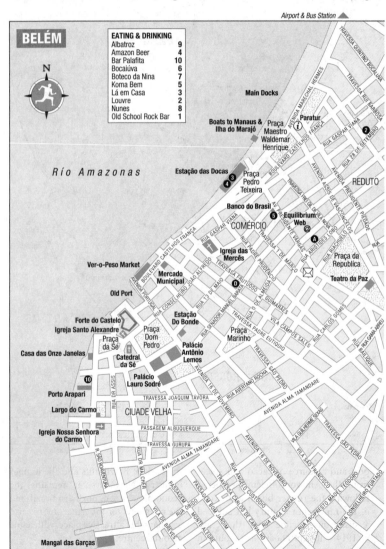

BELÉM

EATING & DRINKING	
Albatroz	9
Amazon Beer	4
Bar Palafita	10
Bocaiúva	6
Boteco da Nina	7
Koma Bem	5
Lá em Casa	3
Louvre	2
Nunes	8
Old School Rock Bar	1

Airport & Bus Station

Río Amazonas

Main Docks

Boats to Manaus & Ilha do Marajó — Praça Maestro Waldemar Henrique — Paratur

Estação das Docas — Praça Pedro Teixeira

REDUTO

Banco do Brasil

COMÉRCIO — Equilibrium Web

Ver-o-Peso Market

Igreja das Mercês

Praça da República

Mercado Municipal

Teatro da Paz

Old Port

Estação Do Bonde

Forte do Castelo
Igreja Santo Alexandre
Praça da Sé
Praça Dom Pedro
Palácio Antônio Lemos
Praça Marinho

Casa das Onze Janelas

Catedral da Sé

Palácio Lauro Sodré

Porto Arapari

Largo do Carmo — CIUADE VELHA

Igreja Nossa Senhora do Carmo

Mangal das Garças

on up the waterfront you reach the **Estação das Docas** cultural centre (Mon–Wed 10am–midnight, Thurs–Sat 10am–3am, Sun 9am–midnight) where some (rather pricey) *artesanato* stalls compete with numerous restaurants, cafés and exhibition spaces in a refurbished warehouse area.

Praça da Republica

Heading inland up Avenida Presidente Vargas, you reach the shady Praça da República, a popular place to stroll. The magnificent **Teatro da Paz** (Tues–Fri 9am–5pm, Sat 9am–1pm; R$4) faces the square. Built on the proceeds of the rubber boom in Neoclassical style, it is one of the city's

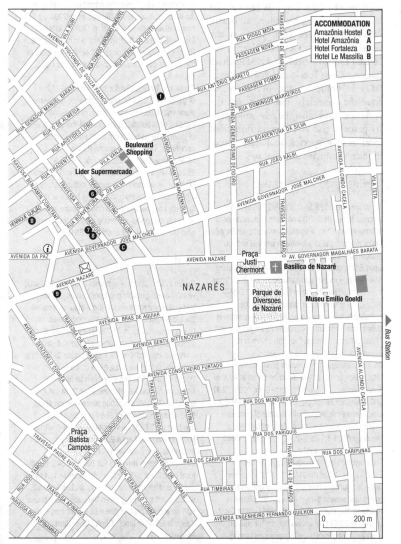

ACCOMMODATION

Amazônia Hostel	C
Hotel Amazônia	A
Hotel Fortaleza	D
Hotel Le Massilia	B

finest buildings; tickets for performances here are very good value.

Basílica de Nazaré and around

Fifteen minutes' walk from the theatre is the **Basílica de Nossa Senhora Nazaré** (daily 6am–7pm), supposedly inspired by St Peter's in Rome. It certainly has a wonderful interior, and is the focal point of the Cirio de Nazaré, the largest religious procession in Brazil, which takes place each year on the second Sunday of October. Nearby, the **Museu Emílio Goeldi** at Av. Magalhães Barata 376 (Tues–Sun 9am–4.30pm; R\$2) is home to one of the major scientific research institutes in the Amazon, and also hugely enjoyable. Its gardens and zoo contain dozens of local animal species, including spider monkeys, caimans and macaws.

Arrival and information

Air Belém Airport (☎91/3266-262) is 12km out of town. Buses (R\$5.60) from here with route card "Marex Arsenal" or "Perpétuo Socorro" pass by all major areas in the city centre. A taxi will set you back around R\$35.

Boat Boats dock on the river near the town centre.

Bus Belém's *rodoviária* is situated some 5km from the centre on Av. Almirante Barroso (☎91/3266-2625); any bus from the stops opposite the entrance to the *rodoviária* will take you downtown. Buses with route card "Canudos Praça Amazonas", "Arsenal" and "Tamoios" all stop at Praça da Republica and the Estaçao das Docas.

Tourist information Belémtur have plenty of information on the city and can be found at Av. Gov. José Malcher 257 (Mon–Fri 8am–6pm; ☎91/3230-3920, ⓦwww.belem.pa.gov.br), while the Paratur offices have information of the state of Pará as a whole and are by the Praça Maestro Waldemar Henrique (Mon–Fri 8am–2pm; ☎91/3212-0669, ⓦwww.paratur.pa.gov.br).

Tour operators Valeverde Turismo, in the Estaçao das Docas (☎91/3218-7333, ⓦwww.valeverdeturismo.com.br) organize good-value river tours around Belém. Amazon Star Turismo, Rua Henrique Gurjão 210 (☎91/3241-8624, 24/7 or 91/9982-7911, ⓦwww.amazonstar.com.br) is an excellent French-run agency specializing in ecotours, including visits to Icoaraci, Ilha Mosqueiro and Ilha de Marajó.

Accommodation

Amazônia Rua Ó de Almeida 548 ☎91/3222-8456, ⓦwww.amazoniahostel.com. Creaky wooden stairs will lead you to the top dorm of this little hostel with small simple rooms lacking in any form of decor. Good value. Dorms R\$13, rooms R\$40.

Amazônia Hostel Av. Gov. José Malcher 592 ☎91/4141-8833, ⓦwww.amazoniahostel.com.br. This spacious YHA-affiliated hostel has beautiful local timber floors, a kitchen, internet facilities, lockers, free wi-fi and a/c in all dorms. Rooms are clean and cosy, although the chairs in the lounge don't scream comfort. Dorms R\$35, rooms R\$76.

Fortaleza Travessa Frutuoso Guimaraes 276 ☎91/3212-1055. Pleasantly colourful, family-run place with lovely wooden floors, in a colonial building on a bustling backstreet of the centre of town. Take care at night as the area can be dangerous. Dorm R\$15, rooms R\$38.

Le Massilia Rua Henrique Gurjão 236 ☎91/3222-2834 ⓦwww.massilia.com.br. This more upmarket French-owned oasis of greenery within the city is a pleasant respite from the stifling heat and the hubbub; the pool alone is worth the extra splurge, although the rooms are pretty dark as they all give onto the shady interior courtyard. R\$135.

Eating

Belém boasts plenty of excellent cheap restaurants, which have especially good deals at lunchtime. You can also eat cheaply at the restaurants within the Lider Supermarket on Av. Visconde de Souza Franco, which is open 24/7. There's also excellent street food by the main docks, and good *tacacá* (shrimp soup) stalls on Av. Nazaré, close to Quintino Bocaiúva. In the evenings, head to the Estaçao das Docas where all places stay open till late.

Albatroz Av. Nazaré 194, corner of Dr Moraes ☎91/3223-8440. A bustling place with excellent food, and outside tables. Good selection of per kilo food (R\$24.99), all washed down well with a bottle of the local Cerpa (R\$2.50). Food served at lunchtime only. Daily 7am–11pm.

Boteco da Nina Travessa Rui Barbosa 946. Small local restaurant with some tables outside, run by smiley and friendly Katia. Always packed at lunch, which is not surprising given the unbeatable prices: R\$6 for a meat *prato* of the day. Dinner only served if food is left after lunch. Open 10am–3pm and 6pm–late.

Lá em Casa Estação das Docas ☎91/3212-5588. Locals rave about this place as it's reputedly the best for *paraense* (southern) nosh, with a buzzing atsmophere at all times of day. Lunchtime all-you-can-eat R$28, à la carte in the evenings. Sun–Wed noon–midnight, Fri & Sat noon–3am.

Nunes Travessa Rui Barbosa 974 ☎91/3083-9611. You can't get any more traditional than this – the owner has pretty much set up shop in his living room. Superb soups for a bargain R$2, while the *prato* of the day ranges from R$3.50 to R$5. Food only served at lunchtime, drinks only thereafter. Daily 11am–10pm.

Drinking and nightlife

Belem has some pretty upbeat nightlife. Even during the week you'll see plenty of people hanging out having drinks until late; you'll find many bars along Av. Almirante Wandekolk and in the Estação das Docas.

Amazon Beer In the Estação das Docas ☎91/3212-5401. Beer-lovers will be in heaven at this bar with an in-house brewery; try the Amazon Weiss for R$4.70. Mon–Fri 5pm–midnight, Sat & Sun 10am–midnight.

Bar Palafita Rua Siqueira Mendes 264, Cidade Velha ☎91/3224-3618 One of Belém's hidden little treasures: an atmospheric bar on stilts right on the Amazon River with truly incredible views, especially at sunset. There's great live music (R$5 cover) too, and if you're peckish you must try the exquisite crab soup (R$15). Daily noon–late.

Louvre Travessa Benjamin Constant 303, Reduto ☎91/3234-7943, ⊛www.louvreclub.com. Fridays and Saturdays are the big nights at this dance club playing electro. Tickets are R$30, if you buy them in advance (around 8pm), otherwise R$50. As ever, the night doesn't get going till at least after midnight. Fri & Sat 11pm–6am.

Directory

Banks and exchange There are plenty of banks on Av. Presidente Vargas, including Turvicam Cambio at 640, Banco do Brasil at 248, and HSBC at 800.

Hospital Hospital Guadalupe, Rua Arcipreste Manoel Teodoro 734 (☎91/4005-9877 or 9820).

Internet Equilibrium Web, Rua Ó de Almeida 533 (Mon–Fri 8am–9pm, Sat 8am-6pm; R$2.50 per hr) has flat-screen computers, excellent broadband connection and Skype; A.S. Net, Travessa Frutuoso Guimaraes 276 (in the same building as *Hotel Fortaleza*; Mon–Sat 8am–10pm,

Sun 8am–noon; R$1.50 per hr Mon–Fri, R$2 Sat & Sun) also has Skype.

Laundry Lav e Lev, Rua Doutor Moraes 576, Batista Campos (Mon–Sat 8am–6pm).

Post office The central post office (Mon–Fri 9am–5pm, Sat 9am–noon) is at Av. Presidente Vargas 498. However, as this is frequently crowded, it's often quicker to walk to the small post office at Av. Nazaré 319, three blocks beyond the Praça da República.

Shopping Belém is one of the best places in the world to buy hammocks (essential if you go upriver) – the best place is at the Ver-o-Peso market, where you can also buy beautiful local crafts.

Taxi Cooperdoca ☎91/3241-3555 or 3099; Cooperduque ☎91/3226-3300.

Telephones There are a number of cheap calling places on Av. Presidente Vargas between Rua Riachuelo and Travessa Ó de Almeida.

Tourist police Policia Militar do Estado do Para, Travessa Francisco Caldeira Castelo Branco 239 or 393 (☎91/3236-2122 or 2223); also at Travessa Castelo Branco 1029 (☎91/4006-9002 or 9037).

Moving on

Air There are daily flights from Belém to most major Brazilian cities, including Boa Vista and Manaus. There are also several flights a week to Fort de France (Martinique), Cayenne (French Guiana), Paramaribo (Suriname) and Georgetown (Guyana).

Boats The port is just east of the Estação das Docas; boats leave Belém for Santarém and Manaus Tues, Wed & Fri at 6pm; for Macapá on Wed, Thurs, Fri & Sat at 10am; for Ilha do Marajó Mon–Sat 6.30am & 2.30pm, Sun 10am. Amazon Star and Navio Rondonia have the most comfortable boats. Buy your ticket in one of the ticket booths in the departure lounge at the port and not off someone on the street.

Bus Connections from the *rodoviária*, 3km east of the centre (Praça do Operário; ☎91/246-8178) to Fortaleza (24hr; R$202), Recife (36hr; R$295), Brasília (33hr; R$235) and Belo Horizonte (43hr; R$396) with Transbrasiliana (⊛ww.transbrasiliana.com.br), Itapemirim (⊛www.itapemirim.com.br) and Expresso Guanabara (⊛www.expressoguanabara.com.br).

ILHA DO MARAJÓ

The **ILHA DO MARAJÓ** is a vast island in the Amazon delta, opposite Belém, consisting of some forty thousand square kilometres of largely uninhabited mangrove swamps and beaches.

Created by the accretion of silt and sand over millions of years, it's a wet and marshy area, the western half covered in thick jungle, the east flat savanna, swampy in the wet season (Jan–June), brown and firm in the dry season (June–Dec). It is home of the giant *pirarucu* fish, which, growing to over 180kg, is the largest freshwater breed in the world. The island is a popular resort for sun-seekers and ecotourists alike.

What to see and do

The main port of **Soure** is a growing resort offering pleasant beaches where you can relax under the shade of ancient mango trees. Magnificent empty **beaches** can be found all around the island – the **Praia do Pesqueiro**, about 13km from Soure, is one of the more accessible. If you want to see the interior of the island – or much of the wildlife – you have to be prepared to camp or pay for a room at one of the *fazendas*: book with travel agents in Belém or take your chance on arrival. **Joanes**, with another tremendous beach, is much quieter.

Island practicalities

Boats leave Belém Monday to Saturday at 6.30am and 2.30pm, and Sunday at 10am, returning 3pm (3hr 30min; R$15.70); there is also a faster ferry boat (Henvil ☏91/3247-0400; 2hr) that leaves at 6.30am and returns at 4pm. Boats dock at **Porto Camará**, about 30km from Soure, and Salvaterra, further south, about 26km away, from where you can grab a bus to any of the island's towns. A good **accommodation** choice is the beautiful French-owned *Pousada O Canto do Francês,* in Soure on Sexta Rua at the corner with Travessa 8 (☏91/3741-1298, ⓦwww .ocantodofrances.blogspot.com; R$100). Alternatively, in Salvaterra, you can stay at *Pousada e Camping* Boto (☏91/3765-1539, ⓦwww.pousada ventaniaboto.com.br; doubles R$94,

camping space R$30, hammocks R$20), where you can also organize a number of activities and excursions. It's wise to take some cash with you from Belém as there's only one ATM on the island. Both *Ponto Certo* (Quarta Rua between Travessa 15 and 16; mains R$5) and *Patú Anu* (Rua Segunda, corner of Travessa 14; R$12) in Soure serve excellent local food. In Salvaterra, head to Praia Grande, where these are cheap places to eat spread along the beach.

MACAPÁ AND THE ROAD TO FRENCH GUIANA

The main reason to pass through **MACAPÁ**, capital of the impoverished state of Amapá, on the north side of the Amazon across from Ilha do Marajó, is to get to French Guiana. You'll need to take a boat from Belém or fly to get here: the key road in the state then heads north, connecting Macapá with **Oiapoque**, on the river of the same name which delineates the frontier. The road isn't asphalted all the way, but mostly it's pretty good quality; Amazontur run regular buses to Oiapoque (daily at 2pm & 7pm; R$52; ☏96/3251-3435 or 96/9112-0892 ⓦwww.amazontur.com .br). These are scheduled to take around twelve hours, though the journey can be nearer twenty in the worst of the rainy season.

MANAUS

MANAUS is the capital of Amazonas, a tropical forest state covering around one-and-a-half million square kilometres. Manaus actually lies on the Rio Negro, six kilometres from the point where that river meets the Solimões to form (as far as Brazilians are concerned) the Rio Amazonas. Arriving in Manaus may at first seem overwhelming given its two million inhabitants, noise and confusion, but you will soon discover some of the city's pluses.

Towards the end of the nineteenth century, at the height of the rubber

ENTERING FRENCH GUIANA

If you are not a citizen of a European Union country, the USA or Canada, you will need a visa to enter French Guiana. There is a French consulate in Macapá at the *Pousada Ekinox*, Rua Jovina Dinoa 1693 (☎96/3223-7554), though it's better to arrange visas before you leave home. Buy euros at the Casa Francesa Turismo either in Belém (at the airport or at Travessa Padre Prudencio 40) or in Macapá (Rua Binga Uchoa 236); you can get them in Oiapoque but the rates are worse, and you can't depend on changing either Brazilian currency or US dollars for euros in Saint-Georges-de-l'Oyapok.

Dug-out taxis are the usual means of transport between Oiapoque and Saint-Georges-de-l'Oyapok (see p.758), about ten minutes downriver. Brazilian exit stamps can be obtained from the Polícia Federal at the southern road entrance into Oiapoque; on the other side you have to check in with the *gendarmes* in Saint-Georges.

Flights from Macapá to French Guiana ceased in 2008. Your only option is travelling in a pick-up 4x4. Most travellers, in fact, cross the border the easy way – by flying from Macapá to the capital at Cayenne (TAF Airlines, from around US$200). Otherwise, once you're across the border you'll probably want to fly from the border settlement of Saint-Georges to Cayenne in any case – or else catch a boat – since overland transport is atrocious.

boom, architects were summoned from Europe to redesign the city, which rapidly acquired a Western feel – broad Parisian-style avenues were laid down, interspersed with Italian piazzas centred on splendid fountains. Innovative Manaus was one of the first cities in Brazil to have electricity, trolley buses and sewage systems. However, by 1914 the rubber market was collapsing fast, yet preserving the glories of the past. Today, Manaus is thriving again: an aggressive commercial and industrial centre for an enormous region.

What to see and do

To start with the real flavour of Manaus, head for the riverfront and the **docks**, a constant throng of chaotic activity set against the serenity of the moored ships as they bob gently up and down. During the day there's no problem wandering around the area, and it's easy enough to find out which boats are going where just by asking around. At night, however, the port is best avoided: many of the river men carry guns.

Customs house and market

Known locally as the Alfândega, the **Customs House** (Mon–Fri 8am–noon & 2–4pm) stands overlooking the floating docks. To cope with the river rising over a 14m range, the concrete pier is supported on pontoons that rise and fall to allow even the largest ships to dock all year round. Across the main road from the port is the **Praça Adalberto Valle**, where there are several craft stalls selling indigenous Amazon tribal *artesanato*. The main **market**, the Mercado Municipal Adolfo Lisboa, is further round the riverfront. It is best visited early in the morning when freshly caught fish of all sizes are laid out on display; by afternoon, most merchants have closed shop.

Teatro Amazonas

The sumptuous **Teatro Amazonas** (Mon–Sat 9am–5pm; R$10 including guided tour; ☎92/3622-1880), inaugurated in 1896, is the most extreme example of Manaus's rubber boom: built with materials brought from Europe and entirely decorated by European artists. The Opera House

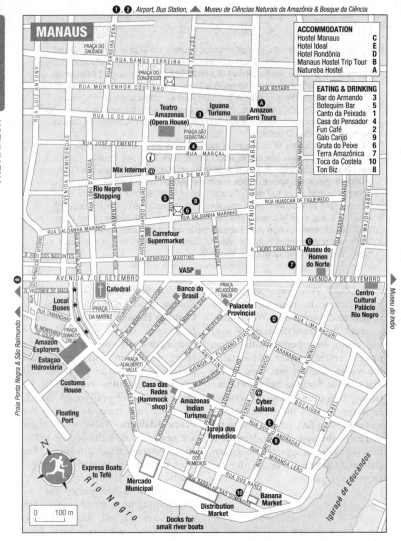

MANAUS

ACCOMMODATION
Hostel Manaus	C
Hotel Ideal	E
Hotel Rondônia	D
Manaus Hostel Trip Tour	B
Natureba Hostel	A

EATING & DRINKING
Bar do Armando	3
Botequim Bar	5
Canto da Peixada	1
Casa do Pensador	4
Fun Café	2
Galo Carijó	9
Gruta do Peixe	6
Terra Amazônica	7
Toca da Costela	10
Ton Biz	8

hosts regular concerts, including in April the **Festa da Manaus**, initiated in 1997 to celebrate thirty years of the Zona Franca.

The beautiful little **Igreja de São Sebastião**, on the same *praça*, was built in 1888 and only has one tower, the result of a nineteenth-century tax payable by churches with two towers.

Museu do Índio

The excellent **Museu do Índio**, at Rua Duque de Caxias 356 (Mon–Fri 8.30–11.30am & 2.30–4.30pm, Sat 8.30–11.30am; R$5), lies a little way east of the centre off Avenida Sete de Setembro. Run by the Salesian Sisters, who have long-established missions along the Rio Negro, especially with the Tukano tribe, it features excellent, carefully presented exhibits ranging from sacred ritual masks and inter-village communication drums to fine ceramics, superb palm-frond weavings and even replicas of Indian dwellings.

Palacete Provincial

Housed in the former military police headquarters, the Palacete Provincial on Praça Heliodoro Balbi (Tues–Thurs 9am–5pm, Fri & Sat 9am–8pm, Sun 4–9pm; free; ☎92/3622-8387, ⊛www .cultura.am.gov.br;) is a cultural and educational centre housing a number of curious museums and exhibition halls; amongst these are the Museum of Image and Sound, the Numismatic Museum and the Archeological Exhibition. The pleasant leafy square and the building itself are also worth checking out.

Museu de Ciências Naturais da Amazônia

The **Museu de Ciências Naturais da Amazônia** (Mon–Sat 9am–noon & 2–5pm; R$12; ☎92/3644-2799) on Estrada dos Japoneses s/n, Colcachoeira Grande, is an interesting little museum that's home to various well-preserved insects as well as some rare species of fish, including *piracuru*, the largest scaled freshwater fish in the world.

Bosque da Ciência

Occupying an area of approximately thirteen hectares, the **Bosque da Ciência** (Tues–Fri 9am–noon & 2–5pm, Sat & Sun 9am–5pm; R$5; ☎92/3643-3135) on Av. André Araújo 1756, Aleixo, is a plot of forest home to plenty of animals that roam freely within the area, such as monkeys and sloths. A fun way to see the park is with one of the *pequenos guias* (free), children who participate in environmental programmes and act as guides.

The meeting of the waters

The most popular and most widely touted day-trip from Manaus is to the

meeting of the waters, some 10km downstream, where the Rio Negro and the Rio Solimões meet to form the Rio Amazonas. For several kilometres beyond the point where they join, the waters of the two rivers continue to flow separately, the muddy yellow of the Solimões contrasting sharply with the black of the Rio Negro, which is much warmer, and more acidic. All tour operators organize day-trips (R$110 upwards; see p.342).

Parque Ecológico Janauary

Most tours to the meeting of the waters stop in at the **Parque Ecológico do Janauary**, an ecological park some 7km from Manaus on one of the main local tributaries of the Rio Negro. Usually you'll be transferred to smaller motorized canoes to explore its creeks (*igarapés*), flooded forest lands (*igapós*) and abundant vegetation. One of the highlights of the area is the great quantity of *Victoria Amazonica*, the extraordinary giant floating lily for which Manaus is famous, and which reaches a diameter of two metres.

Praia Ponta Negra

At weekends, the river beach at **Praia Ponta Negra**, about 13km northwest of Manaus, is packed with locals. It's an enjoyable place to go for a swim, with plenty of bars and restaurants serving freshly cooked river fish nearby. The bus to Ponta Negra (#120) leaves every half-hour; catch it by the cathedral on Praça da Matriz.

Arrival and information

Air The airport (Aeroporto de Eduardo Gomes; ☎92/3652-1212) is on Av. Santos Dumont, 17km north of town. It is served by bus #306 (first bus 5.30am, last bus 11.30pm; 40min); alternatively, take a taxi (R$50). Many tour operators will offer airport pick-up if you're booked with them; and Antônio Gomes (☎92/3234-1294) also offers airport pick-up.
Boat Boats dock right in the heart of the city, either by the Mercado Municipal or a short way along in the floating port. If you're arriving from Peru

or Colombia, don't forget to have your passport stamped at Customs House, if you haven't already done so in Tabatinga.

Bus The *rodoviária* is 7km north of the centre; numerous buses pass nearby heading into the centre (including #300, #301, #306, #500, #580 and #640); taxis cost around R$25.

Tourist information The tourist office is close to the back of the Opera House at Av. Eduardo Ribeira 666 (☎92/3182-6250, Mon–Fri 8am–6pm, Sat 8am–noon); it has helpful, friendly staff who can supply town maps. There is also a tourist office at the airport (☎92/3182-9850, daily 6am–midnight).

Accommodation

There is plenty of affordable accommodation in Manaus, albeit not too much choice in terms of hostels. It's best to avoid the *Hotel Dez de Julho* as there have been reports of theft.

🚶 **Hostel Manaus** Rua Lauro Cavalcante 231 ☎92/3233-4545, ⓦwww.hostelmanaus .com. Aussie-owned HI-affiliated hostel with firm comfortable dorm beds with lockers (some with a/c), lovely views of the Palácio Rio Negro from the breakfast table and an eccentric and eclectic bunch of staff. There's a laundry service, wi-fi, TV lounge

JUNGLE TRIPS FROM MANAUS

The nature and quantity of the wildlife you get to see on a standard jungle tour depends mainly on how far away from Manaus you go and how long you can devote to the trip. Birds like macaws, *jabarus* and toucans can generally be spotted, and you might see alligators, snakes and a few species of monkey on a three-day trip. For a reasonable chance of glimpsing wild deer, tapirs, armadillos or wild cats, a more adventurous trip of a week or more is required. On any trip, make sure that you'll get some time in the smaller channels in a canoe, as the sound of a motor is a sure way of scaring every living thing out of sight. The Rio Negro region has water with high acidity because of the geology of its main sources in the Guyana Shield. Because of the acid water, it tends to have fewer mosquitoes which is an obvious bonus; but it also tends to have less abundant wildlife than some of the lakes and channels around the Rio Solimões. Plenty of tours combine both the Solimões and Negro rivers in their itineraries.

Tour itineraries

The one-day river trip, usually costing around R$140 per person, generally includes an inspection of the famous meeting of the waters, some 10km downriver from Manaus (see p.344). The other most popular jungle river trips tend to be the three- to five-day expeditions. If you want to sleep in the forest, either in a lodge, riverboat or, for the more adventurous, swinging in a hammock outside in a small jungle clearing, it really is worth taking as many days as you can to get as far away from Manaus as possible. The usual price for guided tours, including accommodation and food, should be between R$100 and R$200 a day per person (no matter the sales pitch). As well as the itinerary, check that you're getting what you need in terms of security, health and safety, food, sleeping arrangements, guide quality and transfers.

The most commonly operated tours are three-day trips combining both the Rio Negro and Rio Solimões, although some trips only cover the former, as it is more accessible from Manaus. Four-day trips should ideally also include the Anavilhanas Archipelago on the Rio Negro, the second-largest freshwater archipelago in the world with around four hundred isles, as well as a good day's walk through the jungle. On the Solimões, some of the three- to five-day options include trips to Lago Mamori or Manacapuru.

If you want to forgo organized tours entirely and travel independently, note that milk boats are a very inexpensive way of getting about on the rivers around Manaus. The best place to look for these is down on Flutuante Três Estrelas, one of the wooden wharves behind the distribution market, further along the river edge from the Hidroviária (waterway) at the back of the Mercado Municipal.

and kitchen, and they can also organize tours. Dorms R$23, rooms R$55.

Ideal Rua dos Andradas 491 ☎ 92/3622-0038, ⓦ www.hotelidealmanaus.com.br. Not as ideal as the name might suggest, with dark rooms with no ventilation, most of which give onto the interior corridor. Ask for rooms 101, 201 or 301, which have a balcony and views over the Rio Negro. They also organize tours. R$46.

Manaus Hostel Trip Tour Rua Costa Azevedo 63 ☎ 92/3231-2139, ⓦ www.manaushostel.com.br. Pleasant bright-pink hostel with clean rooms and bathrooms, a little TV area, a kitchen for guests and internet facilities. Dorms R$20, rooms R$65.

Natureba Hostel ☎ 92/3233-1903, ⓦ www .naturebahostel.com. Under construction at the time of research, this new addition to town has male and female dorms sleeping four (R$30), six (R$26) and eight (R$20), as well as a large outdoor communal area. Best make sure you've got some spare change, however, as it's R$5 for hot showers, R$5 to iron and R$5 for use of hairdryer, but, on the upside, free drinking water and internet. R$70.

Rondônia Av. Joaquim Nabuco 703 ☎ 92/3234-5412. The windowless basement rooms here are rather prison-like, with spongy mattresses and creaky beds. The dorms on the ground floor are slightly better with some light coming through. Dorms R$20, rooms R$50.

Eating

There is plenty of cheap street food everywhere, especially around the docks, the Mercado Municipal and in busy downtown locations like the Praça da Matriz, where a plate of rice and beans with a skewer of freshly grilled meat or fish costs about R$5. One traditional dish you should definitely try here is *tacacá* – a soup that consists essentially of yellow manioc root juice in a hot, spicy dried-shrimp sauce. It's often mixed and served in traditional gourd bowls, *cuias*, and is usually sold in the late afternoons by *tacacazeiras*. There's a Carrefour supermarket on Av. Eduardo Ribeiro.

Galo Carijó Rua dos Andradas 536 ☎ 92/3233-0044. One of the best places for fresh fish with plenty of dishes to choose from – try the *pirarucu* (R$27 for two), the largest freshwater scaled fish in the world. Mon–Sat 10.30am–4pm.

Gruta do Peixe Rua Saldinha Marinho 609 ☎ 92/3234-2047. A fish-lover's paradise in a cave-like den (oddly divided with glass partitions) which keeps cool thanks to its location. R$19.90 per kg. Mon–Sat 11am–2pm.

Terra Amazônica Av. Joaquim Nabuco 887. Colombian-owned and family-run, this no-frills place has per kg food (R$16.99), a bargain *prato* (R$6) that changes daily, and Peruvian and Colombian dishes that can be cooked upon request. Live music in the summer on Fridays 5–11pm. Mon–Sat 6am–6.30pm, Fridays till 11pm.

Toca da Costela Rua Barão de São Domingos 268 ☎ 92/3622-0230. Only open at lunchtime and always packed, this is a great location from which to watch the daily mayhem of the banana market as you feast on superb meat and fish dishes. R$15.99 per kg. Daily 7am–5pm.

Drinking and nightlife

There are some good bars in the centre of town, but if you really want to get immersed in Manaus nightlife, the bulk of the action is on Estrada do Turismo, northwest of the city (taxi for four R$35), where bars line the Avenue. Alternatively, try Praça do Caranguejo in El Dorado (taxi R$23), also home to many bars and restaurants.

Bar do Armando Rua 10 de Julho 593 ☎ 92/3232-1195. This is where everyone heads for an ice-cold beer (R$4.50) after a tough day's work. Tables spill out onto the pavement and look onto the square and the Opera House. Mon–Sat 4pm–midnight.

Botequim Bar Rua Barroso 279 ☎ 92/3232-1030. Laidback bar with live music, mainly alternative rock and Brazilian pop, perfect to suss out Manaus's bar scene – either sit indoors or in the patio at the back. Thurs–Sat 7pm–3am.

Ton Biz Av. do Turismo 4004 ☎ 92/3239-0202. In a two-floor straw *cabanha* with bamboo motifs downstairs, this club attracts a chilled crowd who enjoy dancing to reggae sounds. On Thurs, Fri & Sun it's mainly *forró*, *ache* and *pagode*. Entry R$10.

Shopping

Artesanato is available from the Museu do Índio (p.340) and several shops around the square in front of the Teatro Amazonas. The best selection (and the most fun way to shop) is at the Sunday morning street market that appears out of nowhere in the broad Avenida Eduardo Ribeira, behind the Teatro Amazonas. Indian crafts are also sold at the Mercado Municipal (under renovation at the time of research) and *artesanato* (including handmade jewellery) at the stalls on Praça Terreira Aranha. Interesting *macumba* and *umbanda* items, such as incense, candles, figurines and bongos, can be found at Cabana São Jorge at Rua da Instalação 36 and at Cabana Pomba Gira on Rocha dos Santos 92, corner of Rua Miranda. A good hammock shop is Casa das Redes on Rua dos Andradas.

Directory

Banks and exchange There are several banks on Av. Eduardo Ribeiro, just a block or two down the street from the tourist office.

Consulates Chile, Rua Marquês de Caravelas, casa 08, Parque das Laranjeiras (⌾92/3236-6888); Colombia, Rua 24 de Maio 220, Ed. Rio Negro Centre, Centro (⌾92/3234-6777); UK, Rua Poraquê 240 (⌾92/6132-1819); Ecuador, Rua 6 n.16, Conj. Jardim Belo Horizonte, Parque 10 (⌾92/3236-3698); Venezuela, Rua Rio Jutaí 839 Vieiralves (⌾92/3584-3828).

Health For tropical complaints the best is the Instituto de Medicina Tropical, Avenida Pedro Teixeira 25 (⌾92/3238-2801). The Drogueria Nossa Senhora de Nazaré, 7 de Setembro 1333 (⌾92/3215-2844) is a well-stocked pharmacy.

Internet Cyber Juliana, Corner of Av. Joaquim Nabuco & C. Bocaiúva (Mon–Sat 8am–11pm, Sun noon–11pm; R$2 per hr), is air-conditioned and has a good connection; Mix Internet, Rua 24 de Mayo 345 (Mon–Fri 8.30am–7pm, Sat 9am–2pm; R$2 per hr).

Police The tourist police are in the same building as the tourist office, Av. Eduardo Ribeiro 1000 (Mon–Fri 8am–6pm, Sat 8am–noon; ⌾92/3233-0739), and also at the airport (Mon–Fri 8am–6pm; ⌾92/3652-1656).

Post office Rua Monsenhor Coutinho 90, by Praça do Congresso; Rua Barroso 226, corner of Rua Saldanha Marinho (both Mon–Fri 8am–4pm, Sat 8am–noon).

Taxis Amazonas Rádio Taxi ⌾0800/280-8228 or 92/3658-5888; Executivo Rádio Taxi ⌾92/3633-5000; Tucuxi Rádio Taxi ⌾92/2123-9090.

Moving on

Air To get to the airport, catch bus #306 (every 30min; R$2.85) from the terminal in front of the floating harbour. Alternatively, the executive red and white minibus #813 (R$3) can be taken from any bus stop in the centre and will drop you off at the airport. TAM and Trip operate domestic flights from Manaus's Eduardo Gomes Airport to numerous destinations, including Boa Vista (2 daily), Santarem (2 daily), Belém (4 daily), Rio (2 daily), São Paulo (3 daily), Fortaleza (2 daily) and Miami (1 daily). Trip also flies to São Gabriel da Cachoeira.

Bus To get to the *rodoviária* catch bus 205, 209, 311, 315, 440, 449 or 452 from the Terminal Central opposite the port. EUCATUR buses depart Manaus for Boa Vista daily at 10am, 6pm, 7pm, 8pm & 11pm (16hr; ⌾92/3301-5800); the 6pm and 7pm are direct, and the first continues to Porto La Cruz in Venezuela (34hr. For Santa Elena, grab a taxi from Boa Vista's *rodoviária* – it's actually cheaper and less time-consuming than the bus (2hr 30min; R$25) as there are plenty of drivers keen to fill up with cheap fuel in Venezuela. All tourists going to Venezuela must have a yellow-fever vaccination card to buy their tickets – you can get the injection and card at the *rodoviária* or at the main floating harbour for free.

Boat There are regular passenger boat services to Belém (4 days; Wed & Fri), Santarém and all ports along the Amazon (36hr; daily except Sun); along the Rio Solimões to Tabatinga (7 days; Wed & Sat); and up the Rio Madeira to Porto Velho (4 days; Tues & Fri). Tanaka has boats heading up the Rio Negro to São Gabriel da Cachoeira (3 days) every Friday at 6pm; there is also an express boat leaving Fridays at 3pm (26hr). In the express boat you have to sit

---

RIVERBOAT PRACTICALITIES

Tickets for the regular services on the Amazon (see p.331) can be bought from the ticket windows inside the port building off Praça da Matriz, next to where the boat departure list is posted. Before buying your ticket, ask for a **pass** (*papel do permissão*), which allows you into the docks (you'll need your passport, too) where the bigger, long-distance riverboats are moored; here you can have a look at the boats before deciding which you want to travel on. It's sensible to buy tickets in advance, for which you can often get a reasonable discount, and always to get on your boat at least two hours before it's due to depart to secure a decent berth. Make sure you ask if the ticket price includes meals.

Standard boats from Manaus to Belém **cost** around R$260 and take three to five days, often stopping off in Santarém. Smaller boats with no regular schedules are found in São Raimundo, ten minutes out of town. Their destinations are usually marked on signboards. For a fast boat to Tefé, it's best to take the fast Lancha Ajato (13hr; R$190; ⌾92/9984-9091) from near the Mercado Municipal.

upright in your seat for the whole journey – many end up sleeping in the aisle. With all boat journeys, make sure you ask how long the previous journey took as boat durations can change depending on the height of the river (and may end up lasting much longer than planned).

THE RIO SOLIMÕES: CROSSING TO PERU AND COLOMBIA

From Manaus to **Iquitos** in Peru (see p.899), the river remains navigable by large ocean-going boats as well as the occasional smaller, more locally oriented riverboats. In spite of the discomforts, such as long delays and frequently broken-down boats, travellers still use this route as it's the cheapest way of travelling between Brazil and Peru.

There are reasonable facilities for visitors in the border town of **Tabatinga**, though most people prefer to stay in the adjacent Colombian town of **Leticia** (see p.611). All boats have to stop at one of these ports, and most will terminate at the border, whichever direction they've come from. If you want to break the journey, you can do so at **Tefé**, around halfway; but the main reason to call here is to visit the **Mamiraua Sustainable Development Reserve**, an accessible, beautiful and wild area of rainforest upstream from the town. Entering the reserve is pricey though – a three-day pass costs R$1200. Another reason for stopping here might be that you really can't face the boat journey any longer: there are several flights a week from Tefé to Manaus and Tabatinga. There's also an express boat service (13hr; US$40) connecting Tefé with Manaus.

River practicalities

The boat trip from **Manaus to Tabatinga** – five to seven days upstream – leaves twice a week (Wed & Sat) and costs around R$340 inclusive of food (though bring some treats as the food

on board, though good, does get a bit monotonous). There's also a fast *lancha* (speedboat) leaving on Tuesdays at 7am (2 days; R$420). The downstream journey, which is often very crowded, takes three to four days and costs upwards of R$250. On the other side of the border, there are super-fast powerboats connecting **Tabatinga to Iquitos** (10hr; around US$50). Small planes also connect Iquitos with Santa Rosa, an insignificant Peruvian border settlement just a short boat ride over the river from Tabatinga and Leticia; there is at least one flight a week operated by the Peruvian airline TANS.

Brasília

In the savanna-like *cerrado* of the Brazilian highlands, almost 1000km northwest of Rio, **BRASÍLIA** is the largest and most fascinating of the world's "planned cities". Declared capital in 1960 and a UNESCO World Heritage Site in 1995, the futuristic city was the vision of **Juscelino Kubitschek**, who realized his election promise to build it if elected president in 1956. Designed by **Oscar Niemeyer**, South America's most able student of Le Corbusier, it is located in its own federal zone – Brasília D.F. (Distrito Federal) – in the centre of Goiás state.

Intended for a population of half a million by 2000, today the city is Brazil's fastest-growing, with 2.5 million inhabitants. At first glance the gleaming government buildings and excellent roads give you the impression that this is the modern heart of a new world superpower. Look closer and you'll see cracks in the concrete structures; drive ten minutes in any direction and you'll hit miles of low-income housing in the *cidades satellites* (poorer satellite cities). This is a city of diplomats, students,

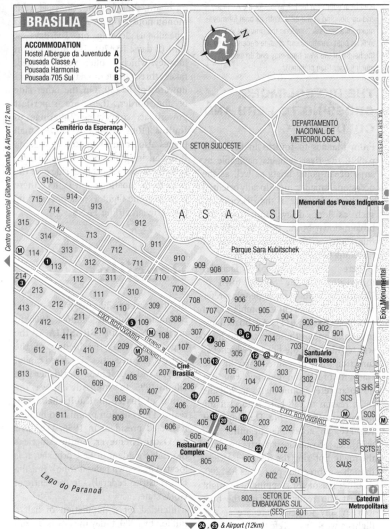

▲ Stadium

BRASÍLIA

ACCOMMODATION
Hostel Albergue da Juventude	A
Pousada Classe A	D
Pousada Harmonia	C
Pousada 705 Sul	B

Centro Commercial Gilberto Salomão & Airport (12 km)

Cemitério da Esperança

DEPARTAMENTO NACIONAL DE METEOROLOGICA

SETOR SUDOESTE

A S A   S U L

Memorial dos Povos Indígenas

Parque Sara Kubitschek

Ciné Brasília

Santuário Dom Bosco

Restaurant Complex

Lago do Paranoá

SETOR DE EMBAIXADAS SUL (SES)

Catedral Metropolitana

▼ 24 , 25 & Airport (12km)

government workers and the people who serve them. Prices are high. Still, there are beautiful sunsets, two or three days' worth of things to see, and exuberant bars and restaurants.

What to see and do

Brasília's layout was designed to resemble an airplane (some say a bird, others a bow and arrow). At its centre is a sloped, grassy plain and two central traffic arteries, the **Eixo Monumental** (north/south) and the **Eixo Rodoviário** or **Eixão** (east/west), which neatly divide the centre into sectors: administrative, shopping, banking, commercial and embassy. These are the treeless (and thus shadeless) parts of Brasília where you can actually walk, and which contain many of the

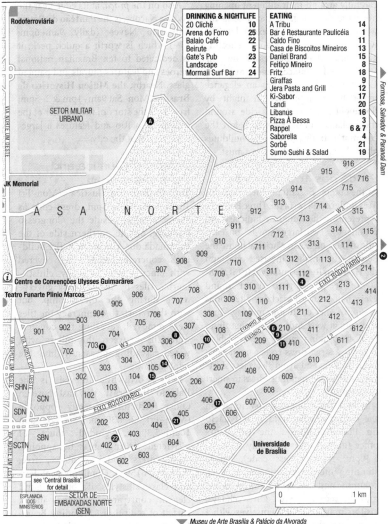

▲ Parque Nacional de Brasília

DRINKING & NIGHTLIFE
20 Clichê	10
Arena do Forro	25
Balaio Café	22
Beirute	5
Gate's Pub	23
Landscape	2
Mormaii Surf Bar	24

EATING
A Tribu	14
Bar é Restaurante Paulicéia	1
Caldo Fino	11
Casa de Biscoitos Mineiros	13
Daniel Brand	15
Feitiço Mineiro	8
Fritz	18
Giraffas	9
Jera Pasta and Grill	12
Ki-Sabor	17
Landi	20
Libanus	16
Pizza À Bessa	3
Rappel	6 & 7
Saborella	4
Sorbê	21
Sumo Sushi & Salad	19

▼ Museu de Arte Brasília & Palácio da Alvorada

sights. North and south of the centre are self-contained **residential areas** – each with its own shopping, restaurants and nightlife. It's easy to burn cash on taxis in Brasília because the city is designed for the car but further out in the city's wings you'll be rewarded by better and cheaper food; pick an area with several restaurants and bars, take a bus there and walk between *quadras* (blocks).

Esplanada dos Ministérios

The heart of Brasília, and its *raison d'être*, is the government complex known as the **Esplanada dos Ministérios**, focused on the iconic 28-storey twin towers of the **Congresso Nacional**, the Congress building (the nose of the plane or the bird's "beak"). The buildings here, designed by Niemeyer, can all be seen in a day for free (though you'll need to plan carefully around their different opening hours) and are regarded as among the world's finest modernist examples. The white marble, water pools, reflecting glass and flying buttresses on the **Presidential Palace** and **Supreme Court** lend the buildings an elegance made more impressive at night by floodlights. A taxi or bus ride around the Esplanada in the evening before the commuter traffic, when the buildings glow like Chinese lanterns, is a must.

Praça dos Três Poderes

At the complex's centre is the **Praça dos Três Poderes** (Plaza of the Three Powers), representing the Congress, judiciary and presidency. Two large "bowls" on each side of the Congresso Nacional house the **Senate** (the smaller, inverted one) and the **House of Representatives** (☏61/318-5092). Free guided tours depart around every half-hour on weekday afternoons (1–5pm) and at 10am, midday, 2pm and 4pm at weekends (ask at what times English-speaking guides are available). There is a strict dress code – men must wear trousers and avoid sleeveless shirts and sandals; women must dress in smart casual attire.

Behind the Congresso Nacional on the *praça*'s northern side, the **Palácio do Planalto** houses the president's office (guided tours Sun only 9.30am–1.30pm; formal dress code), whose stunning interior is dominated by sleek columns and a curving ramp down into the reception area. On weekdays, visitors must content themselves with a changing of the guard out front (daily at 8.30am & 5.30pm).

Also on the *praça*, at its edge near the Av. das Naçoes, is the **Panteão da Pátria Tancredo Neves** (daily 9am–6pm; free) which is worth a quick peek; it is dedicated to ten Brazilian national heroes and features murals and painted glass. Nearby, the **Museu Histórico de Brasília** (Mon–Sat 9am–1pm & 2–5pm; free) tells the story of the transfer of the capital from Rio and features a large-scale model of the city.

Palácio da Justiça and Palácio Itamarati

The **Palácio da Justiça** (Mon–Fri 10am–noon & 3–5pm; dress code as above; free) is beside the Congresso building, on the northern side of the Esplanada dos Ministerios. The building's concrete facade was covered with fancy – and, to many, elitist – marble tiles by the military government during the dictatorship, but with the return to democracy the tiles were removed, revealing the concrete waterfalls between the pillars with water cascading pleasantly into the pools below.

More worthwhile to visit is the **Palácio Itamarati**, the vast Foreign Office structure directly opposite (Mon–Fri 2–4.30pm, Sat & Sun 10am–3.30pm, guided tours of restricted visiting areas by appointment, dress code as above; free; ☏61/411-6159;). Combining modern and classical styles, it's built around elegant courtyards, gardens, and a surfeit of sculptures, including Bruno Giorgi's stunning marble *Meteor*. Inside, the building's spaciousness, set off by modern art and wall hangings, is breathtaking.

Catedral Metropolitana and the Museu Nacional

Between the ministries and the downtown *rodoviária* (within walking distance of either), the striking **Catedral Metropolitana Nossa Senhora Aparecida** (daily 7am–6.30pm; no shorts allowed) marks the spot where the city was inaugurated in 1960. Built in the form of an inverted chalice and crown of thorns, its sunken nave puts most of the interior floor below ground level. It's well lit, though, and the statues of St Peter and the angels suspended from the ceiling combine to create a feeling of airiness and elevation.

Just to the north, also on the Esplanada, the domed **Museu Nacional** Honestino Guimãraes (Tues–Sun 9am–6.30pm; free), with its suspended curved walkway, looks something like a crashed, white Saturn half-submerged in concrete, and houses art exhibitions.

Teatro Nacional

Heading up towards the *rodoviária*, on the northern side of the Eixo Monumental, you'll reach the **Teatro Nacional** (Mon–Fri 3–5pm). Built in the form of an Aztec temple, it's a largely glass-covered pyramid angled to allow light into the lobby, where there are often art exhibitions. Inside are three halls: Martins Pena, Villa-Lobos (the largest) and the smaller Alberto Nepomuceno. Most productions are in Portuguese, but the venues are also used for **concerts** by Brasília's symphony orchestra and pop stars.

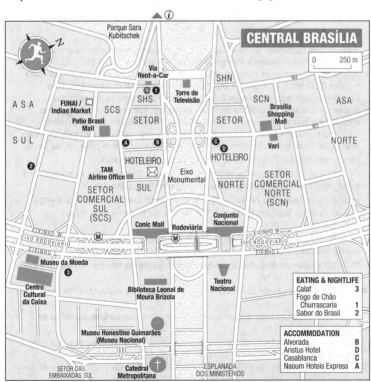

Torre de Televisão

The landmark TV Tower, the **Torre de Televisão**, makes a good place to start a city exploration, 1km north of the *rodoviária* (easily reached on foot or by bus #131). The viewing platform (Tues–Sun 9am–9pm; R$2) atop the 218m-high tower puts Brasília into perspective, and there's no better spot to watch the sunset. On weekends the base of the tower is popular for its craft market – great for clothing and souvenirs.

JK Memorial and Memorial dos Povos Indígenas

For the **Juscelino Kubitschek (JK) Memorial** (Tues–Sun 9am–5.45pm; R$6), another 1.5km further out on the Eixo Monumental, you'll need to take the bus – dozens head up in this direction. Here, a Soviet-like statue of Brasília's founder stands inside a giant question mark, pointing towards the heart of government. The museum has many personal mementos and books of Kubitschek, the extraordinary force behind much of Brazil's twentieth-century development, and features a fascinating display on the construction of the city. JK himself lies in state in a black marble sarcophagus, backlit by purple, violet and orange lights.

Across the road is another Niemeyer building, the **Memorial dos Povos Indígenas** (Tues–Fri 10am–4pm; R$2), which houses a good collection of Brazilian indigenous art, much of it from the inhabitants of the surrounding *planalto* and the headwaters of the Xingú River. Highlights are the ceramic pots of the Warao, beautifully adorned with figures of birds and animals, and vivid,

---

CRACKING THE ADDRESS CODES

While initially confusing, Brasília's address system does eventually make finding places easier than in cities with named streets. For example: SQN 210, Bloco B – 503, means *superquadra* north no. 210, building B, apartment 503. The *superquadra* number (210) is the location, the first digit the direction east or west of the Eixo Rodoviário, with odd numbers to the west and even numbers to the east; the numbers increase as you get further from the centre. The final two digits give the distance north or south of the Eixo Monumental. The logic also applies to roads: even numbers apply east of the Eixão, odd to the west; a letter in front indicates the side of the Eixão it runs, eg L for east (*leste*) or W for west. Some other helpful terms:

Asa Norte/Asa Sul The city's two "wings" (*asas*), north and south.

CLN/CLS or **SCLN/SCLS** *Comércio Local Norte/Sul*. Shopping blocks interspersed throughout the residential *superquadras* of Asa Norte and Asa Sul.

EQN/EQS *Entrequadras Norte/Sul*. The area between *quadras* at Eixinhos's edge.

SBN/SBS *Setor Bancário Norte/Sul*. Two bank districts, either side of Eixo Monumental.

SCN/SCS *Setor Comercial Norte/Sul*. Two commercial office areas set back from the shopping centres.

SDN/SDS *Setor de Diversões Norte/Sul*. Two shopping centres (*conjuntos*) on either side of Eixo Monumental.

SEN/SES *Setor de Embaixadas Norte/Sul*. The embassy areas east of the bank sectors.

SHIN/SHIS *Setor de Habitações Individuais Norte/Sul*. Two peninsulas jutting into Lago Paranoá.

SQN/SQS or **SHCN/SHCS** *Superquadras Norte/Sul*. Individual *superquadras* in the residential wings Asa Norte and Asa Sul.

ESCAPING THE CITY

If you sicken of all the concrete, visit the Sarah Kubitschek National Park, sprawling west of the TV Tower, which has ponds and walking trails for a quick and easy escape. There are more parks and gardens on the outskirts of the city, and some wilder natural attractions a little further out require renting a car. Entrance to most places is free, but there is occasionally R$3 fees.

Botanical Garden Setor de Mansões Dom Bosco, Module 12 (entrance by QI-23 of South Lake) ☎61/3366-3007. Gardens with more than 100 species of native herbs, a 9km taxi-ride (R$25) southwest of the city centre. Tues–Sun 8.30am–5.30pm; free.

Brasília Nacional Park EPIA Highway, North Exit ☎61/465-2016. Trails and two swimming pools with running mineral water, about 6km northwest of the city centre. Take bus #128 from the *rodoviária*. Daily 8am–4pm; free.

Chapada Imperial ☎61/9984-4437, ⊛www.chapadaimperial.com.br. Locals rave about spending weekends camping at this park, which has walking trails and more than thirty natural waterfalls. It's about 50km from the city so renting a car is your best bet.

Goiás Velho One of the prettiest colonial towns in all Brazil, entirely unhurried and surrounded almost completely by steep hillsides. Two buses per day operate the 6-hr route from the *rodoviária* in Brasília. A night or two's stay in a pousada to take in the streets, museums and hiking trails here is well worth the effort.

Jardim Zoológico de Brasília Avenida das Nações, South Exit, Via L4 Sul ☎61/245-5003, ⊛www.zoo.df.gov.br. The zoo has more than 250 species of birds, reptiles and mammals. Take one of the buses running along Av. das Nações. Tues–Sun 9am–5pm; R$2.

Olhos d'Água Park Asa Norte, entrance by Bloco 414 ☎61/340-3777. Trails and playgrounds at this park within the residential wing. Take one of the buses running along Eixo Rodoviária Norte to Bloco 213 and walk one block to the park. Daily 6am–7pm; free.

Pirenópolis In the Serra dos Pireneus mountains, a 5-hr drive from Brasília (regular buses ply the route). This attractive market town is a popular weekend retreat with cobbled streets, pousadas, river swimming, and numerous arts, crafts and hippy/alternative-lifestyle stores.

Pontão Lago Sul The beautiful people come to this lakeside area to eat, drink and be seen. They've got the right idea. Walk along the lake and check out the JK Bridge, a series of spectacular modernist arcs. There's no bus so take a taxi (20min; R$40); a line of waiting cabs are there for your return.

---

delicate featherwork. The gallery is set in a long curve around a circular courtyard, the smoked glass set against Niemeyer's trademark white exterior. Opening hours here are sporadic; if the main entrance at the top of the ramp is shut, go to the right of the ramp on ground level and bang hard on the large metal door for security to let you in – it's worth it.

Palácio da Alvorada

To complete your Niemeyer tour take a short taxi or bus ride to the president's official residence, the **Palácio da Alvorada**, about 3km away by the banks of Lake Paranoá (bus #104 from Platform A at the *rodoviária*). Some consider this building, with its brilliant-white exterior nestled behind an emerald-green lawn and carefully sculpted gardens, to be Niemeyer's most beautiful – note the distinctive slender buttresses and blue-tinted glass. If you go by taxi, make sure it waits for you.

Santuário Dom Bosco

Brasília attracts cults and New Agers of all sorts. One of the prime reasons for this is that in 1883 the canonized Italian priest **Don Bosco**, founder of the Salesians, foresaw the appearance of a "great civilization" here between "Parallels 15º and 20º South". Even if the doors of perception thing isn't for you, the **Don Bosco Sanctuary** (easily walkable at W-3 South, Bloco 702; Mon–Sat 7am–7pm), built to honour him, is worth visiting for the atmosphere created by brilliant blue floor-to-ceiling stained glass.

Arrival and information

Air Aeroporto Internacional de Brasília – Presidente Juscelino Kubitschek is about 12km south of the city. Bus #102 runs from the airport to the downtown *rodoviária*, hourly (R$3.50). A taxi from the airport to the hotel sector costs around R$45.

Bus Long-distance buses arrive at the *rodoferroviária* (where there's no longer a train station), at the tail of the Eixo Monumental. From here bus #131 runs down the Eixo to the city centre *rodoviária*.

Tourist information The official Brasíliatur (☎61/3322-6611, ⊛www.brasiliatur.com.br) office is located north of the TV Tower on the second floor of the enormous *Centro de Convenções Ulysses Guimarães* (entrance on northern side) – they're friendly and helpful. At the airport the first-floor office (at departures) is more helpful than that on the arrivals floor, and has free maps. Pick up the daily *Correio Brasiliense* newspaper, with its daily listings supplement on films, exhibitions and live music.

City transport

Bus City buses are based at the downtown *rodoviária*. Useful services include the #131, which goes up Eixo Monumental past the TV Tower and JK Memorial to the *rodoferroviária*, and #108 and #104, which run frequently past the Museu Nacional, cathedral, ministries, Praça dos Tres Poderes, Congresso Nacional, Palácio do Planalto and the Supremo Tribunal Federal.

Car Lúcio Costa didn't seem to design the city's layout with stoplights in mind; the incredible rush hour traffic and getting the hang of roundabouts and tunnels may make renting a car more trouble than it's worth. If you do drive, take care, as there are speed cameras everywhere.

Metro Unless you're planning on going to one of the satellite cities (Guarái, Águas Claras, Samambaia, Taguatinga or Ceilándia) the metro (R$2.30) is only useful for getting to the end of Asa Sul. Starting from the *rodoviária* there are seven city stops.

Taxi Metered and expensive (especially at night and on Sundays); expect to pay R$15–20 for quick trips and R$30 wing to wing.

Accommodation

The centrally located hostels you'll find everywhere else in Brazil must be making up for the lack of them in the capital. The hotel sectors are aimed at diplomats and expense accounts, though some do offer good discounts at weekends (be sure to ask). In general, the taller the hotel, the more expensive, so go for the squat, ugly ones. The more reasonably priced (though often of poor quality or even semi-legal) pousadas are located in the wings.

Hotels

Alvorada SHS Q.4 ☎61/3222-7068, ⊛www.alvoradahotel.com.br. One of the cheapest central options, a little faded but good value for the area. Can be noisy. R$180.

Aristus Hotel SHN Quadra 2, Bloco O ☎61/3328-8675, ⊛www.aristushotel.com.br. Small, clean rooms with awkwardly mounted TVs, 1970s design and paintings of boats in the hallways. R$190.

Naoum Hoteis Express SHS Quadra 03, Bloco J ☎61/3212-4545, ⊛www.naoumplaza.com.br. A very good deal, proving that low-rise is the way to go: friendly staff, luxurious rooms, breakfast included. R$200.

CLAIMING THE RIGHT OF WAY

Brasília has many cars, few traffic lights and an endless number of roundabouts. At most road crossings you'll see a yellow sign on the asphalt near the curb depicting an outstretched hand with the words, "*Dê sinal de vida*", a prompt to claim right of way. If you see approaching cars a fair distance away do as the locals do and raise your hand with authority. As long as you don't do it at the last second drivers are well trained to cede the road to you. Trying this elsewhere in Brazil may be your last act.

Hostel and pousadas

Hostel Albergue da Juventude SRPN Quadra 2, Lt. 2, Camping de Brasília ☎61/3343-0531, ⓦ www.brasiliahostel.com.br. A bit of a trek from town (bus #143) but this HI hostel is Brasília's only decent budget accommodation; book well in advance. Dorms R$52, rooms R$100.

Pousada Classe A SCLRN 703, Bloco H, Entrada 56 ☎61/3327-3339. The cleanest pousada in Asa Norte, just off the W3. Yellow-curtained rooms are crisp if bare. R$90.

Pousada Harmonia W3 Sul, Quadra 705, Bloco A, Casa 3 ☎61/3443-6527. This pousada has a good atmosphere and its own attached barbershop as well as gated parking; rooms have cots and fans. R$110.

Pousada 705 Sul Bloco M, Casa 184 ☎61/3244-6672. Marginally better than surrounding "low-budget" options, there's no breakfast served here but rooms are reasonably spacious and the place clean. R$80.

Eating

There's a concentration of good restaurants in Brasília, though they're certainly pricey. Eating and drinking is often done in tandem, with restaurants open until at least midnight. Asa Sul is especially popular, peppered with places ranging from Mexican and Chinese to Italian or fondue; good areas are around 206/205, 204/203 and 405/404. Most places close on Monday night, not Sunday.

Restaurants

A Tribu 105 Norte. Excellent vegetarian food including a *por kilo* buffet Tues–Sun lunch, with a couple of fish/meat options thrown in. Expect to pay around R$20 including a fresh juice.

Bar é Restaurante Paulicéia CLS 113, Bloco A, Loja 20 ☎61/3245-3031. A cheap, local dive excellent for *picanha*, salty snacks and for sipping ice-cold beer as smoke from charring meats wafts over the patio. Patrons range from old men to students and office workers.

Feitiço Mineiro CLN 306, Bloco B, Lojas 45/51 ☎61/3272-3032. Even without the live music at weekends this place would be worth patronizing for the food; a buffet of *comida mineira*, heavy on pork, beans and vegetables, served the traditional way on a wood-fired stove (R$30).

Fritz SCLS 404, Bloco D, Loja 35 ☎61/3226-8033. The German food is good and reasonable (from R$30), if a little heavy, at this corner restaurant.

Jera Pasta and Grill SCLS 304 Bloco D Loja 02 ☎61/ 3223-3332. Great upscale-ish people-watching pavement patio; you can't beat a beer and a crêpe or pasta dish in the shade of its beautifully manicured, parasol-shaped tree.

Ki-Sabor SHCN 406, Bloco E, Lojas 20/30/34 ☎61/3036-8525. Popular student self-service buffet with patio-seating. Salads, *feijoada*, grilled meats and decent desserts (from R$18).

Libanus CLS 206, Bloco C, Loja 36 ☎61/3597-7575. Perennially crowded spot serving up good-value, hearty Lebanese food. A young and humming scene at night.

Pizza À Bessa CLS 214, Bloco C, Loja 40 ☎61/3345-5252. This excellent pizza *rodizio* serves forty different slices including dessert pizza. It's all-you-can-eat for R$22 so you can try each kind if you dare – though that would be some achievement.

Sabor do Brasil 302 Sul. On the edge of the centre, this place offers a bargain evening unlimited buffet for R$18, including salads, soups, *mineira* and Northeastern dishes, and fruits. There's usually a veggie option or two; also has a *por kilo* option at lunch.

Cafés, snacks, ice cream

Casa de Biscoitos Mineiros 106 Sul, Bloco A, Loja 7. Decent bakery with bread, cakes, great biscuits and coffee served outside at the rear.

Caldo Fino SQN b/n 409/410, Bloco B. Great soup served nightly under an open tent that workers put up and take down each night. Try the pumpkin and gorgonzola or the *verde* (potato, leek and sausage).

Daniel Brand 104 Norte, Bloco A, Loja 26, Asa Norte. Patisserie/teahouse serving

Brasília's best quiche. Great for coffee, cake, late weekend breakfast or afternoon tea.

Feira de Artesanato TV Tower base. Saturdays and Sundays this area bursts into life, becoming a paradise of very cheap street food ranging from tapioca rolls, sugar-cane juice and *pastels* to full buffets.

Landi 405 Sul. Hot dogs are taken to a new level here, with fresh bread and toppings including tomato, corn and *catupiry* cheese.

Rappel CLN 210, Bloco B, Loja 73 or CLS 306, Bloco B, Loja 10. Very respectable coffee and a good selection of sweets, *salgados* and ice cream. A nice place to start the day.

Saborella 112 Norte, Bloco C, Lojas 38/48. Exquisite ice cream; you'll want to taste several before deciding, sadly, on just two flavours.

Sorbê CLN 405, Bloco C, Loja 41 or CLSW 103, Bloco A, Loja 74, Sudoeste. Artesanal *sorveteria* that has exotic fruit sorbets and unusual, enticing flavours like tapioca, toasted coconut and cheese.

Drinking and nightlife

Brasília has plenty of nightlife, most of it scattered throughout each wing. Remember, the university is in Asa Norte.

20 Clichê CLN 107, Bloco C, Loja 57. Around 300 different kinds of *cachaça* line the walls of this *cachaçeria* which has funky music. Terrific on Sat, when drinks are half price.

Arena do Forro Setor de Clubes Sul trecho 3, near the AABB ⊛ www.arenadoforro .com.br. Get your dancing feet on to enjoy this ram-packed barn of a place showcasing the best in swing from the Northeast of Brazil. Could well be Brasília's best place to go out.

Balaio Café CLN 201 Bloco B Loja 19/31 ⊛ balaiocafe.com.br. Artsy place for a drink and live music until 1am, from samba to jazz.

Beirute 109 Sul, Bloco A, lojas 2 e 4 and 107 Norte, Bloco D, lojas 19 e 29. Two branches of this all-ages institution where you'll have to wait for a table; the Asa Sul bar has been open for 44 years. Try the best *kibe* (Lebanese lamb) in Brasília and if you're feeling adventurous the dangerous "Green Devil" cocktail. Daily until 1am, until 2am Thurs–Sat.

Calaf Edifício Empire Centre, Quadra 2, Bloco S, Sétor Bancário Sul ⊛ www.calaf.com.br. Busy after work until very late (10pm only Sat), this is *the* place in Brasília on Mon, with *Veja* magazine naming it the best place in town to flirt.

Gate's Pub 403 Sul, Bloco B, Loja 34 ⊛ www .gatespub.com.br. This dark London-esque pub has two stages and is bigger inside than it seems, with

live rock, pop and blues most nights. Tues–Sun 10pm until late.

Landscape SHIN CA 07, Bloco F1, Loja 33 ⊛ www .landscapepub.com.br. Hopping alternative/ electronic dance club with a trendy yet friendly feel, a bit of a trek (by taxi) on a hilltop in the north lake district. Closed Sun and Thurs.

Mormaii Surf Bar Pontão Lago Sul. It might be far from the waves but it's still great to scope the scene on a weekend night with cocktail in hand. Food is decent but pricey.

Shopping

Brasília Shopping Setor Comercial Norte, Quadra 05. Centrally located mall with a food court, a short walk from the TV Tower. Mon–Sat 10am–10pm.

Conic Opposite Conjunto, parallel and adjacent to the *rodoviária*. This 24hr "alternative" rough-around-the-edges shopping mall has joke T-shirts, comics and much much more, including bars, though it's best avoided late at night.

Conjunto Nacional Opposite Conic parallel and adjacent to the *rodoviária*. Not as flashy as Brasília Shopping but more upmarket than Conic. Open 24hr (Sun until midnight).

Feira de Artesanato The market at the base of the TV Tower sells clothes and crafts, from hammocks to meticulously pin-pricked dried leaves and *capim dourado*, attractive golden-grass jewellery. Stalls and food stands open every day but busiest weekends 8am–6pm.

Pier 21 Setor de Clubes Esportivo Sul, Tr. 02, Conjunto 32. Take a taxi to this lakeside mall which has cinemas and upscale restaurants. Daily 11am–11pm.

Directory

Banks and exchange Most ATMs take foreign cards; try the numerous branches of Bradesco. There's a centrally located *Citibank* near Brasília Shopping. Cambios are located at the airport and at Pátio Brasil Shopping, 1st Floor, Loja 202, Asa Sul.

Car rental Airport branches include: Avis (☏ 61/3365-2782); Hertz (☏ 61/3365-4425); Interlocadora (☏ 61/3365-3656); and Locadora (☏ 61/3327-4792).

Crime You'll feel pretty safe walking the streets by day, but at night the central area, with its strikingly lit Niemeyer buildings, is mostly deserted, so take care. Remember, there are few if any traffic lights outside the centre and crossing main roads north to south requires either entering the dodgy tunnels underneath or getting through gaps in traffic. Lastly, take care in the *rodoviária* and when using public transport at rush hour.

Embassies and consulates Australia, SES Quadra 801, Conjunto K, Lote 7 ☎61/3226-3111; Canada, SES, Av. das Nações, Quadra 803, Lote 16 ☎61/3424-5400; Ireland, SHIS QL 12, Conjunto 05, Casa 09, Lago Sul ☎61/3248-8800; South Africa, Av. das Nações, Lote 6 ☎61/3312-9500; UK, Setor de Embaixadas Sul, Quadra 801, Conjunto K ☎61/3329-2300; US, Av. das Nações Quadra 801, Lote 03 ☎61/3312-7000.

Hospitals Hospital de Base do Distrito Federal, SMHS 101, Bloco A ☎61/3325-5050 (Emergency 24hr).

Internet All shopping malls have internet cafés, which change location rapidly.

Laundries No self-service laundries in town but there are *lavanderias* in residential *quadras*, which wash clothes for R$5 per item. Try the ubiquitous 5 à Sec, at CLS 309 BL D, s/n Loja 35.

Left Luggage The airport has lockers and baggage storage open 24hr (R$9 per day).

Post office SHS 2 Bloco B, Asa Sul (Mon–Fri 9am–5pm); SDN CNB Bloco A, 2nd Loja 2010 (Mon–Fri 9.30am–10pm, Sat 9am–9pm). Branches also at most shopping malls.

Moving on

Air For the airport it's cheaper to call Rádio Táxi Brasília (☎61/3323-3030; 24hr), which gives a 30 percent discount.

Belém (4 daily; 5.5 hr); Belo Horizonte (12 daily; 2hr); Campo Grande (3 daily; 3hr); Rio (12 daily; 3hr); Salvador (4 daily; 4hr); São Paulo (15 daily; 3.5 hr).

Bus Belém (daily; 36hr); Belo Horizonte (4 daily; 13hr); Recife (daily; 48hr); Rio (daily; 20hr); Salvador (daily; 26hr); São Paulo (daily; 16hr).

The Pantanal

An open, seasonally inundated wetland larger than France, extending deep into the states of Mato Grosso and Mato Grosso do Sul, **THE PANTANAL** is one of the best places in Brazil for watching wildlife. The word Pantanal is derived from the Brazilian word *pantano* (meaning marsh) reflecting its general appearance, but originally it was the site of a giant, prehistoric, inland sea. Today, with an area of 195,000 square kilometres, it represents the world's largest wetland and is one of the most ecologically important habitats in Brazil.

Travelling alone in the Pantanal is difficult and the easiest way to experience it is by taking an economical **organized tour** or, if your budget stretches far enough, spending a night or two at a **fazenda-lodge** (called pousadas in the north). The *fazenda*-lodges are generally reached by jeep; those deeper in the interior require access by boat or plane. At least one night in the interior is essential if you want to see animals; three- or four-day excursions will greatly increase your chances of seeing the more elusive species. Most tours enter the Pantanal by road and spend a couple of days exploring in canoes, small motorboats or on horseback from a land base.

There are three main entry points to the Pantanal: **Cuiabá** in the north, **Corumbá** in the west and **Campo Grande** in the east. The **best time** to explore the Pantanal is towards the end of the rainy season, around April, when your chances of spotting wildlife are high. Renting a car is not recommended unless you hire a local guide who knows the area well to accompany you – you will need a 4x4.

CORUMBÁ

CORUMBÁ was founded as a military outpost in 1778 and rose to prominence due to its strategic location on the Paraguay River. Located in the western Pantanal, today it dedicates itself to the more peaceful pursuits of ranching, mining and ecotourism. Of the three main Pantanal towns, **Corumbá** is best placed for getting right into the Pantanal by bus or jeep, and has more than its fair share of guides and agencies to choose from, as well as boats for hire. Oddly enough, the town is more accessible from Bolivia than from Brazil. The town is not safe at night, so you do need to take care and avoid walking the streets after 10pm.

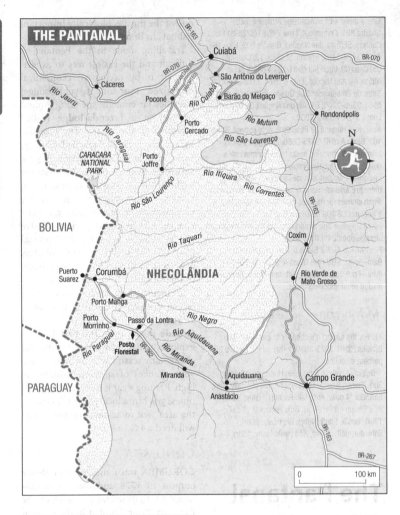

THE PANTANAL

Cuiabá
São Antônio do Leverger
Cáceres
Poconé
Barão de Melgaço
Rio Cuiabá
Rondonópolis
Porto Cercado
Rio Mutum
Rio São Lourenço
CARACARA NATIONAL PARK
Porto Joffre
Rio Itiquira
Rio Correntes
BOLIVIA
Rio São Lourenço
Rio Taquari
N
Coxim
Puerto Suarez
Corumbá
NHECOLÂNDIA
Rio Verde de Mato Grosso
Porto Manga
Porto Morrinho
Passo da Lontra
Rio Negro
Rio Aquidauana
PARAGUAY
Posto Florestal
Rio Paraguai
Rio Miranda
Miranda
Aquidauana
Campo Grande
Anastácio

0   100 km

What to see and do

One of the city's highlights is undoubt-edly the **Museu de História do Pantanal** on Rua Manoel Cavassa 275, Porto Geral (Tues–Sat 1–6pm; ☏67/3232-0303 ⓦwww.muhpan .org.br). The museum, designated a national heritage building in 1992, was erected in 1876 when Corumbá was Latin America's third major river port; curiously, most of the materials used for its construction were imported from England. The museum covers over 8000 years of the region's human history in a highly interactive manner, with a variety of archeological and ethnological artefacts complemented by modern resources in a high-tech setting.

Arrival and information

Air The airport (☏67/3232-1876 or 3231-3322) is located 3km from the centre on Rua Santos Dumont. Trip and TAM both operate flights to

Corumbá from Rio, Sao Paulo, Campo Grande and Foz do Iguaçu. To get into town, catch bus with route card "Popular Nova".

Bus An hourly bus (R$3) runs from the Bolivian border to the *rodoviária* (☎67/3231-2646), five blocks north of the centre at Rua Porto Carrera. There are regular buses to Campo Grande (5–7hr), and daily buses to São Paulo (21hr) and Rio de Janeiro (26hr).

Tourist information There is a tourist information point (☎67/3231-6054, ✆www.corumba.com.br) at the international airport.

Accommodation

Hotels in Corumbá vary considerably but their sheer quantity means you should have no problem finding a room. Out of season, especially January to Easter, there are heavy discounts and prices can be bargained even lower. The clutch of cheap lodgings around Rua Delamare tend to be popular with backpackers.

Corumbá Hostel Rua Colombo 1419 ☎67/3231-1005, ✆www.corumbahostel.com.br. The city's only (HI) hostel has clean simple doubles and single-sex dorms with lockers, some with a/c. There are laundry facilities, kitchen and a pool, but you'll need to rent a towel. Free airport pick-up. Dorms R$30, rooms R$65.

Laura Vicuna Rua Cuiabá 775 ☎67/3231-5874, ✆www.hotellauravicuna.com.br. A peaceful place, very neat and tidy with clean rooms (all with TV, a/c and wifi), although the breakfast area is a little old-fashioned, with flowery tablecloths and unappealing decor. $100.

Pousada do Cachimbo Rua Alan Kardec 4, Bairro Dom Bosco ☎67/3231-4833, ✆www.pousadadocachimbo.com.br. On the site of a former cattle farm, this delightful colonial pousada is located five minutes' from Corumbá on the edge of the Bay of Tamengo. It's ideal for a small taster of what the deeper Pantanal will be like, with birds tweeting about as well as the occasional duck strolling around the garden. All rooms have a/c, there's a pool and even a football pitch. R$90.

Eating and drinking

There's no shortage of restaurants in Corumbá. There are plenty of cheap snack bars throughout town, especially on Rua Delamare west of the Praça da República, serving good set meals for less than R$7. Being a swamp city, fish is the main local delicacy, with *pacu* and *pintado* among the favoured species. You'll find bars all over town – the more relaxed are those down on the riverfront, where you can usually get a game of pool with your drink.

Galpão Rua 13 de Junho 797 at the corner of Rua Antônio Maria Coelho. A no-frills local serving a huge choice of inexpensive meat and fish in vast portions (R$25/kg). Daily 11am–4pm.

Fiorella Pizza On the eastern corner of Praça da República and Rua Delamare. If you're after some European grub, you'll find pizzas (R$26) here, with local toppings including plantain. Daily 6pm–midnight.

TOUR OPERATORS

Organized tours inevitably include at least some water-based transport and a guide who can tell you about what you see. Numerous tour companies are based out of the main access towns Corumbá, Campo Grande and Cuiabá.

Corumbá

Aguas do Pantanal Av. Afonso Pena 367, Miranda ☎67/3242-1242, ✆www.aguasdo pantanal.com.br. This company organizes programmes in the southern Pantanal, as well as fishing trips and visits to traditional local farms where you can stay overnight. They also own a pleasant pousada offering both upscale and economical rooms in Miranda, between Corumbá and Campo Grande. A great location for those wanting to also visit Bonito.

Campo Grande

Pantanal Tours Rua Guia Lopes 150 ☎67/3042-4659, ✆www.pantanaltours.com.

Dutch-run company offering a wide range of activities and packages from one-week-long 4x4 trips exploring the Nhecolândia region to tours of the southern Pantanal combined with Foz do Iguaçu and Bonito; email responses are rapid.

Cuiabá

Joel Souza Ecoverde Tours Av. Getúlio Vargas 155 or at *Pousada Ecoverde* ☎65/3624-1386 or 9638-1614 ✆www.ecoverdetours.com.br. Well-established company keen to foster sustainable ecotourism offering a variety of nature tours, from birdwatching to jaguar treks deeper into the Pantanal. Stay at a *fazenda*-lodge or camp.

Directory

Banks and exchange There's a host of banks including HSBC, some with ATMs, on Rua Delamare west of Praça da República.

Car rental Localiza is at Rua Edu Rocha 969 (☎67/3231-6000) and at the airport (☎67/3232-6000).

Consulates Bolivia, Rua Cabral 1607 (☎67/3231-5605); Paraguay, Av. Rio Branco 182B (☎67/3232-5203).

Customs The Brazilian customs point is at the *rodoviária* so do not forget to get your entry stamp here. Note that the office is open for only a few hours each day, so if you intend to leave Brazil get your exit stamp the day before you cross.

Health Clinica Samec on Rua Colombo 1249 (☎67/3231-3308).

Internet *Nett Internet Café*, Rua Frei Mariano 635.

Police Rua Luiz Feitosa Rodrigues 664 (☎67/3232-2867).

Post office The main post office is at Rua Delamare 708, opposite the church on Praça da República.

Moving on

Air To get to the airport catch bus with route card "Popular Nova" from Rua Ciríaco de

Toledo in the centre. TAM (☎67/3231-7099) and Trip (☎67/3231-1818) fly regularly from Corumbá to Campo Grande, Rio, Sao Paulo and Foz do Iguaçu.

Bus The *rodoviária* (☎67/3231-2033) on Rua Porto Carrero is a ten-minute walk south of the city centre. Regular buses depart for Campo Grande (5–7hr); there are daily buses to Sao Paulo (21hr) and Rio de Janeiro (26hr).

CAMPO GRANDE

Capital of the state of Mato Grosso do Sul, **CAMPO GRANDE** is the most popular gateway into the Pantanal on account of its excellent transport links with the rest of Brazil, plethora of tour companies and good facilities for visitors. The city itself was only founded in 1877 but its growth has been rapid, and today it is a large city with some 800,000 inhabitants

Arrival

Air Campo Grande's international airport, the Aeroporto Antonio João (☎67/3368-6000) is at

---

PANTANAL WILDLIFE

First-time visitors to the Pantanal will be struck by the sheer quantity of animals that populate the region, allowing for some great photo opportunities. Undoubtedly the most visible inhabitants of the region are the waterbirds, vast flocks of egrets, cormorants and ibises that flush in the wake of your boat as you cruise the channels – an unforgettable spectacle. The most spectacular of the region's waterbirds is the immense Jabiru, a prehistoric-looking snow-white stork as tall as a man and the symbol of the Pantanal.

Another species that will undoubtedly catch your eye is the Spectacled Caiman (*jacare*), a South American alligator whose regional populations are estimated at more than ten million. The mammal you'll see most of is the Capybara, a rodent resembling a huge guinea-pig that feeds in herds on the lush plant life, but you will need a bit more luck to see the rare Marsh Deer or the endangered Giant Armadillo. Listen out too for the squeaky calls of the Giant Otter, a species that inhabits the more isolated parts of the Pantanal, but which is often overcome by its own curiosity when approached by a boat-load of tourists.

Jaguar and Puma are present in the area but are active mainly at night; you will need a huge dose of luck to see either, and you shouldn't count on seeing Maned Wolf or Bush Dog either. Lowland Tapir, looking something like a cross between a horse and a short-nosed elephant, are sometimes seen bathing in streams. You will likely be serenaded each morning by the far-carrying song of the Black Howler Monkey, often observed lying prone on thick branches, whilst the gallery forests are the preserve of the Black Spider Monkey, considerably more svelte and active as they swing acrobatically through the trees.

Av. Duque de Caixas. Bus 408 will take you into town to central Av. Afonso Pena.

Bus Buses arrive at the *rodoviária* at Av. Gury Marques (☎67/3026-6789), twenty minutes south of town. There are regular services from most major cities in Brazil including Foz do Iguassu, Rio de Janeiro and Brasília.

Tourist information There is a tourist information office (☎67/3318-6060) at the airport. The very helpful downtown Morada dos Bais tourist office is at Av. Noroeste 5140, on the corner with Av. Afonso Pena (Tues–Sat 8am–6pm, Sun 9am–noon; ☎67/3314-9968).

Accommodation

There are reasonable budget choices around the junction of Rua Barão do Rio Branco and Rua Allan Kardek, although this area is a bit sketchy with seedy characters and prostitutes roaming about.

Anache Rua Marechal Cândido Rondon 1396 ☎67/3383-2841, ✉hotelanache2007@hotmail .com. This centrally located and superb value hotel has immaculate rooms, some with a/c, TV and fridge. There's a communal area on the first floor landing, and parking facilities are available. R$59.

Hostel Campo Grande Rua Joaquim Nabuco 185 ☎67/3321-0505, ⊛www.pantanaltrekking .com. The leafy courtyard here is decorated with vivid animal murals and has a small pool with an adjoining breakfast area. The clean, comfy rooms accommodate up to four people, and there's free internet and free airport and bus pick-up. However, there have been some reports of theft and dodgy management. R$60.

Vale do Sol Av. Calógeras 1803 ☎67/3324-4552. A long blue and orange corridor here leads to various rooms opening onto a courtyard. You definitely get what you pay for – basic amenities and dark and stuffy rooms. R$50.

Eating

Eating out is an important part of the local lifestyle and this is reflected in the diversity of restaurants. There are scores of *lanchonetes*, especially east along Rua Dom Aquino.

Casa do Peixe Rua João Rosa Pires 1030 ☎67/3382-7121. A very popular spot for delicious regional dishes, with fish as the main speciality; a *prato* for two will set you back R$60. Exceptional value and excellent service. Daily 11am–3pm and 6–11pm.

Comitiva Pantaneira Rua Dom Aquino 2221 ☎67/3383-8799. Buzzing per kilo restaurant (R$29.90 weekdays, R$34.90 weekends) with seriously good grub sizzling away on the open stove while waiters in cowboy outfits roam around serving customers. Mon–Fri 11am–2pm, Sat & Sun 11am–3pm.

Fogo Caipira Rua José Antônio 145 ☎67/3324-1641. Pleasant and ever so slightly rustic restaurant, with an old stove and oxen skulls decorating the walls; sit in the intimate patio-cum-garden at the back as you feast on the exquisite *guisado pantaneiro* (R$36 for two) accompanied by the *feijão tropeiro* (R$10); less adventurous types can go for a stroganoff (R$30). Tues–Fri 11am–2pm and 7–11pm, Sat 11am–midnight, Sun 11am–4pm.

Sabor EnQuilo Av. Afonso Pena 2223 ☎67/3321-4726. Good-value, friendly family-run per kilo restaurant (R$26.90 weekdays, R$34.20 weekends) with a variety of fish dishes on offer (including sushi on Tues, Thurs, Sat and Sun) and free dessert on Mon, Fri & Sat. Mon–Fri 10.45am–2.30pm, Sat & Sun 10.45am–3pm.

Directory

Banks and exchange There are ATMs at the airport and at strategic points in the city.

Car rental Lider, Av. Afonso Pena 954 (☎67/3029-9009); Renascença Rent A Car, Rua Joaquim Murtinho 4701 (☎67/3348-3400); YES, Av. Afonso Pena 829 (☎67/3324-0055).

Consulates If you're heading into either Paraguay or Bolivia from Campo Grande, you should check on border procedures and visa requirements. The Paraguayan consul is at Rua 26 de Agosto 384 (☎67/3324-4934), and the Bolivian consul at Rua Cobral 1607 (☎67/3231-5605).

Hospital Emergency number ☎192. The Santa Casa hospital is at Rua Eduardo Santos Pereira 88 (☎67/3322-4000).

Internet Matrix, Av. Calógeras 2069 (R2.50 per hr; Mon–Sat 8am–8pm).

Laundry Planet Clean, Rua Joaquim Murtinho 135, close to the Praça dos Imigrantes.

Pharmacy Rua Barbosa, on the corner of the main square by Rua 14 de Julho and Av. Afonso Pena.

Police Emergency number ☎190. Rua Padre João Crippe 1581 ☎67/3312-5700 or 2417.

Post office Av. Calógeras 2309, on the corner with Rua Dom Aquino.

Moving on

Air To get to the airport catch the Indubrasil bus from the *rodoviária*. TAM, OceanAir, Azul Airlines and Gol serve Campo Grande, with direct flights to most state capitals and daily flights to São Paulo and Rio, Cuiabá, Belo Horizonte and Brasília.

Bus Daily buses depart from the *rodoviária* at Av. Gury Marquis 1215 (⊕67/3026-6789). There are daily services to most major cities including Foz do Iguaçu (daily; 14hr), São Paulo (5 daily; 13hr), Rio (5 daily; 24hr), Brasília (2 daily; 22hr) and Cuiabá (10 daily; 10hr).

CUIABÁ

Capital of Mato Grosso, **CUIABÁ** is a city of half a million people located at the dead centre of the South American continent. The city's unusual name is of disputed origin but probably comes from an indigenous term meaning "arrow-fishing", a reference to the local Bororo Indian hunting technique. The installation of Brasília as the nation's capital in 1960 revived Cuiabá's fortunes and its recent growth has been rapid. The city is the main gateway to the northern Pantanal, and is the least frequently used of the three main access points.

Arrival and information

Air Marechal Rondon International Airport (⊕65/3614-2557), at Rua Gov. Ponce de Arruda en Varzea Grande, receives flights from all major Brazilian cities and regional capitals. To get into town, take bus #24 (R$2.40) with route card "Shopping Pantanal" and hop off at Av. Getúlio Vargas.

Bus Buses arrive at the *rodoviária* (⊕65/3621-3629) outside town at the end of Av. Marechal Deodoro, Km 3. There are regular bus services from most major Brazilian cities including Rio de Janeiro and Brasília. To get into town catch a bus with route card "Centro" from just outside the station, which will drop you along Av. Isaac Póvoas.

Tourist information There's a CAT office at Praca Rachid Jaud, Av. Isaac Póvoas (Mon–Fri 8am–12pm & 2–6pm; ⊕65/3313-3328). There are also branches at the *rodoviária* (daily 8am–6pm; ⊕65/3621-1500) and at the airport (daily 8am–6pm; ⊕65/8419-8310).

Accommodation

Mato Grosso Rua Comandante Costa 643 ⊕65/3614-7777, ⊕65/614-7053, ⊛www .hotelmatogrosso.com.br. With 63 rooms set over three floors, the Mato Grosso has a somewhat institutional feel (the cleaners' ward-like outfits don't help either) but rooms are functional, comfy and clean, and some have cable TV and a/c (R$99). There's a big hearty breakfast buffet included. R$79.

Portal do Pantanal Av. Isaac Póvoas 665 ⊕65/3624-8999, ⊛www.portaldopantanal.com .br. Dark and dreary HI hostel lacking in communal areas and painted with primary colours that gives it the feeling of a closing-down school. They can help you arrange affordable trips into the Pantanal with bilingual guides. Dorms R$43, doubles R$70.

Pousada Ecoverde Rua Pedro Celestino 391, centro ⊕65/9638-1614 or 65/3624-1386, ⊛www.pousadaecoverde.com.br. Welcoming, atmospheric, pousada in the city centre with five rooms, all with fans, giving onto a leafy courtyard. Bric-a-brac – including a collection of antique radios – is dotted around the communal area which has a library with a book exchange; there's also a chill-out area at the back with hammocks and a garden with birds pecking from feeders. Laundry, cooking facilities and internet (all free) are also available, as well as free airport and *rodoviária* transfers. Tours to the Pantanal can be organized. R$50.

Eating

For cheaper lunchtime eating and *lanchonetes*, there are plenty of places in the area around Praça Alencastro, at the north end of Travessa João Dias near Rua Comandante Costa, and in the shopping zone between Rua Pedro Celestino and Rua Galdino Pimentel. For dinner, head to Getúlio Vargas between Rua Comandante Costa and Praça 8 de Abril. Praça Popular also has plenty of restaurants and bars that get busy in the evenings.

Choppão Praça 8 de Abril, Goiabeiras ⊕65/3623-9101. Traditional and hugely popular open-fronted restaurant-bar ten-minutes' walk from the city centre; they serve huge portions of delicious local food as well as pizzas (R$30). Follow local tradition and have an *escaldado* (egg and chicken soup; R$10) to perk you up when you've had a *chopp* too many (draft beer; R$4). They also serve deliciously refreshing jugs of fresh juice (R$5). Daily 11am–1pm & 6–11pm.

Mistura Cuiabana Rua Pedro Celestino 8 ⊕65/3624-1127. Set in an airy colonial

Patriota Praça Popular 20
℡65/3622-0081 or 65/9237-9769. Restaurant-bar popular among the wealthier *cuiabano* set, with a smart and sleek black interior and a stylish outdoor wooden terrace. Set menus (R$24.90) are available for lunch and there's a variety of luscious dishes to choose from for dinner, including the much sought-after paella (R$68). Wines from R$47 a bottle, cocktails R$15. Daily 11am–2am.

mansion on the corner of Praça Alencastro, this excellent per kilo restaurant (R$17.90) hums at lunchtime, with locals nattering away as they feast on the tasty nosh. Mon–Fri 11am–2.30pm.
Telepizza Av. Issac Póvoas 1003 ℡65/3624-2400. A pleasant wood-fire pizza (R$23-35) place with artefacts and memorabilia decorating the walls, from antique squash rackets to nineteenth-century irons. Daily 3pm–midnight, delivery 6pm–midnight.

Directory

Banks and exchange Cuiabá is the only place in the region where you're likely to be able to change travellers' cheques. Visa card cash advances can be obtained and cheques and notes exchanged in the banks on Av. Getúlio Vargas.
Car rental Localiza, Av. Dom Bosco 965 (℡65/3624-7979); Unidas, Praça do Aeroporto (℡65/3682-4052).
Internet Onix, Rua Pedro Celestino, inside the colonial mansion by Mistura Cuiabana (R$2.50 per hr; Mon–Fri 8.30am–6pm).
Police Av. Tenente Coronel Duarte 1044 (℡65/3901-4809; 24hr).
Post office Praça da República.

Moving on

Air To get to the airport catch Bus 24 with route card "Aeroporto" from the corner of Av. Coronel Duarte and Av. Getúlio Vargas. TAM, Trip, OceanAir and Gol all serve Cuiabá; there are direct flights to São Paulo, Campo Grande, Brasília and Iguaçu.
Bus To get to the *rodoviária* catch a bus with route card "Rodoviária" either from Av. Getúlio Vargas, close to Praça Alencastro, or from Av. Mato Grosso at the end of Rua Pedro Celestino. There are buses

to Porto Velho (2 daily; 24hr daily; 12hr), Brasília (5 daily to Santa Cruz in Bolivia via

São Paulo

South America's largest city, **SÃO PAULO** – or "Sampa", as the locals call it – makes up for a lack of beach and leisure culture with all the urban buzz and modern grandeur that you would expect from a place that's home to a staggering half of Brazil's industrial output. With an exceptionally vibrant cultural scene, the city boasts 150 theatres and performance spaces, more than 250 cinemas, countless nightclubs and no fewer than ninety museums. São Paulo is Brazil's New York, and there are echoes of that city everywhere: in Avenida Paulista, it has South America's Park Avenue; in the Edifício Banespa its Empire State Building. It's a city of immigrants, too, with a heritage of Italian and Japanese influx – it has the largest Japanese population outside Japan – which also makes it easily the best place to eat in Brazil.

São Paulo's denizens, known as *Paulistanos*, inevitably live partly in Rio's shadow, but they too like to live the good life and party hard at night. While many people will always want to contrast workhorse Sampa with the beauty of Rio, the city somehow manages its underdog status well, and its friendly population simply gets on with making money – and spending it. If you're someone who gets a thrill out of buzzing cosmopolitan streets and discovering the hottest bar, club or restaurant, then you'll love São Paulo – a city of both pure grit and sophisticated savoir-faire.

What to see and do

São Paulo is a vast city but the central neighbourhoods and metro lines are fairly

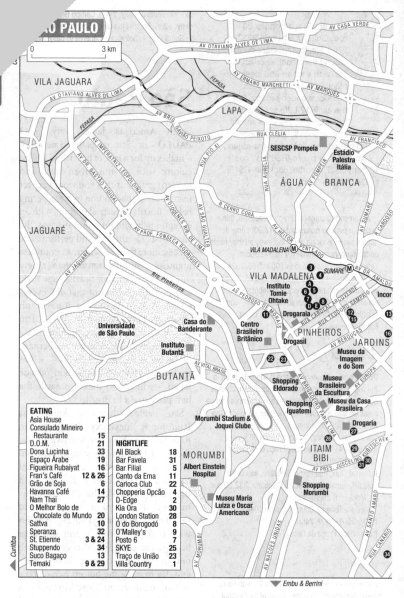

AV CASA VERDE

AV OTAVIANO ALVES DE LIMA

VILA JAGUARA

AV OTAVIANO ALVES DE LIMA

FEPASA

AV ERMANO MARCHETTI

AV MARQUES

LAPA

RUA CLÉLIA

AV BRIG. GASTÃO PEIXOTO

RUA PIO XI

AV FRANCISCO

SESCSP Pompeia

Estádio
Palestra
Itália

ÁGUA   BRANCA

AV IMPERATRIZ LEOPOLDINA

AV DR. GASTÃO VIDIGAL

R CERRO CORÁ

AV SUMARÉ

AV DIÓGENES RIB. DE LIMA

AV SÃO GUALTER

AV HEITOR PENTEADO

AV CARDOSO

JAGUARÉ

AV PROF. FONSECA RODRIGUES

VILA MADALENA Ⓜ

AV JAGUARÉ

Rio Pinheiros

VILA MADALENA

❸
❹

SUMARÉ Ⓜ

AV DR. AMALDO

AV PEDROSO DE MORAIS

Instituto
Tomie
Ohtake

Ⓐ
❻ ❺
❼ Ⓓ
❾ Ⓔ ❽

RUA CARLOS CARDOVERDE

Incor

Drogaraia

RUA TEODORO SAMPAIO

❶❷
❶❺

❶❸

Universidade
de São Paulo

Casa do
Bandeirante

❶❶

Centro
Brasileiro
Britânico

PINHEIROS

RUA REBOUÇAS

❶❻

JARDINS

Instituto
Butantã

Drogasil

AV REBOUÇAS

Museu da
Imagem
e do Som

AV VITAL BRASIL

❷❷ ❷❸

BUTANTÃ

AV BRIG. FARIA LIMA

AV EUROPA

Shopping
Eldorado

Museu
Brasileiro
da Escultura

Morumbi Stadium &
Joquei Clube

Shopping
Iguatemi

Museu da Casa
Brasileira

Drogaria

❷❼

MORUMBI

ITAIM
BIBI

❷❽

❷❾

AV PRES. JUSCELINO KUBITSCHEK

❸❶ ❸❷

Albert Einstein
Hospital

❸❶

Shopping
Morumbi

AV SANTO AMARO

Museu Maria
Luiza e Oscar
Americano

AV NAÇÕES UNIDAS

AV MORUMBI

RUA CANÁRIO

❸❹

Curitiba

▲

▼ Embu & Berrini

EATING	
Asia House	17
Consulado Mineiro	
Restaurante	15
D.O.M.	21
Dona Lucinha	33
Espaço Árabe	19
Figueira Rubaiyat	16
Fran's Café	12 & 26
Grão de Soja	6
Havanna Café	14
Nam Thai	27
O Melhor Bolo de	
Chocolate do Mundo	20
Sattva	10
Speranza	32
St. Etienne	3 & 24
Stuppendo	34
Suco Bagaço	13
Temaki	9 & 29

NIGHTLIFE	
All Black	18
Bar Favela	31
Bar Filial	5
Canto da Ema	11
Carioca Club	22
Chopperia Opção	4
D-Edge	2
Kia Ora	30
London Station	28
Ó do Borogodó	8
O'Malley's	9
Posto 6	7
SKYE	25
Traço de União	23
Villa Country	1

easy to get a handle on. The focal points downtown are the large squares of **Praça da Sé** and faded **Praça da República**, separated by the wide stretch of **Vale do Anhangabaú**. Just north of Praca da Sé is the seventeenth-century monastery of

São Bento, and beyond lively shopping streets lead to the unmissable **Mercado Municipal** and the partly cleaned-up red-light district of **Luz**. **Bixiga** (also called Bela Vista) and **Liberdade**, to the south, are immigrant neighbourhoods,

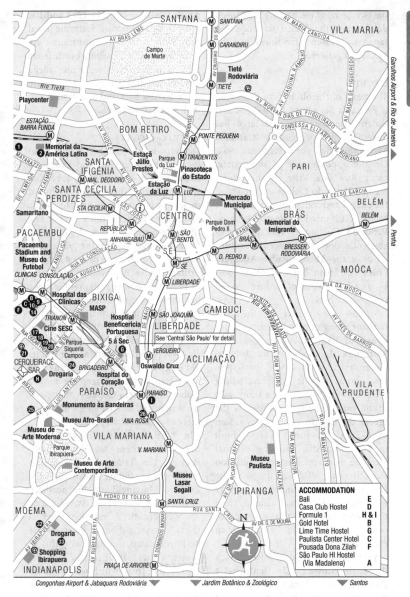

ACCOMMODATION

Bali	E
Casa Club Hostel	D
Formule 1	H & I
Gold Hotel	B
Lime Time Hostel	G
Paulista Center Hotel	C
Pousada Dona Zilah	F
São Paulo HI Hostel	A
(Vila Madalena)	

Congonhas Airport & Jabaquara Rodoviária ▼   ▼ Jardim Botânico & Zoológico   ▼ Santos

home to a sizeable chunk of São Paulo's Italian and Japanese immigrants respectively. Rua Augusta is the city's primary nightlife centre, leading southwards onto the imposing commercial artery of **Avenida Paulista**, with its sprawling upscale suburb gardens descending the hill on the far side. Heading back uphill west of here is Vila Madalena, another fashionable district with numerous bars and restaurants and an artistic feel. The best museums are scattered right across the city: some of the best are the **Museu do Futebol**, the Museu da Imigração **Japonesa, Museu Afro-Brasil** and the **MASP art gallery**.

Centro

The heart of the old part of São Paulo is **Praça da Sé,** a busy, palm-tree-lined square dominated by the large but unremarkable neo-Gothic **Catedral Metropolitana**, completed in 1954. On the opposite side of the square, along Rua Boa Vista, is the white-washed **Pátio do Colégio**, a replica of the chapel and college founded in 1554 by the Jesuit mission. Nearby at Largo Pátio do Colégio 2, the unremarkable collection of seventeenth-century relics at the **Museu Padre Anchieta** (Tues–Sun 9am–5pm, R$6) is best bypassed in favour of its lovely patio café out the back.

Around the corner is the sole remaining eighteenth-century manor house in São Paulo, the **Solar da Marquesa de Santos** (Rua Roberto Simonsen 136; Tues–Sun 9am–5pm; free), home to a few displays telling the story of the city, while a short walk south, on Av. Rangel Pestana, is the **Igreja do Carmo** (Mon–Fri 7–11am & 1–5pm, Sat–Sun 7–11am), built in 1632 and still retaining original Baroque features. Further south on the other side of Praça da Sé is the **Igreja de São Francisco**, another well-preserved colonial church from the latter part of the seventeenth century (daily 7.30am–7pm), with an elaborate high altar.

A ten-minute walk northeast of Praça da Sé, the **Mosteiro São Bento** has a church that dates back to 1598, though most of the complex has been renovated multiple times, and is still home to a community of Benedictine monks. Take in a block of busy market street Rua 25 de Março before moving onto Rua da Cantareira, where you'll find the city's **Mercado Municipal** (daily 7am–5pm),

which was completed in 1933 and has stained-glass windows featuring rural plantation scenes. Downstairs are countless food stalls selling exotic fruits plus trademark thick-wedge mortadella sandwiches and *pasteis*. Upstairs are some terrific bars and restaurants – a mob scene at weekends.

Centro Novo

Downtown São Paulo's other main focal point is around the **Praça da República**, a once-affluent area that was originally the site of high-end mansions belonging to wealthy coffee plantation owners during the late nineteenth century, though almost all have been lost. Just off the *praça*, take the elevator to the top of the 42-storey **Edifício Italia** (Av. Ipiranga 344), built in 1956; the rooftop restaurant is tacky but there are spectacular vistas from the outside viewing platform (R$10). South of the Edifício Italia is **Av. São Luis** which was once lined with high-class shops and still retains some of its old elegance, though the building that most stands out is Oscar Niemeyer's S-shaped **Edifício Copan** – an experiment in mixed urban living with apartments available at all prices.

In the opposite direction, to the north, there are more high-rises in the **Triângulo**, São Paulo's traditional banking district. The **Edifício Martinelli**, on the northern edge of the district at Av. São João 35, was the city's first skyscraper at thirty storeys, although the views are best from atop the 36-floor **Edifício Banespa** (Rua João Bricola 24; Mon–Fri 10am–5pm; free), which was modelled after New York's Empire State Building. Nearby, the grand **Teatro Municipal** is an enticing mix of Art Nouveau and Renaissance styles, the city's premier venue for classical music, and decorated with mirrors, Italian marble and gold leaf (unfortunately only viewable during performances).

Luz

Immediately north of Centro is **Luz**, a formerly upscale area that fell on hard times and although now a red-light district is in the process of a huge government clean-up. The **Parque da Luz** (daily 10am–6pm) was São Paulo's first public garden, and its bandstands and ponds are proof of a ritzy past – today, it's not the safest place after dark. The area is also home to São Paulo's two train stations: **Estação da Luz**, across from the park on Av. Cásper Líbero, which opened in 1901 and lost many of its original decorations in a fire in 1946, though elegant touches can still be appreciated; and **Estação Júlio Prestes**, two blocks west across from Praça Júlio Prestes, built in 1926 and said to be modelled after Grand Central and Pennsylvania Stations in New York. Sadly, the latter is only used for suburban services these days, but its Great Hall has been transformed into **Sala São Paulo**, a 1500-seat concert hall hosting performances by the Orquestra Sinfônica do Estado de São Paulo. Nearby, adjacent to the park, is the **Pinacoteca do Estado** (Av. Tiradentes 141; Tues–Sun 10am–6pm; R$5), which houses nineteenth- and twentieth-century works of Brazilian art by Cavalcanti, Segall, Portinari and Almeida Junior.

Liberdade and Bixiga

Japo ha1

South of Centro, **Liberdade** is the home of São Paulo's Japanese community, its streets lined on either side with overhanging red lampposts. You'll find great traditional Japanese food here on the streets off **Praça da Liberdade** (site of a good Sunday market), as well as lots of Chinese and Korean eateries and stores. There is even a **Museu da Imigração Japonesa** (Rua São Joaquim 381; Tues–Sun 1.30–5.30pm; R$5), whose three floors document the contributions Japanese immigrants have made in Brazil in the hundred years since

they first arrived to work on the coffee plantations. The neighbourhood west of here, the Italian enclave of **Bixiga** or Bela Vista, is also a fantastic place to eat, coming to life at night with great restaurants, bars and clubs, especially on Rua 13 de Maio and the surrounding streets. The **Museu Memória do Bixiga** (Rua dos Ingleses 118; Wed–Sun 2–5pm; R$5) provides the lowdown on the Italian community here in a traditional early twentieth-century house.

Museu do Futebol

The most interesting addition to São Paulo's attractions is undoubtedly the superb **Museu do Futebol** (daily 10am–6pm, closed match days; R$7), located at Estádio do Pacaembu, the home of Sampa's largest soccer club, Corinthians. To get there, take bus #917M from Av. Paulista or #177C-10 from Vila Madelena, or walk for fifteen minutes from Clinicas metro. The impressive 40,000-seat stadium was designed by Lúcio Costa (of Brasília fame) at one end of a large square – Praça Charles Miller – which was named after the Englishman who introduced football to Brazil. The museum's appeal goes far beyond the game itself, offering an enthralling multimedia insight into the history, players, fans and commentators, and piecing together how it became Brazil's greatest national obsession. Allow three hours to make the most of the interactive collection.

Av. Paulista and Jardins

South of Bixiga, **Avenida Paulista** is central São Paulo's third major focal point, a 3-km stretch that in the early 1900s was lined with Art Nouveau mansions owned by coffee barons. Redeveloped in the 1960s, it's now lined with skyscrapers topped by helipads and TV antennas dramatically lit by different colours at night. The **Casas das Rosas** (Av. Paulista 35) gives some sense of what the avenue once looked like, a

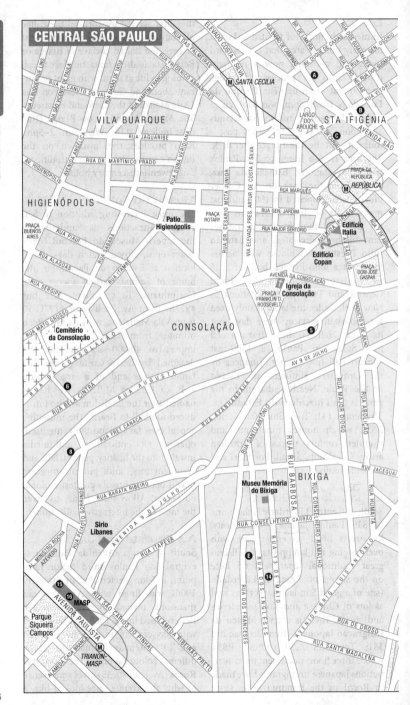

CENTRAL SÃO PAULO

VILA BUARQUE

(M) SANTA CECILIA

STA IFIGÉNIA

LARGO
DO
AROUCHE

AVENIDA SÃO

HIGIENÓPOLIS

PRAÇA
BUENOS
AIRES

RUA ALAGOAS

RUA SERGIPE

RUA JAGUARIBE

RUA DR. MARTINICO PRADO

RUA DONA VERIDIANA

Patio
Higienópolis

PRAÇA
ROTARY

PRAÇA DA
REPÚBLICA
REPÚBLICA

RUA MARQUÉS

RUA GEN. JARDIM

RUA MAJOR SERTÓRIO

Edifício
Italia

Edifício
Copan

PRAÇA
DOM JOSÉ
GASPAR

AVENIDA DA CONSOLAÇÃO

PRAÇA
FRANKLIN D.
ROOSEVELT

Igreja da
Consolação

Cemitério
da Consolação

CONSOLAÇÃO

AV 9 DE JULHO

RUA AUGUSTA

RUA FREI CANECA

BIXIGA

Museu Memória
do Bixiga

RUA BARATA RIBEIRO

RUA CONSELHEIRO CARRÃO

Sírio
Libanes

RUA ITAPEVA

MASP

Parque
Siqueira
Campos

AVENIDA PAULISTA

(M)

*TRIANON-
MASP*

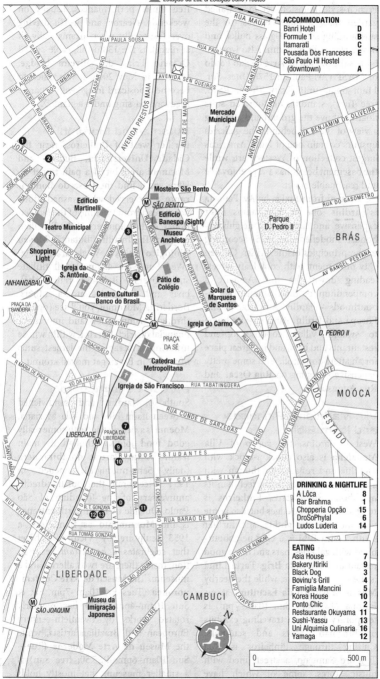

Estação da Luz & Estação Júlio Prestes

ACCOMMODATION

Banri Hotel	**D**
Formule 1	**B**
Itamarati	**C**
Pousada Dos Franceses	**E**
São Paulo HI Hostel (downtown)	**A**

RUA MAUA

RUA PAULA SOUSA

RUA PAULA SOUSA

AVENIDA SEN QUEIROS

RUA DA CANTAREIRA

RUA AURORA

RUA DOS TIMBIRAS

AVENIDA RIO BRANCO

RUA SANTA IFIGÊNIA

RUA GASPAR LIBERO

AVENIDA PRESTES MAIA

Mercado Municipal

RUA BENJAMIM DE OLIVEIRA

AVENIDA DO ESTADO

JOÃO

RUA 25 DE MARÇO

❶

❷

ℹ

RUA CRISPINIANO

JOSÉ DE BARROS

Edifício Martinelli

RUA TOLEDO

Mosteiro São Bento

RUA DO GASOMETRO

SÃO BENTO Ⓜ

Edifício Banespa (Sight)

Parque D. Pedro II

BRÁS

Teatro Municipal

RUA LIBERO BADARÓ

RUA BOA VISTA

❸

RUA 15 DE NOVEMBRO

Museu Anchieta

VIADUTO DO CHÁ

RUA ALVARES PENTEADO

Shopping Light

RUA SÃO BENTO

❹

Pátio de Colégio

RUA 25 DE MARÇO

AV RANGEL PESTANA

Igreja da S. Antônio

RUA DIREITA

ANHANGABAÚ Ⓜ

Centro Cultural Banco do Brasil

RUA ROBERTO SIMONSEN

Solar da Marquesa de Santos

PRAÇA DA BANDEIRA

SÉ Ⓜ

RUA BENJAMIN CONSTANT

Igreja do Carmo

Ⓜ D. PEDRO II

R RIACHUELO

RUA FEIJÓ

PRAÇA DA SÉ

RUA DO CARMO

AVENIDA DO ESTADO

MOÓCA

R MARIA DE PAULA

Catedral Metropolitana

VD DA PAULINA

Igreja de São Francisco

RUA TABATINGUERA

RUA CONDE DE SARZEDAS

VIADUTO SOBRE RIO TAMANDUATEÍ

RUA SANTO AMARO

LIBERDADE Ⓜ

PRAÇA DA LIBERDADE

❼

❾

RUA DOS ESTUDANTES

RUA GLICÉRIO

❿

AV COSTA E SILVA

RUA DA GLORIA

RUA DA GLORIA

RUA CONSELHEIRO FURTADO

DRINKING & NIGHTLIFE

A Lôca	8
Bar Brahma	1
Chopperia Opção	15
DroSoPhylal	6
Ludos Luderia	14

RUA VICENTE E PRADO

AVENIDA 23 DE MAIO

D

R.T. GONZAYA

⑫ ⑬

RUA GALVAO BUENO

⑪

RUA BARÃO DE IGUAPE

RUA TOMÁS GONZAGA

RUA FAGUNDAS

RUA OTTO DE ALENCAR

LIBERDADE

RUA SÃO JOAQUIM

EATING

Asia House	7
Bakery Itiriki	9
Black Dog	3
Bovinu's Grill	4
Famiglia Mancini	5
Korea House	10
Ponto Chic	2
Restaurante Okuyama	11
Sushi-Yassu	13
Uni Alquimia Culinaria	16
Yamaga	12

Ⓜ SÃO JOAQUIM

Museu da Imigração Japonesa

CAMBUCI

RUA DO LAVAPES

RUA TAMANDARÉ

N

0   500 m

French-style mansion set in a walled garden that's a huge contrast to the surrounding steel-and-glass hulks, and now a state-run museum. Also worth a look is the **Museu de Arte de São Paulo** or **MASP** (Av. Paulista 1578; Tues–Sun 11am–6pm, until 8pm Thurs; R$15, free Tues), standing on four red stilts floating above the ground and allowing a view of the city behind. The galleries upstairs contain one of Latin America's largest collection of Western art, while the basement below has a very enjoyable and reasonable buffet.

Separated from Bixiga by Av. Paulista is **Jardins**, one of São Paulo's most expensive and fashionable neighbourhoods, modelled in 1915 according to the principles of the British Garden City movement, with cool, leafy streets leading down the hill. Actually a compendium of three smaller neighbourhoods – Jardim America, Jardim Europa and Jardim Paulista – it's home to swanky villas, condos, top-end restaurants and bars, and is a great place for an afternoon stroll, with some pretty expensive shopping on **Rua Oscar** and **Rua Augusta**.

Vila Madalena, Pinheiros and Itaim Bibi

West of Jardins, the *bairro* of **Vila Madalena** is also chock-a-block with nightlife and restaurants, though with a younger, more bohemian feel than its neighbour. Southwards, **Pinheiros** is rougher around the edges but also home to some decent nightlife, and further south, **Itaim Bibi** is a chic neighbourhood with galleries, bars and more good restaurants. **Avenida Brig. Faria Lima** is the main drag here, while the nearby **Museu Brasileiro da Escultura** at Av. Europa 218 (Tues–Sun 10am–7pm) is temporary home to travelling exhibits of Brazilian artists and sculptors. Cutting through Pinheiros is **Rua Teodoro Sampaio**, a street lined with music stores, some of which have free music performances, usually on weekends. Nearby, and worth driving over (especially when dramatically lit at night), is the 138m-tall, cable-stayed **Octavio Frias de Oliveira bridge**. Opened in May 2008, it was quick to become a postcard image with separate roadways passing under a giant "X".

Butantã and Morumbi

Further west of Pinheiros, near the **Cidade Universitária,** Butantã and Morumbi are a bit of a pain to get to. Here you'll find the **Casa do Bandeirante**, a preserved, whitewashed adobe homestead from the time of the *bandeirantes*, early colonizers of the Brazilian interior. The Instituto Butantã's **Museu Biológico** at Av. Vital Brasil 1500 (Wed–Sun 9am–4.30pm) will titillate snake-lovers – it houses rattlesnakes, boas and anacondas among others. Bordering Morumbi, you'll see (or pass through) Sampa's new and impressive financial district, **Berrini**, within whose towering skyscrapers the largest sums of money in Brazil get moved around.

Parque do Ibirapuera

South of Jardins and sandwiched between Itaim Bibi and Vila Mariana, **Moema** is a rich district with some really good food joints, although its main feature is the **Parque do Ibirapuera** (daily 5am–midnight), opened in 1954 to celebrate the four-hundredth anniversary of the founding of São Paulo. Outside its main north entrance is the **Monumento às Bandeiras**, a 1953 sculpture by Victor Brecheret that celebrates a *bandeirante* expedition; inside there are two galleries and a museum. The **Museu de Arte Contemporânea** (Tues–Fri 10am–7pm, Sat & Sun 10am–4pm; R$6) has regularly rotated works by twentieth-century European and Brazilian artists, while the **Museu de Arte Moderna** (Tues–Sun 10am–6pm; R$5.50; free Sun) is a smaller museum that mostly holds temporary exhibits of Brazilian artists. The **Museu Afro-Brasil** in the northern part of the park at Pavilhão Manoel da Nóbrega, on Avenida Pedro Álvares Cabral, Gate 10 (daily 10am–5pm), is an interesting (though limited) collection exploring the African-Brazilian experience through paintings and artefacts, with sections on religion, slavery and oral history, as well as regular visiting exhibitions and theatrical productions.

Vila Mariana and Ipiranga

East of the park is the **Museu Lasar Segall**, at Rua Berta 111 (Tues–Sat 2–7pm, Sun 2–6pm; free), which houses the work of the Latvian-born, naturalized-Brazilian painter, originally a member of the German Expressionist movement. In nearby Ipiranga (avenidas Dom Pedro and Nazareth) is the impressive **Museu Paulista** (Tues–Sun 9am–5pm; R$4, free Sun), with paintings and furniture that once belonged to the Brazilian royal family. The park the museum stands in was the place where Brazilian independence was declared in 1822.

Arrival and information

Air São Paulo has two airports: Congonhas, which is in the city, and Guarulhos, about 25km from downtown. From Congonhas taxis to downtown cost about R$50; from Guarulhos about R$100. An airport bus service (⊛ www.emtu.sp.gov.br) runs the following routes to and from Guarulhos (R$28): Paulista/Augusta hotel circuit (hourly; 6.10am–11.10pm); Praça da República (every half-hour all day); Itaim Bibi/Faria Lima (hourly; 6.10am–11.10pm); Tietê Rodoviária (hourly; 24hr); Barra Funda (hourly; 5.45am–10.15pm); Congonhas (every half-hour).

Bus Inter-state and international buses arrive at the vast Tietê Rodoviária terminal north of the centre, which lies on the metro line. Three other *rodoviárias* – Jabaquara, Barra Funda and Bresser – serve towns throughout São Paulo State.

Tourist information Available at the Tietê Rodoviária, Congonhas and Guarulhos, though these desks are not especially helpful. You're better off buying a *Mapa Turístico* (R$14.99) at the Laselva Bookstore or heading to the central information

booth at Av. São João 473, Centro, near Praça da República (Mon–Fri 6am–10pm, Sun 8am–8pm; ⊛ www.cityofsaopaulo.com), where they're friendly and have excellent pamphlets and free maps.

City transport

The city is huge but more or less manageable to get around, with the exception – and this can't be emphasized enough – of 4–7pm, when the rush hour brings both roads and metro to a virtual halt. Travel earlier or later to reach your destination.

Bus A dozen private companies make up Sampa's public transport and navigating the 1500 routes can be complicated – though at R$2.30 per trip it's certainly cheap. You can load up a *bilhete único* and ride up to four buses within two hours and pay only one fare (on Sun and holidays, up to 8 buses with a single fare). The card can be used on any bus and the metro. Buses run from 4am–midnight.

Metro (subway) Three lines: Linha Azul (blue, north–south) from Tucuruvi to Jabaquara; Linha Vermelha (red, east–west) from Barra Funda to Corinthians-Itaupera; and Linha Verde (green, east–west) under Av. Paulista from Ana Rosa to Vila Metro. A one-trip ticket costs R$2.40. If you buy a *Cartão Fidelidade*, you get 20 trips for R$44 (saving R$0.30 per trip). Trains run from 5am–midnight. Buses and trains run from the end of most lines.

Taxi Taxis are metered and start at R$3.50. You can also call the following cab companies: Coopertaxi (☏ 11/6195-6000), Ligue Táxi (☏ 11/3866-3030), Especial Rádio Taxi (☏ 11/3146-4000).

Tours Turis Metro (☏ 0800/770-7722, ⊛ www .metro.sp.gov.br) runs free 3-hr city tours (Sat & Sun 9am & 2pm; English spoken), which depart from the Anhangabaú and Trianon-MASP stops, relying on the metro for transport – your only expense. Also check out City Tour São Paulo (☏ 11/5182-3974, ⊛ www.circuitosaopaulo .com.br), whose a/c bus city tours and historic, shopping, culinary and night-walking tours start at R$40. For football/soccer matches Futebol Experience (☏ 11/3167-7905, ⊛ www.fxp.com.br) runs expert trips to all three major city clubs: São Paulo, at Estádio Morumbi Butantã; Corinthians, at Estádio Pacaembu, Consolação; and Palmeiras, at Estádio Parque Itália, Barra Funda.

Accommodation

Note that all options serve breakfast unless otherwise indicated.

Hostels and pousadas

Casa Club Hostel Rua Mourato Coelho 973, Vila Madelena ☎ 11/3798-0051, ⊛ www.casaclub .com.br. One of the better "house" hostels in this upscale, artsy *bairro*, a 25-min walk from the metro Vila Madelena. Great downstairs bar/kitchen under the mango tree. Dorms a little crowded, but wi-fi included. Dorms R$35.

Lime Time Hostel Rua Treze de Maio 1552, Bixiga ☎ 11/2935-5463, ⊛ www.limetimehostels.com. Super-friendly place, that won't win awards for its dorms but more than makes up for it with its vibe: great *caipirinhas*, free use of Macs and wi-fi, kitchen (no breakfast), PlayStation, and guided nights out. Between Liberdade and Bixiga, yards from Paulista. Dorms R$35, rooms R$100.

Pousada Dona Zilah Alameda Franca 1621, Jardim Paulista ☎ 11/3062-1444, ⊛ www.zilah.com. São Paulo's only "proper" pousada, in a good location near Av. Paulista and with friendly, family touches and superb breakfast buffet. Double/twin/quad rooms are on a par with a good hotel, though singles are overpriced. Wi-fi and excellent *Zilah Gourmet* restaurant downstairs. Rates include tax. R$210.

Pousada Dos Franceses Rua dos Franceses 100, Bixiga ☎ 11/3288-1592, ⊛ www.pousada dosfranceses.com.br. More hostel than pousada, in an ideal spot near Av. Paulista and Bixiga. Fresh, blue rooms, small garden, guest kitchen and a mix of dorms (R$40) and doubles (R$100). Wi-fi R$5/day.

São Paulo HI Hostels (Downtown) Rua Barão de Campinas 94 ☎ 11/3333-0844, ⊛ www.hostelsp .com.br; (Vila Madelena) Rua Girassol 519, Vila Madelena ☎ 11/3031-6779, ⊛ www.hostelsampa .com.br. The downtown area is grimy but this gigantic hostel is near the metro, safe, friendly and with numerous facilities, including a roof terrace. HI-discounted dorms R$33, good-value doubles/ triples from R$76; Vila Madalena is smarter and cosier with consummate facilities and close to great bars (HI-discounted dorms R$36, rooms R$90).

Hotels

Bali Rua Fradique Coutinho 740, Pinheiros ☎ 11/3812-8270, ⊛ www.hotelbali.com.br. The mirrors behind the beds make you wonder if it's not a "love motel" at first, but it stands up to scrutiny. Near Vila Madalena. R$70.

Banri Hotel Rua Galvão Bueno 209, Liberdade ☎ 11/3207-8877. There may be cracking plaster in the hallways but this is one hotel where the rooms are better than the public spaces – good value, almost stylish, and near great Japanese restaurants. R$105.

Formule 1 Rua Vergueiro 1571, Paraiso 1571 ☎ 11/5085-5699, ⊛ www.hotelformule1.com. Right by the metro near Paulista, it's very good value but the last word in characterless. All rooms sleep up to three for the same price; no breakfast. Has three other locations around central São Paulo. R$110.

Gold Hotel Alameda Jaú 2008, Jardins ☎ 11/3085-0805, ⊛ www.hotelgold.com.br. On a noisy corner two blocks from Paulista, but has some serious personality, with decor that's Greek diner meets kitsch Taj Mahal. Funky red rooms with doors with room service openings. R$90.

Itamarati Av. Dr. Vieira de Carvalho 150, Centro Novo ☎ 11/3474-4133, ⊛ www.hotelitamarati.com. br. The area is fairly seedy at night and the formica furniture won't make you feel warm and fuzzy, but it's clean and reliable. There are numerous near-identical options nearby, such as the *Riviera* at Al. Barão de Limeira 117 (☎ 11/3221-8077). R$80.

Paulista Center Hotel Rua da Consolação 2567 Consolação ☎ 11/3062-0733, ⊛ www .paulistacenterhotel.com.br. A crisp business hotel just off Paulista, with free wi-fi. R$143.

Eating

São Paulo hosts by far Brazil's best selection of restaurants, and you'll want to splurge at least once. Self-caterers should take advantage of the excellent quality Mercado Municipal (don't neglect the upstairs food court, nor the city's best *pasteis*). A range of cheap *por kilo* restaurants are located along Rua Augusta, north of Av. Paulista. Also keep in mind that at night all bars also serve food, with Vila Madalena known for high-quality options.

Cafés, bakeries, snacks

Bakery Itiriki Rua dos Estudantes 24, Liberdade. Brazilian and Japanese pastries and savoury snacks, with upstairs seating.

Black Dog Rua Alameda Joaquim Eugênio de Lima 612; Rua Líbero Badaró 456 (and other locations, see ⓦ www.blackdog.com.br). The pressed hot dogs here (around R$10), with oozing *catupiry* cheese and other strange fillings, are perfect after-drinks food but they taste really good sober too.

Fran's Cafe Praça Benedito Calixto 191; Rua Cubatão 1111, Vila Mariana, Jardins. Excellent coffee, and free wi-fi access.

Havanna Café Rua Bela Cintra 1829. An airy café perfect for lounging around and reading the paper, with high-quality coffee and free wi-fi. Try the *empanadas* or foil-wrapped *alfajor* cookies.

O Melhor Bolo de Chocolate do Mundo Rua Oscar Freire 125, Jardins. Its name ("the world's best chocolate cake") gives it away – and after tasting their creations here, modelled on those of a renowned Lisbon bakery, you may well agree.

St. Etienne Al. Joaquim Eug. de Lima 1417, Jardins; Rua Harmonia 699, Vila Madalena. A busy, unpretentious café/bar with pavement seating, great sandwiches and a R$16 soup buffet.

Stuppendo Rua Canário 1321, Moema. A great place for top-notch ice cream, with flavours galore rivalling Italy's best.

Suco Bagaço Rua Haddock Lobo 1483, Jardins. Get your *açaí* (or other frozen fruit) fix or grab a quiche and a salad for just R$8.60.

Brazilian

Bovinu's Grill Alameda Santos 2100, Jardim Paulista. Cheap-ish *churrascaría* and *por kilo* restaurant; very often packed out. Spend around R$28 for an evening all-you-can-eat buffet with numerous meats, salads, stews and fish.

Consulado Mineiro Restaurante Praça Benedito Calixto 74, Pinheiros ☎ 11/3064-3882. Great food from Minas Gerais at this popular choice in the Jardins/Pinheiros area. Crowded at weekends; expect to pay R$50 for two.

Dona Lucinha Av. Chibarás 399, Moema ☎ 11/5051-2050. Excellent unlimited R$35 lunch buffet (Tues–Sun) at the best *mineiro* restaurant in São Paulo. Try the full range of typical meat and vegetable dishes (vegetarians catered for), *cachaças* and desserts. Be warned: it's double the price at night.

Ponto Chic Largo do Paissandu 27, Centro Novo ☎ 11/3222-6528. Established in 1922, this low-key sandwich shop does a scrumptious *bauru* with roast beef, four cheeses, tomato and pickle on baguette, plus other meaty goodies.

D.O.M. Rua Barão de Capanema 549 ☎ 11/3088-0761, ⓦ www.domrestaurante .com.br. One of Brazil's best restaurants, starring celebrated chef Alex Atala. If you are going, there's no other way to do it than by working your way through the tasting menu, around R$100. Mon–Fri noon–3pm & 7pm–midnight; Sat 7pm–1am; closed Sun.

Figueira Rubaiyat Rua Haddock Lobo 1738, Jardins ☎ 11/3063-3888. Built around a massive, golden-lit, 130-year-old majestic fig tree, this place serves the city's best steak, *feijoada* and Brazilian specialities. Around R$100 per person (unlimited food); great for a splurge. Mon–Sat noon–3.30pm & 7pm–midnight; Sun noon–6pm.

Uni Alquimia Culinaria MASP, Av. Paulista 1578 ☎ 11/3253-2829. This basement buffet is not the typical museum cafeteria. For R$28 you can endlessly sample the more than sixty types of salads, hot dishes and desserts (lunch only).

Italian and Arabic

For decent Italian food, head to *bairro* Bixiga, where you can take your pick of at least ten budget places; try Rua 13 de Maio.

Espaço Árabe Rua Oscar Freire 168, Jardins ☎ 11/3081-1824. This large and welcoming restaurant does great, tasty chargrilled chicken and steak kebabs, hummus and other excellent Middle Eastern food (from R$25).

Famiglia Mancini Rua Avanhandava 81, Bixiga ☎ 11/3256-4320. Great antipasti, lasagne and other pasta at this mid-priced and highly popular restaurant, with another branch serving high-quality pizza just opposite.

Speranza Av. Sabiá, 786, Moema ☎ 11/5051-1229. This labyrinthine pizza house with balcony seating has been open since 1958, and successfully replicates genuine Neapolitan pizza (from R$30).

Japanese, Korean and Thai

In addition to those below, seek out traditional Korean food along Rua Correia de Melo in *bairro* Bom Retiro.

Asia House Rua da Glória 86, Liberdade and Rua Augusta 1918, Jardins. Great-value *por kilo* lunch buffet, with a range of Japanese soups, sushi, and noodle dishes; expect to pay up to R$18 for a big meal.

Korea House Rua Galvão Bueno 43, Liberdade ☎11/3208-3052. One of São Paulo's few Korean restaurants, with great soups for R$20 and barbecue for R$30 – a nice haven from the busy street downstairs.

Nam Thai Rua Manuel Guedes 444, Itaim Bibi ☎11/3168-0662, ⬤www.namthai.com.br. Great Thai food is hard to find in South America, but this smart restaurant serves an authentic range of dishes, including excellent *tom-yum* soup, succulent ginger fish and delicious curries (mains from R$40).

Restaurante Okuyama Rua da Glória 553 ☎11/3341-0780. Probably the best value of the cheaper Japanese places in Liberdade, open for lunch but most popular late at night until 3 or 4am. Sushi *executivo* lunches for R$15, plus excellent platters for two.

Sushi-Yassu Rua Tomas Gonzaga 98, Liberdade ☎11/3209-6622; Rua Manoel da Nóbrega 199/209 ☎11/3288-2966, ⬤www.sushiyassu.com.br. Great mid-priced sushi, sashimi and other dishes on a barely decipherable menu (ask staff to help), in a very traditional Japanese environment.

Temaki Rua Iguatemi 265 Itaim Bibi, ☎11/3168-5202; Rua da Consolação 3113 ☎11/3088-3719. Fast-food sushi handrolls, R$8 each, from several locations around town.

Yamaga Rua Thoaz Gonzaga 66, Liberdade ☎11/3275-1790. Great Japanese food in an inviting setting, and also reasonably priced (though not budget); lunch specials bring the cost of good-quality sushi down to R$18 for a full plate of sashimi. Excellent ramen dishes too.

Vegetarian

Grão de Soja Rua Girassol 602, Vila Madalena ☎11/3813-2166. One of the *bairro*'s best bohemian eating spots, with soya replacing meat in most dishes, from pasta to Brazilian *feijoada*.

Sattva Alameda Itu 1564, Jardim Paulista ☎11/3083-6237. A lunchtime *prato de dia* is served here for R$12, including a juice, though it's in an otherwise expensive part of town. Full evening vegetarian menu; mains from R$25.

Nightlife and entertainment

São Paulo's nightlife is fantastic; a good enough reason alone for visiting the city. Options are scattered all over, with Rua Augusta north of Paulista the unofficial nightlife (and red-light) centre, while Vila Madalena (corners of Morato

Coelho and Aspicquelta) is a more upscale drinking hotspot, Pinheiros great for Brazilian down at-heel-places, and Barra Funda for big dance music clubs and more. Bixiga/Bela Vista and Itaim Bibi have good live music, while Jardins has the smartest bars for the deepest pockets. Pick up *Guia da Folha* (every Fri) at the tourist office or *Divirta-Se* (weekly) at news-stands for music, theatre, dance and film listings. The listings below detail a few of the best options right across Sampa's varied scenes.

Bars and pubs

All Black Rua Oscar Freire 163, Jardins ☎11/3088-7990, ⬤www.allblack.com.br. São Paulo's best Irish pub for those dying for a Guinness.

Bar Brahma Av. São João 677, Centro ☎11/3333-3030, ⬤www.barbrahmasp.com. Yellow-vested waiters serve good food and beer at this famous daytime bar where Caetano Veloso wrote his song "Sampa". Live music upstairs; decent Brazilian menu.

Bar Favela Vila Olímpia, Rua Professor Atílio Innocenti 419 ☎11/3848-6988, ⬤www.barfavela.com.br. Live music daily until late covering rock, Brazilian pop music (MPB) and samba, at this hip spot on the edge of Itaim Bibi.

Bar Filial Rua Fidalga 254, Vila Madalena ☎11/3813-9226. Order a *caipirinha vermelha* from a bow-tie-wearing waiter at this smart and busy chequered-floor bar.

Chopperia Opção Rua Carlos Comenale, 97 ☎11/3288-7823. Yards from Avenida Paulista and MASP, this is a really popular daytime/after-work place, with an outdoor terrace that's great for watching workhorse Sampa go by.

DroSoPhylal Rua Pedro Taques 80, Consolação ☎11/3120-5535. The strange art and bizarre decor contribute to making this funky bar a popular spot, but the good food and drink are what bring people back.

Kia Ora Rua Dr. Eduardo de Souza Aranha 377, Itaim Bibi ☎11/3846-8300, ⬤www.kiaora.com.br. A little bit of "down-under" in Brazil; the spacious, wooden bar here has a pool table, live music, cover charge, and a dancing, flirty crowd till late.

London Station Rua Tabapuã 1439, Itaim Bibi ☎11/3368-8300. Chic bar/lounge with DJs and live music. Wear that collared shirt or little black dress. Cover R$15–25. Happy hours early evening.

Ludus Luderia Rua Treze de Maio 972, Bixiga ☎11/3253-8452, ⬤www.ludusluderia.com.br. Rainy days (or nights) frequently afflict Sampa, so if you don't fancy damp bar-hopping, check out this place with an (almost) human-sized chessboard and 450 other games, plus a bar and cheap bites. Open noon until 11pm Sun–Thurs, until 3am Fri & Sat.

O'Malley's Alameda Itú 1529, Jardins ☎11/3086-0780, ⓦ www.omalleysbar.net. This cavernous Irish pub has a great happy hour (6–8pm) including food, plus pool, darts, free wi-fi, and live music.

Posto 6 Rua Aspicquelta. This big corner bar is one of the four mammoth standbys in Vila Madalena and central to Sampa's night scene. Get some chop with your *picanha* and cook it at your table.

🏃 SKYE *Hotel Unique*, Av. Brigadeiro Luis Antônio 4700, Jardim Paulista ☎11/3055-4700, ⓦ www.hotelunique.com.br. This is the place to start your night, on the roof of the "watermelon hotel" sipping a cocktail along with the beautiful people and a 360-degree view of the skyline. Chic and luxurious.

Clubs

A Lôca Rua Frei Caneca 916, Consolação ⓦ www.aloca.com.br. Crazy-busy, this place gets crammed with people (gay and straight) looking to dance to techno, house and electronica. There's a second bar upstairs but it is sometimes reserved for VIPs. Cover varies. Open Tues–Sun from midnight.

Canto da Ema Av. Brig. Faria Lima 364, Pinheiros ⓦ www.cantodaema.com.br. You can hear the *forró* outside despite the airlock entrance. Inside, it's all dancing fun and *cachaça*. Cover charge R$7 women, R$10. Open Wed–Sun from 11pm.

Carioca Club Rua Cardeal Arcoverde 2899, Pinheiros. Great dance hall in a slightly seedy area, that often feels more Northeastern-Brazil in atmosphere than *carioca* (from Rio); featuring live *forró*, funk or samba nightly, and with friendly people not averse to showing newcomers the ropes. From 11pm; very busy on Mon. Cover R$25.

D-Edge Al. Olga 170, Barra Funda ⓦ www .d-edge.com.br. Takes its name as Sampa's premier electronica hotspot seriously, with nightly DJs playing anything from techno to (*baile*) funk, and a mixed crowd ready to dance. Mon–Sat from midnight (check programme); entry from R$40.

Ó do Borogodó Rua Horácio Lane 21. This is the real Brazil: a gritty, authentic samba bar where everybody dances with everybody. R$20 cover.

Traço de União Rua Claudio Soares, Pinheiros ⓦ www.tracodeuniao.com.br. One of the city's top Samba venues, mainly famous for its brilliant Saturday *feijoadas* (R$20–30) from 2pm until late, with entrance including food and great music – but it's busy on Wed and Fri nights, too, with a good vibe.

Villa Country Av. Francisco Matarazzo 774, nr. Barra Funda ⓦ www.villacountry.com.br. *Serteneja* (Brazilian Country Music) may not be everyone's choice but it's huge across São Paulo state and

this 1800-capacity venue needs to be seen to be believed. Expect masses of seriously up-for-it guys in cowboy hats and girls in cowgirl hotpants.

Directory

Banks and exchange There are cambios at the airports and sprinkled throughout the city, including Banco do Brasil, at Rua São Bento 465, Centro, and Bradesco and HSBC along Av. Brigadeiro Faria Lima and Av. Paulista.

Car rental Hertz, Rua Da Consolação 431, Centro ☎11/3258-9384; Localiza, Rua da Consolação 419, Centro ☎11/3231-3055; Movida, Rua da Consolação 271, Centro ☎11/3255-6870.

Consulates Argentina, Av. Paulista 2313, ☎11/3897-9522; Australia, Alameda Santos 700, 9th floor, ☎11/2112-6200; Canada, Av. das Nações Unidas 12901, 16th Floor ☎11/5509-4321; Ireland, Al. Joaquim Eugênio de Lima 447 ☎11/3147-7788; South Africa, Av. Paulista 1754, 12th Floor ☎11/3285-0433; UK, Rua Ferreira de Araujo, 741, 2nd floor ☎11/3094-2700; US, Rua Henri Dunant 500 ☎11/5186-7000.

Crime and police São Paulo has high crime, and though most dangerous areas are on the city's outskirts you should be careful everywhere and keep valuables hidden. At night, downtown and the red-light district around Luz should be avoided. The area around Praça da República gets seedy after dark. Police emergencies ☎190. DEATUR (tourist police) at Av. São Luís 91, near Praça da República ☎11/3214-0209.

Hospitals Best hospital is Einstein, at Av. Albert Einstein 627, Morumbi ☎11/3747-1233, ⓦ www .einstein.br. For dental work, Dental Office Augusta, at Rua Augusta 878, Cerqueira César ☎11/256-3104; the largest central public hospital with A&E is Clínicas, at Av. Dr. Enéas Carvalho de Aguiar 255 ☎11/3887-6611.

Laundries Lavesec, Praça Julio Mequita 13, at Sta. Efigênia & Av. Castro Alves 437, Aclimação; 5 à Sec, at Rua José Maria Lisboa 1079, and Brigadeiro Luis Antonio 2013, Loja 4.

Left luggage Guarulhos, Congonhas and Tietê Rodoviária have 24hr lockers available (R$10–30/day).

Post offices See ⓦ www.correios.com.br. Praça Correio, corner Av. São João (Mon–Fri 8am–7pm); Av. Brigadeiro Luis Antonio 996, Bixiga (Mon–Fri 9am–5pm).

Visas To extend a tourist visa, go to the Polícia Federal, at Rua Hugo D'Antola 95, 3rd floor, Lapa de Baixo (Mon–Fri 8am–2pm; ☎11/3616-5000). To get there go to Metro Barra Funda and then take a taxi (R$15–20).

Moving on

Air As Brazil's main transport hub, domestic flights leave Congonhas and Guarulhos airports for all Brazilian destinations, with international departures from Guarulhos only.

Belo Horizonte (20 flights per day; 1hr 30min); Foz de Iguassu (6 daily; 3hr); Rio de Janeiro (every 30min; 1hr); Salvador (8 daily; 4hr).

Bus Buses leave from Rodoviária Tietê to points throughout Brazil and to neighbouring countries.

Belo Horizonte (hourly; 9hr); Curitiba (hourly; 5hr); Foz do Iguassu (5 daily; 19hr); Rio de Janeiro (every 15min; 6hr); Salvador (4 daily; 24hr).

The South

The southern states of Brazil – **Paraná**, **Santa Catarina** and **Rio Grande do Sul** – are generally considered to be the most developed in the country and show little of the obvious poverty found elsewhere. The smallest of Brazil's regions, the South maintains an economic influence completely out of proportion to its size, largely the result of an agrarian structure that is based on highly efficient small and medium-sized units and an economically over-active population that produces a per capita output considerably higher than the national average. For these reasons the south remains an expensive place to travel and hotel and restaurant prices are equivalent to those in Rio de Janeiro. Choose wisely, though, and you can still find good value places to eat out, especially buffets.

The **southern coast** has a subtropical climate that in the summer (Nov–March) offers welcome respite from the oppressive heat of the Brazilian cities. Much of the Paranaense coast is still unspoilt by the ravages of mass tourism, and building is virtually forbidden on the beautiful islands of the **Bay of Paranaguá** – the most frequently visited being the gorgeous **Ilha do Mel**. By way of contrast, tourism has encroached along Santa Catarina's coast, but development has been restrained and resorts such as most of those on the **Ilha de Santa Catarina** around **Florianópolis**, particularly in the south of the island, remain small and in tune with the region's natural beauty.

Despite the appeal of the coast, the spectacular **Iguaçu Falls** are deservedly the South's most visited attraction, the powerful waters set against a background of unspoiled rainforest. The rest of the interior is less frequently visited. Much of it is mountainous, the home of people whose way of life seems to have altered little since the arrival of the first Europeans. The highland areas and the grasslands of southern Rio Grande do Sul are largely given over to vast cattle ranches, where latter-day **gauchos** – who share many cultural similarities with their Uruguayan and Argentine neighbours – keep alive many of the skills of their forebears. To the north the remnants of the **Jesuit missions** pay homage to their brief but productive occupation of the area.

CURITIBA

Founded in 1693 as a gold-mining camp, **CURITIBA** was of little importance until 1853 when it was made capital of Paraná. Since then, the city's population has risen steadily from a few thousand to 1.8 million; its inhabitants are largely descendants of Polish, German, Italian and other immigrants. On average, *curitibanos* enjoy Brazil's highest standard of living and the city boasts facilities that are the envy of other parts of the country. Its eco-friendly design, abundant with green spaces, is a model that many urban planners would like to emulate, although apart from the old town it's not the most beautiful of cities.

What to see and do

Most of Curitiba's main attractions can be visited relatively easily in a day or so on foot. However, if you have limited time, take the Linha Turismo **bus tour**, which departs from Praça Tiradentes

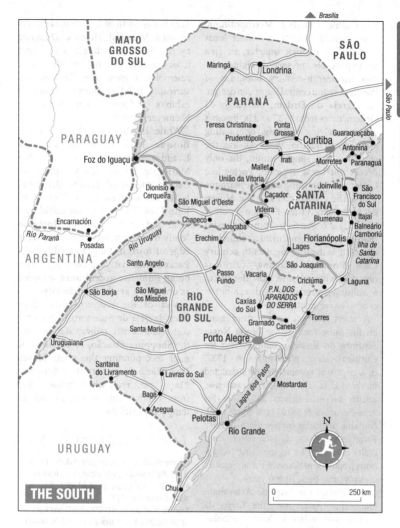

THE SOUTH

(every 30min Tues–Sun 9am–5.30pm; R$20). Stopping at 25 attractions around the city centre and suburbs, it takes 2hr 30min to complete the full circuit. Tickets allow passengers five hop-on hop-off stops.

Rua das Flores

The **Rua das Flores** – a pedestrianized precinct section of the Rua XV de Novembro, lined with graceful, pastel-coloured early twentieth-century buildings – is the centre's main late afternoon and early evening meeting point. Few of the surrounding streets are especially attractive, but the former city hall, at **Praça José Borges**, across from the flower market, is well worth a look.

Praça Tiradentes and the historic quarter

A couple of blocks north from Rua das Flores is **Praça Tiradentes**, the site where the city was founded and home to the neo-Gothic **Catedral Metropolitana**. From here a pedestrian tunnel leads to Curitiba's **historic quarter**, an area of impeccably preserved eighteenth- and nineteenth-century buildings of Portuguese and central European design. The **Igreja da Ordem**, on Largo da Ordem, dates from 1737 and is the city's oldest surviving building, dominating the historic quarter. Plain outside, the church is also simple within, the only decoration being typically Portuguese blue and white tiling and late Baroque altars. The church contains the **Museu de Arte Sacra** (Tues–Fri 9am–noon & 1–6pm, Sat & Sun 9am–3pm; free), with relics gathered from Curitiba's churches. Opposite is the mid-eighteenth-century **Casa Romário Martins**, Curitiba's oldest surviving house, now the site of a cultural foundation and exhibition centre for regional artists.

A short distance uphill from here, on the same road, is the **Igreja Nossa Senhora do Rosário**, built by and for Curitiba's slave population in 1737, though it was completely reconstructed in the 1930s. The **Museu Paranaense**, nearby on Rua Kellers 289 (Tues–Fri 9am–5pm, Sat & Sun 11am–3pm; free), contains paintings by twentieth-century Paranaense artists, as well as arts and crafts made by the region's first indigenous population. Some of the antiquities on show date back 10,000 years.

On Sundays the **Feira de Artesanato** (9am–2pm) takes over the Largo da Ordem and adjacent Praça Garibaldi, with stalls selling local and regional handicrafts – look out, too, for Polish and Ukrainian items, including simple embroideries and intricately painted eggs.

Modern Curitiba

Some of Curitiba's more unusual and impressive attractions are more contemporary, and easily accessible by foot from the centre. Among the largest museums in Latin America is the futuristic **Museu Oscar Niemeyer** (Tues–Sun 10am–6pm; R$4), about 3km to the north of Curitiba's old town, on Rua Marechal Hermes. Designed by the Brazilian architect after whom it was named, its most notable feature resembles a giant eye. This bizarre surrealist building houses modernist exhibits, including many works by Niemeyer himself.

While in the area check out the **Bosque João Paulo II** on Rua Euclides Bandeira, just off Rua Mário de Barros (daily 6am–8pm; free) a memorial garden dedicated to Polish settlers, opened by Pope John Paul II in 1980. You could also head out to the **Jardím Botânico** (daily 6am–8pm; free) on the eastern edge of town at Rua Ostoja Roguski. Packed with native plants, it centres on an immense **greenhouse**, adopted as one of the symbols of the city.

West of the *rodoferroviária* along Avenida Sete de Setembro is the city's converted former railway station, now the **Shopping Estação**, an atmospheric mall incorporating the small **Museu Ferroviária** (Tues–Sat 10am–6pm Sun 11am–7pm; free), which houses relics from Paraná's railway era as well as temporary exhibits.

Arrival and information

Air The ultramodern airport (℡ 41/3381-1153) is about 30min from the city centre. Taxis from the airport to the centre charge about R$55; there is also a bus service (R$8).
Bus The main bus (℡ 41/3320-3232) and train (℡ 041/3888-3488) stations – the *rodoferroviária* – are next to one another in the southeast of town, about ten blocks from the city centre.
Tourist information There's a year-round tourist information booth at the *rodoferroviária* (daily 8am–6pm; ℡ 41/3320-3121, ⓦ www.viaje.curitiba .pr.gov.br).

City transport

Curitiba's centre is small enough to be able to walk to most places within the city centre.
Bus City buses stop at the strange glass boarding tubes you see dotted around town. Pay at the turnstile on entering the tube, not on the bus.

Accommodation

There are numerous cheap and secure hotels near the *rodoferroviária*. Places in the city centre are within walking distance of most attractions and are generally excellent value.

Elo Hotel Universidade Rua Amintas de Barros 383 ☎ 41/3028-9400, ⓦ www.hoteiselo.com.br. Modern, rather characterless hotel with a pool, next to the university's main administrative building. Rooms are clean and comfortable and the staff are very helpful. R$135.

Lumini Rua General Carneiro 1094 ☎ 41/3264 5244, ⓦ www.hotellumini.com.br. Near the *rodoferroviária*, this retro hotel has simple but clean rooms with wi-fi access, minibar and cable TV. Breakfast included. R$95.

Nikko Rua Barão do Rio Branco 546 ☎ 41/2105-1808, ⓦ www.hotelnikko.com.br. Modern hotel with Japanese-influenced interior. The small rooms are simply and attractively furnished, with mineral water supplying the bath and shower, and there's a Japanese garden, a tiny swimming pool and a restaurant serving Brazilian food. R$135.

Plaza Rua Luiz Xavier 24 ☎ 41/3888-0900. A good, affordable choice, more for its excellent location at the end of the Rua de las Flores than for its minimalist rooms. R$90.

Rheno Pedro Ivo 538 ☎ 41/3224-0412. A clean and perfectly acceptable budget option with modern, no-frills rooms and tiled bathrooms. Easily the best of the numerous cheap options on this street – some of the others charge by the hour. R$45.

Roma Hostel Rua Barão do Rio Branco 805 ☎ 41/3224-2117, ⓦ www.hostelroma.com.br. A block from the Shopping Estação, midway between the *rodoferroviária* and the centre, this is a standard HI hostel with dorms, private rooms and an attractive courtyard and garden. Dorms R$30, rooms R$75.

Eating and drinking

Curitiba's prosperity and its inhabitants' diverse ethnic origins have given rise to a good range of restaurants, with the most interesting located in the historic centre. For the cheapest eats check out the food court in Shopping Estação.

Mein Schatz Rua Jaime Reis 18 ☎ 41/3076-0121, ⓦ www.meinschatz.com.br. Next door to the Igreja do Rosário, offering a variable and affordable menu of German and Brazilian dishes in quasi-Bavarian surroundings. You can order a duo of German sausages for R$24. Open Mon–Fri 11.30am–2.30pm & Sun until 6.30pm.

No Kafé Fest Rua Duque de Caxias 4 ☎ 41/3223-9534, ⓦ www.nokafefest.com.br. In an alley next to the Igreja do Rosário, *No Kafé Fest* offers an excellent and reasonably priced *por kilo* lunchtime buffet of hot and cold dishes (R$23.90 per kilo). A German-style high tea is served in the afternoon in a very pleasant building shared with a gallery. Open for lunch Sun–Fri 11.30am–2pm and German high tea Tues–Sat 3.30–8.30pm.

Oriente Arabe Rua Kellers 95 ☎ 41/3224-2061. Excellent, reasonably priced Arabic food, with main meals starting from R$18. If you want to try a bit of everything go for the *rodízio* (lunch R$19.90; dinner Tues–Fri R$29.90). Open Mon–Sat 11.30am–2pm & 6pm–11pm, Sun 11.30am–3pm.

Schwarzwald Rua Claudino dos Santos 63 ☎ 41/3223-2585, ⓦ www.bardoalemaocuritiba.com.br. Also known as the *Bar do Alemão* (German bar), this pub and restaurant has outdoor seating and a spacious, kitsch interior. A popular evening student meeting point in Largo da Ordem, at the heart of the old town, it serves excellent German food with cold beer. A pork joint with sausages for two will set you back R$37. Open daily 11am–2am.

Directory

Banks and exchange Main offices of banks are concentrated at the Praça Osório end of Rua das Flores.

Consulates Argentina, Rua Benjamin Constant 67, 15th floor (☎ 41/3222-0799); Paraguay, Rua Gen. Osório 400 (☎ 41/3222-9226); UK, Rua Presidente Faria 51, 2nd floor (☎ 41/3023-6728).

Hospitals In emergencies use the Nossa Senhora das Graças hospital at Rua Prof Rosa Saporski 229, which has a 24hr hotline ☎ 41/3240-6555.

Internet Widely available throughout the city. A convenient internet café near the *rodoviária* is on

> ### TREAT YOURSELF
>
> **Durski** Rua Jaime Reis 254 ☎ 41/3225-7893, ⓦ www.restaurantedurski.com.br. Curitiba's only Ukrainian restaurant, located in a renovated house in the heart of the historic centre, looking onto Largo da Ordem. The food (including Polish and Brazilian dishes) is attractively presented and very tasty. Try the shrimp stroganoff with blinis for R$69. Open Mon & Wed–Sat 7.45pm–11pm and Sat & Sun noon–3pm.

Av. Presidente Afonso Camargo, next to the *Grand Hotel Itamaraty*.

Laundry Auto Serviço Gama at Rua Tibagi 576, near the intersection with Rua Nilo Cairo, is a good central option.

Post office The main offices are next door to each other at Rua XV de Novembro 700, by Praça Santos Andrade.

Moving on

Air Curitiba's airport has frequent flights to all major cities in Brazil and international flights to Uruguay and Argentina. Buses to the airport from the centre leave about every hour from Rua Visconde de Nacar in front of the old Rua 24 Horas (name of the stop) and the journey costs R$8.

Bus Buses run to Florianópolis (8 daily; 4hr), Foz do Iguaçu (8 daily; 10hr), Paranaguá (hourly; 1hr 30min), Rio de Janeiro (5 daily; 12hr), São Paulo (hourly; 7hr), and other major Brazilian cities.

Train The only remaining passenger train from Curitiba is the Serra Verde Express (see box below), which runs from the *rodoferroviária* to Morretes and Paranaguá.

PARANAGUÁ

Brazil's second most important port for exports, **PARANAGUÁ**, 91km east of Curitiba, has lost some of its former character, though the pastel-coloured buildings along the waterfront retain a certain charm. It was founded in 1585, making it one of Brazil's oldest cities, but only recently have measures been undertaken to preserve its colonial buildings.

What to see and do

The appeal of Paranaguá lies in wandering around the cobbled streets and absorbing the faded colonial atmosphere of the town. Almost everything worth seeing is concentrated along **Rua XV de Novembro** a block inland from the waterfront. At the corner of Avenida Arthur de Abreu is the very pretty **Igreja São Francisco das Chagras** (☎41/3422-8553), a small and simple church built in 1784 and still containing its Baroque altars. Further along is the **Mercado Municipal do Café**, an early twentieth-century building that used to serve as the city's coffee market. Today the Art Nouveau structure contains handicraft stalls and simple restaurants serving excellent, very cheap seafood.

Just beyond the market is Paranaguá's most imposing building, the fortress-like **Colégio dos Jesuítas**. Construction of the college began in 1698, sixteen years after the Jesuits were invited by Paranaguá's citizens to establish a school for their sons. Because it lacked a royal permit, however, the authorities promptly halted work on the college until 1738, when one was at last granted and building recommenced. In 1755 the college finally opened, only to close four years later with the Jesuits' expulsion from Brazil. Today it is home to the **Museu de Arqueologia e Etnologia** (Tues–Fri 9am–noon &

SERRA VERDE EXPRESS

The Serra Verde Express (☎41/3323-4007, ⒲www.serraverdeexpress.com.br) is one of the most scenic train rides in Brazil, winding around mountainsides, slipping through tunnels and traversing one of the largest Atlantic Forest reserves in the country. It is undoubtedly the most atmospheric way to travel between Curitiba and Paranaguá (for the Ilha do Mel); make sure to sit on the left-hand side of the train for the best views (or on the right if you're not good with heights). The complete five-hour run to Paranaguá departs only on Sundays, leaving Curitiba at 8.15am and returning at 2pm; during the rest of the week the service only goes as far as Morretes. A variety of tickets are available, with coach class from R$30 return (one-way is more expensive), through to luxury class at R$200. For cheaper tickets book several days in advance, as they are limited and sell out quickly.

1.30pm–6pm, Sat & Sun noon–6pm; R$1; ☏41/3423-2511, ⊛www.proec.ufpr.br). Exhibits concentrate on prehistoric archeological finds, indigenous culture and popular art, and the poor old Jesuits don't even get a mention. Three blocks inland from here is the town's oldest church, **Igreja Nossa Senhora do Rosário**, dating from 1578 (daily 8am–6pm; free).

Arrival and information

Bus Buses arrive at the *rodoviária*, in the southwest of town on the waterfront.
Tourist information The municipal tourist office is on Rua Padre Albino 45, next to the *rodoviária* (Mon–Fri 8am–7pm; ☏41/3420-2940).
Train The *ferroviária* is three blocks from the waterfront on Av. Arthur de Abreu.

Accommodation

There is no real reason to hang around in Paranaguá, but should you need to, you can choose from a cluster of reasonably priced hotels within walking distance of the major transport terminals.
Hostel Continente Rua Gral. Carneiro 500 ☏41/3423-3224, ⊛www.hostelcontinente.com.br. Handy HI hostel in front of the Estação Nautica. Standard dorms and doubles with reductions for HI members. Dorms R$25, rooms R$70.
Palácio Rua Correia de Freitas 66 ☏41/3422-5655, ⊛www.hotelpalacio.com.br. Centrally located hotel with clean, but spartan rooms for up to four people. A good option for families on a budget. Breakfast, parking and wi-fi included. R$80.
Serra do Mar Rua XV de Novembro 588 ☏41/3422-8907. Don't be put off by the rather dozy service at this hotel, a block behind the Praça de Junho. It represents excellent value for money with modern rooms and spacious bathrooms. R$50.

Eating

Cheap seafood and the local speciality, *barreado* (stew baked in clay vessels), are the order of the day at most restaurants. There are some excellent inexpensive seafood places in the Mercado Municipal do Café, though they are open at lunchtimes only.
Casa do Barreado Rua Antonio da Cruz 78 ☏41/3423-1830, ⊛www.casadobarreado.com.br. The best place to try the regional speciality *barreado*,

a type of beef stew (R$22, with dessert included); the lunchtime buffet of Brazilian dishes is also good. Open Sat & Sun noon–3pm.
Lar do Ma Praça de Junho ☏41/3425-2156. Next to the Colégio dos Jesuítas, this place offers a reasonably priced Chinese lunch buffet, as well as à la carte seafood in the evenings. A portion of succulent prawns for two costs R$35. Open Sun–Tues 10.30am–2.30pm & 10pm–midnight.

Moving on

Bus Curitiba (hourly; 1hr 30min).
Ferry Services depart from the Estação Nautica (Rua General Carneiro 258) to the bay islands, include Ilha do Mel (summer: 4 daily; winter: reduced service; 1hr 30min).
Train The Serra Verde Express to Curitiba departs from the *ferroviária* (Sun only at 2pm; 5hr; see box, p.378).

ILHA DO MEL

Famed for its golden beaches and tranquil setting, the idyllic **ILHA DO MEL** in the Bay of Paranaguá is a hit with backpackers and surfers looking to enjoy the simpler things in life and the island's waves. It's an unusually shaped island, to say the least. Its bulbous northern half, a protected Atlantic forest ecological station (entry is prohibited), is joined to the slender south by a bridge of land where the lively main area **Nova Brasilia** is located. The island's other major settlement, **Encantadas**, near the southwest corner, has the atmosphere of a sleepy fishing village. It's little more than 12km from north to south, but given the relief of the island most walks hug the coast. Bear in mind that there are no cars, no public transport and no shops on the island and electricity for only a short period each day – so come prepared.

What to see and do

Praia do Farol is the closest beach to Nova Brasilia, curving a wide arc around the northeastern part of the island. It's a 4-km walk north along these sands to the Portuguese fort

Fortaleza which once guarded the bay from invaders. Encantadas' nearest beach is **Praia de Fora**. The entire stretch of coastline along the southeast side between Praia de Fora and Praia do Farol is dotted with enchanting coves, rocky promontories and small waterfalls. The rocks are slippery here, so care should be taken, and the three-hour walk along the beach from Praia de Fora as far as Fortaleza should only be attempted at low tide or you risk being stranded. The southern tip of the island, known as **Ponta Encantada**, is where you will find the **Gruta das Encantadas** (Enchanted Cave), focal point for a number of local legends.

Arrival and information

Boat In summer four daily ferries (1hr 30min; R$20–27) link Ilha do Mel with Paranaguá. You can also catch the bus from Paranaguá to Pontal do Sul, from where boats leave every 30min from the beach to the island (7am–7pm; 20–40min). There are fewer boats to the island in winter.

Tourist information There is a tourist information booth at the dock in Nova Brasília (summer: daily 7.30am–8pm).

Accommodation

If you plan to visit in the height of summer, it's best to arrive during the week and as early as possible, as accommodation books up quickly during the weekends. The island is always full to capacity over New Year and Carnaval, when reservations are essential and are accepted only for minimum stays of four or five nights.

A Ilha Verde Hotel Pousada Praia das Encantadas ✆ 41/3426-9036, 🌐 www.ailhaverde.com.br. The only real hotel on the island. Staff will meet you in Encantadas and carry your belongings to the hotel with prior notice. R$150.

Caraguatá Pousada Praia das Encantadas ✆ 41/3426-9097, 🌐 www.caraguata-ilhadomel .com.br. Full of character, with spacious rooms; some offer balconies with glorious sea views. R$190.

Pousada Praia do Farol Praia do Farol ✆ 41/3426-8222, 🌐 www.praiadofarol.com.br. Located right by the dock, this wood cabin-style

pousada is a good bet if you arrive tired, and includes an excellent, ample breakfast to get you started in the morning. R$140.

Pousadinha Praia do Farol ✆ 41/3426-8026, 🌐 www.pousadinha.com.br. Popular backpacker hangout with leafy gardens and relaxing hammocks for chilling out. Rooms are simple but good value and multilingual staff can assist with booking activities. Rooms with shared bathroom are half the price of others. R$120.

FOZ DO IGUAÇU

A classic stop on the backpacker trail, the city of **FOZ DO IGUAÇU** is the Brazilian gateway to the magnificent **Iguaçu Falls**, one of the world's greatest natural wonders, which lie 20km south. Much larger than its Argentine counterpart **Puerto Iguazu** (see p.97), it makes a better base for exploring the falls, with the advantage of decent restaurants and a livelier nightlife.

What to see and do

Foz do Iguaçu is a modern city, with no real sights of its own, but there are a couple of attractions on the road to the falls that are worth checking out. The **Parque das Aves** (daily 8.30am–5.30pm; US$15; 🌐 www.parquedasaves .com.br) maintains enormous walk-through aviaries in dramatic forested surroundings as well as smaller breeding aviaries. There is also a large walk-through butterfly cage – butterflies are bred throughout the year and released when mature. All the butterflies and eighty percent of the eight hundred bird species are Brazilian, many endemic to the Atlantic forest. Across the road is the **Parque Acuatico Cataratas** (Tues–Fri 8am–5pm, Sat & Sun 8am–7pm; R$15; ✆ 45/3529-6016), which maintains a series of thermally heated pools supplied with water springing directly from the underground Guaraní aquifer, the largest natural freshwater source in the Americas. It features a series of giant slides, children's pools and a decent grill restaurant.

Arrival and information

Air The airport (☎45/3521-4200), 16km outside town on the road to the falls, is served by flights from Curitiba, São Paulo, Rio de Janeiro, Brasília, Salvador and Belém. A taxi into town costs around R$45, or take a bus from outside the airport, which goes to the local terminal in town on Av. Juscelino Kubitschek (every 25min 5.30am–7pm, then hourly until midnight; 45min; R$2.20).

Bus The *rodoviária* (☎45/3522-2590) is on the northern outskirts of town; buses #105, #115 and #145 from here, marked "Rodoviária" can take you to the local bus terminal on Av. Juscelino Kubitschek in the city centre (R$2.40); taxis cost around R$12.

Tourist information There are tourist offices at the airport (daily 9am–9pm), the *rodoviária* (daily 6.30am–6.30pm), and the local bus terminal in town (daily 8am–6pm). For information by phone call the main Foz tourist office, Praça Getúlio Vargas 69 (8am–6pm; ☎45/3521-1455).

Tour operators Martin Travel, Travessa Goiás 200 (☎45/3523-4959), is a reliable local travel agency that specializes in ecotourism and puts together groups to go canoeing or mountain biking along forest trails. Macuco Safari (☎www.macucosafari .com.br), based within the national park, offers a guided forest safari and a boat trip into the Devil's Throat (see p.383) among its varied programmes.

Accommodation

When choosing where to stay your main decision will be whether to pick a central option or to go for a place closer to the falls. Central options have the advantage of proximity to good restaurants and bars, while those closer to the falls cut down your travelling time and include a number of excellent hostels. There's a great campsite run by the *Camping Clube do Brasil* (☎45/3529-8064; R$12 per person) at Km17 on the road to the falls; the site is surrounded by jungle, and facilities include a laundry area and a clean swimming pool.

Central

Foz Presidente I Rua Xavier da Silva 1000 ☎45/3572-4450, ☎www.fozpresidentehoteis .com.br. Old-fashioned but comfortable hotel in the centre of town. Its newer, smarter and slightly pricier sister hotel, *Fox Presidente II*, is on Rua Marechal Floriano Peixoto. R$150.

Paudimar Centro Rua Antonio Raposo 820 ☎45/3028-5503, ☎www.paudimarfalls .com.br. Run by the same people as the *Paudimar* (see below), this gives you the same great service

and facilities in a central location, and free internet. R$90.

Pousada Evelina Navarrete Rua Kalichewski 171 ☎45/3574-3817. Extremely friendly place with a youth hostel atmosphere that mainly attracts foreign backpackers. Rooms are simple but spotless, breakfasts are adequate, there's internet access and multilingual Evelina goes out of her way to be helpful. Well located for buses to the falls. R$100.

Pousada El Shaddai Rua Engenheiro Rebouças 306 ☎45/3024-4493, ☎www.pousadaelshaddai .com.br. A good, central, hostel-type establishment; rates include a sumptuous Brazilian buffet breakfast. The multilingual staff, pool, internet access and on-site travel agency all help make your stay comfortable. R$85.

San Remo Rua Xavier da Silva 563 ☎45/3523-1619. Though the spartan rooms could do with an upgrade, this economical hotel is within a couple of blocks of the local bus terminal and the Avenida Brasil. Trips to the falls and surrounding attractions can be arranged if you prefer not to go it alone. R$80.

Road to the falls

Paudimar Av. das Cataratas Km12.5 ☎45/3529-6061, ☎www.paudimar.com .br. A favourite with backpackers, this excellent HI

Tropical das Cataratas Eco Resort Parque Nacional do Iguaçu ☎45/2102-7000, ☎www.hoteldascataratas .com.br. The only hotel within the Brazilian national park, discreetly located just out of sight from the falls. With views of the park's lush, tropical vegetation from all sides, the hotel also offers extremely easy access to the falls and is a far more romantic location than staying in either of the rather non-descript Brazilian or Argentine towns nearest to the falls. The rooms are comfortable with colonial-style furnishings. Even if you can't afford to stay here, you should take a wander around the grounds or eat in the restaurant (see p.382). Reservations are usually required, but check the website for special offers. R$630.

establishment has superb facilities. Choose from basic shared dorms sleeping six to eight people, family apartments (with double bed, bunk bed, a/c and private bathroom) and pretty cabins for two. The extensive grounds include a swimming pool and bar. Kitchen facilities are available, and they also serve evening meals. The hostel organizes daily trips to the Argentine side of the falls. Dorms R$25, private cabin R$90, family apartment R$190.

Eating and drinking

Whilst it's no gastronomic paradise, Foz do Iguaçu is a good place to eat cheaply, with a proliferation of buffet-style *por kilo* restaurants.

La Bella Pizza Rua Xavier da Silva 648 ☎45/3574-2285. The best of several pizza *rodízios* on this block, where you can gorge yourself on endless servings of pizza and pasta for just R$12.99. An added attraction are the "sweet pizzas", including white chocolate and caramelized banana flavours. Open daily 6pm–11.40pm.

Boi Dourado Rua Quintino Bocaiúva 963 ☎45/3523-2115. Excellent quality all-you-can-eat meals for R$35 per person (both lunch and dinner) make this popular with visitors and locals alike. Open daily 11.30am–4pm & Mon–Sat 6.30pm–11pm.

Clube Maringá Rua Dourado 111, Porto Meira ☎45/3527-3472. Justly popular among locals for its superb *rodízio de peixe* (R$27) and stunning views of the Iguaçu River. Apart from a selection of local freshwater fish, there's an excellent salad bar and you can pay a little extra for some of the freshest sashimi you're likely to come across (a portion for 2–3 people costs R$25). Take the "Porto Meira" bus and ask for directions, or a taxi (R$10–15). Open Mon–Sat 8am–11pm; Sun till 4pm; reservations advised on Sun.

O Capitão Rua Jorge Shimelpfeng & Almirante Barroso ☎45/3572-1512. One of a series of lively bars on this stretch, this is a particularly popular nightspot with the local youth on account of its loud music, extensive cocktail menu and affordable pizzas. Outdoor tables fill quickly so arrive early in summer if you want to sit outside. Cocktails from R$9.50. Open daily 5pm–3am.

Recanto Gaúcho Av. das Cataratas, Km15, near the Brazilian park entrance ☎45/3572-2358, ⓦwww.recantogaucho.com. A favourite Sunday outing for locals: the atmosphere's lively, the meat's excellent and cheap (R$25 for all-you-can-eat) and the owner (who dresses in full gaucho regalia) is a real character. Short afternoon horse rides are also included in the price. Turn up soon after 11am; food is served until 3pm. Reservations advised. Open Sun 10.30am–6pm. Closed Dec & Jan.

Trigo & Cia Av. Parana 1750 ☎45/3025-3800. Ten minutes by bus from the centre of town, this busy café serves tasty savoury snacks, good coffee and the best cakes in Foz. White coffee costs R$2.80 and orange cake R$5. Open daily 24hr.

Tropical das Cataratas Parque Nacional do Iguaçu ☎45/2102-7000, ⓦwww.hoteldas cataratas.com. The only hotel restaurant worth trying. They offer an excellent buffet dinner of typical Brazilian dishes for R$93. Lunch is à la carte. Open daily 12.30–3pm & 7.30–11pm.

Directory

Banks and exchange Dollars (cash or traveller's cheques) can be easily changed in travel agents and banks along Avenida Brasil; the banks have ATMs.
Consulates Argentina, Eduardo Bianchi 26 ☎45/3574-2969; Paraguay, Rua Marechal Deodoro 901 ☎45/3523-2898.
Hospital Ministro Costa Cavalcanti, Av. Gramado 580, ☎45/3576-8000 is a good private hospital.
Police Tourist police ☎45/3523-3036.
Post office Praça Getúlio Vargas near Rua Barão do Rio Branco (Mon–Fri 9am–5pm).
Taxi Coopertaxi Cataratas ☎45/3524-6016.

CROSSING THE BORDER TO PARAGUAY

International buses leave every 15min from the *rodoviária* via the local bus terminal, bound for Ciudad del Este in Paraguay (25min; R$3.30), which is 7km northwest of Foz do Iguaçu. You need to disembark at the Brazilian customs for your exit stamps – the bus will not wait but your ticket is valid for the next one. You will then cross the Friendship Bridge to the Paraguayan customs, where you will again be asked to disembark. Buses for Puerto Iguazu (40min; R$4) leave every 20min from the *rodoviária*; you will have to get your passport stamped to enter Argentina – the bus will stop at customs on the way and wait for you.

Taxis from central Foz to Ciudad del Este cost R$30. A taxi to Puerto Iguazu will set you back R$60.

Moving on

Air Buses marked "Aeroporto Parque Nacional" leave the local terminal on Av. Juscelino Kubitschek, passing via the airport on the way to the falls (every 25min; 5.30am–7pm, then hourly until midnight; 45min; R$2.20). Flights serve all the major Brazilian cities.

Bus Campo Grande (1 daily; 15hr), Curitiba (8 daily; 10hr), Florianópolis (1 daily; 16hr), Porto Alegre (5 daily; 16hr), Rio de Janeiro (4 daily; 23hr), São Paulo (2 daily; 17hr).

THE IGUAÇU FALLS

The **IGUAÇU FALLS** are, unquestionably, one of the world's great natural phenomena and form the centrepiece of the vast bi–national reserve **Iguaçu National Park**. First designated in 1936, the park was declared a UNESCO World Heritage Site fifty years later, a long time coming given that the falls were discovered as early as 1542 by the Spanish explorer Alvar Nuñez Cabeza de Vaca. To describe their beauty and power is a tall order, but for starters cast out any ideas that Iguaçu is some kind of Niagara Falls transplanted south of the equator – compared with Iguaçu, Niagara is a ripple. The falls are formed by the Rio Iguaçu, which has its source near Curitiba. Starting at an altitude of 1300m, the river snakes westward, picking up tributaries and increasing in size and power during its 1200km journey. About 15km before joining the Rio Paraná, the Iguaçu broadens out, then plunges precipitously over an 80m-high cliff in 275 separate falls that extend nearly 3km across the river. To properly experience the falls it is essential to visit both sides. The Brazilian side gives the best overall view and allows you to fully appreciate the scale of it; the Argentine side, which makes up most of the falls, allows you to get up close to the major individual falls.

The falls are mind-blowing whatever the season, but they are always more spectacular following a heavy rainstorm. Weekends and Easter are best avoided if you don't want to share your experience with hordes of Brazilian and Argentinian holidaymakers.

What to see and do

At its best in the early morning, a 1.5-km cliffside trail runs alongside the falls, offering breathtaking photo opportunities. A stairway leads down from the bus stop to the start of the trail. The path ends by coming perilously close to the ferocious "**Garganta do Diabo**" (Devil's Throat), the most impressive of the individual falls. Depending on the force of the river, you could be in for a real soaking, so if you have a camera with you be sure to carry a plastic bag. From here, you can either walk back up the path or take the elevator to the top of the cliff and the road leading to the *Tropical das Cataratas Eco Resort* hotel. You'll undoubtedly come across coatis on the trails (though raccoon-like they are not raccoons, whatever the local guides may say) – don't be fooled by their cute and comical appearance, these little creatures are accomplished food thieves with long claws and sharp teeth.

Every 15min the **Helisul helicopter** (☎45/3529-7474, ⓦwww.helisul.com) takes off just outside the park entrance, offering 10-min flights over the falls for US$100 per person, or a 35-min flight over the falls and the Itaipú Dam, the world's largest hydroelectricity scheme, for US$1000 (minimum four people). The Argentines refuse to allow the helicopter to fly over their side of the falls as they do not wish to disturb the wildlife.

Arrival

Bus Buses from Foz do Iguaçu terminate at the entrance to the falls. It costs foreigners R$37.15 to enter (concessions available for MERCOSUL residents), after which a shuttle bus will deliver you to the trails.

ILHA SANTA CATARINA

ILHA SANTA CATARINA is noted throughout Brazil for its gorgeous scenery, ideal climate, attractive fishing villages and the city of **Florianópolis**, the small and prosperous state capital, half of which lies on the mainland and the other half on the island. The island is peppered with resorts – from built-up areas in the north to the more tranquil south – and **Centro do Lagoa** is a great spot for good-value accommodation and bar hopping. Locals often refer to the whole island as Florianópolis, with the city known simply as the *centro*.

Joined to the mainland by two suspension bridges (the longest, British-designed, open only to cyclists and pedestrians is due to re-open in 2011), the island retains a natural beauty that even some questionable developments in the capital itself have failed to diminish. Fifty percent of the island has been placed under a permanent national preservation order, ensuring that its timeless appeal will survive at least for the foreseeable future.

FLORIANÓPOLIS

FLORIANÓPOLIS was founded in 1700 and settled fifty years later by immigrants from the Azores. Since then, it has gradually developed from a sleepy provincial backwater into a lively state capital. With the construction of the bridges linking the island with the mainland, Florianópolis as a port has all but died, and today it thrives as an administrative, commercial and tourist centre. Land reclamation for a multi-lane highway and new bus terminals may have eliminated the character of the old seafront, but the late nineteenth-century pastel-coloured, stuccoed buildings of the old town still have a whiff of old-world appeal, and it's worth taking time to have a walk about. Few people visit Ilha Santa Catarina for the express purpose of seeing the city, however, and to truly experience the natural beauty for which the island is renowned, it's best to head out of the urban centre.

What to see and do

On the former waterfront, you'll find two ochre-coloured buildings: the **Mercado Público** (Mon–Fri 9am–8pm & Sat 8am–1pm), which contains some excellent bars and small restaurants, and the **Alfândega** (Mon–Fri 9am–6pm), a former customs house that has been converted for use as a crafts market. Most sights of interest, however, are centred on the lushly vegetated square, the **Praça XV de Novembro**, at the centre of which is the enormous, gnarled "Centenary Fig" tree. According to legend, walking three times around the tree will guarantee you fame and fortune.

On one side of the square is the **Palácio Cruz e Souza**, an imposing pink building built between 1770 and 1780 as the seat of provincial government – it houses the **Museu Histórico de Santa Catarina** (Tues–Fri 10am–6pm, Sat & Sun till 4pm; R$2) whose nineteenth-century interior is more engaging than its collection of military memorabilia. The **Catedral Metropolitana**, overlooking the square, is surprisingly modern; the only church in the city centre dating back to the colonial era is the mid-eighteenth-century **Igreja de Nossa Senhora do Rosário**, best approached by a flight of steep steps from Rua Marechal Guilherme, two blocks north of the Praça.

Arrival and information

Air The airport (☎48/3331-4000) is 12km south of the city. You can get into the centre by taxi (20min; R$30–35) or "Aeroporto" buses (30min; R$2.95).

Bus Buses arrive at the *rodoviária* (☎48/3212-3100) at the foot of the road bridge that links the island to the mainland. Cross the dual carriageway and it's a short walk to the centre and the local bus terminal, which serves the rest of the island with buses (R$2.95). Faster, air-conditioned yellow minibuses – called *executivos* (R$5) – serve the whole island. Those departing from the Terminal do Centro near the Mercado Público go to the south and east of the island. Those heading north depart from Terminal Rita Maria.

Tourist information There's a tourist information kiosk (daily 8am– 6pm; ☎48/3228-1095, ⓦwww.guiafloripa.com.br) at the *rodoviária*. Santa Catarina's state tourist board is based at Rua Felipe Schmidt 249, on the 9th floor ((Mon– Fri 8am–7pm; ☎48/3212-6300; ⓦwww.santur.sc.gov.br).

Accommodation

Most tourists choose to stay at the beaches and resorts around the island (see p.386), but staying in Florianópolis itself has the benefit of direct bus services to all parts of the island. It's not cheap, though, and accommodation is snapped up quickly in high season.

Central Sumaré Rua Felipe Schmidt 423 ☎48/3222-5359. The cheapest of the central hotels, in a secure area of town. The minimal rooms are nothing to write home about, but will do if you'd rather spend your money on enjoying yourself than on your digs. R$90.

Floripa Hostel Rua Duarte Schutell 227 ☎48/3225-3781, ⓦwww.floripahostel.com.br. Everything you would expect from an HI hostel, though as in the rest of town, you'll find yourself paying more than elsewhere. It fills rapidly in summer, so get here early. Dorms R$45, rooms R$105.

Valerim Center Rua Felipe Schmidt 554 ☎48/3225-1100, ⓦwww.hotelvalerim.com.br. The largest of the mid-range hotels, with perfectly comfortable rooms (some of which sleep up to six people), all with a/c, TV and minibar. R$90.

Eating and drinking

Getting a snack in Florianópolis is no problem, but finding a decent meal sometimes can be, and many of the better restaurants are some way from the centre along Avenida Beira Norte (take bus #134 from the local bus terminal). Whatever you choose to eat, be prepared to pay a little more than you might normally, with prices similar to upmarket areas of Rio de Janeiro like Leblon or Ipanema.

Botequim Floripa Av. Rio Branco 632 ☎48/3333-1234, ⓦwww.botequimfloripa.com.br. Pub-style place with a lively happy hour and cold beer on tap. Serves up Brazilian classic *feijoada* on Saturdays (R$25). Open Mon–Fri 6pm–1am and Sat 11.30am–3pm & 6pm–1am.

Box 32 Mercado Público ☎48/3224-5588, ⓦwww.box32.com.br. Seafood specialist and meeting place of the local glitterati who come to slurp oysters and munch prawns. That said, it's not as expensive as you might fear, with a decent plate of garlic prawns setting you back R$46 (enough for two people). Open Mon–Fri 10am–8pm and Sat till 3pm.

Mini Kalzone Rua Felipe Schmidt 706 ☎48/3024-3106, ⓦwww.minikalzone.com.br. If you're hungry, broke and in a hurry, *Mini Kalzone* is the answer to your prayers. Top-notch, bite-sized fold-over pizzas come with a wide variety of meat and vegetarian fillings. For a good healthy bet try the *Joaquina*: spinach, ricotta and parmesan in a wholemeal casing, for R$4.25. Open Mon–Fri 9am–10pm and Sat till 6pm.

Scuna Bar Rua Forte Santana 405 ☎48/3225-3138, ⓦwww.scunabar.com.br. A smart bar in the shadow of the road bridge that links the island to the mainland. Live music and a dancefloor – though this is not the place to look for an all-night rave. Open Tues–Fri from 10pm.

Vida Natural Rua Visconde de Ouro Preto 298 ☎48/3223-4507. Vegetarian buffet (R$12) for those who like their food to be predominantly green. Open Mon–Fri 11.30am–3.30pm.

Directory

Banks and exchange Banks are located on Rua Felipe Schmidt and by Praça XV de Novembro.

Boat trips Scuna Sul, Av. Osvaldo Rodrigues Cabral s/n (☎48/3225-1806, ⓦwww.scunasul.com.br) offer boat trips around the island for around R$50 per person.

Car rental Avis, Av. Deputado Diomicio Freitas s/n ☎48/3331-4176; Hertz, Rua Bocaiuva 2125 ☎48/3224-9955; Localiza, Rua Henrique Valgas 112A ☎48/2107-6464; YES, Av. Deputado Diomicio Freitas ☎048/3236-0229. Advance reservations recommended in summer.

Consulates Argentina, Av. Rio Branco 387 ☎48/3024-3036; Uruguay, Rua Walter de Bona Castelon 559 ☎48/3222-3718.

Internet Adrenaline Lan House at Rua Ten Silveira 155 has a decent, cheap connection (R$3 per hour; daily 8am–8pm).

Pharmacies Farmacia Bela Vista, Rua Tenente Silveira 110. For homeopathic remedies try Farmacia Homeopática Jaqueline, Rua Felipe Schmidt 413.

Post office The main post office is on Praça XV de Novembro (Mon–Fri 9am–5pm and Sat 8am–noon).

Moving on

Air Daily flights to São Paulo and Porto Alegre with onward connections.

Bus Inter city buses depart from the *rodoviária*. Curitiba (hourly; 5hr), Foz do Iguaçu (5 daily; 14hr), Porto Alegre (8 daily; 7hr), São Paulo (6 daily; 12hr).

THE REST OF THE ISLAND

With 42 beaches around the island to choose from, even the most crowded are rarely unbearably so. The **north** of the island is the most developed whilst the extreme **south** remains the quietest and most unspoilt. Though anywhere on the island can be reached by bus within an hour or so from Florianópolis, **renting a car** (see "Directory", p.385) is a good idea if you have limited time, allowing you to explore the island more thoroughly.

Centro da Lagoa

CENTRO DA LAGOA, a bustling little town at the southern end of the lagoon, is both an attractive and convenient place to stay: there are good bus services from here into the centre of Florianópolis and to the east coast beaches, and the main road is lined with restaurants and bars. This is arguably the liveliest nightspot on the island during the summer and at weekends throughout the year, with restaurants always crowded and people overflowing into the streets from the bars. A large saltwater lagoon in the centre of the island, **Lagoa Da Conceição** is popular for swimming, canoeing and windsurfing. The lagoon's beaches are close by; cross the small bridge on the road leaving Centro da Lagoa and it's a 40-min walk to Praia Mole.

Accommodation

Centro da Lagoa has plenty of good-value options, although you'll need to book ahead in high season. There's also a decent campsite at Av. das Rendeiras 1480 (☎48/3232-5555; ⓦwww .apartamentosecampinglagoa.com.br), costing R$15 per person.

Don Zepe Av. Afonso Delambert Neto 740 ☎48/3232-1507, ⓦwww.donzepehotel.com.br. One of the classier options in the heart of Lagoa, with bright, light-filled rooms and flat-screen TVs. R$170.

Duna'Sol Rua Osni Ortiga 2433 ☎48/3232-6666, ⓦwww.dunasol.com.br. A decent option for those wanting a more tranquil stay on the island, located on the road towards Barra da Lagoa. There are doubles in the main house with views of the lagoon (R$110), but the chalets, which sleep up to six people, complete with kitchen and outdoor hammocks are best (R$120–200 per chalet). There's also a swimming pool and small gym.

Estrela do Mar Rua Antônio da Silveira 282 ☎48/3232-1079, ⓦwww.estreladomar.net. Bright and kitsch *residencial* complete with Disney character gnomes in the garden. The apartments, which all have kitchens, are named after different species of fish. R$140.

Lagoa Hostel Rua José Henrique Veras 469 ☎48/3234-4466, ⓦwww.lagoahostel.com.br. Friendly hostel where staff make you feel part of the extended family. There's a sundeck, jacuzzi, pool table and huge widescreen TV for rainy days. Dorms R$50, rooms R$110.

🏃 **Tucano House Backpackers** Rua das Araras 229 ☎48/3207-8287, ⓦwww .tucanohouse.com. Popular place with six dorms (R$40) and five doubles (R$90), some with lagoon views. The hostel serves meals (R$15) every night in an outside patio area, a great place to meet fellow travellers. There are also half-price drinks at the bar between 5pm and 7pm. Other services include a pool and free surfboard hire.

Way2Go Hostel Rua Rita Lourenço da Silveira 139 ☎48/3364-6004, ⓦwww.hostelway2go.com. Well-located hostel near the bridge at the end of Lagoa. Washing machines available for guests' use and excellent kitchen space. Doubles (R$100) are rather boxy, but functional. Dorms R$45.

Eating and drinking

The Black Swan Rua Manoel Severino de Oliveira 592 ☎48/3234-5682, ⓦwww.theblackswan .com.br. Faux-English pub run by a British expat, popular with Brazilians and an international crowd. Standard priced local beer on tap, plus a range of expensive imported beer from Europe. Open Sun–Thurs noon–midnight and Fri & Sat noon–2am.

Confraria Chopp da Ilha Av. Afonso Delambert Neto 671 ☎48/3334-3696, ⓦwww .confrariachoppdailha.com.br. A bar that regularly offers live Brazilian music and often does promotions on beer (eg two *chopps* for R$4.50).

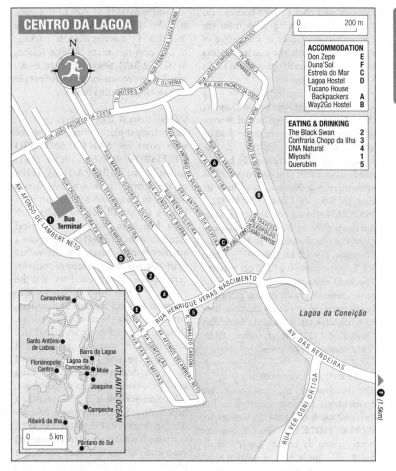

CENTRO DA LAGOA

0   200 m

ACCOMMODATION
Don Zepe	E
Duna'Sol	F
Estrela do Mar	C
Lagoa Hostel	D
Tucano House Backpackers	A
Way2Go Hostel	B

EATING & DRINKING
The Black Swan	2
Confraria Chopp da Ilha	3
DNA Natural	4
Miyoshi	1
Querubim	5

Bus Terminal

Lagoa da Coneição

Canasvieras

Santo Antônio de Lisboa

Floriánopolis Centro   Lagoa da Conceição   Mole

Barra da Lagoa

Joaquina

Campeche

Ribeirã da Ilha

Pântano do Sul

ATLANTIC OCEAN

0   5 km

F (1.5km)

A decent place to watch sports matches too. Open daily 7.30pm until late.

DNA Natural Rua Manoel Severino de Oliveira 360 ☎48/3207-3441, ⊕www.dnanatural.com .br. Specializing in natural, healthy foods, including tasty wraps and huge mixed salads. There's also an exhaustive range of tropical juices and shakes (from R$4). Open daily 8am–midnight.

Miyoshi Av. Afonso Delambert 215 ☎48/3232-5959, ⊕www.miyoshi.com.br. One of the finest restaurants for sushi on the island. It's not cheap, but sushi is self-service and weighed by the kilo (R$6.92 per 100g), so exercise some restraint and you can eat cheaply. There's an all-you-can eat promotion on Monday nights (R$55 per person). Open daily 6.30–11.30pm.

Querubim Av. Henrique Veras do Nascimento 255 ☎48/3232-874. Arguably the best-value place to have lunch in Lagoa. The delicious buffet includes chicken, beef, shrimp and salads (R$24.90 per kilo or R$15.90 all-you-can-eat). Open for lunch 11.30am–3.30pm and afterwards for snacks until 4am.

Canasvieras

The island's built-up **north coast** offers safe swimming in calm, warm seas and is popular with families. The long, gently curving bay of **CANASVIERAS** is the most crowded of the northern resorts, largely geared towards Argentine families who own or rent houses near the beach. By walking away from the concentration of bars at the centre of the beach, towards the east and **Ponta das Canas**, it's usually possible to find a relatively quiet spot.

Unless you're renting a house for a week or more (agencies abound, among them ⓦ www.ibiubi.com.br and ⓦ www .aluguetemporada.com.br), finding **accommodation** is difficult, as the unappealing hotels are usually booked solid throughout the summer. That said, there is a *Floripa Hostel* here on Rua Dr João de Oliveira (☎48/3225-3781; R$34–75) it's run along the same lines as the one in the city. For **campers**, *Camping Canasvieras* is at Rua Mario Lacombe 179 (☎48/3266-0457; cabins R$75 for two; camping R$20 per person). The local **restaurants** mostly offer the same menu of prawn dishes, pizza and hamburgers. If you fancy learning how to scuba-dive try Aquanauta Mergulho (☎48/3266-1137) which offers PADI scuba courses for all levels.

East coast beaches

The beaches of the east coast are accessed via the bus terminal in Rio Tavares, south of Lagoa da Conceição. **PRAIA MOLE** (a few kilometres from Centro da Lagoa) is particularly beautiful, slightly hidden beyond sand dunes and beneath low-lying cliffs. Mole is extremely popular with young people but, rather surprisingly, commercial activity has remained low-key, probably because there's a deep drop-off right at the water's edge. Approached by a road passing between gigantic dunes, the next beach as you head south is at **JOAQUINA**, attracting serious surfers. The water's cold, however, and the sea rough, only really suitable for strong swimmers. If you have the energy, climb to the top of the dunes where you'll be rewarded with the most spectacular views in all directions – Lagoa is only a few minutes away by taxi or bus.

If you're looking to **stay** in this area, try *Cris Hotel* at Estrada Geral da Joaquina 1 (doubles R$135; package of five days minimum in high season; ☎48/3232-5104, ⓦ www.crishotel.com), which offers rooms for up to five people overlooking Joaquina beach.

West coast beaches

The principal places of interest on the west coast are **SANTO ANTÔNIO DE LISBOA** to the north of Florianópolis and **RIBEIRÃO DA ILHA** to the south. These are the island's oldest and least spoilt settlements their houses almost all painted white with dark blue sash windows, in typical Azorean style, and both villages have a simple colonial church. Fishing, rather than catering to the needs of tourists, remains the principal activity, and the waters offshore from Santo Antônio are used to farm mussels and oysters, considered the best on the island. Because the beaches are small and face the mainland, tourism has remained low-key. The few visitors here tend to be on daytrips, staying just long enough to sample oysters at a local bar.

Accommodation is limited, your best hope being in Santo Antônio: the *Pousada Mar de Dentro* (R$195; ☎48/3235-1521, ⓦ www.pousadamardedentro.com.br) has a lovely setting and a tiny pool, right on the beach. In the heart of Ribeirão da Ilha, try the simple *Pousada do Museu* (R$135; ☎48/3237-8148, ⓦ www .pousadadomuseu.com.br) which has

> **TREAT YOURSELF**
>
> For a splash-out meal, the rather kitsch Ostradamus (☎48/3337-5711, ⓦ www .ostradamus.com.br) serves up creative dishes such as oysters with martini and lemon (R$25), as well as delicious mains. Try the seafood risotto (R$88 for two), washed down with local wine. Open Tues–Sat noon–11pm & Sun noon–5.30pm.

some rooms with glorious sea views and a decent restaurant.

BALNEÁRIO CAMBORIÚ

If you are travelling in search of the Santa Catarina party scene, look no further than **BALNEÁRIO CAMBORIÚ**, an effervescent resort town 80km north of Florianópolis with a distinctly hedonistic approach to life. A popular summer destination with young Brazilians, Paraguayans and Argentines, the town is packed out during the peak season, guaranteeing fun in the sun for those who prefer the lighter side of life.

What to see and do

Camboriú has something of a Mediterranean holiday resort feel to it, with its high-rise buildings and pedestrian streets lined with artists peddling souvenirs, and walking around town you could be forgiven for thinking that you were on the Portuguese Algarve. That said, the place is not without its charms – not least its seven kilometre-long **Praia Central**, offering safe swimming and golden sand. **Praia do Pinho**, on the other side of the peninsula west of town, is the site of Brazil's first nudist beach for those adventurous enough to go for an all-over tan.

Camboriú even has its own 33m-high Rio-style Christ statue, the **Cristo Luz**, illuminated at night and casting a faint greenish glow over the town. On summer evenings the park at the foot of the statue is the site of concerts, theatre and poetry recitals. The forested hillside in the south of town is a nature reserve, the **Parque Unipraias** (ⓦ www.unipraias.com.br; R$30). You can reach it via a cable car (9.30am–6pm) that passes through three stations, the first an **ecological park**, the second an **adventure park** and the third, the summit, offering glorious views over the town, beaches and out to sea. Buses between the Cristo Luz and Parque Unipraias run along the seafront

Avenida Atlantica every thirty minutes in summer.

Arrival and information

Bus Camboriú is served by buses (50 times a day; 1hr 30min) from the state capital. Buses arrive at the *rodoviária* (☎ 47/3367-2901) on Av. Santa Catarina, at the edge of town close to the highway.
Tourist information There is a tourist information office at Rua 2950 771 (☎ 47/3367-8005, ⓦ www.guiacamboriu.com.br).

Accommodation

You'd be wise to book ahead in the peak season when block bookings take up the majority of the more affordable hotels. That said, there is always the possibility of reductions if you ask around during late afternoon, with hotels desperate to be full to capacity. If you're in a group ask at the tourist office about renting a house – it's cheaper than you might think.
Hostel Rezende Rua 3100 780 ☎ 47/3361-9815, ⓦ www.hotelpousadarezende.com.br. Standard HI hostel a few blocks back from the beach. It's decent value for money, and dorms are small and uncrowded, with just four beds each. Dorms R$50, rooms R$130.
Pousada Maria da Praia Av. Atlântica 4118 ☎ 47/3367-4365, ⓦ www.mariadapraia.com.br. Well-situated family-run pousada with simple but clean apartments and suites, some with balconies overlooking the beach. R$200.
Pousada Villa Germania Rua 1021 322 ☎ 47/3363-3147, ⓦ www.pousadavillagermania .com.br. Attractive pousada with simple but elegant rooms, each with a balcony, in a quiet area of town. Rates include a sumptuous breakfast buffet. R$160.

Eating

In addition to the proliferation of fast-food joints and *lanchonetes* that you might expect in a town populated by twenty-somethings, there are also some excellent restaurants around if you look hard enough, with seafood platters featuring heavily on most menus.
Guacamole Av. Beira Rio 1122, Barra Sul. Charismatic Mexican restaurant with live music, *mariachis* and *"tequileros"* who are only too happy to wet your whistle. Cultural attractions every Tues night add to the experience. Spicy mains from R$25). Open daily 7.30pm–2am.

O Pharol Av. Atlântica 5740 ☎ 47/3367-3800, ⊛ www.pharol.com.br. Smart seafood restaurant, well worth the extra reais. The seafood *rodizio* (R$46.90 per person) is something special and includes prawns, lobster, oysters and more. Open daily 11.30am–midnight.

Drinking and nightlife

Camboriú has a vibrant nightlife aimed mainly at a young crowd who seek loud music, bare flesh and lots of dancing. Most places are on or around the Av. Atlântica, especially at the southern end, the Barra Sul, where you'll find a huge array of beach bars and discos. Things don't start to get lively until well after midnight and the action continues until after the sun comes up.

Cachaçaria Uai Av. Atlântica 2334 ☎ 47/3367-4978. Bar-style hangout on the beach, specializing in *caipirinhas*, the Brazilian carnival cocktail made with *cachaça* and crushed limes. Open daily 6pm–late.

Djunn Music Place Rua 4500, Barra Sul ☎ 47/3361-1516, ⊛ www.djunn.com.br. Featuring visiting DJs and live music, this is a plush nightclub with table service and a bouncing dancefloor. Not cheap, but always full. Cover charge R$20 (women) and R$30 (men). Open Tues–Sun 10pm–4am.

Enjoy Av. Atlântica 5200 ☎ 47/3360-8097, ⊛ www.enjoy.art.br. Smart club facing the beach playing mainly electro beats. Popular with twenty-somethings. Entry R$30 (women) and R$50 (men). Open Sat & Sun 11.30pm–6am.

Woods Av. Atlântica 4450, Barra Sul ☎ 47/7812-3475, ⊛ www.portalwoods.com.br. This popular country-style pub is a good place to start the evening off, with cold beers served in a beachfront location. Live music most nights. Entry is R$10 (women) and R$15 (men). Open Tues–Sat from 8pm.

Moving on

Bus Florianopolis (18 daily; 2hr); São Paulo (14 daily; 9hr).

THE ILHA DE SÃO FRANCISCO

Just beyond Camboriú at the town of Itajaí, the highway gradually turns inland towards Joinville. Some 45km east of here is the **ILHA DE SÃO FRANCISCO**, a low-lying island separated from the mainland by a narrow strait, which is spanned by a causeway. As Joinville's port and the site of a major Petrobras oil refinery, it might be reasonable to assume that São Francisco should be avoided, but this isn't the case. Both the port and refinery keep a discreet distance from the main town, **São Francisco do Sul**, and the beaches blend perfectly with the slightly dilapidated colonial setting.

São Francisco do Sul

Though the island was first visited by French sailors as early as 1504, it was not until the middle of the following century that the town of **SÃO FRANCISCO DO SUL** was established. One of the oldest settlements in the state, it is also one of the very few places in Santa Catarina with a well-preserved historic centre.

What to see and do

Dominating the city's skyline is the **Igreja Matriz**, the main church, originally built in 1699 by Indian slaves, but completely reconstructed in 1926. The **Museu Nacional do Mar** on Rua Babitonga in the historic centre (Tues–Sun 10am–6pm; R$5; ⊛ www.museunacionaldomar.com.br) has a maritime collection with an emphasis on southern Brazil and its people. The prettiest beaches, **Paulos** and **Ingleses**, are also the nearest to town, just a couple of kilometres to the east. Both are small, and have trees to provide shade. Surprisingly few people take advantage of the protected sea, which is ideal for weak swimmers.

On the east coast, **Praia de Ubatuba** 16km from the centre, and the adjoining **Praia de Enseada**, 20km from town, offer enough surf for you to have fun but not enough to be dangerous. A ten-minute walk across the peninsula from the eastern end of Enseada leads to **Praia da Saúdade** (or just Prainha), where the waves are suitable for only the most macho surfers.

Arrival

Bus The *rodoviária* is inconveniently located a few kilometres outside of town; you'll need to catch a local bus to the market in the town centre. Buses to the beaches at Enseada and Ubatuba leave from the market, with the last services in both directions departing at about 9.30pm.

Accommodation

Most of the island's visitors bypass the town altogether and head straight for the beaches to the east, so, even in midsummer, there's rarely any difficulty in finding a central hotel.

Kontiki São Francisco do Sul, Rua Babitonga 33, near the market ☏47/3444-2232, ⓦwww .hotelkontiki.com.br. Located in the heart of the old town directly in front of the bay, this comfortable hotel has wonderful views and a "colonial-style" (which basically means indulgent) breakfast. R$118.

Pousada Farol da Ilha Enseada, just behind the beach on Rua Maceió 1156 ☏47/3449-1802, ⓦwww.pousadafaroldailha.tur.br. This little family-run place, only 300m from the beach, also has its own pool. The rooms are decorated in a rustic style and it's particularly popular with couples. R$150.

Zibamba São Francisco do Sul, Rua Fernando Dias 27 ☏47/3444-2020; ⓦwww.hotelzibamba.com .br. Relatively luxurious, this attractive colonial-style hotel has its own pool and restaurant. R$180.

Eating and drinking

Eating out holds no great excitement, with the *Zibamba*'s restaurant the best of a generally poor bunch serving up a seafood buffet at lunch and typical Brazilian dishes á la carte in the evenings. Enseada does have a lively nightlife though.

Canoas Bar Prainha, Av. Brasil. Popular with twenty-somethings looking for reasonably priced drinks and fun by the sea.

Surf Bar Prainha, Av. Brasil. Unpretentious and popular bar hosting regular live music acts.

Moving on

Bus Curitiba (daily; 3hr); Joinville (hourly; 1hr 20min); São Paulo (daily; 8hr).

PORTO ALEGRE

The capital of Rio Grande do Sul, **PORTO ALEGRE** lies on the eastern bank of the Rio Guaiba. Despite an attractive core, Porto Alegre gives the impression of a hard-working industrial city, grinding out a living. But it also has a run-down charm – and a lively bar and restaurant scene. It's best to avoid the business centre and area around the bus terminal after dark and take taxis at night. Try to coincide your visit with one of the main **festivals**: Semana Farroupilha (Sept 13–20) features traditional local folk dancing and singing, while the highlight of Festa de Nossa Senhora dos Navegantes (Feb 2) is a procession of fishing boats.

What to see and do

The city centre is a little shabby but everything worth seeing is within an easy walk, and a half-day or so is enough to visit most places of interest. For city tours, the tourist board operates "Linha Turismo", an open-top double decker bus with circuits that take in the historic centre and southern zone. Tours leave from outside the main office, Travessa do Carmo 84 (ⓦwww .portoalegre.travel; R$8-15).

Mercado Público and around

The golden-coloured **Mercado Público** (Mon–Sat 7.30am–7.30pm) stands at the heart of the lower town, located alongside Praça Rui Barbosa and Praça XV de Novembro. A replica of Lisbon's Mercado da Figueira, this imposing building contains an absorbing mix of stalls selling household goods, food and regional handicrafts. Upstairs are restaurants offering traditional Brazilian all-you-can-eat lunch buffetss which stay open after the market stalls shut. Much of the maze of streets around the market is pedestrianized. Next to the market is the ochre **Palácio Municipal**, the old *prefeitura* (town hall), built in Neoclassical style between 1898 and 1901, its impressive proportions an indication of

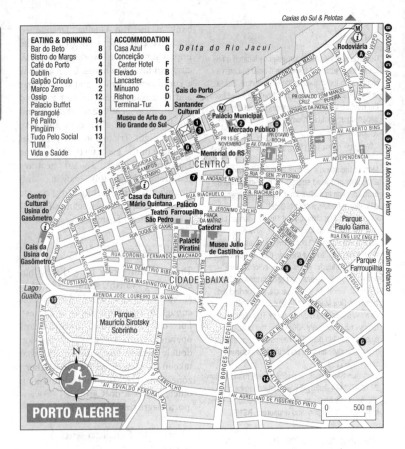

Caxias do Sul & Pelotas ▲

EATING & DRINKING

Bar do Beto	8
Bistro do Margs	6
Café do Porto	4
Dublin	5
Galpão Crioulo	10
Marco Zero	2
Ossip	12
Palacio Buffet	3
Parangolé	9
Pé Palito	14
Pingüim	11
Tudo Pelo Social	13
TUIM	7
Vida e Saúde	1

ACCOMMODATION

Casa Azul	G
Conceição Center Hotel	F
Elevado	B
Lancaster	E
Minuano	C
Rishon	D
Terminal-Tur	A

PORTO ALEGRE

0   500 m

civic pride and self-confidence during the period when Porto Alegre was developing into an important city.

West of here along Rua Sete de Setembro is the pleasantly verdant **Praça da Alfândega**, home of the **Museu de Arte do Rio Grande do Sul** (Ⓦwww .margs.rs.gov.br; Tues–Sat 10am–7pm; free). You can spend an hour or so here, including a visit to the grand **Memorial Rio Grande do Sul** next door (Ⓦwww.memorial.rs.gov.br; Wed–Sat 10am–6pm; free), which houses pictorial exhibitions on the history of the state.

Praça da Matriz

If you walk uphill from the Praça da Alfândega along Rua General Câmara, you will come to the **Praça da Matriz**.

Porto Alegre's oldest buildings are concentrated here, though they have been so heavily altered over the last few centuries that few retain their original character. The **Palácio Piratini** (the state governor's residence) dates from only 1909, and, across from it, is the **Teatro São Pedro** inaugurated in 1858. Surprisingly, its Portuguese Baroque appearance has remained largely unmolested, and the theatre is an important venue for local and visiting companies.

Along the waterfront

There are two cultural centres along Porto Alegre's waterfront that are worth a quick look. The **Casa de Cultura Mário Quintana**, Rua dos Andradas

736 (Tues–Fri 9am–9pm, Sat & Sun noon–9pm; free; ⓦwww.ccmq.rs.gov.br) was a hotel until 1980; the poet Mário Quintana was a long-time resident. Pride of place is given to his room, which is maintained in the state it was in when he lived here. At the western tip of the peninsula, housed in a converted 1920s power plant, is the **Centro Cultural Usina do Gasômetro** (Tues–Sun 9am–9pm; free; ⓦwww.portoalegre.rs.gov.br/smc) which hosts frequent exhibitions, recitals and shows.

Outside the centre

Those wanting to escape the oppressive heat of the city should head to the **Jardim Botánico** on Rua Salvador Franco (Tues–Sun 8am–5pm; free), large enough to justify having a whole suburb named after it. More than 1500 native plant species are represented here, in over forty hectares of gardens that also support a seed bank and research centre. There is also an excellent **zoo,** 24km outside of town along the BR116 (Tues–Sun 8.30am–5pm; R\$4; ⓦwww.fzb.rs.gov.br). South of the centre, the **Fundação Iberê Camargo**, on Av. Padre Cacique 2000 (Tues–Sun 12–7pm, & Thurs 12–9pm; free; ⓦwww.iberecamargo.org.br), has an impressive range of artwork from the renowned Brazilian artist, occupying a modernist building designed by Portuguese architect Álvaro Siza.

Arrival and information

Air The airport (☎51/3358-2000) receives flights from all major national destinations and nearby capitals. A taxi from the airport to the centre costs about R\$25, or you can take the metro (5am–11.20pm; R\$1.70), which joins the airport, *rodoviária* and Mercado Público on its single line.
Bus The *rodoviária* (☎51/3210-0101) is in the northeast of town, within walking distance of the centre; after dark it's safer, and easier, to ride the metro to the Mercado Público.
Tourist information The main municipal office is in the city centre (daily 8am–6pm; ☎51/3289-6700). There are also tourist information offices at

the airport (daily 8am–10pm; ☎51/3358-2048), Usina do Gasômetro (Tues–Sun 9am–6pm; ☎51/3289-8146) and Mercado Público (Mon–Sat 9am–6pm; ☎51/3211-5705). State tourist info is available at the *rodoviária* (Mon–Fri 7am–10pm, Sat & Sun 8am–10pm).

City transport and tours

Boat tours Excursions on the Rio Guaiba with Barco Cisne Branco leave from the tour-boat berth (Cais do Porto) on Av. Mauá 1050, near the train station (Tues–Sun 10.30am, 3pm, 4.30pm & 6pm; ⓦwww.barcocisnebranco.com.br). There are also similar excursions from the Cais da Usina do Gasômetro (Tues–Fri 3.30pm & 5.30pm; Sat & Sun seven daily).
Taxi It's best not to walk around quiet areas or the *rodoviária* at night, so call a taxi (☎51/3352-6166 or ☎51/3319-5100).

Accommodation

Most hotels are scattered around the city centre, but it's a relatively small area and it's possible to walk to most places – though you should take a cab after dark.
Casa Azul Rua Lima e Silva 912 ☎51/3084-5050, ⓦwww.casaazulhostel.com. Newly opened hostel in Cidade Baixa with bar open to the public. There's a spacious outside area, flatscreen TV, pool table and friendly staff who can organize excursions. Dorms R\$35, rooms R\$80.
Conceição Center Hotel Av. Salgado Filho 201 ☎51/3227-6088, ⓦwww.conceicaocenter.com.br. Good value and centrally located apartments with helpful staff. Located near main museums and opposite shopping centre. R\$140.
Elevado Av. Farrapos 63 ☎51/3224-5250, ⓦwww.hotelelevado.com.br. This friendly hotel represents excellent value for homely, and well-equipped, if slightly small rooms. R\$75.
Lancaster Travessa Acelino de Carvalho 67 ☎51/3224-4737, ⓦwww.hotel-lancaster-poa.com.br. Located in one of the liveliest commercial areas of downtown Porto Alegre, this modern 2-star hotel is set behind an imposing 1940s facade. The rooms are small but well equipped, and offer decent value. R\$125.
Minuano Av. Farrapos 31 ☎51/3226-3062, ⓦwww.minuanohotel.com.br. Despite the ugly high-rise building in which they are housed, rooms here are pleasant and surprisingly modern, and the sound-proof windows ensure a good night's sleep regardless of the traffic on the busy avenue outside. R\$90.

Rishon Rua Dr Flores 27 ☎ 51/3228-1387,
Ⓦ www.hotelrishon.com.br. Basic but comfortable
rooms, all equipped with a fridge you're allowed to
stock with your own food, plus microwaves. R$95.
Terminal-Tur Largo Vespasiano Júlio Veppo 125
☎ 51/3061-0447. Box-like in every respect, both
architectural and in room design. But this is a
secure option right next to the *rodoviária* – ideal if
you are planning an early escape. R$110.

Eating

Porto Alegre has some great places to eat,
especially in the Cidade Baixa and Moinhos de
Vento neighbourhoods. As with all major Brazilian
towns, the best value places to eat are buffets,
serving a plentiful range of food and usually offering
good lunchtime deals.

Bar do Beto Av. Sarmento Leite 811 ☎ 51/3332-
9390, Ⓦ www.bardobeto.com.br. Cidade Baixa
restaurant that heaves at lunchtime due to its
R$13.90 buffet special, when waiters walk round
tables offering different cuts of beef and chicken.
Dinner is à la carte only. Open daily 11am–2am.
Bistrô do Margs Praça da Alfândega ☎ 51/3227-
2311, Ⓦ www.margs.rs.gov.br. In the Museu de
Arte do Rio Grande do Sul and with tables on the
praça itself, this is one of the few restaurants
in the area. Food is simple – pastas, steak and
salads – but pretty good, with mains starting from
R$17. Open Tues–Fri 11am–10pm and Sat & Sun
noon–2pm.
Café do Porto Rua Padre Chagas 293 ☎ 51/3346-
8385, Ⓦ www.cafedoporto.com.br. Excellent light
meals, sandwiches, cakes and wine are served
in this pleasant Moinhos do Vento café; there are
plenty of similar places to choose from in the
area. Try the roast beef and artichoke wrap for
R$21. Open Mon–Wed 8am–11pm, Thurs–Sat till
midnight, Sun 10am–midnight.
Galpão Crioulo Parque da Harmonia ☎ 51/3326-
8194, Ⓦ www.churrascariagalpaocrioulo.com.br.
An excellent, very reasonably priced city-centre
churrascaria offering a bewildering selection of
meats in its *rodízio* (R$34–39), along with 18
different types of salad. In the evenings there's
gaucho music and dance performances. Open daily
11.30am–3.30pm & 7pm–midnight
Marco Zero Mercado Público Loja 72 a 78
☎ 51/3226-0551, Ⓦ www.restaurantemarcozero
.com.br. One of several restaurants located around
the upper level of the historic market in the town
centre. The restaurant has high ceilings, big French
windows and old-fashioned charm. Lunchtime
buffet R$13 per person and live music daily from
7pm. Open 11.30am until late.

Palacio Buffet Rua Gral Câmara 78 ☎ 51/3286-
8027. High-quality buffet (R$12.50), featuring
everything from stuffed chicken and pizza to sushi.
Open Mon–Fri lunch only.
Tudo Pelo Social Rua João Alfredo 448
☎ 51/3226-4405, Ⓦ www.restaurantetudopelosocial
.com.br. Hugely popular restaurant that serves
Brazilian classics like rice, beans and meat.
Lunchtime buffet is a bargain at R$6 per person,
while the à la carte *picanha* "for two" (steak; R$26)
comes with huge portions of chips, rice and salad,
and easily feeds three to four people. Open daily
11am–2.45pm & 6pm–11.45pm.
Vida e Saúde Rua Gral. Câmara 60 ☎ 51/3012-
5841. Vegetarian, lunchtime-only buffet, offering
all the healthy vegetable options you may well be
craving in a town obsessed with beef. Buffet R$11,
including fruit juices. Open Mon–Fri 11am–3pm.

Drinking and nightlife

Porto Alegre redeems its lack of obvious tourist
attractions with its lively nocturnal scene. There
are two main centres for nightlife: the more
flashy action revolves around Moinhos de Vento,
and the hub of Rua Padre Chagas; the Cidade
Baixa offers more traditional samba joints and
bohemian bars in the streets around Ruas da
República and João Pessoa. Porto Alegre also
boasts a good popular music scene and a
considerable theatrical tradition.

Dublin Rua Padre Chagas 342, Moinhos de Vento
☎ 51/3268-8835. Every city must have one: this
is your standard faux-Irish bar and the current
place where well-to-do "gauchos" look to enjoy
themselves. Live bands play daily and an entry fee
is charged after 9pm (Thurs–Sat R$7 for women,
R$15 for men; Sun–Wed R$7 for men and women).
Open Sun–Wed 6pm–3am and Thurs–Sat till 5am.
Ossip Rua da República 677, Cidade Baixa
☎ 51/3224-2422. Lively and colourful Cidade Baixa
hangout, with samba and bossa nova most nights.
Open daily 6pm–1.30am.
Parangolé Rua General Lima e Silva 240, Cidade
Baixa ☎ 51/3224-0560. Lovely little bar that has
live music most nights, including samba and tango
with R$5 cover charge to watch music inside.
Also has an impressive range of artisan beers.
Closed Sunday.
Pé Palito Rua João Alfredo 577 ☎ 51/9962-8851,
Ⓦ www.pepalitobar.com.br. Colourfully decorated
club hosting Brazilian live music sessions, from
samba-rock to bossa nova. The more chilled
out sister bar next door, *Boteco do Pé* is just
as colourful and popular (but shuts earlier, at
midnight). Open Thurs–Sat 11pm–6am.

Pingüim Rua General Lima e Silva, Cidade Baixa 505 ☎51/3221-3361. Popular with a youthful party crowd this is a pub-style hangout where things get rowdy once the beer starts flowing. Half a litre of beer costs R$4.90 and a dozen cheese pasties R$13. Open daily 3pm–5am.

TUIM Rua General Câmara 333 ☎51/9962-8851, Ⓦwww.barchopptuim.kit.net. Just off Praça de Alfândega, this pocket-sized pub in the centre is ideal for a cool, quiet beer. *TUIM* also has an impressive variety of spirits, including quality *cachaça*. Try their famous anchovy and mustard sandwich. Open Mon–Fri 9am–9pm.

Directory

Banks and exchange There are banks and casas de câmbio (Mon–Fri 10am–4.30pm) along Rua dos Andradas and Av. Senador Salgado Filho near Praça da Alfândega, and there are ATMs everywhere.
Bookshops Rua Gral. Câmara is lined with secondhand bookshops.
Consulates Argentina, Rua Coronel Bordini 1033 (☎51/3321-1360); Paraguay, Av. Loureiro da Silva 2001 (☎51/3025-1900); Uruguay, Av. Cristóvão Colombo 2999 (☎51/3325-6200); UK, Rua Antenor Lemos 57 (☎51/3232-1414); USA, Rua Riachuelo 1257 (☎51/3226-3344).
Hospital Complexo Hospitalar Santa Casa, Rua Prof Annes Dias 285 ☎51/3214-8080.
Post office Branches at Rua Siqueira Campos 1100 ☎51/3220-8800.

Moving on

Air Porto Alegre is southern Brazil's major transport nexus. There are daily flights to all major Brazilian cities and nearby capitals such as Buenos Aires, Montevideo and Santiago de Chile.
Bus Canela (hourly; 2hr), Florianópolis (5–8 daily; 7hr), Gramado (hourly; 2hr), Rio de Janeiro (1–2 daily; 24hr), São Paulo (1–2 daily; 22hr).

GRAMADO

Some 130km north of Porto Alegre, **GRAMADO** is Brazil's best-known mountain resort. At 825m you're unlikely to suffer from altitude sickness, but Gramado is high enough to be refreshingly cool in summer and positively chilly in winter. Architecturally, Gramado tries hard to appear Swiss, with "alpine" chalets and flower-filled window boxes the norm. It's a mere affectation, though,

since hardly any of the inhabitants are of Swiss origin – and only a small minority is of German extraction. The most pleasant time to visit the area is in spring (Oct and Nov) when the parks, gardens and roadsides are full of flowers.

What to see and do

For most visitors, Gramado's appeal lies mainly in its clear mountain air and generally relaxed way of life – something that inhabitants of Brazil's major cities rarely get to enjoy. There really isn't much to do in town, but a stroll around the large and very pretty flower-filled **Parque Knorr** (home to the kitsch Santa Claus village – a rather random Father Christmas theme park with rides and carol singing during the festive season; daily 10.30am–9.30pm), and secluded **Lago Negro**, surrounded by attractive woodland, are welcome respites from urban stress. The surrounding region is magnificent, and the **Vale do Quilombo**, settled in the nineteenth century by German and Italian farmers, is especially verdant. Although just 6km from town, it's a difficult trek and you'll need a good map to identify the incredibly steep unpaved approach road, Linha 28. Due to the incline, much of the original forest cover has survived intact and can be best appreciated at the **Ecoparque Sperry** (entrance just off Av. das Hortênsias on the way to Canelas; Tues–Sun 9am–5pm; R$10; ☎54/9629-8765; Ⓦwww .ecoparquesperry.com.br) where you'll be guided along forest trails and past waterfalls, by the English-speaking owner who is a font of knowledge on the local flora. Roads in the mountainous areas around Gramado are unpaved and can be treacherous after rain, so **guided tours** are a safe bet – ask at the tourist office for recommendations.

Arrival and information

Bus Buses from Porto Alegre arrive every hour and a half at the *rodoviária* (☎54/3286-1302) on

Av. Borges de Medeiros 2100, a couple of minutes' walk south from the town centre.

Tourist information The tourist office at Av. Borges de Medeiros 1674 is open daily (9am–7pm; ☎54/3286-1475, ⚲www.gramado.rs.gov.br).

Accommodation

Accommodation is expensive and you should book ahead during peak periods. Outside busy times many hotels offer discounts during the week.

Casa da Juventude Rua 25 de Julho, 833 ☎54/3286-1811, ⚲www.brasilalemanha.com.br/acq. This German-style house has simple dorms (R$40) and doubles (R$80) with old-fashioned wood furnishings. Located 2km from the centre, the youth hostel has wonderful views of the Lago Negro.

Hostel Viajante Av. Das Hortências 3880 ☎54/3282-2017, ⚲www.pousadadoviajante.com.br. About 1.5km outside town on the road to Canela, this HI hostel is decent value with dorm rooms (R$30) and some doubles (R$120).

Eating

Gramado has some reasonably good restaurants, but expect to pay through the nose for anything resembling a good meal.

🏃 **La Caceria** Av. Borges de Medeiros 3166 ☎54/3295-7575, ⚲www.casadamontanha.com.br. An interesting but expensive restaurant in the classy *Hotel Casa da Montanha*, specializing in game dishes (R$60) with unusual tropical fruit sauces that complement the often strong-tasting meat. Open daily 7pm–midnight.

Tarantino Ristorante Av. das Hortênsias 1522 ☎54/3036-0057, ⚲www.tarantino.com.br. Fairly authentic and very reasonably priced northern Italian dishes from R$42. Open daily 11.30am–11pm.

Moving on

Bus Porto Alegre (every 30min; 2hr).

CANELA

Marginally cheaper than Gramado, but arranged very much along the same lines, **CANELA** (which means "cinnamon"), 8km further east, is another mountain retreat popular with holidaying Brazilians. The town originally grew as a centre for the local logging industry, but today its main source of income is from the streams of tourists who come to exploit the natural resources of the region in a rather different way. Better located for visits to the nearby national parks than Gramado, it's preferred by many people as a base for exploring the surroundings.

Arrival and information

Bus Canela is served by hourly return buses from Porto Alegre – a spectacular journey winding around forested mountainsides and snaking through valleys – sit on the left-hand side of the bus for the best views. Buses arrive at the *rodoviária* (☎54/3282-1375), a short walk from the centre.

Tourist information The tourist office, at Largo da Fama 227 (☎54/3282-2200; ⚲www.canela.rs.gov.br) in the town centre, can put you in touch with a host of tour companies arranging adventure-style trips to the national parks; buses to Parque Estadual do Caracol also run from here. Open daily 8am–7pm.

Accommodation

Accommodation can be hard to come by during peak periods, when you should book ahead. Though it's cheaper than Gramado, it is not cheap per se, and the town can be easily visited on a day-trip from Porto Alegre.

Hostel Viajante Rua Ernesto Urbani 132 ☎54/3282-2017, ⚲www.pousadadoviajante.com.br. Right next to the *rodoviária* and under the same ownership as the hostel of the same name in Gramado, this is the best budget choice, with economical dorms (R$55) and neat and tidy doubles (R$130) – perfect for travellers winding down after a hard day's bungee jumping.

Eating

You can forget about finding cheap eats in Canela but there are some interesting restaurants around town that make it worth investing the extra few reais.

Churrascaria Espelho Gaúcho Av. Danton Corrêa and Baden Powel 50 ☎54/3282-4348, ⓦwww.espelhogaucho.com.br. Meat, meat and more meat. In fact all the meat you can eat for a one-off R$28.90. Open daily 11.30am–3pm & 6pm–11pm.

Toca da Bruxa Praça da Matriz 25 ☎54/3282-9750, ⓦwww.tocadabruxa.com.br. A pizza house styled like a witch's den. Serves a series of savoury and sweet pizzas with haunting names such as the "Furiosa" and the "Sinistra", the latter with a healthy serving of chilli peppers. The *rodízio* will set you back R$26.90. Tues–Sun 7pm–11pm.

Moving on

Bus Porto Alegre (15 daily; 2hr).

PARQUE ESTADUAL DO CARACOL

Just 7km outside Canela, the highlight of the **PARQUE ESTADUAL DO CARACOL** (Thurs–Tues 9am–5pm; R$10) is the spectacular 131m-high **Cascata do Caracol** waterfall that gives the park its name. The water cascades down over basaltic rock formations and forms a natural feature of stunning beauty. For the best views of the waterfall take the nerve-jangling **cable car** (R$18; ☎54/3504-1405, ⓦwww.canelateleferico.com.br). More accessible than other nearby reserves, Caracol is a popular weekend destination and is a great place to embark on hiking expeditions. While here don't forget to climb the 27m high **Observatorio Ecológico** (ⓦwww.observatorioecologico.com.br), which will give you a 360-degree bird's-eye view of the park over the tree-tops. Binoculars are available for close-up sightings of flora and fauna.

Arrival and information

Bus Buses run from the *rodoviária* in Canela to the park entrance (departs daily at noon; R$1.70) or take a taxi.
Tourist information The admission fee (R$10) should be paid at the excellent visitors centre

(☎52/3278-3035; daily 8.45am–5.45pm). Here you will find details about walking trails and adventure activities such as rock-climbing, abseiling and bungee jumping.
Tours A number of tour companies in Canela can arrange guided visits and adventure tours to the park. Ask in the tourist office for details.

PARQUE NACIONAL DOS APARADOS DA SERRA

The dominant physical feature of south central Brazil is a **highland plateau**, the "Planalto", the result of layer upon layer of ocean sediment piling up and the consequent rock formations being lifted to form the Brazilian Shield. Around 150 million years ago, lava slowly poured onto the surface of the shield, developing into a thick layer of basalt rock. At the edge of the plateau, cracks puncture the basalt and it is around the largest of these that the **Parque Nacional dos Aparados da Serra** (Wed–Sun 9am–5pm; R$6), 100km east of Canela, was created.

Approaching the park from any direction, you pass through rugged cattle pasture, occasionally interrupted by the distinctive umbrella-like araucaria pine trees and solitary farm buildings. As the dirt road enters the park itself, forest patches appear, suddenly and dramatically interrupted by a canyon of breathtaking proportions, **Itaimbez-inho**. Some 5.8km in length, between 600m and 2000m wide and 720m deep, Itaimbezinho is a dizzying sight. The canyon and its immediate surroundings have two distinct climates and support very different types of vegetation. On the higher levels, with relatively little rainfall, but with fog banks moving in from the nearby Atlantic Ocean, vegetation is typical of a cloudforest, while on the canyon's floor a mass of subtropical plants flourishes.

Three trails are open to visitors, the most difficult of which is the **Trilha do Rio do Boi** (8hr) – an option for experienced hikers that must only be attempted with a guide. It involves a 5m vertical descent of a rock face by rope and a complete descent to the rocky river in the canyon floor. Rather easier is the **Trilha do Vértice** (1.4km), which affords views of Itaimbezinho and the two spectacular waterfalls **Véu da Noiva** and **Andorinhas**. If this isn't challenging enough for you try the **Trilha do Mirante do Cotovelo** (6.3km) which runs along the rim of the canyon and provides some glorious photo opportunities.

Arrival and information

Bus To get to the park on public transport, take a bus from Gramado or Canela to São Francisco de Paula, 69km from the park's entrance. From São Francisco you need to take another bus northeast to Cambará do Sul and ask to be let off at the entrance to the park. From here it's a further 15km to Itaimbezinho. Buses occasionally run between São Francisco or Cambará and Praia Grande (which has a couple of basic hotels, one on the main square and the other at the *rodoviária*), on the Santa Catarina side of the state line. These will drop you just 3km from Itaimbezinho but you'll need to walk the difference – there is no bus service to the canyon. Camping is prohibited in the park, though there is a visitors' centre (☏54/3251-1262) and a snack bar.
Car If you intend to make the trip in your own vehicle it is imperative that you call ☏54/3251-1230 for up-to-date information on local road conditions.
Tourist information Only 1000 visitors are permitted to enter the park each day, so it's advisable to phone the visitors' centre (☏54/3251-1262) in advance to reserve a place.
Tours If you don't have your own transport, visiting can be complicated and it is worth bearing in mind that trying to visit the park on your own is much more difficult and barely cheaper than doing it with a tour. Try ecotourism specialists Canyons do Sul (ⓦwww.canyonsdosul.com.br).

JESUIT MISSION LANDS: SANTO ANGELO

Though less well known than those in Argentina and Paraguay, Rio Grande do Sul is home to no fewer than seven **Jesuit Missions** in an excellent state of preservation. Unfortunately, because of their isolated location and difficulties of access, very few foreign tourists ever make it out to visit them – which is not to say that it is not worth making the effort to do so. The best place to base yourself is the town of **SANTO ANGELO** in the northwest of the state, where there is a cluster of accommodation options around Praça Rio Branco. Eight daily buses run from Porto Alegre to Santo Angelo (7hr 30min).

The most accessible of the missions is **SÃO MIGUEL ARCANJO** (ⓦwww.missoesturismo.com.br), declared a UNESCO World Heritage Site and the best of the Brazilian ruins. Guided tours are available, and a nightly light show brings the story of the Jesuits to life. Four daily buses run the 53km southwest from Santo Angelo to São Miguel. Next to the ruins is an excellent themed hostel, *Missões Hostel* (☏55/3381-1202, ⓦwww.pousadatematica.com.br; R$106), which has dorm rooms (R$52 per person) as well as doubles and a relaxing pool.

WHEN TO VISIT

The Parque Nacional dos Aparados da Serra can be visited throughout the year, but is at its best during spring (Oct and Nov) when the blooming flowers create a spectacular effect. In the winter (June to Aug), it can get very cold, though visibility is often excellent. Summers are warm, but heavy rainfall sometimes makes the roads and trails impassable and fog and low-level cloud often completely obscure what should be spectacular views. Avoid April, May and September, the months with the most sustained rain.

CROSSING THE BORDERS TO URUGUAY AND ARGENTINA

To Uruguay

There are three major border crossings to Uruguay in Rio Grande do Sul. By far the most travelled route is via Chuí, 527km south of Porto Alegre. Buses entering and leaving Brazil stop at an immigration office a short distance from town for customs formalities. The Uruguayan immigration post is 3km outside town – you'll either have to walk or take a taxi.

Santana Do Livramento, 497km west of Porto Alegre in the heart of gaucho country, is a less-used but more atmospheric crossing point into Uruguay. There's no duty-free here, just gaucho memorabilia and *mate*. Before leaving Livramento you'll need a Brazilian exit (or entry) passport stamp from the Polícia Federal, at Rua Uruguai 1177, near the central park, and a stamp from Uruguay's Dirección Nacional de Inmigración, at Av. Presidente Viera s/n. If you have any problems, head for the Uruguayan consulate in Livramento at Av. Tamandaré 2101, 4th floor (☏55/3242-1416).

The third, and most complicated, border crossing is at Aceguá (to Melo in Uruguay). You'll need to have your passport stamped in the town of Bagé (see below), 60km north of the frontier, at the Policia Federal office located in Bagé at Rua Barão do Trunfo 1572 (☏53/3242-2668), a few blocks north of the Praça General Osório. Aceguá is little more than a conglomeration of buildings, so make sure you check your onward journey connections before you arrive as you don't want to get stuck here.

To Argentina

Most people heading to Argentina from Brazil cross the frontier at Foz do Iguaçu (see p.380), but if you find yourself in the south of the country, Uruguaiana, 694km west of Porto Alegre, is the most convenient crossing – with Paso de los Libres on the other side. Customs formalities take place at either end of the 1400m-long road bridge across the Rio Uruguai. Accommodation and restaurant options are both better on the Argentine side of the border. The Argentine consulate is at Rua 13 de Mayo 1674 (☏55/3412-1925).

BAGÉ

BAGÉ, 374km west of Porto Alegre, is first and foremost a cattle and commercial centre, rather than a tourist town, but unlike most of the other towns in the area it possesses a certain rural charm that makes it worth a visit if you are passing through the region.

What to see and do

Like all towns in the *campo* (countryside), Bagé has its own lively events, which attract people from the surrounding cattle ranches. The most important **festival**, held every April, is the **Semana Crioula Internacional** (a celebration of country life, with horse and sheep competitions as well as artistic events), though the **Semana de Bagé** (a folklore festival held annually from July 11–17), or even the **Exposição** (first half of Oct), will give you a taste of the area. For an understanding of the region's history, a visit to the **Museu Diogo de Souza**, Av. Guilayn 5759 (Tues–Sun 10am–5.30pm; R$3 although free Sun 10am–2pm; ⊛mdds .imc-ip.pt) is a must.

Arrival and information

Bus Buses arrive at the *rodoviária* (☏53/3242-9090) outside the town centre at Rua Dr Freitas 146.

Tourist information Bagé's tourist office at Praça Silveira Martins (Mon–Sat 8am–2pm;

☎ 53/3247-1395) has details of local festivals and other events.

Accommodation

Fenícia Rua Juvêncio Lemos 45 ☎ 53/3242-8222, ⓦ www.feniciahotel.com.br. This smart hotel in the centre of town offers comfortable standard and luxury apartments. A good option if you're looking for something a little refined. R$130.

Hangar Av. Espanha 257 ☎ 53/3241-6975. This simple hotel is among the cheapest options here; the no-frills rooms are clean and staff are friendly. R$74.

Obino Av. Sete de Setembro 901 ☎ 53/3242-8211, ⓦ www.hoteisobino.com.br. The best, largest and oldest hotel in town, dating from 1850. Generally considered to be the best hotel in Bagé. R$151.

Moving on

Bus Porto Alegre (5 daily; 4hr).

Chile

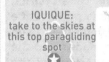
HIGHLIGHTS ✪

ROUGH COSTS

DAILY BUDGET Basic US$40
DRINK Pisco sour US$3
FOOD *Pastel de choclo* US$7
CAMPING/HOSTEL/BUDGET HOTEL
   US$8/16/20/40

FACT FILE

POPULATION 17 million
AREA 576,950 sq km
OFFICIAL LANGUAGE Spanish
INDIGENOUS LANGUAGES Aymará,
   Huilliche, Kawéscar, Mapudungun,
   Quechua, Rapanui and Yámana
CURRENCY Chilean Peso (CH$)
CAPITAL Santiago (population:
   5.3 million)
INTERNATIONAL PHONE CODE ☏ 56
TIME ZONE GMT -4; GMT -3 from
   second Sunday in October to
   second Sunday in March

Introduction

Chileans will tell you that when God created the world, he had a little bit of everything left over, and put pieces of desert, rivers, lakes and glaciers together to make Chile. From the world's driest desert – the Atacama – in the north to the volcanic peaks and verdant landscapes of the Lake District, down to the icy wilderness of Patagonia, this is perhaps the most geographically diverse and fascinating country in Latin America. Snaking between the snow-capped Andes and the Pacific Ocean, it's a fantastic playground for lovers of the outdoors, and for adrenalin junkies, with world-class skiing, surfing, white-water rafting, climbing and paragliding, while the country's plentiful national parks and nature reserves also boast an astounding array of plant and animal life.

Today, in spite of its troubled past, Chile is among the most politically and economically stable of all Latin American countries, and the memory of the tainted Pinochet dictatorship is gradually fading. For the most part, it is westernized and affluent, and its excellent bus network makes it an easy country to navigate.

Cosmopolitan **Santiago** is a very manageable starting point, with plentiful excellent bars, hostels and restaurants, as well as easy access to superb ski resorts and the vineyards of **Middle Chile**. In the nearby coastal city of **Valparaíso**, ride the *ascensores* (funiculars), or relax on the sandy beaches of neighbouring **Viña del Mar**. Head further north to the **Norte Chico** to knock back a pisco sour in the sublime **Elqui Valley**, or gaze at the stars in some of the world's clearest skies, while further north still the **Norte Grande** is where the strong breaks of the Pacific Ocean meet the moonscape scenery of the Atacama Desert. Visit gleaming lagoons and steaming geysers in the backpacker oasis of **San Pedro de Atacama**, and get your fill of sun and surf in the beach towns of **Iquique** and **Arica**.

South from Santiago, the **Lake District** – a region of lush forests and snow-capped volcanoes – exudes opportunities for rafting, cycling and mountaineering, while the mysterious island of **Chiloé** has beautiful wooden churches. Towering granite pillars and blue-tinged glaciers draw thousands of visitors to **Chilean Patagonia**, and the excellent trekking routes of **Parque Nacional Torres del Paine**. Last, but definitely not least, for serene beauty, ancient mystery and giant Moai statues, head to the world's most remote island of **Rapa Nui** (Easter Island).

CHRONOLOGY

1520 Ferdinand Magellan is the first European to sail through what is now the Magellan Strait.

1536 Expedition from Peru to Chile by conquistador Diego de Almagro and his four hundred men ends in death for most of the party.

1541 Pedro de Valdivia, a lieutenant of Francisco Pizarro, founds Santiago de Chile; a feudal system in which Spanish landowners enslave the Indian population is established.

1808 Napoleon invades Spain and replaces Spanish King Ferdinand VII with his own brother.

1810 The *criollo* elite of Santiago de Chile decide that Chile will be self-governed until the Spanish king is restored to the throne.

1817 Bernardo O'Higgins defeats Spanish royalists in the Battle of Chacabuco with the help of Argentine general José San Martín, as part of the movement to liberate South America from colonial rule.

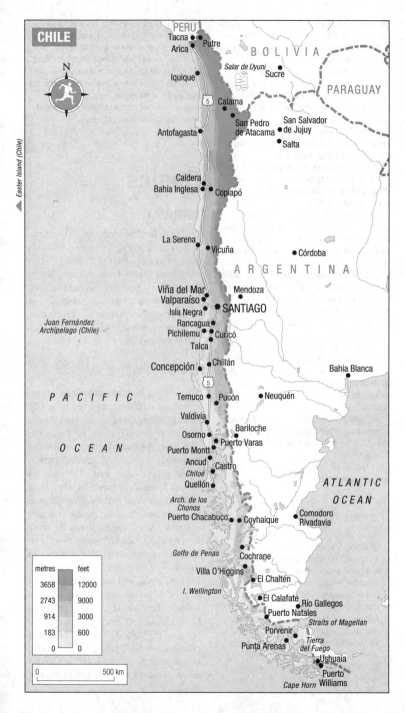

CHILE

N

Easter Island (Chile)

PERU
Tacna
Putre
Arica
Iquique
Calama
San Pedro
de Atacama
Antofagasta
Caldera
Bahía Inglesa
Copiapó
La Serena
Vicuña
Viña del Mar
Valparaíso
Isla Negra
Rancagua
Pichilemu
Curicó
Talca
Concepción
Chillán
Temuco
Pucón
Valdivia
Osorno
Puerto Varas
Puerto Montt
Ancud
Castro
Chiloé
Quellón
Arch. de los
Chonos
Puerto Chacabuco
Coyhaique
Golfo de Penas
Cochrane
Villa O'Higgins
I. Wellington
Puerto Natales
Porvenir
Punta Arenas
Puerto
Williams

BOLIVIA
Salar de Uyuni
Sucre
PARAGUAY
San Salvador
de Jujuy
Salta
Córdoba
ARGENTINA
Mendoza
Bahía Blanca
Neuquén
Bariloche
ATLANTIC
OCEAN
Comodoro
Rivadavia
El Chaltén
El Calafate
Río Gallegos
Straits of Magellan
Tierra
del Fuego
Ushuaia
Cape Horn

PACIFIC

OCEAN

Juan Fernández
Archipelago (Chile)

SANTIAGO

metres	feet
3658	12000
2743	9000
914	3000
183	600
0	0

0   500 km

1818 Full independence won from Spain. O'Higgins signs the Chilean Declaration of Independence.

1829 Wealthy elite seizes power with dictator Diego Portales at the helm.

1832–60s Mineral deposits found in the north of the country, stimulating economic growth.

1879–83 Chilean troops occupy the Bolivian port of Antofagasta, precipitating the War of the Pacific against Bolivia and Peru.

1914 With the creation of the Panama Canal, shipping routes no longer need to pass via the Cape, thus ending the nitrate boom.

1927–31 Carlos Ibáñez del Campo becomes Chile's first dictator, founding the corps of *carabineros* (militarized police); Chile is badly affected by the economic crash of 1929.

1932–52 Period of political instability: land belongs largely to the elite, while US corporations control Chile's copper production. Seeds are sewn of a political divide between left and conservative right.

1946 Gabriel González Videla becomes president of a broad coalition of parties; bowing to pressure from the US, he outlaws the Communist Party.

1970 Socialist leader Salvador Allende becomes the first democratically elected Marxist president by a slim margin.

1973–89 General Augusto Pinochet seizes control of the country with the support of the Chilean armed forces and the CIA. Intense repression of the regime's opponents follows, including arrests, torture and "disappearances"; thousands flee the country.

1990 Christian Democrat Patricio Aylwin is elected president and Pinochet steps down peacefully, though not before securing constitutional immunity from persecution.

2004 The Chilean Supreme Court strips Pinochet of immunity from prosecution.

2006 Socialist leader Michelle Bachelet, former torture victim of the Pinochet regime, is elected president. Pinochet dies under house arrest.

2010 Conservative businessman Sebastián Piñera named president by a narrow margin. On February 27, Middle Chile is hit by a massive earthquake that reaches 8.8 on the Richter scale. In October, 33 Chilean miners are rescued after 69 days trapped underground in a mine near Copiapó.

Basics

ARRIVAL

Chile has land borders with Argentina, Bolivia and Peru. Santiago is Chile's main transportation hub with numerous flights from Europe, North and South America, Australia and New Zealand. You can also fly to Chile's neighbours from several smaller airports such as Arica, Punta Arenas and Puerto Montt.

From Argentina

Numerous **border crossings** from Argentina to Chile are served by public buses, though those in the high Andes are seasonal and some in Patagonia may close for bad weather. Besides the frequently used Mendoza–Santiago crossing via the Los Libertadores tunnel, popular routes in the Lake District include Bariloche–Osorno, San Martín de Los Andes–Temuco and Bariloche–Puerto Varas by ferry across Lago Todos Los Santos. Southern Patagonian routes include Comodoro Rivadavia–Coyhaique, El Calafate–Puerto Natales and Río Gallegos–Punta Arenas, plus frequent (though highly weather-dependent) boat crossings from Ushuaia to Puerto Williams; for more on the Villa O'Higgins–El Chaltén crossing see box, p.503. In the north, the popular Jujuy and Salta–San Pedro de Atacama bus crossing is best booked in advance.

> ### WHEN TO VISIT
>
> If you want to experience the whole of Chile in all its diversity you'll need to come prepared for both extreme cold and extreme heat. The Lake District, Patagonia and Tierra del Fuego are best explored from October through April, since the Chilean winter effectively shuts down much of the south and transport can be very limited. Norte Grande, Norte Chico, Middle Chile and the Pacific island territories, however, can be accessed all year-round.

From Bolivia

The year-round crossing from La Paz to Arica is particularly easy, with a good paved highway running between the two cities. There are infrequent buses from Uyuni to San Pedro de Atacama via the Portezuelo del Cajón.

From Peru

Frequent trains, buses, *colectivos* and taxis serve the year-round crossing from Tacna to Arica.

VISAS

Citizens of the European Union, the United States, Canada, South Africa, Australia and New Zealand do not require **visas**, though citizens of the United States (US$131), Canada (US$132) and Australia (US$61) are subject to **one-off arrival fees**, valid for the life of the passport. Tourists are routinely granted 90-day entry permits and must surrender their tourist cards upon departure. In theory, visitors can be asked to produce an onward ticket and proof of sufficient funds, though that rarely happens. Ninety-day **visa extensions** can be granted by the Departamento de Extranjería, San Antonio 580, Piso 2, Santiago Centro (Mon–Fri 8.30am–2pm, calls taken 9am–4pm; ☎600/626-4222, ⓦwww .extranjeria.gov.cl/ingles) at a cost of US$100, although it may be cheaper and easier simply to cross the border into a neighbouring country and back again. If you lose your tourist card, you can get a replacement from the Policía Internacional, General Borgoño 1052, Independencia, Santiago (☎2/737-1292).

GETTING AROUND

The majority of the population in Chile travels by bus, and it's such a reliable and inexpensive option that you'll probably do the same. However, domestic flights are handy for covering long distances in a hurry.

By plane

Several airlines offer frequent and reasonably priced flights within Chile. You'll often find better fares by booking locally, rather than in advance from home. The flight from Santiago to Arica (2hr 30min) costs around CH$60,000, and the Santiago–Puerto Montt flight (1hr 30min) around CH$30,000. Return tickets are often much cheaper than two singles. **LAN** (☎600/526-2000 in Chile, when abroad call ☎56/2687-2400, ⓦwww.lan.com) is the most established airline with efficient online booking, last-minute discounts and a good-value "Visit South America Air Pass". **Sky Airline** (☎600/600-2828, ⓦwww .skyairline.cl) competes with LAN price-wise, with daily flights between Chile's major cities. Punta Arenas-based **Aerovías DAP** (☎61/616-100, ⓦwww.aeroviasdap.cl) flies to various destinations in Chilean and Argentine Patagonia and Tierra del Fuego; it's best to book tickets directly at the airline offices as their website is inefficient.

By bus

Bus travel is popular, affordable and convenient. The level of comfort depends on how much you are prepared to pay for your ticket, with the *cama* buses being the plushest, their seats reclining almost horizontally. The cheapest seats from Santiago to Arica cost around CH$37,000, from Santiago to Puerto Montt CH$24,000, and from Santiago to Mendoza CH$14,000. Bus tickets are valid only for specified buses, and the major bus companies, such as **Tur Bus** (☎600 660-6600, ⓦwww .turbus.cl) and **Pullman** (☎600 320-3200, ⓦwww.pullman.cl), require you to buy your ticket before you board – though for the majority of routes you'll have no trouble purchasing tickets at a bus station kiosk shortly before your departure. That said, south of Puerto Montt, and especially during the peak months, demand outstrips supply, so it is advisable to book in advance if you are on a tight schedule. Bus station kiosks are the easiest option – online booking services are available but cannot usually process foreign credit cards. If crossing **international** borders by bus, remember that it's prohibited to transport animal and plant matter to neighbouring countries, and luggage searches are frequent.

Smaller **local buses** and minibuses (*micros*) connect city centres with outlying neighbourhoods and smaller towns with villages. In some parts of Chile, especially in the north, *colectivos* (shared taxis with fixed fares) provide a faster and only slightly pricier service between towns than local buses.

By train

Travelling by **train** is a good option if you plan to stop off in Middle Chile. A reliable and comfortable service operated by Terra Sur (ⓦwww.terrasur .cl) usually runs several times a day between Santiago and Chillán, with stops at intermediate stations including Rancagua, and Talca. Following the 2010 earthquake, however, it was at the time of writing only running as far south as Talca – work was being done to restore the line. On the cheapest seats, the three-hour trip from Santiago to Talca costs about CH$5000, and from Santiago to Rancagua (1hr) around CH$3600.

By car

Car rental is costly (CH$19,000–35,000 per day) and complicated, with expensive insurance due to the varying condition of the dirt roads. Carrying spare tyres, a jack, extra petrol and plenty of drinking water is essential for driving around more remote parts of Chile, and punctures are frequent. Since public transport is perfectly adequate in most parts of the country, the only places where it may make sense to rent a 4x4 vehicle is on Easter Island, and perhaps to some national parks. To rent a car, you need to be over 21 years old; take your passport as ID, and have a national driver's licence and major credit card on hand.

By bike

Cycling can be a good way of getting to the more remote national parks, some of which are inaccessible by public

---

PACHAMAMA BY BUS

This hop-on, hop-off **Pachamama by bus** service is especially tailored for independent travellers and designed to cover the most scenic spots in the Lake District and the Atacama Desert. You purchase a pass for the number of days you wish to travel – a seven-day pass costs CH$119,000 – and you can stay at any of the given stops for as long as you want. You are responsible for booking your own accommodation, which the guides can assist with. There are weekly departures on both routes; check the website for exact dates. To book a pass, contact the office inside the *Casa Roja* hostel in Santiago at least 48 hours in advance (see p.422; ☎2/688-8018, ⓦwww.pachamamabybus.com).

transport. It's a good idea to carry spare parts, although bike repair shops are found in most medium-sized towns. While in the south of Chile **drinking water** can typically be acquired from streams, in the northern half of the country it is highly advisable to carry your own, and essential if cycling anywhere in the arid Atacama region. There are few cycle lanes and for the most part cyclists share the road with motorists; at least traffic outside cities tends to be light. Stray dogs can also be a nuisance in populated areas. See p.411 for more on cycling.

By ferry

South of Puerto Montt, where Chile breaks up into a plethora of islands and fjords, you will have to take a **ferry**, whether to continue along the Carretera Austral or to work your way down to Southern Patagonia. Travelling south by boat is more expensive than going by bus, but it allows you access to some of the remotest and most beautiful parts of Chile. Popular routes include Puerto Montt to Puerto Natales, Puerto Montt to Chacabuco and Chacabuco to Laguna San Rafael.

Hitching

Hitchhiking is popular in Chile and widely practised by locals, especially in rural areas. While it's never an entirely safe method of travel, Chile is the safest country in Latin America in which to hitch, although it's always best to do so at least in pairs.

ACCOMMODATION

Chile has a wide range of **budget accommodation**, often of great quality, occasionally not so great. Prices are highest during the peak season from December to February, when Chileans go on summer holiday; in shoulder seasons, they generally drop by around twenty percent. Many lodgings in the south of Chile close down during the winter months, so check ahead. Prices are normally listed inclusive of tax but it is best to establish this at the start of your stay.

Residenciales, cabañas and refugios

Residenciales are the most commonly available budget lodgings, found in both large cities and villages. Typically they consist of furnished rooms in someone's home, often with breakfast included; not surprisingly, the quality varies enormously. A basic double room would cost about CH$12,000–20,000; single rooms can cost as much as two-thirds the price of doubles.

Cabañas are usually found in well-visited spots, particularly by the ocean. They tend to come with a fully equipped kitchen, bathroom and bedrooms, and can be a great option for those travelling in groups. Depending on the time of year, a cabaña for two people costs about CH$20,000–30,000. Lower rates can be negotiated for larger groups.

Refugios are cheap (except those in Torres del Paine National Park), bare-bones lodgings found in national parks, usually consisting of several bunk beds in a wooden hut. Most have clean bedding, showers and flushable toilets; some require you to bring your own sleeping bag. Costs are around CH$8000–10,000 per person. Many *refugios* stay open year-round, but if you are planning on wilderness trekking, or on travelling in the south of Chile in the winter, try to arrange lodgings by calling the local **Conaf** office (ⓦwww.conaf.cl), Chile's national forestry service, in advance; individual offices are listed on its website.

Hostels and camping

Hostel and camping options are plentiful across the country, especially in well-visited cities and popular outdoor destinations. Some independent hostel groups compile booklets listing the best hostels, which are worth picking up. **Backpackers Chile**, for example, who have both a booklet and website (ⓦwww .backpackerschile.com), offer a reliable benchmark for high-quality hostels. The booklet is available from any of the hostels listed on the site, and at major information offices. Also worth picking up is the **Get South** booklet (ⓦwww .getsouth.com), which offers discounts and freebies for various hostels across Chile, as well as Argentina and Uruguay.

Most major cities and key tourist centres have a **Hostelling International**-affiliated hostel (ⓦwww .hihostels.com), for which member discounts will be available. The quality of HI hostels is not necessarily better than independent hostels, though they do tend to meet basic standards, so can be preferable to some budget hotels.

Note that in some widely visited places, such as Pucón and San Pedro de Atacama, a **hostal** may not necessarily mean a bona fide youth hostel – in many cases they simply turn out to be family homes.

Chile has marvellous opportunities for **camping**, with a proliferation of both fully equipped campsites (which can be somewhat pricey) and beautiful wilderness spots. There is ample free camping on empty beaches, although in most national parks you should only camp in designated spots. *Campings y Rutas Chile*, published only in Spanish by Turistel, and updated annually, has an extensive, though not entirely complete, list of campsites around Chile.

FOOD

Despite the abundance of fresh produce, **food** in Chile can seem somewhat bland as few spices are used; exceptions are *pebre* (a spicy salsa served with bread) and *ají chileno*, served with barbecued meat. **Breakfast** (*desayuno*) consists of coffee and the ubiquitous pockmarked bread with butter and jam. **Lunch** (*almuerzo*) is the main meal of the day, typically made up of three courses; at lunchtime most restaurants offer a good-value fixed-price *menú del día*. **Dinner** (*cena*) is usually served late, rarely before 9pm, and in Chilean households is often replaced by a lighter **evening snack** (*once*). Restaurants open from around 7pm but don't start to fill up until around 9pm.

Chicken and beef are the commonest **meats**, the latter often served boiled or grilled with a fried egg on top (*lomo a lo pobre*) or as part of a *parillada* (mixed grill). Two dishes found on menus across the country are *cazuela*, a hearty meat casserole, and *pastel de choclo*, a sweet-tasting corn and beef pie. When in Patagonia, do not miss the *asador patagónico*, spit-roasted lamb (*cordero*) and wild boar (*jibalí*) steaks, while llama and alpaca steaks and stew are a staple of *altiplano* cuisine in the north of Chile. Both the island of Chiloé and Easter Island serve up *curanto*, an elaborately prepared dish of meat and seafood.

There is a fantastic range of **fish and seafood**, and trendy sushi bars are springing up everywhere. Fish are typically served *frito* (battered and deep-fried), or *a la plancha* (grilled) with different sauces. Alternatively, try the *ceviche* – raw fish marinated in lemon juice with cilantro. Excellent seafood dishes include *machas a la parmesana*, baked razor clams covered with parmesan cheese, *chupe de locos*, creamy abalone casserole topped with breadcrumbs, and *paila marina*, seafood soup.

Excellent **fruit and vegetables** are abundant in most parts of Chile, barring Patagonia and Tierra del Fuego. The north of the country grows exotic delights like scaly green *chirimoya* (custard apple), papaya, *tuna* (cactus fruit) and melon-like *pepino dulce*. Easter Island cuisine incorporates Polynesian tubers such as the *camote* (sweet potato).

EATING ON A BUDGET

Prices at some upmarket restaurants in Santiago and Valparaíso could give the impression that you have to break the bank to enjoy good food in Chile, but there are cheaper options.

In coastal towns, you can pick up superb fish at bargain prices at little marisquerías, rustic fish eateries usually found at the busiest point of the seafront. In most large cities, look out for the market area where you'll get excellent deals on fruit and vegetables.

Small kiosks along city streets and country roads will often sell delicious and filling snacks like *empanadas* (savoury pasties filled with meat or fish) and *humitas* (ground corn wrapped in leaves).

American-style diners, and home-grown fast-food chains across Chile sell huge *completos* (hot dogs), and *italianos*, hot-dogs covered in mayonnaise, ketchup and avocado, as well as a range of sandwiches, like *Barros Jarpa* (melted cheese and ham), as alternative cheap eats.

DRINK

Tap water is generally drinkable all over Chile, with the exception of the Atacama, though Santiago tap water may upset some stomachs unaccustomed to the high mineral content. **Mineral water** is inexpensive and comes *sin gas* (still) or *con gas* (carbonated). **Soft drinks** (*gaseosas* or *bebidas*) are plentiful and very popular, and freshly squeezed **fruit juices** (*jugos*) are abundant, especially in the fertile region of Middle Chile; beware that most Chileans like their juice sweetened, so if you don't want a half-juice, half-sugar concoction, ask for it *sin azúcar* (without sugar). *Licuados* are fruit smoothies mixed with water or *leche* (milk). *Mote con huesillo*, a drink made from boiled, dried apricots, is popular, especially in Middle Chile.

It can be difficult to find real **coffee** (*café de grano*) in smaller towns, as Nescafé seems to be the drink of choice, but coffee bars are appearing thick and fast across Santiago and other cities. In the Lake District and Patagonia, due to the proximity to Argentine culture, you are likely to encounter *yerba mate*, an antioxidant-rich, energizing herb drunk from a gourd through a metal straw.

Chile has several generic lager **beers** including Escudo, Cristal and Austral; the best beers come from microbreweries, with Kunstmann being the pick of the bunch. Chileans often start meals with a refreshing **pisco sour**, the national drink (see box, p.441).

Chilean **wine**, renowned worldwide, features on many restaurant menus. Wine tourism is also on the rise, with the Rutas del Vino (Wine Routes) in the Maule and Colchagua valleys giving visitors easy access to both the process of wine-making and the sampling of many different varieties.

CULTURE AND ETIQUETTE

Chilean city lifestyle, superficially at least, has more similarities with Europe than with neighbouring Bolivia. When eating out, a ten-percent **tip** in restaurants is normal and appreciated. Bargaining is not common and rarely done, even in marketplaces, though Chileans are often excellent at seeking out bargain prices.

Chileans are family- and **child-oriented**, and young people tend to live with their parents until they get married. The predominant religion is **Catholicism**, though the Church is not as influential as it used to be. Machismo is not as prevalent here as in other parts of Latin America; **women** are more respected and a lone woman travelling around the country is not likely to encounter any trouble beyond catcalls. While **homosexuality** is still frowned upon, it is tolerated, and there is a thriving gay scene in larger cities.

Chileans are very **sociable** people and will go out of their way to greet you in the street if they know you. If arranging to go out with Chileans, be aware that they may turn up later than the arranged time. When it comes to topics of conversation, Pinochet's rule is still very much a divisive subject, so unless you wish to be drawn into a heated discussion, steer clear.

SPORTS AND OUTDOOR ACTIVITIES

While Chile is not quite in the same league when it comes to **football** as Argentina or Brazil, the game is taken very seriously and attending a live match in Santiago (CH$4000–13,000) is very worthwhile for the atmosphere alone. Be aware, though, that the passion for football can turn aggressive, and be ready to make an exit. Santiago team Colo Colo has the largest and most enthusiastic following.

Every year, over three hundred **rodeos** are staged during the season (Sept–May) in Middle Chile and Aisén in particular. Evolved from the rural *huaso* (cowboy) culture, the rodeo is a spectacle worth going out of your way for.

La cueca, Chile's national **dance**, is also firmly rooted in *huaso* culture; it re-enacts the courting ritual between a rooster and a hen. Men and women clad in traditional outfits dance largely to guitar-led ballads, though the tempo and the instruments vary from region to region. *La cueca* is most commonly seen during the Chilean independence celebrations in September, when troupes perform on streets and stages across the country, though Chileans often take little persuading to show off their beloved dance whatever the opportunity.

Watersports

The mighty rivers of the Lake District and Patagonia offer excellent **white-water rafting** and **kayaking**, with Río Trancura, Río Petrohué and Río Futaleufú offering level 5 challenges. Futaleufú in particular is hailed as one of the top white-water runs in the world.

Sea kayakers can choose between multi-day paddling in the Patagonian fjords, shorter trips to small islands off the coast of Chiloé and wildlife-viewing on Isla Damas near La Serena.

Surfers head to Chile's top spot, Pichilemu, just south of Santiago, though there are excellent surfing and **windsurfing** opportunities all along the coast north of the capital, around Iquique in particular, and year-round swells on Easter Island.

In the northern half of the country, lack of rain makes for good visibility and abundant marine life for **divers** and **snorkellers**, while Easter Island and the Juan Fernández Archipelago both have world-class dive spots.

Hiking, climbing and skiing

Hiking in the Torres del Paine National Park, on Isla Navarino or anywhere in the south is limited to the summer, spring and autumn, but the rest of Chile can be visited at any time of year. There are currently 55 **Rutas Patrimoniales** (ⓦwww.turismochile.cl/rutas -patrimoniales) covering the whole of Chile as part of a government initiative to preserve and develop land that has natural and historical value. These can all be explored on foot, by bike or on horseback. Another ambitious project, **Senderos de Chile** (ⓦwww .senderodechile.cl) consists of 35 trail sections intended to span the whole of Chile, including its Pacific islands. Once completed, it will become the longest trekking route in the world, but progress on the project is currently slow.

Ice climbers will find excellent **climbing** routes in the Central and Patagonian Andes from November to March, with plenty of accessible glaciers, while the granite towers of Torres del Paine rank among the world's most challenging rock climbs. Middle Chile and the Lake District, however, have the greatest variety of climbing and mountaineering spots.

Along with Argentina, Chile has world-class powder snow, with some of the best **skiing** spots found in easy reach of Santiago (see p.426). The Lake District's Villarica-Pucón and Osorno give you the opportunity to whizz down the slopes of volcanoes.

Biking

Spectacular **biking** terrain can be found from Norte Grande to Tierra del Fuego, though you will need a sturdy mountain bike to cope with the potholed trails. While the best time to cycle around much of Chile is between October and March, Norte Chico and Norte Grande can be explored year-round, though altitude is often a consideration, especially if you're planning on exploring Parque Nacional Lauca. Norte Chico offers easy and enjoyable coastal rides, while the Lake District and Chiloé have the greatest variety of cycling routes, and the Carretera Austral is a challenging undertaking that rewards with amazing scenery.

COMMUNICATIONS

Overseas mail sent from any part of Chile via Correos de Chile, Chile's **postal service**, generally takes two or three weeks to reach its destination. Important shipping to Chile is best sent via registered mail. The larger post offices have a *lista de correos* (alphabetical list) for collecting *poste restante* (general delivery).

Chile has a number of different telecoms operators, and in order to make an **international call**, you dial the three-digit carrier code of the telecom, followed by 0, then the country code and finally the phone number itself. Most local numbers consist of six or seven digits, preceded by the city/area code; if dialling from the same area, drop the city or area code and dial the six or seven digits directly. Mobile phone numbers start with 07, 08 or 09, followed by seven digits; drop the 0 when calling mobile-to-mobile. Calls abroad from the numerous **centros de llamadas** to most European countries and North America cost around CH$150, although prices vary from area to area. Setting up a **Skype** account is cheap and convenient, as many internet cafés in Chile are Skype-equipped. Alternatively, get a Chilean **SIM card** for an "unlocked"

CHILE ON THE NET

ⓦ www.chile.travel The international section of the official website of Sernatur – Chile's government-run tourist board – covers regional attractions, places to stay and restaurants.

ⓦ www.conaf.cl Information on Chile's protected natural areas (in Spanish only).

ⓦ www.gochile.cl Online travel agency covering the whole of Chile (available in English).

ⓦ www.santiagotimes.cl Online version of the capital's English-language newspaper.

ⓦ www.dondesalgo.cl Chilean site offering recommendations for good nights out.

ⓦ www.turismochile.cl Descriptions of regional attractions (mostly in Spanish).

ⓦ www.conadi.cl Site for indigenous affairs (Spanish only).

ⓦ www.puntogay.cl Information on gay nightlife and more.

ⓦ www.dibam.cl Plenty of detail on cultural attractions and museums.

mobile phone for around CH$6000, and all incoming calls are free.

Internet is widely available across Chile. Most towns and villages have broadband-equipped **internet cafés**, where access costs around CH$500 per hr, although on Isla Navarino and Easter Island it is considerably pricier.

CRIME AND SAFETY

The risk of **violent crime** in Chile is very low; in larger cities pickpocketing and petty thievery are minor concerns, but assaults are practically unknown, and there is very little corruption among Chilean police.

HEALTH

There are no compulsory **vaccinations** for Chile, though there have been reported incidents of mosquito-borne **dengue fever** on Easter Island; use insect repellent. **Hantavirus**, caused by inhaling or ingesting rat droppings, is uncommon but deadly: when staying in rural buildings that could potentially have rodents, air them out thoroughly and do not sleep on the floor. Chile has two species of **spider** with a venomous and potentially dangerous bite: the black widow (found in parts of Torres del Paine National Park, among other areas) and the Chilean recluse spider (found throughout Chile). The recluse – or *araña del rincón,* literally "corner spider" – is commonly found in houses. Though bites from either spider are relatively rare, they can prove fatal – if you think you may have been bitten, seek medical help immediately.

INFORMATION AND MAPS

Official **Sernatur** tourist offices (Servicio Nacionál de Turismo; Ⓦwww.sernatur .cl) are found in all the major cities and towns. They produce a plethora of brochures on local attractions, accommodation and outdoor activities, though some are better stocked than others. Some regions may also have a **municipal tourism office** run by the regional authorities. For information on Chile's natural attractions, as well as maps and up-to-date trekking conditions for specific areas, you should head to the local **Conaf** office (Corporación Nacionál Forestál, Ⓦwww.conaf.cl), again found in most towns.

JLM Cartografía maps are usually accurate and helpful, and can be found in most bookshops; they cover both cities and trekking routes in Chile. The Instituto Geográfico Militar (Ⓦwww .igm.cl) produces detailed topographic maps of the entire country, but they can be pricey. **TurisTel guidebooks**, published by Telefónica Chile, are an excellent source of information on the country (in Spanish); they come in three volumes, covering the south, Middle Chile and Santiago, and the north, and are updated annually.

MONEY AND BANKS

The **peso** is the basic unit of Chilean currency, and it comes in 1000, 5000, 10,000 and rare 20,000 denomination notes, and 10, 20, 50, 100 and 500 peso coins. It is usually represented with the $ sign, not to be confused with US$. Few places will accept US dollars or other foreign currencies, though some hostels and hotels may suggest you pay in dollars to avoid the nineteen percent IVA tax (value added tax) on accommodation, from which foreigners are exempted when paying in dollars. Chile is fairly expensive compared to its Latin

---

EMERGENCY NUMBERS

Air rescue ☎138 (for mountaineering accidents)
Ambulance ☎131
Coast Guard ☎137
Fire ☎132
Investigaciónes ☎134 (for serious crimes)
Police ☎133

American counterparts (besides Brazil), with prices comparable to those in North America and Europe.

Large and medium-sized cities have plentiful **banks** and **ATMs**; Banco de Chile and Santander are good bets for withdrawing cash with debit cards. Santiago and most of the more visited destinations have casas de cambio which can change traveller's cheques and foreign currencies at a reasonable rate. Some smaller towns (and Easter Island) only have Banco Estado ATMs, which accept just Cirrus and MasterCard. If you are heading to small towns off the beaten track, it's wise to carry enough cash to cover a few days as ATMs are not always reliable. **Credit cards** can also be widely used to pay for purchases, especially in larger towns, though budget lodgings and eating places rarely accept them.

OPENING HOURS AND HOLIDAYS

On weekdays, most services and **shops** tend to be open from 9 or 10am to 6 or 7pm; Saturday hours are usually 10 or 11am to 2pm. In smaller towns, **restaurants** are often closed in the afternoon, between the lunchtime hours of 1 to 3pm and the dinnertime hours of 8 to 11pm. An increasing number of restaurants, bars and shops open on Sundays but smaller places, particularly in more rural areas, generally remain closed. **Banks** typically operate from 9am to 2pm on weekdays only, while post offices generally open Monday to Friday from 9am to 6pm; in larger towns, they also open Saturdays from 9am to 1pm. Monday is a day off for most **museums**;

they are, however, usually open on Sundays, often with free entry. Shops and services are closed during national holidays, local festivals and on local and national election days.

PUBLIC HOLIDAYS

Jan 1 New Year's Day (*Año Nuevo*)
Easter (*Semana Santa*) national holidays on Good Friday, Holy Saturday and Easter Sunday
May 1 Labour Day (*Día del Trabajo*)
May 21 Navy Day (*Día de las Glorias Navales*) marking Chile's naval victory at Iquique during the War of the Pacific
June 29 St Peter and St Paul (*San Pedro y San Pablo*)
July 16 Our Lady of Mount Carmel (*Solemnidad de la Virgen del Carmen, Reina y Patrona de Chile*)
Aug 15 Assumption of the Virgin Mary (*Asunción de la Virgen*)
Sept 17 If it falls on a Monday, an extension of Independence celebrations.
Sept 18 National Independence Day (*Fiestas Patrias*) celebrates Chile's proclamation of independence from Spain in 1810
Sept 19 Armed Forces Day (*Día del Ejército*)
Sept 20 If it falls on a Friday, an extension of Independence celebrations
Oct 12 Columbus Day (*Día del Descubrimiento de Dos Mundos*) celebrates the European discovery of the Americas
Nov 1 All Saints' Day (*Día de Todos los Santos*)
Dec 8 Immaculate Conception (*Inmaculada Concepción*)
Dec 25 Christmas Day (*Navidad*)

Santiago

Towered over by the snow-streaked Andes, the buzzing metropolis of **SANTIAGO** has a distinctly European feel. Its rich pockets of culture and history are often overlooked by travellers frustrated by a lack of iconic sights, and put off by the smog that hangs over the city. Yet those prepared to venture beyond the grid of central shopping streets will be rewarded with quirky, vibrant neighbourhoods filled with a huge variety of lively bars and excellent restaurants. Streetscapes flit between elegant colonial buildings and high-rise office blocks. The city is a microcosm of the country's contrasting ways of life, with ramshackle markets, smart office buildings, rough-and-ready bars and plush shopping malls all just a short metro ride from the main square.

Home to more than a quarter of Chile's population, the capital is crowded but easy to navigate with a clean and efficient metro system. And even if the city itself fails to impress, Santiago is an excellent base from which to explore, with world-class ski resorts, sun-kissed beaches and beautiful vineyards all within easy reach.

What to see and do

Downtown Santiago is loosely bordered by the **Río Mapocho** to the north, and the central thoroughfare of Avenida Libertador Bernado O'Higgins – commonly known as **La Alameda** – to the south. The city's accommodation and most inviting *barrios* are all a short distance from this central section. Bohemian **Barrio Lastarria** is home to a wealth of art museums and characterful boutique shops. North of the river, **Barrio Bellavista** offers trendy cafés as well as the funicular to the city's best viewpoint at **Cerro San Cristóbal**. In the west, down-to-earth **Barrio** **Brasil** and **Barrio Yungay** are home to many budget hostels and good restaurants, while out east, upmarket Providencia and plush Las Condes make up in shopping malls what they lack in character.

Plaza de Armas

Pedro de Valdivia, the city's founder, intended the lush tree-studded **Plaza de Armas** to be the epicentre of Chile, surrounding it with splendid colonial architecture. The oldest building on the west side of the plaza is the **Catedral Metropolitana** (1748), its Neoclassical facade designed by the Italian architect Joaquín Toesca. To the north is the **Palacio de la Real Audiencia** (1804), housing the Museo Histórico Nacional, and the **Correo Central**. A lively gathering point since the mid-1800s, the plaza's flower gardens and the fountain in the centre honouring Simón Bolívar attract a multitude of chess players, mimes, buskers, vagrants, stray dogs, soap-box preachers, strolling families and giggling children, making the square an ideal place to linger on a bench and people-watch.

Mercado Central and La Vega

By the south bank of Río Mapocho lies the lively **Mercado Central** (daily 6am–4pm), a mass of stalls spilling over with wondrous fish and seafood, dotted with busy little *marisquerías* whose delicious smells draw crowds of customers at lunchtime. All of this is gathered inside an elaborate metal structure prefabricated in Birmingham, England, and erected in Santiago in 1868. Cross the Río Mapocho and you reach **La Vega** (daily: roughly 6am–5pm), an enormous roofed market surrounded by outdoor stalls, selling all kinds of fresh produce, with fruit and vegetables at rock-bottom prices. La Vega is full of local character, giving you a glimpse of "real" Santiago: fragrant, pungent and chaotic. It is also the best place in town to grab a giant fruit smoothie, as well as excellent seafood.

Museo Chileno de Arte Precolombino

The excellent **Museo Chileno de Arte Precolombino** (Tues–Sun 10am–6pm; CH$3000, guided tours must be pre-booked, call ☏2/928-1522, ⓦwww.museoprecolombino.cl), at Bandera 361, is housed in the elegant late-colonial Real Casa de Aduana (Royal Customs House, 1807). The unparalleled collection of pre-Columbian artefacts spans a time period of around ten thousand years and covers the whole of Latin America, from Mexico down to the south of Chile. More than 1500 examples of pottery, finely woven textiles and jewellery are on display, including permanent collections from the Andes, Mesoamerica, the Amazon and the Caribbean, and there are outstanding temporary exhibitions.

La Moneda

The restored **Palacio de la Moneda**, on the large **Plaza de la Constitución**, is the presidential palace and site of the dramatic siege that brought Pinochet to power on September 11, 1973, and led to the death of President Salvador Allende. A wide, squat Neoclassical construction, originally built to house the Royal Mint, the palace stages an elaborate **changing of the guard** every other day at 10am, featuring white-jacketed officers, cavalry and an inspired brass band. The palace's inner courtyards can be accessed through the North Gate (Mon–Fri 10am–6pm) and the basement features a huge relief map of Chile that allows visitors to get an accurate impression of the country's size. The **Centro Cultural Palacio La Moneda** (daily 9am–9pm; exhibitions CH$1000; ⓦwww.ccplm.cl), a smart, arty space home to exhibitions, craft shops, and cafés, is accessed by steps to the left and right of the palace's main frontage.

Cerro Santa Lucía

Six blocks east of Palacio de la Moneda along the Alameda, Santiago's main thoroughfare (officially Av. Libertador Bernardo O'Higgins), the splendidly landscaped **Cerro Santa Lucía** (Dec–Feb 9am–8pm; rest of the year 9am–7pm; free; register passport details at the entrance) is the historically significant promontory where Pedro de Valdivia defeated the indigenous forces (to whom it is known as Huelén – "the curse"), and where Santiago was officially founded on February 12, 1541. The barren hill was transformed into a lush retreat through the labour of 150 prisoners in the 1870s. The park's tranquil winding footpaths and the ornate Terraza Neptuno fountain draw amorous couples, while visitors take the steep footpaths to the top to be rewarded with **panoramic views** of the city.

Parque Forestal

It's hard to believe that the tranquil green space of the **Parque Forestal**, stretching along the Río Mapocho's south bank, was once a floodplain covered in rubbish dumps. Top attraction here is the grand and airy Neoclassical **Palacio de Bellas Artes**, housing the **Museo de Bellas Artes** (Tues–Sun 10am–7pm; CH$600, students CH$400), which features paintings, sculptures, prints and drawings by predominantly Chilean artists. The **Museo de Arte Contemporáneo**, or **MAC** (Tues–Sat 11am–7pm, Sun 11am–6pm; CH$600, students CH$400; ⓦwww.mac.uchile.cl), next door, offers temporary modern art exhibitions, some of them interactive, by cutting-edge national and international artists.

Barrio Bellavista

Crossing the Pío Nono bridge brings you to **Barrio Bellavista**, the trendy

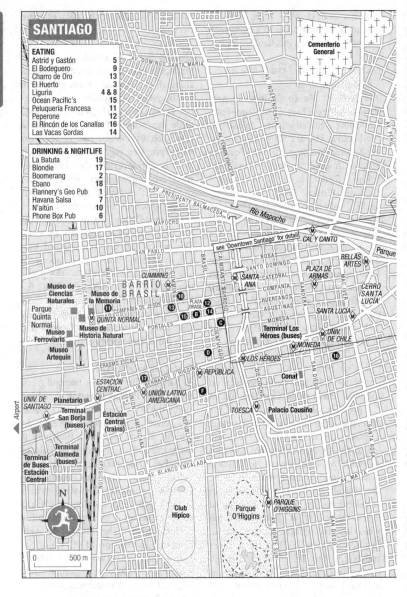

SANTIAGO

EATING
Astrid y Gastón	5
El Bodeguero	9
Charro de Oro	13
El Huerto	3
Liguria	4 & 8
Ocean Pacific's	15
Peluquería Francesa	11
Peperone	12
El Rincón de los Canallas	16
Las Vacas Gordas	14

DRINKING & NIGHTLIFE
La Batuta	19
Blondie	17
Boomerang	2
Ebano	18
Flannery's Geo Pub	1
Havana Salsa	7
N'aitún	10
Phone Box Pub	6

bohemian neighbourhood at the foot of **Cerro San Cristóbal**, the city's second largest hill. Bellavista really comes into its own on weekends; it's home to some of Santiago's best **bars** and **restaurants**, which sit along tranquil, tree-lined streets. There are also several good nightclubs and raucous beer-and-burger joints lining Pío Nono, the main street. You'll find **La Chascona**, one of the three residences of Chile's most famous poet,

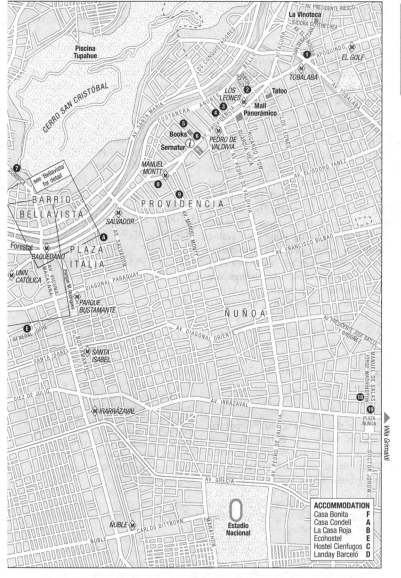

Villa Grimaldi ▶

ACCOMMODATION	
Casa Bonita	F
Casa Condell	A
La Casa Roja	B
Ecohostel	E
Hostel Cienfuegos	C
Landay Barceló	D

Pablo Neruda, down the little side-
street of Márquez de la Plata (Tues–
Sun: Jan–Feb 10am–7pm, March–Dec
10am–6pm; tours CH$3500; ☎2/777-
8741, ⒲www.fundacionneruda.cl).
Named after Neruda's wife Matilde,
"the tangle-haired woman", the house
is faithful to the nautical theme that
characterizes all his residences, its
creaking floorboards resembling those
of a ship and strangely shaped rooms
filled with a lifetime of curios. You can

only visit as part of a tour, which is extremely worthwhile.

Cerro San Cristóbal

From Barrio Bellavista's Plaza Caupolicán, the **Funicular San Cristóbal** runs up to the Terraza Bellavista, high in the hills above the city (Mon 1–8pm, Tues–Sun 10am–8pm; return trip CH$1600). From Terraza Bellavista you walk up to the hill's summit, crowned with a huge statue of the Virgen de la Immaculada Concepción and offering excellent views of the city, though the outlying neighbourhoods might be clouded in a gentle haze of smog. The many dirt tracks running along the forested hillsides offer excellent mountain-biking opportunities, while walking down the spiralling road brings you to **Piscina Tupahue** (Nov–March Tues–Sun 10am–7pm; CH$5000), a popular open-air swimming pool and picnicking spot amidst monkey puzzle trees. You can either return by the same route or continue down to the Estación Pedro de Valdivia in Providencia.

Barrio Brasil

West of the Vía Norte Sur, downtown's western boundary, **Barrio Brasil** is centred around the nicely landscaped Plaza Brasil, with a surreal-looking playground and a tall monkey puzzle tree reaching for the sky. In the early twentieth century this was a prestigious residential neighbourhood; now its elegant streets have faded and it has morphed into a lively area with good restaurants and bars, popular with backpackers and Santiago's students.

Ñuñoa

Southeast of central Santiago, the laidback neighbourhood of **Ñuñoa**, with the attractive **Plaza Ñuñoa** at its heart, is overlooked by many visitors to the city, though it has a lively **nightlife** due to the proximity of two university campuses. Football fans also flock here to watch the matches at the **Estadio Nacional**, at Av. Grecia 2001. The stadium has a grim past – it was once used by Pinochet as a torture centre and prison.

Arrival

Air Aeropuerto Arturo Merino Benítez (℡2/690-1752, ⓦwww.aeropuertosantiago.cl), 30min from the city centre, has useful facilities including ATMs, currency exchange, tourist information kiosk and mobile phone rentals. The blue Centropuerto bus (every 20min: daily 6am–10.30pm; CH$1400 one-way), just outside the terminal doors, is the cheapest way to get to the city centre and stops at the Los Héroes metro station. Tur Bus has transfers to the Terminal Alameda (every 30min: daily 6.15am–midnight; CH$1700), while TransVip (℡2/677-3000) and Transfer Delfos (℡2/913-8800) charge from CH$5500 to drop you off at your destination.

"NEVER AGAIN" – REMEMBERING THE CRIMES OF THE PINOCHET ERA

The excellent Museo de la Memoria y los Derechos Humanos at Matucana 501; Tues–Sun 10am–6pm; free; ⓦwww.museodelamemoria.cl; Metro Quinta Normal) documents the chilling human rights' abuses, repression and censorship that occurred between 1973 and 1990 under the Pinochet dictatorship. Another memorial to the victims of the regime is Villa Grimaldi, Av. José Arrieta 8401, a secret torture and extermination centre now transformed into a Park for Peace (daily 10am–6pm; free; ⓦwww.villagrimaldi.cl). The buildings here were destroyed in an attempt to erase any evidence of the centre's existence, but among a series of memorials to its victims are explanations of the site's original layout. To get there, take bus 513, or D09, or go to Metro Plaza Egaña and get a taxi (about CH$6000).

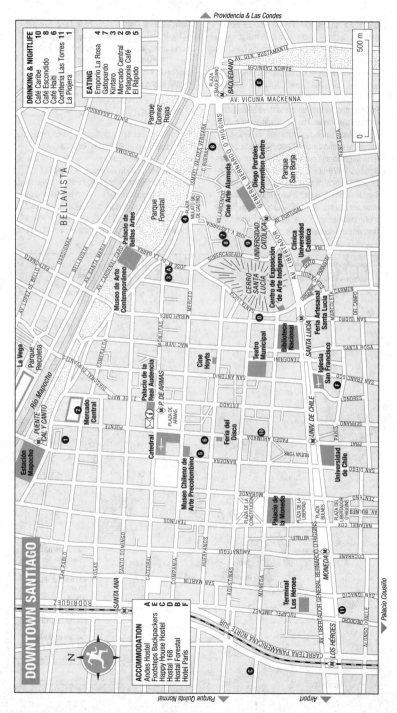

DOWNTOWN SANTIAGO

▲ Providencia & Las Condes

DRINKING & NIGHTLIFE
Café Caribe	10
Café Escondido	8
Café Haiti	6
Confitería Las Torres	11
La Piojera	1

EATING
Emporio La Rosa	4
Gatopardo	7
Kintaro	3
Mercado Central	2
Patagonia Café	9
El Rápido	5

ACCOMMODATION
Andes Hostel	A
Footsteps Backpackers	E
Happy House Hostel	C
Hostal 168	D
Hostal Forestal	B
Hotel Paris	F

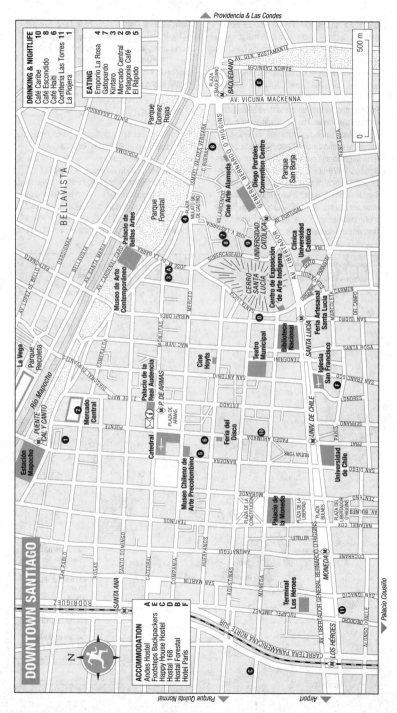

CHILE

SANTIAGO

Bus The main bus station is the Terminal Buses Estación Central – also known as Terminal Santiago –(☎2/376-1755), at Alameda 3850, near the Universidad de Santiago metro station, which handles international routes, and journeys to the west and south. The Terminal Alameda, next door at Alameda 3750 (☎2/822-7400), is served by Pullman and Tur Bus, who also have some international departures. The two terminals have ATMs, snack shops and luggage storage, as well as easy access to public transport along Alameda. Buses from northern and central Chile use Terminal San Borja (☎2/776-0645), at San Borja 184, near the Estación Central metro station, while the smaller Terminal Los Héroes (☎2/420-0099), at Tucapel Jiménez 21 (☎2/420-0099), near the Los Heroés metro station, serves a range of destinations in both northern and southern Chile.

Train Estación Central, at Alameda 3322 (☎2/376-8415, ⊛www.efe.cl), is served by TerraSur trains from various destinations in Middle Chile. Trains were still affected by the 2010 earthquake at the time of writing but may be running from Santiago to Chillán by the time you read this.

Information

Listings For entertainment listings, check Friday's "Recitales" page in *El Mercurio* or in *La Tercera*, Santiago's main newspapers.

Tourist information An excellent source of tourist information (with bilingual staff) is the municipal tourism office found on the north side of the Plaza de Armas (Mon–Fri 9am–6pm, Sat & Sun 10am–4pm, ☎2/713-6745). There is also a small municipal office at the foot of Santa Lucia

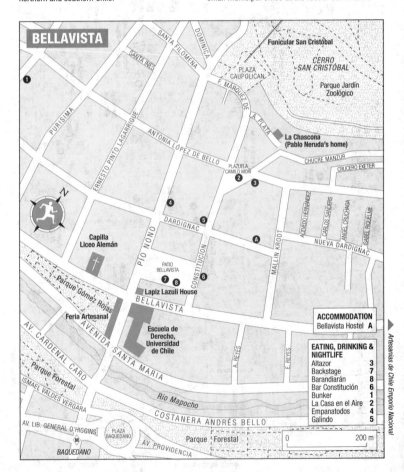

BELLAVISTA

Funicular San Cristóbal

CERRO SAN CRISTÓBAL

Parque Jardín Zoológico

La Chascona (Pablo Neruda's home)

Capilla Liceo Alemán

Lapiz Lazuli House

Feria Artesanal

Escuela de Derecho, Universidad de Chile

ACCOMMODATION
Bellavista Hostel   A

EATING, DRINKING & NIGHTLIFE
Altazor   3
Backstage   7
Barandiarán   8
Bar Constitución   6
Bunker   1
La Casa en el Aire 2
Empanatodos   4
Galindo   5

Río Mapocho

COSTANERA ANDRÉS BELLO

Parque Forestal

0   200 m

Artesanías de Chile Emporio Nacional

on Terraza Neptuno. The main Sernatur office is at Av. Providencia 1550, near the Manuel Montt metro station, east of the city centre (Mon–Fri 9am–6.30pm, Sat 9am–2pm; ☎2/731-8300). It provides maps of the city and is well stocked with brochures on the surrounding area. Conaf has an office at Av. Bulnes 285 (Mon–Fri 9am–1pm & 2–4.30pm; ☎2/390-0282, ⊛www.conaf.cl), which provides information on national parks and reserves, as well as some pamphlets and inexpensive maps.

Tours Free walking tours of the city start in front of the cathedral, and are a good way to take in the city's main sights (Mon–Sat 10am; 4hr; free though tips appreciated); see the box on p.425 for bike tours.

City transport

Bus Fleets of white-and-green "TranSantiago" (⊛www.transantiago.cl) buses run around the city. To use them, you need to purchase a "BIP" transit card (CH$1300), sold in most metro ticket booths, which you can then add credit to (at the same booths, and at BIP centres across the city). Bus destinations are posted on window signs and at marked stops; a standard fare is CH$380.

Colectivo Slightly pricier than buses, *colectivos* have their destinations displayed on their roofs and carry passengers on fixed itineraries, reaching their destination slightly quicker than regular transport, though you need to know where you are going; useful for destinations outside the city centre.

Metro Metro (Mon–Sat 6.30am–10.30pm, Sun 8am–10.30pm; ⊛www.metrosantiago.cl) is the quickest way to get around the city, with just five lines that are easy to navigate, though it gets rather cramped during rush hour. BIP cards (see above) are the easiest way to use the metro, with each journey costing CH$490–600 depending on the time of day. Single-use tickets are also available at metro stations.

Accommodation

There are a number of accommodation options in Santiago to suit budget travellers although really cheap places are scarce. Good inexpensive lodgings are mostly to be found in the city centre and Barrio Brasil.

Central Santiago

Andes Hostel Monjitas 506, Metro Bellas Artes ☎2/632-9990, ⊛www.andeshostel.com; see map, p.419. Centrally located hostel with modern decor, bright dorms complete with individual lockers, and

a whole range of facilities – guest kitchen, lounge with pool table and cable TV, free internet, laundry service and a fully-stocked bar. Dollars preferred. Can get noisy. Dorm CH$8450, rooms CH$20,860.

Casa Condell Condell 114, Metro Baquedano ☎2/717-8592, ⊛www.casacondell.com. Brightly coloured and spotlessly clean guesthouse with very good breakfast included, and a congenial hostess. Situated on a quiet street just off the bustling Alameda. CH$26,000.

EcoHostel General Jofré 349B, Metro Universidad Católica ☎2/222-6833, ⊛www.ecohostel.cl; see map, p.416. With its clean and spacious dorms, chilled-out common areas and fully-equipped guest kitchen, this hostel and its environment-friendly ethic attracts mostly younger travellers. Lockers, internet, good breakfast and knowledgeable bilingual staff are a big plus. Dorms CH$6500, rooms CH$18,000.

Footsteps Backpackers Almirante Simpson 50, Metro Baquedano ☎2/634-7807, ⊛www .footsteps.cl; see map, p.419. Well located for downtown and Bellavista, this cheerful hostel offers colourful dorm rooms and relaxed communal spaces. Internet included. Dorms CH$8000, rooms CH$13,000.

Hostal 168 Santa Lucía 168, Metro Santa Lucía ☎2/664-8478; see map, p.419. Welcoming hostel just beneath Cerro Santa Lucía with excellent facilities, free internet and breakfast included. Dorms CH$8000, rooms CH$22,000.

Hostal Forestal Coronel Santiago Bueras 122, Metro Baquedano ☎2/638-1347, ⊛www .hostalforestal.cl; see map, p.419. Perpetually popular, *Hostal Forestal* throws impromptu barbecues and the bilingual staff can advise on sightseeing. Luggage storage, outdoor patio, guest kitchen and lounge with cable TV are some of the perks. Dorms CH$5500, rooms CH$18,000.

París París 813, Metro Universidad de Chile ☎2/664-0921, ⊛carbott@latinmail.com; see map, p.419. Atmospheric, centrally located budget hotel with cheaper rooms to suit backpackers and a newer annexe featuring comfortable rooms and spotless bathrooms. Continental breakfast CH$1500 extra. CH$16,000.

Bellavista

Bellavista Hostel Dardignac 184, Metro Bellavista ☎2/732-8737, ⓦwww.bellavistahostel.com; see map, p.420. It's easy to see why this hostel is extremely popular with younger travellers – a stone's throw from some of Santiago's best eating and nightlife, it's cosy, colourful, run by helpful bilingual staff and has all the standard backpacker conveniences. Dorm CH$7000, rooms CH$20,000.

Barrio Brasil

La Casa Roja Agustinas 2113, Metro República ☎2/696-4241, ⓦwww.lacasaroja.cl; see map, p.416. Sprawling, Aussie-owned converted mansion firmly established as backpacker party central, with spacious dorms and rooms, and complete with jacuzzi, poolside barbecues, large common areas, free internet, kitchen, on-site travel agency and Spanish language school. A top budget choice, though not a place to catch up on your sleep. Dorms CH$8000, rooms CH$21,000.

Happy House Hostel Moneda 1829, Metro Los Héroes ☎2/688-4849, ⓦwww.happyhousehostel .cl; see map, p.419. Travellers are made to feel really welcome at this beautifully decorated, spacious hostel, with large private rooms, attractive common areas, large kitchen, terrace bar and jacuzzi. Breakfast and internet included. Dorms CH$7000, rooms CH$34,000.

Hostel Cienfuegos Cienfuegos 151, Metro Los Héroes ☎2/671-8532, ⓦwww.hostelcienfuegos.cl; see map, p.416. Large, professionally run, HI-affiliated hostel with clean dorms, plush bunk beds, spacious dining room and bonuses including on-site travel agency, internet and wi-fi, book exchange, breakfast and laundry service. Dorms CH$7000, rooms CH$20,000.

Landay Barceló Erasmo Escala 2012, Metro Los Héroes ☎2/671-0300, ⓦwww.landaybarcelo .cl; see map, p.416. Beautifully renovated house with gleaming bathrooms, wooden floors, colourful rooms with lockers, and a comfy DVD room. Breakfast and internet included. Dorms CH$7900, rooms CH$19,780.

Eating

Santiago has a proliferation of good restaurants. Most are concentrated in Downtown, Bellavista and Providencia, with some good options, popular with backpackers and students, in Barrio Brasil and up-and-coming Barrio Yungay.

Downtown

Emporio La Rosa Merced 291, near the corner of Lastarria; see map, p.419. Café and ice-cream haven with tables out onto the street. Good coffee, too, and the hot chocolate comes highly recommended. One ice-cream scoop CH$1800.

Gatopardo Lastarria 192; see map, p.419. Excellent Chilean and Mediterranean cuisine, good value at lunchtimes, served in an attractive interior. The stuffed calamari are particularly tasty. Closed Sun. Fixed-price lunch CH$7000.

Kintaro Monjitas 460; see map, p.419. Tasty and authentic sushi, along with teriyaki and udon dishes, all at very reasonable prices. Very popular at lunchtimes. Closed Sun. Chicken katsu CH$3900.

Mercado Central See p.414; see map, p.419. The best place for large portions of inexpensive fish and seafood, the fish market's bustling eateries offer such delights as sea bass in seafood sauce (CH$5000), and *machas a la Parmesana* (CH$4500); *Donde Augusto* is a popular spot. Lunch only.

Patagonia Café Lastarria 96; see map, p.419. Well-prepared Patagonian-style lamb and other tasty dishes served within a cosy, rough-hewn wood interior; the weekend buffet brunch is a bargain, as is the fixed-price lunch menu. Smoked salmon salad CH$4500.

TRAITORS' CORNER

For an unusual eating experience, try **El Rincón de los Canallas** ("Traitor's Corner"), at Tarapacá 810 (entry only by prior reservation on ☎2/632-5491; see map, p.416). It was once a secret meeting place for the opposition during Pinochet's dictatorship, and though this is not the original site, you still need a password to enter. When asked, "Quién vive, canalla?", respond "Chile libre, canalla." (Pinochet called his detractors "canallas", so the exchange roughly means: "Who's there, traitor?" "Free Chile, traitor.") Against a nostalgic backdrop including wall-to-wall rallying slogans, this intimate bar offers traditional Chilean grub served up under names like Pernil Canalla ("Traitor's Ham", a roasted leg of pork). Mains CH$4000–7000.

Astrid y Gastón Antonio Bellet 201 ⚓2/650-9125, ⊛www .astridygaston.com; see map, p.416. Flawless fusion cuisine with Peruvian, Spanish, French and Japanese influences by Lima's famous chef, Gaston Acurio. The tuna steak (CH$16,800) borders on divine. Reservations required.

El Rápido Bandera 371; see map, p.419. Established *empanadería* serving perfectly prepared *empanadas* and sandwiches; a snack counter rather than a restaurant. *Empanadas* from CH$850.

Bellavista and Providencia

Backstage Patio Bellavista; see map, p.420. Half bar, half decent pizzeria, popular *Backstage* has an open-air patio, perfect for enjoying live jazz on Sat nights. Pizza from CH$4000.

Barandiarán Patio Bellavista; see map, p.420. Spicy and flavourful Peruvian concoctions, including superb *ceviche* and sea bass dishes; the pisco sours stand out, too. Ceviche CH$5700.

El Bodeguero Manuel Montt 382; see map, p.416. Rough-and-ready bar with cheap lunch deals: an excellent place to experience eating and drinking like a Santiago student. *Pollo al pil pil* (spicy chicken dish) CH$3950.

Empanatodos Pío Nono 153; see map, p.420. Bustling takeaway doing brisk business, turning out 31 types of delicious *empanadas* including delicious *manjar*-filled ones. From CH$900.

Galindo Constitución; see map, p.420. Perpetually packed spot serving traditional Chilean food, such as hearty *pastel de choclo*, *cazuela* and *lomo a la pobre*, along with beers until late, even on weekdays. If sitting outside, you *will* be entertained by street musicians. *Pastel de choclo* CH$4500.

El Huerto Orrego Luco 54; see map, p.416. An excellent choice for a wide variety of lovingly prepared vegetarian dishes, such as hearty burritos. Omelette CH$4100.

Liguria Av. Providencia 1373; see map, p.416. Large portions of Chilean and Italian dishes are on offer in this ever popular and charming bar-bistro, as well as large sandwiches, good salads and superb pisco sours. *Merluza al pil pil* CH$4800. Also has a sister restaurant at Pedro de Valdivia 47.

Barrio Brasil and Barrio Yungay

Charro de Oro Av. Ricardo Cumming 342A; see map, p.416. Spicy and inexpensive Mexican tacos and burritos served in an intimate, no-frills setting. Open until 1.30am Fri & Sat; closed Sun. Tacos from CH$1000.

Ocean Pacific's Av. Ricardo Cumming 221; see map, p.416. Popular restaurant serving consistently good fish dishes (though not the cheapest), including an excellent salmon platter for two. Check out the elaborate puffer fish decorations. Mains CH$5000–7000.

Peluquería Francesa Compañia de Jesús 2789 ⚓2/682-5243; see map, p.416. Take a trip back in time at this charming restaurant above a nineteenth-century hair salon, where each table literally bursts with quirky memorabilia. Excellent French cuisine, and good cocktails. Coq au vin CH$6500.

Peperone Huérfanos 1954; see map, p.416. Excellent *empanadería* dishing out baked *empanadas* with myriad fillings, including scallops. Cheese and crab *empanada* CH$1400.

Las Vacas Gordas Cienfuegos 280; see map, p.416. Probably the best restaurant for carnivores in the city, with steaks grilled to perfection at very reasonable prices. Extremely popular, especially on weekends. Veal medallions with pancetta CH$5290. Closed Sun night.

Drinking and nightlife

Santiago is not a 24-hour party town, and compared to other Latin capitals can seem rather tame. However, Thursdays, Fridays and Saturdays are lively, with crowds pouring into the streets and bars of the nightlife *zonas*.

Downtown

Café Escondido Pasaje Rosal 346; see map, p.419. If you want cheap beer and bar snacks in a less than raucous environment, this intimate bar is the perfect spot. Closed Sun. Open until 2am.

La Piojera Aillavilú 1030; see map, p.419. Carve your name into the wooden tables at this rough-and-ready bar with a loyal clientele, and knock back a *terremoto* (earthquake) – a powerful wine and ice cream mix. Drinks CH$1800.

Bellavista and Providencia

Altazor Antonia López de Bello 189; ⚓02/732-3934; see map, p.420. Popular bar packed on weekends, often featuring live folk music and blues. Cover CH$1500.

Bar Constitución Constitución 61, near Patio Bellavista ☎ 2/244-4569, Ⓦ www.barconstitucion.cl; see map, p.420. A friendly international bar-cum-club with a dancefloor that fills up every Fri and Sat night to an eclectic choice of music. Free entry until 12.30am, and then CH$3000. Open Tues–Sat until 5am.

Boomerang Holley 2285 ☎ 2/334-5457; see map, p.416. Lively Australian-run watering hole with nightly drinks specials, popular with foreign travellers and locals alike. Opens late.

Bunker Bombero Núñez 159 ☎ 2/737-1716; see map, p.420. Giant dancefloor with varied alternative music events. A devoted young following make this one of the most popular places on the gay night scene. Cover CH$5000.

La Casa en el Aire Antonia López de Bello 125 Ⓦ www.casaenelaire.cl; see map, p.420. Inviting candle-lit venue offering poetry reading, contemporary theatre performances, film screenings and folk music; check the website for listings.

Flannery's Geo Pub Encomenderos 83 ☎ 2/233-6675, Ⓦ www.flannerys.cl; see map, p.416. Extremely popular with expats, this pub has authentic Irish charm and a welcoming staff. While the exotic cocktails are not their strong suit, it's a great spot for a beer and surprisingly tasty fajitas. Mon–Fri noon–2.30am, Sat 5.30pm–3am, Sun 5.30pm–12.30am.

Havana Salsa Dominica 142 ☎ 2/737-1737, Ⓦ www.havanasalsa.cl; see map, p.416. If you want to shake your hips to some salsa beats, this is the place. Open until 5am Fri & Sat. Cover and Cuban-style buffet dinner CH$9000.

Phone Box Pub Av. Providencia 1670 ☎ 2/235-9972, Ⓦ www.phoneboxpub.cl; see map, p.416. Relaxed and lively pub, popular with expats, offering a wide selection of beers, including the delectable Kunstmann. Open till 1am Mon & Tues, 2am Wed & Thurs and 3am Fri & Sat; closed Sun.

Barrio Brasil

Blondie Alameda 2879 Ⓦ www.blondie.cl; see map, p.416. Large and popular four-floor dance club featuring techno, goth, indie and other musical styles (depending on the night), as well as occasional live music. Admission CH$3000.

Confitería Las Torres Alameda 1570 ☎ 2/668-0751; see map, p.419. Elegant, nineteenth-century building hosting spellbinding live tango shows on weekends to accompany the expertly cooked traditional Chilean dishes. Closed Sun. Dishes CH$5000–10,000.

N'aitún Av. Ricardo Cumming 453; see map, p.416. An activist bookshop since the 1970s features gritty folk music, attracting bohemian types.

Plaza Ñuñoa

La Batuta Av. Irarrázaval 3500 Ⓦ www.batuta.cl. A thriving gem of Santiago nightlife, where Chilean and British rock music attract a dedicated following. Open Thurs–Sat. Vodka and Red Bull CH$4000.

Ebano Jorge Washington 176 ☎ 2/453-4665, Ⓦ www.ebanococinasoul.cl. Upmarket bar with smart wooden tables; staff make great cocktails and there is an excellent choice of wine. Open Mon–Fri 7pm–2am. Mojito CH$3500.

Entertainment

Cine Arte Alameda Alameda 139, Ⓦ www.centroartealameda.cl, Metro Baquedano; see map, p.419. An arts cinema showing independent and avant-garde films.

Cine Hoyts Huérfanos 735, Metro Santa Lucía Ⓦ www.cinehoyts.cl; see map, p.419. Multiplex cinema showing the latest releases; English-language films tend to be subtitled.

Teatro Municipal Agustinas 749, Metro Universidad de Chile ☎ 2/463-1000, Ⓦ www.municipal.cl; see map, p.419. You can find the best of Chile's classical music inside this magnificent historical building. Special productions take place throughout the year.

Shopping

Artesanías de Chile Av. Bellavista 357, Ⓦ www.artesaniasdechile.cl. High-quality crafts from Chile's indigenous communities, including Aymará textiles, Mapuche silverwork and wood carvings. There is also a small outlet within Patio Bellavista (see p.425).

COFFEE WITH LEGS

In downtown Santiago you may encounter the strange phenomenon of café con piernas, or "coffee with legs" – cafés where besuited businessmen are served coffee by skimpily clad waitresses. *Café Caribe*, at Ahumada 120, and *Café Haiti*, at Ahumada 336, are both tamer examples of the genre. At the raunchier cafés, customers are offered more than just coffee.

Books Av. Providencia 1652. good selection of English-language books, to exchange or to buy.

Centro de Exposición de Arte Indígena Alameda 499. Alongside Cerro Santa Lucía, this *feria artesanal* stocks some excellent Mapuche, Rapanui and Aymará crafts.

Feria Artesanal Santa Lucía, Cerro Santa Lucía. Large crafts market stocking indigenous crafts, tie-dyed clothing and T-shirts featuring the Chilean flag. Mon–Sat 10am–7pm.

Feria del Disco Ahumada 286. A large branch of the ubiquitous music store stocking a wide variety of Chilean music as well as international rock and pop.

Lapiz Lazuli House Bellavista 14, Barrio Bellavista. One of the better places to buy the expertly crafted lapis lazuli jewellery for which Chile is famous.

Patio Bellavista Between Constitución and Pío Nono, Barrio Bellavista, @www.patiobellavista.cl. Open-air space with a concentration of gift shops selling high-quality crafts and clothing, postcards, jewellery and home-made honey. A bookshop by the Constitución entrance stocks a plethora of guidebooks and maps. Open Sun–Wed till 9pm, Thurs–Sat till 10pm.

Tatoo Av. Los Leones 81 ☎2/294-6008. Adventure shop specializing in trekking and climbing gear as well as sleeping bags and backpacks. They also have a store at Av. Las Condes 13451.

La Vinoteca Av. Isidora Goyenechea 2966, @www .lavinoteca.cl. Great if you're looking for some of Chile's best wines to take home with you – the knowledgeable staff here can help locate some of the rarer vintages, and will even wrap up a case so that you can check it in at the airport.

Directory

Banks and exchange There are plenty of ATMs downtown, especially along Huérfanos, Agustinas, Bandera, Moneda and Av. Alameda, as well as at the large bus terminals. There are several exchange houses on Agustinas, between Ahumada and Bandera, which give a reasonable rate on foreign currencies and traveller's cheques (Mon–Fri 9am–2pm & 4–6pm, Sat 9am–2pm).

Embassies and consulates Argentina, Vicuña Mackenna 41 ☎2/582-2606, @www.embargentina .cl; Australia, Isidora Goyenechea 3621 ☎2/550-3500, @www.chile.embassy.gov.au; Bolivia, Av. Santa María 2796, Providencia ☎2/232-8180, @www.consuladobolivia.cl; Brazil, MacIver 225, 15th floor ☎2/425-9230, @www.embajadadebrasil .cl; Canada, Nueva Tajamar 481, 12th floor ☎2/362-9660,@www.canadainternational .gc.ca/chile-chili; New Zealand, Av. El Golf 99, Oficina 703 ☎2/290-9800, @www.nzembassy.com/chile; Peru, Padre Mariano 10, Oficina 703, Providencia ☎2/235-4600, @www.conpersantiago.cl; South Africa, Av. 11 de Septiembre 2353, 17th floor, Providencia ☎2/820-0300, @www.embajada-sudafrica .cl; UK, Av. El Bosque Norte 125 ☎2/370-4100, @ukinchile.fco.gov.uk/en; US, Av. Andrés Bello 2800 ☎2/232-2600, @chile.usembassy.gov.

Hospitals Clínica Las Condes, La Fontecilla 441 ☎2/210-4000; Clínica Universidad Católica, Lira 40, downtown ☎2/633-4122, Clínica Alemana, Av. Vitacura 5951, Vitacura ☎2/210-1111.

Internet There are plenty of internet cafés, and most youth hostels also offer free internet use. Try

---

SANTIAGO TOUR OPERATORS

Attractions around Santiago include wineries, thermal baths, the outdoor enthusiast's paradise of the mountainous Cajón del Maipo valley and more.

La Bicicleta Verde Av. Santa María 227, oficina 406, Bellavista ☎2/570-9338, @labicicletaverde.com. See Santiago at a different pace with a range of bike tours in the city, and around nearby vineyards. Also arranges bike hire. Morning tour of Santiago's sights CH$18,000 per person.

Fueguinos ☎2/737-3251 or 9/162-4707, @www.fueguinos.cl. Full-day nature tours around Santiago; destinations include the Cajón del Maipo valley, Parque Nacional La Campana and the San Francisco glacier. CH$50,000 per person includes transportation, meals and entry to national parks. English and French spoken.

Monteagudo Aventura ☎2/346-9069, @www.monteagudoaventura.cl. Experienced outfit running full-day horseriding and white-water rafting trips in the Cajón del Maipo, as well as treks to the San Francisco and Morado glaciers and night excursions to the Colina thermal baths. Full-day horseriding including an *asado* (barbecue) CH$70,000.

Rockside Expediciones Constantino 96 ☎2/779-6366, @www.rockside.cl. Adrenaline-filled outdoor adventure, including rafting, kayaking, rock climbing and mountain biking in the Cajón del Maipo. Half-day rafting trip to Maipo River CH$17,500 per person.

Café.com, at Alameda 143, or Ciber Librería Internacional, at Merced 324 (☎2/638-6245).

Language schools Bridge Linguatec Language Center, at Los Leones 439, Providencia (☎2/233-4356 or 800/724-4216 in the US, ⓦwww .bridgechile.com), offers intensive immersion Spanish courses, group tutorials and private lessons. Instituto Chileno-Suizo de Idioma, at José Victorino Lastarria 93, 2nd floor (☎2/638-5414, ⓦwww.chilenosuizo.tie.cl) combines Spanish language courses of varying intensity with homestays, city tours and introduction to Chilean culture.

Laundry Try Lavandería Autoservicio, Monjitas 507, or Lavandería Lolos, Moneda 2296, Barrio Brasil.

Pharmacies There are plenty of Farmacias Ahumada and Cruz Verde pharmacies all over Santiago; Farmacia Ahumada at Av. El Bosque 164 is open 24hr.

Post offices Correo Central, Plaza de Armas 559 (Mon–Fri 8.30am–7pm, Sat 8.30am–1pm). Other branches are at Moneda 1155, near Morandé; Local 17, Exposición 57 Paseo Estación; and Av. 11 de Septiembre 2092.

Telephone centres There are numerous *centros de llamados* run either by Entel, whose largest branch is at Morandé, between Huérfanos and Compañía, or by Telefónica CTC Chile, located inside metro stations, such as Universidad de Chile and Moneda, and on the streets.

Moving on

Air LAN, Aerolíneas del Sur and Sky Airline have multiple daily flights to all major Chilean destinations: Arica (hourly; 2hr 45min); Calama (every 30min; 2hr 5min); Iquique (hourly; 2hr 25min); La Serena (hourly; 1hr 5min); Puerto Montt (every 30min; 1hr 40min); Punta Arenas (every 30min; 3hr 25min).

Bus Arica (8 daily; 28hr); Chillán (8 daily; 6hr); Copiapó (5 daily; 10hr); Iquique (10 daily; 24hr); La Serena (15 daily; 7hr); Pucón (every 30min; 12hr); Puerto Montt (8 daily; 13hr); Rancagua (every 15min; 1hr); Valparaíso and Viña del Mar (every 10min; 1hr 45min). Terminal Buses Estación Central has international departures to various South American countries including Argentina (Buenos Aires, Mendoza), Brazil (São Paulo, Río de Janeiro) and Peru (Lima, Cuzco, Tacna, Arequipa).

Train At the time of writing, trains were not running beyond Talca but normal services run as follows: Chillán (6 daily; 4hr 30min); Curicó (6 daily; 2hr); Rancagua (6 daily; 1hr); Talca (6 daily; 3hr); all are served by TerraSur (ⓦwww.terrasur.cl). A slower Metrotrén has hourly departures to Rancagua (7am–10pm).

SKIING NEAR SANTIAGO

It's easy to arrange day-trips from Santiago to experience some world-class powder snow. The **ski season** lasts from mid-June to early October. All resorts rent ski equipment and clothing, and day passes cost CH$20,000–33,000. At the upper end of the Cajón del Maipo valley, east of Santiago, three large **ski resorts** are clustered in the Tres Valles area: El Colorado, La Parva and Valle Nevado; all three can be accessed from Farellones, a village at the foot of Cerro Colorado (3333m). A fourth resort, Portillo, is set on the banks of the stunning Laguna del Inca on the Argentine border, a two-hour drive from Santiago.

Ski Van (☎2/192-672, ⓦwww.skivan.cl) has daily departures to El Colorado, Valle Nevado and La Parva; **Ski Total**, Av. Apoquindo 4900 (☎2/246-0156, ⓦwww .skitotal.cl), operates daily departures for all four resorts, and is a good choice for renting equipment and clothing.

El Colorado ⓦwww.elcolorado.cl. The resort boasts nineteen chairlifts and 22 runs, most of intermediate level, between elevations of 2430m and 3333m.

La Parva ⓦwww.laparva.cl. The Cerro Franciscano (3608m) and Cerro La Falsa Parva here offer thirty runs for skiers of all abilities, with some excellent long advanced runs, as well as extensive backcountry skiing and heli-skiing.

Portillo ⓦwww.skiportillo.com. Chile's most exclusive resort boasts 23 runs between altitudes of 2590m and 3322m that cater to intermediates and experts alike, along with ample backcountry terrain and heli-skiing opportunities.

Valle Nevado ⓦwww.vallenevado.com. With the best skiing conditions in Tres Valles and geared towards foreign visitors, this luxury resort has a good mixture of advanced and intermediate runs, as well as a snowboard park and half-pipe along with extraordinary terrain for heli-skiing.

Valparaíso and Viña del Mar

Draped in a crescent shape around the Bahía de Valparaíso, the UNESCO World Heritage listed city of **Valparaíso** is just 120km from Santiago. "Valpo" – as it's affectionately known – is Chile's principal port and naval base, and also perhaps the country's liveliest and most vibrant city. The **nightlife** and excellent seafood attracts much of Santiago to its bars and restaurants at the weekend, as does the nearby beach resort of **Viña del Mar**. Viña's attractions are wide, white beaches surrounded by expensive high-rise apartments, casinos and pricey, touristy restaurants. It has none of the character that distinguishes Valparaíso – the good news is that since they're so close together, it's easy enough to stay in Valparaíso and visit Viña's beaches for the day.

VALPARAÍSO

Few travellers can fail to be inspired by the ramshackle beauty of **VALPARAÍSO**, whose mish-mash patchwork of brightly coloured houses is built across a series of hills; steep stairways and the city's famous **ascensores** (elevators) link the hills to the port area. Still a major port today, the city came into its own during the California Gold Rush, and in the mid-nineteenth century was the main hub for ships crossing between the Atlantic and Pacific oceans. Valparaíso's narrow labyrinth of atmospheric alleyways offers glimpses of the city's decline from the grandeur of its former glories.

What to see and do

Valparaíso is effectively split into two halves: the hills (*cerros*), and the flat El Plan. Most restaurants and hostels can be found on **Cerro Concepción** and

Cerro Alegre. Visitors usually spend their time here meandering along the winding passageways, and enjoying the spectacular views from the rickety *ascensores*. **El Plan**, which includes the busy port area, is home to an extensive nightlife quarter as well as the shopping and administrative districts, all linked by traffic-choked narrow streets.

The hills

Without a doubt, Valparaíso's biggest attraction is its **hills**. Few pastimes are as enjoyable as meandering up and down the area's winding narrow streets, or riding its antique funiculars (see box, p.430). Visitors can stop to marvel at the impressive views of the city from a multitude of **miradores** (viewpoints), or duck into little shops and cafés to admire the colourful **murals** – a striking example of the city's bohemian culture. It is easy to see how Valparaíso has produced more writers, artists and poets than any other Chilean city.

Cerro Concepción and **Cerro Alegre** are the best known of the hills, with the highest concentration of churches and museums, but they are by no means the only gems. Nearby **Cerro Panteón**, reached by a network of winding paths, is home to three colourful cemeteries, the most interesting of which is the **Cementerio de Disidentes**, resting place of non-Catholic European immigrants. Nearby **Cerro Cárcel** is the site of a former prison, now decorated with colourful graffiti and a hangout for artists and thespians. Its **Parque Cultural** (Mon–Fri 9am–7pm, Sat & Sun 11am–7pm; ☏322/258-567) sometimes hosts outdoor theatre performances.

La Sebastiana

La Sebastiana, Ferrari 692, off Alemania (Tues–Sun: Jan & Feb 10.30am–6.50pm; March–Dec 10am–6pm; CH\$3000; ☏322/256-606, Ⓦwww.fundacionneruda.org), was the

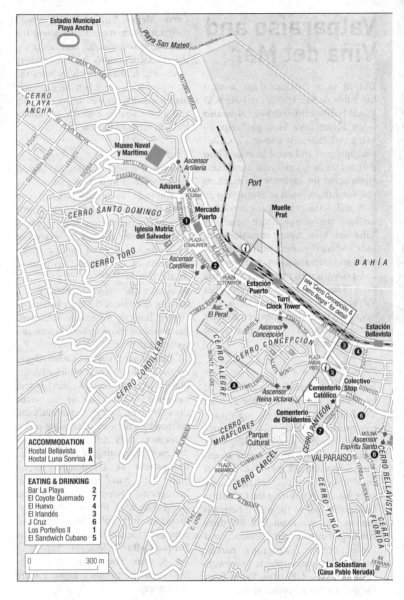

Playa San Mateo

CERRO
PLAYA
ANCHA

AV. GRAN BRETAÑA

ANTONIO VERA

AGUAY

AV. PLAYA ANCHA

QUEBRADA VERDE

LEVARTE

SIGNO

Museo Naval
y Marítimo

ARTILLERÍA

Ascensor
Artillería

CARAMPANGUE

Aduana

PLAZA
ADUANA

Port

CERRO SANTO DOMINGO

Mercado
Puerto

Muelle
Prat

Iglesia Matriz
del Salvador

PLAZA
ECHAURREN

CERRO TORO

Ascensor
Cordillera

PLAZA
SOTOMAYOR

Estación
Puerto

BAHÍA

TOMÁS RAMOS

PRAT

Turri
Clock Tower

see 'Cerro Concepción &
Cerro Alegre' for detail

Asc.
El Peral

URRIOLA

ESMERALDA

Estación
Bellavista

Ascensor
Concepción

CERRO CONCEPCIÓN

CERRO
CORDILLERA

CERRO ALEGRE

MONTE ALEGRE

TEMPLEMAN

ELIAS

MONTI

PLAZA
ANÍBAL
PINTO

El Huevo

Colectivo
Stop

DONOSO

Ascensor
Reina Victoria

CERRO
MIRAFLORES

Cementerio
Católico

Cementerio
de Disidentes

CONDELL

CERRO PANTEÓN

MOLINA

Ascensor
Espíritu Santo

CERRO BELLAVISTA

Parque
Cultural

ECUADOR

VALPARAÍSO

ACCOMMODATION
Hostal Bellavista   **B**
Hostal Luna Sonrisa **A**

AV. ALEMANIA

PLAZA
BISMARCK

CUMMING

CERRO CÁRCEL

AV. YERBAS BUENAS

HÉCTOR CALVO

CERRO YUNGAY

EATING & DRINKING
Bar La Playa   **2**
El Coyote Quemado   **7**
El Huevo   **4**
El Irlandés   **3**
J Cruz   **6**
Los Porteños II   **1**
El Sandwich Cubano **5**

PÉREZ

C. LYON

AV. ALEMANIA

0   300 m

La Sebastiana
(Casa Pablo Neruda)

AV.
FERRARI

CERRO
FLORIDA

least lived-in of the poet **Pablo Neruda**'s three residences, but it offers incredibly picturesque views of the city and the interior design reflects the poet's quirky tastes. Like his other homes, the five-storey house has a nautical theme and is crammed with random knick-knacks that Neruda picked up on his travels; unlike the others, you can explore this one without a guide. The vista from his bedroom window is nothing short of spectacular. To get here, take a short

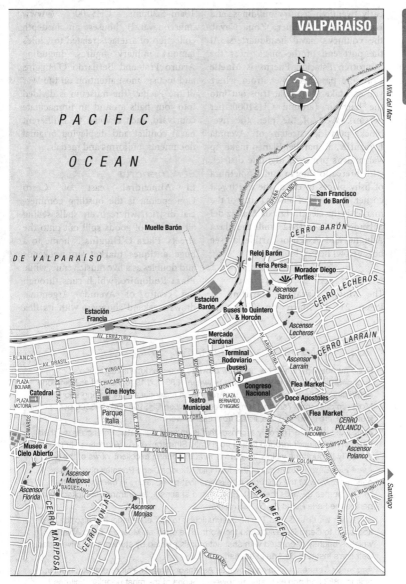

ride on *colectivo* #39, or catch the bus, Verde "D", from Plaza Ecuador.

Barrio Puerto

El Plan consists of long east–west streets, crossed by shorter north–south streets leading into the hills, and is divided into two halves, with **Barrio Puerto** located northwest of Cerro Concepción. Its centrepiece, the pedestrianized **Plaza Sotomayor**, is lined with a mixture of modern concrete blocks and grand early twentieth-century buildings, and is home to the **Primera Zona Naval**, the country's naval headquarters. At the port end of the plaza, near the Metrotrén Estación Puerto, is **Muelle Prat**, the passenger pier, from where you can take short boat trips out into the harbour (around CH$1000 per person). West of the pier, the five-block portside stretch of Avenida Errázuriz and parallel Blanco make up Valparaíso's principal nightlife district, with **Mercado Puerto** and its plethora of fishy places to eat at the northwest corner. A couple of blocks south of the market is the elegant **Iglesia Matriz del Salvador**, built in 1842, while the **Plaza Aduana** and Ascensor Artillería (see box, below) lie two blocks west.

Museo Naval y Marítimo

The **Museo Naval y Marítimo** at Paseo 21 de Mayo s/n (Tues–Sun 10am–5.30pm; CH$700; Ⓦwww.museonaval.cl) houses an in-depth collection of artefacts related to Chile's famous military figures, including Arturo Prat and Bernardo O'Higgins and focuses most attention on the War of the Pacific. The museum is divided into four halls around an immaculate courtyard, each devoted to a different naval conflict and displaying original documents, uniforms and medals.

El Almendral

El Almendral, east of Cerro Concepción, is the bustling commercial district, where lively stalls selling all manner of goods spill out onto the streets. **Plaza O'Higgins** is home to a huge **antiques market** on weekends and doubles as a live music venue, while **Plaza Rodomiro**, which runs through the centre of Avenida Argentina, draws weekend shoppers with its **flea**

LOS ASCENSORES DE VALPARAÍSO

Once numbering thirty-three and now down to about a dozen, Valparaíso's ascensores, or funiculars, were built between 1883 and 1916. As well as being one of the city's enduring attractions, they remain an essential way of getting about. Most run daily from 7am to 11pm and cost between CH$100 and CH$300 per journey. Here is our top five, listed from east to west:

Ascensor Polanco The only *ascensor* that is an actual elevator, Polanco is reached through a long underground tunnel from Calle Simpson, off Av. Argentina. It rises vertically through the yellow tower to a *mirador* offering excellent views of the port.

Ascensor Barón At the top of this funicular, Mirador Diego Portales gives you a panoramic view of the city from its easternmost point, taking in the port and the hillside homes towards the west. Best visited at sunset, its entrance is tucked away behind the Feria Persa Barón flea market.

Ascensor Espíritu Santo The nearest funicular to La Sebastiana, it is also the best approach to Cerro Bellavista and the worthwhile open-air Museo a Cielo Abierto which is brightly decorated with abstract murals painted by students of Universidad Católica's Instituto de Arte in the early 1970s.

Ascensor Concepción (also known as Ascensor Turri). The city's oldest funicular, built in 1883 and originally steam-powered, is one of the most popular. It climbs up to Paseo Gervasoni on Cerro Concepción, a delightful residential area and the start of many walking tours that cover Cerro Alegre as well. The lower entrance is opposite the Relój Turri clock tower.

Ascensor Artillería Extremely popular with visitors, this funicular rivals Ascensor Barón for views. It runs from Plaza Aduana up to Cerro Playa Ancha, and offers a beautiful panoramic view of the city and coastline, with Viña del Mar in the distance. The Museo Naval Marítimo (see above) is nearby.

CERRO CONCEPCIÓN & CERRO ALEGRE

EATING
Alegretto	4
Café Con Letras	7
Caruso	10
El Desayunador	9
Destajo	5
Epif	11
Le Filou de Montpellier	8
Pasta e Vino	3

DRINKING & NIGHTLIFE
Bitácora	6
Salvatorre	2
Valparaíso Eterno	1

ACCOMMODATION
Álecon FineHostel	C
Casa Aventura	E
Hostel Casa Valparaíso	B
La Maison du Filou	A
Residencia en el Cerro	D

market. Across from the square is the main **Terminal Rodoviario**, with the monolithic **Congreso National** building directly opposite it.

Arrival

Bus Long-distance buses arrive at the Terminal Rodoviario, Pedro Montt 2800 (☎322/216-568), a 20min walk from Cerro Alegre and Cerro Concepción. There are snack shops, an ATM and luggage storage inside.

Train Frequent trains from Viña del Mar stop at the stations along the waterfront. Barón is the closest station to Terminal Rodoviario, while Bellavista and Puerto are the handiest for Cerro Alegre and Cerro Concepción.

Information

Tourist information There are tourist information kiosks in the centre of Plaza Aníbal Pinto (Mon–Fri 10am–2pm & 3.30–5.30pm, Sat & Sun 10.30am–5.30pm; ☎322/939-365, ⓦwww .ciudaddevalparaiso.cl), and at the Muelle Prat. Several private kiosks can be found at the bus station but be aware that they are not necessarily impartial. Fundación Valparaíso, Héctor Calvo 205, Cerro Bellavista (☎322/593-156, ⓦwww .fundacionvalparaiso.cl), runs various restoration projects around the city; its "Bicentennial Heritage Trail" guide is full of curious trivia about the city.

City transport

Bus, colectivo and micro Frequent transport of all sorts runs to and from Viña del Mar; look for "Viña" displayed in the window. In El Plan, buses labelled "Aduana" run west towards the centre along Pedro Montt while "P. Montt" buses run back to the bus station; fares range between CH$230 and CH$400.

Metrotrén Fast, frequent, air-conditioned commuter trains run to Viña del Mar and beyond from the stations along the harbour (Mon–Sat every 12min, Sun every 18min; 15min; 6.15am–10.30pm; ⓦwww.merval.cl); you have to make a one-off purchase of a swipe card (CH$1200) on top of the fares. Viña del Mar (Runs from 6.30am–10.15pm; 15min).

Tram Antique German trams offer limited but cheap service around El Plan; just look for the rails (CH$200).

Accommodation

Álecon FineHostel Abtao 684, Cerro Concepción ☎322/491164, ⊛www.alecon.cl. Wonderfully friendly family-run guesthouse with airy single rooms, doubles, triples and quads; excellent breakfast and internet are included and the hostel offers a free Spanish language course to long-term guests. Rooms CH$22,000.

Casa Aventura Pasaje Gálvez, Cerro Alegre ☎322/755963, ⊛www.casaventura.cl. Hostel with friendly and knowledgeable staff, spotless dorms, a sunny lounge, kitchen privileges and internet; popular with backpackers. Dorms CH$9000, rooms CH$19,000.

Hostal Bellavista Pasaje Santa Lucia 5, Subida Ferrari, Cerro Bellavista ☎322/121-544, ⊛www.arthostalbellavista.cl. Arty hostel covered with murals with rooms named after painters. Internet and breakfast included. To reach it, walk up Av. Ferrari for about 300m and take the stairs going up to your right, or take Ascensor Espíritu Santo and walk downhill for 200m. CH$20,000.

Hostal Luna Sonrisa Templeman 833, Cerro Alegre ☎322/734117, ⊛www.lunasonrisa.cl. Professional hostel run by *Footprint* guide author; fully equipped kitchen, tranquil lounge with book exchange and large rooms with tall ceilings in a central location make it a top choice. Good breakfast included. Dorms CH$8000, rooms CH$21,000.

Hostel Casa Valparaíso Pasaje Gálvez 173, Cerro Alegre ☎323/194072, ⊛www.casavalparaiso hostel.blogspot.com. Cheerful, family-run hostel with homely communal spaces, wi-fi and a hearty breakfast included. Dorms CH$7000.

La Maison du Filou Papudo 579, Cerro Concepción ☎322/124681 or 09/8622-0456,

⊛www.lamaisondufilou.overblog.com. Colourful double and twin rooms with high ceilings and wonderful views; kitchen privileges, laundry service, book exchange, wi-fi and breakfast included. French and a smattering of English spoken. Doubles CH$20,000.

Residencia en el Cerro Pasaje Pierre Loti 51, Cerro Concepción ☎322/495298, ⊛www.residenciaenelcerro.cl. Large, wonderfully friendly family-run place, with a good breakfast, internet and a number of cats to keep you company. Dorms CH$6000, rooms CH$22,000.

Eating

Alegretto Pilcomayo 529, Cerro Concepción. Complete with an entertaining vintage jukebox, this Italian spot serves good pizza and excellent gnocchi. Medium pizza CH$5800.

Café Con Letras Almirante Montt 316, Cerro Alegre. A popular artsy café with quirky decor and a book exchange; serves a good range of real coffee, too. Espresso CH$1500.

Caruso Cumming 201, Cerro Cárcel. A superb take on Peruvian and Chilean specialities with added twists. Service is excellent, and dishes very good value for money. *Calugas de pescado* (fried pieces of fish) CH$5200.

El Desayunador Almirante Montt 399, Cerro Alegre. This informal eatery offers generous servings of all-day breakfast from 9am onwards. *Energetico* breakfast CH$3000.

Destajo Cumming 55. Takeaway offering excellent *empanadas* with myriad meat, fish and vegetable fillings – perfect for a late-night snack. Open all eve except Sun. *Empanada* CH$700–950.

Epif C Dr. Grossi 268, Cerro Concepción. A great little restaurant run by a young Chilean-American couple, with plenty of choices for vegetarians and vegans: the gazpacho and veggie burgers are excellent. Open Thurs–Sat 7pm–late; Sun 1–4pm. Dishes CH$3000–5000.

Le Filou de Montpellier Almirante Montt 382. Cerro Alegre. Consistently imaginative meat and fish dishes are served at this well-established and popular French spot. Fixed-price lunch menus are particularly good value (CH$5000). Closed Mon.

Los Porteños II Cochrane 102. Specializing in fresh fish and seafood, this cheerful eatery is an extension of the equally popular *Los Porteños* across the street. *Pastel de jaiba* (crab pie) CH$5200.

El Sandwich Cubano O'Higgins 1221. Small and very popular lunchtime stop serving excellent-value plates of tasty *ropa vieja* (beef dish) with *moros y cristianos* (rice and beans). CH$2000.

Drinking, nightlife and entertainment

Bar La Playa Serrano 567 ☎322/259-4262. This historic bar with a wood-panelled interior is an excellent spot for a quiet beer in the afternoon, and at night transforms into a buzzing dance spot. Open Thurs 10am–2am, Fri & Sat 10am–5am.

Bitácora Cumming 68 ☎09/200-0601. A popular bar that is also a cultural centre and gathering place for local artists and thespians. Open Mon–Thurs noon–1am, Fri & Sat noon–5am.

Cine Hoyts Pedro Montt 2111 ⊛www.cinehoyts .cl. A five-screen cinema showing the latest blockbuster releases.

El Coyote Quemado Subida Ecuador 144 ☎322/249-3478, ⊛www.coyotequemado.cl. Dark two-tiered bar playing heavy rock. Packed with a younger crowd.

El Huevo Blanco 1386, ⊛www.elhuevo.cl. Huge five-level nightclub with different music on each one, packing a student crowd. Entry CH$3000–5000.

El Irlandés Blanco 1279 ☎322/543-592. A fairly raucous Irish pub run by an actual Irishman, and offering a large selection of beers. Chilean pale ale Guayacán CH$2500.

J Cruz Condell 1466 ☎322/211-225. Along a graffiti-covered passageway lies a somewhat legendary bar with glass cabinets filled with all kinds of strange memorabilia. It's an excellent place to enjoy a glass of wine and share a greasy pile of *chorrillana* (meat with fries, onion and fried egg). Open Mon–Sat noon–late.

Salvatorre Almirante Montt 51, Cerro Alegre. A popular bar in the evenings with cheap drink deals; also serves good pizza. Open Wed–Sun until late. Beer CH$1500.

Valparaíso Eterno Señoret 150, 2nd floor ☎322/228-374. Besides offering reasonably priced meals and beers, this joint has heaps of personality; some Sat nights a singer-songwriter belts out Communist tunes. Open Fri & Sat 9.30pm–4am.

Directory

Banks and exchange Prat has a number of banks, ATMs and cambios; Banco de Chile, at Condell 1481, also has an ATM and there is a cambio on Plaza Sotomayor which offers a decent exchange rate.

Hospital Hospital Carlos van Buren, San Ignacio 725, has modern facilities (☎322/204-000).

Internet There are several internet cafés on Cerro Concepción and Cerro Alegre; most hostels have access as well.

Language courses Interactive Spanish School, Calle Elias 571, Cerro Cárcel ☎9/286-4973, ⊛www .interactive-spanish.cl. Spanish lessons of varying intensity offered with or without homestay options.

Laundry Lavandería Jerusalem, Condell 1176, Local 3. Efficient launderette which washes by the kilo. Five kilos wash and dry CH$3700.

Post office Prat 856 on Plaza Sotomayor (Mon–Fri 9am–6pm).

Moving on

See "City transport", p.431, for details of transport to Viña del Mar.

Bus Arica (5 daily; 24hr); Iquique (5 daily; 24hr); Isla Negra (every 30min; 1hr 30min); La Serena (5 daily; 7hr); Puerto Montt (6 daily; 16hr); Santiago (every 10min; 1hr 45min).

VIÑA DEL MAR

Though only fifteen minutes from Valparaíso by public transport, **VIÑA DEL MAR** could hardly be more different from its grittier neighbour. Purpose-built in the late nineteenth century as a weekend getaway for wealthy Santiago and Valparaíso residents, it draws thousands of local holidaymakers during the summer and on weekends. Viña makes for an enjoyable day-trip to the beach, and is especially worth a visit during the week-long **Festival de la Canción**, held in the second or third week of February which draws top Latino and international artists. The city also hosts spectacular Año Nuevo (New Year) celebrations, drawing thousands of Chileans. Other festivals include the two-week long Feria del Libro (Jan), which attracts important literary figures and hosts live readings, and the acclaimed Festival Cine Viña del Mar film festival (held in Oct or Nov; ⊛www .cinevina.cl).

What to see and do

The city is split in two by the broad, none-too-clean **Marga Marga** estuary,

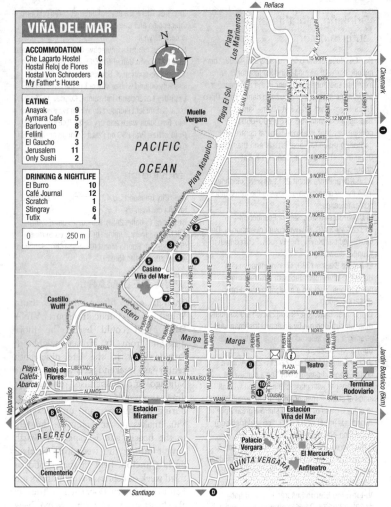

VIÑA DEL MAR

ACCOMMODATION
Che Lagarto Hostel	C
Hostal Reloj de Flores	B
Hostal Von Schroeders	A
My Father's House	D

EATING
Anayak	9
Aymara Cafe	5
Barlovento	8
Fellini	7
El Gaucho	3
Jerusalem	11
Only Sushi	2

DRINKING & NIGHTLIFE
El Burro	10
Café Journal	12
Scratch	1
Stingray	6
Tutix	4

0   250 m

with a largely residential area to the south and most of the beaches in the northern half. **Avenida San Martín**, parallel to the beach, and the side streets off it feature numerous dining and nightlife options. At the heart of Viña lies the large, shady **Plaza Vergara**, a popular spot with the occasional busker or *capoeira* demonstration and horse-drawn carriages parked around it. Several blocks of **Avenida Valparaíso**, Viña's main thoroughfare, which runs from the square's southwest corner, have

been pleasantly pedestrianized with a number of shops and places to eat.

The beaches

Playa Caleta Abarca lies in a sandy cove south of **Castillo Wulff**, an impressive castle-like structure built on a rocky outcrop at the mouth of the estuary by a Valparaíso businessman in 1906. Located next to the large **Reloj de Flores** ("flower clock"), the beach draws a lively picnicking crowd on weekends. Just north of the estuary, Avenida Perú runs parallel to the sea, past the brash **Casino Viña del Mar**. Beyond you will find an almost unbroken line of sandy beaches, backed by high-rise apartment buildings, stretching all the way to the smaller resort of **Reñaca**, which itself has more good beaches and nightlife.

Quinta Vergara

The one spot besides the beaches where you might want to spend some time in Viña del Mar is the lovely **Quinta Vergara** park (daily 7am–7pm), where the manicured grounds are home to a vast array of exotic imported plants. It is located a couple of blocks south of Plaza Vergara behind the Metrotrén Estación Viña, with the futuristic-looking **Anfiteatro**, home to the annual music festival, as its centrepiece.

Arrival and information

Bus Long-distance buses pull up at Terminal Rodoviario (☎322/752-000) at Av. Valparaíso 1055; it has a tourist information booth and an ATM.
Metrotrén The commuter train from Valparaíso stops at Estación Miramar, Estación Viña del Mar and Estación Hospital along Alvares; Miramar is the closest station to the beaches. You need to buy a metro card (CH$1200).
Tourist information The main tourist office is at Arlegui 715 (Mon–Fri 9am–2pm & 3–7pm, Sat & Sun 10am–2pm & 3–7pm; ☎322/269-330, ⓦwww.visitevinadelmar.cl). Staff are helpful and can provide maps, and advise on accommodation and camping options.

Accommodation

Che Lagarto Hostel Diego Portales 131 ☎322/625-759, ⓦwww.chelagarto.com. Clean dorms, a pleasant garden, kitchen use, communal lounge, free internet and wi-fi are all pluses at this hotel – but it attracts a young backpacker crowd, and can get noisy. Dorms CH$6200; rooms CH$26,000.
Hostal Reloj de Flores Los Baños 7 ☎322/485-242, ⓦwww.hostalrelojdefloresbb.com. This popular and welcoming family-run guesthouse has a good location a block from the beach, comfortable single, double and triple rooms (some en-suite), guest kitchen, free internet, cable TV in the rooms

and a good breakfast. Dorms CH$8900, rooms CH$23,750.
Hostal Von Schroeders Von Schroeders 104 ☎323/170-392, ⓦwww.hostalvonschroeders.cl. In an excellent location a short walk from both town and beach, this place has good-value, no-frills rooms, though some have slightly shabby bathrooms. CH$14,000.
My Father's House Gregorio Marañón 1210 ☎322/616-136, ⓦwww.myfathershouse.cl. Spacious, quiet single, double and triple rooms, swimming pool, internet and gracious owners. The only drawback is that it's about 2km from the centre of town; catch *colectivo* #31, 82 or 131. CH$28,000.

Eating

Anayak Quinta 134. A good, unpretentious spot for cake, light snacks and real coffee. Large coffee CH$1400.
Aymara Café Av. Peru, off Plaza Columbia. Simple café with seating outside offering very good value lunch deals. Sandwich, ice cream, soft drink and coffee CH$3500.
Barlovento 2 Norte 195. Trendy minimalist decor, good salads, wraps and appetizer platters draw a younger crowd. Great spot for a cocktail, too. Eve only. Wraps CH$4000.
Fellini 3 Norte 88 ☎322/295-742. Bustling Italian serving up exquisite pasta dishes in an intimate setting with superb presentation and service. Worth booking ahead. Mains CH$6000–8000.
El Gaucho San Martín 435 ☎322/693-502. The ideal place to satisfy your carnivorous cravings, this Argentine-style steakhouse doesn't come cheap but serves succulent steaks, chorizo and sweetbreads, among other offerings. Steak CH$7900.
Jerusalem Quinta 259. Tasty Middle Eastern cuisine is dispensed from this tiny food counter; the falafel is excellent (CH$1500).
Only Sushi San Martín 560. This simple sushi bar offers reasonable Japanese cuisine at affordable prices, and offers delivery across town. Eighteen-piece *tabla* CH$5100.

Drinking, nightlife and entertainment

El Burro Pasaje Cousiño 12 C, off Av/ Valparaíso. Dark and atmospheric pub-disco popular with local youth and foreigners alike; very busy on weekends. Free entry until 10pm.
Café Journal Agua Santa 2. ☎322/666-654, ⓦwww.cafejournal.cl. Thriving university student

haunt, complete with pub grub and regular live music. Open Mon–Thurs 10am–4am, Fri & Sat 10am–5am, Sun 7pm–4am.

Cinemark 15 Norte 961, Local 224. Multiplex cinema showing the latest releases.

Scratch Quillota 898, near 5 Oriente ⓦwww .scratch.cl. Established favourite on the disco scene, perpetually packed on Fri and Sat nights; nothing happens before midnight.

Stingray 5 Poniente 362. With space to drink, and a dancefloor, this is the latest place to bring in the weekend, party-going crowds. Entry CH$1500–3000.

Tutix 6 Poniente, corner with 5 Norte, next to *Starbucks* ⓦwww.tutixclub.com. White leather sofas, and wooden tables adorn the bar area; the dancefloor gets heaving later on.

Directory

Banks, and exchange Numerous banks, most with ATMs and cambios, are found along Av. Arlegui.

Hospital Hospital Gustavo Fricke is on Álvarez at Simón Bolívar (☏ 322/675-067); for emergencies call ☏ 322/652-328.

Internet access and telephone centre There are several internet cafés and telephone centres along Valparaíso.

Post office Plaza Latorre 32, just off the main square.

Moving on

Bus Arica (5 daily; 24hr); Iquique (5 daily; 24hr); La Serena (5 daily; 7hr); Osorno (6 daily; 14hr); Puerto Montt (6 daily; 16hr); Santiago (about 20 daily; 1hr 45min).

Metrotrén Valparaíso (every 12–18min 6.15am–10.30pm; 15min).

ISLA NEGRA

The seaside village of **ISLA NEGRA** (which, incidentally, is not an island), about 80km south of Valparaíso, was the site of Pablo Neruda's favourite and most permanent home. The **Casa Museo Pablo Neruda**, at Calle Poeta Neruda s/n (Tues–Sun: Jan & Feb 10am–8pm; March–Dec 10am–2pm & 3–6pm; CH$3500 including tour in English, or CH$3000 in Spanish, reservations essential in summer; ☏ 35/461-284, ⓦwww.fundacionneruda.org), lies down a wooded trail by the sea, a short walk

from the main road. Larger than his other two homes, Isla Negra is fascinating for the sheer amount of **exotic objects** that Neruda accumulated here, and the amount of thought that went into every aspect of the design – from the arrangement of wooden ships' figureheads in the living room, to the positioning of blue glass bottles along the seaward side of the house. The poet's exotic collection of objects includes African wooden carvings, ships in bottles, a gigantic *moai kavakava* (a statue from Easter Island, see p.521) and an amazing array of seashells, housed in a purpose-built room that Neruda designed but never completed. A strong nautical theme runs throughout; there is even a small boat out on the terrace so that the poet could be "a sailor on land".

Arrival and moving on

Bus Pullman Peñuelas run from Valparaíso to San Antonio (every 30min: 6.35am–9pm); ask to be dropped off in Isla Negra. To return to Valparaíso, wait at the bus stop on the other side of the road, and buy your ticket on the bus. Pullman buses also pass by Isla Negra direct from Santiago.

Norte Chico

Dominated by dry scrubland and sparse vegetation, the **Norte Chico** region, which stretches roughly from the northern tip of Santiago to the southern reaches of the Atacama, might seem unremarkable from a bus window. Visitors are, however, drawn here for its stargazing, long sandy beaches, and trips to its far-flung national parks. The biggest population centre is the relaxed seaside town of **La Serena** with its bustling market and colonial-style architecture, while the fertile **Elqui Valley**, which once inspired Nobel-Prize-winning poet Gabriela Mistral, is now the focal point for the country's favourite tipple, pisco. The islands of **Isla Damas** and **Choros** brim over with seals, penguins and cormorants. Further north, the relaxed mining town of **Copiapó** is the jumping-off point for the stunning kaleidoscopic landscapes of **Parque Nacional Nevado de Tres Cruzes**, and **Parque Nacional Pan de Azúcar**. Horseriding, trekking, and kayaking are all attractions which are likely to keep tourists in this region longer than they expected.

LA SERENA

LA SERENA, 474km north of Santiago, is considered one of Chile's prime **beach resorts**, though its charms also include an impressive number of churches and several worthwhile museums. It is also an excellent base for exploring the surrounding countryside. The city was founded in 1544, and during the seventeenth century it was the target of multiple raids by the French and English, including the pirate Francis Drake.

Downtown La Serena

With a tranquil vibe to its central streets, La Serena is an easy place to get to know on foot. Exploring its peaceful churches is a good way to get to know the town. The largest church is the Neoclassical **Iglesia Catedral**, at the corner of Los Carrera and Cordovez, off the Plaza de Armas, which has a beautiful, marble-decorated interior. **Iglesia de San Francisco**, Balmaceda 640, was the first church to be built out of stone, and **Iglesia Santo Domingo**, Cordovez s/n, dates back to 1673.

The **Casa Gabriel González Videla**, Matta 495, on the west side of the Plaza de Armas (Mon–Fri 10am–6pm, Sat 10am–1pm; CH$600) is well worth a visit. Originally the home of former president González Videla, who was born in the town, it is now a museum housing an impressive collection of fine art and contemporary painting.

About two blocks west from the square, the tranquil and beautifully sculpted Japanese-style **Jardín El Corazón** (daily 10am–6pm; CH$1000) is the perfect place to while away a sunny afternoon.

At the junction of Cienfuegos with Cordovez, the recently renovated **Museo Arqueológico** (Tues–Fri 9.30am–5.50pm, Sat 10am–1pm & 4–7pm, Sun 10am–1pm; CH$1000, Sun free, ticket also valid for Museo Gonzáles Videla) displays elaborate Diaguita ceramics, as well as a 2.5-metre *moai* statue from Easter Island and lapis lazuli jewellery.

The beaches

While quite crowded in the summer, you have the **beaches** pretty much to yourself for the rest of the year. The nearest beach area is a half-hour walk west from the city centre from Jardín El Corazón along Francisco de Aguirre.

Between La Serena and the town of Coquimbo, a **cycle lane** runs beside a dozen or so wide, sandy beaches lined with pricey condominiums, hotels and restaurants – an easy and enjoyable day-trip. **Bikes** are available for rent in the city centre at Vicente Zorilla 990 (☎51/227-939). Most of the beaches are suitable for swimming and windsurfing, although Playa Cuatro Esquinas is known to have strong rip currents.

Arrival and information

Air Aeropuerto La Florida is 5km east of town along Ruta 41; catch a taxi or *micro* to the centre (CH$2000–2500).

Bus The main bus terminal is located at the corner of Amunátegui and Av. El Santo, a 20-min walk south of the centre.

Tourist information Sernatur, Matta 461, Plaza de Armas (Mon–Fri 9am–5.30pm, Sat 10am–2pm; ☎51/225199, ⊛www.turismoregiondecoquimbo .cl). Conaf has an office at Regimiento Arica 901, Coquimbo (☎09/544-3052).

Accommodation

Cabañas y Camping Hipocampo Los Lucumos, off Av. Del Mar ☎51/230-968 or 8/793-3761,

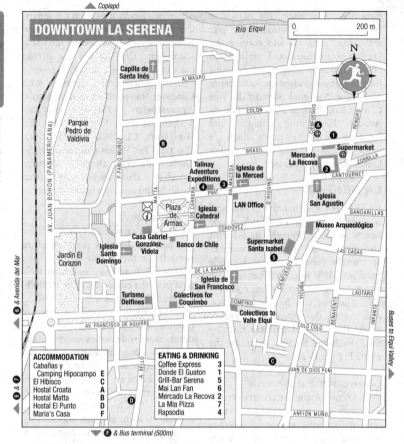

DOWNTOWN LA SERENA

Copiapó

Río Elqui

0   200 m

N

Capilla de Santa Inés

ALMAGRO

COLÓN

CIENFUEGOS

RENGIFO

Parque Pedro de Valdivia

BRASIL

Supermarket

Mercado La Recova

ZORRILLA

CANTOURNET

AV. JUAN BOHON (PANAMERICANA)

P. PABLO MUÑOZ

Talinay Adventure Expeditions

Iglesia de la Merced

MATTA

BALMACEDA

PRAT

O'HIGGINS

LAN Office

Iglesia San Agustín

GANDARILLAS

LOS CARRERA

Plaza de Armas

Iglesia Catedral

Museo Arqueológico

LAS CASAS

Jardín El Corazón

Iglesia Santo Domingo

Casa Gabriel González-Videla

Banco de Chile

CORDOVEZ

Supermarket Santa Isabel

CIENFUEGOS

& Avenida del Mar

DE LA BARRA

Iglesia de San Francisco

VICUÑA

LAUTARO

BENAVENTE

INFANTE

Turismo Delfines

Colectivos for Coquimbo

DOMEYKO

Colectivos to Valle Elqui

COLO COLO

AV. FRANCISCO DE AGUIRRE

Buses to Elqui Valley

ACCOMMODATION
Cabañas y Camping Hipocampo	E
El Hibisco	C
Hostal Croata	A
Hostal Matta	B
Hostal El Punto	D
Maria's Casa	F

EATING & DRINKING
Coffee Express	3
Donde El Guaton	1
Grill-Bar Serena	5
Mai Lan Fan	6
Mercado La Recova	2
La Mia Pizza	7
Rapsodia	4

A BELLO

JUAN DE DIOS PEÑI

ANFIÓN MUÑOZ

& Bus terminal (500m)

Ⓦ www.hipocampolaserena.cl. A good set-up of sixty camping spots with hot showers, and picnic tables in an open space dotted with trees. A 5-min walk to the beach. Well-equipped luxury cabins are also available. Pitches CH$3000 per person.

El Hibisco Juan de Dios Peñi 636 ☎ 51/211-407, Ⓔ mauricioberrios2002@yahoo.es. Guesthouse with a relaxed family atmosphere and wood-floored rooms, kitchen access, laundry service and good breakfast; excursions organized. CH$12,000.

Hostal Croata Cienfuegos 248 ☎ 51/216-994, Ⓦ www.hostalcroata.cl. Cosy rooms, some en suite, all with internet, breakfast and cable TV, in a warm setting. Central location; bike rental available for CH$5000 a day for guests. Rooms CH$15,000.

Hostal Matta Matta 234 ☎ 51/210-014, Ⓦ www.hostalmatta.cl. Large and airy family-run house

with comfortable rooms around a patio, some windowless; includes library, cable TV and grill; tours organized. Breakfast CH$1000 extra. CH$14,000.

Hostal El Punto Andres Bello 979 ☎ 51/228-474, Ⓦ www.hostalelpunto.cl. German-run hostel with friendly and knowledge-able staff, daily excursions, on-site café, wi-fi in the courtyard, laundry service and spotless rooms; popular with travellers of all ages. Call ahead if arriving later than 10pm. Dorms CH$7500, rooms CH$16,000.

Maria's Casa Las Rojas 18 ☎ 51/229-282 or 8/218-9984, Ⓦ www.hostalmariacasa.cl. Small guesthouse with an effusive hostess, kitchen access, free internet, breakfast and a relaxing garden; popular with backpackers. A 3-min walk from the main bus station – good for late arrivals. Dorms CH$6000, rooms CH$14,000.

Eating and drinking

The city's main places to eat are along Calle Prat. Coquimbo, however, is livelier for drinking and nightlife.

Coffee Express On Balmaceda at Prat. A large and popular spot for coffees and sandwiches. Coffee and cake CH$2790.

Donde El Guaton Brazil 750. Popular *parilla* serving excellent grilled meat. *Parillada* for two CH$10,800.

Grill-Bar Serena Eduardo de la Barra 614. For excellent and reasonably priced seafood dishes, look no further. Lunchtime specials CH$4000.

La Mia Pizza Av. del Mar 2100. Seafront pizzeria that offers excellent fish dishes as well as large portions of tasty pizza. Family-sized pizza CH$10,000.

Mai Lan Fan Av. Francisco de Aguirre 109, about three blocks west of the Parque Jardín del Corazón. This restaurant has a plush interior, serving generous portions of well-prepared Chinese food; noodle dishes are particularly good. CH$6000.

Mercado La Recova Though touristy, the upstairs eateries serve excellent seafood *empanadas*, cheap fish dishes and *cazuela*. Try *3 As* restaurant for superb fish. *Corvina* (sea bass) CH$4000.

Rapsodia Prat 470. Jazz bar serving expertly prepared meat and fish dishes. Closed Sun. Grilled fish CH$4000.

Moving on

Air Antofagasta (1 daily); Copiapó (1 daily); Iquique (1 daily); Santiago (4–5 daily).

Bus Via Elqui serves: Pisco Elqui (6 daily; 2hr) and Vicuña (8 daily; 1hr); 24hr Elqui Valley pass costs CH$4500. Other destinations: Antofagasta (8 daily; 13hr); Arica (7 daily; 23hr); Copiapó (8 daily; 5hr); Iquique (7 daily; 19hr); San Pedro de Atacama (1 direct Tur Bus overnight; 17hr), Santiago (7hr; 8 daily); Valparaíso (6 daily; 6hr 30min).

Colectivo Coquimbo (frequent daily departures from Av. Francisco de Aguirre, between Los Carrera and Balmaceda; CH$700); Elqui Valley (several departures daily from Domeyko in the centre; CH$1700).

COQUIMBO

A 15-minute *colectivo* ride south from La Serena lies its rougher, livelier twin: **Coquimbo**, the region's main port. The beautifully restored historical district of **Barrio Inglés** comprises several lively plazas, and has a far more exciting eating and nightlife scene than La Serena. Coquimbo's only real drawback is the lack of budget accommodation, though there is one exception.

The most striking landmark, looming over town, is a huge 93-metre cross, the **Cruz del Tercer Milenio** (Ⓦwww .cruzdeltercermilenio.cl). This slightly bizarre construction, the base of which provides a great viewpoint over town, was funded by the King of Morocco

---

STARGAZING IN CHILE

With an average of 360 cloudless nights per year, northern Chile has some of the clearest skies in the world, so it's little wonder that it's home to some of the world's most powerful telescopes. The larger observatories allow public visits free of charge during the day, allowing you to view the equipment, though not to use it. There are an ever increasing number of small centres offering nocturnal stargazing facilities expressly for tourists, though the best set up for visits are **Cerro Mamalluca** (see p.441) and Cerro Collowara in the Elqui Valley, and **Cielo Austral** (see box, p.450) near San Pedro de Atacama.

Following is the pick of the big Elqui observatories – there is no public transport other than organized tours, and you need to reserve in advance.

Cerro Paranal Ⓣ55/435-335; Ⓦwww.eso.org. 126km south of Antofagasta, the observatory sports four VLTs (Very Large Telescopes), each with an 8m mirror. Open for visits the last two weekends of every month except Dec 2–4pm. **Cerro Tololo** Office at Casilla 603, La Serena Ⓣ51/205-200, Ⓦctio.noao.edu. Some

70km east of La Serena, this Inter-American observatory features an impressive 8.1m Gemini telescope. Open Sat 9am–noon & 1–4pm. **La Silla** Ⓦwww.eso.org. 147km northeast of La Serena, and home to 14 telescopes. Visits Sept–June Sat at 1.30pm; to register, contact recepstg@eso.org.

for the benefit of the town's Lebanese Muslim community.

Accommodation

Hostal Nomade Calle Regimento Coquimbo 5 ☏51/315665 or 9/369-5885, ✆www.hostal nomade.cl. HI-affiliated hostel in the large and rambling former residence of the French ambassador, which has a slight haunted house feel. It has friendly and informative staff, large rooms with exceptionally high ceilings, internet, kitchen facilities and other backpacker conveniences. Dorms from CH$8000.

Eating, drinking and nightlife

With many fish restaurants, Coquimbo is a seafood lover's paradise, and also comes alive at night with lively pubs and clubs – a popular drinking area is along Alduante between Freire and Argandoña. **La Barceloneta** Alduante 726 ☏51/317-205. Offers an exquisite menu featuring fish dishes with a Mediterranean flavour, and transforms into a trendy bar at night, opening until late. Set lunch CH$3500. **Caleta Pescadores** Av. Costanera, about three blocks down from the Plaza de Armas. Bustling, loud and smelly: a superb fish market on the seafront. Fish dishes from CH$2000. **Restaurant Coquimbo** Bilbao, between Varela and Alduante. Serves giant portions of excellent-value fish, as well as superb seafood *empanadas*. *Merluza* and chips CH$2850.

ELQUI VALLEY

East of La Serena, the 62km journey to **Vicuña** is a scenic trip with breath-taking vistas of the tranquil **Elqui Valley**. Its fertile greenery contrasts greatly with the valley's sandy sides, its slopes a spectrum of red, green and gold due to the mineral-rich soil. The ribbon of the highway, lined with pink pepper-corn trees, runs along the valley floor, past vineyards and grapes drying on canvas sheets by the roadside. Tours of the valley typically take in the giant dam and man-made Lago Puklara, popular with windsurfers and kitesurfers, the historical village of **Vicuña**, the laidback community of **Pisco Elqui** and a pisco-tasting distillery, before finishing with stargazing at the **Observatorio Mamalluca**.

Vicuña and the Observatorio Cerro Mamalluca

Sleepy **Vicuña** makes a convenient stopover for exploring the Elqui Valley. Formerly home to Nobel Prize-winner **Gabriela Mistrál**, it has a **museum** at Gabriela Mistrál 759 (Jan & Feb Mon–Sat 10am–7pm, Sun

TOUR OPERATORS

From La Serena, a number of tour companies run excursions in the surrounding area. Popular tours of the Elqui Valley include *pisco*-tasting (around CH$20,000), stargazing at the Observatorio Mamalluca (CH$15,000) and penguin-watching at Isla Damas (CH$30,000).

Daniel Russ ☏9/9454-6000, ✆www .jeeptour-laserena.cl. One experienced and extremely knowledgeable man (with a jeep) runs standard excursions for small groups, as well as trips to Paso del Agua Negra (CH$50,000) and tailor-made outings. German and English spoken. Elqui Total Km 27, along the road between La Serena and Vicuña ☏9/219-7872, ✆www .elquitotal.cl. Stables 20km outside La Serena offering various horseriding trips, including one at night (CH$20,000). Best contacted by phone. Kayak Australis ☏2/334-2015, ✆www .kayakaustralis.com. Specializes in multi-day sea-kayak trips around Chile, including one to

Isla Damas. Book through their Santiago office at El Bosque Sur 65, Piso 2, Oficina 3, Las Condes, or by email. Talinay Adventure Expeditions Prat 470 Local 22 ☏9/8360-6464, ✉contacto@talinaychile .com. Horseriding, diving, sea kayaking and multi-day trekking and volcano-climbing expeditions, as well as visits to observatories including La Silla. Turismo Delfines Matta 655 ☏51/223-624, ✆www.turismoaventuradelfines.cl. Established operator specializing in bilingual guided trips to Isla Damas.

10am–6pm; March–Dec Mon–Fri 10am–5.45pm, Sat 10.30am–6pm, Sun 10am–1pm; CH$600) dedicated to her. **Planta Capel** (daily: March–Nov 10am–12.30pm & 2.30–6pm; Dec–Feb plus public hols the rest of the year 10am–6pm; CH$1000; ☎51/411-251, Ⓦwww.piscocapel.cl), the valley's largest **pisco distillery**, lies just south of town, and has half-hourly bilingual tours tracking the Muscatel grape's journey from the vine to the pisco bottle, culminating in a small free sample at the end.

The **Observatorio Cerro Mamalluca** is located 9km northeast of Vicuña. Compared to those in other observatories in the area, its 30cm telescope is tiny, but still offers magnification of 150 times – sufficient to look closely at the craters on the moon and to view nebulas, star clusters and Saturn. There are two tours offered (both CH$3500; 2hr; 4 nightly in summer from 8.30pm, 3 nightly in winter from 6.30pm): "Basic Astronomy" and "Andean Cosmovision", looking at the night sky as seen by the pre-Columbian inhabitants of the area. Shuttles to and from the observatory (CH$1500 return) depart from the Cerro Mamalluca office in Vicuña (Gabriela Mistrál 260; Mon–Sat 9am–late, Sun 10am–late; ☎51/411352, Ⓦwww.mamalluca.org) half an hour before the tour starts. Reserve tickets in advance, especially in the peak months from December to February.

Arrival and information

Bus The main terminal is one block south of the Plaza de Armas, on O'Higgins at Prat (☎51/411-348).
Colectivo from La Serena stop across the street from the main bus terminal.
Tourist information Inside the Torre Bauer, San Martín s/n, in the northwest corner of the Plaza de Armas (daily 8.30am–5.30pm, Sat 9am–6pm, Sun 9am–2pm; ☎51/209125)

Accommodation

Hostal Donde Rita Condell 443 ☎51/419-611, Ⓦwww.hostaldonderita.com. A homely set of rooms surrounded by a leafy garden, complete with pool and terrace area. Overseen by a charming German hostess, who prepares delicious breakfasts. CH$20,000.
Hostal Valle Hermoso Gabriela Mistrál 706 ☎51/411-206. Family-run, beautifully refurbished colonial-style house with small, clean rooms, some without windows. Excellent fresh breakfasts included. CH$20,000.

Eating

Halley Gabriela Mistrál 404. Vicuña's best eating option, serving inexpensive roast *cabrito* (baby goat; CH$6500) in a rather formal setting.
Halley Pronto Just along from *Halley*, on the east side of the plaza. Fast-food branch of *Halley* dishing out delicious *empanadas* and chicken with chips (CH$2200).
Restaurant Solar de Villaseca Punta Arenas s/n, Villaseca. This famous place, 6km from town in the village of Villaseca (take a *colectivo* from the bus station; about CH$700), cooks up traditional cuisine in ten solar ovens – for obvious reasons, daylight hours only. Closed Mon.

PISCO

The climatic conditions in the Elqui Valley are ideal for growing the sweet Muscatel grapes from which the clear, brandy-like pisco, Chile's national drink, is derived. Pisco is a constant source of dispute between Chile and Peru. Peru claims that the drink originates from the Peruvian port of the same name, and some historical records demonstrate that pisco has been consumed in that area since the Spaniards introduced vineyards in the early 1600s. Chileans claim that they have also been producing pisco for centuries, that their *pisco* is of better quality and that it plays a greater role in Chilean society. In both Chile and Peru, pisco is normally consumed in a pisco sour – a mix of *pisco*, lemon juice, sugar syrup, egg white, crushed ice and a drop of angostura bitters. It goes down deceptively smoothly, but packs a real punch.

For Santiago and other major cities, it is easiest to return to La Serena.

Bus Via Elqui buses go to La Serena (20 daily; 1hr 15min); Coquimbo (20 daily, 1hr 30min); and Pisco Elqui (20 daily; 1hr).

Colectivo to La Serena and Coquimbo leave from the bus station when full (daily 7am–9pm).

Pisco Elqui

The green and laidback village of **PISCO ELQUI** boasts a beautiful hillside setting alongside the Río Clara, with unparalleled views of the Elqui Valley. The shaded **Plaza de Armas**, with its brightly painted Gothic church, hosts the **Mercado Artesanal** in the summer. A block away, the Solar de Pisco Tres Erres – now called **Pisco Mistral** – is Chile's oldest pisco distillery, and offers guided tours (daily: Jan–Feb 11am–1.30pm & 2.30–8pm; March–Dec 10am–12.30pm & 2.30–6pm; CH$5000) complete with tastings. **Los Nichos** (daily: March–Oct 10am–1pm & 2–6pm; Nov–Dec 11am–7pm; free tours) is an old-fashioned distillery 3km south of Pisco Elqui, and worth visiting to see pisco processed by hand.

Be warned there are no ATMs in town, so bring plenty of cash.

Bus Via Elqui buses stop in front of the Plaza de Armas.

Tourist information Hostel owners will be able to help you with information but an excellent option for local knowledge of the area is the tour agency Turismo Migrantes, O'Higgins s/n (☎51/451-917 or 9/829-5630, ⊛ www.turismomigrantes.cl), where Bárbara and Pablo organize pisco tours, horseriding, and bike rides in the surrounding area, and even stargazing tours at their own home.

Horseriding *Alcohuaz Expediciones*, Pasaje Copihues, just beyond the Pisco Mistral distillery (☎51/451-168 ⊛ www.caballo-elqui.cl) is run by a genuine *huaso* (Chilean cowboy) and offers excellent horseriding trips in the area.

Hostal Triskel Baquedano s/n ☎9/4198-8680, ⊛ www.hostaltriskel.cl. Lovingly decorated rooms with a decent breakfast; can arrange hiking, biking and horse-riding. CH$18,000.

El Tesoro de Elqui Prat s/n ☎51/451069, ⊛ www.tesoro-elqui.cl. Cosy adobe dorms and rooms – one with a skylight for stargazing – and excellent food. The owners can help organize motorbike hire and tours. Dorm CH$8500, rooms CH$13,500.

Los Jugos Plaza de Armes. Offers delicious fruit juices and large portions of pizza (CH$3000).

El Ranchito de Don René Centenario s/n, just up from the church. Serves Chilean classics, such as *pastel de choclo* (CH$4000) on a shaded patio.

Bus Via Elqui run to La Serena and Coquimbo (more than 20 daily; 2hr 15min) via Vicuña.

RESERVA NACIONAL PINGÜINO DE HUMBOLDT

The **Reserva Nacional Pingüino de Humboldt** is a remarkable marine wildlife reserve 110 kilometres north of La Serena, which comprises three islands jutting from the cold Pacific waters: Isla Chañaral, Isla Choros and Isla Damas. The islands are home to *chundungos* (sea otters), a noisy colony of **sea lions**, the **Humboldt penguin**, four species of cormorants, clamouring **Peruvian boobies** and countless seagulls.

Unless you plan to stay the night at Punta de Choros (see p.443), it is much easier to visit as part of a tour (see box, p.444). **Boats** sail (CH$8000 per person; sailings dependent on conditions) from **Caleta de Choros**, the small fishing community closest to the islands, along the steep jagged coastline of **Isla Choros**. You get close enough to see the wildlife in great detail and on the way to the island, pods of curious **bottle-nosed** dolphins often frolic around the boat; it's also possible to spot humpback, blue and killer **whales**. On the way back, visitors are allowed a short ramble on sandy **Isla Damas**, whose pristine beaches are home to a smaller penguin population.

Information

Tourist information There is a Conaf-run Centro de Información Ambiental (Mon–Thurs, Sat & Sun 8.30am–5.30pm, Fri 8.30am–4.30pm) at Caleta de Choros, with informative displays on local flora and fauna, and another smaller one at Caleta Chañaral.

Accommodation

There are opportunities for wild camping at Punta de Choros in the summer (mid-Dec to mid-March); reserve in advance with Conaf (℡09/544-3052). Be sure to give names, dates (the maximum stay is three days and two nights) and the number of campers (CH$12,000/site for up to six people). Bring all necessary supplies, including water.

COPIAPÓ

The prosperous mining town of **COPIAPÓ**, 333km north of La Serena, was founded in 1744 and benefited greatly from the **silver boom** of the 1830s. Today, Copiapó still makes its living from mining, nowadays for **copper**. It will forever be linked in many people's minds with the 2010 rock collapse at the nearby San José mine, which left 33 miners ("Los 33") trapped underground for 69 days before the world cheered their safe rescue.

At the heart of Copiapó is the large **Plaza Prat**, dotted with pepper trees; handicraft stalls line the plaza's east side, facing the mall. The Neoclassical **Iglesia Catedral Nuestra Señora de Rosario** graces the southwest corner, while half a block from the northwest corner of the square, at the corner of Colipí and Rodriguez, is the worthwhile but poorly labelled **Museo Mineralógico** (Mon–Fri 10am–1.30pm & 3.30–7pm, Sat 10am–1.30pm; CH$500), with an impressive mineral collection including copper, silver ore, part of a meteorite which landed in the Atacama Desert, and massive chunks of semi-precious stones, such as malachite, onyx, jasper and amethyst.

Arrival

Air Aeropuerto Desierto de Atacama is 45km west of the city; take Transfer Casther (CH$5000) to Copiapó or a *colectivo* (CH$3000) to Caldera.
Bus The Tur Bus terminal is at Freire and Colipí; Terminal Torreblanca, with numerous carriers, is directly opposite. The Pullman bus terminal is a block south, at Colipí 109; buses Casther and Recabarren leave from Caldera stop just east of the Hiper Lider supermarket at Buena Esperanza 552.

Information

Tourist information Los Carrera 691 (Mon–Fri 8.30am–6pm, ℡52/231-510, @infoatacama @sernatur.cl). Extremely helpful staff, and good stock of maps and leaflets. Conaf has an office at Juan Martínez 55 (Mon–Thurs 8.30am–5.30pm, Fri 8.30am–4.30pm; ℡52/237-042, @atacama @conaf.cl). Excellent source of information on Nevado de Tres Cruces and Pan de Azúcar.

Accommodation

Residencial Ben Bow Rodriguez 541 ℡52/238-872. Clean, no-frills rooms around a narrow courtyard. CH$18,000.
Residencial Chañarcillo Chañarcillo 741, a block from the Tur Bus bus station ℡52/238-872. A convenient stopover, with dark but tidy rooms and friendly owners. CH$16,000.

Eating

Bavaria Chacabuco 487. Centrally located eating option, though it lacks atmosphere. A reliable choice for meat dishes and cold beer.
Café Columbia On Plaza Prat at Colipi with Carrera. Pricey but excellent, this place serves good coffee and delectable cake. Breakfasts from CH$3500.
Okasama Av. O'Higgins 799. This intimate, multi-roomed restaurant serves surprisingly good sushi. Six California rolls, CH$3400.

Moving on

Air Antofagasta (2 weekly); Arica (2 weekly); Calama (2 daily); Iquique (2 weekly); Santiago

(10 daily). Airport transfers are operated by Buses Casther (☎ 52-235891).

Bus Antofagasta (6 daily; 5hr); Arica (5 daily; 16hr); Calama (about 5 daily; 10hr); Iquique (6 daily; 13hr); La Serena (5 daily; 5hr); San Pedro de Atacama (at least 6 daily; 11hr).

AROUND COPIAPÓ

The landscape surrounding Copiapó is astonishingly varied, with the salt flats of the **Parque Nacional de Tres Cruces**, mesmerizing **Laguna Verde**, active volcano **Ojos de Salado** and, to the west, the fine white sands of **Bahía Inglesa** and **Caldera**.

Parque Nacional Nevado de Tres Cruces

Remote and ruggedly beautiful **Parque Nacional Nevado de Tres Cruces** is located east of Copiapó via Ruta 31, which winds through the mercilessly desolate desert landscape. The road climbs steeply before reaching the **Salar de Maricunga** – a great field of white crystals on the edge of the park, dotted with emerald-coloured salt pools – and continuing on towards **Paso San Francisco** on the Argentine border.

The park consists of two separate parts. The larger is the 49,000-hectare **Laguna Santa Rosa** sector, 146km east of Copiapó at an altitude of 3700m, which comprises half of the salt flat and

the namesake lake, with roaming herds of **vicuñas** and **guanacos** feeding on the abundant grasslands. The pale blue lagoon, dotted with flamingos and giant coots, is set against a backdrop of snow-streaked volcanoes, including the grand **Nevado Tres Cruces** (6749m). On the west side of the lake is a small and very rustic Conaf-run *refugio*, consisting of bare floorspace, basic cooking facilities and a privy out back.

Cutting across a vast expanse of parched brown land, dotted with hardy yellow altiplano plants, you reach 12,000-hectare **Laguna del Negro Francisco** sector, around 85km south. In summer it becomes a sea of pink and beige thanks to the presence of eight thousand or so Andean, Chilean and James **flamingos** that migrate here from neighbouring Argentina, Bolivia and Peru. On the west side of the lake, Conaf's *Refugio Laguna del Negro Francisco* has beds and kitchen facilities; make reservations with Copiapó's Conaf office (CH$8000 per person).

Laguna Verde and Volcán Ojos de Salado

The magnificent spectacle of the misnamed **Laguna Verde** lies 65km beyond Laguna Santa Rosa, at a whopping altitude of 4325m. The first flash of its brilliant turquoise waters, around a bend in the road, is breathtaking. On the lake's salty white shore are some rustic and relaxing **hot springs** inside a little wooden shack. It's possible to camp here: you must bring all necessary supplies with you, including water, and remember that night-time temperatures drop well below freezing. Beyond the lake loom three volcanoes, including the second-highest peak in Latin America – **Ojos de Salado**. At an elevation of 6887m, it trails just behind Argentina's 6962m Aconcagua as the tallest mountain in the Americas. It is also the world's highest active volcano, with recent eruptions in 1937 and 1956.

Caldera and Bahía Inglesa

The towns of Caldera and Bahía Inglesa, 7km apart and 75km west of Copiapó, are both popular **beach resorts** famous for their large, delicious **scallops**. **Caldera** itself is an unremarkable little town, though the Gothic **Iglesia San Vicente** (1862) on the pretty Plaza Condell is worth a look. Pedestrian **Gana**, lined with craft stalls in the summer, makes for a nice stroll between the square and the waterfront **Costanera** (pier) – home to the oldest railway station in Chile, dating back to 1850, and now a museum and events centre. The pier is the best place to sample inexpensive seafood *empanadas* and other fishy delights.

Caldera's main beach, small seaweed-tinted Copiapina, is not the best in the area; for crystal-clear turquoise waters and long stretches of fine white sand, head to nearby **Bahía Inglesa**, either by *colectivo* or along the cycle path parallel to the road. Bahía Inglesa is immensely popular with locals in the summer, and it's easy to see why: the laidback atmosphere, the proximity of the ocean and an abundance of cheap seafood *empanadas* sold by vendors along the seafront entice you to linger longer. There are several small and sheltered beaches along the main Avenida El Morro, with the wide crescent of **Playa Las Machas** stretching into the distance.

Arrival and information

Bus Buses arrive at the main plaza in Caldera; *colectivos* from the plaza regularly make the 15-min journey to Bahía (CH$1000).

Tourist information On the plaza in Caldera (daily 9am–2pm & 4–7pm; ☎52/316-076, ⓦwww .caldera.cl).

Accommodation and eating

All these options are in Bahía, which has a greater selection of accommodation than Caldera, though it tends to be overpriced during peak season.

Camping Bahía Inglesa off Playa Las Machas, just south of the town ☎52/316-399. An excellent place to camp, with hot showers, picnic tables and cooking facilities. CH$9000 per pitch for up to six people.

Domo Bahía Inglesa Av. El Morro 610, on the waterfront ☎52/316168, ⓦwww.domobahia inglesa.cl. Has bizarre but comfortable tent-like dome rooms (private or shared). CH$28,000.

El Plateao El Morro. Restaurant-bar with a terrace overlooking the beach, good service and an innovative menu offering exceptional seafood dishes.

Moving on

Bus Copiapó-bound Casther and Recabarren buses stop at Ossa Varas 710 (every 30min; 1hr 30min).

Colectivo Those to Copiapó leave from Cifuentes, just south of Ossa Varas.

PARQUE NACIONAL PAN DE AZÚCAR

About 180km north of Copiapó, **Parque Nacional Pan de Azúcar** entices visitors with its spectacular coastal desert landscape, which alternates between steep cliffs, studded with a multitude of cactus species, and pristine white beaches. A small gravel road leads into the park from the compact town of Chañaral and continues past Playa Blanca and Playa Los Piqueros to **caleta pan de azúcar**, a small fishing village inside the park. **Isla Pan de Azúcar**, home to **Humboldt penguins**, **sea lions**, sea otters and a wealth of marine birds, lies a short distance offshore. Although landing on the island is forbidden, fishing boats (March–Nov 9am–6pm; Dec–Feb 9-am–7pm; CH$50,000 for up to ten people, or whatever deal you can strike) get visitors close enough to see (and smell) the wildlife at close quarters. A 9-km trail runs north from the village to the **Mirador Pan de Azúcar**, a lookout point offering staggering panoramic views of the coastline. Also heading north from the village, towards Ruta 5, is a dirt road with a 15-km trail branching off to the west that leads you through the arid landscape to **Las Lomitas**, an outlook point often visited by inquisitive **desert foxes** and shrouded in rolling *camanchaca* (sea mist), the main water source for all the coastal vegetation.

Arrival and information

Bus There are no public buses to the park, though northbound buses from Copiapó can drop you off in Chañaral, the nearest town. Ask around at the bus terminal in Chañaral, and you should be able to get someone to take you to the park. Taxis cost CH$10,000 each way – worth it for a group. Alternatively, take a day-trip tour from Copiapó (see p.444).

Tourist information Conaf's Centro de Información Ambiental (daily 8.30am–12.30pm & 2–6pm) is opposite Playa Los Piqueros and has maps and information on the park, as well as a display of local cacti. The park fee of CH$3500 is payable here; no fee is charged if entering the park from the east.

Accommodation and eating

Camping is available at several sites in the park (☎52/219-271, ☎9/444-5416), costing CH$3500–5000 per person, and includes twenty litres of drinking water, picnic tables, showers and WC use. Groups of four to six people may prefer to rent beachside *cabañas* complete with kitchen facilities (CH$30,000 for two). Both *cabañas* and camping can also be reserved through the Conaf office in Copiapó. For food, there are a number of places in the village cooking up the day's fresh catch.

Norte Grande

In some parts of the vast Atacama Desert, which covers almost all of the Norte Grande region, there are areas where no rainfall has ever been recorded. With such an inhospitable landscape, it is no wonder that most of the population is squeezed into the more moderate climes along the coast. The sprawling port city of **Antofagasta** is the largest population centre, while other major towns include the beach resort of **Iquique** – popular with surfers and paragliders – and **Arica**, home to the iconic cliff of El Morro, a fantastic viewpoint from which to survey the area's long stretches of sandy beach. The best base from which to enjoy the spectacular desert scenery is the laidback backpacker haven of **San Pedro de Atacama**, where visitors flock to whizz down dunes on sandboards, admire the steam rising from geysers in the early morning sun, and spot flamingos on Chile's largest salt flat.

ANTOFAGASTA

ANTOFAGASTA is the biggest city in northern Chile; a busy industrialized port and major transportation hub, it has few attractions to detain travellers, though it's a good place to stock up on necessities. James Bond fans may recognize flashes of the city from the 2008 film *Quantum of Solace*, part of which was filmed here.

What to see and do

Antofagasta's compact centre boasts the surprisingly lovely **Plaza Colón**, the apparent British influence accentuated by its centrepiece, the **Torre Reloj**, a small-scale Big Ben replica. To the north, three blocks of Arturo Prat are pedestrianized and feature shops and cafés, while three blocks south along Matta is a large pedestrian square presided over by the impressive pink, grey and cream **Mercado Central**, with its wafting smells of fish and cooking food.

At the port end of Bolívar, you'll find the oldest building in the city, the former **Aduana**, now housing the **Museo Regional** (Tues–Fri 9am–5pm, Sat & Sun 11am–4pm; CH$600), with exhibitions on regional natural history, archeology and the War of the Pacific, and an outstanding mummified babies exhibit. *Colectivos* (CH$700) run along Matta to the often-crowded Balneario Municipal, and further south to the Balneario El Huáscar and Caleta Coloso. These are Antofagasta's better **beaches**, lined with places to eat, bars and discos, though not really suitable for swimming.

La Portada

Much featured on postcards, the natural monument of **La Portada**, 15km north of Antofagasta, is a giant rock eroded into a natural arch. To get there, take a Mejillones-bound bus and ask to be dropped off at the junction (10min), from where it is a half-hour walk towards the ocean.

Arrival and information

Air The airport is 25km north of the city on Ruta 1; the Aerobús shuttle will drop you off at your destination. Alternatively, take a bus into the city centre.
Bus Most buses now come through the modern Terminal de Buses Cardenal Carlos Oviedo Cavada at Pedro Aguirre Cerda and Paihuano.
Tourist information Prat 384, on Plaza Colón (Mon–Fri 8.30am–5.30pm; ☎55/451818, ⓔinfoantofagasta@sernatur.cl); helpful staff provide city maps and information on local attractions.

Accommodation

Hostal del Norte La Torre 3162 ☎55/251-265 or 8/8692570. Spotless place with pleasant rooms and a family atmosphere, located just a few blocks from the centre. Breakfast available if requested night before. Rooms CH$16,000.
Residencial El Cobre Arturo Prat 749 ☎55/225-162. Centrally located option with a grubby-looking

exterior and no-frills rooms, with shared bathrooms. CH$12,000.
Rocomar Hotel Baquedano 810 ☎55/261-139, ⓔhotelrocomar@hotmail.com. Pricier, but this place offers clean, cosy rooms with private bathroom and cable TV, and a basic breakfast included. Rooms CH$26,000.

Eating and drinking

Bavaria Latorre 2618. Two-tiered grill-caféteria, the latter serving inexpensive fast food, and the former specializing in tasty *panrilladas* and German-style meat-and-vegetable dishes. Lunch special CH$3500.
Mercado Central Matta, between Maipú and Uribe. Besides fresh produce, the market's eateries cook up fishy delights for a reasonable price. *El Sureño* comes recommended. Grilled fish CH$3000.
Raconto Arturo Prat 645. Very popular restaurant offering good steaks, pizzas, sandwiches and ice creams. Lasagne CH$3990.
Wally's Pub Antonino Toro 982. A cosy pub with a chilled-out ambience serving exotic international food and a wide range of drinks, including imported beers. Beer CH$1500. Closed Sun.

Moving on

Air Arica (1 daily); Calama (2 daily); Iquique (1 daily); Santiago (10 daily). Buses to the airport are infrequent. Airport transfers (☎55/262-727) will pick up across town.
Bus Arica (6 daily; 10hr); Calama (about 8 daily; 3hr); Copiapó (8 daily; 7hr); Iquique (6 daily; 6hr); La Serena (8 daily; 12hr); San Pedro de Atacama (at least 6 daily; 5hr); Santiago (10 daily; 18hr).

CALAMA

The busy city of **CALAMA**, at the heart of the Atacama **copper mining** industry, is a convenient transportation hub and an almost inevitable stop for travellers heading to San Pedro de Atacama.

Arrival

Air Aeropuerto El Loa (☎55/342-348) is 6km south of the city. Transfer Licancabur (☎55/543-426) will take you from the airport direct to San Pedro (CH$10,000 one way). To get into Calama, a taxi (about CH$5000) is the only option.
Bus There is no central bus terminal – Turbus and Pullman arrive at separate terminals – and

bus companies are either clustered near the train station to the east of the city centre, or lie to the north of it. No passenger trains now run from Calama to Bolivia.

Accommodation

Hostal El Loa Abaroa 1617 ☎55/341-963. Simple rooms though they're worth booking ahead as they fill up fast – the town lacks budget options. CH$16,000.

Residencial Toño Vivar 1970 ☎55/341-185. Secure and spacious rooms with cable TV. The walls are thin so it can get noisy. CH$13,000.

Eating

Restaurant Palador Vivar con Sotomayor. A meat eater's paradise in quite a plush setting. Offers an excellent two-course lunch and drink deal for lunch (CH$3900).

Salon de Te Abaroa 1688-A. Delightful little tearoom with a laidback feel: a perfect spot for recovering after a long bus journey, with coffee, cake and sandwiches. Large latte CH$1100.

Moving on

Air Antofagasta (1 daily); Copiapó (1 daily); Santiago (10 daily).

Bus Antofagasta (6 daily; 3hr); Arica (5 daily; 9hr); Iquique (5 daily; 7hr); Santiago (8 daily; 22hr); San Pedro de Atacama (every 30min; 1hr 30min). The lack of a central terminal makes bus travel in Calama slightly chaotic. All major cities are covered by Tur Bus (tickets at Granderos 4219), and Pullman, who have their own terminal at Granaderos 3048, out of town. Buses Atacama 2000 (Abaroa 2106; ☎55/314-757) and Buses Frontera (Antofagasta 2046; ☎55/828-828) run to San Pedro de Atacama. Frontera go to Ollagüe (2 weekly; 7hr) on the Bolivian border, from where it's possible to get an ongoing connection to Uyuni. Géminis, at Antofagasta 2239 (☎55/341-993) and Pullman have Tues, Fri and Sun morning departures for Salta and Jujuy between them.

SAN PEDRO DE ATACAMA AND AROUND

SAN PEDRO DE ATACAMA, a little oasis town of single-storey adobe houses and unpaved streets, is situated 75 kilometres east of Calama, the nearest city. No other northern destination can compete with the sheer number of natural attractions in the surrounding area: the stunning *altiplano* scenery draws scores of travellers year-round, while volcanoes, sand dunes, geysers and lagoons will keep any nature lover busy.

One of the oldest settlements in Chile, San Pedro was originally a stop on a pre-Columbian trade route between the highland and coastal communities; in 1547, the Spanish established their first mission here and subjugated the locals. The town later became an important rest stop for cattle drives from Salta, Argentina, when the nitrate industry took off in Chile and fresh meat was needed for the workers.

Despite being somewhat crowded during the peak season, San Pedro retains a friendly and relaxed vibe, and has an excellent assortment of budget accommodation and facilities for visitors, as well as the widest range of cuisine north of Santiago.

What to see and do

Centre of town is the cheery little **Plaza de Armas**, framed by *algarrobo* and pink peppercorn trees. The whitewashed **Iglesia de San Pedro** (1641) stands on the west side of the square, while most places to eat and other services are found along nearby Caracoles.

Museo Arqueológico Gustavo Le Paige

The intriguing **Museo Arqueológico Gustavo Le Paige** (Jan–Feb daily 10am–1pm & 3–7pm; March–Dec Mon–Fri 9am–noon & 2–6pm, Sat & Sun 10am–noon & 2–6pm; CH$2000), located northeast of the square, is well worth a visit, though it no longer displays its famous prehistoric mummy exhibit. Founded by a Belgian Jesuit, after whom it is named, it is home to more than 380,000 clearly labelled

SAN PEDRO DE ATACAMA

Pukará de Quitor

Termas de Puritama & El Tatio Geysers

Calama

Valle de la Luna

Food Stalls
Buses Géminis
★ Buses Atacama 2000

Buses Frontera
LICANCÁBUR
CALAMA
Tur Bus

DOMINGO ATIENZA
N

Museo Arqueológico

GUSTAVO LE PAIGE
Municipalidad

A
Know Chile

Banco Estado (ATM)
PLAZA DE ARMAS
Iglesia de San Pedro
B

Hospital

Observación del Cielo Austral
1
Les Copains
Maxim Experience
Estrella del Sur
CARACOLES
ATM
Cosmo Andino
2
3 4 5
C
7

Azimut 360
F 6

TOCOPILLA

TOCONAO

DOMINGO ATIENZA

PALPANA

G

0   100 m

EATING, DRINKING & NIGHTLIFE		ACCOMMODATION	
Blanco	2	Hostal Elim	G
Cafe Esquina	1	Hostal Florida	B
La Cave	7	Hostal Sonchek	A
La Estaka	3	Hostelling San Pedro	C
Rincón Pintado	6	Hotel & Camping	
Sala de Té 02	5	Takha Takha	F
Tierra Todo Natural	4	Mama Tierra	D
		Oasis Alberto Terrazas	E

D E Customs Post & Argentina

pre-Columbian artefacts, perfectly preserved in the dry desert air, including ceramics, gold work and a wide range of tablets and straws for the ritual inhalation of hallucinogenic cacti.

Arrival and information

Bike rental Bikes can be rented from the internet café at the southeast corner of Plaza de Armas, as well as from most hostels. Rental costs around CH$1000 per hr.

Bus Tur Bus terminal (℡55/851-549) is at the corner of Domingo Atienza and Licancábur; Buses Frontera, Buses Atacama 2000, Buses Géminis and Pullman stop further east on Licancábur.

Money Bring plenty of cash as the ATMs along Caracoles are frequently out of order. Money exchanges on Toconao change foreign currency at a poor rate; tour agencies running trips to Salar de Uyuni can provide better rates for Bolivianos.

Tourist information Toconao s/n, northeast corner of Plaza de Armas (Mon–Fri 9.30am–1pm

& 3–7pm, Sat 10am–2pm; ℡55/541-420). The office provides maps of the town centre, and the visitor book is a good source of gleaning info from other travellers. Also check out ⊛www .sanpedroatacama.com, an excellent source of information on the area.

Accommodation

Hostal Elim Palpana 6 ℡55/851-567, ⊛www .hostalelim.cl. Quiet hostel whose friendly owners offer ten lovingly decorated and furnished doubles, quads and family rooms, with private bathrooms, in a garden setting with fruit trees and hammocks. Prices include breakfast and internet; laundry service available. CH$39,000.

Hostal Florida Tocopilla 406 ℡55/851-021, ⓔ hostalflorida@sanpedroatacama.com. Central backpacker spot, with small rooms around a hammock-festooned courtyard, intermittent hot water, kitchen use, free internet and frequent barbecues. Advance payment required. Dorms CH$7000, rooms CH$18,000.

Hostal Sonchek Gustovo Le Paige 198 ☎55/851-112, ✉sonchcksp@hotmail.com. With a welcoming and helpful English- and French-speaking hostess, this extremely popular and conveniently located hostel has cosy rooms, kitchen use, a courtyard with hammocks, laundry service and an excellent café next door. Dorms CH$7000, rooms CH$16,000.

Hostelling San Pedro Caracoles 360 ☎55/851-426, ⓦwww.hostellingsanpedro .cl. Bustling HI branch with member discounts, three-tiered bunk beds in dorms, clean singles and doubles, a shaded courtyard, free internet and breakfast. It also organizes a plethora of tours in the area and rents out bikes and sandboards. Dorms CH$8000, rooms CH$17,000.

Hotel & Camping Takha Takha Caracoles 101 ☎55/851-038, ⓦwww.takhatakha.cl. Camping sites in a shaded area and clean rooms with private or shared bathrooms, set in a tranquil oasis of vegetation. Popular with travellers of all ages, and there's also a good café on the premises. Camping CH$8000 per person, rooms CH$19,500.

Mama Tierra Pachamama 615 ☎55/851-418, ✉mamatierra@sanpedroatacama.com. Popular with backpackers and a 10-min walk from the centre, this tidy hostel offers dorms, singles and doubles with private or shared bathrooms. Extras include laundry service, and the congenial hostess

can help organize volcano climbs in the area. Dorms, CH$8000, rooms CH$20,000.

Oasis Alberto Terrazas Pozo 3 ☎55/851-042. About 4km out of town, this campsite boasts the best views in all of San Pedro, with the volcanoes in the distance. Ask around at the bus terminal for a taxi to take you there (CH$5000). A pool (CH$3000 for non-guests) with hot showers, picnic tables and barbecue facilities are pluses. Camping CH$5000 per person with pool use included.

Eating, drinking and nightlife

The no-frills food stalls by the Atacama 2000 bus stop on Licancábur s/n are a good place to fill up on *cazuela*, fried chicken, hot dogs and other budget options. Meals are all under CH$3000.

Blanco Caracoles s/n. Although fairly pricey, the imaginative chicken and salmon dishes in this trendy bar-restaurant are worth the splurge. Fixed-price lunch menu CH$5500.

Café Esquina Caracoles s/n. Small cafe dishing out delicious *empanadas* (CH$1300) and wonderfully refreshing ginger lemonade (CH$2200), among other simple sandwiches, and snacks.

La Cave Toconao s/n. Popular French-run restaurant famous for its large crêpes with a myriad of sweet and savoury fillings. Good two-for-one deals on cocktails at night, too. Set menu CH$5,500.

SAN PEDRO TOUR OPERATORS

Choosing a reputable tour operator in San Pedro can be difficult, but at least the intense competition keeps prices fairly stable. Talk to other travellers who have done the tours recently, and look at the comment book in the tourist information office. Expect to pay around CH$28,000 for a tour of the *altiplano* lagoons and villages, CH$7000 to visit Valle de la Luna, CH$18,000 to visit El Tatio geysers and CH$10,000 for a three-hour sandboarding trip (including an instructor and board rental); trip prices normally exclude entrance fees. The following are reliable:

Azimut 360 Caracoles 195 ☎55/851-469 ⓦwww.azimut.cl. Multi-day treks, camping and volcano ascents in the area are offered by this long-standing Santiago-based outfit.

Cosmo Andino Caracoles s/n ☎55/851-069, ⓦwww.cosmoandino-expediciones.cl. Established and reliable bilingual operator running standard trips to El Tatio geysers, Valle de la Luna and the *altiplano* villages.

Estrella del Sur Caracoles 238 ☎9/8516-6032. One of the better operators offering all-inclusive three-day trips across the Salar de Uyuni (around CH$60,000).

Know Chile Gustavo Le Paige 181 ☎9/498-1280, ⓦwww.knowchiletour.com. Cheery and

knowledgeable Erich prides himself on seeking out the less well-trodden path. English spoken.

Maxim Experience Caracoles 174C ☎55/851-952, ✉maximexperience@hotmail.com. Sandboarding and trips to volcano Ojos de Salado, among others.

San Pedro de Atacama Celestial Explorations Caracoles 166 ☎55/851-935, ⓦwww.spaceobs.com. French astronomer Alain Maury brings the night sky to life during the tours at his home in the desert, where he has set up several powerful telescopes (times vary, 2hr 30min; CH$15,000 per person). Tours are conducted in English, French and Spanish. Warm clothes are essential.

La Estaka Caracoles 259. A rustic bar-restaurant that features nightly live music, complementary pisco sours and a range of expertly prepared meat and vegetarian dishes. Cannelloni with wine CH$4000.

Rincón Pintado Caracoles 101B. In the grounds of *Camping Takha Takha*, this small café with outside seating opens at 7.30am for breakfast, and also provides simple lunches. Breakfasts from CH$2000.

Sala de Té 02 Caracoles 295B. Unpretentious place serving excellent quiches alongside standard fast food, as well as a range of teas, and the best breakfasts in town. Quiche, salad and drink CH$3850.

Tierra Todo Natural Caracoles 46. Fantastic daily set menus that always include imaginative vegetarian dishes. Evening service can be slow. Fixed menu CH$6000.

Moving on

Bus Antofagasta (6 daily; 5hr); Arica (1 daily; 14hr); Calama (6 daily; 1hr 45min); Salta and Jujuy (Tues, Fri & Sun 7am & 11am; 14hr); Santiago (1 daily; 22hr); Socaire (1 daily at 7.30pm; 2hr); Toconao (4 daily; 1hr 30min). Most travellers will choose to cross the border to Uyuni in Bolivia on a tour, though it's possible to do so by public transport on a bus from Calama to the border town of Ollagüe (see Calama, "Moving on", p.448).

DAY-TRIPS FROM SAN PEDRO

Beyond San Pedro, the scenery is dramatic, dominated by large volcanic peaks, **Valle de la Luna**'s magnificent lunar landscape, the red rock of the **Valle de la Muerte**, the famous **El Tatio geysers**, Chile's largest salt flat **Salar de Atacama** and dazzling **lagoons**. With the exception of the village of **Toconao**, and Valle de la Muerte and Valle de la Luna, both of which can be visited by bike, these places are only accessible on a tour.

Valle de la Muerte

The easiest attraction to cycle to – only 3km from San Pedro – is the **Valle de la Muerte**, with its narrow gorges, peculiar **red rock formations** and 150-metre high **sand dunes**. It is also a prime **sandboarding** destination, with scores of enthusiasts whizzing down the slopes in the early mornings and late afternoons. The rest of the time an exquisite silence reigns over the still sand and rocks, and you can often enjoy the views of the snow-peaked volcanoes in the distance entirely undisturbed.

Valle de la Luna

Most people come here at sundown with one of a plethora of tour groups, but the lunar landscape of **Valle de la Luna** (Moon Valley; entry CH$2000), at the heart of the Cordillera del Sal, is equally impressive at sunrise, when the first rays of sunlight turn the surrounding jagged red peaks various shades of pink and gold. Though the effect is even more intense at sunset, at dawn there are far fewer spectators, and after making your way up the giant sand dune along a marked trail, you can walk up the crest of the dune for a better vantage point. If cycling the 14km to the valley, go west along Caracoles out of town, turn left at the end and carry straight on; plenty of water, sunscreen and a torch are essential.

Toconao

Toconao, 38km from San Pedro, is a small village nestled in an idyllic spot surrounded by sandy hills, with houses built entirely of volcanic liparita stone. A cool stream runs through the valley and the surrounding fertile soil supports lush vegetation, including fig, pear and quince trees, as well as a hallucinogenic type of cactus. The site has been inhabited since 11,000 BC, and its present population of around seven hundred villagers make traditional crafts. It is possible to stay in several rustic *hospedajes* here, and there are delicious *humitas* (corn paste wrapped in corn leaves) for sale. Buses Atacama and Buses Frontera each run twice-daily bus services to Toconao from San Pedro.

Salar de Atacama

The edge of Chile's largest salt flat, the **Salar de Atacama**, lies 50km south

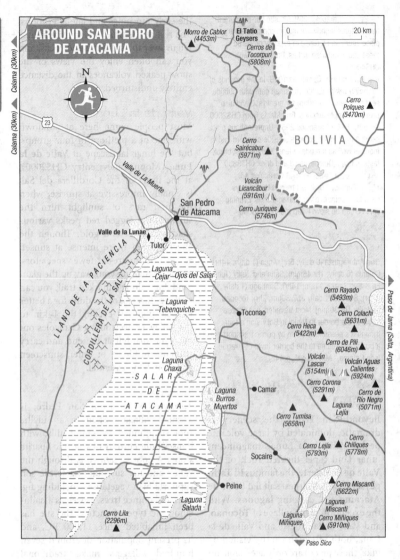

AROUND SAN PEDRO DE ATACAMA

Calama (30km) ◀
Calama (30km) ◀
Calama (30km) ◀

N

23

Morro de Cablor
(4453m) ▲

El Tatio Geysers ▲

0 — 20 km

Cerros de Tocorpuri
(5808m) ▲

Cerro Polques
(5470m) ▲

BOLIVIA

Cerro Sairécabur
(5971m) ▲

Volcán Licancábur
(5916m) ▲

Valle de La Muerte

San Pedro de Atacama

Cerro Juriques
(5746m) ▲

Valle de la Lunae ▲

Tulor ▲

Laguna Cejar—Ojos del Salar

LLANO DE LA PACIENCIA

CORDILLERA DE LA SAL

Laguna Tebenquiche

●Toconao

Cerro Rayado
(5493m) ▲

Cerro Colachi
(5631m) ▲

Paso de Jama (Salta, Argentina) ▶

Cerro Heca
(5422m) ▲

Cerro de Pili
(6046m) ▲

Laguna Chaxa

S A L A R

D E

A T A C A M A

Laguna Burros Muertos

●Camar

Volcán Lascar
(5154m) ▲

Volcán Aguas Calientes
(5924m) ▲

Cerro Corona
(5291m) ▲

Cerro de Río Negro
(5071m) ▲

Laguna Lejía

Cerro Tumisa
(5658m) ▲

Socaire●

Cerro Lejía
(5793m) ▲

Cerro Chiliques
(5778m) ▲

●Peine

Cerro Miscanti
(5622m) ▲

Laguna Salada

Cerro Lila
(2296m) ▲

Laguna Miñiques

Laguna Miscanti
Cerro Miñiques
(5910m) ▲

▼ Paso Sico

of San Pedro. It may disappoint those expecting a sparkling white field, but still makes an unforgettable spectacle: a jagged white crust, resembling dead coral, created by water flowing down from the mountains, stretches as far as the eye can see. Several shallow lakes dot the Salar, including **Laguna Chaxa**, made bright by the resident Andean, Chilean and James flamingos, which spend up to fourteen hours a day feeding on tiny saltwater shrimp. Many excursions will also take in **Laguna Cejar** (CH$2000) – where salt content is so high that you can float on the surface – and gleaming **Laguna Tebenquiche**. Also look out for the two **Ojos del Salar** (entry CH$2500) – two small, and almost perfectly round cold-water pools set amid the arid plain.

El Tatio geysers

The **El Tatio geysers**, 90km north of town, are a morning attraction, with tours setting off at 4am in order to reach them by sunrise, when the fumaroles that spew steam and the jets of scalding water that shoot up from the geysers are at their most impressive. At dawn, there is a surreal quality to the plateau: dark shadowy figures move through the mist and the sunlight glints on patches of white ground frost. When walking around, stick to marked paths, since the ground crust can be very fragile – breaking it might result in a plunge into near-boiling water. The temperature here, at the world's highest geothermal field (4320m), is often below freezing, so warm clothes are essential. A soak in the nearby thermal pool is a must.

Lagunas Miscanti and Miñiques

These two *altiplano* **lagoons** (entry CH$2500) lie 134km from town, at an elevation of around 4200m. Visitors here are left breathless not just by the altitude, but also by the first sight of the huge shimmering pools of deep blue, ringed with white ribbons of salt. There's abundant bird and animal life as well, and it is possible to see both flamingos and the inquisitive *zorro culpeo*, a type of **fox** that often approaches the area's picnic site to look for scraps.

IQUIQUE

The approach to the busy coastal city of **iquique** is unforgettable, especially if coming from the east. The highway along the plateau suddenly gives way to a spectacular 600m drop, looking down onto the giant **Cerro Dragón** sand dune which in turn towers over the city. At sunset, the dune and the surrounding cliffs turn various shades of pink and red, giving the city an almost unearthly feel. Almost 500km north of Antofagasta, Iquique prospered in the nitrate era, between 1890 and 1920. Most of the grand old buildings in the city's historical centre date back to that heyday. The town's biggest draws nowadays are its **beaches**, though the huge duty-free Zona Franca in the north of the city also draws locals and visitors alike. The city is also one of the top destinations in Latin America for **paragliders**.

Plaza Prat

At the heart of Iquique's historic centre lies **Plaza Prat**, lined with banks and restaurants, with the tall white **Torre Reloj**, the city's symbol, built in 1877, as centrepiece. On the south side of the square stands the Neoclassical **Teatro Municipal**. The **Casino Español**, a 1904 Moorish-style wooden building with an opulent interior, graces the northeast corner of the square and is worth a visit both for the interior decorations and the delicious pisco sours.

Calle Baquedano

Heading south from Plaza Prat towards Playa Bellavista, quiet pedestrianized **Calle Baquedano**, with its elevated boardwalks and grand wooden buildings, is strikingly different from the modern parts of Iquique, with a faded colonial feel about it. The **Museo Regional**, at no. 951 (Tues–Fri 10am–6pm, Sat & Sun 9.30am–6pm; CH$1000), is home to a number of curious pre-Columbian artefacts, the most impressive of which are the Chinchorro mummies and skulls, deliberately deformed by having bandages wrapped tightly around them. The natural history section features a sea lion embryo pickled in formalehyde and an informative exhibition on nitrate extraction in the area, along with a scale model of the ghost town of Humberstone.

DOWNTOWN IQUIQUE

0   200 m

N

Caleta Pesquera

Bus Terminal

SOTOMAYOR

Tur Bus Terminal

ESMERALDA

Civet Adventure

BOLIVAR

SAN MARTIN

Casino Español ❶

Sky Airline Office

SERRANO

PLAZA CONDELL

Municipalidad

TARAPACA

LAN Office

Teatro Municipal ❷

LATORRE

THOMPSON

other bus offices

Crafts Market ❻

Turismo Santa Teresita ❸

Tur Bus Office

SARGENTO ALDEA

Mercado Centenario ❼

Museo Regional

Ⓐ

Pullman Office

LATORRE

Avitours

ZEGERS

Palacio Astoreca

Ⓑ

O'HIGGINS

BULNES

EATING, DRINKING & NIGHTLIFE

Canto del Mar	2
Casino Español	1
Doña Lucy	5
M.Koo	3
Mercado Centenario	7
Otaku	10
Paninis	6
Puerto Camarón	4
Sala Murano	9
El Tercer Ojito	8

ORELLA

RIQUELME

Swimming Pool

Ⓒ

J J PEREZ

MANUEL RODRIGUEZ

ACCOMMODATION

Backpacker's Hostel Iquique	D
Casa de Huespedes "Profesores"	A
Flight Park	E
Hostal Cuneo	B
Hostel La Casona 1920	C

Supermarket

Ⓓ, Ⓔ, ❾, ❿ & Beaches ▼

The beaches

Iquique's most popular beach, **Playa Cavancha** is sheltered in a bay alongside the busy main thoroughfare of Avenida Arturo Prat, about 2km from the main plaza. It is particularly popular with sunbathers and boogie-boarders and is safe for swimming. The boardwalk, which winds along the beach amidst the palm trees and giant cacti, is always teeming with bikers, rollerbladers and scores of sun worshippers; in the evenings a relaxed atmosphere prevails. At the north end of Playa Cavancha lies rocky **Playa Bellavista**, with several good surf breaks, while the large stretch of **Playa Brava**, lined by fun fairs and themed restaurants, is south of the Peninsula de Cavancha, and is a popular landing spot for paragliders. The less crowded **Playa Huayquique** is located to the very south of the city; it also has good waves for surfers and can be reached by *colectivos* from the centre.

Arrival and information

Air Aeropuerto Diego Arecena (✪ www.aero puertoiquique.com) lies 41km south of Iquique; Aerotransfer (☎ 57/310-800) drops you off at your door for CH$6000.

Bus The main terminal is inconveniently located at the north end of Patricio Lynch; numerous *colectivos* run to the city centre (CH$1500) and some bus companies pick up passengers at their central offices around Mercado Centenario. The Tur Bus terminal is slightly more central, at the corner of Esmeralda and Ramírez.

Tourist information Anibal Pinto 436 (mid-March to mid-Dec Mon–Thurs 9am–5pm, Fri 9am–4.30pm;

TREAT YOURSELF

Few things compare to the sheer rush of running off the cliff at **Alto Hospicio** on the plateau above Iquique. Once the butterflies settle, you find yourself soaring gently with white-headed eagles as tiny houses with minute turquoise swimming pools, oceanside high-rises, beaches and the giant sand dune of Cerro Dragón spread out beneath you. **Paragliding** feels entirely different from flying in an airplane, and the views from above are nothing short of incredible. You fly in tandem with an experienced instructor, who guides you through the entire procedure, from take-off to landing. Recommended operators are **Altazor Sky Sports** (℡57/380110, Ⓦwww.altazor.cl), and **Puro Vuelo**, Baquedano 1440 (℡57311-127 or 9/829-0805, Ⓦwww.purovuelo .cl), which both offer paragliding courses as well as tandem flights. Puro Vuelo also provide a CD of pictures of you during, before and after your flight. Flights typically cost CH$30,000–35,000 for half an hour; transport to and from the paragliding site is included. If you want to enjoy a beer with some of the world's best paragliding talent, consider staying at *Flight Park Altazor* (see below). For the more faint of heart, tour companies will also help you organize a **sandboarding** trip on the dunes.

mid-Dec to mid-March Mon–Sat 9am–8pm, Sun 9am–2pm; ℡57/419-241, Ⓔinfoiquique@sernatur .cl). Staff can advise on city attractions and provide maps of the city.

Accommodation

🏃 **Backpacker's Hostel Iquique** Amunátegui 2075, about 2km south of Plaza Prat ℡57/320-223, Ⓦwww.hosteliquique.cl. With English-speaking staff who help organize trips in the area, a friendly atmosphere and a superb beachside location, this hostel remains a firm backpacker favourite. Kitchen facilities, free internet and frequent barbecues are part of the draw. Dorms CH$6500, rooms CH$15,000.

Casa de Huéspedes "Profesores" Ramírez 839 ℡57/314-475, Ⓔinostrozafloresltda@gmail.com. Friendly guesthouse with internet and wi-fi, laundry service, bike rental and a tour agency. Rooms by the patio have been recently refurbished. Dorms CH$6000, rooms CH$14,000.

Flight Park Via 6, Manzana Am Sitio 3, Bajo Molle, about a 15-min bus ride from town ℡57/380110, Ⓦwww.altazor.cl. Built almost entirely of ship containers, the rooms at this international parag-liding centre are surprisingly inviting, with shared kitchen, internet access and chilled-out communal areas. See their website for directions. Rooms CH$12,000, camping CH$4000 per person.

Hostal Cuneo Baquedano 1175 ℡57/428-654, Ⓔhostalcuneo@hotmail.com. Cosy, quiet and conveniently located family-run *residencial*, with tidy rooms for up to four and dorms, many with cable TV, some en suite; breakfast included. CH$18,000.

Hostel La Casona 1920 Barros Arana 1585 ℡57413-000, Ⓦwww.casonahosteliquique.cl. Excellent and welcoming hostel in the childhood home of charming owner Isabel, offering spotless rooms with good lockers, spacious communal areas and a family atmosphere. No private bathrooms. Dorms CH$8000, rooms CH$18,000.

Eating

Canto del Mar Baquedano/Thompson. Popular and bustling restaurant on the plaza, serving filling meat and fish dishes and good daily specials. Grilled fish CH$4000.

Doña Lucy La Torre/Vivar. Pleasant café to while away an afternoon or wait for a bus, with huge slices of cream-filled cake (CH$1500).

Mercado Centenario Barros Arana. This market is *the* place for fresh produce and generous helpings of fish and seafood for lunch; *Sureña II* and *La Picada* are very popular. Fish with side dish CH$3000.

M.Koo Latorre 596. An excellent central spot for takeaway *pastel de choclo* and *humitas*, as well as tasty *empanadas* and *chumbeques* (local sweet biscuits). *Empanada* CH$1500.

🏃 **Otaku** Av. Arturo Prat 2089, ℡57/542-850. Small but excellent and reasonably priced sushi restaurant with takeaway on Playa Brava; open late. Six California rolls CH$2500.

Paninis Baquedano s/n, opposite *Puerto Camarón*. Tiny café in front of the Fería Artesanal, good for morning coffee, fresh juices and croissants. Juice CH$1200.

Puerto Camarón On Baquedano at Gorostiaga. Brightly painted restaurant with a fishing net suspended above the tables, outdoor seating and excellent seafood *empanadas* as well as cheap set menus. Two *empanadas* with drink CH$2500.

El Tercer Ojito Patricio Lynch 1420, between Perez and Riquelme ☎57/426-517. One of the best restaurants in town, set in a pretty courtyard, with sublime fish dishes, delicious bread and sushi in the evenings. Swordfish CH$3500.

Drinking and nightlife

Casino Español Plaza Prat 584. The food here is pricey, but it's worth a visit for some of the best pisco sours in Chile. Pisco sour CH$2000.
Sala Murano Bajo Molle Km7 ⓦwww.salamurano .com. Two-tiered dancefloor with a number of different ambiences. Open midnight–5am. Entry CH$3000–5000.

Moving on

Air Arica (3 daily); La Paz (4 weekly); Santiago (4 daily).
Bus Arica (10 daily; 4hr); Calama (4 daily; 6hr); Colchane (2 daily; 6hr); Copiapó (6 daily; 15hr); La Serena (6 daily; 18hr); Pica (13 daily; 1hr 30min); San Pedro de Atacama (1 daily; 8hr); Santiago (8 daily; 24hr).

AROUND IQUIQUE

The nitrate pampas inland from Iquique are dotted with **ghost towns** left over from the area's mining heyday, with the biggest and best-preserved example being **Humberstone** (daily: March–Nov 9am–6pm; Dec–Feb 9am–7pm; CH$1000), 45km to the east. Established in the middle of parched desert land in 1862, this once-thriving mining town bears the name of its British manager, James Humberstone. Visitors can wander the eerie streets where squalid and partially wrecked worker barracks contrast sharply with the faded glamour of the theatre and the well-maintained church. Workers here, mostly Chilean but some foreign, earned a pittance by putting in long hours in a hot and dangerous environment.

The thermal springs at **Pica**, 114km southeast of Iquique, are well worth a visit for a relaxing splash around; the most popular is **Cocha Resbaladero** (daily 8am–9pm; CH$1000). The small, pre-Hispanic town is also famed for producing limes widely believed to make the perfect pisco sour, and the pretty **Iglesia de San Andrés**.

ARICA

ARICA, Chile's northernmost city, 316km north of Iquique, benefits greatly from tourism, with foreign visitors flocking to its pleasant sandy beaches in the summer and a smattering of good museums. The city was the principal port exporting silver from Bolivia's Potosí mines until 1776, and

IQUIQUE TOUR OPERATORS

Apart from sandboarding and paragliding on Cerro Dragón, and surfing all along Iquique's coast, the area around the city has a wealth of attractions on offer, including trips to the ghost town of Humberstone, the Gigante de Atacama geoglyph, the hot springs of Mamiña and the Pica oasis, the burial site of an Inca princess at the village of La Tirana and the sobering mass graves from the Pinochet era at the tiny settlement of Pisaqua. The cheapest – though perhaps not the most satisfying – tours combine a whistle-stop trip through all these attractions in a day (about CH$20,000). We recommend the following operators:

Avitours Baquedano 997 ☎57/473-775, ⓦwww.avitours.cl. Day-trips to the local hot springs, geoglyphs and ghost towns as well as longer excursions to Parque Nacional Volcán Isluga and multi-day trips to Parque Nacional Lauca and Reserva Las Vicuñas, finishing either in Arica or Iquique.
Civet Adventure Bolívar 684 ☎57/428-483, ⓔecivetcor@vtr.net. Customized 4x4 and biking trips to altiplano destinations with an expert guide and an all-new desert buggy.
Turismo Santa Teresita Ramírez 839 ☎57/314-475 or 9/465-3259. Arranges paragliding sessions and runs day-trips to the hot springs, Pisagua, La Tirana and other regional attractions.

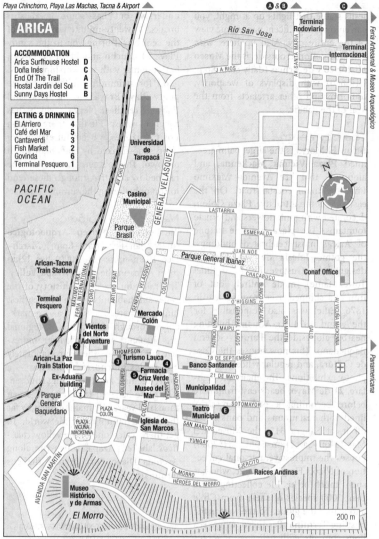

Playa Chinchorro, Playa Las Machas, Tacna & Airport

ARICA

ACCOMMODATION
Arica Surfhouse Hostel   **D**
Doña Inés   **C**
End Of The Trail   **A**
Hostal Jardín del Sol   **E**
Sunny Days Hostel   **B**

EATING & DRINKING
El Arriero   **4**
Café del Mar   **5**
Cantaverdi   **3**
Fish Market   **2**
Govinda   **6**
Terminal Pesquero   **1**

Feria Artesanal & Museo Arqueológico

PACIFIC OCEAN

Río San José

Terminal Rodoviario

Terminal Internacional

AV SANTA MARIA

J A RIOS

Universidad de Tarapacá

Casino Municipal

Parque Brasil

GENERAL VELÁSQUEZ

AV CHILE

LASTARRIA

ESMERALDA

JUAN NOE

Parque General Ibañez

CHACABUCO

BLANCO ENCALADA

Conaf Office

Arican-Tacna Train Station

Terminal Pesquero

Vientos del Norte Adventure

Arican-La Paz Train Station

Ex-Aduana building

Parque General Baquedano

PLAZA VICUÑA MACKENNA

FERIA INTERNACIONAL

PEDRO MONTT

MAXIMO LIRA

ARTURO PRAT

GENERAL VELÁSQUEZ

COLÓN

Mercado Colón

THOMPSON

Turismo Lauca

BOLOGNESI

Farmacia Cruz Verde

Museo del Mar

BAQUEDANO

PLAZA COLÓN

Iglesia de San Marcos

O'HIGGINS

MAIPU

PATRICIO LYNCH

GENERAL LAGOS

21 DE MAYO

18 DE SEPTIEMBRE

Banco Santander

Municipalidad

SOTOMAYOR

Teatro Municipal

SAN MARCOS

YUNGAY

SAN MARTIN

GALLO

AV VICUÑA MACKENNA

Panamericana

EJERCITO

Raices Andinas

EL MORRO

HÉROES DEL MORRO

AVENIDA SAN MARTIN

Museo Histórico y de Armas

El Morro

0   200 m

Playa El Laucho, Playa La Lisera, Playa Brava, Playa Arenillas Negras & Playa Los Corazones

only became part of Chile in the 1880s after the War of the Pacific. Aside from its own attractions, Arica makes a good base for the beautiful Parque Nacional Lauca (see p.461).

What to see and do

The compact city centre is easy to explore on foot, though a visit to Arica isn't complete without climbing **El Morro**, the dramatic cliff that looms high over the city.

El Morro

A steep path leads to the top of **El Morro** from the southern end of Calle Colón. From the clifftop, home to a number of turkey vultures and a giant

Jesus statue that lights up at night, you can enjoy a magnificent panoramic view of the entire city. Also up here, with cannons stationed outside, is the **Museo Histórico y de Armas** (daily 8am–8pm; CH$600) with displays of weaponry, uniforms and other artefacts from the War of the Pacific.

The city centre

Below El Morro is the large, palm-tree-lined **Plaza Vicuña Mackenna**, and alongside that lies Avenida Máximo Lira, the main coastal road. On the east side is the attractive **Plaza Colón**, decorated with pink flowers and ornate fountains. The plaza is home to one of Arica's most celebrated buildings, the gothic **Iglesia de San Marcos**, designed by Gustave Eiffel (of Eiffel Tower fame), made entirely out of iron and shipped over from France in 1876. Eiffel was also responsible for the grand 1874 **Ex-Aduana** building nearby, alongside the Parque General Baquedano. This now houses the Casa de Cultura, and regularly hosts art and photo exhibitions. The main through-fare, **21 de Mayo**, heads east from here before becoming a pedestrian strip, lined with restaurants and banks. Just off it, at Sangra 315, the Museo del Mar (Mon–Sat 11am–5pm, CH$2000) houses the impressive, personal collection of Nicols Hrepic Gutunic, who has spent much of his life collecting more than 1000 species of shells from Chile and across the globe. To the west is the bustling **Terminal Pesquero**, where sea lions compete with pelicans for scraps from the dockside fish stalls.

The beaches

North of the centre and west of the bus terminals lies the popular **Playa Chinchorro**, which is ideal for swimming, sunbathing and body-boarding. The city's northernmost beach, **Playa Las Machas**, is not suitable for swimming due to the strong undertow but has some good surf breaks. A twenty-minute walk south of the centre will bring you to the sandy **Playa El Laucho** and **Playa La Lisera**, both popular with sun worshippers and good for swimming, followed by the pretty **Playa Brava** and the dark-sand **Playa Arenillas Negra**, which has rougher waves. Finally, there's **Playa Los Corazones**, a beautiful expanse of clean sand flanked by cliffs 8km south of town. The southern beaches can be reached by *colectivo*, though these tend to run only during the summer season.

Museo Arqueológico

The excellent **Museo Arqueológico** (daily Jan–Feb 9am–8pm; March–Dec 10am–6pm; CH$2000) lies 12km from Arica in the green **Azapa Valley**. The museum traces the history of the valley's inhabitants, from the earliest hunter-gatherers, via a remark-ably thorough collection of regional pre-Hispanic artefacts. Most impressive of these are the four elaborately prepared **Chinchorro mummies** – a male, a female and two young children, which are believed to be around seven thousand years old, making them by far the oldest mummies in the world. To get there, catch one of the yellow *colectivos* labelled "Azapa" which run along Avenida Diego Portales past the bus terminals.

Arrival

Air Aeropuerto Internacional Chacalluta is 18km north of Arica; a radio taxi downtown costs around CH$6000, or a *colectivo* CH$4000.

Bus Terminal Rodovario, at Diego Portales 948, is the main stop for local arrivals, plus a few international; inside there are cash machines and snack kiosks. Terminal Internacional is immediately adjacent, with arrivals from La Paz and numerous *micros* and *colectivos* crossing the border from Tacna, Peru.

Train The Arica–Tacna train station is located at Máximo Lira 889, on the northwest edge of the city centre.

Information

Tourist information The tourist office is at San Marcos 101 (March–Nov Mon–Fri 8.30am–5.20pm, Dec–Feb daily 8.30am–7pm; ☎58/252054, ⓔinfoarica@sernatur.cl). Helpful staff provide maps of town and a plethora of brochures on local attractions.

Conaf has an office at Av. Vicuña Mackenna 820 (Mon–Fri 8.30am–5.15pm; ☎58/201200). Staff provide information on, and maps of, local national parks; reserve beds at regional Conaf *refugios* here.

Accommodation

You camp for free at the Playa Las Machas.

Arica Surfhouse Hostel O'Higgins 661 ☎58/312-213, ⓦwww.aricasurfhouse.cl. This centrally located hostel has spacious rooms, and caters well to its surfer clientele, as well as organizing other activities including horse-riding and paragliding. Dorms CH$8500, rooms CH$20,000.

Doña Inés Manuel Rojas 2864 ☎58/248-108, ⓔhiarica@hostelling.cl. The inconvenient location of this hostel is compensated for by the owner's hospitality, knowledge and insatiable enthusiasm. Pluses are free internet, bike rental, and a cosy common room with TV. To get there, take *colectivo* #4 from the bus station to Chapiquiña (corner of Blest Gana); the hostel is on the left. Dorms CH$5800, rooms CH$12,500.

End of the Trail Esteban Alvarado 117 ☎58/314-316 or 9/7786-3972, ⓦwww.endofthetrail-arica.cl. A congenial American owner runs this brand-new hostel, which has comfortable, quiet rooms around an indoor courtyard, amazing showers and a specially designed roof that keeps the house cool. Breakfast included. To get there from the bus station, walk two blocks west on Diego Portales, then four blocks south on Pedro de Valdivia. Dorms CH$8000, rooms CH$18,000.

Hostal Jardín del Sol Sotomayor 848 ☎58/232-795, ⓦwww.hostaljardindelsol.cl. Central *hostal* run by a very helpful and welcoming couple who organize all manner of outdoor activities for guests. Most rooms are en suite; shares arranged. Kitchen, lounge, wi-fi, cable TV, bicycle rent and laundry service are some of the bonuses. Breakfast included. Rooms CH$22,000.

Sunny Days Hostel Tomas Aravena 161, ☎58/241-038, ⓦwww.sunny-days-arica .cl. Extremely friendly and knowledgeable Kiwi-Chilean hosts preside over travellers of all ages in this custom-built hostel. Free internet, excellent breakfast, kitchen and lounge facilities and a relaxed communal atmosphere all add to its appeal. Dorm CH$8000, rooms CH$18,000.

Eating and drinking

El Arriero 21 de Mayo 385. Atmospheric steakhouse with fantastic grilled meat and expertly prepared fish dishes; slightly pricier than the competition. Grilled fish CH$5500.

TOUR OPERATORS

A number of tour companies offer trips into the national parks outside Arica. The standard three- to four-day trip takes in Parque Nacional Lauca, Reserva Nacional Las Vicuñas, Salar de Surire and Parque Nacional Volcán Isluga, with overnight stops in the *altiplano* villages of Putre and Colchane. Most tours either return to Arica or drop passengers off in Iquique. Normally, a minimum of two people is required per tour and a three-day all-inclusive package costs around CH$165,000, the price coming down the more people join on the trip. Tour operators do offer day-trips taking in Parque Nacional Lauca, and Putre but this is not recommended as the altitude change is extreme, and is at best likely to make you feel queasy.

Raices Andinas Héroes de Morro 632, ☎58/233-305, ⓦwww.raicesandinas.com. Tour operator with close links to the local Aymará communities, promoting ecotourism and Aymará culture. Also operate Parinacota Expediciones (ⓦwww.parinacotaexpediciones.cl), who offer a trip through Parque Nacional Lauca into Bolivia. **Turismo Lauca** Thompson 20, corner with Bolognesi ☎58/252-322, ⓦwww.turismolauca.cl.

Standard trips around the national park circuit, as well as city tours, and archeological interest trips.

Vientos del Norte Adventure Prat 430, ☎58/231-331, ⓦwww.vientosdelnorte adventure.cl. Experienced, bilingual guide offering trips to Bolivia and Peru, as well as the option of tours finishing in the San Pedro area.

Café del Mar 21 de Mayo 260. Popular restaurant with a bargain *menú del día*, plus large salads and good quiches. Quiche CH$2500.

Cantaverdi Bolognesi 453. Attractive, much frequented pub with a pleasant buzz, serving snacks and pizzas along with a wide range of drinks. Salads CH$3100.

Fish market Avenida Máximo Lira at Calle 21 de Mayo. Excellent place to pick up some inexpensive sea bass *ceviche* (CH$1000).

Govinda Blanco Encalada 200. Top vegetarian lunch option, with fresh organic produce used to create imaginative dishes. Set three-course lunch CH$2500.

Terminal Pesquero Off Avenida Máximo Lira, across from entrance to Calle 21 de Mayo. Several no-frills oceanside eateries here cook up hearty portions of inexpensive fish dishes; *Mata Rangi*, in particular, stands out. Set lunch CH$3800.

Moving on

Air Iquique (8 daily); La Paz (5 weekly); Santiago (10 daily).

Bus Antofagasta (6 daily; 10hr); Arequipa (daily 8am; 12hr), Cusco (daily 10am; 20hr) and Lima (daily at noon; 20hr); Calama (several daily; 9hr); Copiapó (several daily; 16hr); Iquique (frequent daily departures; 4hr); La Paz (4–5 daily, morning departures; 7hr); La Serena (6 daily; 19hr); Parinacota (1 daily Tues–Fri; about 5hr); San Pedro de Atacama (1 overnight; 11hr); Santiago (4–6 daily; 28hr), Salta and Jujuy, Argentina (Mon, Thurs & Sat at 10pm; 25hr).

Colectivo Those to Tacna, Peru depart frequently from Terminal Internacional.

Train Tacna, Peru (Mon–Sat at 9.30am and 7pm; 1hr).

PUTRE

The highland village of **PUTRE** sits at an altitude of 3500m and provides an ideal acclimatization point for venturing into the Parque Nacional Lauca. Populated by the indigenous Aymará people, Putre consists of basic stone houses centred around a square. It is a tranquil place to spend a few days, and is becoming an increasing must-see on the backpacker trail, with an growing number of accommodation options. Note that the only bank, in the square's southeast corner, does not accept Visa.

Arrival and information

Bus La Paloma buses (☏58/222-710) depart daily from Arica to Putre at 7am, returning to Arica from in front of Putre's *Hotel Kukuli* at 2pm (CH$3000).

Tourist information The tourist office is on the south side of the square (Mon–Thurs 8am–1pm & 2.30–7pm, Fri 8am–2pm). The Conaf office is at Teniente Del Campo, between La Torre and O'Higgins (☏9/7773-3032).

Accommodation

La Chakana A 10-min walk from the plaza; head downhill past the church ☏9/9745-9519, ⊛www.la-chakana.com. German-Chilean-run option, with comfy beds, filling breakfasts and a homely atmosphere. Dorms CH$8000, rooms CH$16,000.

Hostal Pachamama Lord Cochrane s/n ☏58/228564. Rustic yet cosy rooms in a colonial-style house with knowledgeable owners. Highly recommended. CH$16,000.

Eating

Cantaverdi east side of the square. Simple and centrally located restaurant, serving up large, inexpensive meals, often accompanied by a football game on TV.

ALTITUDE SICKNESS

Known here as *puna* or *soroche*, altitude sickness affects roughly a quarter of all travellers who venture above the altitude of about 2500m, regardless of age or fitness, though people with respiratory problems tend to suffer more. It is rarely life-threatening, though is dangerous for people suffering from hypothermia. Symptoms include vertigo, headaches, nausea, shortness of breath, lethargy and insomnia. Keeping properly hydrated and taking aspirin can alleviate some of the symptoms; mate de coca (tea brewed from coca leaves) is also widely believed to help. Avoid alcohol consumption, over-eating and over-exertion; if symptoms persist, try to move to a lower elevation. The best way to avoid altitude sickness is to acclimatize gradually by breaking up your journey to higher regions into segments.

Kuchu Marka Baquedano. Homely stews and filling dishes are on offer at this traditional restaurant.

PARQUE NACIONAL LAUCA

From Putre, Ruta 11 leads up onto the *altiplano* to the **Parque Nacional Lauca**, a region of rich flora and fauna, shimmering lakes and snow-capped volcanoes 4300m above sea level. The most visited village at these dizzying heights is the little whitewashed settlement of **Parinacota**, accessible by public transport, though it's far easier to see the sights of Lauca on an organized tour.

Las Cuevas

The Conaf-run **Las Cuevas** *refugio* is located 9km into the park, and the nature trail near it is the best place to see **viscachas**, the long-tailed, rabbit-like relatives of chinchillas, as they use their powerful hind legs to leap from boulder to boulder. The well-watered *bofedal* (alluvial depression) here provides permanent grazing for herds of **vicuñas**, the wild relatives of llamas and alpacas, which are also commonly seen. In addition, you'll find numerous examples of the *llareta* plant, which takes three hundred years to grow to full size; the plant looks like a pile of oddly shaped green cushions but is actually rock-hard. The local Aymará break up the dead plants with picks for use as firewood. Just off the *refugio*'s nature trail are some rustic thermal baths.

Parinacota

The **Conaf** headquarters (daily 9am–12.30pm & 1–5.30pm) are located in the tiny Aymará village of **parinacota**, 19km east of the Las Cuevas *refugio*. Parinacota is worth a stop for its cheerful, whitewashed little **church**, reconstructed in 1789, and for the stalls opposite, selling colourful local **artesanía**. Besides a fetching bell tower with a tiny doorway, the church (ask around for the guardian of the key) has

murals depicting scenes of Jesus being borne to the cross by soldiers resembling Spanish conquistadors, as well as sinners burning in hell. A small wooden table is tethered to the wall to the left of the altar; legend has is it that the table wandered around the village, causing the death of a man by stopping in front of his house – the chain prevents the table from escaping again.

Parinacota can be reached by **public bus** from the Terminal Internacional in Arica (departs Tues–Fri at 11am, returning at 9am the following day; ☎58/260-164). It may be possible to rent a very basic **room** from a villager, or stay in the basic hostel opposite the church (ask at Raíces Andinas in Arica).

Lago Chungará

Some 18km east of Parinacota, at a breathtaking altitude of 4600m, lies the stunning **Lago Chungará**. With its brilliant blue waters perfectly reflecting the towering snow-capped cone of **Volcán Parinacota** (6350m), this is undoubtedly one of the highlights of the national park. The roadside **Conaf refugio** here has six basic beds (CH$6000 per person), kitchen facilities and three **camping** spaces (CH$5500 per site). There is a short lakeside **nature trail**, which provides a good vantage point for viewing the giant coots, flamingos and Andean geese that nest here.

RESERVA NACIONAL LAS VICUÑAS AND SALAR DE SURIRE

A southbound turn-off from Ruta 11 by Lago Chungará heads through the 209,131-hectare **Reserva Nacional Las Vicuñas** towards the Salar de Surire salt lake. The *reserva* is made up of seemingly endless marshes and grasslands where herds of vicuñas can be seen grazing in the distance.

At an altitude of 4295m, the enormous, dirty-white **Salar de Surire** is home to up to ten thousand **flamingos** – mostly Chilean, but with a smattering of James and Andean species. Surire means "place of the rhea" in Aymará, and it's also possible to catch glimpses here of these swift, ostrich-like birds. On the southeast side of the salt flat are the **Termas de Polloquere**, several hot thermal pools amidst a small geyser field, which are a good spot to soak and pamper yourself using the mud at the bottom of the pools. It is possible to **camp** at a rustic site near the pools.

There is no public transport to either the *reserva* or *salar*, and a tour is the easiest option.

PARQUE NACIONAL VOLCÁN ISLUGA

South of Las Vicuñas, the dirt track drifts eastwards, passing by large herds of **llamas** and their shorter and hairier **alpaca** cousins, as well as tiny, seemingly deserted Aymará hamlets. All these are overshadowed by the towering **Volcán Isluga** (5218m), from which the park takes its name. The little village of **Enquelga** is home to a small Conaf-run **refugio** with five beds and hot showers (CH$5500 per person), as well as a free **campsite** (1km east of town) with Conaf-maintained shelters alongside a stream and some hot springs. One warm pool here, against the impressive backdrop of the volcano, is large enough for swimming.

Just outside the park, the small farming settlement of **COLCHANE**, surrounded by fields of bright red quinoa and *kiwicha* (a highly nutritious local staple), has several basic **guesthouses** providing simple home-cooked food. It is possible to get on a bus from Iquique to Colchane (daily 1pm & 9pm; 3hr), and get dropped off at the park but it is best to contact Conaf in advance for advice. For drivers, the road condition is poor and requires a 4x4.

Middle Chile

As the southernmost reaches of Santiago's sprawling suburbs fade away, a vast expanse of fertile fields, orchards and vineyards serves as a transition area between the bustling metropolitan borough and the natural landscapes of the Lake District. This is Chile's most fertile region, and home to the country's world-famous **wineries**, which are accessible by day-trip from Santiago but are much less rushed if taken from the quaint town of **Santa Cruz**. West of Santa Cruz is the country's surf capital of **Pichilemu**, where some of the world's biggest breaks crash along vast sandy beaches. Further south, **Concepción**, Chile's second largest city, was the epicentre of a massive **earthquake** in 2010, which left more than 500 dead across the country. The worst affected towns were **Talca** and **Curicó**, which are likely to show the scars of the destructive quake for some years to come. They both serve as good bases for some excellent wine tours, however, and for trips to see the waterfalls and lush forests of the **Parque Nacional Radal Siete Tazas**, and the diverse wildlife of **Parque Nacional Nahuelbuta**.

RANCAGUA

RANCAGUA is a busy agricultural city that lies 87km south of Santiago. The best time for a day-trip here is either in April, to witness the **National Rodeo Championships**, or the last weekend in March, during the **Fiesta Huasa**, a three-day celebration of cowboy culture held in the main square, involving traditional food and wine. Alternatively, if coming in November, try to catch the **Encuentro Internacional Criollo**, a demonstration of spectacular horse-breaking and lassoing skills from expert riders from all over Latin America.

Arrival and information

Bus The Terminal O'Higgins, hub for long-distance destinations, lies northeast of town, just off Ruta 5. Tur Bus, at O'Carrol 1175 (⊕72/241-117), has a more convenient, central location. Expreso Santa Cruz and Pullman Del Sur run buses on to Santa Cruz.

Tourist information The helpful Sernatur office at Germán Riesco 277, 1st floor (Dec–Feb Mon–Fri 8.30am–5.15pm, Sat 9am–1pm; rest of the year Mon–Fri 8.30am–5.15pm; ⊕72/230-413, ⊛www .turismoregiondeohiggins.cl), can provide plenty of information on the city and its festivals.

Train The hourly Metrotrén from Santiago and the faster train to Chillán stop at the Estación Rancagua (⊕72/225239), on Av. Estación, between O'Carrol and Carrera Pinto, at the western edge of downtown.

SANTA CRUZ

About 90km southwest of Rancagua, the attractive little town of **SANTA CRUZ** lies at the heart of the fertile Colchagua Valley, home to Chile's best-organized *Ruta de Vino*. The hot climate here has proved to be perfect for growing Carmenère, Cabernet, Malbec and Syrah grapes. The ideal time to visit is during the first weekend in March, when the **Fiesta de La Vendimia del Valle de Colchagua** (grape harvest festival) is held, allowing you to sample the best wines and the region's typical dishes.

What to see and do

The heart of Santa Cruz is the gorgeous **Plaza de Armas**, dotted with araucarias, conifers and palm trees, with an ornate fountain at its centre and drinking fountains around its periphery. Within a couple of blocks of the plaza are numerous places to eat and *hospedajes*.

The excellent, privately run **Museo de Colchagua**, at Errázuriz 145 (Tues–Sun: Dec–Feb 10am–7pm; rest of the year 10am–6pm; CH$3000, students CH$1000; ⊛www.museocolchagua.cl), displays the unmatched private collection of Carlos Cardoen, which includes pre-Columbian artefacts from around Latin America, conquistador weaponry, exquisite gold work, Mapuche weavings, a collection of antique carriages and much more. Cardoen himself is a highly controversial figure: still wanted by the FBI for allegedly selling weapons to Iraq in the 1980s, the former arms dealer has transformed himself into a successful businessman and philanthropist with extensive interests in wine and tourism.

Arrival and information

Bus Terminal Municipal is on Casanova, four blocks southwest of the Plaza de Armas.

Tourist information There is a small Sernatur office in the clock tower on the plaza (Mon–Fri 10am–1pm & 3–6pm, Sat 10am–2pm), where you might get a basic map. The Ruta de Vino headquarters on the east side of the plaza (Mon–Fri 9am–11.30am, 2.30pm–6pm, Sat & Sun 10am–2pm; ⊕72/823199, ⊛www.rutadelvino.cl) is an excellent source of information on the Valle Colchagua (see box, p.464).

Accommodation

D'vid Hostal Edwards 205 ⊕9/812-0068 or 7/282-1209, ⊛www.dvid.cl. Just a 10-min walk from the town, this tranquil guesthouse has cosy rooms with comfortable beds, cable TV, wi-fi, a pleasant garden with a pool, and a good continental breakfast. Rooms CH$22,000.

Gomero Capellania 327 ⊕7/282-1436, Unremarkable hotel with clean but not particularly inviting rooms, and friendly staff. Breakfast included. Rooms CH$26,000.

Eating and drinking

Café Sorbo Casanova 158, on the 2nd floor of a cultural centre. Extremely friendly café/restaurant with quality coffee, and great choice for vegetarians. Veggie omelette CH$3800.

Pizzeria Refranes Orlandi/21 de Mayo. Traditional Chilean dishes combine with an excellent range of *empanadas* and divine slabs of pizza in a pleasant ambiance. Large pizza CH$5300.

Sushi and Coffee Sanfurgo 84. As the name suggests, this bizarre wooden hut serves up hot drinks as well as reasonable sushi dishes. Closed Sun. *Gyozas* CH$1900.

Moving on

Bus Pichilemu (10 daily; 2hr); Santiago (more than 10 daily; 2hr 30min).

RUTA DEL VINO DE COLCHAGUA

The Colchagua Valley has some of the best red wines in the world, not to mention the best-organized wine route in Chile. There are fourteen wineries in all, including both large, modern producers and small-scale, traditional bodegas; many of them can be visited on a drop-by basis or at short notice. The Ruta del Vino headquarters in Santa Cruz organizes full-day and half-day tours that commence at 10.30am, taking in two or three wineries, along with lunch and a visit to either the beautiful seventeenth-century Hacienda del Huique, or the Museo de Colchagua. Rates depend on the number of people and type of tour; a half-day tour without lunch will cost around CH$27,000, while full-day tours start at CH$60,000. Another enjoyable way to do the Ruta de Vino is aboard the leisurely Santa Cruz Wine Train (from CH$22,000 per person; ☎2/470-7403, ⓦwww.trendelvino.cl), a steam engine that leaves the agricultural town of San Fernando, 37km northwest of Santa Cruz, at 10.30am every Saturday – though services had been suspended at the time of writing. Excellent wineries include:

Viña Casa Silva Hijuela Norte s/n Angostura, Km 132, Ruta 5, San Fernando ☎72/710-204, ⓦwww.casasilva.cl. Award-winning winery set in a colonial-style hacienda, using modern technology to produce Carmenère, as well as the less common Viognier, Sauvignon Gris and Shiraz.
Viña Laura Hartwig Camino Barreales s/n ☎72/823-179, ⓦwww.laurahartwig.cl. Small,

family-owned, boutique winery producing only reserve-quality wines; the owners directly oversee each stage of production. Book in advance. Tours CH$8000 per person.
Viña Viu Manent Carretera del Vino Km 37 ☎72/858-751, ⓦwww.viumanent.cl. Family-owned winery famous for its excellent reds, especially Malbec, offering horse-drawn carriage tours as part of its attraction.

PICHILEMU

The drive to the surfing magnet of **PICHILEMU**, 90km west of Santa Cruz, is particularly scenic. The road meanders past sun-drenched vineyards before snaking in and out of patches of pine forest. "Pichi", as it's known, was originally planned as an upmarket vacation spot by the local land baron Agustín Ross Edwards, though in recent years it's become ever more popular with a motley crew of **surfers** and local beach bums.

What to see and do

A spread-out town, Pichilemu has numerous guesthouses and places to eat concentrated along the east–west Avenida Ortúzar, and the north–south Aníbal Pinto, a couple of blocks from the sea.

Playa Las Terrazas

Avenida Costanera Cardenal Caro runs alongside the black sand expanse of **Playa Las Terrazas**, Pichilemu's principal beach. Good for both sunbathers and surfers, it has a cluster of places to eat and **surf schools** concentrated towards its southern end, at the rocky promontory of La Puntilla. Steps lead up to the meticulously landscaped **Parque Ross**, dotted with palm trees and boasting an excellent view of the coast.

Punta de Lobos

Chile's most famous wave, **Punta de Lobos**, where the National Surfing Championships are held every summer, can be found six kilometres south of downtown Pichilemu; to get there, take a *colectivo* along Jorge Errázuriz (CH$800), or cycle down Comercio until you reach the turn-off towards the coast and make your way to the end of the jutting, cactus-studded headland. At the tip of the promontory, intrepid surfers descend via a steep dirt path before swimming across the short churning stretch of water to **Las Tetas**, the distinctive sea stacks, and catching the powerful, consistent left break just beyond.

Arrival and information

Bus The main Terminal Municipal is located at Millaco and Los Alerces, though unless you're staying in Pichi's southeastern quarter it's more convenient to disembark at the bus stop on Angel Gaete.

Spanish school Pichilemu Languages Institute (☎ 72/842-449, ⓦ www.studyspanishchile.com) offers short and longer-term Spanish classes.

Tourist information There is a helpful booth on Angel Gaete, between Montt and Rodríguez (Mon–Fri 8am–1pm & 2.30–7pm; ⓦ www.pichilemu.cl), which gives out maps of town and can help with accommodation.

Accommodation

Hostal Casa Verde Pasaje San Alfonso s/n; walk up the track opposite Verde Mar supermarket ☎ 9/299-8866, ⓦ www.hostalcasaverde.cl. About 3km from town, this small but popular hostel has good breakfasts, bike hire, and a chilled-out vibe. Dorms CH$8000, rooms CH$25,000.

Hotel Chile España Av. Ortúzar 255 ☎ 72/841-270, ⓦ www.chileespana.cl. Smart, central guesthouse with clean and comfortable rooms; breakfast is included and there's a pleasant patio area. Rooms CH$20,000.

La Higuera Angel Gaete 467 ☎ 72/841-321, ⓦ www.hospedajelahiguera.tk. This long-standing guesthouse in town has a messy-looking courtyard with basic rooms but it is well located just up from the bus drop-off point. Dorms CH$5000.

Eating, drinking and nightlife

El Balaustro Av. Ortúzar 289. Conveniently located, two-tiered pub which serves excellent lunchtime specials, both meat and fish, and has nightly drinks deals. Mains CH$4500.

Café Alto Primer Cenenario 91. Chilled-out arty café with nachos, sushi and pancakes as well as superbly mixed cocktails. Try their mojitos (CH$2000).

La Casa de las Empanadas Aníbal Pinto, between Aguirre & Acevedo. Takeaway with amazing range of excellent *empanadas* (CH$1000).

Disco 127 Av. Angel Gaete s/n. Pounding venue that acts as a magnet for Pichilemu's youth and surfing population. Doesn't kick off until after midnight.

Waitara Av. Costanera 1039 ☎ 72/843-026, ⓦ www.waitara.cl. The restaurant here is more appealing than the cabañas – its lunchtime menu features tasty and well-cooked fish dishes. Mains CH$4000.

Moving on

Bus There are hourly departures to Santiago (daily 4.30am–6.40pm; about 3hr 30min; with Buses Cruz Mar and Buses Nilahue, stopping in Santa Cruz and Rancagua). Buy your ticket at the bus offices on Angel Gaete at Aníbal Pinto, and catch them at the bus stop on Santa María, four blocks northeast.

CURICÓ

The garden city of **CURICÓ**, 56km south of Santa Cruz along the Panamericana highway, makes for a good brief stop if you want to visit the nearby wineries or the Reserva Nacional Radal Siete Tazas. The **Plaza de Armas** is shaded by a variety of native trees, with several modern sculptures to add character. The **Vinícola Miguel Torres** (daily autumn and winter 10am–5pm, spring and summer 10am–7pm; CH$7000; ☎ 75/564-100,

ⓦ www.migueltorres.cl), a Spanish-owned vineyard just south of Curicó, is a good spot for a drop-in visit, with an informative video on wine production followed by a sampling of the many wines available; there is also an excellent restaurant on-site. Molina-bound *colectivos* can drop you off very near the entrance.

Arrival and information

Buses Most long-distance carriers arrive at the Terminal de Buses Rurales, on Montt and O'Higgins.
Train The station for services between Talca and Santiago is at Maipú 657 (ⓣ 75/310-028).
Tourist information A new and enthusiastic municipal tourist information office has opened at Av. Manso de Velasco 744, Corporacion Cultural building 2nd floor. Information on the Ruta del Vino Curicó is available at the helpful office at Prat 301-A (ⓣ 75/328-972, ⓦ www.rutadelvinocurico.cl).

Accommodation and eating

Hotel Prat Peña 427 ⓣ 75/311-069. Clean and comfortable rooms around a courtyard, free internet access, breakfast and cable TV. CH$20,000.
Plaza Bonissimo Yungay 615. Just off the plaza, this place serves up an excellent three-course lunch (CH$2500), and transforms into a busy bar in the evenings with good drinks deals.

Moving on

Bus Chillán (6–8 daily; 2hr 30min); Santiago (every 30min; 3hr); Talca (every 15min; 1hr); Temuco (5 daily; 8hr). Minibuses shuttle to Santa Cruz run every 30min (2hr).
Train Santiago (6 daily; 2hr); Talca (6 daily; 50min).

PARQUE NACIONAL RADAL SIETE TAZAS

Some 73km southeast of Curicó, the **Parque Nacional Radal Siete Tazas** (April–Nov 8.30am–6pm; Dec–March 8.30am–8pm; CH$1600) is named after an astonishing natural phenomenon in which the crystalline Río Claro has carved the basalt rock-face into a series of "cups", interconnected by seven **waterfalls**, plummeting from high above. Though the waterfall

run is a favourite of expert **kayakers** during the spring snowmelt, the reserve otherwise gets few visitors outside the summer holidays and weekends. From the Conaf Administration, a short trail runs through a lush forest to a **mirador** overlooking the "teacups". Longer hikes to Cerro El Fraile and Valle del Indio are also possible.

Arrival and information

Bus Public buses run year-round from Curicó to Radal, at the western tip of the park, via the village of Molina (Mon–Sat 8am–5.30pm). In summer, Buses Radal 7 Tazas runs to Parque Inglés (mid-Dec to Feb: 8 services daily Mon–Sat 10am–8pm; 6 on Sun, 7.45am–9pm).
Conaf Conaf Administration is located in the western Parque Inglés Sector, where the park fee of CH$1600 is collected. There are talks on the flora and fauna at the Centro de Información on Sat.

TREAT YOURSELF

The best place to stay in the area by far is the Casa Chueca, Camino Las Rastras s/n (ⓣ 71/197-0096 or 9/419-0625, ⓦ www.trekkingchile.com; dorms CH$9000, rooms CH$38,000; closed June–Aug). Located on the banks of the Río Lircay, a short distance out of Talca, this German/Austrian-run guesthouse is a tranquil retreat with comfortable and charmingly decorated rooms for one to three people, delicious, home-cooked, mainly vegetarian meals and a swimming pool set amidst its lush gardens. Franz Schubert, its knowledgeable owner, also runs excellent guided excursions into the little-visited and underappreciated protected areas nearby.

To get here, take a "Taxutal A" bus from the bus stop at the southeast corner of the main bus terminal to the end of the route; if possible, call the guesthouse beforehand so that they can pick you up. Otherwise, follow the dirt road from Taxutal for about twenty minutes.

Accommodation

Of several campsites, the large *Camping Los Robles* (☎71/228029; CH$12,000/site) at Parque Inglés is the pick, with hot showers, toilets, picnic tables and fire pits in an attractive spot, surrounded by native forest and within walking distance of several waterfalls; the site at Radal tends to be rather dirty during peak season.

TALCA

The agricultural city of **TALCA** makes a good base for exploring the nearby **Valle del Maule** and its **Ruta de Vino**, though the town itself has few attractions and was severely damaged in the February earthquake.

The city's streets are on a numbered grid, making it very easy to navigate. Most of the commercial activity revolves around the **Plaza de Armas**, dominated by the cathedral, between 1 Norte, 1 Sur, 1 Poniente and 1 Oriente. Banks and pharmacies line 1 Sur, and there are numerous inexpensive places to eat and *completo* stands within a couple of blocks of the square. It is worth checking out the **Museo O'Higgiano**, at 1 Norte 875, where the national hero Bernardo O'Higgins spent his childhood and signed the Declaration of Independence in 1818; there's an impressive collection of Chilean art, though the building was seriously damaged in the 2010 quake.

Arrival

Bus Most long-distance and local buses arrive at the Terminal Rodoviario at 2 Sur 1920 (☎71/243-270), ten blocks east of the Plaza de Armas; the Tur Bus terminal (☎71/265715) is one block south, at 3 Sur 1940. Frequent *colectivos* go back and forth along 1 Sur to and from the train and bus stations.
Train The station (☎71/226-254) is at 11 Oriente 1100; there is no luggage storage. At the time of writing, work was being done to restore the line running south to Chillán.

Information

Tourist information The well-stocked and very helpful Sernatur office is found in the Correos, on the east side of Plaza de Armas, at 1 Oriente 1150 (Mon–Fri 8.30am–5.30pm; ☎71/233-669, ⓔinfomaule @sernatur.cl). The helpful Conaf office, at 2 Poniente/3 Sur (☎71/209-510), has information on the Reserva Nacional Altos de Lircay and Radal Siete Tazas.

Accommodation

Hostal Lonconao 6 Norte 777 ☎71/231-955, ⓦwww.hostallonconaotalca.superwebchile.com. Ex-teachers Javier and Adela make you feel at home here, with comfy beds and cable TV in clean rooms with private bathrooms. CH$16,000.

RUTA DEL VINO DEL MAULE

Valle Maule is rapidly developing a Ruta del Vino involving fifteen wineries, most of which require reservations to visit. The Ruta del Vino del Maule headquarters, at Plaza Cienfuegos 1 Sur/4 Oriente in Talca (Mon–Fri 8.30am–1pm & 2.30–6.30pm, Sat & Sun noon–6pm; closed weekends in winter; ☎9/8157-9951, ⓦwww .valledelmaule.cl) can help to arrange full-day and half-day visits to the nearby wineries. Good picks include:

Viña Balduzzi Av. Balmaceda 1189, San Javier, ☎73/322-138, ⓦwww.balduzzi.cl. Operating since the seventeenth century, this family winery runs interesting guided tours and tastings in English, and is the easiest to visit by public transport: take the San Javier bus from Talca. No need to reserve. Open Mon–Sat 9.30am–5.30pm.
Viña Gillmore Camino a Constitución Km 20, San Javier ☎73/197-5539, ⓦwww.gillmore.cl.
A boutique winery producing Cabernet Franc, Carignan, Malbec, Syrah, Carmenère and Merlot that doubles as a luxury agro-tourism resort, complete with a "winotherapy" spa.
Viña Hugo Casanova Fundo Viña Purísima, Camino Las Rastras Km 8 ☎71/266-540, ⓦwww.hugocasanova.cl. Family-run four-generation winery with attractive colonial buildings that turns out Cabernet Sauvignon, Merlot, Carmenère, Sauvignon Blanc and Chardonnay.

Hostal Los Castaños ☎ 9/959-2210, ✉ loscastanostalca@gmail.com. Former backpacker favourite which was seriously damaged in the earthquake and was looking to relocate in the town centre during 2011. Rooms around CH$17,000.

Refugio del Tricahue ⊛ www.refugio-tricahue.cl. Run by French-Belgian couple Betty and Dimitri, this nature lover's retreat has simple wooden chalets set against a beautiful backdrop of tree-covered mountains, with opportunities for fishing, trekking and cycling. Take Bus Interbus from Talca terminal towards Armerillo (7 buses daily; 1hr 30min). Email ahead to make a reservation. CH$14,000; camping CH$3500 per person.

Eating

Fuente de Soda Germana 3 Oriente 1105. Popular place that opens late and serves up sandwiches, burgers (CH$3700) and *completos*.

Restaurant Via Lactea 1 Sur Local 10 1339. Has a good-value set menu for CH$3800, and an excellent selection of ice cream. Tables fill up in the evenings.

Moving on

Bus Chillán (every 30min; 2hr), Puerto Montt (5 daily; 10hr); Santiago (hourly; 3hr 30min); Temuco (8 daily; 6hr).

Train Curicó (6 daily; 45min); Santiago (6 daily; 3hr).

CHILLÁN

CHILLÁN lies 150km south of Talca in the middle of the green **Itata Valley**. A nondescript town rebuilt time and time again after earthquake damage and Mapuche attacks, Chillán is famous as the birthplace of Chile's national hero and founding father, Bernardo O'Higgins. It also boasts an excellent market, overflowing with an abundance of fresh produce and authentic Mapuche handicrafts. The centre of town is the **Plaza Bernardo O'Higgins**, featuring a towering 36-metre cross commemorating the thirty thousand victims of the 1939 earthquake, which largely destroyed the city. **Escuela Mexico**, a school built with Mexico's donations in the wake of the earthquake, draws visitors with its frescoes, painted by the famous **Mexican muralists** David Alfaro Siqueiros and Xavier Guerrero. They depict famous figures from Latin American history.

Arrival and information

Bus Most long-distance buses arrive at the Terminal María Teresa at Av. O'Higgins 10 (☎ 42/272103), though some still use the grotty Terminal de Buses Interregionales, Constitución 1 (☎ 42/221014). Buses from local destinations, such as the Valle Las Trancas, arrive at the rural bus terminal at the market.

Tourist information The helpful and well-stocked Sernatur office is located at 18 de Septiembre 455 (Dec–Feb Mon–Fri 8.30am–7pm, Sat & Sun 10am–2pm; rest of the year Mon–Fri 8.30am–1pm & 3–6pm; ☎ 42/223272).

Train At the time of writing, train services to Santiago were not running to Chillán but work was being done to restore the line. The station is at Av. Brasil s/n (☎ 42/222267).

Accommodation

Hostal Canadá Av. Libertad 269 ☎ 42/234515. A welcoming hostess presides over spotless rooms with cable TV. Rooms CH$14,000.

Residencial 18 18 de Sept 213 ☎ 42/221102. Family-run hotel with friendly owners offering slightly tatty but clean rooms with a simple breakfast included. CH$12,000.

Eating

Arcoiris Roble 525. Excellent vegetarian specializing in delicious juices, crêpes and salads. Veggie burger CH$2500.

Mercado Municipal bordered by Roble, Riquelme, Prat and 5 de Abril. Inexpensive, traditional Chilean dishes, such as *pastel de choclo* and *completos*, are served at the multitude of *cocinerías* here.

Moving on

Bus Concepción (8 daily; 1hr 30min); Curicó (every 30min; 2hr); Santiago (every 50min; 6hr); Talca (8 daily; 3hr).

Train At the time of writing, trains were not running from Chillán. Normally, services would run to Santiago (6 daily; 4hr 30min) and Talca (6 daily; 2hr 20min).

AROUND CHILLÁN

One of the biggest attractions of the area is the hot springs resort of **Termas**

de Chillán (☏ 2/557-8112, ⊛ www
.termaschillan.cl), which with 29 runs,
most of intermediate level, becomes a
bona fide **ski resort** in the winter. There
is also ample off-piste terrain, ideal for
snowboarders, who are not allowed on
some of the resort's runs. During the
summer, in the valley overlooked by
the looming **Volcán Chillán** (3212m),
hiking, horseriding and downhill
biking are all popular activities.

Arrival

Bus Regular Rem Bus (☏ 42/229377) services
go to nearby Valle Las Trancas between 7.50am
and 7.20pm from Chillán's rural bus terminal in
high season (May–Sept); the last bus departs Las
Trancas at 5.30pm.

Accommodation and eating

The majority of holidaymakers stay at the cheaper
lodgings in Valle Las Trancas, which offers a
scattering of *hospedajes*, campsites and restaurants, surrounded by immense mountains.
Chill'In Km 72.1, Valle Las Trancas ☏ 42/247-075.
Brand-new place with its own pizzeria, attractive
dorms and Skype-equipped free internet. Dorms
CH$8000.
HI Las Trancas Km 73.5, Valle Las Trancas
☏ 42/243-211, ✉ hilastrancas@hostelling.cl.
Cosy dorms and on-site bar popular with younger
travellers. Dorms CH$8000.

CONCEPCIÓN

CONCEPCIÓN is Chile's second-
largest city, a bustling sprawl some
112km southwest of Chillán. It has little
in the way of tourist sights, though its
huge student population ensures a high
concentration of lively bars. Founded
in 1550, the city was the administrative
and military capital of colonial Chile. It
suffered considerable structural damage
in the huge 2010 earthquake.

What to see and do

The heart of Concepción's walkable city
centre, lined with a mixture of elegant
old buildings and modern concrete
blocks, is the carefully landscaped
Plaza de la Independencia. Partially
pedestrianized Barros Arana, the
main thoroughfare, has shops and
places to eat, while at the western end
lies the lively **Barrio Estación**, whose
trendy bars and restaurants are centred
around **Plaza España**, across Calle Prat
from the new **train station**. A four-
block walk south from the Plaza de
la Independencia along Aníbal Pinto
brings you to the long green stretch of
Parque Ecuador.

Galería de la Historia

Three blocks west of the Parque
Ecuador, at the corner of Lamas and
Lincoyán, is the **Galería de la Historia**
(Mon 3–6pm, Tues–Fri 10am–1.30pm
& 3–6.30pm, Sat & Sun 3–7pm; free),
which showcases the region's turbulent
history through a series of interactive
dioramas, with voice-overs dramatizing
the scenes. There's also a large collection
of ornate silver maté gourds.

Casa del Arte

Three blocks south of the Plaza de la
Independencia, you can catch a *colectivo*
eastwards to the **Casa del Arte** (Tues–
Fri 10am–6pm, Sat 11am–5pm, Sun
11am–2pm; free), on the corner of Plaza
Perú. This museum displays a modest
collection of Chilean art and hosts capti-
vating modern art exhibitions in its
basement, but its highlight is the giant
mural, *La Presencia de América Latina*,
by Mexican muralist Jorge Gonzáles
Camarena. Latin America – its conquest,
its cultural and agricultural wealth – is
captured in a series of densely packed
images oriented around the main figure
of an *indígena* (a native woman). Inter-
woven throughout are colourful ribbons
representing every Latin American flag
and numerous national symbols.

Arrival and information

Air Aeropuerto Internacional Carriel Sur
(☏ 412/732000) is 5km northwest of downtown;

a door-to-door airport transfer service is available (CH\$5000; ☎412/239-371).

Bus Most long-distance buses arrive at the Terminal de Buses Collao, Tegualda 860 (☎412/749000), from where numerous local buses run downtown.

Tourist information The Sernatur office is at Aníbal Pinto 460 (Mon–Fri 8.30am–1pm & 3–6pm; ☎412/741-337, ✪www.descubrebiobio .cl) and has plenty of information on the region surrounding Concepción. Conaf has an office at Barros Arano 215.

Train Estación Concepción (☎412/227-777) is located across Prat from Barros Arana. Fast commuter trains run to nearby Talcahuano, Hualqui and Lomas Coloradas.

Accommodation

Apart Hotel Don Matías Colo Colo 155 ☎412/256-846, ✪www.aparthoteldonmatias.cl /inicio.html. An attractive B&B with friendly service, large rooms, some with private bathrooms, and a good breakfast. CH\$32,000.

Hostal San Martín San Martín 949 ☎412/981-282, ✪www.hostalsanmartin.net. Smart and slightly sterile hotel with professional service, spacious rooms and breakfast included. CH\$30,000.

Residencial O'Higgins O'Higgins 115, 2nd floor ☎412/221-086. Centrally located guesthouse with basic but clean rooms. Dorms CH\$6000.

Eating, drinking and nightlife

Hiper Lider, Prat/Freire, is a massive supermarket with an excellent selection of fresh produce, as well as rare Thai and Chinese cooking ingredients.

Barrabirra Plaza España. To catch the latest match and knock back a beer, try this popular bar with nightly drink specials and pizza. Beers CH\$1500.

Mercado Central Rengo, between Maipú and Freire. The informal *cocinerías* here are a good spot for inexpensive Chilean standards, such as *cazuela* (CH\$3000).

Olivo Cervantes 482. Tasty dishes including flavoursome veggie curries are a bargain price, with a superb lunch menu choice (CH\$3750).

Il Padrino Barros Arana/Plaza España. Bustling Italian restaurant and bar, serving generous portions of pasta and pizza. Closed Sun. Mains CH\$6000–8000.

La Suite Barros Arana/ Serrano. Cafe/restaurant with *tablas*, beers and live music, offering *chorrillanas* (a huge portion of chips, covered with sausagemeat and fried onions).

Directory

Banks and exchange There are numerous banks with ATMs on Barros Arana and O'Higgins; Afex, at Barros Arana 565, Local 7, changes foreign currencies.

Hospital Hospital Regional is at San Martín and Av. Roosevelt (☎412/237445).

Internet access There are several internet cafés around Concepción's centre; Fonossa Internet, at the corner of Freire and Lincoyán, has broadband and Skype-enabled computers.

Laundry Try Limposco y Lavenderia, Colo Colo 148.

Pharmacy Numerous pharmacies can be found along Barros Arana.

Post office O'Higgins 799.

Telephone centres Entel, Barros Arana 541, Local 2, is the best phone centre.

Moving on

Air Puerto Montt and Temuca (several weekly flights) and Santiago (3–4 daily) with LAN (☎412/248-824) and Sky Airline (☎412/218941).

Bus Angol (6–8 daily; 2hr); Chillán (every 50min; 1hr 30min); Los Ángeles (hourly; 1hr 30min); Santiago (every 30min; 7hr); Talca (6–8 daily; 4hr).

PARQUE NACIONAL NAHUELBUTA

High in the Cordillera de Nahuelbuta, 35 kilometres west of the frontier town of Angol, lies the remote **Parque Nacional Nahuelbuta** (daily Jan–Feb 8.30am–8pm; March–Dec 8.30am–6pm; CH\$4000). The park is 1600m at its highest point and benefits from coastal rainfall, creating a **rare ecosystem** that sustains both *coigüe* and *lenga* trees, common to temperate coastal areas, and the araucaria trees of the mountains. The area is a haven for **diverse wildlife**, including *pudú* (pygmy deer), Chilote fox and puma, not to mention many species of birds.

From the park administration at Pehuenco, 5km from the park entrance, a dirt trail snakes its way through monkey puzzle trees to the 1379m pinnacle of **Piedra de Aguila**, presenting awesome panoramic views of the distant volcanoes to the north and the endless blue of the Pacific to the west. From the *Refugio Coimallín*, 3km north of the park administration, a shorter trail leads up to the *mirador* **Cerro Anay**, at the top of a 1450m peak, which offers similarly impressive views of the park and the wilderness beyond. Best time to visit is from October to April, when there is less rainfall.

Arrival and information

Bus To access the park, you'll need to reach the Angol first. Daily buses go from Angol's Terminal Rural, Ilabaca 422 (☎45/712-021) to Vegas Blancas, a village 7km from Portones at the park's eastern boundary, and in Jan and Feb Buses Angol have a Sunday return service to Pehuenco. In Angol, Terminal Rodoviario, Oscar Bonilla 428 (☎45/711854) serves long-distance destinations; Terminal Rural (☎45/712021), at Ilabaca 422, serves local destinations.

Conaf There are five Conaf *guarderías* (ranger stations) in the park, at Portones (where the entrance fee is paid; ☎02/196-0245), Pehuenco, Coimallin, Pichinahuel and Cotico. In Angol, the office is at Prat 191, 2nd floor (☎45/711-870), and has up-to-date information on the park.

Accommodation

Camping You can camp in relative isolation, either by the park administration at Pehuenco, where there are eleven pitches with picnic tables, fire pits, showers, and rustic toilets (CH$12,000/pitch for up to six people; ☎2/196-0244 ext 245), or at a smaller campsite by Coimallín's Centro de Información Ambiental; you'll need to bring all your food and supplies with you.

The Lake District

One of the last parts of Chile to be colonized by Europeans, thanks to fierce resistance by the Mapuche, **THE LAKE DISTRICT** stretches south from the end of the Río Biobío as far as the large port of **Puerto Montt**, just before the land breaks up into a mass of fjords. While not as challenging as Patagonia, the area's multitude of snow-capped **volcanoes**, sparkling **lakes**, mighty rivers and acres of thick **forest** make it a vastly rewarding place to explore and experience the wilderness, attracting thousands of outdoor enthusiasts every year. And after you've hiked, kayaked, climbed and rafted yourself to a state of exhaustion, you can soak your weary bones in the numerous **hot springs** here, sipping Kunstmann, Chile's best beer, brewed in Valdivia.

TEMUCO

TEMUCO, a busy market city, was founded in 1881, towards the end of the "pacification" of the Mapuche, the indigenous minority who are still very much present in the area. You may well have to change buses here, but there's little of interest in the city itself, besides the lively and extensive **market** that stretches four blocks near the eastern end of Avenida Balmaceda. Fresh produce sold here includes *piñones*, the

> **TREAT YOURSELF**
>
> An excellent place to stay in the area, to such an extent that it's become a destination in itself, is the wonderful *La Suizandina* (☎45/197-3725, ⓦwww.suizandina.com; camping CH$6000, rooms CH$41,000). The multilingual and knowledgeable owners can organize horseback excursions and hiking trips into the Reserva Nacional Malalcahuello, and provide detailed information on the best mountain-biking routes and hot springs in the area. The rooms are plush, warm and spacious, while the hearty portions of imaginative food rival cuisine served in Chile's better restaurants. Take any Lonquimay- or Malalcahuello-bound bus from Temuco and get off at the roadside bus stop at Km 83, just in front of the hostel.

pointed nuts of the araucaria tree, once the principal staple of the Mapuche diet. The **Mercado Municipal** (daily 8am–6pm), at the corner of Aldunate and Rodríguez, also stocks a wide array of Mapuche **crafts**, ranging in quality from tacky to exquisite.

PARQUE NACIONAL CONGUILLÍO

A vast expanse of old lava fields, extending from the very active Llaima volcano, pristine lakes and araucaria forest, the **PARQUE NACIONAL CONGUILLÍO** (entry CH$4000) is all the more rewarding because of the difficulty of access by pitted dirt road. If you make it that far, you're rewarded with a variety of hiking trails, ranging from short day-hikes to wilderness expeditions of several days. From Laguna Captrén, take the eight-kilometre Los Carpinteros trail that winds its way through primary forest; halfway along, you'll come across Araucaria Madre – an impressive giant tree that's nearly 2000 years old. Another good day hike is the 10-kilometre Sierra Nevada, which leads you along the shores of Lago Conguillío through different types of local vegetation and allows you to appreciate fine views of nearby glaciers and of the volcano.

In terms of **accommodation**, you can pitch your tent at Laguna Conguillío or at Laguna Captrén (CH$10,000 per tent space for up to 6 people; open Nov–March) and it's also possible to stay in the cabañas and ecolodge run by the La Baita ecotourism project in the southern pasrt of the park (☎045/416-410, ✪www .labaitaconguillio.cl; CH$35,000); meals are available during high season. To **get to the park**, it's best to rent a 4x4, but failing that, you can take Nar Bus from Temuco to Melipeuco (several daily; 2hr), where in high season, the tourist office can help arrange transport to the southern entrance of the park.

Out of season, your only option is to rent a car. To reach the northern entrance at Laguna Captrén, take Buses Flota Erbuc from Temuco's rural bus terminal to Curacautín (several daily; 1hr 30min), from where a shuttle runs to the *guardería* (ranger station) at Captrén (Dec—Feb, Mon & Fri only at 6am and 5pm). You can pick up maps of the park at the Conaf-run Centro de Información Ambiental (✪www .parquenacionalconguillio.cl) by Lago Conguillío.

VILLARRICA

VILLARRICA, 87km southeast of Temuco, is one of Chile's oldest towns, although it may not feel like it – it has been destroyed several times by volcanic eruptions and skirmishes with the Mapuche. While the town has traditionally attracted wealthy Chilean holidaymakers with its beautiful lakeside views of the Volcán Villarrica, foreign visitors are now coming in greater numbers, drawn by the slower pace of life here than in nearby Pucón (see p.473). Next door to the tourist office, the **Fería Artesanal** is considered to be the best Mapuche craft market in the region. Here you can view a *ruka* – a traditional dwelling with walls and roof tightly woven from reeds. The **Museo Histórico y Archeológico** (Mon–Sat 9am–1pm & 3.30–7pm, CH$200), next to the market, showcases Mapuche artefacts, including wooden masks and musical instruments.

Arrival and information

Bus A block south of Avenida Pedro de Valdivia, several bus terminals face each other across Anfion Muñoz, a couple of blocks from the centre of town.
Tourist information The helpful tourist office, at Avenida Pedro de Valdivia 1070 (Mon–Fri 8.30am–1pm & 2.30–6pm; Sat & Sun 9am–1pm & 3.30–5.30pm; ☎45/206-619, ✉turismo @villarica.org), has attentive staff who offer maps of the town and brochures on various attractions and accommodation.

Accommodation, eating and drinking

La Cava de Roble Letelier 658. If you're after meat and more meat, look no further. Not only are the steaks excellent, but you'll also find imaginative game dishes, though the pleasure does not come cheap. Mains CH$6500–10,500.

Hostal Don Juan Körner 770 ☎45/411-833, ⓦwww.hostaldonjuan.cl. Boasting great views of Volcán Villarica, this cosy hostel has an assortment of rooms and cabañas, plus table tennis and table football for the guests. CH$22,000.

La Torre Suiza Bilbao 969 ☎45/411-213, ⓦwww .torresuiza.com. The Swiss owners here welcome you into their wood-panelled haven for outdoor lovers, particularly cyclists. There's a book exchange, kitchen privileges, bike rental, good breakfast and tons of helpful advice. Dorms CH$8000, rooms CH$16,000.

The Travellers Letelier 753. A top spot for coffee or meals of any description – the eclectic menu features dishes from all over the world, from Mexican burritos to Thai curry. Mains CH$6500.

Moving on

Bus: Tur Bus and Pullman serve all major Middle Chile destinations on the way to Santiago. Buses JAC serve Lake District destinations, while Igi Llaima and Buses San Martín cross the border to San Martín de Los Andes and Bariloche, with connections to other Argentine destinations. Bariloche (daily; 5hr); Osorno (4–5 daily; 3hr 30min); Pucón (every 30min; 45min); Puerto Montt (4–5 daily; 5hr); Santiago (3–4 daily; 12hr); San Martín de Los Andes (daily; 6hr); Temuco (6–7 daily; 1hr 30min); Valdivia (3–4 daily; 2hr 30min).

PUCÓN

On a clear day, you will be greeted by the awe-inspiring sight of the **Volcán Villarrica** smouldering in the distance long before the bus pulls into **PUCÓN**, 25km east of Villarrica. This small mountain town, awash with the smells of wood smoke and grilled meat, has firmly established itself as a top backpacker destination in the last decade. Each November–April season brings scores of fresh-air fantatics looking to climb the volcano, brave the **rapids** on the Río Trancura and Río Liucura or explore the nearby Parque Nacional Huerquehue. A day outdoors is usually followed by eating, drinking and partying in the town's restaurants and bars, or by a soak in the nearby **thermal springs**.

Pucón's wide, tree-lined streets are arranged in a compact grid, and most tour companies, supermarkets, banks and bars are located along bustling **Avenida O'Higgins**, which bisects the town. O'Higgins ends by **La Poza**, a black-sand beach on the dazzling blue Lago Villarica. If you follow Calle Lincoyán to its northern end, you will reach **Playa Grande**, with a multitude of pedalos, jet-skis and rowing boats for hire.

What to see and do

VOLCÁN VILLARRICA is undoubtedly Pucón's biggest attraction; in the winter it becomes a **ski and snowboard** destination for the daring. To do the climb, unless you have mountaineering experience, you have to go with a **guide**; they will provide all the necessary equipment. It's a fairly challenging five-hour ascent, starting at the chairlift at the base of the volcano, with much of the walking done on snow. If the chairlift (CH$5000) is running, it cuts an hour off the climb. At the top, by the lip of the smoking crater, you'll be rewarded with unparalleled views across

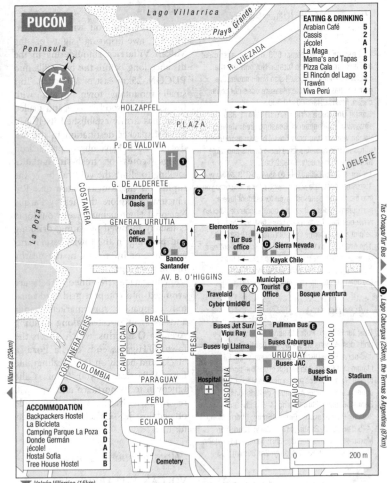

PUCÓN

Lago Villarrica

Playa Grande

R. QUEZADA

Peninsula

N

HOLZAPFEL

PLAZA

P. DE VALDIVIA

J.DELESTE

G. DE ALDERETE ❶

Lavandería Oasis ❷

COSTANERA

La Poza

GENERAL URRUTIA

Elementos

Conaf Office ❹

Tur Bus office

Aguaventura ❸

Sierra Nevada Ⓒ

❻ ❺

Banco Santander

Kayak Chile

AV. B. O'HIGGINS

Municipal Tourist Office ❽

❼ Travelaid @Ⓘ

Cyber Umid@d

Bosque Aventura

BRASIL

Ⓘ

CAUPOLICAN

LINCOYAN

FRESIA

PALGUIN

Buses Jet Sur/ Vipu Ray

Buses Igi Llaima

Pullman Bus Ⓔ

Buses Caburgua

COLO-COLO

URUGUAY

Buses JAC

Buses San Martin

Stadium

COSTANERA GEISS

COLOMBIA

PARAGUAY

Hospital

ANSORENA

ARAUCO

PERU

ECUADOR

Cemetery

0   200 m

EATING & DRINKING
Arabian Café 5
Cassis 2
¡ecole! .... A
La Maga 1
Mama's and Tapas 8
Pizza Cala 6
El Rincón del Lago 3
Trawén 7
Viva Perú 4

ACCOMMODATION
Backpackers Hostel .... F
La Bicicleta C
Camping Parque La Poza .... G
Donde Germán .... D
¡ecole! .... A
Hostal Sofia .... E
Tree House Hostel .... B

Villarrica (25km)

Tas Choapa/Tur Bus

0, Lago Caburgua (25km); the Termas & Argentina (87km)

▼ Volcán Villarrica (15km)

the Lake District, with Lago Villarrica, Lago Caburgua and distant volcanoes stretching out before you. The sulphuric fumes mean you cannot linger long over the spectacle though. Check the **weather forecast** before embarking on the climb, as many tour companies take groups out even in cloudy weather, only to turn back halfway.

Arrival and information

Bus Buses from destinations around Chile and from the Argentinian Lake District stop at various terminals, all within three blocks or so of the centre of town.

Tourist office The Oficina de Turismo Municipal is on the corner of O'Higgins and Palguín (March–Nov daily 8.30am–7pm; Dec–Feb daily 8.30am–10pm; ℡ 45/293-002, ⊛ www.pucononline.cl). The helpful staff speak some English and dish out a plethora of brochures on local attractions.

Travelaid Ansorena 425, Local 4 (Mon–Sat 10am–2pm & 3.30–7pm; ℡ 45/444-040, ⊛ www .travelaid.cl). Knowledgeable Swiss-run travel agency that sells guidebooks and maps of Chile, and can help you book passage on the Navimag tour boat (see box, p.487). English and German spoken.

Accommodation

Backpackers Hostel Palguín 695 ☎ 45/441-417, ⑩ www.backpackerspucon.com. This friendly, efficiently run hostel has clean (though somewhat dark) dorms and private rooms, as well as an on-site laundry service and free internet in the homely lounge. Their own tour company offers a variety of excursions, including canopy tours, white-water rafting and volcano climbs. Breakfast included. Dorms CH$7500, rooms CH$16,000.

La Bicicleta Palguín 361 ☎ 45/444-583, ⓔ labicicletapucon@gmail.com. The owners go out of their way to make you feel welcome at this family-run hostel right in the centre of town. You can organize all your tours, dine at the on-site cafe and use the free internet; the only downsides are the queues to the shared bathrooms and the noise at times. Dorms CH$8000.

Camping Parque La Poza Costanera Roberto Geis 769 ☎ 45/444-982. Large, shaded campsite near the lake with hot showers, a well-equipped cooking hut/dining area, and a picnic table per camping site. Popular with overland expeditions, cycling tourists and backpackers. CH$3,500 per person.

Donde Germán Las Rosas 590 ☎ 45/442-444, ⑩ www.dondegerman.cl. Excellent beds in cosy rooms with rustic wooden decor, a fully equipped kitchen, an inviting common area with satellite TV and an in-house tour agency are just some of perks at this welcoming guesthouse. Walk four blocks south of the centre until you see people relaxing on the outdoor terrace and by the pool. CH$25,000.

¡école! Urrutia 592 ☎ 45/441-675, ⑩ www .ecole.cl. Very popular guesthouse with an excellent restaurant and spotless small rooms and dorms. The knowledgeable owners organize trips to the nearby Santuario Cañi, as part of the conservation project they are involved in. Dorms

---

OUTDOOR ACTIVITIES AND TOUR OPERATORS

The nearby **Río Trancura** offers a popular Class III run on the lower part of the river, with the more challenging Class VI, upper Trancura run made up almost entirely of drop pools; some operators allow you to combine the two. The loop to **Ojos del Caburgua** makes an excellent day-trip for **bikers**; follow the paved road out of town towards Caburgua, cross the bridge over the Río Liucura, then take a left turn along the dirt road by the "El Cristo" cross, 18km away. The signposted dirt trail winds along the Río Liucura, past the azure Ojos de Caburgua pool, fed by several small waterfalls (entry CH$1500), before emerging at the Pasarela Quelhue (hanging bridge) 8km later, and just 2km from the paved road back to Pucón.

Since the activities on offer involve an element of risk, it is important to use a reliable operator like those listed below. We don't recommend Trancura, the largest agency, due to its poor safety record.

Aguaventura Palguín 336 ☎ 45/444246, ⑩ www.aguaventura.com. Established French outfit specializing in rafting trips, canyoning and watersports (eg hydrospeed for CH$40,000), as well as winter activities.

Antilco ☎ 9/713-9758, ⑩ www.antilco.com. 15km out of town. This operator is recommended for horse treks in the valleys around Pucón with bilingual guides. Half-day CH$22,000; two days' riding with barbecue CH$80,000.

Bosque Aventura Arauca at O'Higgins ☎ 45/444-030, ⑩ www.canopypucon.cl. The most reliable operator for zip-lining tours, with an emphasis on safety. Whiz around one of seven circuits, including the largest one in South America. Canopy tour with transfer CH$40,000.

Elementos Ansorena 340 ☎ 45/441-750, ⓔ info@elementos-chile.com. This new, friendly, German-run operator offers tours with

an emphasis on small group size and safety, offering mini-volcano trekking as well as the standard volcano tour and half- and full-day rafting. Volcano tour CH$50,000.

Kayak Chile O'Higgins 524 ☎ 45/441-584, ⑩ www.kayakchile.net. Established American-run outfit specializing in kayaking trips on the Río Liucura. Learn the Eskimo roll in Lago Villarica (CH$35,000 half-day/CH$55,000 full day), take to the Class III rapids in a double kayak with a guide (CH$45,000) or run the river in a ducky (CH$20,000).

Paredon Andes Expeditions ☎ 45/444-663, ⑩ www.paredonexpeditions.com. A small team of expert trekking and mountaineering guides lead small group ascents up Volcán Villarrica and other Lake District volcanoes, and also offer tailor-made excursions around Chile. English and French spoken. Volcano ascent CH$45,000.

CH$6000/8000 (with/without own sleeping bag); rooms CH$26,000; 19 percent discount if you pay with US dollars.

Hostal Sofia Brasil 625 ☎ 45/443-567, Ⓔ hostal sofiapucon@gmail.com. Staying here is like staying with your favourite Chilean aunt: Janette fusses over you and goes out of her way to make you feel welcome. The four rooms and the dorm are bright and decorated with homely touches, though if you go for a room with shared bathroom, go for the one with a window. Wi-fi and fully equipped kitchen available as well as discounts for longer stays. Dorms CH$8,000, rooms CH$18,000.

🏃 **Tree House Hostel** Urrutia 660 ☎ 45/444-679, Ⓦ www.treehousechile.cl. Run by two knowledgeable, bilingual Journey Latin America guides, this chilled-out hostel is the place to organize all manner of outdoor activities, particularly the volcano ascent, and get a good night's sleep on the orthopaedic beds. Relax in the garden hammocks with Kia and Cortito, the resident dogs, or join in an impromptu barbecue. Dorms CH$9000, rooms CH$29,000.

Eating and drinking

Arabian Café Fresia 354. For those who've eaten their fill of Chilean staples, this authentic Middle Eastern restaurant offers falafel, hummus, tasty stuffed vegetables and nicely grilled kebabs. Stuffed aubergines CH$5000.

Cassis Fresia at Alderete. This trendy cafe is often full; the clientele come not just for the free wi-fi, but also for the filling multigrain sandwiches and the impressive array of desserts. Try the Crêpe Cassis – a pancake you'll have to excavate from under a caramel brownie piled high with chocolate and *dulce de leche* ice cream. Desserts CH$3500.

🏃 **¡école!** Urrutia 592. Established vegetarian restaurant serving consistently superb, hearty dishes made from local organic produce, accompanied by home-made multigrain bread. Try the sublime vegetable lasagne, or the yellow Thai vegetable curry with quinoa. Mains CH$4500.

La Maga Fresia 125. Sate all your carnivorous cravings here. While not the cheapest, this Uruguayan steakhouse really delivers when it comes to expertly cooked *bife de chorizo*, and the service is excellent. Steak from CH$10,000.

Mama's and Tapas Av. O'Higgins 587. A well-established watering hole that consistently entices a large clientele nightly with their excellent selection of beers (from CH$1200), nightly drinks specials and not-half-bad Mexican food.

Pizza Cala Lincoyán 361. Hands down the best pizzeria in town, specializing in sizeable portions of thin-crust pizza with imaginative toppings, baked in a wood-fired oven. Relaxed ambience and good music to boot. Small pizza CH$4800; large pizza CH$8500.

El Rincón del Lago Urrutia 657. Fill up on ample portions of hearty Chilean specialities in the spacious, airy interior or out on the patio. The grilled trout and the *lomo* are particularly good. Mains CH$5000.

🏃 **Trawén** O'Higgins 311. One of the friendliest places in town, this offbeat café tantalizes your taste buds with inexpensive and imaginative dishes such as Antarctic krill ravioli with shitake mushroom sauce, excellent wholewheat *empanadas* and large fresh fruit juices. Mains CH$4800; juices CH$1500.

Viva Perú Lincoyán 372. Bringing a welcome touch of spice to Pucón's culinary cornucopia, this restaurant is the place to come for such Peruvian staples as *ají de gallina*, *yuquitos* (fried cassava) and *ceviche* – served Peruvian-style with *ají rocoto*, corn and sweet potato. Mains CH$7000.

Directory

Banks and exchange There are several banks with ATMs and money exchange places along Av. O'Higgins, towards the end closest to the lake. The best exchange rate for US dollars and Euros is inside Supermercado Eltit.

Bike rental Sierra Nevada on O'Higgins 524a (☎ 45/444-210) rents mountain bikes in good condition. Full day (9am–8pm) CH$7000; 5hr CH$5000.

Hospital Hospital San Francisco, Uruguay 325 (☎ 45/441-177).

Internet Cyber Unid@d on Av. O'Higgins 415 has fast and reliable connections (CH$700/hr).

Laundry Lavandería Oasis on Lincoyán 272 (Mon–Sat 10am–1.30pm & 4–7pm); CH$3900 for 1–3 kilos. There's an excellent bakery attached.

Post office Fresia 183 (Mon–Fri 9am–1pm & 3–5pm; Sat 9am–1pm).

Moving on

Air There are twice-weekly flights to Pucón with both LAN and Sky Airlines between December and February.

Bus The three main long-distance carriers have separate terminals: Buses JAC, Palguín 505 (☎ 45/990-880); Pullman Bus, Palguín 555 (☎ 45/443-331); Tur Bus, O'Higgins 910 (☎ 45/443-328). Smaller carriers such as Igi Llaima and Buses San Martín have services to Argentina and are within a couple of blocks of the main bus terminals; Buses Caburgua serves Parque Nacional Huerquehue.

Buses JAC to: Puerto Montt (4 daily; 5hr 30min); Puerto Varas (4 daily; 5hr); Temuco (every 20min; 1hr); Valdivia (6 daily; 3hr); Villarica (every 20min; 45min). Buses Vipu Ray to: Curarrehue (every 30min; 45min). Buses San Martín to: San Martín de Los Andes (Tue–Sun 10.35am; 5hr). Igi Llaima to: San Martín de Los Andes (daily at 9.45am; 5hr). Pullman Bus to: Santiago (2 nightly at 9pm and 9.30pm; 11hr). Tas Choapa to: Bariloche (every other day at 8.30am; 10hr). Tur Bus to: Santiago (9 daily; 11hr).

PARQUE NACIONAL HUERQUEHUE

Though small compared to neighbouring national parks, the lovely 125-square-kilometre **PARQUE NACIONAL HUERQUEHUE** (daily 8.30am–6pm; CH$4000) comprises densely forested **precordillera** (foothills), highland araucaria groves, several waterfalls and many beautiful **lakes**, making it an excellent destination for day-hikes.

The largest of the lakes – Chico, Toro and Verde – are accessed via the popular **Sendero Los Lagos** trail, which climbs to a height of 1300m, past two waterfalls (9km, 3hr one-way). From there, you can take in the tiny Lago de los Patos and Lago Huerquehue (2hr) before rejoining the Los Lagos loop, or you can continue along the **Sendero Los Huerquenes** to Termas de San Sebastián via a basic camping site (CH$10,000 per site; pay Conaf at the park entrance) and the stunning Renahue viewpoint overlooking the lakes below. It's possible to hike to the Termas in one day (23km, 8–9hr), since much of the **Sendero Los Huerquenes** is downhill, and you can either stay at the excellent Cabañas San Sebastián (☎045/341961, cabañas from CH$35,000), or arrange a ride out to the nearest town of Renahue (CH$20,000) from where you can catch a bus back to Pucón.

About 30km northeast of Pucón, Huerquehue is easily reached by public transport (CH$3400 return). During peak season, Buses Caburgua runs there four times daily (8.30am–7pm); less frequently out of season. At the Conaf *guardería* at the entrance, you'll find a trail map; all the trails are clearly signposted. You can either camp at the Conaf-run campsite (CH$10,000 per site) or try the excellent *Refugio Tinquilco* (☎9/539-2728, ⓦwww .tinquilco.cl), an airy wooden guesthouse in a beautiful streamside location (bunks CH$10,000, rooms CH$22,900) with home-cooked meals, a sauna and even a book exchange.

CURARREHUE

This small Mapuche settlement 40km east of Pucón, the last stop before the Argentine border, feels like a frontier town, with its *huasos* (Chilean cowboys) riding by, clad in traditional ponchos and hats. Those interested in **Mapuche culture** will want to stop by the Aldea Intercultural Trawupeyüm (Mon–Sun 10am–8pm; CH$1000), the museum found behind the bright green Municipalidad buildings on the plaza. An enthusiastic guide is on hand to talk you through the exhibits and, if you're lucky, you may find Mapuche chef Anita Epulef in residence. Buses Vipu Ray runs from Pucón to Curarrehue every thirty minutes.

VALDIVIA

VALDIVIA is an energetic university city of German influence that lies at the confluence of the Río Valdivia and Río Calle Calle, 145km southwest of Pucón. Founded in 1552 by Pedro de Valdivia, it is one of Chile's oldest cities. Valdivia was razed to the ground by the Mapuche in the sixteenth century and largely destroyed by the devastating earthquake of 1960, which accounts for the hotchpotch of buildings from every era and architectural style here.

The best time to visit is during the **Verano de Valdivia** – several weeks of

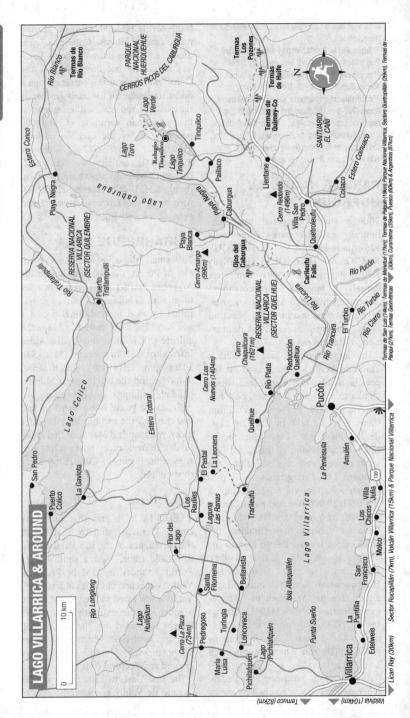

LAGO VILLARRICA & AROUND

0   10 km

Río Blanco

Termas de Río Blanco

PARQUE NACIONAL HUEROUEHUE

CERROS PICOS DEL CABURGUA

Estero Cunco

Lago Verde

Termas Los Pozones

Termas de Huife

Tinquilco

Tinquilco

Refugio Tinquilco

Lago Toro

Lago Tinquilco

Paillaco

Termas de Quimey-Co

Playa Negra

RESERVA NACIONAL VILLARICA (SECTOR QUILEMBE)

Caburgua

Llentane

SANTUARIO EL CANI

Estero Coinuaco

Coilaco

Cerro Redondo (1496m)

Villa San Pedro

Quetroleufu

Río Trafampulli

Puerto Trafampulli

Playa Blanca

Piedra Negra

Ojos del Caburgua

Cerro Amargo (996m)

RESERVA NACIONAL VILLARICA (SECTOR QUELHUE)

Carileufu Falls

Río Liucura

Río Pucón

Termas de San Luis (14km); Termas de Menetué (17km); Termas de Palguin (19km); Parque Nacional Villarica, Sectors Quetrupillán (26km); Termas de Parqui (27km); Termas Geométricas (30km); Curarrehue (35km); Parque Nacional Villarica, Sectors Quetrupillán (26km); Puesco (60km) & Argentina (87km)

Estero Totoral

Cerro Chaguilcura (1621m)

Reducción Quelhue

Río Trancura

El Turbio

Río Turbio

Río Claro

Lago Colico

Cerro Los Nuevos (1404m)

Cerro Plata

Pucón

San Pedro

Puerto Colico

La Gaviota

El Pastal

La Leonera

Quelhue

La Península

Amulén

Río Longong

Flor del Lago

Los Raulíes

Laguna Las Ranas

Trarileufú

Edelweis

Santa Filomena

Bellavista

Lago Villarrica

Isla Allaquilñen

La Puntilla

San Francisco

Molco

Los Chicos

Villa Julia

Lago Huilipilun

Cerro La Plaza (734m)

Pedregoso

Turíngia

Loncovaca

Pichilafquén

Lago Pichilafquén

Punta Sueño

199

Villarrica

María Luisa

Lican Ray (30km)

Sector Rucapillán (7km); Volcán Villarrica (15km) & Parque Nacional Villarrica

Valdivia (104km)

Temuco (82km)

festivities beginning in January, including a parade of decorated boats and floating candles down the Río Valdivia, and fireworks on the **Noche Valdiviana** on the third Saturday in February; be sure to book accommodation in advance. Otherwise the action in this lively town centres on its **waterfront**; you'll smell the fishy **Mercado Fluvial** and hear the noise before you reach it. A resident family of crafty sea lions compete with the clamouring seagulls and cormorants for fish scraps. The waterfront is also a departure point for several boats offering entertaining half-day cruises to the fort ruins (CH$8500–15,000) as well as nature excursions to the **Carlos Anwandter nature Sanctuary**, home to more than eighty species of water fowl, including the graceful black-necked swan.

What to see and do

In the mid-seventeenth century, the Spanish built elaborate fortifications at **Corral**, **Niebla** and **Isla Mancera**, where Río Valdivia and Río Tornagaleones meet the Pacific Ocean, to protect Valdivia from opportunistic attacks by the British, French and Dutch privateers. To get to them, take the Niebla-bound bus #20 from the corner of Carampanque and O'Higgins (25min) and get off at the little ferry port, from where frequent

boats ply their way to Isla Mancera and the ruins of the **Castillo San Pedro de Alcántara** (daily 10am–7pm; CH$600). You can also take a ferry ($700) to **Castillo San Sebastián de la Cruz** (daily 10am–6.30pm; CH$600), constructed in 1645 and reinforced in 1764; it's the most intact of all the forts, and a short walk from the pier in Corral. The ferry trips give you plenty of opportunity to enjoy the views of the brightly coloured houses clustered along the green hillsides. To reach **Fuerte Niebla**, which comprises the original 1645 battlements and the **Museo de Sitio Fuerte Niebla** (Tues–Sun 10am–5.30pm), ask the bus driver to be drop you off further up the road through Niebla.

Arrival and information

Air Aeropuerto Pinchoy lies 32km northeast of the city; a Transfer Valdivia minibus (T 63/225-533) into town will set you back CH$3500.
Bus The main Terminal de Buses (T 63/212-188) is located at Anfión Muñoz 360, by Río Calle Calle.
Tourist informaton There is a helpful Sernatur office in its new temporary headquarters at Yerbas Buenas 181, 1st floor (Mon–Thurs 8.30am–5.30pm, Fri 8.30am–4.30pm; T 63/239-060, W www .valdiviachile.cl).

Accommodation

Airesbuenos Hostel García Reyes 550 T 63/222-202, W www.airesbuenos.cl. Well-run HI-affiliated

---

TOP THREE HOT SPRINGS IN THE LAKE DISTRICT

Termas Geométricas 16km east of Coñaripe towards Palguín T 9/7477-1708 or 2/214-1214 in Santiago, W www.termasgeometricas.cl. With a Japanese feel to the beautiful design, there are seventeen thermal geometrical pools here, connected by winding boardwalks around a ravine overflowing with greenery, as well as three cold plunge pools, two waterfalls, and an excellent café. Open Dec 21–Feb 28 10am–9pm; rest of the year 11am–7pm; CH$14,000.
Termas de Panqui 58km east of Pucón T 45/442-039, E panquihotsprings@hotmail .com. Unconventional hot springs offering three pools of varying temperature, as well as relaxing

mud baths, a vegetarian restaurant, a chance to join in full-moon celebrations, and camping spots and tepees to stay in (CH$6000; more with accommodation).
Termas Los Pozones 34km east of Pucón, past Termas de Huife T 9/197-2350. Probably the most-visited thermal baths near Pucón, especially on night tours, these consist of hot riverside pools at the end of a steep and sometimes muddy descent (bring a torch); there are wooden changing rooms above the pools from which you descend via a trapdoor (open 11am–6pm; day use CH$4000; night use CH$5000).

VALDIVIA

Río Calle Calle

Isla Teja

❷ & Niebla (20km) ◀

Río Valdivia

Plaza

Mercado Municipal

Mercado Fluvial

Scotia Bank

Banco de Chile

Catedral

PLAZA DE LA REPÚBLICA

LAN

Banco Santander

Plaza de Los Ríos

Supermarket: Unimark

Bus Terminal

Torreón de los Canelos

Iglesia de San Francisco

AV ALEMANIA

AV RAMÓN PICARTE

CHACABUCO

ARAUCO

BEAUCHEFF

LORD COCHRANE

ANÍBAL PINTO

RIQUELME

0   200 m

hostel, bustling with younger travellers, with bright, cheery dorms at their new central location, complete with internet, TV lounge and guest kitchen, as well as friendly staff on hand to help and advise. Dorms CH$8000, rooms CH$22,000.
Albergue Latino General Lagos 1036 ☎63/229-364, ⓦwww.alberguelatino.cl. Cheerful cheapie consisting of a large, rambling old house decorated with colourful murals, with resident Choripan the sausage dog. The staff are laidback, and you get to use the kitchen and the internet room. Dorms CH$7000 (CH$2000 reduction with own sleeping bag), rooms CH$20,000.
Hostal Borde Río Henríquez 746 ☎63/214-069, ⓦwww.valdiviacabanas.cl. Most of the colourful rooms have small sofas, the bathrooms are larger than in most hostels, and you can arrange kayaking trips here. CH$28,000.
Hostel Bosque Nativo Fresia 29 (off Janequeo) ☎63/433-782, ⓦwww.hostelnativo.cl. New hostel in a beautifully restored 1920s house with cosy rooms, kitchen, lounge and rooftop terrace. Profits

go towards the preservation of native Chilean forest and foreigners get discounted room prices. The staff couldn't be lovelier. Dorms CH$7500, rooms CH$20,000.
Hostal Totem Carlos Anwandter 425 ☎63/292-849, ⓦwww.turismototem.cl. Quiet guesthouse with clean, spacious, en-suite rooms. Cable TV, wi-fi and breakfast are included. CH$25,000.

Eating and drinking

Café Hausmann O'Higgins 394. Café harking back to Valdivia's German roots, with its specialities of *crudos* (steak tartare) on toast, excellent cakes and *apfelstrudel*. Crudos CH$1500.
La Calesa O'Higgins 160. Peruvian restaurant putting some spice in your life with its *ají de gallina* (spicy garlic chicken stew), and excellent *ceviche*. Mains CH$6000–9000. Closed Sun.
Cervecería Kunstmann 950 Ruta T-350. Come hungry, as this Bavarian beerhall-style restaurant-brewery serves monster portions

of meat, sauerkraut and potatoes to accompany its range of beers; try the honey-tinted Miel or the darker Torobayo, and finish off with tasty beer ice cream. Mains CH$7000–8500; beers CH$1500. To get here, take bus #20 or any *colectivo* bound for Niebla.

Clover Irish Pub Esmeralda 691. Popular with travellers and local students alike, this lively joint has nightly 2-for-1 happy hour drinks specials, and, of course, Guinness.

El Llegado Esmeralda 657. Busy bar featuring live jazz and acid jazz performances, as well as weekend soul nights. Music kicks off at 11.30pm nightly.

Mercado Municipal Prat s/n. Try the large servings of fish, razor clam or mussel dishes at these busy little eateries inside the market overlooking the river. Mains CH$4000.

La Última Frontera Pérez Rosales 787. Laidback café popular with bohemian types. It's decorated with local artwork and serves excellent sandwiches and tasty crêpes with a variety of fillings (including vegetarian options) late into the evenings; wash them down with fresh fruit juice or a Kunstmann beer. Crêpes CH$4000.

Moving on

Air Puerto Montt (weekly); Santiago (twice daily).
Bus Bariloche (2 daily at 8am; 7hr); Osorno (4–5 daily; 1hr 45min); Pucón (3–4 daily; 3hr); Puerto Montt (5–6 daily; 3hr 30min); Santiago (5–6 daily; 11hr); San Martín de Los Andes, Argentina (3 weekly in the morning; 8hr); Villarica (3–4 daily; 2hr 15min).

OSORNO

OSORNO is a bustling city 107km south of Valdivia whose main industries are agriculture and forestry; for travellers it's primarily a busy transport hub, acting as a gateway to the **Parque Nacional Puyehue** and Argentina's Lake District. The two bus terminals are within a block of each other, three blocks from the **Plaza de Armas**, the heart of the city. The helpful **Sernatur office** (Mon–Thurs 8.30am–1pm & 2.30–5.30pm, until 4.30pm on Fri; ☎64/237-575) is located at O'Higgins 667, on the ground floor of the Gobernación building at the west side of the plaza; they can advise on accommodation. **Conaf**, at Martínez de Rosas 430 (Mon–Thurs 9.30am–1pm

& 2.30–5.30pm, Fri 9.30am–1pm & 2.30–4:30pm; ☎64/234-393), provides basic information on the Parque Nacional Puyehue, as well as rudimentary maps of the park.

If you have to **stay** overnight, *Hostal Reyenco*, at Freire 309 (☎64/236-285, ⓔreyenco@surnet.cl; CH$16,000) is a good budget option, with friendly service, several clean rooms (mostly en-suites), breakfast in a cheery dining room and wi-fi, while *Hospedaje Sanchez*, at Los Carrera 1595 (☎64/422-140; CH$5000), is the rock-bottom option a couple of blocks from the bus station, run by a friendly old couple. Osorno's cuisine displays strong German influence; fill up on cheap and hearty portions of sausages, potatoes and sauerkraut at *Bavaria*, O'Higgins 743; their three-course weekday *menu del día* is a bargain at CH$4200. The cheapest eats are the hole-in-the-wall eateries in front of the **Mercado Municipal**, serving freshly baked *empanadas*; alternatively, try the market's busy *marisquerías* for fresh fish and seafood dishes (avoid the fried fish). The main **Terminal de Buses**, at Avenida Errázuriz 1400 (☎64/234149), has frequent daily services to destinations all over Chile, as well as Bariloche in Argentina, while the **Terminal de Buses Rurales**, behind the Mercado Municipal at Avenida Errázuriz 1300 (☎64/232073), serves local destinations.

Moving on

Bus Bariloche (2–3 daily; 5hr); Coyhaique (3 weekly; 26hr); Puerto Montt (5–6 daily; 1hr 30min); Punta Arenas (3 weekly; 33hr); Santiago (5–7 daily; 12hr); Valdivia (4–5 daily; 1hr 45min); Valparaíso (2–3 daily; 14hr).

LAGO LLANQUIHUE

Sixty-five kilometres south of Osorno, on the east side of the Panamericana highway, you are greeted with the dazzling sight of **LAGO**

LLANQUIHUE, the second-largest lake in Chile, its shimmering blue waters framed by thick forest, with the peaks of volcanoes visible in the distance. The lake draws local and foreign visitors alike to its appealing **beaches**, the best found in the German lakeside town of **Frutillar**. People also come for the ample natural attractions around the bustling little town of **Puerto Varas**, and to experience the laidback lifestyle of lakeside villages such as **Puerto Octay**, where the Swiss-Chilean-run *Hostal Zapato Amarillo* (☏64/210-787, ⊛www.zapatoamarillo.cl; dorms CH$9500, rooms CH$28,000) is a huge budget-traveller draw in itself, providing a welcoming place to stay amid stunning scenery. The owners can arrange Volcán Osorno climbs, visits to the nearby hot springs and hikes in the surrounding area; they also rent bikes and canoes.

PUERTO VARAS

PUERTO VARAS, on the southern shore of pristine Lago Llanquihue, is a popular backpacker haunt with unparalleled sunset views of the two nearby volcanoes, Osorno and Calbuco, and attractive Germanic colonial architecture. Rivalling Pucón in terms of nearby **outdoor attractions**, Puerto Varas does not feel too crowded despite its popularity, and makes an excellent base for volcano-climbing, white-water rafting, kayaking and cycling; it also serves as a popular stopover on the way to Patagonia. Though this charming little town is fairly spread out, most services, hostels and restaurants are located within a couple of blocks of the little Plaza de Armas.

Arrival and information

Air The nearest airport is at Puerto Montt, but you can book your flights with LAN at Av. Gramado 560 (☏65/234-799) or Sky Airline at San Bernardo 430 (☏65/231-039).

Bus Buses Norte International (with services to Bariloche, Argentina) and Cruz del Sur (serving Chiloé and the Lake District up to Santiago) share a bus station at San Francisco 1317 (☏65/236-969), a few blocks south of the centre. Pullman has its own downtown terminal at Portales 318 (☏65/237-255) with frequent services to Santiago. Tur Bus, Intersur, Buses JAC, Tas Choapa, Andersmar and Cóndor Bus all share the terminal at San Pedro 210 (☏65/234-163) and each has an office in the centre.

Tourist information The Casa del Turista is found at the foot of a pier, on Av. Costanera (Mon–Fri 9am–6.30pm, Sat & Sun 10am–7pm; ☏65/237-956, ⊛www.puertovaras.org); helpful staff provide maps of town and a plethora of leaflets.

Accommodation

Casa Azul Manzanal 66 ☏65/232-904, ⊛www.casaazul.net. Firm backpacker favourite a short walk from the centre, run by a German-Chilean couple who offer comfortable rooms, kitchen privileges and an excellent breakfast that includes muesli and home-made bread (CH$3500 extra). Dorms CH$8000, rooms CH$18,000.

Casa Margouya Santa Rosa 318 ☏65/237-640, ⊛www.margouya.com. Lively backpacker favourite with guest kitchen, comfortable lounge area and a big emphasis on outdoor adventures. Bathroom queues are the only drawback. Dorms CH$9000, rooms CH$20,000.

Casa Margouya II Purísima 681 ☏65/237695, ⊛www.idiomas-sin-fronteras.com. Doubling up as a language school, the second branch of *Casa Margouya*, housed in a historic 1932 building, offers spacious, quiet rooms, with priority given to those wishing to study Spanish. CH$18,000.

Compass Del Sur B&B Klenner 467 ☏65/232-044, ⊛www.compassdelsur.cl. Large wooden guesthouse with airy dorms and rooms, communal breakfast (muesli, eggs and real coffee; CH$1500 extra), internet, book exchange, kitchen use and laundry service. The helpful staff are happy to organize all manner of tours. Camping CH$6000, dorms CH$9500, rooms CH$25,000.

Hospedaje Ellenhaus San Pedro 325 ☏65/233-577, ⊛www.ellenhaus.cl. Central location and rock-bottom prices make this warren of immaculately clean, tiny rooms a top budget choice. The only drawbacks are not being able to find your way out and the lack of central heating. Dorms CH$5000, rooms CH$13,000.

Hostal Melmac Walker Martínez 561 ☏65/230-863, ⊛www.melmacpatagonia.com. New self-proclaimed

PUERTO VARAS

EATING & DRINKING
Las Buenas Brasas	7
Caffé El Barista	3
Dane's Café	9
Donde El Gordito	4
El Barómetro	8
Garage	2
Sirocco	6
Southport Brewpub	1
Trattoria di Caruso	5

ACCOMMODATION
Casa Azul	B
Casa Margouya	C
Casa Margouya II	F
Compass Del Sur B&B	A
Hospedaje Ellenhaus	D
Hostal Melmac	E

Puma Verde

Train Station

Lago Llanquihue

Cruz del Sur Office

Casa de Turista

Pullman Bus Station

Tur Bus Office

JAC & Condór Bus Offices

Ciber Patagonia

Tas Choapa & Andesmar Bus Offices

Buses to Petrohue ★

Aquamotion @ Expediciones

Puelo Adventure

Banco de Chile

Casino

Lavandería Alba

Troco Money Exchange

Buses to Llanquihue ★ Sky Airlines

Buses to Puerto Montt

LAN

Shopping Gallery

Fruit Stalls

Mercado

Banco Santander

Supermarket Santa Isabel

Supermarket Express Lider

Buses to Puerto Montt ★

N

Iglesia del Sagrado Corazón de Jesús

Tur Bus/Tas Choapa/ Buses JAC terminal

0   300 m

Panamericana & Cruz del Sur Bus Terminal ▼

"hostel from another world" offering yoga and painting workshops, as well as the standard outdoor excursions. The beds are brand new and comfortable, there are lockers for your valuables and kitchen access, and the owner sometimes throws barbecues in the garden. Dorms CH\$9000, rooms CH\$20,000.

Eating and drinking

Las Buenas Brasas San Pedro 543. It may look like a steakhouse, but what this place really does best are the fish dishes. Try any of the *congrio* (conger eel) dishes and you will not go away disappointed. Mains CH\$6000 upwards.

Caffé El Barista Martínez 211. Bright, trendy café serving excellent Italian coffee (CH\$1500), sandwiches and cakes. Wi-fi access available.

Dane's Cafe Del Salvador 441. This established favourite reflects the town's hybrid history, their *empanadas de horno* sitting alongside the superb apfelstrudel. A great spot for coffee with cake (around CH\$1700) or an inexpensive lunch.

Donde El Gordito San Bernardo 560. Busy little café inside the market serving large portions of inexpensive fish and seafood to hungry locals. Try the *paila marina* (seafood soup) for CH\$3500.

Garage Martínez 220. A bar/club that's located in an, erm, garage, that comes alive after 11pm, with its mixture of jazz and rock or wherever the mood takes them.

Sirocco San Pedro 537. You're in for a treat at this elegant restaurant, which serves Patagonian specialities with an international twist. Try the seafood platter for two, with the locally smoked salmon, or feast on the melt-in-your-mouth Patagonian lamb with rustic mash. Mains CH\$ 6000–10,000.

Southport Brewpub Santa Rosa 218. Puerto Varas's only microbrewery feels like a friend's house: a soundtrack of chilled beats, photos of grinning people pinned above the bar, eclectic food (including paella) and the barman stops to chat to you when handing you a frothy pint. Add a message to the scribbles on the wall. Beer CH\$1800.

Trattoria di Caruso San Bernardo and San José. Family-run restaurant with chequered tablecloths and heaped portions of delicious home-made pasta for CH\$4000 approx.

Directory

Banks and exchange There are several banks with ATMs downtown, including the reliable Banco de Chile at Del Salvador 201 and Santander at San Francisco and Del Salvador. You can change foreign currency at Troco Money Exchange, Del Salvador 314 (Mon–Sat 9.30am–2pm & 3–7pm).

Hospital Centro Médico Puerto Varas is at Walker Martínez 576 (☎65/232792).

Internet and telephone Try Ciber Patagonia inside the shopping gallery off Del Salvador, half a block from the Plaza; open until 10pm.

Laundry Lavandería Alba at Walker Martínez 511; self-service CH$1400 or CH$1800 per kilo.

Post office San José 242.

Moving on

Bus Ancud (several daily; 2hr 30min); Bariloche (2 morning departures daily; 8hr); Castro (4–5 daily; 4hr); Petrohué (5–7 daily; 45min); Pucón (3 daily; 6hr); Puerto Montt (4–5 daily; 30min); Santiago (3–4 daily; 14hr); Valdivia (2–3 daily; 3hr).

Minibus Those for Petrohué leave from in front of *Don Jorge* on Walker Martínez; frequent minibuses to Puerto Montt stop along San Francisco.

SALTOS DE PETROHUÉ

The **Saltos de Petrohué** (daily: summer 8.30am–9pm; winter 9am–6pm; CH$1500), a series of impressive waterfalls formed by an extremely hard layer of lava that has been eroded into small channels by the churning water, lie 10km northeast of Ensenada, off a gravel road that leads through dense forest. Los Enamorados and Carilemu are two marked nature trails which make for a pleasant ramble through native flora, while Sendero Saltos leads you straight to the falls. According to local legend, these rapids are the home of a monster, Cuchivilu, which resembles a giant puma with a claw on the end of its tail. Regular minibuses run here from Puerto Varas (every 30min; 45min).

PUERTO MONTT

PUERTO MONTT is beautifully situated on the **Seno de Reloncaví** (Strait of Reloncaví) at the end of the

---

PUERTO VARAS TOUR OPERATORS

The area around Puerto Varas offers a variety of outdoor adventures, from challenging climbs up the nearby volcanoes Osorno and Calbuco to rafting on the turbulent turquoise waters of the Río Petrohué and exploring the surrounding wilderness on horseback. Those operators listed below are reputable.

Campo Aventura ☎65/232-910, ☺www
.campoaventura.cl. The place to go for horse-trekking, from one day to ten days into the foothills of Cochamo valley near the Estuario de Reloncaví. Customized options, like veggie meals, are available and canyoning and rafting are also among activities on offer. Day horseback rides from CH$45,000; the 6 day/5 night "Paddles, Saddles, Pedals and More" tour is highly recommended.

Ko'Kayak Ruta 225, Km 40, Casilla 896, Ensenada ☎9/9310-5272, ☺www.kokayak
.com. Excellent outfit with fun-loving bilingual guides and an emphasis on safety, specializing in half- to four-day rafting trips in the Lake District as well as one- or three-day sea-kayaking trips, and more challenging multi-day expeditions in the Patagonian fjords. Half-day rafting on Río Petrohue CH$33,000.

Pachamagua ☎65/542080 ☺www
.pachamagua.com. A reliable and professional canyoning specialist arranging adrenaline-filled excursions; half-day from CH$33,000; full day from CH$54,000. Can also arrange ascents of the Osorno volcano, horseriding and rafting on Río Petrohue.

Puelo Adventure San Pedro 311 ☎9/799-1920, ☺www.pueloadventure.cl. Reputable operator offering multi-day bike tours in the Lake District and Chiloé, as well as kayaking in the Chilean fjords, multi-day hikes and horseriding excursions. Osorno volcano trek from CH$50,000.

Yak Expediciones ☎9/8/332-0574, ☺www
.yakexpediciones.cl. Long-standing operator specializing in outstanding sea-kayaking excursions – from 1-day trips to Lago Todos Los Santos (CH$59,000) to multi-day adventures in the fjords around Parque Pumalín.

Puerto Varas lies on the well-beaten path between Puerto Montt and Bariloche in Argentina. If you're Argentina-bound, a lake crossing that allows you to experience the beauty of Chile's oldest national park – Parque Nacional Vicente Pérez Rosales – is an excellent alternative to a long bus journey. Starting out at 8.30am, you are first driven along the banks of Lago Llanquihue to Petrohué, before boarding the ferry that takes you across Lago Todos Los Santos, a spectacular expanse of clear blue-green water. As you sail along the densely forested shores, the volcanoes Osorno (2660m) and Puntiagudo (2190m) loom to the north, with the majestic Tronador (3491m) to the east. After going through Chilean customs at Peulla, you then cross the Argentine border at Paso Pérez Rosales, and get stamped in at tiny Puerto Frías. At this point you'll board the ferry again for the short crossing of Laguna Frías, then transfer by bus to your final nautical leg of the journey, a boat across the stunningly beautiful Lago Nahuel Huapi, arriving at your destination around midnight. Book in advance, especially during the peak season, with Turismo Peulla (☎65/437-127, ◍www.traveladventure.cl; CH$120,000).

Panamericana highway, with snow-capped mountains clearly visible beyond the sound on a good day. Though perhaps not deserving its "Muerto Montt" ("Dead Montt") moniker, Puerto Montt is a large, busy city with traffic-choked streets; a place to stock up on provisions and equipment on the way to Patagonia and a major transport hub, but little else.

The town stretches along the bay, with Avenida Diego Portales running east along the seafront towards the **Plaza de Armas** – the centre, surrounded by bars and restaurants. West of the main bus terminal, Avenida Costanera takes you to the busy passenger port with a **fería artesanal** (craft market) and the Angelmó fishing district.

Arrival and information

Air Aeropuerto El Tepual (☎65/486-200) is located 16km west of the city along the Panamericana. Buses ETM (☎65/256-253, ◍www.busesetm.cl) meets flights and drops you off at the main bus terminal.

Bus Both long-distance and local buses arrive at the large, completely refurbished Terminal de Buses (☎65/283-000), at Av. Portales s/n on the waterfront, a 10-min coastal walk from the city centre. The bus station has an information office, ATMs, café and luggage storage.

Ferry The Terminal de Transbordadores lies at Av. Angelmó 2187, several blocks west of the main bus terminal; Navimag (☎65/432-300, ◍www.navimag.cl) and Naviera Austral (☎65/270-430, ◍www.navieraustral.cl) ferries have offices here.

Tourist information There is a small tourist information kiosk at the main bus terminal and a well-stocked and helpful Turismo Municipal office on the Plaza de Armas, on Varas at San Martín (Dec–March daily 9am–9pm; April–Nov Mon–Fri 8.30am–1pm & 3–5.30pm, Sat 9am–1pm; ☎65/223-027).

Accommodation

Casa Perla Trigal 312 ☎65/262-104, ◍www.casaperla.com. The uphill walk is worth it: this is one of the friendliest homes in town, where you're treated like one of the family. The owners speak good English and German, you can use their kitchen and even camp in the yard. Camping CH$5500, rooms CH$10,000.

Hospedaje Rocco Pudeto 233 ☎65/272-897, ◍www.hospedajerocco.cl. Enjoy a warm welcome from the Argentine hostess and her two lap poodles called Cookie and Shakira. The dorms and rooms are cosy, though overpriced for what they are, and they charge for internet use, but the breakfast is excellent and you can use the kitchen. Located just five blocks from the Navimag. Dorms CH$12,000, rooms CH$25,000.

Hostal Vista Hermosa Miramar 1486 ☎09/9888-1548, ◍www.hostalvistahermosa.cl. Though the name is somewhat ironic, given that a new office building now blocks much of the sea view, the rooms have thin walls and some of the singles are not big enough to swing even a very

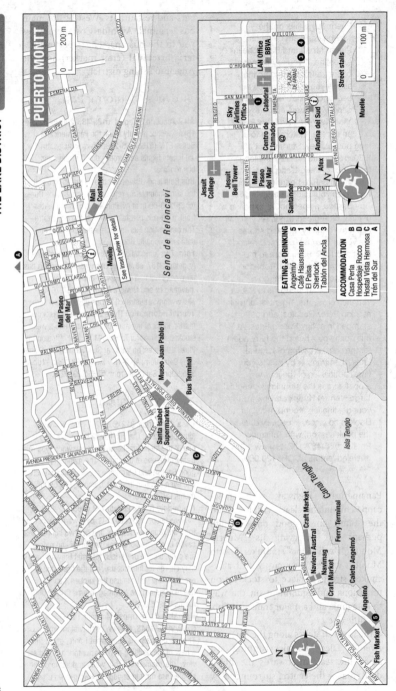

PUERTO MONTT

0   200 m

See inset below for detail

Seno de Reloncaví

Isla Tengio

Canal Tengio

EATING & DRINKING
Angelmó	5
Café Hausmann	1
El Paisa	4
Sherlock	2
Tablón del Ancla	3

ACCOMMODATION
Casa Perla	B
Hospedaje Rocco	D
Hostal Vista Hermosa	C
Trén del Sur	A

Inset map labels:

Jesuit College
Jesuit Bell Tower
Mall Paseo del Mar
Santander
LAN Office
BBVA
O'Higgins
QUILLOTA
San Martín
Catedral
Sky Airlines Office
RANCAGUA
Centro de Llamados
BENAVENTE
GUILLERMO GALLARDO
PEDRO MONTI
Afex
Andina del Sud
PLAZA DE ARMAS
URMENETA
ANTONIO VARAS
AVENIDA DIEGO PORTALES
Street stalls
Muelle

0   100 m

Main map labels:

PHILIPPI
ESMERALDA
EGAÑA
HUASCO
COPIAPÓ
SERENA
ILLAPEL
AVENIDA JUAN SOLER MANFREDINI
AVENIDA ESPAÑA
Mall Costanera
QUILLOTA
O'HIGGINS
SAN MARTÍN
RENGIFO
RANCAGUA
ANTONIO VARAS
Muelle
Mall Paseo del Mar
GUILLERMO GALLARDO
PEDRO MONTI
CAUQUENES
BENAVENTE
URMENETA
CHILLÁN
BALMACEDA
ANÍBAL PINTO
BENGIFO
QUILLOTA
FREIRE
ANCUD
LOTA
Museo Juan Pablo II
Bus Terminal
Santa Isabel Supermarket
AVENIDA DIEGO PORTALES
ANDRÉS BELLO
O'HIGGINS
SAN MARTÍN
AVENIDA PRESIDENTE SALVADOR ALLENDE
VICENTE PÉREZ ROSALES
ECUADOR
CHORRILLOS
AUGUSTO TRAULMANN
BUENOS AIRES
MIRAFLORES
CHILE
RUBLE
SCHWERTER
ANGELMÓ
MARTÍ
CENTRAL
MIRADOR
PUERTO
LINARES
COPIAPÓ
DR FONCK
EBENSPERGER
ANTONIO
TRIGAL
MANZANA
SALVADOR
BELLAVISTA
FEDERICO
VICENTE PÉREZ ROSALES
SEGUNDO DECKERS
CA BULG
VARAS
VERA
BARAG
TRIGUAL
IBAÑEZ
LOS CERROS
AVENIDA CARDONAL
AVENIDA PRESIDENTE
ITALIA
LOS SAUCES
LAS DELIAS
ABENTIANA
NEVADA
LOS ANDES
SERRA NEVADA
PEDRO DE VALDIVIA
CALLE SUR
YATES
SAN JOSE DE LA
SERENA
DIEGO PORTALES
SAN LUIS
TAPIA
HONORATO
TANTA PA
LAS CRUCES
AVENIDA PACHECO ALTAMIRANO
Fish Market
Angelmó
Caleta Angelmó
Ferry Terminal
Naviera Austral
Navimag
Craft Market
Craft Market

small cat, this friendly guesthouse is just a short, steep walk from the bus station and guests get kitchen privileges, free wi-fi, and cable TV in the rooms. CH$9000.

Tren del Sur Santa Teresa 643 ☏65/343-939, ⊛www.trendelsur.cl. Uphill from the port you'll find this adorable train-themed boutique hotel, where guests are referred to as "passengers" and much of the furniture is made from railway trestles. The sixteen en-suite rooms are supremely comfortable and centrally heated, making you wish you didn't have to leave. CH$32,000.

Eating and drinking

Angelmó Av. Angelmó, to the west of the ferry terminal; catch any of the Angelmó-bound *colectivos* along Av. Diego Portales if you don't want to walk (CH$400). This lively fish market sells fresh produce, as well as locally smoked salmon, while the nearby two-storey cluster of cheap *marisquerías* is an ideal place to sample super-fresh fish and seafood dishes, such as *chupe de locos* (abalone chowder; CH$5000). *Señorita Teresa* (Local 14) is an excellent choice; mains CH$3500.

Café Hausmann San Martín 185. This perpetually busy café is a good spot to sample *crudos* (steak tartare on toast with lemon juice, capers and minced onion; CH$1500), or indulge in some of the delicious cakes on display. Smoking is permitted.

El Paisa Varas 326. Adding a welcome bit of spice to the somewhat bland local cuisine, this Colombian hole-in-the-wall specializes in *tamales* (CH$3500), superb deep-fried meat *empanadas* (CH$400) and *pasteles de pollo* (CH$600), accompanied by three delicious home-made salsas. Wash it all down with a fresh pineapple juice (CH$600) and beware the deceptively mild-looking avocado salsa.

Sherlock Varas 542. Named after the fictional detective who supposedly paid Puerto Montt a visit, this is the best pub in town, serving excellent Chilean food, good sandwiches and a wide range of Kunstmann beers in a dark, cosy setting. At lunchtimes there's a good *menú del día* for CH$3400.

Tablón del Ancla Varas and O'Higgins. Slide into a booth at this sports diner decorated with caricatures, and fill up on massive hamburgers and grilled meats. Or if you're particularly hungry, a *pichanga*– mountain of chips strewn with bits of meat and chorizo – should sort you out. Three-course *menu del día* CH$3500.

Directory

Banks and exchange There is an ATM at the main bus terminal and several banks with ATMs downtown; try BBVA at Urmeneta and O'Higgins or Santander at Urmeneta and Montt. La Moneda de Oro, inside the main bus terminal, is a reason-

---

NAVIMAG: THE GOOD, THE BAD AND THE JUST PLAIN HIDEOUS

The Navimag trip from Puerto Montt to Puerto Natales is an incredible introduction to Patagonia. Lasting four days and three nights, the trip takes you through pristine and deserted waterways, past uninhabited islands and Chile's largest glacier, the Piu XI, with frequent sightings of marine life. It passes by Puerto Edén, the last remaining settlement of the Kawéscar people, before sailing into the cold and little-explored fjords of the south, and finally docking in Puerto Natales on the Seno Última Esperanza. If you're lucky with the weather, you'll not want to leave the deck for the duration of the trip, except to drink at the bar and to take part in a raucous game of bingo on the last night with a crowd of new friends. The flipside is a cruise entirely shrouded in mist and fog, topped with a sleepless night as the ship navigates the turbulent waters of the open ocean, followed by the equally sickness-inducing waves of the Golfo de Penas, while you spend your trip stuck in the bar or the dining room, watching re-runs of films with people you have grown mightily tired of by the end of the trip. In the off-season, you will also be sharing the boat with cattle. "C" is the cheapest category of cabin: you get a room divided into several lots of four bunks, each equipped with curtains, its own light and a large luggage locker. Bathroom facilities are shared; bring your own towel. The food is basic, but the staff are extremely helpful. Book your passage several weeks in advance during the peak months of January and February.

able currency exchange; also try Afex, at Portales 516 (Mon–Fri 8.30am–5.30pm, Sat 10am–2pm), which accepts American Express travellers' cheques.

Hospital Clinica Puerto Montt, at Panamericana 400 (☎65/484-800), and Hospital Regional, Seminario s/n (☎65/490-213) handle medical emergencies.

Internet and telephone Try Centro de Llamadas, at Urmeneta 457 (Mon–Fri 8am–10pm, Sat 9am–9pm, Sun 3–9pm; internet CH$600/hr).

Laundry Lavandería Fast Clean, at San Martín 167, Local 6.

Pharmacy There are numerous pharmacies along Urmeneta and inside the malls.

Post office Rancagua 126.

Shopping The best shopping mall is the towering Mall Costanera by the pier, with its extensive food court, multi-screen cinema and an "Andesgear" outlet, which stocks high-quality (though not cheap) outdoor and camping gear.

Moving on

Bus companies include: Buses Cruz del Sur (☎65/254-731); Buses Transchiloé (☎65/254-934); Buses Turibus (☎65/254-731); Tur Bus (☎65/253-329); Pullman Bus (☎6/531-6561); Buses Tas-Choapa (☎65/254828); and Buses Inter (☎65/259-320).

Air Daily flights to Santiago, Punta Arenas, Balmaceda (Coyhaique) and Temuco with LAN, at O'Higgins 167 (☎600/526-2000, ⓦwww.lan .com), and Sky Airline, at Benavente 405, Local 4 (☎600/6002828, ⓦwww.skyairline.cl).

Bus Ancud (several daily; 2hr 30min); Bariloche, Argentina (several daily, morning departures; 6hr); Castro (several daily; 3hr 30min); Coyhaíque (Wed, Fri, Sun at 11.30am; 28hr); Futaleufú (Fridays at 7am; 12hr); Osorno (several daily; 1hr 45min); Pucón (several daily; 6hr); Puerto Varas (every 20min; 30min); Punta Arenas (several weekly; 36hr); Santiago (several daily; 14hr); Villarica (several daily; 5hr 30min).

Ferry Navimag has departures to Puerto Chacabuco (Fri evening; 24hr; CH$55,000 and upwards) and Puerto Natales (Monday at 4pm; 4 days & 3 nights; CH$307,000 upwards; CH$208,000 in low season). Check ⓦwww .navimag.cl for updated timetables and prices.

MYTH AND BLACK MAGIC

Chiloé's mythology is populated with colourful characters. Here are a few that you might encounter:

El Basilisco A cross between a serpent and a rooster, he steals into people's houses at night to suck the phlegm from his victims' throats and lungs, after which they inexplicably sicken and die unless the house is burnt down.

Brujos A cult of male witches who reside in the Cueva de Quicaví, the legendary cave located on Chiloé's eastern coast, reportedly containing a book of spells given to them by a Spanish warlock. *Brujos* have to undergo dark rituals to be accepted as part of the coven; they wield black magic and have the power to do great harm.

El Caleuche A glowing ghost ship that appears out of the sea mist, used by the witches; it can travel at great speed and underwater. It helps those who are on good terms with the *brujos*, but sometimes entices new crew members; those beckoned turn into mere shadows of themselves, leaving their homes forever, with a sack of gold left behind as payment for taking them.

El Invunche The hideously deformed guardian of the witches' cave, raised on cats' milk and human flesh stolen from graveyards, who terrorizes anyone unfortunate enough to catch a glimpse of him.

La Pincoya A beautiful naked woman who lives in the sea, who personifies Chiloé's natural bounty, and to whom fishermen attribute a good catch.

El Trauco A repulsive little forest troll, blamed for unexplained pregnancies on the island. He has an insatiable appetite for young virgins and his gaze has an irresistible power over women.

La Voladora A female messenger of the witches, she vomits up her intestines to turn into a black bird and deliver the *brujos'* messages by night. She must recover her insides to regain human form.

Chiloé

As the ferry ploughs through the grey waters of the Canal de Chacao that separates the **CHILOÉ** archipelago from the mainland, an island appears out of the fog. **Isla Grande de Chiloé** is the second-largest island in South America, covered in a patchwork of forests and fields, with traditional villages nestling in sheltered inlets. Its residents still largely make a living from fishing and farming, as they have done for centuries.

Chiloé draws visitors with the accessibility of its two main towns, **Ancúd** and **Castro**, and the pretty villages with their relaxed pace of life. The rich and diverse food, remote national parks sheltering wildlife unique to the island, and wealth of architecturally unique eighteenth- and nineteenth-century **wooden churches** (UNESCO monuments) are also major attractions. Originally populated by the Huilliche (southern Mapuche) Indians, most of whom died from a smallpox epidemic shortly after European contact, Chiloé was colonized by the Spanish as early as 1567. Scores of refugees fled the fierce Mapuche on the mainland to the island, and Chiloé's very distinct culture evolved in relative isolation, resulting in a diverse and rich mythology that permeates people's lives to this day.

ANCÚD

A small town on Chiloé's northern coast, **ANCÚD** is the island's largest settlement and a pleasant place to linger. Its importance as a Spanish fortification was highlighted when it became the royalists' last stronghold, holding out against hostile forces for a decade after Chile's declaration of independence in 1818. Ancúd is bordered by the white-sand **Playa Gruesa** to the north and much of the action centres on the lively little **Plaza de Armas**, where there are crafts and book stalls in the summer and locals chill out in the evenings. At the Mercado Municipal, a block north, there are numerous bustling *marisquerías* and craft stalls. Avenida Costanera culminates in a busy fishing port at its northern end, beyond which Cochrane leads uphill to the ruins of the 1770 **Fuerte de San Antonio**, built on a promontory with excellent views of the Canal de Chacao and the Golfo de Quetalmahue.

What to see and do

In the southwest corner of the Plaza de Armas, the well-organized **Museo Azul de las Islas de Chiloé** (Jan–Feb Mon–Fri 10.30am–7.30pm, Sat & Sun 10am–7.30pm; March–Dec Tues–Fri 10am–5.30pm, Sat & Sun 10am–2pm; CH$800) features a relief map of Chiloé and the surrounding islets and excellent displays on local wildlife, history and culture, as well as interactive displays. Don't miss the wooden carvings of Chiloé's folkloric figures on the outdoor patio or the blue whale skeleton laid out by the outdoor geological exhibit.

Arrival and information

Buses Most long-distance buses arrive at the conveniently located Cruz del Sur bus terminal (☏65/622249, ⓦwww.busescruzdelsur.cl) at Los Carrera 850; bus tickets to and from the mainland include ferry passage between the mainland and Chiloé's northern shore. Buses from different parts of Chiloé pull up at the Terminal de Buses Rurales on Colo Colo, above the Full Fresh supermarket.

Tourist information The well-stocked Sernatur office is at Libertad 665, on the west side of the Plaza de Armas (Jan–Feb daily 8.30am–7pm; March–Dec Mon–Thurs 8.30am–5.30pm, Fri 8.30am–4.30pm; ☏65/622-800), has very helpful staff, maps of town and lists of accommodation and attractions, as well as a list of families participating in Agroturismo Chiloé, the opportunity to stay in rural family homes. Alternatively, check out ⓦwww.chiloe.cl.

Accommodation

Balai Pudeto 169 ☏65/622-541, ⓦwww .hotelbalai.cl. "Quirky and whimsical" comes to

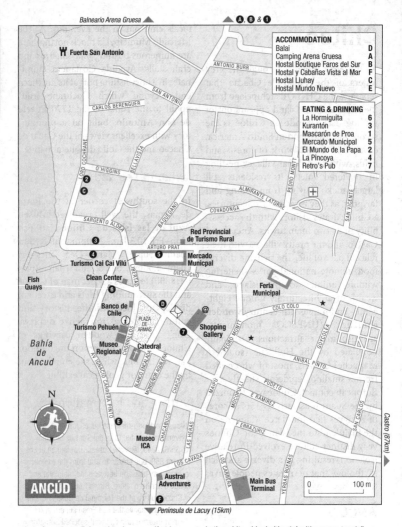

ANCÚD

mind when you walk in and make yourself at home among the boat figureheads, wooden carvings and models of ships. The en-suites are spacious and spotless, the location couldn't be more central and given the extras thrown in – breakfast, wi-fi – the prices are a steal. CH$24,000.

Camping Arena Gruesa Costanera Norte 290 ☎65/623-428, ✆www.arenagruesa.cl. At this great clifftop location, a few minutes' walk from the Arena Gruesa beach, there are three choices of accommodation: a large campsite with excellent sea views, hot water and individual shelters with lights for each site; several fully equipped cabañas for two/four/six/eight people; and well-kept rooms

in the white-shingled hostel with access to wi-fi. Camping CH$3500, rooms CH$20,000, cabañas CH$30,000.

Hostal Boutique Faros del Sur Costanera Norte 320 ☎65/625-799, ✆www.farosdelsur.cl. Superb clifftop views and a stunning lounge with tall ceilings characterize this new guesthouse. The comfortable rooms are thoughtfully located in a separate wing so as not to be disturbed. Perks include a Chilote breakfast (coffee, bread, local jam) and wi-fi; the owner goes out of his way to make you feel welcome. CH$30,000.

Hostal y Cabañas Vista al Mar Av. Costanera 918 ☎65/622617, ✆www.vistaalmar.cl. Another excellent choice with an ocean view, this hostel has something for everyone: clean dorms for younger travellers and spacious en-suite rooms with cable TV. Internet and breakfast are included and if you're travelling with friends, a fully euipped 2- or 4-person cabaña is an ideal choice. CH$28,000.

Hostal Lluhay Lord Cochrane 458 ☏65/622-656, ⓦwww.hostal-lluhay.cl. With extremely warm and welcoming owners who offer you home-made *empanadas*, this hostel comes with its own well-stocked bar and wonderfully plush en-suite rooms with cable TV. Breakfast and wi-fi included. Dorms CH$9000, rooms CH$24,000.

Hostal Mundo Nuevo Av. Costanera Salvador Allende ☏65/628-383, ⓦwww .newworld.cl. An impeccable waterfront location, friendly and knowledgeable staff, truly excellent breakfast, kitchen use for self-caterers, book exchange, wi-fi, and spotless airy rooms and dorms all make this Swiss-owned hostel the most popular choice for backpackers. Dorms CH$9000, rooms CH$24,000.

Eating and drinking

La Hormiguita Pudeto 44. Excellent spot for a three-course bargain lunch including soup, fried fish and pudding (CH$2100). The giant sandwiches also merit praise. Open 24hr.

Kurantón Prat 94. The slogan on the wall reads: "Curanto: helping people to have good sex since 1826". When the bow-tied waiter places the best *curanto en olla* in town in front of you, you'll be wondering whether those people had to wait to digest the mountain of shellfish, meat and potato dumplings first. Don't forget to drink your "liquid Viagra" – the potent shellfish stock that comes with your dish. *Curanto* CH$6000.

Mascarón de Proa Baquedano s/n, on the premises of *Cabañas Las Golondrinas*. This unpretentious restaurant on a clifftop to the north of town has a limited menu, but what it does, it does very well. The generous portions of exceptionally fresh fish are excellent – try the hake. Mains CH$5500.

Mercado Municipal The no-frills eateries in the courtyard at the market tend to be packed at lunchtime if the weather's good. They all serve a variety of inexpensive fish and seafood dishes; *El Sancho* and *La Corita* are good bets. Mains CH$3000–4000.

El Mundo de la Papa Cochrane 412. There is no better place to enjoy all things spud-related than this friendly little café/shrine to the Chiloé potato, overlooking the ocean. Try the superb potato-flour pizza with smoked salmon or treat yourself to chocolate-and-potato pie (tastes better than it sounds). Potato pizza CH$2700; cake CH$1700.

La Pincoya Prat 61. Opposite *Kurantón*, *La Pincoya* overlooks the fish harbour and serves excellent salmon *ceviche*, *curanto* and delicious *cancato* (steamed salmon stuffed with sausage, cheese and tomatoes). *Ceviche* CH$4000; *curanto* CH$6000.

Retro's Pub Maipú 615. Come to this dark, candlelit pub to rub shoulders with strangers and enjoy a lively drink. Those in danger of overdosing on *curanto* should try the pizza and Chilean take on Mexican food; draw your own conclusions. Beer CH$1800; fajitas CH$5000.

Directory

Banks and exchange There is an ATM at Banco de Chile at 621 Chorillos (Plaza de Armas).

Hospital Almirante Latorre 301 (☏65/622-355). 24hr medical service.

Internet and telephone Most hostels now offer internet access and wi-fi. The internet café/call centre inside the shopping gallery on Pudeto has brand-new computers and keeps the longest hours (Mon–Sat 8am–7.30pm, Sun 11am–11pm; CH$700/hr).

Laundry Clean Center, Pudeto 45 (Mon–Sat 9am–1pm & 3–7.30pm).

CURANTO – WHAT'S IN A DISH?

Chiloé's signature dish, curanto, has been prepared for several centuries using cooking methods very similar to those used in Polynesia. First, extremely hot rocks are placed at the bottom of an earthen pit; then, a layer of shellfish is added, followed by chunks of meat, *longanisa* (sausage), potatoes, *chapaleles* (potato dumplings) and *milcaos* (potato dumplings). The pit is then covered with *nalca* (Chilean wild rhubarb) leaves and as the shellfish cooks, the shells spring open, releasing their juices onto the hot rocks, steaming the rest of the ingredients. *Curanto en hoyo* is slow-cooked in the ground for a day or two, but since traditional cooking methods are only used in the countryside, you will probably end up sampling *curanto en olla*, oven-baked in cast iron pots. The dish comes with hot broth, known to the locals as "liquid Viagra", that you drink during the meal.

Shopping The Feria Municipal and then Feria
Rural y Artesanal at the Mercado Municipal have a
number of stalls selling woollen goods and wood
carvings, as well as home-distilled liqueurs such as
the bright golden *licór de oro* – a traditional Chilote
drink, the recipe for which is guarded jealously.

Moving on

Bus Castro (hourly; 1hr); Puerto Montt (several
daily; 2hr 30min); Quellón (4 daily; 2hr 30min);
Santiago (4–6 daily in the afternoon; 16hr).

AROUND ANCÚD

The three islands off the western
coast of Chiloé, 27km southwest of
Ancúd, are breeding grounds for both
Magellanic and Humboldt penguins.
A half-day tour of the **penguin
colony** (CH$10,000; for operators see
above) will take you along a dirt road
through picturesque, hilly country
and along the rugged coastline to
the little fishing village of **Puñihuil**.
From there it's a half-hour return trip
to the offshore islands, where you are
likely to catch sight of sea lions and
sea otters, as well as the penguins and
a wealth of seabirds. Though there are
no scheduled whale-watching trips
as yet, a large pod of **blue whales** has
been spotted in Chiloé's coastal waters,
and local fishermen occasionally take
groups of visitors in search of the
magnificent mammals; ask around. For
more information on the blue whales,
check out ⊕www.ballenazul.org.

Eastern Chiloé

If Chiloé's towns are too "modern" for
you, the eastern coast, just north of
Castro, is the place to witness traditional
village life. Here you can wander around
the Sunday market in coastal **Dalcahue**,
watching fishermen from outlying
islands unload their produce, take a
ferry to the elongated Isla Quinchao to
see the island's **oldest church** in Achao,
or travel up the coast to Tenaún to
enjoy some spectacular coastal hiking.
Look for the legendary **witches' cave**
near tiny Quicaví, near the village of
Quemchi (see box, p.488), or spend
several days camping and **sea kayaking**
between Isla Mechuque and the Islas
Chauques. Buses JM have daily departures for Quemchi and Quicaví from
Ancúd's Terminal de Buses Rurales
(one daily; 12.45pm; CH$1500), but it's
easier to reach Dalcahue from Castro.

Valle de Chepu

Around 25km south of Ancúd, a turn-off
leads to the **Valle de Chepu**, a large stretch
of wetlands created during the 1960
tsunami, whose sunken forest provides
a thriving habitat for hundreds of bird
species. *Chepu Adventures* is a superb, self-
sufficient eco-campsite (camping/dorm/
en-suite cabaña CH$4000/5000/30,000);
you can either cook for yourself or be
directed to two nearby *agroturismo*
homes for some superb home cooking.
The welcoming owners run Chepu

Adventures (☎09/9379-2481, ⊛www
.chepuadventures.com), which offers
dawn kayaking trips as well as ecologically sensitive nature walks along the
coast to the large Ahuenco penguin
colony, access to which is not properly
regulated by Conaf at the present time. To
get here, take any Castro-bound bus, ask
to be dropped off at the Cruce de Chepu
and call Chepu Adventures to arrange
pick-up.

CASTRO

The third-oldest continuously inhabited
city in Chile, **CASTRO** was founded
in 1567 on the Fiordo de Castro and
survived a number of calamities
through the centuries: being pillaged by
English and Dutch pirates, numerous
fires and the great earthquake of 1960,
which largely destroyed it. These days
it's the bustling capital of Chiloé.

What to see and do

A large **Plaza de Armas** surrounded
by bars and restaurants is Castro's
focal point; in summer, outdoor
musical events are staged here. The
yellow-purple neo-Gothic **Iglesia San
Francisco** (1911), one of Chiloé's fabled
wooden churches, stands on the northeastern corner of the plaza. The **Museo
Regional** (Jan–Feb Mon–Sat 9.30am–
8pm, Sun 10.30am–1pm; March–Dec
Mon–Sat 9.30am–1pm & 3–6.30pm;
donations), closed for renovation at the
time of writing, is found on Esmeralda,
just half a block south of the plaza,
and features a collection of black-and-
white photos of the 1960 earthquake
and its devastation. Two blocks from
the plaza, steeply downhill, lies the
Lillo, the coastal road that's home to a
number of **seafood restaurants**, with
the large **Feria Artesanal** by the water
selling all sorts of woollen goodies and
other crafts; though not as famous as
the Sunday market at Dalcahue, this
one is almost as good.

Palafitos

Though deemed unsanitary by some
locals, Chiloé's famous **palafitos** are
still found at several locations around
Castro. Perched precariously on
stilts above the water, these brightly
painted, traditional wooden fishermen's
dwellings are an unforgettable sight. The
idea was that you could moor your boat
at your back door and walk out onto the
street through the front one. The most
impressive examples are found at the
north end of town, off Pedro Montt,
where they are perfectly reflected in
the mini-lake by the roadside. More
palafitos are found slightly south along
the same street, while others are used as
restaurants at the southern end of town,
by the Feria Artesanal. A final batch can
be seen from the western end of Lillo,
across the Río Bamboa, and you can
even stay in one (see "Accommodation",
p.494).

Arrival and information

Bus Most long-distance buses, such as Cruz del
Sur (☎65/632389), Transchiloé (☎65/635152) and
Turibus (☎65/632389) use the Cruz del Sur bus
terminal at San Martín 486 (☎65/632389), which
serves numerous long-distance destinations up to
and including Santiago, as well as Punta Arenas in
the south, Bariloche in Argentina, and Ancúd and
Quellón in Chiloé. Terminal de Buses Municipal, at
San Martín 667, has services to smaller destinations around Chiloé, including Cucao (Parque
Nacional Chiloé).
Tourist office The new tourist information centre
(Dec–Feb only Mon–Fri 9am–7pm, Sat 10.30am–
7pm, Sun 11am–7pm) on the Plaza de Armas has
plenty of information on the area (though it's all
behind the counter, so you have to know what
to ask for) and scale models of Chiloé's famous
wooden churches.

Accommodation

Hospedaje El Mirador Barros Arana 127
☎65/633-795, ⓔmaboly@yahoo.com. The best
choice of guesthouse on this steep pedestrian
street, with immaculate rooms and a friendly
proprietress. Kitchen privileges, wi-fi and good
breakfast are included. CH$20,000.

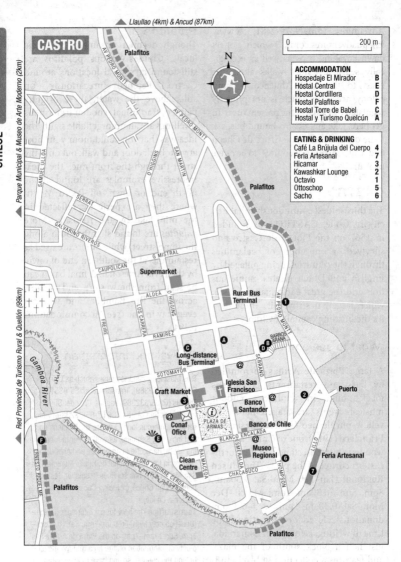

CASTRO

Palafitos

0   200 m

ACCOMMODATION
Hospedaje El Mirador   B
Hostal Central   E
Hostal Cordillera   D
Hostal Palafitos   F
Hostal Torre de Babel   C
Hostal y Turismo Quelcún A

EATING & DRINKING
Café La Brújula del Cuerpo 4
Feria Artesanal   7
Hicamar   3
Kawashkar Lounge   2
Octavio   1
Ottoschop   5
Sacho   6

◀ Parque Municipal & Museo de Arte Moderno (2km)

◀ Red Provincial de Turismo Rural & Quellón (99km)

Palafitos

Palafitos

Supermarket

Rural Bus Terminal

Long-distance Bus Terminal

Craft Market

Iglesia San Francisco

Banco Santander

Conaf Office

PLAZA DE ARMAS

Banco de Chile

Clean Centre

Museo Regional

Fería Artesanal

Puerto

Gamboa River

Palafitos

Palafitos

Hostal Central Los Carrera 316 ☎ 65/637-026,
© hostelcentralpm@hotmail.com. Quiet central
hostel with brightly painted bathrooms and spotless
rooms, some en-suite, all with cable TV and wi-fi,
though some are windowless. Ask for a room on the
top floor, with the best view. CH$16,000.

Hostal Cordillera Barros Arana 175 ☎ 65/532-
247, © hcordillera@hotmail.com. Run by a
gregarious hostess who really make you feel at
home, this central hostel has clean, cosy rooms
and an outdoor deck with sea views to chill out on.

Breakfast, internet/wi-fi and luggage storage are all
included, and the owners can help organize tours of
the island. CH$9000.

Hostal Palafitos Riquelme 1210 ☎ 65/531-
008, © palafitohostel@gmail.com. Staying
in this revamped *palafito* feels like being in a boat:
the eight plush, well-furnished en-suites have
curved walls and there's a little deck at the back
of the dining area. Breakfast includes delicious
home-made bread, the staff can help organize
horseriding in Parque Nacional Chiloé and there's

wi-fi throughout. The only downside is the hill you have to walk up to get into town. Dorms CH$12,500, rooms CH$25,000.

Hostal Torre de Babel O'Higgins 965 ☎65/534-569, ⓦ www.hostaltorredebabel.com. Large, attractive house attracting a mixed Chilean and international clientele. The rooms, panelled with local *mañío* wood, are spacious and clean (most of the time), the owner throws in all-you-can-eat breakfast and wi-fi and organizes group trips into the countryside. You may have to queue for the bathroom as there are only two for the eight rooms. CH$9000.

Hostal y Turismo Quelcún San Martín 581 ☎65/632-396, ⓔ quelcun@telsur.cl. This excellent guesthouse not only has its own tour agency, catering to outdoor enthusiasts, but lovingly decorated, centrally heated, comfortable rooms – the ones in a separate building across the garden are larger and quieter. Breakfast, internet and wi-fi are some of the other perks. CH$13,000.

Eating and drinking

Café La Brújula del Cuerpo O'Higgins 308. Popular, bustling diner on the plaza, serving milkshakes, sandwiches, pizza and decent burger-and-fries combos – a welcome sight for travellers who can't bear to look at another plate of mussels. The fajitas may not be terribly Mexican, but they're certainly palatable. Burger and fries CH$1800; fajitas CH$4500.

Feria Artesanal Lillo s/n. Behind the crafts market you'll find several *palafitos* housing eateries that fill up with locals at lunchtime. Try *El Caleuche*

for inexpensive fish, seafood and *curanto*. Mains CH$4000.

Hicamar Gamboa 413. Ambitious and unusual fare is on the menu here, such as wild boar steaks, as well as other meat and fish dishes; the portion sizes are just right and the meat is expertly prepared. Mains from CH$7000. The less upscale *Hicamar Express* a couple of doors down is a popular takeaway spot for fried chicken and hot dogs.

Kawashkar Lounge Blanco Encalada 35. Trendy café-lounge with a relaxed ambience and good beats, extensive cocktail list and plenty of tasty vegetarian options, including crêpes with sweet and savoury fillings (CH$3800), and large sandwiches.

Octavio Pedro Montt 261. With exemplary service, an excellent location in a *palafito* right over the water and a simple but expertly executed menu, this has been the best place in Castro for *curanto en olla* (CH$5500) for many years now.

Ottoschop Blanco 356. Dark, cosy and popular with a younger crowd, this bar serves a good selection of beers, including Kunstmann. Beers CH$1500.

Sacho Thompson 213. This old favourite still draws both locals and travellers in the know with its mix of friendly service, sea views and, of course, excellent seafood. Try the *pulmay* (like *curanto* but with more shellfish) or anything with clams. Mains CH$5500.

Directory

Banks and exchange There are several banks within a block of the Plaza de Armas, all with

---

CHILOTE CHURCHES

It is impossible to visit Chiloé and not be struck by the sight of the archipelago's wooden churches. In the early nineteenth century these impressively large buildings would have been the heart of a Chilote village, and in 2001 UNESCO accepted sixteen of them on to its prestigious World Heritage list.

The churches generally face the sea and are built near a beach or safe landing place with a plaza in front of them. The outside of the churches is almost always bare, and the only thing that expresses anything but functionality is the three-tiered, hexagonal bell tower that rises up directly above an open-fronted portico. The facades, doors and windows are often brightly painted, and the walls clad with plain clapboard or wooden tiles. The roofs, built like traditional Chilote boats and then turned upside down, create a feeling of space and tranquility. All the churches have three naves separated by columns, which in the larger buildings are highly decorated, supporting barrel-vaulted ceilings. The ceilings are often painted too, with allegorical panels or golden constellations of stars painted on an electric blue background.

Distinctive churches on Chiloé include those in Nercón, Rilán, Llau-Llau and Detif. For more information on Chiloé's churches, check out the informative ⓦ www.interpatagonia.com/iglesiaschiloe.

ATMs. Try Banco de Chile at Blanco Encalada and Serrano.

Festivals Festival Costumbrista Chilote takes place the third week in February – it's a feast of enormous proportions featuring traditional dishes as part of a celebration of Chilote culture and mythology.

Hospital Hospital Augusta Rifat, on Freire 852 (☎65/632-445), has basic medical facilities.

Internet The internet café on Blanco Encalada, half a block from the Plaza, and at Gamboa and Serrano are both open late.

Laundry Clean Center, at Balmaceda 220, does laundry (CH$1200/kilo).

Post office O'Higgins 388, Plaza de Armas.

Tours Altué Expeditions in Dalcahue (☎9/419-6809, ⓦwww.seakayakchile.com) offer multi-day trips around the Chiloé archipelago complete with lodging at their kayak centre near Dalcahue. Multi-activity combination trips in the Lake District and Patagonia are also on offer. Turismo Pehuén on Esmeralda 198 (☎65/635-254, ⓦwww .turismopehuen.cl) organizes city tours, summer boat-trips to the uninhabited islets off the east coast, day-trips around Chiloé as well as in-depth multi-day programmes.

Moving on

Bus Cruz del Sur terminal to: Ancúd (hourly; 1hr 30min); Puerto Montt (11 daily; 5hr); Santiago (4 daily; 18hr). Terminal Municipal to: Chonchi (several daily; 30min); Cucao (4–6 daily; 1hr); Punta Arenas (1 weekly on Monday at 6.25am; 42hr); Quellón (every 30min; 2hr).

Ferry There are currently no passenger boat services from Castro, though this may change when the new passenger port opens in early 2012.

PARQUE NACIONAL CHILOÉ

On the island's western coast, the **PARQUE NACIONAL DE CHILOÉ** comprises vast areas of native evergreen forest, covering the slopes and valleys of the **Cordillera de Piuchen**, as well as wide deserted beaches and long stretches of **rugged coastline**, home to dozens of seabird species, penguins and sea lions. The dense vegetation hides the elusive *pudú* (pygmy deer) and the shy Chilote fox. The park is divided into three sectors, as detailed below.

Sector Chepu

This sector can be reached via several hours' walk along the coast from Chepu Valley (see p.492). Though in future it's due to be incorporated into the Sendero de Chile (see box, p.492), a section of which stretches all the way along the coast from the village of Guabún, near Ancúd, the rugged trail here is difficult to access; you have to arrange for a local fisherman to take you across Río Lar and collect you on the way back. If you do venture this far, you will be rewarded with solitude and some great views of the coast.

Sector Abtao

The most difficult to reach of the three, this section of the park comprises dense woodland and bogs, and hiking here is as wild as it gets. A trail runs through the park to an old Conaf *refugio* on the coast, but it's overgrown and very difficult to follow, so a guide is essential. Experienced guide Sebastián "Bata" Kruger in Ancúd (☎9/509-3741, ⓦwww.chiloeindomito.com) specializes in trekking in Chiloé's remotest parts, including Sector Abtao; he speaks Spanish only, but can arrange for an English-speaker to come along if given some warning.

Sector Anay

To reach Sector Anay, take a bus to the tumbledown village of **Cucao** from Castro's Terminal Municipal (seven daily in peak season; 1hr). Pay the park entrance fee at **Chanquín** (daily 9am–7pm; CH$2000), across the river from the village, where Conaf's **Centro de Visitantes** provides visitors with a detailed map of the park. *Camping Chanquín* (☎9/644-2489), 200 metres beyond the visitor centre, has fully equipped sites, and there are several **guesthouses** of varying quality in Cucao itself. Wild camping is free on the beach and along the trails. Though you can pick up some supplies at Cucao and buy fresh catch from the fishermen, you'll need adequate food to explore the park properly.

There are some attractive **short walks** from the visitors' centre – the 750-m Sendero El Tepual winds its way through humid, slippery *tepú* woods, and the Sendero Dunas de Cucao switches between patches of dense vegetation and sand dunes, before arriving at a white beach. The 25-km Sendero Chanquín—Cole Cole runs to the Conaf *refugio Cole Cole*, alternating between stretches of beach and forest, with dramatic views of the coastline, pounded by the fierce Pacific surf. Another 8-km walk brings you to the Río Anay, with a chunk of largely unexplored wilderness beyond.

PARQUE TANTAUCO

At the very south of Chiloé, the remote private reserve of **PARQUE TANTAUCO**, created by the current president of Chile, Sebastián Piñera, and at least double the size of Parque Nacional Chiloé, is completely uninhabited apart from the fishing hamlet of **Caleta Inío** on the southern coast. The park consists of Zona Norte, accessible only by 4x4, and Zona Sur, accessible only by boat from Quellón, with 150km of trails between the two. While it's possible to do some **day-hikes** in Zona Norte, such as the 6-km Sendero Lagos Occidentales through evergreen forest between Lago Chaiguata and Lago Chaiguaco, it's more rewarding to spend a week, hiking all the way from the first campsite at Lake Chaiguata, 20km from the ranger station (Dec—Feb 9am—8pm) at the entrance of the park, down to Caleta Inío. Here you can camp or stay in some family-owned accommodation (full board CH$18,000), explore the coastal caves and trails and then catch a weekly boat back to Quellón, spotting local marine life such as sea lions and sometimes even blue whale along the way.

The park's infrastructure is well designed, with hikes of moderate length and difficulty along well-signposted trails between fully equipped campsites and unmanned basic *refugios*. Due to the park's remoteness, it's not overrun by day-trippers in the summer. There are extensive beaches near Inío, protected from the rough waters of the Gulf of Corcovado by small offshore islands, so besides the ample hiking terrain, the numerous coastal inlets are ideal for **kayaking**. For more **information** on the park, contact the Oficina de Parque Tantauco in Quellón, at Av. La Paz 68 (☎65/685-064, ⓦwww .parquetantauco.cl), which can help to arrange 4x4 transportation to Zona Norte and book your boat passage to or from Caleta Inío.

Northern Patagonia: Aisén

Comprising the northern half of Patagonia, **AISÉN** is the wildest, least populated and least visited of all of Chile's provinces. **Carretera Austral**, the partially paved, partly dirt-and-gravel "Southern Highway", stretches for 1240km down from Puerto Montt to tiny **Villa O'Higgins** – a popular destination for cyclists – interrupted in places by various bodies of water and supplemented by short ferry rides. The only town of any size is **Coyhaique**, a good base for exploring the surrounding area and for taking a boat excursion to the **San Rafael Glacier**. The area around the town of Chaitén, at the northern end of the Carretera Austral, was evacuated in 2008 following an unforeseen **volcanic eruption** and remains largely uninhab-ited; much of the traffic has been redirected via the white-water rafting base of **Futaleufú** instead. Aisén is best explored between November and March, as transport tends to be scarce at other times of year, and travel is very susceptible to changes in the weather at all times.

PARQUE PUMALÍN

Owned by American Douglas Tomkins, this 2900-square-kilometre chunk of almost pristine wilderness is Chile's largest **private park**, stretching from Hornopirén to the now almost uninhabited town of Chaitén. Before the volcanic eruption in 2008, the park attracted more than ten thousand visitors per year with its well-maintained hiking trails and campsites, but at the time of writing, Pumalín was closed to visitors (check ⓦ www.pumalinpark.org for updated information).

FUTALEUFÚ

The fast-flowing, crystal-clear waters of Río Futaleufú have made this modest village, nestling between snow-tipped mountains, one of the top **white-water rafting** destinations in the world. Though threatened by the Spanish-owned hydroelectricity company ENDESA's proposed plans to dam Río Futaleufú, at the moment, the challenging Class III—V rapids still draw the crowds here from December to February; outside those months, the place can feel like a ghost town.

Arrival and information

Bus Most buses drop passengers off at the corner of Prat and Balmaceda, while some stop by the post office on the Plaza de Armas.

Information Visitor services, such as the tourist office (open only in high season), ATM (which doesn't accept Visa) and post office are all located around the Plaza de Armas.

Accommodation, eating and drinking

Adolfo's B&B O'Higgins 302 ⓣ 65/721-256. Popular family home offering warm, clean rooms. Breakfast includes home-made bread. CH$16,000.

Burger stand Next to the Telefónica Sur on Cerda. If you happen to be passing through during the off-season, this is one of the very few places open. Huge burger CH$1800.

Camping Puerto Espolón Ruta 231, by the town entrance ⓣ 09/9695-0324.Fully equipped campsite in a stunning spot by the river, with its own small beach. Pitch CH$5500.

Martín Pescador Balmaceda 603. The best restaurant in town, serving excellent salmon dishes among others, in a mountain lodge living-room-style atmosphere. Mains CH$7000.

Residencial Carahue O'Higgins 332 ⓣ 65/721-221. The wooden floors may be uneven and creaky, but the family that runs this budget spot is very welcoming and helpful. CH$12,000.

Sur Andes Cerda 308. Real coffee, freshly squeezed juice and good vegetarian options contribute to this café's popularity. Mains CH$3000.

Moving on

Bus Most buses depart from the corner of Prat and Balmaceda. Buses Becker to Coyhaique (Sun

---

RAFTING OPERATORS

The following reputable operators offer half- and full-day rafting trips down the Futa and the less challenging Río Espolón.

Austral Excursions Hermanos Carrera 500 ⓣ 65/721-239. A specialist in river descents down the Espolón, as well as trekking and canyoning.

Expediciones Chile Mistral 296 ⓣ 65/721-386, ⓦ www.exchile.com. Experienced operator that specializes in multi-day rafting and kayaking

on the Futa, though day-excursions are also possible.

Futaleufú Explore O'Higgins 772 ⓣ 65/721527, ⓦ www.futaleufuexplore.com. Established outfit that runs rafting trips from its own luxury riverside camp.

at 8am, more frequently in peak season; 12hr); Buses Transaustral to Puerto Montt via Argentina and Osorno (Mon at 8am; more frequently in peak season; 12–14hr). Buses Transaustral may not let you off in Argentina; during peak season, their twice-weekly buses leave for Esquel from in front of the post office on the Plaza.

COYHAIQUE

The town of **COYHAIQUE**, 634km south of Puerto Montt, is nestled in the shadow of the great slab of Cerro Macay, at the confluence of the Simpson and Coyhaique rivers. It is the region's capital and a welcome pocket of civilization compared to the smaller hamlets and villages along the Carretera Austral. The **transport hub** for the entire area, Coyhaique has departures to destinations up and down the Carretera Austral, as well as neighbouring Argentina.

The heart of the city is the hexagonal **Plaza de Armas**, which resembles a wheel with ten spokes stretching out in various directions, making navigation confusing even for people who have maps. Most places to eat and drink are to be found within a few blocks of the plaza, and the small **Feria de Artesanos**, between Dussen and Horn, on the plaza's western side, sells regional handicrafts. The **Monumento al Ovejero**, three blocks up Condell and one block east along the main thoroughfare of Avenida Baquedano, immortalizes the region's pastoral roots in the form of a sculpture of a sheep farmer herding his flock. Across the street, the small **Museo Regional de la Patagonia** (Mon–Fri 8.30am–6pm; CH$500) has displays on the region's history, mineralogy and flora and fauna, featuring stuffed wildlife and a worthwhile collection of historical photographs, including some of the workmen who built the Carretera Austral highway, commissioned by Pinochet.

Arrival and information

Air Aeropuerto de Balmaceda, 55km south of town, serves LAN flights from Santiago, Punta Arenas, Puerto Montt and Temuco; the flights are met by minibuses that do door-to-door drop-offs (CH$8000–10,000). Aeródromo Teniente Vidal, 7km out of town, handles charter flights from Villa O'Higgins, Cochrane and Chile Chico.
Bus Most buses arrive at the main Terminal de Buses, on the corner of Lautaro and Magallanes, five blocks from the Plaza de Armas.
Conaf There is an office at Los Coigües s/n (Mon–Fri 8.30am–5.30pm; ☎67/212-125), offering information on the Laguna San Rafael Glacier as well as rudimentary maps of Parque Nacional Queulat.
Ferry Navimag ferries from Puerto Montt arrive at Puerto Chacabuco's Terminal de Transbordadores, 82km from Coyhaique and served by frequent buses via Puerto Aisén.
Tourist office The well-stocked and super-helpful Sernatur office at Bulnes 35, just off the Plaza de Armas (Dec–Feb Mon–Fri 8.30am–9pm, Sat & Sun 10.30am–6pm; March–Nov Mon–Fri 8am–1pm & 2.30–5.30pm; ☎67/240-290, ⓦwww .recoreeaysen.cl), dishes out detailed maps of town and is able to advise on accommodation and travel in the area.

Accommodation

HI Albergue Las Salamandras Carretera Teniente Vidal, km 1.5, towards the airport ☎67/211-865, ⓦwww.salamandras.cl. The friendly owners of this large, attractive lodge can assist with planning your outdoor adventures. Comfortable rooms and fully equipped cabañas come complete with breakfast, laundry service, use of a kitchen, a TV loft and ample common spaces. Camping CH$5000, dorms CH$7000, rooms CH$18,000, cabañas CH$25,000.
Hospedaje Gladys Ignacio Serrano 91 ☎67/231-189. Welcoming, quiet, central guesthouse with spotless rooms, complete with cable TV, run by a friendly family. Breakfast CH$1500 extra. CH$10,000.
Hospedaje María Ester Lautaro 544 ☎67/233-023. Compact, bright, spotless rooms in a friendly environment; breakfast CH$2000 extra, as are kitchen privileges. The barking of the toy poodle can be annoying and there's no heating in the rooms. CH$8000.
Hospedaje Natti Almirante Simpson 417 ☎67/231-047. Guesthouse popular with backpackers and bikers, with small rooms, some windowless. There's a separate guest kitchen and eating area, space for a couple of tents and a handy laundry service next door. Camping CH$5000, rooms CH$8500.
Kooch Hostel Camino Piedra El Indio 2 ☎67/527-186, ⓦwww.koochhostel.com. New

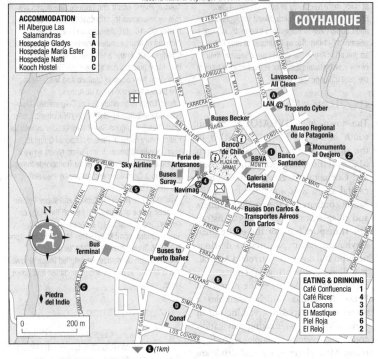

COYHAIQUE

ACCOMMODATION
HI Albergue Las Salamandras	E
Hospedaje Gladys	A
Hospedaje María Ester	B
Hospedaje Natti	D
Kooch Hostel	C

EATING & DRINKING
Café Confluencia	1
Café Ricer	4
La Casona	3
El Mastique	5
Piel Roja	6
El Reloj	2

0 ——— 200 m

E (1km)

backpacker favourite in a quiet, attractive spot overlooking the Piedra del Indio gorge, with reliable hot showers and a fully equipped kitchen. The congenial owner takes good care of you and offers tours to Parque Nacional Queulat, among others. Camping CH$4000, dorms CH$9000, rooms CH$24,000.

Eating and drinking

Café Confluencia 25 de Mayo 548. The menu at this arty bistro actually features fresh vegetables, not to mention imaginative dishes, such as *ají relleno* (stuffed hot pepper) and Spanish-style tortillas. On Fridays and Saturdays, live music kicks off at 11pm. Mains CH$4000–6000.

Café Ricer Horn 48. Perch on a sheepskin-covered chair at this gringo-friendly wi-fi-enabled café-restaurant and enjoy ample portions of Chilean staples, sandwiches and pasta. None of the dishes are outstanding, and the Arabic ones are often non-existent, but it's all competently cooked and filling. Grilled salmon CH$5500.

La Casona Obispo Vielmo 77. Popular with both tour groups and locals, this white-linen restaurant counts delicious grilled lamb and *pastél de*

jaiba (crab souffle) among its specialities. Mains CH$6000.

El Mastique Bilbao 141. Highly recommended for its good home-cooked Chilean food, this place is particularly busy at lunchimes. Try the hearty *cazuela de pollo* (chicken stew) for CH$3500.

Piel Roja Moraleda 495. An excellent spot for a beer and snack, this lively pub with a quirky interior serves up good burgers and quesadillas. Strut your stuff on the upstairs dancefloor (bar and disco open until 4am).

El Reloj Baquedano 828. This may be an elegant upscale restaurant, but it serves excellent, creative dishes at lower prices than more downscale central options. Try the "frutas del mar" – a quartet of salmon *ceviche, centolla* (king crab), prawns and local smoked salmon, or the *congrio al ajillo* (conger eel in garlic sauce) and wash it all down with an expertly prepared pisco sour. Mains from CH$6000.

Directory

Banks and exchange Banco de Chile, BBVA and Santander, all located along Condell, have global ATMs.

Hospital Jorge Ibar 168 (☎67/219-100) for 24hr emergencies.

Internet and telephone *Café Ricer* has free wi-fi access; also try Trapando Cyber opposite *Hospedaje Gladys*.

Post office Cochrane 226.

Moving on

Air Daily flights to Puerto Montt and Santiago with LAN and Sky Airline, and weekly flights to Punta Arenas. Transporte Aéreo Don Carlos has weekly charter flights to Cochrane and Villa O'Higgins, though its safety record leaves something to be desired.

Bus Buses Acuario 13 (☎67/522-143), Bus Sabra (☎67/524-543) and Buses Don Carlos (☎67/232-981) run to Cochrane; Buses São Paolo (☎67/255-726) serves Cochrane and Puerto Aisén; Buses Becker (☎67/232-167) serves Futaleufú; Queilén Bus (☎67/240-760) serves Santiago, Osorno, Puerto Montt, Ancúd and Castro; Transaustral (☎67/232-067) goes to Puerto Montt and Comodoro Rivadavia, Argentina.

Cochrane (daily at 8am; 10hr); Comodoro Rivadavia, Argentina (Mon & Fri at 9am; 9hr); Futaleufú (weekly on Sat at 8am; more departures Dec–Feb; 12hr); Osorno, Puerto Montt, Ancúd and Castro (Mon & Fri at 4pm; 20/24/24/28hr); Puerto Aisén (hourly; 1hr).

Ferry The Navimag office is at Paseo Horn 47-D (☎67/223306). Navimag has three weekly departures to Puerto Montt during high season; C berths, high season/low season CH\$40,000/33,000; check ⓦwww.navimag.cl for updated timetables.

PUERTO CHACABUCO AND PUERTO AISÉN

The port and ferry terminal of **PUERTO CHACABUCO** lies 82km west of Coyhaique, and 16km south of **PUERTO AISÉN** (also a port). While the road to the two ports cuts through the stupendous scenery of the **Reserva Nacional Río Simpson**, there is little to see in the towns themselves. If you're planning on taking a trip to **Laguna San Rafael**, however, you have little choice but to spend a night or two here due to the early departure and late arrival of the catamaran. *Residencial El Puerto*, at O'Higgins 80 (☎67/351-147; CH\$8000), has unremarkable rooms with shared bathroom and breakfast.

TREAT YOURSELF

If you only see one glacier in Latin America, make it Laguna San Rafael, 200km southeast of Coyhaique and only accessible by boat or plane. It is estimated that in the next twenty years or so, it will be completely gone.

As you pass through the tight squeeze of Río Témpanos ("Iceberg River"), and sail past the silent, densely forested shores of the long, narrow inner passage of Estero Elefantes, you catch numerous glimpses of marine wildlife. Nearing the impossibly huge glacier, over 4km in width and 60m in height, the boat dodges massive bobbing icebergs, some the size of small houses. From time to time you'll hear a loud crack as a massive slab of blue ice calves from the glacier face, temporarily disturbing the still waters. Most boat trips allow the passengers to get close to the glacier in inflatable Zodiacs, and one of the trip's highlights is drinking whisky on the rocks – using the millennia-old ice, of course.

Catamaranes del Sur (☎67/351112 ⓦwww.catamaranesdelsur.cl) runs high-speed catamaran day-trips from Puerto Chacabuco's *Hotel Loberías del Sur* to the glacier (Dec–Feb every Saturday and on several other days; fewer days Sept–Nov & March–April 7.30am–10pm; CH\$185,000); book several weeks in advance.

A new gravel road is currently in construction, running from Puerto Río Tranquilo, south of Coyhaique, towards Bahía Exploradores, which should eventually shorten the boat trips.

PARQUE NACIONAL QUEULAT

A five-hour drive north of Coyhaique lies the little-explored **PARQUE NACIONAL QUEULAT** (entry CH\$3000). The park's crowning feature is the stunning **Ventisquero Colgante**, or "hanging glacier", a frozen blue-white mass spilling over a rock face, while a mighty **waterfall** fed by the melting ice roars into the Laguna Los Tempanos below. You can stay at the fully equipped **campsite** (℡67/314-250; CH$10,000 per site) by the *guardería* at the park's southern entrance. Two trails run from here – a 2-km trail to the *mirador* overlooking the hanging glacier, and a hopelessly overgrown path on which you may catch sight of the elusive *pudú* (pygmy deer). There is no **public transport** to the park; you can ask any northbound bus to drop you off at the park entrance, though it can be difficult to hitch a lift onwards.

SOUTH OF COYHAIQUE

From Coyhaique, the Carretera Austral runs south, interrupted by the dark blue Lago General Carrera, then passes the attractive village of Puerto Río Tranquilo, on the lake's northern shore, and **Puerto Bertrand**, popular with cyclist and fly-fishermen. Fifty kilometres south, the only settlement of any size on the remaining chunk of the road is **Cochrane**, where you are likely to have to stop overnight, as buses in Northern Patagonia run only during daylight hours. *Residencial Cero a Cero*, at Lago Brown 464 (℡67/522-158; CH$20,000), is a wonderfully cosy, family-run guesthouse that serves good breakfast, while *Café Ñirrantal*, on the corner of Avenida O'Higgins and Esmeralda, a block south of the Plaza de Armas, whips up excellent vegetarian crêpes, fish and meat dishes.

Beyond Cochrane, the paved road becomes a dirt-and-gravel track that makes its way through a dense carpet of evergreens and giant wild rhubarb plants. After around two hours, a track splits off to the west, leading you to the picturesque hamlet of **Caleta Tortél**, where a few houses on stilts sit at the mouth of Río Baker and there is fishing-boat access to both the Northern and Southern Patagonian ice fields. Continuing south to the last stop of **Villa O'Higgins**, the Carretera Austral

narrows to a single lane, ribboning its way around hairpin bends as the terrain becomes even hillier, with sheer drops on the side of the track revealing spectacular vistas of glacial rivers cutting through endless forest, and distant mountains shrouded in mist.

VILLA O'HIGGINS

Until 1999, **VILLA O'HIGGINS**, a cluster of wooden houses huddled against a sheer mountain face, was accessible only by a small prop plane from Coyhaique or by boat from Argentina. Once here, there are two choices: turn back or cross the lake into Argentina. You are likely to linger longer than intended, partly because of the scarcity of public transport, and partly to enjoy the relaxed pace of life, small-town hospitality and the hiking and horseriding opportunities the rugged scenery provides.

The town is built on a simple grid around the Plaza de Armas. The Carretera Austral runs along the western side of the village all the way down to the boat landing on **Lago O'Higgins**, several kilometres away. A footpath off Calle Lago Cisnes runs through Parque Cerro Santiago up to a *mirador* overlooking the village; from there, the path continues on towards the ice "tongue" of the **Ventisquero Mosco**, the nearest hanging glacier, though the trail is sometimes impassable.

Arrival and information

Air The twice-weekly flights from Coyhaique arrive on Mondays and Thursdays at the airstrip just to the west of town.

Bus The twice-weekly bus from Cochrane arrives at the Supermercado San Gabriel on Mondays and Thursdays.

Ferry The boat from Argentina docks at the Bahía Bahamóndez, 7km east of town; a private pick-up is available.

Tourist information Helpful staff run the small tourist office on the plaza (Mon–Fri 9am–5.30pm; no tel, ⊛ www.villaohiggins.com) and provide plenty of information on the town and the surrounding area. The public library, just off the plaza, has free **internet**. There are no **banks** in town, so bring plenty of cash with you. Hielo Sur (☎67/431-821, ⊛www.hielosur.com), on a nameless side street off the west end of Calle Mosco, has up-to-date timetables for the Lago O'Higgins crossing (CH$40,000) as well as day-trips to the Glaciar O'Higgins (CH$75,000).

Accommodation, eating and drinking

Camping Los Ñires Carretera Austral s/n. Just south of *Hostal Runín*, this spacious, tree-lined campsite has indoor cooking facilities and hot showers, though the ground can be muddy. CH$3000 per tent.
Entre Patagones Carretera Austral s/n. Excellent family-run restaurant, busy after 8pm, serving tasty Patagonian favourites such as *asadór patagónico* (spit-roasted lamb) and hearty *cazuela* in a homely environment. To reach it, follow Carretera Austral to the north end of town. Dinner CH$6000.

Hospedaje Patagonia Río Pascua 191 ☎67/431-818. A comfortable, family-run choice by the plaza that offers clean, basic rooms with shared bathroom. Rooms CH$7000. Breakfast CH$1500 extra; lunch or dinner CH$5000.
Hostal Runín Pasaje Vialidad s/n ☎67/431-870. Tranquil, popular guesthouse with welcoming rooms, hot showers, tasty home-cooking and the occasional BBQ. It may be possible to camp outside. Meals extra. Dorms CH$8000, rooms CH$28,000.

Moving on

Air Transportes Aéreos Don Carlos has charter flights to Coyhaique on Mon and Thurs; confirm the departure time at the office on Lago O'Higgins.
Bus Buses Los Ñadis run two weekly trips to Cochrane (Tues & Fri at 10am; 7hr); buy tickets in advance from the Supermercado San Gabriel, as the bus is usually full. *Hostal El Mosco* sometimes runs services to Caleta Tortel.
Ferry The ferry to Argentina docks at the Bahía Bahamóndez, 7km east of town; a private minibus charges CH$1500 per person from Villa O'Higgins. See box below for departure info.

TO CROSS OR NOT TO CROSS?

The crossing between Villa O'Higgins and Argentina's El Chaltén is still remote and challenging, yet more and more hardy travellers are prepared to take on the lake crossing, followed by a strenuous hike over the border. The sixty-passenger *Quetru* leaves Bahía Bahamóndez at 8.30am (Dec Wed & Sat; Jan–Feb Mon, Wed & Sat; Nov & March Sat only; April every other Sat; CH$40,000) and arrives at the hamlet of **Candelario Mancilla** at around 11am. Here there's no-frills accommodation (CH$8000) and camping spots (CH$3000 per tent), and you'll get your passport stamped by **Chilean border control**. Beyond, a wide gravel track runs slightly uphill through patches of woodland to the international border; on the way, you will have to either ford the shallow, glacial **Río Obstáculo**, or cross it on some rickety planks. Beyond the border, the 7.5km stretch of trail to the **Argentine border control** on the banks of the **Laguna del Desierto** becomes a narrow, muddy footpath snaking its way through hilly forest and scrubland; cyclists have to push and sometimes carry their bikes.

After being stamped into Argentina, you can either pitch a tent at *Camping Laguna del Desierto* (CH$3500), catch the *Viedma* motor launch across the lake (daily at 1.30pm, 4.45pm & 6.45pm; 30–45min; CH$13,000, bicycles CH$5000 extra) or hike the remaining 15km (5hr) along a thickly forested path on the left side of the lake, emerging at the *guardería* by the pier on the south side. Minibuses to **El Chaltén** meet the arriving boats, the last one leaving for town at 7.45pm (CH$14,000).

While it is possible to complete the border crossing in a day, boat schedules are weather-dependent, so pack enough food for several days. To book a guide and pack horses (CH$15,000 per pack horse), and for up-to-date information on the trek, visit the helpful website ⊛www.villaohiggins.com. Do the crossing while you can: there are plans to make it more accessible by creating a proper road between the lakes and using larger boats to carry vehicles, which, while making it easier to go from Villa O'Higgins to Puerto Natales, will destroy the frontier feel that currently exists.

Southern Patagonia

Enormous glaciers calving icebergs the size of houses, pristine fjords and dozens of islands make up the otherworldly vistas of Magallanes province, or **SOUTHERN PATAGONIA**. Add in forbidding craggy peaks, impossibly blue glacial lakes, a wealth of wildlife and the sheer size and majesty of the internationally renowned **Torres del Paine** national park, and it's easy to see why Patagonia captures the imagination of travellers and explorers. Sparsely inhabited, the region is buffeted by storms from the Pacific and is subject to a powerful wind, known as the "escoba de Díos" ("God's broom"), that is capable of snapping large trees in two, and winters are exceptionally harsh. Cut off from the rest of Chile by the giant Campo de Hielo Sur (Patagonian Ice Fields) to the northeast, the locals have a strong camaraderie with their counterparts across the Andes; many consider themselves to be Patagonians first, Chileans or Argentines second.

PUNTA ARENAS

On the shores of the turbulent Magellan Strait, 241km southeast of Puerto Natales, **PUNTA ARENAS** is Patagonia's largest and southernmost city. Originally a remote military garrison know to British sailors as "Sandy Point", the city provided a convenient stopover for ships heading to California during the gold rush of 1849, and then grew in size and importance with the introduction of sheep from the Falkland Islands to the Patagonian plains. Punta Arenas emerged as a wool empire, drawing migrant workers from Croatia, Italy, Spain and Britain, among others, and evolved into a thriving port. Following the decline of the wool economy after World War II, the city benefited from the discovery of petroleum in Tierra del Fuego in the 1940s, and now makes its living from a combination of petroleum production, commercial fishing and tourism.

What to see and do

The city centre is compact and easy to navigate, its streets laid out in a grid, and most services and conveniences lie within a few blocks of the main square.

Plaza Muñoz Gamero

The heart of the city is this tranquil, shady square lined with lofty Monterrey cypresses and craft stalls, hosting occasional live music. In the centre stands a fierce-looking statue of **Ferdinand Magellan**, donated by wool magnate José Menéndez in 1920 to commemorate the 400-year anniversary of the explorer's voyage. A statue of a **Tehuelche Indian**, symbolizing Patagonia, sits at the foot of the monument; it is believed that if you touch or kiss his big toe, you will one day return to Punta Arenas. Around the square you can also see a number of ornate buildings, such as the Sara Braun mansion, dating back to its wool-producing heyday.

Mirador Cerro La Cruz

A five-block walk along Calle Fagnano from the southeast corner of the square brings you up to the *mirador*, offering an excellent view of the brightly coloured, galvanized metal rooftops of Punta Arenas and the deep blue Magellan Strait beyond. Nearby, at España 959, stands a red-brick tower with gothic windows – **Castillo Milward**, the house that formerly belonged to the eccentric explorer Charley Milward, relative of the writer Bruce Chatwin and described in his travel memoir *In Patagonia*.

Casa Braun-Menéndez

Casa Braun-Menéndez (Tues–Sun 10.30am–12.30pm & 3–5.30pm;

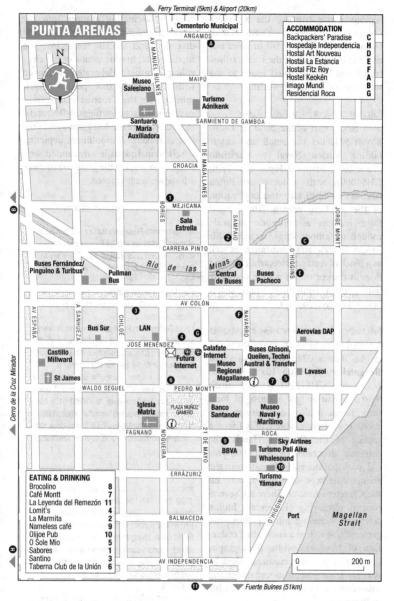

Ferry Terminal (5km) & Airport (20km)

PUNTA ARENAS

N

Cementerio Municipal
ANGAMOS

Museo Salesiano

MAIPÚ

Turismo Aónikenk

Santuario María Auxiliadora

SARMIENTO DE GAMBOA

CROACIA

MEJICANA

Sala Estrella

CARRERA PINTO

Buses Fernández/ Pingüino & Turibus'

Pullman Bus

Río de las Minas

Central de Buses

Buses Pacheco

AV COLÓN

Bus Sur

LAN

JOSÉ MENÉNDEZ

Castillo Millward

St James

WALDO SEGUEL

PEDRO MONTT

Futura Internet

Calafate Internet

Museo Regional Magallanes

Buses Ghisoni, Queilen, Techni Austral & Transfer

Aerovías DAP

Lavasol

Iglesia Matriz

PLAZA MUÑOZ GAMERO

Banco Santander

Museo Naval y Marítimo

FAGNANO

ROCA

BBVA

Sky Airlines

Turismo Pali Aike

Whalesound

ERRÁZURIZ

Turismo Yámana

BALMACEDA

Port

Magellan Strait

AV INDEPENDENCIA

0   200 m

Fuerte Bulnes (51km)

ACCOMMODATION

Backpackers' Paradise	C
Hospedaje Independencia	H
Hostal Art Nouveau	D
Hostal La Estancia	E
Hostal Fitz Roy	F
Hostel Keokén	A
Imago Mundi	B
Residencial Roca	G

EATING & DRINKING

Brocolino	8
Café Montt	7
La Leyenda del Remezón	11
Lomit's	4
La Marmita	2
Nameless café	9
Olijoe Pub	10
O Sole Mio	5
Sabores	1
Santino	3
Taberna Club de la Unión	6

Cerro de la Cruz Mirador

CH\$2000), the former family residence of the marriage that united the two wealthiest and most powerful families in Punta Arenas, is located half a block northeast of the plaza at Magallanes 949, and is divided between perfectly preserved living quarters, featuring superb French Art Nouveau family furnishings, and the **Museo Regional Magallanes**. The museum features displays on the maritime and farming history of the region, as well as the region's native tribes – the Kawéscar (Alacalúf) and the Selk'nam (Ona). Ironically, the displays fail to point out that the destruction of the native tribes' traditional lifestyle owed much to the wool barons' pursuit of wealth.

Museo Naval y Marítimo

Two blocks east of the plaza, at Pedro Montt 981, lies the small and entertaining **Museo Naval y Marítimo** (Tues–Sat 9.30am–12.30pm & 2–7pm; CH$1000), with a focus on Punta Arenas's naval history and exploration of the southern oceans. The ground floor features a multitude of scale models of famous ships, including Sir Ernest Shackleton's *Endurance*, as well as a block of Antarctic ice, while the first floor is decked out as a ship, complete with nautical equipment, maps, charts and interactive displays.

Museo Salesiano Borgatello

Located seven blocks north of the plaza, at Av. Bulnes 336, **Museo Salesiano Borgatello** (Tues–Sun 10am–12.30pm & 3–6pm; CH$1500) is very much worth a visit to get a sense of local flora, fauna, geology and history. One room is entirely devoted to a life-size replica of the **Cave of Hands**; the original, decorated with 11,000-year old rock paintings, is found near the small settlement of Chile Chico, off the Carretera Austral. There are several rooms displaying Kawéscar Indian artefacts, including hunting tools and garments, as well as a fascinating collection of black-and-white photographs documenting native cultures, taken by Alberto D'Agostini, a mountaineer and missionary who spent much of his life in Patagonia.

Cementerio Municipal

A stroll through the darkly impressive **Cementerio Municipal** (daily 7.30am–8pm), its straight alleys lined with immaculately sculpted cypresses,

offers a fascinating glimpse into the city's immigrant history, cultural diversity and social hierarchy. The monumental marble tombs of the city's ruling families, elaborately engraved with the English and Spanish names, mingle with the Croatian and Scandinavian names of immigrant labourers, etched on more modest grave spaces the size of lockers. A monument depicting a **Selk'nam Indian** is surrounded with plaques conveying the gratitude of those whose wishes it granted.

Arrival and information

Air Aeropuerto Presidente Ibáñez is 20km north of town. Flights are met by Buses Fernández (CH$2500) and taxis (CH$10,000). Transfers to Puerto Natales meet flights arriving during day time hours.

Bus There is no central bus station, though all buses arrive within four or five blocks of the Plaza de Armas.

Ferry Ferries from Puerto Williams and Porvenir arrive at the Terminal Tres Puentes on the north side of town; frequent *colectivos* (CH$600) shuttle between the docks and the city centre.

Tourist office There's a tourist information kiosk on the east side of Plaza Muñoz Gamero (Mon–Sat 8am–6pm, Sun 9am–6pm; ☎61/200-610), and a helpful and well-stocked Sernatur office at Navarro 999, at Pedro Montt (Mon–Fri 8.30am–6pm, Sat 10am–6pm; ☎61/241-330, ⓦwww.sernatur.cl).

Accommodation

Backpackers' Paradise Ignacio Carrera Pinto 1022 ☎61/240-104, Ⓔbackpackersparadise @hotmail.com. Run by an effusive hostess and perpetually popular with younger travellers, this hostel offers cheap bunks in two large, open-plan rooms. Laundry service, free hot drinks, secure luggage storage, kitchen facilities, internet access and bike rentals are among the extras. Dorms CH$7000.

Hospedaje Independencia Av. Independencia 374 ☎61/227-572, ⓦwww.chileaustral.com /independencia. This hostel, six blocks from the centre, is popular with hikers and bikers; there's a homely feel to the dorms and rooms, which are small but warm and comfortable. The friendly young family has camping spaces in their front yard and rent camping equipment; they also organize tours of the area and let you use their kitchen. Camping CH$2000 per person, dorms and rooms CH$5000 per person.

Hostal Art Nouveau Navarro 762 ☏61/228-112, ⓦwww.hostalartnouveau.cl. Owned by *Brocolino*'s effusive chef, this quiet guesthouse decorated in, erm, Art Nouveau style is a godsend in colder weather, when you'll truly appreciate having central heating. The rooms are compact en-suites with buffet breakfast included, and there's a gazebo in the back yard for relaxing in. CH$25,000.

Hostal La Estancia O'Higgins 765, ☏61/249-130, ⓦwww.backpackerschile.com/en/hostel-estancia .php. At this perpetually popular hostel, you're well looked after by the bilingual Alex and Carmen, who can arrange your outdoor adventures. The restored 1920s house has spacious rooms and comfortable common areas. Book in advance, even in the off-season. Foreigners paying with US$ are exempt from tax. Dorms CH$10,000, rooms CH$30,000.

Hostal Fitz Roy Lautaro Navarro 762 ☏61/240-430, ⓦwww.hostalfitzroy.com. This old-fashioned guesthouse has large, rambling rooms with shared bathrooms, kitchen privileges and continental breakfast included. The owner is a former Torres del Paine guide and can help you organize all manner of outdoor trips. Dorms CH$8500, rooms CH$24,000.

Hostel Keokén Navarro 762 ☏61/226-507, ⓦwww.hostelkeoken.cl. Comfortable rooms, a book exchange and kitchen privileges are all on offer at this welcoming family-run guesthouse right by the cemetery; ask about camping in the back yard. English, French and Italian is spoken and the owners can help you with further travel arrangements. CH$24,000.

🏃 **Imago Mundi** Mejicana 252 ☏61/613-115, ⓦwww.imagomundipatagonia.cl. Environmentallyconscious travellers and outdoor junkies alike flock to this popular little hostel run by a brother-sister team. There are just eight cosy bunk beds in two en-suite rooms, as well as an on-site climbing gym for pros and beginners alike, an excellent café (full-board is possible) and an attached cultural centre that often features live music. Dorms CH$12,500.

Residencial Roca Magallanes 888, 2nd floor ☏61/243-903, ✉franruiz@entelchile.net. If all you're after is a central location and a bed for the night, this rambling guesthouse, run by a friendly family, has large, spartan rooms at a bargain price. Basic breakfast included. CH$12,000.

Eating

🏃 **Brocolino** O'Higgins 1055. The unassuming exterior hides some of the best food in Patagonia; don't miss "aphrodisiac soup", made with the freshest seafood and *centolla* (king crab) or steak "in the style of Paris Hilton", whatever that means. Mains CH$5500–9000.

Café Montt Pedro Montt 976. A book exchange and wi-fi are available in this cosy coffee shop, as well as a good selection of teas and coffees. Particularly good is the caffeine-fuelled creation with condensed milk (CH$1700).

La Leyenda del Remezón 21 de Mayo 1469. On a par with *Brocolino* (see above) when it comes to creativity, chef Luís takes a walk on the wild side, his ingredients being as diverse as beaver and venison. The salmon smoked with black tea also comes highly recommended. Mains from CH$10,000.

Lomit's Menéndez 722. Dependable diner, open until the wee hours even on Sundays, that serves a good variety of sandwiches as well as nicely cooked burgers. The staff live on zen time, so be prepared for a wait. Mains from CH$4000.

🏃 **La Marmita** Plaza Sampaio 678. If you can tear your gaze away from the decor, order one of the imaginative dishes made from organic produce, such as the exotic *ceviche* with coconut milk, or the tasty *caldillo de congrio* (conger eel soup). The pisco sours, served in martini glasses, are the best in Patagonia and the calafate berry and chocolate dessert is a work of art. Mains from CH$6500.

Nameless café Fagnano 875. Elbow your way to the counter at this tiny nameless joint packed with locals and grab a banana milkshake or *choripan con queso* (bread with chorizo and cheese); CH$600.

O Sole Mio O'Higgins 974. An informal Italian restaurant decorated with classic movie posters, serving tasty home-made pastas, gnocchi and other fare for around CH$6000.

Sabores Mejicana 702. Cosy spot offering such bargains as the four-course "Magellanic menu" (CH$12,000), which includes the local speciality of *centolla* (king crab), ample portions of home-made pasta and hearty seafood stews.

Drinking

Olijoe Pub Errázuriz 970. Decked out like an upscale English pub, with its leather and dark wood, this pub serves a good selection of beers, though its speciality is the *glaciar*: a potent mix of pisco, milk, *horchata* and curaçao. It may take a while to catch the barman's eye.

Santino Colón 657. Spacious, welcoming pub offering typical Chilean food, such as *lomo a* *la pobre*, as well as good sandwiches. Beers CH$1200; mains CH$5000.

Taberna Club de la Unión inside the Sara Braun mansion, Montt at Nogueira. Travellers can't resist this darkly elegant basement drinking venue – a former gentlemen's club and gathering point for the town's most powerful men.

Directory

Banks and exchange There are several banks with global ATMs located around the Plaza Muñoz Gamero, including Banco Santander and BBVA. There are cambios along Roca and Lautaro Navarro.
Hospital Hospital Regional at Angamos 180 (☎61/205-000) deals with 24hr emergencies.
Internet and phone Try *Hostal Calafate*, at Magallanes 922, which has an excellent phone centre and internet café (daily 9am–11pm; CH$700 per hr); or the similarly priced Futura Internet around the corner (daily 9am–midnight).
Laundry Autoservicio Lavasol, at O'Higgins 969 (open daily; CH$3500 per load).
Pharmacy There are several well-stocked pharmacies along Bories.
Post office Bories 911.

Moving on

Air LAN and Sky Airline offer daily flights to Santiago and frequent flights to other parts of Chile. Aerovías DAP has frequent flights to Puerto Williams and Porvenir, as well as twice-weekly flights to Ushuaia.
Bus The Central de Pasajeros, on Av. Colón and Magallanes (☎61/245-811), sells tickets for several companies.

Queilen Bus, Buses Pacheco, Bus Sur and Turibus to Puerto Montt and Chiloé (daily; 34–36hr); Buses Fernández, Buses Pacheco and Bus Sur to Puerto Natales (several daily; 3hr); Buses Pacheco, Bus Sur, Tecni Austral to Ushuaia via Río Grande (daily morning departures around 8am; 12–14hr); Pinguino, Buses Ghisoni, and Buses Pacheco to Río Gallegos (daily at around 11am; 5–7hr).
Ferry Transbordadora Austral Broom, at Av. Bulnes 5075 (☎61/218-100, ⊛www.tabsa.cl) operates the ferry *Cruz Australis* to Puerto Williams (Wed only; CH$110,000 for a berth, CH$91,000 for a Pullman seat; 38hr, subject to weather conditions), while the *Melinka* sails to Porvenir (daily; 2.5–4hr; CH$5100).

AROUND PUNTA ARENAS

In the middle of the stormy Magellan Strait lies **Isla Magdalena** – the largest Magellanic **penguin colony** in all of Chile, with an estimated 100,000 nesting birds residing on a one-kilometre-square cliff by the historical lighthouse. The monogamous birds spend the September to March breeding season here, living in burrows in the ground. The female lays two eggs in October, with both parents taking turns looking after the chicks once they've hatched in December, while the other fishes for food. In early February you'll find the grown chicks huddled near the sea, as large as their parents but still growing the adult feathers necessary for swimming.

PUNTA ARENAS TOUR OPERATORS

Turismo Aónikenk Magallanes 619 ☎61/221-982, ⊛www.aonikenk.com. Multi-day hiking excursions in southern Patagonia and Tierra del Fuego as well as local day-trips to the penguin colonies and Pali Aike National Park. Multi-day Dientes de Navarino hike from US$999.
Turismo Pali Aike Navarro 1125 ☎61/233-301, ⊛www.turismopaliaike.com. A variety of nature-watching trips, including daily trips to Isla Magdalena, Seno Otway and Estancia Lolita, as well as full-day canopy trips, transfers to the nearby Reserva Nacional Magallanes and excursions to the historical Fuerte Bulnes. Day-trip to Pali Aike park CH$45,000.

Turismo Yámana Errázuriz 932 ☎61/710-567, ⊛www.yamana.cl. Intrepid single- and multi-day kayaking trips on and around the Strait of Magellan, taking in seal and penguin colonies, as well as multi-day trekking and riding excursions in Tierra del Fuego. Nine-day kayak expedition from US$2995.
Whalesound Navarro 1163, 2nd floor ☎61/221-076, ⊛www.whalesound.com. Responsible operator offering study-based kayaking trips to the Coloane Marine Park and humpback whale-watching trips from December to May. All-inclusive trip (2 day, 1 night) US$1100.

The **best time to visit** the colony is January, when the population is at its largest. Though you have to stick to the designated walking routes, the penguins don't fear humans and will come quite close to you. You can visit the colony with the large ferry *Melinka*, run by **Turismo Comapa** (Magallanes 990 ☎61/200-200, Dec daily at 3pm, Jan & Feb daily at 7.30am & 3pm, with around 90 minutes on the island; CH$25,000) or with **Turismo Aonikenk** (see p.508), which has daily excursions to the island in a small Zodiac boat (7.15am daily, depending on weather conditions; CH$35,000), passing Isla Marta on the way (home to a colony of sea lions who use nearby Isla Magdalena as their local takeaway).

Pingüinera Seno Otway

If you can't make the boat trip to Isla Magdalena, then don't miss the land-based excursion to the colony of **Seno Otway**, 70 kilometre northwest of Punta Arenas. Hosting around eight thousand Magellanic penguins at its peak, the breeding site is fenced off and visitors are obliged to stick to the wooden boardwalk that runs between the penguin burrows. While not as up-close-and-personal as Isla Magdalena, you still get excellent views of the penguins, especially at the viewpoint by the beach, where you can watch them frolic in the waves just a few metres away. Several tour operators run tours at 4pm daily (CH$15,000; CH$2500 entry charge not included).

Cabo Froward

Around 90 kilometre south of Punta Arenas lies **Cabo Froward** – the southernmost point on the continent, marked with an enormous cross erected in honour of the 1987 visit by Pope John Paul II, which can be reached via a starkly picturesque two-day hike along the weather-beaten cliffs. While the 50-kilometre trail is now well signposted and no longer as wild as it used to be, this is still a challenging hike that requires you to be prepared for any weather that Patagonia may throw at you, and to ford several rivers along the way.

There are **camping facilities** along the way, as well as a rustic *refugio* and the upmarket *Hostería San Isidro* at the San Isidro lighthouse (☎09/9349-3862, ⓦhosteriafarosanisidro.cl), halfway along the trail. You can either join a guided expedition (see box on Puerto Natales tour operators, p.512) or do it alone, taking all necessary supplies with you and catching a ride to the start of the trail, past Fuerte Bulnes.

PUERTO NATALES

The town of **PUERTO NATALES** is situated in relative isolation on the **Seno Última Esperanza** ("Last Hope Sound"). Officially founded in 1911, it was used primarily as a port for exporting wool and beef from the nearby Puerto Prat cattle *estancia*, built by German explorer **Hermann Eberhard** in 1893. Though the export trade has since declined, the town's proximity to one of the continent's most popular national parks – Torres del Paine – as well as Argentina's Parque Nacional Los Glaciares, combined with daily buses to various Chilean and Argentine cities and a popular Navimag cruise from Puerto Montt, has led to a tourist boom that has firmly established Puerto Natales as one of Patagonia's top destinations for outdoor enthusiasts.

Faced with a motley collection of tin and wooden houses, a visitor's first impression of Puerto Natales is invariably coloured by the weather. On a clear day, Seno Última Esperanza, bordering the town's west side, is a remarkably vivid, tranquil blue, with magnificent views of the snow-capped **Cordillera Sarmiento** and **Campo de Hielo Sur** visible across the bay. Bad weather can be very bad indeed.

What to see and do

The town is built on a grid pattern and very easy to navigate. It is centred on the **Plaza de Armas**, with a multitude of guesthouses, restaurants and services located along nearby streets, and its main commercial thoroughfares are north-south Baquedano and east-west Bulnes. The plaza is overlooked by the colonial church – **Iglesia Parroquial María Auxiliadora**, and has an old **locomotive engine** formerly used in the Puerto Bories abattoir as its centrepiece, an evening magnet for lovers and drunken teenagers.

Museo Histórico Municipal

The worthwhile little **Museo Histórico** at Bulnes 285 (Dec–Feb Mon–Fri 8.30am–1pm & 3–8pm, Sat & Sun 2.30–6pm; rest of the year Mon–Thurs 8am–5.30pm, Fri 8am–4.30pm; CH$1000), less than two blocks from the plaza, has attractive bilingual exhibits on the region's **native tribes**, illustrated with black-and-white photos of Aónikenk and Kawéscar Indians, as well as on European settlement and natural history, including the story of the Milodon's cave. A room is dedicated to Hermann Eberhard, the intrepid German explorer responsible for early settlement in the region; the most compelling exhibit is his collapsible boat that turns into a suitcase.

Arrival and information

Air The tiny airport is 5km out of town.
Buses Puerto Natales has no central bus station but all buses stop within a couple of blocks of each other.
Ferry The Navimag ferry (Bulnes 533 ☎61/414-300, ⓦwww.navimag.cl) docks at the pier five blocks west of the Plaza de Armas.
Tourist information Sernatur is at Pedro Montt 19, on the shore of the Seno Última Esperanza (Dec–Feb Mon–Fri 8.15am–7pm, Sat & Sun 10am–1pm & 3–6pm; rest of the year Mon–Fri 8.30am–1pm & 2.30–6pm; Sat 10am–1pm & 2.30–5.30pm; ☎61/412-125, ⓦwww.sernatur.cl), with very

Airport, Punta Arenas, ▲ Parque Nacional torres Delpaine (111km) & Cueva De Milodón (24km)

PUERTO NATALES

ACCOMMODATION

Alma Gaucha	F
Casa Cecilia	A
Erratic Rock II	G
Hostal Kawashkar	H
Hostal Lili Patagonicos	E
Patagonia Adventure	B
Residencial Los Inmigrantes	C
Yagan House	D

EATING & DRINKING

40 y 20 Fruta Seca	10
Afrigonia	7
El Asador Patagónico	3
Baguales	1
El Bar de Ruperto	8
Base Camp	11
El Living	2
Mesita Grande	5
Patagonia Dulce	6
La Picada de Carlitos	9
Última Esperanza	4

helpful staff. Erratic Rock at Baquedano 719 holds excellent daily talks at 3pm at "Base Camp" on hiking in Torres del Paine, covering logistics as well as park etiquette and required gear.

"Black Sheep", a monthly freebie widely available around town, contains entertaining articles and lots of useful information about the surrounding area. If you want anything booked, from bus tickets to tours to accommodation in Argentina, look no further than the Austral Glacier office at Baquedano 695 (℡09/9357-8558, ⓦwww.australglacier.com).

Accommodation

Alma Gaucha Galvarino 661 ℡61/413-243, ⓔalmagauchacl@hotmail.com. Rustic backpacker joint with cowboy paraphernalia adorning the walls, run by a genuine gaucho. Dorms are basic but spacious and the owner sometimes throws a Patagonian BBQ on the patio. Dorms CH$8000.

Casa Cecilia Tomás Rodgers 60 ℡61/613-560, ⓦwww.casaceciliahostal.com. The rooms at this long-established guesthouse are on the small side, but the helpful owners are good for trekking info. Guests have use of the kitchen and the good breakfast includes home-made bread. CH$20,000.

Erratic Rock II Zamora 732 ℡61/414317, ⓦwww.erraticrock2.com. A good choice for those wanting a quiet stay with all the creature comforts; the rooms are plush, the bathrooms sparkling and the breakfast ample. CH$30,000.

Hostal Kawashkar Encalada 754 ℡61/414-553. Incredibly laidback backpacker haunt, run by the knowledgeable Omar. Kitchen privileges and lockers are included; it's possible to camp out back and Omar helps to organize your stay. Dorms CH$7000.

Hostal Lili Patagonicos Prat 479 ℡61/414-063, ⓦwww.lilipatagonicos.com. The new contender for the best hostel in town, this lively place features an indoor climbing wall, an excellent breakfast, wi-fi and book exchange, and the owners organize half- and full-day trips into the surrounding area. The doubles are particularly plush. Dorms CH$7000, rooms CH$16,000.

Patagonia Adventure Tomás Rogers 179 ℡61/411028, ⓦwww.apatagonia.com. Brightly decorated central hostel run by young owners; a good breakfast is included and other bonuses include internet, a camping gear outlet next door and the hostel's own adventure outfit for kayaking enthusiasts. Dorms CH$8000, rooms CH$20,000.

Residencial Los Inmigrantes Carrera Pinto 480 ℡61/413-482. An excellent choice for hikers; the congenial owner – a former guide – is a treasure trove of information on the surrounding area.

Kitchen privileges are included. Dorms CH$8000, rooms CH$20,000.

Yagan House O'Higgins 584 ℡61/414-137, ⓦwww.yaganhouse.cl. Highly recommended hostel, with comfy beds, a fire blazing in the welcoming lounge and owners who can arrange all manner of tours. Dorms CH$10,000, rooms CH$25,000.

Eating and drinking

40 y 20 Fruta Seca Baquedano 443. The place to stock up on a bewildering array of dried fruit and nuts for the forthcoming hike. Dried mango is especially good. CH$500 per 100g.

Afrigonia Eberhard 343. The place to splurge, this trendy little restaurant titillates with its imaginative, flavourful African-Patagonian fusion dishes. Try the ceviche with mango or the seafood curry with *wali* (rice with almonds and raisins), and follow it down with a decadent chocolate dessert. Service can be slow when the place is full. Mains CH$6500.

El Asador Patagónico Prat 158. Like most hikers, you'll be drawn into this excellent restaurant catering primarily to carnivores by the sight of the *asador patagónico* – a lamb being spit-roasted in front of you, Patagonian style. The expertly cooked steaks are just as good; bring your appetite, as the portions are ample. Mains CH$8500.

Baguales Bories. If the one thing that would make your Patagonian hiking experience complete is returning to a cosy brewery that serves ample platters of tasty Buffalo wings, quesadillas, tacos and other assorted Tex-Mex food, accompanied by rice and beans and home-made guacamole, then you're in luck: look no further than this new Californian-Chilean pub on the Plaza de Armas. Beers CH$1700; quesadillas CH$4400.

El Bar de Ruperto Bulnes 310. Popular bar with loud music, Guinness and pool tables, drawing a younger crowd – a good spot for a post-hike beer. Open until 4.30am on weekends.

Base Camp Baquedano 719. This new pub is set to draw the crowds, with the backpackers from next door raising the roof during the odd rock and reggae gig, or enjoying a post-hike beer or three.

⚞ **El Living** Prat 156. Not just an excellent vegetarian restaurant, with changing daily specials, but also the town's most popular café/lounge, playing chilled-out tunes, and featuring the best book exchange in town. Smoothies, sandwiches and salads stand out, and the proprietress makes excellent cakes, too; the only drawback is that it seems to close too early. Daily specials CH$4500. Closed mid-April to October.

⚞ **Mesita Grande** Prat 196. Hordes of hungry hikers stage a daily invasion of the best pizzeria in Patagonia, drawn by the generous portions of superb thin-crust pizzas (CH$5000), home-made pasta and sumptuous desserts (including sweet pizza with *dulce de leche*). Customers sit along two long wooden tables, which encourages conversation and creates a communal dining experience.

Patagonia Dulce Arana 233. Those with a sweet tooth shouldn't miss out on the home-made chocolates and ice cream in this little gingerbread-house-like café, though it's not the cheapest. They say that if you eat calafate berries, you'll return to Patagonia; whether the same is true of calafate berry ice cream (CH$1700) is not clear, but it's worth a try.

La Picada de Carlitos Encalada 444. Ever-popular place famed for its hearty Chilean dishes, such as the *cazuela de pollo* (chicken stew), as well as the big sandwiches. *Menú del día* CH$3000.

Última Esperanza Eberhard 354. Come early to get seats in this extremely popular restaurant, which serves some of the tastiest fish and seafood in southern Chile. Try the *chupe de locos* (abalone chowder) for CH$8000.

Directory

Banks and exchange Banco Santander, on Blanco Encalada at Bulnes, and Banco de Chile, at Bulnes 544, both have ATMs. Casa de Cambios at Bulnes 692 gives reasonable exchange rates.

Camping equipment Rent camping gear at Patagonia Adeventure, Tomás Rogers 179; or Base Camp, Baquedano 719. Buy camping essentials at La Maddera, Prat 297, or at the Survival Outdoor Store, Baquedano 622.

Hospital Hospital Puerto Natales (☎61/411-583), at Pinto and O'Higgins, handles basic medical emergencies, but the facilities in Punta Arenas are better.

Internet and phone Call centres tend to be expensive, so it's better to use Skype at one of the many Skype-equipped internet cafés. *Hotel Reymar*, Esmeralda at Baquedano, has good connections.

Laundry Lavandería Milodon, Baquedano 642 (daily 10am–noon & 2.30–8pm).

Pharmacy Farmacía Cruz Verde, Bulnes at Blanco Encalada.

Post office Eberhard 429.

Moving on

Air El Calafate (daily departures with Aerovías DAP).

Bus Bus Sur, Turismo Zaahj, Cootra and Transportes JB to El Calafate (daily morning departures during high season; 5hr 30min); Buses Fernández, Bus Sur and Puses Pacheco to Punta Arenas (several daily; 3hr); Transportes JB, Bus Sur, Buses Gómez and Turismo Zaahj to Torres del Paine (daily Dec–Feb at 7am, 8am & 2.30pm; fewer departures other

---

PUERTO NATALES TOUR OPERATORS

Baqueano Zamora Baquedano 534 ☎61/613531, ✪www.baqueanozamora.com. Horse-trekking trips of varying length in Torres del Paine National Park. Half-day horseriding CH$25,000; full-day CH$45,000.

Erratic Rock Baquedano 719 ✪www .erraticrock.com. Equipment rental, informative talks on Torres del Paine and multi-day trekking expeditions to Cabo Froward and Isla Navarino, among others.

Indómita Bories 206 ☎61/414-525, ✪www .indomitapatagonia.com. Kayaking adventures, from half-day trips around Last Hope Sound (CH$50,000) to multi-day expeditions in northern Patagonian fjords.

Rutas Patagonia Blanco Encalada 353 ☎61/613-874, ✪www.rutaspatagonia.cl. Up-and-coming operator offering ice-hiking and kayaking trips in Torres del Paine National Park (Ch$45,000 for a half-day ice hike).

> ## HIKING THE "W"
>
> Though Torres del Paine offers numerous hiking trails, the most popular is undoubtedly the "W", a four- to five-day hike that takes in the park's highlights: the massive Glacier Grey, steep Valle Francés, and finally, the *miradór* Las Torres. It makes sense to hike the "W" from west to east, tackling the steepest ascent first, especially if you're carrying camping gear, as you will have eaten most of your provisions by the time you approach the challenging *mirador*, and will have grown used to the rigours of the hike.

months; 2hr); Bus Sur and Buses Pacheco to Ushuaia (four weekly at 7am; 14hr).

Ferry The Navimag ferry *MV Magallanes* sails to Puerto Montt (weekly on Fri mornings; from CH$180,000, see box, p.487; 4 days). Book a couple of weeks in advance in summer.

PARQUE NACIONAL TORRES DEL PAINE

Your first glimpse of **PARQUE NACIONAL TORRES DEL PAINE** comes after a 112km drive northwest of Puerto Natales through an interminable stretch of brown scrubland, enlivened only by a few **ñandú** (small ostriches). The park teases you with the sheer granite towers of **Las Torres** to the east, and the multicoloured **Los Cuernos** to the west, dominating the startling emerald-green waters of **Laguna Amarga** at the park entrance.

The park offers incomparable opportunities for backcountry hiking, as well as animal spotting; you are likely to see **guanacos** – wild relatives of llamas – that dwell here in large numbers. Pumas also live in the park, though they're shy, as well as foxes, the elusive *huemúl* deer and condors. There are also challenging scrambles to the park's *miradores* and a host of other outdoor activities – from ice-trekking on the Glacier Grey to horseriding in the outlying hills.

Lago Pehoé

After Laguna Amarga (see "Arrival and information", p.517), the bus stops at the northern tip of **Lago Pehoé**, near the catamaran pier. From here it's a fifteen-minute walk uphill to **Salto Grande**, a thundering waterfall fed by melting glacial waters, with views of Los Cuernos in the distance. There's also an easy hour's walk along the lakeside to another **viewpoint**, offering a spectacular vista of the Cuernos del Paine, reflected in the icy blue waters of Lago Nordenskjöld. You can commence on the "W" by taking the Hielos Patagónicos catamaran (see p.518) across Lago Pehoé to the *Paine Grande Lodge* (see p.518).

Glacier Grey

From *Hostería Pehoé*, a clearly marked trail runs north through the scrubland, partially shaded by clusters of *ñirre* (a native Chilean plant), past a small lagoon and into a *lenga* forest, crisscrossed with narrow, icy streams. During this leg of the hike you don't have to worry about carrying enough water, as you can top up with some of the cleanest drinking water on earth. The trail meanders before emerging at the **Quebrada de los Vientos** ("Windy Gorge"), an hour or so into the hike, where your first glimpse of **Glacier Grey** stops you in your tracks. For the next couple of hours, you walk across exposed terrain, beside the pale water of Lago Grey and its house-sized chunks of blue ice. The glacier peeks from behind the dark rock of **La Isla Nunatak** on the lake's far side.

The trail then descends steeply through the silent *lenga* woods, almost doubling back on itself and crossing a wooden bridge over a gushing torrent, before emerging on the lakeshore. Ten

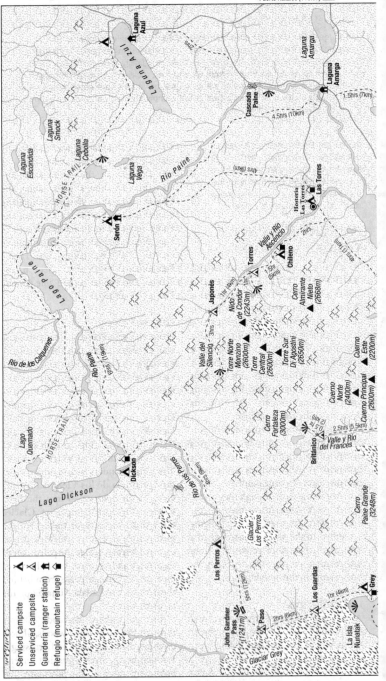

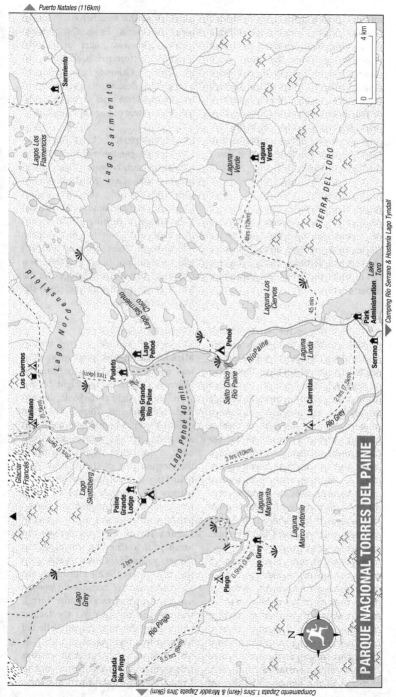

PARQUE NACIONAL TORRES DEL PAINE

Puerto Natales (116km)

Sarmiento

Lagos Los Flamencos

Lago Sarmiento

Laguna Verde

SIERRA DEL TORO

Lago Nordenskjöld

Lago Chico

Lago Sarmiento

Laguna Los Ciervos

45 min

4hrs (12km)

Camping Rio Serrano & Hostería Lago Tyndall

Park Administration

Lake Toro

Serrano

Laguna Linda

Río Paine

Pehoé

Lago Pehoé

Puerto

1hrs (4km)

Salto Grande Río Paine

Salto Chico Río Paine

Las Carretas

Río Grey

2 hrs (7.5km)

Los Cuernos

Italiano

(5.5km)

Glaciar Frances

2hrs (9km)

Lago Skottsberg

Lago Pehoé 40 min

Paine Grande Lodge

3 hrs (10km)

Laguna Margarita

Laguna Marco Antonio

Lago Grey

3 hrs

Pingo

0.5hrs (3 km)

Lago Grey

Río Pingo

5.5 hrs (8km)

Cascada Río Pingo

N

Compamento Zapata 1.5hrs (4km) & Mirador Zapata 3hrs (9km)

515

minutes before arriving at a shaded lakeside clearing housing the **Refugio y Camping Grey**, another short trail branches off from the main path, leading you to a rocky outcrop with a spectacular close-up of the glacier's gigantic ice crystals. The hike lasts three or four hours; *Refugio y Camping Grey* marks the end of the first leg of the "W", from where you either double back to Lago Pehoé or continue north if doing the "Circuit" (see p.517).

Lago Grey

From the *Hostería Lago Grey* it's possible to take a spectacular three-hour **boat ride** up Lago Grey to the glacier, or kayak right up to it, past the massive blue icebergs. Rutas Patagonia can organize the latter; check ahead for departure times.

Valle Francés

A two-hour long, eastbound trail heads through scrubland and prickly calafate bushes along Lago Pehoé before leading north with glimpses of **Lago Skottsberg** on your right-hand side. As you round the imposing 3050-metre Paine Grande massif, look up, as there is a known condor nest near the peak. A wobbly hanging bridge brings you to the *Campamento Italiano*, where you can leave most of your gear before scrambling up the steep rocky path leading up the **Valle Francés**, the middle part of the "W". The turbulent **Río del Francés** churns on your left-hand side and there are spectacular views of Glacier Francés and Glacier Los Perros.

After two hours hiking through enchanted-looking woods, you reach the very basic *Campamento Británico*, from where it's an hour's hike up to the steep lookout that gives you an excellent close-up view of the multicoloured Los Cuernos, rising from dense forest to the east, as well as the aptly named 2800-metre-high **Fortaleza** ("fortress"), northeast of the *mirador*. The descent can be somewhat treacherous, so hiking poles are useful. From *Campamento Italiano*, allow two hours for the hike through the forested backcountry to the *Refugio y Camping Los Cuernos*; it's a long steep descent on a scree-strewn trail followed by a brief stretch along the pale blue waters of Lago Nordenskjöld.

Los Cuernos to Las Torres

From the *refugio*, the trail runs through hilly scrubland, crossing several small streams, with Lago Nordenskjöld on your right. Shortly after you depart Los Cuernos, you come to the **Río del Valle Bader**, a rushing glacial stream that can be difficult to cross without hiking poles. This sector of the hike takes around four hours and there is a clear track that crosses a bridge over the Río Asencio just before you reach the *Hostería Las Torres*.

Mirador Las Torres

To see the sunrise at the famous **Mirador Las Torres**, some make their way up the Valle Ascencio from the *Hostería Las Torres* the night before, spending the night at the basic, unserviced *Campamento Torres*. The hike itself is a steep, 3 hour 30 minute ascent alongside the Río Ascencio. You'll need to rise before daybreak to tackle the steepest part of the journey – an hour-long scramble up boulders – to witness the spectacle of the sun's first rays colouring the magnificent Torres, perfectly reflected in the still waters of **Laguna Torres**. Alternatively, you can break your journey by staying at the *Refugio y Camping Chileno*, halfway up the trail. Or take the hike further up the Valle Ascencio to *Campamento Japonés*, used by climbers tackling the Torres, then up another steep yet spectacular climb along the aptly named **Valle del Silencio** to a less-visited *mirador*. The "W" ends with a short trek or minibus ride from *Hostería Las Torres* back to Laguna Amarga and the park entrance.

The "Circuit"

The "Circuit" is an extended version of the "W", a seven- to ten-day hike that leads you around the back of the Torres, giving you respite from the inevitable crowds during peak season, and offering unique glimpses of the park, which you may be able to experience in complete solitude. You can either start from the *Paine Grande Lodge* and head straight for the Valle Francés, or you can stay on the bus past Lago Pehoé, get off at the Park Administration, and do the scenic five-hour walk before commencing on the Circuit (this is called "doing the Q"). Alternatively, you can follow the trail directly from **Laguna Amarga**, from where it's a mostly flat five-hour hike along Río Paine to *Camping Serón*. You can also pick up the trail from the *Hostería Las Torres*.

From *Serón*, the trail climbs a hill and meanders along Lago and then Río Paine for six hours before descending steeply to the shores of **Lago Dickson**. You can spend the night at the *Refugio y Camping Dickson*, or press on southwards along the **Río de Los Perros**, crossing the bridge over the Río Cabeza de Indio and passing the beautiful Salto Los Perros on your right, before reaching *Camping Los Perros* on the far side of a small lagoon, three or

four hours later. Then comes the most challenging part of the Circuit: the crossing of the rock and snow of the **John Gardner Pass**, which takes five hours, leading you to *Campamento Paso* alongside the impossibly massive Glacier Grey. You may have to wait for favourable weather conditions at Los Perros, as crossing the pass in inclement weather can be fatal. You rejoin the "W" after a two-hour hike along the glacier, passing *Campamento Los Guardas* just an hour from the *Refugio y Camping Grey*. Since there is only one *refugio* along the Circuit, you will have to stop at unserviced campsites most of the way, bringing food and camping supplies with you.

Arrival and information

Bus Buses from Puerto Natales stop at the Laguna Amarga park administration building, then at Pudeto (the catamaran departure point) and finally at the Administration building. Out of season, when the catamaran is no longer running, the buses stop first at Administration and then at Laguna Amarga. Minibus transfers (CH$2500) meet the buses at Laguna Amarga and run to *Refugio y Camping Las Torres*.

Conaf The Conaf *guardería* at Laguna Amarga has information on the park's fauna and flora, as well as basic trekking maps. You must register and pay your CH$15,000/8,000 peak/off-peak entrance fee here. Ranger stations at Lago Sarmiento, Laguna Azul, Lago Grey and Laguna Verde also have basic

---

REFUGIOS IN TORRES DEL PAINE

Most of the park's campsites and refugios are open only from October to April, as winter weather makes them inaccessible. The campsites are run by Conaf, while the *refugios* belong either to Andescape (Eberhard 599 ⊕61/412-592, ⓦwww .andescapepatagonia.com), or Fantástico Sur (Magallanes 960 ⊕61/710-050, ⓦwww.lastorres.com), both in Puerto Natales. At the *refugios* you can rent bedding and enjoy pricey hot meals (around CH$5500 for breakfast, CH$7500 for lunch and CH$10,000 for dinner). Though it is widely suggested that you book your *refugio* space in advance, especially in the peak season from December to February, high prices mean that many hikers opt for camping instead, so it's often possible to just turn up and get a bed. You can rent camping equipment at Las Torres, Chileno, Los Cuernos and Serón: tents CH$6000; sleeping bags CH$3500; mats CH$1500. There are several unserviced campsites in the park which are free of charge and consist of a clearing with a fire pit; these include *Campamento Paso*, *Campamento Italiano*, *Campamento Británico* and *Campamento Torres*. Wild camping inside the park is not permitted.

information on the park. The Conaf-run Centro de Informaciones Ecológicas (Dec–Feb daily 8.30am–8pm; ☎61/691931, ✉ptpaine@conaf.cl) at the Lago del Toro Park Administration building has extensive displays on the park fauna and flora.

Ferry A Hielos Patagónicos catamaran (☎61/411-380; CH$11,000 one-way, CH$18000 return) crosses Lago Pehoé from Pudeto, returning from Paine Grande 30min later. Pudeto departures are at 9.30am, noon and 6pm (Nov 16–March 15); noon & 6pm (March 16–March 31 & Oct 16–Nov 15); or noon only (Oct 1–Oct 15 & April 1–April 30); there is no service the rest of the year.

Accommodation

Campamento Los Perros (Andescape). Halfway between the John Garner pass and the *refugio Dickson*, this campsite comes equipped with hot showers, a food shop and equipment rental; meals have to be reserved in advance. Camping CH$4000.

Campamento Serón (Fantástico Sur). Partially shaded campsite on the Circuit beside the Río Paine; hot showers, toilets, and a *guardería* on-site. Camping CH$4000.

Refugio y Campamento Chileno (Fantástico Sur). A popular stop halfway along the Valle Ascencio, this *refugio* offers kitchen privileges after certain hours as well as hot meals. Camping CH$4000, rooms CH$20,000.

Refugio y Campamento Los Cuernos (Fantástico Sur). *Refugio* serving good meals, with kitchen privileges after 10pm; campers share bathroom facilities with *refugio* guests. Camping spots are sheltered among vegetation. Camping CH$5000, rooms CH$20,000.

Refugio y Campamento Dickson (Andescape). On the shore of Lago Dickson, this *refugio* offers hot showers and hot meals, and has a small grocery kiosk and equipment rental. Camping CH$4000, rooms CH$21,000.

Refugio y Campamento Grey (Andescape). A small popular *refugio* a stone's throw from Glacier Grey; book meals in advance. Campsite includes hot showers and a small on-site grocery store. Camping CH$4000, rooms CH$21,000.

Campamento Paine Grande /Paine Grande Lodge (Andescape). The campground, where you can rent gear, has an indoor cooking area, hot showers and bathrooms. The popular lodge has great views of Lago Pehoé, as well as a small grocery store, café-bar and restaurant, though the food is decidedly uninspiring. Camping CH$4000, rooms CH$25,000.

Refugio y Campamento Las Torres (Fantástico Sur). Near the entrance to the park, this *refugio* is split between two buildings and has comfortable bunks as well as decent food. Camping spots have hot showers, picnic tables and fire pits. More upmarket eating can be found at the excellent restaurant at nearby *Hostería Las Torres*. Camping CH$4000, rooms CH$20,000.

Tierra del Fuego

TIERRA DEL FUEGO, the most remote of Chile's land territories, was named "Land of Fire" by Fernando Magellan, who sailed through the strait that now bears his name, and saw a multitude of cooking fires lit by the native hunter-gatherers who made this inhospitable terrain their home. Prior to the creation of the Panama Canal, the frigid waters around Cape Horn – the largest ship graveyard in the Americas – formed a link in the perilous yet lucrative trade route from Europe to the west coast of the Americas.

Tierra del Fuego's Isla Grande is split between Chile and Argentina; the Chilean half features the nondescript town of **Porvenir**, settled by a mixture of Chilote and Croatian immigrants in the late nineteenth century, as well as a number of remote sheep-rearing *estancias*. The Argentine half includes the lively town of **Ushuaia**, the base for Antarctic voyages. The region's biggest natural draw is southern Tierra del Fuego – a scattering of rocky islands, separated by labyrinthine fjords, home to the craggy Darwin Range and the southernmost permanently inhabited town in the world – Isla Navarino's **Puerto Williams**.

PUERTO WILLIAMS

Although Argentine Ushuaia, on the north side of the Beagle Channel, loudly proclaims its "end of the world" status, that title rightfully belongs to **PUERTO**

THE YÁMANA, THE SELK'NAM AND THE KAWÉSCAR

The unforgiving lands of Tierra del Fuego and Isla Navarino were originally home to three tribes: the Yámana (Yahgan), the Selk'nam (Ona) and the Kawéscar (Alacalúf), all of whom lived along the coast and subsisted on a diet of fish, shellfish and marine animals. Though dismissed by European explorers as savages (Charles Darwin famously commented that the "Canoe Indians" were "among the most abject and miserable creatures I ever saw"), and now largely culturally extinct, the tribes had complex rituals. The Selk'nam, for example, performed a sophisticated male initiation ceremony, during which young male initiates confronted and unmasked malevolent spirits they had been taught to fear since their youth, emerging as *maars* (adults). Father Martín Gusinde was present at the last such ceremony in 1923, and managed to capture the event in a series of remarkable photographs, copies of which circulate as postcards today.

WILLIAMS. Home to just over two thousand people, the windblown town has a desolate quality to it even in the height of the brief summer and is completely at the mercy of the elements. In contrast to the weather, the people of Puerto Williams are exceptionally warm and welcoming; you get a real sense of a close-knit community, brought together by isolation from the rest of Chile. The isolation is occasionally broken by the arrival of an Antarctica-bound ship of researchers, or international hikers looking to tackle the arduous Dientes de Navarino circuit.

What to see and do

The post office, Aerovías DAP office, a call centre and internet café are concentrated in the **Centro Comercial**, by Plaza O'Higgins. There's a global ATM at the Banco de Chile towards the waterfront and several small **supermarkets** along Piloto Pardo. Parallel Yelcho leads uphill to the colourful, wind-blown **cemetery**, while Avenida Costanera takes you past a cluster of beached fishing boats, and the rusted hulk of a half-sunken barge loaded with *centolla* traps, towards the indigenous community of **Villa Ukika**. In the other direction, it leads you towards the **airport** and the *Club Naval de Yates Micalvi*, past the **Mirador Plaza Costanera**, the bright-red pier leading up to the channel, from which you get

a wonderful view of the town against a backdrop of forest-covered mountain peaks beyond.

Museo Martín Gusinde

This worthwhile **museum**, at Aragay 1 (Mon–Fri 9am–1pm & 2.30–7pm, Sat & Sun 2.30–6.30pm; donations), is named after a clergyman and anthropologist who spent a great deal of time among the native tribes of Tierra del Fuego. Located on the west side of town, it features informative and well-laid-out displays on the native Kawéscar, Selk'nam and Yámana Indians, complete with a replica of a Selk'nam ritual hut, as well as exhibits on local geology, flora and fauna.

Arrival and information

Air The tiny airport receiving Aerovías DAP flights from Punta Arenas and chartered flights from Ushuaia lies a short distance from Puerto Williams; flights are met by local minivans that double as taxis.

Boat The Transbordadora Austral Broom (Ⓦwww .tabsa.cl) ferry arrives at Puerto Williams on Friday nights. Speedboats from Ushuaia dock at tiny Puerto Navarino, on the eastern end of the island, where visitors have to check in with Chilean immigration authorities; minibus transfers take passengers to their *residenciales* in Puerto Williams, an hour's drive across the island.

Tourist information There's a booth in the Centro Comercial that acts as a tourist information office (when it's actually open) and hands out photocopied maps of Los Dientes de Navarino. If the information booth is closed, ask the proprietress at the nearby yellow bakery to open it. Check out ⓦwww .imcabodehornos.cl for more information.

Accommodation

Hostal Bella Vista Teniente Muñoz 118 ☏61/621-010, ⓦwww.victory-cruises.com. A new hostel with incredible views of the Beagle Channel, run by an American-Chilean family. Warm rooms (some en-suite), with laundry service, wi-fi and discounts at the internet café and the minimart. Sailing trips to Cape Horn and Antarctica on their yacht *S/V Victory* are on offer. CH$34,000.

Hostal Coirón Ricardo Maragaño 168 ☏61/621-150, ⓔhostalcoiron@tie.cl. Knowledgeable and helpful young owner runs a friendly hostel popular with backpackers, with a dorm, a couple of en-suite twin rooms, kitchen use and intermittent internet. Dorm CH$10,000; rooms CH$25,000.

Hostal Patagonia Yelcho 230 ☏61/621-075, ⓔpedroortiz@chilesat.net. Owned by the proprietor of *Club Naval de Yates Micalvi*, this guesthouse has several clean and cosy singles and doubles; there is satellite TV and internet, and the owners cook up traditional Chilean food. Rooms CH$25,000 (full board CH$10,000 extra).

Residencial Pusaki Piloto Pardo 222 ☏61/621-116, ⓔpattypusaki@yahoo.es. Another backpacker favourite run by an extremely hospitable family, this hostel has warm, cosy rooms with shared bath as well as a common lounge and kitchen. CH$22,000.

Eating and drinking

Café Ángelus Centro Comercial Norte 151. A beacon of light in the early darkness, this inviting café lures you in with a range of alcoholic coffees, cakes, decent sandwiches and pasta. The friendly proprietress is a good source of local information and speaks fluent English and French. Pasta dishes CH$4000; coffee CH$1200.

Club Naval de Yates Micalvi Seno Lauta Costanera s/n. The former Navy ship is a nightly gathering point for travellers, local sailors and Antarctic explorers; open late. Drinks are not cheap, but the atmosphere can be priceless.

Los Nonos Pizzeria Presidente Ibañez 147. Pizzeria popular with locals serving Navarino takes on the Italian idea: expect lots of cheese and seafood toppings. Pizza for one CH$4000.

🏃 Residencial Pusaki Piloto Pardo 222. Even if you're not a guest here, give the owner a couple of hours' warning and come try some of her delicious home-cooking at dinnertime; *centolla* night is the best, when Patty makes filling king-crab stew. CH$5000.

Moving on

Air Aerovías DAP, Centro Comercial Sur 151 (☏61/621-051, ⓦwww.aeroviasdap.cl), has flights to Punta Arenas (Nov–March daily; April–Oct 3 weekly); reserve several weeks in advance if flying between Dec and Feb. One-way/return CH$70,000/110,000; luggage restriction 10–15kg.

Boat The Transbordadora Austral Broom ferry (☏61/621015 ⓦwww.tabsa.cl) sails to Punta Arenas (every Sat night; seat/berth CH$91,000/110,000; 38hr). Ushuaia Boating, at Maragano 168, Ushuaia (☏+54/061-221-227), runs small zodiac boats to and from Puerto Navarino (Sept–March daily at 9am & 4.30pm, depending on the weather; 30min; one way/return CH$60,000/110,000). The boats do not sail in extreme conditions, so be prepared to spend an extra day or two on Isla Navarino.

ISLA NAVARINO TOUR OPERATORS

Outdoor activities on and around Isla Navarino tend to be on the expensive side and not for the faint-hearted, but if you've had fantasies about yachting to Cape Horn or tackling some of the most challenging hiking in Latin America, several experienced tour operators in Puerto Williams can help you realize your dream.

Sea & Ice & Mountains Adventures Unlimited Austral 74 ☏61/621-227, ⓦwww .simltd.com. Intrepid German-Venezuelan operator organizing hiking and horseriding on Isla Navarino and Cordillera Darwin, as well as sea-kayaking trips and multi-day yacht excursions around Cape Horn and even to Antarctica.

Shila Turismo Aventura O'Higgins 322 ☏61/621-366, ⓦwww.turismoshila.cl. Luis and family run trekking trips around Isla Navarino (including the Dientes circuit) and fishing excursions to Lago Windhond, Lago Navarino and Laguna Rojas; they also rent outdoor gear.

AROUND PUERTO WILLIAMS

Many travellers come to Puerto Williams to complete the challenging 70-km **Los Dientes de Navarino Circuit** – a strenuous four- to seven-day clockwise trek in the Isla Navarino wilderness for experienced hikers only. Follow Vía Uno west out of town; the trail starts behind the statue of the Virgin Mary in a grassy clearing. The road leads uphill up to a waterfall and reservoir, from where a marked trail climbs steadily through the *coigüe* and *ñirre* forest. It's a two-hour ascent to **Cerro Banderas**, a *mirador* with a wonderful view of the town, the Beagle Channel and the nearby mountains; a climb that is definitely worthwhile even if you're not thinking of doing the circuit.

The rest of the trail is not well marked, and leads you past the starkly beautiful **Laguna El Salto**, then crosses a fairly steep pass to **Laguna de los Dientes**. Continue west past Lagunas Escondido, Hermosa and Matrillo before reaching the particularly steep and treacherous descent of **Arroyo Virginia**; beware of loose rocks. The trail officially finishes behind the **Centolla Factory**, from where you can follow the main road back to Puerto Williams. Before setting out, ensure you have plentiful food and water supplies, a good map (you can pick up rudimentary photocopied maps of the trail at the tourist kiost, but it's far better to get the JLM Beagle Channel Trekking Map no. 23 in Punta Arenas or Santiago), sunscreen and warm and waterproof outdoor gear. Be prepared for inclement weather – it can snow even in summer – and inform people in town of your plans before leaving.

Ukika and beyond

A 15-minute coastal walk east along the waterfront brings you to the hamlet of **Villa Ukika**, home to the last remaining descendants of the Yámana people. Here you'll find a replica of a traditional Yámana dwelling – the **Kipa-Akar** (House of Woman) – which can be unlocked and viewed on request, and you can purchase handicrafts such as reed baskets and miniature canoes. From Villa Ukika, the road runs south-east through the dense forest for 26 kilometres before ending at **Puerto Toro**, a tiny fishing post frequented by *centolla* fishermen. Beyond lies the cold expanse of the Atlantic Ocean, the treacherous Cape Horn, and Antarctica – the final frontier.

Easter Island

One of the most remote island territories on earth, over 2000km from the nearest inhabited part of the world, **EASTER ISLAND** entices visitors with the enduring mystery of its **lost culture**. A remarkable civilization arose here, far from outside influence on an island only 163 square kilometres in extent. It apparently declined rapidly and had all but disappeared by the time Europeans first arrived here. Originally known as "Te Pito O Te Henua", or "the navel of the world", due to its isolation, and now called "Rapa Nui" by its inhabitants (*Pascuenses*), the island is home to a culture and people with strong Polynesian roots and a language of their own, which sets it well apart from mainland Chile. Archeological mysteries aside, the island has much to offer: year-round warm weather, excellent diving and surfing conditions and plenty of scope for leisurely exploration of the more out-of-the-way attractions, both on foot and on horseback. Welcoming people, excellent food and a laidback atmosphere seal the deal.

HANGA ROA

The island's only settlement and home to around four thousand people,

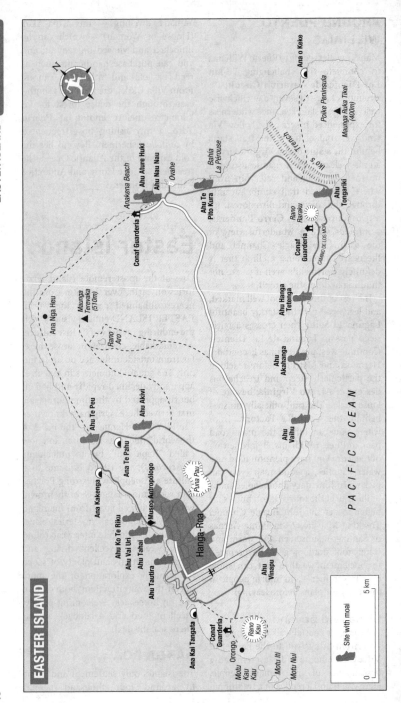

EASTER ISLAND

PACIFIC OCEAN

Ana o Keke

Poike Peninsula

Maunga Ruka Tikei (400m)

Ahu Tongariki

Trench

27°S

Bahía La Pérouse

Ahu Te Pito Kura

Ovahe

Ahu Nau Nau

Ahu Ature Huki

Anakena Beach

Conaf Guardería

Rano Raraku

Conaf Guardería

CAMINO DE LOS MOAI

Ahu Hanga Tetenga

Ahu Akahanga

Ahu Vaihu

Maunga Terevaka (510m)

Ana Nga Heu

Rano Aro

Ahu Te Peu

Ahu Akivi

Ana Te Pahu

Ana Kakenga

Museo Antropológico

Puna Pau

Ahu Ko Te Riku

Ahu Vai Uri

Ahu Tahai

Hanga Roa

Ahu Tautira

Ana Kai Tangata

Conaf Guardería

Orongo

Rano Kau

Ahu Vinapu

Motu Kau Kau

Motu Iti

Motu Nui

◣ Site with moai

0 _____ 5 km

522

HANGA ROA is a dusty village spread out along the Pacific coast. At night there is limited street lighting and the sky, lit with endless stars, is spectacular. North–south Atamu Tekena is the main road, lined with small supermarkets, cafés and tour agencies. Much of the action is centred on the pier, Caleta Hanga Roa, overlooked by **Ahu Tautira**, the only *moai* site in the town proper. Restaurants spread from here along oceanside Policarpo Toro and east–west Te Pito O Te Henua, which takes you past the small Plaza Policarpo Toro before ending at the Iglesia Hanga Roa, a Catholic **church** decorated with elaborate wood carvings.

What to see and do

Just south of the pier and opposite the tourist office lies tiny **Playa Pea**, a rock pool safe for swimming, cordoned off from the stretch of ocean popular with surfers and bodyboarders. Avenida Policarpo Toro heads north, past the Hanga Roa **cemetery** with its colourful crosses, to three main sites, particu-

---

A BRIEF HISTORY OF EASTER ISLAND

500–800 AD Easter Island is settled by King Hotu Matu'a and his extended family, who come from either the Pitcairn Islands, or the Cook or Marquesas Islands in Polynesia. The island is divided between *mata* (tribes), each led by a male descendant of the original king.

800–1600 Population grows to an estimated 20,000–30,000. Island culture evolves into a complex society and flourishes; *ahu* (ceremonial platforms) are built and *moai* (stone statues) are erected all over the island.

1600–1722 Natural resources are depleted and deforestation takes its toll. Two warring factions form: the Ko Tu'u Aro, who rule the island's western half, and the Hotu Iti, who populate its eastern half. *Moai* construction stops, the population declines and the Birdman cult develops.

1722 Dutch admiral Jacob Roggeveen lands and names the island after the day of his arrival – Easter Sunday.

1770 The expedition of Felipe Gonzáles de Haedo claims Easter Island for King Carlos III of Spain.

1774 Captain James Cook visits; he finds the *moai* in ruins and the population bedraggled.

1862 Nearly one thousand islanders are kidnapped to work as slaves in the guano mines of the Chincha Islands off the coast of Peru, including the island's king and all the priestly elite. Later, one hundred islanders are shipped back to Easter Island; the final fifteen survivors of this voyage infect the islanders with smallpox and the population is reduced to a few hundred.

1870 The island is purchased for a pittance by Frenchman Jean Baptiste Dutroux-Bornier, who wages war on missionaries. Most islanders agree to be shipped to Tahiti rather than work in indentured servitude.

1888–1953 Easter Island becomes part of Chile and is leased to the Compañía Explotadora de la Isla de Pascua, a subsidiary of the sheep-rearing Scottish-owned Williamson, Balfour and Company. Villagers are confined to Hanga Roa.

1953 Company's lease is revoked; Easter Island comes under the control of the Chilean Navy.

1967 Mataveri Airport is built. Islanders are given full rights as Chilean citizens.

1967–present day The island undergoes material improvement and the Rapa Nui language is no longer suppressed. Disputes with the Chilean government over ancestral land rights, however, continue.

larly spectacular at sunset. First is **Ahu Tahai**, with a single large *moai*, then **Ahu Vai Uri**, with five standing *moai* in various states of repair, and finally the much-photographed **Ahu Ko Te Riku**, a single *moai* with a *pukao* (topknot) and intact, pensive-looking coral eyes. Also in this direction, amid gentle hills dotted with numerous *hare paenga* (boat-shaped foundations of traditional houses), lies the **anthropological museum** (see below). To the south, Policarpo Toro heads towards the extinct Rano Kau volcano.

Museo Antropológico Padre Sebastían Englert

Off the coastal road just north of Ahu Tahai, this excellent **museum** (Tues–Fri 9.30am–5.30pm, Sat & Sun 9.30am–12.30pm; CH$1500; ☎322/551020, ⦵www.museorapanui .cl, Spanish only), is not to be missed, as it gives a thorough and informative

introduction to the island's geography, history, society, Birdman cult (see box, p.526) and the origins and significance of the *moai*. The well-labelled displays are in Spanish, with English-language handouts, and include a rare female *moai*, a wooden carving of a *moai kavakava* – a gaunt figure, believed to represent the spirits of dead ancestors, and replica *rongorongo* tablets (no original examples remain on the island). *Rongorongo* script is one of only four written languages in the world that developed independently of outside influence; the tablets were first mentioned in the nineteenth-century accounts of French missionary Eugene Eyraud, and their purpose remains unclear. It seems that only a small priestly elite was literate and that the knowledge perished with them during the slave raids and smallpox epidemic of the early 1860s. The script remains undeciphered to this day.

HANGA ROA

PACIFIC OCEAN

0   500 m

Caleta Hanga Piko

Orongo & Rano Kau (4km)

Caleta Hanga Roa

Orca Diving Centre

Playa Pea

Banco Santander $

AV. APINA

AV. POLICARPO TORO

Banco Estado (ATM)

AV. POLICARPO TORO

Makemake Rentabike

Taura'a Tours

LAN Chile

Kia Koe Tour

Insular Car Rental

Oceanic Rent A bike

AV. ATAMU TEKENA

Farmacia Cruz Verde

Supermerket Kai Nene

AV. AVAREIPUA

Feria Municipal

Man@net

Policarpo Toro

Mike Rapu Diving Centre

Banco Estado

Football Field

Cemetery

Entel

AV. TE PITO O TE HENUA

AV. ATAMU TEKENA

Omotohi Cybercafe

Lavandería Rapa Nui

Aku Aku Turismo

Plaza Policarpo Toro

Mercado Artesanal

Iglesia Hanga Roa

Jail

Aeropuerto Mataveri

AV. HOTU MATUA

AV. PONT

AV. TUUKOIHU

AV. SIMON PAOA

Hospital

Tahai & Museo Antropológico

ACCOMMODATION
Ana Rapu	B
Apina Tupuna	C
Camping Mihinoa	A
Hostal Aukara	E
Inaki Uhi	D
Residencial Kona Tau	F

EATING, DRINKING & ENTERTAINMENT
Ahi Ahi	5
Au Boût du Monde	3
Café Ra'a	6
La Esquina	8
Kite Mate	7
Matato 'a	3
Merahi Ra'a	4
Mikafé	1
La Taverne du Pêcheur	2

▼ Anakena (22km)   Ahu Akivi ▼

THE RISE AND FALL OF THE MOAI OF EASTER ISLAND

The giant stone statues, around 887 of which litter the island, are a unique symbol of a lost civilization, whose existence raises many questions. Why were they made? By whom? How were they transported around the island and erected without the benefit of machinery? Why was their construction suddenly abandoned?

Believed to be representations of ancestors, the statues range from two to ten metres in height, with an average weight of twelve tons. The majority of the *moai* share a similar appearance: elongated features and limbs, prominent noses, heavy brows and rounded bellies. Most are male, and some wear *pukao*, topknots carved of red stone in a separate quarry. Most *moai* once had coral-and-rock eyes, though now the only intact example is Ahu Ko Te Riku.

Carved from the slopes of the Rano Raraku quarry, the *moai* were buried upright in earthen pits so that their sculptors could shape their facial features with basalt *toki* (chisels), and then lowered down the volcano's slopes, presumably using ropes. Most archeologists believe that to transport them to the coastal *ahu* (platforms) the islanders used wooden rollers or sledges – a practice which resulted in complete deforestation – and that once at the foot of the *ahu*, the *moai* were lifted into place using wooden levers. All *moai*, apart from those at Ahu Akivi, were positioned around the coast facing inland, so as to direct their *mana* (life energy) towards their creators and to bless them with plentiful food and other bounties.

It is known that at the height of Easter Island's civilization (800–1500 AD), the tiny island supported a large and complex multi-tiered society, with a ruling class who worshipped Make-Make, the creator, and oversaw the construction of these statues. A phenomenal amount of energy must have gone into their creation and transportation, fatally depleting the island's resources and causing acute food shortages. Full-scale warfare erupted when farmers and fishermen couldn't or wouldn't support the *moai*-carving workforce any longer. The carving ceased and the *moai* were toppled from their pedestals. That which gave the civilization purpose was ultimately also its undoing.

Rano Kau crater and Orongo ceremonial village

South of Hanga Roa, a dirt road climbs steeply past a *mirador* offering an excellent panoramic view of the island, to one of Easter Island's most awe-inspiring spots – the giant crater of the extinct **Rano Kau volcano**. The dull waters of the volcano's reed-choked lake contrast sharply with the brilliant blue of the Pacific, visible where a great chunk of the crater wall is missing. You pay the CH$5000 entry fee at the Conaf ranger station just before you reach **Orongo ceremonial village**; it is valid for one visit each to the two main sights of **Parque Nacional Rapa Nui** which comprises much of the island: Orongo and Rano Kau.

The Orongo site of the Birdman cult consists of 53 restored houses with tiny doorways, made of horizontally overlapping flat stone slabs, hugging the side of the cliff. A winding labelled footpath leads past them to the edge of Rano Kau, where a cluster of **petroglyphs** depicting the half-bird, half-human Birdman, as well as Make-Make, the creator, overlook a sheer drop, with the islets Motu Kao Kao, Motu Iti and Motu Nui jutting out of the azure waters below.

THE SOUTHERN COAST

Heading east out of Hanga Roa, Hotu Matu'a leads you towards the **southern coast**. A right turn at the end, followed by an almost immediate left by the fuel storage tanks, takes you to **Vinapu**, an important site consisting of three *ahus* (stone platforms) with a number of broken *moai* scattered around. The *ahus* are made of overlapping stone slabs, seemingly similar in construction to those built by the Inca in Cusco, Peru, leading some archeologists to believe that Easter Island culture has Latin American roots. Continuing east along this coast you reach **Ahu Vaihu**, with its eight toppled *moai* and their scattered *pukao* (stone topknots). Up the road, the large **Ahu Akahanga** is widely believed to be the burial place of Hotu Matu'a, the first king of the island. The site features a dozen *moai*, lying face down, with petroglyphs carved into one of the platforms. There are also the remains of a village, consisting of *hare paenga* outlines, as well as a number of *pukao*.

Another 3km east, the almost utterly ruined **Ahu Hanga Tetenga** consists of two toppled and shattered *moai*. Beyond, the road forks, the northern branch looping inland toward Rano Raraku, while the east-bound branch continues to **Ahu Tongariki**, one of the island's most enduring and awe-inspiring images. Consisting of fifteen *moai*, one significantly taller than the rest and another sporting a topknot, the island's largest *moai* site was destroyed by a tsunami in 1960, and re-erected by the Japanese company Tadano between 1992 and 1995.

Rano Raraku

Just inland of Ahu Tongariki lies the unforgettable spectacle of **Rano Raraku** – the gigantic quarry where all of Easter Island's *moai* were chiselled out of the tuff (compressed volcanic ash) that makes up the sides of the crater. From the Conaf ranger station, a dirt path leads up to the volcano's slopes, littered with dozens of completed *moai*, abandoned on the way to their *ahus*. The right branch meanders between the giant statues, buried in the ground up to their necks, their heads mournfully looking out to sea. You pass *moai* in various stages of completion, including the largest one ever carved, **El Gigante**, 21m tall and 4m wide, its back still joined to the stone from which it was carved. The east end of the path culminates in the kneeling, round-headed **Moai Tukuturi**, the only one of its kind, discovered by Thor Heyerdahl's expedition in 1955.

To the west, the trail winds its way up between wild guava trees into the crater itself, with a dirt path running through knee-high shrubbery alongside the large reed-strewn lake. You may take the footpath up to the crater's eastern rim for unparalleled views of the bay and Ahu Tongariki in the distance, but only if accompanied by a ranger or a guide. There has been increased concern regarding visitor behaviour ever since a Finnish tourist was caught in 2008 while trying to break an ear off a moai to take home as a souvenir.

THE CULT OF THE BIRDMAN

The Birdman cult venerating the creator Make-Make flourished in the eighteenth and nineteenth centuries, up until the 1860s. An important element of the religion was a brutal and dangerous competition staged each year between July and September to pick the Tangata Manu, or Birdman. Only military chiefs were allowed to compete; they would send their representatives, or *hopu*, on a swim through shark-infested waters to the *motu* (islets) off the coast. The *hopu* would often attempt to stab their rivals on the way. Once on the *motu* the competitors would wait for days to retrieve the first Manutara (sooty tern) egg of the season; the winner would then communicate his victory to those waiting in Orongo. The chosen Birdman then spent the year in complete seclusion, either in one of the houses in the Orongo village or in Anakena, attended to only by a priest, while his family enjoyed an elevated social status and special privileges.

Ovahe Beach

This small, sheltered **beach** is located off a dirt road just before Anakena Beach, on the other side of the Maunga Puha hillock. Backed by tall cliffs, its pristine sands are very popular with locals who come here to picnic, swim and snorkel. It's best earlier in the day, before the cliff blocks the afternoon sun.

Anakena Beach

Easter Island's largest and most popular beach is found on the northeast side of the island, and can be reached directly by the paved, cross-island road. A white-sand beach dotted with coconut trees, it has picnic tables and fire pits, public toilets and showers, as well as food stands offering drinks and snacks. The beach is also home to the largest *hare paenga* (boat-shaped house) on the island and is believed to have been the landing point for the legendary King Hotu Matu'a. To the east stands the large, squat *moai* on **Ahu Ature Huki**, re-erected by Thor Heyerdahl's expedition of 1955 with the help of some islanders, while nearby stand the seven *moai* of **Ahu Nau Nau**, four sporting *pukaos* and two badly damaged. The best time for photographers to visit is in the mid-afternoon.

THE NORTHERN COAST AND THE INNER LOOP

Heading up the coast from the north end of Hanga Roa, a rutted dirt-and-gravel road takes you past **Ana Kakenga**, or Caverna Dos Ventanas – a cave set in the cliff with a spectacular view of the coast. Look for two offshore **islets**, Motu Ko Hepko and Motu Tautara; the cave is directly opposite them, with a cairn indicating the location. Bring a torch if you wish to explore. Further along, at the site of Ahu Tepeu, the road turns inland while a path carries on up to a copse of trees. The inland road leads you along fenced-off pasture land to **Ana Te Pahu** on your right-hand side – one of many underground **lava caves** on the island, used as a *manavai* (underground garden) to cultivate bananas, sweet potatoes, taro and other tropical plants due to its moisture and fertile soil.

At the southwestern base of **Maunga Terevaka**, the island's highest point (507m), is **Ahu Akivi**, with seven intact *moai*, the only ones on the island to be looking out to sea. As the road heads south to link up with the island's main thoroughfare, a dirt track to the west takes you to **Puna Pau**, the quarry where the *pukao* were carved.

Arrival and information

Air Aeropuerto Mataveri (☎ 322/100-277) is located on Hotu Matu'a, southeast of Hanga Roa; most *residenciales* provide free transfers. Flights to Easter Island tend to be in the region of US$700–900, unless you buy your ticket very much in advance and also in conjunction with a long-distance LAN flight.

Conaf Mataveri Otai s/n, south of Hanga Roa (Mon–Fri 8.30am–5pm; ☎ 322/100-236, ⊛ www.conaf .cl), has information on the Rapa Nui National Park. Conaf ranger stations are found at Rano Raraku, Anakena Beach and Orongo ceremonial village.

Tourist office Policarpo Toro at Tu'u Maheke (Mon–Fri 8.30am–1.30pm & 2.30–5.30pm; ☎ 322/100-255). Helpful staff provide detailed information on the island's attractions and can help you organize camping, activities such as horse-riding and vehicle rental; some English and French is spoken. There is a tourist information booth at the airport providing brochures on the island.

Accommodation

Ana Rapu Apina Iti s/n ☎ 322/100-540, ⊛ www .anarapu.cl. Accommodation at this seafront guesthouse, set in a garden overflowing with lush vegetation, ranges from camping spots to large, airy en-suites and cabañas. It's possible to arrange horseriding and scuba-diving with Ana herself and her son Joaquín. Camping CH$7500, rooms CH$27,000, cabañas CH$40,000.

Apina Tupuna Policarpo Toro s/n ☎ 322/100-763. Oceanside *residencial* popular with backpackers and surfers, offering six bright rooms around a large communal area, decorated with the owner's own artwork; alternatively you can rent one of the 2–3 person cabañas. Breakfast and fully equipped kitchen included; camping allowed on the lawn. Camping CH$7000, rooms CH$21,000, cabañas CH$30,000.

Camping Mihinoa Pont s/n ☎ 322/551-593, ⓦ www.mihinoa.com. Large campsite with an excellent ocean view, run by a friendly family, with adjoined showers, kitchen facilities, dining room, internet access and scooter and bike rental; complete lack of shade is the only drawback. Adjoining guesthouse has basic, clean rooms and a five-bed dorm; it's also possible to rent camping equipment. Camping CH$5500, dorms CH$7000, rooms CH$20,000.

Hostal Aukara Av. Pont s/n ☎ 322/100-539, ⓦ www.aukara.cl. Follow the signs for the Aukara art gallery, which showcases the owner's pieces, to this small guesthouse, lost in the midst of the beautiful garden. The rooms are basic but comfortable, there's a small kitchen for guests and guided tours of the gallery are available. CH$37,000.

Inaki Uhi Av. Atamu Tekena s/n ☎ 322/551-160, ⓦ www.inakiuhi.com. As central as it gets, this guesthouse consists of two self-contained appartments (for 2 and 4 people) and sixteen pristine rooms and fully equipped kitchens in two low-slung buildings, with an attractive garden/sitting area in between. What the rooms lack in character, the owners more than make up for by being extremely accommodating. There is currently a café/internet area being built. CH$35,000.

Residencial Kona Tau Avareipua s/n ☎ 322/100-321, ⓦ www.hostelz.com/hostel/44363-Kona-Tau. HI-affiliated hostel in a large family home with a friendly atmosphere, with sixteen comfortable dorm beds, as well as basic en-suite rooms set in a mango-strewn garden. Large breakfast a bonus, but the staff can be hard to find. Dorms CH$10,000, rooms CH$30,000.

Eating

Ahi Ahi Off Av. Policarpo Toro, next to the football field. Enjoy a spirited Sunday football game over a fresh fruit juice and a sandwich at this informal shack.

Café Ra'a Atamu Tekena s/n, near Plaza Policarpo Toro. Popular café with outdoor terrace, excelling in light dishes. The tuna *ceviche* is divine and the fresh fruit juices are excellent (if pricey). *Ceviche* CH$9000.

La Esquina Te Pito O Te Henua and Tu'u Koihu. For epic fruit juices, come to this chilled-out place popular with locals. The pizza and the *empanadas* aren't half bad either. Fresh fruit juice CH$2000; pizza CH$4500.

Kite Mate Plaza Policarpo Toro. This bright-green shack serves some of the best *empanadas* on the island (CH$1400–2000); try the *surtido de mariscos* or the *atún y queso*.

Merahi Ra'a Te Pito O Te Henua s/n. This is the place to come for large servings of the freshest grilled fish, the *mahi mahi* (dorado) being particularly tasty; the local speciality is *rape rape* (spiny lobster). Fish dishes from CH$9000.

Mikafé Caleta Hanga Roa s/n. Tiny café with outdoor seating overlooking the bay featuring the tastiest home-made ice cream on the island, as well as exotic fruit juices from CH$1700 (try the guayaba), and banana cake to die for.

La Taverne du Pêcheur Av. Te Pito O Te Henua s/n. Sit on the attractive terrace at the (formerly) best restaurant in town and dig into expertly prepared fish, accompanied by island tubers. The desserts are also superb, though the pleasure doesn't come cheaply, and the quality of the service depends on the mood of the chef. Mains from CH$12,000; desserts CH$6000.

Drinking and entertainment

Kari Kari Atamu Tekena s/n, opposite Tuku Haka He Vari. Extremely entertaining traditional dance-and-music show, featuring talented young dancers and musicians in elaborate costumes. Be warned that there is usually some audience participation. Tues, Thurs and Sat at 9pm; CH$12,000.

Matato'a Av. Policarpo Toro s/n. At a venue next to Au Bout Du Monde, this internationally renowned band with vividly painted bodies and faces turns up the heat with its energetic music and dance - a mix of traditional and modern, accompanied by "umu", or typical Rapa Nui cuisine. Mon, Thurs and Sun at 9.30pm.

Piditi Av. Hotu Matua s/n, by the airport. Smaller club that gets packed with an older crowd on weekends; action kicks off after midnight. Open until 6am.

Te Ra'ai ☎ 322/551460. Highly recommended island banquet, accompanied by a traditional singing and dancing performance of the Haha Varua

TREAT YOURSELF

Au Boût du Monde Policarpo Toro s/n, north of Caleta Hanga Roa. Enjoy excellent sunset views from the extensive upstairs terrace while tucking into inspired dishes such as tuna steak in Tahitian vanilla sauce accompanied by island vegetables. The chocolate mousse is also superb. Mains CH$10,000–13,000; cake CH$5000.

dance group on Mon, Wed and Fri nights. Book ahead for pick-up from your guesthouse.

Toroko Av. Policarpo Toro s/n, near the cemetery. Popular disco with a mellow atmosphere that seems to draw all the young islanders on a Saturday night.

Directory

Banks and exchange There are two banks on the island: Banco Estado, at Tu'u Maheke s/n (Mon–Fri 9am–1pm), with an adjoining ATM which only accepts MasterCard. Another Banco Estado ATM can be found at the Puna Vai gas station which doubles as another exchange office, at the west end of Av. Hotu Matu'a. Banco Santander, at Av. Apina s/n, (Mon–Fri 9am–1pm), just south of the Sernatur office, has an ATM that accepts Visa cards. You can change US dollars at both banks. Many establishments accept US dollars and credit cards.

Car, scooter and bicycle rental Most agencies and bike rentals are found along Av. Atamu Tekena and Av. Te Pito O Te Henua. Oceanic Rent a Car and Insular rent hardy 4x4s (from CH$30,000/24hr), as well as quad bikes (CH$30,000/24hr), motorbikes (CH$25,000/24hr), scooters (CH$20,000) and mountain bikes (CH$10,000). Makemake Rentabike, at Atamu Tekena s/n, rents well-maintained bikes (CH$10,000/24hr) and gives out handy maps of various bike routes around the island. There is no insurance on the island, and to rent a scooter, dirt bike or motorbike, you need a valid motorbike licence.

Festivals Tapatai Rapa Nui, a ten-day cultural celebration in February, involving traditional dance and music, statue-carving competitions, canoe races and more, is the most popular time to visit Easter Island. Semana Santa (Easter week) has lively celebrations at Hanga Roa's Iglesia Parroquial de la Santa Cruz. The Ceremonia Culto al Sol is a feast that takes place on June 21 for the winter solstice, and Día de la Lengua Rapa Nui, a celebration of the Rapa Nui language, is held in late November.

Hospital Hospital Hanga Roa on Simón Paoa s/n (☎322/100-215), southeast of the church, has basic medical facilities.

Internet and phone Internet cafés in Hanga Roa tend to be expensive, charging CH$1500 per hour. Man@net on Akamu Tekena s/n (Mon–Sat 9am–10pm, Sun 10am–10pm), has wi-fi, while similarly priced Omotohi Cybercafé on Te Pito O Te Henua s/n doubles as a call centre and you can hook up your laptop to a cable, though you won't get charged any less. When dialling a Rapa Nui number, all local numbers are preceded by a "2", making them seven-digit numbers.

Laundry Lavandería Rapa Nui, on Te Pito O Te Henua s/n, near the church (Mon–Sat 9.30am–1pm & 4.30–7pm).

Pharmacy Farmacía Cruz Verde, Akamu Tekena s/n, opposite Tu'u Maheke (Mon–Sat 9am–1pm & 4.30–8pm).

Post office Te Pito O Te Henua s/n (Mon–Fri 9am–1pm & 2.30–6pm).

Shopping There are two crafts markets in town: Feria Municipal, at Tu'u Maheke at Atamu Tekena,

EASTER ISLAND TOUR OPERATORS

There is a proliferation of tour operators in Hanga Roa, and touring the archeological sites with a knowledgeable guide, especially if you have limited time on Easter Island, can be very worthwhile. If you are not thrilled at the idea of being cooped up in a minivan, horseriding can be an excellent way of seeing the sites instead. A full-day car tour costs around CH$30,000, while a day's horseriding can set you back CH$45,000 or so.

Aku Aku Turismo Av. Tu'u Koihu s/n ☎322/100-770, ⊛www.akuakuturismo.cl. Established operator offering standard guided day- and half-day tours of the island's sites, both in 4x4s and on horseback.

Cabalgatas Pantu ☎322/100-577, ⊛www .pantupikerauri.cl. Reputable operator offering half- and full-day horseback tours of the west and north coasts, including the ascent of Maunga Terevaka, the island's highest point. Includes grilled fish cooked in the traditional

Rapa Nui manner, or *curanto*, seafood and meat slow-cooked in an earth oven.

Kia Koe Tour Atamu Tekena s/n ☎322/100-852, ⊛www.kiakoetour.cl. Bilingual archeological tours of the island.

Taura'a Tours Atamu Tekena s/n ☎322/100-463, ⊛www.tauraahotel.cl. Excellent operator offering full-day, small-group tours of the south coast, including Anakena Beach as well as the principal sites, or the west coast, incorporating the inland *moai* site of Ahu Akivi. English and French spoken; tailor-made tours possible.

and Mercado Artesanal, at Tu'u Koihu at Ara Roa Rakei; the latter is larger and better-stocked. Local crafts, and wood carvings in particular, tend to be expensive; a cheaper option is to seek out the local jail (off Manutara, behind the airport), as local craftsmen sometimes outsource to inmates.

Surfing and diving Surfing schools near Playa Pea offer lessons to beginners, and Hare Orca, next to the Orca Diving Centre, rents surf- and boogie boards (CH$12,000/9000). The established and reputable Orca Diving Centre on the Caleta Hanga Roa (T 322/550-877, W www .seemorca.cl) and Mike Rapu Diving Centre next door (T 322/551-055, W www.mikerapu.cl) both offer day and night dives (CH$30,000–45,000), as well as introductory dives for complete beginners (CH$40,000).

Moving on

Air LAN (T 322/100-920) is the only airline with commercial flights to Easter Island, and flies to Santiago every day (twice on Wed) except Mon; there are also two weekly flights on Wed and Sun to Papeete, Tahiti. Flights to Santiago are often full, so book well in advance. Some travellers have complained that due to overbooking, they have been bumped off their return flight, so it may be worth confirming flights at Hanga Roa's LAN office or check in for the afternoon flight in the morning.

Colombia

Introduction

HIGHLIGHTS

PARQUE NACIONAL TAYRONA: a paradise of white sandy beaches and falling coconuts

CARTAGENA'S OLD CITY: Spain's most enduring architectural legacy in Latin America

LA ZONA CAFETERA: stay on an authentic coffee plantation and indulge in caffeine-fuelled activities

BOGOTÁ: see one of Latin America's largest collections of art at the Donación Botero museum

CALI: Colombia's salsa capital

SAN AGUSTÍN: ponder the mystery behind the Parque Arqueológico's curious statues

ROUGH COSTS

DAILY BUDGET Basic US$40/ occasional treat US$75

DRINK Aguardiente (big bottle to share) US$14

FOOD *Pargo frito con arroz con coco* (fried snapper with coconut rice) US$7

HOSTEL/BUDGET HOTEL US$15/ US$30

TRAVEL Bogotá to Cartagena (663km): 19hr by bus, US$65

FACT FILE

POPULATION 45.9 million

AREA 1,141,748 sq km

LANGUAGES Spanish (official), plus various indigenous languages

CURRENCY Colombian peso (C$ or COP)

CAPITAL Bogotá, DC (Distrito Capital; population:8.8 million)

INTERNATIONAL PHONE CODE ☏57

TIME ZONE GMT -5hr

Introduction

Home to a rich history, stunning scenery and some of the continent's most welcoming and sophisticated people, Colombia is a natural draw for travellers to South America. Despite its four-decade-long civil war and reputation for violence, improved security conditions have led to a sharp increase in tourism. Foreigners and Colombians alike are now far more able to explore this thrilling paradise of cloud forested mountains, palm-fringed beaches and gorgeous colonial cities. The only country in South America to border both the Pacific and the Caribbean, Colombia offers a huge range of ecosystems, from the Amazon rainforest near Leticia to the snowcapped mountains of the Sierra Nevada de Santa Marta.

Cosmopolitan **Bogotá** is, like most capitals, a busy commercial centre, with a vibrant cultural scene and festive nightlife. The two other major cities, **Medellín** and **Cali**, are also lively but less overwhelming. Better still are the small towns scattered throughout the country that could turn out to be the highlight of your visit. **Popayán** and **Mompox**, for example, are famed for raucous

Semana Santa (Easter week) celebrations. Colombia's coffee-growing region, the **Zona Cafetera**, offers breathtaking walks in the foothills where the bean is grown, accommodation in authentic *fincas* and excellent trekking.

Most visitors make time – and rightfully so – to head north to the Caribbean for the sun. Just a stone's throw away from the beach, the walled city of **Cartagena** is the biggest Spanish colonial port in South America. A few hours east, the less scenic **Santa Marta** and fishing village of **Taganga** are near **Parque Nacional Tayrona**, whose picturesque sandy beaches are unrivalled. Santa Marta is also the base for a five-day trek to the archeological ruins of **La Ciudad Perdida**, the Lost City.

As you head north from Bogotá through the Andes to **Bucaramanga**, quaint colonial villages like **Villa de Leyva** give way to more tropical, river-fed bastions of adventure tourism such as **San Gil**.

In the southeast, Colombia's stake of the Amazon, centred on **Leticia**, may not be as well known as Peru's or Brazil's but is just as lush and far more peaceful. The southwest, near Popayán, boasts some wonderful scenery as well as the monumental stone statues and burial chambers of **San Agustín** and **Tierradentro**.

WHEN TO VISIT

Colombia's proximity to the Equator keeps regional temperatures stable throughout the year, around 24°C (75°F) along the coast and 7–17°C (45–63°F) as you move higher inland. However, seasons do vary in response to rainfall. In the Andean region there are two dry and two wet seasons per year, the driest months being from December to March and July to August. In low-lying areas, especially southern Colombia, rainfall is more constant but showers never last very long. The Amazon climate is uniformly wet the entire year. Bear in mind that the most intense tourist seasons, with the highest prices, are from December to February and Semana Santa (Easter Week), the week before Easter.

CHRONOLOGY

1200 BC–1525 AD Indigenous cultures – including the Tayrona, Calimas, Sinú, Muisca, Pastos, Nariño, Tierradentro and San Agustín – live scattered across the country's narrow valleys and isolated cloudforests.

1525 Rodrigo de Bastides establishes the first Spanish settlement in Santa Marta, kicking off the hunt for El Dorado.

1533 The Spanish gain control of Cartagena.

1538 Spanish conquistador Gonzalo Jiménez de Quesada wrests power (and staggering amounts of gold and emeralds) from the native Chibchas and founds Santa Fe de Bogotá, now known simply as Bogotá, the nation's capital.

1717 The Spanish consolidate their colonial holdings, creating the viceroyalty of Nueva Granada from the land now occupied by the independent nations of Colombia, Ecuador, Panama and Venezuela.

1819 Simon de Bolívar overthrows Spanish rule and founds Gran Colombia, comprised of Colombia, Ecuador, Venezuela and Panama. He becomes its first president, thus fulfilling his desire for a united, independent South America.

1853 Colombia adopts a constitution that includes a prohibition against slavery.

1886 Nueva Granada is renamed Colombia, after Christopher Columbus.

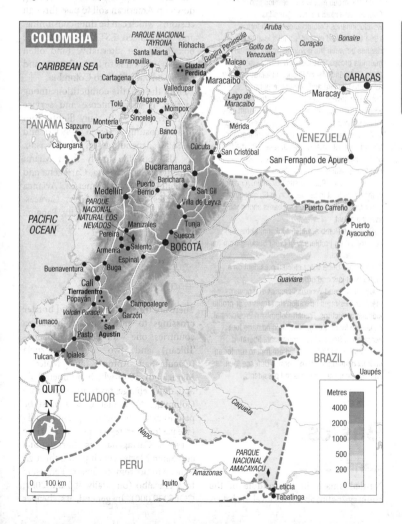

1902 End of The War of a Thousand Days, the bloody three-year-long civil war born of escalated antagonism between the Conservative and Liberal political parties.

1903 With the support of the US Navy, Panama secedes from Colombia.

1948 The assassination of the working class's greatest advocate, Bogotá's populist mayor, Jorge Eliécer Gaitán, begins the massive rioting known as *El Bogotazo*, which catalyzes a decade of partisan bloodletting, *La Violencia*, leaving 300,000 dead.

1953 General Rojas Pinilla leads a military coup and begins negotiations to demobilize armed groups and restore peace and order.

1954 The group that would develop into Communist-linked Fuerzas Armadas Revolucionarios Colombianos (FARC) forms.

1964 US-backed military attacks lead to violent clashes between the government and armed guerrilla groups. The Leftist National Liberation Army (ELN) and Maoist People's Liberation Army (EPL) are founded and civil war erupts.

1984 The government intensifies efforts to do away with drug cartels, as violence by narco-trafficker death squads and left-wing terrorists escalates.

1985 Members of radical leftist guerrilla group Movimiento 19 de Abril (M-19) take over the Palace of Justice, killing eleven judges and nearly a hundred civilians.

1986 Pope John Paul II visits Colombia. A grandiose cathedral is built in preparation in Chiquinquirá.

1993 Drug kingpin Pablo Escobar is shot dead evading arrest.

1999 Plan Colombia, which took aim at the country's drug problem with great backing from the US, is launched.

2002 Álvaro Uribe Vélez elected president on a platform of law and order.

2008 The US and Venezuela assist in a government-orchestrated operation that frees high-profile kidnapping victims. French-Colombian Presidential candidate Ingrid Betancourt, held hostage for six years, and fifteen other captives are liberated.

2010 Following Uribe's failed attempt to run for an unprecedented third term, former Defence Minister Juan Manuel Santos is elected president.

Basics

ARRIVAL

Nestled smack in the middle of the country 2640m above sea level, Bogotá is the best entry point for visitors arriving **by air**. Direct services from Europe to Bogotá are offered by Iberia (Madrid), Air France (Paris), Avianca (Barcelona and Paris) and Lufthansa (Frankfurt). Avianca also operates flights from Madrid to Cali and Medellín. Return fares start around £500/US$780 and increase to £750/US$1170 in high season (Dec–Feb, Easter & July–Aug). You might find cheaper flights that connect via Miami, though remember that the US requires all those touching down on American soil to pass through customs, which can be time-consuming, and you'll need ESTA clearance (see box, p.27). An alternative (and often cheaper) option is to fly to Caracas and buy an onward flight to Colombia.

From the US, the competition among carriers is more intense and service more frequent, with daily flights from Miami costing between US$320 and US$600 depending on the season. It's also possible to fly from Miami directly to Santa Marta, Cartagena and Medellín. In South America, Avianca also flies to Buenos Aires, Caracas, Guayaquil, Lima, Mexico City, Panama City, Quito, Río de Janeiro, Santiago (Chile) and São Paulo.

Overland to/from Ecuador and Venezuela

There are three official overland **border crossings** to and from neighbouring countries, one with Ecuador (Ipiales–Tulcán) and two with Venezuela (Cúcuta–San Antonio and Maicao–Maracaibo), all of which are open daily and don't charge taxes for entry into Colombia. Note that US$10 must be paid to exit Venezuela. Expreso Brasilia (see p.536) operates a coastal bus service between Cartagena, via Barranquilla and Santa Marta, which passes through Maicao in the remote Guajira Peninsula to Maracaibo (one daily at 7am; 20hr; COP$220,000). In general, it's cheaper to take buses at the border and travel on more frequent national lines. One bus company (Ormeño) covers several international routes to and from Bogotá, including Quito (COP$180,000), Caracas (COP$120,000) and Lima (COP$340,000).

By boat to/from Brazil, Peru and Panama

From the Amazon region it's possible to cross to or from Colombia into Brazil and Peru by taking a **riverboat** between Leticia and Manaus (departs Wed & Sat around 2pm; 3.5 days; COP$550,000 for a cabin or COP$200,000 if you bring your own hammock) or Iquitos (daily; 10hr; COP$160,000). If you're travelling from Colombia and plan to return, be sure to have your passport stamped at Leticia's airport before departing.

Sailboats also run between Cartagena and Puerto Lindo or Colón in Panama via the remote tropical islands of the San Blas archipelago. Trips take four to five days and cost around COP$750,000 per person. Rough seas can make travelling between November and February dangerous. There is no overland crossing between Colombia and Panama due to the presence of drug traffickers, paramilitaries and smugglers, and the threat of kidnapping in the Darién Gap.

VISAS

A passport and onward ticket (though this is checked only patchily) are the sole entry requirements for nationals of most of Western Europe, Canada, the US, Australia, New Zealand and South Africa.

Upon arrival, you'll normally either be ushered straight through if you're staying for less than two months or be given a **sixty-day tourist visa**, though it's possible to request up to ninety days if you have proof that you plan to stay that long. For those staying less than sixty days, no visa is issued. Once in the country,

you can stay a maximum of ninety days continuously and 180 days in any single calendar year. Thirty-day **extensions** cost COP$70,100 and can be obtained at any DAS (Departamento Administrativo de Seguridad) immigration office in Colombia. You'll need two passport photos with a white background and copies of your passport and entry stamp as well as the original. Visa extensions can only be issued four days in advance.

Airport **taxes** of COP$63,000 are sometimes charged on exit for international flights (Air France, American Airlines and Avianca include this in the cost of your ticket). If you stay sixty days or more a tax will certainly be levied upon your departure.

GETTING AROUND

Colombia's generally reliable and numerous **buses** are your best bet for intercity travel. Domestic **flights** are also very affordable and for longer journeys it is likely to be cheaper to fly, with one-way flights from Bogotá to the Caribbean coast starting around COP$115,000 in high season.

By bus

Learning how to travel **by bus** in Colombia is an art perfected only over time and not really necessary for short visits. The wide range of options in comfort and quality is compounded by the size and diversity of the country; it's a good idea to shop around at different companies' kiosks within larger stations. Generally, the larger, long-distance buses have reclining seats, toilets, loud cheesy music and videos; wear warm clothing as air conditioning is guaranteed to be on full blast. Service is usually direct and the ride comfortable, though prices tend to be higher and service less frequent on these buses. Some recommended companies are Expreso Bolívariano (ⓦwww.bolivariano.com.co), Expreso Brasilia (ⓦwww.expresobrasilia.com), Expreso Palmira

(🌐www.expresopalmira.com.co), Berlinas (🌐www.berlinasdelfonce.com), Copetran (🌐www.copetran.com.co) and Flota Magdalena (🌐www.flotamagdalena.com).

For shorter trips, you're better off sacrificing comfort and price for speed by buying a ticket on a *buseta*, *colectivo* or any similarly sized minibus or minivan that departs on demand. Within this category, prices and quality fluctuate but at a minimum are the same price as the more luxurious larger buses. Velotax and Taxiverde are two companies with a nationwide presence and a reputation for modern vehicles.

By car

Renting a **car** is a reasonable option for short distances and several international chains operate in Bogotá and other major cities, with prices starting at around COP$95,000 a day for unlimited mileage. If you are driving, be prepared for occasional roadblocks and passport checks by police and the military. Although the sight of young men with machine guns can be intimidating, most are friendly and more interested in making sure you're not involved in arms trafficking than trying to squeeze small bribes out of you for imagined road violations. Driving with a foreign licence is allowed, though it's highly advisable to have an international driver's licence to avoid harassment.

By plane

There are five domestic commercial airlines: Avianca (🌐www.avianca.com), serving more than twenty cities, Copa Airlines Colombia (🌐www.copair.com), the second largest, Aires (🌐www.aires.aero), Satena (🌐www.satena.com) and EasyFly (🌐www.easyfly.com.co). Avianca offers a **five-stop airpass** called Avianca AirPass for travel within the country over a thirty-day period. Prices start at US$50 for three flight coupons when bought in combination with an international ticket on Avianca; the price is nearly double in conjunction with another carrier. Although theoretically a good deal, the cumbersome restrictions and high penalties charged for changes make it worthwhile only if you plan to keep a rigid itinerary. A US$30 fee (and $30 more if your itinerary change puts you in a higher fare class) is charged per alteration. Also, some popular destinations like San Andrés and Cartagena cost US$20–30 extra.

Booking in advance doesn't guarantee a low fare (except during Semana Santa), so keeping your schedule open is a viable option. A one-way fare between Santa Marta and Bogotá purchased a day – or a month – in advance costs about COP$115,000–125,000 (in high season). When travelling by plane, be sure to arrive at the airport well in advance as vigilant security controls can extend check-in times.

ACCOMMODATION

Accommodation ranges considerably, but given the country's relative prosperity you'll be pleasantly surprised at the bargains available. **Backpacker hostels** start at around COP$18,000 for dorms and COP$40,000 for double rooms. Comfortable beds, shared kitchens, wi-fi, book exchange, laundry, cable TV, colourful murals and stacks of DVDs are common and hostels are often the best places to find out about local attractions, as well as explore them; some rent bicycles and even horses. More comfortable lodgings rarely cost more than COP$70,000 for a double room with private bathroom.

Camping is an option in more rural areas, and can be an affordable, fun way to meet locals (lots of high school and university students camp). Be aware that many campsites don't rent tents, so it's best to bring your own if you plan to camp regularly.

In the coffee-growing region, you can stay on one of the stately **fincas**, coffee-growing plantations that have barely changed over the decades. Though these farms range from tiny to sleek, modernized operations, the majority are small estates that offer comfortable accommodation for a moderate price (COP$20,000–40,000). Meals prepared from locally grown food as well as numerous outdoor activities, like farm tours and horseriding, are often included or available.

FOOD AND DRINK

Whether it's a platter full of starch or a suckling pig stuffed with rice, Colombian **food** is anything but light. Not even the heat of the coast seems to impinge on the country's obsession with fried foods.

The carbo-loading begins with breakfast, which usually consists of *huevos pericos*, scrambled eggs with onion and tomatoes, accompanied by a fried maize pancake, known as an *arepa* or a *tamale*, stuffed with chopped pork, rice, potatoes and anything else under the sun. The most important meal of the day is the midday *almuerzo* or *comida corriente*, consisting of soup, a main course and dessert. Dinners, after 6pm, are somewhat lighter but also consist of chicken or meat.

In Bogotá and other major cities there are a high number of fashionable restaurants of the same quality you'd expect in any major European or US city but at a fraction of the price. Bogotá also offers an excellent array of Western and international cuisine, especially Arabic food.

Local specialities

Traditionally, each region in Colombia had its own local speciality, though now many of these are available across the country. One of the most widespread is the *bandeja paisa*, which consists of a cafeteria-sized tray filled to the brim with ground beef, chorizo sausage, beans (*frijoles*), rice, fried banana (*plátano*), a fried egg, avocado and fried pork. You can usually find one served at inexpensive **market stalls** known as *fondas*, or at restaurants catering to local palates.

In rural areas, vegetarians will be hard-pressed for options, but medium and large cities cook up a decent spread of vegetarian dishes, with savoury crêpes and pastas being the most regular menu items. Many restaurants also whip up excellent *cremas,* which are simple pureed vegetable soups and usually don't contain dairy.

One of the tastiest Colombian dishes is *ajiaco*, a thick chicken stew replete with vegetables, maize, three types of potato, cream, capers and sometimes avocado. Despite its peppery-sounding name (*aji* is Spanish for chilli peppers), it's a surprisingly mild dish, ideally suited for the high Andean climate around Bogotá. *Mazamorra* is a similar meat and vegetable soup but with beans and corn flour. Both are often served with *patacón*, a mashed and heavily salted cake of fried plantain. Don't leave Colombia without trying one.

The most sophisticated of the regional specialities, and not for the faint-hearted, is called *hormigas culonas*, which consists of fried black ants and comes from Bucaramanga and the Santander area. In Cali and southern Colombia, grilled guinea pig, known as *cuy* or *curí*, is popular. On the coast, fish – especially shellfish and whitefish, like *pargo* (snapper) – is more common and often served with aromatic *arroz con coco*, rice with coconut. Rotisserie chicken is also widely consumed.

Drinking

For a country that produces some of the world's finest beans, **coffee** is of a remarkably poor quality in most places other than speciality cafés and the ubiquitous Juan Valdéz chain. In any case, the only thing Colombians have adopted from the art of espresso making is the demitasse cup, from which they drink heavily sugared, watered-down black coffee known as *tinto*. Colombians also consume large amounts of herbal infusions, called **aromáticas**, made from plants like *yerbabuena* (mint) and *manzanilla* (camomile). A good combatant against altitude sickness is *agua de panela*, hot water with unrefined sugar.

If there's one thing you'll pine for when you've returned home it's Colombia's exotic variety of **fresh fruit juices**, found for as little as COP$1000 a glass, especially on the coast. Many are completely foreign to western palates and lack English translations. Worth trying are *guanábana*, *lulo*, mango, *feijoa*, *maracuyá*, *mora* and *guayaba*.

While **beer** is reasonably good and inexpensive (try light, fizzy lagers like Dorado, Club and Aguila), the locally produced wine tends to be of the boxed variety. Far more popular among locals is the anise-flavoured *aguardiente*, pure grain alcohol, and rum (*ron*), both of which are drunk neat. Each *departamento* takes pride in its particular variant of the former, most commonly referred to as *guaro*. Brave souls won't want to pass up any offer to try *chicha*, a frothy drink, often prepared with maize or yuca, which is found in rural areas and made with the fermenting enzyme found in saliva: pieces of the peeled root are chewed, spat into a bowl and the juice is left to ferment.

CULTURE AND ETIQUETTE

As in much of South America, family plays a central, guiding role in the lives of Colombians of all socio-economic levels. You'll find Colombians to be quite courteous; when visiting someone's home, it's customary to bring a small gift, such as chocolates or flowers.

When it comes to **table manners**, common-sense rules apply: no elbows on the table, be free with compliments regarding the food and eat with decorum. Westerners will note that sincerity in expression, often expressed via good eye contact, is valued more

---

TROPICAL FRUIT

Dotting the country's streets are vendors who will happily blend drinks for you from the juicy bounty in their baskets. Some of the varieties below are especially good with milk (*con leche*), some tastier with the standard ice and sugar (*con agua*). Contamination concerns are unfounded as the water used in the fruit drinks comes from a bag: filtered water packaged in thin plastic instead of a bottle.

Corozo A round, maroon-skinned fruit, not unlike a cranberry in tartness and robust flavour. The building block of a bracing breakfast.

Guanabaná Pulpy, yellow fruit that tastes like a mild guava, with a refreshing touch of grapefruit. Perfect antidote to humid afternoons.

Lulo Resembling a vivid yellow persimmon, this tangy fruit ranks among the most popular with Colombians. Perfectly balanced sweetness and tartness make for a delicious taste.

Mora Close cousin of the blackberry.

Níspero This combination of pear and papaya is intensely rich and musky, and goes really well with milk.

Tomate de árbol Literally, "tree tomato", this orange-red fruit blurs the line between fruit and vegetable, being sharp and only faintly sweet. A common breakfast juice.

Zapote Though resembling a wrinkly sweet potato, this luscious orange fruit's uncanny resemblance to sherbet is confirmed by the tendency of some locals to freeze its pulp to eat as dessert.

LOCAL SLANG

Colombians take much joy in their particular style of linguistic acrobatics and slang. Using typical words and phrases is sure to get you a smile – perhaps of the incredulous variety. Keep in mind that, like most Spanish-speakers, Colombians freely convert verbs to nouns and vice versa, so take each word as a fluid concept. A Spanish language guide can be found on p.1016.

Un camello (n), **camellar** (v) Work, or working. A good way to refer to a particularly trying task.

La/una chimba (adj) Used to describe a situation or thing that is wonderful. Roughly synonymous with the youthful American usage of "awesome." Variations include "Qué chimba!" ("Nice!").

Chucha (n) Body odour. A crass but still useable term.

Elegante (adj) "Cool", loosely. Used to describe the subset of cool things – or happenings – that's particularly classy, well-executed or elegant. Think football passes or a good outfit. *Chevere* and *bacán* are other words for "cool".

Paila (adj) "That really sucks." Used in response to a comment or situation that's aggressively bad or heavy.

Perico (n) Cocaine. Regional translations include scrambled eggs, coffee with milk or (as here) a parakeet.

Al pelo (adj) Common response to a question like "How was your day?" that means "Good!" or "Perfect!"

highly than the typical steady stream of pleases and thank-yous.

Tipping about ten percent at mid-range restaurants is the norm, although some Colombians don't tip at all. As a general rule of thumb, the nicer the establishment, the greater the tip expected (capped at about fifteen percent), though check to see if the tip has already been included, as is sometimes done at more touristy cafés and restaurants. For reasonably short taxi trips, round up to the nearest thousand pesos. The best way to show your appreciation can be to take the driver's phone number and call him when you next need a ride.

The **machismo** often ascribed to Latin American culture is largely absent from Colombia, and there is some flexibility – and contradiction – in views toward gender and sexual orientation. Young straight men tote traditionally woven bags across their chests, but *marica* or *maricón* (homosexual) are among the most common insults. Gay clubs catering largely to men are common, especially in bigger towns like Bogotá and Medellín. Otherwise, the country's Catholic roots run quite deep and are apparent in sexual attitudes among both men and women.

There is a good deal of variety regarding formality of dress, with skin-tight leggings and shoulder-baring tank tops as ubiquitous as more elegant daywear. If you feel good in what you're wearing, you're not likely to turn heads for the wrong reasons.

SPORTS AND OUTDOOR ACTIVITIES

Adventurous types might hyperventilate when they discover Colombia. From almost every vantage point there's a snowcapped peak to climb, an untamed river to ride or some sunken coral reef to explore. The country's impressive cliffs and shorelines are guaranteed to provide more than enough adventure to satisfy even the most hardened adrenalin addict.

Football is the national sport and Colombians have a reputation for being some of South America's most skilled if untidy players. Going to see any of the big teams play in Bogotá,

Medellín or Cali is an unforgettable experience. **Cycling** is also a common passion – the mountainous land here is made for rugged biking – and Colombians regularly compete in the Tour de France.

Among the most popular activities for travellers is **scuba-diving**. Colombia's waters may not be the most impressive place in the world to learn, but they're certainly cheap. All along its 3000km of coastline, but especially around Santa Marta and Taganga, operators offer week-long PADI certification courses for around COP$600,000. Be sure to enquire about the reputation of dive operators before signing up, check their PADI or NAUI accreditation, the instructor-to-student ratio and ask for recommendations from other divers. Be aware that it is your responsibility to ensure that equipment is well maintained: check the side of the tank to make sure a hydrostatic test has been carried out in the last five years and that the air inside is pure (it should be odourless). Also check your instructor's credentials carefully and make sure that he/she is the same person you dive with and who signs your forms and certification.

Snorkelling and sailing are two other popular waterborne activities. There is a concentration of Class II–IV rapids among the many rivers in the *departamento* of Santander – three intersect near San Gil – that are gaining attention from **river-rafting** enthusiasts (see p.562).

COMMUNICATIONS

Sending a postcard or a **letter** abroad can be done for COP$5000–6000 from almost anywhere in the country, using ADPOSTAL or 4-72 (La Red Postal de Colombia). Standard service isn't reliable, however, and packages or important documents should be sent *certificado* (certified mail) or through one of the international couriers available in major cities.

Local phone calls cost around COP$200–300 and **international calls** COP$200–600 per minute, depending on whether you are calling a landline or a mobile phone; phonecards are commonly sold at local kiosks for as little as COP$5000. **Domestic long-distance calls** are best made using the mobile phone of someone selling their minutes piecemeal, a widespread practice that's delightfully Colombian in its rogue capitalism. Look for any sign – and they are often scrawled crazily in marker on a piece of cardboard in front of an unlikely doorway – including the word "minutos". The person you speak to will happily lend you their mobile phone for about COP$1000 a minute. They generally have at least three handsets, for different networks, and will be able to determine which one you need from the number you are calling. A more formal and less ubiquitous alternative is to visit one of the call centres called *telecentros* – you can choose between Orbitel (05), ETB (07) and Telecom (09) before dialling the country code or national area code (*indicativo*) followed by the local number.

COLOMBIA ON THE NET

ⓦ www.colombia.com A mega-portal with links to the most popular Colombian websites.

ⓦ www.colombiareports.com Latest news, sports, culture and travel in English.

ⓦ www.eltiempo.com Colombia's leading newspaper (Spanish only).

ⓦ www.hosteltrail.com/colombia Budget accommodation and local attractions.

ⓦ www.turismocolombia.com Colombia's official tourism site, with plenty of photos, good background and some practical information.

Internet cafés can be found everywhere, even in small towns, and wi-fi is available in most hostels. Rates start at around COP$3000 per hour.

CRIME AND SAFETY

Colombia today is far safer and more accessible than it has been in decades. That said, the civil war is ongoing and, although danger is largely confined to the most remote rural areas and jungles, it is unlikely to end in the near future. Renewed efforts by the government have struck significant blows to the country's major rebel groups, FARC (Fuerzas Armadas Revolucioanrios Colombianos) and ELN (Ejército Liberación Nacional), although the government has been criticized for using techniques as dirty as those employed by the rebels and not cracking down hard enough on the ultra-conservative paramilitary groups.

Kidnappings have declined a staggering 95 percent from their peak of 3700 in 2000 and the homicide rate has halved, though 2010 saw a marked increase, with rising murder rates, mostly attributed to gang warfare, concentrated in and around Cali and Medellín. Although, reassuringly, tourists have not been targeted specifically in the country's civil war, **certain areas should be avoided**, including the Chocó, parts of Nariño, Putumayo and Arauca and rural parts of Cauca. Most guerrilla activity is confined to rural areas near the border with Panama and Venezuela. If you are crossing into Venezuela by land, take care, and minimize your time in Cúcuta. Be sure to stay abreast of current events and for up-to-date travel advice check Ⓦwww.travel.state.gov/colombia or www.fco.gov.uk.

Drugs are widely available in Colombia, cocaine and marijuana in particular, and you're likely to be offered something at some stage. Possession of either is illegal and could result in

a prison sentence. The police may on occasion turn a blind eye to a discreet joint being smoked but being caught with drugs while trying to cross a border can have serious consequences. If you do decide to take drugs, be very careful: they are much stronger than in the UK and the US. Do not accept drinks, snacks or cigarettes from strangers as there have been reports of these being spiked with the tasteless and smell-free drug *burundanga*, leaving victims senseless and susceptible to robbery and rape.

HEALTH

Vaccinations against hepatitis A, hepatitis B and typhoid are strongly recommended and rabies should also be considered – visit your doctor or a travel health clinic six to eight weeks before you travel for advice. It is also advisable to get vaccinated against yellow fever; carry a doctor's certificate as you may be required to show this when entering national parks. Insect-borne diseases such as **malaria** and **dengue fever** are present, particularly in the Chocó, Antioquia, Córdoba, Sucre, Bolívar and Atlántico departments – bring plenty of mosquito repellent with a high DEET level and cover up with long sleeves and trousers. **Altitude sickness** may affect travellers at altitudes over 2500m, including those flying directly to Bogotá – take time to acclimatize before continuing your journey, drink plenty of water and avoid alcohol.

All major cities have **hospitals** and offer medical services. In the case of serious health issues, you may be transferred to a larger hospital with more specialized doctors and facilities. Simply dial 123 for all health concerns; you will be connected to the national

COLOMBIA BASICS

541

police who will ask a few basic questions before dispatching help. For less time-sensitive issues, contact your country's embassy for help.

INFORMATION AND MAPS

Despite the significant rise in tourism to Colombia in recent years, the practical information available at tourist offices can be lacking and they tend to focus more on promoting Colombia abroad than on assisting travellers inside the country. Almost every town has a tourist office, although their relative merit varies and staff often don't speak English. You're more likely to pick up useful information at your accommodation.

There are a good number of quality **road maps** available. The *Auto Guia,* updated annually, and available in bookstores for COP$15,000, has detailed departmental maps with hotels and attractions listed. The best guidebook available (Spanish only) is the annually updated *Guía de Rutas,* which also costs COP$15,000 and can be found in tourist offices in larger cities. The book is divided up into potential road-trip routes, and offers extensive local listings amidst the uniformly gushing prose.

MONEY AND BANKS

Colombia's national currency is the **peso (COP)**, divided into 100 centavos. Coins are for 50, 100, 200, 500 and 1000 pesos and notes for 1000, 2000, 5000, 10,000, 20,000 and 50,000 pesos. As elsewhere in Latin America, changing large notes can be problematic.

The easiest way to obtain cash is through **ATMs**, which you'll find pretty much everywhere. Check with your bank regarding fees for withdrawing funds abroad, which can be from two to fifteen percent. For **changing money**, casas de cambio offer similar rates, have more flexible hours and provide quicker service than most banks. Traveller's cheques can also be exchanged at casas de cambios and banks, but are generally frowned upon by most businesses other than hotels. Using moneychangers on the street is not recommended.

In terms of **costs**, your largest expense is likely to be transport, as Colombia is a big country. Still, there's stiff competition in road transport and most bus ticket prices can be negotiated down easily. Rising fuel costs worldwide have caused a surge in the price of domestic airfares, though they remain enticing given how many of the country's main

---

PLAN COLOMBIA

On 7 August 2010, Juan Manuel Santos was inaugurated as the fortieth president of Colombia, following a failed attempt by former President Álvaro Uribe to run for an unprecedented third term in office. Uribe was first elected in 2002 on a platform of law and order and turned to the US for help in dealing with the country's perpetual cycle of violence by tipping the military balance in their favour. Under Plan Colombia, the US has committed US$1.6 billion in foreign aid, most of it to the military, to root out illegal drug trafficking and the guerrilla protectors that allow it to blossom. Also intended to eradicate the growing of coca, Plan Colombia has recently seen a dramatic decline in coca cultivation and subsequently violence; in 2010 the country reduced production by sixty percent, relative to the peak in 2000, and Peru surpassed Colombia as the world's main producer of coca leaves. Uribe's strategy proved immensely popular, both at home with war-weary Colombians and with the US, and Santos has vowed to continue his predecessor's hardline security policies. As well as committing to make continued gains in security, Santos has also pledged to tackle Colombia's high unemployment rate (currently around twelve percent) and to improve relations with neighbouring Venezuela and Ecuador.

CALENDAR OF PUBLIC HOLIDAYS

Note that when holidays do not fall on a Monday, the public holiday is often moved to the following Monday.

January 1 New Year's Day (*Año Nuevo*).

January 6 Epiphany (*Día de los Reyes Magos*).

March 21 St Joseph's Day (Father's Day).

March or April Easter (*Semana Santa*), with national holidays on Good Friday, Holy Saturday and Easter Sunday.

May 1 Labour Day (*Día del Trabajo*).

May Ascension Day, observed on the Monday six weeks and a day after Easter Sunday.

May/June Corpus Christi, observed on the Monday nine weeks and a day after Easter Sunday.

June 29 Saint Peter and Saint Paul (*San Pedro y San Pablo*).

July 20 Independence Day. Celebrates Colombia's first attempt at independence from Spanish rule in 1810.

August 7 Battle of Boyacá. Commemorates the 1819 battle in which Colombia acquired its independence from Spain.

August 15 Assumption of the Virgin Mary (*Asunción de la Virgen*).

October 12 Columbus Day (*Día de la Raza*). Celebrates the European discovery of the Americas.

November 1 All Saints' Day (*Día de Todos los Santos*).

November 11 Independence of Cartagena.

December 8 Immaculate Conception (*Inmaculada Concepción*).

December 25 Christmas Day (*Navidad*).

routes take upwards of eighteen hours. A typical meal costs no more than COP$8000, but for lighter, healthier meals expect to pay more. For a standard meal, modest lodging and sightseeing, it's possible to survive on less than COP$70,000 a day.

OPENING HOURS AND FIESTAS

The **opening hours** for most shops are 8am until 6pm, Monday to Friday. Many businesses also often open on Saturdays until mid-afternoon. Outside Bogotá it's common for businesses to close at noon for a two- or three-hour siesta. Commercial hours in cities in warmer areas such as Cali often get started and end earlier. Government offices often follow the same pattern. Banks tend to open around 9am and close at 4pm, though casas de cambio stay open later.

Colombia's calendar is awash with **festivals and public holidays** (see box above), which all demand the ability to survive long days and nights of music, dancing and processions, fuelled by tons of street food and booze. The biggest events take place around Christmas, New Year and Easter (Semana Santa). Barranquilla's two-week long Carnaval, second in importance in Latin America after Río's, kicks off in the last half of February.

Bogotá and around

Colombia's capital, **SANTA FÉ DE BOGOTÁ**, is a city that divides opinion. Its detractors cite poverty, gridlock traffic and crime, as well as depressingly regular rain, and with 7.5 million tightly packed inhabitants and some decidedly drab neighbourhoods, Bogotá rarely elicits love at first sight. Given a day or two, however, most people do fall for this cosmopolitan place with its colonial architecture, numerous restaurants and raucous nightlife.

Situated on the **Sabana de Bogotá**, Colombia's highest plateau at 2600m, the city was founded on August 6, 1538 by Gonzalo Jiménez de Quesada in what was a former citadel belonging to the Muisca king **Bacatá**, from whom the city's name is derived. For many years, Bogotá's population did not expand in step with its political influence, and even in the 1940s the city had just 300,000 inhabitants. That all changed in the second half of the twentieth century, thanks to industrialization and civil war, which prompted a mass exodus of peasants from rural areas. Today, Bogotá is South America's fourth-largest city and home to one of the continent's most vibrant cultural scenes. Tourism has expanded dramatically in the last couple of years, while a municipal regeneration campaign has brought cleaner streets, improved security and new public spaces. After years in the doldrums, Bogotá is palpably on the up.

What to see and do

The city's historic centre, **La Candelaria**, is full of colourfully painted colonial residences. It begins at Plaza de Bolívar and stretches northward to Avenida Jiménez de Quesada, and is bordered by Carrera 10 to the west and the mountains to the east. **Downtown Bogotá** is the commercial centre, with office buildings and several museums, while **North Bogotá**, a catch-all term for the wealthier neighbourhoods to the north of the centre, offers stylish shopping districts and enough dining options to suit most palates and wallets.

Plaza de Bolívar

The heart of La Candelaria is the pigeon-filled **Plaza de Bolívar**. A statue of El Libertador himself stands in the centre of the square, which is surrounded by monumental buildings in disparate architectural styles spanning more than four centuries. The district is renowned for its churches (see box, p.548), few more historic than Bogotá's **Catedral** (Tues–Sun, noon–1pm & 5–6.30pm; free), completed in 1823. Its opulent gold-laced interior is a tribute to the Baroque religious art popular during the colonial era.

On the west side of the cathedral stands the Neoclassical **Capitol,** with its imposing, colonnaded stone facade. Congress meets here, and visitors can get inside by prior appointment only

---

(to make one, head to the Biblioteca del Congreso on C 6 No. 8–34). On the plaza's north side, is the modern **Palacio de Justicia** which was reconstructed in 1999 after the original was damaged during the Army's much-criticized storming of the building in 1985, in response to the M19 guerrilla group taking it over. More than a hundred people, including twelve Supreme Court justices, were killed in the raid.

Every Friday from 5pm, Cra 7 is closed to traffic from Plaza de Bolívar all the way to C 26, and the streets fill instead with performers, food vendors, families of *cachacos* (Bogotá natives) and groups of friends. The **Septimazo**, as it is called, is people-watching at its best, and a good-natured start to any weekend in the Colombian capital.

Palacio (or Casa) de Nariño

A block south of the plaza on Cra 8, the heavily fortified presidential palace and compound, **Palacio (or Casa) de Nariño**, is done in the style of Versailles. Because of security concerns, the palace's gaudy interior is not open to the public. However, it's possible to watch the ceremonial changing of the guard three times a week (Mon, Fri & Sun at 4pm) from the adjacent streets.

Biblioteca Luis Angel Arango

Biblioteca Luis Angel Arango (☎1/343-1212, ⓦwww.lablaa.org) is the umbrella name given to a cultural complex that spans both sides of C 11 between carreras 4 and 5 and encompasses some of Bogotá's most important museums. The **Manzana Norte** (Mon–Sat 8am–8pm, Sun 8am–4pm; free) features an extensive library, a collection of musical instruments and a bookshop with English-language paperbacks. Of more interest to most visitors, however, is the **Manzana Sur** (Mon & Wed–Sat 9am–7pm, Sun 10am–5pm, closed Tues; free), a slightly confusing modern construction that connects the **Museo Botero**, **Casa de Moneda** and **Museo**

de Arte del Banco de la República (see below) plus two cafés.

Museo Botero

Housed in a fine colonial mansion, the **Museo Botero** (enter via the main Manzana Sur entrance or from C 11) contains one of Latin America's largest collections of modern and Impressionist art, donated in 2000 by Colombian's most celebrated artist, Fernando Botero.

On display across two floors are paintings by Picasso, Miró, Monet, Renoir and Dali, as well as a sculpture room featuring works by Henry Moore and Max Ernst. At the heart of the museum, however, are no fewer than 123 paintings and sculptures by Medellín-born Botero himself. The Colombian's trademark is the often satirical depiction of plumpness, and in this most comprehensive of exhibitions you will find fatness in all its forms, from chubby parrots to rotund guerrilla fighters.

Casa de Moneda

Once you've had your fill of Botero, head next door to the adobe and stone-built **Casa de Moneda**, or mint, one of the city's most elaborate colonial edifices. Here you'll find displays chronicling the history of money in Colombia from the barter systems of indigenous communities to the production of modern bank notes.

Colección de Arte

Behind the Casa de Moneda is the **Colección de Arte**, a series of rooms featuring a permanent exhibition of works owned by the Banco de la República. The predominant focus here is on Colombian artists, but the pieces on display range from seventeenth-century religious art through to modern canvases by twentieth-century painters. Behind the permanent collection is the **Museo de Arte**, a modern, airy building that houses free, temporary exhibitions of art, photography and culture.

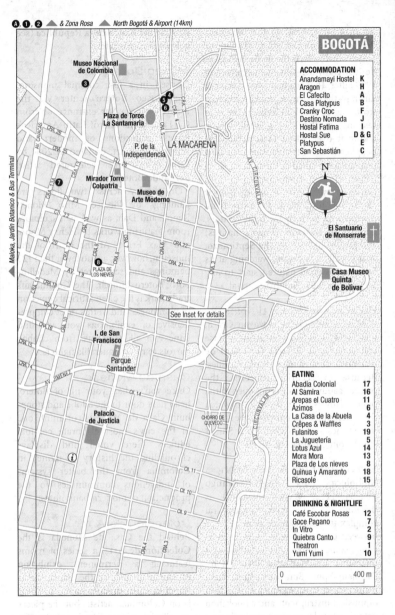

BOGOTÁ

ACCOMMODATION
Anandamayi Hostel	K
Aragon	H
El Cafecito	A
Casa Platypus	B
Cranky Croc	F
Destino Nomada	J
Hostal Fatima	I
Hostal Sue	D & G
Platypus	E
San Sebastián	C

EATING
Abadia Colonial	17
Al Samira	16
Arepas el Cuatro	11
Ázimos	6
La Casa de la Abuela	4
Crêpes & Waffles	3
Fulanitos	19
La Juguetería	5
Lotus Azul	14
Mora Mora	13
Plaza de Los nieves	8
Quinua y Amaranto	18
Ricasole	15

DRINKING & NIGHTLIFE
Café Escobar Rosas	12
Goce Pagano	7
In Vitro	2
Quiebra Canto	9
Theatron	1
Yumi Yumi	10

0   400 m

Centro Cultural Gabriel García Márquez

The spacious **Centro Cultural Gabriel García Márquez**, at C 11 No. 5–60 (Mon–Sat 9am–7pm, Sun 10.30am–5pm; ☎1/283-2200, ⓦwww.fce.com.co), is the city's newest cultural precinct, with rolling art exhibitions, an inviting plaza and a book and music store.

Museo Arqueológico

The **Museo Arqueológico**, at Cra 6 No. 7–43 (Tues–Fri 8.30am–5pm, Sat 9.30am–5pm, Sun 10am–4pm;

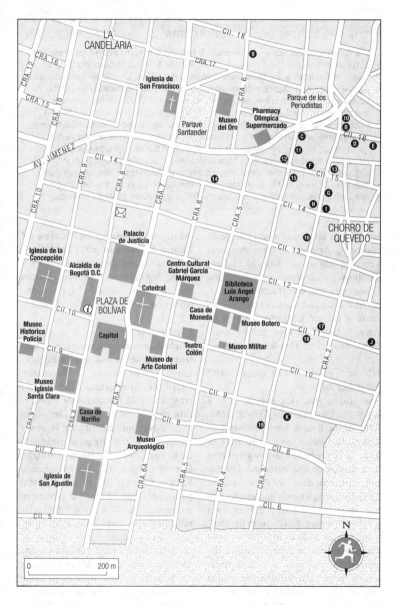

COP$3000 ☎1/243-0465, ⓦwww .museoarqueologicomusa.com;) is housed in a restored colonial townhouse. The museum aims to give an overview of Colombia's various pre-Columbian cultures, primarily through an extensive collection of pottery gathered from around the country.

Museo de Arte Colonial
The **Museo de Arte Colonial** (Tues–Fri 9am–5pm, Sat & Sun 10am–4pm, ☎1/341-6017; COP$2000), Cra 6

THE CHURCHES OF LA CANDELARIA

In addition to its cathedral, La Candelaria is teeming with some of the best-preserved colonial-era churches and convents found in Latin America. Overlooking Palacio Nariño at Cra 8 No. 8–91, the austere exterior of the Iglesia Museo de Santa Clara (Mon–Fri 9am–5pm, Sat–Sun 10am–4pm; COP$2000), built in the early part of the seventeenth century and formerly part of the convent of Clarissa nuns, contrasts sharply with its garish gold-plated interior. The Iglesia de San Francisco (Mon–Fri 6am–7pm, Sat–Sun 7am–1pm; free), facing the Museo del Oro on Parque Santander, appropriately enough is noted for its ornate golden altar, while the soaring vault at Iglesia de la Concepción (Mon–Sat 8am–6pm, Sun 6.30am–1pm; free) at C 10 No. 9–50 is a fine example of the Moorish-influenced Mudéjar style popular in the sixteenth century. Another noteworthy colonial-era church is the domed Iglesia de San Ignacio, on C 10 No. 6–35 (Mon–Sat, 9am–4.30pm, Sun 11am–1pm; free), which was begun in 1605 and became the first Jesuit church in Nueva Grenada.

No. 9–77, is set around a beautiful, leafy courtyard. Among the three thousand items on display are fine colonial-era paintings, sculptures and furniture. Upstairs is a well-constructed exhibition about the life and work of seventeenth-century painter Gregorio Vásquez de Arce y Ceballos. Free guided tours (Spanish only) on Tues & Fri at 3pm.

Museo Histórico Policía and Museo Militar

The **Museo Histórica Policía**, at C 9 No. 9–27 (Tues–Sun 8am–5pm; ☎1/233-5911; free), houses some uniforms of Colombia's police force, plus a lot of guns. The basement is largely given over to a display on the notorious 499-day police hunt for drug lord Pablo Escobar. Friendly young English-speaking police offer free guided tours, and there's a great view across the city from the roof.

The **Museo Militar**, at C 10 No. 4–92 (Tues–Sun 9am–4.30pm; free) is the equivalent museum for Colombia's armed forces, but without the guided tour to provide context it amounts to little more than several rooms full of guns and medals.

Plazoleta del Chorro de Quedevo

Nowhere is La Candelaria's grittier, bohemian side better captured than on the streets surrounding the **Plazoleta del Chorro de Quevedo**, at C 13 and Cra 2. Scholars say the tiny plaza was the site of the first Spanish settlement, though the tiled-roof colonial chapel on the southwest corner was built much later.

Monserrate

Perched above La Candelaria is the rocky outcrop that is one of Bogotá's most recognizable landmarks: **Cerro de Monserrate**. The hilltop, crowned by **El Santuario de Monserrate** church, offers spectacular views back down on the city. It is easily reached by the frequent *teleférico* cable car (Mon–Sat noon–midnight, Sun 9am–5pm; COP$14,000 before 5.30pm, COP$17,000 after, COP$8000 Sun; ☎1/284-5700, ⊛www.cerro monserrate.com) or by funicular railway (Mon–Sat 7.45am–11.45pm, Sun 6am–6.30pm; prices same as *teleférico*) up the road from the Quinta de Bolívar (see p.549). Alternatively, it's a 1-hour 30-minute trek along a stone path that begins at the base of the hill and leads to the summit 600m above.

If you do go on foot, leave all but essentials at the hotel as tourists are frequently **robbed** both on the way up the hill and on the walk between the Quinta and its base. The safest time to go is Sunday, when you'll be accompanied by thousands of pilgrims hoping for miracles from the church's dark-skinned Christ. Atop are snack bars and a couple of pricey **restaurants**, including the French-inspired *Casa San Isidro* (℡1/281-9309; mains around COP$60,000).

Casa Museo Quinta de Bolívar

At the foot of Monserrate is the **Casa Museo Quinta de Bolívar** (Tues–Fri 9am–4.30pm, Sat & Sun 10am–3.30pm; ℡1/284-6819, ⓦwww .quintadebolivar.gov.co; COP$3000), a spacious colonial mansion with beautiful gardens where Simón Bolívar lived sporadically between 1820 and 1829. The informative museum retells the story of Bolívar's final, desperate days in power before being banished by his political rivals. One object you won't find among the plethora of El Libertador paraphernalia is the sword he used to free the continent from four centuries of Spanish rule. It was stolen in 1974 from the collection that contained his bedpan, military medals and billiard table in the now legendary debut of urban guerrilla group **M-19**. When they handed in its arsenal in 1991, the sword was quickly shuttled into the vaults of the Banco República for fear of another embarrassing burglary.

Museo del Oro

On the northeastern corner of Parque de Santander, at Cra 6 and C 16, is the must-see **Museo del Oro**, or Gold Museum (Tues–Sat 9am–6pm, Sun 10am–4pm; COP$3000, Sun free; ℡1/343-2221, ⓦwww.banrep.gov.co /museo). Most of Colombia's gold was hauled away by its Spanish plunderers, but the leftover scraps were still sizeable enough to assemble the world's largest collection of auriferous ornaments, some 35,000 pieces strong, not all of which are on exhibition. A maze of informative displays on Colombia's indigenous cultures culminates in the Salón Dorado, where eight thousand

gold objects dazzle in an otherwise pitch-dark bank vault brought to life by Andean pipe music and moody jungle sounds. Self-guided audio tours in English are available (COP$6000), although there is plenty of English explanation on the walls.

Museo Nacional de Colombia and Mirador Torre Colpatria

As exhaustive as the Museo de Oro, the **Museo Nacional de Colombia**, at Cra 7 at C 28 (Tues–Sat 10am–6pm, Sun 10am–5pm; COP$3000; ℡1/334-8366, ⓦwww .museonacional.gov.co;), provides a detailed look at the country's tumultuous history. The converted jailhouse's most impressive exhibits relate to the conquest and the origins of the beguiling El Dorado myth that so obsessed Europe. The second floor houses an extensive collection of paintings by modern Colombian artists, including Fernando Botero. There is a free **guided tour** in English on Wednesday at 4pm. Near the museum, at the top of Bogotá's tallest building, fantastic views can be had from the **Mirador Torre Colpatria** (Sat & Sun 11am–5pm; COP$3000).

Museo de Arte Moderno

The **Museo de Arte Moderno**, at C 24 at Cra 6 (Tues–Sat 10am–6pm & Sun noon–5pm; COP$2000 ℡1/286-0466, ⓦwww.mambogota.com) has the largest collection of contemporary Colombian art in the country, although most of the museum space is often taken up with temporary exhibitions. There's also a bookshop here and a *cinemateca* that projects art films.

Plaza de Toros La Santamaría

The **Plaza de Toros La Santamaría** on Cra 6, two blocks north of the Museo de Arte Moderno, is the Moorish-style bullring where the Temporadas Taurinas take place each January and February with the enthusiastic support of well-heeled *cachacos*. To sneak a peek inside when the bullring is closed, ring the doorbell and ask the guard nicely. The small museum should be open Mon–Fri 9.30am–12.30pm & 2–5.30pm, but ring ahead if you're particularly keen to see it (☏1/334-1482).

North Bogotá

North of C 60, the museums peter out and are replaced by leafy neighbourhoods peppered with gourmet restaurants, lively bars and modern shopping malls. An exception is the cobblestoned *barrio* of **Usaquen**, which was a small village before being swallowed up by the capital's expansion. On weekends the central plaza hosts the **Mercado de las Pulgas** antiques fair (see "Shopping", p.555). To get to Usaquen, catch a bus heading north along Cra 7.

Maloka and Jardín Botánico

Bogotá's science and technology museum, **Maloka**, at Cra 68D No. 24A–51 in the west of the city (Mon–Fri 8am–5pm, Sat & Sun 10am–7pm; ☏1/427-2707, ⓦwww.maloka.org; COP\$9000), is an interactive extravaganza of hands-on exhibition rooms about biodiversity, space and the human body, plus a 3D cinema (COP\$10,500). Ideal for kids of all ages, particularly on a rainy day.

The **Jardín Botánico José Celestino Mutis**, also in West Bogotá at C 63 No. 68–95 (☏1/437-7060, ⓦwww.jbb.gov.co; COP\$2000) has a greenhouse full of colourful orchids and jungle plants, and good sections on the flora of *páramo* and cloudforest regions.

Neither Maloka nor the Jardín is particularly convenient to get to. There are *busetas* (small buses) that run along the airport road to the latter, but by far the easiest option for both is to take a **taxi** (approx COP\$12,000 to either).

Arrival

Air Most international flights land at El Dorado International Airport, 14km northwest of the city centre, though some use Puente Aéreo domestic terminal, 1km away. A taxi downtown costs about COP\$20,000; be sure to buy a ticket at one of the authorized stands instead of arranging directly with the driver, who's likely to charge you more. Bus rides into town cost COP\$1300 and can take about an hour; at the time of research, the electric Trans-Milenio bus network (see "City transport", p.551) was being expanded to connect with the airport.

Bus The huge long-distance bus terminal, Terminal de Transporte (☏1/423-3600, ⓦwww.terminalde transporte.gov.co), is on the southwest edge of Bogotá near Av. Boyacá (C 72) between El Dorado (Av. 26) and Av. Centenario (C 13). It's divided into four hubs, serving destinations north, south, east or west of the city. A taxi to the centre costs about COP\$12,000. You can also get into town by hailing any *buseta* from Cra 10 or along Cra 7, marked "Terminal" (roughly COP\$1200).

BOGOTÁ FESTIVALS

Partly thanks to the municipal authorities' determination to reclaim public space for the law-abiding majority, Colombia's capital has no shortage of public events and festivals. The year begins with the Bogotá Bullfighting Festival (Jan–Feb), with stars from Spain flown in for the occasion, while Holy Week (March or April) brings processions, re-enactments and religious pomp. Perhaps the highlight of the annual calendar is Rock in the Park (June), a three-day bonanza of guitar music featuring Colombian and international bands, before the Summer Festival (Aug) to commemorate Bogotá's founding. September heralds the International Jazz Festival at the *Teatro Libre*, followed by the Film Festival (Oct), which includes open-air screenings. Soon after that, the citiy begins gearing up for a truly South American Christmas.

ACTIVITIES AROUND BOGOTÁ

Climbing The Gran Pared climbing wall (C 50 & Cra 7 ☎1/285-0903, ⊛www
.granpared.com; COP$25,000 per day) is a good place to try out rock climbing
before heading to Suesca (see p.556). There are classes and courses on offer.

Cycling Every Sunday morning (until 2pm), there is much good-natured fun to be
had as many of Bogotá's main roads close to traffic in a civic attempt to get people
cycling, known as *Ciclovía*. Thousands of locals take to their bikes and tour the city,
seemingly as much to flirt with each other as to exercise. Bogotá Bike Tours (Cra
3 No.12–72 ☎1281-9924, ⊛www.bogotabiketours.com) rents bikes so that you
can join the fun (COP$15,000/25,000 per half/full day), and runs informative guided
tours of the city (COP$25,000, 4hr approx).

Horseriding You can get in the saddle with Cabalgatas Carpasos (☎1/368-7242,
⊛www.carpasos.com), which offer rides by day or night (around COP$35,000 per
hr depending on route).

Languages There is no shortage of Spanish courses to choose from, including one
at International House in La Candelaria (⊛www.ihbogota.com), which offers both
one-on-one and group lessons.

Information

National park information For up-to-date safety
information on Colombia's 51 national parks and
protected areas, visit the ecotourism office of
Unidad de Parques Nacionales at Cra 10 No. 20–30
fourth floor (☎1/353-2400, ⊛www.parques
nacionales.gov.co; Mon–Fri 8am–5.45pm).

Publications Be sure to pick up a copy of *Plan B*, a
monthly publication listing cultural events, restaurants, theatres and clubs; also see its excellent
website ⊛www.planb.com.co. On Fridays, Bogotá's
leading newspaper, *El Tiempo*, publishes a weekend
entertainment guide. For non-Spanish speakers, the
free English-language *The City Paper* (⊛www
.thecitypaperbogota.com) is a useful resource.

Tourist information Bogotá's tourist bureau
produces helpful guides, many in English, to the
city's main churches, museums and other historical
attractions. There are no fewer than sixteen *Puntos
de Información Turística* around the city, including at
the airport, bus station and the southwest corner of
Plaza Bolívar (Mon–Sat 8am–6pm, Sun 10am–4pm;
☎1/283-7115) at Cra 8 No. 10–65. You can use the
internet here for 15min free of charge.

Tour operators Ecoguías, Cra 7 No. 57–39 office
501 (call first for appointment; ☎1/212-1423,
⊛www.ecoguias.com); Sal Si Puedes, Cra 7
No. 17–01, office 739 (☎1/283-3765, ⊛www
.salsipuedes.org).

City transport

Most sightseeing can be done on foot, as most of
Bogotá's attractions are in or near La Candelaria.

Bus For moving around the city your best public
transport option is the clean and efficient
TransMilenio (5am–11pm, Sun 10am–6pm), an
electric bus system with a flat fare of COP$1600
per journey. The most popular line follows Av.
Caracas from La Candelaria all the way to the city's
northern edge, El Portal del Norte. Crowded and more
confusing to the uninitiated, but covering a wider
range of routes, are gas-guzzling *busetas*, which
charge around COP$1500 per ride. Note that Cra 7 is
closed off to southbound traffic every Sun until 2pm.

Taxi Taxis in Bogotá are relatively inexpensive, with
a trip across the city usually costing COP$10,000–
15,000. They are yellow, have meters and levy a
small surcharge at night; be sure to check the fare
table before paying as some drivers overcharge. At
night, it's better to use a radiotaxi; when you call,
the dispatcher will give you a confirmation number
that you must verify with the driver. Try Radio Taxi
(☎1/288-8888), Taxi Real (☎1/333-3333) or Taxi
Express (☎1/411-1111).

Accommodation

Budget accommodation is concentrated in La
Candelaria, where hostels are proliferating. Most
have private rooms with either shared or private
bathrooms; prices below are for the former, cheaper
option in high season.

Anandamayi Hostel C 9 No. 2–81 ☎1/341-7208,
⊛www.anandamayihostel.com. This hostel is pure
Zen, set in a restored colonial house around two
flower-filled, hammock-strung courtyards. Rustic
dorms and private rooms come with lockers, and
shared bathrooms have spacious stone showers.

At night, guests huddle around the woodfire stove in the communal kitchen. Includes internet and wi-fi, plus free tea and coffee. Dorms COP$30,000, rooms COP$100,000.

Aragon Cra 3 No. 14–13, La Candelaria ☎1/342-5239. Cheap, clean and popular with young travellers. The double rooms all have shared bathrooms. Has a TV room but no other services. COP$40,000.

El Cafecito Cra 6 No.34–70, La Merced ☎1/285-8308, ⓦwww.cafecito.net. Out on a limb on a residential street just north of the centre, but set in a nice old English-style mansion and perfect for anyone who wants to avoid the gringo-tastic streets of La Candelaria. Some rooms are a little spartan for the price. Downstairs is an excellent bar and restaurant serving mostly vegetarian food. Dorms COP$20,000, rooms COP$50,000.

Cranky Croc C 15 No. 3–46 ☎1/342-2438, ⓦwww.crankycroc.com. A friendly, Australian-run place with sparklingly clean dorms, a great shared kitchen and good-value communal dinners, including Friday night barbecue. Free wi-fi plus computer terminals (COP$1800/hr). Dorms COP$20,000, rooms COP$60,000.

Destino Nomada C 11 No. 00–38 ☎1/352-0932, ⓦwww.dnhostels.com. A compact place with simple but good-value double rooms and pristine dorms, plus a small bar, kitchen, table football and blackboards in the courtyard listing daily suggestions for things to do around the city. Dorms COP$20,000, rooms COP$40,000.

Hostal Fatima C 14 No. 2–24, La Candelaria ☎1/281-6389, ⓦwww.hostalfatima.com. Popular with a young party crowd, this 31-bed hostel has a large courtyard, TV lounge, games room, kitchen and free internet, plus a bar next door that sometimes has live music. Shared rooms are cramped. Dorm COP$15,000, rooms COP$50,000.

Hostal Sue Cra 3 No. 14–18, La Candelaria ☎1/341-2647, ⓦwww.suecandelaria.com. This well-maintained hostel with a party vibe has just about everything a backpacker could want: neat dorms, three doubles with TV, on-site bar, bean-bag-stacked TV lounge, kitchen, free coffee, laundry service, ping-pong table, computers and wi-fi. Has a second location in La Candelaria at C 16 No. 2–55 (☎1/334-8894). Dorms COP$20,000, rooms COP$50,000.

Platypus C 16 No. 2–43, La Candelaria ☎1/341-3104, ⓦwww.platypusbogota.com. An institution, mostly because the English/German-speaking owner warmly shares knowledge accumulated from extensive travels. Comfortable shared and private rooms with kitchen facilities. Dorms COP$20,000, rooms COP$48,000.

San Sebastián Av. Jiménez No. 3–97, La Candelaria ☎1/243-8937. Some of the double rooms here are more like suites, complete with lounge area, private bathroom, TV and kitchenette. The brightly painted lobby gives way to bland 1970s decor in the rest of the building. Includes wi-fi. Rooms COP$75,000.

Eating

While the traditional highlander diet consists of vegetables and starch, middle-class *cachacos* prefer the same cosmopolitan cuisine as their counterparts in London or New York. Bogotá has four main restaurant zones; from south to north they are: touristy La Candelaria; yuppie La Macarena (Cra 4 between calles 23 & 28); gay-friendly Chapinero, also called the "G-Zone" (between calles 58 & 72 and carreras 3 & 7); and upmarket Zona Rosa (concentrated in the "T Zone" at C 82 and Cra 12).

Cafés, markets and light meals

Al Samira Cra 3 No.13–55, La Candelaria. A compact Middle Eastern café with small wooden tables and low painted ceilings. The *shawarma* (from COP$5500) are served with an assortment of accompaniments including falafel, babaganoush and tabbouleh, and are fantastic value. Open 10am–9pm daily.

Arepas el Cuatro Cra 4 just off Parque de los Periodistas. This bare-bones café also has a hole in the wall selling excellent *arepas* with delicious shredded meat (COP$3000) or cheese (COP$1600). Be sure to season yours with some spicy *ají* sauce from the counter. Open until midnight, and great for soaking up that one beer too many.

Ázimos Cra 5 No. 26A–64, La Macarena. An enticing organic foodshop and bakery with a chilled café out back, serving good coffee and excellent cake (around COP$3000). Also has wi-fi. Mon–Sat 8am–8pm, Sun until 2pm.

Crêpes & Waffles Av. Jimenez No.4–55 plus Cra 12 No. 83–40 in the Zona Rosa and more than 30 other city outlets (see ⊛www.crepesywaffles.com). A hugely popular chain restaurant that fulfils every savoury and sweet craving with a monster menu of crêpes and waffles, plus naughty ice-cream sundaes. Savoury crêpes range from COP$9000–30,000, sweet treats start at $3800.

Mora Mora Cra 3 No. 15–98, La Candelaria. A funky juice and sandwich bar that's ideal for breakfast and people-watching. Good smoothies. Closed Sun.

Plaza de los Nieves C 19 & 20 between Cra 8 & 9, Downtown Bogotá. A covered outdoor market where you can pick up fantastic fruit and veg or sit down at one of several canteen-style places serving inexpensive but filling *comida corriente* such as *arepas* or *caldo de res* (hearty beef soup, COP$3400) and fresh fruit juices.

Ricasole Cra 4 No. 14–83, La Candelaria ☎1/910-4707. This fast-service pizza joint in the heart of the historic centre is open until midnight (10pm Sun) and serves portions from slices (COP$2000) to an XL feast (COP$16,000).

Restaurants

Abadía Colonial C 11 No. 2–32, La Candelaria ☎1/341-1884. This Italian restaurant in an attractive colonial hotel (double room COP$220,000) has upmarket decor (think linen napkins and flowers on tables) and slick service but reasonable prices. Pizzas (around COP$14,000) are of the thin-crust variety and toppings, including anchovy, artichoke and authentic Parma-style ham, are high quality. Open noon–9.30pm daily.

La Casa de la Abuela C 27 No. 4–75 La Macarena. A popular diner serving excellent (and cheap) *ajiaco* (a chicken stew blended with maize, potatoes, avocado and capers), but only on Fri (COP$8500). Lunch only; closed Sun.

El Corral Gourmet C 81 No. 13–05 in Atlantis Shopping Centre, Zona Rosa, North Bogotá. Looks like any other unappetising fast-food chain, but its beefy burgers (around COP$14,000 with fries) are a cut above.

Fulanitos Cra 3 No. 8–61, La Candelaria ☎/352-0173. Typical Valle del Cauca fare such as lentils

with spicy meatballs (mains COP$12,000–20,000) is served in an atmospheric colonial house with sensational views over the rooftops of the old city. Delightful, old-fashioned service and different dishes for each day of the week. Open Mon–Thurs noon–4pm, Fri & Sat noon–9pm, Sun noon–6pm.

La Juguetería C 27 No.4A–03, La Macarena ☎1/341-1188. Decked out like a children's fairground on acid – complete with distortion mirrors, carousel horses and somewhat creepy plastic dolls dangling from the ceiling – this restaurant serves plenty of fun with its barbecued meat. Mains, with names like Miss Piggy *parrillada*, cost COP$22,900–29,800. Closed Mon, lunch only Sun.

Lotus Azul Cra 5 No. 14–00, La Candelaria. A Hare Krishna-run vegetarian café that does a roaring trade in set lunches for COP$6600, plus decent lentil burgers (COP$6000). Low tables upstairs are nicer than the canteen-style ground floor. Closed Sun.

Museo del Tequila Cra 13A No. 86–18, Zona Rosa, North Botoga ☎1/256-6614. Photographs of Bogota's beautiful people cover the walls near the entrance to this two-storey restaurant; the rest of the place is full of cabinets containing part of its 2400-bottle tequila collection. The menu features eighty Mexican dishes (mains around COP$25,000), plus the obligatory margarita (COP$19,800). Lunch only Mon & Sun, until 1am otherwise.

🏃 **Quinua y Amaranto** C 11 No.2–95, La Candelaria. A tiny place with an open kitchen and delicious, largely organic and vegetarian set lunches (COP$10,000). Sample dishes include black bean soup and mushroom risotto. Also sells wholewheat *empanadas*, bread, eggs and coffee. Mon–Fri 7.30am–7.30pm, Sat 7.30am–5pm.

Wok Cra 13 No. 82–74, Zona Rosa, North Bogotá and several other locations. This small chain of trendy restaurants has all-white modern decor and a menu that was clearly constructed by someone who knows about Asian food. The staples are all there – Pad Thai, green curry, sushi and great tempura – but there are also some less obvious offerings. Spice fans should ask for extra chilli. Mains start around COP$16,000.

Drinking and nightlife

Rumbear, literally to dance the rumba, is how locals refer to a night's partying, which invariably involves heavy doses of dancing. Bars and discos in La Candelaria attract a somewhat bohemian, often studenty crowd, while their fluorescent-lit counterparts in the Zona Rosa in North Bogotá (around C 83 and Cra 13) appeal to the city's beautiful people. Virtually everywhere shuts down at 3am. It is always safer to take taxis to and from your destination.

Bogotá Beer Company Cra 12 No. 83–33, Zona Rosa and around the city ⓦwww .bogotabeercompany.com. Artisan brews including stout and wheat beer, served in bottles and on tap, plus excellent pub grub to soak them up (burger and fries COP$19,000). One of the few places that is busy even on a Monday night.

Bolera San Francisco Av. Jimenez No. 6–71, La Candelaria ⓣ1/342-3232. There's heaps of good-natured fun to be had at this subterranean bowling alley where a sign above the door proclaims "*fundada en 1941*". Not a great deal has changed since then: scores are kept on paper and teenagers rather than high-tech machines pick up the pins. A game costs just COP$3200 per person (COP$3800

Andrés DC Calle 82 No. 12–21, Zona Rosa ⓦwww .andrescarnederes.com. The central Bogotá incarnation of the suburban legend *Andrés Carne de Res* must be seen to be believed. A 1000-capacity restaurant and salsa club that looks like something from a Tim Burton movie, it is the biggest all-singing, all-dancing party in the Colombian capital. The four floors (Hell, Earth, Purgatory and Heaven, the last with large roof terrace) are decked out in a kind of gothic burlesque, with live salsa music and staff dressed as circus performers and coquettish chamber maids who parade around dragging non-dancers to their feet. The menu has the design and length of a newspaper, and features no fewer than nine pages of alcoholic drinks as well as countless eating options (eg tenderloin COP$42,900). There's live music, and the party runs until 3am Fri & Sat (cover $20,000), finishing a bit earlier the rest of the week (COP$10,000 after 10pm Thurs). An unforgettable if expensive night out, although some locals swear that the original *Andrés*, on a rancho in the suburb of Chía (40min from downtown Bogotá by taxi) is still the best.

at peak times) including hire of some pretty antique bowling shoes. Open Mon–Sat until around 10pm.

Café Escobar Rosas C 4 No.15–01, La Candelaria. The infectious funk music spun at this former pharmacy makes it nearly impossible not to dance and intermingle with locals. COP$15,000 cover, though that gets converted to a drinks voucher.

Goce Pagano Cra 13A No. 23–97, Downtown. Less is more in this legendary watering hole, which has a simple dancefloor and Bogotá's largest rack of golden-era salsa LPs. Sapient owner Gustavo is a throwback to the era when the revolution was fought listening to salsa; you won't soon forget your visit. No cover. Take a taxi as the area is unsafe at night. Thurs–Sat only.

In Vitro C 59 No. 6–38 ⓦwww.invitrovisual.com. Popular with studenty locals, this aquamarine-lit lounge changes moods with the hour, from quiet cocktail bar early on to late-night dance joint embracing diverse musical styles on different days of the week, including electronica on Thurs and salsa on Fri. Shows locally produced short films on Tues & Thurs.

The Irish Pub Cra 12A No. 83–48, Zona Rosa, North Bogotá. Gringo expats and yuppie Colombians sink pints of Guinness (COP$13,900) and tuck into "Celtic fish and chips" (COP$23,900) at this upmarket Irish bar. Pub quiz on the last Thurs of the month.

Quiebra Canto Cra 5 No. 17–76, Downtown ⓦwww.quiebracanto.com. Quiebra's two floors provide salsa like it's meant to be – hot and sticky. The funk night on Wed is extremely popular with expats and locals alike. Cover COP$8000–30,000.

Theatron C 58 No. 10–42, Chapinero ⓦwww .theatrondepelicula.com. A neon-lit wonderland, this colossal gay club is spread over three floors and six rooms, some of which are men only. Also hosts live shows, which attract a mixed audience. The COP$22,000 cover charge on Sat night gets you a cup and access to an open bar (until 2am).

Yumi Yumi Cra 3A No.16–40. A pint-sized cocktail bar on Parque de Los Periodistas offering delicious but potent drinks. Try the coconut mojito or the *maracuyá caipiroska*. Dangerously, cocktails are always 2-for-1 (around COP$16,000). Also does food until 9pm, including cheap, tasty Thai curry on Tues & Wed. Has a second branch in the Zona Rosa on the corner of Cra 13 and C 84.

Shopping

Artesanías de Colombia Cra 2 No.18A–58 ⓣ1/286-1766, ⓦwww.artesaniasdecolombia.com. co. Not cheap, but has beautiful, high-quality handicrafts and jewellery from all over Colombia that's far nicer than the tat you'll find in the tourist traps around the Museo del Oro. Has two other branches in north Bogotá.

Authors C 70 No.7–53 ☎1/217-7788, ⓦwww .authors.com.co. A bookstore with a café and two floors of English-language books. Open daily 10am–8pm (until 6pm Sun).

Flea markets In addition to the antiques and handicrafts of the upmarket Mercado de las Pulgas in Usaquen (see p.550), there are more rough-and-ready Sunday flea markets at Parque de los Periodistas and opposite the Torre Colpatria on Cra 7 (between calles 24 & 26).

Paloquemao C 19 & Cra 24. The largest and most bustling market in the city, where you can stock up on supplies to cook at your hostel. Fantastic veg and tropical fruit, a somewhat gory meat section and plenty of dry goods. Fri and Sun are when the flower-sellers show up: get there by about 8am to catch the best of their displays. It's safe enough to take a camera if you are sensible with it: be discreet and ask permission before taking photos of people.

San Andresito Cra 38 between calles 38 & 39. This district is the place to come in Colombia for cheap electronics; just don't ask where your vendor got his stock from. *Busetas* run here from C 19, or take a taxi.

UN La Librería C 20 No.7–15 ☎1/342-7382, ⓦwww.unalibreria.unal.edu.co. The National University bookshop has volumes in English, French and German as well as beautiful photography books on Colombia and a nice coffee bar with terrace on the second floor. Open Mon–Fri 9.30am–7pm, Sat 10am–3pm.

Directory

Banks and exchange ATMs are available throughout the city. Several currency exchanges, charging 2–3 percent commission, can be found at most shopping centres, hotels and the city's airports, as well as near the Museo de Oro.

Car rental Most rental agencies have offices at the airport. Hertz, at Av. Caracas No.27–17 (☎1/327-6700, ⓦwww.hertz.com) is a decent bet, costing from US$54 per day.

Embassies Australia, Cra 18 No. 90–38 (☎1/636-5247); Brazil, C 93 No. 14–20, 8th floor (☎1-218-0800); Canada, Cra 7 No. 114–33, 14th floor (☎1/657-9800); Ecuador, C 67 No. 7–35 (☎1/317-5328); Peru, C 80 No. 6–50 (☎1/257-0505); UK, Cra 9 No. 76–49, 9th floor (☎1/326-8300); US, Cra 45 No. 24B–27 (☎1/315-1566); Venezuela, Cra 11 No. 87–51 (☎1/644-5555).

Hospital Clínica Marly at C 50 No. 9–67 (☎1/343-6600) is a modern medical facility accustomed to attending foreigners. Dial ☎125 for an ambulance.

Immigration For visa extensions (COP$70,100) visit the DAS (Departamento Administrativo de Seguridad) at their Dirección de Extranjería office at C 100 No. 11B–27 (Mon–Thurs 7.30am–4pm, Fri 7.30am–3.30pm; ☎1/601-7269). You can apply for a one-month visa extension in DAS offices in most Colombian cities.

Internet Virtually all hostels have internet access (frequently free) and there are plenty of internet cafés across the city, charging around COP$1500 per hr. One option is Internet de La Vieja Candelaria, next door to *Ricasole* (see "Eating", p.553), open 9am–9pm daily.

Pharmacy There is a pharmacy in the Olimpica supermarket at Av. Jimenez No. 4 (Mon–Sat 7am–9pm, Sun 9am–4pm).

Police Headquarters of the tourist police is at Cra 13 No. 26–62 (daily 7am–noon & 2–7pm; ☎1/337-4413). In an emergency dial ☎123 from any phone.

Post The main post office in La Candelaria is on Cra 8 between calles 12 and 13, but locals often use private postal services. A popular option is 472 (☎1/4199-299, ⓦwww.4-72.com.co), which has offices around town including at Cra 7 No.12–13.

Moving on

Air Multiple flights daily to Bucaramanga (1hr); Cali (1hr); Cartagena (1hr 20min); Leticia (1hr 50min); Manizales (50min); Medellín (40min); Pasto (1hr 30min); Pereira (50min); Popayán (1hr 15min); San Andres (2hr); Santa Marta (1hr 30min). International direct flights to: Buenos Aires (6hr), Caracas (2hr), Guayaquil (1hr 50min), Lima (3hr), Santiago (6hr), São Paulo (5hr).

Bus Cali (hourly; 10hr); Cartagena (14 daily; 19hr); Manizales (10 daily; 18hr); Medellín (hourly; 10hr); Pasto (8 daily; 21hr); Pereira (hourly; 8hr); Popayán (7 daily; 13hr); San Agustin (11 daily; 12hr); Santa Marta (11 daily; 16hr); Villa de Leyva (4 daily; 4hr). International buses to: Buenos Aires (4 weekly; 7 days); Caracas (2 weekly; 28hr); Lima (4 weekly; 3 days); Quito (4 weekly; 32hr); Santiago (4 weekly; 5 days).

DAY-TRIPS FROM BOGOTÁ

The **Zipaquirá salt cathedral** and the up-and-coming adventure sports town of **Suesca** are both within easy day-trip distance of the capital.

The Zipaquirá salt cathedral

The most obvious day-trip from Bogotá is a visit to the salt cathedral of **ZIPAQUIRÁ** (Daily 9am–6pm; ☎1/852-4030, 🌐www.catedraldesal .gov.co; COP$17,000), some 50km north of the city. Inaugurated in 1995 to great fanfare – having replaced an earlier one that closed because of collapse – the cathedral lies completely underground, topped by a hill that was mined by local Indians even before the Spaniards arrived in the seventeenth century. As you descend 180m into the earth, you'll pass fourteen minimalist chapels built entirely of salt that glow like marble in the soft light. The main nave is a feat of modern engineering, complete with the world's largest subterranean cross, although the quiet majesty of the place is diminished by the photographer waiting in front of the altar to charge COP$10,000 per snap and the large gift shop to the right of the aisle.

Above ground, there's a **museum** (same hours as cathedral) explaining the history of salt extraction, plus a somewhat tacky plaza with *arepa* outlets and, bizarrely, a climbing wall. Mass is held on Sundays at noon. A **guided tour** of the cathedral is included in the entrance fee (ask at the ticket desk if you want the English version). To get there from Bogotá, take the TransMilenio to the Portal del Norte station at the end of the #2 or #3 line and from here a *buseta* (COP$3500) to Zipaquirá. From the centre of Zipaquirá, it's a short cab ride or 15-min walk to the entrance.

Suesca

Some 70km north of Bogotá, the small town of **SUESCA** has become one of Colombia's top rock-climbing destinations. Adventure sports enthusiasts of all persuasions will feel at home here, with mountain biking, paragliding, white-water rafting, caving, horser-iding and good trekking all on offer, but it is the sandstone cliffs on the town's doorstep that steal the show, offering traditional and sport rock-climbing with more than six hundred routes including multi-pitch.

The majority of the rock-climbing and adventure sports operators are located at the entrance to the rocks, a 15-min walk from the town centre. Try Vamonos Pa'l Monte (☎1/274-4649, 🌐www .escaladaencolombia.com; half-day COP$70,000, full day COP$100,000;). A further 15-min on is the *El Vivac Hostal*, at Autopista Norte (☎1/284-5313, 🌐www.vamonospalmonte.com/ Hostal/hostal-el-vivac.html), a cosy place to stay and recharge, with a communal kitchen, fireplace and good mattresses in the shared rooms (COP$20,000, also private doubles COP$55,000). Campers can pitch out back, and the hostel rents mountain bikes (COP$10,000 per day). To get to Suesca from Bogotá, take the Trans-Milenio to the northern terminus at Portal del Norte and then jump on one of the regular buses for Suesca (40min).

North of Bogotá

Just a few kilometres from Bogotá, the smog and busy streets quickly give way to the bucolic countryside of Colombia's Central Andean departments. Boyacá, Cundimarca and Santander mark the geographical heart of the country. First inhabited centuries ago by the gold-worshipping Muisca Indians, these mountainous highlands played a pivotal role in forging Colombia's national identity. Near **Tunja**, one of Colombia's oldest cities, stands the bridge where Bolívar defeated the Spanish army in 1819, clearing the way for independ-ence. An hour further northwest is one of Colombia's best-preserved colonial towns, **Villa de Leyva**, with its cobbled streets, mild climate and beautiful surrounding countryside.

Tiny **Barichara** offers an even more genteel atmosphere, just a steep 22km from the burgeoning adventure town of **San Gil**. Further north again, the modern city of **Bucaramanga** or the colonial town of Girón are both decent midway points if you're heading to Venezuela or the coast. Follow a different road from Tunja, and eight hours later you arrive at the high-altitude splendours of **Parque Nacional El Cocuy**, with its glacial lakes and snowcapped peaks. All these destinations are easily accessed by **bus**.

TUNJA

TUNJA, capital of Boyacá department, has a reputation for dullness that is neither wholly undeserved nor an adequate picture of this friendly city. Founded in 1539 on the ruins of the ancient Muisca capital of Hunza, Tunja's historic centre is one of the foremost preserves of the country's colonial heritage while its sizeable student population gives it a youthful atmosphere. Once you've gotten beyond that, however, there is little to distinguish it from most other functional, mid-sized urban centres and with Villa de Leyva just 45min further down the road from Bogotá, not many bother to stop here. Nevertheless, Tunja is a pleasant place to spend a few hours, and is also the most convenient base from which to visit **El Puente de Boyacá** (see below).

What to see and do

The majority of the sights are gathered around **Plaza de Bolívar**, including the **Casa del Fundador Suárez Rendón** (Wed–Sun 8.30am–12.30pm & 2–6pm; free to walk the grounds, COP$2000 for upstairs museum), home of the town's founder. Dating from 1540, it was built in the Moorish Mudéjar style and contains some colonial artwork, as well as the local tourism office. At C 20 and Cra 8, the **Casa de Don Juan de Vargas** (Tues–Fri 9am–noon & 2–5pm, closes at 4pm Sat & Sun; COP$2000) stands out for its eighteenth-century interior frescoes.

Like much of the town's architecture, Plaza Bolívar's **Catedral** (open all day weekends, roughly 5–6pm weekdays), built in 1569, contains Islamic motifs. More ornate are the **Santo Domingo** and **Santa Clara** churches. The former, on C 11 between carreras 19 and 20, is known for its Rosario Chapel, which exhibits religious paintings and woodwork by Gregorio Vásquez de Arce y Ceballos. The latter, on Cra 7 and C 19 (7.30am–6pm; ring bell if door closed; COP$3000), was part of the first convent in South America, and combines indigenous and Catholic imagery in its elaborate decor. It is now a religious museum.

El Puente de Boyacá

About 16km south of Tunja on the main road back to Bogotá is a reconstructed colonial-era bridge, **El Puente de Boyacá,** commemorating the Battle of Boyacá of August 7, 1819, which cleared the way for Bolívar and his freedom fighters to march triumphantly into Bogotá. The trickling river's trivial girth lends a new perspective to the popular myth of Bolívar's bravery – perhaps at the time of the battle it formed a more substantial natural barrier. There's a monument to El Libertador here as well as a restaurant and small museum. *Busetas* leave from Tunja's conveniently located bus terminal every 30min.

Arrival and Information

Bus Plaza Bolívar is just a short walk northwest from the city's bus terminal. To get to the plaza, head up the steps at the back of the terminal building and head right along Cra 7 (there are signs). After two blocks, turn left along C 19 for two blocks until you hit the southern border of the square. There is a left luggage office at the terminal, open 24hr (COP$700 per hr).

Taxi A taxi from the front of the bus terminal should cost no more than COP$3000.

Tourist information The Boyacá office, which has plenty of information to help you get off the beaten track, is located within the Casa de la Cultura on the west side of the Plaza de Bolívar (Mon–Fri 8am–noon & 2–6pm, Sat & Sun 9am–4pm). The local Tunja information office is inside the Casa del Fundador Suárez Rendón, on the east side of the square.

Accommodation

Alicante Cra 8 No. 19–15 ☎8/744-9967. A new hotel from the same owners as *Casa Real* (see below), with the same keen prices, good facilities and friendly service as the original but a totally different, modern and minimalist design. COP$50,000.

Casa Real C 19 No. 7–65 ☎8/743-1764, ✉hotelcasareal@yahoo.es. An atmospheric hotel in an old colonial building with attractive rooms (en-suite, TV) set around a lovely courtyard. Wi-fi, laundry service and free hot drinks; breakfast from COP$5000. Prices drop twenty percent in low season; it's worth asking about discounts all year. COP$50,000.

Dux C 19 No. 10–78 ☎8/742-5736. An old colonial home converted into an inn with nine rooms, which are basic (though each has private bath) and have a slightly funny smell. Nevertheless, this place is cheap, clean and located very close to the main square. Also has a café downstairs. COP$36,000.

Eating

Café República West side of Plaza de Bolívar. Excellent coffee and great views of the square, plus simple food including omelettes for breakfast, sandwiches, *empanadas* and brownies. Open until 7.30pm weekdays, 7pm weekends.

El Maizal Cra 9 No. 20–30. A stark, two-storey place open from breakfast until 9pm. The menu includes specials for each day of the week, such as *ajiaco* (potato soup; COP$4000) or fish soup (COP$8500). A simple breakfast of bread, butter and cheese costs just COP$700.

Shalom Pasaje de Vargas (C 19A, through gates on west side of Plaza Bolívar). A very popular place with friendly staff selling good-value set lunches for COP$6500. Despite the name the food is very much local: lots of soups, meat, yuca and rice, and good fresh fruit juices.

Moving on

Bus Buses north to Bucaramanga, the main jumping-off point for the trips to the Caribbean coast, leave about every hour (6–7hr). You can get off in San Gil (4hr 30min) to head on to Barichara (see p.563). Small buses – some direct, some not – to Villa de Leyva leave every 15min (45min) until about 6pm.

VILLA DE LEYVA

Just four hours by bus from Bogotá and an hour from Tunja, tucked against the foot of spectacular mountains, scenic **VILLA DE LEYVA** is the hub of tourism in the high Andes heartland. Founded in 1572, the town is a must-see showcase of colonial architecture and was declared a national monument in 1954. Whether you're hunting for fossils, enjoying the countryside on horseback or just sitting around the 400-year-old plaza drinking sangria, the untroubled ambience and mild, dry climate make it a perfect place to relax before or after tackling Bogotá.

What to see and do

Villa de Leyva looks and feels immaculately preserved, right down to hand-painted tiles prohibiting horseback riding and car traffic along the main plaza. As most tourists come at the weekend, some restaurants, sights and the tourist information office close on Mondays. A lively **market**, mostly featuring fruit, veg and clothing, is held in the Plaza de Mercado on Saturday morning.

Plaza Mayor and around

The impressive **Plaza Mayor** is one of the largest in Colombia, paved over in large cobblestones and centred on a stone well. Dominating the plaza is the huge stone portal of the seventeenth-century **Catedral**, rebuilt after an 1845 earthquake. Directly in front across the plaza is the **Casa-Museo Luis Alberto Acuña** (daily 10am–6pm; COP$3000) which houses sculptures and large murals by the avant-garde twentieth-century artist.

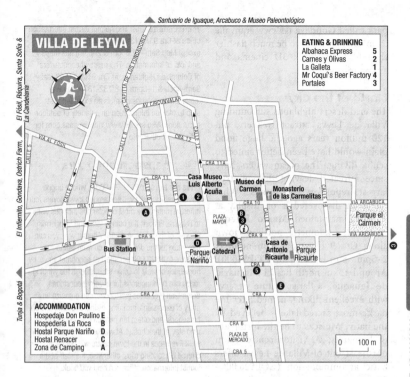

VILLA DE LEYVA

EATING & DRINKING
Albahaca Express	5
Carnes y Olivas	2
La Galleta	1
Mr Coquí's Beer Factory	4
Portales	3

ACCOMMODATION
Hospedaje Don Paulino	E
Hospedería La Roca	B
Hostal Parque Nariño	D
Hostal Renacer	C
Zona de Camping	A

0   100 m

Facing the imposing **Monasterio de las Carmelitas** and its attached church is the **Museo del Carmen** (Sat, Sun & holidays only, 10am–1pm & 2–5pm; COP$2500), containing large numbers of wooden icons from the Church's early years of proselytizing in the New World.

A few blocks south, at Cra 8 and C 15, the **Casa de Antonio Ricaurte** (Wed–Fri 9am–noon & 2–5pm, Sat–Sun 9am–1pm & 2–6pm; free) was home to a national hero who fought for Bolívar. Operated by the Colombian armed forces since 1970, the house contains objects belonging to Ricaurte plus modern military paraphernalia, but the best reason for coming here is the beautiful garden.

West of the city

El Fósil (daily 9am–5pm; COP$4000), 5km out of town along the road to Santa Sofía, is a low-key museum featuring the fossilized remains of a Kronosaurus, a prehistoric marine lizard found by a *campesino* here in 1977. The 12.8m-long lizard is one of only two in the world excavated in its entirety. At the nearby **Ostrich Farm** (Mon–Fri 9am–4.30pm, Sat & Sun 9am–5pm; COP$8500) you can see these elegantly grizzled creatures strut and then sample a bird burger at the on-site restaurant, though it's not cheap.

Around 2km on from El Fósil, you'll find **El Infiernito**, a Muisca observatory made famous in tourist photos because of its large, phallic stone monoliths. Tiny **Ráquira**, 25km from Villa de Leyva to the west, makes a good stop only if you're looking to buy some crafts – hammocks, jewellery and terra-cotta pottery spill from storefronts onto its single main street. On the way to Ráquira, about 15min by bus from Villa de Leyva, is a new dinosaur-themed

park called **Gondava** (Ⓦwww.granvalle
.com) that promises to be much flashier
than El Fósil (think 3D cinema and
animatronics).

North of the city

The arid desert highlands surrounding
Villa de Leyva attract trekkers, but
120 million years ago the huge flood
plain would have been better suited to
scuba diving. The ocean waters have
since retreated, leaving the country's
largest repository of **fossils**. What
has been discovered is on display at
the well-maintained **Museo Paleontológico**, a kilometre north of town
along Cra 9 (Tues–Sat 9am–noon &
2–5pm, Sun 9am–3pm; COP$4000).
Around 15km north lies **El Santuario
de Iguaque**, a large nature reserve
with excellent hiking, named after the
park's most sacred lake – believed by
the native Muiscas to be the birthplace
of humanity. A visitor centre 12km
northeast out of Villa de Leyva offers
basic accommodation (COP$26,000–
33,000 per person depending on
season), a camping area (COP$5000–
7000 per person) and food. The
entrance fee for the reserve is a steep
COP$31,000 for foreigners. Take one of
the buses that leave for Arcabuco four
times a day and pass the turn-off for the
park en route; check with the driver as
there are two roads to Arcabuco.

Arrival and information

Bus The bus stop is a short walk southwest from
the city centre, towards the road to Tunja.

Tourist information The helpful tourist information
office at Cra 9 No. 13–04 (☎8/732-0232, daily
except Mon 8am–12.30pm & 2–6pm) has maps
and lots of information. The nearby headquarters
of Colombian Highlands, at Cra 9 No. 11–02 (daily
9am–noon & 1–8pm; ☎8/732-1379, Ⓦwww
.colombianhighlands.com), is an excellent first
stop to pick up information on a variety of outdoor
excursions. Also see Ⓦwww.villaleyvanos.com for
listings and other info.

City transport and tours

Chiva bus tours (☎311/475-8681), whose brightly
painted vehicles you will see around town, covers four
different routes. The most popular one includes visits
to Ráquira, El Fósil, the ostrich farm and El Infiernito,
all west of the city (see p.559). Alternatively, you can
hire a taxi for the day to drive you from site to site
(approx. COP$20,000 per site, but negotiate), travel by
horseback or walk to some sites, though the winding
roads can be dangerous for unwary pedestrians.
Colombian Highlands (see above) can organize an
array of excursions, including hiking, abseiling and on
horseback, and offers ten percent discounts to those
who stay at their hostel. At weekends, you can barely
walk five paces in the town centre without being
offered horseriding trips; otherwise, the staff at the
tourist Information office can help you book.

Accommodation

Villa de Leyva has a wide range of quality hotels,
many of them former colonial residences. Various
campsites with basic bathrooms make the best
true budget options, though a lot of them cater
to young *Bogotános* arriving by car and are
BYO tent. Discounts of up to thirty percent are
often available during the week; book early for
weekends and holidays.
Hospedaje Don Paulino C 14 No. 7–46 ☎8/732-
1227. Chintzy decor and no additional services
but cheap, spotless rooms with private bathrooms
and cable TV. An especially good deal for single

LOCAL FIESTAS

The city plays host to two spectacular annual festivals. The larger is the
Festival of Lights (Dec 6–8), a fireworks extravaganza that gathers the best
of the region's pyrotechnicians, while the popular Kite Festival (Aug) sees the
country's finest kite-flyers compete in a variety of categories as spectators shout
encouragement. Smaller festivals, including celebrations of gastronomy (end
Oct) and of cinema (Sept), occur at other times during the year: ask at the tourist
information office for details.

travellers, who can get a private en-suite room for COP$25,000 (and a 20 percent discount on that in low season). COP$50,000.

Hospedería La Roca Plaza Mayor ☎8/732-0331. This place has a fantastic location on the main square, plus a pretty courtyard and 23 rooms (including for up to 6 people) with private bathrooms and TV. Breakfast COP$5000. Prices drop twenty percent outside high season. COP$100,000.

Hostal Parque Nariño Parque Nariño ☎311/251-5194. A great-value hostel hidden behind an unassuming little door set on the very pretty Parque Nariño. Upstairs rooms with shared bathrooms have more natural light than those with private bath on the ground floor. Kitchen but no internet. COP$40,000.

Hostal Renacer ☎8/732-1201. Owned by Oscar Gilède, the English-speaking biologist behind Colombian Highlands (see opposite), *Hostal Renacer* is a haven surrounded by trees and mountain views. A TV room, hammocks, free wi-fi and hot drinks, a fridge full of beer and heaps of information, plus rooms with huge windows and comfortable beds, make it popular with backpackers unsurprisingly. You can also camp here. The location, about 1km uphill from the centre, is a bit of a pain, but if you call when you arrive in town they'll pay for your cab. Camping COP$9000 per person with own tent (COP16,000 without), dorms COP$16,000, rooms COP$60,000.

Zona de Camping Corner of C 10 and Cra 10 ☎311/530-7687. No-frills camping, with a wall set up around a large patch of grass and a basic toilet/shower block. Great mountain views. COP$10,000 per person.

Eating and drinking

The greatest density of restaurants lies in the vicinity of the intersection of C 11 and Cra 9. Most are busier for lunch than dinner, since people seem to spend their evenings congregating in the Plaza Mayor. In terms of organized nightlife, weeknights can be a bit subdued, although you should be able to find live guitar music In one of the bars around the main square.

Albahaca Express Cra 8 No. 13–46 ☎313/844-6613. A very attractive restaurant that's bustling by day, romantic and candlelit with a roaring fire by night. Offers a *menu del día* (COP$7000) plus great *ajiaco con pollo* (chicken stew with capers and avocado; COP$14,000) and local Villa de Leyva sausage with chips. Live music events are scheduled for the garden, which has sweet-smelling flowers and orange trees. Open 9am–9pm daily.

Carnes y Olivas Cra 10 No.11–55 ☎8/732-1368. Offers a fantastic value, three-course *menu del día* (COP$7000), including traditional dishes such as tender braised *sobrebarriga* (flank steak), cooked with considerable skill and flair. Also has a lengthy menu of regional and international dishes featuring pizza and hamburgers. Open 9am–9pm daily.

La Galleta Cra 10 No. 11–33. Serves up wedges of delicious baked cheesecake topped with local fruits such as *mora*, plus chocolate cake and other extremely unhealthy treats. Also does good coffee, and has a second branch at C 13 No. 7–03. Open from 11.30am daily, closes at 7pm weekdays and 9pm weekends.

Mr Coqui's Beer Factory Corner of Calle 13 and Plaza Mayor. This huge indoor-outdoor place on the corner of the main square has its own micro-brewery, a big screen showing sports or music videos, a DJ until 3am on Sat nights and a food menu that includes hamburgers and burritos (both COP$10,000). Open from 8am daily for breakfast.

Portales Plaza Mayor. Outdoor tables on the main square make this a good place for people-watching. Serves up Italian staples such as spaghetti bolognaise (COP$13,500) and pizzas (COP$12,000–39,000).

Moving on

Bus The two main bus companies are Reina and Libertadores. Six buses a day (3 on Sun and holidays) leave for Bogotá (4–5hr) between 5am and 5pm. To continue north to San Gil and Barichara, or further on to Bucaramanga and Cúcuta, you typically must first take a bus south to Tunja (every 15min; 45min) or to Chinquinquira (6 daily; 1hr) and transfer.

SAN GIL

Thanks to its developing reputation as an adventure-sports hotspot, **SAN GIL** has recently become one of the biggest backpacker draws in northern Colombia. The compact town is an ideal base for taking part in the various adrenaline-heavy activities that take place in the surrounding country-side, and has a certain grubby charm of its own. For those that fancy a spot of culinary adventure sport, fried *hormigas culonas*, or fat-bottomed ants, a Santander delicacy, can be bought from a few places around town including the market.

What to see and do

The main attraction in town is the sylvan, riverside **Parque Gallineral** (8am–5.30pm; COP$5000). There's a natural swimming pool, and the entrance fee gets you a wristband that means you can go in and out of the park all day. To get here, head to the river and turn left along the Malecón to its end.

Two other popular spots for swimming and general lounging about are **Pescadarito** and the **Juan Curí waterfalls**, both about 30min from San Gil. To reach the former, take a bus to Curiti from San Gil's local terminal on the corner of Cra 11 and C 15; from there it's a 40-min walk. You can also camp for free at Pescadarito, though you will need to hike 30min upriver from the first pool and there are no facilities. To get to Juan Curí, catch a bus from the terminal heading to Charalá and get off when you see signs for *Las Cascadas* (the bus driver will stop here expectantly if he knows there are tourists on board). From here it's a 25-min walk to the waterfalls; you might be asked to pay COP$5000 by the owners of the land.

About an hour from San Gil on the road to Bucaramanga is **Parque Nacional del Chichamocha** (Tues–Sun 9am–6pm; ☎7/657-4400, ⓦwww.parquenacionaldelchicamocha.com), a collection of tacky attractions situated next to a beautiful canyon. The *teleférico*, a cable car which runs down into the canyon and over to the other side, is the best route to sweeping views (park entrance COP$12,000, with *teleférico* COP$36,000). You can also come here from San Gil to paraglide, though it is far more expensive than at Curiti, which is nearer town and not so heavily marketed.

Arrival and city transport

Bus The bus terminal is 2km southwest of town; a taxi to the centre costs COP$3000.

Taxi If you are heading out of town in a group, it can sometimes be cheaper and easier to negotiate with a taxi driver than to take the bus. A return taxi to the Juan Curí waterfalls, for example, should cost about COP$35,000 including waiting time.

Accommodation

Hostel Santander-Aleman C 12 No. 7–63 ☎7/724-2535, ⓦwww.hostelsantanderaleman .com. Perhaps the best budget place in town for a quiet stay, this small place has airy rooms, an open-air shower and a DVD player plus film collection (including in English). Also serves breakfast (from COP$5000). Dorms COP$15,000, rooms COP$35,000.

Macondo Guesthouse C 12 No. 7–26 ☎7/724-4463, ⓦwww.macondohostel.com. Australian-owned *Macondo* has such a homely, laidback atmosphere that you forgive the ramshackle rooms in the main

---

ADVENTURE SPORTS

Adrenaline junkies are spoilt for choice by the array of adventure sports on offer in San Gil. There are two main white-water rafting routes; a hair-raising day-trip down the Class IV/V (depends on the season) Río Suarez costs about COP$125,000, while a more sedate half-day on the Río Fonce is COP$30,000. Abseiling down the Juan Curí waterfalls will set you back COP$40,000, or you can take flight with a tandem paraglide (COP$60,000–170,000 depending on location). Spelunkers have the choice of several caves to explore (around COP$25,000). Other sporty options include kayak and bike-hire, paintballing and horseriding.

Most accommodation can arrange any of the above, and you should pay the same as if you book direct. The staff at *Macondo Guesthouse* (see above) are particularly helpful if you're trying to decide what to opt for. Alternatively, recommended operators are Colombia Rafting Expediciones, who have an office at Cra 10 No.7–83 (☎311/291-2870, ⓦwww.colombiarafting.com) and Páramo Santander Extremo (☎7/725-8944, ⓦwww.paramosantanderextremo.com).

building, although those in the second building two doors down are decidedly soulless. Loads of info on sports and the area. Dorms COP$15,000, rooms COP$30,000. The owner has recently opened a second place, *Hormiga Hostel*, on Cra 8.

Sam's Hostel Cra 10 No. 12–33 ☏7/724-2746, ⓦwww.samshostel.com. This new hostel is a young party animal's dream, with a balcony overlooking the main square, poker table and even a small swimming pool. Rooms themselves are cramped, although the double rooms downstairs should be great when finished. Dorms COP$15,000, rooms COP$50,000.

Eating and drinking

By far the liveliest place to drink on most evenings is the main plaza, which is usually full of groups of young people swilling beer purchased from one of the obliging shops around the square. The central market between calles 13 and 14 is the best bet for self-catering supplies, including great fruit, and is open until 2pm daily.

Café Con-Verso C 12 No. 7–63. Those with a sweet tooth should be sure to try the café frappe with ice-cream at this candlelit café bar, which has a jazz-and-blues soundtrack plus board games to enjoy over beer or cocktails. Also serves pizza (COP$20,000) and pasta (COP$8000). Open 4pm–midnight, depending on the punters.

El Maná C 10 No. 9–12 Ask a local for advice on restaurants and you'll probably be directed here: *El Maná* is extremely popular for its dependable set meals (COP$9000), which come with dessert, salad and drink as well as soup and a choice of main course. Open Mon–Sat 11am–2.30pm & 6–9pm, Sun 11am–3pm.

Moving on

Bus Bogotá (several daily; 6–8hr); Bucaramanga (every 30min; 2hr 30min).

BARICHARA

With its undulating stone-slab roads, clay-tiled *tejas* roofs draped in bougainvillea blossoms and single-storey adobe homes, the sedate hamlet of **BARICHARA** looks like it probably hasn't changed much in its 250 years. So well-kept is the town that it was declared a national monument in 1978. Barichara is considerably less crowded than similarly picturesque

Villa de Leyva, making it a peaceful, if expensive, resting spot for weary travellers on the way to Venezuela. Indeed, the town's name comes from an Indian word, *Barachala*, meaning "a good place to rest". Alternatively, it makes for a very pleasant day-trip from San Gil.

What to see and do

There isn't an enormous amount to do in Barichara itself other than admire the general charm of the place. Once you've checked out the striking **Catedral de la Inmaculada Concepción** on the Parque Central, which stands on fluted sandstone columns, and the small collection of photos and ceramics in the **Casa de la Cultura** (Wed–Mon 9am–noon & 2–5pm, closed Tues; COP$500), the best way to sample a bit of local culture is by treating yourself to a delicious lunch at *Color de Hormiga* (see p.564).

Another very pleasant option is the 2-hr (one-way) walk to the tiny village of **Guane**, which follows the old, rocky *camino real* through rolling countryside with great mountain views. To join the path, head uphill along C 5 from the cathedral before taking a left along Cra 10 to the edge of Barichara.

When planning a trip to Barichara, bear in mind that some restaurants only open at weekends, and that everything is shut on Tuesdays. **Buses** run between Barichara's Parque Central and San Gil's local bus terminal every half-hour until 6.30pm (30–45min; COP$3500).

Accommodation

Although prices listed here are for high season, and costs drop considerably at other times, accommodation in Barichara is expensive all year round. A day-trip from San Gil is probably a better option for those who are really watching their wallets.

Casa de Hercilia C 3 No. 5–33 ☏7/726-7450 ⓦwww.lacasadehercilia.com. A light and airy place that oozes tranquility, with hammocks, beanbags and leafy pot plants liberally scattered throughout. Also has a well-equipped communal kitchen. No dorms, but in low season it's worth asking about renting a single bed in one of their bigger rooms. COP$95,000.

Hostal Aposentos C 6 No. 6–40 ☎ 313/264-2962. Situated right on the main plaza, with polished beams, red-tiled floors, TV and private bathrooms, *Aposentos* is good value compared with much of the competition. COP$90,000.

Eating

Color de Hormiga C 8 No.8–44 ☎ 7/726-7156, ✉ colordehormiga@hotmail.com. Yes, they make food with ants in it, but this is far from a gimmicky tourist trap. Dishes such as *medallones de lomito en salsa de hormiga culona* (essentially steak in ant sauce, COP$23,000) are beautifully cooked and elegantly presented, and there are insect-free options too. A lovely spot for a classy lunch. Open noon–4.30pm, closed Tues.

El Compa C 5 No.4–48. A popular canteen dishing up standard set lunches for COP$8000 and other no-frills meals. Think soup, grilled meat and plenty of rice. Open until 8pm.

Panadería Central Corner of C 6 & Cra 6. This bakery on the main square selling bread, cheese, ham and cakes is a useful spot for walkers in search of picnic provisions, and self-caterers. Open 7am–9pm daily. Several other shops around the square sell basic dry goods.

BUCARAMANGA

Founded in 1622, **BUCARAMANGA** has shed much of its colonial heritage and evolved into one of Colombia's largest, most modern cities. There's little to detain visitors, but it makes a convenient stopover for anyone travelling to the coast or Venezuela.

Simon Bolívar (El Libertador) spent a grand total of seventy days living in Bucaramanga in 1828; enough for the locals to rename the beautiful house where he stayed, at C 37 No. 12–15, **Casa de Bolívar** (Mon–Fri 8am–noon & 2–6pm, Sat 8am–noon; COP$1000). It now contains a small historical museum and research centre. Across the street another colonial mansion houses the **Casa de la Cultura** (Mon–Fri 8am–noon & 2–6pm, Sat 8am–noon; COP$1000), which holds displays of regional art. Catching

any *buseta* heading to Floridablanca (30–45min; COP$1400), a neighbourhood to the northeast, will take you near the **Jardín Botánico Eloy Valenzuela** (daily 7.30am–6pm; COP$5000), where the Río Frío runs through the verdant gardens.

Bucaramanga is taking off as a **paragliding** destination, thanks to Colombia Paragliding (☎ 312/432-6266, ⓦ www.colombiaparagliding.com), which now offers everything from one-off tandem flights to 15-day courses for those who want their international licence. The owners, who also run *Kasa Guane* (see "Accommodation", see below) have a hostel at their flight site outside town, which means you can be airborne within about ten minutes of getting out of bed.

Arrival

Air Palonegro International Airport lies about 30km southwest of the downtown area. The taxi fare to downtown is fixed at COP$27,000.
Bus The Terminal de Transportes is about 5km southwest of the city, and is accessible by city bus or taxi. A night journey (most leave between 7pm and 10pm) can be preferable for longer-haul trips if you're willing to forgo the beautiful scenery. Bring a blanket or have a jumper to hand as the buses get chilly.

Accommodation

Steer clear of the Parque Centenario neighbourhood near C 31 and Cra 17–24. C 34 offers some upper mid-range options in the carrera 20s, also near the city's concentration of discos.
Balmoral Corner C 21 & Cra 35 ☎ 7/630-4663. Lacking in style or soul, but has very cheap double rooms which are clean, secure and have private bath and TV. Many also have fridges, and there's internet and a restaurant serving cheap breakfasts and lunches on the ground floor. COP$35,000.
Kasa Guane C 49 No. 28–21 ☎ 7/657-6960, ⓦ www.kasaguane.com. The backpacker hostel that Bucaramanga desperately needed, *Kasa Guane* has airy dorms, basic doubles, a good communal kitchen, TV area, hammocks, a pool table, free wi-fi and loads of info. The top-floor bar is great if you want to socialize – less good if you're trying to sleep in one of the nearby double rooms. Dorms COP$20,000, rooms COP$50,000.

Eating and drinking

Strip clubs have taken over much of the once-fashionable Zona Rosa. The nightlife scene has shifted to the nearby Cabecera district, with Cra 33 holding the top clubs.

La Calle C.C. Cabecera Et IV L-505 ⊤7/647-8673. Located atop one of the city's shopping centres, this local favourite has great views of the city and a young clientele which likes to party late into the night.

Colombia en Sazón C 43 No. 32–50. A popular, squeaky-clean spot for simple but well-cooked set lunches (COP$7500); there is a different menu for every day of the week. Open 10.30am–2pm daily.

Pan Pa' Ya C 49 No. 28–48. This bakery-café perpetually emits hunger-inducing smells of fresh bread. As well as loaves, pastries and decent coffee, it sells pizza (from COP$8500) and sandwiches to eat in or take away, and provisions such as eggs and juice. Open Mon–Sat 8am–10pm, Sun 9am–2pm & 4–8pm.

Rio Palma Cra 29 at C 48. An extremely popular two-storey bar with live music upstairs at weekends and canned tunes the rest of the week. Full of lively groups swigging beer from early in the evening. Open until 2am.

El Viejo Chiflas Cra 33 at C 34. *Comida típica* including *cabro en salsa* (goat in sauce; COP$18,000) and nibbles such as chorizo or *papas criollos* (COP$5000). Open 24hr, as is *Tony*, a similar restaurant over the road.

Moving on

Air Bogotá (10 daily; 1hr).
Bus Bus companies Berlinas and Copetran offer the most comfortable and frequent trips. Bogotá (every 15min; 8–9hr); Cartagena (8 daily; 13–16hr, often via Barranquilla); Santa Marta (2 daily; 9hr).

GIRÓN

With its whitewashed colonial buildings, leafy main square and elegant churches, pretty **GIRÓN** makes for a more genteel stopover destination than nearby Bucaramanga, and is particularly worthwhile for those who don't have time to visit other colonial gems like Villa de Leyva and Barichara. The pace of life here is extremely relaxed, and there is not much to do other than wander around the colonial centre,

making it a good spot to recharge the batteries if you want to break the journey to or from the Caribbean coast.

Accommodation

Girón Chill Out Cra 25 No. 32–06 ⊤7/646-1119, Ⓦwww.gironchillout.com. Advertises itself as a boutique hostel and has stylish touches to fit the billing. The Italian owner runs a restaurant for guests only, and can organize tours including barbecues by the river. COP$74,000.

Las Nieves Main square ⊤7/681-0144, Ⓦwww .hotellasnievesgiron.com. Spotless rooms with private bath and TV; good value given its location. COP$66,000.

Eating and drinking

Restaurante Balcón Real de Girón Across the square from Las Nieves. A good place for people-watching over big portions of local or international food (goat with yuca COP$18,000) or a cold beer. Alternatively, there are plenty of cafés and stalls nearby selling *arepas*, *empanadas*, fruit and juices.

Moving on

Bus Bucaramanga (every 15min; 30min).
Taxi A taxi from Bucaramanga's bus terminal to Girón costs COP$10,000; from the airport it's around COP$20,000.

PARQUE NACIONAL EL COCUY

Rising to a high point of 5330m above sea level, and taking in 32 glacial lakes and 22 snowcapped peaks on the way, **PARQUE NACIONAL EL COCUY** (entrance for foreigners COP$34,000) is a walker's dream come true. Tourism is increasing here but for now at least, you can hike for a week surrounded by natural splendours with little to no contact with other people.

The starting points for any trip to the park are the towns of **El Cocuy** and **Guicán**, and one of the most popular hikes is to walk south to north between the two (or vice versa), which normally takes six or seven days. A milk truck departs from El Cocuy every morning at 6am; visitors can hitch a ride up the mountain to the park (45min; COP$7000) to begin their walk. Alternatively, private transport to and from the park (at a steep COP$80,000 per car) can be arranged through Cooperativa Serguias (☎311/855-4263, Ⓔ coopserguias@hotmail.com), which can also arrange guides (COP$100,000 per day) and has limited supplies of camping gear for rent. *Posada del Molino* (Cra 4 No. 7–51; ☎310/494-5076), which has rooms with private bath for COP$20,000 per person, is also the best place in town to eat.

Accommodation in the park itself is extremely limited, but there are a few cabañas that can be used as bases for day walks, or as a place to acclimatize to the altitude before embarking on a longer hike. *Cabañas Sisuma* (☎311/557-7893; COP$30,000 per person), near Las Lagunillas at the south end of the park, is a good base for walks to the beautiful **Laguna de la Plaza**, a beautifully situated glacial lake, and **El Pulpito del Diablo** (The Devil's Pulpit), a column of rock that sits dramatically in the middle of a glacier.

Bear in mind that the **weather** in the region is often poor and can change quickly; all but very experienced walkers should consider hiring a guide. By far the best weather is in December to February, when the park is predictably, at its busiest.

The **bus** to El Cocuy from Bogotá takes around eleven hours; it's another 30min on to Guicán. Although on a map the national park appears close to Bucaramanga and San Gil, a lack of roads means – frustratingly – that you have to go to Tunja (8hr from El Cocuy) and change.

CROSSING INTO VENEZUELA: CÚCUTA

The only reason to visit **CÚCUTA**, capital of Norte de Santander department, is if you're heading by land to Venezuela. The city offers precious few attractions and the outlying area has been the focus of intense guerrilla and paramilitary activity in recent years. Tensions between Venezuela's vehemently anti-US head of state, Hugo Chávez, and Colombia, which has close, if problematic, ties to the United States, present another reason for minimizing time here.

If you do spend time in the city, take a peek inside the ornate Neoclassical **Palacio de la Gobernación**, the department's main administrative building on Avenida 5 between calles 13 and 14, and the **Casa de la Cultura**, at C 13 No. 3–67, which contains a museum recounting the city's history.

BORDER CROSSING

The border is open 24hr, though it can become unexpectedly backed up or closed at short notice. Visitors should exercise utmost caution, as muggings are not uncommon on both sides of the border. At the time of writing, Americans, Canadians and Europeans don't need to purchase visas for surface travel, but make sure all is in order with your passport to ensure a smooth passage through the various checkpoints. For the most up-to-date information, contact the Venezuelan consulate (Mon–Fri 8am–noon; ☎7/579-1954) at Avenida Camilo Daza in Zona Industrial. Entering into Venezuela from Cúcuta, the first town you reach is San Antonio, but it's advisable to take the bus directly to the larger San Cristóbal if you want to make connections to Caracas (see p.955). You can catch a bus or take a *colectivo* into Venezuela from Cúcuta's bus terminal, but you must temporarily disembark at the DAS post just before the bridge to get your Colombian exit stamp. Once over the border, remember to put your watch forward thirty minutes.

Although a little on the expensive side for true budget travellers, by far the best affordable accommodation in town is *Hotel Cinera* (C 11 No. 3–49 ☎7/572-3710, ⊛www.hotelcinera .com; COP$100,000). Alternatively, try one of several basic *residencias* situated along Avenida 7, though this area can be somewhat dangerous at night. *Hotel Mary*, at Av. 7 No. 0–53 (☎7/572-1585; COP$42,000), is one option.

Cartagena and the Caribbean

Ever since Rodrigo de Bastidas became the first European to set foot on Colombian soil in Santa Marta in 1525, there's been a long history of foreigner fascination with the country's Caribbean coastline, and hundreds of thousands – Colombian holidaymakers chief among them – follow in his footsteps annually. In addition to hot weather and cool breezes, Cartagena boasts splendours from the town's past role as the main conduit for the Spanish crown's imperial plundering. For its extensive fortifications and colonial legacy, the walled city was declared a UNESCO World Heritage Site in 1984.

The 1600-km coast holds a wide variety of landscapes from the inaccessible dense jungles of the **Darién Gap** on the border with Panama to the arid salt plains of the **Guajira Peninsula**. If it's a tropical paradise you're after, try the white, jungle-fringed beaches of **Tayrona National Park** near Santa Marta. The translucent waters around **Santa Marta** and the nearby fishing village of **Taganga** number among the most inexpensive places in the world to learn to scuba-dive. Inland, travel back to the sixteenth century in sleepy **Mompox** and cross paths with coca-chewing Kogis on a mesmerizing five-day trek to the **Ciudad Perdida**.

CARTAGENA DE INDIAS

Without a doubt one of the Caribbean's most beautiful cities, the tourist gold mine of **CARTAGENA DE INDIAS** offers all-night partying, colonial architecture, gourmet dining and beaches. Cartagena literally embodies Colombia's Caribbean coast, with many of the city's colourful, weathered buildings built using coral from the surrounding reefs.

Founded in 1533, Cartagena was one of the first Spanish cities in the New World and served as the main port through which the continent's riches were shipped off to the mother country. Not surprisingly, the city proved an appetizing target for English pirates prowling the Caribbean, and it suffered several dreadful sieges in the sixteenth century, the most infamous led by Sir Francis Drake in 1586, during which he held the town hostage for more than a hundred days. After "the Dragon" withdrew, the Spaniards began constructing the elaborate network of fortifications that are now the city's hallmark.

Little of the city's aristocratic ways remain, though its attractiveness does. **San Diego**, home to a good number of mid-priced hostals and hotels, offers a more mellow, though still lively, version of the pricey, pretty **Old City**. Grittier **Getsemaní**, in pockets of which shirtless men play dominoes and *cumbia* music blasts from open plazas, lacks some of the architectural grandeur of the walled city but offers a better taste of local life. The most raucous nightlife and nearly all budget accommodation are found here. South of the Old City is **Bocagrande**, Cartagena's modern sector, a thin isthmus dotted with high-rise hotels and timeshare apartments catering to Colombian holidaymakers.

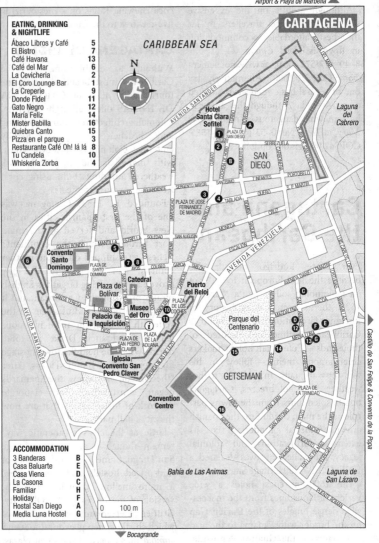

CARTAGENA

EATING, DRINKING & NIGHTLIFE

Ábaco Libros y Café	5
El Bistro	7
Café Havana	13
Café del Mar	6
La Cevicheria	2
El Coro Lounge Bar	1
La Creperie	9
Donde Fidel	11
Gato Negro	12
María Feliz	14
Mister Babilla	16
Quiebra Canto	15
Pizza en el parque	3
Restaurante Café Oh! lá lá	8
Tu Candela	10
Whiskería Zorba	4

ACCOMMODATION

3 Banderas	B
Casa Baluarte	E
Casa Viena	D
La Casona	C
Familiar	H
Holiday	F
Hostal San Diego	A
Media Luna Hostel	G

CARIBBEAN SEA

Laguna del Cabrero

Hotel Santa Clara Sofitel

SAN DIEGO

Convento Santo Domingo

Catedral

Plaza de Bolívar

Puerto del Reloj

Museo del Oro

Palacio de la Inquisición

Parque del Centenario

Iglesia Convento San Pedro Claver

GETSEMANÍ

Convention Centre

Bahía de Las Animas

Laguna de San Lázaro

0   100 m

Castillo de San Felipe & Convento de la Popa ▲

▼ Bocagrande

CARTAGENA AND THE CARIBBEAN   COLOMBIA

What to see and do

Bursting with history and generally aglow with Caribbean langour, Cartagena's walled **Old City** is where the bulk of the sightseeing is. Expect to get lost – as if the labyrinth of narrow, winding streets isn't disorienting enough, each block bears a different name. As such, the city's many **plazas** can guide you, acting not only as convenient landmarks but as distinct social hangouts. Take a shady afternoon break on a polished wood bench or enjoy people-watching while sipping a beer in the evening. You can take in the city by strolling the 11km of stone **ramparts** that encircle it, though it's best to avoid this late at night.

Plaza de los Coches and around

The city's main entranceway is the triple-arched **Puerta del Reloj**, which gives way to the **Plaza de los Coches**, a former slave-trading square. Today, it's the area where horse-drawn carriages can be hired at night for romantic tours around the city and the stage for a variety of street performances. Equally entertaining are the no-nonsense vendors at the plaza's covered arcade, **Portal de los Dulces**, who adeptly pluck bite-sized sweets of your choice out of a sea of huge glass jars. In the evening, several lively bars open up above the arcade.

Plaza de la Aduana and around

Half a block south of the Puerta del Reloj is the **Plaza de la Aduana**, the administrative centre during the colonial era, with a statue of Columbus at its centre. A few steps in the same direction and you'll bump into the imposing **Iglesia Convento San Pedro Claver** (daily 8am–5pm; free), on the quiet plaza of the same name. Built by Jesuits in 1603, this is where Spanish-born priest Pedro Claver lived and died, in 1654, before his canonization some two centuries later. Called the "slave of the slaves" for his door-to-door fundraising on behalf of the city's slaves, the ascetic monk's skull and bones are guarded in a glass coffin at the church's altar. The well-preserved church has a religious art museum, where you can park yourself on the same throne that Pope John Paul II sat on during his 1986 visit to Cartagena.

Plaza de Bolívar and around

A popular meeting place for locals is the flower-filled **Plaza de Bolívar**, perhaps the most opulent in town. On its west side stands the **Palacio de la Inquisición**, a block-long example of late-colonial architecture, the city's finest remnant of the era. It was completed in 1776 and is believed to be the site where at least eight hundred people were sentenced to death. Scenes from the 2009 movie adaptation of García Márquez's *Love and Other Demons* were shot at the torture museum within. To the right of the Palacio, is the **Museo de Oro** (Tues–Sat 10am–1pm & 3–6pm, Sun 10–4pm; free) specializes in ornaments which from the pre-Columbian Sinú culture and is well worth seeing if you don't have time to visit the museum of the same name in Bogotá. On the northeast corner of the plaza is the **Catedral**, whose construction began in 1575, was almost derailed by cannon fire in 1586 by Drake, and was finally completed in 1612.

Plaza de Santo Domingo

Head a block west past a series of nicely preserved balustrades to the lively **Plaza de Santo Domingo**. The **Iglesia y Convento de Santa Domingo**, with Botero's satirical sculpture *La Gorda* as de facto sentinel, constitutes the plaza's main draw. Completed in 1579, the fortress-like structure's austere interior belies its status as Cartagena's oldest church. On the Baroque altar there's a Christ carved in the sixteenth century.

East of the Old City

For a bird's-eye view of Cartagena, take a cab (30–45min; COP$50,000 return) up to the **Convento de la Popa** (Mon–Fri 8am–5pm; COP$9000), outside the city's walls. Don't walk: the area around it is unsafe. The restored whitewashed chapel, built in 1608, is clearly visible from almost anywhere in the city. In addition to offering spectacular panoramic views of the city, photos of Pope John Paul II's 1986 visit to Cartagena are also on display in the small chapel. On February 2, when the city celebrates the day of its patron saint, the **Virgin of Candelaria**, protector against pirates and the plague, a candle-lit procession of pilgrims storms the hill.

The fortresses

More than a single, uniform wall, Cartagena is surrounded by a series of impressive fortresses, most of which are still standing. The largest and most important was **Castillo de San Felipe de Barajas** (daily 8am–6pm, COP$15,000), a towering stone fort just east of the walled city along Avenida Pedro de Heredia. Built between 1656 and 1798 with plans from a Dutch engineer, the castle is an ideal spot from which to watch the sunset or tour the maze of underground tunnels connecting the various areas of the fort. The utter lack of information placards in and around the castle has to do with keeping the freelance tour-guide industry afloat, so if you'd like detailed information on the various cannons, passageways and the architectural strategy at work, you may want to hire one of the guides (they speak Spanish or English).

The majority of Cartagena's other remaining defences, most of them nearer to the sea than San Felipe, were built much later, during the dawning of the Spanish Empire in the late eighteenth century. Visible on excursions to Islas del Rosario (see below), the **Fuerte de San Fernando** on Tierrabomba Island was built to seal off Bocachica, which, after a sandbar blocked Bocagrande in 1640, was the only access to the city's harbour. As part of the complex engineering feat, a heavy bronze chain was dangled across the entrance, beneath the water, to the restored fort **Batería de San José**. Boats to Tierrabomba Island depart every 30–45min from the Muelle Turística (10min; COP$6000).

Boat trips

At least fifty minutes out to sea from Cartagena (the bigger the boat, the faster the trip) lies an archipelago of small coral islands known as the **Islas del Rosario**, sunk in transparent turquoise waters. In total there are more than forty islands, many of them private islets barely large enough for a bungalow. Not technically part of the chain, **Playa Blanca**, on Barú island, is one of the more popular beach spots.

For **day-trips by boat**, all of which depart in the morning around 8am, you can either book through your accommodation or head straight to the **Muelle Turística**, the wharf across from the Convention Center, and approach anyone with a clipboard. For COP$60,000 you can get a round-trip boat ride to Playa Blanca with about twenty others, plus a messy, tasty lunch of fried fish, *patacones* (smashed, fried plantains), rice and salad. Avoid larger boats, such as the *Alcatraz* – although cheaper (COP$35,000), the trip is unbearably slow and you will spend most of your day on the boat, with only a couple of hours of beach time.

If you want to **stay** on the island and enjoy the peace once day-trippers return to Cartagena around 3pm, there are a few basic accommodation options, with hammocks available for around COP$10,000. Snorkelling costs COP$20,000 extra – COP$5000 if you bring your own gear – and entrance to the open-water aquarium that's a stop on some trips (ask ahead) is COP$15,000. A COP$12,000 park fee is extracted from all those leaving from the port, since the entire island area is protected by the Corales del Rosario National Park.

Some boats stop at Fuerte de San Fernando (where it's too polluted to swim) on **Tierrabomba Island** and offer brief stops at other nearby islands, so be sure to clarify the itinerary before handing over cash or hopping aboard. At all beaches, islanders offering beaded jewellery and massages are tough to rebuff, but the water is blue and crystal clear and the beaches clean.

Arrival and information

Air Cartagena's Rafael Nuñez International Airport is 10min by taxi (COP$12,000) or a slightly longer bus ride (COP$1500) from the city centre.

Bus The city's large bus terminal is some 45min away by bus from the city centre; a taxi will set you back COP$15,000.

Tourist information Turismo Cartagena de Indias (daily 9am–1pm & 2–6pm, ☎5/660-1583, ⓦwww .turismocartagena.com) is located in Plaza de la Aduana and is dedicated primarily to selling excursions to the outlying beaches.

City transport

Most visitors will get around by foot, though the streams of available taxis make a trip to the other end of town after a long night out easy. Local city buses aren't as inexpensive as their peeling paint exteriors would indicate (COP$1500 for most one-way trips).

Accommodation

Finding comfortable accommodation at an affordable price is easier than you might think. Handsome San Diego offers many nicely outfitted mid-range options, while Getsemaní, a short walk from the Old City, holds the lion's share of cheap hostels along and around Calle Media Luna. Prices during the summer high season (Dec–Feb) usually surge ten to twenty percent.

3 Banderas C Cochera del Hobo 38–66, San Diego ☎5/660-0160, ⓦwww.hotel3banderas.com. Just a block from Plaza San Diego, this is a reasonably priced option if you want to stay in the walled city and features quiet rooms (with a/c) that ring flower-draped patio. COP$185,000.

Casa Baluarte C Media Luna No. 10–81, Getsemaní ☎5/664-2208, ⓔadmin@hostalbaluarte.com One of the more airy and upmarket options in the area, housed in a colonial building. The atmosphere is pleasant, and terracotta-tiled floors contrast nicely with the white-laquered external staircase. The 24 well-kept rooms in this quiet, family-run hostel all come with a/c and private bathroom and there is a decent restaurant on-site. COP$35,000.

Casa Viena C San Andres no. 30–53, Getsemaní ☎5/664 6242, ⓦwww.casaviena.com /cartagena-hostel.html. Your typical shabby backpacker paradise. Great potential to meet up with other travellers and has some of the cheapest shared rooms in town, plus free coffee and internet. Dorms COP$19,000, rooms COP$38,000.

La Casona Cra 10–31–32 (at Cra 10), Getsemaní ☎5/664-1301, ⓦwww.lacasonahostel.com. Rooms in this bric-a-brac-filled hostel are on the small side, but the private bathrooms, plant-filled courtyard and price make it a stellar deal. Dorms COP$20,000, rooms COP$40,000.

Familiar C del Guerrero, no. 29–66, Getsemaní ☎5/664 2464. This friendly family-run hostel, covered in pretty tiles and balconies, is a good choice if you're after somewhere cheap, quiet and clean, and is off the main Media Luna drag. Dorms COP$22,000, rooms COP$38,000.

Holiday C Media Luna no. 10–47, Getsemaní ☎5/664-0948, ⓦwww.hotelholidaycartagena .com. Seventeen modest, clean rooms ring a breezy outdoor patio at this popular hostel, known for its friendly, sociable traveller scene. Dorms COP$20,000, rooms COP$30,000.

Hostal San Diego C de las Bóvedas no. 39–120, San Diego ☎5/660-1433, ⓦwww.hostalsandiego .com. Medium-sized and modern, with a/c in all rooms and a delicious breakfast, this is among the best deals near the centre. Paintings of intriguingly misshapen figures intended to conjure Botero's voluptuous style adorn the walls. COP$109,000.

Media Luna Hostel C Media Luna no. 10–46, Getsemaní ☎5/664-3423, ⓦwww .medialunahostel.com. Popular with young travellers, this smart super-hostel (with 160 beds) has quickly established itself on the backpacker scene. Frequent parties on the enormous roof terrace (overlooking Castillo San Felipe) – with a late night bar open until 4am – go on until the early hours and pool-side sun loungers are the perfect remedy for your hangover. Has 27 spotless dorms and two private rooms. Dorms COP$22,000, rooms COP $40,000.

Eating

Among Cartagena's greatest charms is its array of fine restaurants – nowhere else in Colombia is the urge to splurge so intense, perhaps partly because inexpensive options are so few and far between. For cash-conscious dining, grab some pizza and take a seat in the nearest plaza for prime people-watching. Alternatively, buy from street vendors who sell everything from hot dogs and hamburgers to griddle-cooked corn *arepas*.

El Bistro C de Ayos No. 4–46, the Old City ☎312/666-3550, ⓦwww.el-bistro-cartagena .com. German-owned bistro and bakery, serving a French-leaning set menu of soup and a main course as well as curries prepared by the excellent Bangladeshi chef; a fantastic deal at COP$11,000–13,000. Mon–Sat 8am–11pm.

La **Ceviceria** C Stuart No. 7–14, San Diego. Lively outdoor seating, with music from the *Santa Clara* (see below) across the road and passing street musicians filing the air. Deliciously fresh *ceviche* with shrimp, snails, octopus and squid combos in coconut-lime and mango sauces. Expect to pay around COP$40,000 for two.

La **Creperie** No. 3–110 Plaza de Bolívar ⓦwww .creperiecafe.com. A variety of crêpes sweet and savoury, plus meat and fish dishes and pasta, at reasonable prices for the plaza. Mains COP$10,000–25,000. Mon–Wed 10am–9pm, Thurs–Sat 10am–midnight, Sun 11am–7pm.

Gato Negro C San Andrés No. 30–39, Getsemaní. ⓦwww.gatonegrocartagena.com. Take a welcome break from the standard *arepa* breakfast and start the day with delicious muesli, crêpes, omelettes or toast for around COP$6000. Mon–Sat 7am–2pm, Sun 8am–2pm.

Pizza en el Parque Plaza de Jose Fernández de Madrid, C Segunda de Badillo No. 36–153, San Diego ⓦwww.pizzaenelparque.com. People flock here after dark for tasty, inexpensive pizza (from COP$7000) and to check each other out. Enjoy your dinner sitting on a bench in the picturesque plaza. Daily until 1–2am.

 Restaurante Café Oh! lá lá C de Ayos Cra 5 No. 4–49, the Old City ☎6/660-1757.

TREAT YOURSELF

Lounge on a luxurious white leather sofa with an exclusive cocktail at **El Coro Lounge Bar** at the *Santa Clara Sofitel* (C del Torno No. 39–29, San Diego; ☎5/650-4700, ⓦwww .sofitel.com). Housed in a former 1621 monastery, *El Coro* (the Choir), named after its original use where nuns performed their daily chanting, is a chic bar where you can immerse yourself in the architectural splendour of the city. The room itself evokes the sense of a grand library, with a majestic vaulted ceiling and giant wooden doors, and is the perfect place to curl up with a book during the day. At night, trendy locals arrive for the quality live music from Thursday to Saturday and regular house DJs. A super-stylish spot with excellent service; well worth splashing out on. Expect to pay around COP$20,000 per cocktail.

Attentive Colombian/French couple Carolina and Gilles serve fresh, innovative food that reflects their respective cultural backgrounds, including outstanding soups and robust meat dishes, plus fish and vegetarian options. The stylish decor conjures up a lively Parisian pavement café, complete with cobbled floor, a soothing wall of water and bustling open kitchen. Easily the most exciting affordable meal in the city. Mains COP$12,000–30,000. Closed Sun.

Drinking and nightlife

When the sun sinks into the ocean, Cartagena gets its second salsa-filled wind. A concentration of tourist bars and dance clubs above the Portal de los Dulces overlooks the Plaza de los Coches. Depending on business and the season, most will charge a small cover. Locals tend to gather at the cheaper but no less rowdy clubs in Getsemaní along Calle del Arsenal or to hang out with a beer or fruit juice in Plaza de la Trinidad. Another option for a night out is a *chiva* ride – essentially a party bus in an old-fashioned, luridly decorated trolley that takes you on a late-night city tour fuelled by rum or red wine, fried regional finger foods, and *vallenato* music. *Chivas* depart at 8–8.30pm from Bocagrande locations such as *Hotel Capilla del Mar,* at Cra 1 No. 8–12 (☎5/650-1500; rides around COP$25,000, return at midnight).

Ábaco Libros y Café Corner of C de la Iglesia & C de la Mantilla No. 3–86 ⓦwww.abacolibros .com. This quaint café/bar/bookshop has a decent selection of travel, photography and fiction books in English. A good place to cool down and browse over a coffee or glass of wine. Mon–Sat 9am–8.30pm, Sun 4.30–8.30pm.

Café Havana Corner of C de la Media Luna and C del Guerrero, Getsemaní ⓦwww.cafehavana cartagena.com. You'll be transported to Old Havana at this packed Getsemaní hotspot, where black-and-white photos of Cuban music legends line the walls and thumping live Cuban beats get the crowd's hips swinging. Excellent mojitos (COP$12,000). Thurs–Sun 7pm–4am.

Café del Mar Baluarte de Santo Domingo, Old Town ⓦwww.cafedelmarcartagena.com. Perched on the city's stone fortress walls, with spectacular 360-degree views of the Caribbean and the Old City's elegant colonial buildings, this is the perfect spot to lounge on an open-air couch with a sunset martini (COP$12,000) surrounded by cool locals. No flip-flops or sandals after 7pm, food served until 1am (mains from COP$30,000) and late-night DJs from 10pm. Sun–Wed 5pm–3am, until 5am Fri & Sat.

Donde Fidel Portal de los Dulces No.32–09, Old Town. These outdoor tables are the place to chill out and order a beer between the city wall and the Plaza de los Coches. Pounding Cuban music from the comparatively tiny indoor portion of the bar reaches the tables outside. Open until 2am.

María Feliz C de la Media Luna No. 9–36, Getsemaní ☏312/615-6029. For a relaxed start to the evening or a break from partying, cosy up on a sofa at this cinema/bar/café and settle down to an arthouse film. Well-priced beer (COP$2700) and no cover charge. Open Tues–Sun; films start at 7.30pm.

Mister Babilla Av. del Arsenal No. 8B–137, Getsemaní ✆www.misterbabilla.com. It's impossible not to dance in this club, where the party usually extends until dawn. Entry COP$10,000.

Quiebra Canto Camellon de Los Martires No. 25–110 (2nd floor), Getsemaní ✆www.quiebracanto .com. A local mainstay where old-school salsa mixes with endless shot glasses of locally distilled *ron*. The second-floor balcony offers a great view of Puerta del Reloj and the Old City. Open until late.

Tu Candela Above the Portal de los Dulces No. 32–25, Old City. Cartagena's wildest and most popular salsa club is frequented by tourists and Colombian jet-setters, who dance the night away packed tightly in this second-floor club. Daily 8pm–4am. Entry COP$10,000.

Whiskeria Zorba Plaza de Jose Fernández de Madrid, C Segunda de Badillo No. 36–96, San Diego. A lively spot to watch the world go by or play chess with locals. Daily 9am–midnight/1am.

Directory

Banks and exchange Several banks with 24hr ATMs and casas de cambio are on the Plaza de la Aduana and adjoining streets, as well as along Av. San Martín in Bocagrande.

Embassies and consulates Canada: Cra 3 No. 8–129 (☏5/665-5838); UK: Edificio Inteligente Chambacú, Cra 13B No. 26–78 (☏5/664 7590); US: Centro, Cra 3 No. 36–37 at C de la Factoría (☏5/660-0415).

Immigration For visa extensions, DAS has an office in the airport and at Calle Gastelbondo near the ramparts. Otherwise dial ☏153 for any immigration-related emergencies.

Internet There are a couple of internet cafés on Calle Media Luna in Getsemaní. Expect to pay around COP$2000 per hour.

Medical Hospital Bocagrande ☏5/665-5270 on C 5 and Cra 6.

Police Dial ☏112 for the Policía Nacional.

Moving on

Air Multiple flights daily to Bogotá (1hr 20min), Cali (1hr 25min) and Medellín (1hr 20min).

Bus Barranquilla (every 30min 5am–10pm; 2hr); Bogotá (every 2hr 6am–7pm, 22hr); Caracas (1 daily at 7am: 20hr); Medellín (6 daily 5am–9pm; 13hr); Mompox (1 daily at 7.30am; 8hr); Riohacha (every 2hr 5am–8pm; 7hr); Santa Marta (every 1–2hr 4.30am–8pm; 4hr).

Boat Sailboats run between Cartagena and Puerto Lindo or Colón in Panama via the remote islands of the San Blas archipelago. Trips take 4–5 days and cost around COP$750,000 per person. Rough seas can make travelling between November and February dangerous. Ask at your hostel for more information or check hostel noticeboards.

MOMPOX

Marooned on a freshwater island in the vast low-lying wetlands of the Rio Magdalena's eastern branch, **MOMPOX** – also spelt Mompós and originally known as Santa Cruz de Mompox – was founded in 1537 by Don Alonso de Heredia (brother of Cartagena's founder). It served as the lynchpin for the mighty river's trade network between coastal Cartagena and the country's interior, and remained one of Colombia's most prosperous commercial centres until the silt-heavy river changed its course in the late nineteenth century and Mompox was left to languish as a forgotten backwater. Simon Bolívar raised an army here and Mompox was later the first town in Colombia to declare complete independence from Spain in 1810.

Its beauty has remained practically untouched ever since and wherever you go, vestiges of former Spanish domination are ubiquitous. **UNESCO** declared it a World Heritage Site in 1995 in recognition of its outstanding colonial architecture, and it was also the setting for **Gabriel Garcia Márquez**'s classic novella *Chronicle of a Death Foretold*. The town's remoteness has kept it out of the mainstream of backpacker travel but improved transport links and a fresh batch of hostels has seen a recent influx of visitors.

What to see and do

Mompox is easy to explore on foot and its sprawl of grand Catholic churches and elaborate colonial mansions are a constant reminder of the town's faded glory and wealth. Of its six churches, the finest is **Iglesia de Santa Bárbara**, at the end of Calle 14 on the riverfront plaza of the same name, with its Baroque octagonal bell tower and Moorish balcony adorned with ornate mouldings of flowers and lions. **Iglesia de San Agustín**, on Calle Real del Medio, houses several richly gilded religious objects, most notably the Santo Sepulcro, used in the traditional Semana Santa processions. Wander on and around **Calle Real del Medio** to see whitewashed colonial houses with wrought-iron grilles, intricately carved doorways, clay-tile roofs and fragrant flower-draped balconies. Mompox is also famous for its **wooden rocking chairs** – residents drag these onto the streets in late afternoon to watch the world go by – and **filigree silver and gold** work; jewellery is sold at various workshops around Calle Real del Medio. If your Spanish is reasonable, ask the knowledgeable owner at **Jardín Botánico El Cuchubo** on C 14 to fill you in on the medicinal properties of his exotic plants. The **Museo Cultural**, at Cra 2 No. 14–15 (Mon–Fri 8am–noon & 2–5pm, Sat & Sun 8am–5pm; COP$3000), where Simon Bolívar once stayed, has a small collection of religious art.

If you're interested in local birds and wildlife, it's worth hiring a guide and taking a **boat trip** through the backwaters to nearby lakes, such as the **Ciénaga de Pjinon**. Tours leave around 3pm, generally take four hours and cost approximately COP$30,000 depending on the number of people. Returning by boat to Mompox after a quick sunset dip,

you'll be greeted by a sixteenth-century vision of how this once-thriving town would have appeared to new arrivals, with all six of its imposing churches facing the river to welcome you. Guides can be found at the riverfront, or ask at *La Casa Amarilla*.

Arrival and information

Bus Buses arrive and depart from the Brasilia terminal, next to *La Casa Amarilla*, on the riverfront.
Tourist information There is no tourist office but Richard Mcoll at *La Casa Amarilla* is very knowledgeable about the area. The ATM on Plaza Bolívar often runs out of money so arrive with plenty.
Van A door-to-door van (*"puerta a puerta"*) can be arranged from Cartagena (6–8hr; COP$60,000), Santa Marta (8–10hr; COP$40,000) and Taganga (8–10hr; COP$50,000). Call *La Casa Amarilla* to book or ask for more information at your hostel.

Accommodation

La Casa Amarilla Cra 1 No. 13–59 ☎5/685-6326, ✆www.lacasaamarilla mompos.com. This scenic hostel in a charmingly restored, riverfront colonial building has ten clean and stylish rooms, ranging from dorms to luxury suites, with comfortable beds and colourful murals. The bright, plant-filled courtyard is great for an afternoon hammock snooze and the open-air shared kitchen, rooftop terrace, bike hire, book exchange, cable TV and stacks of DVDs make backpackers feel welcome. Helpful owner Richard Mcoll is an excellent source of information and can arrange transport and tours. Dorms COP$15,000, rooms COP$50,000.
Casa Hotel La Casona Cra 2 (Calle Real del Medio) No.18–58 ☎5/685-5307. Atmospheric colonial building with a maze of communal areas, including pretty courtyards, lots of scattered rocking chairs and a large living room with piano and loud TV. COP$40,000.
Hostal La Reina Cra 2 (Calle Real del Medio) No. 20–85 ☎5/685-6689. The only place in town where you can rent hammocks for the night, this Republican-style hostel is small and peaceful, with a spacious book-filled front room. Hammocks COP$10,000, dorms COP$15,000, rooms COP$60,000.

Eating and drinking

The pace of life in Mompox is slow and best enjoyed by sipping a cold juice on a tree-shaded plaza or heading to the riverfront for a cheap beer (COP$1000) at dusk to watch swooping bats and lizards skimming the water's surface; bars start blaring *vallenato*, reggaeton and salsa music later on. Bustling Plaza Santo Domingo has stands selling beer, pizzas, hot dogs and the usual grilled meats. Plaza de la Concepción is good for a traditional breakfast of *arepas con huevos* (COP$800) and freshly squeezed fruit juice (COP$1200).

Comedor Costeño Cra 1 (Calle de la Albarrada) No.18–45 ☎ 5/685-5263. Beautiful location on the breezy riverfront with outdoor seating and excellent-value set meals. Try the mouth-watering *bagre* (catfish) with coconut rice, fried plantain and yuca, which comes with a fish soup starter and refreshing iced tea (COP$10,000). Lunch only.

Dely Bros C 18 No.2B–19 (opposite Colegio Pinillos) ☎ 5/685-5664. Colombian classics at a reasonable price. Try the tender steak served with salad and plantain (COP$12,000). The air-conditioning is a welcome respite from the stifling heat. Daily 8am–10pm.

Fuafua's Plaza Bolívar. Housed in a section of the impressive Iglesia de la Concepción, the outdoor patio has tables overlooking Parque Bolívar. Serves decent *comida corriente* from COP$8000. Daily 7am–9pm.

Luna de Mompox Cra 1, Albarrada de Los Angeles. This lively bar on the riverfront can get cramped but has tables outside and is fun for a late-night drink. Daily until 1am, later on weekends.

Vinimompox C 18 No. 2B–74. Sample and buy fruit wines made from banana, guava, orange and tamarind at this shop of a local wine producer.

Moving on

Bus/water taxi/4x4 To Barranquilla (6hr): take a *colectivo* to Bodega (50min) and then a *chalupa* water taxi to Magangué (30min) – they leave when full but you won't have to wait long – followed by a direct bus to Barranquilla (4–5hr). To Bogotá (14hr): take a 4x4 to El Banco Magdalena (1hr) and change for a bus to Bogotá (1 daily at 4pm). To Bucaramanga: 3 buses daily; 8hr. To Cartagena: a direct bus leaves at 6am from the Brasilia terminal, next to *La Casa Amarilla* (8hr); for a faster route (5–6hr), take a *colectivo* to Bodegá (50min) and then a *chalupa* water taxi to Magangué (30min), followed by a direct bus to Cartagena (4–5hr).

Van A direct van ("*puerta a puerta*") service can be arranged to Cartagena (6–8hr; COP$60,000), Santa Marta (8–10hr; COP$40,000) and Taganga (8–10hr; COP$50,000); ask Richard at *La Casa Amarilla* for more information.

BARRANQUILLA

Despite being Colombia's fourth-largest city and main port, **BARRANQUILLA**, on the mouth of the Río Magdalena, about three hours by bus from Cartagena, would be all but overlooked if it were not for its annual **Carnaval** (☻ www.carnaval debarranquilla.com). For four days at the start of each March, this miserably hot, industrial city drapes itself in a riot of vibrant colours, playful costumes and pulsating music – salsa, *cumbia*, *vallenato* and African drumming. Preparations begin much earlier, in mid-January, with the public reading of a municipal diktat ordering residents to have fun. Once the festivities begin, the town converts into one huge street party, kicked off by traditional parades like the "Battle of the Flowers" and "Dance of the Caiman". Parallel to the festivities, the city-sponsored gay Carnaval, though less publicized, is equally bacchanalian. Although barely known outside Latin America, Barranquilla's festivities are second only to Rio's Carnaval in size.

Be sure to arrange **accommodation** well in advance if you visit during Carnaval. The centre can be unsafe at night but this is where you'll find the cheapest options. *Hotel Colonial Inn* (C 42 No. 43–131; ☎ 5/379-0241; COP$40,000) is a reasonable bet, with clean and simple rooms; carnival parades pass nearby. As for a more relaxed stay, head to the upmarket neighbourhood of El Prado – a taxi from the centre costs around COP$7000. Rooms at the *Hotel Barahona 72* (Cra 49 No. 72–19; ☎ 5/358-4600; COP$111,000) are well priced for the area and comfortable. As for food, *Sancochos y Asados de la 74* (C 74 No. 49–10; ☎ 5/358-7762; mains COP$12,000–15,000) serves generous portions of Colombian favourites; try the thinly sliced *punta gorda* grilled beef with yams, boiled potatoes and salad.

SANTA MARTA AND AROUND

Although Colombia's oldest city, founded in 1525, **SANTA MARTA**'s colonial heritage was all but swept away at the hands of English and Dutch pirates. The result is a friendly, understated beach city geared to middle-class Colombians on holiday. Large investment and restoration in the city centre over the past few years has started to return Santa Marta to its former colonial glory. An international marina, due to be completed in 2011, will is hoped it attract international sailing boats from the Caribbean, especially during hurricane season, as the bay is protected by the surrounding sierra. The simple pleasures predominate here: strolling along the waterfront and enjoying a stunning sunset; purchasing snacks from one of the many itinerant vendors peddling cigarettes, sweets and super-sweet *tinto* (brewed coffee) served in tiny plastic cups; entering the fray in the indoor and outdoor markets to find a local souvenir; taking a shady break in sleepy Parque Santander.

Not far away are some of the country's most tranquil beaches, particularly **Parque Nacional Tayrona**, Colombia's premier Caribbean paradise. Close by but a world away, is the quiet fishing village of **Taganga** which has unpaved dirt streets and a small bay clustered with petite wooden boats. Santa Marta also acts as the hub for organizing hikes to the ruins of the **Ciudad Perdida**.

What to see and do

Although better-known for drawing sun-worshippers, Santa Marta does have a few worthwhile museums. A striking building with wooden garrets underneath a pitched tile roof, the well-maintained **Casa de la Aduana** (Customs House), on the corner of C 14 and Cra 2, is the city's oldest building, dating from 1531. Simon Bolívar stayed here briefly, and his body lay in state in an upstairs gallery after his death. On its ground floor, the **Museo Antropológico y Etnológico** (Mon–Fri 8.30am–3.30pm; free) has extensive displays on ancient Tayrona culture and its modern-day descendants – the Kogis, Arhuacos and Arsarios. A large replica of the Ciudad Perdida provides a valuable introduction for anyone planning to visit the ruins.

The sun-bleached **Catedral**, at Cra 4 and C 17, is the oldest church in Colombia but has received successive facelifts. The current structure, with its bulky bell tower and stone portico, dates mostly from the seventeenth century. Bolívar's remains were kept here until 1842, when they were sent off to his native Venezuela.

An obligatory stop for history enthusiasts is the **Quinta de San Pedro Alejandrino** (daily 9.30am–4.30pm; COP$10,000), the sugar plantation 5km south of town where Bolívar spent his last agonizing days. The hacienda's peaceful grounds and exotic gardens are worth a visit, but the displays are more an exercise in Libertador fetishism – an Italian marble toilet bowl, military badges, a lock of hair – than items of interests biographical. Guided tours (in Spanish) are included in the price of admission. There's also a contemporary art museum on the premises. Buses leaving the waterfront main drag (Cra 1) for the Mamatoco suburb will drop you off at the Quinta if you ask the driver (COP$1200). Or take a taxi for around COP$3500.

Arrival and information

Air Santa Marta's Simon Bolívar airport is 16km south of the city centre. A taxi from here will set you back around COP$15,000.

Bus The bus station lies 5km to the southeast of the city centre and taxis cost in the region of COP$4000; negotiate the price before getting in.

Tourist information There is a tourist office at C 17 No. 3–120 (Mon–Fri 8am–1pm & 2–6pm; ☎5/438-2587, ⓦwww.turismocartagena.com), just off Plaza de la Catedral. You can pick up free maps here but note that the staff don't speak much English.

Accommodation

Following renovations in the historic centre, a good range of backpacker hostels have sprung up, taking the focus away from the old cheap lodgings around seedy Calle 10C. In January, prices can double and reservations are recommended.

Aluna C 21 No. 5–72 ☎ 5/432-4916, ⓦ www.alunahotel.com. Feel well looked-after and rested at this peaceful hostel, beautifully designed by Dublin-born architect and owner Patrick Flemming. Paintings by local artists line the walls, rooms are spotless and fresh, thanks to wooden slats that allow air to circulate, and a bamboo roof offers welcome shade from the blazing midday sun. Great if you need to rejuvenate. Dorms COP$20,000, rooms COP$60,000.

La Brisa Loca C 14 No. 3–74 ☎ 5/431-6121, ⓦ www.labrisaloca.com. This sprawling converted mansion, named after Santa Marta's wild coastal winds, is owned by two party-loving Californian dudes and has firmly established itself as a backpacker haven, with spacious dorms, a roof terrace, lively late night bar, billiards and a well-used pool. Attracts a mostly younger crowd and the helpful bilingual staff are a big plus. Dorms COP$18,000, rooms COP$60,000.

Casa Familiar C 10C No. 2–14 ☎ 5/421-1697. The cleanest and best-serviced of the old Calle 10 backpacker dens. Rooms have private bath, and the fourth-floor terrace has views of the harbour. Hammocks COP$10,000, dorms COP$15,000, rooms COP$27,000.

Hostal El Noctámbulo C 20 No. 6–55 ☎ 5/431-7643, ⓦ www.hostalelnoctambulo.com. After years of backpacking, the French owners of this small hostel have figured out what people really want. Their attention to detail creates a relaxing, sociable atmosphere. Tables are clustered together on the patio to encourage lone travellers to grab a cocktail from the outdoor bar and get chatting to guests. Dorms COP$18,000, rooms COP$43,000.

Eating, drinking and nightlife

A number of bustling restaurants with outdoor seating line Carrera 1, the city's main thoroughfare, which runs parallel to the beach. Santa Marta's nightlife really heats up once the sun goes down. Be prepared to dance to reggae remixes, traditional offerings like *chumpeta* and popular international hits at clubs in both Santa Marta proper and nearby Taganga (see below).

Agave Azul C 14 No. 3–58 ☎ 317/585-9598. New York-trained chef Michael McMurdo uses locally sourced ingredients to prepare a quality spin on Mexican food at reasonable prices. The *ceviche* platter (COP$17,000), fresh langoustines with coconut (COP$24,000) and red snapper dishes are excellent. Start with a frozen margarita. Tues–Sat noon–10pm.

Café El Santo C 21 No. 2A–52 ☎ 5/423-6170, ⓦ cafeelsanto.blogspot.com. Juicy steaks, fresh bread and fine red wine in a relaxed setting. A great spot to know about on Sundays when many places close. Wed–Sun from 6pm.

Crêpes Expresso Cra 2 No. 16–33 ⓦ www .crepesexpresso.com. Gorge on tasty sweet and savoury crêpes (from COP$6000) at this authentic French-owned crêperie. Mon–Sat from 4pm.

Lulo Café + Bar Cra 3 No. 16–34 ⓦ www .lulocafebar.com. Friendly owners Melissa and David whip up fantastic breakfasts for around COP$8000 at this much-needed, excellent new café. Try the delicious "Lula la Ranchera" *arepa* made from natural corn, served with egg, beans and chorizo. Great smoothies from COP$3500, happy hour cocktails Mon–Fri 5–7pm and free wi-fi. Mon–Fri 8am–10pm, Sat 9am–11pm. Breakfast served until 11am.

La Puerta C 17, No. 2–29 ⓦ www.ohlalalapuerta .com. Colombians and foreign travellers in their twenties and thirties frequent this jam-packed, sexy club. Salsa, electronica, and American club hits will have you sweating on the narrow dancefloor that snakes into one of the club's many nooks and crannies. Cool off on the outdoor patio if the crowd gets too much, as it does on weekends. Open until late.

Moving on

Air Bogotá (12 daily; 1hr 30min); Medellín (3 daily; 1hr 30min).

Bus Brasilia and Berlinas are two of the biggest coastal bus companies, both with a comfortable and modern fleet. Bananquilla (hourly; 2hr); Bogotá (hourly 2–8pm, 17hr); Bucaramanga (3 daily, 10hr); Cartagena (hourly 5am–8pm; 4hr); Medellín (12 daily; 15hr). Buses run between Taganga and Cra 1C in Santa Marta every 10min from 5am–10pm.

Taxi Taking a taxi 16km to the airport costs COP$15,000. A taxi to Taganga costs COP$7000.

TAGANGA

Although no longer as pristine as it used to be, **TAGANGA** retains much of the spirit of the quiet fishing village it was before being absorbed in recent years by Santa Marta's expansion. Only fifteen minutes from Santa Marta by frequent public buses along the boardwalk on Carrera 1C, Taganga offers a wholly different vibe. Built on the side of a mountain, the town has an uncanny Mediterranean feel, with incongruously pleasant unpaved dirt streets. For budget travellers, it's an ideal base for exploring the surrounding area's attractions.

What to see and do

One of the cheapest spots in the world for **scuba** certification, both PADI and NAUI, Taganga has so many dive shops that the prices and services offered by each are pretty competitive. A four- to six-day certification course costs about COP$600,000 and often includes basic accommodation, English or Spanish-speaking dive masters, and six dives (four open water, two pool). Quality-focused Aquantis Dive Center (C 18 No. 1–39 ☏5/421-9344, ⊛www .aquantisdivecenter.com) offers the best service in town, with the highest standard of professional instruction and a great awareness of the needs of both new and experienced divers. If you decide to opt for one of the other schools, don't just be tempted by cheap deals: check their PADI or NAUI accreditation, your instructor's credentials, the instructor-to-student ratio and ensure that equipment is well maintained. For more tips on what to look out for when choosing a dive school, see p.540.

Everything else here is pretty much water-related too. Fishermen ply an easy alternate access route to Tayrona National Park's southern beaches, the most popular being the crystalline waters of **Bahia Concha**, about an hour away by boat. Costing at least COP$120,000, this is a good excursion for a small group rather than an individual. Accessible by boat (5min, COP$5000) and foot (20min) is the

much closer **Playa Grande**, which is modestly sized, heavily touristed and a bit pebbly, but still has the makings for a day of sun and sand. Keep in mind that Taganga's main beach is awash in small boats, many available for hire, and not fit for swimming.

Conveniently, Ciudad Perdida treks (see p.580) and a whole manner of adventure travel options are on offer, too, at bigger shops on the main drag, along the beach.

Arrival and information

Air A taxi from Santa Marta's Simon Bolívar Airport (14km) will cost around COP$30,000.
Bus Taganga is easily accessible from Santa Marta, where buses (COP$1200) depart every 10min from Cra 1C (daily 6am–9pm; 15min).
Taxi A taxi from the centre of Santa Marta to Taganga costs COP$7000. If you're coming from the bus terminal, it will be around COP$10,000.
Tourist information Hostel owners are a good source of information. The ATM on Cra 2 next to the police station often runs out of money, so it's best to load up in Santa Marta.

Accommodation

Casa de Felipe Cra 5A No. 19–13 ☏5/421-9101, ⊛www.lacasadefelipe.com. Three blocks uphill from the beach, with beautiful views of the bay, the rustic rooms at this long-time backpacker fave fill up quickly so book in advance if possible. Good tourist information. Dorms COP$16,000, rooms COP$45,000, private apartments for 2 people COP$80,000.

Casa Holanda C 14 No. 1B–75 ☏5/421-9390, ⊛www.micasaholanda.com. Quiet terraces with hammocks and bay views, perfect for reading, and bright, spotless rooms with comfortable beds. A 2-for-1 happy hour in the bar daily from 9–10pm livens things up and the restaurant serves local speciality mains, such as fried *pargo* (red snapper) from COP$12,000. Breakfast included. COP$40,000.

Hostel Divanga B&B C 12 No. 4–07 ☏5/421-9092, ⊛www.divanga.com. This French-run hostel has a small pool lined with hammocks, an upstairs bar and a distinct party vibe. Rooms are small and can be noisy but the proximity to *El Garaje* (see p.579) is a bonus. Dorms COP$29,000, rooms COP$74,000.

Pelikan Hostal Cra 2 No. 17–04 ☎ 5/421-9057. Comfy leather couches greet you upon entering this character-drenched spot, a favourite hangout of salty locals and even saltier ex-pats. A shared kitchen and cosy hammock out front sweeten the deal. Dorms COP$15,000, rooms COP$45,000.

Eating, drinking & nightlife

For dining, you need look no further than the road gently curving with the line of the shore, which is chock-full of restaurants specializing in seafood.

Los Baguettes de María C 18 No. 3–47 ⓦ www.losbaguettesdemaria.com. Stuff yourself on giant foot-long baguettes and thirst-quenching peach iced tea before stumbling into one of the hammocks at this backpacker treat. The chicken-loaded *Bahia Concha* (COP$10,000) is excellent. Sun–Thurs 10am–10pm, Fri 10am–6pm.

Bitácora Cra 1 No. 17–13. Serves up a very veggie-laden signature salad, as well as carefully prepared meat and chicken dishes that complement locally caught *robalo* (sea bass) and *mero* (grouper fish). The breezy porch has nice sea views and is good for people-watching. Mains COP$8000–22,000. Daily 7am–11pm (opens 11am in low season).

Café Bonsai C 13 No. 1–7 ⓦ www.cafebonsai.com. This cool Swedish-run café serves delicious home-made treats (around COP$2000), including brownies in chocolate sauce and sticky peanut butter, fresh sandwiches on crusty home-baked bread, healthy muesli breakfasts with yogurt and blackberry jam (from COP$9000), and organic coffee from the surrounding foothills of the Sierra Nevada. Happy hour cocktails 5–8pm and Rock Fridays with pizza and beer for COP$5000. Mon–Sat 9am–9.30pm.

El Garaje C 8 at Cra 3, Taganga. The frisson sparked by the mix of locals and foreigners that fill the place and the low, tropical lighting make this place taxi-worthy even if you're staying in Santa Marta. A raised, palm-fringed *palapa* acts as a dancefloor while club classics, traditional Colombian music and reggae rotate through. Wed–Sat 8pm–3am.

Moving on

Bus Frequent buses (every 10min 6am–9pm; 15min) run from the junction near Poseidon dive school and the police station to Cra 1C in Santa Marta.

Taxi A taxi to the centre of Santa Marta costs COP$7000. Expect to pay around COP$10,000 to the bus terminal and COP$30,000 to Simon Bolívar Airport.

PARQUE NACIONAL TAYRONA

Colombia's most unspoilt tropical area, **PARQUE NACIONAL TAYRONA**, a 45-min drive east of Santa Marta, is a wilderness of jungle-fringed beaches, archeological ruins and lush forest, with maddeningly elusive howling spider monkeys and falling coconuts. Silhouettes of swaying palm trees set against sunsets complete the cinematic image. The laidback attitude of the place makes it feel like a paradisiacal summer camp.

The park gets its name from the Tayrona Indians, one of South America's greatest pre-Columbian civilizations. This area was a major trading centre for the Tayrona, whose population once exceeded a million. With the arrival of the Spanish, however, their peaceful existence came to an end. The Spanish governor ordered their annihilation in 1599 on the trumped-up charge that the Tayrona men practised sodomy; the brutal massacre that followed forced the remaining Tayronas to seek refuge high in the Sierra Nevada de Santa Marta, whose foothills flank the park to the south. Rising from sea level, these snowcapped sierras reach their apex just 42km from the coast, at the 5775m-high **Cristóbal Colón**, Colombia's tallest peak.

Pueblito

A clear and physically demanding uphill path leading from Cabo San Juan brings you to the archeological site of **Pueblito**, a former Tayrona village with a large number of terrace dwellings, sometimes called a mini Ciudad Perdida. Although it's possible to complete an Arrecifes–Cabo San Juan–Pueblito circuit in one long, strenuous day, the trip is better made as part of a multi-day stay in the park. From Pueblito, you can also hike two hours through the jungle back down to the road and catch a bus back to Santa Marta from that park exit point, instead of traversing your original route back to Cabo San Juan. That said, you may be better off hiring a guide for this less trafficked hike out, which has no signs and is quite taxing.

Beaches

Besides Pueblito, Tayrona's beaches and the jungle that edges them are the irrefutable stars of the park. Note that although Arrecifes has a gorgeous sea-green layer cake of waves, it also has notoriously lethal rip tides; more than two hundred overconfident tourists have drowned here over the years. The nearest swimming beach, **La Piscina**, is a 15-min walk away.

Wander another half-hour to reach **Cabo San Juan**, a tranquil swimming beach with a hammock-strung gazebo peached atop a rocky outcrop. Further into the park you'll stumble onto an endless variety of beaches studded with hulking rocks, the first being a **nudist beach** that's followed, about ten minutes on by a beach with pretty decent waves for body surfing. There's not much to do but hike, eat, drink and sleep, but don't be surprised if the place grows on you in a way that makes getting on with the rest of your journey oddly tough.

Arrival and information

Bus You'll probably come from Santa Marta, where buses (every 30min; 1hr) leave the market at the corner of Cra 11 and C 11 for El Zaino, 35km away. They'll gladly drop you off at the Tayrona Park entrance, where your passport will be checked, and entrance fee (COP$34,000) collected. From here, take one of the jeeps that regularly traverse the 4km to the entrance proper for COP$2000, or walk if you enjoy hikes on paved roads.
Park information The 45-min walk west from the drop-off point at Cañaveral goes through alternating patches of forest to Arrecifes, the first in a string of gorgeous beaches. At the park entrance, you may be asked for your yellow-fever certificate (though the checking is haphazard). Be sure to bring plenty of cash – only the Aviatur-run restaurant and accommodations accept credit cards – and lots of insect repellent.

Accommodation and eating

The two beaches offering accommodation are Arrecifes and Cabo San Juan; both offer the option of renting tents and hammocks, and cabañas are an indulgent alternative for medium to large groups at Arrecifes. Lockers are available too.

Arrecifes

Aviatur A hammock/camping/cabaña (COP$25,000, COP$30,000 and COP$335,000–569,000 respectively) operation, with luxury bathrooms. Also has a well-priced restaurant – the only one in the park that accepts credit cards. It looks expensive but don't be intimidated: the food is consistently top-notch and mains are around COP$15,000.
Finca El Paraíso Rents hammocks (COP$16,000) and tents (COP$50,000 for 2 people, COP$12,000 if you bring your own tent) close to the beach, and has a basic restaurant and shop.
Panadería Vere Further along Arrecifes beach from Finca El Paraíso, towards La Piscina. Serves delicious fresh chocolate and cheese buns for COP$2500.

Cabo San Juan

Cabo San Juan de la Guía The downside to the hammocks here (COP$15,000 on beach, COP$30,000 in gazebo) is that they offer no mosquito netting – and it can get quite chilly at night. Seek out the information hut next door to the restaurant (mains from COP$12,000), the only real building in sight. Camping is also available (COP$20,000).

Moving on

Bus Buses run from the El Zaino park entrance to the market at the corner of Cra 11 and C 11 in Santa Marta (every 30min; 1hr).

CIUDAD PERDIDA

The "Lost City" of the Tayronas, **CIUDAD PERDIDA** ranks among South America's most magical spots. More than a lost city, it's a lost world. Although its ruins are less spectacular than those found at Machu Picchu in Peru, thanks to its geographic isolation the once-teeming city perched high in the Sierra Nevada de Santa Marta manages to preserve the natural allure that the overrun Inca capital lost years ago to tourism. While steadily climbing the sierra's luxuriant foothills, you'll get a chance to bathe under idyllic waterfalls, visit inhabited indigenous villages and marvel at the swarms of monarch butterflies and abundant jungle wildlife.

Built sometime after 500 AD, the Tayrona capital is less than 50km southeast of Santa Marta. It wasn't discovered until 1975, when a few of the more than ten thousand *guaqueros* (tomb raiders) from Santa Marta chanced upon it while scavenging for antiquities. Perched atop a steep slope 1300m high in the vast jungle, the site consists of more than a thousand circular **terraces** – with more still being uncovered – that once served as foundations for Tayrona homes. Running throughout the city and down to the Buritaca river valley is a complex network of paved footpaths and steep stone steps – more than 1350, if you're counting – purportedly added later to obstruct the advance of Spanish horsemen.

Hiking practicalities

While the hills around Ciudad Perdida are considered safe by Colombian standards, it's easy to lose the trail, so go with an organized tour group. You can book tours through any hostel or hotel, or middle-man operators you encounter on the streets of Santa Marta, the most reputable being **Magic Tour** (☎5/421-9429, ⓦwww.hosteltrail.com/magictour). Prices for the five-to six-day-long hike start around COP$450,000 and include all meals, hammock lodging at farmhouses, the entrance fee to the ruins and transport to and from the trailhead. The hike can be done all year, although during the wet months from May to November the trail can get quite muddy. In any case, expect to get and stay wet at any time of the year and don't forget to bring a torch and plenty of insect repellent.

RIOHACHA AND AROUND

Founded in 1539 by German explorer Nicolás de Federmán, **RIOHACHA** is the capital of the little-explored Guajira Peninsula, an arid spit that juts into the Caribbean to form the northern tip of South America. The city itself offers few attractions other than its fine white **beaches**, but makes a comfortable base from which to explore the surrounding badlands. *Hotel Gimaura*, at C 1 Avenida La Marina (☎5/727-0009; COP$116,000), is a peaceful if somewhat decadent resort on the beach just a short walk from downtown Riohacha.

THE KOGI INDIANS

Although now uninhabited, Ciudad Perdida is in many respects a living monument. It's surrounded by villages of Kogi Indians, who call the revered site Teyuna. By far the biggest highlight of any visit is the chance to interact with the Kogis as they drift on and off the main trail you'll traverse as part of a tour. As it comprises only a fraction of the wilderness they call home, they are increasingly less present on this popular tourist trail. The men are recognizable by their long, ragged hair, cream-coloured smocks and trusty *poporo*, the saliva-coated gourd holding the lime that activates the coca leaves they constantly chew. About nine thousand Kogis are believed to inhabit the Sierra Nevada.

When flower power was in full bloom in the US in the 1970s, the Sierra Nevada became a major marijuana factory, and an estimated seventy percent of its native forests were burned to clear the way for untold amounts of the lucrative Santa Marta Gold strand. As the forest's prime inhabitants, the Kogis suffered dearly from the arrival of so many fast-buck farmers, one of the reasons why they're sceptical of the outside world: don't take pictures without their permission.

Guajira Peninsula's hostile, desert climate has kept it largely isolated since colonial times. As a result it's one of those special places where independent travellers can still feel as if they're leaving fresh tracks. Some 240km long and no more than 50km wide, the barren peninsula is empty except for the semi-nomadic Wayúu, or Guajiro, Indians – and **drug smugglers**. The numerous sheltered coves from which drugs leave for the US has earned Guajira Peninsula a reputation as Colombia's contraband capital. Most illicit activity, however, is kept hidden and, as in any frontier area, the absence of the law doesn't pose any risks so long as you don't seek out trouble.

Frequent **buses** run from Riohacha to Santa Marta, Barranquilla and Cartagena, and twice-daily buses make the 2-hr trip along the northern coast from Riohacha to **Manaure**, where traditionally dressed Wayúu extract salt manually and pile it in mounds. Otherwise, catch a *colectivo* from C 5, Cra 15 to Uribia (1hr), followed by a 4x4 to the beautifully remote **Cabo de la Vela** (2–3hr), which is famous for its large flamingo population and long sunsets.

Tierra Paisa

Nominally a slang term to describe anyone from the region of Antioquia, **paisas** are alternately the butt of jokes and the object of envy for many Colombians. What makes them stand out is their rugged individualism and reputation for industriousness. Their fame dates back to the early nineteenth century, when they cleared Colombia's hinterland for farming in exchange for the government's carrot of free land. Their rapid progress over the next century earned the mostly European colonists a reputation for hard work, exaggerated frugality and an unequalled

skill at turning a profit from any enterprise, legal or otherwise. Perhaps the biggest *paisa* contribution to Colombia is its role in the spread of coffee.

The heart of *paisa* country is the burgeoning metropolis of **Medellín**, which has made a remarkable turnaround since its days as Colombia's murder capital in the early 1990s, although murder rates were on the rise again in 2010. The picturesque coffee-growing *fincas* near the modern cities of **Manizales** and **Pereira** were almost all established by *paisa* homesteaders and some growers have opened their estates to tourists, who during harvest time can partake in the picking process. The so-called **Zona Cafetera**, or "Coffee Zone", is Colombia's fastest-growing tourist attraction. The zone is also the base for exploring one of Colombia's most postcard-perfect national parks, **Parque Nacional Natural Los Nevados**.

MEDELLÍN

It's hard to think of a city that was more in need of a public relations makeover than **MEDELLÍN**. When turf wars between rival drug gangs became public in the 1980s and 1990s, Colombia's second-largest city was rampaged by teenage hitmen, called *sicarios*, who, for as little as US$30, could be hired to settle old scores. The bloodthirst earned Medellín the world's highest murder rate.

But when cocaine kingpin **Pablo Escobar** was snuffed out in 1993, Medellín began to bury its sordid past. These days, the increasing number of travellers who come here find a safe and inviting, modern city with one of the country's best climates – year-round temperatures average 24ºC.

What to see and do

Pleasant green spaces, interesting museums, a bustling centre and thriving commercial areas make Medellín an exciting place to explore, while top-notch

COFFEE AND COCAINE

It's hard to say which of Colombia's two cash crops garners more international attention, the white or the black one. One thing is for certain: both are synonymous with quality. The country's first bumper crop was coffee. Colombia is the second-largest producer of hand-picked mild Arabica coffee after Brazil and the third-largest overall coffee producer in the world (behind Vietnam and Brazil). High temperatures, heavy rainfall and cool evening breezes make Colombia the bean's ideal habitat, though changes in weather patterns of late have led to poor crops in recent years; 8.9 million bags were produced in 2010 following torrential downpours and flooding, below the average of around 12 million.

Cocaine was perceived as an innocuous stimulant until the twentieth century. Two US presidents, several European monarchs and even a pope were early addicts (and vocal advocates) of Vin Tonique Mariani, a nineteenth-century liqueur made from coca extract. The "real thing" that Coca-Cola initially pushed on its customers was cocaine. For Sigmund Freud, a spoonful of coke each day was the cure for depression. Today around ninety percent of the world's cocaine is grown and manufactured in Colombia. Plan Colombia (see p.542) has recently seen a dramatic decline in coca cultivation; in 2010 the country reduced production by 60 percent, relative to the peak in 2000, and Peru surpassed Colombia as the world's main producer of coca leaves.

restaurants, vibrant bars and a pumping club scene provide non-stop fun until the early hours. The clean and reliable metro means it is easy to get around and to get out and discover the soaring peaks and parks that surround the city.

Pablo Escobar's grave

Much to the displeasure of the well-intentioned tourist board, the former stomping grounds of **Pablo Escobar** – his homes, the modern buildings he built, the country-club mountain jail he was ambushed at – are becoming a minor draw for curious visitors. The former godfather of the Medellín cartel is still very much venerated for his extensive philanthropy by the city's poorer residents, who've even named a *barrio* after him. To make your own pilgrimage, visit his austere grave-stone at the **Jardines de Montesacro cemetery** at Cra 42 No. 25–51, near Itagüí metro station.

Basílica Nuestra Señora de la Candelaria

A few churches from the late colonial era survive. The most important is the **Basílica Nuestra Señora de la Candelaria**, whose Baroque interior dates from 1776. The whitewashed, flat-naved chapel, which overlooks the centrally located **Parque Berrío**, was Medellín's cathedral until 1931.

Catedral Metropolitana

The current cathedral is the fanciful **Catedral Metropolitana**, four blocks away from Basílica de la Candelaria, along a pedestrian walkway, at **Plaza Bolívar**. The fortress-like structure was constructed between 1875 and 1931 and claims to be the largest church in the world built entirely of bricks – 1.2 million, if you're counting. A large **handicraft fair** is held on the first Saturday of every month in the plaza.

Museo de Antioquia

Medellín is the birthplace of sculptor and painter **Fernando Botero**, known for his satirical representation of all things fat – oranges, priests, even the Mona Lisa. Although Medellín residents felt miffed by Botero's donation of his extensive European art collection to a Bogotá museum (see

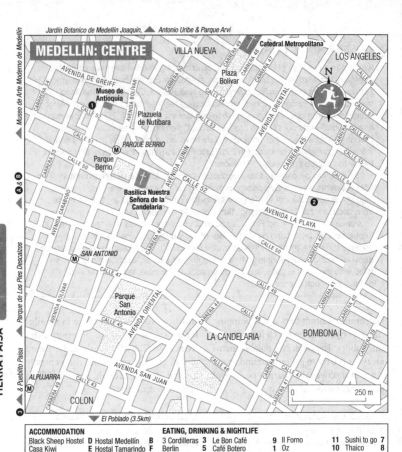

MEDELLÍN: CENTRE

Jardín Botánico de Medellín Joaquín, ▲ Antonio Uribe & Parque Arví

Catedral Metropolitana

VILLA NUEVA

LOS ANGELES

Plaza Bolívar

AVENIDA DE GREIFF

Museo de Antioquia

Plazuela de Nutibara

PARQUE BERRIO

Parque Berrio

Basílica Nuestra Señora de la Candelaria

AVENIDA LA PLAYA

SAN ANTONIO

Parque San Antonio

LA CANDELARIA

BOMBONA I

AVENIDA SAN JUAN

ALPUJARRA

COLON

Museo de Arte Moderno de Medellín

Parque de Los Pies Descalzos

& Pueblito Paisa

0   250 m

▼ El Poblado (3.5km)

ACCOMMODATION

Black Sheep Hostel	**D**	Hostal Medellín	**B**
Casa Kiwi	**E**	Hostal Tamarindo	**F**
Casa Maydé	**C**	Palm Tree Hostal	**A**

EATING, DRINKING & NIGHTLIFE

3 Cordilleras	**3**	Le Bon Café	**9**	Il Forno	**11**	Sushi to go	**7**
Berlin	**5**	Café Botero	**1**	Oz	**10**	Thaico	**8**
El Blue	**4**	El Eslabón Prendido	**2**	Sandwich Qbano	**6**		

▲ Centre (3.5km) & Jardines de Montesauro cemetery

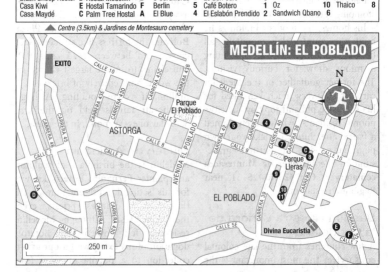

MEDELLÍN: EL POBLADO

EXITO

Parque El Poblado

ASTORGA

Parque Lleras

EL POBLADO

Divina Eucaristía

0   250 m

TIERRA PAISA   COLOMBIA

Donación Botero, p.545), the largest collection of his works is housed in the modern **Museo de Antioquia** at Cra 52 No. 52–43 (Mon–Sat 10am–6pm, Sun 10am–5pm; ⓦwww.museodeantioquia .org; COP$8000). Another twenty sculptures are on display outside the museum in the busy **Plaza Botero**.

Parque San Antonio

If your appetite for Botero isn't sated, check out his *Pájaro de Paz* (Bird of Peace) sculpture at **Parque San Antonio**, on Carrera 46 between calles 44 and 46. When a guerrilla bomb destroyed the bronze sculpture in 1996, Botero ordered the skeleton to be left in its shattered state and placed alongside it a replica of the original as an eloquent protest against violence.

Museo de Arte Moderno de Medellín

The **Museo de Arte Moderno de Medellín**, at Cra 44 No. 19A–100 (Tues–Fri 9am–5.30pm, Sat 10am–5.30pm, Sun 10am–5pm; ⓦwww.elmamm.org; COP$5000; Metro Poblado) is housed in an attractively restored industrial warehouse in the Ciudad del Río neighbourhood. It features an impressive selection of contemporary art by international and national artists, including prolific Medellín painter Débora Arango.

Pueblito Paisa

The geographical limitations of so many people living in a narrow valley have forced residents to live in overcrowded conditions, with many homes literally running up 45-degree slopes. At the same time, within the city centre itself there's a huge shortage of open recreational spaces. An exception is **Pueblito Paisa** at C 30A No. 55–64 (daily 6am–midnight; free), a replica of a typical Antioquian village that's situated atop Cerro Nutibara, a hilly outcrop downtown that offers panoramic views of the city. It's a pleasant place in which

to people-watch, go for a stroll, nibble on fast food and enjoy the view. The closest metro station is Industriales, from where it's a 10-min uphill walk.

Parque de los Pies Descalzos

A symbol of Medellín's renaissance is the **Parque de los Pies Descalzos**, a Zen-inspired playground where children of all ages are encouraged to take off their shoes and tread barefoot through a series of sand, water and pebble mazes. It is at Cra 57 No. 42–139; take the metro to Alpujarra.

Jardín Botánico de Medellín Joaquín Antonio Uribe

The city's other diminutive green space is the **Jardín Botánico de Medellín Joaquín Antonio Uribe** (daily 9am–5pm; ⓦwww.botanicomedellin .org; free; Metro Universidad), located in the city's northern sector at C 73 No. 51D–14. The lush botanical garden is one of Colombia's oldest, dating from 1913. Don't miss a visit to the stunning Orchideorama – a weaving structure of steel trunks and towering wooden petals – where plants are showcased and the Jardín's annual orchid exhibition is held in August during the Feria de las Flores flower festival.

Parque Arví

On the eastern slopes of the Aburrá Valley, **Parque Arví** (Tues–Sun 9am–6pm; ⓦparquearvi.wordpress .com) is an ecological nature reserve and archeological site. It forms part of the network of pre-Hispanic trails of Parque Ecológico Piedras Blancas (see p.588), which can be reached from the park in an hour on foot. Alternatively catch a bus (COP$1000) or rent a horse for COP$5000. Directly connected to downtown Medellín via the new Metro-cable (opened March 2010), the park is a valuable addition to the city's green spaces. The 15-min ride from Metro

Santo Domingo (COP$2500) glides over the mountain ridge and into the park, affording spectacular views of the city.

Arrival and information

Air Medellín's futuristic José María Córdova Airport (☎4/562-2828) lies a hilly 28km from the city along a scenic highway; it services all international and most domestic flights. Taxis to the city cost COP$52,000, or you can get a seat in a shared taxi for COP$15,000 – turn right outside baggage reclaim and look for a green and white bus (service runs 6am–10pm). The city's smaller second airport is Olaya Herrera (☎4/365-6100), located beside the southern bus terminal; taxis to El Poblado are COP$5000.

Bus Depending on which part of the country you're coming from, long-distance buses arrive either at the Terminal del Norte (Metro Caribe) or Terminal del Sur, both almost equidistant from the centre. A taxi from the northern terminal to El Poblado, where most of the hostels are, costs about COP$11,000, but it is cheaper and easy to get the metro. A taxi from the southern terminal to El Poblado is COP$5000.

Immigration For visa extensions (COP$70,100) visit the DAS (Departamento Administrativo de Seguridad) at C 19 No. 80A–40 (Mon–Fri 7–11am & 2–4pm; ☎4/238-9252.

Tourist information There are information stands at both airports as well as at Pueblito Paisa at

C 30a No. 55–64 (daily 6am–midnight; ☎4/235-8370) and in the Plaza Botero at Cra 51 No. 52A–48 (Mon–Fri 9am–7pm, Sat 9am–6pm, Sun 10am–1pm & 2–5pm; ☎512-3508).

City transport and tours

Most sightseeing in the centre can be done on foot. Taxis are cheap and plentiful and there is no surcharge for journeys to the bus terminal, airports or at night. Better yet is the city's excellent metro system (Mon–Sat 4.30am–11pm, Sun 5am–10pm; COP$1550), among the cleanest and most efficient in the world; included in the price of a metro ride are cable cars that leave from Acevedo, Santo Domingo and San Javier metro stations, carrying passengers high above the city for remarkable views (COP$2500 from Santo Domingo to Parque Arví). The safety and efficiency of the metro has rendered buses mostly redundant; at COP$1400 a ride they're a cheap – though not recommended – option after the metro closes. Bus #133 runs between Parque Berrío and Calle 10 in El Poblado.

City tours For an overview of the city, Turibus (☎4/371-5054, ⓦwww.seditrans.com) hits all the main sights, allowing you to jump on and off throughout the day (COP$15,000).

Accommodation

Inexpensive, if run-down, lodging tends to be located in the centre, which becomes a ghost town and therefore dangerous at night. Most of the hostels and more modern hotels can be found closer to the night-time action in El Poblado and Patio Bonito.

Hostels

Black Sheep Hostel Transversal 5A No. 45–133, Patio Bonito ☎4/311-1589, ⓦwww.blacksheep medellin.com. This sociable backpacker's pad has all bases covered, including Spanish classes, high-pressure showers and weekly barbecues. The affable Kiwi owner has travelled extensively in Colombia and is happy to share his knowledge. Dorms COP$19,000, rooms COP$40,000.

Casa Kiwi Cra 36 No. 7–10 ☎4/268-2668, ⓦwww.casakiwi.net. Owned by a motorcycle-loving American, this excellent 55-bed hostel has clean dorms, DVD room, pool table, kitchen, bicycles for rent, laundry service, wi-fi and an adjoining luxury wing with fancy doubles, some en suite. Dorms COP$20,000, rooms COP$40,000.

Casa Maydé C 10 No. 37–39 ☎4/312-0254, ©casamayde@yahoo.com. A low-key spot, run by welcoming Maydé Gonzales, to relax in and feel cosy. Swap stories with other travellers in the patio area filled with flowers and bonsai trees. Dorms COP$18,000, rooms COP$50,000, studio apartment (for four) COP$80,000.

Hostal Medellín Cra 65 No. 48–144 ☎4/230-0511, ⓦwww.hostalmedellin.com; Metro Suramericana. Owner Claudia's laidback attitude creates a pleasant atmosphere and the pool table, barbecue area and scattered hammocks encourage guests to get to know each other. Well located, within easy reach of the city centre and nightlife on Calles 70 and 33. Dorms COP$18,000, rooms COP$25,000.

Hostal Tamarindo C 7 No. 35–36 ☎4/268-9828, ⓦwww.hostaltamarindo.com. Tranquil hostel run by a warm Colombian-American with kitchen, DVD lounge, wi-fi, internet, laundry service, dance classes and great tourist information. Dorms COP$20,000, rooms COP$40,000.

Palm Tree Hostal Cra 67 No. 48D–63 ☎4/260-2805, ⓦwww.palmtreemedellin.com. Comfortable, quiet youth hostel with internet, cable TV and guest kitchen. Private or shared rooms are available. Three blocks from Suramericana metro stop. Dorms COP$18,000, rooms COP$27,000.

Eating

Paisa cuisine, among Colombia's most distinctive, is heavy on the *frijoles* (black beans), grilled meat, plantains and rice. Perhaps no dish is more characteristic of the region than the *bandeja paisa*, a large bowl filled with ground beef, chorizo sausage, *frijoles*, rice, fried green bananas, a fried egg, avocado and fried pork. The city's trendiest restaurants are around leafy Parque Lleras in El Poblado, also known as the Zona Rosa.

Le Bon Café C 9 No. 39–09. Excellent pastries and 32 types of coffee are on offer at this El Poblado café, which has several other locations throughout the city.

Café Botero Cra 52 No. 52–43 inside Museo de Antioquia. Excellent salads and international cuisine, popular with a business lunch crowd. Mains around COP$25,000.

Il Forno Cra 37A No. 8–9. A modern, open-air Italian eatery and El Poblado institution with plenty of mood lighting and satisfying pizza, pasta and salads. Mains COP$12,000–18,000.

Sandwich Qbano C 10, No. 38–32. Giant, cheesy grilled sandwiches for COP$7000–18,000 go down a treat the morning after a late night.

Sushi To Go C 9A No. 38–26 local 107 ☎4/311-0652. For a taste of raw fish, try this spacious sushi restaurant. Plenty of Asian noodle and rice dishes too. Plates COP$9000–32,000.

Thaico C 9 No. 37–40 ☎4/311-5639. Overlooking Parque Lleras, this restaurant is full of *paisas* eating appetizing (if slightly inauthentic) Thai food and getting steadily drunk on three-for-one cocktails. Mains around COP$13,000 before 7pm or COP$23,000 after.

Drinking and nightlife

A cluster of thumping bars and clubs – most of them catering to a young clientele – are in El Poblado. If you fancy something a bit more authentic, start with a beer on Calle 70 (Metro El Estadio) and listen to local musicians playing *vallenato* before heading on to Calle 33 (Metro Floresta) for a dance. Bars usually close around 2am Mon–Wed and 4am Thurs–Sat.

3 Cordilleras C 30 No.44–176 ☎4/444-2337. If you take beer seriously and want to learn a thing or two about how it's made, this brewery offers weekly tours (COP$15,000), including five free beers, to help you appreciate Medellín's finest. Thurs only 5.30–9pm.

Berlin C 10 No. 41–65 ⓦwww.berlin1930 .com. Laidback drinking hole with quirky wall art and an indie rock soundtrack ideal for nursing a beer, shooting some pool or playing cards with friends. Thurs–Sat until 3am.

El Blue C 10 No. 40–20. Giant speakers pump hard electro beats to a student and backpacker-centric crowd who wave along to flashing green laser lights. Thurs–Sat until late. Entry COP$5000–10,000.

El Eslabón Prendido C 53 No. 42–55. Renowned for its live music on Tuesday nights, when the tightly packed crowd goes wild to Colombia salsa. Tues–Sat 8pm–2am. Entry COP$5000.

Oz Cra 38, No. 8–8. There's plenty of eye candy at this satin-draped club that attracts a young crowd. Cocktails COP$10,000. Thurs–Sun 9.30pm–3am. Entry COP$15,000–$20,000.

Moving on

Air Conbuses, at Cra 50a No. 53–13 (☎4/311-5781) leave every 20min from 4.20am to 7.30pm from the *Nutibara Hotel*, across the street from Plaza Botero, to José María Córdova Airport (1hr; COP$6500). International: Caracas (daily; 2hr); Lima (daily; 4hr 30min); Quito (1–2 daily; 1hr 30min). Domestic: Barranquilla (14 daily; 1hr 45min); Bogotá (31 daily; 50min); Bucaramanga (5 daily; 50min); Cali (2 daily; 50min); Cartagena (3 daily; 1hr 20min); Manizales (2 daily; 30min); Monteria (6 daily; 50min); Pereira (7 daily; 35min); Quibdó (6 daily; 35min); San Andrés (1 daily; 1hr 50min).

Bus Bogotá (every 30min; 9–10hr); Cali (50 daily; 8–9hr); Buenaventura (2 daily; 10hr); Cartagena (14 daily; 13hr); Guatapé (every 30min; 2hr); Ipiales (5 daily; 20–22hr); Magangué for Mompox (2 daily; 12hr); Manizales (hourly; 4–5hr); Pasto (5 daily; 18hr); Pereira (more than 50 daily; 5–6hr); Popayán (3–4 daily; 10hr); Santa Fe de Antioquia (every 30min; 1hr 30min); Santa Marta (12 daily; 15hr); Tolu (14 daily; 10hr); Turbo (hourly; 10hr).

DAY-TRIPS FROM MEDELLÍN

A few nearby parks make good if not absolutely essential stops within range of Medellín; the attractions around the lake Embalse del Peñol come close to qualifying.

Parque Ecológico Piedras Blancas

The **Parque Ecológico Piedras Blancas** (daily 9am–5pm; ☎4/262-0592; free), 26km east of the city, serves as the lungs of Medellín. Set at the cool height of 2500m, much of this nature reserve has been reforested with native species, attracting butterflies and birds such as the brilliant blue soledad and the toucanet. Well-preserved pre-Columbian stone trails constructed between 100 BC and 700 AD weave through the park, while there is a butterfly gallery and a slick **insect museum** close to the official entrance. **Camping** is permitted (COP$14,400; bring your own tent) and a **hotel** (☎4/460-1100, ⊛www.comfenalcoantioquia.com/piedrasblancashotel) offers beds from COP$120,000 per person.

To **get to the park**, board a bus from the corner of Ayacucho and Córdoba in the city centre (leaves every 30min) to the village of Santa Elena (30min), where another bus runs every 30min to the park. The metro cable car that runs from Santo Domingo to Parque Arví (see p.585) also connects the city to the park. Eco Rutas (see p.585) offers full-day park tours with a multilingual anthropologist guide.

Piedra del Peñol and Guatapé

Bearing a freakish resemblance to Rio de Janeiro's Sugar Loaf Mountain, **Piedra del Peñol**, or simply "the rock", rises spectacularly from the edge of Embalse del Peñol, an artificial lake some 70km east of Medellín. Locals may tell you that the 200m granite and quartz monolith is a meteorite. Whatever geological or intergalactic anomaly brought it here, it's well worth climbing the 649 stone steps to the rock's peak for phenomenal 360-degree views of emerald green peninsulas jutting into the azure Embalse del Peñol – a hydroelectric dam that submerged the original town of El Peñol in the 1970s.

There are a handful of restaurants and tourist stalls at the base of the rock, but it's better to walk or take a jeep (COP$3000 per person) to the delightful lakeside village of **Guatapé**, 3km away, which is full of restaurants serving trout fresh from the lake. The palm-lined main square, Plaza Simón Bolívar, is well preserved, with its crowning glory the Iglesia La Inmaculada Concepción; throughout the town you'll find colourful colonial houses adorned with intricate artistic motifs. A few blocks away by the lake, you can opt for one-hour cruises, boat hire or zip-line rides.

If you want to **stay the night**, the scrubbed-to-a-pulp *Hospedaje Familiar*, at Cra 27 No. 31–58 (☎4/861-0574; COP$35,000), is a good bet; it has more than thirty simple rooms with TV and private bathrooms. The best places to eat are along the lakefront Avenida Malecón (also known as Calle 32) and include *Vaso é Leche, at* C 32 No. 26–35 (☎4/861-0622), where you'll get filling trout mains with a salad, plantain and fries for COP$10,000. **Buses** leave for Guatapé roughly every half-hour from Medellín's northern bus terminal (2hr). Ask the driver to let you off at "La Piedra".

MANIZALES AND AROUND

Founded in 1849 by migrating *paisas*, **MANIZALES** developed in the late nineteenth century with the growth of the coffee industry. One legacy is the numerous Neoclassical buildings from the era found in the city centre, which has been declared a national monument. This high-mountain city (altitude 2150m) sits at the base of the snowcapped Nevado del Ruiz volcano (see p.591), which, on a clear day you can sometimes see burping vapour from the bridge in front of the Teatro Los Fundadores. Manizales owes its hilly topography to the geologically volatile earth beneath it, and earthquakes occur with some frequency.

What to see and do

Although half a day is enough to take in the sights, Manizales is a pleasant place to while away a few days. Much of its charm lies in its large student population that creates a festive atmosphere – centred mostly on Cable Plaza, the main focus of night-time entertainment – which other large cities in the region lack. The party comes to a head in the first weeks of January during the **Fería de Manizales**, when there are colourful parades, a beauty pageant in search of a new Coffee Queen and bloody bullfights staged in the Plaza de Toros (C#8 and Cra 27). Manizales also makes an excellent base for exploring the surrounding **coffee farms** (see p.593) and the **Parque Nacional Natural Los Nevados** (see p.591).

Monumento a Los Colonizadores

In the northwest suburb of Chipre, on a high bluff at the end of Av. 12 de Octubre, the **Monumento a Los Colonizadores**, is a 25-tonne bronze sculpture reliving the trials and triumphs of the Antioquian mule drivers who founded the city. It's the city's best viewpoint and on a clear day you can see seven *departamentos* and three mountain ranges.

Estación del Cable Aéreo

In the well-manicured Cable neighbourhood, you'll find the **Estación del Cable Aéreo**, the well-conserved end station for the 73km, suspended funicular (once the world's longest), which linked Manizales with the Magdalena River port of Honda (and hence the Atlantic Ocean) from 1910 to 1961. This incredible monument to *paisa* ingenuity, with a little help from migrant Australian engineers, is at Carrera 23 (also called Av. Santander) and Calle 65.

Jardín Botánico

A short stroll down the hill from El Cable on the campus of the Universidad de Caldas, the **Jardín Botánico**, at C 65 No. 26–10 (Mon–Fri 8am–5pm, Sat by appointment only; COP$5000; ☏6/878-1588), offers a peaceful place to walk among orchid gardens, Andean forests and endangered native tree species.

Reserva Ecológica Río Blanco

Around 3km northeast of Manizales, the **Reserva Ecológica Río Blanco**, home to 256 bird species, 350 butterfly species and more than forty mammals, is one of the best places for birdwatching in Colombia. Tranquil orchid-lined uphill hikes through impressive cloudforest reveal dense jungle flora entwined in a battle for a place in the sun and if you are lucky, may end with a glimpse of the reserve's endangered spectacled bear. There is also a hummingbird farm. You'll need to request permission to enter the reserve from the Aguas de Manizales office (Avda Kevin Angel No. 59–181, Mon–Fri 8am–4.30pm). They will organize transport (20min; COP$20,000) and guides are compulsory (COP$18,000 for up to ten people).

Recinto del Pensamiento

Butterflies and birds are the main attraction at **Recinto del Pensamiento** (Tues–Sun 9am–4pm; COP$8000 or COP$13,000 including cable car ride; ☏6/874-4157; ⊛www.recintodel pensamiento.com), 11km from Manizales. As well as visiting the colourful butterfly enclosure, you can also wander through a medicinal herb garden, relax in the Japanese Zen garden, enjoy a stroll through the orchid forest and marvel at the gigantic *guadua* bamboo gazebo, used for conventions and wedding ceremonies. Guides are compulsory and included in the admission price. Buses (marked Sera Maltería; 30min; COP$1200) leave Cable Plaza every 15min; or you can catch a taxi (10min; COP$7000).

Arrival and information

Air La Nubia Airport is 8km southeast of the city centre. A taxi costs COP$8000–9000 or you can jump on one of the frequent buses for COP$1200.

Bus The new bus terminal (☏6/878-5641 ext.118, ⊛www.terminaldemanizales.com) is at Cra 43 No. 65–100. Ride the cable car to the centre of town from where regular buses (COP$1200) run to Cable Plaza or jump in a taxi (COP$5000).

Cable car The city's flashy new cable car line runs from the bus station (Cambulos stop) to Cra 23 in the centre of town (Fundadores stop) in less than 10min and costs COP$1200.

Immigration For visa extensions (COP$70,100) visit the DAS (Departamento Administrativo de Seguridad) at C 53 No. 25A–35 (☏6/810-0600).

Tourist information The tourist office at Cra 21 No. 22–23 (Mon–Fri 8am–noon & 2–6pm; ☏6/884-9280) is good for city maps but not much else. There's another tourist office at Parque Benjamin López on the corner of Cra 22 and C 31 (daily 7.30am–7.30pm; ☏6/873-3901).

Accommodation

🏃 **Base Camp** Cra 23 No. 32–20 ☏6/882-1699, ⊛www.basecamphostel.com. Just steps from the cable car's Fundadores stop, this spacious hostel is a great city centre option, immaculately clean and with a stylish retro design. The roof terrace has stunning views across the city and is perfect for a sunset beer. Owners Carolina and Victor are outdoor enthusiasts and can organize multiple-day hikes to Los Nevados. Dorms COP$20,000, rooms COP$50,000.

Manizales Hostel C 67 No. 23A–33 ☏6/887-0871, ⊛www.manizaleshostel.com. *Mountain House*'s sister hostel has the same friendly management, facilities and excellent tourist information but its smaller capacity makes it more low-key and a good choice if you want to wind down. Helpful owner Cristina Giraldo goes out of her way to enhance your stay in the city and several tours can be booked through both hostels. Dorms COP$20,000, rooms COP$45,000.

🏃 **Mountain House** C 66 No. 23B–137 ☏6/887-4736, ⊛www.mountainhouse manizales.com. On a quiet suburban street just two blocks from the buzzing Zona Rosa, this lively backpacker's hostel has comfortable dorms, a cosy TV room stocked with DVDs, free breakfast, kitchen, a large backyard with a barbecue area, pool table, bike and mountain gear hire, laundry service and helpful staff. Dorms COP$20,000, rooms COP$40,000.

Pit Stop Hostel C 65 No. 23B–19 ☏6/887-3797, ⊛www.pitstophostelmanizales.com. This new hostel likes a party and its on-site jacuzzi, large terrace and popular bar with regular DJs draws an energetic bunch. Dorms COP$20,000, rooms COP$55,000.

Eating, drinking and nightlife

The city centre clears out at night and most eating and drinking is done in the suburbs. The liveliest area, popular with students, is around Cable Plaza, between calles 60 and 75 along Cra 23 (the Zona Rosa), where you'll find the best selection of restaurants, bars and places to dance.

101 Perros C 51 No. 22A–07. This hot dog and hamburger stand, part of a chain, is a decent late-night bet. Hot dogs COP$3900, hamburgers COP$6300. Daily until 5am.

🏃 **La Clave del Mar** C 69A No. 27–100, Barrio Palermo ☏6/887-5528. Excellent fresh seafood delivered from Tumaco or Buenaventura on the Pacific coast. Try the delicious *Cazuela de mariscos* seafood casserole (COP$24,000) or the *Sancocho del bagre* (COP$17,000), a potato, cassava and catfish soup. Mon–Sat 10am–9.30pm, Sun 10am–4.30pm.

Las Cuatro Estaciones C 65 No. 23A–32 ☏6/886-0676. A stylish Italian restaurant that does a fine trade in tomato soup, tasty pizzas (small, COP$16,000, extra large COP$32,000), cheese-smothered steak

(COP$25,000) and vegetarian-friendly pastas (up to COP$22,500). Mon–Thurs noon–10.30pm, Fri & Sat until 11pm, Sun until 9.30pm.

Juan Sebastian-Bar Cra 23 No. 63–66. Charismatic owner Elmer Vargas has a passion for jazz and an awesome CD collection. Popular with artists, writers and university lecturers, this intimate spot has great views of the city and fine cocktails – try the dry martini (COP$12,000). Mon–Sat 7pm–2am.

Manimez Cra 22 No. 24–24. Handy for the main plaza, this health-food store and bakery does a COP$6000 vegetarian set lunch including soup and main course. Mon–Sat noon–2.30pm.

Restaurante y Asadero Típico El Zaguán Paisa Cra 23 No. 31–27 ☏6/882-1395. Enter through the never-ending bamboo corridor for a hearty *menu del día* (COP$4500) before boarding the cable car at Fundadores opposite to the bus station. Daily 11.30am–9pm.

Santelmo Cra 23B No. 64–80. Heaving with students who down cocktails (COP$12,000) and jugs of sangria (COP$30,000), then dance the night away between the tables. Wed–Sat until late.

Valentino's Gourmet Cra 23 No. 63–128. Excellent hot chocolates (COP$3500) and an extensive coffee, cocktail and ice-cream menu. Mon–Fri 9.30am–midnight, Sat & Sun until 2am.

PARQUE NACIONAL NATURAL LOS NEVADOS

Indisputably one of the crown jewels in Colombia's national parks system, the **PARQUE NACIONAL NATURAL LOS NEVADOS** (entry COP$57,000, including guide), 40km southeast of Manizales, protects some of the last surviving snowcapped peaks in the tropics. Three of the five volcanoes are now dormant, but Nevado del Ruiz – the tallest at 5321m – remains an active threat, having killed 22,000 people and buried the now extinct town of Armero when it erupted in 1985. Sadly, though, for a park whose name, Nevado, implies perpetual snow, climate change has lifted the snow line to almost 5000m on most peaks. The best months to visit are January and February – clear days make for spectacular views of the volcanic peaks. March, July, August and December can also be ideal, while the rest of the year sees a fair amount of rain.

What to see and do

The park's **northern sector** is the more touristy and is easily accessible from Manizales. Though it's of little compensation, because of the severe melt, it's now possible for even moderately fit armchair adventurers to reach Nevado del Ruiz's summit in a long day's journey from Manizales. Although not technically difficult – with good weather you can climb in regular hiking shoes – a **guide** is required to navigate the confusing path and assist in the event of altitude sickness (for tour operators, see p.592).

The dramatic **southern end**, where a dense wax-palm forest slowly metamorphoses into *páramo* near the cobalt-blue **Laguna del Otún** (3950m), can only be accessed on foot. Reaching Laguna del Otún from Manizales involves an initial 4-hr drive, taking in park highlights such as the extinct Olleta crater, Laguna Verde and Hacienda Potosí, before culminating in a 2-hr trek to the trout-stuffed lagoon (fishing permitted). You can also approach from either the Valle de Cocora in Salento (see p.595) or via an 18-km uphill hike from *La Pastora* in Parque Ucumarí near Pereira (see p.594).

Accommodation and information

Visitors with time will want to spend at least a couple of nights inside the park exploring the boggy *páramo* landscape, an important freshwater reserve dominating the high massifs. There's a campsite (COP$10,000 if you bring your own tent, COP$60,000 for two people including tent hire) and an upmarket hotel (COP$145,000 with breakfast) at El Cisne, the base for exploring the park's less-visited interior, including the hidden mountain pond Laguna Verde and the cloud-covered Nevado de Santa Isabel. For further information, a map and good logistical advice on camping or hiking, call *Concesiones Confamiliares* (Mon–Fri 8am–noon & 2–6pm; ☏6/881-2065,

(Ⓦconcesionnevados.com) at Cra 19B No. 54–52 La Leonora.

Tour operators

Destinos y Rutas de Colombia Cra 43B No. 11A–10 Istambul Ⓣ6/884-6788. Runs standard day-trips for COP\$120,000, including transport, medical insurance, meals, entrance fee and a guide, plus a visit to *Tierra Viva* hot springs.
Ecosistemas Cra 21 No. 23–21 Local 108 Ⓣ6/880-8300. Runs a daily 12-hr trip from Manizales, leaving at 7.30am, for COP\$125,000, including transport, breakfast, lunch, park entrance, the ascent of Ruiz and a visit to the thermal baths at the park's entrance.
O.X. Expeditions Ⓣ321/756-6176 or ask at *Base Camp* hostel (see p.590), Ⓦwww.oxexpeditions .com. The focus is on pure hiking and trekking, with excellent advanced multi-day hikes and bike tours on offer. Gear hire available and pick-up can be arranged from any hostel in town. Tours are tailored to suit your physical fitness level (graded from easy to OX-treme) and start from COP\$88,000.

Moving on

Air Bogotá (12 daily; 50min); Cartagena (daily, 1hr 20min); Medellín (2 daily; 30min).
Bus Bogotá (hourly; 8–9hr); Cali (hourly; 5hr); Medellín (hourly; 4hr 30min); Pereira (every 5min; 1hr 20min).

PEREIRA

Just 56km south of Manizales, **PEREIRA** makes an equally suitable base for exploring the Zona Cafetera. The region's largest city, it shares Manizales' history as a centre for the coffee industry but lacks its sister city's youthful energy. Its historic centre has been repeatedly destroyed by earthquakes, the most recent striking in 1999. However, it's closer to many of the region's coffee *fincas* and thermal springs.

Pereira's **Plaza de Bolívar** is unique among the uniformly named central plazas of Colombia for its modern sculpture of the El Libertador nude on horseback, a controversial pose when it was unveiled in 1963 but now a beloved city symbol. Also on the plaza is the town's magnificent **Catedral**, built in

1875. Nondescript from the outside, the Catedral's single-nave interior is supported by an elaborate latticework of twelve thousand wooden beams forming a canopy like a spider's web.

Arrival and information

Air Pereira's airport (Ⓣ6/314-2765, Ⓦwww .aeromate.gov.co) is 5km west of the city centre. A taxi downtown costs COP\$5000–6000, or jump on one of the frequent buses for COP\$400.
Bus The bus terminal (Ⓣ6/315-2323; Ⓦwww .terminalpereira.com) lies 1.5km south of the city centre at C 17 No. 23–157. A taxi to the centre is COP\$3000; a bus will set you back COP\$400.
Tourist information The tourist office (Mon–Fri 8.30am–noon & 2–6pm; Ⓣ6/325-8753, Ⓦwww .pereira.gov.co) is on the corner of C 17 and Cra 10 on the first floor of the Centro Cultural Lucy Tejada.

Accommodation

Pereira's accommodation is fairly uninspiring, with few options for budget travellers. If possible, it's worth staying at one of the converted *fincas*, many of them former coffee plantations, between 5km and 35km from the city (see p.593). Most have swimming pools, offer meals and are accessible by bus from Pereira. Tourist agency TurisCafe (Mon–Fri 8am–noon & 2–6pm, Sat 9am–noon; Ⓣ6/325-4157, Ⓦwww.turiscafe.net), at C 19 No. 5–48 office 901 in the Centro Comercial Novacentro, can organize stays.
Cataluña C 19 No. 8–61 Ⓣ6/335-4527, Ⓔhotelcataluna@hotmail.com. Close to the Plaza de Bolívar, this recently refurbished hotel has large, spartan rooms (some with external windows) with hospital-style beds, TV and private bath. Breakfast included. Dorms COP\$25,000, rooms COP\$40,000.
Del Café C 20 No. 4–60 Ⓣ6/334-7871, Ⓦwww .hoteldelcafe.com. Centrally located with comfort-able rooms. Coffee region-themed art and *guadua* bamboo furniture brighten the communal areas. Dorms COP\$28,000, rooms COP\$35,000.
Mi Casita C 25 No. 6–20 Ⓣ6/333-9995, Ⓔhotelmicasita@yahoo.es. Close to Parque El Lago Uribe and used to dealing with tourists, this no-frills option is your best bet in town, with reasonable rates, cable TV and clean rooms. COP\$59,000.

Eating and drinking

Some late night bars are also clustered on Cra 6, between C 23 and C 25.

STAYING ON A COFFEE FARM

Coffee is the planet's most-traded commodity after oil and Colombia is one of its largest producers, with 500,000-plus growers and the unique benefit of two annual harvests. Recognized for producing world-class coffee, coffee fincas in the Zona Cafetera are now following in the footsteps of the wine industry and opening their doors to curious tourists.

Fincas range from traditional estates still attended by their owner to deceptively modern rural hotels where the only coffee you'll find comes served with breakfast. Scenically, the farms look out on lush slopes, overgrown with the shiny-leaved coffee shrubs and interspersed with banana plants and bamboo-like *guadua* forests. Many will also arrange horseriding and walks, and they make an ideal base to explore the region's many attractions.

To locate the best *fincas* for your needs, ask other travellers or a trusted travel agency like Ecoguías in Bogotá (see p.551). You can also enquire at the local tourist offices or hostels in Manizales or Pereira (see p.590 & p.592).

Finca El Ocaso Vereda de Palestina Km 4, 15min by Jeep Willys (ex-US military 4x4; COP$2000) from Salento ☏ 310/451-7194, ✉ fincaelocaso@hotmail.com. Offers guided tours (COP$5000) of a riverside coffee farm and overnight stays with breakfast in a colonial-style farmhouse. Dorms COP$20,000, rooms COP$40,000.

Hacienda Guayabal Cra 3 No. 15–72 Chinchiná ☏ 6/840-1463, ⊛ www.haciendaguayabal.com. Runs tours, in English, of their postcard-perfect coffee farm (COP$25,000). Guests can stay in the main house, and the price includes a tour, three meals and use of the swimming pool. To get there, take a bus from Manizales or Pereira to Chinchiná (30min) and then travel the last 3km by taxi or catch a bus from in front of the church to the farm. COP$45,000.

Hacienda Venecia C 59 No. 24A–18 Of.301 ☏ 6/885-0771, ⊛ www .haciendavenecia.com. This fourth-generation, family-owned working coffee farm is an essential stop for anyone who wants to learn more about coffee production, roasting techniques, trade and aromas. Proud owner Juan Pablo exports coffee as well as roasting for the domestic market. Tours (COP$25,000 including 8.15am pick-up from Manizales) of his sprawling plantation allow visitors to observe the production process from start to finish. Spend a night at the guesthouse, swinging in a hammock on the veranda, firefly-spotting and listening to the croaks of happy frogs in the swimming pool. Breakfast included. To get there, catch a taxi (COP$30,000) or take a jeep from the Plaza de Mercado in Manizales (3 daily at 6am, midday and 5pm; COP$2500). COP$30,000.

La Pequeña Granja de Mamá Lulú ☏ 312/831-9359, ✉ granjaluluquimbaya @yahoo.es. Although it no longer grows coffee, this is a model ecological farm and guest lodge, where everything from animal manure to rainwater is recycled. For non-guests, a guided tour of the tiny farm patch costs COP$7000. Mamá Lulú and her children warmly receive tourists in a house built entirely of *guadua* bamboo. To get there, take a taxi (COP$10,000) or Jeep Willys (ex-US military 4x4; COP$2000) to Vereda Palermo from the village of Quimbaya, 31km south of Pereira, COP$30,000.

El Aperito Paisa C 17 No. 7–62 ☏ 6/334-9522. Breezy second-floor restaurant serving tasty regional dishes, including an excellent *bandeja paisa*. Mains from COP$9000. Daily 7.30am–8pm.

G&G Cra 8 No. 19–17. Buffet-style food and a good salad bar. Lasagne COP$6000, steak COP$8500. Open 24hr.

Le Gascon Cra 7A bis No. 18B–09 ☏ 6/335-0866. An outdoor French bistro and café on the pedestrian walkway near Plaza de Bolívar. Does a filling set lunch for COP$10,000. Open 8am–8pm Mon–Thurs, 8am–1am Fri, 9am–4pm Sat.

El Mesón Español C 14 Cra No. 25–57 ☏ 6/321-5969, ⊛ www.elmesonespanol.com. This Spanish restaurant is Pereira's top eatery; bring an appetite and order the paella (COP$23,000). Closed Sun.

Parnaso Bar Cra 6 No. 23–35. European-style bar covered in French posters. Enjoy a cocktail (COP$10,000) in the lively outdoor garden, with fairy lights strung between guava trees. Open until late.

Moving on

Air Bogotá (8 daily; 50min); Cali (4 daily; 30min); Medellín (5 daily; 35min).

Bus Armenia (every 10min; 1hr); Bogotá (hourly; 9hr); Cali (hourly; 3hr 30min); Manizales (every 15min; 1hr 20min); Medellín (hourly; 5hr 30min); Salento (5 daily, hourly on weekends; 50min); Santa Rosa de Cabal (every 10min; 30min).

DAY-TRIPS FROM PEREIRA

Pereira itself is not a place in which you'll spend a lot of time; if you do base yourself here, you'll likely be striking out on numerous ventures to the nearby hot springs, hiking trails and coffee *fincas*.

Termales San Vicente

The lavishly landscaped **Termales San Vicente** (daily 8am–1am; COP$20,000; ☏6/333-6157; ⓦwww.sanvicente.com .co), 35km northeast of Pereira via the town of Santa Rosa de Cabal, features a selection of steaming medicinal thermal pools scattered across some five square kilometres of cloudforest, river, waterfalls and luxuriant country-side. At 2330m, it gets pretty chilly up here, so it helps that the average pool temperature is 38°C. A variety of spa treatments are offered, including massage (COP$35,000) and mud therapy (COP$15,000). If you want to **spend the night** at the springs, the most cost-effective option is camping (COP$85,000 including entrance fee and breakfast). Further up the accommodation ladder are cabañas (COP$110,000–200,000) or, for the height of romantic luxury, honeymoon-worthy cottages with private thermal pools (COP$400,000 per couple).

The easiest way to get to San Vicente is with one of the direct daily buses that leave at 9am from the thermal springs' office in Pereira at Cra 13, No. 15–62, returning at 5pm. This service only runs during the week if there is a minimum of ten people. The price, including entrance, transport and lunch, is COP$10,000. Spa treatments are extra. Alternatively, you can make your own way to the spa by catching a bus to Santa Rosa from the bus terminal in Pereira and grabbing a seat on a Jeep Willys (ex-US military 4x4) for Termales San Vincente.

Parque Ucumarí

The lush and wild **Parque Ucumarí**, 22km southeast of Pereira, forms a seamless biological corridor with the western side of Parque Nacional Los Nevados. The 42-square-kilometre reserve, established in 1984, acts as a refuge for the endangered Andean spectacled bear as well as tapir, deer and puma. Around two hundred bird species have been spotted here, including condors, eagles and hummingbirds. A steep 18km trail leads from the reserve's Andean tropical forest to the *páramo* landscape of the little-visited southern sector of Parque Nacional Los Nevados before culminating at Laguna del Otún. Due to the poor condition of the trail, a guide is recommended.

Transporte Florida (C 12 No. 9–40; ☏6/334-2721) operates daily *chiva* buses (9am & 3pm Mon–Fri; also at 7am and midday Sat & Sun; 1hr) from Pereira to **El Cedral**, the entrance to the park; a 7am *chiva* runs Mon–Fri but only as far as Otún Quimbaya. It's then a 6-km walk (2hr) from El Cedral to *La Pastora* (altitude 2600m), where you can stay in a cabin overnight (COP$17,000) or camp (COP$5000) and also buy meals. From here it's a breathtaking 6-hr uphill hike to Laguna del Otún in Los Nevados, where most trekkers spend a chilly night camped just beneath the snow line. Fecomar (Av. de las Américas, C 46; ☏6/312 200-7711, ⓦwww.fecomar.com.co) is in charge of the park and can book accommodation at *La Pastora* or organize a guide.

SALENTO

In the heart of coffee country, the quaint hamlet of **SALENTO** is one of the region's earliest settlements, and its slow development has barely altered the original lifestyle or buildings of the *paisa* journeymen who settled here in 1842. Rural workers clad in cowboy hats and *ruanas*, the name for Colombian ponchos, are a common sight. The colourful, one-storey homes of thick adobe and clay-tile roofs that surround the plaza are as authentic as it gets.

What to see and do

Although an afternoon visit is worthwhile, Salento is a popular destination for weary backpackers who linger here to soak up the town's unpretentious charms and hike in the spectacular Valle de Cocora or to use the town as a base to explore the rest of the Zona Cafetera. Salento is a busy weekend destination for Colombians, and on Saturdays and Sundays the main plaza hosts a **food and handicrafts fair** catering to the day-trippers. During the rest of the week, though, the town is as sleepy as ever. Salento's annual fiesta falls in the first week of January, when the town kicks up its heels for a week of horse processions, mock bullfighting and folk dancing.

The main street, Carrera 6, also known as Calle Real, is full of handicraft stalls and restaurants. From the top of the street, steps lead to **Alto de la Cruz**, a hilltop *mirador* offering unbeatable vistas of the Valle de Cocora and, on a clear day, the peaks of snow-clad volcanoes in Parque Nacional Natural Los Nevados (see p.591).

Arrival and information

Bus Buses arrive and depart from Salento's main plaza. Jeep Willys (3 daily; 20min) runs between Salento and Cocora.
Bank The ATM on the main square often runs out of money and will charge you even if you can't make a withdrawal. A currency exchange service is available at *SuperCocora* supermarket, also on the main square, but it's best to arrive with cash.
Tourist information Hostel owners are the best source of information. The English-speaking staff at *Plantation House* (see p.596) are very knowledgeable about the area.

Accommodation

The number of hostels here has mushroomed over the last few years and Salento now has some of Colombia's prettiest and most peaceful accommodation. Book ahead if you plan to visit during the annual fiesta at the start of January.

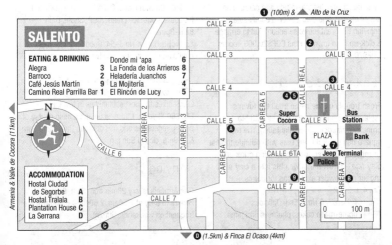

SALENTO

EATING & DRINKING
Alegra   3
Barroco   2
Café Jesús Martín   9
Camino Real Parrilla Bar   1
Donde mi 'apa   6
La Fonda de los Arrieros   8
Heladería Juanchos   7
La Mojitería   4
El Rincón de Lucy   5

ACCOMMODATION
Hostal Ciudad de Segorbe   A
Hostal Tralala   B
Plantation House   C
La Serrana   D

Armenia & Valle de Cocora (11km)

(100m) & Alto de la Cruz

Super Cocora • Bus Station • PLAZA • Bank • Jeep Terminal • Police

0   100 m

(1.5km) & Finca El Ocaso (4km)

Hostal Ciudad de Segorbe C 5 No.4–06
☎6/759-3794, ⊛www.hostalciudaddesegorbe
.com. Stunning views of the Valle de Cocora and
stylish rooms. Balconies overlook the spacious
flower-filled central courtyard, which is a great
place to unwind with a book, and there's also
a Spanish bar with a good selection of wine.
Breakfast included. Dorms COP$20,000, rooms
COP$40,000.

Hostal Tralala C 7 No.6–45 ☎314/850-
5543, ⊛www.hosteltralalasalento.com.
Friendly Dutch owner, Hemmo Misker, has worked
hard to convert this traditional *paisa*-style house
into a beautiful, modern hostel. The spotless
rooms and smart bathrooms retain original
features, like the wooden floors with furnishings made by local artisans. Socialize on the sun
terrace or if you fancy some time on your own,
grab a hammock. You're guaranteed a great
night's sleep in a comfortable bed here. Dorms
COP$18,000, rooms COP$45,000.

Plantation House C 7 No.1–04 ☎316 285 26
03, ⊛www.theplantationhousesalento.com. An
old colonial house set on a picturesque coffee
plantation, this British/Colombian-run hostel
is a good place to meet fellow travellers and
provides excellent tourist information. An adjacent
building accommodates guests when the main
house is full and the owners run regular tours
of their nearby coffee farm, Finca Don Eduardo.
Dorms (COP$18,000) are plain and some rooms
(COP$40,000) are en suite.

La Serrana Via Palestina Km 1.5,
☎6/296-1890, ⊛www.laserrana.com.co.
Eco-friendly working farm and hostel, 1.5km from
Salento, with spectacular views of the surrounding
Cocora mountains and valleys. Horseriding,
mountain biking, fishing, rafting and paragliding
are all offered. End your day on a comfy sofa
enjoying the great music selection. Call to arrange
a pick-up from town. Dorms COP$20,000, rooms
COP$70,000.

Eating and drinking

Fresh trout is on the menu in all the town's
restaurants and is usually served with big
crunchy *patacones* (fried plantains). The main
square has several lively bars with outside tables.
Or meet locals over an early evening drink and
play *tejo* – throw metal weights into a clay pit to
trigger gunpowder explosions for points – at
Cra 4, C 3–32.

Alegra C 6 No. 7 Esq. Delicious
home-made cakes, chutneys and jams.

Owner Jaime Eduardo has a passion for local
organic produce and paintings by Salento artists.
Pasta, pizza and salad mains COP$8000.
Thurs–Mon 11am–7.15pm.

Barroco Cra 6 No. 2–51. Low-key Latin grooves,
hammocks and eclectic art set the scene for this
relaxed bar-cum-restaurant with excellent baked
trout. Service is slow, but it's a beautiful place
to wait. Mains COP$12,000–15,000. Thurs–Tues
11am–9/10pm.

Café Jesús Martín Cra 6 No. 6–14. This
candle-lit café with cosy sofas is perfect for a
warming *canelazo* (hot sugar cane, cinnamon and
anise-flavoured *aguardiente*) after a long day hiking
in the Valle de Cocora. Serves excellent locally
grown coffee too. Daily 8am–9pm.

Camino Real Parrilla Bar Cra 6 No. 1–35.
Known locally as bar "OPEN" because of the
sign above the entrance. The lush garden is a
highlight, with giant tree-trunk furniture and
evening bonfires. Mon–Fri 10am–midnight, Sat &
Sun until 2am.

Donde mi 'apa Cra 6 No. 5–24, main
square. Perfect for people-watching on the
square and hanging out with drunk locals. The
interior is packed with stacked vinyls, old photos
and a glaring stuffed bull's head. Mon–Thurs
4pm–midnight, Fri 4pm–2am, Sat 1pm–2am, Sun
11am–midnight.

La Fonda de Los Arrieros Cra 6, No. 6–02
☎6/759-3466. This plaza-side restaurant does a
divine *trucha criolla a la plancha* (trout topped with
onion and tomato) served with a gigantic *patacón*
(COP$15,000). Mon–Fri 9am–10pm, Sat & Sun
7.30am–11pm.

Heladería Juanchos Main plaza, southeast corner.
A wide selection of exotic tropical fruit juices
(COP$1500 with water, COP$2000 with milk) and
fruit salads with ice cream (COP$3500). Daily
8am–8pm.

La Mojitería C 4 No.5–54. Good for a late night
mojito and 80s remixes. Daily noon–midnight; Sat
until 2am.

El Rincón de Lucy Cra 6 No. 4–02
☎313/471-5497. A whizz in the kitchen,
Lucy serves the best set lunches in town. For
COP$6000 you get juice, soup and a main course of
beans, vegetables and fish or meat. Daily 6am–3pm
& 5–9pm; closed Sun pm.

Moving on

Bus Armenia (every 20min from 6am–9pm; 1hr);
Pereira (3 daily at 7.50am, 2.50pm & 5.50pm, more
frequent on weekends; 50min).

DAY-TRIP FROM SALENTO: VALLE DE COCORA

Salento sits atop the **VALLE DE COCORA,** which contains a thick forest of the skyscraper wax palm, Colombia's national plant, which grows up to 60m high. The valley, which offers picturesque hikes, is easily explored in a day-trip from Salento. The hamlet of Cocora, with a handful of restaurants, small shops and hotels, lies 11km east of Salento. From Cocora a well-trodden path leads into misty, pristine cloud-forest, scattered with the remains of pre-Columbian tombs and dwellings. Orchids, bromeliads and heliconias are just some of the plant species that thrive here, and the fauna includes spectacled bear, native deer and puma, along with hundreds of bird species such as toucans, eagles and motmots.

A five-to-six-hour **loop walk** starts from the blue gate in Cocora, passing a trout farm and, a couple of kilometres on, the Reserva Acaime (entrance COP$3000), home to eighteen species of hummingbirds. The trail crosses nine rickety wooden Indiana Jones-style bridges over the Río Quindío before culminating at a mountaintop viewing platform with exhilarating valley views (as long as there's no cloud cover).

To **get to Cocora**, take one of the three Jeep Willys (ex-US military 4x4s) that leave daily from Salento's main plaza (COP$3000 one-way). Jeeps can also be hired for COP$23,000 one-way.

The southwest

Leaving the snowy white caps of the "Coffee Zone" behind, the Cauca River Valley descends south and widens until you reach **Cali**, gateway to Colombia's southwest and the self-proclaimed world capital of salsa music. Further south, the Panamerican Highway stretches past steamy fields of sugar cane to the serene, colonial town of **Popayán**, Colombia's *joya blanca*, or white jewel, known for its blindingly white Rococo colonial architecture. The verdant rolling countryside around **San Agustín** is some of Colombia's finest, and would be worth a visit even without the enigmatic stone monoliths that pepper the hillsides. **Tierradentro**'s ancient tombs are less well known but no less fascinating. Heading further south from the overlooked town of **Pasto**, you ascend a ridge dominated by volcanoes all the way to Ecuador.

CALI

Colombia's third-largest city, with a population of 2.3 million, **CALI** was founded in 1536 but only shed its provincial backwater status in the early 1900s, when the profits brought in by its sugar plantations prompted industrialization. Today it's one of Colombia's most prosperous cities, in part because of its central role in the drug trade since the dismantling of the rival Medellín cartel in the early 1990s.

The low-lying and extremely hot city (with temperatures routinely surpassing 40°C) straddles the **Río Cali**, a tributary of the Río Cauca, surrounded by the sugar plantations of the marshy Cauca Valley. The large numbers of African slaves brought to work the sugar mills left a notable impact on Cali's culture, nowhere more so than in its music.

Parts of central Cali are **unsafe** to walk around; be sure to get up-to-date advice on where not to go.

What to see and do

The city stakes a powerful claim to being Colombia's party capital, and if you walk its steamy streets any time of the day or night you'll hear Cuban-style **salsa**

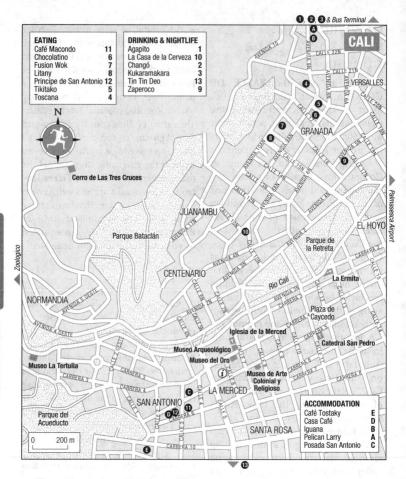

EATING

Café Macondo	11
Chocolatino	6
Fusion Wok	7
Litany	8
Principe de San Antonio	12
Tikitako	5
Toscana	4

DRINKING & NIGHTLIFE

Agapito	1
La Casa de la Cerveza	10
Changó	2
Kukaramakara	3
Tin Tin Deo	13
Zaperoco	9

CALI

VERSALLES

GRANADA

Cerro de Las Tres Cruces

JUANAMBU

EL HOYO

Parque Bataclán

Parque de la Retreta

CENTENARIO

La Ermita

Río Cali

NORMANDIA

Plaza de Caycedo

Iglesia de la Merced

Catedral San Pedro

Museo Arqueológico

Museo del Oro

Museo La Tertulia

Museo de Arte Colonial y Religioso

LA MERCED

SAN ANTONIO

Parque del Acueducto

SANTA ROSA

0   200 m

ACCOMMODATION

Café Tostaky	E
Casa Café	D
Iguana	B
Pelican Larry	A
Posada San Antonio	C

Zoológico

Palmaseca Airport

music blaring from the numerous clubs. It also has several splendid colonial churches and makes an ideal base for exploring the riverside community of **San Cipriano** or the region's beautiful haciendas.

Plaza de Caycedo and around

The city's centre is **Plaza de Caycedo**, which has a statue of independence hero Joaquín de Caycedo y Cuero in the middle. On the plaza's south end is the nineteenth-century **Catedral San Pedro**, with its elaborate stained-glass windows. Walk north along C 12 and

you'll run into the Río Cali. On your right, at Cra 1 and C 13, is the Gothic-style **Iglesia de la Ermita** with its tall spires and powder-blue facade.

Iglesia de la Merced

The oldest church in the city is the **Iglesia de la Merced**, on the corner of Cra 4 and C 7, built from adobe and stone shortly after the city's founding. In the adjoining former convent is the **Museo Arqueológico la Merced** (Tues–Sat 9am–1pm & 2–6pm, Sun 10am–4pm; ☎2/889-3434, ⓦwww .musarq.org.co/fpc/museo_merced .htm; COP$4000), which has displays of pre-Columbian pottery including funerary urns and religious objects unearthed throughout central and southern Colombia.

Museo del Oro

The **Museo del Oro**, in the Banco de la República building at C 7 No. 4–69 (Tues–Fri 9am–5pm, Sat 10am–5pm; ☎2/684-7754, ⓦwww .banrep.org/museo; free), has a collection of gold and ceramics from the Calima culture from the region northwest of Cali. Across the road, the **Museo de Arte Colonial y Religioso** (Mon–Fri 9am–noon & 1–5pm, Sat 9–1pm; free; ☎2/881-8643) features an extensive collection of New World religious relics.

Museo de Arte Moderno La Tertulia

The **Museo de Arte Moderno La Tertulia** at Av. Colombia No. 5–105 Oeste (Tues–Sun 9am–6pm; ☎2/893-2941; COP$4000), has rolling exhibitions of modern art, sometimes featuring high-profile international names, and screens arthouse films in the adjoining *cinemateca* (Tues–Sat 7pm & 9.15pm, Sun 4pm & 7pm; COP$5000).

Zoológico

Cali residents are very proud of their **zoo** (daily 9am–5pm or until 4.30pm in low season; ☎2/892-7474, COP$9800; ⓦwww.zoologicodecali.com.co), which focuses (though not exclusively) on South American species. It's located on spacious grounds on the south bank of the Río Cali, on Cra 2A West and C 14, about 3km from the city centre. By far the easiest way to get there is by taxi (about COP$5500).

Arrival and information

Air The best way into town from Cali's Palmaseca Airport (☎2/275-7414), 20km northeast of the city, is to catch the Rápido Aeropuerto bus, which leaves frequently and takes about 45min (COP$4000). This will drop you at the bus terminal.

Bus The city's gigantic bus terminal (☎2/668-3655) at C 30N No. 2AN–29, is a 30-min walk following the river along Av. 2N. A taxi into downtown costs COP$5000. There is a left luggage office at the terminal open 24hr (COP$2300 per 12hr).

Tourist information There's a tourist information stand in the bus terminal (Mon–Fri 7am–9pm, Sat & Sun 9am–noon & 3–7pm; ☎2/668-3655) and another in the Centro Cultural de Cali at Cra 5 No.6–05 (Mon–Fri 8.30am–4pm; ☎2/885-8855).

City transport

Most local sightseeing can be done on foot; buses including the new Mio network of electric buses cost COP$1500. A taxi is the best option for trips to the zoo (see above); always take a taxi at night. Try Taxi Libre (☎2/444-4444) or Taxi Libre Aeropuerto (☎2/555-5555).

Accommodation

Cali's backpacker hostels are concentrated in two clusters, one around the Granada neighbourhood with good access to nightlife on Avenida 6N and the restaurants around Avenida 8N, and the other in the more characterful (but slightly less secure at night) colonial neighbourhood of San Antonio.

Café Tostaky Cra 10 No.1–76 ☎2/893-0651, ⓦcafetostaky.blogspot.com. There's a more refined atmosphere here than you'll find in most hostels, which probably has something to do with the coffee bar complete with chess sets in the front room. Long-stay rates are available in the second building next door. Dorms COP$17,000, rooms COP$35,000.

Casa Café Cra 6 No.2–13 ☎2/893-7011, ⓦwww .lacasacafecali.blogspot.com. This tiny, arty place above a pizzeria has cold showers and a capacity of just ten. The extremely friendly owners make you feel like you're a visiting relative rather than a paying customer. Dorms COP$15,000, rooms COP$30,000.

Iguana Av. 9N No. 22N–46 ☎2/661-3522, ⓦwww .iguana.com.co. A friendly, Swiss-run youth hostel with all the vital backpacker facilities (including wi-fi) plus loads of information on the region. Can arrange salsa classes and paragliding. Dorms COP$18,000, rooms COP$40,000.

Pelican Larry C 23N No.8N–12 ☎2/396-8659, ⓦwww.pelicanlarrycali.com. The somewhat utilitarian building doesn't live up to this hostel's flashy website, but the big beds, DVD room and twice-weekly barbecues make it understandably popular with young backpackers who are in Cali to party. Dorms COP$16,000, rooms COP$40,000.

Posada San Antonio Cra 5 No.3–37 ☎ 2/893-7413, ⓦ www.posadadesanantonio.com. A peaceful posada in a colonial building that's a wallet-friendly step up in class for those who need a break from hostels. Rooms with private bath are set around a courtyard complete with fountain. Rates include breakfast. COP$88,000.

Eating

The local cuisine consists of heavy portions of chicken and pork. Food stalls around town often sell *mazorcas*, baked corn on the cob, as well as fresh fruit. *Manjar blanco*, made from sugar and served with a biscuit, is a popular dessert. The city's gourmet zone is concentrated around avenidas 8N, 9AN and 9N in Granada, where there are oodles of chic restaurants dishing up fusion and ethnic cuisine.

Café Macondo Cra 6 No.3–03 ☎ 2/893-1570, ⓦ www.macondocafe.blogspot.com. This cosy café with a jazz and blues soundtrack offers sandwiches, salads and burgers with the works (COP$8000–14,000) plus delicious carrot muffins with an oozy *mora* centre (COP$2000) and a decent list of coffees and alcoholic drinks. Open Mon–Thurs 11.30am–11pm, Fri & Sat 11.30am–11pm, Sun 4.30–11pm.

Chocolatino Av. 8N No.17N–01 ☎ 2/401-4494. Marvel at the elaborate cake slices in their chilled counter, order á la carte (mains around COP$25,000) or enjoy a better class of set lunch (COP$12,000–15,000) at this minimalist café. Also does brunch at weekends. Open 11am–11pm daily.

Fusion Wok Av. 9AN No. 15A–30 ☎ 2/661-0302. Asian food that's not overly authentic, but with minimalist Japanese decor and staff dressed like they're about to pull karate moves, it at least looks the part. The menu includes staples like Pad Thai (around COP$20,000) and gyoza (from COP$7900) plus sushi. Open Mon–Wed noon–11pm, Thurs–Sat noon–midnight, Sun noon–10pm.

Litany C 15AN No. 9N–35 ☎ 2/661-3736, ⓦ www.restaurantelitany.com. Flavour-starved foodies should make a beeline for this acclaimed Lebanese restaurant which serves up mouth-watering platters featuring *tabouli*, falafel, vine leaves (COP$22,000) and top-notch *shawarma* (around COP$17,000). Better still, you can BYO alcohol for no charge. Excellent value. Closed Fri & Sun night.

Principe de San Antonio Cra 6 No.2–89 Decent, cheap *menus del día* with a range of options (COP$4500) are the order of the day at this popular

neighbourhood joint. Also does breakfast (from COP$3000). Open 8am–10pm daily.

Tikitako Av. 9N No.17A–36 ☎ 2/660-1389. A Mexican restaurant with extremely friendly staff and a menu that includes a dazzling array of tasty burrito/taco/nacho options (COP$12,000–20,000), as well as burgers with guacamole and more refined dishes. A pleasant place to sit outside, though the beer's expensive. Until 10.30pm Mon–Thurs, midnight Fri & Sat.

Toscana Av. 9A No.20N–45. A bakery-café offering great bread (baguettes, wholemeal, jalapeño) and pastries to take away plus eat-in breakfast options and a good set lunch (COP$10,000). Has wi-fi. Open Mon–Sat 7.30am–8pm.

Drinking and nightlife

Much of the late-night action is just beyond the city limits, in suburbs like Menga and Juanchito. This puts clubs beyond Cali's strict laws on closing times and allows them to open well into the night, often past 3am. Cover charges, where they exist, are usually converted into drinks vouchers. The clubs around Avenida 6N rarely have cover charges and get started early in the afternoon, but are liveliest at the weekends. Single male travellers should find themselves a mixed group to go out with or risk being refused entry. For up-to-date information about what's hot and what's on, see the excellent website ⓦ www.planb.com.co.

Agapito Vía Cavasa Km 2, Juanchito. An institution for salsa fanatics of all ages where, even if you can't hold your own on the dancefloor, you should at least dress like you can.

La Casa de la Cerveza Av. 8N No. 10N–18 ⓦ www.casadelacerveza.com.co. A raucous beer hall serving cheap booze in boot-sized glasses, this is the sort of place you visit to begin your night out and end up staying all evening. The dancefloor gets packed after 10pm, and there are regular events and promotions.

Changó Vía Cavasa Km 2, Juanchito ⓦ www .chango.com.co. Named after the African god of virility and leisure, *Changó* overlooks the Río Cauca at the entrance to Juanchito. Skilled salsa dancers regularly fill its two dancefloors, and the clientie are less forgiving of gringos with two left feet than at some other places, so this is perhaps not the best spot for rank amateurs.

Kukaramakara C 28N No. 2bis–97 ☎ 2/653-5389. There's rock, pop and electronica to be had at this rowdy spot, but the live bands, who usually blast out salsa, are the biggest draw. Open Thurs–Sat, cover COP$10,000.

Tin Tin Deo C 5 No. 38–71 ⓦ www
.tintindeo.com. A fun and unpretentious
salsa temple where the odd reggae tune also
sneaks onto the playlist and dancers sing along to
the music as they sway. Particularly popular with
foreigners on Thursdays. Entrance is COP$5000 for
women, COP$10,000 for men. Inside the city limits,
so closes at 1am.

Zaperoco Av. 5N No.16N–42 ☎ 2/661-2040,
ⓦ www.zaperocobar.com. Photos of salsa stars
plaster the walls of this long-standing club, which is
particularly popular with a thirty-something crowd.
There's live music every Thurs; things really get
going after midnight. Open Thurs–Sat until 3am.

Moving on

Air Bogotá (daily; 50min); Cartagena (daily; 1hr
25min); Ipiales (daily; 50min); Medellín (5 daily;
40min); Pereira (4 daily; 30min); Pasto (2 daily;
1hr); San Andrés (2 daily; 2hr).
Bus Armenia (hourly; 3hr); Bogotá (hourly; 10hr);
Manizales (hourly; 5–6hr); Medellín (8 daily; 8hr);
Pasto (hourly; 9hr); Popayán (every 30min; 3hr).

DAY-TRIPS FROM CALI

Cali offers numerous day-trip opportunities, including visits to former suger-
cane plantations and the remote jungle
community of San Cipriano.

El Paraíso

A number of historic sugar-cane
plantations that have been converted
into museums lie just north of Cali and
make for a pleasant day excursion. The
most famous is **El Paraíso** (Tues–Sun
9am–4pm; ☎ 2/514-6848; COP$4500),
the colonial hacienda that served as
the backdrop for Jorge Isaacs's *María*,
considered the apogee of nineteenth-
century Latin American literary
romanticism. The well-maintained
house is decorated as it would have
been when Isaacs lived here, with
bedpans, candlestick chandeliers and
a working aqueduct that delivers water
throughout the estate. More impressive
is its location, on a gentle slope halfway
between a verdant mountain chain
rising directly from the backyard and
an immense spread of sugar-cane fields.

To **get to El Paraíso** take any bus from
Cali north that passes El Cerrito (40km
away) and ask the driver to let you off
at Amaime, just before El Cerrito, from
where you can share a taxi to the estate
for about COP$2000 per person. Note
also that, on Sundays *busetas* shuttle
picnickers every two hours between El
Paraíso and Palmira, 18km from Cali.

San Cipriano

Set in the sweltering tropical jungle
128km northwest of Cali, the straggly
riverside community of **San Cipriano**
offers an entertaining change of pace
for those who need time out from city
life. The crystalline river here provides
plentiful secluded cooling-off opportunities, but it is the unique journey to the
300-strong community of African slave
descendants that has put San Cipriano
on the traveller's map. There are no roads
into San Cipriano, just a forest-flanked
railway line linking the community
with the town of Córdoba, 6km away.
Nowadays the railway sees very little
train action, so to bring visitors to their
community from Córdoba, inventive
locals have attached motorcycle-
powered wooden carts to the tracks. The
carts leave when they are full of people
(max COP$10,000 return). Unfortu-
nately, rising tourist numbers have led
to incidences of overcharging and offers
of unnecessary guide services; agree the
price of your cart trip before setting off.

San Cipriano lies at the confluence
of the Escalarete and San Cipriano
rivers and there are nine sites for safe
river swimming, as well as opportunities for tubing (COP$5000). Follow the
only road out of the settlement (the
river will be on your right); well-signed
tracks positioned every few hundred
metres lead down to the river. Some
7km of nature trails branch off into
the surrounding forest. A number of
restaurants serve meals and many also
offer basic **accommodation**. If you do
plan to spend the night here bring a

mosquito net, as malaria is an issue. The rooms at *Posada Don José* (☎311/318-9831; COP$25,000) come with fans and mosquito nets, and shared or private bathrooms with cold water only.

To **reach San Cipriano**, catch any Buenaventura bus from Cali's bus terminal and ask to be let out in Córdoba (2hr). Walk down the hill (10min) to the train tracks from where carts leave roughly every hour. San Cipriano is just inland from the port city of **Buenaventura**, making it a convenient stop-over for adventurous souls heading to the Pacific coast.

POPAYÁN

Although less illustrious than Cartagena, Colombia's other open-air colonial museum, **POPAYÁN**, has little reason to envy its more celebrated rival. Founded in 1537 by Sebastián de Belálcazar on his march northward from Quito, the town was a powerful counterweight to Bogotá's dominance during the colonial era and a bastion of Spanish loyalty during the wars of independence. Unlike Cartagena, which saw its influence wane after independence, Popayán's aristocrats remained very active in politics, and no fewer than eleven presidents have emerged from their ranks.

Civic pride runs high in Popayán. When a disastrous earthquake destroyed most of the historic centre in 1983 residents banded together to rebuild, and the result is one of the most attractive cities in Colombia, with cobblestone streets and whitewashed mansions that in many ways look better and more uniformly conserved than before the quake. Popayán is also uniquely tranquil and traditional for a city of its size. Not a single traffic light pervades the quiet centre, which still comes to a complete standstill during the midday siesta. During Easter week the city is cordoned off to make way for thousands of parading worshippers brandishing candles and colourful flowers. Popayan's Semana Santa celebrations are the second-largest in the world, after Seville in Spain.

What to see and do

Most of what there is to see in Popayán itself revolves around the city's rich colonial heritage. Further afield there are natural splendours to enjoy too.

The cathedral and other historic churches

The best way to appreciate Popayán's Rococo riches, including its historic

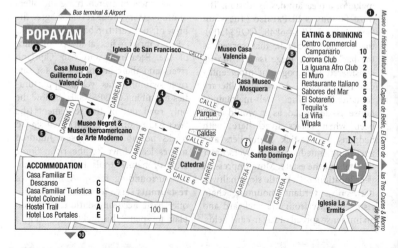

churches, is to wander the streets radiating from the town's main square, Parque Caldas, which is overlooked by the whitewashed **Catedral**. Although the biggest and most frequently used of the churches architecturally it's the least important, built around 1900 on the site where two earlier structures stood. Four blocks east, on C 5 and Cra 2, is the city's oldest standing church, **La Ermita**, which features an austere single-naved chapel comprised of wooden ribbing and a golden altar dating from 1564.

On C 4 and Cra 5, the **Iglesia de Santo Domingo**'s Baroque stone portal is an excellent example of Spanish New World architecture. Equally ornate is the staircased pulpit of **Iglesia de San Francisco**, situated on a quiet plaza on C 4 and Cra 9, where several of Popayán's patrician families are buried.

Casa Museo Mosquera

Several colonial homes have been donated to the government and converted into museums, offering a rare glimpse into the salon society of the colonial and early independence era. One of the best-maintained is the **Casa Museo Mosquera** on C 3 No. 5–14 (Tues–Sun 8am–noon & 2–6pm; ✆2/820-9900; COP$2000), which was the childhood residence of Tomás Cipriano de Mosquera, four times Colombia's president. There's a room dedicated to General Carlos Albán, who died a hero resisting Panama's secession from Colombia.

Museo Negret and Museo Iberoamericano de Arte Moderno

The **Museo Negret** on C 5 No. 10–23 (Tues–Sun 8am–noon & 2–5pm; ✆2/824-4546; COP$2000) was the home of modernist sculptor Edgar Negret and is now a museum exhibiting his work. Next door the **Museo Iberoamericano de Arte Moderno** (included in entry to Museo Negret) exhibits Negret's private collection of works by Picasso and other important artists from Spain and Latin America.

Museo Casa Valencia and Casa Museo Guillermo León Valencia

The **Museo Casa Valencia**, on Cra 6 at C 3 (Mon–Fri 10am–noon & 2–5pm, Sat 10am–noon; ✆2/820-6160; free), is an eighteenth-century home belonging to the city's most famous bard, Guillermo Valencia. The somewhat scruffy central courtyard belies a well-conserved interior, kitted out with elegant period furniture and colonial paintings. The life story of his son, a former Colombian president, is recounted through interesting photographs at the **Casa Museo Guillermo León Valencia** at C 5 No. 9–82 (Tues–Sun 8am–noon & 2–5pm; free). His grave is in the courtyard.

Museo de Historia Natural

A few blocks east of the historic centre at Cra 2 No. 1A–25, in a drab three-storey building, is the **Museo de Historia Natural** (daily 9am–noon & 2–5pm; COP$3000; ✆2/820-1952; ⊛museo .unicauca.edu.co;). Various themed rooms feature an array of interesting insect specimens plus stuffed animals and birds, many of which are endemic to Colombia. There is also a modest display of pre-Columbian artefacts from Tierradentro and San Agustín.

Capilla de Belén, El Cerro de las Tres Cruces and Morro de Tulcán

For a scenic two-hour leg stretch that offers tremendous views over Popayán and the surrounding verdant country-side, walk to the eastern end of C 4 and follow the steep cobbled path up to the hilltop chapel **Capilla de Belén**. From here, a path continues to the three crosses of **El Cerro de las Tres Cruces** and on to **Morro de Tulcán**, once the site of a pre-Columbian pyramid and now capped by an equestrian statue of

Sebastián de Belalcázar, who founded Popayán in 1537. There have been robberies on this route in the past so leave valuables behind. Near to El Morro is **Pueblito Patojo**, a slightly bizarre set of buildings that are smaller copies of Popayán's most famous landmarks.

Arrival and information

Air Popayán's airport is just a 20-min walk north of the centre of town, opposite the bus terminal.

Bus The bus station is a 15min walk north of the centre along Autopista Norte and opposite the airport.

Tourist information The tourist office is at Cra 5 No. 4–68 (claims to be open Mon–Fri 9am–6.30pm, although can be unexpectedly closed; ☎2/824-2251, ✉oficinaturismopopayan@hotmail.com). Staff hand out a good free city guide, plus maps of the city, bus and flight timetables, and can help arrange guided tours in the region.

Accommodation

Popayán boasts a plethora of colonial residences tastefully converted into hotels and small B&Bs, many of which are ridiculously inexpensive. Book well ahead, and expect to pay considerably more, if you plan on being here during Semana Santa.

Casa Familiar El Descanso Cra 5 No. 2–41 ☎2/822-4787; ✉sepp78@latinmail.com. A clean and secure but chintzy back-up option in the same building as the owner's family home. Any enquiries about discounts will be met with a tirade about penny-pinching backpackers. Dorms COP$15,000, rooms COP$30,000.

Casa Familiar Turística Cra 5 No. 2–11 ☎2/824-4853. Simple shared rooms plus one private double, all with shared bath, in a colonial house on a quiet street. There's a kitchen, laundry service and wi-fi. Popular with backpackers. Dorms COP$12,000, rooms COP$30,000.

Colonial C 5 No.10–94 ☎2/831-7848, ✉hotelcolonial@hotmail.es. A comfortable budget option with clean and bright double rooms with private bath and cable TV. Free Internet, wi-fi and local calls. COP$55,000.

HostelTrail Cra 11, No. 4–16 ☎314/696-0805, ⊛www.hosteltrail.com. Friendly Scottish owners Tony and Kim have transformed an odd, modern building into an excellent hostel with clean, bright rooms, free wi-fi and coffee, DVD room and a sociable atmosphere. There's heaps of information about Popayán and the region,

plus English-language books for sale. Dorms COP$16,000, rooms COP$40,000.

Los Portales C 5 No. 10–125 ☎2/821-0139, ⊛www.losportaleshotel.com. A great-value hotel in an attractive colonial building. The 29 rooms all come with cable TV and private bathrooms, and are nicely set around three pretty patios. Free internet and wi-fi. Considerably more expensive if you pay on a card. COP$50,000 (cash).

Eating

Centro Commercial Campanario Cra 9 No.23 N-21 ⊛www.campanariopopayan.com. Popayán's gleaming new shopping mall has a sizeable food court with a range of outlets including popular burger chain *El Corral*, as well as a glass-roofed drinking hall. Regular events and live music make it a very popular weekend hangout. There's also a Carrefour supermarket. A taxi from the town centre should cost COP$3000–4000.

El Muro Cra 8 No.4–11. This cosy, family-run vegetarian joint is deservedly popular for its tasty set lunches (COP$5000) and friendly service. Customers are given a scrap of paper and asked to select seven items (eg soya meatballs, brown rice) from a list on the wall. Also sells good wholemeal bread to take away. Mon–Sat 10.30am–3pm, though the owners have plans to open all day.

Restaurante Italiano C 4 No. 8–83 ☎2/824-0607. A two-floor, Swiss-owned restaurant serving good Italian standards as well as fondues (around COP$23,000) and more unusual European dishes. Service can be poor and waits long at busy times. Set lunch COP$9000, pizza from COP$13,500. Open Mon–Sat noon–3pm & 5.30pm–10pm (11pm if busy), Sun noon–11pm.

Sabores del Mar C 5 No.10–97. Another provider of cheap set lunches, but this one has nautically themed decor and – unusually for a *menú del día* – you can enjoy decent fish or seafood rather than yet more grilled meat. Lunch COP$5000. Mon–Sat 11am–7pm, Sun 11am–4pm.

Tequila's C 5 No.9–25 ☎2/822-2150. A jaunty Mexican café that is not going to win any fine dining awards, but does get a prize for hearty fare (burritos COP$6000), cheap beer, lively music and very friendly service. The spicy *salsa verde picante* is a good addition to any dish. Open Mon–Thurs 5–10pm, Fri & Sat 5pm–midnight.

La Viña C 4 No. 7–79. Does a good breakfast complemented by fresh fruit juices and a cheap set lunch (COP$6500). In the evening, a bewildering array of meat, chicken and fish options, most involving a grill and some kind of sauce, range from COP$8000–27,000. Open daily 9am–midnight.

Drinking and nightlife

Corona Club Inside Hotel La Casona del Virrey, C 4 No.5–78. A multi-roomed salsa/electronica club where the modern decor jars with its colonial setting and spirits are bought by the bottle. Also hosts karaoke and "ladies' nights." Cover is usually COP$10,000, more for special events. Thurs–Sat until 3am.

La Iguana Afro Club C 4 No. 9–67. This dimly lit bar has a good cocktail list (around COP$10,000), funky salsa soundtrack and trendy clientele.

El Sotareño Cra 6 No. 8–05. Head through *El Sotareño*'s swing doors and the first thing you'll see is the owner quietly sitting behind his compact bar, surrounded by a vinyl collection of vintage salsa, tango and other Latin music. Order a cheap, cold beer, bag one of the booths then sit back and listen as the tunes are spun. Until 1am Mon–Sat.

Wipala Cra 2 No. 2–38. An arty café-bar that promises different musical styles for each night of the week (classic rock on Mon, jazz on Wed) as well as artisan wine and organic coffee. Attracts a studenty crowd. Also has a shop selling crafts. Open Mon–Sat 4–11pm (shop 9am–7pm).

Moving on

Bus Bogotá (5 daily; 12hr); Cali (every 10min; 3hr); Pasto (hourly; 6hr; for safety reasons it is inadvisable to take a bus departing before 5am or after 2pm, see p.610); San Agustín (11 daily; 6–7hr); Silvia (every 30min; 1hr 30min); Tierradentro (1 daily plus 3 to El Cruce, see below; 4hr 30min–6hr).

DAY-TRIPS FROM POPAYÁN

The colourful market village of Silvia, an outstanding national park and some invigorating thermal springs are all within 60km of Popayán.

Silvia

Well worth a detour is the rural village of **Silvia**, 60km northeast of Popayán, which fills up with Guambiano Indians in colourful blue and fuchsia dress every Tuesday for market day. The market itself focuses on fruit, veg and basic household goods rather than tourist-friendly handicrafts, but the presence of the Guambiano, who arrive from their homes in the mountain villages above Silvia, makes it a great opportunity for people-watching. **Buses** (COP$5000) leave for Silvia every 30min from Popayán's bus terminal. Once here, it's possible to hire horses (COP$6000 per hour) and ride up to the village of Guambia (1hr) where the Guambiano cook up fried trout, plucked fresh from nearby trout farms. Silvia's tourist information office, on the corner of the main square, is open 9am–4pm Tues, Sat & Sun.

Parque Nacional Natural Puracé

The high-altitude **Parque Nacional Natural Puracé** (daily 8am–5pm; COP$19,000), 58km east of Popayán, encompasses 860 square kilometres of volcanoes, snowcapped mountains, sulphurous springs, waterfalls, canyons, trout-stuffed lagoons and grasslands. The park's literal high point is **Volcán Puracé** (4700m), which last blew its top in 1956. It's a lung-straining 4-hr climb to the steaming crater where, on a clear day, there are sensational views of Cadena Volcánica de Los Coconucos – a chain of forty volcanoes. There are also less strenuous trails, including an orchid walk, and thermal baths. Enquire at the visitor centre near the park entrance if you want to hire a guide. The weather is best for climbing the volcano in December to January; it is worst in June to August.

Four **buses** daily leave Popayán for the park entrance at El Cruce de San Juan (2hr), though if you're planning a day-trip you should catch the bus at 4.30am or 6.45am. The last bus back to Popayán passes El Cruce at 5pm. For those wanting to make an early ascent of the volcano, it is possible to **overnight** in the park in basic cabañas (☎2/823-1279; COP$26,000; order meals in advance) or camp (COP$4000), which includes use of a bathroom with hot showers.

Thermal springs at Coconuco

The village of **Coconuco**, 26km from Popayán, is a short hop to two rudimentary outdoor thermal baths. The better-maintained and more pleasant of the two is **Termales Agua Tibia** (daily 8am–6pm; ☎2/824-1161; COP$8000), 5km southwest of Coconuco on the road to San Agustín. Set at the base of a steep-sided valley with great views, the complex has three lukewarm pools, a waterslide and a basic mud pool rich in rejuvenating minerals. Facilities are scant and there is no place to lock up valuables.

The indigenous-run **Agua Hirviendos** (Tues–Sun 24hr; COP$6000), 3km east of Coconuco, is less picturesque than Agua Tibia but its sulphur-reeking pools are far toastier, with temperatures around 38ºC. The on-site waterfall is a refreshing shock to the system.

To **get to either baths**, take the bus from Popayán to Coconuco (every 30min; 45min; COP$3000), from where it's a short walk to Agua Hirviendos and about 30min to the Termales Agua Tibia; a *mototaxi* will take you for COP$2000, or hire a jeep for COP$7000. The owners of *HostelTrail* in Popayán will drive you and a rented bicycle to the thermal baths for COP$30,000. Having enjoyed the waters you can then pedal your way, mostly downhill, back to town, stopping for lunch and photographs on the way.

SAN AGUSTÍN AND PARQUE ARQUEOLÓGICO

The thoroughly laidback little town of **SAN AGUSTÍN**, 140km southeast of Popayán, has everything a hippie could want – awesome landscape, cryptic ruins and bargain-basement prices. If that's not enough, there's also the **San Isidro mushroom**, a powerful hallucinogenic fungi that grows especially well in the surrounding area's perennially green pastures. But even if you're not part of the rainbow culture, there's still plenty to discover here, in particular the **archeological park**. Some 3300 years ago the jagged landscape around the town was inhabited by masons, whose singular legacy is the hundreds of monumental stone statues comparable in detail to the more famous Moai statues found on Chile's Easter Island.

Much mystery still surrounds the civilization that built the monoliths, though the surreal imagery of sex-crazed monkeys, serpent-headed humans and other disturbing zoomorphic glyphs suggests that San Isidro may have already been working its magic when the statues were first created. What is known is that the priestly culture disappeared before the Spanish arrived, probably at the hands of the Inca, whose empire stretched into southern Colombia. The statues weren't discovered until the middle of the eighteenth century.

It's a good 7-hr journey by bus from Popayán via the small town of Coconuco along a mostly unpaved road, but the beautiful scenery more or less redeems the bumpy ride. For those going on to Bogotá, or coming from the capital, it makes sense to exit San Agustín via the paved road to Neiva rather than backtrack to Popayán.

Parque Arqueológico

The nearest archeological sites are 2.5km west of San Agustín in the **Parque Arqueológico** (daily 8am–6pm; except museum until 5pm, Alto del Lavapatas until 4pm; COP$15,000), which was declared a UNESCO World Heritage Site in 1995. The park contains over a hundred statues, the largest concentration of statues in the area. Many of them are left as they were found, while others, like the ones in the wooded sector known as the **Bosque de las Estatuas**, are rearranged and linked by an interpretative trail. There's also a museum in the park that displays Indian earthenware. To tour the park you'll need at least two hours and if you don't want to spend COP$40,000 for a guide, you can buy an English-language guidebook for about COP$12,000 (the tourist information office in town also sells guidebooks in English or Spanish).

Other statue sites and activities

Hundreds more statues are littered across the colourful hillside on either side of the Río Magdalena, the source of which can be visited in a strenuous five-day hike. For most visitors, walking, horseriding or motorcycling through the verdant, unspoiled landscape is more impressive than the ruins themselves. The numerous trails could keep you busy for more than a week but the most popular destinations, all which are within a day's return hike from town, are **El Tablón**, **La Chaquira**, **La Pelota** and **El Purutal**. While none of these requires a guide, it is advisable to walk in groups or with a guide when visiting **El Tablón** and **La Chaquira** as there have been robberies on this route in the past.

Alto de los Idolos (daily 8am–4pm; COP$15,000 or combination ticket with Parque Arqueológico COP$25,000) is the area's second most important archeological site after the Parque Arqueológico, and is home to the region's tallest statue, 7m high. It can be reached via a 3-hr hike from San Agustín, on horseback or by driving to San José de Isnos, 30km along the road to Popayán and another 5km along a side road. The tourist information office, and most accommodation options, can organize full-day **jeep tours** (around COP$30,000 per person), which include Alto de los Idolos. If you do venture into the hills on foot, take rain gear and good boots as the weather near San Agustín often changes throughout the day. A recommended guide for **horse trips** is Pacho (℡311/827-7972; ℮pachito campesinito@yahoo.es), who offers

everything from the standard 4-hr trip around outlying statues (standard price is COP$21,000 per horse plus COP$40,000 for the guide, but negotiate) to month-long rides all the way to Ecuador.

As well as from archeological attractions, **white-water rafting** and **kayaking** are also popular in San Agustín, thanks to ready access to the Class II–IV Río Magdalena. Magdalena Rafting (℡311/271-5333, ℗www .magdalenarafting.com) offers excursions (COP$45,000 for a half-day).

Arrival and information

Bus Buses arrive and depart in the centre of town near the corner of C 3 and Cra 11, where there is a cluster of bus company offices.

Tourist information The helpful tourist office (daily 6–11am & 1–6pm; ℡8/837-3940) is near where the buses stop at C 3 No. 10–84.

Accommodation

There is an abundance of budget accommodation in San Agustín, including some fantastic-value *fincas* in stunning locations just outside town. Most of these are foreign-owned, which, perhaps predictably, creates a bit of tension with some locals. If you're heading to a *finca*, don't be surprised if taxi drivers exaggerate the distance and try to overcharge you, and don't listen to the touts who tell you that it is closed or the owner is dead/in prison/a serial killer and then helpfully offer alternative accommodation.

La Casa de Francois 250m along Vía El Tablón ℡8/837-3847, ℗www.lacasadefrancois.com. Situated on a bluff overlooking the city, this long-standing and sociable place offers airy dorms (one with fantastic views), an excellent new communal kitchen and a couple of private doubles. The enthusiastic owner offers home-made bread, jam and other goodies, plus hearty breakfasts (COP$7000). There's also a camping area. Camping COP$7500, dorms COP$15,000, rooms COP$30,000.

Casa de Nelly Vía la Estrella 1.5km along Av. 2 ℡311/535-0412, ℗www.hosteltrail.com/ hotelcasadenelly. Tricky to find, as the route along a poorly lit dirt track from town is not brilliantly sign-posted, but lovely once you've made it. Romantic cabins surrounded by trees make this a great spot for those who want to hide away and relax for a couple of days. Has a restaurant serving breakfasts and "whatever's available" for dinner. COP$40,000.

El Hogar de San Agustín Cra 14 No. 4–03 ☎8/837-3185; ⊛www.hotel-san-agustin.com. The beautiful garden at this homely new posada makes it a good option for those who want both greenery and an in-town location. The enthusiastic French owners have plans for a living room with TV/DVD and book exchange, and the on-site restaurant serves up cuisine from their homeland (open to the public but reserve ahead). COP$30,000.

Hostal Maya Cra 13 No. 6–78 ☎314/392-0089; ⓔwww.hostalmaya@gmail.com. Excellent-value doubles and dorms in an attractive colonial building, with free fruit juice as well as the standard complementary coffee. Communal kitchen, plus top-floor terrace with hammocks. There have been some reports of valuables going missing. Dorm COP$10,000, rooms COP$20,000.

🏃 **Finca Ecológica El Maco** 750m along the road to the Parque Arqueológico and then 500m up a rough road ☎8/837-3437, ⊛www.elmaco.ch. This working organic farm offers a range of sleeping options from camping and simple dorms to luxurious *casitas* (literally "small houses"). The restaurant serves up good-value Thai curries, great crêpes and massive breakfasts. Alternatively, you can buy home-made bread, cheese, pasta sauces and yoghurt and make your own meals in the basic communal kitchen, then retire to a hammock and admire the surrounding hills. Camping COP$8000, dorms COP$15,000, rooms COP$24,000.

Hospedaje El Jardín Cra 11 No. 4–10 ☎314/488-6220, ⊛www.hosteltrail.com/eljardin. Reliable and cheap, if uninspiring, town-centre option set around a courtyard. The beds are droopy and the en suites tiny, but the owner is friendly and will drown you in free coffee if you let her. COP$24,000.

The town's fruit and veg market on the corner of C 2 and Cra 11, where self-caterers can stock up, is open daily but liveliest Sat–Mon when the *campesinos* come to sell their wares.

Donde Richard 750m along the road to the Parque Arqueológico at C 5 No. 23–45 ☎312/432-6399. High-quality, carnivore-friendly food such as barbecued pork, chicken, beef and fish, all cooked on a big grill at the front of the restaurant (mains COP$18,000). Good selection of Chilean and Argentinian wine. Closes at 8pm.

El Fogón C 5 No. 14–30. Extremely popular restaurant that serves up a better-than-average *menú del día* (COP$6000) to scores of hungry locals every day of the week. Daily 6am–11pm.

Limonetto's C 5, No.16–38. Cheap burgers (from COP$5000 with fries) and hot dogs plus larger plates, served with a jaunty salsa soundtrack and very cheap beer (COP$1700). Open 11am–11pm daily.

🏃 **Nakanda** 500m from town on the road to Parque Arqueológico ☎320/480-6736. Tasty pizza (COP$10,000–16,000), cheap beer, good music and friendly service make this new restaurant/bar a great place to sate your appetite and then linger on the terrace for a sociable drink or two. Open until 2.30am (custom depending), pizza until 10pm (midnight at weekends). Also does takeaway.

Bus Bogotá (5 daily; 10–12hr); Neiva (5 daily; 4–5hr); Pitalito (several daily; 45min); Popayán (at least 7 daily; 6–7hr). Getting to Tierradentro from San Agustín involves two bus transfers, which can extend the journey time to around 7hr. The first transfer is at Pitalito, then at La Plata (after 3hr). From La Plata it's 2hr 30min to El Cruce de San Andrés, then a 20-min walk to the museum in Tierradentro. There are many more buses to destinations (including Bogotá) from Pitalito.

TIERRADENTRO

After San Agustín, **Tierradentro** is Colombia's most treasured archeological complex. Its circular burial caverns, some as deep as seven metres, are decorated with elaborate geometric iconography and are at least as impressive as San Agustín's statues. Monumental statues have also been found here, indicating a cultural influence from San Agustín, yet, like the latter, little is known about the Tierradentro civilization other than that it flourished around 1000 AD.

No large population centres have been discovered, lending credence to the belief that the original inhabitants belonged to a dispersed group of loosely related farmers. The tomb-dwellers' modern descendants are the **Paez Indians**, 25,000 of whom live in the surrounding hillside. During the colonial era, the Paez were known as a ruthless warrior tribe, and they remained free of Spanish subjugation until well into the seventeenth century.

TATACOA DESERT

The bizarre Tatacoa Desert makes for a worthwhile detour en route from Bogotá to San Agustín or Tierradentro. Measuring just 300 square kilometres, tiny Tatacoa's arid topography – complete with cracked earth, giant cacti, orange-and-grey soil and towering red rock sculptures – is all the more astonishing because it lies only 37km northeast of Neiva, a city encircled by fertile coffee plantations. Scorpions, spiders, snakes, lizards, weasels and eagles have all found a home here, while fossils indicate that the area was an ancient stomping ground for monkeys, turtles, armadillos and giant sloths.

Some of the fossils are on display at the paleontology museum on the main plaza in the village of Villavieja, 4km from the desert. Villavieja has a few basic hotels and restaurants, but since one of Tatacoa's chief attractions is the amazing night sky, it pays to stump up for one of the cabins in the desert itself. *Noches de Saturno* (⊕313/305-5898) has very basic rooms and ambitious tariffs; with some negotiation you shouldn't need to pay more than COP$15,000 per person (same price for campers), and there's a small swimming pool. It's also not far from the observatory (open weekends 7–9.30pm or by appointment), where there's a restaurant (lunch COP$10,000). A number of locals offer guided desert tours by car, *mototaxi* or horseback, although it is possible to reach some of the highlights on foot.

Villavieja is an hour by bus from Neiva, which in turn is 6hr by bus from Bogotá and 4hr 30min from San Agustín on the main Bogotá to San Agustín road. A *mototaxi* from Villavieja to the desert costs COP$5000–7500 per person depending on group size; from Neiva you can often find transport straight to Tatacoa for about COP$10,000 per person. The best time to explore the desert is early morning before the heat becomes intolerable (temperatures frequently reach 43˚C).

What to see and do

Tierradentro means "Inner Land", an appropriate nickname to describe the rugged countryside of narrow valley and jagged summits. Few visitors make it here, thanks to the poor quality of the road from Popayán and the presence of guerrillas in the relatively recent past. With the area now safe and with roadworks improving access, however, it won't be long before Tierradentro is firmly established on the backpacker circuit.

Before visiting any of the burial sites which make up the **Parque Arqueológico Tierradentro**, you must first head to the **Tierradentro Museum** (halfway along the road to El Cruce; daily 8am–4pm) to pay the COP$15,000 park entry fee and receive a wristband, which is valid for two days. There are in fact two museums; one has an archeological display including pottery urns and information about the park's tombs; the other focuses on the history and customs of the indigenous Paez. The park itself contains one statue site (El Tablón) and four **cave sites** – Segovia, El Duende, Alto de San Andrés and El Aguacate – spread across a sublime landscape. All can be visited in one long day; the best tombs are at Segovia, so don't rush through this first stop. Be sure to bring your own torch to explore the tombs, as most are unlit, and wear sturdy shoes as the walk is long and at times very steep. The guards at each site who open the tombs for you can answer most questions (in Spanish) and will expect and appreciate a small tip. There have been some reports of robberies on the lonely walk back from El Aguacate; be sure to allow plenty of time to get back to the main road in daylight.

The nearest village to Tierradentro is tiny **San Andrés de Pisimbalá**, 4km from El Cruce de San Andrés, which is on the main Popayán–La Plata road. It has a picturesque thatched-roof chapel that dates from the seventeenth-century mission, and is within walking distance of most burial sites.

Hikes to outlying Indian villages, cascading waterfalls and high-altitude *páramos* could easily keep walkers busy for more than a week.

Arrival

Bus Tierradentro is 113km from Popayán along a rough mountain road. There is one direct bus at 10.30am daily (5–6hr) from Popayán and an additional three daily that pass El Cruce de San Andrés. From here it's a 2-km walk to the museums and 4km to San Andrés de Pisimbalá.

Accommodation and eating

Hospedaje Ricabet ☎312/279-9751 Slightly further uphill than *Pisimbalá*, *Hospedaje Ricabet* has small, basic rooms with shared or private bath, set around a pretty cobbled courtyard. COP$22,000.

La Portada ☎311/601-7884, ✉restaurante-la-portada@hotmail.com. Located 2km from the museums in San Andrés de Pisimbalá, *La Portada* has slightly nicer, more expensive rooms with hot showers. Its chief advantages, however, are the excellent, home-cooked food on offer in the pretty restaurant (breakfast COP$4500, lunch and dinner COP$5500), and the hospitality. For those not staying here, this is a great lunchtime pit stop on the route around the Parque Arqueológico: you should also try the home-made ice cream. COP$35,000.

Residencias Pisimbalá ☎311/612-4645. This orange building is one of a clutch of simple options lining the road for 250m uphill from the museum. Also has a basic restaurant serving breakfast, lunch and dinner (COP$4000–7000). COP$24,000.

PASTO

Capital of Nariño *departamento*, **PASTO** is the commercial hub of southern Colombia. Although the surrounding foothills of the Galeras Volcano are attractive, the bustling town is devoid of major sights and likely to be visited only in passing on the way to Ecuador, 88km further south along the Panamerican Highway. The southern stretch of the highway between Pasto and Popayán has been unsafe in the past; to err on the side of caution, avoid travelling overland at night.

Founded in 1537 by Sebastían de Belalcázar on his march from Quito, Pasto sided with Spain during the wars of independence and later tried to fuse with Ecuador when Bolívar's Nueva Granada confederation split up in 1830. Successive earthquakes have destroyed most of Pasto's colonial architecture but a few churches still recall its past glory.

CROSSING INTO ECUADOR

The Colombian town of Ipiales, a 2-hr bus ride from Pasto, is 2km from the Rumichaca Bridge, which has Colombian and Ecuadorian border control offices on either side. You will need to cross into Ecuador on foot and take new transport from there; the town of Tulcán is 2km from the bridge (see p.639), and from there you can connect to Quito, Otavalo and elsewhere. There are money changers on both sides of the border on and close to the bridge. From Ipiales, you can catch a taxi or a *colectivo* (COP$1500) to the border, which is normally open 6am to 10pm.

The neo-Gothic cathedral Santuario de Las Lajas (daily 6am–6pm; free), spectacularly situated on a stone bridge straddling a canyon, is a very worthwhile diversion. You can leave your bags at the Ipiales bus terminal's left luggage office (COP$2000 per bag) and take a taxi to Las Lajas (15min; COP$7000) before returning an hour or so later to continue your journey into Ecuador. Regular *colectivos* (COP$1500) also make the 7km journey to and from Las Lajas, departing from the corner of Cra 6 and C 4 in Ipiales town centre.

AMAZONIAS

Colombia's share of the Amazon basin occupies a third of the nation's territory, although it remains only loosely integrated with the rest of the country and has very little in the way of infrastructure. While much of the region remains off-limits thanks to cocaine production and guerrillas, the town of Leticia is a safe base from which to explore the area's incredible biodiversity, as well as to cross into Brazil or Peru. The only way to get to Leticia from elsewhere in Colombia is to fly; both Aerorepública and Satena have several flights a week from Bogotá.

There are numerous tour agencies in town that can organize jungle and river trips of virtually any length, taking in flora, fauna and the area's indigenous communities; when choosing, be sure to ask questions about what an operator does to protect all three. One recommended budget operator is Omshanty (☎311/489-8985, ⓦwww.omshanty.com), a jungle lodge 11km from Leticia that gives a taste of the wild and offers beds from COP$10,000. Omshanty also runs tours, from around COP$120,000 for a day-trip for two people. Alternatively, you can make your way independently to Puerto Nariño, an appealing little town of 2000 residents 2 hours 30 minutes upstream from Leticia, from where you can take trips to see pink river dolphins. The boat to Puerto Nariño passes Parque Nacional Amacayacú, 90min from Leticia, which is home to some 500 bird and 150 mammal species. It is pricey to get in (COP$31,000) and extremely expensive to stay the night.

Many people come to Leticia en route to Brazil or Peru. To get to the former, you need only head to the port of Tabatinga, just across the border, which has virtually fused with the Colombian town; there are no checkpoints between the two. If you want to continue further into Brazil, by catching a plane or boat (4 days) from Tabatinga to Manaus, you will need to get a Colombian exit stamp from DAS at Leticia Airport and an entry stamp from the Brazilian federal police in Tabatinga; also check in advance whether you need a Brazilian visa. From Leticia there are also speedboats (10hr) and slow barges (3 days) to Iquitos in Peru.

Each year in early January, the politically incorrect **Carnaval de Blancos y Negros** (ⓦwww.carnavaldepasto .org) presents one of Colombia's most traditional celebrations. The festival's racist roots date from the colonial period when, once a year, slaves would paint themselves white and their masters, in approval, would parade the next day in blackface.

What to see and do

The **Cristo Rey** at C 20 and Cra 24, noted for its stained-glass windows and beautiful paintings, is the best-preserved church in town. The pulpit at the city's oldest church, **San Juan Bautista**, on C 18 and Cra 25 – the city's principal plaza – was built in the Arabesque Mudéjar style. At C 19 No. 21–27, the **Museo de Oro** (Mon–Fri 8am–6pm; free), has a small exhibition of art from the region's pre-Columbian cultures.

Pasto is known for its handicrafts, especially the *barniz de pasto*, a china-like finish used to decorate wooden objects. Examples can be bought at the **Mercado de Bombóná**, an artisan market on C 14 and Cra 27.

Arrival and information

Air Pasto's airport is 29km north of the city. There are no buses to downtown, but you can bag a seat in a *colectivo* for COP$5000–7000. A private taxi will cost COP$30,000–35,000.

Bus The bus terminal (☎2/732-4935) lies 2km south of downtown at Cra 6 No. 16D–50. A bus to the centre (take #1, 6, 9 or 15) is COP$1100, while a taxi is COP$4000.

Tourist information The Pasto tourist office, which also has information on the whole of the Nariño department, is at C 18 No. 25–25 (Mon–Sat

8am–noon & 2–6pm; ☎2/723- 4962; ⓦwww
.turismonarino.gov.co).

Accommodation

Koala Inn C 18 No. 22–37 ☎2/722-1101, ⓦwww
.hosteltrail.com/koalainn. Two blocks from the
main square, this long-established backpackers'
hostel has 15 private rooms (some with cable TV)

arranged around a central courtyard, plus plenty of
information on the region. COP$28,000.
Metropol C 15 No. 21–41 ☎2/720-0245. Decent
budget hotel where the rooms have private
bathrooms, cable TV and wi-fi. COP$35,000.

Moving on

Bus Cali (hourly; 9hr); Ipiales (every 30min; 2hr);
Popayán (hourly; 6hr).

Ecuador

HIGHLIGHTS

QUITO: explore the capital's preserved colonial squares, churches and monasteries

CANOA: The Coast's most relaxed suffer hang-out

THE NORTHERN ORIENTE: vast areas of rainforest filled with diverse wildlife and indigenous cultures

VOLCÁN COTOPAXI: a magnificent cone-shaped volcano

BAÑOS: thermal baths, adventure sports and a stunning location at the foot of Tungurahua

GALÁPAGOS ISLANDS: witness the miracle of evolution

ROUGH COSTS

DAILY BUDGET Basic US$25/ occasional treat US$40

DRINK Cerveza Pilsener US$1

FOOD Set menu two-course lunch US$2

HOSTEL/BUDGET HOTEL US$5–10

TRAVEL Quito–Baños: 4hr, US$5

FACT FILE

POPULATION 14.7 million

AREA 283,000 sq km

LANGUAGE Spanish

CURRENCY US dollar

CAPITAL Quito (population: 1,400,000)

INTERNATIONAL PHONE CODE ☏593

TIME ZONE GMT -5hr

Introduction

In Ecuador it's possible to wake up on the Pacific coast, drive through the snow-capped Andes and reach the edge of the Amazon jungle by sundown. Although Ecuador is only slightly larger than the UK, its wildly different terrains have more than enough to keep visitors occupied for months. It's one of the world's most biodiverse countries with some 25,000 species of plants, more than the total species found in all of North America, and 1600 species of birds. It's entirely fitting, therefore, that the Galápagos Islands, where Charles Darwin developed his theory of evolution, belong to Ecuador.

Mainland Ecuador is divided into three geographically distinct regions: coast, jungle and highlands. The most popular region is the highlands, with **Quito** the most convenient starting point. The Ecuadorian capital's historic sights, range of day-trips and excellent tourism facilities can keep you busy for a week or more.

To the northwest of Quito lie the cloudforest reserves around **Mindo** and to the northeast the bustling indigenous market town of **Otavalo**, whose *artesanía* crafts are a shopper's dream.

South of Quito is Ecuador's most dramatic mountain scenery, including **Volcán Cotopaxi**, the highest active volcano in the world, and the extinct volcanic lake **Laguna Quilotoa**. Further south is the popular spa town of **Baños** and **Riobamba**, the best base to explore Ecuador's highest mountain, **Chimborazo** (6310m), and the **Nariz del Diablo** train ride. In the southern highlands are Ecuador's best-preserved Inca ruins, **Ingapirca**, its beautiful third city **Cuenca** and the relaxing "Valley of Longevity", **Vilcabamba**.

Excursions deep into wildernesses of primary jungle, including **Cuyabeno Natural Reserve** and **Yasuní National Park**, can be arranged via the unsightly oil towns of **Lago Agrio** and **Coca**, while shorter trips and stays with indigenous communities are best via

Puyo and **Tena**, Ecuador's white-water-rafting capital.

On the coast, visit **Guayaquil** to see how the waterfront of Ecuador's largest city has been regenerated, then head for the beach. From the high-class hotels of **Salinas** and **Bahía de Caráquez** to the surfer hangouts of **Montañita** and **Canoa** and the unspoilt beaches of **Parque Nacional Machalilla** and **Mompiche**, there are resorts to suit everyone.

Some 1000km west of mainland Ecuador lie the country's tourism crown jewels, **the Galápagos Islands**. Although sadly on the UNESCO Danger List, they remain among the world's top destinations for watching wildlife and are increasingly easy to explore independently.

CHRONOLOGY

4000 BC The first evidence of humans in Ecuador is the Valdivia culture in Santa Elena.

1460 AD Tupac Yupanqui leads the first Inca invasion of Ecuador.

1495 Huayna Capac conquers Ecuador, establishing centres in Quito and Ingapirca.

1526 Civil war erupts between Huayna Capac's sons Huascar and Atahualpa; the latter triumphs.

1532 Spaniard Francisco Pizarro arrives in Ecuador, captures and executes Atahualpa the next year, and completes the conquest of Peru in 1535.

1541 Francisco de Orellana journeys down the Amazon and reaches the Atlantic.

1820 On October 9, Guayaquil declares independence, supported by Simón Bolívar.

1822 On May 24, Quito wins its independence at the Battle of Pichincha. Bolívar's dream of a united continent dies and Ecuador becomes fully independent in 1830.

1861 Conservative Gabriel Garcia Moreno seizes power, quashes rebellions and makes Catholicism a prerequisite for all citizens. He is assassinated in Quito in 1875.

1895 Liberal Eloy Alfaro becomes president and introduces sweeping reforms, ending the connection between church and state and legalizing divorce. He is assassinated in 1912 by angry conservatives.

1941 Peru invades Ecuador and forces through a treaty giving Peru a 200,000-square-kilometre section of Ecuadorian jungle.

1967 Oil is discovered in the Ecuadorian Oriente, prompting an oil boom in the 1970s.

1979 Left-winger Jaime Roldós is elected president, ending a long period of military rule. He confronts the oil-rich hierarchy and dies in a mysterious plane crash two years later.

1996 Self-styled *loco* (crazy) Abdalá Bucharam wins the presidency then raises taxes and records an album. He is ousted by Congress a few months later for "mental incapacity" and goes into exile in Panama.

1998 President Jamil Mahuad and Peruvian President Fujimori sign a peace treaty, which finally ends the long-running border dispute.

2000 The sucre plummets from 6000 to 25,000 to the dollar in less than a year. President Mahuad is ousted in a coup but his successor Gustavo Noboa presses ahead with a radical dollarization plan.

2001 Ecuador qualifies for the FIFA Football World Cup for the first time, sparking wild national celebrations.

2002 Former coup leader Lucio Gutiérrez wins the presidency but is removed in 2004 after infuriating his left-wing base by adopting neo-liberal policies and attempting to increase his presidential powers.

2007 Rafael Correa, a friend of Venezuelan President Hugo Chavez, becomes Ecuador's seventh president in ten years. He refuses to pay Ecuador's national debt, engages in a war of words with the rich classes, replaces Congress with a newly elected Assembly and introduces a new constitution.

2010 Following his re-election in April 2009, Correa endures a series of crises, including a scandal involving his brother and an energy crisis causing two months of power cuts. On September 30 a police protest escalates into an attempted coup. Six people are killed as the president is dramatically rescued by his own army from a police hospital in Quito.

Basics

ARRIVAL

Arriving by **air**, most travellers enter Ecuador via Quito's Mariscal Sucre airport, though Guayaquil's new José Joaquín de Olmedo is more convenient for the Galápagos and the beach. Airlines with regular services from Europe include: Air Europa, Air France, Avianca, Iberia, KLM, LAN and Lufthansa. From North America: Air Canada, American Airlines, Continental Airlines, Delta and COPA (see listings in Guayaquil and Quito sections for contacts). Note that when flying out of Ecuador, you must pay departure tax in cash. In Quito, it's

WHEN TO VISIT

Because of Ecuador's diverse landscapes, the best time to visit varies by region. On the coast, temperatures are typically 25–35°C. The rainy season is most dramatic, with downpours between January and April. This is the hottest time of the year, with the weather often uncomfortably humid inland. These are also the best months for visiting the beach. It's cooler and cloudier between June and December. In the highlands, the temperature is on average 15°C but it gets hot at midday due to the altitude and cold at night, particularly above 2500m. The driest, warmest season is June to September. In the Oriente the temperature Is generally 20–30°C with high levels of rainfall and humidity. The driest season is December to March. In the Galápagos, the temperature peaks at over 30°C in March and cools to the low 20s in August. It's best to avoid the roughest seas between June and September.

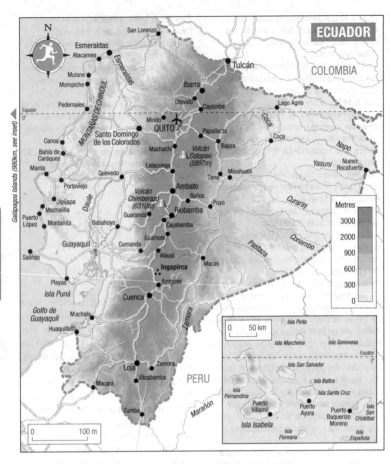

$40.80 (to help pay for a new airport) and in Guayaquil $28.

Overland from Peru

You can reach Ecuador by **bus** from Peru via Tumbes and Huaquillas on the coast. It's also possible to cross via Macará in the highlands. Both routes are safe and several companies including CIFA can take you across.

Overland from Colombia

Travelling to and from Colombia overland is only possible via Tulcán in the northern highlands. The border region has a troubled history, however, so many travellers fly to Cali from Tulcán with TAME (☎02/2397-7100, ⓦwww.tame.com.ec).

PASSPORTS AND VISAS

Visitors to Ecuador require a passport valid for over six months and can stay for up to **ninety days** on an automatic 12-X tourist visa. Visitors receive a T3 tourist card, which must be kept with your passport until you leave. Officially, you should bring proof of sufficient funds to support yourself and a return ticket or proof of onward travel, but it's rarely demanded in practice.

It's possible to get an extension to 180 days but you must go to the immigration office on the day the visa expires and the decision is at officials' discretion. If the visa expires, it's a $200 fine. Given this, it's probably better to leave the country within ninety days and then re-enter.

GETTING AROUND

By bus

Ecuador's inexpensive and generally reliable **buses** are the preferred form of public transport, reaching just about everywhere there's a road. The **Panamericana** forms the backbone of the road network, linking all major highland towns. The government is pouring huge investment into the roads and many have improved markedly in recent years.

Poor quality of the roads, particularly in the rainy season, often result in **delays**; the worst roads tend to be in Esmeraldas, the southern highlands and Oriente. Public buses are very cheap though – typically about $1 per hour of travel, but quality varies so if possible check the bus you're going to travel on before buying a ticket.

If you're lucky the stereo will be pumping out a salsa soundtrack; if you're unlucky there'll be a loud macho action movie ruining the trip. For longer bus rides at peak periods, buy tickets in advance. Avoid bus travel at night if possible as **crime** is more common. Also note that pickpocketing is rife on public buses, especially on popular tourist routes out of Quito. Never stow valuables in your bag above your head or under your seat but keep them on your person.

By car

Hiring a car is possible but not recommended because of the expense, combined with poor roads. It costs $300–500 per week, depending on the size of vehicle, with an alarming excess of $1000 in case of damage. A better option is a **taxi**. In bigger cities this is certainly the best way to get around, though always check credentials, avoid unmarked cabs and use the meter (if there isn't one, negotiate in advance). Taxi drivers in tourist towns will often offer longer trips, but rates are obviously far higher than buses.

By air

It's tempting for those pushed for time or weary of long bus rides to **fly**. TAME (☏02/2397-7100, ⊛www.tame.com.ec) offers reasonably priced flights from Quito to Coca, Cuenca, Esmeraldas, Galápagos, Guayaquil, Lago Agrio, Loja, Machala, and Cali, Colombia. There are flights from Guayaquil to Coca, Cuenca, Galápagos, Loja and Cali. Prices start at about $60 one-way. Icaro (☏02/244-8626/ 02/245-0928) and Aerogal (☏02/294-2800) both serve Quito, Guayaquil and Cuenca, and are cheaper than TAME. A new option is Chilean airline LAN (☏02/299-2300, ⊛www.lan.com), which offers the cheapest flights from Quito to Guayaquil ($40 one-way).

ACCOMMODATION

Ecuador has a wide variety of **accommodation**, from dirt-cheap rickety shacks to comfortable mid-range hotels – and then a big jump in price to the luxury options. You can pay as little as $4–5 per person for a basic dorm in a cheap *pensión*, *residencial* or *hostal*. The mid-range is where Ecuador offers best value. In most destinations $20–30 gets you a good-sized double room with comfortable beds, private bathroom, hot water and cable TV. In the $50–100 range, you can stay at a swankier international city hotel, a colonial hacienda or a secluded jungle lodge.

Cities such as Quito, Guayaquil and Cuenca are slightly more expensive but competition keeps the prices down. On the coast, air conditioning costs extra, and budget places sometimes have no hot water, although the climate renders it unnecessary. Consider bringing your own mosquito net if you plan to spend time in the jungle or the coast during the rainy season. Deep in the jungle, budget options are harder to find so expect to pay more (usually as part of a tour). **Camping** is not widely available but possible in some areas for $3–5 per person, but you must usually bring your own gear unless you book a tour.

FOOD AND DRINK

There's a lot more to Ecuadorian cuisine than roasted guinea pig. Rice and beans are the staple, so don't be surprised to be served rice with everything, even with pasta or potatoes, in a carbohydrate extravanganza. Budget travellers can enjoy cheap set menu *almuerzos* (lunches) and *meriendas* (dinners), which serve a soup, main course and drink for $1.50–3. *Sopa* (soup), *caldo* (broth) and *seco* (stew) are healthy, cheap ways to stay full. Try *locro de papa*, a blend of cheese, pasta and potato; or *chupe de pescado*, a thick fish-and-vegetable soup. *Caldo de pata* (cow's foot soup) is for the more adventurous. For main course, try *seco de pollo* (chicken stew with coriander) or *lomo salteado* (salted beef steak). In the highlands and Oriente the fish of choice are tilapia and river trout. The famous *cuy* (guinea pig) and *hornado* (giant pigs) are sights to behold, roasted whole on a spit.

On the Ecuadorian coast, the **seafood** is among the best in the world. *Ceviche*, a cold seafood dish marinated with lemon and onion, is excellent. *Encebollado*, a fish and onion soup, is often eaten to stave off a hangover. A more interesting option is *cazuela*, a seafood and vegetable broth made with plantains and peanut. In Manabi try *biche*, a sweeter fish soup with corn and *maduros* (sautéed plantains). You won't find a better fresh white fish than *corvina* (sea bass), which can be *frito* (fried), *apanado* (breaded), *a la plancha* (grilled) or *al vapor* (steamed) Note that shellfish is a common cause of illness, so take care.

If you're on a tight budget, **snacks** come in handy but make sure street food is sizzling and avoid hot snacks sold on public transport. Popular treats from bakeries include *empanadas* (meat or cheese-filled pastries), *tortillas de verde* (fried mashed green bananas) or *yucca* (a local root vegetable) and delicious *humitas* (mashed corn with cheese wrapped in a corn husk and steamed). *Pan de yucca* (yucca bread), eaten with yogurt, is a common snack.

Always buy **bottled water** and never drink from the tap. It's best to avoid ice in cheaper places. Ecuador's abundant tropical fruits make fresh *jugos* (juices) and *batidos* (milkshakes) great breakfast options. As well as pineapple, melon, papaya and banana, try unusual fruits such as *naranjilla* (a sour orange) or *tomate de árbol* (a sweet tomato). Sodas are everywhere, while coffee is of variable quality, annoying in a country which produces so much. The most common beers are the standard local Pilsener and slightly more expensive Club Verde, but beer connoisseurs will be disappointed. Whisky, rum and the local firewater *Agua Ardiente* are cheap and strong enough to give you a stonking hangover. *Chicha*, made from fermented corn or potato, is drunk by indigenous people in the jungle. If you don't try it, don't worry – you won't be missing much.

CULTURE AND ETIQUETTE

One of the best aspects of Ecuador is the hospitable, fun-loving people. Ecuador's population of more than fourteen million is divided equally between the coast and highlands, with only 5 percent in the Oriente. Most of the population,

65 percent, are *mestizo* (mixed race), 25 percent indigenous, 3 percent Afro-Ecuadorian and 7 percent white. While many of the Indians hold on to the traditional customs and dress, the mainstream population dress like Americans in jeans and designer labels. This aspiration has led to nearly two million emigrants in recent years.

Around ninety percent of Ecuadorians are Roman Catholic, although evangelical Christianity is increasing rapidly. Rivalry between the mountains and coast, particularly between Quito and Guayaquil, is fierce. *Costeños* consider *Serranos* (mountain people) to be conservative, uptight and two-faced. *Serranos* call *Costeños* "monos" (monkeys) and consider them rude, uncultured, immoral gossips. The rivalry ranges from banter to deep resentment, so it can be a touchy subject.

Ecuadorians' lax attitude to time is legendary. At social gatherings, add at least an hour to the agreed meeting time or bring a book and patience. That said, scheduled departures such as buses and tours are usually punctual, so don't be caught out.

Greetings are essential for Ecuadorians – a kiss on each cheek for women and a handshake between men. If you don't know any Spanish, at least make the effort to learn the basic greetings and pleasantries.

Tipping is not essential in most situations but advisable in higher-end hotels for bellboys (50 cents to $1). If your guide is particularly good, show your appreciation with an extra few dollars. Supermarket bag carriers and parking attendants require a tip (up to $1).

SPORTS AND OUTDOOR ACTIVITIES

Football

Football is undisputedly the number one sport in Ecuador and watching a local match at a stadium in Quito Guayaquil is unforgettable. If there is a national team match or a *clásico* (local derby) between Quito or Guayaquil teams, the cities grind to a halt with everyone glued to the television. Quito has three major teams: Liga, Nacional and Deportivo Quito, while Guayaquil has two: Emelec and Barcelona.

Hiking and climbing

The highlands' open spaces offer the widest range of **hiking** options – the Quilotoa Loop, Parque Nacional Cotopaxi, Mindo cloudforest, the hills around Baños, Parque Nacional Cajas and Vilcabamba are just a few that stand out. On the coast, Parque Nacional Machalilla and Cordillera Chongón near Montañita also offer good hiking. The best **climbing** is on Cotopaxi and Chimborazo, although ensure you are fully fit, properly acclimatized and travelling with a qualified guide.

Watersports

For watersports, including **rafting** and **kayaking**, Tena and Baños are the best bases for trips on fast-flowing rapids and gentler tributaries to suit all levels. The best **surfing** is at the beach resorts of Montañita, which holds a famous surfing competition around Carnival, or Canoa and Mompiche. **Scuba-diving** and **snorkelling** opportunities are limited on the mainland. Parque Nacional Machalilla has a few reputable operators but the best place by far is the Galápagos Islands, whose amazing marine life makes it one of the world's top underwater destinations.

Wildlife

Birdwatching enthusiasts should head to the cloudforests of Mindo, which have more than 400 bird species and 250 species of butterfly. The tiny hummingbirds are a highlight, most commonly seen in the cloudforests and the jungle. The Andean condor is a rare but unforgettable sight, occasionally seen in Parque Nacional Cotopaxi and other areas of the highlands. For other **wildlife-watching**, the Oriente offers great opportunities to watch sloths, otters, caymans, tapirs and many species of monkey. The Galápagos is of course unbeatable for close encounters with wildlife.

COMMUNICATIONS

The **postal** system in Ecuador is very unreliable; your postcard will either reach its destination late or never. Receiving mail is worse, so if you need to send or receive something, use an international courier service such as DHL or Fedex, but bear in mind there is a minimum charge of about $40.

Ecuador's **phone** system is improving and international calls are cheaper than they used to be. There are countless phone offices in towns, most commonly Andinatel. These are the best places for conventional calls, useful for calling hotels or tour operators. There are also cellular public phones, which use prepaid phone cards available at shops or kiosks. Calling North America costs as little as $0.10–0.20 per minute and Europe $0.30–0.40 per minute, but there is usually a connection charge. Most travellers staying longer than a few weeks invest in a mobile phone from Porta or Movistar. Phones start at $35 and SIM cards from $4.

The **internet** is the cheapest and easiest way to keep in touch. You're never far from internet cafés in tourist towns and even remote places have a connection somewhere. Expect to be charged $1 per hour, although prices can be higher. Many good hotels have free wi-fi.

CRIME AND SAFETY

Sneak theft is the most common crime for travellers around Ecuador. In Quito, in particular, tourists are targeted by expert pickpockets. Be vigilant in crowded areas and on public transport, keep your money out of sight and be wary of strangers engaging you in conversation on the street, as this is a common diversionary tactic. Don't carry large amounts of cash.

Armed robbery is less common but it is increasing. Sadly the tourist district of Mariscal Sucre in Quito is now the most common place to be mugged in Ecuador. There have also been some reports of violent attacks on tourists. Gangs look for easy targets, so don't wander around alone and always take a licensed taxi back to your hotel at night, no matter how close it is. Other crime hotspots in Quito include parts of the Old Town, the walk up to El Panecillo (take a taxi) and Parque Carolina.

In Guayaquil, be extra vigilant at night, particularly downtown. Esmeraldas and Atacames also have problems with theft and robbery; avoid the northern coastal town of San Lorenzo completely. Avoid arriving at Esmeraldas bus station at night. Drug smuggling and Colombian guerrilla activity in the northern border areas have made areas of Sucumbíos (capital Lago Agrio), Carchi (capital Tulcán) and Esmeraldas (capital Esmeraldas) provinces unsafe. On the southern border, the Cordillera del Cóndor, southeast of Zamora, contains landmines from the conflicts with Peru.

By law you must carry identification – for foreigners this means your passport. If you can't produce identification, you may be detained by the police. Carry drugs in Ecuador and you may end up in jail – for up to fifteen years, so avoid any contact with drug dealers. Foreigners are vulnerable to set-ups and bailing you out is an easy way for corrupt police officials to make some serious money.

HEALTH

Vaccinations which are strongly recommended include typhoid, hepatitis A and yellow fever. Others to consider are hepatitis B and rabies. **Malaria** is present (but rare) in the Oriente and on the northern coast. Wear long sleeves, light-coloured clothes and use repellent to avoid mosquito bites. The best anti-malarial medication is Malarone, which must be taken daily. **Dengue fever** is spread by day-biting mosquitoes, mainly during the rainy season, and is becoming more of a problem in coastal areas on the coast. There is no vaccine, so seek medical help as soon as possible if you show symptoms (high fever, aching limbs, vomiting and diarrhoea).

The most common problem is the dreaded **travellers' diarrhoea**. Minimize the risks of bacterial and parasitic infections by avoiding bus vendor/street food that's not sizzling hot; also try to eat in clean restaurants. Tap water, ice, salad, ice cream, unpeeled fruit and seafood are common culprits. Eat plenty of carbohydrates, drink water and pack oral rehydration and Imodium.

Another common problem is **altitude sickness**, which can be dangerous. At altitudes over 2000m (most of the highlands), don't overexert yourself, avoid alcohol and don't attempt to climb mountains without sufficient time to adjust to the altitude.

Sunburn and **sunstroke** are also very common because the Ecuatorial sun is fiercely strong. On the beach you burn in half an hour at midday without sunblock, so apply regularly. Don't be fooled by the cool temperatures in the mountains. Because of the altitude, the sun is far stronger.

Note that Ecuador's health system is poor and **emergency care** particularly bad. Travelling with valid insurance is essential. If you have an emergency, try to head for a private hospital. In Quito, Hospital Metropolitano is good and in Guayaquil, Clínica Kennedy has several branches. Pharmacies are plentiful and will dish out medicines without prescription, so you are responsible for knowing what you're taking.

INFORMATION AND MAPS

Ministry of Tourism iTur offices (ⓦ www.ecuador.travel) in provincial capitals and the main tourist centres, supply maps, as well as lists of hotels, restaurants and sights. Some are better than others. Also, mid-range hotels often have leaflets and brochures in reception.

El Instituto Geográfico Militar in Quito, at Senierges and Paz y Miño, sells topographical maps for just $2 and a giant map of Quito for $8 (bring your passport as ID to enter the institute). The best general map of Ecuador is the 1:1,000,000 International Travel Maps Ecuador map (ⓦ www.itmb.com). There are also maps of the Galápagos Islands and Quito available.

MONEY AND BANKS

Ecuador replaced the plummeting sucre with the **US dollar** as its official currency following an economic crisis in 2000. There are 1, 5, 10, 25, 50 cent and 1 dollar coins. Notes come in 1, 5, 10 and 20. Avoid 50 and 100 dollar bills, and even 20 dollar bills cause problems in small towns. Dollarization has made Ecuador more expensive but it's still a cheap country; you can get by on $20 per day staying in budget hotels, eating off set menus and taking public buses. For $30–40 per day you'll get a higher level of accommodation, restaurants and taxi rides. The climbing, birdwatching and jungle-trekking tours push costs up to $50–100 per day.

Carry enough cash for at least a few days; a credit card is highly recommended as backup. Visa, MasterCard,

ECUADOR

BASICS

Cirrus and Maestro are commonly accepted at ATMs. In larger agencies, you can pay for tours with a credit card but you may be charged 5 to 10 percent extra. Note that rates of exchange for currencies outside South America (eg British pounds) are often poor, so bring cash and travellers' cheques in US dollars wherever possible.

OPENING HOURS AND HOLIDAYS

Most shops and public offices are open Monday to Saturday 9am to 5pm or 6pm, although family-owned businesses open and close at the owner's discretion. Banks open 8 to 9am Monday to Friday and close 2 to 4pm. Some extend hours to 6pm but it's preferable to go before 2pm. Telephone call centres open 8am to 10pm. Restaurant and bar opening hours vary widely. Museums are usually open at weekends and closed Mondays. On Sundays and public holidays you may find yourself in a ghost town.

Most national holidays mark famous historical events as well as Catholic festivals. Ecuadorians love to party with lots of food, drink and late nights, so it's a great experience. Note that tourist resorts, especially beach towns, are usually extremely busy on national holidays, with sky-high prices to boot. Most of the following are national holidays, although some are only celebrated in certain areas of the country. Note that the government habitually changes the dates of national holidays, often to tag them onto the weekend.

PUBLIC HOLIDAYS

January 1 New Year's Day (*Año Nuevo*). This is recovery day with millions nursing hangovers.

January 6 Epiphany (*Reyes Magos*). Celebrated mainly in the highlands.

February/March Carnival (*Carnaval* – literally "goodbye to meat"). The week before Lent is Ecuador's biggest party. Usually Monday and Tuesday are holidays. The beaches are packed and in the highlands Ambato and Guaranda are famous for their celebrations. Don't be surprised to get wet, as throwing water is an essential part of the fun.

March/April Holy Week (*Semana Santa*). The big processions in Quito are on Good Friday, which is a public holiday.

May 1 Labour Day (*Día del Trabajo*).

May 24 Battle of Pichincha (*La Batalla del Pichincha*). Celebrating the decisive battle for independence in 1822 (highlands only).

July 24 Birthday of Simón Bolívar, the man who dreamed of a united South America and helped to liberate Ecuador.

August 10 Quito Independence Day (*Día de la independencia*).

October 9 Independence of Guayaquil (Guayaquil only).

October 12 Columbus Day (*Día de la Raza*).

November 2 All Souls' Day or Day of the Dead (*Día de los Muertos*).

November 3 Independence of Cuenca (Cuenca only).

December 6 Foundation of Quito. Bullfights are the order of the day (Quito only).

December 25 Christmas Day (*Navidad*). Most Ecuadorians celebrate Christmas on Christmas Eve night and relax on Christmas Day.

December 31 New Year's Eve (*Nochevieja* or *Años viejos*). New Year rivals Carnival as the country's biggest party. Locals burn effigies of well-known characters – everyone from the president to Homer Simpson. Note that safe use of fireworks is not high on the agenda.

Quito

At a dizzying elevation of 2850m, Quito is the second-highest capital city in the world after Bolivia's La Paz. It has a dramatic location with the active Volcán Pichincha, which covered the city in ash in 1999, looming to the west and Valle de los Chillos descending east towards the Amazon basin. If the altitude doesn't leave you breathless then the architecture surely will. Founded by the Spanish in 1534, Quito rapidly became a major colonial centre and its churches, monasteries, cobbled streets and wide plazas have been beautifully preserved. The warmest, driest time is June to September, but the rest of the year can be very chilly, especially at night, with frequent rain in the afternoons.

What to see and do

Although most visitors stay in the New Town, the **Old Town**, also known as "El Centro Histórico", is what makes Quito special in terms of sightseeing. Sights not to be missed are the two main squares **Plaza Grande** and **Plaza San Francisco**, the **Palacio del Gobierno**, the **Catedral**, the gaudy gold church **La Compañia** and the **Church of San Francisco**. For great views of the city, take a taxi up to the top of **El Panecillo** or climb the stairs of the gothic **Basílica del Voto Nacional**.

The **New Town** has a huge range of accommodation, restaurants and bars around Avenida Amazonas in Mariscal Sucre. This thriving tourist district is where most visitors base themselves and has such an international feel that it's nicknamed "gringolandia", although safety is a problem, especially at night. The New Town has plenty of attractions, although they are spread out, which makes sightseeing more complicated than in the compact Old Town. Highlights include Ecuador's best museum, **El Museo del Banco Central**, Oswaldo Guayasamín's extraordinary work of art **La Capilla del Hombre** and a trip to an altitude of 4100m on the **Teleférico**.

Plaza Grande and around

This picture-perfect sixteenth-century plaza, formally known as Plaza de la Independencia, forms the political and religious focal point of Quito, containing the cathedral, Presidential Palace, Archbishop's Palace and alcaldia municipal (city hall). Visitors can only enter the **Palacio del Gobierno** (Presidential Palace; tours 10am–4pm Tues–Sun; free) on one of the guided tours (there are five per day, the last at 4pm), but it's worth the wait to see the state rooms, a stunning mosaic and various indigenous artefacts. On the other side of the square is the **Catedral**, which is entered through the museum (entrance on Venezuela, 9.30am–4pm Mon–Fri, 10am–4pm Saturday; $1.50, Sunday services free). Inside is a collection of seventeenth- and eighteenth-century religious art, the tomb of liberator Mariscal Sucre and

---

SIX OF THE BEST VIEWS OF QUITO

Quito's stunning location in a valley surrounded by hills and volcanoes means that you are spoilt for choice for where to get the finest views of the city. Here are six of the best options. All are best visited by taxi (except La Basílica which is easily accessible).

1. El Panecillo, Old Town
2. La Basílica, Old Town
3. Centro Cultural Itchimbia, Old Town
4. Guápulo, New Town
5. Parque Metropolitano, New Town
6. El Teleférico, North of the city

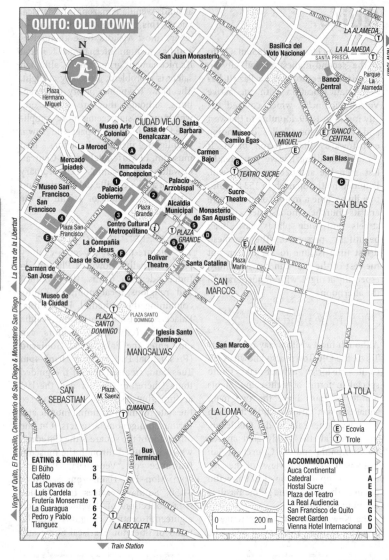

QUITO: OLD TOWN

N

New Town

Plaza Hermano Miguel

San Juan Monasterio

Basílica del Voto Nacional

LA ALAMEDA
LA ALAMEDA
SANTA PRISCA
Parque La Alameda

Banco Central

CIUDAD VIEJO
Santa Barbara
Museo Arte Colonial
Casa de Benalcázar

Museo Camilo Egas

HERMANO MIGUEL

BANCO CENTRAL

La Merced

Carmen Bajo

San Blas

Mercado Ipiades
Inmaculada Concepcion

Palacio Arzobispal

TEATRO SUCRE

SAN BLAS

Museo San Francisco
San Francisco

Palacio Gobierno

Plaza Grande

Sucre Theatre

Monasterio de San Agustín

Plaza San Francisco

Alcaldia Municipal

Centro Cultural Metropolitano

PLAZA GRANDE

LA MARÍN

La Compañía de Jésus

Plaza Marín

Casa de Sucre

Bolivar Theatre

Santa Catalina

Carmen de San Jose

SAN MARCOS

Museo de la Ciudad

PLAZA SANTO DOMINGO

Iglesia Santo Domingo

San Marcos

LA TOLA

PLAZA SANTO DOMINGO

MANOSALVAS

SAN SEBASTIAN

Plaza M. Saenz

CUMANDÁ

LA LOMA

Ⓔ Ecovía
Ⓣ Trole

Bus Terminal

LA RECOLETA

EATING & DRINKING
El Búho	3
Caféto	5
Las Cuevas de Luis Cardela	1
Frutería Monserrate	7
La Guaragua	6
Pedro y Pablo	2
Tianguez	4

ACCOMMODATION
Auca Continental	F
Catedral	A
Hostal Sucre	E
Plaza del Teatro	B
La Real Audiencia	H
San Francisco de Quito	G
Secret Garden	C
Vienna Hotel Internacional	D

0   200 m

Virgin of Quito, El Panecillo, Cementerio de San Diego & Monasterio San Diego ◄   La Cima de la Libertad ◄

ECUADOR

QUITO

▼ Train Station

a memorial to conservative president Gabriel García Moreno.

On the corner of García Moreno and Espejo is the **Centro Cultural Metropolitano**, with regular exhibitions and performances in its impressive courtyard. The centre also houses the **Museo Alberto Mena Caamaño** (Tues–Sun 9am–4.30pm; $1.50), which has waxwork depictions of Quito life from 1700 to 1830, including the battles for independence.

Walk half a block south from Plaza Grande along Calle García Moreno to reach Quito's most extravagant church, **La Compañía de Jesús** (Mon–Fri 9.30am–5.30pm, Sat 9.30am–4.30pm; $2), built by Jesuits in the seventeenth and eighteenth centuries. It took 163 years to construct, with seven tons of gold to cover the interior from top to bottom. Although it's an extraordinary achievement, it borders on opulence gone mad.

Continue south down García Moreno to reach the **Museo de la Ciudad** (Tues–Sun 9.30am–5.30pm; $2). If you can navigate the somewhat confusing layout, it's a rewarding experience, depicting life in Quito through the centuries in a series of scale models.

Plaza San Francisco

From La Compañía head northwest to reach Plaza San Francisco, one of Ecuador's most beautiful squares. The sixteenth-century **Iglesia de San Francisco** is Quito's oldest church and its twin bell tower is one of the city's most famous sights. At the time of writing the altar of the church was being restored, but the rest of the interior is visible. Behind the impressive facade of the church and monastery on the northwest side is the largest religious complex in South America. The **Museo de San Francisco** (Mon–Sat 9am–1pm & 2–6pm, Sun 9am–noon; $2) is housed among the cloisters of the complex and has an impressive collection of religious sculptures, paintings and furniture. Through the museum, you can enter the choral room of the church with a statue of the "dancing virgin" and depictions of planets revolving around the sun on the ceiling.

Plaza Santo Domingo and La Ronda

Walk east along Simón Bolívar down to Quito's third impressive square, Plaza Santo Domingo, dominated by the sixteenth-century **Iglesia Santo Domingo**. Walk further down Guayaquil to reach the narrow alley of **La Ronda**, one of Quito's oldest streets. This working-class neighbourhood has been completely renovated; the result is a pleasant walkway of tiny art galleries, bakeries and traditional cafés.

El Panecillo

Old Quito's skyline is dominated by the 40m-high statue of **the Virgin of Quito**, high up on the hill known as El Panecillo ("little bread loaf") to the southwest. It's not safe to walk up the hill so take a taxi (about $3 single from the Old Town or $8 return including waiting time). There are regular buses at weekends between El Panecillo and Mitad del Mundo. From the top, the view over the city is spectacular and the close-up of the statue with a chained dragon at her feet is equally impressive. Although she's nicknamed "la Bailarina" (the dancing virgin), she's actually preparing to take flight. You can climb up the statue for $1.

Basílica del Voto Nacional

Walk uphill northeast on Calle Venezuela from Plaza Grande to admire the gothic grandeur of the **Basílica del Voto Nacional** (open daily 9am–5pm; $2). Construction has taken place over the past century, beginning in 1892. Instead of gargoyles, the church has iguanas and Galápagos tortoises protruding from its sides. Climbing the steep stairs and ladders up the 74m-high towers is an unnerving experience, so take the lift if you're afraid of heights. The views across the city are fantastic.

La Casa de La Cultura

Next to the Parque El Ejido, the large oval building of **La Casa de la Cultura** (Patria between 6 de Diciembre and 12 de Octubre ☎02/222-3392, ⓦwww.cce .org.ec) has the appearance of a convention centre. Within the complex are cinemas, theatres, auditoriums and, of most interest to tourists, the **Museo del Banco Central** (Tues–Fri 9am–5pm, Sat & Sun 10am–4pm; $2). This is arguably Ecuador's best museum, with an astonishing collection of pre-Columbian ceramics and artefacts as well as colonial, republican and modern art. The museum is divided into four rooms:

archeology, colonial art, contemporary art and the Gold Room, which displays the majestic Inca sun-mask, the symbol of the Banco Central.

Museo Fundación Guayasamín and the Capilla del Hombre

Oswaldo Guayasamín is Ecuador's most famous contemporary artist and Quito's Bellavista district, where he used to reside, houses two collections of his art. The **Museo Fundación Guayasamín** (Jose Bosmediano 543, Mon–Fri 10am–5.30pm, closed weekends; $3; ⓦwww.guayasamin.org) has a large collection of the artist's work as well as his enormous collection of pre-Columbian ceramics and colonial religious art. A further ten-minute walk up the hill is the far more impressive **Capilla del Hombre** or "Chapel of Man" (Tues–Sun 10am–5pm; $3, or $2 with museum entrance ticket). This is one of South America's most important works of art. This was Guayasamín's last great project, initiated in his last years and not fully completed until after his death in 1999. From the museum you can walk up to the garden of Guayasamín and see where his ashes are buried under the "Tree of Life". Just up from the Capilla del Hombre is the **Parque Metropolitano**, Quito's largest park, with forested trails, picnic areas and sweeping views. There are occasional buses up to Bellavista but it's best to take a taxi ($2).

Parque Carolina

The best place to relax in Quito's New Town is **Parque Carolina**. This is where locals come to walk, play sports and eat from the food stalls. The park contains a beautiful set of **Botanical Gardens** (Tues–Sun 9am–5pm; $3.50), which showcases Ecuador's biodiversity with a vast array of plants and trees, including more than five hundred orchid species in greenhouses. Next door, the **Museo de Ciencias Naturales** (8.30am–4.30pm Mon–Fri; $2) has a huge collection of dead insects and arachnids. The park also contains **The Vivarium** (Tues–Sun 9.30am–5.30pm; $2.50) with more than forty species of reptiles including caimans, frogs, turtles and snakes. The highlights are the six-metre-long python and the boa constrictor which you are invited to hold while you/your have photo taken ($3).

The Teleférico

Quito's most dizzying tourist attraction is the **Teleférico** (Sun–Thurs 9.45am–9pm, Fri–Sat 9am–9pm; $4 or $7 express line), a cable-car ride high above the city. There's a rather tacky theme park with discos, bars and handicraft stores at the entrance but the main attraction is the 15-minute ride up to a height of 4100m, from where the views are spectacular on a clear day. At the top, take in the views, relax in the café or tackle the half-hour hike to Ruca Pichincha, 3km away, but do not attempt this walk alone, as robberies have been reported. Bring warm clothes and take care not to overexert yourself at this altitude if you've just arrived in Quito. It can get very busy on weekends so come early. Teleférico shuttles run from Rio Coca y 6 Diciembre (Ecovía) and Estación Norte (Trole).

Arrival

Air Aeropuerto Internacional Mariscal Sucre (☎02/294-4900, ⓦwww.quiport.com), serving national and international flights, is 6km north of the New Town. The airport has a casa de cambio in the international terminal and several ATMs outside. Taxis outside the arrivals gate charge $3–4 to the New Town (about $1 more at night), or you can pay a $6 fixed fare at the taxi desk in the airport just beyond customs. For public buses to the New Town, walk to Av. 10 de Agosto, about 150m from the terminal entrance, from where regular buses travel on Amazonas to the Mariscal hotel district. Note that at the time of writing a new airport is under construction 25km east of the city, which will considerably lengthen transport to and from Quito.

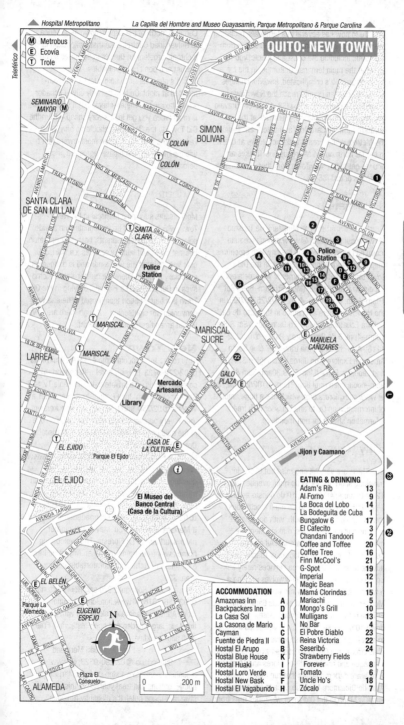

QUITO: NEW TOWN

M Metrobus
E Ecovía
T Trole

EATING & DRINKING

Adam's Rib	13
Al Forno	9
La Boca del Lobo	14
La Bodeguita de Cuba	1
Bungalow 6	17
El Cafecito	3
Chandani Tandoori	2
Coffee and Toffee	20
Coffee Tree	16
Finn McCool's	21
G-Spot	19
Imperial	12
Magic Bean	11
Mamá Clorindas	15
Mariachi	5
Mongo's Grill	10
Mulligans	13
No Bar	4
El Pobre Diablo	23
Reina Victoria	22
Seseribó	24
Strawberry Fields Forever	8
Tomato	6
Uncle Ho's	18
Zócalo	7

ACCOMMODATION

Amazonas Inn	A
Backpackers Inn	D
La Casa Sol	J
La Casona de Mario	L
Cayman	C
Fuente de Piedra II	G
Hostal El Arupo	B
Hostal Blue House	K
Hostal Huaki	I
Hostal Loro Verde	E
Hostal New Bask	F
Hostal El Vagabundo	H

0   200 m

Bus Quito now has several bus terminals, replacing the old Cumandá station. For all destinations from the south, including the coast and jungle, you arrive at the main terminal, Quitumbe, in the far south of Quito. It's complicated, involves changes and takes over an hour to reach the New Town by trolleybus, so consider a taxi ($8–10). From Otavalo and the northern highlands, you arrive at the northern terminal Carcelén, at the northern end of the Metrobus line. From Mindo, you arrive at Ofelia in the far north on the Metrobus line. It takes an hour to get to the New Town from these stations by Metrobus or taxi ($5–7).

Information

Tourist information The Ministerio de Turismo (ⓦ www.quito.com.ec, ⓦ www.experiencequito .com) has several offices in the city with brochures, maps and information on Ecuador. In the Old Town the office is at the corner of Venezuela and Espejo on Plaza Grande (Mon–Fri 9am–8pm, Sat 10am–8pm, Sun 10am–4pm, ☎02/257-0786). In the New Town there's an office in the Casa de La Cultura Ecuatoriana (Mon–Fri 9am–5pm, Sat & Sun 10am–4pm, 6 de Diciembre y Patria, ☎02/222-1116). Also check out the travellers' club South American Explorers on Jorge Washington 311 and Leonidas Plaza (Mon–Fri 9.30am–5pm & Sat 9am–noon, open until 8pm Thurs; ☎02/222-5228, ⓦ www.saexplorers.org), which has a huge amount of information on Quito and Ecuador with free information sheets for non-members.

City transport

Bus These are very hit and miss but useful for travelling short distances up main avenues such as 12 de Octubre, Amazonas, 10 de Agosto and Colón. Electric bus There are three main electric bus routes running north to south, with designated stations and car-free lanes, making them the most efficient way to get around. All charge $0.25 flat fare (bought at kiosks or machines in advance). Note that the three services rarely link up, so changing routes often involves walking a few blocks. They generally run every ten minutes Mon–Fri 6am–midnight, weekends 6am–10pm. El Trole is the modern trolleybus system that runs down 10 de Agosto to the Old Town; stops are easy to spot because of their distinctive green raised platforms. In the Old Town buses travel south along Guayaquil and return north on Flores and Montufar. Ecovía are dark red buses that run mainly along Av. 6 de Diciembre from Río Coca in the north to Plaza la Marín in the Old Town. Metrobus runs from Carcelén, north of the airport, down Av. América to Universidad Central. Note that pickpocketing is a chronic problem on Quito's trolleybuses so be vigilant and don't carry valuables.

Taxi It's often easier to take a taxi and recommended at night. Quito is the only city in Ecuador where taxis use a meter–check that it's the meter is reset when you get in. It's very cheap – from the Old Town to the New Town should be only $2–3. Fares increase at night, when most drivers don't use the meter (in which case, agree the price beforehand).

Accommodation

Most visitors stay in La Mariscal in the New Town, which is geared up for tourists with a wide selection of hotels, restaurants, bars, tour operators, internet cafés and laundry services. La Mariscal gets very noisy at the weekends and is dangerous, especially at night. There are quieter, safer alternatives in Guapulo and La Floresta. Staying in the Old Town is a better option than it used to be and very convenient for sightseeing – though there are fewer tourist amenities, especially at night.

New Town

Amazonas Inn Joaquín Pinto 471 y Av. Amazonas ☎02/222-5723. Friendly hotel with comfortable if compact rooms with private bath and cable TV. $26.

Backpackers Inn Juan Rodríguez 245 and Reina Victoria ☎02/250-9669, ⓦ www.backpackersinn .net. A very popular budget option situated on one of the quieter, more pleasant streets in Mariscal. Dorms $8, rooms $16.

La Casa Sol Calama 127 ☎02/223-0798, ⓦ www .lacasasol.com. Cosy, quiet, brightly coloured guesthouse with comfortable rooms set around an attractive courtyard. Breakfast included. $68.

La Casona de Mario Andalucia 213 y Galicia ☎02/254-4036, ⓦ www.casonademario.com. If Mariscal is not for you, stay in the quieter neighbourhood of La Floresta. This welcoming home away from home run by an Argentine has a communal kitchen and comfortable lounge area. $20.

Cayman Juan Rodríguez 270 and Reina Victoria ☎02/256-7616, ⓦ www.hotelcaymanquito .com. Attractive renovated old house with a huge fireplace, large garden and good restaurant. Free wi-fi and breakfast. $53.

Fuente de Piedra II Juan Mera and Baquedano ☎02/290-0323, ⓦ www .ecuahotel.com. Take a step up from Mariscal's budget options and treat yourself at this colonial-style mid-range hotel. It's elegantly furnished and has attentive service, wi-fi and a gourmet restaurant (breakfast is included). A sister hotel is in Tamayo and Wilson. $56.

Hostal El Arupo Juan Rodriguez E7-22 y Reina Victoria ☎ 02/255-7543, ⊛ www.hostalelarupo .com. An attractive renovated house with TV room, free internet and colourful rooms. Breakfast included. $40.

Hostal Blue House Pinto and Diego de Almagro ☎ 02/222-3480, ⊛ www.bluehousequito.com. Very popular new backpacker hostel with a kitchen, bar, free internet and breakfast included. Dorms $8, rooms $30.

Hostal Huauki Joaquín Pinto E7-82 y Diego Almagro ☎ 09/811-2270, ⊛ www.hostalhuauki .com. A converted 1940s residence with comfortable rooms and a very good Japanese sushi restaurant. Dorms $6, rooms $20.

Hostal Loro Verde Juan Rodriguez and Diego de Almagro ☎ 02/222-6173; $30. A hotel as colourful as its name (green parrot) with indigenous artefacts and comfortable rooms.

Hostal New Bask Lizardo Garcia and Diego de Almagro ☎ 08/188-5575. The cheapest, friendliest place in the New Town. A great deal but fills up fast. Dorms $6, rooms $14.

Hostal El Vagabundo Wilson E7-45 ☎ 02/222-6376; $27. A dependable budget option with a friendly atmosphere, small café and table tennis.

Old Town

Auca Continental Sucre OE-414 y Venezuela ☎ 02/255-3953. Clean, no-frills budget option with firm beds, private bath and TV. $20.

Catedral Mejia 638 y Benalcazar ☎ 02/295-5438, ⊛ www.hotelcatedral.ec. Recently upgraded hotel in the heart of the old town with comfortable rooms, cable TV, sauna and steam room. $40.

Hostal Sucre Bolivar and Cuenca ☎ 02/295-4025. The cheapest option in the old town by a long way. Basic, tatty rooms but a friendly atmosphere, lounge area and great views of Plaza San Francisco. Dorms $8.

Plaza del Teatro Guayaquil and Esmeraldas ☎ 02/295-9462. Great value mid-range choice with a plush reception and charming if slightly worn rooms. $24.

La Real Audiencia Bolívar 220 y Guayaquil, ☎ 02/295-0590, ⊛ www.realaudiencia.com. Try this for a more upmarket Old Town option with stylish rooms, black-and-white photography and a fabulous view of Plaza Santo Domingo from the restaurant (open to non-guests). Breakfast included. $55.

San Francisco de Quito Sucre 217 and Guayaquil ☎ 02/228-7758, ⊛ www.sanfranciscodequito.com.

ec. The pick of the Old Town mid-range options with pleasant rooms set around a cosy courtyard, a fountain, rooftop patio and great views. Breakfast included. $47.

🏃 **Secret Garden** Calle Antepara E4-60 y Los Rios, ☎ 09/602-3709, ⊛ www.secretgarden quito.com. Hidden away southeast of the historic centre in a listed building, this is a great Aussie-run budget hostel set on five floors with a rooftop terrace serving big breakfasts. Basic but always bustling with backpackers. There's also a Spanish school and tour operator. Dorms $9, rooms $24.

Vienna Hotel Internacional Flores and Chile ☎ 02/295-4860. A good-quality three-star hotel with well-appointed rooms set around an enclosed courtyard. $40.

Eating

Quito boasts the best selection of international restaurants in Ecuador – from Asian to Middle Eastern and Mediterranean. Most are found in the New Town, with Old Town eating options restricted. For those on a budget, fill yourself up at lunch, as most restaurants offer lunch specials for $2–4.

New Town

Adam's Rib Calama and Reina Victoria. The best place for barbecued meat – ribs, steak, kebabs and even sautéed chicken livers if that floats your boat. Mains $6–8.

Al Forno Moreno and Diego de Almagro. Seek out the biggest choice of perfectly cooked pizzas in town ($5–10) with an incredible fifty different varieties.

La Bodeguita de Cuba Reina Victoria N26-105. Tasty Cuban specialities ($4–5) with live Cuban music on Thurs nights, when drinking and dancing continues well into the early hours.

El Cafecito Luis Cordero 1124, New Town. Cosy café with great coffee, home-made cakes, crêpes and vegetarian meals for around $3–5.

Chandani Tandoori Juan Mera and Luis Cordero. Head here for authentic, spicy Indian food at low prices. Masala, korma, dupiaza, balti and hot vindaloo – all the classics are done well for only $3–5.

Coffee and Toffee Calama y Diego Almagro. Start the day with breakfast or the evening with cocktails, lounging on armchairs and surfing the net in this relaxed café.

Coffee Tree Foch and Reina Victoria. A long-standing café on Plaza Foch, great for people-watching over a coffee or cocktail.

G-Spot Diego de Almagro and Calama. Its name may leave you nonplussed but this fast-food joint

La Boca del Lobo Calama 284 y Reina Victoria, New Town. With a brightly coloured glass-encased patio, flamboyant decor and Mediterranean menu, this is a place to indulge yourself. You'll be amazed at how many ways they cook mushrooms. Mains $8–12.

has cheap, imaginative burgers with trimmings galore ($2–3).

Imperial Juan Rodriguez and Reina Victoria. Eat al fresco in this restaurant's garden terrace. Choose from an imaginative menu of mainly chicken and meat dishes ($5–6) and a great-value set lunch ($2). Simple rooms with bath upstairs for $20.

Magic Bean Foch and Juan Mera. Hugely popular café with a small garden where you can sit out until late. Great breakfasts, pancakes and fresh juices from $3–6.

Mamá Clorindas Reina Victoria 1144. Well-prepared but quite pricey Ecuadorian specialities. Try half a guinea pig (cuy) for $9.

Mariachi Foch and Juan Leon Mera. A good Mexican place – burritos, chimichangas, fajitas, etc, for $5–8, all washed down with cocktails and sangria.

Mongo's Grill Calama. This hugely popular Mongolian barbecue has a great atmosphere, offering sizzling meat and vegetable dishes such as chicken teriyaki and lamb in spicy yogurt, all cooked in front of you. Excellent-value buffets from $4–6.

Tomato Juan León Mera y Calama. A great place for pizza ($5–7) and pasta. The calzone is particularly good.

Uncle Ho's Calama 166-E8-29. Vietnamese restaurant run by a friendly Irish guy who serves up a range of great cocktails, followed by a feast of Asian food – from coconut curry to Imperial rolls and beef noodle soup. Mains $5–7.

Old Town

El Búho Jose Moreno and Espejo. Inside the Centro Cultural Metropolitano, this is a pleasant stop for soups, salads, sandwiches and pasta. $3–6.

Caféto Chile and Guayaquil. Little gem of a café at the entrance to San Agustín Monastery specializing in coffee and hot chocolate served with humitas, tamales, empanadas and cakes for $3–5.

Las Cuevas de Luis Candelas Benalcazar and Chile. One of the best restaurants in the Old Town, snuggled in a cosy basement offering gourmet Ecuadorian and International food. Paella and Fondu Bourguignonne are two specialities. Mains $6–10.

Frutería Montserrate Espejo 0e2-12. The perfect place to take a break from sightseeing with an extravagant helping of fruit salad and ice cream ($2–3). Cheap almuerzos and sandwiches also available.

La Guaragua Espejo 0e2–40. Appealing little restaurant just down from Plaza Grande. Ecuadorian specialities such as seco de pollo (chicken stew) and chuleta (fried pork chops); the great-value set lunches will set you back $2–4.

Pedro y Pablo Chile and Plaza Grande. Just one of the many cafés in a delightful food court hidden in a historic building on Plaza Grande, serving mainly seafood ($4).

Tianguez Plaza de San Francisco. Under the church on the plaza, this is a perfectly situated café in which to take a break from sightseeing. Well-prepared local specialities and indulgent desserts are slightly pricey ($5–8) but worth it.

Drinking and nightlife

Mariscal in the New Town has a vibrant nightlife scene and gets packed on weekends. The most happening area is along José Calama and Foch between avenidas Amazonas, Juan León Mera and Reina Victoria. Bars are busy from 8pm onwards with the clubs filling up towards midnight and things wind down by 3am. Remember to take a taxi at night. Mariscal is dead and feels dangerous on Sundays, when most police take the day off.

Bungalow 6 Calama y Diego Almagro. A mixture of locals and tourists flock to enjoy the great atmosphere and dance to Latin and pop classics in this hugely popular bar/disco (entrance $5 including one drink).

Finn McCool's Pinto 251 y Reina Victoria. The most popular expat pub with draught beer, pool, quiz nights, movie nights and plenty of rock music.

Mulligans Calama and Reina Victoria. Very popular Irish bar with draught beer, football on the big screen and traditional gut-busting food. Guinness is extortionate though, at $12.

No Bar Calama 380. Raucous Mariscal disco with a large dancefloor. It gets very loud and crowded at weekends (entrance $5 including one drink).

El Pobre Diablo Isabel La Católica and Galavis. A Quito institution in La Floresta with a bohemian atmosphere, cocktails, a good restaurant and live music.

La Reina Victoria Reina Victoria 530 and Roca. Seek out this British pub with dart board, open fire and the obligatory fish and chips on the menu. Quiet during the week.

Seseribó Edificio El Girón, Veintimilla and 12 de Octubre. A long-time Quito favourite and the best place to dance salsa and merengue, or just stand back and watch the experts. Thursday nights are particularly good.

Strawberry Fields Forever Calama E5-23. A world away from *No Bar* next door, this tiny rock bar, brimming with Beatles memorabilia, is great to escape the disco craziness.

Zócalo Corner of Reina Victoria and Calama. This Mexican restaurant/bar has live music most nights and is a popular place to start the evening. Tacos and other Mexican dishes are served up alongside cocktails.

Directory

Banks and exchange There are plenty of banks near Av. Amazonas in the New Town but fewer in the Old Town. They are normally open Mon–Fri 8.30am–4pm and Sat mornings. Try Banco de Guayaquil on Reina Victoria and Colón or Banco del Pacífico, on 12 de Octubre y Cordero.

Books The English Bookshop, at Calama and Diego de Almagro, is the best place in Mariscal to pick up fiction and travel books, to buy, sell or borrow.

Car rental Many reputable international companies have offices outside the international terminal of the airport, including Avis (℡02/244-0270) and Hertz (℡02/225-4258).

Embassies and consulates Argentina, Amazonas 21–147 and Roca ℡02/250-1106; Bolivia, Eloy Alfaro 2432 and Fernando Ayarza ℡02/244-6652; Brazil, Amazonas 1429 and Colón, Edificio España ℡02/256-3086; Canada, 6 de Diciembre 2816 and Paul Rivet, Edificio Josueth González ℡02/250-6162; Chile, Juan Pablo Sanz 3617 and Amazonas ℡02/224-9403; Colombia, Colón 1133 and Amazonas, Edificio Arista ℡02/222-2486; Ireland, Antonio de Ulloa 2651 and Rumipamba ℡02/245-1577; Peru, República de El Salvador 495 and Irlanda ℡02/246-8411; UK, Naciones Unidas and República de El Salvador, Edificio Citiplaza, 14th floor ℡02/297-0801, ⓦwww.britembquito.org .ec; US, 12 de Octubre and Patria ℡02/256-2890, ⓦwww.usembassy.org.ec; Venezuela, Cabildo 115 and Quito Tenis ℡02/226-8635.

Hospitals Hospital Metropolitano, Av. Mariana de Jesús and Av. Occidental ℡02/226-1520, emergency and ambulance ℡02/226-5020.

Internet Quito's New Town is full of internet cafés, charging about $0.70–$1 per hour. Friendly, comfortable places include Papaya Net (Calama y JL Mera, ℡02/255-6574) and Sambo.net (JL Mera and J Pinto, ℡02/290-1315).

Police La Policía de Turismo (Reina Victoria and Roca ℡02/254-3983).

Post offices The most convenient office for La Mariscal is on the corner of Reina Victoria and Colón (℡02/250-8890; Mon–Fri 8am–7pm, Sat & Sun 8am–noon).

Shopping Mercado Artesanal (Juan Leon Mera and Jorge Washington, New Town), weekend market at Parque El Ejido, and Mercado Ipiales (Chile and Imbabura, Old Town).

Taxis Reliable 24hr services include Central Radio Taxis (℡02/250-0600) and Teletaxi (℡02/222-2222).

Telephones Andinatel (ⓦwww.andinatel.com) has its main office on Eloy Alfaro near 9 de Octubre and branches around the city. In Mariscal there are offices in JL Mera and Reina Victoria. You can also buy Porta and Bell South phonecards at most larger shops.

Moving on

Air Quito's international airport has regular flights to Europe, North America, Central America and other destinations in South America. (See p.617 for list of airlines).

Bus Go to Quitumbe bus station for destinations south, the coast and the jungle; Carcelén in the north of Quito for Otavalo, Ibarra and Tulcan; Ofelia (also in the north of Quito) for Mindo. All the bus stations are about an hour from Mariscal by metrobus or trolleybus or by taxi, $8–10 so it's easier to book at a private bus company in the New Town. The biggest company is Panamericana (Reina Victoria and Colon, ℡022557-133).

Atacames (8 daily; 6hr); Baños (every 15–30min; 4hr); Cuenca (every 15–30min; 10hr); Guayaquil (every 10–20min; 10hr); Manta (every 30min; 8hr); Puerto Lopez (2 daily; 10hr); Riobamba (every 15min; 4hr).

Train Trains from Quito leave from Chimbacalle station, south of the old town, which can be reached on the trolleybus or via a taxi from Mariscal ($4–5). Advanced booking is advised as the services are very popular. At the moment the train service from Quito only runs to Latacunga (Thurs–Sun at 8am; $10). This service passes through Machachi and Boliche, but there are separate services to each of these towns on weekends (see ⓦwww.ferrocarrilesdelecuador.gob.ec).

DAY-TRIPS FROM QUITO

There are many interesting destinations which can be reached on a day-trip from Quito – Otavalo, Mindo and Cotopaxi are all less than three hours from the city.

ACTIVITIES IN QUITO

After a few days of sightseeing and acclimatization, you will be ready to take advantage of the huge range of activities in the mountains near the city. The most popular one-day tours are cycling and horseriding. For cycling, Cotopaxi National Park and Ilinizas are firm favourites (average cost $65 per day). There are numerous locations south of Quito offering horseriding (average cost $45 per day). For rafting and kayaking, day tours in valleys north and west of Quito cost $70–80. The most popular trekking route is around Lake Quilotoa (see p.644). One- and two-day tours can be booked from Quito. If you fancy climbing, the easier peaks include Pasochoa (4199m), El Corazón (4788m) and the more challenging Iliniza Norte (5126m). All cost $65 for a one-day tour. Cotopaxi (5897m), Cayambe (5790m), Antisana (5755m) and Chimborazo (6310m) are tough and can all be climbed by well prepared, fit people on two-day tours ($175–215).

Tour operators

The following tour operators offer many of the above tours as well as a range of other tours throughout Ecuador:

Alta Montaña Jorge Washington 8–20 ☏ 02/252-4422. Climbing and trekking.

Biking Dutchman Foch 714 and Juan León Mera ☏ 02/256-8323, ⊛ www.biking-dutchman.com. Mountain-biking tours.

Ecuadorian Alpine Institute Ramírez Dávalos 136 and Amazonas ☏ 02/256-5465, ⊛ www.volcanoclimbing.com. Top-class climbing tours.

Enchanted Expeditions De las Alondras N45-102 y Los Lirios ☏ 02/334-0525, ⊛ www.galapagosenchantedexpeditions.com. Wide range of tours. Specialists in Galápagos yachts and haciendas in the highlands.

Gulliver JL Mera and Calama ☏ 02/252-9297, ⊛ www.gulliver.com.ec. Popular Mariscal operator with climbing, hiking, biking and jungle tours as well as Galápagos visits.

Sierra Nevada Expeditions J Pinto and Cordero E4-150 ☏ 02/255-3658, ⊛ www.hotelsierranevada.com. Climbing and river-rafting specialist.

Yacu Amu Foch 746 and Juan León Mera ☏ 02/290-4054, ⊛ www.yacuamu.com. White-water rafting and kayaking specialist.

Mitad del Mundo

The most popular day-trip is the **Mitad del Mundo** tourist complex ("The Middle of the World"; 9am–6pm daily; $2) on the Equator, 22km north of Quito. The centrepiece is the 30m-high **monument** ($3 to go inside), topped by a brass globe. Climb to the top and then descend the stairs through the **Ethnographic Museum,** which has fascinating displays of Ecuador's richly varied indigenous populations. There are various other small exhibitions dotted around the complex and the **plaza** is a pleasant place to relax and have lunch, with music and dance at weekends. Although everybody wants to get a photo of themselves straddling the Equator in front of the monument, this is not actually the real Equator, which lies approximately 300m along

the main road to the east at the **Museo Solar Inti Ñan** (9.30am–5.30pm; $3). This is definitely worth visiting, particularly to see the fun experiments to prove you are standing on the Equator – such as water rushing down a plug in the opposite direction on either side. There's an interesting exhibition of indigenous housing and, bizarrely, a step-by-step guide on how to make a shrunken head. To get to Mitad del Mundo, take the Metrobus north to Cotocollao and then a green Mitad del Mundo **bus** ($0.50). The trip takes an hour.

Papallacta

About 65km (two hours) from Quito, the road leading to Lago Agrio and Tena passes through the town of **Papallacta**, home to probably the best thermal baths in Ecuador. The entrance to

Las Termas de Papallacta (7am–10pm, $7) is a 20-minute walk up a dirt road, so consider taking a taxi. The complex is very impressive, with 25 baths of different temperatures up to a scalding 60 degrees (you can cool off with an exhilarating plunge in the river nearby). On clear days there are great views over the town and snowcapped Volcán Artisana. Note that at 3300m it gets very cold, so bring warm clothes.

Termas de Papallacta (☎02/250-4787, ⓦwww.termaspapallacta.com; from $110), a spa hotel next to the complex, is a luxurious option to stay the night, with spacious rooms and cabins, a private jacuzzi and free use of the baths. A great budget option in town is the *Choza de Don Wilson* (☎06/232-0627; $24 including breakfast), which has decent rooms, great views and a good restaurant serving a $4 set menu. Trout is a speciality.

The Northern Highlands and Western Andean slopes

To the north of Quito lie two dramatically different regions. To the northwest are verdant **cloudforests**, teeming with birdlife. The small town of **Mindo** is the best base to explore the forest's huge biodiversity and indulge in adrenalin-pumping adventure sports. To the northeast, magnificent Andean scenery populated by proud indigenous cultures extends to the Colombian border. Passing the snow-capped **Volcán Cayambe**, the most popular destination is **Otavalo**, whose colourful Saturday market is one of the largest in South America and heaven for lovers of

indigenous crafts and clothing. Some 30km north are the stately squares of La Ciudad Blanca, **Ibarra**, the largest city in the region and an important transport hub. North of Ibarra is the road less travelled, mainly visited by those crossing into Colombia via **Tulcán**.

MINDO

Snuggled in a cloudforest at a pleasant elevation of 1200m, **MINDO** is a truly idyllic destination. Whether you want to watch for some of the four hundred species of birds and 250 species of butterfly, swing above the forest canopy on zip-lines, plunge down the rivers on rubber tubes or simply gaze at the wonderful waterfalls, there's something for everyone here. The cool climate means that this is a far more comfortable region to explore pristine forest than the Oriente. Tourism has developed relatively slowly in Mindo so you can usually avoid the crowds in this endearingly sleepy town, although weekends get busy with day-trippers.

Mariposas de Mindo

The town is surrounded by the Bosque Protector Mindo-Nambillo cloudforest but most of the accessible areas are due south. The dirt road leading out of town forks after about 1km. To the left is the butterfly farm **Mariposas de Mindo** (9am–6.30pm; $3, ⓦwww.mariposasdemindo.com), which breeds 25 species, including the Brown Owl Eye and the Peleides Blue Morpho, the latter with a wingspan of 20cm. The guide shows the lifecycle from eggs to caterpillars, pupae to butterfly. Come in the early morning and you may be lucky enough to see them hatch.

Mindo Canopy Adventure

Take a right where the road forks and this will lead you to **Mindo Canopy Adventure** (☎08/542-8758; $15, ⓦwww.mindocanopy.com,). Adrenalin lovers

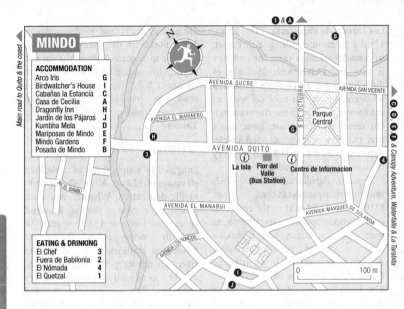

MINDO

ACCOMMODATION

Arco Iris	G
Birdwatcher's House	I
Cabañas la Estancía	C
Casa de Cecilia	A
Dragonfly Inn	H
Jardín de los Pájaros	J
Kumbha Mela	D
Mariposas de Mindo	E
Mindo Gardens	F
Posada de Mindo	B

EATING & DRINKING

El Chef	3
Fuera de Babilonia	2
El Nómada	4
El Quetzal	1

Main road to Quito & the coast

& Canopy Adventure, Waterfalls & La Tarabita

AVENIDA SUCRE
AVENIDA SAN VICENTE
AVENIDA EL WARINERO
9 DE OCTUBRE
Parque Central
AVENIDA QUITO
La Isla Flor del Valle (Bus Station) Centro de Informacíon
AV EL BANIU
AVENIDA EL MANARUI
AVENIDA MARQUES DE SOLANDA
AVENIDA LOS YUNCOS

0   100 m

can get their fix by zinging along cables from 20m to 400m in length, high above the forest. Go solo or be accompanied by a guide. It's great fun – the lines and harnesses are designed and tested by experts so they're very safe.

About 1km up the hill is a more relaxed way to travel across the treetops. **La Tarabita** cable car cruises 150m above a river basin. On the other side are trails leading to seven waterfalls. The paths are confusing in places but you can't really get lost as there is only one exit. The entire circuit takes two hours and is muddy so bring boots, but it's worth it to get deep inside the cloudforest. Hire a guide for $25 per day to gain a better insight. Guides with specialist bird knowledge cost $35 per day.

Tubing and canyoning

For adventure-sports lovers, there's plenty to keep you occupied in Mindo. As an unusual alternative to rafting you can tumble down the river rapids in an inflatable **tube** ($5 for a couple of hours including transport). **Canyoning** is also available ($10 for a half-day). Recommended tour operators, who

can organize all of the above, include La Isla Mindo (☎02/217-0481, ⓦwww .laislamindo.com) and Mindo Bird (☎09/735-1297, ⓦwww.mindobirds .com.ec), both on the main Avenida Quito. Most of the attractions listed above are a 1–2hr walk away from town. To save time you can share a taxi for $5–10.

Arrival

Bus From Quito's Ofelia bus station, Cooperativa Flor de Valle (☎02/252-7495) goes to Mindo at 8am and 3.45pm Mon–Fri, returning at 6am and 2pm. There are more regular services at weekends. Tickets cost $2.50 and the journey takes just under two hours. There is no official tourist office, so stop by Mindo Bird or La Isla Mindo for information (see above).
Taxi From Quito's New Town this should cost $5–7.

Accommodation

Mindo has a wide selection of accommodation and while it has some good hotels, it's a more enjoyable and authentic experience to stay in one of the lodges on the edge of town, surrounded by cloudforest. There's also a good selection of cabins south towards the waterfalls and Tarabita.

Arco Iris Quito and 9 de Octubre ☎ 02/390-0405. A dependable option in town, with comfortable rooms and a central location on the main square. $18.

Birdwatcher's House Los Colibres ☎ 02/217-0204; ⊛ www.birdwatchershouse.com. On the western edge of town, this homely place has stunning photography in the rooms, hummingbirds in the gardens and an outdoor jacuzzi. $30.

Cabañas la Estancia ☎ 098/783-272; ⊛ www.mindohosterialaestancia.com. Cross the rickety bridge to these spacious cabins, set in landscaped gardens with outdoor restaurant, a swimming pool and even a waterslide. $36, camping from $3.

Casa de Cecilia End of 9 de Octubre ☎ 0933/45393. On the eastern edge of town, these great value rustic cabins stand on the banks of a roaring river. $10.

Dragonfly Inn Quito and Sucre ☎ 02/217-0426, ⊛ www.dragonflyinn-mindo.com. This wooden cabin-style hotel is one of the best options in town, with balconies overlooking a garden patio along the river and a very good restaurant. $43.

Jardin de los Pájaros Los Colibres ☎ 0917/56688. Well-presented hotel with carpeted rooms, and a balcony lounge with hammocks and outdoor swimming pool. $26.

Kumbha Mela ☎ 094/051-675; $42. Deep in the forest with a selection of cabins and rooms nestled in extensive gardens. There's a good restaurant, swimming pool and even a private lagoon. Dorms $16, rooms $42.

Mariposas de Mindo ☎ 02/224-2712, ⊛ www.mariposasdemindo.com. Pleasant cabins 2km from town near the butterfly farm (entrance included in price, as well as breakfast). $58.

Mindo Gardens ☎ 09/733-1092, ⊛ www.mindogardens.com. One of Mindo's most popular mid-range hotels, 1km past the butterfly farm and set in a private reserve of forest and waterfalls. Brightly coloured cabins sit beside the river and there's a comfortable lounge and games area. Breakfast included. $65.

Posada de Mindo End of Vicente Aguirre ☎ 02/217-0199. One of the most comfortable options in town, these new spotless cabins have a good restaurant attached. $40.

Eating and drinking

There are plenty of restaurants on the main street in the centre of town offering Ecuadorian standards for around $5. Many of the lodges out of town listed above also have good restaurants attached. Most restaurants are open noon–2pm for lunch and 6–10pm for dinner, often staying open all day at weekends. Mindo has very little nightlife so it's a case of having a few beers in a restaurant after dinner.

El Chef Quito. One of the best restaurants in town and usually full at lunchtime. The set lunch ($2.50) is outstanding value. To treat yourself, try the speciality *lomo a la piedra* (barbecued steak). Mains $5–8.

Fuera de Babilonia 9 de Octubre. An alternative bar with assorted Indian artefacts on the walls, misshapen tables, a wide-ranging menu (dishes $4–7) and live music at weekends.

El Nómada Quito. On the eastern edge of town, this is the best place to fill up on carefully prepared pizza and pasta dishes, from $6–10.

El Quetzal 9 de Octubre. Head to this new restaurant for organic specialities, big breakfasts, fresh juices and tasty snacks. Mains $6–8.

OTAVALO

If you love wandering around markets and picking up *artesano* bargains, then **OTAVALO** is your town. The famous **Saturday market** (from 7am) is easily the best in Ecuador and possibly in South America, spreading out across town from the Plaza de Ponchos. Here you can find a wide range of handicrafts, clothing, hammocks, weavings, carvings, jewellery, ceramics and even oddities such as fake shrunken heads. The *Otavaleño* traders are very friendly and will greet you as "amigo"; behind the smiles, they're savvy salespeople and foreigners are habitually offered inflated prices. Take your time gauging the prices and then knock them down by a few dollars, but bear in mind that while this is all part of the fun, the extra dollar means more to the locals than it does to you.

During the week the town is quieter but the market is still open. Apart from shopping, soaking up the atmosphere of a vibrant indigenous culture is another key attraction of Otavalo. Outside the market, the **Museo de Tejidos el Obraje** (Mon–Sat 9am–1pm and 3–5pm, $2) is worth a visit for its demonstrations of textile production. Otavalo's surroundings are also impressive – the town is nestled between the extinct volcanic peaks of Imbabura

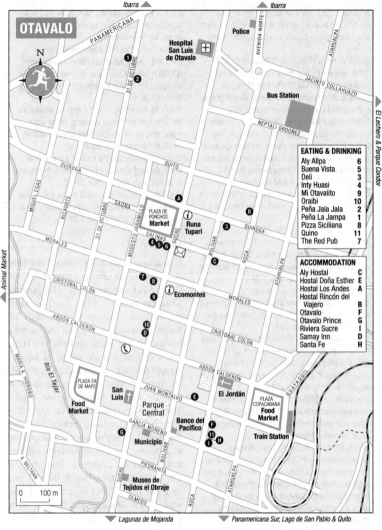

OTAVALO

Ibarra

Ibarra

Police

PANAMERICANA

31 DE OCTUBRE

Hospital
San Luis
de Otavalo

AVENIDA NORTE

ATAHUALPA

JACINTO COLLAHUAZO

Bus Station

NEPTALI ORDONEZ

El Lechero & Parque Condor

QUITO

QUIROGA

MIGUEL EGAS

BOLÍVAR

RICAURTE

SADNA

31 DE OCTUBRE

MODESTO JARAMILLO

SALINAS

SUCRE

PLAZA DE
PONCHOS
Market

Runa
Tupari

QUIROGA

ROCA

ATAHUALPA

MORALES

CRISTÓBAL COLÓN

Ecomontes

MORALES

ABDÓN CALDERÓN

CRISTÓBAL COLÓN

MARÍA A. HIDROBO

Río El Tejar

ABDÓN CALDERÓN

PLAZA 24
DE MAYO

Food
Market

San
Luis

JUAN MONTALVO

Parque
Central

El Jordán

PLAZA
COPACABANA
Food
Market

GUAYAQUIL

GARCÍA MORENO

Banco del
Pacífico

Train Station

A. BELTRAN

Municipio

BOLÍVAR

PIEDRAHITA

SUCRE

Museo de
Tejidos el Obraje

ATAHUALPA

ROCA

OLMEDO

0   100 m

Lagunas de Mojanda

Panamericana Sur, Lago de San Pablo & Quito

EATING & DRINKING

Aly Allpa	6
Buena Vista	5
Deli	3
Inty Huasi	4
Mi Otavalito	9
Oraibi	10
Peña Jala Jala	2
Peña La Jampa	1
Pizza Siciliana	8
Quino	11
The Red Pub	7

ACCOMMODATION

Aly Hostal	C
Hostal Doña Esther	E
Hostal Los Andes	A
Hostal Rincón del Viajero	B
Otavalo	F
Otavalo Prince	G
Riviera Sucre	I
Samay Inn	D
Santa Fe	H

ECUADOR

THE NORTHERN HIGHLANDS AND WESTERN ANDEAN SLOPES

Animal Market

and Cotacachi, looming on opposite ends of town. Some 4km out of town is the **Parque Condor** (☎02/292-4429, ⍟www.parquecondor.org; $2.50, 9.30am–5pm Tues–Sun), which rehabilitates owls, eagles, falcons and – you guessed it – condors. On the way to the park is **El Lechero**, a tree revered by locals for its healing powers, so named because of the milky liquid found in its leaves. It makes for a pleasant walk for views over

Otavalo. Start the walk from the south end of town along Piedrahita and follow the signs past a eucalyptus grove and up a hill. Note that robberies have been reported on this route so consider taking a taxi ($2–3).

The town's biggest festival is **La Fiesta del Yamor** in the first week of September, which celebrates the corn harvest with processions, a beauty contest and boisterous revelry.

Arrival and information

Bus Buses to Otavalo leave Quito's new Carcelén terminal several times per hour (1hr 50min). There are also regular services from Ibarra (35min). The bus station is on Atahualpa and Neptalí Ordoñez, a couple of blocks northeast of the central Plaza de Ponchos market.

Tourist information For information and maps, try the Cámara de Turismo office (Quiroga y Modesto Jaramillo, ☎06/292-7230; Mon–Fri 8.30am–12.30pm & 2–5.30pm).

City transport

Otavalo is small and compact enough to walk around but a taxi across town costs just $1 and is recommended at night.

Accommodation

Otavalo has a lot of hotels for such a small town, most of which are empty during the week but fill up at weekends (it's recommended to book ahead for Friday or Saturday night). The area near the market can be noisy and the best hotels are found in the south part of town.

Aly Hostal Bolivar and Salinas ☎06/292-1831. Slick business-like exterior but inside there are cheap, basic rooms. $16.

Hostal Doña Esther Montalvo 4-44, ☎06/292-0739, ⓦwww.otavalohotel.com. Owned by a Dutch family, this small colonial-style hotel has friendly service, a verdant courtyard and a great restaurant with Mediterranean specialities. $36.

Hostal Los Andes Roca and Juan Montalvo ☎06/292-1057. One of the cheapest options in

SPORTS AND ACTIVITIES AROUND OTAVALO

Otavalo is surrounded by stunning scenery that can be explored independently or on guided tours organized from town. While most travellers only come to Otavalo for a day or two, you could easily fill a week exploring the surrounding mountains and valleys, trying out various adventure sports and activities.

The nearest attraction is the Laguna de San Pablo, 15min from town by bus from the terminal (take any bus heading to Araque). You can hike around the lake, visit small indigenous communities or arrange some watersports on site. It's very popular with locals at weekends.

Of the many indigenous communities near Otavalo, the best known is Peguche, a 5-min journey by bus (Coop Imbaburapac at the terminal does this route). The town is famed for its weavers and musicians, and for a 20m-high waterfall. Peguche, the waterfall and surrounding communities can be visited on a tour ($35) with Runa Tupari (☎06/292-5985, ⓦwww.runatupari.com).

Further afield are the three Lagunas de Mojanda, considered sacred by many locals. There are trails around the lakes and up to the peak of Fuya Fuya (4275m), which is good practice for climbing higher peaks. Another popular trip is the stunning Laguna Cuicocha, a 3km-wide extinct volcanic crater lake with steep forested islands in the middle. It sits at the foot of Cotacachi Volcano and can be reached by taxi from Cotacachi (a 30-min bus ride from the Otavalo terminal). Tours to Mojanda and Cuicocha can be organized with tour operators in Otavalo for $25. Hiking or cycling tours cost $30–40.

The valleys and rivers around Otavalo offer great adventure-sports opportunities. Canyoning is possible in Peguche and in Taxopamba ($30–35). There is class 3–4 white-water rafting in Río Chota, Río Mira and Río Intag ($30). The best mountain-biking tour descends into the Intag Valley to the west ($50).

For those who are well acclimatized and fit, the mountains around Otavalo offer unforgettable climbing. Imbabura (4690m, $60) is the easiest climb, Cotacachi (4944m, $80) has technical climbing at the summit, and Cayambe (5789m, $190) is Ecuador's third-highest peak and takes a minimum of two days.

Most of the hiking, rafting and adventure-sports tours listed above can be booked with local tour operators Ecomontes (Sucre and Morales ☎6/292-6244, ⓦwww.ecomontestour.com) or Runa Tupari (Plaza de Ponchos ☎6/292-2320, ⓦwww.runatupari.com).

town, overlooking the market. Great view but the simple rooms can be noisy. $15.

Hostal Rincón del Viajero Roca 11-07 ☎06/292-1741. This is a hospitable option for budget travellers, with artwork on the walls, a TV lounge with fireplace, rooftop terrace with hammocks, games room and restaurant. Includes breakfast. $25.

Otavalo Roca and Juan Montalvo ☎06/292-3712. Quiet, colonial-style hotel with a spacious peach-coloured interior and immaculate rooms for a great price. $36.

Otavalo Prince Sucre and Garcia Moreno ☎06/292-3200. Extravagant exterior but cosy interior with low ceilings. The low prices mean this place fills up fast. $18.

Riviera Sucre Roca and Garcia Moreno, ☎06/292-0241, ⊛www.rivierasucre.com. Relaxing lounge area, beautiful garden and colourful, comfortable rooms. $26.

Samay Inn Sucre and Colon ☎06/292-1826. One of the best options in the centre with hot water, firm beds, cable TV, small balconies and a family atmosphere. $20.

🏃 **Santa Fe** Roca and Garcia Moreno ☎06/292-3640, ⊛www.hotelsantafe otavalo.com. The quiet location, excellent-quality rooms furnished in pine and eucalyptus, good restaurant and reasonable prices make this one of the best deals in town. $26.

Eating

Aly Allpa Plaza de Ponchos and Salinas. Endearing little café with great value Ecuadorian meals and fresh lemonade. Three-course set lunch $4.

Buena Vista Plaza de Ponchos and Salinas. From the balcony you can observe the market from afar and choose from a wide-ranging menu. The brownies are a speciality.

🏃 **Deli** Corner of Quiroga and Bolivar. Little gem of a café a block from the market specializing in Tex Mex and Italian (main dishes $4–8). Also crepes, desserts and delicious hot chocolate with marshmallows.

Inty Huasi Plaza de Ponchos and Salinas. Locals head to this well laid-out, large restaurant to fill up on meat and seafood dishes priced around $5–7.

Mi Otavalito Sucre near Morales. The best place in town to enjoy well-presented Ecuadorian dishes ($5–7) in an elegant but cosy setting. Live Andean music at weekends.

Oraibi Sucre and Colon. Enjoy veggie specialities – soups, salads, pasta and pizza for $3–5 – in a leafy garden setting.

Pizza Siciliana Morales and Sucre Out of all the pizza places in town, this has the best reputation with a rustic atmosphere and roaring fire. Pizzas $5–10.

Quino Roca near García Moreno. If you're craving seafood, try the *ceviche* and fresh mountain trout here. Juices, cocktails and mulled wines are also worth a try. Mains $5–8.

Drinking and nightlife

Peña Jala Jala 31 de Octubre. Head north of the centre to catch live music and dance the night away to a mix of local and international tunes.

Peña La Jampa 31 de Octubre. Three blocks north of the market, this is another great place to catch energetic live performances from traditional Andean bands.

The Red Pub Morales and Jaramillo. English-style pub with plenty of beer, rock music and live bands at weekends.

IBARRA

Half an hour by bus northeast of Otavalo lies **IBARRA**, the largest town in the northern highlands, known as La Ciudad Blanca (white city). Ibarra's status as the region's commercial hub means it's less of a draw for tourists but it does have some beautiful squares and a fantastic ice-cream store.

What to see and do

Parque La Merced is impressive, fronted by the nineteenth-century Basilica La Merced, but eclipsed in terms of beauty by **Parque Pedro Moncayo**, dominated by the Baroque-influenced **cathedral** adorned with a golden altar. The **Museo Banco Central** on Sucre and Oviedo (Mon–Fri 8.30am–1.30pm & 2.30–4.30pm, $0.50) has an exhibition of archeology from prehistory to Inca times. A **train service** used to run all the way to San Lorenzo on the north coast but it's been defunct for years and now only runs 45km from Ibarra's train station (☎06/295-0390) to Primer Paso at 7am (8am weekends) and returning at 2pm (4pm weekends). A return costs $7.60.

Arrival and information

Bus The terminal is 1km out of town, so take a bus to the centre ($0.25) or a taxi ($1).
Internet Zonanet, Moncayo 5-74 ($1/hr).
Tourist information García Moreno on Parque La Merced (Mon–Fri 8.30am–1pm & 2–5pm; ☎06/295-5711) supplies free maps and general information.

Accommodation

Most tourists stay at hotels in the historic centre of town, which are more pleasant than the cheap hotels near the train station, an area that feels unsafe at night.
Hostal Imbabura Oviedo 9-33 and Chica Narváez ☎06/295-0155. A good budget choice with laundry service, internet and clean rooms set around a pleasant courtyard. $10.
Hostal El Ejecutivo Bolívar 969 ☎06/295-6575. Another dependable option with private bath and cable TV. Some rooms have balconies. $12.
Madrid Pedro Moncayo 7-41 and Olmedo ☎06/295-6177. This quiet hotel feels slightly more upmarket with slickly decorated, well-appointed rooms. $16.
Nueva Estancia García Moreno 7-58 and Parque La Merced ☎06/295-1444. Treat yourself at this ideally located hotel across from Basílica La Merced. It has spacious, carpeted rooms, cable TV, laundry service and a good restaurant. Breakfast included. $31.

Eating and drinking

There are plenty of cheap restaurants serving filling *almuerzos* and *meriendas* for $2.
Antojitos de mi Tierra Plaza de la Ibarreñidad. Traditional Ecuadorian dishes and tasty snacks such as *humitas* and *quimbolitos* ($1–3).

Cafe Arte Salinas 5-43 and Oviedo. A wide variety of international food – from burgers to tacos to filet mignon – in a vibrant setting, with live music at weekends. Mains $3–6.
Donde El Argentino Plaza de la Ibarreñidad. A tiny place that specializes in barbecued meats, ideal for eating al fresco on sunny days.
Heladería Rosalía Suárez Corner of Oviedo and Olmedo. Ibarra is famous for its sorbet and this is the best place to try it.
El Horno Rocafuerte and Flores. Great pizza (from $5) cooked in a clay oven.

Moving on

Bus Aerotaxi and Expreso Turismo have regular services to Quito (2hr) and Atacames (9hr); Trans Otavalo goes to Otavalo (35min); Expreso Turismo and Flota Imbabura head to Tulcán (2hr).

TULCÁN

The border between Ecuador and Colombia is a problematic region and the only recommended place to cross is via **TULCÁN**. Don't wander out of town and take care at night. There's little reason to stay here very long and, with Otavalo and Ibarra only three hours south of the border by bus, staying in Tulcán overnight is unnecessary. If you do decide to linger however, don't miss the town cemetery near the Parque Ayora, whose **topiary gardens** feature trimmed bushes and hedges sculpted into pre-Columbian figures, animals and geometric shapes.

Arrival and information

Bus There are regular buses to Ibarra (2hr 30min) and Quito (5hr). The bus terminal on Bolívar is 1.5km from the centre so take a taxi (about $1).
Embassies The Colombian Consulate is on Bolívar and Junín (☎ 06/298-0559, Mon–Fri 8am–1pm & 2–3pm).
Money exchange To exchange dollars, you should get a slightly better rate in Tulcán than at the border so try the official moneychangers on Plaza de la Independencia, where there are also ATMs.
Tourist information The Cámara de Turismo office (Mon–Fri 9am–12.30pm and 2.30–6pm; ☎ 06/298-6606) is on Bolívar and Ayacucho.

Accommodation

San Francisco Bolívar near Atahualpa ☎ 06/298-0760. A good budget option with basic but decent rooms, hot water and cable TV. $.
Sara Espindola Sucre and Ayacucho ☎ 06/298-6209. A place to treat yourself with sauna, steam room, disco, restaurant, free internet and laundry service. $70.

Eating

There are several decent restaurants close to the main plaza.
Mama Rosita Sucre at Chimborazo. Filling but simple Ecuadorian staples for $3.
El Patio Bolívar near 10 de Agosto. Large portions of Colombian specialities such as *bandeja paisa* (pork, sausage, egg, fried bananas, avocado, beans and rice).

The Central Highlands

South of Quito lies Ecuador's most dramatic Andean scenery, where the Panamericana winds its way between two parallel mountain chains. Eight of Ecuador's ten highest peaks are here so it's unsurprising that nineteenth-century German explorer Alexander von Humboldt named the region "the Avenue of the Volcanoes". On the eastern side, the most popular peak to visit (and climb if you're fit enough) is **Cotopaxi** (5897m), which dominates the surrounding valley. To the southwest lies the turquoise luminescence of **Lake Quilotoa**, one of Ecuador's most stunning natural sights. The region's principal towns are **Latacunga, Ambato** and **Riobamba**, all of which sit at an altitude of 2800m and provide convenient bases. The little town of **Baños**, with its ideal climate, beautiful setting, thermal baths and adventure sports is a highlight of the region. Nearby **Volcán Tungurahua** is erupting at the time of writing and an attraction in itself. South of Riobamba, the hair-raising **Nariz del Diablo train ride** remains popular, although riding on the roof is no longer permitted.

PARQUE NACIONAL COTOPAXI

About 60km south of Quito, the cone-shaped **Volcán Cotopaxi** (5897m) is everybody's idea of a picture-perfect volcano, its symmetrical cone-shaped peak dominating the region. But Cotopaxi's beauty belies its destructive heritage – it has erupted on more than ten occasions since 1742, destroying Latacunga several times. Luckily for the local inhabitants, it has been quiet since 1904, although it's still officially active, with plumes of smoke visible to climbers who reach the crater. As well as being Ecuador's most photogenic volcano, **Parque Nacional Cotopaxi** (open 8am–5pm, $10) is also Ecuador's most-visited park. The volcano offers a spectacular climb (see box opposite) but for a more relaxed experience, the surrounding *páramo* (Andean grasslands) offers great opportunities for trekking and cycling plus close-up views of the volcano. Inhabitants of the park include deer, rabbits, foxes, pumas and ninety species of birds, among them the elusive Andean condor.

CLIMBING COTOPAXI

Climbing Cotopaxi can be done with little technical mountaineering experience. However, this is not a challenge to be taken lightly. You must be in good physical shape, strong, fully acclimatized and travel with a qualified guide, preferably certified by ASEGUIM (Asociación Ecuatoriana de Guías de Montaña). For a list of tour operators, see below.

The importance of proper acclimatization cannot be stressed enough. If you're pushed for time and feeling bold, it's all too tempting to get up in the morning and think: "let's climb a volcano today". Some unscrupulous guides will have no hesitation in taking your money and going straight up to the high-altitude refuge. But above 3000 metres you need to ascend slowly over a few days. A couple of days in Quito (2800m) is not enough to immediately tackle Cotopaxi (5897m). Lake Quilotoa (3800m) is good preparation and a three-day climbing tour of Cotopaxi is recommended more highly than the two-day tour. From the José Rivas refuge at 4800m, it's six to eight very strenuous hours to the top, negotiating snow, ice and several crevices. The views of Ecuador's other major peaks are truly breathtaking, as is the view down into the steaming crater. The descent takes three to four hours. December to April are usually the best times to climb Cotopaxi, when the snow is hardest, but it can be climbed year-round.

Arrival, information and tours

Most people take a guided tour from Quito, Latacunga, Riobamba or even Baños. A one-day hiking and cycling tour costs $50, taking in the museum, Limpiopungo Lake and the mountain refuge. A two-day climbing tour costs about $160 and the better three-day tour about $200. A good tour operator in Latacunga is Volcán Route (2 de Mayo y Guayaquil ℡03/281-2452, ✉volcanroute@hotmail.com). In Quito, try Gulliver (JL Mera and Calama ℡02/252-9297, ⓦwww.gulliver.com.ec). All of the accommodation options listed below can arrange tours.

Accommodation

Cuello de Luna El Chasqui, Panamerican Highway South Km 44 ℡099/700-300, ⓦwww.cuellodeluna.com. The "neck of the moon" is just 6km from the park entrance and offers simple dorms or private rooms with fireplaces. Dorms $16,rooms $44.
Hostería La Ciénega ℡03/271-9052, ⓦwww.hosterialacienega.com. A 400-year-old hacienda, 2km from Lasso, with period furnishing and a good restaurant. Breakfast included. $88.
Secret Garden Cotopaxi ℡093/572-714, ⓦwww.secretgardencotopaxi.com. An ecolodge set in the foothills of Pasochoa, near the village of Pedregal, overlooking the national park. The price includes three meals, snacks, drinks and use of mountain bikes. Many rooms have their own fireplace to keep warm. Dorms $35, rooms $65.

SAQUISILÍ

Saquisilí is gaining popularity for its bustling Thursday market, a lesser-known and more authentic experience of an indigenous market than Otavalo. On market day, eight plazas in the centre flood with tradespeople selling foodstuffs, herbal remedies, household goods and live animals. It's also a social gathering for the locals, many of whom arrive in their best traditional dress and felt hats. For tourists, the main attraction is the shopping. There are also plenty of tasty *tortillas de maíz* to snack on; if you're feeling adventurous, try the *cuy* (guinea pig).

Saquisilí is a few kilometres off the Panamericana, two hours south of Quito. Ask the bus driver to drop you off at the junction and take another bus – or better, catch a regular bus from Latacunga (30min). If you want to stay the night, your options are limited. *Hotel San Carlos* (Bolivar and Sucre ℡03/720-1981) has very basic rooms for $12–15 but a busy bar and restaurant. Alternatively, stay

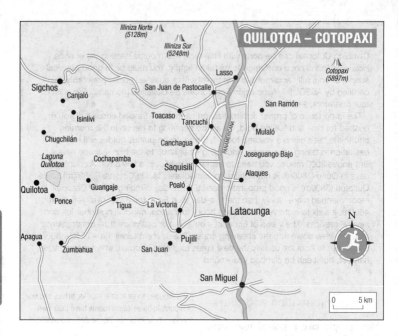

out of town at *Cuello de Luna*, a popular travellers' hub (see p.641).

LATACUNGA

Some 30km south of Cotopaxi National Park, **LATACUNGA** doesn't look very inviting from the highway, but venture towards the centre of town and you'll find quaint cobbled streets and a charming centre bustling with friendly people. There's not a huge amount to do, but the town serves as the best base to explore **Quilotoa** (see p.644) and **Cotopaxi** (see p.640), with good local tour operators and decent accommodation.

(see p.644) and **Cotopaxi** (see p.640)

What to see and do

The town has been rebuilt in colonial style after being destroyed several times by Cotopaxi's devastating eruptions, last time it was rebuilt was 1877. The main square – **Parque Vicente León** – forms the town's focal point, flanked by the cathedral and stately town hall. A few blocks to the west, next to the river

Cutuchi, is the **Museo de la Casa de la Cultura** (corner of Vela and Salcedo, Tues–Fri 8am–noon & 2–6pm; $0.50), which has a small ethnography and art museum. In late September (exact date varies so check), Latacunga parties hard for **La Fiesta de la Mama Negra**, which features a parade of colourful costumed characters and culminates in the arrival of the Mama Negra, a man dressed up as a black woman in honour of the liberation of African slaves in the nineteenth century.

Arrival and information

Bus Latacunga's bus station is on the Panamericana, five blocks west of town. If Latacunga is not the final destination of your bus, you'll be dropped off 400m further west (taxi to the centre $1 or walk over the bridge).

Tourist information Captur (Orellana and Guayaquil ⊕03/281-4968).

Accommodation

Hostal Tiana Guayaquil 5-32 y Quito ⊕03/281-0147, ⓦwww.hostaltiana.com. A friendly backpacker favourite in a converted nineteenth-century hacienda, set around a relaxing courtyard café. Dorms $8, rooms $20.

Central Orellana at Salcedo ☎03/280-2912. This is the best-located budget option in Latacunga and has private bathroom, cable TV and a great view of the main square. $16.

Rodelu ☎03/280-0956, ⓦ www.rodelu.com.ec. This rather upmarket hotel has wood panelling, indigenous motifs, free internet and an excellent restaurant worth visiting even if you don't stay here. $40.

Rosim Quito 16-49 ☎03/280-2172, ⓦ www .hotelrosim.com. A quieter option than the *hostals* on the main square, with well-equipped rooms and high ceilings. Good value. $20.

Eating

El Copihue Rojo Quito 14-38. Charming restaurant tucked away behind the cathedral, specializing in grilled meats for $6–8.

Pizzeria Bon Giorno Corner of Orellana and Maldonado. A friendly place in which to escape the highland staples, with great lasagne and large pizzas ($5) to share.

LAKE QUILOTOA AND THE QUILOTOA LOOP

The luminous turquoise water of volcanic crater lake **Laguna Quilotoa** is one of Ecuador's most awe-inspiring sights. The lake was formed 800 years ago by a massive eruption and subsequent collapse of the volcano. The caldera is two miles wide and the lake 250m deep. You can visit from Latacunga on a day-trip but it's better to at least stay overnight or spend a couple of days hiking parts of the **Quilotoa Loop**.

What to see and do

The first town of note after leaving Latacunga is **Tigua** (3500m), famous for its indigenous arts and handicrafts. Another 30km along the road is **Zumbahua**, a small village that gets rather boisterous at the weekend with its busy Saturday market and accompanying merriment. A further 14km north is the sleepy little village of **Quilotoa** (3800m), the best base to explore, perched as it is above the lake. It costs $1 to enter the village, including unlimited access to the lake. You can hike down into the crater to the waterside in 40min (it's an hour to come back up, or a donkey ride costs $5). The water's high sulphurous content makes it unsuitable for swimming but there are canoes for hire ($2.50). For a longer walk and to appreciate the lake from all angles, allow four hours to walk around the perimeter. The most

If you're travelling alone or want to see Quilotoa without the inconvenience of relying on public transport, take a guided tour from Latacunga. A one-day tour to the lake costs $40, or two days taking in Zumbahua, Quilotoa and Chuhchilán costs $120. Three days to do the entire loop costs $160. Recommended tour operators include Volcan Route (2 de Mayo y Guayaquil ☏03/281-2452; ✉volcanroute@hotmail.com), Tova Expeditions (Guayaquil 5-38 y Quito, ☏03/281-1333) and Tierra Zero (Padre Salcedo y Quito, ☏03/280-4327). All these operators also offer hiking and climbing tours to Cotopaxi.

popular hike on the Quilotoa Loop is the dramatic route from Quilotoa to Chugchilán. It takes about five hours but don't attempt it alone and do not set off after 1pm.

Getting around

The biggest problem in this region is getting around because public transportation is infrequent and often full. During the rainy season, bus routes are sometimes cancelled and roads impassable. It is strongly advised that you don't attempt parts of the loop alone because of the remoteness of the region.

From Latacunga there is a daily bus at midday to Quilotoa via Zumbuhua. It takes about two hours to Quilotoa and continues to Chugchilán at 2.30pm. If you miss it, catch one of the more frequent services to Zumbuhua, from where you can hire a taxi to Quilotoa (about $5 per person). Buses via the northern route through Saquisilí and Sigchos leave Latacunga daily at 11.30am. Coming back from Chugchilán, there are daily buses to Latacunga via the northern route through Sigchos, leaving at the ungodly hour of 3am. The southern route to Latacunga via Quilotoa and Zumbuhua leaves Chugchilán at 4am. There are buses later in the morning on Sundays, otherwise take a taxi to Zumbuhua ($10 from Quilotoa), where there are more frequent buses back to Latacunga.

Accommodation

Quilotoa has a few accommodation options run by friendly indigenous people. All *hostals* provide two meals.

🏃 **Black Sheep Inn** ☏03/281-4587, ⓦwww.blacksheepinn.com. Award-winning American-run ecolodge with organic vegetable gardens, solar power and composting toilets. There are spacious rooms with lofts and stoves, and a bunk house with dorms sleeping up to 10. The restaurant prepares delicious vegetarian food, with all three meals included. Book in advance. Bunks $35, rooms $60.

Hostal Cabanas Quilotoa ☏092/125-962. The best budget option in Quilotoa is owned by local artist Humberto Latacunga. It has comfortable rooms, hot showers and wood burners (it gets very cold at night). $16.

Hostal Cloudforest ☏03/281-4808. A backpacker favourite in Chugchilan with simple rooms and a common room with fireplace to warm up. $16.

Mama Hilda ☏03/281-4814, ⓦwww.hostal mamahilda.org. Another good-value option in Chugchilan with cosy rooms. $20.

Princesa Toa Another simple, budget option in the village of Quilotoa with warm, comfortable rooms just across from the best lake-viewing area. $8.

Quilotoa Crater Lake Lodge ☏02/252-7835, ⓦwww.quilotoalodge.com.ec. The only mid-range accommodation option in Quilotoa is perched above the lake, with spectacular panoramic views. Comfortable rooms, a warm common room area with large fireplace and an international restaurant makes this a well-earned treat after a hard day's hiking. Includes breakfast. $40.

AMBATO

Some 47km south of Latacunga, most tourists merely pass through **AMBATO** en route to Baños or Riobamba. There's little to hold your interest for more than a few hours and the downtown area suffers from traffic problems, which somewhat ruins the experience of wandering around what is, in parts, a beautiful city.

What to see and do

Of most interest in the **Parque Juan Montalvo** is the **Casa de Montalvo**

(Mon–Fri 9am–noon & 2–6pm, Sat 10am–1pm; $1), the former residence of Ambato's most famous literary son. A noted liberal, he was forced into exile by conservative president Gabriel García Moreno in 1869. The house has a collection of photos, manuscripts, clothing and a life-size portrait. Unnervingly, Juan Montalvo's body is on display in the mausoleum. His face is covered by a death mask but his decayed fingers are visible. On the other side of the park is the city's huge but rather ugly modern **cathedral**, rebuilt after the devastating 1949 earthquake. The interior is more impressive with huge bronze statues and fabulous acoustics during mass. On Parque Cevallos, the **Museo de Ciencias Naturales** (Mon–Fri 8.30am–12.30pm & 2.30–5.30pm; Sat 9am–5pm; $2) houses stuffed animals, including a grisly display of freak animals such as six-legged lambs. Escape the city's bustle by visiting **La Quinta de Juan León Mera** (Av Los Capulíes; 9.30am–5.30pm, Wed–Sun; $1), just 2km from the centre (a half-hour walk or $1 taxi ride). Wander through the gardens and relax on the banks of the river.

Arrival and information

Bus Ambato's bus station is 2km north of the centre. Even if you aren't going to Ambato, you may end up here as it is an important bus hub. There are regular services to and from Quito, Guayaquil, Latacunga, Riobamba, Baños, Puyo, Cuenca and Loja. To get to the centre of town, costs $1.50 by taxi or you can catch a local bus.
Tourist information The tourist office on Guayaquil and Rocafuerte (☎03/282-1800, ◍www.ambato .com) is open Mon–Fri 8am–5pm and has maps and brochures.

Accommodation

Pirámide Inn Av. Cevallos y Mariano Egüez ☎03/242-1920. Well-appointed rooms with hot water, private bathroom and cable TV. Breakfast included. $25.
Quinta Loren Calle Los Taxos and Guaytambos ☎03/284-6165, ◍www.quintaloren.com. This

small *hostería*, surrounded by beautiful gardens and fruit orchards, is ideal to escape the crowds. The rooms are elegantly decorated and the gourmet restaurant is top quality. $55.
Residencial San Andres Parque 12 de Noviembre ☎03/282-1604. If you're on a tight budget, these clean, basic rooms are the best of the city's cheap options. $10.
Señorial Cevallos y Quito ☎03/282-5124, ◍www .hotelseniorial.com. Spacious, bright, carpeted rooms with cable TV, telephone and mini-bar. There's a small spa offering massage. $30.

Eating and drinking

Café la Catedral Bolívar. This friendly little place, in a small mall opposite the cathedral entrance, is ideal for good-value lunches ($2.50–4).
La Fornace Av. Cevallos 17-28. Delicious pizza baked in a massive brick oven as well as great pasta dishes ($2.50–4).
Oasis Café Sucre and Mariano Equez. A modern café, great for snacks and famed for its home-made ice cream (snacks $2–5).
Parrilladas El Gaucho Bolívar and Quito. The best place to pig out on huge portions of steak and barbecued meats ($6–10).

SALASACA

On the road between Ambato and Baños, it's worth stopping at **Salasaca**, famous for its tapestries. The indigenous people who live here look noticeably different to those elsewhere, dressed in black ponchos and white hats. They originate from Bolivia, driven here by the Incas in the fifteenth century. There is a craft market every Sunday; on other days, it's best to browse the tapestry stores. About 6km from Salasaca is **Pelileo**, with surely more cut-price jeans per square metre than anywhere in South America. To visit Pelileo and Salasaca, hop off the bus from Ambato to Baños. There are several buses per hour.

BAÑOS

Locals call it "un pedacito de cielo" (a little piece of heaven) and this is no exaggeration because **BAÑOS** is mainland Ecuador's most idyllic destination. If you're only in Ecuador

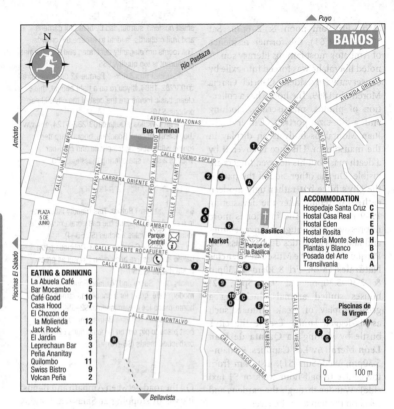

Puyo

BAÑOS

Río Pastaza

N

Ambato ◄

Piscinas El Salado ◄

AVENIDA AMAZONAS

Bus Terminal

CALLE EUGENIO ESPEJO

CARRERA ELOY ALFARO

CALLE 16 DE DICIEMBRE

AVENIDA ORIENTE

AVENIDA ORIENTE

PABLO ARTURO SUAREZ

CALLE JUAN LEON MERA

CALLE PASTAZA

CARRERA ORIENTE

CALLE PEDRO V. MALDONADO

CALLE P. HALFLANTS

❶

❷ ❸

Ⓐ

PLAZA 5 DE JUNIO

CALLE AMBATO

❹
❺

❻

Basílica

ACCOMMODATION

Hospedaje Santa Cruz	**C**
Hostal Casa Real	**F**
Hostal Eden	**E**
Hostal Rosita	**D**
Hostería Monte Selva	**H**
Plantas y Blanco	**B**
Posada del Arte	**G**
Transilvania	**A**

Parque Central

Market

Parque de la Basílica

CALLE VICENTE ROCAFUERTE

CALLE 16 DE DICIEMBRE

CALLE LUIS A. MARTINEZ

❼

❽

EATING & DRINKING

La Abuela Café	6
Bar Mocambo	5
Café Good	10
Casa Hood	7
El Chozon de la Molienda	12
Jack Rock	4
El Jardín	8
Leprechaun Bar	3
Peña Ananitay	1
Quilombo	11
Swiss Bistro	9
Volcan Peña	2

❾

❿ Ⓒ

Ⓓ

Ⓑ

Ⓔ

CALLE ELOY ALFARO

CALLE 12 DE NOVIEMBRE

CALLE RAFAEL VIEIRA

Piscinas de la Virgen

CALLE JUAN MONTALVO

⓫

⓬ Ⓕ

Ⓖ

Ⓗ

CALLE VELASCO IBARRA

0   100 m

▼ Bellavista

for a short time, this is one place that is not to be missed. With an ideally warm climate, a stunning location in a verdant valley surrounded by steep hills, an excellent choice of hotels and restaurants, great walking and adventure sports, plus of course, the thermal baths that give the town its name, don't be surprised if you end up spending longer than planned here. There are four sets of public baths around the town and many of the better hotels have their own, although they don't draw on volcanic spring water. Be aware that Baños is only 8km from the active **Volcán Tungurahua**, which was erupting at the time of writing. Luckily, the crater is on the opposite side to the town and Baños has been relatively unaffected (for further information see p.649).

What to see and do

In town, don't miss the **Basílica de Nuestra Señora de Agua Santa** on the main Ambato street. This massive church is dedicated to the Virgin Mary, credited with several miracles including saving the town from Tungurahua's eruption in 1773. It's spectacular when lit up at night, dominating the town's skyline. Inside the church are ten huge paintings depicting the Virgin saving the town and its citizens from various calamities. Upstairs is a small **museum** (open daily 8am–5pm, $0.50) with a collection of the Virgin's processional clothes, religious art and a bizarre collection of stuffed animals.

Piscinas de la Virgen

The most popular baths are the **Piscinas de la Virgen** (4.30am–5pm & 6–10pm;

$1.60 daytime, $2 at night) at the foot of a small waterfall at the eastern end of Avenida Martínez. The cloudy yellow waters are high in minerals and make for a very relaxing soak. Next to the changing rooms you can see where the boiling waters emerge from the rock face. There are three pools – freezing cold, warm and hot (just a little too hot to linger for more than a few minutes). The baths get very busy at weekends so it's best to go either early morning or early evening to avoid the crowds.

Piscinas El Salado

About 2km out of town, Piscinas El Salado has five pools ranging from 16 to 42°C with the water visibly bubbling up from underground. In August 2008 the complex was damaged by a landslide but has since been rebuilt by the local government, though bear in mind that this area is vulnerable when there is heavy rain. It's a 20-min walk from town or take a taxi ($1.50). Entrance $2.

AROUND BAÑOS

The best way to take in the town's stunning setting is to **walk to** **Bellavista**, high above the town. It's a steep 40-minute climb up a rocky, muddy path, rewarded with spectacular panoramic views over Baños and the Pastaza valley leading down to the Oriente. There are a couple of cafés at the top selling light lunches and drinks. If you're feeling energetic, continue on the path uphill for a further hour to the small village of **Runtun;** you can then loop around to the other side of Baños, passing the statue of La Virgen del Agua Santa and back to town. The entire walk takes about four hours. You can **hire horses** to see this route ($12 for 2hr, $22 for 4hr, including guide).

Arrival and information

Bus Baños's bus terminal is a few blocks north of the main square surrounded by stalls selling *jugo de caña* (sugar cane juice). Baños is so compact that you can walk everywhere. A taxi across town costs $1.

Tourist information You can purchase guidebooks and pick up free maps at the municipal tourist office on Haflants near Rocafuerte (Mon–Fri 8am–12.30pm & 2–5.30pm; ☎03/274-0483, ⓦwww.baniosadn.com.ec) on the east side of Parque Central.

THE ROAD FROM BAÑOS TO PUYO

One of Ecuador's most beautiful routes, the road from Baños to Puyo, drops nearly 1000m following the Río Pastaza down from lush Andean foothills, through cloudforest to the edges of the tropical jungle. It's best admired from the saddle of a bike, which can be hired from any agency in Baños for $5 per day, including helmet, map and repair kit. Leaving Baños you cross the Agoyan hydroelectric project and it's about 40 minutes until you reach the impressive Manto de La Novia (Bride's Veil) waterfall. You can take the cable car ($2) 500m across the river gorge for a closer look. A 25-minute ride then brings you to the village of Río Verde, where you can lock your bike and hike 15 minutes downhill to see the even more spectacular Pailón del Diablo (Devil's Cauldron) waterfall. View it from a rickety suspension bridge or pay $0.50 to get a closer look from the panoramic balcony. Cycling half an hour uphill from Río Verde, you reach Machay. From here, hike a 2.5km trail into the cloudforest past eight waterfalls, the most beautiful of which is Manantial del Dorado. From Machay, it's downhill to Río Negro where the surroundings begin to feel truly tropical with bromeliads, giant tree ferns and colourful orchids. Start early if you want to cover the entire 61km but the route is far more scenic than the end destination of Puyo, a rather ugly jungle town. Most people hop on a bus back to Baños from Río Verde or Río Negro. Note that in February 2010 two locals were killed by a landslide in Rio Verde so exercise caution visiting this area during the rainy season.

Accommodation

Hospedaje Santa Cruz 16 de Diciembre ☎03/274-0648. A funky little place with simple but colourfully decorated rooms. $19.

Hostal Casa Real Montalvo y Pasaje Ibarra ☎03/274-0215, ⓦbanios.com/casareal. This is an excellent-value mid-range option close to the waterfall. Rooms have murals of wildlife and the massages are among the best in town. Breakfast included. $24.

Hostal Eden 12 de Noviembre ☎03/274-0616. This hostel has decent rooms with cable TV facing a pleasant garden courtyard. There's a cheap restaurant next door. $16.

Hostal Rosita 16 de Diciembre near Martínez ☎03/274-0396. This is one of the best-value budget options in town, with free internet. There are two larger apartments for longer stays. $10.

Plantas y Blanco Martínez near 12 de Diciembre ☎03/274-0044. This backpackers' institution is a great place to swap stories with kindred spirits. There's a rooftop terrace, sunloungers, kitchen, Turkish baths, free internet and compact but clean rooms. Dorms $6.50, rooms $19.

Posada del Arte Pasaje Ibarra ☎03/274-0083, ⓦwww.posadadelarte.com. A truly special place

containing a feast of South American art. The plushly decorated rooms have fireplaces with chimneys to keep you warm. They also own the delightful *Casa del Abuelo* up the road which has a free art exhibition but rather basic rooms for the price. $51.

Transilvania 16 de Diciembre and Oriente ☎03/274-2281, ⓦhostal-transilvania.com. Far more welcoming to weary travellers than its bizarre name suggests, this Israeli-owned *hostal* is a backpacker favourite with bright, simple rooms and a colourful café where big breakfasts are served on petrified wooden tables. There's also a pool table and Middle Eastern food is served. Breakfast included. $15.

Eating

Baños has many top-quality **restaurants** and offers some of the best international cuisine outside Quito. Most of the finest are situated away from the main street. The town is also great for those with a sweet tooth, famous for its dozens of stalls selling *membrillo* (a gelatinous red block made with fruit) and *milcocha*, chewy sugar cane bars which you can watch being made, swung over wooden pegs. Outside the market, there's also the memorable sight of *cuy* (guinea pigs) being roasted on a spit.

ACTIVITIES AND TOURS

Adventure sports are popular in the Pastaza valley between Baños and Puyo. **Rafting** is particularly good. A half-day on the class 3 part of the Rio Pastaza costs $30 including transport, equipment, licensed guide and lunch. A half-day on the faster class 4 part of the river costs $45. Other adrenalin-filled activities include **Bridge Jumping** (rather like bungee except you swing like a pendulum) for $10–15 as well as zipping across the valley on **canopy lines** ($3–6). You can also hire *Cuadrones* buggies and motorbikes for about $8 per hour ($20 for 3hr).

Most of the **tour operators** in Baños offer the above activities but some are more experienced than others. Geotours (Ambato and Thomas Haflants ☎03/274-1344) has been in the business for more than fifteen years and is highly recommended. Other agencies to try include Expediciones Pailontravel (12 de Diciembre y Montalvo ☎03/274-0899) and Wonderful Ecuador (Maldonado and Oriente ☎03/274-1580).

Jungle tours can be arranged with several tour operators in Baños, including Geotours and Wonderful Ecuador (see above). You can book tours to many of the jungle destinations including Coca and Lago Agrio but these tours generally go through Quito so you may be better off booking there. For a shorter, more accessible jungle experience, there are good trips via Puyo. For more information on jungle trips, see the chapter on the Oriente (see p.662).

Baños has many skilled professionals and you can get all types of **massage** treatments here from soothing aromatherapy to reflexology, deep tissue treatments and physiotherapy. Most charge around $20 for an hour's massage and $15 for a facial. Stay in Touch (Pasaje Ibarra y Montalvo ☎03/274-0973) is particularly good, as is *Hostal Casa Real* (see above).

La Abuela Café Ambato near 16 de Diciembre. Many of the restaurants on the main street are uninspiring but this is one of the best options, with a wide-ranging menu and a balcony to watch the world go by. Mains $4.

Café Good 16 de Diciembre ☎03/274-0592. Specializes in vegetarian and Asian food. The Indian curry is particularly good. Mains $3–7.

🏃 Casa Hood Martinez and Alfaro ☎09/462-0269. This is a great place for a meal or a drink, with a vibrant atmosphere and an eclectic menu of international food including Mexican, Middle Eastern and Asian dishes, plus smoothies and hot drinks. Mains $3–5.

El Chozón de la Molienda Montalvo y Pasaje Ibarra ☎03/274-1816. Enjoy excellent barbecued dishes such as *lomo volcánico* (steak in ginger sauce) served in a thatched hut set in a large garden. Mains $5–7.

El Jardín 16 de Diciembre. A popular place to eat breakfast or afternoon snacks al fresco in the leafy garden, with a wide selection of dishes and an economical set menu. Mains $4.

Quilombo Montalvo y 12 de Noviembre ☎03/274-2880. A quirky, humorous place set in a wooden cabin decked out with eclectic decor, from hammocks to horseshoes and even a broken bicycle. The menu comes on cubes in little bags and the barbecued steaks and chicken dishes ($6–8) are cooked to perfection.

🏃 Swiss Bistro Martínez y Alfaro ☎094/004-019. The new sensation in town, with cow skins on the walls and even cow-patterned lamp shades that place you in the heart of the Swiss Alps. The cheese and meat fondues ($6–8) are fabulous, rounded off by stewed pears in red wine for dessert.

Nightlife

Nightlife in Baños has improved in recent years. Although it's still rather sleepy during the week, it can get busy at weekends, particularly on Saturday night. Most of the best places are situated on the stretch of Alfaro north of Ambato. Start the evening off with some rock classics at either *Bar Mocambo* or *Jack Rock*, which is decked out with music memorabilia. As midnight approaches, make for *Volcán Peña* bar, which plays mainly Latin music, or *Leprechaun Bar*, which is more popular with backpackers and has a dancefloor and a roaring bonfire in the back garden. To catch some traditional *folklórica* music, go to *Peña Ananitay* (16 de Diciembre and Espejo).

Moving on

Bus There are regular buses to Puyo (1hr 30min), Riobamba (2hr) and Ambato (1hr). For most other destinations, including Quito (4hr) and Guayaquil (7hr), it's usually easier to change at Ambato, but there are occasional direct services. The direct road to Riobamba was closed at the time of writing due to Tungurahua's eruptions.

VOLCÁN TUNGURAHUA

Tungurahua, which means "throat of fire", has a troubled relationship with Baños. The volcano supplies the **hot springs** that make the town famous, but its eruptions have caused regular alerts in recent years. The volcano awoke from years of dormancy in October 1999 with a spectacular eruption that covered Baños in ash. However, because the crater is on the opposite side, the town escaped any further damage. There have been subsequent eruptions in August 2006 and at regular intervals in 2008, 2009 and the latest in May 2010, when a 10km-high ash cloud reached as far as Guayaquil, over 200km away.

Bañeños have been living in Tungurahua's shadow for centuries and nobody in town seems particularly worried about the volcano, though it's important to check on its current state of activity before visiting the town. Check the national press or, for more detailed information, the Instituto Geofísico's Spanish website (ⓦwww.igepn.edu.ec) or the Smithsonian Institute's English site (ⓦwww.volcano.si.edu). When Tungurahua is erupting, it becomes a star attraction. The best views of the volcano are from the town of Runtun above Bellavista (see "Around Baños", p.647). Most agencies in town charge $3 for a night tour but good views are rare.

Riobamba

The main draw of **RIOBAMBA** is that it's the starting point for the dramatic **Nariz del Diablo** (Devil's Nose) train ride, but this traditional town's nineteenth-century architecture and

▲ Bus Terminal

RIOBAMBA

Alta Montaña
DIEGO DE IBARRA
Plaza de Toros
AVENIDA MIGUEL ANTONIA LEON
Parque 21
de Abril
MAYOR RUIZ
VARGAS TORRES
Julio Verne
ESPECTADOR
Train Station
CARABOBO
M. DAVALOS
V. ROCAFUERTE
10 DE AGOSTO
ESPAÑA
GUAYQUIL
Monasterio de
Parque las Conceptas
Sucre
Museo de
Arte Religioso
PLAZA LA
CONCEPCIÓN
La Concepción
CRISTOBAL COLON
Mercado La Merced
Parque
Maldonado
Catedral
EUGENIO ESPEJO
EUGENIO ESPEJO
Museo de la Ciudad
5 DE JUNIO
5 DE JUNIO
Municipio
ARGENTINOS
JUNIN
JOSE DE OROZCO
TARQUI
PLAZA SAN
FRANCISCO
JUAN DE VELASCO
Mercado
San Francisco
Parque de
la Libertad
SEBASTIAN DE BENALCAZAR
SEBASTIAN DE BENALCAZAR
La Basílica
ALVARADO
0   200 m
DIEGO DE ALMAGRO
Parque Nacional Sangay
Terminal Oriental (5 blocks)

ACCOMMODATION
Imperial	D
El Libertador	A
Montecarlo	E
Nuca Huasi	C
Oasis	F
Tren Dorado	B
Troje	G

EATING & DRINKING
El Centadero	2
El Delirio	4
Natural Food Restaurant	6
Pizzería d'Baggio	1
San Valentín	3
Sierra Nevada	5

wide avenues lined with huge palm trees make it a pleasant stopover for a day or so. It's also the best base to climb towering Volcán Chimborazo, Ecuador's highest mountain.

What to see and do

The best sightseeing is centred around **Parque Maldonado**. The **Catedral** is the town's only surviving building from the 1797 earthquake, painstakingly moved and reconstructed when the town was rebuilt in a new location. A couple of blocks further north, inside the Monasterio de las Conceptas, the **Museo de Arte Religioso** has a large collection of religious art (entrance on Argentinos, Tues–Fri 9am–12.30pm & 3–6.30pm, Sun 9am–12.30pm; $2). On Saturdays, Riobamba has one of the largest **markets** in the region, spreading out northeast of Parque de

la Concepción. On clear days, walk up the hill to **Parque 21 de Abril** for good views of Chimborazo.

Arrival and information

Bus Riobamba's main bus terminal is 2km northwest of the centre. From the Oriente (and from Baños if the road passing Tungurahua reopens) you arrive at the Terminal Oriental (corner of Espejo and Luz Elisa Borja), from where you can take a regular bus ($0.25) to the centrally located train station.

Taxi A taxi into town from the Terminal Oriente costs $1.

Train See box, p.651.

Accommodation

Most accommodation is situated close to the train station. The area is vibrant and noisy so it's best to stay just off the main road or ask for a quieter back room.

Imperial 10 de Agosto and Rocafuerte ☎03/296-0429. One of the best deals in town with colourful decor, spacious rooms, friendly service and surprisingly low prices. $12.

El Libertador Av. Daniel León Borja 29-22 ☎03/294-7393. For more comfort, this colonial-style hotel has spacious, tastefully furnished rooms with cable TV. $35.

Montecarlo 10 de Agosto 25-41 ☎03/296-1557, ⓦwww.hotelmontecarlo-riobamba.com. To treat yourself, try this restored historic house around a pleasant flower-filled courtyard. Breakfast included. $33.

Ñuca Huasi 10 de Agosto 10-24 ☎03/296-6669. For those on a very tight budget, try these basic rooms in a tatty but characterful old building. $12.

Oasis Veloz and Almagro ☎03/296-1210. South of the Basílica in a quiet area of town, this is an excellent mid-range choice. Tastefully decorated rooms, a flower-filled courtyard and kitchen. Book in advance as there are only eight rooms. $20.

TREAT YOURSELF

Troje Km 4.5 Via Riobamba a Chambo ☎03/262-2201, ⓦwww.eltroje.com. If you have spare cash, go south of town to enjoy the sauna and spacious grounds of this upmarket *hostería*. Breakfast included. $55.

THE DEVIL'S NOSE TRAIN RIDE

As the name suggests, this train ride is not for the faint-hearted, but it's an exhilarating experience. Riobamba is the starting point and the 100-km line stretches from there southwest via Alausi to Sibambe. The journey is relatively laidback at first, with sweeping views of Andean valleys, but the final part of the ride is the main act – a hair-raising 800-m descent through a series of tight switchbacks carved out of the steep mountainside. Tourists used to ride on the roof to get the full dramatic effect but the authorities have banned this after the deaths of two Japanese tourists in 2007.

The train leaves Riobamba on Wed, Fri & Sun at 7am and takes around five hours to get to Sibambe. Tickets ($11) can be purchased from Riobamba's train station (⊤03/296-1909). At the time of writing the train route was undergoing maintenance work and was only running between Alausi and Sibambe (which is the most interesting part of the trip anyway). Take a bus from Riobamba at 6am (2hr) to catch the train from Alausi. After the ride, get the bus back from Alausi to Riobamba and head south to Cuenca (4–5hr). Alternatively, note that Alausi is the most obvious starting point to do the three-day hike to Ingapirca (see p.652).

Tren Dorado Carabobo 22-35 and 10 de Agosto ⊤03/296-4890. A popular option for travellers, with compact but perfectly adequate rooms and a friendly atmosphere. A filling buffet breakfast ($3) is available in the café at 5.30am on train days. $20.

Eating and drinking

El Centadero Av. León Borja. Nightlife is limited in Riobamba but this club, just up from *San Valentín*, pumps out reggaeton, merengue and salsa until late (Thurs–Sat; $1).
El Delirio Primera Constituyente 28-16 ⊤03/296-6441. This traditional colonial house is the perfect place for a romantic meal accompanied by live music. Book in advance. Mains, including filet mignon, $6–8.
Natural Food Restaurant Tarqui and Veloz. The best option in town for wholesome, tasty vegetarian food with options for carnivores too. Mains (such as filet mignon) $6–8.
Pizzeria d'Baggio Av. Leon Borja 33-24 ⊤03/296-1832. Unbeatable for sumptuous pizzas made by hand in front of you. Pizzas $4–8.
San Valentín Av. Leon Borja and Torres ⊤03/296-3137. For something cheap and cheerful, try the Tex Mex and varied fast food served in an informal atmosphere. Mains $3–4.
Sierra Nevada Primera Constituyente 27-38 ⊤03/295-1542. An excellent value eatery offering imaginative seafood and meat dishes. Mains around $5.

Moving on

Bus Ambato (every 15–30min; 1hr); Baños (every 15–30min; 1hr 30min); Cuenca (hourly; 7hr); Guayaquil (hourly; 4hr 30min); Quito (hourly; 4hr).

VOLCÁN CHIMBORAZO

Just 30km northwest of Riobamba, the extinct **Volcán Chimborazo** looms large. At 6310m, it's Ecuador's highest peak and is the furthest point from the centre of the Earth due to the Equatorial ridge. The mountain has good roads so is easily visited on tours from Riobamba. On a day-trip you can walk from the lower refuge (4800m) to the second refuge (5000m) but bear in mind that the climb in altitude from Riobamba could leave you suffering badly. For experienced mountaineers planning to tackle the summit, there are several tour operators in Riobamba charging approximately $200 for a two-day tour. Recommended operators include: Alta Montaña, at Av. Daniel León Borja and Diego Ibarra (⊤03/294-2215); and Andes Trek, at Colón 22-25 and 10 de Agosto (⊤03/294-0964, ⊛www.andes-trek.com).

The Southern Highlands

South of Riobamba, the majestic mountains of the Central Highlands fade from view to be replaced by undulating green hills. The tourist hub of the region is **Cuenca**, Ecuador's third-largest city and possibly its most beautiful. Cuenca is also the best base to explore **Ingapirca**, Ecuador's only major Inca ruins, and the rugged moors and lakes of **Parque Nacional El Cajas**.

South of Cuenca, distances between towns lengthen and the climate warms up. The historic plazas and award-winning parks of the provincial capital of **Loja** are worth a visit before heading to the relaxing backpacker favourite of **Vilcabamba**, nicknamed the "Valley of Longevity". Recharge your batteries and take advantage of great hiking and horse-riding trails in the surrounding hills.

INGAPIRCA

Between Riobamba and Cuenca lies the site of **Ingapirca** (daily 8am–6pm; $6 including guide), Ecuador's only major Inca ruins. Those who've already visited Peru may be disappointed by this rather modest site. However, it is worth the visit, in particular to see the Inca empire's sole remaining sun temple. The site's strategic position is also impressive, at a height of over 3200m with panoramic views over the surrounding countryside.

Ingapirca was built at the end of the fifteenth century by Huayna Capac on top of the ruins of a Cañari city. The stone of the Cañari moon temple, which the Inca preserved from its earlier construction, is still visible. Sadly, much of the site is now little more than stone foundations and it takes imagination and a guided tour to bring it to life.

What to see and do

Points of interest include the **calendar stone** and sacrificial site, but the highlight is the well-preserved **Temple of the Sun**, constructed with more than three thousand intricately carved blocks. It's entertaining to stand in the sentry posts of the temple and hear your whispers reverberate through the walls. Just outside the complex is a small **museum** (included in the entrance fee), which houses a small collection of

THE INCA TRAIL TO INGAPIRCA

Though by no means as famous or impressive as the trail in Peru, keen hikers can make the most of the countryside between Alausí and Cuenca by hiking this three-day trail. Take plenty of food, water and camping equipment as facilities are thin on the ground.

The start of the trail is at Achupallas. To get there, take a bus from Riobamba towards Cuenca and get off at La Moya, 10km south of Alauso. From there, it's a steep climb or hitch a ride to Achupallas. Alternatively, a taxi from Alausi direct to Achupallas costs $7. On the first day, head south down the Río Cadrul valley and through a narrow gap between two hills, Cerro Mapahuiña and Cerro Callana Pucará. Continue towards Laguna Tres Cruces and camp nearby. This hike is about six hours in total.

On day two, continue southwest and up along Cuchilla Tres Cruces, which commands great views of the valley Quebrada Espíndola. Descend into the valley to the left of the final peak, Quillo Loma. There are remains of an Inca road and the foundations of an Inca bridge. You'll also find a trail to Laguna Culebrillas and more ruins at Paredones.

On day three, head southwest from Paredones on the seven-metre-wide Inca road. After the village of San José turn right to El Rodeo, then follow the road to Ingapirca. It takes nearly five hours in total. The entire trail is not well-marked so ensure you are prepared. Alternatively, take a guided tour. Several tour operators based In Riobamba and Cuenca operate tours (see p.655 for details).

Cañari and Inca ceramics, sculptures, tools and a skeleton found at the site.

Arrival

Bus To get to Ingapirca, take a Transportes Cañar bus from Cuenca's bus terminal (departing 9am and 1pm, returning 1pm and 4pm except weekends when there are no afternoon buses; 2hr).

Accommodation

Options to stay overnight are limited and a day-trip is most common. If you're feeling flush, try *Posada Ingapirca* (☎07/282-7401; $85 including breakfast), a beautiful converted farmhouse overlooking the ruins, adorned with indigenous art and with a decent restaurant. For very basic rooms, stay at *Hostal Inti Huasi* (☎07/229-2940; $10) in Ingapirca village, 5min from the site. Bring warm clothes as it gets cold at night.

CUENCA

CUENCA is Ecuador's third-largest city, with a population of some 400,000, but it doesn't feel that way, retaining the atmosphere of a traditional Andean town. Prior to the Spanish conquest, the Incas established the city of **Tomebamba** in the late fifteenth century, one of the most important cities in the Inca empire. The city was destroyed shortly afterwards by the civil war between brothers Atahualpa and Huascar and the Spanish later founded Cuenca in 1557. Little remains of the city's Inca past, although ruins of Tomebamba have been excavated behind the **Museo del Banco Central** (see p.657). Note that most museums and restaurants are closed on Sundays, which makes it the best day to take a trip outside the city to **Cajas, Ingapirca** or **Baños**.

What to see and do

The cobbled streets, charming squares, colonial architecture and magnificent cathedral make the historic centre a delight to explore; it's not surprising that it was declared a UNESCO World Heritage Site in 1996.

The historic city centre

The focal point of Cuenca's centre is **Parque Calderón**, an elegant square filled with flower beds and palm trees, dominated by the towering eighteenth-century **Catedral Nueva**. The interior is relatively bare except for the stunning gold-leaf altar and the massive sky-blue domes, which are best viewed from the side or rear. To the left of the cathedral entrance, along Calle Sucre on the Plazoleta del Carmen, is a daily flower market. Turn left along Padre Aguirre to the ramshackle clothes market on **Plaza San Francisco** and the slightly battered **Iglesia San Francisco**. Five blocks west is the seventeenth-century **Iglesia San Sebastián** on a quiet square. Opposite is the **Museo de Arte Moderno** (Mon–Fri 9am–1pm and 3–6.30pm, Sat 9am–1pm; free), which houses temporary exhibitions of national and Latin American modern art.

Along the Río Tomebamba

After exploring the historic centre, head south to the riverside. Along Calle Larga, there are several interesting museums. The **Museo Remigio Crespo Toral** (Mon–Fri 8.30am–1pm & 3–6pm, Sat 10am–noon; free) has a collection of pre-Columbian ceramics as well as colonial and modern art in a restored nineteenth-century house. A couple of blocks further east, the **Museo de las Culturas Aborígenes** (Mon–Fri 8.30am–6pm, Sat 9am–1pm; $2) has an enormous collection of pre-Hispanic artefacts – from Stone Age tools to Inca ceramics. Calle Larga has three staircases, the largest of which is **La Escalinata**, down to the banks of the river, which is pleasant to stroll along. East is the landmark **Puente Roto** (Broken Bridge), the remaining third of a bridge which once spanned the river.

Museo Pumapungo

Museo Pumapungo (Calle Larga near Huayna Capac ☎07/283-1155, ✆www.pumapungo.net, Mon–Fri 9am–6pm,

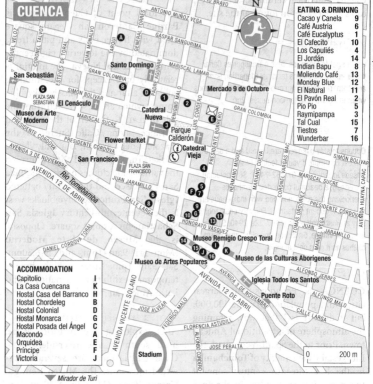

EATING & DRINKING

Cacao y Canela	9
Café Austria	6
Café Eucalyptus	1
El Cafecito	10
Los Capuliés	4
El Jordán	14
Indian Bapu	8
Moliendo Café	13
Monday Blue	12
El Natural	11
El Pavón Real	2
Pio Pio	5
Raymipampa	3
Tal Cual	15
Tiestos	7
Wunderbar	16

ACCOMMODATION

Capitolio	I
La Casa Cuencana	K
Hostal Casa del Barranco	H
Hostal Chordeleg	B
Hostal Colonial	D
Hostal Monarca	G
Hostal Posada del Ángel	C
Macondo	A
Orquídea	E
Príncipe	F
Victoria	J

Mirador de Turi

Sat 9am–1pm; $3) is easily Cuenca's best museum and worth the 20-minute walk east of the centre (taxi $1.50). The museum is spread out across three floors and includes a large collection of colonial art, an archeology room and an exhibition of indigenous costumes and masks. The highlight is the excellent **ethnographic** exhibition of Ecuador's diverse indigenous cultures, with animated dioramas, recreated dwellings and a stunning display of five *tsantsas* (shrunken heads) from the Shuar culture in the Southern Oriente. Entrance includes access to the **Pumapungo archeological site** behind the museum, where the most important buildings of the Inca city of Tomebamba were located, although mainly foundations remain. Below the ruins are landscaped gardens and a bird rescue centre with parrots, hawks and a black-chested eagle.

Mirador de Turi

For the best views over Cuenca, take a taxi ($2.50) to the **Mirador de Turi**, a lookout point on a hill 4km south of the centre. The views are particularly good on evenings when the churches are lit up.

Arrival and information

Air and bus Cuenca's airport and bus terminal are both located 2km northeast of the centre, from where buses run on Av. España to the northern edge of central Cuenca. There are daily flights from Quito and Guayaquil from Tame (Av. Florencia Astudillo ℡07/288-9581, ⊛www.tame.com.ec), LAN (Bolivar 9-18 and Benigno Malo ℡07/282/2783, ⊛www.lan.com) and Aerogal (Av. España 1114

Hotel Victoria Calle Larga 6-93 y Borrero ☎07/282-7401. Splash out on one of Cuenca's finest hotels and stay in a beautifully restored colonial building overlooking extensive gardens. Most of the spacious, elegantly furnished rooms have views of the river. The sister hotel, *Posada Ingapirca*, is also the best place to stay In Ingapirca (see p.653).

☎07/286-1041, ⊛www.areogal.com.ec). Icaro also operates regularly to Quito (Av. España 11-14 ☎07/280-2700, ⊛www.icaro.aero).

Taxi Taxis cost about $2 from the airport to Cuenca.

Tourist information Go to the iTur office on the main square (Mariscal Sucre ☎07/282-1035, ⊛www.cuenca.gov.ec), which has friendly staff providing maps and regional information.

Tour operators The following offer tours to Ingapirca, Cajas and elsewhere: Expediciones Apullacta, at Gran Colombia 11-02 and General Torres (☎07/283-7815, ⊛www.apullacta.com); Metropolitan Touring, at Mariscal Sucre 6-62 and Hermano Miguel (☎07/283-1463, ⊛www.metropolitan-touring.com); Río Arriba Expeditions, at Hermano Miguel 7-14 and Córdova (☎07/283-011); Terra Diversa Travel and Adventure, at Hermano Miguel 5-42 and Honorato Vásquez (☎07/282-3782, ⊛www.terradiversa.com).

Accommodation

Cuenca has a wide range of accommodation with a wealth of hotels in charming colonial buildings. The best area to stay is south of the centre on the north bank of the river. Consider booking ahead at weekends and particularly on national holidays when accommodation fills up quickly.

La Casa Cuencana Hermano Miguel 4-36 ☎07/282-6009. With terracotta walls adorned with artwork and a friendly family atmosphere, these simple rooms with private bathrooms are excellent value for the price. $14.

El Capitolio Hermano Miguel 4-19 ☎07/282 4446. Opposite *La Casa Cuencana*, this is an equally good budget option offering decent, basic rooms with shared bathroom in a quiet, homely ambience. $14.

Hostal Casa del Barranco Calle Larga 8-41 y Cordero ☎07/283-9763, ⊛www.casadelbarranco.com. Many of the hotels on Calle Larga come at a premium but this historic house displaying

paintings by local artists is a great-value mid-range option. Breakfast included. $30.

Hostal Chordeleg Gran Colombia and General Torres ☎07/282-2536. An attractive converted colonial home on a corner in the city centre with decent mid-range rooms set around a pleasant courtyard and garden. Breakfast included. $40.

Hostal Colonial Gran Colombia 10-13 y Padre Aguirre ☎07/2841-644. Comfortable mid-range rooms in an eighteenth-century house set around a small courtyard. Breakfast included. $34.

Hostal Monarca Borrero 5-47 y Honorato Vasquez ☎07/283-6462. Loud, bright decor but a quiet family atmosphere, with great-value budget rooms with shared bathroom. $14.

Hostal Posada del Angel Bolivar 14-11 and Estevez de Toral ☎07/284-0695, ⊛www.hostelposadadelangel.com. It's difficult to paint a hotel orange and blue and still maintain a charming elegance, but this endearing, welcoming place pulls it off. Free internet and breakfast served in the spacious, enclosed courtyard. $57.

Macondo Tarqui 11-64 and Mariscal Lamar ☎07/284-0697. Another colonial-style favourite with artwork on the walls, a spacious lawn in the back garden and a choice of private or shared bathrooms. Breakfast included. $26.

Orquidea Borrero 931 and Bolivar ☎07/282-4511. A converted colonial home in the centre of the city, and one of the cheapest mid-range options. $24.

Príncipe J Jaramillo 7-82 y Cordero ☎07/284-7287, ⊛www.hotelprincipecuenca.com. Charming, elegantly furnished rooms in a traditional colonial house with artwork on the walls of the spacious dining area. Breakfast included. $42.

Eating

The sweetness of the *Cuencanos* temperament extends to their palates. You're never far from a stall or bakery selling a wide range of cakes and

Tiestos Corner of Jaramillo and Borrero. One of Cuenca's best and most popular restaurants. Gourmet dishes cooked to perfection and served in style with a range of side dishes. Try the beef tenderloin or the langoustines followed by one of the indulgent desserts. Book in advance. Shared mains $15.

confectionery, including the ubiquitous *membrillo* (a gelatinous red block made with fruit). Along with Baños in the Central Highlands, Cuenca has the best choice of restaurants outside Quito, offering diverse international and local cuisine. Note that most places are closed on Sundays.

Cacao y Canela Jaramillo y Borrero. Snug little café serving a huge selection of hot chocolate drinks ($2–3) – rum, cinnamon, almonds and mozzarella are just a few of the flavours available. Great cakes and snacks too.

Café Austria Benigno Malo 5-95 and Juan Jaramillo. Tasty Central European specialities such as roulade and goulash plus tasty cakes and ice creams for dessert. Open on Sunday too. Mains $5–6.

Café Eucalyptus Gran Colombia and Benigno Malo. Lively fun café-bar with a diverse tapas menu (dishes $5–6), draught beer, couches to lounge on and live music Wed–Sat.

El Cafécito Honorato Vasquez 7-36 and Luis Cordero. A backpacker hangout, this is a good place to meet like-minded travellers over a coffee and a game of chess. Rooms out back ($15) are very basic.

Los Capuliés Córdova y Borrero. Well-priced Ecuadorian specialities ($3–5) served in a pleasant enclosed courtyard.

El Jordán Calle Larga 6-111 y Borrero ☎07/285-0517, ⊛www.eljordanrestaurante.com. Middle Eastern specialities such as moussaka with falafel, served attentively in a formal setting with French and Moorish decor. Perfect for a romantic meal. Mains $6–8.

Indian Bapu Calle Larga and Benigno Malo. Authentic Indian cuisine is hard to come by in Ecuador but this place does it well at very reasonable prices. Mains $2–4.

Moliendo Café Honorato Vásquez 6-24. Huge selection of cheap Colombian *arepas* (corn tortillas) and filling *almuerzos* ($2–4).

El Natural Miguel 5-62 and Juan Jaramillo. Popular vegetarian café with a filling, healthy set lunch for just $2.

El Pavón Real Gran Colombia. Ecuadorian-American owned restaurant that brings the best of both worlds with big breakfasts, buffet lunches, a range of international and local specialities at low prices ($2–5) and live music.

Pio Pio Borrero and Córdova. Cheap fried chicken and fast food for $2–3.

Raymipamba Benigno Malo and Bolívar, Parque Calderón. Bustling café under the colonnaded arches of the Catedral Nueva, offering large portions of filling Ecuadorian staples for $3–5.

Drinking and nightlife

It's not as raucous as Guayaquil or Quito but there are enough options to enjoy, mostly south of downtown and along Calle Larga.

Monday Blue Calle Larga y Cordero. Funky little bar with walls covered in art and eclectic memorabilia, serving cheap Mexican and Italian food. Closed Sun.

Tal Cual Calle Larga 7-57. This popular bar pulls in the crowds at weekends when it turns into a lively disco, playing mainly salsa and merengue. Closed Sun & Mon.

Wunderbar Escalinata, off Calle Larga. Popular German-owned place in a large red-brick building with a small garden nestled above the river. The bar is lively in the evenings with occasional live music.

Moving on

Air Tame, LAN and Icaro operate regular flights from Quito and Guayaquil (see "Arrival", p.654).
Bus There are regular buses to Quito (10hr), Guayaquil (4–5hr), Ambato (7hr), Riobamba (6hr) and Loja (5hr).

Directory

Banks and exchange Banco de Guayaquil at Mariscal Sucre and Hermano Migue; Banco de Austro at M. Sucre and Pdte A Borrero; Banco de Pacifico at Benigno Malo 9-75.
Hospitals Hospital Santa Ines at Av. Daniel Cordova Toral 2-113 and Augustian Cueva (☎07/281-7888); Hospital Monte Sinai at Miguel Cordero 6-111 and Av. Solano (☎07/288-5595).
Internet Cuenc@net at Calle Larga and Hermano Miguel; ExploreNet at Padre Aguirre 10-96 and Lamar.
Police Main station at Benigno Malo and Antonio Muñoz (☎07/281-0068).
Post offices Main post office at Presidente Borrero and Gran Colombia; Fedex at Miguel Cordero 350 and Alfonso Cordero.
Telephone Pacifictel at Benigno Malo and Cordoba.

BAÑOS

The ideal way to relax after a few days' sightseeing is to visit the small town of Baños, a 15 minute drive southwest of Cuenca, although the mineral content of the baths is debatable and the town certainly doesn't rival its namesake in the Central Highlands (see p.645). There are two sets of baths: the *Balneario Durán* (Av Ricardo Durán) has two warm pools ($2.50); and there are more upmarket facilities up the road at the *Hostería Durán* (Av Ricardo Durán, ☎07/289-2485, ✆www .hosteriaduran.com; $85 including spa access and breakfast). Use of the warm pool (36°C) and steam rooms costs $5.50. Massages cost $25 per hour.

A taxi from Cuenca to Baños costs $4, or catch the bus ($0.25) from Vega Muñoz and Padre Aguirre or Av. 12 de Abril and Av. Fray Vicente Solano, south of the river.

PARQUE NACIONAL EL CAJAS

Just 30km northwest of Cuenca, the enormous **PARQUE NACIONAL EL CAJAS** (daily 6am–5pm; $10) spans nearly 300 square kilometres of spectacular moor-like *páramo*. With more than two hundred lakes shining beneath rugged hillsides, this is one of Ecuador's most compelling wildernesses, offering great hiking and trout-fishing opportunities. However, the wind, rain and fog can often make visits uncomfortable so come prepared with rainproof gear, snacks, warm clothing and walking boots. Most of the park lies above 4000m so ensure you are properly acclimatized before tackling any long hikes.

It's best to visit the park with a Cuenca-based tour operator, costing about $40 per person (see p.655). To get here independently, take a Cooperativa Alianza bus from the terminal (1hr) and walk to the Laguna Toreador refuge station, which has maps and information on popular hiking trails. The station also has a few beds, or you can camp in the recreation area for about $5 per person, but bear in mind that it gets very cold.

LOJA

South of Cuenca, there is little to catch the visitor's attention until the city of **LOJA**, some 200km away. Loja is one of Ecuador's oldest cities, founded in 1548, with a historic centre, thriving music scene and spectacular parks.

What to see and do

Begin at the **Parque Central**, dominated by the towering green and white **Catedral**. On the south side, the **Museo del Banco Central** (Mon–Fri 9am–1pm & 2–4.30pm; $0.40) has a small collection of pre-Columbian ceramics and religious art. Walk south on Bolívar, passing the beautiful **Iglesia Santo Domingo**, which houses more than one hundred oil paintings. A couple of blocks further on is arguably the highlight of the centre, the **Plaza de la Independencia** (also known as Plaza San Sebastián), lined by brightly coloured colonial buildings. On the southwest corner is the **Iglesia San Sebastián**. The focal point of the square is an impressive clock tower with stone depictions of the battles for Ecuador's independence.

After seeing Loja's historic old town, the best thing to do is visit the parks, easily reachable with a short taxi ride ($2). The best option is the **Parque Universitario de Educación Ambiental y Recreación** (PUEAR, daily 9am–4pm; $1), which has trails up through the forest and impressive views over Loja and the valley. Across the road is the **Jardín Botánico Reynaldo Espinosa** (Mon–Fri 9am–4pm, Sat & Sun 1–6pm; $0.60), which has more than two hundred species of orchids.

Arrival and information

Air Flights from Quito and Guayaquil arrive at the Aeropuerto La Toma, 33km west in the town of Catamayo. A shared taxi (about $5 per person) is the only way to get to Loja from the airport.
Bus Loja's bus terminal is 2km north of the centre on Avenida Cuxibamba, with plenty of taxis ($1) and buses ($0.30) to the centre.
Tourist information The city's iTur office is on the corner of Bolívar and Eguiguren (☎07/258-1251; Mon–Fri 8.30am–1pm and 3–6.30pm).

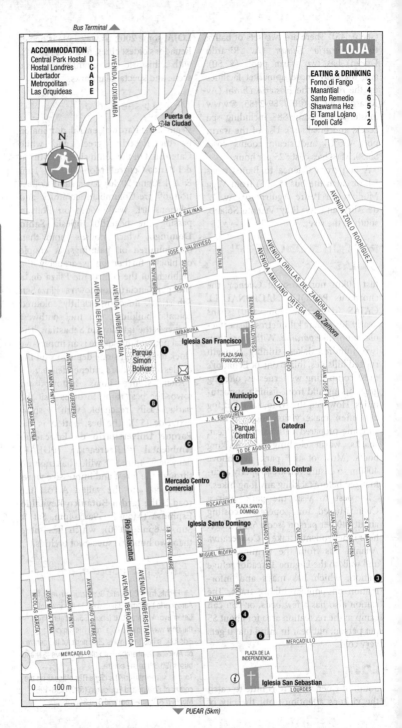

Bus Terminal

LOJA

ACCOMMODATION
Central Park Hostal D
Hostal Londres C
Libertador A
Metropolitan B
Las Orquideas E

EATING & DRINKING
Forno di Fango 3
Manantial 4
Santo Remedio 6
Shawarma Hez 5
El Tamal Lojano 1
Topoli Café 2

N

Puerta de la Ciudad

AVENIDA CUXIBAMBA

JUAN DE SALINAS

JOSE F. VALDIVIESO

18 DE NOVIEMBRE

SUCRE

BOLIVAR

QUITO

AVENIDA IBEROAMERICA

AVENIDA UNIBERSITARIA

IMBABURA

AVENIDA ORILLAS DEL ZAMORA

AVENIDA AMILIANO ORTEGA

Río Zamora

AVENIDA ZOILO RODRIGUEZ

BERNARDO VALDIVIESO

OLMEDO

JUAN JOSE PEÑA

Parque Simón Bolívar

Iglesia San Francisco

PLAZA SAN FRANCISCO

COLON

Municipio

J. A. EGUIGUREN

Parque Central

Catedral

10 DE AGOSTO

Museo del Banco Central

Mercado Centro Comercial

ROCAFUERTE

PLAZA SANTO DOMINGO

Iglesia Santo Domingo

MIGUEL RIOFRIO

SUCRE

BOLIVAR

AZUAY

18 DE NOVIEMBRE

Río Malacatus

RAMON PINTO

JOSE MARIA PEÑA

AVENIDA LAURO GUERRERO

NICOLAS GARCIA

JOSE MARIA PEÑA

RAMON PINTO

AVENIDA LAURO GUERRERO

AVENIDA UNIBERSITARIA

AVENIDA IBEROAMERICA

MERCADILLO

MERCADILLO

PLAZA DE LA INDEPENDENCIA

Iglesia San Sebastian

LOURDES

JUAN JOSE PEÑA

PASAJE SINCHINA

24 DE MAYO

0   100 m

▼ PUEAR (5km)

Accommodation

Central Park Hostal 10 de Agosto y Bolívar ☎07/256-1103. Pink satin bedspreads are not for everyone but otherwise this is one of the best mid-range choices, ideally located on the Parque Central. $35.

Hostal Londres Sucre 07-51 ☎07/256-1936. A dependable option for those on a tight budget, with small but adequate rooms and shared bath. $10.

Libertador Colon 14-30 ☎07/256-0779. The best option to treat yourself, with plush decoration, swimming pool, sauna and steam bath. Breakfast included. $65.

Metropolitan 18 de Noviembre 06-31 ☎07/257-0007. A solid mid-range choice with wooden floors and good-sized rooms with cable TV and private bath. $24.

Las Orquideas Bolivar and 10 de Agosto. Probably the pick of the budget options with clean, neat rooms with TV and private bathroom. $16.

Eating and drinking

Forno di Fango 24 de Mayo y Azuay. Head to this local favourite for great pizza and pasta dishes for around $5.

Manantial Bolívar near Plaza de la Independencia. An informal, cheap place to fill up on Ecuadorian staples for $2–4.

Santo Remedio Plaza de la Independencia. Nightlife is limited in Loja, but this bar with delightful decor themed on the seven deadly sins is a good option for a drink and dance.

Shawarma Hez Bolívar near Plaza de la Independencia. Enjoy something a little different with tasty Arabic food (mains $2–3) served on floor cushions.

El Tamal Lojano 18 de Noviembre. The best place to sample local specialities like *humitas*, *tamales* and *empanadas* for $1–2.

Topoli Café Bolívar y Azuay; $5. Bolivar and Riofrio; $1–2. Sandwiches, burgers, crepes, cakes and ice cream, all for less than $3.

VILCABAMBA

VILCABAMBA has been attracting travellers for years in search of relaxation and the apparent secret to a long, healthy life. Although reports of locals living to 140 years old are wildly exaggerated, there seems to be something in the water in the famous "Valley of Longevity". Backpackers, hikers and hippies flock here to enjoy the region's perfect climate, spectacular scenery and friendly people. The town itself is not brimming with tourist attractions; the main draw is in the surroundings, which offer great **hiking** and **horse-riding** opportunities. Afterwards there are plenty of places to pamper yourself with a relaxing massage. Vilcabamba has also long been associated with the hallucinogenic San Pedro cactus, which grows in this region. Be warned that San Pedro is illegal and local police now deal severely with anyone found taking it.

What to see and do

There are plenty of hiking trails around Vilcabamba to keep you busy for a few days. Perhaps the most impressive is up to the jagged hill **Cerro Mandango**. Walk south of town along Avenida Eterna Juventud to find the trail entrance ($1.50). It's a steep 45-minute climb to the first peak and then an unnerving trek across the very narrow ridgeline to the second peak. You can loop around descending slowly towards town. The entire walk is about four hours. To shorten it, retrace your steps back down from the first peak.

Many hotels have excellent **massage** facilities attached; two great options in town are Piedad Masajes (Calle Agua de Hierro y La Paz ☎09/179-4292) and Karina at Massage Beauty Care (Diego Vaca de Vega y Bolívar ☎07/264-0359). Both charge from $10 per hour.

Northeast of town is the small Rumi-Wilco Nature Reserve ($2 donation) which has a self-guided trail system. To hire **horses**, contact Caballos Gavilán (Sucre y Diego Vaca ☎07/264-0281), which is run by a friendly New Zealander. Half-day/full-day tours with guide cost $20/30.

Arrival and information

Bus Buses run to and from Loja every half an hour from the corner of Av. de la Eterna Juventud and C Jaramillo.

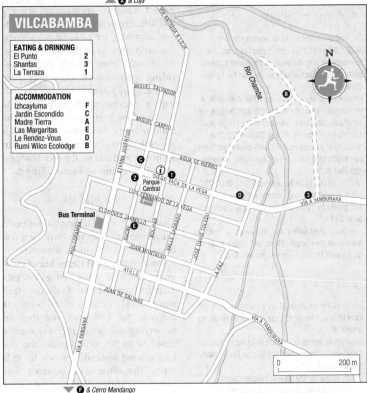

VILCABAMBA

Ⓐ & Loja

EATING & DRINKING

El Punto	2
Shantas	3
La Terraza	1

ACCOMMODATION

Izhcayluma	F
Jardin Escondido	C
Madre Tierra	A
Las Margaritas	E
Le Rendez-Vous	D
Rumi Wilco Ecolodge	B

VIA ANTIGUA A LOJA

Río Chamba

MIGUEL SALVADOR

MIGUEL CARPIO

ETERNA JUVENTUD

AGUA DE HIERRO

DIEGO VACA DE LA VEGA

Parque Central

LUIS FERNANDO DE LA VEGA

VIA A YAMBURARA

Bus Terminal

CLODOVEO JARMILLO

SUCRE

HUILCOPAMBA

BOLIVAR

VALLE SAGRADO

JOSE DAVID TOLEDO

JUAN MONTALVO

LA PAZ

ATILLO

JUAN DE SALINAS

VIA A YANGANA

VIA A YAMBURARA

N

0   200 m

Ⓕ & Cerro Mandango

Money Note that there is a Banco de Guayaquil cash machine in Vilcabamba but no bank; the nearest is in Loja.

Taxi Pick-up trucks act as taxis and charge $1–1.50 to most of the accommodation in and around Vilcabamba.

Tourist information The tourist office, on the northeast corner of Parque Central (open daily 8am–1pm and 3–6pm ☎ 07/264-0090) provides maps and information on hikes and excursions around Vilcabamba.

Accommodation

Expect to pay a little more for accommodation in Vilcabamba than in other parts of Ecuador unless you stay at one of the town's grubbiest dives.

Hostal Jardín Escondido Sucre y Diego de Vaca ☎ 07/264-0281. Simple but spacious rooms around a garden with lemon trees, a small pool and jacuzzi. The hotel's Mexican restaurant is excellent and the service friendly. $25.

Izhcayluma ☎ 07/264-0095, ❼ www .izhcayluma.com. About 2km south of town, this friendly German-owned *hostería*, which means "between two hills" in Inca, has rustic cabins, free use of bikes, buffet breakfasts and one of the best views in town. The owners have mapped out several trails around Vilcabamba for keen hikers. Don't miss the Bavarian stroganoff or the German Weissbier in the fantastic restaurant. Dorms $10, rooms $28.

Madre Tierra ☎ 07/2640269, ❼ www.vilca bambamadretierra.com. For a little luxury, stay at this award-winning spa hotel 1km north of town. Enjoy the view from the balcony of your comfortable cabin and take advantage of the jacuzzi, pool and huge range of spa treatments on offer. Breakfast and soft drinks included. $35.

Las Margaritas Sucre y C Jaramillo ☎ 07/264-0051. This large white house feels like a family residence, with a cosy atmosphere and well-maintained rooms. Excellent value for the price, and breakfast is included. $20.

Le Rendez-Vous Diego Vaca de Vega ☎ 092/191-180, ❼ www.rendezvousecuador.com. East of the

CROSSING INTO PERU

If you're in the southern sierra, it's much better to cross to Peru via Macará, 190km southeast of Loja, than go down to the coast and cross via frenetic Huaquillas. A bus service operated by Cooperativa Loja (☎07/257-9014) travels to Piura in Peru via Macará (8hr) from Loja at 7am, 1pm and 11pm. Buy tickets in advance if possible. The company has offices in Loja bus terminal and next to Vilcabamba's bus terminal. From Vilcabamba take a bus to Loja and change. In Macará the bus stops at the 24-hr *Migración* office for your exit stamp. Walk across the bridge which forms the border to get the entry stamp on the other side and then get back on the bus.

town centre, this French-owned guesthouse has good-value, cosy rooms with hammocks on the terrace overlooking the garden. $18.

Eating

Many hotels have good restaurants attached, particularly *Jardin Escondido* and *Izhcayluma* (see p.660). After dinner, nightlife is almost non-existent in Vilcabamba. Many restaurants outside the hotels are closed on Sundays.

El Punto Sucre and Luis Fernando de Vega. Popular café with expats, ideal to watch the world go slowly by over coffee, juice or dessert ($3–4).

Shantas Diego Vaca de la Vega. Going east out of town, this informal place offers a wide selection of dishes, including trout and frog's legs ($4–6). The more adventurous can try the snake juice ($2), made from pickled coral snake, sugar cane and *aguardiente*.

La Terraza Parque Central. This restaurant serves good *almuerzos* as well as tasty Mexican, Italian and Chinese dishes ($3–4).

The Oriente

East of Quito, the Andes drop dramatically and snow-capped mountains give way to verdant swathes of tropical rainforest stretching some 250km to the Colombian and Peruvian borders. Ecuador's chunk of the Amazon basin, known as the Oriente ("The East"), constitutes almost half of the country's territory, although only five percent of the population lives here in ramshackle towns and remote indigenous communities.

The Northern Oriente offers the most spectacular opportunities for visitors to encounter a bewildering array of flora and fauna in primary rainforest. The highlights are the two huge protected areas – **Parque Nacional Yasuní** and the **Reserva Faunística Cuyabeno**. Unfortunately, reaching these unforgettable wildernesses usually involves travelling through the decidedly forgettable hubs of **Lago Agrio** or **Coca**. For those with limited time seeking an accessible experience, the more pleasant towns of **Tena**, **Puyo** and **Macas** are surrounded by secondary rainforest with chances to stay with **indigenous communities**. The higher elevation of these towns makes **white-water rafting** and **kayaking** popular activities in the rapids tumbling down to the Amazon basin.

Tour operators

It's easiest to book your tour in Quito. The New Town, particularly around Mariscal Sucre, has scores of tour operators and travel agencies offering tours to the main jungle destinations. The following are recommended:

Dracaena J Pinto E4-453 y Amazonas ☎02/254-6590. Offers tours of Cuyabeno, staying at *Nicky Amazon Lodge* (5 days, $280).

Fundación para la Sobrevivencia del Pueblo Cofán Mariano Cardenal N74-153 y Joaquín Mancheno ☎02/247-0946, ⊛www.cofan.org. Stay with the indigenous Cofán community, 25km east of Lago Agrio. Five days from $500 (minimum 4).

Ikiam Expedition ☎08/829-7677, ⊛www.ikiam .info. Community tourism project staying with the Shiwiar people deep in the jungle near the Peruvian border. Fly from Shell near Puyo to Shiona (from $200). Five days from $280.

Kem Pery Tours Pinto 539 and Amazonas ☎02/222-6583, ⓦwww.kempery.com. Offers trips to the Huaorani reserve staying in *Bataburo Lodge* (4 days $340, plus $20 donation to the Huaorani). Trips also on the "Flotel" boat *Jungle Discovery* in Cuyabeno.

Magic River Tours 18 de Diciembre, C Primera and Pacayacu ☎02/262-9303, ⓦwww.magicriver tours.com. German-owned company specializing in canoe trips in the Cuyabeno reserve. Five days from $320.

Neotropic Turis J Pinto E4-340 near Amazonas and Wilson ☎02/252-121, ⓦwww.neotropicturis .com. Four-day tours to Cuyabeno Reserve, staying in *Cuyabeno Lodge* (see p.663) from $250.

Rainforestur Amazonas 410 y Robles ☎02/223-9822, ⓦwww.rainforestur.com. Wide range of jungle tours throughout the Oriente via Lago Agrio, Coca, Puyo and Tena. Four days in Jamu Lodge from $220.

Surtrek Amazonas and Wilson ☎02/223-1534, ⓦwww.surtrek.org. Large tour operator that works with a dozen Amazon lodges plus tours throughout Ecuador. Four days In Cotococha from $670.

Tropic Ecological Adventures Av. República 307 and Almagro, Edif Taurus ☎02/222-5907, ⓦwww .tropiceco.com. Tours and ecotourism projects throughout the Oriente. Four days in Yasuni from

$570 in *Sani Lodge* (see p.663); from $500 in *Huaorani Lodge* (not including flights from Puyo). Indigenous community stays available.

Via Natura Av. Republica del Salvador and Shyris ☎02/246-9846, ⓦwww.vianatura.com. Wide range of tours throughout Ecuador. Four days in Jardin Aleman near Misahualli for $463; four days in Yachana Lodge, three hours from Coca, for $630.

LAGO AGRIO

LAGO AGRIO, also known as Nueva Loja, was used by Texaco in the 1960s as a base for oil exploration in the Ecuadorian Oriente and takes its name (meaning "sour lake") from the company's original headquarters in Texas. In many ways the town epitomizes the power struggle between oil companies keen to get their hands on the "black gold" underneath the jungle and tour operators keen to preserve the once pristine forests of the **Cuyabeno Reserve**. More worryingly, the infiltration of Colombian FARC guerrillas along the border just 21km

---

JUNGLE BASICS

If you dream of striking out on your own and hacking through dense jungle like a modern-day explorer, dream on. Unguided travel is strongly discouraged by the Ecuadorian government and certainly not advisable, considering how inhospitable and inaccessible parts of the Oriente remain. Guided tours are the best option and are relatively cheap, costing $30–50 per person per day. Prices rise if you stay in a more luxurious lodge or on an air-conditioned river cruiser but bear in mind that some discomfort is part of the jungle experience. Always check that your guide has a permit from the Ministry of Tourism. Generally the larger the number of people in your group, the lower the price will be. Tour operators regularly advertise tours leaving imminently with last-minute spaces. Solo travellers usually have to share a cabin or pay a higher rate for a separate room.

Tours range from two to eight days. For tours around Puyo and Tena, a couple of days will give you an insight into life in the Oriente. If you are travelling deep into the jungle, more than four days is recommended, because nearly two days will be spent travelling.

The best place in which to organize a jungle tour is definitely Quito, while Baños, Puyo and Tena have plenty of operators running regular tours. Booking locally is more difficult in Coca and Lago Agrio (although you may be lucky) so it's better to make arrangements beforehand.

You must prepare thoroughly and pack the essentials before heading into the jungle. Be sure to take plenty of insect repellent, long sleeves, trousers, waterproofs, a torch and boots. A first-aid kit is also advisable, although the guide will carry one. See p.620 for information on anti-malarials and yellow fever vaccinations. You must carry your original passport, as copies are not sufficient at military checkpoints.

TEN OF THE BEST JUNGLE LODGES

Prices include all accommodation, food, guides and tours. Transfers are extra. Contact details given are for the Quito offices of each operator.

Bataburo Lodge Ramirez Davalos and Amazonas Edificio Turismundial ☏ 02/250-5600, ⓦ www.kempery.com. Thatched cabins on Tinguino river, eight hours by bus and canoe from Coca, deep in Huaorani territory in primary jungle. Proceeds of tours stay with the local tribe. Four days from $340.

Cotococha Lodge Amazonas and Wilson ☏ 02/223-4336, ⓦ www.cotococha.co. Located on the Napo river between Tena and Puyo, with 21 comfortable bungalows and a large lounge area. Five days from $420.

Cuyabeno Lodge Pinto and Amazonas ☏ 02/252-121, ⓦ www.neotropicturis.com. The first lodge in Cuyabeno Reserve, these simple eco-cabins are still one of the cheapest ways to experience primary jungle. Four days from $250.

Jamu Lodge Calama and Reina Victoria ☏ 02/222-0614, ⓦ www.cabanasjamu .com. One of the best-value budget lodges in the jungle, with nine thatched cabins in the Cuyabeno Reserve. Four days from $200.

Kapawi Lodge Mariscal Foch and Reina Victoria ☏ 02/600-9333, ⓦ www.kapawi.com. High-end ecolodge owned by the Achuar people and

situated on the Pastaza river near the Peruvian border. Five days from $999.

Misahualli Jungle Lodge Ramirez Davalos and Paez ☏ 02/252-0043, ⓦ www.misahuallijungle .com. Comfortable lodge near Tena with swimming pool and restaurant. Five days from $304.

Napo Wildlife Center Av. de la Prensa and Av. de America ☏ 02/289-7316, ⓦ www.napo wildlifecenter.com. Two hours from Coca by boat are these ten deluxe cabins and a 50-ft viewing tower. Part-owned by the Quichua Añargu community. Four days from $760.

Sani Lodge Roca and Amazonas ☏ 02/255-8881, ⓦ www.sanilodge.com. Cabins owned by the Quechua community, set on a secluded lagoon on the Napo river, three hours from Coca. Four days from $570 (camping from $360).

Yachana Lodge Vicente Solano and Oriental ☏ 02/256-6035, ⓦ www.yachana.com. Award-winning higher-end lodge with comfortable accommodation on Napo river near Coca. Four nights from $640.

Yarina Lodge Av. Amazonas and Av. Colon ☏ 02/250-4037, ⓦ www.yarinalodge.com. Ecolodge in Yasuni National Park with 24 huts. Five days from $450.

to the north makes this a **dangerous area**. A FARC leader and 16 rebels were killed in a bombing raid just north of Lago Agrio in March 2008. It's best not to hang around waiting for a tour here; book from Quito instead. If you are staying in Lago Agrio, don't wander from the centre of town and take care at night. Note that at the time of writing, the British Foreign Office advises travellers to avoid Lago Agrio and all areas in Succumbios Province bordering Colombia.

Arrival and information

The **bus station** is 2km northeast and the **airport** 4km east. Take a **taxi** to the town centre ($2) unless your tour operator has arranged a transfer. Most of the hotels, restaurants and tourist agencies are located along the Avenida Quito.

Accommodation

D'Mario Av. Quito 1-171 ☏ 06/283-0172. A popular option with bar, cable TV, swimming pool, a/c and free internet. Breakfast included. $36.

Gran Colombia Av. Quito 265 ☏ 06/283-1032. Well-equipped but rather characterless rooms with fans (a/c extra) and cable TV. $28.

RESERVA FAUNÍSTICA CUYABENO

This beautiful reserve (admission $20) of unique **flooded rainforest** spreads out over more than 6000 square kilometres east of Lago Agrio, extending to the Peruvian border. It contains an astonishing biodiversity of plants, trees, mammals and aquatic wildlife. Meandering down the Rio Aguarico, a tributary of the Amazon, through huge areas of inundated forest and passing countless lagoons, is unforgettable. Pink freshwater **dolphins**, white and black **caiman**, **giant otters** and many species of **monkeys** are commonly seen, while the famous anaconda and jaguar will likely prove elusive. The borders of the reserve were expanded in the early 1990s, partly in response to damaging oil exploration in the region. Sadly, areas of Cuyabeno have been badly polluted but vocal indigenous protest has improved the situation and there remain areas of unspoilt jungle to explore. The remoteness of the region means that you need a guided tour (see p.661 for a list of operators).

COCA

The capital of Orellana province has grown rapidly since the 1970s into an ugly oil town. Similar to Lago Agrio, there's little to tempt you to stay longer than is necessary. **COCA** is, however, the last major town on the Río Napo, the gateway to the enormous **Parque Nacional Yasuní** and also emerging as a route over the border to Peru via **Nuevo Rocafuerte**. Local operators are thin on the ground so it's best to organize a tour from Quito.

Arrival and information

Air Tame (☏06/288-1078) and Icaro (☏06/288-0997) both operate two or three flights daily from Quito to Coca (from $60 one-way), which is tempting to avoid the gruelling bus ride. The airport is 2km north of town (taxi $1).

Boat Coop de Transportes Fluviales Orellana (☏06/288-0087) operates boat services to Nuevo Rocafuerte (8hr; $15) on Mon and Thurs at 7.30am. Advance booking advised.
Bus Coca's bus terminal is 500m north of town but most bus companies have offices in the centre of town. Trans Baños (Napo and Bolívar) offers the best services to Quito (8–10hr) while El Dorado and Transportes Jumandy at the terminal go to Tena (6hr).
Taxi White pick-up truck taxis will take you around town from about $1.

Accommodation

El Auca Eloy Alfaro y Napo ☏06/288-0127. Choose from rustic cabins or upscale hotel rooms with a garden courtyard and good restaurant. $25.
La Misión Camilo de Torrano ☏06/288-0260, Ⓦwww.hotelmision.com. Next to the river, this is one of Coca's more upscale hotels with well-tended rooms, swimming pool, steam baths, good restaurant and monkeys roaming the grounds. $43.
San Fermín Quito and Boliva ☏06/288-1848. Comfortable a/c cabins made from concrete and wood. $22.

Eating and drinking

Emerald Forest Blues Bar Espejo and Napo. A place to drink with fellow jungle-seekers at this backpacker hangout.
Ocaso Eloy Alfaro and Napo. Economical place popular with locals serving the usual Ecuadorian staples such as chicken stew, grilled fish and fried pork chop.
Parrilladas Argentinas Cuenca and Inés. The best place in town for well-prepared but pricey steaks.
Pizza Choza Rocafuerte and Napo. Get your fill of Italian pasta and pizza before heading to the jungle (mains $4–6).

In 2007, Rafael Correa's government launched one of its most ambitious and innovative projects, Yasuní ITT. The basic idea is that Ecuador will be paid around $3.6 billion over thirteen years in exchange for not drilling the estimated one billion barrels of oil in the Ishpingo, Tambococha and Tiputini (ITT) fields under Yasuní National Park, a biodiversity hotspot. The government's reasoning is that oil has been a key income for Ecuador for the past thirty years and, now that supplies are dwindling, there is increasing financial pressure to drill under protected rainforest. To resist this pressure, the country deserves compensation for preserving a unique biosphere, protecting indigenous communities and helping efforts to curb global warming.

Initially, the project received a very favourable response from international media and governments. However, in the global economic crisis, it has proved difficult to get firm commitments to invest. President Correa has also been reluctant to accept conditions on how the money is spent. At the time of writing, the project is at a crucial stage with Correa threatening to exploit Yasuní if funds are not secured, even though constitutional experts claim that any such exploitation would be illegal. For further information, visit ⊕ www.yasuni-itt.gov.ec or www.sosyasuni.org.

PARQUE NACIONAL YASUNÍ

YASUNÍ ($20) is one of Ecuador's last great wildernesses and the country's largest mainland national park. The terrain of nearly 10,000 square kilometres ranges from upland tropical forest to seasonally flooded forest, marshes, swamps, lakes and rivers. This region was untouched by the last Ice Age and has staggering biodiversity – more than five hundred species of **birds** and more than sixty percent of Ecuador's **mammals**, including rarer species such as jaguar, harpy eagle, puma and tapir.

UNESCO declared it an International Biosphere Reserve in 1979 but unfortunately this didn't prevent oil exploration. The construction of a road, Vía Maxus, through the park and pollution from irresponsible oil companies has damaged some areas. However, large sections remain unscathed and Yasuní still offers the best opportunities in Ecuador to experience pristine rainforest. Most tours coming through Coca will include a visit to the park.

TENA

TENA is the most pleasant town in the Oriente to be based for a few days. Rather than being merely a gateway to the jungle, it's a destination in itself, with a slightly cooler climate, good hotels and restaurants, and an impressive setting on the river surrounded by lush forest.

Aside from wandering around the centre and relaxing in a riverside restaurant, the main attraction in town is **Parque Amazónico La Isla** (daily 8.30am–5pm; $2), just south of the main pedestrian bridge. This park has several self-guided forested trails, diverse plants and wildlife including tapirs, toucans, a rather fierce ostrich and various species of monkey who will jump on your back and follow you around with some persistence.

Arrival and information

Bus The terminal is 1km south of the centre. A taxi from here or anywhere in town costs $1.

Tourist information On Agusto Rueda (☏06/288-8046).

Accommodation

A Welcome Break Corner of Agusto Rueda and 12 de Febrero ☏06/2886-6301, ⊕www.awelcome breakecuador.com. A dependable budget option with basic rooms, a cheap restaurant for breakfast and a travel agency. Dorms $6, rooms $12.

JUNGLE TOURS AROUND TENA

The following Tena-based operators offer jungle tours in addition to rafting and kayaking. Most tours are all-inclusive of transport, accommodation, food and guides.

Agency Limoncocha Sangay 533 ☎06/288-7583. Based in the hostal of the same name (see below); offers jungle tours of 1–4 days at $35–45 per day.

Akangau Jungle Expeditions 12 de Febrero and Augusto Rueda ☎08/6175-641, Ⓦwww.akangau.com. Offers four-, five- and six-day tour expeditions to Limoncocha and one-day tours near Tena. From $30 per day.

Amarongachi Tours 15 de Noviembre ☎06/288-6372, Ⓦwww.amarongachi.com. Tours staying in Cabañas Amarongachi or,

preferably, Cabañas Shangri-La, perched 100m above the Napo River commanding wonderful views. From $45 per day.

Ricancie Av. El Chofer y Cuenca ☎06/288-8479, Ⓦricancie.nativeweb.org. Co-ordinates ten indigenous community ecotourism projects in the upper Napo region. Tours cost around $45 per day.

Sacharicsina Tours Montesdeoca 110 and Pano ☎06/288-6839. Run by a local Quechua family, providing jungle tours ($40–50 per day) in cabañas on the Río Illoculín, southwest of Tena.

Brisa del Rio Av. Francisco de Orellana ☎06/288-6444. One of the best-located budget hotels on the river. Pricier rooms have a/c, cable TV and private bath. $16.

La Casa del Abuelo Sucre 432 ☎06/288-8926. This excellent mid-range choice is as cosy and homely as the name ("grandfather's house") with well-furnished rooms, high ceilings and a pleasant rooftop terrace. $20.

Limoncocha Av. de Chofer ☎06/288-7583. A popular backpacker option is this German-run *hostal* on the southeast edge of town (20-min walk from the centre), with a travel agency, guest kitchen and free internet. $16.

🏃 **Travellers Lodging** Av. 15 de Noviembre 438 and 9 de Octubre ☎06/288-7102. Budget travellers will feel right at home here. The good-quality rooms are excellent value for the price, with hot water, private bathroom and cable TV. The reputable Amarongachi travel agency is attached. $14.

Los Yutzos Augusto Rueda 190 y 15 de Noviembre ☎06/288-6717. The riverside location and spacious, tastefully decorated rooms make this the best mid-range place in town. Lounge on the balcony overlooking the river or relax in the verdant gardens. $40.

Eating

Café Tortuga Francisco de Orellana. Travellers' favourite with friendly service, an ideal location on the river and great fresh coffee, snacks and desserts.

Chuquitos Off Parque Central. An excellent riverside position, with a wide-ranging menu and attentive service. The fish is particularly good. Mains $5.

Cositas Ricas Av. 15 de Noviembre and 9 de Octubre. This cheap, cheerful place serves tasty Ecuadorian staples ($2–4) and is a good option for lunch.

The Marquis Grille Amazonas and Olmedo. The ideal choice to treat yourself and one of Tena's few upmarket restaurants. The steak and trout are specialities. Mains $8.

Pizzeria Bella Selva Francisco de Orellana. The best place in town for pizza and large plates of pasta (mains $4–10).

Moving on

Bus There are hourly buses to Quito (5hr) via Baeza, and regular buses to Puyo (3hr) and Baños (4–5hr). Daily buses to Coca (6hr) are a little less frequent.

PUYO

If you're arriving from Baños or even Tena, **PUYO** will at first sight be a disappointment, as the centre is rather ugly. But a few kilometres out of town are some attractions worth seeing, principally the **Jardín Botánico Las Orquídeas** (daily 8am–6pm; $5 book in advance; ☎03/288-4855, Ⓦwww.jardinbotanicolasorquideas.com;), 3km southeast of town (take a taxi for $1). These botanical gardens, set among lush hills, boast more than two hundred species of native Amazonian orchids. Also worth visiting is **Parque Pedagógico Etno-Botánico Omaere** (daily 8am–6pm; $3; ☎03/288-7656),

For adventurers wanting to emulate Francisco de Orellana and float deeper down the Río Napo into the Amazon Basin, improved relations between Ecuador and Peru in the past decade have made it easier to cross the border via Nuevo Rocafuerte. There are even plans afoot to make the trip possible all the way to Brazil's Atlantic coast, although it remains to be seen if and when this will happen. This is not a trip for those who like comfort, as it's some eight hours downstream from Coca. Boats leave Coca at 7.30am Monday and Thursday ($15 one-way), usually stopping off at Pañacocha. From Nuevo Rocafuerte to Coca there are usually departures Wednesday and Sunday. Come prepared with adequate supplies of food, water purification tablets and insect repellent. In Nuevo Rocafuerte there are a few very basic, cheap places to stay but nowhere good enough to linger long. From Nuevo Rocafuerte you receive an exit stamp and boats cross the border to Pantoja, where you get an entry stamp. Pantoja also has a small amount of basic accommodation. Boats leave to Iquitos only once a month, a trip which takes six days.

a ten-minute walk north from the city centre, which has guided tours along forested paths past indigenous dwellings.

Arrival and information

Bus The bus station is 1km west of the centre, a 15-minute walk or $1 by taxi.

Tourist information The Cámara de Turismo office is on Av. Marin and General Villamil (☎ 03/288-3681) and supplies maps and information on attractions in and around Puyo.

Accommodation

You didn't come to Puyo to stay in the bland, central hotels, so it's best to avoid these options and stay on the outskirts of town or head straight to a jungle lodge.

El Jardin Paseo Turistico, Barrio Obrero ☎ 03/288-6101, ⍟ www.eljardin.pastaza.net. North of the centre towards Parque Omaere has this rustic wooden house, set behind a large garden, an award-winning restaurant. Breakfast included. $56.

Hostal Araucano Ceslao Marín and 27 de Febrero ☎ 03/288-5686. Worn, weathered rooms but very friendly service in this cosy, basic budget option in town. $14.

Hosteria Turingia Marin and Orellana ☎ 03/288-5180, ⍟ www.hosteriaturingia.com. German-owned mid-range choice with attractive, wood-panelled bungalows. $40.

Eating

Chifa Ken Wah Atahualpa. Tasty, cheap Chinese dishes – noodles, sweet-and-sour chicken and fried rice. Mains $3–4.

El Jardin In lodge of the same name. Probably the best restaurant in the area with specialities including pollo Ishpingo (chicken with cinnamon). Mains $5–10.

Parrilladas El Vino Tinto Atahualpa. Barbecued meat dishes and jungle specialities, including guanta (a type of Amazonian rodent). Mains $4.

Tour operators

Most travellers book from Quito or Baños but there are a few good tour operators in Puyo offering tours to communities close to town. Other communities, such as the Huaorani, are only reachable by light aircraft from the Shell airport 10km west of town; these tours are more expensive. Further information about Huaorani communities can be obtained from the political body ONHAE (☎ 03/288-6148).

Amazonia Atahualpa y 9 de Octubre ☎ 03/288-3219. Offers a range of tours close to Puyo from $35–50 per day.

Papangu 27 de Febrero and Sucre ☎ 03/288-3875. An indigenous-run agency offering tours to nearby Quechua communities and further afield to Sarayacu and Río Curaray (travel by light aircraft). Tours $45–60 per day not including flights.

Selva Vida Ceslao Marin and Atahualpa ☎ 03/288-9729, ⍟ www.selvavidatravel.com. Light two- and three-day jungle trips, plus five-day trips deeper into the jungle.

Moving on

Bus Baños (every 30min; 1hr 30min); Tena (hourly; 3hr).

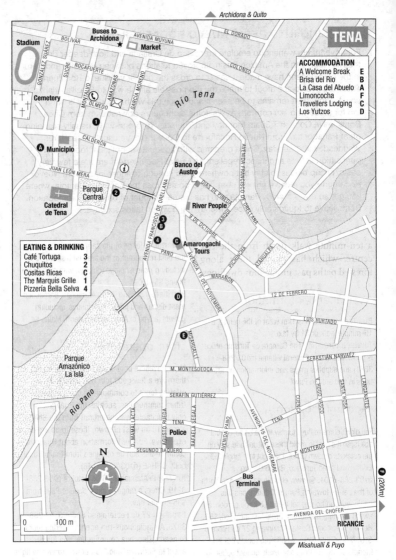

MACAS

MACAS is Ecuador's southernmost and most remote jungle town, five hours south of Puyo and seven hours northeast of Cuenca. Most travellers enter the jungle via the northern towns but quieter Macas has a certain charm that makes it worth visiting. In the midst of Shuar territory, a people once renowned for headhunting, indigenous pride burns strongly here and there have been recent confrontations with the government. Tourists can only visit the traditional villages that surround Macas with approved guides. Local tour agencies also arrange jungle treks.

What to see and do

In the centre of Macas, the main attraction is the large modern **Catedral** on Parque Central, which commands good views of the town. A block southwest of the park is the small **archeological museum** at the Casa de la Cultura (10 de Agosto and Soasti Mon–Fri 8am–5pm; free), which has Shuar exhibits including head-dresses, blowpipes and a replica of a shrunken head. To the north is the **Parque Recreacional**, which has even better views than the cathedral.

Arrival and information

Air Tame (☎02/397-7100) flies Mon–Fri to Macas from $50 one-way.
Bus The bus terminal is on Amazonas and 10 de Agosto.
Tourist information There is a new tourist office on Comin (Mon–Sat 8am–noon; ☎07/270-1606, ⓦwww.macasturismo.gov.ec).

Accommodation

Casa Blanca Soasti and Sucre ☎07/270-0195. Has decent rooms with private bath, cable TV and breakfast included. $25.
La Orquidea 9 de Octubre and Sucre ☎07/270-0970. A basic boarding house with firm beds, run by a friendly family. $18.

Eating and drinking

La Maravilla Soasti and Sucre. Adorned with indigenous artefacts, and serving a variety of meat dishes and snacks (mains $3–6).

La Napolitana Amazonas and Tarqui. Serves pizza, pasta and barbecues as well as great fish dishes, including tilapia and trout. Mains $3–8.

Moving on

Bus Cuenca (several daily; 7hr); Puyo (10 daily; 5hr); Quito (2 daily; 10hr).

The northern coast and lowlands

As you travel north up the Ecuadorian coast, you'll notice that the scenery gets greener and the vibe more Caribbean. The Afro-Ecuadorians that make up a large part of the population of **Esmeraldas** province give the region a different cultural feel to the rest of the country. You'll find the locals exuberant, extrovert and talkative; a refreshing change from the mountains.

The main route from the Sierra descends dramatically via **Santo Domingo de los Colorados**, an unattractive transport hub. Avoid the dangers of **Esmeraldas** town and head south to a string of beach resorts to suit all tastes, whether you're seeking all-night parties or a beach to yourself. **Atacames** is by far the most popular party town. Further down the coast, the beautiful beach at **Mompiche** is emerging as a popular spot for budget travellers. Moving further south into the province of **Manabi**, head to **Canoa**, a haven for surfers and sunseekers, and one of the country's most laidback resorts. Nearby, the elegant resort **Bahía de Caráquez** juts out dramatically on a slim peninsula, close to mangroves and tropical forest. Further south is Ecuador's second largest port, **Manta**, a bustling city with its own beaches.

SANTO DOMINGO DE LOS COLORADOS

This transport hub is the most convenient route from the Sierra to the coast. From here you can head north to Esmeraldas and Pedernales or south to Bahía de Caráquez, Manta and Guayaquil. Parts of town are dangerous so take care at night. Try to begin your journey early so that an overnight stop becomes unnecessary, since Santo Domingo has little to offer.

The **bus terminal** is 1.5km north of the town centre (take a taxi for $1 or a public bus). If you're stuck here, you'll find **accommodation** is unimpressive. Opposite the bus terminal, *Hotel Sheraton* (Av Calazacón 111 ☎02/275-1988; $17) has clean rooms, hot water, cable TV and fans. In town, *Hotel Diana Real* (Corner 29 de Mayo y Loja ☎02/275-1380; $19) has the same facilities and a restaurant attached. For **eating**, try the upmarket *Gran Hotel Santo Domingos* good restaurant or *La Tonga* (Rio Toachi y Galápagos) or *Chifa Happy* (Tulcan 117) for Chinese.

ESMERALDAS

ESMERALDAS is the north coast's most important industrial town, with oil pumped in for refining and cash crops shipped out for export. Little of the wealth stays here, so it's a very poor town and one of Ecuador's most **dangerous**, particularly on the Malecón

Maldonado. Either take a direct bus to the beach resorts or time your journey to arrive in Esmeraldas before nightfall, so that you can change and avoid an overnight stay.

Bus services run by Transportes La Costeñita and Transportes del Pacífico depart regularly to the beach resorts of Atacames, Súa and Same from Malecón Maldonado (6.30am–8pm). The **airport**, served by flights from Quito, is 25km east of town and the only way to get there is by taxi ($18, but $25 will get you direct to Atacames instead). If you really must stay over in Esmeraldas, the best **accommodation** is in the more pleasant suburb of Las Palmas, 3km north of the centre. *Hotel Cayapas* (Av Kennedy 401 ☎06/272-1318; $50) has comfortable rooms with TV and hot water plus a good restaurant. You're best off **eating** in one of the hotels in Las Palmas. There are plenty of cheap eateries downtown but take care after dark.

ATACAMES

ATACAMES is the busiest, brashest beach resort on the north coast and, along with Salinas, the most popular in Ecuador. Most of the hotels, restaurants and bars are situated on the peninsula, which forms the **Malecón**. The long sandy beach is lined with bamboo bars serving up fruit shakes by day and cocktails by night. During the week it's relatively quiet and a bit depressing, with staff desperately trying to lure you into their empty bars, but at the weekends and on national holidays Atacames turns into a heaving party town. Boom boxes pump out ear-splittingly loud salsa and reggaeton, while bars are packed with revellers until dawn.

There are a few interesting excursions, including boat trips to nearby **Isla Encantada** ($3), which has abundant birdlife. From June to September, you can watch humpback whales off the

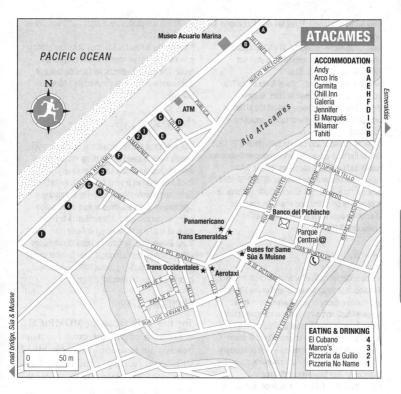

Map labels:

Museo Acuario Marina

PACIFIC OCEAN

ATACAMES

Río Atacames

Esmeraldas

ATM

Banco del Pichincho

Panamericano
Trans Esmeraldas

Buses for Same
Súa & Muisne

Trans Occidentales

Aerotaxi

Parque Central

road bridge, Súa & Muisne

0   50 m

ACCOMMODATION

Andy	G
Arco Iris	A
Carmita	E
Chill Inn	H
Galería	F
Jennifer	D
El Marqués	I
Milamar	C
Tahiti	B

EATING & DRINKING

El Cubano	4
Marco's	3
Pizzeria da Guilio	2
Pizzeria No Name	1

coast; tours can be organized through *Le Castell Hotel*, on the Malecón (℡06/273-1442). The town of Atacames is inland over the bridge but it's a dusty unpleasant place which only necessitates a visit if you need a bank or an internet café. Note that tourists, particularly women, get hassled more here than in the southern resorts. **Muggings** have also been reported so avoid taking valuables onto the beach, take taxis and stay in well-lit areas.

Arrival and information

Bus There are buses at least every hour coming up and down the coast to Atacames. The town is compact enough to walk around but if you're laden with luggage and particularly at night, take one of the motorized tricycle taxis ($0.50).

Internet There are several cafés inland in town on Rua Luis Cervantes and opposite the Parque Central.

Accommodation

Atacames has a vast amount of accommodation ranging from dirt-cheap cabins to luxurious tourist complexes. It can be surprisingly hard to find anything decent during peak periods so book ahead. Note that prices can rise by around fifty percent in high season.

Andy Malecón y Los Ostiones ℡06/276-0221. This beachfront hotel is cleaner than other budget options and has good, well-kept rooms (for the price) with fans and TV, although it gets noisy. $20.

Arco Iris Malecón ℡06/273-1069, ⒲www .arcoirisatacames.com. Here, at the far north end of the Malecón, you'll feel as if you've stepped into the Oriente, lazing on a hammock in rustic cabins tucked away in verdant gardens. $35.

Carmita Las Taguas and Malecón ℡06/273-1784. For a quieter stay just off the seafront, this *hostal* is good value with cable TV and a/c. $20.

Chill Inn Los Ostiones and Malecón ℡06/276-0477, ⒲www.chillinnecuador.com. Comfortable rooms, communal TV, kitchen for guest use and a small bar make for a homely atmosphere at this new Swiss-run hostel. There are only four rooms so book in advance. $20.

Galería Malecón ☎06/273-1149. The cheapest place on the seafront, with friendly staff but decidedly basic rooms. $16.

Jennifer Malecón and Calle la Tolita ☎06/273-1055, ⊛www.hostaljennifer.com. Another dependable budget choice just off the Malecón, with peach-coloured, clean rooms equipped with fans. $15.

Milamar Malecón and Calle la Tolita ☎06/273-1363. One of the best-value mid-range hotels, with spacious rooms and fans. Back rooms are quieter. $20.

Tahiti Malecón and Los Delfines ☎06/273-1078, ⊛www.hotel-tahiti.net. Choose from comfortable cabins or hotel rooms and enjoy the spacious swimming pool terrace and a high-quality restaurant. $40.

Eating

You're spoilt for choice for **seafood restaurants**. The beach stalls at the south end of the Malecón sell cheap *ceviche* (a popular hangover cure for breakfast) and most of the restaurants offer similarly good fish and shellfish dishes. After dinner there are scores of beach bars in which to enjoy cocktails and dancing – they are usually either packed or empty. All restaurants are on the Malecón unless otherwise indicated.

El Cubano Out of the many seafood restaurants along the seafront, this is the most popular budget choice, always jam-packed with locals and tourists wolfing down fish soup and breaded shrimps. Set menu just $3.

Marco's For something a bit more intimate, try *Marco's*, where a delightful old lady serves up large portions of sumptuous seafood dishes such as *encocado* (seafood cooked in coconut and garlic) and *cazuela* (fish and plantain casserole) in an elegantly furnished setting (mains $4–7).

Pizzeria da Giulio For a break from seafood, head to this Italian-Ecuadorian place, which takes pride

in offering sumptuous fresh pizza and pasta dishes (mains $5–12).

Pizzeria No Name Luckily, they put more effort into the food and atmosphere than they do the name. The decor is eclectic and a wide range of dishes (mains $4–10) are served on a bamboo balcony.

Moving on

Bus Atacames has no central bus terminal so you usually need to stand on the dusty main street inland to hail one. Trans La Costeñita and Trans Pacífico buses run several times an hour to Súa, Same and Muisne (1hr 30min). For Mompiche (2hr 30min), there are three or four direct buses a day, or you can catch a bus heading to Pedernales to drop you off nearby. For Quito (7hr), use Trans Esmeraldas, Aerotaxi or Trans Occidentales (offices across the footbridge). Bear in mind that at weekends and during national holidays you must book in advance as demand is high.

MOMPICHE

The tiny little village of **MOMPICHE** is home to one of the most beautiful beaches in Ecuador. This, combined with great surfing conditions, have increased its popularity recently, albeit at a reassuringly slow pace. Things may change, however, with the recent arrival of the luxury hotel *Royal Decameron*. Unless you have hundreds to spend per night, the town has limited **accommodation** options and is booked up during busy periods. The best budget option is *Gabeal* (☎09/969-6543; $15), located up the beach to the right. This ecolodge has 25 rooms in bamboo cabins, each with a private bathroom. An equally good choice is the new Argentine-owned *La Facha* (☎08/8734271; $14), with great-value rooms and pizza and barbecues in the small restaurant. Five minutes' walk inland is one of the few modern budget hotels in town, *Hotel San Marena* (☎09/191-6115; $20) with large rooms and TV. You can get your seafood fill at any of the **restaurants** on the beachfront such as *El Económico* and *El Punto Encuentro*, but head a block inland to the south to *La Langosta* for the best in town (mains $4–7).

There are a few **buses** daily from Esmeraldas via Atacames. If you miss one, either take a bus to Muisne and change at El Salto, or take a bus to Pedernales and ask the driver to drop you off at the entrance to Mompiche. From there, you can hitch a ride or sweat it on a half-hour walk.

CANOA

CANOA is rather like the Montañita of ten years ago – a quiet fishing village that has developed into a laidback resort by virtue of its beautiful beach and great surfing conditions. It has a dramatic setting, with waves crashing upon long stretches of sand flanked by steep cliffs. At present, it just might be Ecuador's best beach resort for budget travellers without the overblown weekend craziness of Atacames or Montañita, but it's changing fast.

An interesting excursion from Canoa is **Río Muchacho Organic Farm**, where you can see sustainable farming in practice and learn about the culture of the *Montubia* (coastal farmers). Guided hikes, horseriding and birdwatching are available, and Guacamayo Bahíatours offers all-inclusive tours (1 day $30, 3 days $115). Its offices are in Bahía de Caráquez (Bolívar 902 ☎05/269-1412) and Canoa (☎091/479-849).

Arrival and information

Bus From Quito there is now a direct bus with Transvencedores from Quitumbe bus station at 2.30pm (8hr), returning at midnight. There are more regular buses from Quito to Bahia de Caraquez; from there, cross the bay on the ferry and take a bus from San Vicente (15min) to Canoa. From Pedernales, there are buses to Canoa every half hour or so.

Tourist information There is no tourist office, though the Rio Muchacho Office a block inland on Av. 3 de Noviembre and Javier Santos has plenty of information and friendly staff. The guys at *Surf Shak* (see p.674) are also full of advice on local tours.

Accommodation

Bambú ☎08/926-5225, ⦿www.hotelbambu ecuador.com. At the north end of the beach is Canoa's most happening hotel. Rooms are small but the vibrant atmosphere and beautiful beachfront gardens make up for it. The restaurant is worth visiting even if you don't stay. Camping available ($3.50) and surfboards for hire. $13.

Canoa's Wonderland Malecón and Calle San Andre ☎05/261-6363, ⦿www.hotelcanoas wonderland.com.ec. This hotel stands out as one of the few plush options in Canoa with a pleasant bar, restaurant, rooftop terrace, swimming pool and a/c rooms. $45.

Coco Loco ☎09/544-7260, ⦿hostalcocoloco .weebly.com. Two blocks left of the junction with the beach are these basic rooms in a large thatched bamboo house with fans, hammocks on a balconies, kitchen, bar with cocktails and a friendly atmosphere. Dorms $6, rooms $18.

Pais Libre ☎05/261-6387. This very popular hotel is run by friendly local surfer Favio Coello. Rooms are well kept, the hotel is decorated with artwork, there's a disco/bar next door and small pool is set in leafy gardens. Dorms $6, rooms $14.

Posada Olmito Javier Santos ☎09/553-3341, ⦿www.olmito.org. An endearing Dutch-owned place with basic rooms in an intricately constructed wooden building. $14.

Sundown Beach Hostel Km 2 Via San Vicente ☎09/981-5763, ⦿www.ecuadorbeach.com. A 20-min walk from town, this quiet beachfront hostel is a good spot to get away from it all with private patio, garden and communal atmosphere. Dorms $6, rooms $12.

La Vista Hotel ☎08/647-0222, ⦿www.lavista canoa.com. Next to *Coco Loco*, this mid-range beachfront hotel offers more comfortable, airy rooms, all with sea view and private bathroom. $24.

Eating and drinking

Canoa has plenty of restaurants – mainly informal beachfront places offering fresh seafood, though some new options have opened recently. Nightlife is restricted but quite busy in the bars on the main street at weekends and on national holidays.

Amalur Calle San Andres. A few blocks from the beach, this is one of Canoa's few upmarket options and specializes in Spanish specialities such as tortillas, meatballs and octopus (dishes $5–8). They've just opened a small but great-value hotel at the back ($20).

Café Flor Malecón. A block or so behind *La Vista Hotel*, this cosy café serves a range of Mexican, Italian and vegetarian dishes ($4–8) in an informal setting. They also have real ales.

Cevicheria Saboreame Malecón. The best seafood in town according to locals – and they should know. Mains $3–5.

Coco Bar Javier Santos. On the main street leading to the beach, this is the hub of Canoa's nightlife – dead during the week but hot at weekends and in high season, with a packed dancefloor and free-flowing cocktails.

Surf Shak Malecón. For a break from seafood, try this American-owned place which offers big burgers and pizzas. Wi-fi is available as well as plenty of advice on tours from the friendly owners.

BAHÍA DE CARÁQUEZ AND AROUND

The most dramatic location of Ecuador's coastal resorts, **BAHÍA DE CARÁQUEZ** sits on a slim sand peninsula jutting out from the mouth of the river Chone into the Pacific. The city, known simply as Bahía to locals, endured two disasters in 1998, when the El Niño rains washed away roads and triggered massive landslides before an earthquake in August destroyed two hundred buildings and left twenty people dead. The city recovered, however, and introduced a wide-ranging environmental programme, converting itself into an "eco-city" with recycling, sustainable development and reforestation. The result is that, unlike many of Ecuador's resorts, which have well-kept Malecóns backed by dirty, shabby streets, Bahía is a clean and pleasant place to stroll around.

What to see and do

The **Museo Bahía de Caráquez** (Tues–Sat 10am–5pm, Sun 11am–3pm; $1) has a small collection of pre-Columbian artefacts, and the **Mirador La Cruz**, a large cross above the south end of town, offers good views over the city and surrounding bay. Some 15km south of town is the **Chirije archeological site**, which has countless ancient artefacts such as ceramics and burial sites dating from 500 BC. The site can be visited through Bahía Dolphin Tours (Bolívar 1004 ☎05/269-2097, ⓦwww.bahiadolphin tours.com). Inland from Bahía, the river Chone has some excellent unspoilt mangroves inhabited by abundant birdlife, including a colony of frigate birds to rival those found in the Galápagos. A half-day tour with Guacamayo Bahia-tours (Bolívar 902 ☎05/269-1412) costs $25 per person.

Arrival and information

Boat It's a short walk to the passenger ferry dock, which has regular boats speeding across the bay to San Vicente, from where you can continue north up the coast.

Bus Buses arrive and leave from the south end of the Malecón. There are regular services to and from Portoviejo, Manta and Guayaquil and four per day from Quito (or travel via Pedernales). Reina del Camino (18 de Septiembre and Av. Patria, Mariscal, Quito) is the biggest bus company.

Taxi There are plenty of tricycle taxis to get around town (most fares $0.50–$1).

Tourist information There's no tourist office in town but the next best thing is to visit Guacamayo Tours (Bolívar and Arenas ☎05/269-1412, ⓦwww .guacamayotours.com).

Accommodation

Most budget travellers prefer to stay in Canoa but Bahia is a pleasant alternative. Accommodation ranges from cheap and basic to rather overpriced at the higher end. Hotels fill up quickly during high season (Dec–April) and on national holidays.

Bahia Bed and Breakfast Inn Ascazubi 316 and Morales ☎05/269-0146. The best rock-bottom budget option in town, with basic rooms with fans and cable TV in the lounge. $10.

Hostal Coco Bongo Intriagi and Arenas ☎08/544-0978, ⓦwww.cocobongohostal .com. Run by a friendly Aussie lady, this converted house overlooking the park has rooms with hot water, private bath, wi-fi and cable TV. It's a good place to hang out and the breakfasts are top-notch. $20.

La Herradura Bolívar and Daniel Hidalgo ☎05/269-0266. At the northwest of town, this charming old Spanish house has a/c rooms with cable TV and a good restaurant attached. $35.

Eating and drinking

Arenabar Pizzeria Marañon and Bolívar. Good pizza and lasagne ($5–7) plus eclectic celebrity decor.

Colombius Bolívar. A cheap place for set lunches of chicken and fish ($2–3).

Muelle Uno Malecón. One of a string of restaurants on the pier near the docks, serving man-sized barbecue platters and seafood dishes for $4–8.

Puerto Amistad Malecón. This place is owned by an American sailor and offers quesadillas and crepes as well as meat and fish dishes ($5–10).

Tropiheados Bolívar. Indulgent ice-cream sundaes and filling fast food ($2–3).

MANTA

MANTA is a thriving commercial centre and Ecuador's second-largest port after Guayaquil. The city used to host an **American air base** that brought riches into the town, but was criticized for drawing Ecuador into the drug war with Colombia. President Rafael Correa refused to renew the contract and the US opened bases instead in Colombia. The departure of US forces has partly been blamed for an increase in crime in Manta.

Although it remains a popular resort with locals, it doesn't have a huge amount to offer foreign tourists. There are better beaches elsewhere and the areas of the city with budget accommodation are **dangerous** at night. You're better off heading south to Machalilla National Park or north to Bahía de Caráquez and Canoa. The main beach, **Playa Murciélago**, north of the centre, is packed with restaurants and snack bars. Note the beach can be dangerous for swimming because of a strong undertow. To the east of town past the fishing boat harbour is **Playa Tarqui**. The waters are calmer but it can be dangerous here at night.

Arrival and information

Air There are daily flights from Quito with Tame (ⓦ www.tame.com.ec).

Bus The bus station in front of the fishing boat harbour on Calle 7 and Av. 8 has regular services to Bahía de Caráquez, Portoviejo, Puerto López and Montañita, as well as hourly departures to Guayaquil and Quito (Reina del Camino) and occasional services up the coast to Esmeraldas.

Tourist information There is a tourist information office on Av. 3 and Calle 11.

Accommodation

The cheapest accommodation is in Tarqui but it's not a very safe area, particularly at night. If you're on a tight budget you should head elsewhere and if you can afford it, stay in the safe, more pleasant northwestern sector of the city behind Playa Murciélago.

Las Gaviotas Malecón de Tarqui 1109 ☏ 05/262-0140, ⓦ www.hotelgaviotasmanta.com. Four-storey mid-range option with pool, game room, internet, bar and restaurant. Breakfast included. $50.

Hostal Manakin Calle 20 and Av. 12 ☏ 05/262-0413. Perfectly positioned between the beach and the nightlife spots, this is a home away from home. With ten comfortable rooms, it retains an intimate atmosphere missing in many other hotels in Manta. $45

Old Navy Calle 104 and Malecón, Tarqui ☏ 05/261-3556, ⓦ www.oldnavyhotel.com. One of the better options in Tarqui with bright rooms and private bathroom. $30.

Eating and drinking

There are plenty of seafood restaurants on the Malecóns, both In Tarqui and Playa Murciélago; they are cheaper in Tarqui but it's not safe at night. The best area for food and nightlife is Avenida Flavio Reyes, inland from Playa Murciélago, which is filled with bars and discos. Always take a taxi back to your hotel.

El Cormoran Av. 24 and Calle M-2. In a large restaurant complex, this is just one of many places offering seafood, meat and pasta ($4–6).

Marisco Flipper Calle 20. Just one of the scores of good restaurants around Flavio Reyes, offering cheap set lunches and a wide range of seafood specialities ($4–6).

Oh Mar Malecón, Playa Murciélago. Dependable seafood chain restaurant which does all the traditional plates well – generous portions of *ceviche*, fish soup, grilled sea bass and breaded shrimps (around $4–6).

Pizzeria Topi Malecón. Near the theatre east of Playa Murciélago, this is one of the best places in town for pizza and pasta (mains $5–9).

Guayaquil

Ecuador's coast feels like a separate country compared to the Sierra and, with regionalist feelings burning strongly, many *costeños* wish it was. **Guayaquil** is Ecuador's largest city and its economic powerhouse, handling most of the country's imports and exports. The heat, dirt and danger used to be reasons enough to stay away, but the city has undergone quite a facelift in the past decade and the waterfront and city centre have enough to keep visitors occupied for a few days.

Arriving from the mountains, the contrast is striking between Quito's cool colonial charms and Guayaquil's hot, humid vivacity. *Guayaquileños* (or *Guayacos*) are fiercely proud of their city and they have a centre that is worth showing off. Guayaquil's 3km-long **Malecón** and renovated artistic district of **Las Peñas** are great achievements, as are the new airport, bus terminal and museums.

What to see and do

Be aware that the heat and traffic pollution can make sightseeing an uncomfortable experience, so get up early. The weekend, when the city is quieter, is the best time to explore. Outside the centre, Guayaquil is not picturesque and remains dangerous, particularly at night.

La Plaza Cívica and Plaza Olmedo

The best point to enter the **Malecón** (a 3-km public space that is easily the highlight of the city – enclosed, pedestrianized and patrolled by security guards; open daily 7am–midnight) is **La Plaza Cívica** at the end of 9 de Octubre. Start at **La Rotonda**, a statue of South America's liberators, José de San Martín and Simón Bolívar, shaking hands in front of a semi-circle of marble columns. Past the plush Guayaquil Yacht Club is the 23m-high Moorish Clock Tower and further south **The Henry Morgan**, a replica of a seventeenth-century pirate ship, is docked. A one-hour trip on the river costs $5 (hourly departures afternoons and evenings).

Further south is **Plaza Olmedo**, with its contemplative monument of José Joaquín de Olmedo (1780–1847), the first mayor of Guayaquil. The southern end of Malecón reaches La Plaza de la Integración and an artesans' market, selling traditional indigenous clothing and crafts.

Botanical gardens

North from La Rotonda is the Jardines del Malecón, a large children's play area packed with families at weekends. Further on is a stunning set of **botanical gardens** with more than three hundred species of coastal vegetation. The gardens are divided into four zones: ornamental trees, humid forest, palms and coniferous. There are two plazas within the gardens: the Pre-Columbian Plaza, with Manteña balsa wood and palm trees, and the Neoclassic Plaza, with a bronze fountain surrounded by lanterns. Above the gardens is a set of 32 transparent panels with the names of some 48,000 citizens who contributed to the construction of the Malecón.

IMAX and Museo Guayaquil en La Historia

At the north end of Malecón is an **IMAX cinema** (☎04/256-3078, ⓦwww.imaxmalecon2000.com) with a 180-degree screen. Below the cinema is **Museo Guayaquil en La Historia** (daily 10am–6.30pm; $2.50), which condenses a compact history of the city, from prehistory to the present day, into fourteen dioramas. Unlike many of the city's museums, the entire tour is available in English.

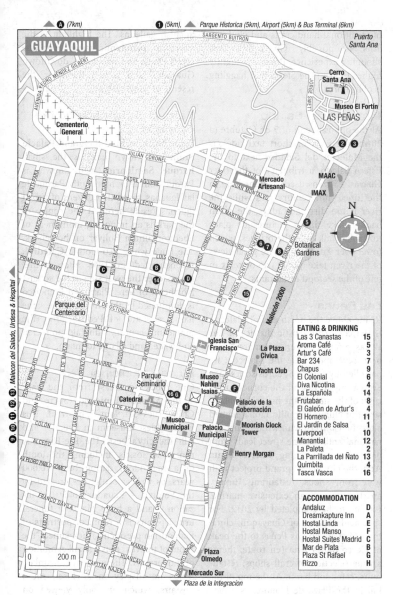

GUAYAQUIL

SARGENTO BUITRÓN

Puerto
Santa Ana

Cerro
Santa Ana

Museo El Fortin

LAS PEÑAS

Cementerio
General

JULIÁN CORONEL

MAAC

Mercado
Artesanal

IMAX

Botanical
Gardens

N

Parque del
Centenario

Malecon 2000

EATING & DRINKING

Las 3 Canastas	15
Aroma Café	5
Artur's Café	3
Bar 234	7
Chapus	9
El Colonial	6
Diva Nicotina	4
La Española	14
Frutabar	8
El Galeón de Artur's	4
El Hornero	11
El Jardín de Salsa	1
Liverpool	10
Manantial	12
La Paleta	2
La Parrillada del Ñato	13
Quimbita	4
Tasca Vasca	16

Iglesia San
Francisco

La Plaza
Civica

Yacht Club

Parque
Seminario

Museo
Nahim
Isaias

Catedral

Palacio de la
Gobernación

Museo
Municipal

Palacio
Municipal

Moorish Clock
Tower

Henry Morgan

ACCOMMODATION

Andaluz	D
Dreamkapture Inn	A
Hostal Linda	E
Hostal Manso	F
Hostal Suites Madrid	C
Mar de Plata	B
Plaza St Rafael	G
Rizzo	H

Plaza
Olmedo

Mercado Sur

Plaza de la Integracion

0   200 m

Museo Antropológico y de Arte Contemporáneo

The north end of Malecón culminates in the spacious **Museo Antropológico y de Arte Contemporáneo** (MAAC) (Tues–Sat 10am–6pm, Sun 10am–4pm; $1.50, Sun free), which has an exhibition on "10,000 years of ancient Ecuador",

a huge collection of pre-Columbian ceramics and modern art exhibition.

Mercado Artesanal (Artisans' market)

A couple of blocks inland along Calle Loja is the huge, enclosed **Mercado Artesanal**, which has a wide selection of traditional handicrafts and clothing. This is possibly Guayaquil's best shopping experience. Prices are slightly higher than in the Sierra and haggling is obligatory.

Malecón del Salado

At the opposite end of 9 de Octubre (a 20-minute walk or short taxi ride), is the **Malecón del Salado**, next to the Estero Salado, a tributary of the river Guayas. Citizens used to bathe here in the nineteenth century and while the river is too dirty nowadays, the green banks make this a picturesque place to stroll. Walk onto the bridges, which tower over 9 de Octubre, for great views of the river, take a boat trip or relax in one of the seafood restaurants.

Las Peñas

Rising above the north end of Malecón is the colourful artistic district of **Las Peñas**, a formerly run-down area that's been revamped. Like the Malecón, it's patrolled by security guards so it's safe, even at night. Round the corner to the right of the steps is the historic, cobbled street of Numa Pompillo Llona, named after the *Guayaco* who wrote Ecuador's national anthem. The street leads from old to new, reaching **Puerto Santa Ana**, the city's latest grand project with waterfront shops, restaurants, luxury apartments and an extensive marina. It's due to be completed by 2012. For spectacular views of Guayaquil, climb the 444 steps up Las Peñas to the peak of **Cerro Santa Ana** (en route, there's a wide selection of craft shops, restaurants, cafés and bars). At the top of the hill in the Plaza de Honores is a new colonial-style chapel and the **Lighthouse** (free), based on Guayaquil's first, built in 1841. Also here is the open-air **Museo El Fortín del Santa Ana**, which holds the foundations of the Fortress of San Carlos. The fortress, which defended the city from pirates, has original cannons and replicas of

Spanish galleons. The highlight is the sweeping panoramic view over the rivers Daule and Babahoyo, downtown Guayaquil and, across the river, the reserve of Santay Island.

Parque Seminario and the Catedral

Three blocks behind the grand **Palacio Municipal** (town hall) is the small **Parque Seminario**, also known as Parque Bolívar or, more aptly, Parque de las Iguanas, given that dozens of urban iguanas reside here. At the centre of the park is an imposing monument of liberator Simón Bolívar on horseback. The huge white neo-Gothic **Catedral**, reconstructed in 1948 after a fire, towers over the west side of the square. Northeast of here, Plaza San Francisco is dominated by the church of the same name, a statue of Pedro Carbo, the nineteenth-century liberal politician and writer, and a large fountain.

Museo Municipal

One block southeast from the park is the **Museo Municipal** (Sucre and Chile, Tues–Sat 9am–5pm; free). This is the oldest museum in Ecuador and still the city's best. The Pre-Hispanic room has fossils, including the tooth of a mastodon, dating back 10,000 years, as well as sculptures created by the Valdivia – Ecuador's oldest civilization – and a huge Manteña funeral urn. Upstairs is a room of portraits of Ecuadorian presidents, nicknamed "the room of thieves", plus a small exhibition of modern art. There are five shrunken heads on display in a closed room upstairs, which are only viewed on guided tours. Free tours in English are recommended because the museum has no English information.

Parque Histórico

Across the bridge in the wealthy district of Entre Rios, the Parque Histórico (Wed–Sun 9am–4.30pm; $3 or $4.50

Sun; ☎04/283-3807) is worth the trip out of town. The park is divided into three zones. Created out of the natural mangroves of the river Daule, the **wildlife zone** provides a snapshot of the Ecuadorian jungle with deer, tapirs, monkeys, sloths, ocelotes, tortoises, parrots, toucans, caimans and fermenting termite mounds. The **traditions zone** depicts the rural way of life via haciendas, "peasant" houses and crops. At weekends, there are boisterous music and comedy shows. In the **urban architecture zone**, some of Guayaquil's late nineteenth-century buildings are reproduced. The colonial-style *Café 1900* is the perfect place to gaze out over the river. To **get there**, catch bus #81 from the terminal or get a taxi from downtown ($4–5).

Arrival and information

Air Guayaquil's José Joaquín de Olmedo airport (☎04/216-9000, ☒www.tagsa.aero) is Ecuador's only other international airport outside Quito, about 5km north of downtown. There are regular flights to and from Quito, the Galápagos, Cuenca and Loja. The airport has an exchange bureau and ATM machines.

Bus The bus terminal is 6km north of downtown, with food courts and shopping malls. The best way to get into town from here is the Metrovia, a rapid transit bus system modelled on Quito's. It runs from Terminal Rio Daule opposite the bus station through downtown to the south. Get off at La Catedral stop for the main tourist sights.

Taxi There are plenty of taxis but few of them use a meter, so negotiate the price first. Taxi drivers In Guayaquil will nearly always try to overcharge foreigners. You should pay $3–4 from the terminal to the centre and $4–5 from the airport. Avoid unmarked cabs. Short taxi rides around the city should cost about $2.

Tourist information The Dirección Municipal de Turismo office at Pedro Icaza 203 (Mon–Fri 9am–5pm; ☎04/259-9100, ☒www.visita guayaquil.com) has friendly staff and up-to-date maps and brochures. The tourist office also produces two guidebooks – a general tourist guide and a gastronomic guide. Another useful website is ☒www.inguayaquil.com.

Tour operators Carlson Wagonlit Travel (4th floor, Edificio El Fortín, Padre Aguirre 104 and Malecón

☎04/231-1800, ☒www.carlsonwagonlit.com); Canodros Urb. Santa Leonor Mz 5 Solar 10 Vía al Terminal Terrestre ☎04/228-5711, ☒www .canodros.com); Cetitur (9 de Octubre 109 y Malecón, Piso 1 ☎04/232-5299); Ecoventura (Miraflores Av. Central 300A ☎04/283-9390, ☒www.ecoventura.com); Metropolitan Touring (Artarazana Calle 11A NE103 ☎04/232-0200, ☒www.metropolitan-touring.com).

Accommodation

Guayaquil has plenty of hotels but is still not well geared up for the backpacker market. Many of the budget hotels are of a very poor standard in unappealing areas, while the top-end hotels charge very high rates for foreigners. It's best to stay near to Parque Bolívar or Parque Centenario. The centre can get very noisy so consider asking for a back room or a higher floor. It doesn't make much sense to stay in the suburbs because there are few tourist sights, although there is one good backpacker hostel, *Dreamkapture Inn* (see below).

Andaluz Baquerizo Moreno y Junín ☎04/230-5796. Located just a few blocks from Malecón and 9 de Octubre, this bright, breezy hotel has comfortable rooms with a/c and hot water, a splash of artwork on the walls, a relaxing rooftop terrace and a lounge area with leather sofas and TV. $40.

Dreamkapture Inn Alborada Doceava Etapa ☎04-224-2909, ☒www.dreamkapture.com. A few miles from the centre, this is one of the city's few backpacker haunts. Secure, well-maintained and friendly, the comfortable rooms have a/c and there's a small pool. The hostel also owns its own travel agency. Dorms $10, rooms $25.

Hostal Linda Lorenzo de Garaicoa 809 ☎04/256-2495. New hotel overlooking Parque Centenario with marble floors and plush, well-furnished rooms. $40.

Hostal Manso Malecón 1406 and Aguirre ☎04/252-6644, ☒www.manso.ec. A slice of Arabian boutique chic in Guayaquil with individually designed rooms, seated cushions and regular performances in the lounge area. $42.

Hostal Suites Madrid Quisquis 305 and Rumicacha ☎04/230-7804, ☒www.hostalsuitesmadrid .com. Not the best location but certainly one of the best-value options in the city, with colourful decor, patterned bedspreads, spacious rooms, background music, a feast of artwork covering the walls and very friendly service. $23.

Mar de Plata Junín 718 y Boyacá ☎04/230-7610. Many of Guayaquil's budget hotels border on intolerable but this is a good deal. Rooms are basic but clean and come equipped with fans, cable TV and private bathrooms (a/c $5 extra). $20.

Plaza St Rafael Chile 414 ☏ 04/232-7140. Smallish but comfortable rooms with a/c, cable TV and hot water. Breakfast included. $35.

Rizzo Clemente Ballén y Chile ☏ 04/232-5210. Adequate rooms, some with small balconies, ideally situated next to Parque Bolívar. $44.

Eating and drinking

Guayaquil has a wide range of restaurants spread around the city. Downtown, there are plenty of cheap, very basic places, while restaurants attached to hotels are rather overpriced. Las Peñas is the most pleasant area to eat, with a cluster of traditional cafés. An alternative is to take a taxi ($2–3) up to the fashionable neighbourhood of Urdesa, where there's a wide range of restaurants along the main street Victor Emilio Estrada.

Las 3 Canastas Velez and Chile. This colourful, informal café specializes in pastries, fruit salads, ice creams and traditional Ecuadorian meals. It's cheap, clean and portions are big (mains $2.50–4). What more could you want? There's a smaller sister café on Pedro Carbo and Clemente Ballen.

Aroma Café Jardines del Malecón 2000. The best place to eat on the Malecón, with a wide selection of Ecuadorian specialities ($5–8) served in the cool, shaded atmosphere of the botanical gardens.

Artur's Café Numa Pompillo, Las Peñas. Dramatically located restaurant perched over the river. The open windows make for a fresh, breezy experience and the menu offers local staples such as grilled fish, *ceviche* and fried pork chops for $5–7.

La Española Junín y Boyaca. Excellent bakery with a wide selection of delicious cakes, pastries, sandwiches and big breakfasts.

Frutabar Malecón y Martinez. Surfboards, tropical murals and a huge selection of *batidos* (fruit shakes) and imaginative burgers and sandwiches make this the perfect repose after a hard morning's sightseeing.

El Galeón de Artur's La Escalinata, Las Peñas. With its maritime decor and live music at weekends, this is a good place for a drink and a light meal.

El Hornero Estrada 906, Urdesa. Delicious pizzas baked in a large clay oven. Portions from $2.

Manantial Estrada 520, Urdesa. Large, popular café with benches, serving a wide range of Ecuadorian specialities and pitchers of beer. Service is a bit surly.

La Parillada del Ñato Estrada and Laureles, Urdesa. Treat yourself to a huge plate of barbecued meats in this enormously popular Urdesa institution. Mains $5–10.

Tasca Vasca Ballén 422 Parque Bolívar. Beautifully laid-out Spanish restaurant with a cosy cellar-like ambience and waiters in traditional dress. Large menu of tapas and Spanish specialities. Mains $6–10.

Nightlife

Guayaquileños love to party, so it's no surprise that the city has a nightlife to rival Quito's. Las Peñas has a wide selection of café-bars and Urdesa is also a good place for a few drinks after dinner. To hit the dancefloor, go to the Zona Rosa, between downtown and Las Peñas, around Rocafuerte and Pánama. Most discos open at 10pm and close around 3am. There's usually a minimum consumption charge of $10, which includes entrance.

Bar 234 Imbabura y Rocafuerte, Zona Rosa. If you've had enough of reggaeton, head to this popular rock bar.

Chapus Estrada, Urdesa. A Guayaquil institution. Have a few drinks on the wooden balcony or hit the dancefloor – one of the few in Urdesa.

El Colonial Rocafuerte y Imbabura, Zona Rosa. A traditional Peñas bar with Ecuadorian specialities and live music at weekends.

Diva Nicotina La Escalinata, Las Peñas. At the bottom of the steps of Las Peñas, you can catch some great live music here – from Cuban Habanera to jazz – accompanied by whisky and cigars.

El Jardín de Salsa Av. Las Américas (near the airport). Swivel those hips or just stand back and watch the experts on one of the biggest dancefloors in Ecuador.

Liverpool Av. Las Monjas 402, Urdesa. Bright, vibrant café-bar packed with Beatles memorabilia. Live music Tues–Sat.

La Paleta Numa Pompillo Llona, Las Peñas. One of the city's most aesthetically pleasing watering holes with a bohemian atmosphere, cosy corners and bars on two floors.

Quimbita Galeria La Escalinata, Las Peñas. At the bottom of the steps, this art gallery doubles as a café-bar with live folk music at weekends.

Directory

Banks and exchange The most convenient downtown banks are Banco del Pacífico on Pedro Carbo and Icaza, and on 9 de Octubre and Ejército; Banco de Guayaquil is on Rendón and Pánama.
Consulates Australia, San Roque and Av. Francisco de Orellana, Ciudadela Kennedy Norte ☏ 04/268-0823; Canada, Edificio Nobis Executive Centre,

702 Av. Joaquin Orranita y Av. Juan Tanca Marengo
☎04/256-3580; UK, General Córdova 623 and
Padre Solano ☎04/256-0400; US, 9 de Octubre
and García Moreno ☎04/232-3570.
Hospital Clínica Kennedy on Av. del Periodista,
Kennedy ☎04/228-6963.
Internet Internet 50C, Rumicacha and Rendon.
Post office The main office is on Pedro Carbo and
Ballén, just off the Parque Bolívar.

The south coast beaches

At weekends, *Guayacos* flee the city's heat in droves and head west to the cooler Pacific beaches of the **Ruta del Sol**. It gets very crowded in peak season between Christmas and Easter, when the weather is hottest. Among the resorts, **Playas** is the closest to Guayaquil, the beach resort of **Salinas** is the playground of wealthy *Guayacos*, and surfer hangout of **Montañita** draws in backpackers. Further north is the beautiful province of Manabí, which contains Ecuador's only protected coastal area, the **Parque Nacional Machalilla**. The port of **Puerto López** is the most convenient base to explore the park and Isla de la Plata, billed as the "poor man's Galápagos" because of its birdlife. **Whale-watching** is a highlight between June and September.

PLAYAS AND PUERTO EL MORRO

Playas, 90 minute from Guayaquil by bus, attracts lower-middle-class *Guayacos* rather than the rich (who generally go to Salinas). Like all south-coast resorts, it's jammed in high season and quiet the rest of the year. The beach is very long but not sheltered and currents are strong, so take extra care in the water. The many cabins that line the beach dole out some great fresh seafood; a cosier alternative is the restaurant *La*

Cabaña Tipica on the Malecón (main dishes $4–6). There are plenty of well-priced hotels on the waterfront should you choose to stay. *Hotel Dorado* (Malecón ☎04/276-0402; $35) is a good mid-range choice with air conditioning, private bath and cable TV. For a cheaper room, try *Hostal Cattan* further along to the right (☎04/276-0179; $20).

A few miles east of Playas, the small port of **Puerto El Morro** is an enjoyable day-trip from Guayaquil. To get there, take a bus to Playas from Guayaquil's terminal, then change (1hr 30min). The main attractions are mangroves, birdlife and dolphins in the estuary. The short tour (1hr 30min; $5) takes in the mangroves, lets you see dolphins and even do a spot of fishing, and the longer route (3hr; $8) includes an extended boat trip and a walk on the Isla de los Pájaros, which has large populations of magnificent frigatebirds and pelicans. Both can be arranged with Ecoclub Los Delfines de Puerto el Morro (☎04-2529496, ⓦwww.puertoelmorro .blogspot.com).

SALINAS

To new arrivals **SALINAS** looks like a wannabe Miami Beach with high-rise apartment blocks and expensive yachts in the harbour. But it's worth stopping here, at least for a day-trip, to walk along the attractive waterfront and swim in the calm waters. The resort has plenty of great restaurants and nightlife for those who want to party with rich kids. West of the Malecón is a second beach, **Chipipe**, which is quieter and has a plaza, church and park.

Arrival

Bus CLP buses run regularly from Guayaquil (every 30min) and have improved dramatically in quality recently; many coaches now equipped with a/c, TV and seat belts. Change at Santa Elena for Montañita.
Tourist information The tourist information office (Enriquez Gallo and Calle 30 ☎09/623-6725) is open sporadically, mainly in high season.

Accommodation

Book hotels ahead in high season, particularly at weekends and on national holidays. Hotels on the waterfront come at a premium, while inland from the waterfront, Salinas is rather ugly.

Cocos Malecón y Fidón Tomala ☏04/277-2609, ⓦ www.cocos-hostal.com/hostel.html. The most economical of the options on the waterfront with a restaurant, bar, disco and games room. $35.

Francisco II Enríquez and Rumiñahui ☏04/277-3544. A dependable mid-range option with a/c and a small pool. The sister hotel, *Francisco*, is located behind. $36.

Hostal Las Palmeras Enriquez Gallo and Rumiñahui ☏04/277-0031. This hotel has good rooms for the price but a rather uninspiring view. $25.

Oro del Mar I Calle 23 and General Enrique ☏04/277-1334. One of the most economical choices, but like most of the cheap accommodation in Salinas, it's a bit shabby. There are three hotels of the same name dotted around town. $25.

Yulee Eloy Alfaro and Mercedes Molina ☏04/277-1334. In the more pleasant area of Chipipe, this brightly painted colonial-style hotel is a break from the high-rise concrete. It has three levels of rooms and you won't find a cheaper option. $16.

Eating and drinking

You're spoilt for choice on where to eat, particularly seafood. Note that you should avoid the seafood stalls, nicknamed "Cevichelandia", on Calle 17 and Enriquez, as sanitation is a problem. Salinas's nightlife hots up in high season when you can take your pick from discos on the waterfront. All restaurants listed are on the Malecón, unless otherwise indicated.

Amazon ☏04/277-3671. International cuisine in a rustic ambience. Mains $6–10.

La Bella Italia ☏04/277-1361. For a break from Ecuadorian fare, watch mouth-watering pasta and pizza prepared in front of you in this comfortable restaurant – and then devour. Mains $4–7.

Holmurguesa ☏04/277-1868. Great value home-made burgers for just $2.

Oh Mar ☏277-2896. A good choice on the Malecón for fresh seafood ($5–10).

La Ostra Nostra Eloy Alfaro and Las Almendras ☏04/277-4028. Choose from a wide range of seafood, soups and meat (mains $5–10) at this extremely popular restaurant out towards Chipipe. Oysters ($12 per dozen) are a particular speciality.

Moving on

Bus Get a bus from Calle Enriquez (one block in from the front) to Libertad; from there, buses run to Guayaquil (every 30min; 2hr 30min) and Montañita (every 30min; 1hr 30min).

MONTAÑITA

Perhaps there should be a sign at the entrance to **MONTAÑITA** that reads: "You are now leaving Ecuador". Such is the international vibe that you could be anywhere in the world. At first sight, the town feels like countless other backpacker havens, but whether you love it or hate it, you can't deny the place's infectious energy. The surfing contingent has been joined in recent years by hippies and partygoers, making it the coast's most buzzing resort for budget travellers. Many people stay for months, while others get out after a couple of excessive nights. If you like to party all night, this is the place to be, but if you're seeking a relaxing beach break, go elsewhere. Surfers can enjoy rideable breaks most of the year, frequently 2–3m on good days. It's not the best place to learn but there are plenty of experienced teachers. There's a renowned international surf competition around Carnival (Feb/March).

Arrival and information

Bus Comfortable CLP buses leave Guayaquil at 5am, 1pm and 5pm (4hr). If you can't catch one of these, take one of the several buses from Guayaquil to Salinas every hour. Ask the driver to drop you at Santa Elena to catch a connection (daytime only). The bus stop is a couple of blocks inland from the beach on the corner of Rocafuerte.

Tour operators Sweet Surf (Calle Quatro ☏09/738-9089, ⓦ www.sweetsurfecuador.com), run by a friendly Swedish-Ecuadorian couple, offers surfboard rentals for $15 per day ($4 per hr) and two-hour lessons for $15, as well as tours ranging from day-trips to a week-long surf tour of the coast. Carpe Diem (Guido Chiriboga and Rocafuerte ☏04/206-0043) is a new tour operator in town and offers a wide range of tours – everything from kayaking, horseriding and snorkelling to organized tours of Machalilla and even the jungle.

Accommodation

Montañita has a huge amount of accommodation and where you stay depends mainly on how much sleep you want to get. If you're not fussy you can find a basic room for $5–7 per person but bear in mind the centre is often very noisy and at weekends the partying continues until after dawn. The north end is quieter with the best quality mid-range accommodation and allows you to enjoy the best of both worlds.

Abad Lounge Avenida Costanera and Malecón ☎4/230-7707. Right on the beach, this new family-run hotel has tidy rooms, many with sea views and balconies. $20.

Casa del Sol ☎09/2488581, ⊛www .casadelsolsurfcamp.com. Walk north all the way to the point to this very popular hangout run by a Californian surfer. The rooms are bright and breezy, and there's a great restaurant and bar area. Sea view costs extra. $40.

El Centro de Mundo Malecón and Rocafuerte ☎0972/82831. Look no further for cheap, basic rooms than this three-storey, wooden beachfront building, just to the right of the junction of Rocafuerte with the beach. Dorms $3.50, rooms $14.

Charos Malecón between 15 de Mayo and Rocafuerte ☎04/206-0044, ⊛www.charoshostal.com. Just inland to the left of the beachfront. This is the most comfortable place to stay in the centre, with a/c rooms, a bar, restaurant and small pool. $45.

Hostal Pakaloro Avenida Costanera at the north end of Chiriboga ☎04/206-0092. A great budget deal, featuring newly refurbished rooms with private bath and cable TV. $18.

Mochica Zumpa Malecón ☎09/938-7483. The rooms – on either side of the junction with the beach – are basic but the location is impressive. Choose from rustic bamboo or multicoloured decors. $20.

Paradise South ☎04/290-1185. For something quieter and more upmarket, go north of town (past the second bridge) to enjoy the comfortable thatched cottages and large lawns of this tranquil, welcoming place. $25.

Eating and drinking

There are scores of good restaurants in the centre of town. Montañita throws quite a party at weekends, particularly in high season (Dec–April). Most bars on the main street, Guido Chiriboga, offer two-for-one happy hours on cocktails ($3) but take it slow until things get going towards midnight.

Cañagrill Avenida Costanera. Round the corner from the main street Guido Chiriboga, this is the town's busiest nightclub, with two dancefloors playing a mix of electronic and latin music. It gets packed in the early hours and the partying continues until after dawn. Open from 10pm at weekends; entrance $5.

Hola Ola 10 de Agosto. Two blocks inland, *Hola Ola* is turning into the centre of the town's social scene. Big breakfasts in the morning, a wide range of cocktails in the evening, parties at weekends and great international food in between – what more could you want?

Karukera Guido Chiriboga. A great choice for breakfast, this place specializes in crepes and also serves up Caribbean specialities such as fish in orange sauce.

Papillon Guido Chiriboga and Rocafuerte, on the corner of the main street. Indulge in a range of sweet and savoury pancakes or relax with an ice-cream sundae.

Tiburon Rocafuerte. It's a spit and sawdust place but that's part of the charm. The menu is surprisingly diverse – *empanadas*, Thai dishes, risotto and more. Sign the wall after eating for a bit of fun – everybody else has.

Tiki Limbo Guido Chiriboga. This backpackers' favourite takes pride in its food and you're bound to find something tantalizing on its imaginative, eclectic menu. Asian and vegetarian dishes ($6–9) are particular specialities. The brightly coloured rooms in the hostel upstairs are very popular ($20).

Moving on

Bus Guayaquil (every 15–30min; 3hr 30min); Puerto Lopez (hourly; 1hr); Manta (hourly via Puerto Lopez; 3hr). For Quito, go to Manta or Puerto Lopez and change.

MANGLARALTO AND DOS MANGAS

Just south of Montañita is the quiet fishing village of **Manglaralto**. The sea is too dangerous for swimming but the estuary where the river Manglaralto flows into the Pacific is safe to bathe. There are few decent hotels in town. *Hostal Manglaralto* (☎04/290-1369, $20) has comfortable rooms, some with a sea view; the slightly cheaper *Sunset Hostel* (☎04/244-0797, $20) has hammocks but an uninspiring view.

By far the most interesting option is *Kamala Hostería* (☎09/942-3754, ⓦwww.kamalaweb.com; $30); the individual cabins are set around a small swimming pool in front of the beach and there's also a bar, restaurant and dive school.

Nearby **Dos Mangas** is the best base to explore the tropical dry forest of the Cordillera Chongón. Dos Mangas is a community of 950 people living from crafts and agriculture. It has a small information centre, and two paths through the forest to waterfalls and natural pools. Trucks from the main coast road head to Dos Mangas every hour and you can hire guides and horses (around $10 per person). The park entrance fee is $1. Alternatively, book a tour in Montañita.

OLÓN

This tranquil village on the other side of the point is developing as a quiet alternative to Montañita; it has a long beach and a few good hotels and restaurants. The sea isn't suitable for surfing but you could just about swim in it. The most interesting accommodation option is *Quimbita* (☎04/278-0204, $20), a charming, colourful hotel with a permanent art exhibition. *Hostería N&J* (☎04/239-0643; $25 with breakfast) on the beachfront is another friendly place. Seafood specialities ($3–4) are dished up at one of the beach huts.

MONTAÑITA TO PUERTO LÓPEZ

Head north from Montañita and cross into the province of **Manabí**. This is probably the most beautiful stretch of Ecuador's coastline – so if you prefer peace to partying and watching wildlife rather than people this is the place to come. On the road to Parque Nacional Machalilla, you'll pass a succession of fishing villages – **Ayampe**, **Las Tunas**, **Puerto Rico** and **Salango**. These villages

are not great destinations in themselves as tourist facilities are still underdeveloped, but the area does contain some good-quality accommodation and the beaches are often deserted.

Between Las Tunas and Puerto Rico, there are a couple of highly recommended *hosterías*. A very popular **accommodation** option is *La Barquita* (☎04/278-0051, ⓦwww .hosterialabarquita.com; $20). The main attraction is the wooden, boat-shaped restaurant, worth a visit even if you don't stay. The rooms are set in idyllic gardens with a small adventure playground and swimming pool. *Hostería Alandaluz* (☎04/278-0690, ⓦwww.alandaluzhosteria.com; $40), near the tiny village of Puerto Rico with an entrance signposted from the highway, is an award-winning eco-resort with a great location in front of the beach, enclosed by a garden, orchard and bamboo forest. Camping ia available for $7 per person. If either of these are beyond your price range, a decent budget alternative is on the Malecón de Las Tunas at *Cabañas Mirada al Mar* (☎09/121-7400; $10). The rooms are perfectly adequate for the price and the view is unbeatable.

Further north, it's worth stopping at Salango to see the small **archeological museum** ($2), which has an exhibition of pottery and sculptures from the Valdivia and Manteña cultures. Salango also has a pleasant beach, although the large factory to the south spoils the view. The town has a couple of decent restaurants, notably *El Pelicano*, but it's better to stay in Puerto Lopez or Puerto Rico.

PUERTO LÓPEZ

Puerto López is the tourism hub for the Machalilla area and the best base to explore **Parque Nacional Machalilla** and **Isla de la Plata**. The town boasts one of the most attractive locations on the coast, set in a wide bay surrounded by the green hills of Ecuador's largest protected coastal forest. The dusty Malecón has a certain beaten-down charm and in the morning the sight of fishermen heading out from the bay gives the town a vibrant feel. Note that the town gets very busy on weekends during the whale-watching season (June–Sept) so booking accommodation in advance at that time is advisable.

Arrival and information

Bus Buses drop passengers on the main road, General Córdova, by the church, from where it's a short walk to the waterfront. Alternatively you can take a tricycle taxi ($0.50).

Tourist information The local iTur office (Av Machalilla and Atahualpa ⓔturismo@puertolopez .gov.ec) is two blocks inland and has plenty of leaflets and attentive service. Open daily.

Accommodation

Hostal Itapoa Malecón ⓣ09/314-5894, ⓦwww .hosteltrail.com/hosteriaitapoa. North of town, these Brazilian-run cabins set in a small garden are an endearing budget hideaway. $20.

Hostería Mandala ⓣ05/230-0181, ⓦwww.hosteriamandala.info. North of town along the Malecón is this very popular travellers' option with beachfront cabins set in beautiful gardens, plus a games room, small library and a good restaurant. $43.

Hostería Nantu Malecón ⓣ09/781-4636. This new hotel is excellent value, offering mid-range level rooms at a low price. Firm beds, hot water as well as a small pool and games room to keep you busy. $30.

Piedra del Mar ⓣ05/230-0011. Boutique style at budget prices at Puerto Lopez's newest hotel. The colonial-style courtyard, pebble-dashed walls and small pool mark this out as the most interesting option in the centre of town. $50.

Ruta del Sol Malecón and Mariscal Sucre ⓣ05/230-0236, ⓔhotelrutadelsol@gmail.com, ⓦwww.puertolopez.net. Comfortable hotel on south end of the Malecón with well-equipped rooms with a/c, hot water, cable TV, restaurant, postal service and friendly staff. $30.

Sol Inn Juan Montalvo y Eloy Alfaro ⓣ05/230-0248. The basic, wooden cabins and laidback vibe are ideal for those on a tight budget. Camping $3, rooms $10.

Eating and drinking

Espuma del Mar The decor is a bit tacky but this spacious restaurant does most things well, from breakfasts to snacks and evening meals. Mains $3–5.

Patacón Pisa'o General Córdoba. For something different, try Colombian specialities such as *arepas* at this friendly little place. Mains $3–5.

Restaurant Carmita Stands out from the cluster of restaurants along the Malecón with a great selection of seafood in a polished setting. Mains $5.

Spondylus This is a cheaper option with an informal vibe and colourful murals, but avoid eating the oyster that gave the restaurant its name as it's endangered. Mains $2–3.

Moving on

Bus Jipijapa (every 30min; 1hr 30min); La Libertad (every 30min; 3hr); Manta (hourly; 2hr). Reina del Camino (ⓣ05/230-0207) offers comfortable secure services to and from Quito at 8am and 8pm (10hr).

PARQUE NACIONAL MACHALILLA

Ecuador's only coastal national park was set up in 1979 to preserve the rapidly disappearing tropical dry forest that once stretched north all the way to Costa Rica. It's a dramatic setting with thickly forested hills crowned by candelabra cacti, dropping down to pristine, peaceful beaches. The park headquarters (8am–5pm; ⓣ05/260-4170) is based in Puerto López, opposite the market, just off the main road running through town. This is where you pay your entrance fee valid for five days. Mainland only is $12; Isla de la Plata only is $15; combined ticket $20.

What to see and do

The best place to explore the park's dry forest is **Agua Blanca**, a village inhabited by some 280 indigenous people and an important archeological site of the Manteño culture that lived here from 800 to 1500 AD. Getting to Agua Blanca involves either taking a bus north from Puerto López and then walking the unpleasant 5-km trail up a dirt track, or hiring a mototaxi ($5 one-way, $10 return). The museum houses an interesting collection of sculptures, funeral urns and pickled snakes. A guided tour ($5) includes museum entry followed by a two-hour forest walk. Highlights include the towering ceibos, barbasco and fragrant Palo Santo trees whose wood is burnt as incense and to repel mosquitoes. Take in the spectacular views up to San Sebastián before a refreshing soak in a pungent but relaxing sulphur pool, considered sacred by local indigenous people.

San Sebastián

The landscape rises to 800m inland, where the dry forest turns into the cloudforest of **San Sebastián**, where the lush vegetation includes orchids, bamboo and wildlife such as howler monkeys, anteaters and more than 350 species of birds. This virgin forest can be explored on a 20-km hike with a mandatory guide hired in Agua Blanca ($20). You can camp overnight or stay with local villagers.

Playa Los Frailes

A few kilometres further north is the entrance to **Playa Los Frailes**, a stunning virgin beach, often deserted in early mornings. Present your park ticket or pay the entrance fee at the kiosk, then either head straight for Los Frailes on a half-hour hike or take the 4-km circular trail via the black-sand cove of La Payita and Playa La Tortiguita. To get straight to the beach, take a taxi from Puerto Lopez ($5 one-way).

ISLA DE LA PLATA

The tag of "poor man's Galápagos" is a rather unfair comparison for this small island 37km from Puerto López. Don't visit the island as a substitute for the world-famous archipelago as it will inevitably come up short, but **ISLA DE LA PLATA** is worth a day-trip to see its birdlife. In the summer months, whale-watching is also excellent. The island is home to numerous blue-footed boobies, masked boobies and frigate birds and these are the species most frequently on view. Red-footed boobies and waved albatrosses are also seen from April to October. The island has a small colony of sea lions, though it's rare to see them. Note that you can only visit the island as part of a tour (for operators, see below).

What to see and do

From the landing point in Bahía Drake, there are two circular **footpaths** around the island, the 3.5km Sendero Machete and the 5km Sendero Punta Escaleras. The hikes are about three hours long and there's no shade, so bring sunscreen and a hat. The close encounters with the friendly boobies, which peer at you with mild curiosity, are the main highlight but also watch out for colourful caterpillars crossing your path. Cool off after the hike with some snorkelling among an array of marine life including parrotfish and clownfish. Peak season is June to September (particularly July–Aug) when humpback whales arrive for the mating season, which is an awesome spectacle.

Tour operators

The day-trip to Isla de la Plata can be arranged at several local tour operators and hotels on the Malecón in Puerto López. It generally costs $35–40 per person including guide and light lunch but not including the park entrance fee. Recommended companies include Bosque Marino (☎09/337-6223, ⓦ www.bosquemarino.com) and Exploramar Diving (☎05/256-3905, ⓦ www.exploradiving .com), which also offers diving trips along the coast. Naturis (☎05/230-0218, ⓦ www.machalillatours .com) specializes in community tourism and offers a wide range of multi-activity trips including kayaking, fishing and snorkelling ($25 per person) as well as tours to San Sebastián.

South of Guayaquil and the Peruvian border

The only significant coastal town between Guayaquil and the Peruvian border is **Machala**, Ecuador's "banana capital". Apart from the World Banana Festival in September, there's not much reason to stop here as Guayaquil and Cuenca are both within five hours of the border by bus. If you're stuck, consider *Hotel Inés* (Juan Montalvo 1509 ☎07/293-2301; $20), or *Oro Hotel* (Sucre and Juan Montalvo ☎07/293-7569; $40 including breakfast); both have good rooms with air conditioning and cable TV. Restaurants include the cheaper *Don Angelo* (9 de Mayo and Rocafuerte) or the more upmarket *Mesón Hispano* (Av Las Palmeras and Sucre).

HUAQUILLAS

Some 75km south of Machala is the grubby border town of **Huaquillas**, the busiest crossing point from Ecuador to Peru. Spend the minimum amount of time here but, for those arriving at night, *Hotel Vanessa* (1 de Mayo 323 and Hualtaco ☎07/299-6263; $24),

and the *Grand Hotel Hernancor* next door (☎07/299-5467; $24) offer decent rooms with bathroom and air conditioning. The restaurant *La Habana* (T. Córdovez and Santa Rosa) serves filling set meals.

Moving on

Bus For those arriving in Ecuador, buses from Huaquillas leave from depots a few blocks from the international bridge. Co-op CIFA (☎07/293-0260, Ⓦwww.cifainternacional.com) has several buses an hour to Machala (1hr), the closest city. CIFA also goes to Guayaquil (4hr 30min), as does Ecuatoriano Pullman (☎07/293-0197) and Rutas Orenses (☎07/293-7661). Panamericana (☎07/293-0141) has six comfortable buses daily to Quito (12hr). For Cuenca (5hr) use Trans Azuay (☎07/293-0539), which has eight daily buses. If you intend to go to Loja, it's better to cross from Peru at Macará.

The Galápagos Islands

Charles Darwin developed his monumental theory of evolution after travelling to the **GALÁPAGOS** in the 1830s, and it's no exaggeration that the creatures of these unworldly volcanic islands, 1000km west of the Ecuadorian coast, were fundamental in changing the way we view ourselves.

CROSSING INTO PERU

Crossing the border is a fraught business but you need to ensure you do it right. If you don't get the correct stamps on your passport, you're in big trouble. Keep your wits about you, a close eye on your belongings and avoid changing money here as the rates are bad. The border crossing is a bridge over the Río Zarumilla, but before crossing the border get the exit stamp from the Ecuadorian immigration office (☎07/299-6755; open 24hr), inconveniently located 3km north. If you're coming from Machala, ask the driver to stop here, otherwise take a taxi ($1.50). Then take a bus or taxi to the bridge, which must be crossed on foot, and get your passport checked by Peruvian officials on the other side. Note that the entry stamp is usually obtained at the main Peruvian immigration office at Zarumilla 2km away ($1 by mototaxi). There are regular direct buses to Tumbes, Piura, Trujillo or Lima. A taxi to Tumbes costs $5–7.

The array of **wildlife** in the Galápagos is spellbinding. From giant tortoises to marine iguanas, sea lions to sharks and blue-footed boobies to magnificent frigate birds, it's hard to know which way to turn. Nowhere else on earth can you view wild mammals, reptiles and birds that are utterly unconcerned by human presence – a legacy of there being few natural predators on the islands.

Visiting the Galápagos independently is now relatively easy and last-minute deals are better than ever. That said, a week in the Galápagos will cost considerably more than one in the Ecuadorian mainland. The **low season** is May/June and September/October, while December to mid-April and July/August is **high season**, though cheap deals can still be found if you look hard enough. The tours, accommodation and cruises are where the prices vary hugely. When booking from abroad, tours **cost** $2000–5000 for a week. Booking last-minute in Quito and Guayaquil brings the prices down to $500–1500 (not including flights). However, the most common way for backpackers to visit is to buy flights, stay in budget accommodation ($10–20 per night), eat at cheap restaurants and pick up day-trips locally ($50–150 per day). Doing it this way, it's possible to spend a week on the islands for less than $1200 total, including flights.

The Galápagos is a year-round destination, but the conditions are best between December and April, with calmer seas and sunny weather with occasional rain on the larger islands. From June to October the weather is cooler and the sea rougher. Whenever you choose to visit, you can only see a tiny percentage of the islands because 97 percent of the area is protected by the national park and the seventy registered visitor sites comprise only 0.01 percent of the landmass; a comforting fact for environmentalists.

Arrival and information

Air Return flights to San Cristóbal or Baltra cost about $350 from Guayaquil and $400 from Quito with TAME (Quito ☎ 02/397-7100, Guayaquil ☎ 04/231-0305) or Aerogal (Quito ☎ 02/294-2800, Guayaquil ☎ 04/231-0346). Chilean airline LAN (☎ 1800-101075, ✪ www.lan.com) has recently launched flights at slightly cheaper rates. In San Cristóbal it's a $2 taxi ride to the port, Puerto Baquerizo Moreno. If arriving on Baltra, it's more

WHERE TO SEE WILDLIFE IN THE GALÁPAGOS

Blue-footed boobies Most easily viewed on North Seymour, Punta Pitt (San Cristóbal), Española or Genovesa.

Frigate birds Try Seymour Norte, Punta Pitt or Española.

Galápagos penguins Colonies on Floreana, Bartolomé, Fernandina and Isabela.

Giant tortoises Try the Charles Darwin Station on Santa Cruz or the larger breeding centres on Isabela and San Cristóbal.

Green sea turtles The best-known nesting sites are Bartolomé, Tortuga Bay (Santa Cruz) and Gardner Bay (Española).

Iguanas The marine variety are found on all major islands; see their land cousins on Seymour Norte, South Plaza or Santa Fé.

Sea lions To see them underwater, the best snorkelling spots are Champion Island (Floreana) and La Isla de los Lobos (San Cristóbal). Or walk among a colony at South Plaza or La Lobería (San Cristóbal). Males are territorial, so keep your distance.

Sharks Docile white-tipped and black-tipped reef sharks are best viewed off Floreana, North Seymour, Bartolomé and Leon Dormido (San Cristóbal), while hammerhead sharks are mainly seen by divers (also at Leon Dorimido).

Waved albatross Exclusively found on Española from April to November.

THE GALÁPAGOS IN DANGER

The boom in tourism to the Galápagos has its downside. Visitors have done huge damage to the fragile ecosystem and the islands were placed on the UNESCO Danger List in April 2007. It was controversially removed from the list in July 2010, a decision met with dismay by scientists and environmentalists. The key problems included: uncontrolled immigration; high traffic levels; an inadequate sewage system; invasive species such as livestock, pets and fruits; and overfishing.

The Ecuadorian government took action by deporting thousands of illegal Ecuadorian immigrants back to the mainland, using satellite technology to stop illegal fishing and restricting tourist arrivals. There are also plans to have 100 percent renewable energy on the islands by 2017. Isabela, Floreana and Santiago have seen goat extermination programmes, with more than 250,000 killed since 2006. Other harmful invasive species are fruit flies, fire ants and rats, the last of which have proved the most difficult to exterminate.

The Galápagos Islands were removed from the UNESCO danger list in July 2010 after the emergency measures were deemed successful. This was significant turnaround, though scientists continue to emphasize that the islands' problems are far from over. Tourists can help by following the strict rules on waste disposal and recycling, reporting malpractice and making donations to the Charles Darwin Foundation (Ⓦwww.darwinfoundation.org).

complicated. To get to the main port Puerto Ayora involves a 10-min bus ride south, a 10-min ferry crossing and then a bus (45min; $2.50) or taxi (40min; $15). Note that to return to the airport from Puerto Ayora, the last bus usually leaves about 9.30am, after which a taxi or private transfer is the only option.

Tourist information Contact the Ministry of Tourism (☏ 05/252-6174, Ⓦ www.turismo.gov .ec), which has iTur offices in Puerto Ayora, Puerto Baquerizo Moreno and Puerto Villamil. Alternatively contact the Galápagos National Park (☏ 05/252-6511, Ⓦ www.galapagospark.org). The Galápagos National Park entrance fee is $100, payable in cash on arrival. There is also a $10 transit card, which must be purchased in Quito or Guayaquil airport, that regulates the length of stay in the archipelago (3 months maximum).

Getting around

Air The small airline EMETEBE (Ⓦ www.emetebe .com.ec) flies between the islands (Santa Cruz ☏ 05/252-6177, San Cristóbal ☏ 05/252-0615 and Isabela ☏ 05/252-9255). Small eight-seater planes fly between San Cristóbal, Baltra and Isabela several times per week. Prices from $160 one-way or $260 return, plus $15 taxes.

Ferry There are daily services on small launches connecting Santa Cruz with San Cristóbal and Isabela. All routes cost $30 one-way and take 2 to 2hr 30 minutes. The ferries leave Isabela at 6am

and San Cristóbal at 7am, and depart Santa Cruz for both islands at 2pm. There are usually two boats, but you should book one day in advance at a registered agent in the main ports. Note that it's a bumpy ride, particularly at 2pm. One launch to San Cristóbal, La Cholita, is comfier, with a/c, reclining seats and TV.

PUERTO AYORA

This is the main port of **SANTA CRUZ**, the most developed island in the Galápagos and the central tourism hub where most visitors arrive. It's by no means the most interesting island, but the central location and wide range of hotels, restaurants and tour operators make it the best base to explore the surrounding islands. It's also the best place to pick up last-minute deals.

There are various attractions close to Puerto Ayora but to see them you need to take the **Bay Tour** ($25 from most local operators). The tour takes in La Lobería, where you can snorkel with sea lions, Playa de los Perros, where marine iguanas and various birds are seen, Las Tintoreras, channels where sharks are often found, and Las Grietas (see p.690).

What to see and do

Puerto Ayora is essentially the best base to arrange tours, though a visit to the Charles Darwin Research Station to see the tortoises is worth it, and there are some interesting short hikes out of town.

Charles Darwin Research Station

A 15-min walk east of town is the **Charles Darwin Research Station** (☎05/252-6146, ⓦwww.darwinfoundation.org), which contains an information centre and a museum. The highlight is the walk-in giant tortoise enclosure where you can meet the Galápagos giants face to face. Of the original fourteen sub-species, eleven have survived; the most famous resident is Lonesome George, once thought to be the last survivor of the Pinta island sub-species. Note that the station gets quite busy with tour groups and you can actually see more tortoises at the breeding centres in San Cristóbal and Isabela.

Tortuga Bay

If you're in Puerto Ayora at the beginning or end of your trip and want to kill a few hours, then the best option is probably Tortuga Bay. Follow the trail from the western edge of town along a paved path through cacti forest (a 45-min walk with little shade). The first bay you reach is not actually Tortuga Bay, but one of the longest beaches in the archipelago, popular with surfers but dangerous to swim. Walk to the end of this beach and cross over to a lagoon to find the bay where marine turtles come to lay their eggs. Note that the beach closes at 5pm so you should leave the port earlier than 3pm to have time to enjoy it.

Las Grietas

Another side trip from the port with a relaxing dip at the end is the walk to Las Grietas, a crevice in the rocks that supplies the port with much of its fresh water. Take a water taxi ($0.50) across the bay towards Playa de Los Alemanes, then venture along rocky trails for a further twenty minutes to reach Las Grietas. Fissures in the lava rocks have created two layers of brackish water – saline and fresh. It's a beautiful, sheltered place for a swim. Note that the rocky trails are a bit tricky; walking shoes will come in handy.

Accommodation

Santa Cruz has the largest selection of accommodation on the islands and it's even possible to find budget rooms in peak periods. If you have your eye on a specific hotel, it's a good idea to book in advance as places fill up fast. Prices start from $15–25 per person for budget and mid-range rooms up to $100–200 per night in the higher-range hotels, which are mainly filled by tour groups.

Casa Natura Petrel and Isla Floreana ☎02/246-9846, ⊛ www.vianatura.com. To enjoy more comfort in charming surroundings, stay at this friendly new hotel ten minutes out of town and enjoy the buffet breakfast and small pool at the back. $125.

España Thomas de Berlanga and 12 de Febrero ☎05/252-6108, ⊛ www.hotelespanagalapagos .com. One of the most popular budget hotels, with neat rooms around a colourful courtyard with hammocks. $30.

Gardner Thomas de Berlanga and 12 de Febrero ☎05/252-6108, ⊛ www.hotelgardnergalapagos .com. Next door to *España*, with elegant decoration, spacious rooms and breakfast included. A/c extra. $35.

Lirio del Mar Islas Plaza and Thomas de Berlanga ☎05/252-6212. Another dependable budget option with a small terrace but basic, no-frills rooms. A/c extra. $30.

Las Palmeras Thomas de Berlanga and Islas Plaza ☎05/252-6139, ⊛ www.hotelpalmeras .com.ec. This is one of the best mid-range options in town. Rooms are plushly decorated and there's a large pool on the terrace and even a small disco downstairs at weekends. $65.

Salinas Islas Plaza and Thomas de Berlanga ☎05/252-6212. Across from *Lirio del Mar*, this is a well-established budget hotel. Ground-floor rooms are very basic with more comfort and higher prices on the upper floors. $35.

Eating and drinking

If you're expecting to be staying in a deserted wildlife paradise, you'll be surprised by the liveliness of Puerto Ayora in the evenings. It's a very pleasant resort with a wide range of restaurants, mostly in the slightly higher range ($15–25 for dinner). There are also quite a few cheap places, particularly the Kioskos along Charles Binford, where you can get a good meal for $5. Some restaurants also do set lunches and dinners for just $3.50.

Café Hernan Av. Charles Darwin and Av. Baltra. This waterfront favourite does the best pizza in town and indulgent desserts such as black forest gateau. Mains $6–10.

Chifa Asia Charles Binford. Backpackers flock to the "Kioskos" restaurants on this street to grab a delicious budget meal. For something a little spicier try this popular Chinese. Mains $4–6.

El Descanso del Guía Av. Charles Darwin (opposite the ferry docks). A popular option for locals to fill up on Ecuadorian staples such as *bolon* (fried plantain ball) for breakfast and chicken stew or a variety of white fish for lunch. The juices are excellent and the two-course set meals are well above average and cost just $3.

Il Giardino Av. Charles Darwin and Charles Binford. The town's newest gourmet restaurant does not disappoint, with a menu featuring home-made panini and crepes, plus delicious ice creams and sorbets. Mains $6–10.

Limón y Café Av. Charles Darwin and 12 de Febrero. Friendly, popular bar to start the evening with music, chat, pool and cards.

La Panga Av. Charles Darwin and Thomas de Berlanga. The town's main disco, which pumps out Latin and international music until 2am. *Bongos*, the bar upstairs, is a more laidback place for a drink.

The Rock Av. Charles Darwin and Islas Plaza. Named after the first Galápagos bar set up on Baltra in the 1940s, this endearing place serves up a feast, from Mexican quesadillas to teriyaki fish fillets ($6–10). The wide variety of juices, shakes and cocktails wash it all down.

Servisabroson Charles Binford. One of the many cheap places on the "Kioskos" – a string of informal restaurants with seating in the middle of the pedestrianized street Charles Binford – offering filling plates of chicken, meat, pork and seafood. The fish in coconut is particularly popular. Mains $4–7.

Tintorera Av. Charles Darwin and Floreana. A great place for a healthy organic breakfast or snack. Vegetarian specialities ($3–6) are popular and the set lunch is a good deal.

AROUND ISLA SANTA CRUZ

The highlands and islands of Santa Cruz offer plenty of opportunities for

CRUISES

Although many budget travellers now choose to travel independently and stay in hotels, in many ways the best way to see the Galápagos is on a cruise. If you can deal with the seasickness, which is likely on all but the most luxurious boats, then you'll be rewarded with more quality time at the sites and be spared the daily return journey to a major port. There are also many sites that are only accessible to cruise boats.

Vessels that tour the Galápagos range from small boats to luxury cruise yachts carrying ninety passengers. Five-day tours allow visitors to explore the islands close to Santa Cruz, while eight-day tours include islands further afield. Single-cabin supplements are usually very high. Note that if you have some flexibility, you can make substantial savings on cruises by booking last-minute in Quito or Guayaquil. Prices are even lower booking last-minute in Puerto Ayora and you could be lucky enough to get the higher-level cruises half price. Always check the official grading of the boat before booking. Prices below are for eight days based on two sharing. Boats listed are not necessarily recommended.

Economy class boats cost around $500–700 or $80–100 per day per passenger. Boats have tiny bunk beds, shared bathrooms, simple food and Class 1 guides with a low level of training. You save money but it's not a comfortable experience and it's best to avoid these.

Tourist class boats cost $800–1100 or $100–125 per day and are slightly bigger, while still not offering a high level of comfort. They have Class 2 guides with a higher level of knowledge and English-language skills. Boats include *Pelikano*, *Rumba*, *Sea Man* and *Yolita*.

Tourist-superior boats cost $1000–1500 or $150 per day and have more comfortable cabins, better food and Class 2 guides. Boats include *Spondylus*, *Free Enterprise*, *Aida Maria*, *Angelique* and *Encantada*.

First-class yachts cost $1500–2500 or $200 per day, can travel faster and have a decent level of comfort, high-quality food and Class 3 guides, the highest level of accreditation. Boats include *Eric*, *Letty*, *Flamingo*, *Galápagos Adventure*, *Monserrat*, *Beagle*, *Tip Top* and *San José*.

Luxury yachts cost $2500–4000 or $300–500 per day. These are the largest yachts with the most stability and have extra facilities such as jacuzzis and more spacious social areas. Boats include *Galápagos Legend*, *Galápagos Explorer* and *Santa Cruz*.

wildlife-watching, snorkelling and a chance to experience the island's curious geological formations.

The highlands

The highlands offer a very different experience to the beaches on Santa Cruz and it's worth venturing inland to see the diversity of the island. At El Chato, you can observe giant tortoises in their natural habitat in the reserve (entrance $3 including guide). Nearby are the lava tunnels, which are naturally formed and have lighting so you can walk through them. Note that you need to crawl under a low wall to get out unless you walk back to the entrance. Either side of the main road which cuts through Santa Cruz are the Gemelos (twins), collapsed 30m-deep craters. The sheer drop into the craters, covered in vegetation, makes them an impressive sight; tour groups often stop on the way to or from the airport. All of the attractions above can be seen on a guided tour with any of the tour operators in Puerto Ayora ($80 for groups up to 14) or to save money, hire a taxi in the port to take you to all of them ($30), which can be done in two or three hours.

Las Bachas

On the north coast, **Las Bachas**, once a base for the US military, is a long white-sand beach often covered in Sally Lightfoot Crabs; flamingos also abound in the lagoons inland. Tour operators often combine a visit here with other excursions such as North Seymour (see below).

Isla North Seymour

Off the north coast of Santa Cruz is the tiny island of **North Seymour**, which offers some of the best opportunities in the archipelago to watch frigate birds and get close to blue-footed boobies. Follow the 2.5-km circular trail around the island to see frigates nesting and the amusing courtship of the boobies. Sea lions and iguanas are also common here. A day tour here is comparatively pricey ($110 per person with Puerto Ayora tour operators) due to restricted access.

Islas Plazas

Off the east coast of Santa Cruz are the two tiny islands of **Plazas**, home to a large sea-lion colony and a great place to observe these animals up close on land. You can only visit the south island, where there is a 1-km trail around the cliffs offering good views of birdlife including pelicans and frigate birds. There's also a sea-lion bachelor colony, where defeated males congregate to plot their next move. Like north Seymour, day tours to Plazas cost $110 per person, combined with Punta Carrion.

Isla Santa Fé

Southeast of Puerto Ayora, the small island of **Santa Fé** has great snorkelling as well as opportunities to see white-tipped reef sharks, marine iguanas, sea lions and stingrays. Santa Fe land iguanas laze around the trails that wind through a forest of 10m-high *Opuntia* cacti. Access to the island's land sites is restricted to cruise boats, but there are day-trips from Puerto Ayora (around $70), which visit selected offshore sites.

Isla Santiago

Northwest of Santa Cruz are the blackened lava fields of **Isla Santiago**, also known as San Salvador. The highlight of this barren, uninhabited island is **Bartolomé**, just off the east coast, which contains the Galápagos's most famous landmark, **Pinnacle Rock**, a partially eroded lava formation. Climb up 108m to a viewpoint commanding spectacular views over the 40m-high rock with two horseshoe-shaped beaches in the foreground and the blackened lava of Santiago's Sullivan Bay beyond. There's very good snorkelling below and opportunities to see the Galápagos penguins and marine turtles. Bartolomé can be visited on a day-trip from Puerto Ayora ($125 per person with Puerto Ayora tour operators).

On the western side of Santiago is Puerto Egas, the best landing point to hike along the lava flow and watch countless crabs and marine iguanas. On the southeastern tip of Santiago, the waters around the volcanic cone of **Sombrero Chino** are also excellent for snorkelling.

Isla Floreana

The southern island of **FLOREANA** has a small population at Puerto Velasco Ibarra and a few high-rise hotels. The infrequent transportation and strict regulations mean that this is an island you can only visit on an organized tour. Post Office Bay is the most common landing point for cruises, with its quirky post office barrel – you leave a postcard, hoping a fellow tourist will post it, while you in turn take letters to post in your country. In the highlands, there is a small tortoise-breeding centre and caves that were inhabited by pirates in the sixteenth century. Punta Cormorant is a good place to observe flamingos and various wading birds. The islands of Enderby and Champion are excellent spots for snorkelling, while nearby Devil's Crown, a half-submerged volcanic cone, is one of the top snorkelling and diving sites in the archipelago, with reef sharks, turtles and rays. A day-trip from Puerto Ayora costs about $75, but only includes the highlands, Enderby and Champion. The tour misses out many of the most famous sites, which are restricted to cruises.

PUERTO BAQUERIZO MORENO

On the eastern side of the archipelago, **SAN CRISTÓBAL** is the administrative centre of the islands. **Puerto Baquerizo Moreno** is the capital and though it is smaller than Puerto Ayora, it has the feel of a tourism hub with plenty of hotels, restaurants and tour operators, and a pleasant waterfront and beach that's usually covered in sealions.

What to see and do

A 15min walk north of town past the small, popular Mann Beach is the Centro de Interpretación, which provides a more in-depth overview than the exhibition at Charles Darwin Station in Puerto Ayora. Here you can learn about the islands' history,

development and current environmental problems, split into three galleries. Continue walking past the centre and you will find a forked path that leads to Las Tijeretas (Frigatebird Hill) to observe the birds and enjoy sweeping views over the bay below. Then take the other path down to Playa Cabo de Horno, which has good snorkelling. On the opposite end of town, it's a half-hour walk to La Lobería, a large sea-lion colony, which is not technically part of the national park. There's also good surfing nearby (taxi from port $2).

Accommodation

Casa Blanca Malecón and Melville ☎05/252-0392, ⌨www.casablancagalapagos.com. This Moorish Moroccan throwback is the most elegant mid-range place in town with rustic a/c rooms, wide balconies and an art gallery downstairs. $50.
Hostal Leon Dormido José de Villamil and Malecón ☎05/252-0169. The best-value budget option – clean rooms with private bath, fans and TV. $30.
Hostal San Francisco Malecón ☎05/252-0304. A cheap option with no-frills, basic rooms, ideal for those on a tight budget. $20.
Suites Bellavista Malecón and Melville ☎05/252-0352. This is an excellent mid-range option with smart, a/c rooms on the waterfront. $40.

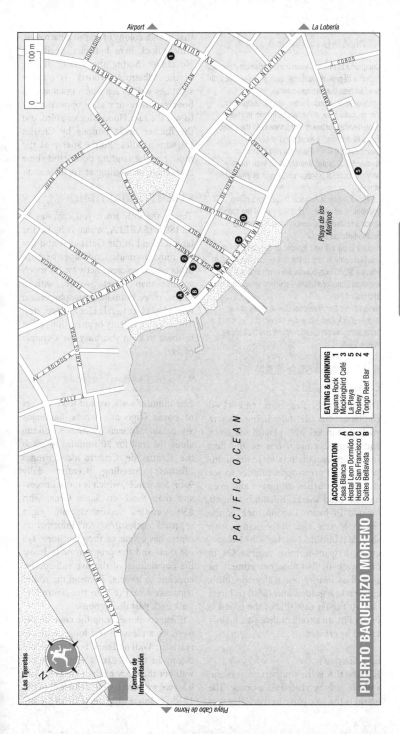

THE GALÁPAGOS ISLANDS

ECUADOR

PUERTO BAQUERIZO MORENO

ACCOMMODATION
Casa Blanca A
Hostal Leon Dormido D
Hostal San Francisco C
Suites Bellavista B

EATING & DRINKING
Iguana Rock 1
Mockingbird Café 3
La Playa 5
Rosley 2
Tongo Reef Bar 4

Airport ▲   ▲ La Lobería

Playa de los Marinos

PACIFIC OCEAN

Las Tijeretas

Centros de Interpretación

Playa Cabo de Horno ▲

Eating and drinking

Compared to Puerto Ayora, it's surprisingly difficult to find a decent cheap meal, unless you're fine with sandwiches, burgers and snacks.

Iguana Rock J Jose Flores and Av. Quito. After dinner, head here, three blocks inland, to shoot pool, have a few beers and dance until the early hours at the town's most popular bar.

Mockingbird Café Española and Ignacio de Hernández. A rustic, homely place with friendly service, ideal for a snack and a spot of internet surfing.

La Playa Av. de la Armada. If you don't mind spending a bit more, this is the pick of the town's upscale restaurants, specializing in delicious seafood (mains $7–12).

Rosley Española and Ignacio de Hernández. This local favourite is one of the few places in town that offers a $2.50 two-course set lunch and dinner of standard Ecuadorian fare – chicken stew, fried beef and grilled fish.

Tongo Reef Bar Malecón. One of many cheap, simple snack bars along the waterfront, serving big breakfasts, burgers, sandwiches and fruit juices. Mains $3–5.

AROUND ISLA SAN CRISTÓBAL

The most popular boat trip ($50) combines Isla de Los Lobos, where you can snorkel with playful sea lions, and Leon Dormido, one of the best snorkelling and diving sites in the archipelago, with great opportunities to see reef sharks, turtles, stingrays and even hammerhead sharks. Inland, highlights include El Junco Lagoon, one of the few freshwater lakes in the islands, with abundant birdlife. Nearby is the Galapaguera, a giant-tortoise reserve set in dry forest. To visit these two attractions as well as nearby beach Puerto Chino, either take a guided tour ($50) or hire a taxi. At the far east side of the island is Punta Pitt, an excellent dive site, mainly visited by cruises.

Isla Española

ESPAÑOLA is the southernmost island and can only be visited via a cruise. The island is the sole place in the Galápagos that hosts a colony of waved albatrosses, which flock here between April and November. Seeing them land at one of the "albatross airports" is quite a sight. As well as sea lions, iguanas and boobies, there are also opportunities to see the rare Hood Mockingbird and the finches made famous by Charles Darwin's studies. Punta Suárez is the most popular landing point, and there is excellent snorkelling at Turtle Island.

PUERTO VILLAMIL

This is the only town you can stay in on **ISLA ISABELA**, which is by far the largest island in the Galápagos and has the most dramatic landscapes because of its recent volcanic activity. It's much smaller than Puerto Ayora, with a sleepy, more intimate atmosphere, and is an ideal place to relax for a longer stay. There are also plenty of attractions close to town to keep you busy for a couple of days.

What to see and do

Five minutes' walk west of town is a set of **pozas** (lagoons), where flamingos are commonly seen. Continue walking along the trail for 20 minutes to reach the Centro de Crianza de Tortugas (Tortoise Breeding Centre; daily 9am–5pm; free), which is more impressive than those on Santa Cruz, with 850 tortoises separated into eight separate enclosures. An information centre has details of the giant tortoise's life cycle and the programme to boost the populations of the five sub-species endemic to Isabela. To avoid the round trip, take a taxi ($2) to the centre and walk back past the lagoons.

If you continue along the coast to the west, it's a pleasant but longer walk to reach the **Wall of Tears**, built by a penal colony in the 1940s. It may be just a wall but the story of the penal convicts who were forced to build the wall in the 1940s is interesting (a taxi here costs

$5). Southeast of town is a set of islets called **Las Tintoreras**, named after the reef sharks that frequent them. This is a very good snorkelling spot, with opportunities to watch sea lions, turtles, penguins and white-tipped sharks, which sometimes rest in the canals. There's also a short trail around the islets.

Accommodation

There is quite a large accommodation offering in town and it may be possible to negotiate because hotels don't fill up that often. Accommodation on the beach tends to be a bit more expensive than inland.

La Casa Rosada Antonio Gil ☎091/454-819. Spacious rooms, a friendly vibe and in the evenings the attached beach bar has become a haven for backpackers, especially at happy hour (5–7pm). $30.

Dolphin House Antonio Gil ☎05/252-9138. Great for dramatic views of the ocean, but beware of the insistent cockerels guaranteed to wake you before dawn. Rooms are adequate – you're paying extra for the location. Breakfast included. $45.

Posada del Caminante Near Cormoran ☎05/252-9407. For those on a tighter budget in search of an informal atmosphere, try this place, a 15-min walk inland. Most rooms have a kitchen and there's a communal fridge and free laundry. $20.

Rincon de George 16 de Marzo and Antonio Gil ☎05/252-9214. Offers comfortably furnished rooms with firm beds, a/c and hot water. $30.

Eating and drinking

Bar Beto Next to *La Casa Rosada*. One of the few open-air bars in town; a place where you can sip pricey cocktails on wooden tables overlooking the beach.

La Choza Antonio Gil in front of the park. Puts on a barbecued feast (mains $8–15) in a colourful, rustic setting.

Tres Hermanos A cheaper option on Antonio with simple but good meals, ranging from breakfasts, burgers and sandwiches to fish with *patacones*, rice and salad ($3–6).

AROUND ISLA ISABELA

A trek around the Volcán Sierra Negra is the highlight of a trip to Isabela; if you're an iguana fan you may also want to visit Isla Fernandina.

Volcán Sierra Negra

You can trek to the volcano yourself, but it's far better and safer to take a guided tour ($35–40); Wilmer Quezada is a particularly good **local guide** (☎086/878-626 or 05/252-9326). There are two routes – the shorter is known as **Volcán Chico** and takes about four hours, usually on foot and horseback. You can see small lava cones and impressive views over the north of the island and Fernandina. The visibility also tends to be better on this side. The longer trek is to **Las Minas de Azufre** (Sulphur Mines), takes around seven hours and is tougher, especially in the rainy season. However, the extra effort is rewarded with a more spectacular experience. The walk around the crater, which is the second-largest in the world after Ngorongoro in Tanzania, is followed by a descent into the yellow hills of the sulphur mines, which spew out pungent sulphuric gas. Note that the longer trek is less popular so you may need to book ahead.

Isla Fernandina and outlying islands

West of Isabela is the equally volcanic **FERNANDINA**, which can only be visited on a cruise. The highlight is the huge population of marine iguanas sunning themselves on the rocks of Punta Espinoza; there are also trails through the recently formed lava fields. Fernaninda's volcano La Cumbre was the most recent eruption in the Galápagos, in April 2009. Further north are the tiny, remote islands of **Darwin** and **Wolf**. These are very difficult to visit and mainly restricted to specialist diving trips attracted by large populations of hammerhead and whale sharks.

The Guianas

KAIETEUR FALLS:
one of the world's
highest single-drop
water falls ✪

**GALIBI NATURE
RESERVE:**
an important turtle-
nesting beach with
hordes of olive ridleyr ✪

ILES DU SALUT:
spot monkeys and
peacocks at these
former French
prison islands ✪

IWOKRAMA: ✪
ecotourism aplenty in
this pristine rainforest

**BROWNSBERG
NATURE RESERVE:** ✪
enjoy a hike and spot
wildlife in Suriname's
forest-covered interior

**CENTRE SPATIAL
GUYANAIS:**
view a space rocket
being launched
into orbit ✪

BASIC DAILY BUDGET G: Basic US$60;
S: US$40; FG: US$150

DRINK G: beer US$1.50; S: beer
US$1.40; FG: beer US$5

FOOD G: Cow-heel soup US$4; S: *Saoto
soep* US$2.70; FG: Blaff (soup) US$14

GUESTHOUSE/BUDGET HOTEL
G: US$15–60; S: US$18–45;
FG: US$65–80

TRAVEL G: Georgetown–Bartica, bus &
water taxi: 2hr, US$12;
S: Paramaribo–Albina, taxi: 2hr,
US$15; FG: Cayenne–St Laurent,
minibus: 2hr 30min, US$65.

G = Guyana S = Suriname FG = French Guiana

POPULATION G: 751,000; S: 524,000;
FG: 203,000

AREA G: 214,970 sq km; S: 163,820
sq km; FG: 84,500 sq km

OFFICIAL LANGUAGES G: English; S:
Dutch; FG: French

CURRENCY G: Guyanese dollar (G$);
S: Suriname dollar (SRD); FG: Euro (€)

CAPITAL G: Georgetown;
S: Paramaribo; FG: Cayenne

INTERNATIONAL PHONE CODE
G: ☏592; S: ☏597; FG: ☏594

TIME ZONE GMT -3hr (-4hr in Guyana)

Introduction

The Guianas, which comprise the independent nations of Guyana and Suriname and the French overseas *département* of French Guiana, feel more Caribbean than South American. As a result of colonial legacies the official languages are English (Guyana), Dutch (Suriname) and French (French Guiana), and each has an ethnically diverse population, a mix of indigenous peoples, descendants of European colonizers and their slaves, East Indians, Indonesians, Southeast Asian refugees and Haitians.

Tucked between Brazil's Amazonian region and the continent's northeast coast, the Guianas are extremely verdant, with rivers running through the region in abundance; indeed, the Amerindian word *guiana* means "land of many waters". Between eighty and ninety percent of the area is covered by dense tropical forests. Jaguars, pumas, caimans, iguanas, ocelots, tapirs and other diverse wildlife thrive in this environment, making the Guianas an ecotourism haven. That said, wildlife can remain stubbornly elusive and though you're bound to see birds, monkeys and small rodents, you'll be very lucky to spot a big cat. It's worth the expense to stay in a **jungle lodge**, to witness **sea turtles** laying their eggs or to take a **river trip** down some of its majestic waterways.

The towns take a backseat to nature in the Guianas, but the capital cities of **Georgetown** (Guyana), **Paramaribo** (Suriname) and **Cayenne** (French Guiana) have a certain dilapidated charm and are worth exploring for a day or two. Of the three, Paramaribo is the best-preserved, Georgetown offers wonderful wooden architecture and sleepy Cayenne, with little in the way of budget accommodation, will probably not detain you long. These three capitals comprise the main **international gateways** from the Caribbean, North America and Europe. Within South America, you can fly directly to Guyana and Suriname from **Belém** and **Boa Vista** in Brazil, but there is little commercial air traffic (with the exception of charter flights) to French Guiana. There are varying **visa** requirements for each country; see p.703, p.723 and p.739 for details.

Borders between the Guianas are marked by imposing rivers, and

---

WHEN TO VISIT

Temperatures in the Guianas vary little from one country to another or from one month to the next: generally 20°C to 33°C, with a mean temperature of around 26°C (slightly hotter in the interior owing to the absence of the cooling coastal trade winds). This makes deciding when to plan a trip much more dependent on the vagaries of the dry and wet seasons. While the tropical forest is undeniably lush and verdant during the wet season, road travel can be extremely difficult to navigate (if not impossible) along the many unsealed roads that govern land access to the interior. The main rainy seasons in the region are generally between mid-April to July and August and from around November to early February. As such, late summer/early autumn and late winter/early spring are the optimum times for a visit – the latter particularly, as this is when many carnival celebrations take place.

crossing involves taking infrequent **ferries** and **motorized boats**. From Guyana to Suriname, you'll need to cross the Corentyne River from **Molson Creek** to **South Drain** near Nieuw Nickerie (see p.734); from Suriname to French Guiana, the Maroni River from **Albina** to **Saint-Laurent du Maroni** (see p.738). Overland travel between the three countries, although lengthy and sometimes tortuous, is relatively straightforward.

Guyana

GUYANA, the largest and most populous nation of the Guianas trio, is a rum-drinking and cricket-loving country, and the only English-speaking nation in South America. **George-town**, the capital, typifies this with its wooden architecture and cosmopolitan mix of black, white, East Indian, Asian and Amerindian ethnicities.

You won't, however, find the white sand and emerald waters of the Caribbean here, and a stroll along Georgetown's sea wall offers views of a murky brown sea beyond a muddy stretch of beach. Instead, Guyana's principal attractions are its rainforests, rivers and indigenous population. One of Guyana's greatest natural wonders is the majestic **Kaieteur Falls** – among the tallest and most powerful in the world – made all the more dramatic by its isolated location in a tree-covered mountain range.

Going down the middle of the country from north to south is the **Iwokrama Rainforest**, where millions of acres of rainforest have been reserved for conservation, research and sustainable ecotourism. Further along, at the edge of the jungle in the far south,

the **Rupununi Savannah** offers a flat landscape, contrasting with the several highland regions in the interior, where you can stay at working ranches, play cowboy (or cowgirl) and see birds, caimans and giant river otters.

CHRONOLOGY

1498 Christopher Columbus first lays claim to the area for Spain.

1580 The Dutch build settlements and trading posts, and import slaves from Africa to work the sugar-cane plantations.

1763 Slave revolt led by Guyana's national hero, Cuffy.

1796 Dutch lose de facto control of colony to the British.

1834 Slavery is abolished. Thousands of indentured labourers from India, China and Portugal are brought to Guyana to work the sugar-cane plantations.

1950 The People's Progressive Party (PPP) is established, with Dr Cheddi Jagan as leader and Forbes Burnham as chairman.

1953 PPP wins first elections allowed by British. Jagan becomes leader. Britain suspends constitution and sends in troops fearing plans to establish Guyana as a communist state.

1955 PPP splits and Burnham forms the People's National Congress (PNC).

1957 Elections permitted and PPP wins. Jagan become first premier in 1961.

1964 PNC wins elections and Burnham becomes prime minister.

1966 Guyana achieves independence.

1978 US Congressman Leo Ryan murdered and more than 900 members of Rev. Jim Jones' People's Temple religious sect commit mass suicide in Jonestown (see box, p.716).

1980 Guyana gets a new constitution and Burnham becomes executive president.

1985 Burnham dies; prime minister Hugh Desmond Hoyte becomes president.

1992 Cheddi Jagan's PPP wins election.

1997 Jagan dies. His American widow, Janet Jagan, is elected president.

1999 Janet Jagan resigns due to ill health and is succeeded by Bharrat Jagdeo.

2009 Norway agrees to invest US$250m to preserve Guyana's rainforests.

2010 Guyana chosen as one of the hosts of the Twenty/20 cricket World Cup.

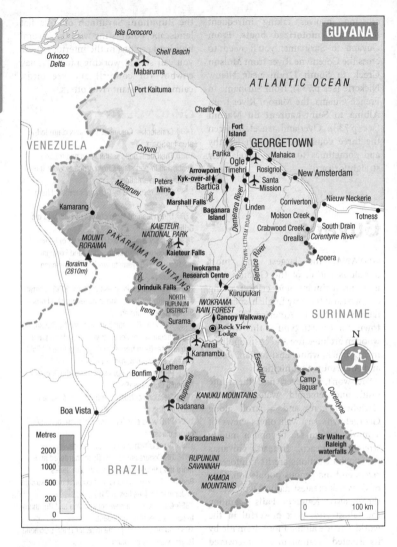

GUYANA

ATLANTIC OCEAN

VENEZUELA

SURINAME

BRAZIL

Isla Corocoro

Orinoco Delta

Shell Beach

Mabaruma

Port Kaituma

Charity

Fort Island

GEORGETOWN

Parika

Ogle

Mahaica

Arrowpoint

Kyk-over-al

Timehri

Rosignol

New Amsterdam

Cuyuni

Peters Mine

Bartica

Santa Mission

Corriverton

Nieuw Neckerie

Mazaruni

Marshall Falls

Baganara Island

Linden

Molson Creek

Totness

Kamarang

KAIETEUR NATIONAL PARK

Crabwood Creek

South Drain

MOUNT RORAIMA

PAKARAIMA MOUNTAINS

Kaieteur Falls

Orealla

Corentyne River

Roraima (2810m)

Iwokrama Research Centre

Apoera

Orinduik Falls

NORTH RUPUNUNI DISTRICT

Kurupukari

Ireng

IWOKRAMA RAIN FOREST

Canopy Walkway

Surama

Rock View Lodge

SURINAME

Annai

Karanambu

N

Bonfim

Lethem

Camp Jaguar

Boa Vista

Rupununi

KANUKU MOUNTAINS

Essequibo

Corentyne

Dadanana

Karaudanawa

Sir Walter Raleigh waterfalls

RUPUNUNI SAVANNAH

KAMOA MOUNTAINS

Demerara River

GEORGETOWN-LETHEM ROAD

Berbice River

Metres

2000
1000
500
200
0

0   100 km

Basics

ARRIVAL

Guyana's main international airport, **Cheddi Jagan International Airport**, located at Timehri, an hour south of Georgetown, receives direct **flights** from Suriname, Brazil, Barbados, Trinidad, New York, Miami and Toronto. As such,

North American travellers will find the widest choice and best deals on flights to Georgetown. Currently, European travellers must fly to New York and then take Caribbean Airlines or Delta to Guyana, or fly to Barbados/Trinidad and take Caribbean Airlines or LIAT to Guyana, via Trinidad. Caribbean Airlines (formerly BWIA) is now considering reintroducing flights from London to the Caribbean and, if all goes to plan, this service will begin in 2012. Some flights (small planes) from Suriname and special domestic charters arrive at the smaller Ogle International Airport, some 7km east of the capital, on the east coast of Demerara.

Overland from Brazil

Travellers arriving overland from Brazil enter Guyana at the town of **Lethem**, about 130km northeast of the Brazilian town of Boa Vista. It is a tiring and bone-jarring Intraserv **bus** ride (see p.720) from Lethem to Georgetown (11–16hr); alternatively you can take a minibus, which is faster but has less leg room.

Overland from Suriname

Travellers from Suriname must board a **ferry** at South Drain, near Nieuw Nickerie, and make the 30-min journey across the Corentyne River to **Molson Creek** on the Guyana border (see p.734). This is followed by a 3-hr ride in a local minibus to Georgetown.

VISAS

You must have a passport with at least six months remaining validity to enter and leave Guyana. If you arrive by air, you must show a return ticket (an online printout is sufficient). Guyanese immigration normally grants visitors a thirty-day stay. To extend your stay, contact the Ministry of Home Affairs at 60 Brickdam St (☎592/226-2444/5, ⓦwww.moha.gov.gy) and the Central Office of Immigration at Camp St (☎592/226-4700).

Visas are required for all visitors except those from Commonwealth and CARICOM countries, plus Belgium, Denmark, Finland, France, Germany, Greece, Ireland, Italy, Japan, Republic of Korea, Luxembourg, The Netherlands, Norway, Portugal, Spain, Sweden and USA. As this list can change, check for updates on MOHA's website or from the Consulate/Guyana Foreign Office

nearest to you. It's possible to apply for a visa for Suriname at the embassy in Georgetown (see p.714).

GETTING AROUND

Licensed and independent **taxi** services abound in Georgetown; outside of the capital taxis are less common and are most likely to be found around main shopping areas. Consult your hotel or tourist information for recommended taxi firms. Always agree the destination and fare before setting off. Privately owned **minibuses** operate to nearly all destinations accessible by road. Route numbers are displayed on the front of the bus. Prices are structured and relatively cheap, though it's best to confirm the fare before entering the vehicle.

There are several **car rental** firms in Georgetown and a few in outlying areas. Ask your hotel to recommend a firm or try Sonic Auto Rentals at 35 Main St, Georgetown; ☎592/226-7755, ⓔsonicautorentals@gmail.com. Expect to pay between G$5000–20,000 per day, depending on vehicle make and size. Roads in and out of the capital to Timehri, Linden (via the Linden Highway), Parika (West Coast) and Corriverton (East Coast) are relatively good, but consider a **4x4** if you are planning trips off the beaten track. Driving is on the left-hand side, seat belts are compulsory and you must obtain a free drivers' permit before you can rent or drive a vehicle; contact customs for this.

It's easiest to use the toll bridges to cross the Demerara and Berbice rivers, though you can take the Demerara River Ferry or the quicker **river taxis** (speedboats) from Stabroek Stelling across to Vreed-en-Hoop. Speedboats also ply routes between Parika, Bartica, other hinterland areas and places of interest in the Essequibo region.

ACCOMMODATION

There are plenty of good, reasonably priced **guesthouses** and **hotels** in

Georgetown, where G$6000 will get you a spacious, clean room with a TV, running water and a fan. Elsewhere, prices will be more like G$2500–5000 per night, which should at least guarantee a mosquito net and a fan. Keep your possessions secure and don't expect too much in the way of service.

There are several **resorts** located on islands in the interior and on the ranches in Rupununi Savannah. Many are ecotourism-focused and offer cultural visits to Amerindian communities as well as outdoor pursuits such as fishing and hunting. Resort accommodation is normally provided on an all-inclusive basis; it's advisable to book in advance.

FOOD

Curries, roti, cassava, rice and coconut milk reign over **Guyanese cuisine**. Chicken, pork and beef are fried Creole-style, curried with East Indian spices or flavoured with Chinese spices. **Rice** is ubiquitous, boiled with coconut milk, black-eyed peas, lentils, channa (chickpeas), okra or calaloo. Other staples include roti and *dhal puri* (softer and more pliant versions of a tortilla wrap) used to envelope and mop up curries and stewed vegetables. *Dhal puris* contain a thin layer of spiced lentils within.

Black pudding (a sausage filled with rice mixed with cow's blood) is popular, and is often eaten with *sour*, a hot, tangy sauce, and *souse*, which is basically pickled pork, pig's skin, chicken's feet, cow's heel, cow's face or fish. The lasting Amerindian contribution to Guyanese cuisine is *pepperpot*, considered Guyana's national dish, traditionally served at Christmas but in reality eaten all year. It's a dark-red dish made with stewed meat (or fish), coloured, preserved and flavoured with *cassareep* (a thick dark sauce made from cassava juice), cinnamon and hot peppers, and served with bread or rice. Other

Amerindian food includes *tumapot* (similar to *pepperpot*), cassava bread and *farine* (grated, parched cassava, a bit like couscous).

Locals consider **wild meat** a delicacy and more adventurous eaters should try deer, iguana, wild pig, *manicou* (opossum) and *labba* or agouti (jungle rat). Locals like to tell visitors that if they eat *labba* and drink creek water they will return to Guyana – though in practice, it's more likely that you'll be returning to the toilet with greater frequency.

Snacks such as patties, buns, potato balls, *pholouri* (seasoned flour and lentil balls), pine tarts (triangular pastries with a pineapple filling), *salara* (red coconut rolls) and *cassava pone* (like bread pudding but made with coconut and cassava) are sold in most bakeries and cost G$160–300 each.

A hot meal **costs** G$300–400 from a market *cook shop*; in local cafés it costs twice that and in more upmarket restaurants you'll spend over G$1000.

DRINK

The local award-winning **Banks Beer** does the job and cheaply from around G$300. Two local **rum** brands are worth trying (neat, if you want to earn the locals' respect): Banks DIH's 10-year-old or Demerara Distillers' El Dorado 15-year-old Special Reserve. You may be offered **high wine** or **bush rum** but these can strip paint and are only for the truly brave.

Fizzy soft drinks are sold everywhere, along with regional brands such as Busta and I-Cee. Chilled drinks like Mauby (a tree bark-based beverage), Cherry and Sorrel (each flavoured with their eponymous ingredient) are very refreshing, though nothing beats drinking **coconut water** straight from the shell and then eating the white jelly with a scoop. **Bottled waters** like Diamond Mineral or Tropical Mist are readily available.

CULTURE AND ETIQUETTE

English is the national **language** but locals tend to converse in Guyanese *Patwah* (patois), an English-based Creole influenced by the Amerindian, African, Dutch and Indian languages. While Guyanese has no official status, it is often regarded as the first language. The nine Amerindian communities speak several dialects including Arawak, Macushi and Warao, while the three predominant **religions** are Christianity, Hinduism and Islam.

Women can expect to get plenty of loud comments and persistent, kissing noises, but this is essentially harmless flirting. Even so it's best not to wear excessively revealing or sexy clothing. Guyanese dress stylishly for work, church, visiting government offices or dining out. Favourite conversation topics are cricket and politics. **Tipping** is not compulsory though it is appreciated; ten percent is the norm.

SPORTS AND OUTDOOR ACTIVITIES

The country may be located in South America where **football** rules, but nobody told the Guyanese, who by far favour **cricket,** considered the national sport. There are cricket grounds around the country and you'll see children playing it everywhere, sometimes with makeshift bats and balls. Guyana's cricketing credentials were boosted by the construction of the national stadium in Providence in time for the 2007 Cricket World Cup.

After cricket and football, young Guyanese follow basketball, boxing, hockey, cycling, badminton and table tennis. Although not technically a sport, a hugely popular pasttime is **dominoes**. **Outdoor activities** such as canoeing, sport fishing, birdwatching, wildlife-spotting and mountain climbing usually involve visits to nature resorts in the interior and quite a bit of expenditure. **Horseriding** in the Rupununi Savannah is more easily accessible and a visit to the annual **Rupununi Rodeo**, held in the border town of Lethem over the Easter weekend, is highly recommended.

COMMUNICATIONS

Sending **letters and postcards** from Guyana is cheap (G$60–150) and fairly efficient. For urgent deliveries, try **private mailing companies** in the capital like FedEx, through Camex Ltd, 125 C Barrack Street (☎592/227-6976) or UPS, via Mercury Couriers, 210 Camp Street and New Market Street (☎592/227-1853).

Phone calls – local, national and international – can be made with cards issued by GT&T and Digicel, available from most stores and pharmacies. If you plan to use your **mobile phone**, get it unlocked before you arrive in Guyana, then purchase a local SIM card and prepaid charge cards. These are available from GT&T or Digicel stores authorized retailers.

Internet service is available in many Georgetown hotels and internet cafés, costing about G$200 per hours though sometimes free in hotels. It is not as readily available outside of the capital. **Wi-fi** is available in some of the larger hotels but in others you may have to queue up to use a designated computer or laptop. **Internet cafés** often provide

> ### GUYANA ON THE NET
>
> ⓦ www.exploreguyana.org
> Directory of accommodation, restaurants, airlines and travel agencies run by the Tourism and Hospitality Association of Guyana.
>
> ⓦ www.guyana-tourism.com
> Similar listings from the Guyana Tourism Authority.
>
> ⓦ www.guyanalive.com Social site providing forums and info on festivals and events.

affordable international phone services, costing G$20–60 per minute.

CRIME AND SAFETY

For the most part, Guyanese are honest, welcoming people and most visits to Guyana are trouble-free. That said, **petty crime** (particularly theft) is a given. Avoid displaying valuable items such as cameras, and ensure that you secure travel documents, jewellery, cash and valuables in hotel safes. Avoid large crowds and demonstrations, and don't give out information about where you are staying. In particular, don't carry any packages for anyone in or out of Guyana, no matter how well you think you know them, as drug trafficking is big business but could earn you serious prison time.

HEALTH

There is one public and several private **hospitals** in Georgetown. Rural and outlying areas are served by municipal hospitals and health centres; Medivac services (emergency air ambulance) are also available in emergencies. The quality of service can be inconsistent and the number of hospital beds is limited. Private ambulances offer a limited service without much medical care and take patients to the Georgetown public hospital (see p.714).

Avoid drinking tap, creek or river **water** and pack at least one long-sleeved top, long socks and protection from the sun and mosquitoes.

Consult your doctor regarding malaria tablets and vaccinations required, which may include hepatitis A and B, yellow fever, typhoid, tetanus-diphtheria and

rabies, depending on your plans. AIDS is a major problem in Guyana so take the necessary precautions.

INFORMATION AND MAPS

There is no tourist information office as such in Guyana but the **Tourism and Hospitality Association of Guyana (THAG)** (157 Waterloo St, Mon–Fri 8.30am–5pm; ☎592/225-0807, ⓦwww.exploreguyana.com) is the umbrella organization of all tourism-related services. THAG also produces an excellent free annual **magazine**, *Explore Guyana*, containing informative articles, maps and **general information** about the country. G.E.M.S. Inc also publishes a pocket-sized guide called *Guyana: where & what*, providing information on "everywhere you need to go and everything you need to know". Both magazines are available at hotels and tourism agents around the city. **Permits** may be required to visit Amerindian villages. Tour operators arrange this for organized trips, but independent travellers should contact the Ministry of Amerindian Affairs, at 251–252 Quamina & Thomas sts (☎592/227-5087, ⓦwww.amerindian .gov.gy).

It's best to buy **maps** of Guyana before you arrive (try a specialist shop such as Stanfords; ⓦwww.stanfords.co.uk). In Guyana, the best city plan of Georgetown is produced by Advertising & Marketing Services Ltd (☎592/225-53834); it can be picked up from THAG and tour operators such as Wilderness Explorers (see p.712).

MONEY AND BANKS

The unit of **currency** is the Guyanese dollar (G$), which comes in 20, 100, 500, and 1000 notes and 1, 5, and 10 coins. Guyana has a floating foreign exchange policy against the US dollar, which causes the foreign exchange rate to fluctuate depending on demand and supply. Licensed currency exchanges

---

EMERGENCY NUMBERS

911 or 564 Police.
225-6411 Police emergency response unit.
912 Fire service.
913 Ambulance.

(cambios) often offer better exchange rates than banks. A few businesses may accept foreign currency (usually US$) but they tend to use the daily bank rate.

While travellers' cheques and major **credit cards** such as MasterCard, Visa and American Express are accepted by most tour operators, car rental agents and in some restaurants and hotels, you may have difficulty paying with them elsewhere. The Bank of Nova Scotia (Scotia Bank) is one of the few banks that accepts some foreign cards; it has some 24hr ATM machines in Georgetown, New Amsterdam, Parika and Bartica. Cash can also be obtained on American Express Cards at the

Demerara Bank (Camp St, Georgetown). Travellers can usually change sterling, euros, Canadian and US dollars without difficulty, but keep any cambio receipts in order to exchange Guyanese dollars on departure. At the time of writing, US$1=G$204, €1=G$280, £1=G$330. Prices throughout this guide are given in Guyanese dollars unless otherwise stated.

OPENING HOURS AND PUBLIC HOLIDAYS

Banks in Georgetown usually open Mon–Thurs 8am–2pm, Fri 8am–2.30pm and are closed at weekends. Hours outside of Georgetown may differ.

PUBLIC HOLIDAYS

January 1 New Year's Day

February Youman-Nabi (Muslim celebration of birth of Prophet Mohammed; date varies) **February 23** Republic Day (Mashramani carnival celebrating the achievement of republic status in 1970).

March Phagwah (date varies). Hindu festival celebrating triumph of good over evil. Participants wear white and cover each other in dye, water, perfume and powder.

March/April (varies) Good Friday

March/April (varies) Easter Monday

May 1 Labour Day

May 5 Indian Heritage Day, commemorating the arrival of indentured servants from India.

May 26 Independence Day

July Caricom Day (First Monday)

August 1 Freedom Day, commemorating the end of African slavery in the British Caribbean.

September Eid ul Fitr (varies). Muslim festival breaking the Ramadan month of fasting.

November Diwali (Festival of Lights). Hindus prepare special foods and decorate their properties with lit *diyas* (clay pots with wicks).

December Eid-ul-Adha (Muslim festival of sacrifice; date varies)

December 25 Christmas Day

December 26 Boxing Day

FESTIVALS AND NATIONAL CELEBRATIONS

National celebrations often involve special food and drink, parties and general revelry. There are sometimes spectacular float parades, masquerade bands and lots of dancing in the streets. Christmas is an excellent time to visit Guyana, to sample traditional festive food and and get-togethers such as the Boxing Day Main Big Lime (street party) and New Year's Eve parties. For more details on annual event-led festivals including Gospel Fest (April), Rupununi Wildlife Fest (April), Guyana Music Festival (August) and the Rockstone Fish Festival (October), check the THAG and GTA websites (see box, p.706).

Government offices open Mon–Thurs 8am–noon and 1–4.30pm, Fri 8am–noon and 1–3.30pm; and shops and other businesses Mon–Fri 8am–4pm, Sat 8am–noon. Supermarkets and small corner shops may have a more relaxed schedule but most businesses (with the exception of eating establishments) are closed on Sundays and public holidays.

Georgetown

GEORGETOWN is the financial, commercial and administrative centre of Guyana. Set on the east bank of the Demerara estuary, the capital is a grid-city designed largely by the Dutch in the eighteenth century. Known as **Stabroek** under the Dutch, it was renamed Georgetown by the British in 1812 after George III. Georgetown was originally nicknamed "The Garden City" because of its botanical parks, wide tree-lined avenues and an abundance of flowers, though today that name seems less appropriate. That said, there is a definite charm to the wild flowers, shaky housing, roti stands and sheer hustle of **Stabroek Market**, the soul of the city.

After dark, take a **taxi** wherever possible and avoid walking on sparsely lit streets like Seawall Road, North Road and around the Promenade Garden and Independence Square areas. Seek local advice about where not to go and avoid meandering into troubled areas such as Albouystown and Tigerbay (near Main Street) at any time.

What to see and do

This small yet interesting city is worth exploring for its diverse cultural, religious and historical landmarks, including unique wooden buildings that date back to the eighteenth and nineteenth centuries. Most of the streets are laid out in perfect rectangles, making it relatively easy to navigate.

The seawall and around

Georgetown is bounded to the north by the Dutch-built **seawall**, which keeps the Atlantic Ocean at bay and protects the city from flooding. The seawall extends some 450km along the Atlantic coast of Guyana and Suriname and is a popular spot for kite-flying, jogging, weekend food stalls, *liming* (hanging out) and romance, although care should be taken here after dark.

Nearby, on the corner of High St and Battery Road is the **Umana Yana** (Mon–Fri 8.30am–4.30pm; free), a large *benab* (Amerindian thatched hut) built by the Wai-Wai people in the 1970s. It's a popular venue for meetings, concerts and exhibitions, and there are plaques on display that provide information on the building's history. Also on High Street is the **Red House** (Mon–Fri 9am–4pm; free; ☎592/223-7524), a nineteenth-century colonial style building famous for its bright red *wallaba* (wood) shingles and for being the former home of Guyana's second President, Dr Cheddi Jagan. Further south on Main Street is **State House**, the official residence of the current President of Guyana and out of bounds to the public.

Main Street and around

The **National Museum** (North Road; Mon–Fri 9am–4.30pm, Sat 9am–noon; free) showcases an eclectic mix of exhibits including flora and fauna, Amerindian craft, precious stones and one of the world's rarest postage stamps – the British Guiana one-cent magenta. The **Walter Roth Museum of Anthropology** (Mon–Thurs 8am–4.30pm, Fri 8am–3.30pm; free), which houses artefacts relating to Guyana's nine Amerindian tribes, is also located on Main St.

The impressive **St George's Cathedral**, on Church Street, is one of the world's tallest free-standing wooden structures at 44m. Guided tours for groups can be booked through the Deanery Office, or ask any available verger for a tour (Mon–Sun 9am–2pm except public holidays; free; ☎592/226-5067, ⓦwww .stgeorges.org.gy).

Markets

Stabroek Market, near Water Street, is dominated by its four-faced, non-functioning clock tower. It's the focal point for Georgetown's merchants, shoppers, minibuses, moneychangers, beggars and pickpockets. You can find anything from canned mackerel and rat poison to gold jewellery and handicrafts. East of Stabroek is Bourda, home to **Bourda Market**, a smaller market though no less lively, and **Merriman's Mall,** a colourful shantytown filled with fruit, vegetable and coconut vendors.

The botanical gardens and around

The **botanical gardens** on Vlissengen Road is a peaceful green space where you can feed manatees and pose on the Kissing Bridge. There are more than one hundred wildlife species in the **zoo** housed within the grounds (daily 9.30am–5.30pm; G$200; ☎592/225-9142).

Also on Vlissengen Road, in Castellani House, is the **National Art Gallery** (Mon–Fri 10am–5pm, Sat 2pm–6pm; free), once the official residence of L.F.S. Burnham, Guyana's first president. The collection inside features the work of celebrated Guyanese artists. Just south of the gallery is the **1763 Monument** is a 5m-high bronze memorial to Cuffy, an African slave who led an unsuccessful slave rebellion in 1763.

Demerara Distillers

Guyana has had over two centuries to perfect its rum, so set aside an hour for a tour of **Demerara Distillers** (G$3000; ☎592/265-5019, ⓦwww.theeldorado rum.com), which shows how rum is made

and stored, and includes free samples of its award-winning premium rums. Definitely worth the 15-min minibus ride out of Georgetown to the DDL factory in Diamond on the East Bank Road.

Arrival

Air Cheddi Jagan International Airport (ⓦwww .cjairport-gy.com) is located at Timehri, 40km south of the city centre. International carriers currently serving CJIA are Delta Airlines, Caribbean Airlines, LIAT, Meta Airlines, Suriname Airways and Blue Wing (the last-named with a poor safety record). Minibus #42 takes 45min to get to Georgetown (G$260); taxis are also available and cost around G$4000– 5000. There's an official cambio at the airport.
Bus The Intraserv bus from Lethem arrives in Georgetown around 1am; it will drop you at the bus terminal outside the *New Tropicana Hotel*, at 177 Waterloo St.
Minibus Minibuses from Molson Creek will generally take you to your accommodation on request; if not, they will drop you near Stabroek Market, where you can pick up a taxi to your accommodation.

City transport

Minibus Privately owned minibuses operate in allocated zones and are both loud and intimate, but rarely cost above G$100 within town. Most start out from the Stabroek Market area but can be stopped

TREAT YOURSELF

Guyana has a number of excellent **resorts** but they can take some time, effort and money to get to, so are best booked through a tour operator. Otherwise, for a fun day out or camping for a few nights that won't break the bank, try **Splashmin's Resort** (☎592/223-73014, ⓦwww.splashmins.com; entry G$580), a water park located a 45-min drive from Georgetown on the Linden/Soesdyke Highway. Take a picnic basket or buy food and drink on site. Swimming, peddle boats, kayaking, jet-skiing, basketball, football, volleyball and table tennis are all available. A night at the hotel here will cost around G$10,000, but you can camp across the lake for as little as G$1100 (entrance fee included).

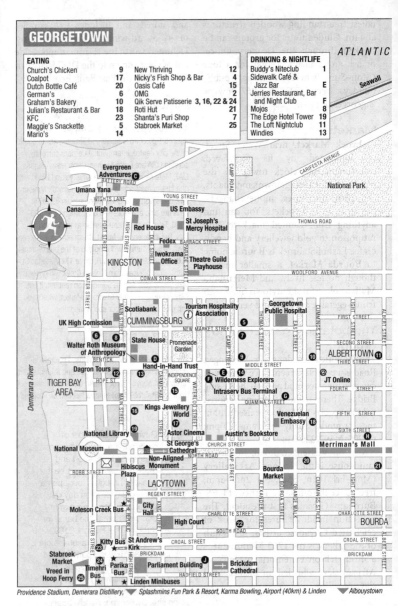

GEORGETOWN

EATING

Church's Chicken	9
Coalpot	17
Dutch Bottle Café	20
German's	6
Graham's Bakery	10
Julian's Restaurant & Bar	18
KFC	23
Maggie's Snackette	5
Mario's	14
New Thriving	12
Nicky's Fish Shop & Bar	4
Oasis Café	15
OMG	2
Qik Serve Patisserie	3, 16, 22 & 24
Roti Hut	21
Shanta's Puri Shop	7
Stabroek Market	25

DRINKING & NIGHTLIFE

Buddy's Niteclub	1
Sidewalk Café & Jazz Bar	E
Jerries Restaurant, Bar and Night Club	F
Mojos	8
The Edge Hotel Tower	19
The Loft Nightclub	11
Windies	13

Providence Stadium, Demerara Distillery, ▼ Splashmins Fun Park & Resort, Karma Bowling, Airport (40km) & Linden   ▼ Albouystown

along the route if space is available. Routes include: #40 to Kitty/Campbellville; #41 to South Ruimveldt; #45 to Alberttown; #47 to West Ruimveldt.

Taxi Taxis are unmetered, everywhere, on constant lookout for passengers and are the cheapest in the Guianas; take advantage of them. Most taxis are painted yellow and display number plates

beginning with the letter "H". They can be found at Stabroek Market and outside most hotels. Always agree to a price before starting your journey. Fares rarely top G$400–500 unless you travel outside of Georgetown. For prompt, courteous service call Dindy of D. Singh's Transport Service (☎ 592/218-1867).

Molson Creek, Corriverton, Ogle Airport, East Coast Highway & New Amsterdam ▲

OCEAN

0   200 m

SECOND AVENUE
THIRD AVENUE
PUBLIC ROAD
FOURTH AVENUE
SUBRYANVILLE
Ⓑ
WILLIAM STREET
FIFTH AVENUE
DAVID STREET
GORDON STREET
KITTY
PIKE STREET
THOMAS STREET
BARR STREET
SHELL ROAD
CAMPBELLVILLE
THOMASLANDS
SANDY BABB STREET
CAMPBELL AVENUE
❶
❷
DOWDING STREET
AUSTIN STREET
❸
STATION ROAD
❹
DUREY LANE
DENNIS STREET
UPPER LAMAHA STREET
GARNETT STREET
CRAIG STREET
ANIRA STREET
D'ANDRADE STREET
JOHN STREET
Topaz
NEWTOWN
WILLIAM STREET
LALUNI STREET
Surinamese
Embassy
DA SILVA STREET
CROWN STREET
DUNCAN STREET
LANCE GIBBS STREET
BARIMA AVENUE
OLEANDER AVENUE
QUEENSTOWN
EPING STREET
FORSHAW STREET
Roraima Tours
BEL AIR PARK
Colombian Embassy
Brazilian Embassy
LAMA AVENUE
CHURCH STREET
NORTH ROAD
Bourda
Cricket
Ground
Zoo
ROBB STREET
REGENT STREET
Botanical
Gardens
National Art Gallery
HOMESTRETCH AVENUE
Ⓘ
Cliff Anderson
Sports Hall
DURBAN PARK
National
Cultural
Centre
1763 Monument
HADFIELD STREET

Camp Ayangana

SEAWALL ROAD
CLIVE LLOYD DRIVE
WIRELESS ROAD
DR J B TACHMANSINGH ROAD
VLISSENGEN ROAD
STANLEY PLACE
ALEXANDER STREET
QUEEN STREET
PEIE STREET
EARLE AVENUE
CHUCK ROAD
SHERIFF STREET
LAMAHA STREET
DELPH STREET
SEAFORD STREET
RAILWAY STREET
VLISSENGEN ROAD
IRVING STREET
REPUBLIC STREET
D'ABREU STREET
MIDDLETON STREET
DELPH STREET
NEW GARDEN STREET
PETER ROSE STREET
ALBERT STREET
LILINI STREET
RUIMVELDT STREET
RUPUNUNI ST
ORONOQUE STREET
ABARY STREET
NEW GARDEN STREET
ORONOQUE STREET

ACCOMMODATION	
Ariantze	E
Cara Lodge	G
New Tropicana Hotel	F
Pegasus Hotel	C
Rima Guest House	D
Sleepin Guest House	H
Sleepin International Hotel	J
Tourist Villa	B
Windjammer International	A
YWCA	I

Accommodation

Note that in Guyana a "single room" will usually have a double or queen-sized bed and a "double room" may come with two beds of varying sizes. Prices quoted below are inclusive of 16 percent VAT, for a standard without a/c, unless otherwise stated. Some establishments accept foreign credit cards but not all, so check when making a booking. Don't rely on email for reservations.

Ariantze 176 Middle St ☎592/227-0152, Ⓦwww .ariantzesidewalk.com. Central hotel offering charming if a little worn facilities with TV, a/c, fridge

TOUR OPERATORS

Tour operators can arrange city tours (from G$7000); aerial tours (G$20,000); day-trips to nearby resorts (around G$20,000); Kaieteur Falls (from G$40,000) and customized excursions into Guyana's vast interior (from G$50,000). Most tour operators specialize in nature and adventure tours throughout Guyana's hinterland.

Bushmasters Lethem ☏ 592/682-4175, ⓦ www.bushmasters.co.uk. Jungle survival, safari, riding and cowboy adventure tours.

Cortours Lot 34 Grant 1651, Crabwood Creek, Corentyne ☏ 592/339-2430, ⓔ cortoursinc @yahoo.com. Tours along the Corentyne River.

Dagron Tours 35 Main St ☏ 592/223-7921, ⓦ www.dagron-tours.com. Tours to ecolodges, ranches and Sloth Island.

Evergreen Adventures Pegasus Hotel, Seawall Rd ☏ 592/225-4484, ⓦ www.evergreen adventuresgy.com. City, nature and adventure tours; Baganara island resort packages and main Intraserv Bus agent.

Roraima Tours Roraima Residence Inn, 8 Eping Ave, Bell Air Park, Georgetown ☏ 592/225-9648, ⓦ www.roraimaairways .com. Linked with Roraima Airways and offers aerial tours, trips to Amerindian settlements and other nature tours.

Wilderness Explorers Cara Suites, 176 Middle St, Georgetown ☏ 592/227-7698, ⓦ www.wilderness-explorers.com; UK rep (Claire Antell) ☏ 0044/7958-218-784, ⓔ claire@wilderness-explorers.com. Offer city, cultural, research, nature and adventure tours around Guyana.

and en-suite facilities, breakfast and nearby pool access (G$13,000). Food and entertainment on site at the *Sidewalk Café & Jazz Club*. Credit cards accepted. G$11,200.

New Tropicana Hotel 177 Waterloo St ☏ 592/227-5701, ⓦ www.newtropicanahotel.com. Central hotel with a Latin vibe, good for backpackers. Rooms have fans, mosquito nets and shared bathrooms (en-suites available at extra cost). There's an all-night café/club downstairs so it can be a bit noisy. Internet café and Intraserv bus terminal on site. G$3600.

🏃 **Rima Guest House** 92 Middle St ☏ 592/225-7401, ⓔ rima@networksgy .com. This centrally located budget option claims to be the "cleanest guesthouse in town" and doesn't lie. Simple rooms have shared bath, fans and mosquito nets, but be prepared for thin walls and cold water. G$5500.

Sleepin Guest House 151 Church St ☏ 592/231-7667, ⓦ www.sleepinguesthouse.com. Reasonably priced lodgings located in a peaceful but fairly central part of the city. Not as fancy as its sister hotel (see below), but clean and comfortable with en-suite rooms, free wi-fi and breakfast. G$7100.

Sleepin International Hotel 24 Brickdam ☏ 592/227-3446, ⓦ www.sleepininternationalhotel .com. A spacious city-centre hotel with comfortable, modern en-suite rooms with balconies, free wi-fi and breakfast included. Outdoor pool and bar. G$8200.

🏃 **Tourist Villa** 95 5th Ave, Subryanville ☏ 592/227-2199, ⓦ touristvillagy.com. Furnished, spacious en-suite rooms and apartments

with a/c, over several floors. Enjoy BBQs and drinks in the roof garden with views of the Atlantic. G$8200.

Windjammer International In the Kitty area near Seawall, 27 Queen St ☏ 592/227-7478, ⓦ www .windjammer-gy.com. Small ensuite rooms with a/c, wi-fi and fridge. On-site café is reasonably priced, with breakfast and dinners ranging from $600–1000 and G$800 lunch specials. G$6000.

YWCA 106 Brickdam ☏ 592/226-5610, ⓔ ywca@sdnp.org.gy. This clean hostel situated near the botanical gardens welcomes both men and women to its dorms (G$2400) and private rooms (G$4000). A great budget option and food is available from a nearby café.

Eating

Georgetown has a wide range of cheap options, including bakeries, snackettes and *cook shops*. Fast-food outlets include *Mario's Pizzeria* and *Church's Chicken* (Middle and Camp sts); *OMG* (Sheriff St) and *KFC* (Vlissingen Rd). Opening hours vary but are generally between 10am–10pm; a few establishments remain open until later, particularly at weekends.

Coalpot 125 Carmichael St ☎ 592/225-8556. Restaurant serving well-balanced Guyanese food with a great balcony view of the cathedral. Mains G$700.

Dutch Bottle Café 10 North Rd ☎ 592/231-6561. Charming establishment in a traditional, colonial-styled house, with a good bar and an outside eating area. Creole and international menu with daily lunch specials (G$1200). Dinners (G$2500–4500) include satays (from G$1800), tamarind-glazed pork chop (G$2000) and *pepperpot* (G$3000). Mon–Sat 11am–11pm, Sun 5pm–11pm.

🏃 **German's** 8 New Market and Mundy sts ☎ 592/227-0079. Busy lunchtime restaurant famed for its legendary cow-heel soup (G$925) and Creole dishes. Located in a sketchy part of town, so take a taxi and discover what all the fuss is about.

Graham's Bakery 345 Cummings St. Tennis rolls (sweet bread rolls best eaten with cheese), bread, buns, cheese pies and excellent *salara* (sweet coconut-filled bread, G$140).

Julian's Restaurant & Bar 331 Cummings St, ☎ 592/227-1319. Quiet, cosy restaurant offering daily lunch specials and dinner from G$800. Wine bar on site.

Maggie's Snackette 224 New Market St. Busy shop with delicious cakes, pastries, black pudding and *souse* (G$160–360) plus lunch specials (G$1000).

New Thriving Restaurant 32 Main St ☎ 592/225-0868. Large, busy Chinese restaurant over three floors, with pastries, ice cream and buffet meals on the ground floor, dim sum, à la carte dining and sushi upstairs, and an open-air bar overlooking Main Street. Lunch specials (G$720), vegetable chow mein (G$580), sweet and sour chicken (G$1100). Mon–Sat 10.30am–11pm, Sun 9.30–11pm.

🏃 **Nicky's Fish Shop & Bar** Durey Lane, Campbellville. Chill out at this relaxed, open-air eatery, very popular with the locals. Wash down the tasty fish and chips (G$800) with a beer, while listening to the latest beats. Daily 9am until late.

Oasis Café 125 Carmichael St ◍ www .oasiscafegy.com. Milkshakes (G$500), a lunch buffet (G$2000) and decent coffee (G$335) makes this a favourite hangout for expats and locals, albeit not the cheapest. Free wi-fi.

Qik Serv Patisserie A popular café chain with four branches in Stabroek, Camp, Main and Sheriff sts . Reasonably priced breakfasts, lunches, pastries, cakes and fast foods (G$140–600). Also does a range of drinks, ice creams and milkshakes (G$100–400).

Roti Hut 18 North Rd. Roti and *puri* accompanied by curry and Creole dishes, cakes, pastries and bread. A roti, vegetable curry and drink will set you back less than G$1000.

🏃 **Shanta's Puri Shop** 225 New Market St. Small shop in the heart of town that serves excellent *dhal puri* with a range of tasty fillings, rice dishes, meat and vegetable stews, pastries, cakes and fruit drinks. Prices range from G$120 for snacks to G$1000 for full meals including rice, stews, curries and *dhal puri*.

Sidewalk Café 176 Middle St. Pleasant café with a lunch buffet (G$300–1000) that includes fish, meat, vegetable, rice, pasta and potato dishes. The dinner menu is printed on an LP record and features fish, meat and seafood dishes from G$1700.

Stabroek Market Head to the enclosed part of the market for cheap, tasty local Guyanese fare (G$300–400) at the many *cook shops*.

Drinking and nightlife

Georgetown's party spirit is focused on the bars and clubs along Sheriff and Main streets. Weekends are the liveliest; the real action starts around midnight.

Buddy's Niteclub 137 Sheriff St ☎ 592/231-7260. A multi-storey, multi-use hot spot with a laser-lit nightclub, pool hall and Chinese restaurant.

Jerries Restaurant, Bar and Night Club 177 Waterloo St. A 24hr venue with a busy nightclub, located below the *New Tropicana* hotel, with a well-stocked bar and tasty snacks including channa, jerk chicken, patties and eggballs. Visitors are encouraged to write a message on the walls.

Mojos 45 Main St. Party with a young crowd to the latest dance music and choose from three bars (one by the poolside). Open Fri–Sun; entry G$1000–2000.

The Edge Hotel Tower 74–75 Main St. Trendy nightspot offering two bars, varied music and free entry for women on Wed. Entry G$2000.

🏃 **The Loft Nightclub** 110 Third St. Spacious venue offering a mix of dance, *soca*, reggae and a mixed crowd. The bar is well stocked and does tasty snacks too. Open Wed–Sat.

Windies 91 Middle St. Watch sport on the big screen, sip iced drinks while surfing the net (free) or relax on the guarded patio while expats party upstairs.

Shopping

Georgetown's main shopping areas run along the bottom of Main St and along Water, Regent and Robb sts. Shopping hours are 8am until 5pm (street vendors keep their own time), though a few stores, particularly in the malls, are open until 7pm.

Arts and crafts Visit the Hibiscus Plaza (in front of the Robb St Post office) for arts and craft items including hammocks, beaded jewellery and other souvenirs.

Jewellery For beautiful gold jewellery visit Topaz, at 143 Crown and Oronoque sts (☎592/227-3968, ⊛www.theonlyjewellers.com) or Kings Jewellery World, on Kings Plaza, Quamina St (☎592226-0704, ⊛kingsjewelleryworld.com).

Directory

Banks and exchange Bank of Nova Scotia, at 104 Carmichael St and at Robb St, has ATMs that accept some foreign cards. There are also ATMs at Pegasus Hotel, Seawall Rd and Courtyard Mall, Robb St. The best rates are on the street and in cambios around town including Fogarty's Store, at Water St; Hand-In-Hand Trust, at 62–63 Middle St; and R. Sookraj & Sons, at 108 Regent St.

Embassies and Consulates Australia, 18 Herbert St, Port of Spain, Trinidad (☎868/628-0695); Brazil, 308 Church St (☎592/225-7970); Canada, High & Young sts (☎592/227-20812); Suriname, 171 Peter Rose & Crown sts (☎592/226-7844, ⊛surnmemb@gol.net.gy); UK, 44 Main St (☎592/226-5881); US, Young & Duke sts (☎592/226-3938); Venezuela, 296 Thomas St (☎592/226-1543).

Hospitals Davis Memorial Hospital, 121 Durban St (☎529/227-20413); Dr Balwant Singh's Hospital, 314 East St (☎592/226-5783); Georgetown Medical Centre, 260 Thomas and Middle sts (☎592/226-72149); Georgetown Public Hospital, New Market St (☎592/227-8210-2); St Joseph's Mercy Hospital, 130–132 Parade St (☎592/227-20725).

Internet *JT Online Internet Café* at 38 Cummings St or *Power Surf Internet Café* at 29 Lombard St (around G$200 per hr). Also, look out for GT&T wi-fi Hot Spot signs in locations around town.

Pharmacies Try Medi-care Pharmacy at 18 Hinck St (☎592/225-9369) or The Medicine Chest at 315 Middle St (☎592/226-4971).

Moving on

Air Several scheduled domestic flights and charters to destinations throughout Guyana depart from Ogle and Cheddi Jagan airports. Airlines include Air Guyana (⊛www.airguyana.biz), Air Services Ltd(⊛www.asigy.com) Roraima Airways (⊛www.roraimaairways.com) and Trans Guyana Airways (⊛www.transguyana.net). There is a G$4000 departure tax for international departures.

Annai (request stop; daily; 1hr 30min); Karanambu (request stop; daily; 1hr 20min); Lethem (daily; 1hr 30min); Mabaruma (4 weekly; 50min). Charter flights are available to Baganara (25min), Bartica (25min) and Kaieteur (50min).

Boat The ferry crosses the Demerara River en route to Vreed-en-Hoop and departs from the Stelling, behind Stabroek Market. For schedules, prices and durations, call ☎592/226-9745 or visit the Stelling, where you will also find faster speedboats.

Bus Intraserv provides an overnight scheduled service to Lethem (for the Brazil border) on Sun, Tues, Thurs & Fri, which departs between 8pm and 9pm from the Intraserv Bus Terminal outside the *New Tropicana* hotel at 177 Waterloo St. The trip includes a pontoon river crossing at Kurupukari at 6am the next morning and unofficial stops at Iwokrama (around 6.45am), Canopy Walkway (about 1hr 30min later), Surama (45min from the Walkway) and a scheduled stop at Annai (for Rock View and the airport), before you arrive in Lethem around 1pm or later. All departure and arrival times are approximate. It's advisable to book your ticket in advance via Evergreen Adventures or directly at the Intraserv Terminal (see p.712).

Minibus All services leave from the Stabroek Market area when full; prices vary depending on fuel costs.

Corriverton and Molson Creek, (for Suriname border; bus #63A, 3hr); Linden (bus #43; 1hr 30min); Parika for Bartica (bus #32; 1hr); Timehri for CJ Airport (bus #42; 45min). Also there are two private minibus services that offer pick-ups from your base in Georgetown to Molson Creek and then on to Paramaribo (Suriname). The trip takes 11–15hr depending on traffic and the ferry departure: P&A Bus Service, 75 Church St (☎592/225-5058, ⊛adele_bellamyward@hotmail.com); Dougla Minibus Service (☎592/226-2843).

West to Venezuela

There is no legal border crossing to Venezuela but there are a few places worth visiting out west along Guyana's coast, such as the hilly town of **Mabaruma**, which is the gateway to Shell Beach. Here you can observe marine turtles by night and tropical birds by day. Other points of interest include **Hosororo Falls** and **Skull Point**. Otherwise, plan a visit to the sleepy mining town of **Bartica**, which comes alive during the Easter Regatta. It is also a good point from which to embark on tours of the Mazaruni area and visits to areas of interest along the river, but make sure you make your travel and accommodation arrangements in advance (see below).

BARTICA

BARTICA, one of the country's oldest settlements, is a mining town situated on the confluence of the **Essequibo**, **Mazaruni** and **Cuyuni** rivers. Its population, a gritty mix of lumberjacks and gold/diamond miners, is rough and raucous but friendly. There's not much to see and do but it's a good base from which to explore places of interest in and around the Essequibo and Mazaruni rivers. These include the remains of **Kyk-Over-Al**, a seventeenth-century Dutch-built fort on an island in the Essequibo and **Marshall Falls,** a pleasant waterfall on the banks of the Mazaruni with good swimming. For guided boat tours of the area (G$32,000 for six; G$80,000 for overnight camping and night fishing), call *D'Factor Guesthouse* (see below), Monty Belle (☎592/695-2617) or Remsford Williams (☎592/629-0956).

Easter is the best time to visit Bartica, when it hosts its annual Easter Regatta. The week-long celebrations include the Miss Bartica Regatta Pageant, talent shows, cricket and football matches, a street parade, watersport events and general revelry around the town. Book accommodation well in advance at this time.

To **get to Bartica**, take Minibus #32 from Georgetown to the town of Parika. Then journey up the Essequibo River to Bartica in one of the many speedboats available at the Parika Stelling, which leave when full but not after 4pm (1hr; G$2000). There's also a slower twice-weekly ferry (9am Thurs & Sat, 4hr; G$500).

Arrival

Boat The Bartica Stelling is not far from the main street and it's easy to get around on foot, although taxis are available near the Stelling and market area.

Accommodation

🛶 **Baganara Island Resort** ⓦwww .baganara.net. A beautiful, tranquil resort located on an island 8km south of Bartica, set among lush greenery and colourful tropical flowers. To book lunch (G$6000), a day-trip or nights at Baganara, or for a relaxing getaway at the nearby Sloth Island, contact Evergreen Adventures or Dagron Tours (see p.712). If you are travelling independently then you must make your own way to Bartica, but contact them in advance to arrange your visit. G$26,000.

D'Factor Guesthouse Lot 2 Triangle St ☎592/455-2544, ⓔcutienadira@hotmail.com. Clean en-suite rooms, fans and nets. Balcony around the hotel; the nicer rooms are downstairs. Tours offered (see above). G$5000.

New Modern Hotel 9 First Ave ☎592/455-2301. Wood-walled en-suite rooms with fans and cable TV. Restaurant on site. (G$5000)

Eating, drinking & nightlife

There's not much variety to the food in Bartica but you can find roti, pastries, supermarkets and fruit stands along First Avenue and in the arcade.

Hong Kong Chinese Restaurant Corner of First & Fourth sts . Chinese meals from G$800.

J&D Spicy Corner & Hangout Bar First Ave. Offers Creole foods including okra, beef curry, black-eye cook-up and *labba* stew at low prices (G$600).

Micky's Hangout Lot 4, First Ave. Has a bar, TV and pool tables, and is popular with locals.

Moving on

Air Air Services Limited (ⓦ www.aslgy.com) and Roraima Airways (ⓦ www.roraimaairways.com) provide regular and charter flights from Bartica (25min) and Baganara (25min) to Ogle Airport. Contact them directly for prices, travel dates and times.

Boat and minibus For visits to Baganara, nearby tourist spots or hinterland areas, you will need a speedboat or 4x4 transport. To return to the capital from Bartica, retrace your steps to Parika by speedboat or ferry and then take a minibus#32 to Georgetown.

MABARUMA

MABARUMA, located about 15km from the Venezuelan border, comprises three villages: **Mabaruma** itself (administrative capital of the region in which the airstrip is located), **Kumaka** (port town, where the boats travel along the Arouca River) and **Hosororo** (a small community known for its stunning panoramic views and the Hosororo Falls).

An hour's boat ride away is **Shell Beach**, which extends from the mouth of the Pomeroon River to the Venezuelan border. It is here that four species of **marine turtle** (leatherback, Olive Ridley, hawksbill and green) come at night to lay their eggs from February to August. During the day, there is good **birdwatching** for scarlet ibis, egrets, herons, flamingos and other fauna including monkeys. Other excursions include swimming at **Hosororo Falls**, observing bats at **Bat Cave**, hiking to **Skull Point** (home to a burial ground, supposedly for the first peoples of Guyana) and the **Kissing Rock** (G$3000–5000). For a reliable tour guide with whom to see these sights contact Mr Chung (☎ 592/616-0832).

Arrival

You can only arrive in Mabaruma by air or by boat. Tour operator GMTCS (see p.712) offers a 6–7hr trip from the capital, which is a combination of overland and water transport (G$70,000), or you can book flights directly with airlines (see below).

Air Air Services Ltd (ⓦ www.aslgy.com) and Trans-guyana Airways (ⓦ www.transguyana.net) each offer 3–4 flights from Georgetown per week (1hr; G$31,000 return).

Boat The ferry *MV Kimbia* leaves Georgetown fortnightly, taking roughly 24–30hr to reach Kumaka. As the Arouca river links to larger rivers and their communities, you could also arrive by speedboat depending on where you're coming from. Prices will vary depending on distance, fuel prices and the number of passengers. If you have not already organized a speedboat to take you to

---

JONESTOWN MASSACRE

The chilling events of November 18, 1978, when more than 900 members of a sect died in an apparent mass suicide in northwestern Guyana, about 80km southwest of Mabaruma, have been the subject of many books and theories. In 1974, Reverend Jim Jones, the leader of a sect called The People's Temple, chose Guyana to establish a self-sufficient community of about 1100 based on utopian socialist ideals, which he humbly named Jonestown. Referring to an unnamed enemy that would come to destroy Jonestown, he told his flock that "revolutionary suicide" was the only way to combat this threat. When Congressman Leo Ryan and a party of journalists and concerned family members visited Jonestown in November 1978 to investigate alleged human rights abuses, the enemy had apparently arrived. Ryan and others were shot and killed at Port Kaituma airstrip as they tried to leave, while back at Jonestown the men, women and children were instructed to drink poison. A total of 913 people died, although a coroner's report suggested that as many as 700 of the victims were forcibly killed. Today the Jonestown site is overrun by bush and there is no monument or other reminders of its existence.

Shell Beach (G$30,000–55,000 return) prior to arriving in Mabaruma, check with the locals in the town of Kumaka to see if any boat is available, or call David Devideen (☏ 591/678-8075).

Minibus While you are unlikely to be arriving by minibus, you will be able to travel around the area using minibus and other transport services that operate between the villages. However, don't expect the same kind of frequency and vehicle numbers that you would find in Georgetown.

Accommodation and eating

Almond Beach Guyana Marine Turtle Conservation Society has a community-managed field station here and organizes small group tours from Georgetown (G$70,000 per person for groups of 6–10; fully inclusive). For further info contact Romeo De Freitas (☏ 592/260-2613, ✉ romeodefreitas @yahoo.com).

Broomes Guest House Perched on a hill halfway between the town centre and Kumaka ☏ 592/777-5118. Pleasant self-contained rooms with fan, net and TV. East-facing rooms have balconies with views of the Kumaka waterfront and the Arouca River. You can get meals from Broomes Shop, about 400m away. G$4500.

Mabaruma Guest House Town centre ☏ 592/777-5091. Eight basic en-suite rooms with fan and net; meals (G$600–800) can be ordered in and staff can organize local trips. G$3500.

South to Brazil

Guyana's most famous attraction, the beautiful but dramatically isolated **Kaieteur Falls**, is the centrepiece of the ancient Pakaraima mountain range in southwestern Guyana. Legend accords its name to Chief Kai of the Patamona tribe, who sacrificed his life to save his people from marauding Caribs.

Further inland, the potholed dirt road from Georgetown to the Brazilian border traverses pristine rainforests and wide-open plains before arriving at the border town of **Lethem**. En route, highlights include the **Iwokrama Rainforest,** the huge, densely forested home of a diverse variety of flora and

fauna, and the **Canopy Walkway,** where you can observe some of this wildlife from bridges suspended above the forest floor. Further along the George-town–Lethem Road is **Surama Village,** a small, progressive Amerindian settlement in the **Rupununi Savannah,** a vast area of wooded hills, dry grassland and cattle ranches that provides excellent possibilities for wildlife watching. After Surama, you can chill out at the beautiful and peaceful *Rock View Lodge* in Annai, take a flight from the nearby Annai Airport or carry on to Lethem.

KAIETEUR FALLS

At 226m tall, **KAIETEUR FALLS,** almost five times the height of Niagara Falls and twice the height of Victoria Falls, stands in a cavernous gorge surrounded by the forests of the **Kaieteur National Park**. Its isolation and trickle of visitors make it one of the world's most impressive waterfalls. There's some interesting **wildlife** to spot too, including the brilliant-orange cock-of-the-rock bird and thumb-sized poisonous golden frogs.

Arrival and information

Most people visit Kaieteur Falls by air, and several tour operators in Georgetown offer day-trip packages that twin the site with Arrowpoint Nature Resort (see p.712), Baganara Resort (see p.715), Orinduik Falls, Rock View Lodge (see p.720) and Karanambu Ranch (see p.720). It's possible to trek to the falls all the way from Georgetown, provided you have the time (at least 4–5 days), money (G$160,000 approx) and the motivation. If so then contact either Dagron Tours (see p.712) or Rainforest Tours (Hotel Tower, 74–75 Main St ☏ 592/227-5632, ✆ www.rftours.com).
Air Day-trips from Georgetown (including flight from Ogle, park entrance fees and lunch) start from G$46,000. Flights can be arranged independently or through tour operators (see p.712).

Accommodation

Kaieteur Guest House Has two bedrooms, hammocks, nets, stove and a fridge. Bring food and water purification tablets for rainwater. At the time of writing there was no way to contact the guesthouse directly but your tour or flight operator should be able to arrange accommodation with the guesthouse if you wish to stay.

IWOKRAMA RESEARCH CENTRE AND AROUND

The pristine, 400-square-kilometre **Iwokrama Rainforest** is home to 474 bird species, 130 different mammals, 420 types of fish and 132 species of reptile. It's possible to stay at the **Research Centre** here (☎592/225-1504, ⓦwww .iwokrama.org; rooms G$20,000), an internationally funded project to promote ecotourism and sustainable development. Tourists share lodgings and meals with visiting biologists, botanists and journalists and can take part in nature walks along the Prince Charles Trail (named after the prince, who is a patron of Iwokrama) and treks to Turtle Mountain. There are also organized trips to a butterfly form, Fairview (an Aerindion village), the canopy Walkway or to see caimove at night. These excursions range from G$2000 to G$10,000 and are all conducted by knowledgeable, well-trained guides.

Canopy Walkway

A 90-min drive from the Research Centre is the **Canopy Walkway, a** 140-metre network of aluminium suspension bridges set amid the treetops. Its four observation platforms provide excellent vantage points to spot birds, monkeys and other fauna within the forest canopy. The bridges wobble but are very solid and have high ropes to hang on to; even so, those afraid of heights might find the experience challenging. An overnight stay at the nearby **Atta Rainforest Camp** costs around G$22,400 including three meals, the canopy user fee and a trained guide. Day visitors pay G$4700 but must

book in advance. Further details are at ⓦwww.iwokrama.org.

Surama Village and Ecolodge

A 45-min drive west of the Canopy Walkway is the turn-off for **Surama Village** (☎001-347-487-8723 US number that connects to village, ⓦwww .suramaecolodge.com). A small Amerindian settlement of some 300 people, it rests on a patch of savanna in the forest and offers individual guesthouses, meals and nature walks/mountain hikes with local guides. A popular activity is an evening hike (G$13,000) through the nearby forest to spend the night camping on the banks of the nearby **Burro Burro River**. Otherwise, overnight stays with meals, guided hikes and boat transportation start at approx G$26,000. You can also just stop by and pay for a specific activity or meal, but in that case you must pay the G$1000 village fee in addition to normal costs.

Arrival and information

Iwokrama strongly encourages visitors wishing to stay overnight to book in advance. If you have done this, then a member of staff will be waiting to collect you at the Iwokrama drop-off point for the drive in to the lodge. Otherwise, it will be a 25–30min walk in, or you will need to ask staff at the Iwokrama Ranger Station located near the junction to radio a message in for someone to collect you. Visitors arriving by plane will land at Annai and are advised to make arrangements in advance to be collected and driven to Iwokrana; failing that, they will need to make their way to the lodge independently by bus or 4x4.

Bus As long as everything is running to schedule, the Intraserv bus will cross the Essequibo River around 6am at Kurupukari and arrive on the other side around 6.30am. There is a police checkpoint just up the road so be prepared to show your passport. You must then gather your belongings and ask the driver to put you off at the Iwokrama junction, which is very near the checkpoint.

Minibus The above information also applies to minibuses, except that their arrival time may differ if they take a later crossing.

Moving on

Bus To continue on from Iwokrama to the Canopy Walkway, Surama Village, Annai (for Rock View Lodge and the airport) or Lethem, you must catch the scheduled Intraserv bus service that arrives on Mon, Wed, Fri and Sat mornings from Georgetown (having departed Georgetown the night before). For journeys back to Georgetown, Intraserv provides one scheduled departure on Sun, Tues, Thurs and Fri, departing around 11am from Lethem (border town for Brazil) to George-town. It's important to remember that the only official Intraserv bus stop between the Kurupukari Crossing and Lethem is at the Oasis Service Centre, Annai. Iwokrama, the Canopy Walkway and Surama are all request stops, so you must arrange with staff for transport out to the appropriate pick-up points and be waiting with your luggage before the bus arrives from either direction. Make sure that you confirm the bus schedule in both directions in advance and be aware that it is possible that you may have to wait for ages as the bus schedule can be severely hampered by vehicle, weather and/or road conditions. Fares are G$8000–10,000 (single) and up to G$19,000 (return) depending on where you join the bus. To guarantee a seat, book your ticket in advance via Evergreen Adventures or directly at the Intraserv Terminal (see p.714).

RUPUNUNI SAVANNAH

Travel in the **RUPUNUNI SAVANNAH** is expensive but provides a welcome break from the rainforest-and-river experience. A few kilometres further south of the turn-off for Surama Village, the dense surrounding vegetation suddenly morphs into flatlands that stretch across southern Guyana (about one-third of the country). Here you'll find cowboys working vast cattle ranches that constitute the lifeblood of the small Amerindian settlements that have formed around them. You can **stay** at some of these (see below); many ranches offer tours in the savanna. Book directly with them (often cheaper) or use a tour operator (see p.712).

Wildlife, including river otters, caiman, giant river turtles, tropical fish, monkeys and tapirs, is relatively easy to spot during boat trips on the nearby Rupununi River. However, during the **wet season**, kaboura flies, sandflies and mosquitoes can be a problem and driving becomes difficult, if not impossible, as much of the savanna is under several metres of water.

Arrival and information

Unless stated otherwise, overnight packages cover accommodation, meals and drinks, boat transportation, porters and local guides but exclude alcoholic drinks and air/road transport, which can be very expensive. Book directly via the lodge itself or via tour operators such as Wilderness Explorers, Bushmasters or Dagron Tours (see p.712).

Air Transguyana offers daily flights from George-town to Annai, and Karanambu (all 1hr 20min) from G$37,000 return. Standby tickets are available if there is space on the flight and the desired stop is scheduled or requested in advance (Annai and Karanambu are by request only). Strict baggage restrictions apply.

Bus The Intraserv bus (see p.714) operates a scheduled service to Lethem, which passes near Iwokrama, Canopy Walkway, Surama and Annai.

Car 4x4 overland transfers to Iwokrana prear-ranged by tour operators will take less time (5–6hr) than the Intraserv bus (11–15hr) but will be much more expensive; for example a return trip from Georgetown to Iwokrama in a 4x4 with driver will cost around G$143,000. Note that there are few passenger services in the savanna but villagers might drive you for a little less if they have the time and a road-worthy vehicle.

Minibus P&A Bus Service runs a daily service to and from Lethem (see p.714).

Accommodation and eating

Dadanawa Ranch ☏ 0044/7961-521-951 (UK number), ⊕ www.rupununitrail.com. This is the largest and most isolated ranch in Guyana, a 3-hr drive southeast of Lethem. The ranch is a good base to see cowboys work the cattle, and for trekking, horseriding, nature walks, birdwatching, swimming and fishing (see website for details of tours). G$24,500 including meals and on-site tours such as horseriding and birdwatching; tours off the ranch cost extra.

Karanambu Ranch @ Andrea.Salvador @karanambulodge.com, Ⓦ www.karanambulodge .com. Owner Diane McTurk is famed for rehabilitating orphaned Giant River Otters into the wild. Tours (G$30,000 approx) include trips to see birdlife and black caiman, helping to care for the otters and a visit to Lake Amaku, said to hold the Lost City of El Dorado. Special rates in wet season and for volunteers. G$40,000 including airstrip transfers, meals, local bar and two guided tours per day.

Oasis Service Centre Annai Ⓦ www .rockviewlodge.com/oasis.html. Conveniently located at a scheduled Intraserv bus stop on the Georgetown-Lethem road, the *Oasis* offers en-suite rooms (G$8000), hammock spaces (G$2000) and a camping area (G$8000 with two meals). There is running water, timed electricity, toilet and bathroom facilities, a laundry room and food for sale (G$100–1200). Nature trail and birdwatching activities available.

Rewa One of the most isolated tourism destinations, Rewa offers beauty and a mix of wildlife including monkeys, jaguars, tapirs and giant armadillos. The journey to Rewa involves a flight (1hr), vehicle transfer (15min) and a boat ride (4–7hr). The total cost is around G$65,000. Add another G$10,000 per day for lodgings (not including tours and one-off fees). To book a trip contact Wilderness Explorers or Bushmasters (see p.712).

Rock View Lodge Annai Ⓦ www.rockviewlodge .com. Owned by the affable Colin Edwards, *Rock View Lodge* is set within palm gardens and offers comfortable en-suite rooms, a swimming pool and excellent food. It's accessible by public transport and the Annai airstrip is practically in its front garden, making it a good base from which to explore the North Rupununi attractions. G$24,000.

LETHEM

Apart from the airstrip, there is not much to detain you in this tranquil town on the Brazilian border, unless you are breaking your journey on the way to or from Boa Vista in Brazil. Visas, if necessary, can be arranged via the Brazilian embassy (Church Street) and take about one to three working days.

Accommodation and eating

Kanuku View Restaurant and Snackette This place next to the roundabout offers Chinese, Indian and Brazilian specialities for G$700–1000.

Savannah Inn ☎ 592/772-2035. @ ramsaran4al @yahoo.com. Comfy, en-suite cabins and rooms with a/c, TV and wi-fi. Has a restaurant, and there's also a supermarket nearby. Offers return tours to Boa Vista in Brazil (G$50,000). G$5000.

Takutu Hotel ☎ 592/772-2034. @ morsha @electricity.gov.gy. Friendly staff and clean rooms, with a patio and garden for barbecues. G$5000.

East to Suriname

The long, winding and reasonably well-maintained East Coast road will take you all the way to **Molson Creek** for the ferry crossing (see p.721). There is not much tourism in this part of Guyana, but if you wish to break the journey

---

CROSSING INTO BRAZIL

To get from Lethem to the Brazilian town of Bonfim, you need to cross the Takutu River Bridge by foot or vehicle, about 1.5km north of Lethem. The local bus services do not cross the bridge and pick-ups from the airstrip to the crossing cost G$1000. Guyanese immigration formalities should be completed either at the airstrip when there are flights, or at the Lethem immigration office. Your passport is stamped on the Brazilian side of the border before you make your way to Bonfim, from where there are buses to Boa Vista, some 150km away. There is a GBTI bank in Lethem (Lot 121; Mon–Fri 8am–1pm), which offers foreign exchange. Moneychangers on the Lethem side of the river will also change Guyanese dollars for Brazilian reis and vice versa. Make sure that you have enough reis to get you to Bonfim, if not Boa Vista.

before crossing over to Suriname, you could stop off in **New Amsterdam** for a meal and a brief wander. Otherwise, the East Coast road passes the Guyana Sugar Corporation at **Albion** (the largest sugar estate in Guyana) and runs parallel to the Atlantic coast, bending southward towards its terminus at the mouth of the Corentyne River. **Corriverton**, the most easterly town in Guyana, faces Suriname across the river. About 10km before Corriverton is **No. 63 Beach**, one of Guyana's most popular beaches despite its muddy stretch of coast more suited to cricket than sunbathing.

Another option is to book a day or overnight trip with Cortours (see p.712) to Crabwood Creek, Cowfalls Resort or **Orealla**, an Amerindian village located on the Corentyne River. Ecotourism activities include nature walks, forest trails, visits to waterfalls and birdwatching, or you could just camp out on a sandy beach and say a final goodbye to Guyana before heading across the river to Suriname.

Arrival and information

Minibus Corriverton/ Molson Creek (3hr); New Amsterdam (1hr 30min). Minibuses to Corriverton and Molson Creek drop you either in the town or at the port. Generally, buses leave when full, though minibuses for Molson Creek leave Georgetown in the early hours to get passengers to the ferry on time. Otherwise, the services operate up and down the East Coast Road all day long. For through services from Georgetown to Paramaribo, see p.714.

Accommodation and eating

Lim Kang 12 Chapel St, New Amsterdam. Large portions of sweet-and-sour pork and fried rice are served up while Indian music plays in the background.
Mahogany Hotel 50 Public Rd, No.78 Village ☎ 592/335-3525. A 15-min drive from Molson Creek, with pleasant, clean rooms and a veranda overlooking the Corentyne River. G$5000.
The Train Next to the Shell service station, Corriverton. A popular place for a curry and roti breakfast before crossing the border.

Suriname

SURINAME, sometimes referred to as Dutch Guiana, is one of South America's smallest nations and shares similar traits with its Caribbean neighbours. Like Guyana, it has the palm trees without the sandy beaches and feels unlike much of the rest of the continent on which it is situated. Suriname only gained independence from the Dutch in 1975 and the vestiges of colonialism – including the language, numerous Dutch tourists and some attractive wooden architecture in the capital, **Paramaribo** – make it a quirky place to include on a pan-South American trip.

Ecotourists will love Suriname, as almost thirteen percent of its land surface area is under official environmental protection. This has led to the creation of a few nature reserves and a park, offering good opportunities for hiking and to observe wildlife such as butterflies, apes, toads, snakes and the red-rumped agouti. **Brownsberg Nature Park** is the most easily accessible from Paramaribo and the **Central Suriname Nature Reserve**, the third-largest of its kind in South America. On the coast, the **Galibi Nature Reserve** offers the chance to observe giant sea turtles laying their eggs.

CHRONOLOGY

Suriname's earliest inhabitants are thought to be the Surinen Indians after whom the country is named.
1498 Columbus sights Surinamese coast.
1602 Dutch begin to settle the land.
1651 England establishes first permanent settlement.
1667 Becomes Dutch Guiana with the Treaty of Breda, a formal exchange with the British for Nieuw Amsterdam (now New York).
1853 Chinese plantation labourers begin arriving.
1863 Abolition of slavery.
1873 Labourers from India, and later Indonesia, begin to arrive.
1949 First elections based on universal suffrage held.
1975 Suriname wins independence.

1980 Military coup led by Sergeant Major Dési Bouterse topples government.

1982 Fifteen prominent leaders of re-democratization movement executed.

1986 At least 39 unarmed inhabitants, mostly women and children, of the N'Dyuka Maroon village, Moiwana, are murdered by the ruling military government. The survivors and other families flee to French Guiana.

1987 Civilian government installed with new constitution for Republic of Suriname.

1990 Military overthrows civilian government.

1991 Under international pressure Bouterse holds elections. The New Front, a coalition of parties, wins and Ronald Venetiaan is elected president.

1996 National Democratic Party (founded by Bouterse in 1987) wins election.

2000 Venetiaan and the New Front coalition regains presidency (and again in 2006).

2007 UN maritime border tribunal awards both Guyana and Suriname a share of the potentially oil-rich offshore basin under dispute.

2008 Trial begins of Bouterse and others accused of involvement in executions of opponents of military regime.

2010 Bouterse elected president after Mega-Combination NDP party secures two-thirds majority in parliamentary elections.

Basics

ARRIVAL

Johan Adolf Pengel International Airport (also known as Zanderij), an hour south of Paramaribo, receives direct **flights** from Aruba, Amsterdam,

Belém and Boa Vista (Brazil), Curaçao, Georgetown, Miami and Port of Spain (Trinidad). **Zorg en Hoop**, a smaller airport about 30min from the capital, receives mainly helicopters and small domestic aircraft, as well as six flights a week from Guyana.

Overland from Brazil

There is no border crossing between Brazil and Suriname. Travellers arriving overland from Brazil enter Guyana at the town of Lethem, before making the 11–15hr **bus** journey to Georgetown and then entering Suriname from there (see p.714 for details).

Overland from Guyana

From Georgetown it's a 3-hr **bus** ride to the **ferry** port at Molson Creek, with one crossing per day, then a 3-hr bus ride from South Drain to Paramaribo. **Rental cars** cannot cross the border.

Overland from French Guiana

Travellers from French Guiana must cross the Marowijne Maroni River from St Laurent du Maroni to Albina by ferry or motorized dugout canoe, before continuing the 2–3hr drive by minibus or taxi to Paramaribo (see p.756). Be aware that prices and journey times can be affected by the condition of the road.

VISAS

At the time of writing, visas are required for all visitors except nationals from CARICOM countries, Brazil, Chile, Gambia, Hong Kong, Israel, Japan, Malaysia, Netherlands Antilles, Philippines, Singapore and South Korea. Visas can only be provided at the airport if organized in advance by a local tour operator or contact. Alternatively, apply for a visa at a Suriname diplomatic mission. For updated information on visa requirements, check ⓦwww .surinameembassy.org. Overland travellers can obtain visas for Suriname at the consulates in Guyana (see p.714) and French Guiana (see p.747) but factor in processing time. Visa **costs** are US$45 upwards, based on citizenship and duration.

GETTING AROUND

While commuting around the capital and outlying areas is reasonably easy, there are no major highways in Suriname except for the Oost–Westverbinding (East–West Highway) that runs between Albina and Nieuw Nickerie; large stretches of this road are still under repair following political unrest in the mid-1980s. For many remote interior destinations you may need to take a vehicle, flight, dugout canoe or a combination of the three; you're often better off going as part of a tour, which will arrange all transport. There are also several **bike rental** companies, which offer affordable rental and cycling tours to various attractions in Suriname.

By air

There are some **scheduled internal flights,** but tour operators tend to charter planes to visit parks and reserves, and this limits their frequency to the number of tourists wishing to make a trip. Suriname Airways (ⓦwww .slm.firm.sr) offers organized tours to Kasikasima, Palumeu and Awarradam through its tour division METS (see p.730).

By boat

The construction of the Paramaribo–Meezorg (J.A. Wijdenbosch) Bridge across the Suriname River has put the local ferry out of business, but you can still cross the Suriname River from Paramaribo to Meerzorg by small motorized boats. There's also a mail boat (Postboot) operated by SMS, which commutes from Paramaribo to the districts of Commewijne and Saramacca.

By bus

Budget travellers will learn to love the crowded and noisy **minibus**, one of the cheapest modes of travel both between the capital and smaller cities near the coast, and to Paramaribo's various neighbourhoods. **Private minibuses** (always brightly decorated) are numbered and run along assigned routes. These are slightly more expensive and display their prices on the door, which is always open. They do not leave until they are full but are more frequent than the official service and stop wherever you want along the road. The less decorated **state-run buses** (*staatsbus*) have a dedicated bus station, follow a formal schedule and use bus stops. See Ⓦ www.nvbav suriname.com.

By car and taxi

In Paramaribo it's fairly easy to get around by **private taxi**, which charge reasonable prices though it's still best to agree the fare before getting in. Registered taxis usually charge a fixed fare for specific city destinations. **Vehicle rental** is also an option, and while roads in the capital are fairly decent and there are now more paved roads in country areas, improvements are still needed – particularly on the unpaved sections of road on the way to the border town of Albina.

ACCOMMODATION

Accommodation in the main towns will normally consist of **guesthouses** (sometimes in private homes and in some cases quite basic) and mid-range **hotels** (generally larger and pricier).

No matter how luxurious or lamentable your lodgings, almost all rooms will come equipped with running water, fans and mosquito nets. A comprehensive list of guesthouses can be found at Ⓦ www.suriname-tourism.org.

There are also several **resorts**, as well as **lodges** in nature parks and reserves. Staying at these is usually on an all-inclusive basis and bookings are best made through tour operators, who will also arrange transport, which can be tricky if attempted independently.

FOOD

The food in Suriname is fairly inexpensive, very tasty and heavily influenced by its ethnically diverse population. Informal Indonesian eateries known as **warungs** (in the Blauwgrond area) and Hindustani **roti shops** are juxtaposed with the ever-present Chinese, European-style and Creole restaurants. Meals are generally around SRD12–20.

Kip (chicken) is very popular and typical Surinamese dishes include *moksie alesie* (rice, beans, chicken, and vegetables) and *pom* (chicken baked with a root vegetable). Indonesian specialities include *saoto* (chicken soup, bean sprouts, potatoes and a boiled egg), *bami* (fried noodles) and *nasi goreng* (fried rice). Two tasty peanut soups are *pindasoep*, made with tom-tom (plantain noodles), and *petjil*, made with vegetables. *Bakabanna* (plantain slices, dipped in a pancake batter and fried) is an established crowd-pleaser. Traditional Dutch favourites like *bitterballen* (breaded and fried minced meat balls) and *poffertjes* (sugared pancakes) are plentiful.

DRINK

Local **rum** does not rival Guyana's 15-year-old El Dorado but both Borgoe and Black Cat hold their own (try the latter with cola or coconut water). Imported and local beer, spirits, soft drinks and bottled water are widely available, as is **dawet**, a very sweet, pink concoction of coconut milk and lemongrass.

CULTURE AND ETIQUETTE

Suriname's diverse population is 27 percent Hindustani (the local term for East Indian); 18 percent Creole (people of African or mixed European and African origin); 15 percent Javanese; 15 percent Maroon (Bush Negro); and 25 percent Amerindian, Chinese, Portuguese and Jewish. The main **religions** are Hinduism, Christianity and Islam.

The official **language** in Suriname is Dutch but the common language is Sranan Tongo (Surinamese Creole). Several Maroon languages, including Saramaccan and Aukan, are spoken, as are Amerindian languages such as Carib. A reasonable number of people speak some English, particularly in Paramaribo. It's respectful to ask permission before taking pictures of people, buildings and sacrificial areas, especially when visiting Maroon villages. Always check with your guide, and if refused, accept this graciously. For **tipping**, ten percent is the norm if a service charge hasn't been included.

SPORTS AND OUTDOOR ACTIVITIES

The Surinamese are not cricket-crazy like the Guyanese. Their passion is **football**. Most good footballers leave to play in the Dutch professional leagues, making them ineligible to play for the national side. Other popular sports include **basketball** and **volleyball**.

Though hardly a conventional sport, competitive **bird-singing contests** are held on Onafhankelijkheidsplein in front of the presidential palace on Sunday mornings. Here, *picolets* and *twa twas* are persuaded to sing in turns, with the winning bird earning a payout for its owner.

COMMUNICATIONS

Postal services are provided by the Central Post Office, Surpost, near RBTT in Kerkplein 1 (☎597/477-524, ⊛www .surpost.com). Internet and phone services are provided by Telesur, Digicel and Úniqa. Public **telephone booths** in Suriname do not accept coins, so the cheapest option for international calls is to buy **phone cards** from newsagents, shops and hotels, which typically come in denominations of US$3, 5 and 10 (for local calls, SRD-denominated cards may be preferable). If you plan to use your **mobile phone**, get it unlocked before you arrive in Suriname, then purchase a Telesur or Digicel SIM card and some prepaid charge cards costing SRD5, 10, 20 or 50. **Internet cafés** are common in Paramaribo but less so elsewhere; generally they charge SRD3–4 per hour. Most Telesur branches offer email, fax, local/international phones and computer services, including internet access.

CRIME AND SAFETY

Locals are proud of saying that tourists can walk safely from one end of Paramaribo to the other at night. Take this with a pinch of salt; there are few reports of criminal incidents but as in any city, burglary, armed robbery and other **petty crime** do take place. Avoid wearing pricey jewellery or flashing money around and keep your possessions safe.

> ## SURINAME ON THE NET
>
> ⊛www.suriname-tourism.org The Suriname Tourism Foundation has info on what to do, where to stay and how to get around in Suriname.
> ⊛www.stinasu.com Before you travel to any of Suriname's parks or reserves, be sure to contact Stinasu, which manages them.

Travel to the interior is usually without incident, although there have been some reports of tourists being robbed. There is not a major police presence outside the capital, so avoid travelling at night if possible. Be careful on the **roads**, as drivers can be reckless and mopeds, scooters and motorcycles always have the right of way. Many of the roads in the interior are dirt roads with little in the way of street lighting or roadside services.

HEALTH

Medical care is limited, as is the small ambulance fleet. **Academisch Ziekenhuis** (Fluestraat ☎597/442-222, ⊛www.azp.sr) has the only 24hr emergency room service in Paramaribo as well as general practitioners who speak English. Tap water is allegedly safe to drink in Paramaribo but where possible, drink bottled water and avoid raw and undercooked foods. Pack at least one long-sleeved top, long socks,

good walking shoes and protection from the sun and mosquitoes. Consult your doctor regarding malaria tablets and the various **vaccinations** required, which include hepatitis A, hepatitis B, yellow fever, typhoid, tetanus-diphtheria and rabies, depending on where your trip activities are based. AIDS is also a problem in Suriname, so take precautions as necessary.

INFORMATION AND MAPS

Paramaribo is the easiest city in the three Guianas in which to find maps, which are generally available in bookshops and at most tour operators. Staff at the Toeristen Informatie Centrum (Tourist Information Centre), at Fort Zeelandia Complex, Waterkant 1 (Mon–Fri 8am–3.30pm; ☎597/479-200) are very helpful and speak English. They provide free maps and information in Dutch and English on transport, restaurants, nightlife, day-trips and tours, as well as the latest copy of *Suriname's Destination*

PUBLIC HOLIDAYS

January 1 New Year's Day

March Holi Phagwa (varies). Hindu festival celebrating triumph of good over evil. Participants wear white and cover each other in dye, water, perfume and powder.

March/April (varies) Good Friday

March/April (varies) Easter Monday

May 1 Labour Day

July 1 Keti Koti. Parades and other activities celebrating emancipation from slavery in 1863.

August 9 Day of the Indigenous People (when permitted)

September Eid Ul Fitr (varies). Muslim festival ending the Ramadan month of fasting.

November 25 Srefidensi. Activities based around Surinamese culture and traditions, including military parades, celebrating Suriname's independence in 1975.

December 25 Christmas Day

December 26 Boxing Day

Festivals and national celebrations

In addition to national holidays, many important events are celebrated among the resident ethnic communities. These include Chinese New Year (Feb); Jewish New Year (Sept); Loweman Dei, celebrating all things Maroon (Oct) and Diwali (Nov). Other festivities include the Brazilian carnival (Feb), French Music Festival (June); Back to School Festival (Sept); Salsuri Music and Suriname Jazz Festivals (Oct) and Surifesta, the end of year festival (Dec). On New Year's Eve (Owru Jari) there is a spectacular fireworks display in the capital.

Guide, which contains maps and tourism information.

MONEY AND BANKS

The unit of **currency** is the Suriname dollar (SRD), which comes in 1, 2.5, 5, 10, 20, 50 and 100 notes and 1, 5, 10, 25, 100 and 250 cent coins. Prices are often given in Euros, which are readily accepted, and street **moneychangers** often offer better exchange rates than banks. Major **credit cards** are accepted by most tour operators and in many restaurants and hotels in Paramaribo, but cash advances are only possible at RBTT Bank (Kerkplein 1 ☏597/471-555). Some **ATMs** in Paramaribo accept foreign bank cards; elsewhere ATMs are sparse, so carry extra **cash**. At the time of writing, €1 = SRD4.40; US$1 = SRD3.25 and £1 = SRD5.20.

OPENING HOURS AND HOLIDAYS

Banks and government institutions open Monday to Friday between 7.30am and 2pm. **Shops** and other businesses open between 8am and 4pm, as well as Saturday morning. Malls open from 9am to 9pm. Friday is the day for late-night shopping, though many Chinese retailers open until at least 9pm throughout the week.

Paramaribo

PARAMARIBO (called "Parbo" by the locals) may have the problems associated with traffic and urban sprawl but it offers a little more for the visitor than either Georgetown or Cayenne. Many of the colonial buildings on **Waterkant** and **Mr F.H.R. Lim A Postraat** have been rehabilitated, and a sunset walk along the river can be quite romantic. It's a tidy place – even the gutters and dirt paths get raked clean in many of the tourist areas – and has great food, some of the best budget accommodation in the Guianas and a buzzing nightlife.

Paramaribo is generally **safe**, but visitors should avoid the unlit Palmentuin (Palm Garden) after dark, as well as the residential area east of Van Sommelsdijkekstrant Straat and its intersection with Kleine Dwarsstraat. It makes sense to use a taxi to see the city after dark.

What to see and do

Paramaribo started life as a Dutch trading post and became the capital in the mid-1600s. Parts of the city were destroyed by fires in 1821 and 1832, but it is still characterized by attractive Dutch, French, Spanish and British colonial architecture, grassy squares and wooden houses. Its historic inner city became a UNESCO World Heritage Site in 2002.

Onafhankelijkheidsplein and around

Onafhankelijkheidsplein (Independence Square) was historically a parade ground and most of the sites worth seeing in Parbo are clustered around its well-manicured green lawns. The **Presidential Palace** and other attractive state buildings overlook the square and the nearby **Mr F.H.R. Lim A Postraat** takes you into the heart of the **Historic Inner City**, now a UNESCO World Heritage Site. Here you'll find a cluster of tree-shaded paths and well-preserved old buildings, including **Fort Zeelandia** (Tues–Fri 9am–2pm, Sun 10am–2pm; SRD10, with free guided tours Sun 10.30am & noon), which contains **the Stichting Surinaams**

SURINAME • PARAMARIBO

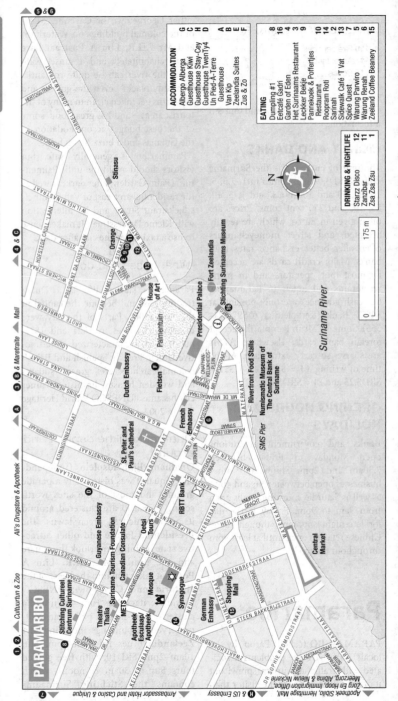

PARAMARIBO

ACCOMMODATION

Albergo Alberga	G
Guesthouse Kiwi	C
Guesthouse Stay-Cey	H
Guesthouse TwenTy4	D
Un Pied-A-Terre	A
Guesthouse	B
Van Kip	E
Zeelandia Suites	F
Zus & Zo	

EATING

Dumpling #1	8
Eetcafé Gadri	16
Garden of Eden	4
Het Surinaams Restaurant	3
Leckker Bekje	9
Pannekoek & Poffertjes	10
Restaurant	
Roopram Roti	14
Sarinah	2
Sidewalk Café 'T Vat	13
Spice Quest	7
Warung Parwiro	5
Warung Renah	6
Zeeland Coffee Beanery	15

DRINKING & NIGHTLIFE

Starzz Disco	12
Zanzibar	11
Zsa Zsa Zsu	1

Suriname River

0   175 m

Museum (same hours). The museum contains exhibitions that focus on modern art, period rooms and colonial relics reflecting Suriname's history. The fort itself has a small café and excellent views of the Suriname River. Rehabilitated colonial buildings can be found south of the square on the streets between Onafhankelijkheidsplein and Kerkplein.

Central Market and around

On Waterkant, past the food stalls, is the vast, two-storey **Central Market**, where you can buy all manner of goods including fruit, vegetables, clothes and fake watches. The nearby **craft market** and **art gallery** at SMS Pier sells handmade crafts and souvenirs. Further west from the market is downtown Paramaribo, full of shopping malls, casinos and gold and jewellery stores.

The **Numismatic Museum of the Central Bank of Suriname** (Mon–Fri 8am–2pm; free), at Mr F.H.R. Lim A Postraat 7, showcases Surinamese coins and banknotes dating from the seventeenth century.

St Peter & Paul's Cathedral

Previously a theatre, the cathedral, **De St Petrus en Paulus Kathedraal** on Henck Arronstraat(free tours Wed & Sat mornings) is a huge yellow edifice made entirely of wood; at the time of writing it was under renovation. Inside are beautiful paintings and its four flanking towers afford excellent views of the city. To the west on Keizerstraat, a **mosque** and **synagogue** sit happily side by side.

Palmentuin Park

The **Palmentuin** is an impressive park (the only one in Paramaribo) full of lofty royal palms. Although a bit run-down, it makes for a pleasant place to sit or stroll during the day under the shade of the trees. At night it's an area to avoid.

Just north of the park, near 'T Vat on Kleine Dwarsstraat 1, is the **House of Art** (daily 10am–3pm; free), with exhibitions of contemporary Surinamese art. The **Paramaribo Zoo** is situated at Sawarienotolaan in Rainville (daily 9am–5pm; SRD3–5; ☏597/545-275).

Arrival and information

Air Johan Adolf Pengel International Airport (Zanderij) receives flights from the Netherlands, Trinidad, Brazil, Curaçao, Guyana and the US. The smaller Zorg en Hoop airport is for domestic and Guyana flights. Airport service buses from JAPI must be booked in advance and will drop you at your hotel (1hr; approx SRD50; ✺ www.legrandbaldew.com). The cheaper state bus (*staatsbus*) will drop you off at the Heiligenweg bus station in Knuffelsgracht (3 daily services except Sun; 1hr 35mins; SRD2.15; ✺ www .nvbnvsuriname.com) or you can catch the more frequent private minibuses, which will drop you in Maagdenstraat (Line POZ, less than SRD10). From Zorg en Hoop, minibus lines #8 and #9 pass near the airport and drop you at Steenbakkerijstraat (less than SRD10). Unmetered taxis from JAPI to the city centre (45min) cost around SRD100–120. Taxis from Zorg en Hoop should cost no more than SRD20 and take about 30min.

Minibus From South Drain (Guyana river crossing) and Nieuw Nickerie (parking lot next to market), private minibuses (2–3hr; SRD50) will offload you at Dr. Sophie Redmondstraat, opposite *Hotel Ambassador*. The state-run bus (2 daily except Sun; 2hr; SRD12.50) drops you at the Heilgenweg bus station in Knuffelsgracht.

From Albina (French Guiana border) fairly frequent minibuses (PA) and two daily state-run minibuses (one service on Sat and Sun; 2hr 30min; SRD8.50) drop you at Waterkant and the Heilgenweg bus station in Knuffelsgracht.

Taxi From South Drain/Nieuw Nickerie (Guyana river crossing) unmetered taxis cost SRD120–200 depending on passenger numbers (2–3hr).

Tourist information The Toeristen Informatie Centrum is at Fort Zeelandia Complex, Waterkant 1 (see p.727 for details).

City transport

Bicycle You can rent bikes from SRD12.50 per day from Fietsen, at Grote Combeweg 13a (☏597/520-781, ✺ www.fietseninsuriname.com) or from SRD20 per day from Cardy Adventures

& Bike Rental, at Cornelis Jongbawstraat 31 (☎597/422-518, ⊛www.cardyadventures.com).

Boat Fast, cheap and fairly regular dugout canoes wait in the Waterkant area to take passengers across the Suriname River to Meerzorg (15min; SRD5).

Kapkar One way to see the city (albeit by weaving in and out of traffic), is to hail a passing motorized *kapkar* (similar to a tuk-tuk) or rent one in advance. Hail one in the street or book through Kapkar Company (☎597/477-788, ⓔkapkarcompany @sr.net).

Bus The larger, cheaper but less frequent scheduled state buses (*staatsbus*) leave from the bus station at Heiligenweg in Knuffelsgracht. Fares in and around Paramaribo cost about SRD1.25. Routes (10-20min) include: Blauwgrond (for *warung* restaurants; Bus #PB); Lallarookhweg (for Hermitage Mall; Bus #1); Maretraite (for shopping mall; Bus #PG); Mahonylaan (Bus #10). For schedules see ⊛www.nvbnvsuriname.com.

Minibus Unscheduled minibuses leave from the car park just past *De Waag* restaurant on Waterkant, Saramaccastraat, Steenbakkerijst and Dr. Sophie Redmondstraat but can be flagged down anywhere along the road. Fares in and around Paramaribo cost between SRD1–5.

Taxi Taxis wait for passengers in front of Central Market (Waterkant). Taxis are usually unmetered but registered taxis tend to use fixed rates. Trips within the city should cost between SRD6–10; always agree a fare with your driver in advance. It's a good idea to use taxis for visiting *warungs* (small, Javanese/Indonesian restaurants, usually outdoors) and several of Paramaribo's other good restaurants in outlying areas of the city. Recommended taxi firms include Djo's Taxi

(☎597/471-048), Romeo's Taxi (☎597/492-956), Sheriff Taxi (☎597/410-241) and Tourtonne Taxi (☎597/475-734).

Accommodation

Albergo Alberga Mr F.H.R. Lim A Postraat 13 ☎597/520-050, ⊛www.guesthousealber goalberga.com. Lovely nineteenth-century wooden house in city centre with clean, bright, en-suite rooms and a small swimming pool. SRD75.

Guesthouse Kiwi Mahonyland 84, ☎597/410-744, ⊛www.guesthousekiwi.com. Basic accommodation, a 10-min taxi ride from the centre, offering 15 rooms, some with en-suite, king-sized beds, TV, fridges, ventilators or a/c. Shared bath and toilet in hallway. Somewhat overpriced for what you get; view before booking. SRD80.

Guesthouse TwenTy4 Jessurunstraat 24 ☎597/420-751, ⊛www.twenty4suriname.com. This homely guesthouse, located in the historical centre, offers rooms with fans and sinks (some a/c and en suite). Enjoy breakfast (SRD7.50) on the covered porch overlooking a rippling stream. Friendly staff can arrange tours from SRD40 and there's a lively bar open until 11pm. SRD65.

Un Pied-À-Terre Guesthouse Costerstraat 59 ☎597/470-488, ⊛www.un-pied-a-terre .com. A quaint guesthouse just blocks away from all the action. Breezy veranda and rooms with four-poster beds draped with mosquito nets, and breakfast from SRD13. For a cheaper option, hang a hammock in the garden (SRD55). SRD115.

Van Kip Gompertstraat 100, Maretraite 4 ☎597/452-408. If you are looking for your own little space, try this secure self-contained studio a 10-min drive from the city centre. Has a/c, wi-fi, and small sitting, dining and kitchen areas. SRD80.

Zeelandia Suites Kleine Waterstraat 1a ☎597/424-631, ⊛www.zeelandiasuites.com. Self-contained rooms and studios in the centre of town with the popular *Sidewalk Café 'T Vat* downstairs. SRD180.

Zus & Zo Grote Combéweg 13a ☎597/520-905, ⊛www.zusenzosuriname.com. This charming central guesthouse facing the Palmentuin is one of the coolest places to stay. It offers shared facilities, a/c and wi-fi, a café, gift shop, bike rental and nightly entertainment. Meals from SRD9.50 and tours from SRD40; one of Paramaribo's best budget options. SRD65.

Eating

There are several restaurants in and immediately around *'T Vat*, the favourite hangout for Dutch tourists due to the patio seating and central location. Alternatively, take a taxi to the Blauwgrond neighbourhood to eat at one of the many *warungs* (Javanese restaurants) there. Check ⊛www.eteninsuriname.com for a restaurant list and online menus.

Dumpling #1 Nassylaan 168 ☎597/477-904. Try this breezy, candlelit, Chinese restaurant on a tree-lined street for good food and its famed king crab legs. Meals from SRD30. Open Tues–Sat 9.30am–3pm & 6–11pm; Sun 8am–1pm & 6–11pm.

Eetcafé Gadri Zeelandiaweg 1 ☎597/420-688. Generous portions of Creole and Indonesian food (SRD14–26), served at tables overlooking the Suriname River. Open Mon–Fri 8am–10pm & Sat 11am–10pm.

Het Surinaams Restaurant Jozef Israëlstraat 27 ☎597/452-700. Tasty Creole lunches like peanut soup, chicken, fish and rice dishes (SRD18–20). Open Mon–Fri noon–6pm.

Leckker Bekje Van Sommelsdijckstraat 1A ☎597/479-014. Near the Torarica and '*T Vat* area. Tasty snacks and meals such as pasta, prawns, fish 'n' chips and hamburgers (SRD11.50–20). Open Mon–Fri 7.30am–11pm & Sat 4.30pm–1am.

Pannekoek & Poffertjes Restaurant Van Sommelsdijckstraat 11 ☎597/422-914. Sweet and savoury Dutch pancakes and crêpes, served with preserves and jams (SRD10–25). Open Sun–Thurs 10am–11pm, Fri & Sat 10am–1pm.

Roopram Roti Several sites across town including Saturnusstraat 44. Visit for generous portions with all the trimmings, including chicken roti and a drink for SRD12.50. General opening hours daily 9am–10pm, though some locations may vary.

Sarinah Verlengde Gemenelandsweg 187 ☎597/430-661. Javanese café on Parbo's outskirts serving staples like *nasi kip, saoto* and *loempia* (spring roll) from SRD8.50. Open evenings until late.

Sidewalk Café 'T Vat Kleine Waterstraat 1A. Popular hangout due to its shady sidewalk terrace, which sometimes features live music and shows. Menu includes sandwiches and burgers (from SRD7), *saoto* soup (SRD9.50), salads (SRD15) and mains (from SRD18). Expect small portions and slow service. Open Mon–Thurs & Sun 9am–1am, Fri & Sat 9am–3am.

Warung Parwiro J. S. Greenstraat 114 ☎597/452-689. This friendly, open-air venue provides quick service and tasty food like *saoto* (SRD9) and *bakabana* (4 for SRD2). Open Mon–Fri 6–10pm & Sat 6–11pm.

Warung Renah J. S. Greenstraat 106 ☎597/450-987. This covered, open-air authentic *warung* is quick and does everything from satay to *dawat*, with prices between SRD3 and SRD15. Open evenings until late.

Zeeland Coffee Beanery Domineestraat 39. Outdoor seating at this corner café, which is a good place to sip espresso and observe the strip. Open Sun–Wed 7am–9pm, Thurs–Fri 7am–11pm.

Drinking and nightlife

Starzz Disco Kleinewaterstraat 5–7 ☻www .clubstarzz.com. Central nightclub near *'T Vat* with a balcony to watch the action on the street below. Open Fri–Sat from 10pm.

Zanzibar Van Sommelsdijkstraat 1. This lively alcoholic outpost with a DJ (Fri and Sat) has outdoor seating and an open-air bar serving food and delicious cocktails from SRD7. Open 6pm until late.

Zsa Zsa Zsu J Pengelstraat 236. Take a cab to this club and enjoy multiple dance areas, varying music styles, a bar and a restaurant. Dress to impress. Open Fri & Sat 11pm–5.30am.

Shopping

Haggle for bargains on gold jewellery in the small stores on Maagdenstraat between Steenbakkeri-jstraat and Heiligenweg, or pick up knick-knacks on Steenbakkerijstraat. For Amerindian, Javanese and Maroon handicraft, try the stores along Domineestraat. A few malls open until 10pm including the Hermitage Mall (Lallarookhweg) and Maretraite Mall (Jan Steenstraat). On Sundays there is a Chinese market on vanSommeldijck-straat, which sells produce and handicrafts.

Directory

Banks and exchange There are many cambios about town, including Surpost Money Exchange, at Kerkplein 1; Multi Track Exchange, at Wilhelmi-nastraat 35 and Kleine Waterstraat 11; Trade Exchange, at Waterkant 78; and Moneyline, at Domineestraat 35c.

Embassies and Consulates Brazil, Marata-kastraat 2 (☎597/400-200); Canada, Wagen-wagstraat 50 (☎597/424-527); France, Henck Arronstraat 5–7 (☎597/476-455); Guyana, Henck Arronstraat 82 (☎597/477-895); Netherlands, Van Rooseveltkade 5 (☎597/477-211); UK, c/o VSH United Bldgs, Van't Hogerhuysstraat 9–11 (☎597/402-558); US, Dr. Sophie Redmondstraat 129 (☎597/472-900).

Internet *Browser Internet Café*, corner of Hoek Wilhelmina/HJ De Vriesstraat, opposite *Pizza Hut*

(SRD4 per hr); Telesur Noord, corner of Jozef Israel and Kristalstraat (Mon–Sat 7am–10pm; SRD1.50 for 30min).

Pharmacies Ali's Drugstore & Apotheek, at Tourtonnelaan 127; Apotheek Sibilo, at Koningstraat 90; Apotheek R. Jamaludin, at Watermolenstraat 8; Apotheek Esculaap, at Zwartenhovenbrugstraat 34.

Moving on

Air Scheduled domestic and charter flights mainly operated by Gum Air (☻www.gumair.com) and Blue Wing (☻www.bluewingairlines.com; note that this airline has a poor safety record) depart from Zorg en Hoop to a few destinations in Suriname including Botopasi (3 weekly; 40min), Kajana (2 weekly on Mon & Fri; 50min) and Palumeu (2 weekly on Mon & Fri; 1hr 5min). These flights are often fully booked by organized tours but it is sometimes possible to book a seat directly with the carrier. Trans Guyana Airways (☻www.transguyana.net) and Blue Wing both operate scheduled flights from Zorg en Hoop to Guyana (daily except Sun; 1hr 20 min).

Bus/minibus Formalized bus info is sketchy: ask at the various start points near Central Market to confirm which buses go where and the fares. Albina (state bus from Heilgenweg, minbus #PA from Central Market; 2hr); Brownweg (state bus/ minibus/Jumbo from Saramaccastraat; 3hr); Commewijne (state bus or minibus #PA from Meerzorg; 25min); Leonsburg (minibus #4 from Central Market; 30min); Nieuw Nickerie and South Drain (state bus from Heilgenweg or minibus #PN from Dr. Sophie Redmondstraat; several daily; 2hr–3hr 30min); Meerzorg (minibus #MHA from Central Market; 20min).

Taxi Taxis to South Drain (for the Guyana border crossing) cost SRD120–200 depending on passenger numbers (2–3hr). Taxis to Albina (for the French Guiana border crossing) wait near the buses at Central Market, Waterkant and cost SRD50–200 depending on passenger numbers (2hr).

Day-trips from Paramaribo

There are a lot of day-trips on offer and these are easily accomplished if you have your own transport or join organized tours (see p.730), which include the Commewijne Plantation Tour (from SRD225), the Commewijne River Cruise (around SRD270) and cycling tours (from SRD180). Day-trips to **Brownsberg Nature Park** (see p.735) are also possible.

Commewijne and Fort Nieuw Amsterdam

The predominantly Javanese district of **Commewijne** is located on the right bank of the Suriname River, directly east of Paramaribo. The area is littered with remnants of plantations and colonial architecture, including the ruins of the old **Marienburg Sugar Factory** on the Marienburg Plantation (daily 9am–6pm; free, guided tours SRD35–40 per group). Other highlights include **Peperpot Plantation** (an old coffee and cocoa plantation) and Frederiksdorp Plantation, whose stone and wooden buildings have been fully renovated and converted into a delightful hotel and restaurant. The star-shaped **Fort Nieuw Amsterdam** (Mon–Fri 9am–6pm, Sat & Sun 10am–6pm; SRD8) is located at the meeting point of the Commerwijne and Suriname Rivers. It houses an open-air museum with a small selection of exhibits including American World War II cannons. The former jail cells are used for local art displays.

Organized bike, vehicle and boat tours to Commewijne and areas of interest are available from SRD200 (for operators, see p.730). To **visit independently**, you will need to take a minibus to Commewijne, then hire a taxi and negotiate the fare with the driver. Alternatively, the state bus provides services from Meerzorg to Peperpot (10min) and Marienburg (45min); see ⓦwww .nvbnvsuriname.com for bus schedules within Commewijne. Boat trips from Paramaribo to the plantations are also possible – for times, prices and embarkation points see ⓦpristineforestcruise .com.

Jodensavanne and Blakawatra

Jodensavanne, 70km south of Paramaribo on the east bank of the Suriname River, is named after the Jews who settled in this savanna area around 1650. Little remains of the village, but ruins of the graveyard and the **synagogue** – said to be the oldest in the Americas – are worth a visit; there is a small museum to give you a sense of its historical importance. You can get here by state bus from the Heiligenweg bus station to the nearby Amerindian village of Cassipora (daily except Sat; 2hr).

About 5km east of Jodensavanne is **Blakawatra**, a small but popular resort that fills with locals at weekends. Here you can camp in the jungle-like setting and splash about in the dark, mineral-rich creek water that runs through it. Public transport is patchy at best; by car the trip takes about three hours from Paramaribo.

West to Guyana

The drive along the coastal belt west of Paramaribo is a scenic one. Around 140km from the capital, the paved road passes through **Totness**, once a Scottish settlement, as it continues towards the district of **Nickerie**, where salt ponds, Dutch-style polders (land reclaimed from water) and, most notably, rice paddies start to appear. **Nieuw Nickerie** is the obvious place to break your journey before the ferry crossing to Guyana (see box, p.734), from **South Drain,** an hour's drive southwest of the town.

NIEUW NICKERIE

If you have just arrived on the ferry from Guyana then your first taste of Suriname will be **NIEUW NICKERIE,** the country's second-largest town. Its main boulevard is lined with palm trees and the town is divided by a grid layout, making orientation easy. There's no reason to stay unless you arrive very late; if you do linger, you may want to organize a day-trip via *Residence Inn* (☎597/210-950, ⊛www.resinn.com) to **Bigi pan**, a mangrove-ridden stretch of swampy coast with excellent birdwatching.

Accommodation

Concorde Hotel Wilhelminastraat 3 ☎597/232-345. This newly renovated budget hotel has en-suite rooms with a/c and breakfast; the on-site restaurant offers cheap meals. SRD65.
River Breeze G. G. Maynardstraat 3 ☎597/212-111. Basic, clean, self-contained rooms with TV, a/c and breakfast. SRD55.

Eating and drinking

In the morning you can find fresh fruit, vegetables, cakes, pastries and small roti stands in the market.
Café de Smuller St Jozefstraat 12. This tiny hole in the wall has burgers, fries and *bitterballen*, along with other Dutch snacks.
De Tropen Bar In *Residence Inn*. A pleasant enough place to have a drink outdoors on the streetside terrace and watch the scooters buzz by.
P & G Rotishop A. K. Doerga Sawhstraat 95. Roti, curried accompaniments, beer and soft drinks on the second floor of the Doerga Mall.
🏃 **Restaurant Melissa's** In *Hotel Concord*, Wilhelminastraat 3 ☎597/232-345. A busy, affordable Indonesian restaurant with a takeaway service. *Saoto soep* SRD7. Open until late.

Directory

Banks and exchange Surinaamsche Bank at Landingstraat and RBTT at Gouverneurstraat 79.

Hospital Nickerie Medical Centre, at A. K. Doerga Shawstraat 80 (☎597/210-700).
Internet Telesur Office at Oostkanaalstraat 3.

Moving on

Boat The ferry for Guyana leaves daily at 11am from South Drain to Molson Creek. For more information call ☎597/231-500 or email ⊛canawaimanick@sr.net.
Bus Paramaribo (minibus or state bus from the parking lot next to the market; several daily; 2hr–3hr 30min); South Drain (minibus from parking lot next to market; 1hr).

South to the interior

You won't have seen the real Suriname until you venture south of Paramaribo into the interior, which has vast areas of pristine rainforest as well as Maroon and Amerindian communities that particpate in ecotourism ventures. Much of the interior is isolated and necessitates either long, challenging boat trips or plane rides, though **Brownsberg Nature Park,** an area of great natural biodiversity, is relatively easy to access. To visit the more isolated areas in the sprawling **Central Suriname Nature Reserve**, as well as **Awarradam** (home to the largest community of Saramaccan Maroons)

CROSSING INTO GUYANA

Getting to Guyana involves crossing the Corantijn (Corentyne) River on the ferry, with daily departures at 11am (SRD8 single) from South Drain, an hour west of Nickerie. You will need time to clear customs and a valid passport and visa for Guyana (the latter can be obtained within two days from the Consulate in Gravenstraat 82; ☎597/475-209). Once you arrive at Molson Creek, Guyana, you must clear customs again and get your passport stamped before taking one of the waiting minibuses for the 3-hr journey to Georgetown (G$2500–3000). There is no cambio or ATM at South Drain or Molson Creek so bring Euros or US$, preferably the latter, to exchange for Guyanese dollars at Molson Creek. There's usually someone around willing to exchange your money for local Guyanese currency and street exchange rates are often better than official ones.

and **Palumeu** (an Amerindian village in the far south of Suriname) you'll need more time and money.

AWARRADAM AND PALUMEU

AWARRADAM is a community made up of eight villages populated by Saramaccan Maroons, descendants of runaway plantation slaves who fled deep into the jungle; it lies in the Gran Rio River near a rapid of the same name. Unless you fancy a long boat journey, you can get here via a flight from Zorg en Hoop Airport (2 weekly on Mon & Fri; 50min) to Kajana airstrip, followed by a 20-min trip in a dugout canoe. Accommodation is usually provided in traditional lodges, while activities include jungle treks, hiking, fishing, river tours, and visits to nearby islands and villages.

PALUMEU is a village located at the beginning of the Tapanahony River, deep within the Amazon rainforest, populated by Trio and Wajana Amerindians. Visitors stay in traditional lodges and activities offered include a boat trip along the Tapanahony River to Poti Hill, hikes in the rainforest and a two-day trip by dugout canoe to Mount Kasikasima. Most visitors will arrive by plane (same details as for Awarradam), though it's possible to get here on an 8- to 12-day river journey from Albina.

Trips to either community are usually booked through **tour operators** such as METS (see p.730), which offers 5-day tours from SRD535. You can also make arrangements direct with the Maroons themselves: try Botopasi (☎597/884-1273, ⓦwww.botopasi.com) or Eco Resort Kosindo (☎597/865-9702, ⓦwww.kajana-kosindo.com).

BROWNSBERG NATURE PARK

About 130km south of Paramaribo on the Mazaroni Plateau, **BROWNSBERG NATURE PARK** is the only protected area in Suriname that can be easily visited from Paramaribo using public transport. On a lucky day, you might see howler and spider monkeys, deer, agouti and birds such as woodpeckers, macaws and parrots. There are also fine views from the plateau of the rainforest and **Van Blommestein Lake**, created to provide electricity for the Alcoa aluminium industry. STINASU (see p.736) operates a lodge on the plateau (rooms from SRD370), as well as hammock and camping facilities (SRD33–45). It also maintains several hiking trails to the impressive **waterfalls**, which, besides its elusive wildlife, are the park's main attractions. If you plan **to stay**, note that *Brownsberg Eco Camp* has hammocks from around US$15 per night and lodges sleeping up to eight from US$120.

The simplest way to visit Brownsberg is on an **all-inclusive tour** arranged by STINASU (around SRD208 for the day, SRD416 overnight) or a tour operator (see p.730). If you plan to go it alone, you must pay for the lodgings in advance at the STINASU office in Paramaribo. Additionally, p**ublic transport** from Paramaribo only runs as far south as Brownsweg, some 13km from the plateau, so you'll need to arrange for a STINASU bus to take you the rest of the way to the park. Note that if you're coming by bus you won't be able to get back to Paramaribo on the same day, as the journey one-way takes 3 hours 30 minutes to 4 hours.

THE CENTRAL SURINAME NATURE RESERVE

Created in 1998 by amalgamating the Raleighvallen, Tafelberg and Eilerts de Haan nature reserves, the **CENTRAL SURINAME NATURE RESERVE** occupies 16,000 square kilometres of southwestern Suriname, some nine percent of the country's total surface area. Most tourists visit **Raleigh-vallen**, where STINASU lodgings start at SRD210 per person or SRD45 to camp. You can swim, relax or do the 3-hr hike to the base of the **Voltzberg mountain**, where there is a jungle camp with hammocks. Then it's another 240 metres or so to the summit, which affords good views of the surrounding forest canopy plus the chance to see the world's largest-known species of the cock-of-the-rock bird.

STINASU runs three-day inclusive **tours** to Raleighvallen for SRD1360, flying from Zorg en Hoop Airport (50min). The tour involves hiking, climbing and swimming. It's obligatory to have a **guide** and this must be arranged in advance.

East to French Guiana

It should only take two hours or so by minibus or taxi to cover the 140km between Paramaribo and **Albina**, the last town of note before crossing the Maroni River to French Guiana. The town was affected by the political upheavals that took place in the district during the 1980s, but it is an important gateway for **Galibi Nature Reserve**, with its population of nesting turtles and nearby **Amerindian villages** and Langamankondre. You can visit **Matapica Beach** to swim and see turtles but there is little access to the **Wia-Wia Nature Reserve,** which lies east of Matapica. Make sure to have cash (ideally Euros) as ATMs are scarce in this part of Suriname.

ALBINA

ALBINA, the capital of the Marowijne District, is a small town on the west bank of the Marowijne (Maroni) River.

There is not much to do here except stock up on essentials and then board a boat or ferry to the French Guiana border town of St Laurent-du-Maroni, directly across the river. Albina is also the gateway for visits to the **Galibi Nature Reserve** (see p.737), where you can observe sea turtles, and to the Amerindion villages of Christiankondre and Langamankondre.

Travellers should note that the journey by road from Paramaribo is long and challenging, as more than half the route is a wide dirt track. The situaton is set to improve, however, as the road is gradually being tarmacked.

Arrival

If you plan to visit Galibi Beach or the Galibi Nature Reserve, it is advisable to book an all-inclusive two-day tour (from SRD625) with Myrysji Tours, the only Amerindian tour operator in Suriname (Griegstraat 41 ☎597/456-611, ⓦwww.myrysjitours-suriname.com), starting with pick-up from your hotel in Paramaribo. The alternative is to base yourself in Christiaankondre or Langamankondre (see p.737) and then walk the few hours to Galibi Beach. Visiting the area independently is possible, but you will have to wait until you find a boat going in that direction and you're unlikely to save much money.

Minibus Minibuses and state buses will drop you off in the town centre near the boats or at the immigration office/ferry terminal.

Accommodation

Guesthouse Albina Breeze Poeloegoedoeweg 8 ☎597/034-2120. Small guesthouse near the fire station with clean, breezy en-suite rooms and shared kitchen. Internet and pharmacy downstairs. Take a taxi back after dark. SRD75.

Eating and drinking

Restaurant Derots Martinstraat 7. This small, clean restaurant serves chicken, beef or pork dishes (SRD 15–25) mixed with rice and noodles. Open Tues–Sat 9am–3pm.

Rotishop Whilhelminastraat 28. A small shop a few roads down from the main street, selling reasonably priced rotis with various fillings including eggs, vegetables and meat. Roti with potato SRD7.

Moving on

Boat Motorized dugout canoes run between Albina and St Laurent in French Guiana (see box, p.738). Christiankondre, Langamankondre and Galibi Nature Reserve are only accessible by boat. If you are not on an organized tour, you'll have to find a boat heading to them and persuade the driver to give you a lift for a negotiated fare.

Bus/minibus Minibuses ply the route to Paramaribo (every 2-3hr); state buses leave twice daily Mon–Fri (every 2–3hr). For schedules see ⓦ www.nvbnvsuriname.com.

Ferry A scheduled ferry operates back and forth between Albina and St Laurent in French Guiana (see box, p.738).

CHRISTIANKONDRE AND LANGAMANKONDRE

CHRISTIANKONDRE AND LANGAMANKONDRE are two fairly large coastal villages (approximately 800 inhabitants each) used to receiving tourists en route to Galibi Nature Reserve, as visits are frequently included in tours. If you're in the area in late August or early September, you may witness the traditional festivities of the Galibi Beach Festival and the election of Miss Galibi. Christiankondre has the small, informal **Galibi Zoo** (SRD6), where you can pet, feed and handle monkeys, sloths, snakes and baby caimans. Independent travel to the villages is not recommended, as it will save you neither time nor money.

GALIBI NATURE RESERVE

Situated in the northeastern corner of Suriname at the mouth of the Maroni River, the **GALIBI NATURE RESERVE** was once one of the main nesting areas of the **Olive Ridley** and **hawksbill** sea turtles. Unfortunately, these species are on the critically endangered list and, according to the villagers, no longer nest at the reserve.

Leatherback and **green turtles** continue to flourish here, however, and their **nesting season** is from March to August. Trips to the reserve are usually part of package tours to the villages and involve about an hour's boat ride to the reserve, travelling along the Marowijne Maroni River and into the Atlantic Ocean. The trip normally takes place at night or in the early morning; once you arrive your guide will lead you on a walk along the sandy beach, looking out for nesting turtles and tiny baby turtles hatching and scampering towards the water. You don't see much of the reserve because of the darkness, but take along a torch and insect repellent, as the mosquitoes are rampant.

MATAPICA BEACH

MATAPICA BEACH, just west of the wild and little explored **Wia-Wia Nature Reserve**, is at the end of a channel that links it to the Commewijne River. This once important reserve was established in 1966 to protect the nesting places of the sea turtles. Nowadays, much of the beach has eroded, though some turtles still visit the shores to lay their eggs and it is also the habitat of many species of waterfowl.

There are no tours just to Wia-Wia, but a two-day tour to Matapica with STINASU (☎597/476-597, ⓦwww .stinasu.com) will cost around SRD680, including ecolodge accommodation. Independent travellers must find their way by boat and bus or taxi to Marienburg, and then take a boat over to Margaretha (10–15min), followed by another boat to Matapica (45min). Be aware, however, that the tide is only high enough for boats to get through the channel twice a day and you really need to plan this trip carefully for it to work well.

French Guiana

FRENCH GUIANA is the oddball of the Guianas. Its laws, customs, language and outlook largely mirror those of metropolitan France, despite many of its citizens coming from Caribbean stock; it's also the most expensive country to visit in South America. Most visitors are French, and as such it will certainly help to speak a little of the language.

Until about sixty years ago, French Guiana's muggy, oppressive climate, malaria-ridden forests and inhospitable terrain were considered an ideal way to punish French criminals. The penal colony on the **Iles du Salut** was subsequently abandoned, and French Guiana next came to international attention in the 1960s, when the European Space Agency cleared a patch of jungle and built a **space centre** to launch satellites into orbit from the town of **Kourou**. Both are within easy reach of the capital **Cayenne**, where mosquitoes, expensive lodgings and a distinct lack of things to do are unlikely to detain you very long.

Pirogue trips along **rivers** such as the Maroni and Oyapok and treks in the Amazonian interior are popular, but the highlight is **Plage Les Hattes**, one of the finest places in the world to observe leatherback turtles laying their eggs on the beach.

CHRONOLOGY

10,000 BC Original inhabitants are thought to have been either the Arawak Indians or Amerindians. Later, Caribs move into the territory.
1496 AD Discovered by the Spanish.
1604 Settled by the French.
1643 Cayenne founded.
1664 Dutch occupy Cayenne.
1667 Awarded to France under the Treaty of Breda. All inhabitants now French citizens.
1676 Dutch expelled.
1763–65 France sends 15,000 immigrants as part of the Kourou Expedition to develop the region, but 10,000 die of yellow fever and typhoid.
1848 Slavery is abolished. The colony's fragile plantation economy begins to collapse.
1852 Region designated a penal colony; more than 70,000 French convicts transported to the area.
1946 Becomes an overseas *département* of France.
1947 Penal colony abolished.
1964 ESA establishes space station in Kourou to launch communications satellites.
1974 Gains own Conseil Régional with some autonomy in social and economic matters.
1997 Independence leader Jean-Victor Castor arrested by police, leading to civil violence in Cayenne.

CROSSING INTO FRENCH GUIANA

When you arrive in Albina, take a local taxi (SRD5) the short distance from the town centre to the Surinamese immigration office (7am–6pm) at the ferry pier, to get your passport stamped before crossing over to French Guiana. The ferry departs from Albina for St Laurent (French Guiana) on Mon, Tues & Thurs at 8am, 10am, 3pm & 5.30pm; Wed at 7.30am, 8.30am & 5.30pm; Fri at 7.30am, 8.30am, 9.30am, 2.30pm, 3.30pm, 4.30pm & 5.30pm; Sat at 8.30am & 9.30am; Sun at 3.30pm, 4.30pm & 5.30pm. Foot passengers pay €4, motorbikes €15 and cars €33 (only euros are accepted as payment). There is a cambio at the ferry terminal, which gives good rates when exchanging Suriname and US dollars for euros.

There is no reason to wait for the official ferry if you don't have a car, as there are many motorized dugout canoes available. The crossing takes 10–15min and costs €3 or SRD10. Dugouts leave from moorings near the town centre, though staff at the ferry terminal can call boat drivers and ask them to pick you up from the pier. Once you cross the river, the boat will tend to drop you off on the beach, but it's best to ask for a drop to the ferry pier near the French Immigration office (6am–7pm), where you can get your passport checked and stamped.

FRENCH GUIANA

Alliance
Plage les Hattes   Awala-Yalimapo
Moengo   Mana
        Albina   Javouhey   Iracoubo   Sinnamary
        St Laurent
        du Maroni
                                    ATLANTIC OCEAN

Apatou   Îles de Salut
                        Kourou
        Voltaire Falls
                                    CAYENNE
Blommestein   Montsinéry   Matoury   Remire-Montjoly
Meer   Tonne Grande
                            Roura
                    Cacao   Cabo
                            Kaw   Orange
        Grand Santi   Regina   Approuague
                                    River
                        Cisame   Ouanary
                                    Saint-Georges-
                                    de-l'Oyapok   Oiapoque
SURINAME
        Maripasoula   Saül

        N   Camopi

                            Metres
                                    2000
                                    1000
                                    500
                                    200
                                    0

            St Maroni
            (635m)
                            BRAZIL   0   50 km

2000 Riots occur in Cayenne following an organized march calling for greater autonomy.
2008 President Sarkozy dedicates 1000 troops to combat growing immigration problems.
2009 The largest space telescope yet created is launched from Kourou.

Basics

ARRIVAL

French Guiana's main international airport, **Aéroport de Rochambeau**, is some 17km south of Cayenne, near the town of Matoury. It receives direct flights from France, Martinique, Guadeloupe, Haiti, Brazil and the Dominican Republic.

Overland from Brazil

Travellers arriving from Brazil enter French Guiana via a boat across the Oyapok River to the town of **Saint-Georges** (see p.758) and then continue their journey via road by bus or car.

Overland from Suriname

Travellers from Suriname must take a **ferry** or **dugout canoe** across the Maroni River to **St Laurent du Maroni** (see p.753), then fly or continue via road by bus or car.

VISAS

As French Guiana is an overseas department of France, **visas** are only required for those travellers who would also need a visa for France. Non-EU nationals unsure of their visa requirements should check Ⓦ www.diplomatie .gouv.fr/en. You may be able to obtain a French visa in Suriname (see p.732), in which case you'll also need to provide evidence of a vaccination against yellow fever.

GETTING AROUND

Public transport in French Guiana is not as extensive as in Guyana or Suriname. **Taxis collectifs** (shared minibuses) offer a limited number of routes to the main towns along the coastal road, although prices are expensive and they only leave when full. **Private taxis**, which are sorely needed, are hard to find, even in Cayenne; hotels or travel agents should be able to book one for you.

Cayenne and its suburbs have a small network of **local state buses** run by SMTC (☏ 594/594-302-100), though information on routes and costs is difficult to find. TIG (Ⓦ www .cg973.fr/Lignes-de-transport-prevues) runs **urban state buses** with eighteen numbered routes in and out of Cayenne. While the buses are not as frequent, they are cheaper than taxis and *taxis collectifs* and at least follow timetables. Be aware that few, if any bus routes operate on weekends, so check the TIG schedules or information at bus stops when planning your journeys.

Renting a car is worth considering, given the limited public transport options and the paved, well-signed roads (see box, p.746 for rental firms). The main highways, which run along the coast, are the RN1 and the RN2, which link Cayenne with St Laurent du Maroni and Saint-Georges. Keep your passport with you when driving, as there are occasional armed checkpoints where police will ask to see it. Once you start venturing further afield, you may find that the quickest way is by **plane**. To negotiate the many rivers in the interior you'll need a **pirogue**, or motorized dugout canoe. There are few scheduled passenger services, so your pirogue travelling will usually be part of an organized tour.

ACCOMMODATION

Accommodation in French Guiana is tailored to businesspeople and package tourists, and extremely limited in extent and variety. There are no HI-affiliated hostels and the few apparent budget options are usually pretty grotty – but still pricey for travellers who have been elsewhere in South America.

The most convenient budget option may be the humble **hammock**. The only real budget lodgings available are *carbets*, wooden huts on the beach or in the forest, with hammocks slung to the rafters and adjacent toilet blocks. Some towns also offer covered concrete areas to rent or hang a hammock for around €10. Unfortunately many *carbets* are inconveniently located and the expense of getting to them may negate any savings made on sleeping costs. Fortunately, hammocks are reasonably priced (€20–60 depending on quality and where you buy it) and often sold by street vendors, at local markets and in general stores.

Some **gîtes** (inexpensive lodgings in rural settings) are also available, though prices vary (visit Ⓦ www.tourisme -guyane.com for further info). You may also want to consider joining an online **hospitality site** such as Ⓦ www.couch surfing.com, whereby you can stay with locals.

FOOD

Restaurant food is generally good, although you may find yourself paying Parisian prices. Those on a tight budget will look to street vendors and small takeaway joints, and there are decent pizzas on offer in the main towns, as well as good coffee, croque monsieurs, crêpes and croissants in the capital's cafés. The best French restaurants are in Cayenne, but you'll also find plenty of Chinese, North African, Indonesian, Brazilian and Creole options here and elsewhere.

Fish dishes are more plentiful than elsewhere in the Guianas, with giant shrimp, grouper, shark and freshwater fish cooked in various ways, one of the more typical being *blaff*: a stock heavily seasoned with onion, garlic, celery, basil and spices. Another popular stock, used mostly at Easter and the Pentecost, is *bouillon d'awara*, made from the *awara* palm tree fruit and cooked with chicken, shrimp, crab and vegetables. *Fricassée* and *colombo* are typical Creole stews, the latter a meat-and vegetable-based curry stew. Wild meat like capybara, peccary and paca are also on the menu.

DRINK

The authentic drink here is the sweet French aperitif **Ti' punch**: lime, sugar-cane syrup and rum – without ice, downed in one and sometimes accompanied by cod rolls and black pudding. There is a better selection of **wines** in French Guiana than you will find in most of the rest of South America, and every now and then you will stumble across a café that would not look out of place in Montmartre, serving short, sharp espressos and shots of pastis. The **tap water** is safe to drink, although most visitors drink bottled water (as they do in metropolitan France).

CULTURE AND ETIQUETTE

Amerindian tribes and Maroons maintain their own cultural traditions, as do the immigrant population of Laotians in towns such as Cacao and Javouhey. The majority of the population is **Creole**, and mixed-Creole culture is dominant in the metropolitan areas, typified by carnival (see p.743). French is the most widely spoken **language**, though a significant proportion of the population also speaks a French-based patois or Creole, with Chinese, Bush Negro (*neg maron*) and Amerindian languages spoken in certain areas.

SPORTS AND OUTDOOR ACTIVITIES

French Guianese are into **football** rather than cricket, with watersports and fishing also popular. Partly because of the high quality of the roads, many serious cyclists come here.

COMMUNICATIONS

The postal system is integrated with that of metropolitan France, which makes deliveries to Europe quick and cheap. There is at least one **post office** (La Poste) in each town, and some have ATM machines that accept major international credit cards (though not American Express). Public **telephone** booths do not take coins, but cards issued by France Telecom can be used to make local calls. For international calls it's better to buy phone cards that work with PINs (*libre service*), available from convenience stores.

If you plan to use your **mobile phone**, get it unlocked before you travel, then purchase a local SIM card and some prepaid charge cards from authorized retailers. Making phone calls to French Guiana from abroad can be confusing because the **international dialling code** for French Guiana is 594 and the same three numbers are also used to form nine digit local numbers. Thus, when calling from abroad you must dial 594 followed by a nine-digit number also beginning 594. Numbers beginning 694 are mobiles.

Internet cafés are not easy to find, particularly outside Cayenne, but they do exist (and charge around €3 per hr). **Local newspapers**, **TV channels** and **radio stations** are in French, although a few hotels do broadcast some international news channels such as BBC and CNN.

CRIME AND SAFETY

While most travellers' visits will be trouble-free, you should use common sense, avoid isolated areas (beaches included) and mind your valuables.

HEALTH

Malaria tablets are recommended if staying close to rivers and a number of vaccinations, including hepatitis A, hepatitis B, typhoid, yellow fever, tetanus-diphtheria and rabies are required, depending on your plans. Vaccination against yellow fever is compulsory, and you may be asked to show your yellow-fever certificate, which is as important as your passport. There have also been outbreaks of dengue fever and Q fever, so enquire about these too.

Tap water is drinkable throughout the coastal area but avoid drinking creek or river water and pack at least one long-sleeved top, long socks and some mosquito protection. **Medical care**, in the form of hospitals, pharmacies and doctors' surgeries is available in Cayenne, Kourou and St Laurent du Maroni. Interior communities have dispensing chemists.

INFORMATION AND MAPS

Printed tourism information (mostly in French) is readily available. In Cayenne, visit the Comité du Tourisme

EMERGENCY NUMBERS

15 ambulance
17 police
18 fire service

de la Guyane, at 12 Rue Lallouette (Mon, Tues & Thurs 7.30am–1pm & 2.30–5.30pm; Wed & Fri 7.30am–1pm; ℡594/296-500, Ⓦwww.tourisme-guyane.com) for brochures, maps, hotel fliers and bus schedules. Elsewhere you'll normally find a tourist office (*office du tourisme* or *syndicat d'initiative*) with relevant local information, mostly in French. Ask for a copy of *Le Guide*, a handy, annual, easy-to-carry guide, which lists hotels, restaurants, bars and clubs throughout French Guiana in both French and English.

MONEY AND BANKS

The currency of French Guiana is the **euro** (€), and credit/debit cards are widely accepted in the urban centres. **ATMs** generally accept Visa, Master-Card and Eurocard (and occasionally American Express) but few banks, if any, have foreign exchange facilities; for that you'll need a bureau de change. That said, only one or two exchanges are in operation in the country and the one in the airport has closed down, so you may want to arrive with currency.

OPENING HOURS AND HOLIDAYS

Many businesses and stores shut for two to three hours over lunch. Most **shops** are open Monday to Saturday 8/9am to 1pm and 3/4 to 6.30/7pm. Grocery stores and supermarkets remain open until around 9.30pm and open on Sunday 9am to 12.30pm. **Banks** open Monday to Friday 7.30am to noon 2.30 to 5.30pm.

PUBLIC HOLIDAYS

January 1 New Year's Day

February Ash Wednesday (varies)

March/April Good Friday (varies)

March/April Easter Monday (varies)

May 1 Labour Day

May 8 WWII Victory (VE) Day

May/June Ascension Day (varies)

May/June Whit Monday (varies)

June 10 Abolition of Slavery Day

July 14 Bastille Day

15 Aug Assumption Day

1 Nov All Saints' Day

October Cayenne festival (varies)

November 11 Armistice (Remembrance Day)

December 25 Christmas Day

Festivals and national celebrations

French Guiana observes the same official public holidays as France but has two additional days, Ash Wednesday and Abolition of Slavery Day. The major festival in French Guiana is Carnival, which begins after Epiphany in the first week of January and goes on for about two months until Ash Wednesday. On Friday and Saturday nights during Carnival you can witness the tradition of Touloulou balls, when women (*Touloulou*), heavily disguised and wearing masks, are given the sole, non-reciprocal right to ask the men to dance; guys are not allowed to refuse. Women disguise their faces, bodies and voices so the men are incapable of recognizing even their own wives. This carousing and subterfuge has been blamed for a number of marriages and relationships ending in tears around this time. Mardi Gras (Carnival Monday and Tuesday) takes place during the last five days of Carnival, which ends on Ash Wednesday. It features colourful street parades with music, dancing, exotic costumes and merriment. They are not official public holidays but tend to be treated as customary days off.

Cayenne

French Guiana is not blessed with a wealth of beautiful towns, and **CAYENNE** is perhaps the best of a rather average bunch. It's compact, easy to walk around and sleepy, with an attractive central square, a colourful market and some decent beaches a few kilometres south of town. None of this will distract you for more than a day or so, and Cayenne should be treated as a base for excursions into the interior rather than a sight in itself.

Cayenne is no more dangerous than any other South American capital, but don't wander about at night on your own, particularly if you are female. While Avenue du Général de Gaulle is busy during the day, the stretch between Place des Palmistes and the cemetery can appear fairly desolate after nightfall. You should also take care around Canal Laussat and the market area at night, and avoid the sketchy Village Chinois, known locally as "Chicago", altogether.

What to see and do

The view overlooking Cayenne and the ocean from the hill at the end of Rue de Rémire, west of the Place des Palmistes, is the best place to establish your bearings before exploring.

Place des Palmistes and around

Place des Palmistes, on Avenue du Général de Gaulle, is a refreshing green space covered sparsely with palms, where much of Cayenne's limited activity is centred. It includes a statue of Felix Éboué (1884–1944), a black French Guianese who governed various French territories in Africa and the Caribbean. Just off the square, the **Musée Départemental**, at 1 Avenue du Général de Gaulle (Wed 8am–1.15pm & 3–5.45pm;

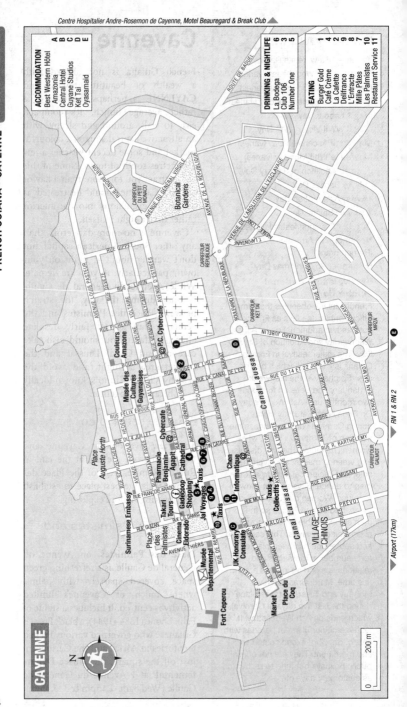

Centre Hospitalier Andre-Rosemon de Cayenne, Motel Beauregard & Break Club ▲

CAYENNE

ACCOMMODATION
Best Western Hôtel — A
Amazonia — B
Central Hotel — C
Guyane Studios — D
Ket Tai — E
Oyasamaid

DRINKING & NIGHTLIFE
La Bodega — 6
Club 106 — 3
Number One — 5

EATING
Burger Gold — 1
Café Crème — 4
La Cafette — 2
Delifrance — 9
L'Entracte — 8
Mille Pâtes — 7
Les Palmistes — 10
Restaurant Service — 11

N

0   200 m

Thurs 8am–1.45pm; Fri 8am–1.45pm & 3–5.45pm; Sat 9am–1.15pm; €3, free for under-18s), offers exhibits on French Guiana's cultural and natural riches, including paintings by local artists and an impressive butterfly collection.

Climb up the hill at the end of Rue de Rémire (ignoring the "no entry" sign like everyone else) and you will find the remains of **Fort Céperou**, the first building to appear in Cayenne after the Compagnie de Rouen purchased the hill from a Galibi Amerindian chief named Céperou in 1643. There is little here but ruins but it does afford a great view of the city.

Markets

Avenue du Président Monnerville leads you to the **fruit and vegetable market** (open Wed, Fri & Sat from dawn until early afternoon), a lively place where most of the produce is grown by the Laotian farmers in Cacao (see p.757). Under the covered market area you can find local handicrafts, rum punches and delicious Vietnamese phô soup. There's also a fish market at Rue du Vieux.

Cayenne Cathedral

La Cathédrale Saint-Sauveur, a landmark building on the corner of Rue François Arago and Rue du Lieutenant Goinet, was built in 1833 and became a cathedral in 1934. The altar, pulpit and confessional are all built from local wood and the building houses a clock dating back to 1871. Sunday Mass is a weekly event and everyone dresses up for it.

Botanical gardens and around

In the northeastern part of town, the **Musée des Cultures Guyanaises**, at 78 Rue Madame-Payé (Mon–Fri 8am–1pm & 3–5.45pm except Wed 8am–1pm, Sat 8am–11.45am; €3), houses Amerindian artefacts, craft, costume and art exhibitions. Further east on Boulevard de la République are the somewhat paltry **Botanical Gardens.** In the centre is the statue of Gaston Monnerville (1897–1991), a French Guianese lawyer who became the first black man to hold a senior position in the French government.

Arrival and information

Air Rochambeau International Airport (@www.guyane.cci.fr/fr/aeroport) in Matoury, 17km south of Cayenne, receives regular flights via Air France (@www.airfrance.com) and Air Caraibes (@www.aircaraibes.com). Air Guyane Express (@www.airguyane.com) provides domestic flights from Grand Santi, Maripasoula, Saul and St Laurent du Maroni. From the airport, a *taxi collectif* will drop you at the bus station opposite Canal Laussat in 20–30min for around €2, though you'll have to wait for it to fill up. TIG Bus #13 services the airport on a Cayenne-via-Matoury route (5 daily; 30–50min; €3.30). Another option is to take a taxi direct to Cayenne (20–30min; €25–30) or to Matoury (5–10min; €10 or less) and then TIG bus #8, 12A, 14, 15R, 16R or 17R to Cayenne.

Bus/minibus TIG buses and *taxis collectifs* arrive at the Cayenne bus station opposite Canal Laussat.

Tourist information The Comité du Tourisme de la Guyane is at 12 Rue Lallouette (see p.742 for details).

City transport

Bus SMTC, at Rue du Lieutenant Brassé (☎594/594-302-100), runs a small network of local buses around Cayenne. Most of the buses leave from Place du Coq near the market. Contact SMTC or check bus stops for details and remember that few, if any, buses operate on Sundays.

Taxi Taxis in Cayenne are metered and generally hard to find. They can be arranged by hotels or are sometimes found at the taxi stand on the corner of Rue Molé and Rue de Rémire, across the street from the Place des Palmistes. Expect to pay over €6 to get anywhere in town.

Accommodation

You will be hard-pressed to find much budget accommodation in Cayenne. Expect to pay through the nose for substandard furnishing, facilities and

CAR RENTALS

French Guiana is fairly small but the places of interest are far away from each other and there is a limited public transport system. As such, it's worth considering renting a car (an international driving licence is useful but not a legal requirement). Many car rental firms have offices in both Cayenne and at Rochambeau Airport (Hertz also has agencies in St Laurent and Kourou). Prices for economy and compact cars range from €22 to €60 per day.

Avis 58 Blvd Jubelin (☎ 594/594-302-522).

Budget 55 Artisanal Zone Galmot (☎ 594/594-351-020).

Europcar ZI Collery Ouest (☎ 594/594 -351-827).

Hertz Auto Guyane Zi Collery Building, Route de la Madeleine (☎ 594/594-296-930).

Sixt 11 Rue du Capitaine Bernard (☎ 594/594-29-80-42).

decor. The voltage is 220V; two-pronged sockets are used so pack an adaptor for your equipment.

Best Western Hôtel Amazonia 28 Ave du Général de Gaulle ☎ 594/594-310-000, ⊛ www .bestwestern.fr. Hotel near Place de Palmistes in need of sprucing up, with restaurant and swimming pool. Becomes a better budget option if you're in a group, as 4–5 people can stay for €120 in a family suite with sitting room and kitchen. €90.

Central Hotel Corner of Rues Molé & Becker ☎ 594/594-256-565, ⊛ www .centralhotel-cayenne.fr. This pleasant, reasonably priced hotel has comfortable rooms with a/c, TV and wi-fi; some also have kitchenettes. *Bar Françoise 1*, on site, is open 6–10pm. €65.

Guyane Studios Corner of Rues Molé & C. Colombe ☎ 594/594-282-929, ⊛ dalmazir.pierre @orange.fr. Musty, dark studio apartments with a/c and basic furnishings near Place des Palmistes. €76.

Ket Tai 72 Blvd Jubelin ☎ 594/594-289-777, Eg.chang@orange.fr. This non-smoking hotel offers clean, pokey self-contained rooms with extremely shabby furnishings. On the plus side, it's the cheapest accommodation in town. €43.

Oyasamaïd No. 2313, Route de la Madeleine 97300 ☎ 594/594-315-684, ⊛ www.oyasamaid.com. Delightful four-bed family pension about 4km from the centre, with a/c, internet, TV, kitchen, garden and swimming pool. Breakfast €5, lunch or dinner €15. Also offers car rental from €35. Reception open Mon–Sat 8am–1pm & 2–5pm; closed Sun. €60.

Eating

Eating in French Guiana is not cheap, though budget travellers will find many affordable Chinese takeaway spots dotted around the market area, as well as in the market itself (meals €5–10). Self-catering is also easy as there are numerous grocery shops and a few supermarkets around. Most restaurants are closed on Sundays and a ten percent tip is the norm.

Burger Gold Corner of Jubelin & Ave du Général de Gaulle. It's only a small mobile shop but locals line up until late for sandwiches and burgers (€5) with all the trimmings.

Café Crème 44 Rue J. Catayée. A great place to start the day with a café, croissant or croque-monsieur (from €3). Pavement tables and friendly service. Mon–Sat 7.30–1am.

La Cafette 120 Ave du Général de Gaulle ☎ 594/594-307-392. On the east side of town, this is a good low-key restaurant-café that serves *moules frites*, *salade niçoise* (€11) and has a fine selection of whiskies. Open Mon–Fri 7.30am–1am; until 2am on Sat.

Delifrance 26 Ave du Général de Gaulle. Pastries, cakes, sandwiches (from €3) and hot and cold drinks, all right next door to *Hôtel Amazonia*. Open Mon–Fri 7am–6pm & Sat 8am–2pm.

L'Entracte 65 Rue Justin Catayée ☎ 594/594-300-137. Cosy and busy restaurant with a theatrical and cinematic decor. Book in advance to dine on salads, pizzas, grilled platters and French specialities (daily noon–2.30pm & 6–10.30pm). Small pizza from €5, pasta and salads from €9.

Mille Pâtes 52 Rue Justin Catayée ☎ 594/594-289-180. Busy sit-down and takeaway pizzeria with a/c that serves up good thin-crust pizza (from €6) plus soufflés, pastas, calzones, shellfish, grilled meat and salads. Open daily midday–11pm.

Les Palmistes 12 Ave du Général de Gaulle ☎ 594/594-300-050. On Place des Palmistes, with a chic wooden-beamed dining room and outdoor café. Breakfast €7, lunch and dinner €13–22. Menu includes soups, salads, pasta and fish dishes. Daily 6.30am–midnight, Fri & Sat until 1am.

Restaurant Service 23 Rue Molé ☎ 594/594-293-255. Small, friendly Chinese restaurant and takeaway (with a/c) next to *Central Hotel*. On offer are typical Chinese rice, noodle, meat and vegetables dishes for €3–10.

Drinking and nightlife

La Bodega 42 Ave du Général de Gaulle. This bar with pavement seating is where tourists, journalists and locals looking for a drink and some good banter hang out. Open daily 7am–1am.

Club 106 106 Ave du Général de Gaulle. Disco with a/c that offers reggae, salsa and zouk (music originating from the French Caribbean), plus karaoke and exotic shows nightly from 11pm. Entry €10 for men; women free.

Number One 7 Ave du Général de Gaulle. This two-floor discotheque with a dancefloor and bar on each floor plays techno, salsa and merengue and is popular with a youngish crowd. Open Wed–Mon 10pm until dawn.

Shopping

You won't find the latest Parisian fashion here. Most of the shopping in Cayenne is centred on pirated cheap souvenirs, knockoff shoes and clothing. You can also find shops selling gold jewellery and native handicrafts, including hammocks, sculptures, basketry and pottery. The main shopping streets are Avenue du Général de Gaulle and Rue François Arago but there are lots of Asian shops selling all manner of items along the roads leading to the town market area (near Rue Lieutenant Brassé).

Directory

Banks and exchange Few banks if any exchange money; try the Change Caraïbes bureau de change, at 64 Ave de Général-de-Gaulle (Mon–Fri 7.30am–12.30pm & 3.30–6.30pm, Sat 8am–12.30pm).

Embassies and Consulates Brazil, 444 Chemin Saint-Antoine (☎ 594/594-296-010); Suriname, 3 Ave Leopold Heder (☎ 594/594-282-160); UK, Honorary British Consul, 16 Ave du Président Monnerville (☎ 594/594-311-034).

Hospitals Centre Hospitalier de Cayenne Andrée Rosemon, 3 Avenue des Flamboyants (☎ 594/594-395-050, ⊛ www.ch-cayenne.com); Clinique Saint-Paul Pk 2-5, Route de la Madeleine (☎ 594/594-390-300); Clinique Véronique PK 1453, Route de Baduel (☎ 594/594-281-010).

Internet Copy'Print Cybercafe, at 22 Rue Lallouette; *P.C. Cybercafe*, at 27 Blvd Jubelin.

Pharmacies Pharmacie Benjamin-Agapit, 23 Ave dea Général de Gaulle (☎ 594/594-302-503); Pharmacie Billery, 3494 Route Montabo (☎ 594/594-256-030); Pharmacie Jubelin, 23 Blvd Jubelin (☎ 594/594-311-459).

Post office Opposite Place Léopold Heder near Place des Palmistes (Mon–Fri, opens at 7.30am but note that it closes at 1pm, 2pm or 3pm on weekdays depending on the month and Sat at 11.30am). See monthly timetable posted outside the office.

Moving on

Air Air France (⊛ www.airfrance.com) flies direct to France, Guadeloupe and Martinique. Air Caraibes

---

TOUR OPERATORS

Virtually the only way of getting off the beaten track and out into nature is to join an organized excursion. Prices sometimes depend on numbers and can range from around €35 (one-day trips to nearby places) to as much as €900 for longer trips to places further afield.

Couleurs Amazone 21 Blvd Jubelin, Cayenne ☎ 594/594-287-000, ⊛ www.couleursamazone .fr. The young, dynamic owners provide tours for visitors of a similar nature and you'll need a decent level of fitness for some of the activities on offer.

GuyanEspace Voyages 39 Ave Hector-Berlioz, Kourou ☎ 594/594-223-101, ⊛ guyane @guyanespace.com. Tours of up to 14 days include a range of activities from river excursions to guided visits to the space centre in Kourou.

JAL Voyages 26 Ave du Général de Gaulle, Cayenne ☎ 594/594-316-820, ⊛ www .jal-voyages.com. Specializes in birdwatching river trips to Kaw and the Maroni aboard floating *carbets*, but also arranges trips to attractions across French Guiana.

Takari Tour 2 Rue Lallouette, Cayenne ☎ 594/594-311-960, ⊛ takari.tour@orange .fr. Good river tours, overnight expeditions on the Maroni and Oyapok, and white-water rafting.

(Ⓦwww.aircaraibes.com) flies to Brazil and France and connects French Guiana with other parts of the Caribbean including Haiti, Martinique, Guadeloupe and the Dominican Republic. Air Guyane Express (Ⓦwww.airguyane.com) flies to Grand Santi, Maripasoula, Saul and St Laurent du Maroni.

Bus Cacao (bus #16; 1hr 15min); Iracoubo (bus #9; 2hr); Kaw (bus #15; 1hr 50min); Kourou (bus #5B; 1hr 15min); Matoury (bus #12B; 45min); Régina (bus #17; 1hr 30min); Rémire Montjoly (bus #11B; 45min); Roura (bus #15; 40–50min); Saint-Georges de l'Oyapock via Régina (bus #17 to Regina, 1hr 30min; then bus #18 to Saint Georges, 1hr); Saint Laurent du Maroni via Iracoubo (1hr 30min); Sinnamary (bus #9, 1hr 30min). For more info and prices visit Ⓦwww .cg973.fr/ligner-de-transport-prevues.

Minibus Minibuses (*taxis collectifs*) leave when full from the bus station opposite Canal Laussat. They are faster but usually more expensive than public buses, and do not cover as many routes as the TIG bus service. Destinations include Kourou (1hr; €10); Matoury (20min; €2); Rémire Montjoly (30min; €3); St Laurent du Maroni (2hr 30min; €40–50). Always agree on a price before entering the vehicle.

DAY-TRIPS FROM CAYENNE

There are a couple of outlying areas of Cayenne that are worth visiting. Some public transport is available, though if you are travelling in a group you should consider renting a car for a day-trip. Rémire-Montjoly is a nicer place to stay than Cayenne.

Rémire-Montjoly

Rémire-Montjoly, 8km from Cayenne, is actually two separate sprawling towns that spread into each other near the coast. The area alternates between unattractive malls and asphalt roundabouts before turning into deserted coastline with sparse roadside restaurants and hotels. On the flip side, the area provides some of the best opportunities for sunbathing and swimming in French Guiana. The ocean water is not clear but the beaches themselves, dotted with palm trees, are often quite picturesque. **Plage Montjoly** is the longest stretch of beach in these parts:

a pleasant-enough spot spoiled slightly by stiff breezes and occasional rumours of sharks.

To **get here** from Cayenne, drive along the RN1 following the signs to Rémire-Montjoly or take TIG bus #11B (45min) or a *taxi collectif* from the bus station opposite Canal Laussat.

Montsinéry Tonnégrande

Montsinéry Tonnégrande, about 40km southwest of Cayenne, has two things to offer: a remote, peaceful setting to collect your thoughts and the nearby zoo, the **Réserve Animalière Macourienne** in Macouria (Wed–Sun 9.30am–5.30pm, last entrance 4.30pm; adults €15, children 3–12 €9; ☎594/594-317-306, Ⓦwww.zoodeguyane.com), home to spider monkeys, anteaters, jaguars and tapirs. The main attraction is the feeding of caimans.

From Cayenne, bus #12B will take you to Matoury (45min), where you must change to bus #8R, which goes to Tonnégrande (20min) before arriving in Montsinéry (another 20min).

Accommodation and eating

L'Auberge Du Lotus Montsinéry Tonnégrande, PK2, 5 Rue Tonnégrande ☎594/594-315-008. Nothing fancy here but this little *carbet* serves good Vietnamese specialities.

La Kaz a Gusto CD 5, Route de Montsinéry, 15 Jardins de Sainte-Agathe, Macouria ☎594/694-407-532, Ekazsoleil@hotmail.fr. Two self-contained studios with a/c, TV and kitchen, a 5-min walk from the zoo. Breakfast included. €50.

Mille Pâtes Rémire-Montjoly, 1 Lot Colline ☎594/594-382-903, Ⓦwww.millepates.fr. Like its Cayenne sister, with decent pizza (from €7), pasta and salads (from €9), grills (from €13) and a Brazil dance showcase every Tuesday night. Open Mon–Sun.

Motel Beauregard Rémire-Montjoly, 2 Route de Rémire ☎594/594-354-100. Comfortable rooms with a/c but try one of the palm-surrounded cabanas (from €57). Hotel guests get discounted access to the nearby *Break Club*, which has a gym, tennis courts, swimming pool, bowling and food on site. €70.

West to Suriname

The coast between Cayenne and Suriname contains French Guiana's most-visited attractions, including the **Centre Spatial Guyanais** in Kourou, the focal point of the European space programme, and the **Iles du Salut**, a former penal colony. The RN1 road continues west past the small towns of Sinnamary and Iracoubo to the turtle-nesting beach at **Plage Les Hattes** and **St Laurent du Maroni**, the last town before the border.

KOUROU

KOUROU was not designed with tourists in mind. It's a hopelessly sprawling place with no defined centre, is difficult to get around on foot and has no public transport to speak of. Accommodation is more limited than in Cayenne and is just as expensive.

What makes Kouru special is the **Centre Spatial Guyanais**, where rocket-launch towers, silos and high-tech machinery help to send satellites into orbit from a massive clearing in the jungle. The majority of its ever-growing population have something to do with the space centre.

Arrival and information

Bus TIG bus #5B runs from Cayenne to Kourou (1hr 15min); from St Laurent take bus #10 to Iracoubo (1hr 30min) then bus #4 from Iracoubo to Kourou (1hr 30min).

Minibus *Taxis collectifs* operate to Kourou from Cayenne (1hr) and St Laurent (1hr 30min). Negotiate with your driver to take you directly to your hotel.

Tourist information Place de l'Europe, C2 Rue Palika, Kourou (☎594/594-329-833, Etourisme @kourou.info). Impressive collection of information in French and English on the space centre, Iles du Salut, Kourou and French Guiana generally. More useful than the equivalent office in Cayenne.

What to see and do

This once sleepy coastal town has transformed itself into a fairly modern residential area, complete with night-clubs and shopping areas. Most visitors come to Kourou to visit the Centre Spatial Guyanais (CSG), which is outside the town, or to board catamarans bound for the Iles du Salut (see p.751).

Centre Spatial Guyanais

The sight of the launch towers surrounded by tropical forest at the **CENTRE SPATIAL GUYANAIS** (3-hr guided tours Mon–Thurs 8am & 1pm, Fri 8am; free but must be reserved by phone/email; ☎594/594-326-123, ✉visites.csg@orange.fr) is like something out of a Bond film. The CSG occupies an area of 850 square kilometres and has sent more than five hundred rockets (most carrying satellites) into orbit since *Véronique* blasted off on April 9, 1968. Visitors must be over 8 years old and provide ID. **Tours** include a film charting the site's history and a visit to the Jupiter Control Centre, though no tours take place on launch days. The actual Ariane 5 launch site itself is 15km up the road.

The **Musée de l'Espace** (Mon–Fri 8am–6pm, Sat 2–6pm; €7 or €4 if on a guided tour of the CSG; ☎594/594-335-384), next to the CSG welcome centre, provides a general overview of space exploration, the site's history and its activities. It features multimedia animations, collections of objects and models, educational activities and temporary themed exhibitions.

Unless visiting the CSG via a tour operator, you'll need to make your own way to Kourou via car, taxi or *taxi collectif*, then sort out local transport (taxi or private minibus) to the site.

Ariane 5 Space Launch

There are around four to six launches per year, usually scheduled on weekday nights (visit ⓦwww.cnes-csg.fr for details). If you are fortunate enough to be here when a launch is due, jump in a taxi and hightail it to **Carapa** (the free, unrestricted public observation site, about 12.5km from the Ariane launch pad) for the 30-minute experience.

The view is even more impressive from the two other official launch viewing sites, **Agami** and **Toucan**, which are closer but have restricted public access. For an invitation to these sites (limited places and you must be over 16), send a written request by post or email, giving your full name, date/place of birth and contact details, including address, email and telephone number to: CNES, Centre Spatial Guyanais, Communication Service, BP 726, 97387 Kourou Cedex. Check the website (ⓦwww.cnes-csg.fr) for specific details.

There are no formal **public transport** links to the three observation sites so you must rent a car, hire a taxi or join a tour to get to them. If you go by taxi, you will need to arrange for collection after the launch or you will be stranded in the countryside. Don't worry if you can't get there, though; after the drama of the countdown and ignition, the rocket gives off enough light that you can see the launch from almost anywhere in Kourou.

Accommodation

Budget travellers who are into hammocks can stay at the *carbets* on the beach, though be warned that the areas surrounding Lac Bois Diable and Lac du Bois Chaudat are mosquito-ridden. If you plan to arrive late, reserve a room in advance. Minibus drivers will take you directly to your hotel and often know residents who will put tourists up in their homes for a fee (likely to be less than local hotels).

Association Taliko Village Amerindien de Kourou ☎594/594-325-927. Hang a hammock on a beach under an Amerindian *carbet*. Cheap but mind your things. €6.

Ballahou 1–3 Rue Amet-Martial ☎594/594-220-022, ⓦwww.ballahou.com. Situated on the way into Kourou, fairly near to McDonalds and the beach. Family hotel offering five rooms and nine studios with en-suite, TV, fridge, microwave and kitchen facilities. Reservations recommended. Reception open noon–2pm & 6–8pm. €45.

Monsieur Ringuet 3 Rue Jules Séraphin ☎594/594-320-895. Two clean self-contained rooms with a/c, just a few blocks from the restaurants along Ave du Général de Gaulle, make this one of the better budget options. €40.

Typic Accueil No.1, Résidence St Exupéry 97310, Kourou ☎594/594-324-370, ⓔtypic.accueil@orange.fr. Friendly alternative to the usual hotel offering, this quiet, secure, family-run establishment has five studios with a/c, TV, microwave and en-suite facilities, and is just outside the city centre. €45 (minimum 2 nights).

Eating and drinking

The best places to eat and drink are in Le Vieux Bourg (the old village), along Ave du Général de Gaulle.

Le Baraka 37 Ave du Général de Gaulle ☎594/594-323-323. This inviting spot lit with Christmas lights serves Moroccan tagines and the like from €13.

Le Cupuacu 38 Ave du Général de Gaulle ☎594/694-912-146. Colourful Brazilian *churrascaria* in Le Vieux Bourg, with charming owners. Meals from €15.

N'Jifa 21 Ave du Général de Gaulle ☎594/594-328-701. Little Creole restaurant in Le Vieux Bourg that serves hearty cook-up and fish dishes for around €10.

Le Relais Du Bourg 77 Ave du Générale de Gaulle. Popular sports bar with a pool table and projection TV with satellite hook-up.

Directory

Banks and exchange BFC at Place Jeanne-d'Arc; BNP at Ave des Roches; BRED at 85 Ave Gaston-Monnerville; La Poste at Ave des Frères-Kennedy.
Internet Webcom, at CV 14, Simarouba (ⓦwebcom.pk973.org; €3 per hr).
Pharmacies Pharmacie du Bourg, at Ave Thomas Guidiglio (☎594/594-321-366); Pharmacie de l'Anse, at Ave Gaston Monnerville (☎594/594-326-373).
Post Office 4 Ave des Frères-Kennedy.

Moving on

Bus Cayenne (bus #5A; 1hr 15min); Iracoubo (bus #4R; 1hr 30min).

Minibus Cayenne (1hr); St Laurent (2hr). For *taxi collectif* services from Kourou to Cayenne contact Saint CY, at 8 Rue Henri Matisse (☎594/594-223-849) or Davilars Dalger, at 1 Rue Devèze (☎594/594-221-869). For services from Kourou to St Laurent contact Service Transport Vayaboury Charles (☎594/594-321-336).

ILES DU SALUT

The **ILES DU SALUT** (Salvation Islands), 15km off the coast, comprise three islands – **Ile Royale, Ile Saint-Joseph** and **Ile du Diable** – infamous for their use as a penal colony from 1852 to 1953. Thanks to Henri Charrière's book *Papillon*, which recounts the horrors of life in the colony and his various attempts at escape (which finally succeeded), the islands have become a major tourist attraction. You can sign up for a guided tour of Ile Royale (in French) or check out the quaint museum, but the main appeal is in wandering the paths among the lush green vegetation and observing the fearless wildlife.In stark contrast to the coastline of French Guiana, the islands are surrounded by clear blue water.

What to see and do

Ile Royale, the main island and the one most visited by tourists, was used for administration and housing common-law criminals. You can visit some of the ruins of old buildings or peep over the walls of the ones that are restricted. There is also a working prison and mental hospital on site.

"Incorrigible" convicts and those who tried to escape were sent to **Ile Saint-Joseph**. While Ile Royale has been restored, the ruins of the penal colony on Ile Saint-Joseph are overgrown with vegetation and arguably offer a more authentic and atmospheric experience. However, be aware that once you get here, you're stuck until the return trip to Kourou later in the afternoon.

The virtually inaccessible **Ile du Diable** is off-limits to tourists and was once reserved for political prisoners – most famously Alfred Dreyfus, who was arrested but later cleared for passing military secrets to the Germans.

Arrival

There are two ways to make the one-hour trip across the choppy Atlantic to the islands – the noisy, daily ferry or the more enjoyable catamaran.

Catamaran/yacht Except for the vessels operated by Tropic Alizés, boats leave from the *appontement des pecheurs* (fisherman's jetty) at the end of Ave du Général de Gaulle, departing from Kourou around 8–8.30am and leaving the islands around 4pm. One-day tours (from €39) include visits to Ile Royale and Saint-Joseph and you must make reservations in advance. The crossing from Ile Royale to Ile Saint-Joseph is around €5. On the return, make sure that you are at the pier 30min before you are told, as boats often depart early for Kourou. For longer stays contact the operator.

Operators include: Albatros (☎594/594-321-612, ✉halliercatherine@orange.fr); La Hulotte (☎594/594-323-381, ☷www.lahulotte-guyane.fr); Royal Ti'Punch (☎594/594-320-995, Eactiv.snc @orange.fr); Tropic Alizés (☎594/694-402-020, ☷www.ilesdusalut-guyane.com).

Ferry The 200-seater ferry departs for Ile Royale (€35, cash only) from the landing opposite the Kourou fish market in the old town. Make reservations via a tour operator (see p.747) or call ☎594/594-320-995.

Accommodation

You can pretty much sling a hammock anywhere on Ile Saint-Joseph and Ile Royale. If you're on an overnight guided tour then you'll probably end up spending the night near its small beach. You can camp independently on both islands but you'll need to bring all your supplies, including food, water and camping gear, and will have no access to the hammocks and facilities at Auberge des Iles.

Auberge des Iles Ile Royale ☎594/594-321-100, ☷www.ilesdusalut.com. Offers delightfully clean, bright and breezy rooms (from €166) or in the renovated former guards' barracks (from €60). Hammock spaces are also available (€10) with access to toilet and shower facilities in the hotel grounds. The on-site restaurant provides good meals, including excellent fish soup.

SINNAMARY

The coastal town of **SINNAMARY** lies on the Sinnamary River between

Kourou and Iracoubo, around 110km from Cayenne along the RN1. Sinnamary was the second French settlement in French Guiana, founded in 1664, and is a charming town that merits a quick view on the way to St Laurent or Cayenne. Among its population of fewer than 3500 are an Indonesian community and a Galibi Amerindian community, which both produce artwork and jewellery for sale. There is also the chance to see large populations of Scarlet Ibis in their natural habitat. Around 10km from town, along the RN1 to Iracoubou (it's well signposted) is **La Maison de la Nature** (Wed & Sat–Sun 9am–noon & 1.30–2.30pm; ☎594/594-345-856, ⓦmaison.nature.free.fr), where you can tour, wander or canoe through several ecosystems including the Pripri de Yiyi marsh (tours €2).

The riverside deck of *Le Pakira* restaurant, at 14 Rue Constantin Verderosa, has a tasty Creole and wild meat menu (dishes €15–25). For information on *carbets*, gîtes and hotels in the area call ☎594/594-346-883.

IRACOUBO

French police will check your passport at their outpost in IRACOUBO, which lies 30km west of Sinnamary on the RN1. While here, visit **L'Eglise Saint-Joseph d'Iracoubo** (daily 7am–6pm; free), a church famed for its amazing interior covered with brightly coloured frescoes, painted by French convict and painter Pierre Huguet between 1892 and 1898. The frescoes depict a variety of holy images as well as, pleats and flower garlands set upon blue backgrounds and cover much of the interior, including the wooden ceiling, plastered walls, pillars, chancel and choir area. For a bite to eat, stop at *Restaurant Floria* on the main road, where the friendly hostess offers wholesome Creole meals for around €13.

PLAGE LES HATTES

From roughly April to July, **PLAGE LES HATTES**, situated at the mouth of the Maroni River a few kilometres from the Suriname border, is French Guiana's best place to view **leatherback turtles** laying their eggs. Leatherbacks are massive – they can grow up to two metres in length and weigh almost 900kg. During the peak of the egg-laying season, it is estimated that more than two hundred of these giant, grunting, shell-less turtles crawl up onto the beach each night. From August to October, you can witness thousands of baby turtles hatching at night and their mad dash towards the water to escape predators.

Plage Les Hattes is some 260km from Cayenne, accessible by road along the RN1 via the pleasant town of Mana and then a single-track access road for about about 20km to the small Amerindian village of **Awala-Yalimapo**, situated 4km away from the beach. Unless you are part of an organized tour, it may be cheaper to rent a car and to base yourself in the village or on the beach itself (in which case bring food, water, a hammock and mosquito protection). **Boat tours** also access the beach from St Laurent; check with tourist information in St Laurent (see p.753) for details.

Arrival

Transport may involve a combination of car, taxi collectifs or TIG bus and changes at Iracoubo and Mana may be required.

Bus Bus #1R goes from St Laurent to Awala-Yalimapo (55min) via Mana; bus #9 from Cayenne goes to Iracoubo (2hr), then take the #2 to Mana (40min). For more information and prices visit ⓦcg973.fr/Lignes-de-transport-prevues.

Minibus *Taxi collectifs* offer services in both directions between Cayenne and St Laurent via Iracoubo and Sinnamary. However, you may have to pay the full fare between the two destinations and wait a long time, as the driver will only leave when the vehicle is full.

Accommodation and eating

Chez Judith et Denis Ave Paul Henri, Awala-Yalimapo ☏ 594/594-342-438. Provides catered *carbet* facilities 100m from the beach. €23.

Simili Youth Hostel Route de Yalimapo; 97319 Awala Yalimapo ☏ 594/594-341-625. Near beach. Basic bungalow accommodation sleeping 2–6 people (€12 per bed), plus a collective *carbet* with hammocks (€9). Mosquito nets provided. Breakfast and lunch can be provided (from €5).

Yalimalé Pointe des Hattes, 97319, Awala-Yalimapo ☏ 594/594-343-432. Another collective *carbet* with toilets, showers and mosquito nets. The nearby restaurant serves Creole-Amerindian dishes. Breakfast included. €20.

Moving on

Transport to destinations such as St Laurent, Iracoubo, Sinnamary, Kourou and Cayenne may involve a combination of car, *taxi collectif* or TIG bus. For the latter, changes at Iracoubo and Mana may be required.

Bus Cayenne (bus #9 from Iracoubo via Sinnamary and Kourou (2hr); Iracoubo (bus #1 from Awala-Yalimapo, 15min; then bus #2 from Mana, 40min; then bus #9 from Sinnamary, 35min); Kourou (bus #4 or #9 from Iracoubo; 1hr 30min); Saint Laurent (bus #1 from Awala-Yalimapo via Mana, 45min–1hr; then bus #2R, #3R or #10 from Iracoubo (1hr 40min); Sinnamary (bus #4 or bus #9 from Iracoubo (35min). For more information and prices visit ⓦ www.cg973.fr/Lignes-de-transport-prevues.

SAINT LAURENT DU MARONI

One of French Guiana's larger towns, with a population of around twenty thousand, **SAINT LAURENT DU MARONI** (often shortened to St Laurent) lies on the east bank of the Maroni River some 260km from Cayenne. A quiet, down-at-heel place, St Laurent was originally conceived as an agricultural penal colony, where convicts were put to work managing forests or cultivating bananas and sugar cane. The town's principal highlight is the former **penitentiary**, and it makes a good base for trips to a nearby **Hmong community,** excursions on the **Maroni River**, the beautiful Voltaire Falls or

the Saint-Maurice Rum Distillery, the only rum distillery still in operation in French Guiana.

Arrival and information

Boat If you arrive via boat from Suriname and are not dropped off at the official ferry pier, walk about 400m down Ave Hector Rivierez to the pier to get your passport stamped at the French Immigration office (6am–7pm). There is no bus service to town, so you can either walk (about 2km) or take a local taxi (€3–5).

Bus TIG buses arrive at the bus station (*gare routière*) on Rue Léa Chapelin, near the stadium in the centre of the town.

Minibus *Taxis collectifs* from Kourou or Cayenne will drop you at the bus station.

Tourist information The Office du Tourisme at 1 Esplanade Laurent Baudin (Mon 2.30–6pm, Tues–Sat 8am–12.30pm & 2.30–6pm, Sun 9am–1pm; ☏ 594/594-342-398, ⓦ www.ot-saintlaurent dumaroni.fr) provides lots of useful information in English and French on St Laurent's restaurants, lodgings, activities and excursions up the Maroni River (see box, p.755). Some staff speak English.

Tour operators Amazonie Accueil, at 26 Rue Colonel Chandon or 3 Rue Barrat (☏ 594/594-344-145, ℮ am.ac&orange.fr); Havas Voyages 336, at Christophe Columb (☏ 594/594-278-000); Maroni Tours, at Village St Jean (☏ 594/694-408-040, ℮ maronitours@orange.fr); Ouest Voyages Guyané, at 10 Ave Félix Eboué (☏ 595/594-344-444); Tropic Cata, at 1 Esp Laurent Baudin (☏ 594/594-342-518).

What to see and do

Saint Laurent has some fine colonial architecture and a well-planned town divided into three districts: the triangular Officer District which faces the river; the Colonial City (village area) gathered around the market and extending towards Rue Theirs; and the Prison Town, bordered in the west by the river and the east by the village.

Camp de la Transportation

The **Camp de la Transportation**, the former prison, is St Laurent's main tourist draw (1hr 15min guided tours daily at 9.30am, 11am, 3pm & 4.30pm except Mon 3pm & 4.30pm only and

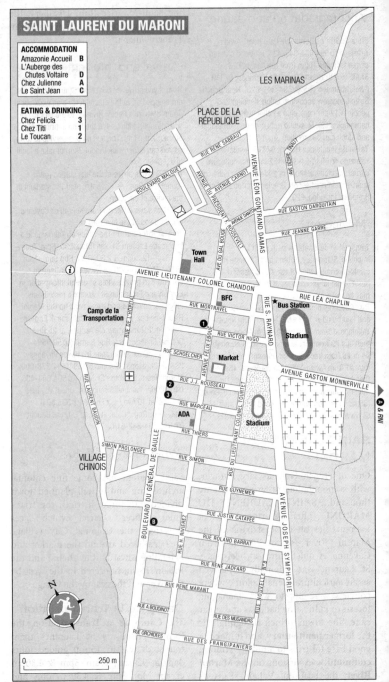

SAINT LAURENT DU MARONI

ACCOMMODATION
Amazonie Accueil **B**
L'Auberge des
  Chutes Voltaire **D**
Chez Julienne **A**
Le Saint Jean **C**

EATING & DRINKING
Chez Felicia **3**
Chez Titi **1**
Le Toucan **2**

LES MARINAS

PLACE DE LA
RÉPUBLIQUE

RUE RENE SABBAUT
BOULEVARD MALOUET
AVENUE DU PRESIDENT ROUSSELET
AVENUE CARNO
AVENUE DANTON
AVENUE LÉON GONTRAND DAMAS
AVE DESSE ANAUT
RUE GASTON DARQUITAIN
RUE JEANNE GARRE

Town Hall

AVENUE LIEUTENANT COLONEL CHANDON
AVE DU GAL BOUGE
RUE LÉA CHAPLIN

BFC
RUE MORTRAVEL
★ **Bus Station**
RUE S. RAYNARD

Camp de la Transportation
RUE DE L'HOPITA
RUE VICTOR HUGO
Stadium

RUE SCHOELCHER
AVENUE FELIX EBOUE
Market
AVENUE GASTON MONNERVILLE

RUE J.J. ROUSSEAU
RUE LAURENT BAUDIN

RUE MARCEAU
ADA
Stadium
RUE DU LIEUTENANT COLONEL TOURTET

RUE THIERS

SIMON PROLONGEE
VILLAGE CHINOIS
RUE SIMON
BOULEVARD DU GÉNÉRAL DE GAULLE

RUE GUYNEMER

RUE JUSTIN CATAYEE
AVENUE JOSEPH SYMPHORIE
RUE H. RIVIEREZ
B

RUE ROLAND BARRAT

RUE RENE JADFARD

RUE RENE MARANT

RUE A BOUDINOT

RUE ORCHIDEES
RUE DES MUSANDAS
RUE DES FRANGIPANIERS

N

0   250 m

& RN1

Official Ferry Crossing, Immigration & Hertz ▼ **C**, **D**, Airport, Paul Island, Saint-Maurice & Rum Distillery, ▼ Apatou, Voltaire Falls & Saint-Jea

EXCURSIONS FROM ST LAURENT

River trips
Most tour operators (see p.753) offer a variety of pirogue river trips, which often focus on visits to the nearby Amerindian and Maroon villages. As well as learning about the traditions and subsistence lifestyle of these groups, you can swim, fish, go wildlife-spotting or try jungle treks.

Javouhey
Javouhey is a traditional Hmong village (of refugees from Laos), a 20-min drive from St Laurent. You can rent a bike to ride around the village or into the forest, and there is a Sunday market with traditional craftwork including basketry, carvings and embroidery. Either rent a car or take bus #1R from St Laurent (30min).

Saint-Maurice Rum Distillery
This rum distillery lies in the small village of Saint-Maurice, around 3km south of St Laurent. There is no official tour but you can visit to learn a little about the distillery process and purchase rum at cheaper prices than those at the supermarkets. Open Mon–Fri 7.30–11.30am. There's no public transport, so you'll need a car to get there (10min).

Apatou
Apatou, an Aluku Maroon village, is about 70km upriver from St Laurent, and is a great way to experience Maroon culture, food and lifestyle. Although now accessible by road, there is no public transport. Most visitors reach Apatou by pirogue on organized tours; note also that, pirogues leave daily around 11am from La Glacière (in the Charbonniére quarter, near where the boats cross over to Albina) arriving in Apatou at around 2pm (around €15 one-way). You return the next morning at 7am. For specific details, prices and tours, contact Tropic Cata (see p.753) or the tourist office in St Laurent.

Voltaire Falls
While not as large and powerful as Guyana's Kaieteur Falls, Voltaire Falls, about 42km east of Apatou, is worth a visit. Getting there involves a 4x4 journey through dense forest via the Route de Paul Isnard and Route d'Apatou forest roads, followed by a 1hr 30min hike (if you're going independently, check with the tourist office in St Laurent to see if the road is passable). The falls can also be reached by river in a pirogue. Picnic and lodging facilities are nearby (see below).

Sun 9.30am & 11am only; €5). You can walk round the grounds and check out the permanent free exhibition of photos in the camp's former kitchen and chapel, though the French-only guided tours of the cells and other installations put everything into its chilling context and should not be missed. Tickets for the tour are sold at the tourist office (see p.753).

Accommodation

Amazonie Accueil 3 Rue R Barrat ☎594/594-343-612. Two guarded *carbets*, which come with a hammock and mosquito net (€15 or hang your own for €10). Shared bathroom. Breakfasts, snacks and meals available (€5–20).

L'Auberge des Chutes Voltaire PK 73, Route de Paul Isnard Eaubergevoltaire@hotmail.com, ⓦwww.aubergechutesvoltaire.com. Located about 73km from St Laurent following Route de Paul Isnard (2hr 30min). The lodge sits on the banks of the Voltaire River, close to Voltaire Falls. Rent a hammock with a mosquito net in the *carbet* (€20) or a room for two in the lodge (€50). Bookings must be made in advance by email. Meals €5–30, ranging from sandwiches to breakfasts and main meals.

Chez Julienne Rue Gaston Monnerville ☎594/594-341-153. Six basic en-suite rooms with a/c, TV but no fridge, just a few blocks out of town past the football field. €39.

Le Saint Jean 3 Chemin du Parc ☎594/594-341-422. Take a hammock and net to this *carbet* near the Maroni River, with three bedrooms, shared bathroom and space for twelve hammocks (€10). Food available but hammocks not provided.

Eating and drinking

Chez Felicia 23 Ave deu Général due Gaulle. A small, bustling place with open-shuttered windows that serves *fricassée* and other Creole dishes (€9–12). Closed Sun afternoon.

Chez Titi 18 Ave Félix Eboué. Open-air pizzeria with outdoor tables, which serves decent food including French, Creole and grilled dishes (mains €9–19). A bakery attached to the restaurant does tasty snacks. Closed Sun and Mon.

Le Toucan 17 Ave du Général de Gaulle. Salads and daily menus for €13–17. Closed Tues.

Directory

Banks and exchange BFC, at 11 Ave Félix Eboué; BRED, at Banque 30 Rue Thiers.

Internet Infocentre SARL, at 16 Rue Hugo; Upgrade Computer, at 25 Rue Félix Eboué.

Pharmacies Pharmacie Centrale, at 22 Ave du Général de Gaulle; Pharmacie du Maroni, at 56 Ave Hector Rivierez.

Post Office Ave du Général de Gaulle.

Moving on

Boat Get your passport stamped at the immigration office (6am–7pm) at the ferry pier, then cross the Maroni River to Albina in Suriname by ferry or wooden speedboat (see box below).

Bus Awala-Yalimapo (bus #1 via Mana; 45min–1hr 10min); Cayenne (bus #2, #3 or #10 to Iracoubo, 1hr 25–40min; then bus #9 from Iracoubo to Cayenne via Sinnamary and Kourou, 2hr); Javouhey (bus #1 via Mana (1hr 10min); Kourou (bus #2, #3 or #10 to Iracoubo, 1hr 25–40min; then bus #4 or 9 from Iracoubo to Kourou, 1hr 30min). For more info and prices visit ⓦwww.cg973.fr/Lignes-de-transport-prevues.

Minibus *Taxis collectifs* congregate around the bus station on Rue Léa Chapelin, near the stadium, waiting to fill up with passengers before departing for Kourou (2–3hr) or Cayenne (3–4hr).

South to Brazil

The settlements in the southern part of French Guiana are few and far between compared with the relatively populous north coast and tourism here is mainly nature-oriented. Interesting side trips can be made to the Hmong (Laotian) village of **Cacao** and the swamp of **Kaw**. At the end of the paved section of the RN2, **Régina** is the departure point for excursions on the **Approuague River**, but the road continues on the opposite bank of the river as an unsealed track all the way to **Saint-Georges de l'Oyapok** on the Brazilian border. Various tour operators (see p.747) offer organized tours to these areas. Independent travel may be cost effective if you're travelling in a group,

---

CROSSING INTO SURINAME

The **ferry** departs from St Laurent for **Albina**, Suriname on Mon, Tues and Thurs at 7am, 9am, 2pm & 5pm; Wed 7am, 8am & 5pm; Fri 7am, 8am, 9am, 2pm, 3pm, 4pm & 5pm; Sat 8am & 9am; Sun 3pm, 4pm & 5pm. The fee is €4 one-way for foot passengers; a motorbike or car will cost €15 or €33 respectively. Only euros are accepted as payment.

Unless you have a car, the quickest and easiest way to cross the Maroni River to Albina is to take one of the many **motorized dugout canoes** waiting on the beach about 500m from the ferry pier. The crossing takes 10–15min and costs €3 or SRD10. When you arrive in Albina, ask the boat driver to put you off at the **Surinamese immigration office** (6am–7pm) to get your visa checked and passport stamped. There is a **cambio** at the ferry terminal, which gives good rates when exchanging euros and US dollars for Suriname dollars.

There is no reason to linger in Albina so once you have cleared immigration you can either take a local taxi (SRD5) or walk into the centre of town (10–15min). The state bus (SRD8.50), minibus (SRD50–70) or a taxi (SRD50–200 depending on passenger numbers) will take you to Paramaribo (2–3hr).

but otherwise unlikely to save you much time or money.

CACAO

A once-abandoned little town along the River Comté, about 75km southwest of Cayenne, **CACAO** was resettled in 1977 by refugees from Laos. Since then, this small Hmong community (fewer than 1500 inhabitants, most of whom are farmers) has become the fruit and vegetable basket of the *département* due to the extensive cultivation of Cacao's steep hillsides. There's a picturesque local **market** on Sunday mornings where you can find good produce, soups and handicrafts; otherwise there isn't much to do except admire the Laotian-styled houses and church. Those interested in insects should visit **Le Planeur Bleu** (Sun only; ☎594/594-270-034; €2), a museum of sorts that houses a collection of living and preserved rare butterflies and spiders. To view the collection on any other day, call ahead and arrange it.

Arrival

Independent travellers can rent a car and drive along the RN2 before turning off about 40km before the town of Régina, on to the extremely bad road that leads to the village.
Bus There is a Mon–Fri service between Cayenne and Cacao via Matoury (bus #16; 2 daily; 1hr 15min). Buses will drop you in the centre of town.

Accommodation and eating

Quimbe Kio ☎594/594-270-122, ☻www .quimbekio.com. Hang or rent a hammock (€12–16) in a *carbet* on a wooded hill near the centre or stay in one of the en-suite rooms (€40 including breakfast). Kayaking, boat and quad tours available from €5.
Restaurant Cacaoyer 111 Bourg de Cacao. The best Laotian restaurant in Cacao has dishes such as pork steamed in a banana leaf or chicken with Laotian caramel, served on a shady terrace in a pretty flower garden. Main dishes €12–19. Open daily 11am–8pm.

Moving on

From Cacao, take the bus or drive back to Cayenne, turning left at the junction with the RN2. Otherwise,

turn in the opposite direction and head to Régina and Saint-Georges de L'Oyapok.

KAW

Some 50km east of Cacao, across the heavily forested Kaw Hills, is an Everglades-style swamp called **MARAIS DE KAW**, which covers around one thousand square kilometres. The surrounding hills make for some stunning vistas – especially when covered with mist during the wet season – and this is an excellent place to spot water birds, including flamingos. Tour operators such as JAL Voyages (see p.747) offer wildlife-spotting boat trips along the river, after-dark pirogue trips to spot black caiman and overnight stays in a floating carbet. It's also possible to take a pirogue trip to the island of Kaw, at the centre of the swamp, where you can spend a pleasant half-hour exploring the tiny deserted village. Surprisingly, mosquitoes are not a problem on the swamp itself; there are more on the banks and in the hills around it.

Arrival

Visitors to Kaw arrive either as part of an organized tour, by renting a car or via the limited TIG bus service.
Bus Bus #15 goes to Kaw from Cayenne via Roura (2 daily; 1hr), and there are two additional daily services from Roura (1hr). Services do not run on the weekend.

Accommodation

Auberge de Camp Caïman PK 36, Route de Kaw 97311 Roura ☎594/594-307-277. Large wooden hostel that offers eight rooms and *carbet* accommodation housing thirty hammocks. Solar-powered shared toilets and showers. Butterfly-catching, marsh walks and caiman-spotting trips offered. Breakfast available from €6; more for main meals. €23.50 per person.

Moving on

Bus Bus #15R will take visitors back to Roura (4 daily; 1hr), with two of those services continuing for 1hr to Cayenne. Check the schedules as they are limited and do not run on the weekend.

CROSSING INTO BRAZIL

From Régina, you can take the #18 bus or a *taxi collectif* to Saint-Georges de l'Oyapok and the Brazilian border (1hr 15min). The immigration office can also be found near the Oyapok River; you'll need to have your passport stamped or at least checked before crossing over to Brazil. From Saint-Georges de l'Oyapok, boats cross the Oyapok River to Oiapoque in Brazil (15–20min; €8). Once in Brazil you should go to the Federal Police to get your passport stamped. With the river on your right, follow the main street until you see a road to your left with a church in its middle. The office is on the right side of this road past the church.

Moneychangers operate on the Brazilian side of the river, but not in Saint-Georges. If you are just travelling overland from Suriname through to Brazil, budget for between €60–100 in transport costs depending on which methods you use.

SAINT-GEORGES DE L'OYAPOK

SAINT-GEORGES L'OYAPOK is a small town on the French Guiana border with a considerable indigenous population. Apart from organized excursions on the river (for tour operators see p.747), there is little to do but get your passport stamped and cross into Brazil. If you need a place **to stay**, *Chez Modestine* (☎594/594-370-013) try which offers clean en-suite rooms (€35), air conditioning and an on-site café in a traditional house on the main square. It can also arrange hammock lodgings on Ilet Sophia, 30min upstream, for less than €10 per person. Alternatively, take a boat to Ilha do Sol, a small islet on the river facing Saint-Georges, which provides hammocks for negotiable prices. The Oyapock River Bridge is currently under construction and when this is completed (potentially in 2011), travellers should be able to commute without too much trouble between Cayenne and Macapa (Brazil),

Paramaribo (Suriname), Georgetown (Guyana) and Boa Vista (Brazil).

You will need to pass through the town of **Régina**, about 122km from Cayenne, to get to Saint-Georges de L'Oyapok. Regina is a small town of no particular note, where you join pirogue trips up the Approuague River and embark on travel to the Cisame camp. Cisame, probably French Guiana's most comfortable jungle camp, has good sanitary facilities, constant electricity, tasty meals and good outdoor activities including gold-panning (2 days; €164). For further information contact Couleurs Amazone (see p.747).

Moving on

Boat Boats take 15–20min to cross the Oyapok River to Brazil (€8).

Bus Bus #18 from Saint-Georges to Régina (4 daily Mon–Fri; 1hr 10min). Travellers must then connect with bus #17 from Régina to Cayenne (4 daily Mon–Fri; 1hr 30min).

Minibus *Taxis collectifs* provide an occasional, irregular service to Régina (2hr).

Paraguay

HIGHLIGHTS ✪

THE CHACO:
wildlife abounds in this
immens wilderness

LAGUNA BLANCA:
a crystal-clear lake,
perfect for birdwatching ✪

**THE ITAIPÚ HYDRO-
ELECTRIC PROJECT:**
the world's second-biggest
dam an extraordinary feat
of engineering design ✪

ASUNCIÓN:
visit Paraguay's most
famous monument, the
Panteón de los Héroes ✪

SAN RAFAEL PARQUE NACIONAL:
Paraguay's most biodiverse reserve, a
must for nature lovers ✪

ENCARNACIÓN:
glimpse Jesuit life at nearby
missions or party at the
vibrant February Carnaval ✪

ROUGH COSTS

DAILY BUDGET basic US$25,
occasional treat US$35

DRINK 1 litre Pilsen Beer US$1.50

FOOD *chipa* US$0.25, *asado
completo* US$10

HOSTEL/BUDGET HOTEL US$8–12/
US$15–25

TRAVEL Asunción–Encarnación
(365km): bus US$15

FACT FILE

POPULATION 6.4 million (2009)

AREA 406,750 sq km

LANGUAGE Guaraní and Castellano
(Spanish)

CURRENCY Guaraní (GS)

CAPITAL Asunción (population of
Greater Asunción: 1.48 million)

INTERNATIONAL PHONE CODE ☎595

TIME ZONE GMT -4hr

Introduction

Paraguay is billed by the tourist board as the "Heart of South America", but perhaps "South America's forgotten corner" is more appropriate. Despite being one of the most traditional countries on the continent and the only one with an indigenous tongue as its official language (Guaraní), Paraguay is far too often passed over by travellers rushing from one long bus journey to another in search of the next well-known sight. Those who do make it may find themselves pleasantly surprised by the rich culture, host of under-promoted natural attractions, fascinating and bloodthirsty history and real feeling of being "off the beaten track".

Paraguay combines the scorching, arid wilderness of the **Chaco** – remarkably, one of the best places in South America to see large mammals – with the wet and humid **Atlantic forests** of eastern Paraguay; the rampant commercialism of **Ciudad del Este** with the muted, backwater feel of colonial towns like **Concepción**. It is part-owner of the second-largest hydroelectric dam in the world – **Itaipú** – and home to a superbly preserved series of **Jesuit ruins**. Thanks to its extraordinary biodiversity and varied natural habitats, **ecotourism** is developing fast here. Tourism in general is still in its infancy so this is not the place for pampered travellers, but if you crave a sense of adventure and a real, uncommercialized South American experience, then Paraguay is your spot.

CHRONOLOGY

1537 The Spanish found the city of Nuestra Señora de Asunción.

1609 The Jesuit missionaries arrive with the aim of converting indigenous tribes.

1767 The Jesuits are expelled from Paraguay by King Carlos III of Spain.

1811 Paraguay declares its independence from Spain in a bloodless revolution.

1814 Dr José Gáspar Rodriguéz de Francia is chosen as the first president and takes Paraguay into a period of isolation and industrialization.

1816 Francia declares himself "El Supremo" – dictator for life, becoming progressively more

arbitrary through his reign, suppressing the church and oppressing the population.

1844 Francia is succeeded by Carlos Antonio López and Paraguay enters its period of greatest prosperity, becoming the most prosperous country on the fledgling continent.

1862 Mariscal Carlos Antonio López takes over as president from his ailing father, who leaves him with the deathbed advice that the pen is mightier than the sword.

1865–1870 Mariscal López launches Paraguay into the disastrous War of the Triple Alliance against Brazil, Argentina and Uruguay, which saw the country lose much of its territory and male population.

1902 The first Mennonites arrive in Paraguay, part of a campaign to colonize the Chaco.

1932–37 With the Bolivian army encroaching on the Chaco for many years, rumours of undiscovered oil reserves provoke a violent reaction from the Paraguayan government and the start of the Chaco War, with both sides secretly funded by international oil companies.

1954 After 22 presidents in 31 years, General Alfredo Stroessner seizes power and goes on to become the longest-lasting dictator in South American history, holding power for 34 years.

1989 Stroessner is driven into exile and Paraguay declares itself a Republic.

1993 The first democratic elections are held, and are won by the quasi-liberal Colorados, effectively returning Stroessner's political party to power. Their unpopular reforms lead to a general strike the following year.

2003 Nicanor Duarte-Frutos is elected president, promising to put an end to corruption. In fact his period in office is dogged by allegations of extreme corruption; he unsuccessfully attempts to change

the constitution, implemented after Stroessner, preventing any president from serving more than one term in office.

2008 Fernando Lugo defeats Colorado Party candidate Blanca Ovelar, ending 61 years of Colorado party rule, the longest reign by any one political party anywhere in the world.

Basics

ARRIVAL

A **passport** valid for six months after entry is required by all visitors, except residents of Argentina or Brazil who can use their national identity documents. Australian, Canadian, and US citizens are required to have

an **entry visa** that must be obtained prior to travelling; other Western European, UK and Japanese citizens do not (see ⓦwww.worldtravelguide.net /paraguay/passport-visa for a full list of countries not requiring visas).

If you're **arriving by land**, be aware that buses frequently cross the border without stopping at the customs post. It is your responsibility to get exit stamps from Bolivia, Brazil and Argentina upon departure and to obtain the required entry stamp when entering Paraguay, or you risk a substantial fine – inform your driver that you need your stamps and take your bags with you to passport control as the bus won't always wait. The entry stamp usually entitles you to a ninety-day stay in Paraguay and this can be renewed once without cost. Also make sure that you have a **yellow-fever certificate** before entering Paraguay – it is occasionally asked for. There is a US$25 **departure tax** if leaving the country by air.

From Argentina

The border city of Encarnación sits across the River Paraguay from Posadas, the capital of Argentina's Misiones province. International buses connect the terminals on each side of the border via the San Roque González bridge (see p.779). Also, local buses also run between Ciudad del Este and Puerto Iguazú.

From Bolivia

Land crossings from Bolivia are fairly straightforward in favourable weather conditions, less so during heavy rains. A paved road branches off from the Trans-Chaco to cross the border at Fortín Infante Rivarola; international buses stop here en route from Santa Cruz to Asunción.

From Brazil

The busiest border crossing with Brazil is the Puente Amistad ("friendship bridge") linking Ciudad del Este with Foz do Iguaçu. Regular buses make the short crossing, and it is also possible to cross by taxi or even on foot (see p.774). Many other border crossings with Brazil, such as that at Pedro Juan

Caballero, are popular smuggling routes and considered unsafe.

GETTING AROUND

Travelling around Paraguay is generally cheap and easy, if less than comfortable. There are currently no passenger train services in Paraguay, making buses the best way to get around.

By plane

Though most visitors arrive in Paraguay crossing by land from neighbouring Brazil or Argentina, those arriving on international flights will land at Pettirossi International Airport (☎021/645-444), 15km northeast of the centre in Luque, a satellite town of Asunción. The main **airlines** operating in and out of Paraguay at the time of writing are TAM (⦿www .tam.com.py) and Aerosur (⦿www .aerosur.com), although there are also flights within South America via Pluna (⦿www.pluna.aero) and Aerolineas Argentinas (⦿www.aerolineas.com.ar). It's a good idea to confirm your flight 24 hours in advance, as they can be subject to last-minute changes.

By bus

The easiest and cheapest way to get around Paraguay is by **bus**; there are frequent and affordable services daily between the major cities. Visiting areas away from the major cities is more difficult and bus

---

WHEN TO VISIT

Paraguay is an extremely hot country for most of the year. Eastern Paraguay (Orient) can be very humid, while western Paraguay (Chaco) is dry. The hottest time of year is from November to February, when daytime temperatures can peak around 45°C and high atmospheric pressure makes just walking along the street a tough task. Winter (June–Aug) is often pleasantly warm during the day (around 20–25°C), generally sunny and dry, though frequently chilly. There is no real rainy season, but from September to November spectacular electric storms become more frequent and travelling off-road can be difficult. The climate is governed by the prevailing winds: *viento sur* (southerly winds) bring cooler temperatures from Patagonia and *viento norte* (northerly winds) bring hotter weather from the tropics.

services – when they exist – are uncomfortable. Journey durations and departure times tend to be erratic, as buses leave when they are full and may pick further passengers up en route.

Unsurprisingly, Asunción is the country's major transport hub. A large number of companies compete for business at the central bus terminal, at Argentina y Fernando de la Mora (☎021/551-740), ensuring that outside of the holiday seasons there is no need to book tickets in advance. The quality of service provided by the different companies varies greatly – in general, you pay for what you get. During the hot summer months a bus service with air-conditioning will make for a more pleasant experience and is worth the extra expense.

City buses are cheap, with a set fare of Gs2300 regardless of how far you go. Services tend to tail off around 10pm.

By car

Renting a **car** is possible only in Asunción or Ciudad del Este, and a 4x4 is required for the dirt roads that crisscross the country away from the main national Ruta system, as many roads are impassable after rain. Rental is expensive (around Gs450,000 per day for a 4x4) and there is a charge for extra kilometres, making it difficult to see more remote areas of the country cheaply. On the other hand petrol costs are low (a little over Gs4500 a litre for unleaded).

An **international driving licence** is required to rent a car. If you plan on going deeper into the Chaco than the Mennonite colonies in the Central Chaco, you should take a guided tour (see p.784) rather than drive – many tourists come to grief by embarking on poorly planned journeys in an effort to save a little money. Even on the Ruta Trans-Chaco (which is now fully paved), once past the Mennonite colonies there is nowhere to stay or buy food, and very few places to refuel.

Heading off the Ruta Trans-Chaco on your own is strongly discouraged.

By taxi

Taxis are reasonably priced but only use those from marked taxi ranks and insist that the meter is switched on. Within Asunción you should not pay more than Gs50,000 for a journey to the suburbs, or Gs25,000 for a trip within the centre. In smaller towns such as Encarnación and Ciudad del Este maximum fares for city journeys should be around Gs25,000.

ACCOMMODATION

On the whole **accommodation** in Paraguay represents good value for money, though away from major towns it can be difficult to find. It's not usually necessary to book in advance, although it is a must in Caacupé during the weeks surrounding the feast of the Día del Virgen (Dec 8), during the Carnival in Encarnación (Feb) and in the Mennonite colonies during the Trans-Chaco Rally (Sept–Oct). Prices are correspondingly higher during these events.

All but the very cheapest of hotel rooms are en-suite and in most places, it's possible to get a decent double room for as little as Gs130,000, usually with TV and breakfast. Budget travellers should have no problem finding a good deal, and should not necessarily be scared off by very cheap rooms – though it's wise to ask to see the room before paying. There are next to no **youth hostels** in Paraguay and campsites are few and far between. Do not expect to camp in rural areas; the vast majority of the land is in private hands and if you do not have the permission of the landowner you risk being accused of trespassing.

FOOD

At first glance **Paraguayan cuisine** may appear to be based entirely on junk-food joints selling hamburgers, *milanesas* (breaded meat fillets) and pizza. However, a little exploring will uncover a number of excellent restaurants, at least in the major cities. The mainstay of the Paraguayan diet is the **asado** – essentially grilled meat, almost always accompanied by *mandioca* (manioc), the staple food plant. The best cuts are *tapa de cuadril*, *corte Americano* and *colita de cuadril*. If you don't like to chew too hard avoid *costillas* (ribs). *Vacio* (flank steak with a layer of softening fat) is extremely tasty at its best, but at its worst is like boot leather – ask for a decent piece. Those with a weak stomach should avoid *mondongo* (tripe), *lengua* (tongue), *chinchulín* (small intestine) and *tripa gorda* (large intestine). *Morcilla* is black pudding and *chorizo* is sausage – but no relation to Spanish chorizo. *Pollo asado* (grilled chicken) is often sold on roadside grills, and don't forget to try *corazoncitos* (chicken hearts).

Fish is generally expensive and at least twice the price of beef, *surubí* being the most frequently available. For a cheap, tasty snack *empanadas* (pasties) are widely available and there is almost always somebody selling **chipa** (cheese bread made with manioc flour) – it is best when hot. Oddly, *chipa* in Asunción is frequently disappointing, so don't let it put you off trying it elsewhere. *Sopa Paraguaya* is not soup, but a cornmeal and cheese bread, delicious when warm. *Chipa Guazu* is similar, but made with fresh corn.

Ask around for unmarked eating houses, which local people always know about but tourists always miss. Here you may be able to find home-cooked Paraguayan fare such as *vori-vori* (soup with corn balls), *guiso de arroz* (a sort of Paraguayan paella) and *so'o apu'à* (meatball soup).

Paraguayan **desserts** include the sandwich spreads *dulce de leche* and *dulce de guayaba*, as well as *dulce de batata con queso paraguayo* (a candied sweet potato accompanied with cheese).

DRINK

Undoubtedly the most widely consumed drink is **tereré**, or ice-cold *yerba mate*, a herbal tea that is surprisingly refreshing and addictive. Paraguayans are not averse to experimenting with their *yerba mate*, and locals will even drink it mixed with fruit juice (*tereré Ruso*) or milk with dessicated coconut (*tereré dulce*). Look out for street vendors with baskets of "**yu-yos**" – native plants with medicinal properties. Whether you have a hangover or want to lose weight, let the vendor know and he'll add the appropriate plant mix to your *tereré*.

Mosto is a sickly sweet juice made from sugar cane, while *caña* is a distilled alcoholic spirit from the same source. **Local beers** Pilsen and Baviera are both good. *Chopp* is a generic term for draught beer, although beer is more widely available in returnable litre bottles.

CULTURE AND ETIQUETTE

Paraguay is generally an informal and laidback country. Men greet each other with a shake of the hand and women are greeted with a fake kiss on each cheek (unless they first offer you their hand). The main **religion** is Roman Catholicism. As in many Latin American countries, there is a typically macho attitude to **women**, who may be seen as "fair game" when travelling alone; women should try to avoid any behaviour or clothing that may be misconstrued as "flirty", especially away from the major cities. Equally, it's not considered normal or appropriate for respectable women to be drunk in public. Men wishing to talk to a Paraguayan woman should take care that she is not already accompanied. Even if your intentions are perfectly innocent, it may be considered disrespectful to approach her instead of her escort. If you wish to take a photo of somebody, ask permission and don't offer payment if it's not asked for.

Tipping is not expected but is always appreciated. A tip of Gs2000–3000 is appropriate for a snack or ordinary meal.

SPORTS AND OUTDOOR ACTIVITIES

As in most South American countries, **soccer**, or *fútbol*, is the main sporting obsession. Matches are played on Sundays and the two biggest clubs are Olimpia and Cerro Porteño. Tickets to see games are bought at the stadium upon entry. **Volleyball** is also a popular sport, at least to play, and the Chaco is home to the **Trans-Chaco Rally** – usually held in September or October – one of the most demanding motor races on earth.

Fishing is becoming increasingly popular, and undoubtedly the biggest prize for any angler is the *dorado* of the Paraguay, Paranà and Tebicuary rivers: a monster fish weighing up to 30kg. A permit is required for fishing, obtainable from SEAM (Av. Madame Lynch 3500 ☎021/614-687, ⓦwww.seam.gov .py).

Ecotourism is a growing industry in this country blessed with large unspoilt areas of natural habitats. The Chaco is one of the best places in South America to see large mammals such as jaguar, tapir and puma, while the Atlantic Forests of eastern Paraguay are officially the most threatened natural habitat on the planet, with an interesting endemic birdlife. Paraguay's vast tracts of wildlife-rich terrain are best explored via organized tours, which will include transport, lodgings and permits, all of which can be tricky to arrange independently. One reliable company is Paraguay Natural Ecotourism (ⓦwww.paraguaynatural .com.py/english/html/home.html).

COMMUNICATIONS

Postal services are unreliable, so important mail should always be sent registered (*certificado*) despite the slightly higher cost, or else by international courier. **Telephone services** are provided by COPACO, and there are numerous *cabinas telefónicas* in the major cities. Directory enquiries can be reached by dialling 112. SIM cards for the local **mobile phone** companies Tigo and Personal can be purchased very cheaply with free credit usually part of the package.

Internet access is ubiquitous in the major cities and is very cheap (around Gs4000 per hr), with generally good connections. The most popular **newspapers** (*diarios*) are the tabloids *Crónica* and *Popular*, both written in a mixture of Spanish and Guaraní and typically sensationalist in their approach to reporting. For a more serious read try *ABC* or *Ultima Hora*.

CRIME AND SAFETY

Paraguay is generally a safe country to visit, and with so few tourists around they are rarely targeted by thieves. As such the usual precautions regarding personal safety and protecting your belongings should be taken, and it's unwise to wander alone after dark in unpopulated areas of the capital. Though crime against tourists is rare, do not expect the **police** to offer more assistance than the taking of your statement for insurance purposes.

The border area in **Ciudad del Este** is occasionally unsafe and you should take a taxi if you have all your belongings with you. Further afield, the vast, largely unpopulated wilderness of the **Chaco** is an extremely desolate and hostile environment, and you should not go off the beaten track without a local guide and/or substantial preparation and supplies.

HEALTH

Travellers coming to Paraguay should be **vaccinated** against dyptheria, yellow fever and hepatitis A. Your doctor may also recommend malaria, rabies, hepatitis B, tuberculosis and typhoid vaccines, depending on your travel plans. It is not advisable to drink **tap water** in Paraguay – although chlorinated in cities and major towns, bottled or sterilized water is preferable and essential in more rural areas. Peel fruit and vegetables before eating; salads in restaurants may cause stomach upsets.

INFORMATION AND MAPS

The tourist office in Asunción at Palma y Alberdi (☏ 021/494-110) is a useful source of information. Be sure to drop in, as this is likely to be the only functional tourist office that you will come across in Paraguay. **Permits**, required to visit many of the national parks, are available from the government ministry SEAM at Av. Madame Lynch 3500 (☏ 021/614-687, ⊛ www .seam.gov.py). These will be arranged for you if you take organized tours.

Good national and local **maps** are available from the Servicio Geográfico Militar in Asunción at Artigas 920. Fauna Paraguay (⊛ www.faunaparaguay .com) provides a huge amount of information in English about the country's wildlife and natural habits, including accurate lists and image galleries of the majority of the species present here.

MONEY AND BANKS

The **guaraní** has been relatively stable in recent years, despite a history of devaluation and high inflation. Notes are issued in denominations of 1000, 5000, 10,000, 20,000, 50,000 and 100,000. Coins are in short supply but come in denominations of 50, 100, 500 and 1000. It is almost impossible to change the guaraní outside Paraguay, and you should attempt to get rid of any spare currency before crossing the border. **Credit cards** are not widely accepted outside the capital and incur a charge of five to ten percent – plan on paying in cash wherever you go. **ATMs** are widely available in the cities and most accept foreign cards such as Visa and MasterCard, though an administration charge of Gs20,000–30,000 is sometimes applied.

Do not use street **moneychangers**; one of their classic tricks is to miss a zero off the end while performing the calculation in front of you – easily missed when you are dealing with hundreds of thousands of guaraníes.

OPENING HOURS AND HOLIDAYS

Opening hours for shops are generally Monday to Friday 8am until 6pm, plus Saturday until early afternoon. Many businesses observe a siesta from noon to 2pm. Banks are typically open Monday to Friday 8am to 3pm and closed at weekends, though ATMs can be used at any time. In addition to the national holidays listed below, some local anniversaries or saints' days are also public holidays, when everything in a given town may close down.

January 1 New Year's Day (Año Nuevo)
February 3 Day of San Blas, patron saint of Paraguay (Día de San Blas)
March 1 Death of Mariscal Francisco Solano López (Cerró Corà)
March/April Easter and Holy Week (Pascua y Semana Santa)
May 1 Day of the Worker (Día del Trabajador)
May 15 Independence Day (Día de la Independencia Patria)
June 12 Commemoration of the end of the Chaco War (Paz del Chaco)
August 15 Founding of Asunción (Fundación de Asunción)
August 25 Victory in the Battle of Boquerón (Victoria del Boquerón)
December 8 Immaculate Conception (Día del Virgen)
December 25 Christmas Day (Navidad)

Asunción

Less intimidating than many other South American capital cities, **ASUNCIÓN** sits astride a broad bay on the Rio Paraguay. Once the historic centre of government for the Spanish colonies of Rio de la Plata, the city declined in importance with the founding of Buenos Aires, while the impenetrable Chaco prevented it from becoming the envisioned gateway to the riches of Peru. The centre of the city is based on a grid square system, a leftover from the days of the paranoid despot **Dr Francia** who, convinced of plots to kill him, declared that the buildings had to be short enough that he could see who was on the roof while riding his horse, and that at every street corner he should be able to see in all four directions so that would-be assassins would have nowhere to hide. The destruction of colonial buildings that didn't fit with this vision robbed Asunción of some architectural gems.

What to see and do

Modern Asunción is a strange city; with a crumbling historical centre and modern, trendy suburbs, the city encapsulates the extremes and contrasts that visitors will find throughout Paraguay. The old colonial centre, which is deserted at weekends when office workers retire to their suburban homes, provides enough cultural attractions to fill a day or two of wandering. The action is centred in the area around the **Plaza Uruguaya** and **Plaza de los Héroes,** as well as the **Waterfront**. Those seeking more tranquil surroundings will find solace in the numerous green spaces that surround the city. The best of the city's **restaurants** have now relocated to the suburbs, especially in the area around the mammoth **Shopping del Sol** complex, but central Asunción is still the best base to look for cheap accommodation and nightlife.

The Waterfront

El Paraguayo Independiente, and its continuations, Avenidas República and Mariscal Francisco S. López, run along the **Waterfront**. At the western end, set among highly manicured gardens, is the stunning president's residence, the **Palacio de Gobierno** (Palacio López). The marble building was completed in 1892 to a design based on the Palace of Versailles. Across the street is the **Manzana de la Rivera** (daily 8am–6pm; free), a series of restored houses dating from 1750, some of which house small museums depicting life in the 1700s.

Plaza de la Independencia

The **Plaza de la Independencia** is marked largely by balding lawns, and is dominated by the ageing, pink-lit **Cabildo** (Mon–Fri 7am–3pm; free), the former seat of government. Constructed by Carlos Antonio López in 1844, it now houses the **Centro Cultural de la República**, which hosts regular art and photography exhibitions and occasional live classical music events (daily 10am–5pm; free). On the southeastern corner of the plaza stands the Neoclassical **Catedral**, a rather disappointing structure that fails to capture the imagination. The western side houses the **Casa de la Cultura** (Mon–Fri 10am–2pm & 6–9pm, Sat noon–2pm; free), a former Jesuit College now hosting a military museum.

A few blocks south of here, along 14 de Mayo, the eighteenth-century **Casa de la Independencia** (Tues–Fri 7am–noon & 2–6pm, Sat & Sun 7am–noon; free) is one of the oldest and most important buildings in the country. It was here that the architects of Paraguayan independence met to discuss their plans. Today it houses a museum with period artefacts from the time of the declaration of independence.

CENTRAL ASUNCIÓN

⑩, La Quinta Avenida & Bus Terminal ▼

Plaza de los Héroes

The **Plaza De Los Héroes** is a huge and verdant square filled with *lapacho* trees that bloom a dramatic pink in July and August. A lively and vibrant place, and frequent concert venue, it attracts tourists and pedlars alike.

In the northwestern corner of the plaza, the **Panteón de los Héroes** (daily 8am–6pm; free) is Paraguay's most instantly recognizable monument. This great domed memorial to Paraguayan heroes was begun in 1863 but not completed until 1937. Permanently guarded by foot soldiers, it contains the remains of former presidents Carlos Antonio López and his son Mariscal Francisco Solano López, as well as Mariscal Estigarribia, a hero of the Chaco War. West of here, you'll find the busy commercial and shopping street of **Calle Palma**, where high-street shops and boutiques rub shoulders with street traders peddling counterfeit wares.

Further east along Mariscal Estigarribia is the **Museo de Bellas Artes** (Tues–Fri 8am–6pm, Sat & Sun 8am–noon; free). Minor works by Tintoretto and Courbet figure in this large collection of fine arts, as well as numerous pieces by Paraguayan artists including Pablo Alburno and Juan Samudio.

Plaza Uruguaya

The leafy but rather charmless **Plaza Uruguaya** can be a little intimidating after dark, but the surrounding streets have some excellent restaurants and hotels. On the northern edge is the **Estación de Ferrocarril**, the city's railway station, defunct in terms of public transport but now serving as an exhibition centre (Mon–Fri 7am–5pm; free). There are occasional classical music recitals held here at weekends. The one train still in operation departs from a station adjacent to the Jardín Botánico (see below): the old **steam engine** *Sapucai* heads out to the town of Areguá (see p.771) every second Sunday (☎021/447-848; Gs100,000). This enjoyable journey not only transports you to another place but another time, with ticket collectors in period dress and actors posing as passengers.

Outside the city centre

Winding its way northeast from the centre around the bay, Avenida General Artigas arrives at the **Jardín Botánico** (daily 7am–darkness; Gs5000; bus #24 or 35 from Cerro Corá). Once the López family estate, today the gardens are open to the public. Set around the banks of the river, there are trails through the trees and a small, rather distressing zoo of native wildlife. Inside the gardens, the **Museo de Historia Natural** (Mon–Sat 8am–6pm, Sun 8am–1pm; free) houses an unkempt collection of natural history displays in the colonial-style former home of Carlos Antonio López. The nearby house of his son, Mariscal Francico Solano López, contains the **Museo Indigenista** (same hours; free), with modest displays of pre-Colombian tools and other artefacts.

Three blocks from Shopping del Sol at Grabadores del Cabichui, the **Museo del Barro** (Thurs–Fri 3.30–8pm; Gs8000), is jam-packed with fascinating bits and pieces, both historical and contemporary, which give an alternative look at Paraguayan life and culture. Continuing along Avenida Aviadores del Chaco towards the airport, you pass **Parque Ñu Guazu** on the left-hand side, a tranquil park with attractive lakes and excellent walking opportunities.

Arrival and information

Air The international airport, Silvio Pettirossi (☎ 021/645-444), is 15km northeast of the city along Av. España and its continuation Aviadores del Chaco. Note that due to union rules, taxi fares departing from the airport are extremely high (around Gs110,000 to central Asunción). If you arrive by day you may be better walking to the avenue outside the airport and taking a taxi from the rank in front of the airport (Gs60,000 to city centre).

Bus The two-tiered intercity bus terminal (☎ 021/551-740) at Argentina and Fernando de la Mora lies in the southeast of the city. A taxi from the terminal to the centre will cost around Gs40,000.

Tourist information The tourist office (☎ 021/491-230; daily 7am–7pm), at De la Palma 468 and Juan Bautista Alberdi, is packed with maps and information – make the most of it, as it's one of the very few *turismos* in Paraguay.

Tour operators DTP, at Gral. Bruguez 353 and 25 de Mayo (☎ 021/221-816, ⒲ www.dtp.com.py).

City transport

Bus While the city centre is compact and easily walkable, city buses stop at all street corners. Destinations are advertised on the front of the buses and there is a flat fare of Gs2300 for most journeys. Buses #28 and 31 run along Oliva/Cerro Corá to the bus terminal.

Taxi A journey within the centre shouldn't come to more than about Gs25,000; there are ranks at the main plazas.

Accommodation

Accommodation in Asunción is generally good and affordable. The best areas for cheap, central accommodation are in the streets around the two main plazas, de los Héroes and Uruguaya; also ideally located for the main sights.

🏃 **Asunción Palace** Colon 145, corner with Estrella (☎ 021/492-215, ⒲ www.asuncion hotelpalace.com). This ornate, imposing building dates back to 1858 and the elegant rooms, with wi-fi, cable TV and minibar, are far more affordable than the hotel's appearance suggests. Breakfast included. Gs200,0000.

Black Cat Hostal Eligio Ayala 129, between Yegros and Indepencia Nacional ☎ 021/449-827. Paraguay's only bona fide hostel, this newcomer features funky decor, comfy dorm beds, a relaxed bar and welcome extras such as wi-fi, cable TV and DVDs. The friendly staff can arrange trips and tours. Breakfast included. Dorms Gs67,000.

Plaza Dr. Eligio Ayala and Paraguarí ☎ 021/444-196. A well-established hotel with dated but fully equipped rooms, an excellent buffet breakfast and a great location overlooking Plaza Uruguaya, next to the old railway station. GS150,000.

🏃 **Portal del Sol** Av. Dennis Roa 1455 and Sta Teresa ☎ 021/609-395, ⒲ www .hotelportaldelsol.com. Handy for the Shopping del Sol and the Museo del Barro, this is an excellent 4-star hotel with 3-star prices, boasting stone-clad rooms, a pleasant courtyard with waterfall and pool, and free internet access for guests. Gs240,000.

Preciado Dr. Félix de Azara 840 ☎ 021/447-661. Located three blocks southeast of Plaza Uruguaya, the *Preciado* is handily placed for the city's best nightlife, without ever getting noisy. Modern and spotless, and run by friendly, helpful staff, it offers rooms with cable TV, a/c and marble bathrooms. The price also includes a buffet breakfast and use of a small swimming pool. Gs180,000.

Eating

If you want a cheap, filling feed, you'll find that the food in the shopping malls (see below) is often surprisingly good. For cheap eats and *comida típica*, head out to Avenida Francisco Acuña de Figueroa, known locally as La Quinta Avenida, which is lined with enough possibilities to satisfy even the fussiest of eaters – though it's a taxi ride from the centre.

Almicar Estados Unidos 1734 and Quinta Avenida. Serving fast food with a Paraguayan flavour, *Almicar* is the place to head for if you want affordable portions of *comida típica*. Try the *Pajaguá Mascada* (translated from Guaraní it means "what the dog chewed"), a delicious meat pattie that costs Gs5000.

Lido Bar Av. Mariscal José Felix Estigarribia and Chile. Located right in front of the Panteón de los Héroes, *Lido Bar* is a popular meeting place for locals. It has a café-style interior and the menu includes some typical dishes, including *sopa Paraguaya* (Gs7000) and Chipa Guazu (Gs8000). Open daily 7.30am–1am.

Rodizio Palma 591 and 14 de Mayo. Brazilian-style buffet with a huge range of quality grilled meats, salads, pastas and pizzas. A set price of Gs57,000 buys you as much food as you can handle. Open daily 11am–3.30pm & 7.30–10.30pm.

Taberna Española Ayolas 631 ☎021/441-743. Excellent tapas, hearty portions of paella and flowing *sangría* at this extremely welcoming Spanish restaurant. Mains from Gs25,000. Open daily 11.30am–2.30pm & 7.30–10.30pm.

La Vida Verde Palma and 15 de Agosto. Excellent vegetarian Chinese buffet. Interesting tofu dishes, sushi and fresh veggies make it a great place to detox if you have been overdoing the *asados*. Gs28,000 per kilo. Open Mon–Fri 7.30am-2.30pm, Sat until 1.30pm.

Drinking and nightlife

Asunción has a thriving nightlife, especially at weekends. Things only really get going around midnight but a recent change in municipal law means that alcohol is no longer served after 2am. In the centre, the blocks east of Plaza Uruguaya are where most of the action is. For more upmarket options head out to Paseo Carmelitas off Avenida España.

Asunción Rock Mariscal Estigarribia and Tacuary. Wacky rock hangout, packed with revellers at weekends. What with the ample dancefloor and bustling bars, you'll hardly notice the unusual choice of decor, which includes a car apparently crashing out of a wall.

Boehemia Legión Civil Extranjero and Av. España. Trendy and yes, you guessed it, bohemian hangout in Barrio Manorá. Offers a wide cocktail menu and live alternative music most nights.

Britannia Pub Cerro Corá and Tacuary. Ever popular with travellers and locals alike, *Britannia* offers English pub grub, beer and Britpop music to a cosmopolitan crowd and even has its own brand of beer. Unlike most Asunción nightspots it's busy on weeknights and the action starts earlier than elsewhere. While there's also a pleasant outdoor courtyard and bar, the indoor seating is limited – a problem if it rains.

Café Literario Av. Mariscal José Felix Estigarribia and México. A laid-back café-bar in a former convent, this is a chilled place to enjoy a quiet drink during the day, though things liven up after the sun goes down.

Flow Manzana T. and Av. Mariscal Francisco S. López. With a pub-style atmosphere, cheap beer, delicious pizzas and pop music blaring from oversized speakers, *Flow* is popular with a younger crowd. Open daily 6pm–2am.

Kilkenny Paseo Carmelitas and Av. España. Every city must have one, and this is a typical faux-Irish bar with drunken revelry guaranteed. In keeping with its trendy surroundings, though, the prices are higher than in central Asunción.

Shopping

Arts and crafts Try the tourist office on De la Palma or Folklore at Palma and Iturbe.

Shopping malls Asunción has several US-style malls including Shopping del Sol, at Av. Aviadores del Chaco, the largest shopping mall in the country. Alternatively, try Shopping Excelsior, at Nuestra Señora de la Asunción and Manduvirá.

Directory

Banks and exchange Lloyds TSB is at Palma and Juán O'Leary and has an ATM. Palma is full of casas de cambio; shop around for the best rates.

Bookshops A series of bookshops are on the Plaza Uruguaya. Books, in the Shopping del Sol, sells a variety of English-language titles.

Car rental Renta Car, at Aeropuerto Internacional Silvio Pettirossi (℡ 021/646-083, ☺ www.rentacar .com.py).

Embassies and consulates Argentina, Av. España and Perú (℡ 021/212-320); Brazil, Gral Díaz 521 3rd floor (℡ 021/444-088); Canada, Prof. Ramirez y J. de Salazar ℡ 021/227-207); UK, Av. Boggiani 5848 (℡ 021/612-611); USA, Av. Mariscal Francisco S. López 1776 (℡ 021/213-715).

Internet Countless options all around the city, with several along Palma. Also Cyber-Net Mall, at Chile y Manduvira (9am–9pm); and X-Zone Cyber, at Dr Paiva y coronel Lopez Sanjonia (9am–11pm).

Pharmacy Catedral, on the Plaza de Armas at Palma and Independencia Nacional.

Post office Central branch at Juan Bautista Alberdi and Presidente Franco.

Moving on

Air Brazilian airline TAM (☺ www.tam.com.br) offers flights from Asunción to Buenos Aires, Santiago, Santa Cruz, Cochabamba, São Paulo and Rio de Janeiro, while Bolivian operator Aerosur (☺ www.aerosur.com) has flights, via connections, to many other South American destinations.

Bus Long-distance buses depart from the bus terminal's upper tier to destinations across Paraguay and into Bolivia and Argentina, including Buenos Aires (8 daily; 21hr); Ciudad del Este (hourly; 4hr 30min); Concepción (hourly; 7hr); Encarnación (hourly; 5hr 30min); Filadelfia/Loma Plata (2–4 daily; 8hr); Pilar (13 daily; 5hr).

DAY-TRIPS FROM ASUNCIÓN

Respite from the urban jungle of Asunción is easier than you might imagine, and just a short distance from the city limits the pace of life slows to a more typically Paraguayan tempo.

The lushness of the area is striking, the green vegetation com.. with the brick-red clay soils to create ₋ textbook image of fertile South America. Ruta 2 heads east out of Asunción, passing the cool waters of **Lago Ypacaraí** and its surrounding resort towns, all of which are easily visited on public transport as a day-trip from Asunción.

Itaguá

Straddling the *ruta* east of Asunción, **ITAGUÁ** is a picturesque town and the home of *ñandutí* (spiderweb) lace, fine early examples of which can be seen at the **Museo San Rafael** (daily 8am–6pm; free). Visit in July to catch the annual Festival de Ñandutí. Three blocks east of the plaza is the **Mercado Municipal**, where you can buy quality lace. Buses depart roughly every hour from platforms 31–35 from Asunción's main terminal.

Areguá

A pleasant town located among the cool hills above the lake, 7km north of Ruta 2 at Km 20, **AREGUÁ** is noted for its ceramics, and is the choice destination for Asunción day-trippers; it becomes crowded from December to February. Hourly buses leave from Asunción's main bus terminal, but a more enjoyable way to get here is on the tourist train (see p.768).

San Bernardino

From Areguá, short boat trips run at weekends in summer (times and price depend on demand) to the shady village of **SAN BERNARDINO**, on the eastern shore of the lake. Prices here are higher than elsewhere as it's favoured by Asunción's wealthier residents, but the surrounding mix of valleys and wooded slopes make for some fantastic walking. Buses depart roughly every hour from platform 36 from Asunción's main terminal.

...ón

Central Circuit, Ruta 2 ...east on to the crossroads of ...Oviedo. A major transport cent... and meeting point of four main *rutas*, it is depressingly bereft of interest and not somewhere to be stranded. North of here is the gorgeous, tranquil **Laguna Blanca**, while to the south along Ruta 8 lies the well-kept town of **Villarrica**, and east along Ruta 7 is the consumer-driven mayhem of **Ciudad del Este** – crossing point for Brazil and the Iguazú Falls. Ecotourists will want to seek out the **Itaipú Reserves** and the world-famous **Mbaracayú Forest Reserve**.

LAGUNA BLANCA

The crystal-clear **LAGUNA BLANCA** is named for its white sandy substrate, visible even in the deepest parts of the lake. Completely unspoilt (the water is clean enough to drink), it is one of Paraguay's best-kept secrets, its comparative isolation meaning that few people make it out here to enjoy the white-sand beaches, kayak in the lake or ride a horse over the plains. Over 25 square kilometres of pristine *cerrado* habitat – the native South American grasslands – surround the lake. Though for much of the year *cerrado* vegetation can appear brown and lifeless, it springs to life during the rainy season (Sept–Nov), when plants rapidly come into bloom and a patchwork of colours dots the landscape.

Laguna Blanca is also a must for **birdwatchers**, as no fewer than twelve globally threatened bird species are found here, including the Lesser Nothura (a small partridge-like bird) and the White-winged Nightjar, one of the world's rarest birds. Maned wolves are also present, as are other large mammals such as puma and peccary – your best chances of seeing them are by taking a night drive.

Wildlife enthusiasts may wish to visit **Para La Tierra**, a conservation project led by a team of professional scientists. As well as offering visitors a bed for the night and transport from Santa Rosa del Aguaray (see below for details), the organization runs volunteer and internship programmes. See ⓦ www.paralatierra .org for more information.

Arrival and information

Bus Take any bus from Asunción to San Pedro or Pedro Juan Caballero (4–8hr depending on operator) and get off at the town of Santa Rosa del Aguaray. From here, a local bus (3 daily; 30min–2hr) passes in front of the entrance to Para La Tierra's office.

Tours Guided ecotours are available through the Encarnación-based Fauna Paraguay (ⓦ www .faunaparaguay.com).

Accommodation

Para La Tierra ☏ 0985/260-074, ⓦ www .paralatierra.org. Basic but comfortable accommodation at this conservation project. Beds must be booked at least a day In advance. Gs120,000 per person, including meals and local pick-up. There is also camping at the site (Gs80,000 per tent).

CIUDAD DEL ESTE

Commercial, tacky, frequently intimidating and occasionally sordid, **CIUDAD DEL ESTE** is a shock to the system for many entering Paraguay for the first time – you may be forgiven for considering turning round and heading straight back to Brazil. Founded in 1957 as Puerto Presidente Stroessner (the city dropped the link to the hated dictator almost as soon as he fell from power), it grew rapidly as the control centre for the **Itaipú Dam**. Capitalizing on its position on the Brazilian border, the town provides cheap **duty-free** – and frequently contraband – goods to a public hungry for bargains. In recent years customs has tightened the net on the *contrabandistas*, but Ciudad del Este remains one of the best places on the continent for purchasing cheap electronic goods.

Though the city suburbs are pleasant enough, its relative modernity means that Ciudad del Este has little in the way of sights of it own. The surrounding area, however, contains some of Paraguay's biggest attractions, including the dam and numerous nature reserves (see p.774).

Arrival and information

Air The airport, 30km west of town on Ruta 7, has irregular flights from Asunción, as well as nearby destinations in Brazil and Argentina, but suffers from frequent unexplained cancellations. A taxi to most points in the city will be around Gs60,000.

Bus The bus terminal (☎061/510-421) is some way south of the centre on Chaco Boreal y Capitán del Puerto, adjacent to the Club 3 de Febrero soccer stadium. Taxis from here run into the centre.

Tourist information The tourist office (daily 7am–7pm; ☎061/511-626) is in the Edificio Libano on Coronel Franco and Pampliega. It can provide a map of the city as well as information regarding day-trips to the Itaipú Dam and other nearby attractions.

Accommodation

Mid-range accommodation in Ciudad del Este is widely available, but very cheap options are frequently seedy. Avoid the area around the bus station and head for the cluster of decent hotels that line Emiliano R. Fernández, two blocks north of the *ruta* near the bridge.

Austria Emiliano R. Fernandez ☎061/500-883, ⓦwww.hotelaustriarestaurante .com. Excellent rooms with TV, minibar and a spacious terrace with majestic views out over the river. German is spoken and the price includes a breakfast so mammoth it has to be seen to be believed. Gs160,000.

Munich Emiliano R. Fernández and Capitán Miranda ☎061/500-347. Neat, tidy and efficient, *Munich* offers excellent value and spacious rooms, as well as secure parking. Gs170,000.

Venecia Emiliano R. Fernandez 209 ☎061/500-375. Rooms are basic but spacious and have a/c and cable TV. Buffet breakfast included. Gs135,000.

Eating

Some of the best places to eat are outside the centre in the more attractive suburbs, especially along Avenida del Lago. The city has a proliferation of excellent Asian restaurants and a number of gems offering *comida tipica*.

Al Carbón Av. Teniente Armada, 100m from the bus terminal. Absolutely enormous burgers – the "Extrema" (Gs20,000) is big enough for two. Great place to refuel while you are waiting for a bus. Mains from Gs30,000.

Faraone y Heladería Mitai Av. Rogelio Benítez, in front of the Municipalidad. Actually two establishments under the same management, *Faraone* is an Italian restaurant with one of the best reputations in the city. The adjacent ice-cream parlour is just what the doctor ordered in the midday sun.

Las Delicias Carlos Antonio López and Oscar Rivas. A great place to sample exactly the kind of typical – and cheap – Paraguayan food that can be so hard to find elsewhere, including dishes like *vori vori* (corn ball soup) for Gs14,000. Menu changes daily.

Novo Tokio Pioneros Del Este and Adrian Jara (next to Arco Iris supermarket). Authentic Japanese restaurant with a good-value lunch buffet (Gs29,000 Including fresh juice and fruit salad). Open Mon–Sat 11am–2pm & 5–10pm.

Yrupe Av. Curupayta and Adrian Jara. Good pizzas and pastas, as well as an absolutely delicious *Chipa Guaza* (Gs6000). Open daily 8am–11pm.

Drinking and nightlife

The centre can be a little seedy at night, so you are best taking a taxi out to the suburbs if you are looking to party hard.

Cerca del Río Choperia Av. del Casino and 11 de Septiembre. Air-conditioned bar with a terrace offering fantastic views of the Paraná River and international bridge.

Inside Bar Eugenio A. Garay ⓦwww.insidebar .com.py. A stylish, lively nightspot where all the cool kids in Ciudad del Este hang out. Open Tues–Sat.

Shopping

Not for nothing is Ciudad del Este known as the "Supermarket of South America", and just about everything you can think of can be purchased here at prices well below market rates. The maze of shops and stalls on either side of the main *ruta*, near the border with Brazil, is where the bulk of the bargains are to be found, but the area also

CROSSING TO BRAZIL AND ARGENTINA

The Puente de la Amistad (Friendship Bridge), at the eastern end of the centre Of Ciudad del Este, marks the border with the Brazilian town of Foz do Iguaçu. Immigration formalities take place at either end of the bridge. This is Paraguay's busiest border crossing, and there are frequently huge queues of traffic waiting to cross in either direction. A local bus runs from the bus terminal to the terminal in "Foz", as it's known locally (every 15min; duration varies depending on bridge traffic; Gs6000). In many cases crossing on foot is quicker, but be sure to obtain all necessary entrance and exit stamps – it is not true that you do not need them if you are just visiting the waterfalls. Traffic police do not help matters by putting pressure on pedestrians to speed up their crossing, occasionally directing them away from the customs checkpoint.

To get to Puerto Iguazú in Argentina, catch a local bus run by El Práctico from the bus terminal (every 15min; duration varies depending on bridge traffic; Gs6000). This is an easier border crossing, but, again, be sure that your paperwork is in order.

attracts petty thieves like bees to a honeypot – do not carry valuables with you. Electronics, alcohol and perfumes provide the best deals, but beware of substandard goods and do not be afraid to haggle or barter; it is expected. Compare prices before completing any transaction and ask for the product to be tested; not all dealers are honest.

Directory

Banks and exchange Banco do Brasil at Nanawa 107 and Monseñor Rodríguez; Interbanco at Av. San Blas 122 and Patricio Colmán.
Car rental Avis office at the airport (☎061/504-770).
Hospital Fundación Tesai on Av. Caballero behind the bus terminal.
Post office Alejo Garcia and Centro Democrático (Mon–Fri 7am–6pm, Sat 7am–noon).

Moving on

Air Brazilian airline TAM (ⓦwww.tam.com.br) operates direct flights from Ciudad del Este to São Paulo, Buenos Aires and Asunción.
Bus Asunción (hourly; 4hr 30min); Encarnación (hourly, 4hr 30min); Foz do Iguaçu (every 15min, 1hr); Puerto Iguazú (every 15min, 1hr).

AROUND CIUDAD DEL ESTE

The number-one reason for staying in Ciudad del Este is to visit the **Itaipú Dam**, the second-largest dam in the world and an extraordinary engineering feat. The Itaipú Dam company also oversees the management of eight **small nature reserves** in the area immediately north of Ciudad del Este. Representing the last refuges of the once extensive Alto Paraná Atlantic Forest, most of which was washed away by the dam-related flooding, these reserves harbour important populations of endangered wildlife including jaguar, Bush dog and marsh deer. None, though, are as famous as the **Mbaracayú Forest Reserve**, listed by the WWF as one of the hundred most important natural areas on earth and home to hundreds of bird species.

Salto de Monday

If Iguazú has given you a taste for waterfalls, then you'll **SALTO DE MONDAY** (pronounced Mon-da-oo), 10km south of the city, find worth a visit. At 80m high, the falls here are a stunning natural feature, though they suffer from being so close to their more famous and spectacular neighbours across the border. A return taxi from Ciudad del Este costs around Gs60,000.

Itaipú Dam

Sited 20km north of Ciudad del Este (taxi Gs60,000 return, or take bus marked "Hernandarias" from the terminal, Gs5000), **ITAIPÚ** was once referred to as one of the seven wonders of the modern world. With a maximum height of 195m and generating up to 75,000GWh of energy per year, it's still something to behold. Visits are by **guided tour only** (daily on the hour 8am–4pm; Gs50,000, passport required) and last about 90 minutes. A short documentary is shown before the tour begins.

The highlight of the trip is the opportunity to see the inside of the dam and the colossal 1km-long machine room. The project's backers were forced to invest heavily in ecological damage limitation projects, which led to the establishment of the nature reserves (see below) as well as the **Flora and Fauna Itaipú Binacional** (9am–5pm; free; ☎061/599-8652), a few kilometres south of the dam's entrance and easily reached by taxi. An excellent zoo by South American standards, it was set up to house animals rescued from the flooding, including a rare black jaguar and a breeding colony of Bush dogs. It also contains well-maintained natural history and archeological museums (same hours; free).

Itaipú reserves

The most accessible of the reserves is **Refugio Tati Yupi**, 26km north of Ciudad del Este. Its clear natural pools and waterfalls, bicycle and horse-riding trails and decent tourist infrastructure have made it popular with weekend visitors from the city; as such it's best visited during the week if you actually want to see animals. If you are serious about wildlife a better bet is **Itabó**, some 100km from the city (approximately a third of which is dirt road). This is one of the larger reserves and is one of the last strongholds of the endangered Vinaceous-breasted Amazon parrot.

You will need your own vehicle to get the most out of the Itaipú reserves, as well as **prior permission** from the Flora and Fauna Itaipú Binacional

(see above). It may take a day or two to process your permits, so plan in advance. Basic dorm **accommodation** is available free of charge, but you will have to bring and prepare your own food. Alternatively, all the reserves can be visited on a day-trip from Ciudad del Este, though you will not be allowed to enter before 7.30am and must leave before 10pm if you are not staying the night. For guided day-trips in Spanish only, contact Nelson Pérez of the Itaipú Dam company (✉guajaki@gmail.com).

Mbaracayú Forest Reserve

MBARACAYÚ FOREST RESERVE remains a model for conservation in Paraguay, consisting of a patchwork of Atlantic Forest and *cerrado* habitat, criss-crossed by snaking streams and with populations of large mammals such as jaguars and tapirs. More than four hundred **bird species** have been recorded here, and from September to February the ear-splitting call of Paraguay's national bird, the Bare-throated Bellbird, rings out across the forest canopy.

Prior to travelling you should arrange your visit with the **Fundación Moisés Bertoni** (Prócer Carlos Argüello 208; ☎021/608-740, 🌐www.mbertoni.org.py), which will provide you with the paperwork necessary for entry into the reserve (Gs50,000) and instructions on how to get there. **Accommodation** (Gs150,000) is available at the Jejui-Mi base camp, where there are a couple of double rooms and some dorms, all with shared bathroom and a well-equipped kitchen.

The reserve can be accessed with difficulty by **public transport** – you will need to take an Empresa Paraguarí bus to the town of Ygatimi, where you should arrange to be picked up by FMB forest guards to take you to the reserve. Whether you have your own vehicle or not, you will need to bring all your own food and drink for your stay.

South of Asunción

The main road south of the capital is Ruta 1, following a rather convoluted route to the border city of **Encarnación**. Along the way it passes a number of small towns, some with colourful histories, though none except **Villa Florida** is worthy of more than a passing visit. The south of the country is where the former Jesuit missions were concentrated: several sites are worth exploring, notably the *reducciones* at **Jesús** and **Trinidad**. Wildlife enthusiasts will not want to miss **Parque Nacional San Rafael**, the country's most biodiverse reserve.

VILLA FLORIDA

Located where Ruta 1 crosses a bend in the Río Tebicuary, and en route for buses between Encarnación and Asunción, **VILLA FLORIDA** is the closest that Paraguay comes to a beach resort, since when the river is not in flood, it is flanked by glorious white-sand beaches. Aside from the beaches there's not much to do – unless you visit during Easter week, when the nation's youth gathers to hold impromptu all-night raves.

Cheap if unspectacular **accommodation** is available at *Hotel La Misionera* (☎083/240-215; Gs70,000) near the beach, but a better option if you are in a group is to rent a house along the riverfront (around Gs100,000; ask around for options). You can get a half-decent feed at the *Parador* next to the bridge, which has a pleasant garden with river views.

ENCARNACIÓN

ENCARNACIÓN is Paraguay's wealthiest city outside of the capital and has a laidback modernity that makes it instantly likeable. Founded in 1615 by Beato Roque González under the title of Nuestra Señora de la Encarnación de Itapúa, today – despite a population of just under seventy thousand – Encarnación qualifies as the third-largest city in Paraguay. San Roque had long been considered the Patron Saint of Encarnación, even before he was officially beatified in 1988, becoming Paraguay's first official saint in the process. The city's other famous son was the less than saintly dictator Alfredo Stroessner, born here in 1912. His former residence (now a neurological hospital) is near the bus station at Carlos Antonio López and Jorge Memmel.

What to see and do

Though many visitors use Encarnación as little more than a base to visit the Jesuit ruins, the city has some sights of note and is at its best during the Carnaval in February (see box, p.778), which draws thousands of visitors from across the continent for four weekends of rampant hedonism.

Centre of life in the Zona Alta is the **Plaza de Armas**, a spacious and attractive tree-lined square split into several "gardens" that pay homage to the various immigrant groups in the city. Two blocks further towards the river, the **Casa de la Victoria** at General Artigas and Cerro Corá (Mon–Fri 8–11.30am & 2–5pm; free), is a small but interesting museum displaying artefacts from the Chaco War, with the emphasis on the contribution by local soldiers. The **first railway line in South America** ran between Asunción and Encarnación, and, incredibly, one of the first trains to use it, the *Carlos Antonio López*, is still in active service. Today it is a goods train and the best place to see it is in front of the **Feria Municipal** on Avenida Coronel Luis Irrazábal.

Encarnación's decaying old port area, the Zona Baja, was largely flooded by the Yacyretá dam in 2010, with bars and restaurants expected to spring up along the new waterfront.

EATING & DRINKING

La Estación	4
Hiroshima	2
Karumbé	6
Novo Rodeio	8
La Piccolla Italia	1
Pizza El Crocante	5
Planeta Lomito	3
Casino Carnaval	7

ACCOMMODATION

Hotel Acuario	B
Hotel de la Costa	C
Hotel Germano	D
Hotel Tirol	A
Hotel Vienna	E

0   200 m

▼ **8**, Feria Municipal & Paraguayan Customs

Arrival and information

Bus Most visitors arrive at the bus terminal at General Cabañas y Mariscal Estigarribia – from here it's uphill six blocks to the Plaza de Armas (the town centre). If you're coming from Argentina you'll arrive at the San Roque González International Bridge in the south of the city.

Tourist information There is a tourist information office at customs, but it is rarely open.

Tour operators Fauna Paraguay (ⓦ www.faunaparaguay.com). Professional, expert-led ecotours to nature-rich destinations such as the Chaco and Paraguayan Pantanal.

City transport

Taxi Bordered on three sides by broad avenues, central Encarnación is easily walkable, though if it's hot you may prefer to take a taxi. There is a taxi rank at the bus terminal and another at the Plaza de Armas, or you can call a radio taxi (ⓣ071/202-420). No journey within the city should cost more than Gs25,000.

Accommodation

Book ahead during Carnaval, when prices rise considerably. Avoid the hotels around the bus terminal (except *Germano*) and those along Tómas Romero Pereira in the centre. The former attract an undesirable clientele, the latter have serious noise issues at weekends.

Acuario Juan L. Mallorquín and Villarrica ⓣ071/202-676. Central, secure and offering good value for money, this hotel makes up for its characterless rooms with friendly service and an Olympic-size indoor swimming pool hidden behind a door. Gs110,000.

De la Costa Av. Francia and Cerro Corá ⓣ071/200-590. If you are looking to splash out without breaking the bank then this is your best bet. Has an outdoor pool, pleasant gardens and a distinctly affordable luxury suite (Gs300,000) complete with jacuzzi and breakfast in bed. Gs180,000.

Germano General Cabañas and Mariscal Estigarribia ⓣ071/203-346. Conveniently located right in front of the bus station, this is the city's best-value budget option. It is basic, but with en-suite bath and ceiling fan, it's a good place to get your head down

Around 20km east of Encarnación, just past the town of Capitán Miranda, is Hotel Tirol (☎071/202-388, ⓦwww.hoteltirol.com.py; Gs250,000), a favourite of the King of Spain. The valley of Atlantic Forest within its grounds is home to capuchin monkeys and some 190 bird species. There are four swimming pools, plus a majestic view of the forest canopy from the hotel bar. Even if you don't stay here, you can use the pools and walk around the forest for a minimal fee (Gs10,000). All buses heading between Encarnación and Ciudad del Este pass the hotel entrance, or alternatively take local bus line 1y2 Capitán Miranda, which passes every 15min along General Artigas in Encarnación, terminating 100m from the hotel entrance.

for the night if you've an early bus to catch in the morning. Gs80,000.

Vienna General Pedro Juan Caballero 658 ☎071/203-486. Cheap as chips, but dodgy decor and a location in a distinctly uninteresting part of town mean this hotel is best left to those on a tight budget. Gs70,000.

Eating

There is surprisingly good eating to be had in Encarnación if you look for it. The multi-cultural population offers up a smorgasbord of different eating options, as well as the traditional *asados* and fast food. The Super 6 supermarket does a good range of pay-by-weight salads and mains for around Gs27,000 per kilo. Most restaurants are open 11am–9pm daily.

Hiroshima 25 de Mayo and Lomas Valentinas. This is your chance to sample sushi Paraguayan-style. Good service, fresh ingredients and excellent quality for this price. Mains Gs25–35,000.

Karumbé Mariscal Estigarribia and Tomás Romero Pereira. Named after the traditional yellow horse-drawn cart, a uniquely *Encarnaceno* form of transport that you are likely to see around town, *Karumbé* offers a diverse menu including fish dishes – try the grilled *surubí*. If you're not hungry just chug a beer on the outdoor tables and watch the world go by. Salads from Gs15,000, meat and fish mains Gs45,000–80,000. Open Sun–Thurs 11am–midnight, Fri–Sat 11am–1am.

Novo Rodeio Av. San Roque González, near the international bridge. Brazilian-style all-you-can-eat grill and buffet. If you can resist the allure of the succulent barbecued meats roasting over hot coals on the *parrilla*, give your arteries a rest by sampling some of the huge variety of innovative salads on offer. Price per person around Gs35,000.

La Piccola Italia Ruta 1 and Posadas. Faux Mediterranean surroundings and a cheery Paraguayan/Italian host at this popular trattoria. Pig out on huge portions of quasi-authentic pizza and pasta – one plate is easily enough for two. Mains around Gs15,000.

Pizza El Crocante Tomás Romero Pereira and General Artigas. This place doesn't look like much, but these are some of the best and cheapest pizzas in Paraguay. Pizza for two around Gs20,000.

CARNAVAL

For most Paraguayans, Encarnación is synonymous with Carnaval, a spectacular celebration transforming the city into a whirlpool of frivolity during the first three weekends of February. Things begin to hot up during the week with bands of children roaming the streets armed with spray-snow and water balloons, looking to make a fool out of the unwary, but the main events are the weekend *corsos* (parades) along the Avenida Francia. The *corso* is opened by the *Rey Momo*, an elected local man who is usually tall and fat, and whose job it is to whip the crowd into a frenzy. Each neighbourhood of the city is represented by its *comparza*, a group of dancers, performers and hangers-on, who compete to impress the *jurado* (judges) with the outrageousness of their costumes, the animation of their dancing and overall fluidity of the spectacle. The action begins around 9pm each night and lasts through to the early hours, but tickets, sold at the entrance on Avenida Francia, (Gs20–50,000) sell out rapidly and you'll need to get there early to claim a good seat.

Planeta Lomito Lomas Valentinas y Villarino. Junk food at its best; this place is open until the early hours of the morning and is a popular twilight meeting place for weekend revellers winding down after a night out. Make sure you give the *Lomito Arabe* – essentially a meaty kebab – a try. Mains Gs7000–10,000. Open daily 10am–2am.

Drinking and nightlife

Encarnación suffers from an ephemeral nightlife in which bars open and close with alarming regularity – ask around for the latest hot spot. On warm evenings the local youth gather around the Plaza de la Ciudad on Avenida Francia with cool-boxes full of beers and loud music pumping from their car stereos.

Casino Carnaval Avenida Coronel Luis Irrazábal. Live music every night at this popular bar, music venue and casino. Music genre varies nightly. Open 24hr.

La Estación Avenida Francia. Among a cluster of drinking options on this street, *La Estación* is the most established, and the vast space holds regular high-profile events at weekends, with live big-name DJs attracting a young, dressed-up crowd.

Directory

Banks and exchange Amambay and Interbanco on the Plaza de Armas both have ATMs.
Hospital Clínica Tajy at General Artigas y Constitución.
Internet Countless options around town. Pya'e, where Tomás Romero Pereira meets the Plaza, has a good connection (Gs3000– 4000 per hr).
Post office Central branch opposite the Sanatorio Itapúa on Juan L.Mallorquín and Constitución.
Spanish school Master Key Institute, at Galería San Jorge, Mariscal Estigarribia y Curupayty

---

CROSSING TO ARGENTINA

A bus to the terminal in Posadas, Argentina, runs from Juan L.Mallorquín in Encarnación, one block west from the Plaza de Armas, every 15min (5am–11pm; 1hr; Gs5000). Don't forget to get off the bus at both ends of the bridge for customs formalities. The bus won't wait for you to get your stamps, but your ticket remains valid for the next service.

(☎0985/778-198), runs unique open-air Spanish courses for all levels, with nearby tourist attractions replacing the classroom, and a five-day course coming in at Gs750,000G; pre-booking is essential.

Moving on

Bus Asunción (hourly; 5hr 30min); Ciudad del Este (6 daily; 4hr 30min); Posadas (every 15min; 1hr).

AROUND ENCARNACIÓN

As the heartland of the Jesuit Missions, southern Paraguay is home to some of the best-preserved **Jesuit ruins** (*reducciones*). The most famous of these is **Trinidad**, an easy day-trip from Asunción. The country's largest remaining block of humid Atlantic Forest is at **Parque Nacional San Rafael**, the most biodiverse area in Paraguay and as such its most important protected area. Despite concern over the reserve's future (see below), it remains one of the most beautiful and easily accessed natural areas in the country.

Trinidad

The Jesuit *reducción* of **Trinidad** (daily 7am–7pm; Gs40,000), 28km east of Encarnación, is located on the main *ruta* to Ciudad del Este and any bus between the two cities passes right in front – get off at the slightly out-of-place power station, on your right when heading east. A hilltop settlement and UNESCO World Heritage Site, the partially restored church (which is for the most part roofless) is filled with fantastically ornate stone carvings of religious figurines. Bilingual **guides** are available at around Gs10,000 and are worth paying for, as there is a distinct lack of visitor information.

Parque Nacional San Rafael

Though designated as a national park in 1992, all of the land within **Parque Nacional San Rafael** still remains in private hands. This has created a conflict of interest between landowners, conservationists and indigenous groups in the area, each of which has legitimate claims to the tenure. A government promise to buy out the landowners has not been acted upon due to a perpetual lack of funds, and the long-term conservation of San Rafael is far from secure. Local NGOs such as Pro Cosara – whom you should inform of any visit in advance – try to ensure that environmental law in the area is upheld.

That said, San Rafael remains one of the true highlights of Paraguay, where nature abounds against a spectacularly verdant backdrop. Over four hundred bird species exist here, including many endemic to the Atlantic Forest biome. You can expect to see trogons, toucans, tanagers, tinamous and hummingbirds during walks in the forest, and jaguar and tapir are still present in the area.

Arrival and information

Bus A bumpy bus run by Empresa Pastoreo departs daily from Encarnación at 8am and 11.30am (3hr). Ask the driver to drop you off at the town of Ynambú where, if you've notified Pro Cosara, you will be met by a 4x4 to take you to the reserve.

North of Asunción

Crossing the Río Paraguay, the main route north from the capital is Ruta 1, a long and uneventful drive to the cross-roads of Pozo Colorado at the gateway to the Chaco. Ruta 9 – the "Trans-Chaco" – continues north to Filadelfia and the Mennonite colonies, while the dramatic and beautiful Ruta 5 heads east through glorious countryside in which wildlife abounds. The main towns along here are **Concepción** on the Río Paraguay and **Pedro Juan Caballero** on the border with Brazil. The only reason to visit the latter is as a base for visiting the nearby **Parque Nacional Cerro Corá** – it is not

recommended that you try to cross to Brazil here, as it's a smuggling route.

CONCEPCIÓN

A colourful port town on the eastern bank of the Río Paraguay, **CONCEPCIÓN** is the main trading centre in the north of the country. More recently it has become popular with tourists as a centre for uncomfortable but picturesque **river trips** along the Río Paraguay (see p.781).

What to see and do

The town itself is bisected north to south by **Avenida Agustín Pinedo**, its central reservation filled with a mixed bag of industrial and agricultural machinery (called the Museo al Aire Libre). Most of the interest lies west of the Avenida around **Plaza Libertad**. An eclectic, almost Venetian-style **Catedral** (access after 5pm) overlooks the plaza, and adjacent to it is the **Museo Diocesano** (Mon–Sat 7.30–11.30am; free), packed with religious paraphernalia. Two blocks east along Estigarribia is a series of charming **mansion houses** that now operate as municipal buildings. A pastel blue mansion dating from 1898 houses the council headquarters, while the delightful honey-coloured Mansión Otaño (1940) is used by the public works department.

Arrival and information

Bus Buses arrive at the terminal on Garal, eight blocks north of the town centre. There is no functional tourist office and no map of the town, but the centre is small and you'll soon know your way around.

Accommodation

The best place to look for accommodation is along Franco, west of Avenida Pinedo, which is well located for both the port and the town centre. **Center** Franco and Yegros ℗ 03312/42-360. A really cheap option, if rather unappealing on account of spartan furniture, lumpy beds and a noisy karaoke bar next door. Food at the hotel restaurant is poor. Gs60,000.

Francés Franco and Carlos Antonio López ☎03312/42-383. The best bet in town, with a great swimming pool and a buffet breakfast worthy of the price alone. Gs190,000.

Victoria Franco and Pedro Caballero ☎03312/42-256. This handsome whitewashed building may have seen better days, but it's great value, with spacious communal areas and cable TV, breakfast and a/c all included. Dorms Gs55,000, rooms Gs140,000.

Eating

Places to eat are limited, although fans of spit-roasted chicken have no end of choice.

Francès Franco and Carlos Antonio López. A hotel with a good-value lunch buffet and à la carte evening meals including a couple of soup and pasta options for vegetarians. Mains Gs35,000–65,000.

Toninho y Jandri Mariscal Estigarribia and Iturbe, in front of the plaza. An excellent Brazilian-style *churrascaria*. A set price of Gs45,000 buys you a hearty plateful of either meat or fish, accompanied by rice, beans and salad.

Directory

Banks and exchange Avenida Franco is lined with banks, most of which have ATMs that accept international cards.

Internet Several places along Avenida Franco, including *Cybercom Internet Café*, at the corner with 14 de Mayo.

Moving on

Bus Asunción (hourly; 7hr); Pedro Juan Caballero (hourly; 4hr).

Ferry A number of ferry services leaving from the port run along the Río Paraguay to Fuerte Olimpo and Bahía Negra in the Paraguayan Pantanal. Schedules change regularly and you are advised to check latest departure times with the tourist office in Asunción (see p.769). Boats are uncomfortable, beds little more than hammocks, and you would do well to take your own food with you.

PARQUE NACIONAL CERRO CORÁ

PARQUE NACIONAL CERRO CORÁ lies 35km west of the border town of **Pedro Juan Caballero**. This 220-sq-km-kilometre park was the site

of Paraguay's final defeat in the War of the Triple Alliance and the place where Francisco Solano López (see p.768) finally met his end. The site of López's death is marked by a monument set above a small wooded brook, at one end of a long line of busts of the war leaders. At the opposite end of the line of busts is an abstract **monument to the war dead**, featuring commemorative plaques from groups as diverse as the Uruguayan Rotary Club and Brazilian Air Force. There is ample opportunity to spot rare birds and various species of monkey, but the area is best explored with a guide such as those available with Fauna Paraguay (Ⓦ www.faunaparaguay .com), as there are no marked trails and the park is not particularly visitor-friendly. Bring plenty of food and water for your trip, as there is nowhere to refuel within the park itself.

All buses between Concepción and Pedro Juan Caballero pass the park entrance, where there is an administrative office with a small wildlife museum (free) and information centre where you can ask about **camping**. More comfortable accommodation can be found in Pedro Juan Caballero at *Eiruzú*, at Mariscal López y Estigarribia (☎036/272-435; Gs295,000); there's a small pool, a lively bar/restaurant and the price includes breakfast.

Moving on

Regular buses leave Pedro Juan Cabellero for Concepción, Asunción and Ciudad del Este (duration and departure times vary).

The Chaco

The Chaco's reputation as a hot, dusty, thorny hell is only partially accurate; in reality it consists of two very different ecosystems. The first 300km or so of the **Ruta Trans-Chaco** – the long, straight highway which traverses the region – passes through the **Humid Chaco**, a flat, seasonally flooded palm savanna that teems with waterbirds at certain times of the year. The **Mennonite colonies** of the **Central Chaco** mark the transition zone from Humid to **Dry Chaco** habitat, characterized by high temperatures, a thorny forest environment and hot winds.

Vast swathes of the Chaco are uninhabited and **guided tours** are the easiest way to see the highlights, which include the stunning birdlife of the **Central Chaco Lagoons**, historically important battle sites at **Fortín Boquerón** and **Fortín Toledo**, as well as isolated, wildlife-packed national parks. Independent explorers will need a 4x4 vehicle and enough fuel, food and water for several days.

CRUCE LOS PIONEROS AND FORTÍN BOQUERÓN

The last place on the Trans-Chaco where you can guarantee that you will be able to refuel your vehicle, sleep in a hotel – *Hotel Los Pioneros* (☎04914/32-170; Gs100,000) – and have a half-decent meal is at the tiny crossroads outpost of **Cruce Los Pioneros**. It's also worth stopping to look at **Fortín Boquerón**, accessible via a turn-off on the left just as you reach Cruce Los Pioneros; the site is signposted along the way. Another Chaco War battleground, Fortín Boquerón is particularly worth a visit for its excellent museum (Tues–Sat 8am–6pm; Gs5000), featuring munitions and cannons from the conflict, as well as a poignant display of photographs and writings by the combatants. Of morbid interest is the hollowed-out tree, used as a sniper's nest by the Paraguayan army to pick off the advancing Bolivians.

FILADELFIA

FILADELFIA is the Chaco's most highly populated Mennonite settlement, and its innate "Germanness" is somewhat surprising given its dry and

---

THE MENNONITE COLONIES

The Mennonites first arrived in Paraguay in 1926, having purchased a large area of the central Chaco, which today constitutes the Mennonite colonies. They arrived in the Río Paraguay port of Puerto Casado, where they were received with much pomp and ceremony by the then-president of the Republic, Dr Eligio Ayala, who had campaigned hard to bring them to Paraguay with the aim of settling the Chaco. The following year they began their overland migration to the lands in which they hoped a better life awaited them. Their first encounters with the dry Chaco summer came as a huge shock and of the 1700 or so initial colonists, a large percentage fell victim to the heat, lack of water and disease in the early years. Those that remained suffered enormously as they tried to establish themselves in one of the world's harshest environments. Against all odds, the Mennonites have succeeded in becoming the major providers of dairy produce in the country; their beef is recognized as among the best on the continent and their settlements operate with a clinical efficiency that belies their isolated location.

The easiest way to get to the Mennonite colonies is via the turn-offs at Cruce Los Pioneros (see above) and, 50km or so further on, at Cruce Loma Plata. There are three colonies in all, each with its own administrative capital – Menno (capital Loma Plata) and Fernheim (capital Filadelfia) are the largest and most easily reached from Asunción. Unless you are a motor-racing fanatic, the area is best avoided during September when it becomes gripped with Trans-Chaco Rally fever. Billed as one of the toughest motorized events on earth, it is accompanied by a considerable hike in hotel prices and you will have to book well in advance if you want a room. For more information see ⓦwww.transchacorally.com.py.

dusty location. The perfect lawns and well-trimmed hedges may seem out of place in this harsh climate, but neatly symbolize the triumph over adversity of the original settlers.

What to see and do

Most of the action centres on the dual-laned **Avenida Hindenburg**, which bisects the town. From a tourist point of view there is relatively little to keep you occupied and the main interest lies in absorbing the colonial lifestyle of the people, built largely around dairy farming and cooperation with native populations. The **Unger Museum** (Mon–Fri 9–11.30am & 2–5pm; free) on Avenida Hindenburg is worth a brief visit. Jakob Unger was a collector of animal specimens in the Chaco from 1950 to 1975 and the fruits of his labours are housed on the second floor. The ground floor is given over to artefacts dating from the time of the colonization – the wooden building itself, known as the Casa de la Colonia, was the original headquarters of the colony.

Arrival and information

Banks and exchange There is only one ATM in Filadelfia, at Interbanco in the Portal del Chaco development. Although it accepts some foreign cards, you are strongly advised to bring enough money for your stay with you.
Bus In the absence of a bus terminal, buses arrive and depart from their own offices along Chaco Boreal, off Hindenburg.

Accommodation

Filadelfia offers some surprisingly good accommodation, with the two hotels listed below the pick of the bunch. There are no restaurants in Filadelfia so you will have to eat at one of the hotels, where buffet lunches are the norm.
Florida Hindenburg 165-S ☎ 0491/432-151, ⓦ www.hotelfloridachaco.com. Attractively laid out with a great pool and garden, the *Florida* has a range of rooms: at the higher end are spacious rooms with cable TV and minibar, while the

CROSSING TO BOLIVIA

At the small town of La Patria, a fully paved road (formerly Picada 108) now branches off the Trans-Chaco to the border crossing of Fortín Infante Rivarola. There is a small guard post here that does not have exit stamps (you should attempt to get them prior to travelling or in the small settlement of Mariscal Estigarribia en route) and the Bolivian side of the border remains unpaved and unattended. This border point is extremely isolated and a popular smuggling route so you are not advised to attempt to cross the border here by yourself. International buses (1–3 daily; 30hr) run between Asunción and Santa Cruz in Bolivia via the bus companies Yacyretá, Pycasu and Ester Turismo.

cheapest consist of little more than four walls and a bed. Its restaurant is also excellent, and even offers an entire menu dedicated to gluten-free food. Gs180,000.
Safari Industrial 149E, around the corner from *Florida* ☎ 0491/432-218. A plush option, if slightly retro (the decor is rather 1970s), with rooms boasting cable TV and a/c. Gs170,000.

Moving on

There is no public transport in the Mennonite colonies except for the bus companies that connect the towns with Asunción. Most services from Filadelfia pass through Loma Plata en route to the capital. Taxis are non-existent and there is nowhere to hire a car. Visiting on a guided tour or hiring a car in Asunción gives you much greater flexibility for further exploration.
Bus There are several daily services south to Asunción, all via Pozo Colorado, where it is possible to change for buses to Concepción. Unless you enjoy a leisurely bus ride be sure to take a direct service, as indirect services are extremely slow.

LOMA PLATA

The oldest of the Mennonite towns, **LOMA PLATA** is arranged along a similar pattern to Filadelfia, with a neat grid system of side streets arranged around a dusty central avenue. Loma Plata's main tourist attraction is the **Museo de Historia Mennonita** (daily 7am–noon & 2–6pm; free) on the main avenue. Though small, it is a fascinating documentation of the trials and tribulations that the original settlers had to overcome.

Buses from Asunción to Filadelfia pass through Loma Plata en route. One of the best places **to stay** is at the *Loma Plata Inn* (☎0492/253-235; Gs150,000), which also has a good buffet restaurant, *Chaco Grill*.

FORTÍN TOLEDO

At Km 475 a rough road runs 9km south to **FORTÍN TOLEDO**. An important Chaco war site with a combatants' cemetery and well-preserved vestiges of trenches, it is perhaps more often visited for the peccary breeding project **Proyecto Taguá**. The principal objective of the project – overseen by San Diego Zoo – is the reintroduction into the wild of the Chaco peccary (*taguá*), a pig-like animal that was known only from fossil remains until its remarkable discovery alive and well in the Paraguayan Chaco in 1976. Today all three known species are bred here, the *taguá* being the largest and shyest species, and the other two being the bad-tempered white-lipped (*tañykati*) and the mild-mannered collared (*kure'i*). Check out the aggressive threat displays of the male white-lipped – releasing a foul-smelling fluid before dashing towards and gnashing its enormous jaws together. The project launched in 1985 with just three animals, and more than 250 *taguá* have now been released into the wild.

No public transport passes Fortín Toledo, but drivers will find the site well-signposted off the Trans-Chaco.

CENTRAL CHACO LAGOONS

Correctly known as the Cuenca del Upper Yacaré Sur lagoons, the **CENTRAL CHACO LAGOONS**, as they are more commonly called, are a series of temporary saline lakes east of the Mennonite colonies. Because of their importance for migrating waterbirds they have been declared an "Important Bird Area" or IBA. The amount of water in the lagoons depends greatly on rainfall in previous months; they may be dry for several years before suddenly filling with water again in favourable conditions. In winter they may be occupied by ducks and Chilean flamingos, while during the southbound migration for Nearctic waterbirds (Sept–Dec), huge flocks of sandpipers and plovers are attracted to the water.

Probably the best place to base yourself nearby is Lagung Capitán (☎0991/650-101; Gs60,000 per person), a Mennonite holiday resort around 30km from Lomo Plata, where there is comfortable shared accommodation. The gardens here throng with birdlife and grey brocket deer, while armadillos and capybara are common nearby. To see the lagoons, head to the **Reserva Privada Campo María**, which hosts tapir and peccary as well as birdlife. There is a Gs10,000 entry fee, payable at the house at the entrance to the reserve.

PARQUE NACIONAL TENIENTE ENCISO

In the highest part of the High Chaco, almost at the Bolivian border, **PARQUE NACIONAL TENIENTE ENCISO** (Enciso for short) is the most accessible of the Chaco protected areas. Basic **accommodation** is available at the visitor centre with running water, 24hr electricity, a passable kitchen and even air conditioning in some rooms (Gs100,000) and should be arranged in advance with environment agency SEAM (🌐www.seam.gov.py), or through a tour agency such as Fauna Paraguay (🌐www.faunaparaguay.com).

The reserve consists almost entirely of dense Chaco forest – a dry, stunted and spiny vegetation typical of the area. The park was established to protect a series of trenches dating from the Chaco War and to conserve a healthy population of Chaco peccary (*taguá*). The species is regularly seen in the area along with puma, tapir and a host of Chaco endemic bird species including Black-legged Seriema, Chaco Owl and the turkey-like Chaco chachalaca.

If you are here with a Fauna Paraguay guide, your best chance of seeing mammals is on **night-walks** with a torch – stake out the waterhole and salt lick just after dark to increase your chances of bumping into the more spectacular species. A series of walking trails are well maintained and allow for hiking, but the frequent hot, dry winds can seriously impede your chances of seeing wildlife during the day. The best time of year to visit is during winter (May–Sept), when temperatures are more manageable.

Arrival and information

Bus NASA runs buses (2 daily; 16hr) from the Asunción bus terminal to Nueva Asunción that pass in front of the visitor centre at Enciso, but it's a long and uncomfortable journey.

Car If hiring a car, a 4x4 vehicle is absolutely necessary as the tarmac runs out some 22km before the reserve.

Tours Guided ecotours to Enciso are available through Fauna Paraguay (🌐www.faunaparaguay.com).

PARQUE NACIONAL MÉDANOS DEL CHACO

Around 65km further north from Enciso along the Ruta Trans-Chaco is the vast **PARQUE NACIONAL MÉDANOS DEL CHACO**, an area of thorny, dusty terrain that's home to the last lowland herd of the llama-like guanaco. Beyond Enciso the Trans-Chaco deteriorates into a series of *talcales* (dust baths), which are only occasionally passable in a 4x4. It is not recommended that you attempt this journey unless accompanied by a professional **guide** or somebody with local knowledge. Fauna Paraguay (🌐www.faunaparaguay.com) can provide English-speaking guides. Note also that there are no accommodation or visitor facilities at Médanos del Chaco, and that whether travelling alone or by public transport, you will need to take all food and drink with you, as there is nowhere to buy supplies.

Peru

ROUGH COSTS

DAILY BUDGET Basic US$20 / occasional treat US$35

DRINK Cristal beer US$1–2

FOOD Lunchtime menu US$2–5

HOSTEL/BUDGET HOTEL US$7–12

TRAVEL Tumbes–Lima: 18hr, US$20–40, Lima–Cuzco: 22hr, US$25–55

FACT FILE

POPULATION 29.5 million

AREA 1,285,216 sq km

LANGUAGES Spanish, Quechua, Aymara

CURRENCY Nuevo Sol (S)

CAPITAL Lima (population: 8.5 million)

INTERNATIONAL PHONE CODE ☎51

TIME ZONE GMT -5hr

Introduction

Peru is the most varied and exciting of all the South American nations, with a combination of mountains, Inca relics, immense desert coastline and vast tracts of tropical rainforest. Dividing these contrasting environments, the Andes, with its chain of breathtaking peaks, over 7km high and 400km wide in places, ripples the entire length of the nation. So distinct are these regions that it is very difficult to generalize about the country, but one thing for sure is that Peru offers a unique opportunity to experience an incredibly wide range of spectacular scenery, a wealth of heritage, and a vibrant living culture.

Hedonists will head for the beaches of **Máncora**, the nightclubs of **Lima** and the bars of **Cusco** – the latter a city where a cosmopolitan lifestyle coexists alongside pre-Columbian buildings and ancient festivals. Just as easily, you can retreat from civilization, travelling deep into the remote parts of the **Peruvian Amazon**, searching for jaguars or taking part in hallucinogenic *ayahuasca* (jungle vine) ceremonies. Or you can walk in the footsteps of the Incas, taking on the challenge of the **Inca Trail** to reach the ancient citadel of **Machu Picchu**, take a flight over the **Nazca Lines** to ponder the meaning of the giant figures etched into the desert, or hike the canyons and snow-tipped peaks around **Arequipa** and **Trujillo**.

In the more rural parts of Peru, local life has changed little in the last four centuries and many people lead humble, traditional lives, though roads and tracks now connect almost every corner of the country, making travel around quite straightforward. Nevertheless, you should be prepared to accept the occasional episode of social unrest or travel delays caused by natural disasters with the good humour of the locals.

CHRONOLOGY

c.40,000–15,000 BC The first Peruvians, descendants of nomadic tribes, cross into the Americas from Asia during the last ice age.

WHEN TO VISIT

The best time to visit Peru will depend upon which areas of the country you intend to visit, and what activities you plan on doing. The coast tends to be mostly dry year-round, but sits under a blanket of fog from April to November each year (especially in Lima); the driest, sunniest months here (Dec–March) tend to coincide with the rainiest weather elsewhere.

In the Andes the seasons are more clearly marked, with heavy rains from December to April and a relatively dry period from June to September, which, although it can be cold at night, is certainly the best time for trekking and most outdoor activities. In much of the jungle, rainfall is heavier and more frequent, and it's hot and humid all year. In the lowland rainforest areas around Iquitos water levels are higher between December and January, which offers distinct advantages for spotting wildlife and accessing remote creeks by canoe.

Those wishing to avoid the crowds will prefer to visit during the shoulder seasons of May and September to November, as from May to August many popular tourist attractions are packed with tour groups.

2,600 BC The complex civilization at the site of Caral develops, lasting for an estimated 500 years.

200–600 AD Emergence and growth of the Moche and Nazca cultures.

1200 The Inca Empire begins to emerge.

1438–70 Pachacutec becomes ruler of the Inca Empire. Machu Picchu and the Inca capital of Cusco are constructed.

1500–30 The Inca Empire stretches over 5,500km, from southern Colombia right down to northern Chile.

1532 Francisco Pizarro leads his band of 170 conquistadors from Tumbes to Cajamarca, capturing the Inca ruler Atahualpa and massacring thousands of Inca warriors.

1533 Atahualpa is executed and the Spaniards install a puppet Inca ruler, Manco Inca.

1535 Lima is founded by Pizarro as the "City of Kings".

1538–41 Conquistadors fight for control of the colony. Diego de Almagro is executed by Pizarro, who in turn is assassinated by Almagro's son.

1542 The Viceroyalty of Peru is established by Spain's King Charles I, with Lima as its capital.

1571 Unsuccessful rebellion by the last Inca, Túpac Amaru, results in his execution.

1821 Argentine general José de San Martín declares Peruvian Independence on July 28.

1824 The last of the Spanish forces defeated at the battles of Junín and Ayacucho. Peru becomes an independent state.

1879–83 The War of the Pacific with Chile. Chile is victorious, annexing a large chunk of southern Peru, including the nitrate-rich northern Atacama desert.

1911 Hiram Bingham discovers Machu Picchu.

1948–56 The economy spirals into ruin and a military junta takes control.

1969–75 Massive economic crisis occurs after General Juan Velasco nationalizes foreign-owned businesses, bans foreign investors and gives all the hacienda land to workers' cooperatives.

1980–1992 The Maoist Sendero Luminoso ("Shining Path"), led by Abimael Guzman, carries out terrorist attacks against the government. The conflict causes 69,000 deaths and "disappearances", at least 75 percent of them Quechua-speaking highlanders.

1985 Socialist candidate Alan García comes to power. Financial reforms cause massive hyperinflation and trigger the worst economic crisis Peru has ever experienced.

1990 Surprise presidential victory by Alberto Fujimori over renowned author Mario Vargas Llosa. Privatization of state-owned companies improves economic conditions.

1994 Amnesty offered to Shining Path members; more than 6000 surrender.

2000 Fujimori re-elected amidst alregations of electoral fraud, but flees to Japan shortly after due to revelations of corruption, extortion, arms trafficking and human rights abuses.

2001–06 Alejandro Toledo becomes Peru's first full-blooded indigenous president. Protests against the US-backed eradication of coca plantations and nationwide strikes ensue, but the economy remains stable.

2007 Massive earthquake devastates the coastal province of Ica, killing 520 people.

2007–09 Fujimori extradited to Peru. After a lengthy public trial he is convicted to 25 years in prison for authorizing death squad killings in 1991–92.

2010 Mario Vargas Llosa wins the Nobel Prize for Literature.

Basics

ARRIVAL

Peru has land borders with Chile, Ecuador, Bolivia, Brazil and Colombia. While the borders with Chile, Ecuador and Bolivia are easily negotiated, the borders with Brazil and Colombia are deep in the jungle and less easily reached. Lima is a major transport hub with international flights from the USA and Europe; there are also good connections from Lima to other South American countries. International flights within South America tend to be expensive, while national flights within Peru average around US$90 to any destination. Save money by crossing borders by land and only flying within Peru.

Major operators include LAN Peru and Taca; also American Airlines from the US, Iberia from Europe via Madrid, and KLM from Europe via Amsterdam. Local airlines include Star Peru and Peruvian Airlines. US citizens are required to show a return ticket if flying in.

If crossing land borders from Chile, Bolivia or Ecuador, aim to take a long-distance bus that takes you directly to your destination across the border – it

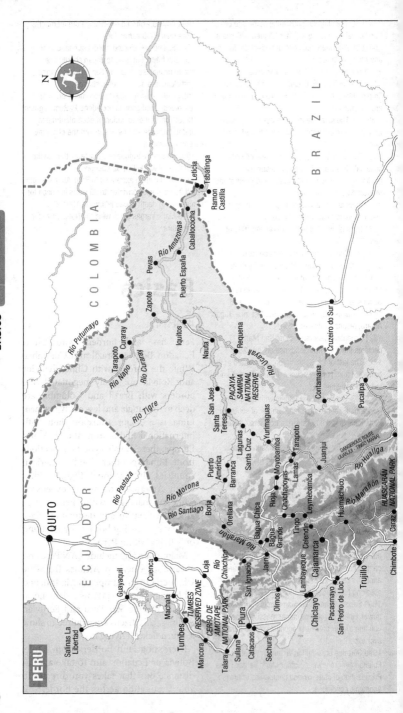

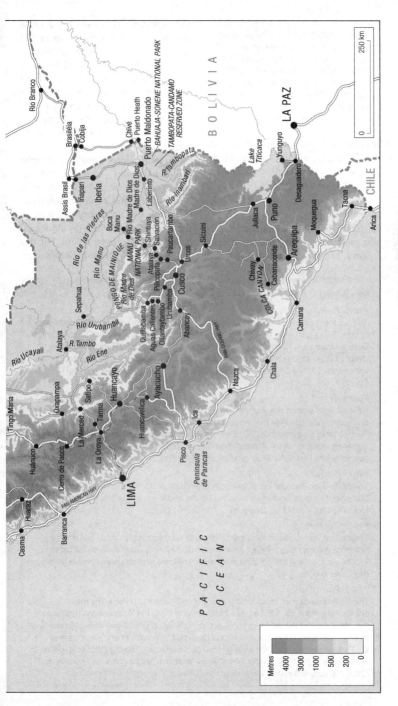

There is a $32 departure tax payable at Lima airport when flying to an international destination. For national flights the fee from Lima is $7, and similar fees apply from regional airports in Peru. Only cash payments are accepted.

may be a little pricier, but that way you avoid hanging around dodgy border crossing areas and the drivers can assist you with border formalities.

VISAS

In August 2008 a new immigration law was passed concerning foreign tourists in Peru. EU, US, Canadian, Australian and New Zealand citizens can now all stay in Peru as tourists for up to 183 days without a visa; for other nationalities, check with the local Peruvian embassy. You're typically given ninety days upon entry, so if you're planning to stay a long time in Peru, make sure to ask for the maximum time allowance, as it is no longer possible to extend tourist visas.

All nationalities need a **tourist or embarkation card** (*tarjeta de embarque*) to enter Peru, which is issued at the border or on the plane before landing. In theory you have to show an outbound ticket (by air or bus) before you'll be given a card, but this is almost never checked. Keep a copy

LAND AND WATER ROUTES TO PERU

From Bolivia
The southern cities of Puno, Cusco and Arequipa are easily reached overland from Bolivia. There are two crossings: Yungayo from Copacabana on Lake Titicaca, and Desaguadero from La Paz; Yungayo is marginally less chaotic. Regular buses run direct to Puno (and some to Cusco) from both destinations. It's difficult, though not impossible, to take a boat to Puerto Maldonado from Bolivia's Puerto Heath via Puerto Pardo. See p.868.

From Brazil
It's a straightforward bus journey along the Interoceanic Highway and across the bridge from the Brazilian border post of Assis Brasil to the Peruvian village of Iñapari, which is three hours by bus from Puerto Maldonado. See p.906. You can also reach Iquitos via the Amazon from the small port of Tabatinga via the border post of Santa Rosa, just like from Colombia's Leticia.

From Chile
The Arica-Tacna border in the far south of Peru causes few problems for travellers. Taxi *colectivos* run regularly across the border and the driver will help with border formalities for a small tip. See p.861.

From Colombia
The easiest way to reach Peru from Colombia is by bus via Ecuador, but if in the Amazon, you can also take a boat from the Colombian border town of Leticia to Iquitos via the small immigration post of Santa Rosa; river journeys take up to two days. See p.906.

From Ecuador
There are three border crossings open between Ecuador and Peru. The most commonly used is the Tumbes–Machala crossing along the Panamerican Highway on the coast, though the crossing from Loja to Piura via La Tina is also straightforward, as there are direct buses between major destinations in each country, stopping at the Peruvian and Ecuadorian immigration offices en route. The third crossing – from Vilcabamba to Jaén – is further inland where roads are not so good, and it involves changing basic transportation several times. See p.889 for more information.

of the tourist card and your passport on you at all times – particularly when travelling away from the main towns. It is very important that you keep your original tourist card safe, since you will be asked to return it to immigration officials when leaving the country. Fines of around S55 are applicable if you lose your card.

GETTING AROUND

Given the size of the country, many Peruvians and travellers fly to their destinations, as all Peruvian cities are within a two-hour flight from Lima. Most budget travellers get around the country by bus, as these go just about everywhere and are extremely good value. There is a limited rail service along some routes, which makes for a change from the monotony of long bus rides, despite being considerably slower and more expensive than the equivalent bus journey.

By bus

Peru's privately operated buses offer remarkably low fares. Long-distance bus services cost from around S5 per hour on the coastal highway and are even cheaper elsewhere. Buses range from the efficient and relatively luxurious *cama* or *semicama* buses with air conditioning, snacks/meals included and on-board entertainment, to the more basic *económico* buses, to the scruffy old ex-school buses used on local runs between remote villages.

Cruz del Sur (Ⓦ www.cruzdelsur.com .pe) and Oltursa (Ⓦ www.oltursa.com .pe) offer the plushest and most reliable buses; Cruz del Sur covers most destinations (though not the Cusco–Puno route), while Oltursa is best for any destination along the Panamericana, followed by Cial (Ⓦ www.expresocial.com). Ormeño (Ⓦ www.grupo-ormeno.com.pe) has routes as far as Colombia, Brazil, Chile, Argentina and Bolivia, though it also has a reputation for lateness and the condition of the buses has declined over the years. Reliable companies covering the north of Peru include Movil Tours (Ⓦ www.moviltours.com.pe) and Tepsa (Ⓦ www.tepsa.com.pe), while the south is covered by the cheaper Flores (Ⓦ www .floreshnos.net), TransMar (Ⓦ www .transmar.com.pe) and Soyuz (Ⓦ www .soyuz.com.pe). For intercity rides, it's best to buy tickets in advance direct from the bus company offices; for local trips, you can buy tickets on the bus itself.

If storing main luggage in the hold, you should get a receipt that you hand in at the end of your journey to collect it. Keep your hand luggage with you at all times, particularly if travelling on cheaper buses.

By taxi, mototaxi and colectivo

Taxis are easily found at any time in almost every town. Any car can become a taxi simply by sticking a taxi sign up in the front window; a lot of people take advantage of this to supplement their income. However, in recent years this has led to an increase in crime, so if possible call a radio taxi from a recommended company. Always fix the price in advance, since few taxis have meters. Relatively short journeys in Lima generally cost around S6, but it's cheaper elsewhere. Taxi drivers in Peru do not expect tips.

In many towns, you'll find small cars and motorcycle rickshaws (*mototaxis* or *motocars*). The latter are always cheaper than taxis, if slightly more dangerous and not that comfortable. Outside Lima, you will almost never pay more than S5 for a ride within a town.

Colectivos (shared taxis) are a very useful way of getting around. They connect all the coastal towns, and many of the larger centres in the mountains, and tend to be faster than the bus, though often charge twice as much. Some *colectivos* manage to squeeze in about six people plus the driver and can be found in the centre of a town or at major stopping-places along the main roads. *Colectivo* minibuses, also known as **combis**, can squeeze in twice as many people, or often more. They cost on average S10 per person, per hour travelled.

In the cities, particularly in Lima, *colectivos* (especially *combis*) have a poor reputation for safety. They frequently crash, turn over and knock down pedestrians, so take extra care.

By train

Peru's spectacular train journeys are in themselves a major attraction. Peru Rail (ⓦwww.perurail.com) runs passenger services from Puno to Cusco, from where another line heads down the magnificent Urubamba Valley as far as Machu Picchu (see p.836). The world's second-highest railway route, from Lima to Huancayo, is considered to be amongst the most scenic in the world, but it only runs once a month or so; check departure dates and times at ⓦwww.ferrocarrilcentral.com.pe.

Trains tend to be slower than buses and considerably more expensive, but they do allow ample time to enjoy the scenery, and are quite comfortable. If you're planning on visiting Machu Picchu but don't intend to hike the Inca Trail, you have no option but to take a tourist train, divided into "backpacker" and "Vistadome" classes that are priced in US dollars.

At the time of writing, the Cusco–Puno service costs S706, while a bus costs S40; a "backpacker" train to Machu Picchu costs US$48. If possible tickets should be bought at least a day in advance, and a week in advance on the Cusco–Machu Picchu route.

By air

Peru is so vast that the odd flight can save a lot of time, and flights between major towns are frequent and relatively inexpensive. The most popular routes usually need to be booked at least a few days in advance (more at the time of major fiestas). For the best fares to popular destinations, either book your flights in advance with Chilean-owned LAN (ⓦwww.lan.com), the main airline, or with the smaller Peruvian subsiduaries of Star Peru (ⓦwww .starperu.com.pe), Peruvian Airlines (ⓦwww.peruvianairlines.pe) or LC Busre (ⓦwww.lcbusre.com.pe).

Some places in the jungle, such as Iquitos, are more easily accessible by plane, as land and river routes take much longer and can cost as much as a plane ticket. More remote jungle areas, such as the Manu National Park, are served by small twin propellor planes; the flights are costly and particularly susceptable to bad weather.

Flights are sometimes cancelled, delayed or leave earlier than scheduled, so it is important to reconfirm your flight 48 hours before departure. If a passenger hasn't shown up twenty minutes before the flight, the company can give the seat to someone on the waiting list.

By boat

There are no coastal boat services in Peru. From Puno, on Lake Titicaca, there are plenty of small boats that will take visitors out to the various islands in the lake for around S30 per person, and while there are no passenger ferries, it's possible to take one- or two-day catamaran tours to Bolivia (see p.868).

In the jungle, river travel is of enormous importance, and cargo boats are an excellent way of travelling along the Amazon – though you have to have plenty of time at your disposal. The facilities are basic (bring your own hammock to hang on deck or rent a cabin), as is the food. The most popular routes are either from Pucallpa or Yurimaguas to Iquitos, from where you can then go on to Colombia or Brazil. On smaller rivers, motorized dugout canoes are the preferred local mode of transport and come in two basic forms: those with a large outboard motor and slow and noisy *peke-peke* (the name describes the sound of the engine).

ACCOMMODATION

Peru has the typical range of Latin American accommodation, from top-class international hotels to tiny rooms at the back of someone's house for around ten soles a night. Virtually all upmarket accommodation will call itself a hotel or, in the countryside regions, a posada. Lodges in the jungle can be anything from quite luxurious to an open-sided, palm-thatched hut with space for slinging a hammock. *Pensiones* or *residenciales* tend to specialize in longer-term accommodation and may offer discounts for stays of a week or more.

Hotels

Budget **guesthouses** (usually called *hospedajes* or *hostales* and not to be confused with youth hostels) are generally old – sometimes beautifully so, converted from colonial mansions with rooms grouped around a courtyard – and tend to be quite central. At the low end of the scale, which can be basic with shared rooms and a communal bathroom, you can usually find a bed for S20–30, the price often including breakfast. Rooms with private bath tend to cost S10–15 more. *Hostales* can be great value if you're travelling with one other person or more; you can often get a good, clean en-suite room for less than two or three bunk beds in a youth hostel. A little haggling is often worth a try, particularly in the low season.

Hostels and camping

A list of the HI-affiliated **youth hostels** in Peru is at ⓦ www.hihostels.com/dba /country-PE.en.htm. These are relatively cheap and reliable; expect to pay around S15–25, more in Lima. All hostels are theoretically open 24hr and most have cheap cafeterias attached. There are also many non-HI-affiliated hostels throughout the country (try ⓦ www.hostels.com or www.hostel world.com). While these are great for meeting people, they are often not the cheapest option, as dorm beds cost from S20-25, the same price as a room at a budget hotel.

Camping is possible all over Peru. In towns and cities you may be charged the same amount to put up a tent in the grounds of a hostel as for a dorm bed. Organized campsites are gradually being established on the outskirts of popular tourist destinations, though these are still few and far between. Outside urban areas, apart from some restricted natural reserves, it's possible to camp amid stunning scenery along Peru's vast coast, in the mountains and in the jungle. It's best not to camp alone and if you are setting up camp anywhere near a village or settlement, ask permission or advice from the nearest farm or house first.

FOOD AND DRINK

Peruvian cuisine is wonderfully diverse, and essentially a *mestizo* creation, merging indigenous Indian cooking with Spanish, African, Chinese, Italian and Japanese influences. Along the coast, *ceviche* is the classic Peruvian seafood dish, consisting of raw fish, assorted seafood or a mixture of the two, marinated in lime juice and chilli and with corn, sweet potato and onions. You'll also find *arroz con mariscos* (seafood-fried rice), *tiradito* (like sashimi, served with a spicy sauce), *conchitas a la parmesana* (scallops baked with cheese) and fish prepared a dozen different ways. In coastal areas you'll also find numerous *chifas* (Chinese eateries) serving ample portions of inexpensive Chinese dishes, including vegetarian options.

Food in the Andes includes delicious, hearty soups, such as *sopa de quinoa* (quinoa soup), *chupe de camarones* (shrimp chowder) and *sopa criolla* (beef noodle soup with vegetables). Peru is home to hundreds of potato varieties, the standout dishes from which include *ocopa* (potato with spicy peanut sauce), *papa a la Huancaína* (potato in a spicy cheese sauce) and *causa* (layers of mashed potato with countless fillings). Other popular dishes include *lomo saltado* (stir-fried beef), *ají de gallina* (chicken in garlic sauce), *arroz con pato* (rice with duck, simmered in dark beer with coriander) and the ubiquitous *cuy* (seared guinea pig).

In the jungle, the succulent local fish, such as *dorado* and *paiche*, comes grilled, as *patarashka* (spiced, wrapped in banana leaves and baked on coals) or as *paca* (steamed in a banana tube). Fried and mashed plantain figures highly, along with *yuca* (a manioc rather like a yam) and *juanes* (banana leaves stuffed with chicken, rice and spices). There is often game on the menu, but beware of eating turtle or other endangered species.

In big cities, there are numerous vegetarian restaurants, though vegetarian food may be quite difficult to find elsewhere. If you ask for your dish *sín carne* (without meat), that may only exclude red meat, but not chicken or fish.

Dessert-wise, Peru offers a wide array of tropical fruit, such as *lúcuma*, *chirimoya* (custard apple) and *grenadilla* (passion fruit) as well as *mazamorra morada* (purple corn pudding with cloves and pineapple) and *suspiro limeño* (caramelized condensed milk topped with meringue).

Drinks

In Peru you can find all the popular soft drink brands, though Peruvians prefer the ubiquitous neon-yellow Inca Kola, which tastes like liquid bubblegum. Fresh fruit juices (*jugos*) are abundant, with *jugerías* (juice stalls) in markets and elsewhere offering a variety of flavours, such as papaya, *maracuyá* (passion fruit), *platano* (banana), *piña* (pineapple) and *naranja* (orange); specify whether you want yours *con azucar* (with sugar) or *sín azucar* (without sugar). Another excellent non-alcoholic drink is *chicha morada*, made from purple corn – not to be confused with *chicha*, home-made corn beer popular in the Andes (look out for a red flag outside homes).

Surprisingly, for a coffee-growing country, Peruvians tend to drink either *café pasado* (previously percolated coffee mixed with hot water to serve) or simple powdered Nescafé, though it is possible to find good coffee in big cities. A wide variety of herbal teas are also available, such as *menta* (mint), *manzanilla* (camomile) and the extremely popular *mate de coca* – tea brewed from coca leaves that helps one acclimatize to high altitude.

Peru brews some excellent beer, the most popular brands being *Cristal*, *Pilsen* and *Cusqueña* – all light lagers, though you can also get Pilsen *cerveza negra* (dark beer). Good regional brews include *Arequipeña* and *Trujillana* (named after the cities they're brewed in). Most Peruvian wine tends to be sweet and almost like sherry. Among brands more attuned to the Western palate are *Tabernero*, *Tacama* and *Vista Alegre*. The national beverage and a source of great pride is pisco, a potent grape brandy with a unique and powerful flavour. Pisco sour – a mix of pisco, lime juice, ice and sugar – is a very palatable and extremely popular cocktail found on menus everywhere.

CULTURE AND ETIQUETTE

Due to the huge variety of geographical conditions found within Peruvian territory, culture and traditions tend

to vary between regions. On the whole, coastal people tend to be more outgoing and vivacious, while the mountain people of Quechua descent are more reserved and modest. The jungle is still home to many indigenous groups who keep their ancestral traditions and way of life. All Peruvians are family-oriented and tend to be close to large extended families. *Machismo* is alive and well in Peru, though women travelling alone are not likely to encounter much trouble. Note that whistling in the north of Peru can be a greeting rather than an attempt at harassment.

One of the most common things travellers do that offends local people is to take their picture without asking – so always ask first, and respect a negative answer. At tourist sites all over Peru, you'll encounter women and children in stunning traditional dress who expect a tip for having their photo taken (2–3 soles is a reasonable amount). In the highlands in particular there is a strong culture of exchange, meaning that if you receive something, you are expected to give in return. This can be as simple as giving someone coca leaves in exchange for directions on a trail.

Tipping is becoming the norm in more upmarket restaurants, where a 10 percent gratuity is expected and sometimes automatically added to the bill; in cheap local eateries, tips are received with surprise and gratitude. It's worth bearing in mind that some unscrupulous travel agencies pay their guides very low wages, meaning that they rely on tips, as do freelance guides in museums (agree on a fee before a tour). You should always tip your guide and porters on the Inca Trail (see box, p.834).

SPORTS AND OUTDOOR ACTIVITIES

When it comes to exploring the wilderness, few of the world's countries can offer anything as varied, rugged and colourful as Peru

Trekking and hiking

Peru offers a spectacular variety of trekking routes; the main hiking centres are Cusco and Arequipa in the south and Huaraz in the north. The most popular trekking route is, of course, the famous Inca Trail, but other trails in and around the Sacred Valley are rapidly gaining popularity, partly because you get to experience fantastic Andean scenery without being overrun by hordes of tourists. From Arequipa, you can descend into two of the world's deepest canyons – Cañón de Colca and the more remote Cañón de Cotahuasi, which are accessible all year, unlike the Sacred Valley. The Cordillera Blanca near Huaraz lures hikers and climbers alike with its challenging peaks, many of them over 5000m high.

Guides are required for some trekking routes, such as the Inca Trail, and for some challenging routes you'll need to hire mules and *arrieros* (muleteers). You can rent trekking gear or join guided treks at all the major hiking centres; good topographic maps are available from the Instituto Geográfico Nacional (IGN) or the South American Explorers' Club (see p.800). Always make sure you're properly equipped, as the weather is renowned for its dramatic changeability, and properly acclimatized.

Mountain biking

Bike shops and bicycle repairs workshops are easy to find throughout Peru, though you should bring your own bike if you're planning on some major cycle touring, as mountain-bike rental is pretty basic. Various tour companies (see p.812) offer guided cycling tours, which can be an excellent way to see the best of Peru. Huaraz and Cusco are both popular and challenging destinations for experienced bikers, while the Colca Canyon is a better bet for novices.

Watersports

Cusco is one of the top white-water rafting and kayaking centres in South America, with easy access to a whole range of river grades, from Class II to V on the Río Urubamba (shifting up grades in the rainy season) to the most dangerous white-water on the Río Apurímac, only safe for rafting during the dry season. Río Chili near Arequipa offers good rafting for beginners, with half-day-trips passing through Class II and III rapids. A superb multi-day rafting expedition from Cusco goes right down into the Amazon Basin on the Tambopata River.

Bear in mind that rafting is still not a regulated sport in Peru, so it's very important to go with a responsible and eco-friendly operator (see p.824). Also see Ⓦ www.peruwhitewater.com.

Surfing

Surfing's a popular sport in Peru, with annual national and international championships held in Punta Rocas, south of Lima. You can find good breaks even in Lima itself, particularly in the Miraflores area, though Punta Hermosa, further south, is less crowded. Peru's north coast offers some world-class breaks, with Puerto Chicano boasting the world's longest left-hand wave, whereas Santa Rosa and Pacasmayo outside Chiclayo also have excellent waves. Equipment rental is abundant and it's possible to take surfing lessons. Check out Ⓦ www.peruazul.com or www.vivamancora.com for more information.

Sandboarding and dune buggying

The best places to ride the sand are in Nazca (see p.851), home of the world's largest dune – Cerro Blanco – and Huacachina, near Ica (see p.850). You can either rent a board from the numerous agencies or go out on the dunes with one of them; snowboarding experience is helpful but not necessary. Also in Huacachina, you can experience the stomach-churning adrenalin rush of dune-buggy rides. While in Nazca they are used as the most efficient means of reaching distant desert sites, in Huacachina they are used for the thrill alone.

COMMUNICATIONS

Postal services are slow and expensive but quite acceptable for normal letters and postcards. All Peruvian towns have *locutorios* (call centres), usually operated by Telefónica del Peru; to make local or international calls, you're allocated a numbered booth from which you dial direct and pay afterwards. These offices also take phone cards, though the rates are far better if you use them to dial from a regular fixed line phone.

All public phones are operated by coins or phone cards (*tarjetas telefónicas*), which are available in 3, 10, 20 and 50 sol denominations. You can buy cards at *farmacias* (corner shops) or on the street from cigarette stalls in the centres of most towns and cities. Both 147 and Hola Peru cards are good for local, national and international calls. Most shops, restaurants or corner shops in Peru have a phone available for public use, which you can use for calls within Peru only. If you need to contact the international operator, dial ☏108. Collect calls are known either simply as *collect* or *al cobro revertido*.

If you have an unlocked mobile phone, it's cheap and easy to get a Peruvian SIM card (S15); alternatively, you can buy a cheap mobile for the duration of your stay (S80). The network with the most extensive coverage of the country is

---

PERU ON THE NET

Ⓦ www.andeantravelweb.com/peru Links to a whole range of travel-related features and listings.

Ⓦ www.perulinks.com English-language pages on a range of Peruvian topics like art, entertainment, and travel.

Ⓦ www.virtualperu.net Peruvian geography, history and people, plus satellite photos, maps and other information.

Claro, which also allows you to send free text messages via their website.

Peru has good internet connections, with internet cafés abundant in big cities and found even in the most unlikely of small towns (though the connection may be slow). Many hotels, hostels and cafés now have free wi-fi as well. The general rate is S2 per hour, though in touristy places you may end up paying as much as S6.

CRIME AND SAFETY

Perhaps the most common irritants are the persistent **touts** found at bus stations and other tourist spots, offering anything from discount accommodation to tours; be very wary of accepting their services, and don't give them money up front. Also don't take **unlicensed taxis** if possible.

You're most likely to come into contact with **police** at the border posts. While they have a reputation for being corrupt, they will mostly leave tourists alone, though some travellers may experience petty harassment aimed at procuring a bribe. If they search your luggage, be scrupulously polite and be aware that possession of any drugs is considered an extremely serious offence in Peru – usually leading to at least a ten-year jail sentence.

Violent crime, such as muggings, is relatively rare. Robberies occasionally occur on overnight buses and there have been isolated attacks on hikers in the area around Huaraz, so it's best not to hike alone. It's not advisable to travel at night between Abancay and Ayacucho, around the Apurímac Valley near Ayacucho or in the Río Huallaga area in the north, between Tingo María and Juanjui, as those areas are notorious for drug trafficking.

If you're unlucky enough to have anything stolen, your first port of call should be the **tourist police** (*policia de turismo*), from whom you should get a written report. Bear in mind that the police in popular tourist spots, such as Cusco, have become much stricter about investigating reported thefts, after a spate of false claims by dishonest tourists. This means that genuine victims may be grilled more severely than expected, and the police may even come and search your hotel room for the "stolen" items. For emergency services, call ☎105.

HEALTH

In most cities there are **private clinics** (*clínicas*) with better medical facilities than general hospitals, and if given the choice in a medical emergency, opt for a *clínica*. The EsSalud national hospitals have undergone drastic improvements in the last few years, and although they are supposed to be for Peruvians who pay into an insurance scheme with them, they can take independent patients (who pay a higher price). Even in relatively small villages there is a *posta médica* where you can get basic medical attention and assistance in getting to a larger medical facility. The South American Explorers' Clubs in Lima and Cusco as well as IPerú offices can provide you with a list of recommended doctors and clinics.

INFORMATION AND MAPS

The government IPerú offices present in every large city are useful for basic information and advice, as well as free local maps and leaflets (24hr hotline: ☏01/574-8000, ⊛www.peru.info/iperu); they are also the place to go if you need to make a formal complaint about dishonest guides, tour companies not meeting their obligations, and so on.

Good bookshops stock the Lima 2000 series, which produces the best maps of the major cities as well as the best road map of Peru. For excellent topographic maps of remote places, try Lima's Instituto Geográfico Nacional (⊛www.ign.es).

MONEY AND BANKS

The current Peruvian currency, the **nuevo sol**, whose symbol is S/, is simply called a "sol" on the streets and has so far remained relatively steady against the US dollar. The bills come in denominations of 10, 20, 50 and 100 soles; there are coins of 1, 2, and 5 soles, and the sol is divided into céntimos, in values of 5, 10, 20 and 50. Beware of counterfeit bills, which feel smooth and glossy to the touch, rather than crisp and coarse; genuine bills should have watermarks and thin ribbons when held up against a light source, and when tilted from side to side, the reflective ink on the number denomination should change colour.

Changing foreign currencies is easy in all major cities; you will find casas de cambio around the Plaza de Armas or along the main commercial streets. They readily change Euros and British pounds, though the preferred currency is US dollars. You'll find that some tour companies and hotels still quote prices in US dollars, and readily accept them as long as the notes are new; few places will accept US$100 bills.

Banks and ATMs are numerous in cities; if travelling to remote villages, take plenty of cash in small denomination bills and coins with you. BCP (Banco de Crédito) accepts all major credit cards and is the best bank for cash withdrawals, as it doesn't charge a fee for the transaction, whereas the Global Net network charges an extortionate S7.50 per withdrawal.

OPENING HOURS AND HOLIDAYS

Most services in Peru open Monday to Saturday 9am to 6pm, although some are open until around 1pm and then close for a long lunch and reopen from 4pm to 8pm. Most shops are open from around 9am to 9pm, and many are open on Sunday as well, if for more limited hours. Peru's more important ancient sites and ruins usually have opening hours that coincide with daylight – from around 7am until 5pm or 6pm daily.

Peruvians love any excuse for a celebration and the country enjoys a huge number of religious ceremonies, festivals and local events. Carnival time (generally late February) is especially lively almost everywhere in the country, with fiestas held every Sunday – a wholesale licence to throw water at everyone and generally go crazy. It's worth noting that most hotel prices go up significantly at fiesta times and bus and air transport should be booked well in advance.

FESTIVALS

Peru is a country rich with culture and traditions, and on any given day there is a town or village celebrating their anniversary or similar occasion. Most festivals consist of processions, usually with live music and dancing, and a proud usage of traditional dress. They can be quite spectacular events and small towns will become completely booked up, transport services stop running or prices double, and often most people will stop work and celebrate (usually by drinking) for a few days either side of the festival. Below are some of the major events:

February Carnival. Wildly celebrated immediately prior to Lent, throughout the whole country.

February 2 Virgen de la Candelaria. Celebrated in the most spectacular way in Puno (known as the folklore capital of the country) with a week of colourful processions and dancing.

March/April Semana Santa (Holy Week). Superb processions all over Peru (the best are in Cusco and Ayacucho), the biggest being on Good Friday and Easter Saturday night.

Late May/early June Q'oyllor Riti. One of the most breathtaking festivals in Peru; thousands of people make the overnight pilgrimage up to Apu Ausangate, a shrine located on a glacier just outside of Cusco.

Early June Corpus Christi. Takes place nine weeks after Maundy Thursday and involves colourful processions with saints carried around on floats and much feasting. Particularly lively in Cusco.

June 24 Inti Raymi is Cusco's main Inca festival.

June 29 St Peter's Day. Fiestas in all the fishing villages along the coast.

July 16 Virgen del Carmen. Celebrated in style in the town of Paucartambo, on the road between Cusco and Manu Biosphere Reserve. Dancers come from surrounding villages in traditional dress for the celebration, which lasts several days. There's a smaller celebration in the Sacred Valley town of Pisac.

August 13–19 Arequipa Week. Processions, firework displays, plenty of folklore dancing and craft markets in Arequipa.

August 30 Santa Rosa de Lima. The city of Lima stops for the day to worship their patron saint, Santa Rosa.

Late September Spring Festival. Trujillo festival involving dancing, especially the local Marinera dance and popular Peruvian waltzes.

October 18–28 Lord of Miracles. Festival featuring large and solemn processions (the main ones take place on October 18, 19 and 28); many women wear purple.

November 1–7 Puno Festival. Celebrates the founding of Puno by the Spanish and of the Inca Empire by Manco Capac. Particularly colourful dancing on the fifth day.

November 1–30 International Bullfighting Competitions. Spectacular in the Plaza da Ancho in Lima.

Lima

LIMA, "City of Kings", was founded in 1535 by **Francisco Pizarro** and rapidly became the capital of a Spanish viceroyalty that included Ecuador, Bolivia and Chile. By 1610 its population had reached 26,000 and it had become an international trading port, the city's centre crowded with stalls selling produce from all over the world and it was one of the most beautiful and wealthy cities in Spanish America. It then grew steadily until the twentieth century, when the population exploded. Today, many of its nine million inhabitants are *campesinos* (rural folk) who fled their homes in the countryside to escape the civil war that destroyed many Andean communities in the 1980s and 1990s.

Some say that Lima is Peru. And given its wealth of museums, nightlife, architecture and world-class food, plus its position as the nation's transport hub, the city makes the perfect base from which to explore the rest of the country. So ignore Lima's grey and polluted facade; avoid the parts that very real poverty has made no-go-zones for visitors and instead ride the *combis* and get stuck in – there is so much to see and do. Truthfully, no visit to Peru is complete without time well spent in Lima.

What to see and do

Lima is very much a city of neighbourhoods, and it's worth visiting several before making up your mind about this huge capital. You can't beat **Central Lima** for sights, architecture or, currently, nightlife. **San Isidro** and neighbouring **Miraflores** are certainly the most modern and commercial areas of the city and you'll find many designer stores, gourmet restaurants and sophisticated lounge bars here, as well as some of the best tourist attractions. Arty and colourful **Barranco** feels like a sleepy seaside town by day, and is fantastic for escaping the chaos of central Lima, but at night comes alive and is packed with bars and clubs. Neighbouring port city **Callao** offers yet more to see, including the charming seaside town of **La Punta**, where you can see marine wildlife, eat fresh *ceviche* and remind yourself of Lima's fantastic location by the Pacific.

The Plaza Mayor

Lima's main square, known as the **Plaza Mayor** or the Plaza de Armas, boasts UNESCO World Heritage status due to its former colonial importance – Lima was capital of the Spanish Empire in South America – and its colours and famous wooden balconies are kept in beautiful condition accordingly. It is one of the largest squares in South America and has some of the most important government and religious buildings in Peru.

On the eastern corner of the plaza the austere Renaissance-style **Catedral** stands (open for Mass Sat 9am & Sun 11am). The interior retains some of its appealing Churrigueresque (highly elaborate Baroque) decor and it houses the **Museo de Arte Religioso** (Mon–Fri 9am–4.30pm & Sat 10am–12.30pm; S10, ☎01/427-9647), which contains paintings from the seventeenth century as well as the remains of Francisco Pizarro.

The original **Palacio del Gobierno** was built on the site of Pizarro's adobe house, where he spent the last few years of his life until his assassination in 1541. The present building was only built in 1938 (the older palace was destroyed by an earthquake). It's possible to arrange a free tour, though it's a bureaucratic nightmare and takes a few days to sort out (contact the Jefatura de Turismo, who speaks English, on ☎01/311-3908). The **changing of the guard** takes place outside (daily 11.45am), which always draws a crowd to watch the marching soldiers and listen to the military brass band.

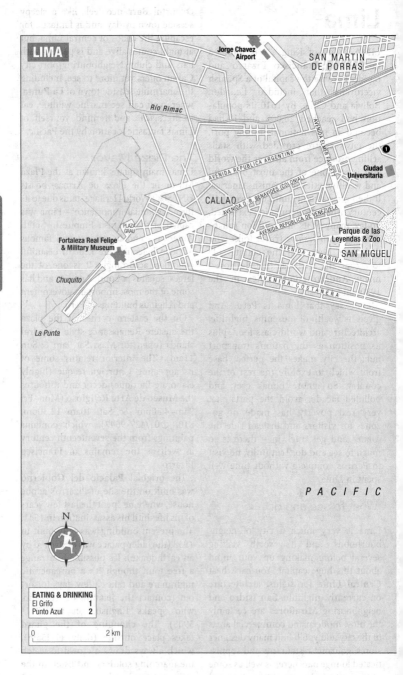

LIMA

Jorge Chavez Airport

SAN MARTIN DE PORRAS

Río Rimac

AVENIDA ELMER FAUCET

AVENIDA REPUBLICA ARGENTINA

Ciudad Universitaria ❶

CALLAO

AVENIDA O. R. BENAVIDES (COLONIAL)

AVENIDA REPUBLICA DE VENEZUELA

Parque de las Leyendas & Zoo

SAN MIGUEL

PLAZA GRAU

Fortaleza Real Felipe & Military Museum

AVENIDA LA MARINA

Chuquito

AVENIDA COSTANERA

La Punta

PACIFIC

N

EATING & DRINKING
El Grifo   1
Punto Azul   2

0   2 km

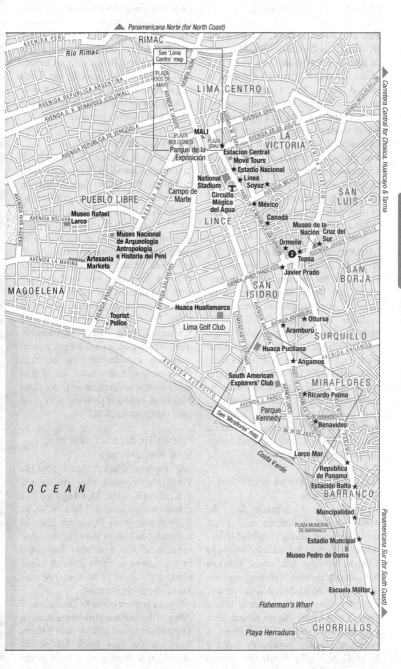

RÍMAC

Río Rímac

See 'Lima Centro' map

AVENIDA PERU

AVENIDA REPUBLICA ARGENTINA

AVENIDA O. R. BENAVIDES (COLONIAL)

AVENIDA REPUBLICA DE VENEZUELA

'PLAZA DOS DE MAYO'

AVENIDA TACNA

AVENIDA A. UGARTE

AVENIDA M. CAPAC

LIMA CENTRO

AVENIDA GRAU

AVENIDA 28 DE JULIO

PLAZA BOLOGNESI

MALI

PLAZA GRAU

Parque de la Exposición

Estación Central
Movil Tours
★ Estadio Nacional
★ Línea
Soyuz ★

LA VICTORIA

AVENIDA AVIACION

AVENIDA MEXICO

National Stadium

Campo de Marte

Circuito Mágica del Agua

★ México

PASEO DE LA REPUBLICA

SAN LUIS

PUEBLO LIBRE

Museo Rafael Larco

Museo Nacional de Arqueología Antropología e Historia del Perú

Artesanía Markets

LINCE

AVENIDA BOLIVAR

AVENIDA RIVA AGÜERO

AVENIDA BRASIL

AVENIDA LA MARINA

Canadá ★

Museo de la Nación Cruz del Sur
Ormeño ★
❷
Tepsa ★

★ Javier Prado

AVENIDA JAVIER PRADO OESTE

SAN BORJA

MAGDELENA

AVENIDA SALAVERRY

AVENIDA BRASIL

Tourist Police

Huaca Huallamarca

Lima Golf Club

AVENIDA JAVIER PRADO ESTE

SAN ISIDRO

AVENIDA AREQUIPA

AVENIDA AREQUIPA

COMANDANTE ESPINAR

AVENIDA ARAMBURU

★ Oltursa

Aramburú ★

SURQUILLO

AVENIDA EJERCITO

Huaca Pucllana

AVENIDA ANGAMOS

PASEO DE LA REPUBLICA

★ Angamos

AVENIDA AROSEMENA

South American Explorers' Club

MIRAFLORES

★ Ricardo Palma

AVENIDA LA PAZ

See 'Miraflores' map

AVENIDA J. PARDO

Parque Kennedy

Costa Verde

AV. BENAVIDES

AV. 28 DE JULIO

★ Benavides

AVENIDA LA REPUBLICA

PANAMA

O C E A N

Larco Mar

República de Panamá ★

Estación Balta ★

BARRANCO

Muncipalidad ★

PLAZA MUNICIPAL DE BARRANCO

Estadio Muncipal ★

Museo Pedro de Osma ★

Escuela Militar ★

Fisherman's Wharf

Playa Herradura

CHORRILLOS

PERU LIMA

Museo de la Iglesia y Convento San Francisco

East of the Palacio del Gobierno along Jr. Ancash is the majestic **Museo de la Iglesia y Convento San Francisco** (daily 9.30am–5.30pm; S5 for 40-min guided tour). The ticket combines seeing the large seventeenth-century church and its attached **monastery**, which contains a superb library, a room of paintings by (or finished by) Pieter Paul Rubens, Jordaens and Van Dyck, some pretty cloisters and the main highlight – vast crypts with gruesome **catacombs**, which contain the skeletons of some seventy thousand people – well worth a visit.

Museo de la Inquisición

A couple of blocks southeast of San Francisco, the **Museo de La Inquisición**, at Jr. Junín 548 (daily 9am–5pm; free, by regular guided tours only, available in English; ☎01/311-7777, Ⓦwww.congreso.gob.pe/museo.htm), was the headquarters of the Inquisition for the whole of Spanish America from 1570 until 1820. The museum includes the original tribunal room, with its beautifully carved mahogany ceiling, and beneath the building you can look round the dungeons and torture chambers, which contain a few gory, life-sized human models.

Mercado Central and Chinatown

Walk South on Av. Abancay from the Museo de La Inquisición, take a left on Ucayali and after a couple of blocks you'll see the fascinating **Mercado Central** on your left, where you can buy almost anything (keeping one eye open for pickpockets). A little further east, an ornate Chinese gateway ushers visitors into Lima's **Barrio Chino**. This pedestrianized section of the street is, rather graphically, commonly referred to as Calle Capón (Castration Street) after some of the practices the Chinese used to fatten up their animals. As you'd expect, this is where many of Lima's best, cheapest, and most swanky Chinese restaurants are, crammed into a few bustling streets. There's also an indoor mall selling Asian goods, and don't forget to look down at the modest walk of fame paying tribute to many Limeños who could afford to pay for a tile.

Jirón Ucayali

Walking back towards the Plaza, you'll find that Jr. Ucayali has a few interesting buildings. The **Iglesia San Pedro**, on the corner with Jirón Azángaro (Mon–Sat 9.30–11.30am & 5–6pm; free) was built by the Jesuits in 1636 and the plain exterior is completely at odds with its richly decorated interior; a world of gold leaf, ornate tiles and impressive altars. A short walk west on the corner with Jr. Lampa is the excellent **Museo Banco Central de Reserva del Perú** (Mon–Fri 9.45am–4.30pm, weekends 9.45am–12.30pm; free; Ⓦmuseobcr .perucultural.org.pe), whose permanent collection includes textiles, ceramics and a security-heavy room full of gold and precious artefacts, as well as a short history of Peruvian painting with good information in English.

Santa Rosa de Lima and Las Nazarenas

Walking west down Jr. Lima from the Plaza Mayor you'll pass the **Iglesia y Convento Santo Domingo** on the corner with Camaná (daily 9.30am–6.30pm; monastery S5, church free). It's here that you can see the skull and other remains of the first saint canonized in the Americas, Santa Rosa de Lima, along with those of another Peruvian saint, Martín de Porres.

If you continue on to Av. Tacna, you'll come to the **Santuario de Santa Rosa de Lima** (daily 9am–12.30pm & 3–5.30pm; free), on the first block behind the church, is a small garden built in the grounds of the saint's former home. It's a

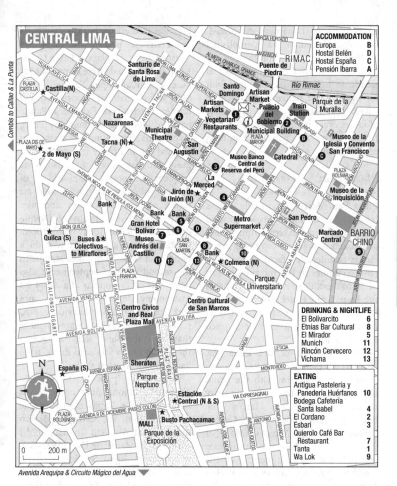

Avenida Arequipa & Circuito Mágico del Agua

pleasant escape from the chaos of Lima and many Peruvians come here to drop cards with their wishes down the well.

A few blocks south on Tacna, at the junction with Huancavelica, is the **Iglesia de Las Nazarenas** (daily 8am–noon & 5–9pm; free), small and outwardly undistinguished but with an interesting history. After the 1655 earthquake, a mural of the crucifixion, painted by an Angolan slave on the wall of his hut, was apparently the only object left standing in the district. Its survival was deemed a miracle – the cause of popular processions ever since – and it was on this site that the church was founded. The

widespread and popular processions for the **Lord of Miracles**, to save Lima from another earthquake, take place every autumn (Oct 18, 19, 28 & Nov 1).

Jirón de la Unión

The stretch between Plaza Mayor and Plaza San Martín is now the main shopping street, with everything from designer brands to thrift stores. Nestled among the modern shops there is, perhaps, the most noted of all religious buildings in Lima, the **Iglesia de La Merced**, on the corner with Jirón Miro Quesada (daily 8am–noon & 4–8pm; free). Built on the site where the first

PERU   LIMA

Latin mass in Lima was celebrated, the original church was demolished in 1628 to make way for the present building. Much of its beautiful colonial facade is not original, but look out for the **cross of Padre Urraca**, whose silver staff is smothered by hundreds of kisses every hour and witness to the fervent prayers of a constantly shifting congregation.

Plaza San Martín and around

Plaza San Martín is virtually always busy, with traffic tooting its way around the square and buskers, mime artists and soapbox politicos attracting small circles of interested faces. It has been (and continues to be) the site of most of Lima's political rallies. Of note is the huge **Gran Hotel Bolívar**, not for its rooms but for its streetside bar *El Bolivarcito*, which serves the best pisco sour in Lima.

One block east of the Plaza, Av. Nicolás de Piérola runs towards the **Parque Universitario**, with the grand old buildings of the first university in the Americas, San Marcos. The buildings now house the **Centro Cultural de San Marcos** (Mon–Sat 9am–6pm; free; @www.ccsm-unmsm .edu.pe), the cultural centre of the modern university, now sited in Pueblo Libre. It hosts many interesting talks and events and also contains a gallery, focusing on Peruvian folk and contemporary art, and an archeological and anthropology museum with rotating exhibits on different aspects of Peruvian history, as well as a permanent collection of textiles and ceramics.

Plaza Grau and around

The Jr. de la Unión becomes Jirón Belén and leads down to the **Plaza Grau** and the **Paseo de la República** (also known as the Vía Expresa), an enormous dual carriageway that cleaves through the city. Underneath the plaza is the Estación Central of the Metropolitano bus service (see p.813).

Just south of the plaza at Paseo Colón 125 is the **Museo de Arte Lima (MALI)** (Tues–Sun 10am–8pm, Sat until 5pm; S12; @www.mali.pe), housed in the former International Exhibition Palace built in 1868 and designed by Eiffel. It contains interesting collections of colonial art and many fine crafts from pre-Columbian times, and also hosts frequent temporary exhibitions of modern photography and other art forms, as well as lectures and film screenings. MALI sits in the **Parque de la Exposición** (daily 8am–10pm; free), a pleasant green space with duck ponds and some pretty bandstands. In the second week of September it also hosts the ever-popular **La Mistura** gastronomy festival (@www.mistura .pe). Created by Gastón Acurio (see box, p.797), this five-day food fest with more than two thousand stalls showcases the best of Peru's food and drink, from haute cuisine to street stalls.

Through the park is the **Estadio Nacional** (National Stadium) and just beyond that lies Lima's most eccentric new attraction, the **Circuito Mágico del Agua**, at Av. Petit Thouars at the corner of Jr. Madre de Dios (Wed–Sun & holidays 4–10pm; S4; @www.circuit omagicodelagua.com.pe). It's a park showcasing thirteen different fountains, including one over 80 metres tall and one sprouting arches you can walk under, all choreographed to pop music and coloured lights.

Museo de la Nación

The **Museo de la Nación**, at Avenida Javier Prado Este 2465 (Tues–Sun 9am–5pm; free; @01/476-9933) in San Borja, a district southeast of the centre, is one of the country's largest and most important museums, though it was being completely overhauled at the time of writing. Currently it has a scattering of galleries still open to the public, including an outstanding and very moving exhibition about the devastation caused by the Sendero Luminoso group, which terrorized the country in the 1980s and 1990s (see p.789). When complete, the museum will act as a useful place to plan your travels within Peru, as its permanent collection includes many artefacts from important archeological sites across the country.

To **get here**, take the Metropolitano bus from the centre or from Miraflores to the huge intersecting Avenida Javier Prado. Then take any bus east marked "todo Javier Prado" and ask for the museum.

Miraflores

Miraflores, its streets lined with cafés and flashy shops, is the major focus of Lima's gastronomy and nightlife as far as affluent locals and most tourists are concerned – along with San Isidro, further north, which has even more exclusive boutiques and lounge bars. To get here from the centre, jump on any of the *combis* yelling "todo Arequipa" from Tacna (just ask to get off at the Parque Kennedy) or take the Metropolitano (see box, p.813) to the Ricardo Palma stop.

The attractive **Parque Kennedy** at the end of Av. Arequipa has a small craft and antiques market every evening (6–10pm). Av. Larco, which runs along the eastern side of the park, leads to the ocean and to **Larcomar** (ⓦwww.larcomar.com), a popular clifftop mall with great sea views. From here you can walk north along the Malecón through the small parks and flower gardens, as many others do at weekends. At the **Parque el Faro** (the lighthouse park) you can take tandem paraglides (S150 for 10min) from the clifftop down to the beach.

Barranco

Barranco, scattered with old mansions as well as colourful smaller homes, was the capital's seaside resort during the nineteenth century and is now a kind of *limeño* Left Bank, with young artists and intellectuals taking over many of the older properties. To get here take any *combi* along the Diagonal beside Parque Kennedy (about 10min), or take the Metropolitano to the Municipalidad stop.

The best museum here is the pleasant **Museo Pedro de Osma**, at Av. Pedro de Osma 421 (Tues–Sun 10am–5.30pm; S10; ⓦwww.museopedrodeosma.org), which houses a good collection of religious art, silver and antique furniture in a stunning French-style mansion with stained-glass windows designed by the eponymous collector. A walk across the **Puente de Suspiros** to the cliffside bars and cafés is a favourite pastime for locals, but otherwise there's little else to see specifically; the main highlight of Barranco is its bars, clubs and cafés clustered around the small but attractive **Plaza Municipal**, which retain much of the area's original charm.

Pueblo Libre

This upcoming neighbourhood, southwest of the centre, hosts two world-class museums. The **Museo Nacional de Arqueología, Antropología e Historia del Perú** (Tues–Sat 9am–4.30pm, Sun & holidays 9am–3.30pm; S11.50; ⓦmuseonacional.perucultural.org.pe), at Plaza Bolívar, has an extensive collection of pre-Hispanic and colonial artefacts, helpfully laid out in chronological order. It also houses the two most important relics from the Chavín de Huántar site near Huaraz: the Raimondi Stela, a 2m-tall piece of granite with intricate carvings, and the Tello Obelisk, which once lurked underground, worshipped by priests of the Chavín cult. Part of the museum is in a mansion once inhabited by the liberators Simón Bolívar and José de San Martín.

Follow the (sometimes worn) blue line outside the museum for a pleasant

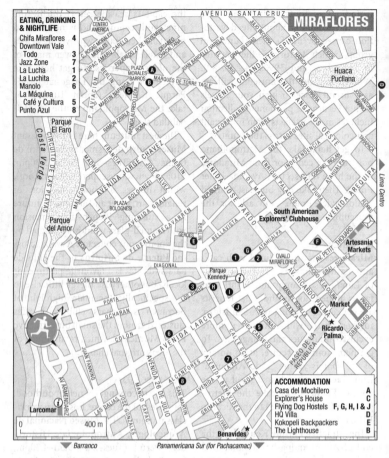

EATING, DRINKING
& NIGHTLIFE
Chifa Miraflores 4
Downtown Vale
    Todo
Jazz Zone 7
La Lucha 1
La Luchita 2
Manolo 6
La Máquina
    Café y Cultura 5
Punto Azul 8

MIRAFLORES

Parque
El Faro

Costa Verde

CIRCUITO DE LAS PLAYAS

Parque
del Amor

PLAZA
CENTRO
AMERICA

AVENIDA SANTA CRUZ

Huaca
Pucllana

Lima Centro

South American
Explorers' Clubhouse

Artesanía
Markets

OVALO
MIRAFLORES

Parque
Kennedy

DIAGONAL

MALECÓN 28 DE JULIO

Market

Ricardo
Palma

Larcomar

0   400 m

Barranco   Panamericana Sur (for Pachacamac)

ACCOMMODATION
Casa del Mochilero   A
Explorer's House   C
Flying Dog Hostels F, G, H, I & J
HQ Villa   D
Kokopeli Backpackers   E
The Lighthouse   B

PERU

LIMA

25-minute walk to the expensive but excellent **Museo Rafael Larco** at Av. Bolívar 1515 (daily 9am–6pm; S30, guided tour in English S20; ☏01/461-1312, ⊛www.museolarco.org). Situated in a viceroy's mansion which in turn was built on a pre-Columbian pyramid, it displays the enormous private collection of Peruvian archeologist Rafael Larco, which includes textiles, jewellery, gold, silver and ceramics. Best of all, you can explore the vast storage rooms, packed to the rafters with more than 45,000 pre-Columbian objects. It's also famous for an extensive erotic ceramics section. Be sure to check out the elegant

café and shops in the beautifully manicured grounds.

These museums are close to both the **artisan markets** on blocks 6–8 of Av. La Marina (considerably cheaper than their equivalent in Miraflores) and the **Parque de las Leyendas** at Av. Las Leyendas 580 (daily 9am–6pm; S10; ⊛www .leyendas.gob.pe), a family-orientated zoo landscaped to represent the three zones in Peru – coast, mountains and jungle. The site also contains more than thirty pre-Columbian *huacas* (see box, p.811), all in differing stages of excavation, as well as a botanical garden and boating lake.

Callao and La Punta

Still the country's main commercial harbour, and one of the most modern ports in South America, **Callao** lies about 14km west of central Lima. Its main attraction is the pentagonal **Fortaleza Real Felipe**, on Plaza Independencia, which houses the **Museo del Ejército** (Military Museum; Tues–Sun 9.30am–4pm; S12 by 1.5-hr guided tour in Spanish; ☎01/429-0532). The collection of eighteenth-century arms and rooms dedicated to Peruvian heroes are interesting, but the real star is the fort itself, a superb example of the military architecture of its age. A short walk from the fort, at the dock on Plaza Grau, you can take **boat tours** out around local islands (for tour operators see p.812). Book ahead for trips further out to the **Islas Palomino** (around 4hr; S105), where you'll see sea birds, dolphins and sometimes whales; you can swim here with sea lions.

A 20-minute walk southwest of the fort are the crumbling but charming neighbourhoods of **Chuquito** and **La Punta**, where you can dream away an afternoon on the pebble beach, eat mouth-wateringly fresh *ceviche* or go for a row-boat ride out to sea.

To **get to Callao** from central Lima, take a bus from Plaza Dos de Mayo running down Av. Oscar R. Benavides, or a bus marked "La Punta" from Av. Arequipa west along either Av. Angamos or Av. Javier Prado. Callao can be dangerous, so make sure the conductor knows where you want to get off.

Arrival

Air From Jorge Chavez Airport (🌐www.lap.com.pe) in Callao, 10km northwest of the city centre, the quickest and safest way to get into central Lima is by taxi (45min). Take an official taxi from one of the three companies with desks at the airport – pay there and you'll be assigned a driver. Green Taxis are the cheapest of the three (S60 to downtown).

Bus Buses to Lima usually arrive at the terminals in the district of La Victoria, near to central Lima, or

---

HUACAS

There are reminders of Lima's pre-Columbian past all over the city in the form of adobe huacas – sacred places – also referred to as pyramids. They are mostly associated with the Lima Culture, which dominated in the area from 200 to 700 AD. Two of the most impressive sit wonderfully at odds with the modern monstrosities around them. The Huaca Pucllana, at General Borgoño block 8, Miraflores (Wed–Mon 9am–4pm; S10; 🌐pucllana.perucultural.org.pe), the larger of the two, was thought to have been a major administrative centre for the Lima. It's a short walk from Av. Arequipa at block 44 (off to the right if you're coming from central Lima). Huaca Huallamarca, at Nicolás de Rivera 201, San Isidro (Tues–Sun 9am–5pm; S7; 🌐www.sanisidrolima.com/distrito/huallamarca) is three blocks from Camino Real along Choquehuanca. It's thought to be a little older than Pucllana and pertaining to the Hualla tribe. The spaceship-like ramp can be scaled to get great views of the neighbourhood. Both tickets include entrance to small site museums.

The most wonderful of all Lima's *huacas*, Pachacamac, lies just outside the city at km31.5 off the Panamericana Sur, Lurín (Tues–Sun 9am–5pm; S7, guides S20; 🌐pachacamac.perucultural.org.pe). It's easily reached by public transport – you can do it in half a day. Get there from Lima centro by catching the brown *combi* marked San Bartolo from outside MALI and double-check that it's going to Lurín. Alternatively, you can get this same *combi* nearer Miraflores by taking any bus marked "todo Benavides" from Miraflores to the Panamericana, go down the steps to the busy motorway and wait at the stop under the bridge. From here it's about 30 minutes away and you can be dropped right outside the Museo de Sitio (site museum).

at the other end of La Victoria on Av. Javier Prado. For full details of Lima bus companies and their terminals, see box, p.817. Whichever terminal you arrive at, your best bet is to hail the first decent-looking taxi you see and fix a price – about S5–7 to anywhere in the centre, or S10–15 for anywhere else in Lima.

Information

Tourist information The municipal tourist office is just off the Plaza de Armas behind the Palacio Municipal (INFO). IPerú is the national tourist info provider, and can also help if you need to make a complaint, visit the police or simply book accommodation. IPerú has desks in Lima airport (open 24hr; ☎01/574-8000), Miraflores (Larcomar, stand 10; daily 11am–8pm; ☎01/445-9400) as well as San Isidro (Jorge Basadre 610 ☎01/421-1627, ✉iperulima@promperu.gob.pe). Callao has a basic tourist information booth on the road between Plaza Grau and Chuquito (daily 10am–5pm), which has information about the museums in the area. The South American Explorers' Club, at C. Piura 135, Miraflores (Mon–Fri 9.30am–5pm, Sat 9.30am–1pm; ☎01/445-3306), has good information including maps, listings and travel reports available to non-members for a fee (see box, p.812). For information specific to gay travellers in Lima see box, p.798.

Tour operators Fertur Peru, at Jr. Junín 211, Central Lima (☎01/427-2626, ⊛www.fertur-travel.com) offers nationwide package tours and some local tours. Better and cheaper for Lima tours, including Pachacamac and the museums, is Lima Vision, at Jr. Chiclayo 444, Miraflores (☎01/447-0482, ⊛www.limavision.com). For open-top bus tours of Lima, Mirabús (☎01/242-6699, ⊛www.mirabusperu.com), which has a stall in both the Parque Kennedy and the Plaza Mayor, runs daily tours of Miraflores, colonial Lima and Lima by day/night, as well as Pachacamac (Tues–Sun 10am), Callao (Sun only), and boat trips to the Palomino Islands (bi-monthly). Other operators to the Islas Palominos include Ecocruceros, at Av. Arequipa 4964 office 202 (☎01/226-8530, ⊛www.islaspalomino.com), with an office in Miraflores and a stand by the port in Callao; and Kolibri Expeditions (⊛www.kolibriexpeditions.com), which is recommended for trips from Callao. Bike Tours of Lima, at Calle Bolívar 150, Miraflores (☎01/445-3127, ⊛www.biketoursoflima.com) does what it says on the tin, as well as bike rentals.

City transport

Bus *Combis* (inner-city buses) race from one street corner to another along all the major arterial city roads. Wave one down and pay the flat fare (S0.50–2 within Lima, depending on distance) to the driver or *cobrador* (conductor). Simply call out "bajo esquina" ("I'm getting off at the corner") when you want to get off, or ask the *cobrador* to advise you ("avisame") when your destination comes up. A fantastic unofficial map of Lima's most useful and safe *combis* (many are more than a little ropey) can be purchased for US$5 at ⊛www.rutasrecomendables.com.

Colectivo These look like private cars or taxis but run a fixed route; each has a small sign in the window with the destination and can squeeze in up to six passengers. They have set starting points, but if there's space the driver will try and catch your attention and will stop almost anywhere to let you in. The price is generally double that of *combis*, depending on distance travelled.

Taxi Taxis can be hailed on any street, and should not cost more than S20 within the city (except to/from the airport). Most are unofficial, although the yellow ones with a licence plate number on the side are, in theory, regulated. It is, perhaps, better to look at the condition of the car and always agree on a price beforehand. As a guide, taxis within a district (eg anywhere within central Lima) should be S4–6, while Miraflores to the centre should be S10–12. Prices also depend on traffic. Private companies are few and far between, change numbers regularly and charge a lot more.

Accommodation

There are good budget options throughout the city, although Central Lima works out slightly cheaper and offers hostels within walking distance of some of the most important tourist sights. Barranco offers a relaxed bohemian atmosphere close to the sea, but the most popular district for tourists is still Miraflores; with bright lights and fast-food joints on every corner it has a cosmopolitan feel, plus plenty of chain backpacker hostels proving mainly dorm-style accommodation. There are no campsites, official or otherwise.

Central Lima

Europa Jr. Ancash 376 ☎01/427-3351. An old, slightly run-down, draughty building opposite the San Francisco church, with a lovely courtyard. The rooms are worthy of a monastery in their simplicity (most have shared bath), but it's more or less clean. Can be cold in winter. S25.

METROPOLITANO

Lima may be one of the largest cities in the world without an underground metro, but it now has the very modern Metropolitano bus service (daily 6am–9.50pm, express service during rush hours 7–9.30am & 5–8.30pm; www.metropolitano .com.pe). This bus runs through the city north to south and connects the main tourist areas of Barranco, Miraflores and San Isidro along the Paseo de la Republica with central Lima. It uses a rechargeable card which subtracts S1.50 per ride, and it's the quickest, easiest and certainly the safest way to get around Lima as the buses use special lanes and the fleet is new. The Estación Central (under Plaza Grau) is the best place to go for any queries, though each station has attendants and a ticket booth. Check the website (under "rutas") for any changes before you use it.

Hostal Belén Nicolás de Piérola 935, Plaza San Martín ☎01/427-7391. One of the best-value budget options in Central Lima – a well-maintained colonial gem with a restaurant serving bargain set lunches to guests and passers-by. Try to get a room with views of the plaza. S40.

Hostal España Jr. Azángaro 105 ☎01/428-5546, www.hotelespanaperu .com. The main courtyard filled with antique oil paintings, marble statues and trailing pot plants is quite stunning; worth sticking your head in for that alone. There's also a verdant rooftop patio where breakfast is served (S5 extra). Service is brusque, but aside from that this is a good place to stay; it's secure and has internet connection, book exchange and a tour operator service. Ask for a room away from the stairs if you want a lie-in, and extra blankets in the winter. Dorms S16, rooms S45.

Pensión Ibarra Av. Tacna 359 apt.1402 ☎01/427-8603. For a different type of experience, try staying with the very welcoming Ibarra couple in their apartment on the fourteenth floor. The rooms are simple but the views are spectacular and the place is kept tidy. Breakfast and laundry can be arranged for a bit extra, use of the kitchen is permitted and there's no curfew. Very cheap rates can be arranged for long stays. S30.

Miraflores

Casa del Mochilero Jr. Cesareo Chacaltana 130a, upstairs ☎01/444-9089. This safe place is remarkably good for the price, with hot water, cable TV and kitchen facilities. It's not right at the centre of Miraflores's action, but it's close enough. Don't confuse it with the similarly named and decorated hostel next door; ask for Pilar (the owner) to be sure. Dorms S15, rooms S35.

Explorer's House Av. Alfredo Leon 158 ☎01/241-5002. Out of the centre of Miraflores but close to the ocean, *Explorer's House* is a good old-fashioned

hostel with a family atmosphere and comfy if worn beds. Breakfast is included and internet, wi-fi, hot water and a rooftop terrace add to the charm; there's also a small kitchen for guests to use. Book ahead as it is small and popular. Dorms S20, rooms S48.

Flying Dog Hostels www.flyingdogperu .com. The Flying Dog empire continues to expand in Miraflores with no less than four locations: *Backpackers*, at Diez Canseco 117 (includes breakfast); *Bed and Breakfast*, at Calle Lima 457; *Hostel*, at Olaya 280; *Long stays*, at Pershing 155. All locations offer cheap accommodation, kitchen use, TV room, storage service and internet access, as well as being hugely popular and therefore a great place to meet people. They also run the small and trendy *Tasca Bar* under their hostel on Diez Canseco. Dorms S30, rooms S66.

HQ Villa Calle Independencia 1288 ☎01/651-2320 www.hqvilla.com. While this is a bit out of the way in a quiet residential neighbourhood – in between Miraflores and San Isidro, parallel to Cuadra 40 of Arequipa and about a 20-min walk to the centre of either neighbourhood – it's worth it. A British/Peruvian-owned boutique hostel with tons of character, including a huge garden and open-plan kitchen/living area with moodily lit bathrooms, chandeliers, photography and a packed social calendar, on top of all the usual extras. Dorms S29, rooms S45.

Kokopeli Backpackers Calle Berlin 259 ☎01/651-2886 www.hostelkokopeli.com. What makes this hostel stand out is the breakfast; it's at hip *Café Z* and instead of the usual rolls with jam you can choose from waffles, granola and fesh coffee/juice. That aside there's a rooftop bar, artwork and plenty of beanbags, as well as all the backpacker favourites. Dorms S30, rooms S75.

The Lighthouse Jr. Cesareo Chacaltana 162 ☎01/446-8397, www.thelighthouse peru.com. This B&B offers perhaps the best-value accommodation in Miraflores in the form of spacious comfortable rooms (one with a balcony) with cable TV. A patio with BBQ plus a communal area with DVDs, books and internet offer the budget traveller some real creature comforts. Kitchen use and a generous breakfast all add to the homely experience. Book in advance as there are only six rooms. S70.

Barranco

La Casona Roja Av. Grau 720 ☎01/256-1789 ⓦwww.casonaroja.com. This huge hostel really is a mansion – you might get lost in its winding corridors. But it offers everything travellers want: breakfast, a bar, DVDs, a pool table and chill-out zones. The friendly French owners sometimes take residents out to experience Barranco's excellent nightlife. Dorms S30, rooms S75.

Domeyer Calle Domeyer 296 ☎01/247-1413, ⓦwww.domeyerhostel.net. Charming and homely hostel with shared kitchen and living room plus laundry service. Rooms include cable and wi-fi, and there are cheaper dorms in a building along the same street. Gay friendly. Breakfast included. Dorms S40, rooms S110.

The Point Malecón Junín 300 ☎01/247-7952, ⓦwww.thepointhostels.com. Has lots of facilities including internet, TV room and kitchen, as well as the on-site *Pointless Bar*, a great place to meet other travellers and have a good time. Relaxed garden with hammocks is a boon. Dorms S26, rooms S68.

Eating

Lima has seen its gastronomy boom in the past few years, partly thanks to Peruvian celebrity chef and international restaurateur Gastón Acurio (see box, p.797); the swell in national pride surrounding Peruvian cuisine is palpable, nowhere more so than in Lima. Many of the more upmarket restaurants fill up very quickly, so it's advisable to reserve in advance; where this is the case the phone number is included.

Central Lima

There is a Metro supermarket on Jr. Cusco between Lampa and Augusto Wiese and two enormous supermarkets opposite each other on Alfonso Ugarte, where it is crossed by Uruguay. Most *chifas* (Chinese restaurants) in Chinatown are good and very cheap. There is also a whole street full of vegetarian restaurants one block from the Plaza de Armas on Camaná.

Antigua Pastelería y Panedería Huérfanos Corner of Azángaro and Puno. This cake shop and bakery really is *antigua* (old) – it's been here for over fifty years– and is easily the best place in central Lima for bread. It also makes its own fresh pasta and you can buy pastries and biscuits by weight. One section of the shop is a great little restaurant with set lunches, huge portions and cheerful waiters. Plate of ravioli with wine S15.

Bodega Cafetería Santa Isabel Jr. Augusto Wiese 520. Recharge after sightseeing in this tiny *huarique* that serves some of the best coffee in Lima. Excellent chocolates and liquors are available, and they also specialize in regional cheeses and hams –their sandwiches and *empanadas* (S6–7) are excellent. Open Mon–Sat 8am–9pm.

El Cordano Jr. Ancash 202. Beside the Palacio del Gobierno, this is one of the city's last surviving traditional bar-restaurants, open since 1905. The food is overpriced, but go for a drink, soak up the atmosphere and feel yourself slip back in time. Open Mon–Sat 8am–8pm.

Esbari Jr. de la Unión 574, Primarily an ice-cream parlour with fabulous flavours (they'll give tasters) and sundaes (S12.50), good coffee and cheap food – look for the "ofertas" section in the back of the menu where everything is less than S10. Daily 8am–11.30pm.

Quierolo Café Bar Restaurant Corner of Camaná and Quilca. Arguably there is no place that better represents old bohemian Lima; this bar has seen every artist and writer in the city come through its doors for lunch or drinks since 1880. They serve a good set lunch (S6), as well as sandwiches and the usual *criolla* favourites. Open daily 9am–2am.

Tanta Pasaje Nicolás de Rivera 142–148 ☎01/428-3115. If you can't afford a whole Gastón Acurio meal, his café chain *Tanta* can give you a taste of what he has to offer. This one, opposite the tourist information office, is a great pleasant place to refuel while sightseeing. Serves breakfasts, sandwiches, soups, salads and mains (S20–40), with sumptuous desserts and other snacks for under S10. Open Mon–Sat 9am–10pm, Sun 9am–6pm.

Wa Lok Jr. Paruro 864, Chinatown ☎01/427-2656. An excellent and traditional Chinese restaurant, consistently recommended by many Peruvians. It offers a range of authentic *chifa* dishes and although it's not the cheapest, there are good vegetarian and dim sum options under S20. Come for an early dinner as it closes at 9pm.

Miraflores

Eating options tend to be a little more expensive out of the centre, but there are a lot of good set menus for S6–10 in the small passage connecting Manuel Bonilla to Esperanza off the Parque Kennedy in Miraflores (go for the ones that are full of locals). There is also a huge food market between the Ovalo Parque Kennedy and Paseo de la Republica at Jr. Eledoro Romero and supermarkets everywhere.

Chifa Miraflores Av. Ricardo Palma 322. This outwardly unremarkable *chifa* is a favourite of celebrated chef Gastón Acurio. Try the enormous *sopa suicao con langostino* (prawn dumpling soup; S22), which can easily be shared between two or three with other starters. Open daily noon–11pm.

La Lucha & La Luchíta Av. Diagonal at the corner with Pasaje Olaya & Pasaje Champagnant 139, Miraflores. These two sandwich joints just around the corner from each other may be diminutive, but their oversized sandwiches with a variety of meaty fillings and sauces certainly aren't – the *chicharrón* (deep-fried pork) is particularly delicious. Open Mon–Fri 8am–3am & Sat–Sun 8am–3am.

Manolo Larco 608 🌐 www.manolochurros .com. The whopping sandwiches on display in the counter may catch your eye, but this Miraflores institution is all about the Spanish-style *churros con chocolate* – a doughnut that comes with hot chocolate for dipping; heaven for just S12. Also does breakfasts, mains, burgers and the like. Open daily 7.15–12.45am, until 1.45am Fri & Sat.

La Máquina Café y Cultura Alcanfores 323, Miraflores. Achingly trendy cafe with reading material, games, rock and electronic music, fairy lights and a huge picture of David Bowie. A great place for sandwiches, snacks and fantastic organic salads (all can be made vegetarian), all under S15. Try the incredible cocktails; the pisco hot chocolate is a must. Open Mon–Sat 10am–midnight, Sun 5pm–midnight.

Punto Azul Benavides 2711 & San Martín 595, Miraflores 🌐 puntoazulrestaurante .com. This *cevichería* is a real gem. As well as *ceviche* (S20) it serves other Peruvian classics involving fish or seafood, such as *causas* (tuna with mashed potato and lime) and *chupes* (chowder). The original site, a *huarique* on the busy Javier Prado in San Isidro, has you sitting on stools outside, while those in Miraflores are more restaurant-like. Open daily, lunchtime only.

Barranco & other suburbs

Anticuchos Tío Jhony Stall on the first block of Catalina Miranda, Barranco. This authentic *huarique* serves us some of the best *anticuchos* (beef heart

kebabs) in the capital. Don't be put off by the unusual meat – *anticuchos* are the most flavourful beef you'll ever try, especially here. "Uncle" Jhony's special chilli sauce is spectacular.

Expreso Virgen de Guadalupe Av. Prolongación San Martín 15-A, next to the Municipalidad, Barranco ☎ 01/252-8907. A unique vegetarian restaurant in an old tram car right on the main square, run by the owners of the *Posada del Angel* trio of bars. Lunchtime buffet S12.50 (S15 at weekends) for a great selection of meat-free and some vegan dishes. The food's a little more expensive á la carte. Open daily 10am–3pm.

Songoro Cosongo Ayacucho 281, Barranco ☎ 01/247-4730, 🌐 www.songorocosongo.com. By the Puente de los Suspiros, this traditional and friendly restaurant offers some of the best seafood and Creole dishes around at very reasonable prices (mains S20). They also often have live music and dancing. Daily 12.30–5pm & 7–11pm.

Drinking and nightlife

The daily newspaper *El Comercio* provides good entertainment listings and its Friday edition carries a comprehensive supplement on Lima's nightlife. The Plaza San Martin is, at present, the newest hotspot for nightlife, with enough bars and clubs there to take you through until dawn. Barranco is also trendy and the liveliest place to hang out at weekends, while Miraflores has the highest concentration of cheap bars around the Parque Kennedy. Good places for live music can be found in all three areas. As you would expect, Friday and

Saturday nights are the most popular, and many bars and clubs only open on those days. Most bars have Facebook pages to check what's on.

Bars and clubs

The distinction between a bar and club in Lima is often blurred, as bars become dancefloors and stay open all night. A good guide as to which is which is the opening times – many of the clubs only open at weekends. Lima has a fun and rapidly growing gay and lesbian scene; see Ⓦ lima.queercity.info for current information about what's on.

El Bolivarcito Jr. de la Unión 926, Central Lima. Come to the "catedral" of pisco sour, part of the Gran Hotel Bolívar, for the best in Lima. Also does an excellent set lunch (S12). Open daily noon–midnight.

Downtown Vale Todo Pasaje Los Pinos 168, Miraflores Ⓦ www.peruesgay.com/downtownvale todo. The name means "everything's allowed downtown" and it certainly is here at Lima's most established gay/lesbian club. Often has live drag or strip shows. Open daily from 9pm. Free Mon–Thurs, entrance fee at weekends.

Etnias Bar Cultural Augusto Wiese 815, Central Lima Ⓦ www.etniasbar.com. A highly atmospheric multipurpose space with muralled walls, folk art and a chequered dancefloor. Etnias is a café/nightclub which often has live world music/reggae or film showings. Try one of their "mystic drinks" for a truly Peruvian cocktail. Open Thurs–Sat 9.30pm until dawn.

🏃 **El Mirador** Jr. de la Unión 892, 7th floor, Central Lima Ⓦ barelmirador.com. Without doubt the bar with the best view in Lima. Walk confidently up to the bouncer and take the lift up to the 7th floor, where you'll find a cool crowd listening to a mix of rock and latin music surrounded by incense and Hindu imagery. Get there before 10pm to grab a table with views of the plaza. Open Thurs–Sat 8pm until dawn. Entry S5–10.

Munich Jr. de la Unión 1044. German-themed underground piano bar with a barrel for a doorway and bar food, a live pianist and nostalgic European landscapes on the walls. Daily from 5pm.

Posada del Ángel I, II & III Pedro de Osma 164 & 222; Av. Prolg San Martín 157, Barranco. This trio of bars are good for those who like a quiet drink – no dancing is one of the rules here, although there's often live acoustic music. All three bars have the owner's special brand of kitsch, chintz, religious iconography and of course angels, topped off with Tiffany-style glass and lamps. Has wi-fi and some food is served. Mon–Sat 7pm–3am.

Rincón Cervecero Jr. de la Unión 1045 Ⓦ www .rinconcervecero.com.pe. Another German-themed bar opposite Munich, where you can order beer in containers of all forms, including a 5-litre barrel of beer (S80), from Peruvian waiters in lederhosen. Open daily from 4pm.

Vichama Augusto Wiese 945, Central Lima. A seriously cool rock bar/club in a huge colonial space, with many small art-filled rooms containing a mix of shabby chic furniture. Thurs–Sat 10pm until very late. Free entry.

Wahio's Bar Pasaje Espinoza 111 on the Plaza de Bomberos. Cosy bar club with several rooms playing different sounds, though you'll mostly hear reggae and electronic pop. Walls are packed with photos and artwork, there's comfy seating and bar food is served. Thurs–Sat from around 9.30pm until the last people leave. Free entry.

Live music

The great variety of traditional and hybrid sounds is one of the most enduring reasons for visiting the capital. The best place to go for an evening's entertainment is a *peña* – a live music spectacular featuring many styles of national song and dance with an MC, live band, some audience participation and much dancing. *Peñas* are great fun for all ages, although they start late and the dancing can last all night, and the Lima versions are very expensive compared to the rest of the country (you can pay up to S60 just to enter) – so if you can't go here, be sure to seek one out elsewhere.

La Candelaria Av. Bolognesi 292, Barranco ☏ 01/247-1314, Ⓦ www.lacandelariaperu.com. Impressive costumes, choreography and plenty of audience participation mark this place out as one of Barranco's most popular *peñas*. The amazingly decorated room adds to the atmosphere. Shows Thurs–Sat starting at 9.30pm. Entrance fee (depending on the show) S25, including a pisco sour.

Jazz Zone Av. La Paz 646, Pasaje El Suche, Miraflores Ⓦ www.jazzzoneperu.com. Live music (most often rock and jazz) from local and international groups in this atmospheric joint upstairs. Open Mon–Sat from 8pm. Entrance fee varies depending on the show.

🏃 **La Noche** Av. Bolognesi 307 at the corner with El Boulevard, Barranco Ⓦ www .lanoche.com.pe. at the top end of the Boulevard, this bar is really packed at weekends and is the top nightspot in the neighbourhood. There's a section with a stage for live music, with free jazz sessions on Mon eve. Fine decor and a good range of snacks. Open daily from 7pm, closed Sun. Free entry to bar, pitcher of beer S15; S10–30 entry for live music.

De Rompe y Raja Calle Manuel Segura 127, Barranco ☏ 01/247-3271, Ⓦ www.derompeyraja .pe. This moodily lit *peña* is especially famous for

Afro-Peruvian rhythms, but you'll hear salsa and *folklorica* too. Open Thurs–Sun from around 10pm. Prices vary, but can be free entry if you arrive early with a minimum spend of S35 per person on food and drink – always check the website as flyers can be printed off for discounts. Lunchtime shows with food included are cheaper.

Shopping

All types of Peruvian *artesanía* are available in Lima, including woollen goods, crafts and gemstones. Some of the best in Peru are on Av. Petit Thouars, which is home to a handful of markets between Av. Ricardo Palma and Av. Angamos, all well within walking distance of Miraflores centre.

Often considerably cheaper are the artisan markets on blocks 9 and 10 of Av. La Marina in Pueblo Libre, as well as the good craft and antique market in the Miraflores Park between Diagonal and Av. Larco, which takes place every evening (6–9pm). In central Lima the Artesanía Santo Domingo, opposite the church of the same name, houses a range of suppliers to suit all budgets, just a stone's throw from the Plaza Mayor; it is especially good for loose beads.

For clothing, Polvos Azules (Av. Paseo de le República, 2 blocks from Plaza Grau) and Gamarra (Prolongación Gamarra, La Victoria) are huge shopping centres/markets where you can pick up very cheap branded clothing and footwear. Both areas can be dangerous and are rife with pickpockets so take only the money you want to spend and try to visit early in the morning.

Directory

Banks and exchange Central Lima, Miraflores, Barranco and San Isidro all have several casas de cambio, and Interbank will change money and travellers' cheques. Moneychangers on the streets will often give a slightly better rate but will try all sorts of tricks, from doctored calculators to fake money. Often the best way to change money in Lima is by buying things in supermarkets with large US$ notes and asking them for the change in soles – they usually give the best rates.

Embassies and consulates Australia, Av. Victor Belaúnde 147, oficina 1301, Torre Real 3 San Isidro (☎01/222-8281); Canada, Bolognesi 228, Miraflores (☎01/319 3200); Ireland (consulate), Av. Paseo de la Republica 5757b, Miraflores (☎01/242-9516); South Africa, Av. Víctor Andrés Belaunde, Edificio Real 3, San Isidro (☎01/440-9996); UK, Torre Parque Mar, Av. Larco 1301, 22nd

floor, Miraflores (☎01/617-3000); USA, Av. La Encalada, block 17, Monterrico (☎01/434-3000).

Internet Internet cafés are available throughout the capital, most equipped for chat, with several 24hr places in Miraflores.

Police Tourist Police, at Jr. Moore 268, Magdalena del Mar (☎01/460-1060 or 980-121-462, ✉divtur@pnp.gob.pe). English spoken.

Postal services Not overly reliable, the principal postal company is SERPOST whose main office is on Pasaje Piura off Jr. de la Unión, one block from the Plaza de Armas (☎01/511-5110; open 8am–8.30pm). SERPOST also has an office in Miraflores at Petit Thouars 5201. FedEx, DHL and UPS all have offices in Lima – check their websites for details.

Moving on

Air Lima Airport applies a flat US$30 departure tax on international flights, paid on departure. For domestic flights the departure tax is around US$7. All airlines fly to and from Jorge Chávez Airport in Callao. Arequipa (10 daily; 1hr 20min); Cajamarca (5 daily; 1hr 20min); Cusco (15 daily; 1hr 15min); Iquitos (8 daily; 1hr 45min); Tumbes (daily; 1hr 50min).

Bus Lima's numerous bus terminals are dispersed throughout the city and, unfortunately, often in dodgy areas. Unless your Spanish is good enough to enquire over the phone, or the bus company is modern enough to have a reliable website, you'll have to trawl around finding times and booking tickets. The following bus companies have terminals in La Victoria (always take a taxi there, as the area's not safe), unless otherwise stated. See p.793 for company information and websites. Cruz del Sur, at Av. Javier Prado 1109 (☎01/311-5050); Línea, at Av. Paseo de la República 941-959 (☎01/424-0836); Movil Tours, at Paseo de la Republica 749 (☎01/716-8000); Oltursa, at Av. Aramburu 1160, San Isidro (☎01/225-4499); Ormeño, at Av. Carlos Zavala 177, Central Lima & Av. Javier Prado Este 1059 (☎01/427-5000); Soyuz Perú, at Av. México 333 (☎01/205-2370); Tepsa, at Av. Javier Prado Este 1091 (☎01/386-5689).

Destinations: Arequipa (15hr): Cruz del Sur (9 daily), Oltursa (4 daily), Ormeño (2 daily), Tepsa (2 daily); Cajamarca (14hr): Cruz del Sur (1 daily), Línea (2 daily), Tepsa (1 daily); Chachapoyas (20hr): Movil Tours (1 daily); Chiclayo (12hr): Cruz del Sur (4 daily), Línea (2 daily), Movil Tours (7 daily), Oltursa (4 daily), Tepsa (3 daily); Cusco (22hr): Cruz del Sur (3 daily), Tepsa (2 daily); Puno (20hr): Ormeño (1 daily); Huaraz (8hr): Cruz del Sur (2 daily), Movil Tours (10 daily); Nazca (7hr): Cruz del Sur (5 daily), Oltursa (3 daily), Ormeño (2 daily),

Soyuz Perú (hourly), Tepsa (3 daily): Tacna (18hr):
Tepsa (1 daily); Trujillo (8hr): Cruz del Sur (5 daily),
Línea (9 daily), Movil Tours (1 daily), Oltursa (3
daily), Tepsa (2 daily); Tumbes via Máncora (all
1 daily; 18–20hr): Cruz del Sur, Línea, Oltursa,
Ormeño, Tepsa.

Train The only train from Lima goes to Huancayo
once a month (see p.794).

Cusco and around

The former capital of the Inca empire,
modern **CUSCO** is an exciting and
colourful city, enclosed between high
hills and dominated by the imposing
ceremonial centre and fortress of
Sacsaywamán. It's one of South
America's biggest tourist destinations,
thanks to its narrow whitewashed
streets, thriving culture, lively nightlife,
substantial Inca ruins and architectural
treasures from the colonial era.

Once you've acclimatized to the
3500m altitude, there are dozens of
enticing destinations within easy reach.
For most people the **Sacred Valley**
is the obvious first choice, with the
citadel of **Machu Picchu** as the ultimate
goal. The mountainous region around
Cusco boasts some of the country's
finest trekking, and beyond the **Inca
Trail** to Machu Picchu are hundreds of
lesser-known paths into the mountains,
including the **Salcantay** and **Ausungate**
treks, which are even more stunning and
challenging. Cusco is also a covenient
jumping-off point for the exploration
of the lowland **Amazon rainforest** in

Madre de Díos, such as the Tambopata-
Candamo Reserved Zone, or the Manu
Biosphere Reverve, among the most
biodiverse wildernesses on Earth.

Some history

Legend has it that Cusco was founded
by **Manco Capac** and his sister **Mama
Occlo** in around 1100 AD. Over the
next two centuries, the **Cusco Valley**
was home to the Inca tribe, but it wasn't
until **Pachacutec** assumed power in
1438 that Cusco became the centre of an
expanding empire. Of all the Inca rulers,
only **Atahualpa**, the last, never actually
resided in Cusco, and even he was en
route there when the conquistadors
captured him at Cajamarca. **Francisco
Pizarro** reached the native capital
on November 15, 1533, after holding
Atahualpa to ransom, then killing him
anyway. The city's beauty surpassed
anything the Spaniards had seen before
in the New World, the stonework was
better than any in Spain and precious
metals were used in a sacred context
throughout the city. As usual, they lost
no time in looting it.

Like its renowned art, the Cusco of
today is dark yet vibrantly coloured,
reflecting its turbulent legacy. It's a
politically active, left-of-centre city
where the streets are often alive with
fiestas and demonstrations.

What to see and do

The city divides into several distinct
zones, with the **Plaza de Armas** at the
heart of it all. Many of the streets now
bear Quechua names due to a recent

WHEN TO VISIT

The best time to visit the area around Cusco is during the dry season (May–Sept),
when it's warm with clear skies during the day but relatively cold at night. During
the wet season (Oct–April) it rarely rains every day or all week, but the heavy
downpours trigger landslides, making it difficult and dangerous to travel in the
nearby mountains.

resurgence of indigenous pride, though some are still referred to by their Spanish names.

The **Boleto Turistico** (Tourist Ticket; see above) will give you an idea of some of the most popular city and sacred valley sites, but does not include entry to the one unmissable Cusco site, the Inca sun temple at **Q'orikancha**. Around the city there are opportunities for tours, hikes and extreme sports, as well as the fascinating Inca sites of **Sacsaywamán** and **Tambomachay**.

Plaza de Armas

Cusco's ancient and modern centre, the **Plaza de Armas**, corresponds roughly to the ceremonial *Huacaypata*, the Incas' ancient central plaza, and is a constant hub of activity, its northern and western sides filled with shops and restaurants. Here you'll be approached by touts, waiters and shoe-shine boys, and here is where you'll come to watch the parades during Cusco's festivities. You'll see two flags flying here – the Peruvian one and the rainbow flag of Tuhuantinsuyo, which represents the four corners of the Inca empire (not to be confused with the gay pride flag). On the northeastern side stands the imposing cathedral, flanked by the Jesús María and El Triunfo churches, with the Compañía de Jesús church on the eastern side.

La Catedral

The plaza's exposed northeastern edge is dominated by the fortress-like Baroque-style **Catedral** (Mon–Sat 10am–5.45pm, Sun 2–5.45pm; S30), which sits solidly on the foundations of the Inca Wiraco-cha's palace. Inside you'll find some of the best examples of art from the *Escuela Cusqueña* (Cusco School): look out for *The Last Supper*, with Christ sitting down to a feast of *cuy* (guinea pig), and the portrayals of the Virgin Mary as Pachamama (Mother Earth), her skirt looking like a mountain, its hem a river. Also check out the cathedral's finely carved granite altar and oldest surviving painting in Cusco, depicting the terrible 1650 earthquake, as well as a Neoclassical high altar made entirely of finely beaten embossed silver. Ten smaller chapels surround the nave, including the Chapel of El Señor de los Temblores (The Lord of Earthquakes) which houses a 26-kilo crucifix made of solid gold and encrusted with precious stones.

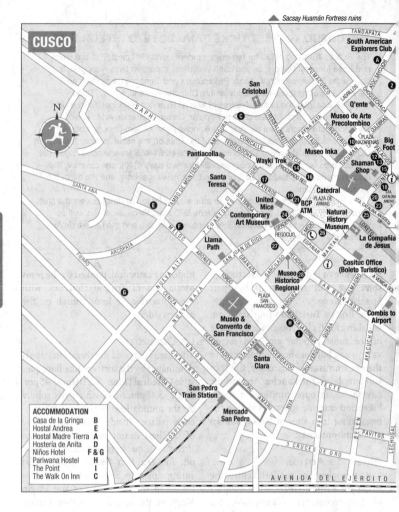

▲ Sacsay Huamán Fortress ruins

CUSCO

N

ACCOMMODATION
Casa de la Gringa	B
Hostal Andrea	E
Hostal Madre Tierra	A
Hostería de Anita	D
Niños Hotel	F & G
Pariwana Hostel	H
The Point	I
The Walk On Inn	C

❧ Iglesia de la Compañía de Jesús

Looking downhill from the centre of the plaza, the **Iglesia de la Compañía de Jesús** (daily 9–11.30am & 1–5.30pm; S10) dominates the skyline, and is often confused with the cathedral on first glance due to the splendour of its highly ornate facade. First built in the late 1570s, it was resurrected after the earthquake of 1650 in a Latin cross shape, over the foundations of Amara Cancha – originally Huayna Capac's Palace of

the Serpents. Cool and dark inside, with a grand gold-leaf altarpiece and a fine wooden pulpit displaying a relief of Christ, its transept ends in a stylish Baroque cupola.

Museo Inka

North of the cathedral, slightly uphill, you'll find one of the city's most beautiful colonial mansions, **El Palacio del Almirante** (The Admiral's Palace), which now houses the **Museo Inka** (Mon–Fri 8am–6pm, Sat 9am–4pm;

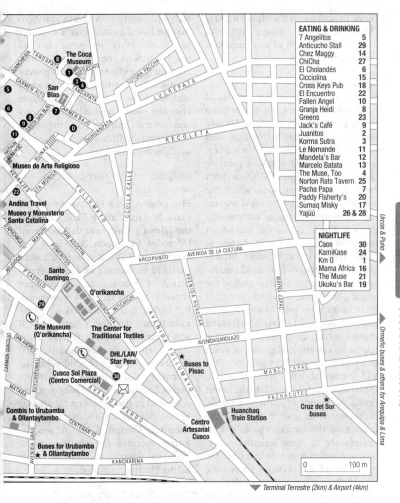

CUSCO AND AROUND

Urcos & Puno ▶

Ormeño buses & others for Arequipa & Lima ▶

EATING & DRINKING

7 Angelitos	5
Anticucho Stall	29
Chez Maggy	14
ChiCha	27
El Cholandés	6
Cicciolina	15
Cross Keys Pub	18
El Encuentro	22
Fallen Angel	10
Granja Heidi	8
Greens	23
Jack's Café	9
Juanitos	2
Korma Sutra	3
Le Nomande	11
Mandela's Bar	12
Marcelo Batata	13
The Muse, Too	4
Norton Rats Tavern	25
Pacha Papa	7
Paddy Flaherty's	20
Sumaq Misky	17
Yajúú	26 & 28

NIGHTLIFE

Caos	30
KamiKase	24
Km 0	1
Mama Africa	16
The Muse	21
Ukuku's Bar	19

▼ *Terminal Terrestre (2km) & Airport (4km)*

0 ———————— 100 m

S10). The museum itself is the best place in Cusco to see exhibits of Inca pottery, textiles, trepanned skulls, finely crafted metalwork (including miniature metal llamas given as offerings to the gods) and the largest range of wooden *quero* vases in the world. The superb room with the adult and child mummies, eerily lit with red lighting, presents you with a scene of macabre domesticity. There's excellent interpretative information in Spanish only, but you can hire a guide at the entrance for a small fee.

Monasterio de Santa Catalina

Leading away from the Plaza de Armas, Callejón Loreto separates La Compañía from the tall, stone walls of the ancient **Acclahuasi**, a temple where the Sun Virgins used to make *chicha* beer for the Inca ruler. Today, the building is occupied by the **Monasterio de Santa Catalina**, built in 1610, with its small but grand side entrance half a short block down Calle Arequipa; just under thirty sisters still live and worship here.

Inside the convent is the **Museo de Arte** (Mon–Sat 8.30am–5.30pm; S10), with a splendid collection of paintings from the *Escuela Cusqueña*.

Q'orikancha

If you visit one site in Cusco it should be **Q'orikancha**. The Convento de Santo Domingo at the intersection of Avenida El Sol and Calle Santa Domingo rises imposingly but rudely from the impressive walls of the Q'orikancha complex (Mon–Sat 8am–5pm; S10/S15 joint entry to Santo Domingo), which the conquistadors laid low to make way for their uninspiring Baroque seventeenth-century church. Before the Spanish set their gold-hungry eyes on it, the temple must have been even more breathtaking, consisting of four small sanctuaries and a larger temple set around the existing courtyard, which was encircled by a cornice of gold made of seven hundred solid gold sheets (Q'orikancha means "golden enclosure"). Below the temple was an artificial garden in which everything was made of gold or silver and encrusted with precious jewels, from llamas and shepherds to the tiniest details of clumps of earth and weeds, including snails and butterflies. The Incas used the Q'orikancha as a solar observatory to study celestial activities, and archeologists believe that the mummies of the previous Incas were brought here and ritually burned.

Visitors need to use their imagination when they enter the courtyard inside the site. The sacrifical font in the centre was once covered with 55kg of gold but the surviving sections of the original Inca wall, made of tightly interlocking blocks of polished andesite, stand as firmly rooted as ever, completely unshaken by the powerful earthquakes that have devastated colonial buildings.

Museo de Sitio del Q'orikancha

The underground **Museo de Sitio del Q'orikancha** (Mon–Sat 9am–6pm, Sun 8am–1pm; entry with Boleto Turístico) may not have the archeological treasures of Cusco's other museums, but it's worth a look. It consists of five rooms, containing various relics such as pottery shards, Inca weaponry, mummies and a section on the practice of trepanning, complete with medical instruments and several examples of trepanned skulls from the Paracas area. Guides are available for a small fee.

Iglesia y Convento de La Merced

Five minutes' walk southwest from the Plaza de Armas along Calle Mantas is the **Iglesia y Convento de La Merced** (Mon–Sat 8am–noon & 2–5pm; S6). Founded in 1536, it was rebuilt after the 1650 earthquake in a rich combination of Baroque and Renaissance styles. While its facade is exceptional, the highlight is a breathtaking 1720s' **monstrance** standing a metre high; it was crafted by Spanish jeweller using more than six hundred pearls, 1500 diamonds and 22kg of solid gold. The monastery also possesses a fine collection of *Escuela Cusqueña* paintings, and entombed in the church on the far side of the cloisters are the bodies of the two Diegos de Almagro, father and son, the former executed for rebelling against Francisco Pizarro and the latter for killing Pizarro in revenge.

Plaza San Francisco

Continue on another block and you'll come to the **Plaza San Francisco**, which comes alive on Sundays with street performers and food stalls selling traditional favourites. The square's south-western side is dominated by the simply decorated **Convento de San Francisco** (Mon–Sat 6.30–8am & 5.30–8pm, Sun 6.30am–noon & 6.30–8pm), completed in 1652. The two large cloisters inside have a large collection of colonial paintings, while the attached **Museo** (Mon–Fri 9am–noon & 3–5pm, Sat 9am–noon; S5) features a work by local master Juan Espinosa de los Monteros, responsible for the massive oil canvas measuring 12 metres by 9 metres – allegedly the largest in South America. Look out also for an unusual candelabra made out of human bones.

San Pedro Market

Stop in at the **San Pedro Market** (daily 8am–5pm) to enjoy a freshly squeezed juice, or to stock up on anything from llama toenail ornaments to herbal potions. Altough it is principally a food market, there are several stalls selling traditional costumes. Leave your valuables behind, as pickpockets are rife here.

Museo Histórico Regional y Casa Garcilaso

At the southern corner of Plaza Regocijo, the **Museo Histórico Regional y Casa Garcilaso** (Tues–Sun 8am–5pm; entry with Boleto Turistico) is home to fascinating pre-Inca ceramics, plus a Nazca mummy with 1.5m-long hair, and a number of Inca artefacts such as bolas, maces, and square water dishes that functioned as spirit levels. The museum also displays some gold and silver llamas found in 1996 in the Plaza de Armas when reconstructing the central fountain, golden figurines from Sacsaywamán and wooden *quero* drinking vessels and dancing masks from the colonial era.

Museo de Arte Precolumbino

On the western side of the small, quiet Plaza Nazarenas, the **Museo de Arte Precolumbino** housed in the Casa Cabrera (daily 8am–10pm; S20) has an open courtyard that's home to *MAP Café*, one of Cusco's finest restaurants, and elegant exhibition rooms displaying some exquisite pre-Columbian works of art, including a fine collection of Nazca and Mochica pottery and ornately carved Mochica ceremonial staffs, all labelled in English, French and Spanish.

San Blas

Just around the corner you come to the narrow alley of **Hathun Rumiyoq**, the most famous Inca passageway of all. Within its impressive walls lies the celebrated **Inca stone**; the twelve-cornered block fits perfectly into the original lower wall of what used to be the Inca Roca's old imperial palace.

Walking up the Cuesta de San Blas, you come to the Plazoleta de San Blas, which hosts a Saturday handicrafts market. Also on the tiny square is the small **Chapel of San Blas** (Mon–Sat 10am–6pm, Sun 2–6pm; S15 or free with Boleto Religioso). The highlight here is an incredibly intricate pulpit, carved from a block of cedar wood in a complicated Churrigueresque style by an indigenous man who allegedly devoted his life to the task and whose skull rests in the topmost part of the carving.

Museo de Coca

Just up Calle Suytuqatu from Plazoleta San Blas lies the fascinating little **Museo de Coca** (daily 9am–8pm; S10), devoted to the history of the coca leaf

---

MOUNTAIN SICKNESS

Soroche, or mountain sickness, is a reality for most people arriving in Cusco by plane from sea level. It's vital to take it easy, not eating or drinking much on arrival, even sleeping a whole day just to assist acclimatization. Coca tea is a good local remedy. After three days at this height most people have adjusted sufficiently to tackle moderate hikes at similar or lesser altitudes. Anyone considering tackling the major mountains around Cusco will need time to adjust again to their higher base camps. *Soroche* needs to be treated with respect.

through the ages. The exhibits explore the significance of the plant in Peru from its first known ceremonial use by the Andean people to the present day through a series of displays, from ancient ceramic figures with cheeks bulging from chewing coca leaves to nineteenth-century texts on research into the medical use of cocaine. The curator is happy to answer any questions you may have.

Arrival

Air Cusco airport (℡ 084/222-611) is 4km south of the city centre. You can either take a taxi from outside the arrivals hall (S10–15 to the city centre), or hop on a Correcaminos *colectivo* (S0.60) from outside the airport car park, which goes along Avenida Sol to Calle Ayacucho, two blocks from the Plaza de Armas.

Bus Most international and inter-regional buses arrive at the Terminal Terrestre (℡ 084/224-471), at Vía de Evitamiento 429, 2km southeast of the centre. You can catch any *colectivo* from the nearby Pachacutec monument uphill towards either the Plaza San Francisco or the Plaza de Armas (S0.60) or take a taxi (S5–8). Cruz del Sur has its own bus depot at Av. Pachacutec 510 (℡ 084/248-255); catch a taxi (S5–8).

Train If you're coming in from Puno by train, you'll arrive at the Huanchac station in the southeast of the city. From here you can hail a taxi on the street outside (around S5 to the centre), catch the airport *colectivo* mentioned above, or walk the eight or nine blocks up a gentle hill to the Plaza de Armas.

If you're coming by train from Machu Picchu, you'll disembark at Estación Poroy, east of the centre; arrivals are met by a bus (S8) that can drop you off at the Plaza Regocijo, or else take a taxi (S15–20).

Information

Tourist information The main tourist office (Dircetur) at Mantas 117-A (Mon–Sat 10am–8pm ℡ 084/223-701) has limited information on the city as well as free maps, though the staff are friendly and helpful. IPerú, at the arrivals hall at the airport (℡ 084/237-364), has free maps and brochures about the area. By far the best source of information about Cusco and around, with trip reports compiled by fellow travellers, as well as good trekking maps and a good book exchange, is the South American Explorers' Club, at Atoqsaycuchi 670 (Mon–Fri 9.30am–5pm, Sat 9.30am–1pm ℡ 084/245-484, ⓦ www.saexplorers .org). Andean Travel Web (ⓦ www.andeantravelweb .com) also has up-to-date information about events and festivities in the Cusco area.

Tour operators

The Cusco area is an adrenaline junkie's paradise, with a huge range of adventure sports on offer. As well as trekking expeditions in the Sacred Valley, there's world-class river rafting on the Apurimac River, climbing and canyoning in the nearby mountains, and mountain biking.

Amazonas Explorer Avenida Collasuyo 910, Miravalle ℡ 084/252-846, ⓦ www.amazonas -explorer.com. Internationally renowned operator offering multi-activity trips, combining hiking and rafting on the Apurimac, as well as mountain biking and horseriding excursions.

TOURS IN AND AROUND CUSCO

Tours in and around Cusco range from a half-day city tour to a full-on adventure down to the Amazon. Service and facilities vary considerably, so check exactly what's provided. **Standard tours** around the city, Sacred Valley and to Machu Picchu range from a basic bus service with fixed stops and little in the way of a guide, to luxury packages including guide, food and hotel transfers. The two to four-day **Inca Trail** is the most popular of the **mountain treks**; many agencies offer trips with guides, equipment and fixed itineraries; see box on p.834 on when and how to do the Inca Trail.

Other **popular hikes** are around the snowcapped mountains of Salcantay (6264m) to the north and Ausangate (6372m) to the south, a more remote trek, which needs at least a week plus guides and mules (see p.843 for more info about these and other alternative Inca trails). You can also rent out **mountain bikes** for trips to the Sacred Valley and around, and some operators arrange guided tours. Many **jungle trip** operators are also based in Cusco (see above).

Andina Travel Plazoleta Santa Catalina 219 ☎084/251-892, ⓦ www.andinatravel.com. A well-established tour operator which specializes in responsible trekking, particularly along the more remote Lares routes (see p.846), where you get to experience traditional Andean life.

Big Foot Triunfo 392, Cusco ☎084/238-568, ⓦ www.bigfootcusco.com. Specialists in multi-day expeditions, such as trekking in Ausangate and to Vilcabamba (see p.844).

Llama Path San Juan de Dios 250, Cusco ☎084/240-822, ⓦ www.llamapath.com. One of the newer Inca Trail trekking operators in town, Llama Path has quickly established itself as a more affordable, high-quality, responsible outfit.

Q'ente Choquechaca 229, Cusco ☎233-722, ⓦ www.qente.com. Responsible adventure travel company specializing in alternative treks as well as the traditional Inca Trail.

United Mice Plateros 351, Cusco ☎084/221-139, ⓦ www.unitedmice.com. One of the original Inca Trail operators; the owner of this company started out as a porter on the trail. Professional service and good English-speaking guides.

Wayki Trek Procuradores 351, Cusco ☎084/224-092 ⓦ www.waykitrek.net. Professional company supporting many community projects in the area and offering some off-the-beaten-trail treks. Also offers a "wayki option" on the Inca Trail whereby groups spend the night in a porter community prior to starting the trail.

City transport

Bus and colectivo The city bus and *colectivo* networks are incredibly complicated, though cheap and fast once you learn your way around, and charge S0.60 per person. If you don't have much luggage, you can take a Correcaminos *colectivo* from the eastern side of Calle Ayacucho, half a block south of Av. El Sol, to the airport and the terminal terrestre.

Taxi Rides within Cusco cost around S3 or S6–10 for trips to the suburbs or up to Saqsaywamán and Q'enqo (some *taxistas* may charge S20 and wait for you, in which case give them half in advance and half later).

Accommodation

There are numerous budget options around the Plaza de Armas and in the quieter San Blas area uphill from the square.

Casa de la Gringa Tandapata and Pasnapacana 148 ☎084/235-473 ⓦ www.casadelagringa.com. Try to stay in the original Casa, with individually decorated rooms, all-day coca tea and a good book exchange, as the overflow house lacks charm. There's free wi-fi and the owner is one of the best people to consult about the Ayahuasca and San Pedro journeys (see box, p.898). S40.

Hostal Andrea Santa Ana 504 ☎084/236-713, ⓔ andreahostal@gmail.com. This family-run cheapie may not look like much from the outside, but its humble exterior hides some of the best bargains in Cusco. The rooms with shared bathrooms are very basic, but if you nab an en-suite room on the first floor, you'll get a superb view of Cusco, along with cable TV. S25.

🏃 Hostal Madre Tierra Atoqsaycuchi 647 ☎084/248-452, ⓦ www.hostalmadretierra .com. This little gem of a guesthouse is located high up in San Blas, with a lovingly decorated interior, seven bright, wi-fi-enabled en-suites and helpful staff on-call 24/7. American-style breakfast is included and the in-house tour agency can help you arrange your time in Cusco. Free airport transfers available. S140.

Hostería de Anita Cuesta de San Blas 541 ☎084/225-933, ⓦ www.amaruhotels.com. One of the popular Amaru guesthouses, this hidden place, arranged around a sunny flowering courtyard, is one of the best budget spots for a good night's sleep. The beds are firm, the hot water reliable, the staff are helpful and amenities include free wi-fi and cable TV. S87.

Niños Hotel Meloc 442 ☎084/231-424, ⓦ www .ninoshotel.com. Not only does this secure colonial-era house have bright, comfy rooms, set around a sunny courtyard café, but the proceeds go to a Dutch-run nonprofit foundation that provides food and education to underprivileged children. The staff are multilingual and very helpful. Other branch at Fierro 476. S44.

Pariwana Hostel Mesón de la Estrella 136 ☎084/233-751, ⓦ www.pariwana-hostel.com. The top choice for party-loving backpackers, this colonial house is perpetually packed with travellers, drawn by the easy-going atmosphere and extras such as reliable hot showers, a fully equipped kitchen, DVD lounge and delicious Peruvian food cooked at the on-site café. Dorms S33, rooms S78.

The Point Mesón de la Estrella 172 ☎084/252-266, ⓦ www.thepointhostels.com. Housed inside a renovated sixteenth-century mansion, *The Point* has a firm following of backpackers who like to party; plan on getting very little sleep and taking part in nightly events held at their very own *Horny Llama Bar*. Other perks include spacious dorms, free internet, kitchen, laundry service and involved staff. Dorms S30, rooms S80.

The Walk On Inn Suecia 504 ☏084/235-065, ⊕www.walkoninn.com. This secure backpacker favourite, a short, breathless walk up from Plaza de Armas, has several spacious rooms and dorms arranged around a large, light common space and an upstairs TV lounge with all-day coca tea. The helpful, informative staff can book your bus tickets with Cruz del Sur and organize all manner of tours in the city and around. Dorms S25, rooms S75.

Eating

For great street food, try the *anticucho* stall on Av. El Sol and Kuychipunku. Self-caterers can stock up on fresh produce at the San Pedro market, the Mega supermarket (Matará and Ayacucho) or the pricey, small Gato's Marker (Portal Belén 115).

Chez Maggy Procuradores 365. Watch your pizza prepared right in front of you in a wood-fired oven at this reliable chain restaurant, or try some of the tasty (if not terribly authentic) Mexican dishes on offer – the quesadillas are particularly good. Pizza for one, S18.

El Cholandés Choquechaca 188. This new Dutch lounge/café is the perfect spot to linger over a beer and home-made snacks, or to take a break from Peruvian cuisine with a Thai green curry or Pad Thai. The cocktails are reasonably priced too (S10–12).

El Encuentro Santa Catalina 384 and Choquechaca 136. These two unpretentious joints are packed full at mealtimes with customers clamouring after their impressively imaginative range of strictly vegetarian fare. The *sorpresa de palta* (avocado surprise) is particularly tasty. Mains from S10.

Granja Heidi Cuesta San Blas 525. A smiling cow greets you at the door and a wholesome Alpine theme is continued within. There's a huge selection of healthy breakfasts with lots of home-made dairy products, as well as a range of sweet and savoury crepes and numerous veggie options. Breakfasts S12—20.

Greens Santa Catalina Angosta 235, 2nd floor. Not only is the pecan/chocolate cake at Cusco's trendiest veggie restaurant something special, but the food is all-organic, the lunchtime buffet is innovative and the maracuyá sours are a great way to kick off any meal. Buffet S25; mains from S30.

Jack's Cafe Choquechaca 509. Probably the most popular gringo joint in Cusco; expect to queue for up to an hour outside at peak times. The food is definitely worth the wait – with a menu packed full of breakfast and sandwich options as well as great coffee and juices, it's just like home – or maybe better. Mains S20.

Juanitos Qanchipata 596. This tiny sandwich joint serves the best sandwiches in Cusco. Everything is freshly cooked to order with your choice of garnishes and sauces and the finished sandwiches (around S10) are so big that they need a small electric saw to cut them in half for you. Closed Sun.

Korma Sutra Tandapata 909, San Blas. Join other homesick Brits at this sultry, intimate dining room for generous helpings of onion bhajis, chicken tikka masala and lamb rogan josh, washed down with fantastic mango lassis. Mains from S22. Daily from 5pm.

Marcelo Batata Palacio 121.Though the coffee machine seems to be perpetually broken, the Andean fusion cuisine here is nothing short of inspired (the pasta with *ají de gallina* comes highly recommended) and the view from the terrace is among the very best in Cusco. Mains from S30.

The Muse, Too Tambopata 917, San Blas. This San Blas branch of the legendary *Muse* is so laidback that you often find customers snoozing on the comfy lounge seats upstairs. The wholesome food is lovingly prepared and the vegetarian lasagne is superb (S25).

Pacha Papa Plaza San Blas 120. If you're craving quality Andean food, such as the nutritious *sopa de quinoa*, *gulash de alpaca* or *lomo saltado*, then this popular restaurant, set around an attractive courtyard, is the place to come. The *chicharrón* (deep-fried pork belly) is superb; wash it down with *chicha morada* (a sweet purple corn drink). Mains S20–40.

🏃 **Sumaq Misky** Plateros 334, 2nd floor. A great place to try some innovative takes on traditional Andean food such as alpaca steaks or curried guinea pig. There's a huge open kitchen so that you can watch the chefs in action. Mains S20–45.

Yajúú Heladeros at Marquez. Stop by this bright and bustling *jugería* for a generous helping of freshly prepared tropical juice (S3) – papaya, banana, orange, mango, etc. Inexpensive sandwiches also served. There's another branch on the Plaza de Armas.

Drinking and nightlife

Apart from Lima, no Peruvian town has as varied a nightlife as Cusco. Clubs open early, around 9pm, but don't start getting lively before 11pm, and close in the wee hours. Pubs and clubs alike often offer 2 for 1 drink deals during happy hour. Beware of your drink being spiked in crowded night spots.

Pubs and bars

7 Angelitos San Blas 638. Up on the hillside, this chilled-out little lounge draws locals and visitors alike with its nightly mix of rock and funk perfromed by local bands and the excellent cocktails. With the motto "Coffee, Music, Cocktails", how can they lose?

Cross Keys Pub Calle Triunfo 350, 2nd floor. With its comfy leather seats, dark wood panels and a slightly formal air, this classic English pub, owned by the British consul, is a good spot for a civilized drink. The extensive beer selection and range of comfort food, such as chile con carne and curries, brings all the Brits to the yard.

🏃 **Fallen Angel** Plazoleta Nazarenas 221. Sip your pricey cocktail amid the inflated heart-shaped cushions, red spikes dangling from the ceiling and bathtub-cum-aquarium tables, filled with fish. Meanwhile mellow, bass-heavy remixes of Bob Marley play on and your waiters ("full of pleasure", according to their T-shirts) bring you desserts which are sublime works of art.

Le Nomade Choquechaca 207 (2nd floor). Relax with a hookah pipe, knock back one of the many flavoured rums and enjoy the varied live bands at this trendy French-run café bar. Music from 9pm.

Mandela's Bar Palacio 121, 3rd floor. Huge bar with cosy corners for couples, lot of cocktails and light snacks on offer. There's a heated outdoor rooftop terrace, so you can sit back and sip while watching the stars (without freezing to death).

Norton Rats Tavern Santa Catalina Angosta 116, 2nd floor, Plaza de Armas. This spacious, unpretencious bar plays rock, blues, jazz and latin music and features a pool table, dartboard and cable TV for sports. There's also a café serving some of the best burgers in Cusco.

Paddy Flaherty's Triunfo 124. This cramped Irish pub draws a lively European crowd with their selection of beers (including real Guinness, of course). Shepherd's pie and various Irish culinary delights are on the menu, as well as excellent sandwiches.

Clubs and live music

Caos So kitsch it's cool, the only swanky nightclub in Cusco boasts lots of neon and a shiny dancefloor, packed with twenty-something locals. Music ranges from electronica to latin pop.

KamiKase Portal Cabildo 274, Plaza Regocijo. One of Cusco's best-established nightspots, with varied live music – anything from Andean folk music to rock to sultry salsa – after 10pm; there's usually a small cover charge.

Km 0 Tandapata 100, Plaza San Blas. Chilled-out bar with nightly live bands, though things don't kick off until late. The Thai dishes are not bad either.

Mama Africa Portal de Harinas 191, 2nd floor, Plaza de Armas. Popular with backpackers, and particularly packed at weekends, this is a great place to grind away to reggae and rock.

The Muse Plateros 316, 2nd floor. An all-round winner, this established café-bar-resturant not only offers a tasty mix of international and Peruvian food, but the service is spot-on, there's some of the best coffee in town and nightly live music.

🏃 **Ukuku's Bar** Plateros 316. One of the most popular venues in town for the past decade, the small dancefloor at this club tends to be packed with locals and tourists alike due to its consistently good mix of Andean folk, latin and Western rock, salsa and reggaeton. Live music from 11pm.

Shopping

The best shopping area is around Plazoleta San Blas – Tandapata, Cuesta San Blas and Carmen Alto.
Books The best bookshops with extensive English-language sections are Jerusalén at Heladeros 143, with a large book exchange (if you give two books

you can take one) and guidebooks, and the smaller SBS Bookshop on Av. El Sol 781A.

Clothing Buy quality T-shirts with unique designs at Andean Expressions on Choquechaca 210; makes for a nice change from the standard T-shrts advertising Inka Kola or Cusqueña beer.

Crafts Mercado Modelo de Huanchac stocks a good range of crafts and you can find quirky gifts at Mercado San Pedro. Try Aymi Wasi on Nueva Alta for handmade fairtrade gifts – anything from jewellery to ceramics to art.

Textiles Centro de Textiles Tradicionales del Cusco on Av. El Sol 603A promotes traditional weaving techniques, so not only can you purchase textiles of excellent quality, but you may also watch weavers demonstrate their skill.

Directory

Banks and exchange BCP has a global ATM at Plateros and Espaderos on the Plaza de Armas, and there are ATMs in the BCP and BBVA bank branches along Av. El Sol. There are several casas del cambio along Av. El Sol that do better exchange rates than banks. *Cambistas* (moneychangers) may offer slightly better rates than foreign-exchange bureaus, but rip-offs are common.

Camping equipment Most tour agencies rent out tents, sleeping bags, sleeping mats and cooking equipment. There are also several shops on Calle Plateros. Try Mañay Wasy at 341 Plateros or X-Treme Turbulencia at 358 Plateros.

Consulates Most embassies are in Lima, though there are several honourary consul representatives in Cusco: UK (☎084/239-974); US (☎084/224-112); France (☎084/233-610); Germany (☎084/235-459).

Hospital and pharmacies Clinica Pardo (☎084/240-997) on Av. de la Cultura 710 is well-equipped to deal with 24hr emergencies. There are also pharmacies along Av. El Sol.

Laundry There are plenty of *lavanderías*, especially along Suecia, Procuradores and Carmen Bajo in San Blas.

Left luggage Most *hospedajes* and tour agencies have luggage storage facilities for travellers taking multi-day tours out of the city.

Post office The main office is at Av. Sol 800 (Mon–Sat 8am–8pm).

Taxis Reliable companies include AloCusco (☎084/222-222).

Telephones and internet Call centres and internet cafés are found all over the centre of Cusco; many hostels also offer free wi-fi.

Tourist police Plaza Túpac Amaru s/n (☎084/235-123); 24hr.

Moving on

At the Terminal Terrestre there is an embarkation tax of S1.20, which you pay before getting on. Recommended bus companies include: Cruz del Sur (☎084/221-909); Ormeño (☎084/241-706); Inka Express (☎084/247-887); Tour Peru (☎084/249-977); Litoral (☎084/281-920); Movil Tours (☎084/238-223); Cial (☎084/221-201); San Martín (☎09/8461-2520).

Bus Terminal Terrestre to: Arequipa (hourly between 6–7am and 7–9.30pm; 9hr); Arica, Chile (twice weekly; 2 days) La Paz, Bolivia (daily at 10pm; 13hr); Lima (at least hourly; 18hr); Nazca (hourly; 12–14hr); Puerto Maldonado (5–6 daily between 3.30–7pm; 10–14hr); Tacna (several daily; 17hr).

Cruz del Sur to: Arequipa (daily at 8pm & 8.30pm; 9hr); Lima via Nazca (daily at 2pm & 6pm; 18hr).

Train Wanchaq station to: Puno (Mon, Wed, Fri & Sat at 8am, April–Oct; Mon, Wed & Sat Nov–March; 10hr). Poroy station to: Machu Picchu (Vistadome daily at 6.53am; Expedition daily at 7.42am; Hiram Bingham daily at 9.10am; 4hr).

Train tickets The Estación Huanchac ticket office (Mon–Fri 7am–5pm, Sat & Sun 7am–noon; ☎084/581-414) sells train tickets to Puno and Machu Picchu, though it's easier to buy tickets directly through Perú Rail (🌐www.perurail.com). For Machu Picchu, it's best to buy a week in advance in peak season.

INCA SITES OUTSIDE CUSCO

There are four major Inca sites, all an energetic day's **walk** from Cusco: The megalithic fortress of **Sacsaywamán**, which looms high above the city, the great *huaca* of **Q'enqo**, the fortified hunting lodge of **Pukapukara** and the nearby imperial baths of **Tambomachay**. To start from the top and work your way downhill, take one of the regular **buses** to Pisac leaving from Av. Tullumayo or Calle Puputi every 20 minutes throughout the day and ask to be dropped off at the highest of the sites, Tambomachay, from where it's an easy two-hour walk back into the centre of Cusco, visiting the above sites in reverse order. The **opening**

times for all the sites below are Mon–Sun 7am—6pm and entry is by Boleto Turistico only (see p.819).

Sacsaywamán

From central Cusco, it's quite a steep 2km climb up to the ruins of Sacsaywamán from the Plaza de Armas. Take Calle Suecia, then the first right along Huaynapata until it meets the even narrower Pumacurco going steeply up (left) to a small café-bar. From there, follow the signposted steps all the way up to the ruins.

Because **SACSAYWAMÁN** was protected by such a steep approach from the town, it only needed defensive walls on one side, and three massive parallel walls zigzag together for some 600 metres. Little of the inner structures remain, yet these enormous ramparts stand 20 metres high, unperturbed by past battles, earthquakes and the passage of time. The strength of the mortar-less stonework – one block weighs more than three hundred tonnes – is matched by the brilliance of its design: the zigzags expose the flanks of any attackers trying to clamber up. The Inca Pachacutec began work on Sacsaywamán in the 1440s, although it took the labour of some twenty thousand men and nearly a century of work to finish it.

A flat expanse of grassy ground divides the fortress from a large outcrop of volcanic rock, called the **Rodadero** ("precipice"), which is used today during the colourful spectacle of the **Inti Raymi festival** held annually during the summer solstice in June.

Q'enqo

From the warden's hut on the northeastern edge of Sacsaywamán, take the track towards the Cusco–Pisac road; **Q'ENQO** is just over the other side of the main road.

This great stone or *huaca* revered by the Inca is carved with a complex pattern of steps, seats, geometric reliefs and puma designs, and illustrates the critical role of the Rock Cult in the realm of Inca cosmological beliefs; the name of the temple means "zigzag" and refers to the patterns carved into the upper western edge of the stone. At an annual festival priests would pour *chicha* or sacrificial llama blood into a bowl at the serpent-like top of the main channel; if it flowed out through the left-hand bifurcation, this was a bad omen for the fertility of the year to come. If, on the other hand, it continued the full length of the zigzag and poured onto the rocks below, this was a good omen.

Pukapukara

A relatively small ruin named **PUKAPUKARA** ("Red Fort", due to the pinkish hue of the rock) is situated right beside the main Cusco–Pisac road, a two-hour cross-country walk uphill from Q'enqo. Although in many ways reminiscent of a small European castle, Pukapukara is more likely to have been a hunting lodge, or out-of-town lodgings for the emperor, than simply a defensive position. Thought to have been built by the Emperor Pachacutec, it commands views towards glaciers to the south of the Cusco Valley.

Tambomachay

TAMBOMACHAY, otherwise known as "El Baño del Inca" ("The Bath of the Inca"), less than fifteen minutes' walk away along a signposted track from Pukapukara, is an impressive temple, evidently a place for ritual as well as physical cleansing and purification.

The ruins consist of three tiered platforms. The top one holds four trapezoidal niches that may have been used as seats; on the next level, underground water emerges directly from a hole at the base of the stonework, and from here cascades down to the bottom platform, creating a cold shower just about high enough for an Inca to stand under. On this platform the spring water splits into two channels, both pouring the last metre down to ground level. The superb quality of the stonework suggests that its use was restricted to the higher nobility, who perhaps used the baths only on ceremonial occasions.

Tipón

Around 25km east out of Cusco, the town of **TIPÓN** is famous for its Sunday lunches, featuring oven-roasted *cuy* (guinea pig), and its ruins – a large structure made up of several terraces and one of the only working examples of Inca irrigation systems, with fountains and water channels covering the area. From the town, it's a steep 1-hour 30-minute climb (or 20-minutes taxi ride) to the ruins. To get here take an Urcos-bound *colectivo* from Av. Tullumayo 207 and ask to be let out at the Tipón turn-off (45min; S3), or else take a less-frequent Tipón-bound bus. To get back, squeeze onto a passing bus on the main road.

Pikillaqta and Rumicolca

One of the few well-preserved pre-Inca sites in the area, **PIKILLAQTA** was built by the Wari culture and comprises a sprawling residential compound surrounded by a defensive wall in the midst of rolling grasslands. It is the earliest example in the region of two-storey buildings. Further on, on the opposite side of the road, is Rumicolca, the huge Inca gateway to Cusco, built on top of what used to be a massive Wari aqueduct. The contrast between the fine Inca stonework and the cruder earlier constructions of the Wari is quite striking. You can easily visit this site together with Tipón in a day-trip from Cusco; otherwise, stay on an Urcos-bound bus for an extra 5km; the site is 1km from the main road.

The Sacred Valley and Machu Picchu

The Río Urubamba valley, also known as El Valle Sagrado or the **Sacred Valley of the Incas**, traces its winding, astonishingly beautiful course to the northwest of Cusco. Standing guard over the two extremes of the Sacred Valley road, the ancient **Inca citadels** of Pisac and Ollantaytambo are among the most evocative ruins in Peru, while the small Andean towns of Pisac and Chinchero really come into their own on Tuesdays and Sundays – market days – when villagers in colourful regional dress gather to sell their crafts and produce.

Beyond Ollantaytambo the route becomes too tortuous for any road to follow, the valley closes in around the rail tracks, and the Río Urubamba begins to race and twist below **Machu Picchu** itself, the most famous ruin in South America and a place that – no matter how jaded you are or how commercial it seems – stops you in your tracks.

A plethora of tour companies run day-trips to Machu Picchu (which have to be booked in advance), as well as whirlwind day tours of the Sacred Valley (from S30 upwards). While guiding standards vary, it's a good way of seeing sights that are far apart, especially if you don't have much time, though it's more rewarding to linger and explore the valley at your leisure.

PISAC

A vital Inca road once snaked its way up the canyon that enters the Sacred Valley at **PISAC**, and the ruined citadel that sits at the entrance to the gorge controlled a route connecting the Inca Empire with Paucartambo, on the borders of the eastern jungle. Nowadays, the village is best known for its Tuesday, Thursday and Sunday craft **market**, held on the town's main square, the Plaza Constitución, though most stalls are open all week, with fewer crowds on non-market days. The main local **fiesta** – Virgen del Carmen (July 16–18) – is a good alternative to the simultaneous but more remote and raucous Paucartambo festival of the same name, with processions, music, dance groups, the usual fire-cracking celebrations, and food stalls around the plaza.

Arrival

Bus From Cusco, Calca-bound buses via Pisac leave from Tullumayo 207 (5am–7pm, every 15min; 1hr), returning from the same small plaza where they drop you off in Pisac throughout the day.

What to see and do

It takes roughly two hours to climb directly to the **citadel** (daily 7am–6pm; entry by Boleto Turístico), heading up through the agricultural terraces still in use at the back of Plaza Constitución. A better option is to take a taxi to the top of the ruins (20min; from S20 one-way, or negotiate a return fare with waiting time) and then walk back down, visiting all four archeological complexes on the way.

Set high above a valley floor patch-worked by patterned fields and rimmed by centuries of terracing amid giant landslides, the stonework and panoramas at the citadel are magnificent. On a large natural balcony, a semicircle of buildings is gracefully positioned under row upon row of fine stone terraces thought to represent a partridge's wing (*pisac* means "partridge"). In the upper sector of the ruins, the main **Temple of the Sun** is the equal of anything at Machu Picchu. Above the temple lie still more ruins, largely unexcavated, and the honey-combed cliff wall opposite the fortress is the handiwork of agile grave robbers who desecrated the cliff tombs.

Accommodation and eating

Blue Llama Plaza de Armas. You'll be drawn in by the quirky decor at this half-shop, half-restaurant, and you won't regret it. There's a range of veggie options, as well as tasty meat dishes, and the desserts come highly recommended. *Menú* S20.

Club Royal Inca ☎084/203-064. An excellent place to camp, 1.5km out of town. Not only do you get access to the *Club*'s facilities, such as the restaurant and Olympic-sized pool, but each fenced-off camping area comes with BBQ, an electricity plug and a light. S20 per tent.

Samana Wasi Plaza de Armas 509 ☎084/203-018. This guesthouse has a decent restaurant that serves ultra-fresh trout dishes and an excellent *cazuela de gallina* (spicy chicken stew), as well as a pleasant courtyard and balcony overlooking the plaza. S40.

Ulrike's Café Plaza de Armas 828. A pleasant place to hang out, with a book exchange and films, as well as excellent vegetarian dishes. The cheese-cake is a must. Mains from S13.

URUBAMBA AND AROUND

Spread-out **URUBAMBA** lies about 80km from Cusco via Pisac or around 60km via Chinchero. Although it has little in the way of obvious historic interest, the town has numerous connections to other parts of the Sacred Valley and is situated in the shadow of the beautiful Chicon and Pumahuanca glaciers.

The attractive Plaza de Armas is laidback and attractive, with palm trees and a couple of pines surrounded by interesting topiary. At the heart of the plaza is a small fountain topped by a maize corn, but it is dominated by the red sandstone **Iglesia San Pedro**. At weekends there's a large **market** on Jirón Palacio, which serves the local villages.

What to see and do

Because of its good facilities and position, Urubamba makes an ideal base from which to explore the mountains and lower hills around the Sacred Valley, which are filled with sites.

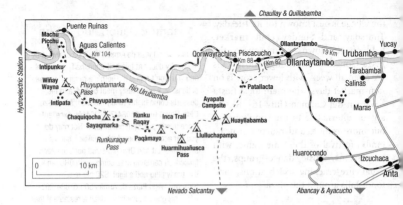

The map shows:

Chaullay & Quillabamba

Puente Ruinas, Machu Picchu, Aguas Calientes Km 104, Intipunku, Wiñay Wayna, Phuyupatamarka Pass, Intipata, Phuyupatamarka, Chaquiqocha, Sayaqmarka, Runkuraqay Pass, Runku Raqay, Paqámayo, Harmihuañusca Pass, Llulluchapampa, Huayllabamba, Ayapata Campsite, Patallacta, Inca Trail, Río Urubamba, Qoriwayrachina Km 88, Piscacucho Km 82, Ollantaytambo, Yucay, Urubamba 19 Km, Tarabamba, Salinas, Moray, Maras, Huarocondo, Huarocondo, Izcuchaca, Anta

Hydroelectric Station

0 — 10 km

Nevado Salcantay ▼   Abancay & Ayacucho ▼

The eastern side of the valley is formed by the **Cordillera Urubamba**, a range of snowcapped peaks dominated by the summits of Chicon and Veronica. Many of the ravines can be hiked, and on the trek up from the town you'll have stupendous views of Chicon. **Moray**, a stunning Inca site, lies about 6km north of Maras village on the Chinchero side of the river, within a two- to three-hour walk from Urubamba. Make a circuit to include the spectacular Maras salt flats.

Arrival

Bus From Cusco, buses leave from Av. Grau 525, while frequent *colectivos* depart from along Pavitos; both arrive at the Urubamba Terminal Terrestre on the main highway, 1km west of town via either Pisac or Chinchero (5am–7pm; every 20min; 1hr–1hr 30min). Regular buses connect Urubamba with Cusco, Pisac, Calca and Ollantaytambo.

Accommodation, eating and drinking

Hostal Los Perales Pasaje Arenales 102 ☎084/201-151. Not far from the bus terminal and featuring several sunny rooms around an overgrown garden. The owners are congenial and speak some English. S35.
Hostal Urubamba Bolognesi 605 ☎084/201-400. This friendly guesthouse, one and a half blocks from the Plaza de Armas, has basic, clean rooms. S25.
The Muse, Too Calle Comercio 347, Plaza de Armas. A relaxed bar with a range of food (mains S18–25) and drinks, and live music in the evenings. A gringo favourite, they often hold pub quizzes.

Tres Keros 500m west of town, off the highway and Señor de Torrechayoc. The best dining experience in town, this restaurant specializes in experimental *novoandina* dishes, as well as superbly cooked steaks and its own smoked trout. Mains from S30.

OLLANTAYTAMBO

On the approach to **OLLAN-TAYTAMBO** from Urubamba, the river runs smoothly between a series of fine Inca terraces that gradually diminish in size as the slopes get steeper and rockier. Just before the town, the rail tracks reappear and the road climbs a small hill into the ancient plaza. Built as an Inca administrative centre rather than a town, it's hard not to be impressed by the two huge Inca ruins that loom above the village, or by the foundations that abound in the cobbled backstreets radiating up from the plaza, especially in Calle Medio. Laid out in the form of a maize corncob – and one of the few surviving examples of an Inca grid system – the plan can be seen from vantage points high above it, especially from the hill opposite the fortress. Ollanta is an attractive, laidback village, and a wonderful place in which to linger.

What to see and do

The hubs of activity in town are the main **plaza** – the heart of civic life and the scene of traditional folk dancing

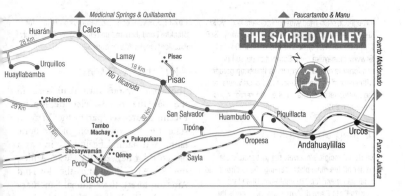

during festive occasions – the Inca fortress and the train station. Off the central plaza, down Patacalle, there's the recently refurbished **Museo CATCCO** (Mon–Sat 9am–6pm; S5), a small but very interesting museum containing interpretative exhibits in Spanish and English about local history, culture, archeology and natural history. It also has a ceramic workshop where you can buy some good pottery.

Downhill from the plaza, just across the Río Patacancha, is the old Inca Plaza Mañya Raquy, dominated by the town's star attraction – the astonishing Inca ruins atop some steep terraces. Climbing up through the **fortress** (daily 7am–5pm; entrance with Boleto Turístico, see box, p.819), the solid stone terraces, jammed against the natural contours of the cliff, remain frighteningly impressive and the view of the valley from the top is stupendous. Not only was this the site of a major battle in 1536 between the Spaniards and the rebellious Manco Inca, who fought them off before being forced to retreat to the jungle stronghold in Vilcabamba, but this was also a ceremonial centre; note the particularly fine stonework towards the top of the ruins.

Directly across, above the town, are rows of **ruined buildings** originally thought to have been prisons but now believed to have been granaries. To the front of these it's quite easy to make out a gigantic, rather grumpy-looking profile of a face carved out of the rock, possibly an **Inca sculpture** of Wiracochan, the mythical messenger from Wiracocha, the major creator god of the Incas. It's a stiff 40-minute climb to the viewpoint; follow the signpost from Waqta, off the Plaza de Armas.

Arrival

Bus and colectivo From Cusco, several buses daily go via Urubamba from Av. Grau 525, as well as numerous *colectivos* and *combis* from Pavitos in Cusco (between 6am–5pm; 1.5–2hr) and Urubamba (30min). From Ollanta, Cusco-bound tourist buses leave from the small yard just outside the railway station, often coinciding with the train timetable, whereas local buses, *combis* and *colectivos* depart from the Mercado Central, off the southeastern corner of the plaza (at least hourly, 1hr 30min).
By train The train station is a 10-min walk along Av. Ferrocarril from the main part of the village. There are at least ten trains daily each way between Cusco and Machu Picchu via Ollanta (check ⓦwww.perurail.com for an updated schedule); book tickets in advance, particularly the return, since trains going back to Cusco fill up with hikers coming off the Inca Trail.

Accommodation

Chaska Wasi Calle del Medio s/n ⓣ084/203-061, ⓔchaskawasihostal@hotmail.com. Warren of colourful rooms and common spaces, popular with backpackers. English spoken. S25.
KT Tambo Hostal Ventiderio s/n ⓣ084/204-035, ⓦwww.kbperu.com. Colourful laidback guesthouse with a jacuzzi on the rooftop terrace and wi-fi

throughout, often filled with backpackers and cyclists (the owner runs cycle tours of the Sacred Valley). S50.

Munay Tika Av. Ferrocarríl 118 ☎084/204-111, ⓦwww.munaytika.com. Somewhat dated but comfortable rooms set around a flowering garden, with welcoming management and good views from the rooftop terrace. The on-site café serves good breakfast. S120.

Eating and drinking

Cactus Principal s/n. Lively bar just around the corner off the main plaza, serving cheap drinks and a bargain *menú* for S10 until 9pm. Open late.

Hearts Café Plaza de Armas s/n. Not only is the "mostly whole food" excellent – from vegetarian burritos to cakes and fresh juices – but the proceeds fund several childrens' projects in the Sacred Valley, improve nutrition in the poorest villages and provide support for maltreated women and the elderly. Mains S14–20.

Puka Rumi Ventiderio s/n. Visitors come here for breakfast and then end up returning for the equally excellent steaks. Mains from S20.

THE INCA TRAIL

The world-famous **Inca Trail** is set in the **Sanctuario Histórico de Machu Picchu**, an area set apart by the Peruvian state for the protection of its flora, fauna and natural beauty. Acting as a bio-corridor between the Cusco Andes, the Sacred Valley and the lowland Amazon forest, the National Sanctuary of Machu Picchu has a huge biodiversity, with species including the cock-of-the-rock (known as *tunkis* in Peru), spectacled bear (*tremarctos ornatus*) and condor (*vultur gryphus*). Although just one of a multitude of paths across

THE INCA TRAIL: WHEN AND HOW TO DO IT

Consider the season when booking your Inca Trail. The dry season runs approximately from May to October – expect blistering sun during the daytime and sub-zero temperatures at night. During the rainy season of November to April the temperature is more constant but, naturally, the path is muddier and can be slippery, and afternoon thunderstorms are the norm. The trail is closed for restoration during the entire month of February.

In recent years, due to the growing popularity of the Inca Trail, the sanctuary authority, the Unidad de Gestión del Sanctuario Histórico de Machu Picchu, has imposed a limit of 500 people a day on the Inca Trail, and they must be accompanied by a registered tour operator. By law, permits must be purchased thirty days before departure on the trail with the name and passport number of each trekker. In practice, however, it is usually necessary to book four to six months in advance to make sure you get a space on the trail. Currently permits cost around US$100 per person, including entrance to Machu Picchu – this permit should always be included in the price of your trek. Always carefully research the tour company (see p.824) that you choose, and make sure you know exactly what you are paying for, as well as what conditions your porters will be working under (see box, p.835).

Prices vary considerably between US$300 to US$750 and although a higher price doesn't always reflect genuine added value, usually the better and more responsible companies will have higher expenses to cover (for better food, equipment, fair wages, and so on). Check what's included in the price: train tickets (which class), quality of tent, roll mat, sleeping bag, porter to carry rucksack and sleeping bag (or if not, how much a personal porter will cost), bus down from ruins, exactly which meals, drinking water for the first two days, and what transport to the start of the trail.

As far as preparations go, the most important thing is to acclimatize, preferably allowing at least three days in Cusco if you've flown straight from sea level, because altitude sickness will seriously ruin your travel plans.

If you don't want to hike for four days, the two-day Inca Trail is a good option. It starts at Km104 of the Panamerican Highway, 8km from Machu Picchu; the footbridge here leads to a steep climb (3–4hr) past Chachabamba to reach Wiñay Wayna (see p.836), where you join the remainder of the Inca Trail.

remote areas of the Andes, what makes the 33km Inca Trail so popular is the fabulous treasure of **Machu Picchu** at the end.

An early departure from Cusco (around 5am) is followed by a 3-hour drive to Ollantaytambo (where you can buy last-minute supplies, including recycled walking sticks). The trail begins at **Piscacucho**, at Km 82, where you cross the Urubamba River after signing in at the first checkpoint on the trail. The first day consists of a 12km stretch, beginning at an elevation of 2600m and gaining 400m during the course of the day. The gentle incline of the trail first follows the river and passes a viewpoint with the terraced Inca ruins of the **Llaqta-pata** fortress below, before it descends past rock formations to the first night's campsite at **Huayllabamba**. Along the way you pass the villages of Miskay and Hatunchaca, where you can buy (overpriced) snacks and water, as well as *chicha* (traditional fermented corn beer).

The campsite at Huayllabamba is very basic, and there are no showers, though you may consider bathing in the icy stream. If you haven't acclimatized and don't feel well, then Huayllabamba is the last place from which it's fairly easy to return to Cusco; beyond, it's nearly impossible.

The second day is the toughest part of the hike – an ascent of 1100m to the Abra Huarmihuañusca, or **Dead Woman's Pass** (4200m), the highest point on the trail, followed by a steep descent to the second night's campsite at Paq'aymayo. There is little shade or shelter, so prepare yourself for diverse weather conditions, as cold mist sometimes descends quickly, obscuring visibility.

After an hour or so, you reach the campsite of Ayapata (where some groups camp on the first night), where there are bathrooms and a snack stall. Another 90min–2hr along a combination of dirt path and steep stone steps through mossy forest takes you up to the second campsite of Llulluchapampa, your last chance to purchase water or snacks.

The views from the pass itself are stupendous, but it gets cold rapidly. From here the trail drops down into the Paq'aymayo Valley. The descent takes up to two hours, but you're rewarded by sight of the attractive **campsite** by the river (3600m), complete with showers (cold water only).

This is the longest day but also the most enjoyable, with some of the loveliest scenery. It takes 40min up the steep,

PORTER WELFARE

Even though the Peruvian government has recently introduced regulations, stipulating that the Inca Trail porters must be paid a set minimum wage and only carry a set amount, abuses of staff by unscrupulous tour agencies still occur, especially on the alternative trails, where you may find your porters eating leftovers, carrying huge weights and sleeping without adequate cold-weather gear. Avoid doing the Inca Trail for the cheapest price possible, and be prepared to pay more by going with a reputable company that treats its staff well (see box, p.824, for recommended operators). When trekking, keep an eye on the working conditions of the porters, offer to share your snacks and water, ask the porters about how they are treated, and don't forget to tip them at the end of the trek (around US$20 per porter is fair; a bit more if you had a personal porter). If you find evidence of abuse, don't hesitate to report it at your nearest IPerú office.

exposed trail to reach the ruins of the Inca fortress of Runkurakay, then another 20min of stone steps and steep dirt track before you pass the false summit with a small lake before arriving at the **second pass** – Abra de Runku-racay (3950m), from which you can see the snow-covered mountains of the Cordillera Vilcabamba.

About an hour's descent along some steep stone steps leads to the Inca ruins of **Sayaqmarka**, a compact fortress perched on a mountain spur, overlooking the valley below. From Sayaqmarka you make your way down into increasingly dense cloudforest where delicate orchids begin to appear among the trees, and then up to the Chaquicocha campsite, where some groups break for lunch. The hour's hike between Chaquicocha and the **third pass** – Abra de Phuyupatamarka (3650m) – is the loveliest bit of the hike; the trail runs through stretches of cloud-forest, with hummingbirds flitting from flower to flower and stupendous views of the valley. The trail winds down to the impressive ruin of **Phuyupatamarca** – "Town Above the Clouds" – where there are five small ceremonial baths and, in the wet season fresh running water. Some groups camp here on the third night, which leaves them at a disadvantage on the last day, as they have to get up at 3am in order to reach the Sun Gate by sunrise.

It's a rough 2–3hr descent to the final campsite. The first section comprises steep stone steps for 40min, followed by gentler stretches of dirt track. When you come to the fork in the trail, take the right branch down to the next ruin, a citadel almost as impressive as Machu Picchu, **Wiñay Wayna** ("Forever Young"), where most groups will spend their third night. There is basic **accommodation** here and a large restaurant/bar area where you can treat your group and porters to a round of drinks. Most groups will **camp** outside the structure, but still enjoy the hot showers.

To reach **Intipunku** ("The Sun Gate") for sunrise the next day, most groups form a bottleneck at the Wiñay Wayna guard post long before it opens at 5.30am; groups are no longer allowed to leave the campsite any earlier. A well-marked track from Wiñay Wayna skirts the mountain, leading you along some gentle ups and downs for about an hour before you reach a spectacularly steep set of stone steps – the last ascent of the hike – which leads to a pathway paved by the Inca. This in turn culminates in a large stone archway, Intipunku, where you catch your first sight of Machu Picchu – a stupendous moment, however exhausted you might be. From Intipunku, to reach the main ruins, it's an easy 30–40min descent.

MACHU PICCHU

The most dramatic and enchanting of the Inca citadels lies suspended on an extravagantly terraced saddle between two prominent peaks. **MACHU PICCHU** (daily 6am–5pm; S120) is one of the greatest of all South American tourist attractions, set against a vast, scenic backdrop of forested mountains that spike up from the deep valleys of the Urubamba and its tributaries.

With many legends and theories surrounding the position of Machu Picchu (meaning "ancient mountain"), most archeologists agree that the sacred geography of the site helped the Inca Pachacutec decide where to build it. Its intactness owes much to the fact that it was never discovered by the Spaniards and the atmosphere, as you wander around, drinking it all in, is second to none.

Some history
Unknown to the outside world, for many centuries the site of Machu Picchu lay forgotten, except by local Quechua

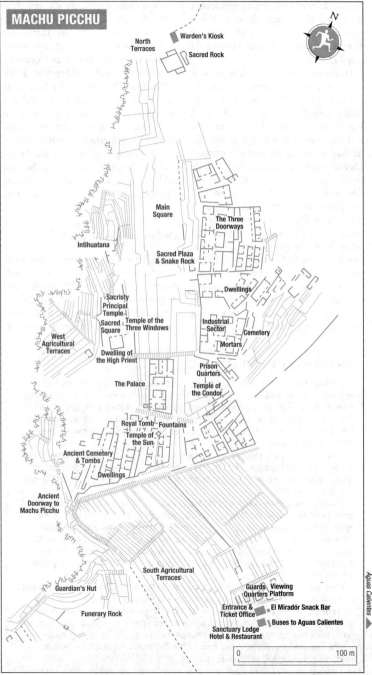

MACHU PICCHU

North Terraces

Warden's Kiosk

Sacred Rock

Main Square

The Three Doorways

Intihuatana

Sacred Plaza & Snake Rock

Dwellings

Sacristy
Principal Temple

Sacred Square

Temple of the Three Windows

Industrial Sector

Cemetery

Mortars

West Agricultural Terraces

Dwelling of the High Priest

Prison Quarters

The Palace

Temple of the Condor

Royal Tomb

Fountains

Temple of the Sun

Ancient Cemetery & Tombs

Dwellings

Ancient Doorway to Machu Picchu

Guardian's Hut

South Agricultural Terraces

Guards Quarters

Viewing Platform

Entrance & Ticket Office

El Miradór Snack Bar

Funerary Rock

Buses to Aguas Calientes

Sanctuary Lodge Hotel & Restaurant

0   100 m

Footpath to Inca Drawbridge

Aguas Calientes

Machu Picchu Mountain, ▼ *Inti Punku gateway, Inca Trail & Wiñay Wayna* people. In the 1860s it was first looted by a pair of German adventurers and then rediscovered by the US explorer **Hiram Bingham**, who came upon it on July 24, 1911.

It was a fantastic find, not least because it was still relatively intact, without the usual ravages of either conquistadors or tomb robbers. Bingham was led to the site by an 11-year-old local boy, and it didn't take long for him to see that he had come across some important ancient Inca terraces. After a little more exploration Bingham found the fine white stonework, which led him to believe (incorrectly, as it transpired) that Machu Picchu was the lost city of Vilcabamba, the site of the Incas' last refuge from the Spanish conquistadors. Bingham returned in 1912 and 1915 to clear the thick forest from the site and in the process made off with thousands of artefacts; the Peruvian government is currently trying to reclaim them from Yale university, where they are kept.

While archeologists are still not clear as to what Machu Picchu's purpose was, there is a general consensus that it was an important religious and ceremonial centre, given the layout and quantity of temples, as well as the quality of the stonework. The citadel may have been built as an administrative, political and agricultural centre, while the existence of numerous access routes to Machu Picchu has led others to believe that it was a trading post between the Andes and the Amazon. Conflicting theories aside, there is no denying Machu Picchu's great importance to the Inca culture.

What to see and do

Though more than 1000m lower than Cusco, Machu Picchu seems much higher, constructed as it is on dizzying slopes overlooking a U-curve in the Río Urubamba. More than a hundred flights of stone steps interconnect its palaces,

ARRIVING AT MACHU PICCHU

If coming from the Inca Trail, you'll need to descend to the main entrance and register your entrance ticket before doubling back to the ruins. Or, if you're arriving from Aguas Calientes, you can either hike up to the ruins (1–3hr, depending on how fit you are) along a clearly marked footpath that's much shorter than following the winding paved road, or take one of the buses that run throughout the day (every 20min, 5.30am–6pm).

If you're travelling independently, it's best to buy your entrance ticket to Machu Picchu at the INC (Instituto Nacional de Cultura) office in the main square before going up to the ruins; that way you'll avoid the long queues at the ticket office at the site itself.

There is no accommodation near Machu Picchu itself apart from the hideously overpriced *Machu Picchu Sanctuary Lodge*, located right at the entrance to the ruins. The lodge serves up a good lunchtime buffet that will set you back $50; otherwise, there are sandwiches to be had at the expensive café by the gate. You may bring your own food, as long as you consume it outside the ruins. You may bring water inside the ruins, but it must be in a proper flask or Sigg bottle; plastic bottles are not allowed.

There are two left-luggage offices: one next to the entrance to the ruins (S5) and one just as you go inside (S3); you must check in any large rucksacks, camping equipment, food and walking sticks (even with rubber tips). There are toilets just outside the entrance (S1) and this is where you can also hire a guide (approximately S100 for a one-hour tour, per group), though they tend to be of varying quality.

When walking around the ruins, stick to the designated trails, or the zealous wardens will blow their whistles at you.

temples, storehouses and terraces, and the outstanding views command not only the valley below in both directions but also extend to the snowy peaks around Salcantay. Wherever you stand in the ruins, spectacular terraces (some of which are once again being cultivated) can be seen slicing across ridiculously steep cliffs, transforming mountains into suspended gardens.

Unless you're coming off the Inca Trail, you'll be following the footpath from the main entrance to the ruins proper. For a superb view of the ruins, take the staircase up to the thatched guardian's hut and the **funerary rock** behind it; this is thought to have been a place where mummified nobility were laid due to its association with a nearby graveyard where Bingham found evidence of many burials, some of which were obviously royal.

Temple of the Sun and the Royal Tomb

Entering the main ruins through the ancient doorway, you soon come across the **Temple of the Sun** on your right, also known as the *Torreón* – a wonderful, semicircular, tower-like temple displaying some of Machu Picchu's finest stonework and built for astronomical purposes. Its carved steps and smoothly joined stone blocks fit neatly into the existing relief of a natural boulder, which served as some kind of altar. During the June solstice, the first rays of the sun shine directly into the window and illuminate the tower perfectly. The temple is cordoned off, but you can appreciate it from above.

Below the Temple of the Sun is a cave with a stepped altar and tall niches, known as the **Royal Tomb**, despite the fact that neither graves nor mummies have ever been found here. Along the staircase leading up to the Temple of the Sun, you'll find sixteen small **fountains**, the most beautiful at the top.

The Sacred Plaza

Another staircase ascends to the old quarry, past the **Royal Area**, so called due to the imperial style Inca stonework. Turn right and cross the quarry to reach the **Sacred Plaza**, flanked by an important temple complex. Dominating the southeastern edge of the plaza, the attractive **Three-Windowed Temple** has unusually large windows, perfectly framing the mountains beyond the Urubamba river valley. Next to it is the **Principal Temple**, so-called because of the fine stonework of its three high main walls; the damage to the rear right corner was caused by the ground sinking, as opposed to a construction flaw. Directly opposite the Principal Temple, you'll find the **House of the High Priest**.

Intihuatana

An elaborately carved stone stairway behind the **Sacristy** brings you to one of the jewels of the site, the **Intihuatana**, loosely translated from Quechua as the "hitching post of the sun". This fascinating carved rock, sometimes mistakenly referred to as a sundial, is one of the very few not to have been discovered and destroyed by the conquistadors in their attempt to eradicate sun worship. Its shape resembles Huayna Picchu and it appears to be aligned with the nearby mountains. Inca astronomers are thought to have used it as an astro-agricultural clock for viewing the complex interrelationships between the movements of the stars and constellations.

Sacred Rock

Following the steps down from the Intihuatana and passing through the Sacred Plaza towards the northern terraces brings you in a few minutes to the **Sacred Rock**, below the access point to Huayna Picchu. A great lozenge of granite sticking out of the earth like a sculptured wall, little is known for sure about the Sacred Rock – though its outline is strikingly similar to the Inca's sacred mountain of Putukusi, which towers to the east.

Eastern side of the ruins

On the other side of the Sacred Plaza lies the secular area, consisting largely of workers' dwellings and the industrial sector. At the back of this area lie some shallow circular depressions, dubbed the **Mortars**, though their real purpose remains unknown. On the other side of the passageway from the Mortars lie the **Prison Quarters** – a maze of cells, the centrepiece of which is the **Temple of the Condor**, named after a carving on the floor that resembles the head and neck of the sacred bird. The rocks behind it bear a resemblance to a condor's outstretched wings.

Huayna Picchu

Huayna Picchu is the prominent peak that looms behind the ruins in every photo you see, at the northern end of the Machu Picchu site, and is easily scaled by anyone reasonably energetic and with no trace of vertigo (allow 40min–1hr). Access to this sacred mountain (daily 7am–1pm; 200 people at 7am and 200 people at 10am; free) is controlled by a guardian from his kiosk just behind the Sacred Rock. To get a ticket you will need to be at the Machu Picchu gate when it opens, which means queueing for the bus in Aguas Calientes as early as 4.30am; if you are coming directly from the Inca Trail, you won't get here early enough. From the summit there's a great overview of the ruins suspended between the mountains among stupendous forested Andean scenery.

Temple of the Moon

From Huayna Picchu, two trails signposted "Gran Caverna" lead down to the stunning **Temple of the Moon**, hidden in a grotto hanging magically above the Río Urubamba. Not many visitors make it this far, but if you do you'll be rewarded with some of the best stonework in the entire site, the level of craftmanship hinting at the site's importance to the Inca. The temple is set in the mouth of a dark cave and there is a flowing, natural feel to the stonework and the beautifully recessed doorway. Its name comes from the fact that it is often lit by moonlight, but some archeologists believe the temple was most likely dedicated to the spirit of the mountain.

The best way to visit the temple is to take the steep downhill trail from the very top of Huayna Picchu (30min, including a near-vertical section involving a lashed wooden ladder) and then follow the other trail from the side of the main cave, which ends part way up Huayna Picchu (1hr).

Intipunku

If you don't have the time or energy to climb Huayna Picchu or visit the Temple of the Moon, simply head back to the guardian's hut on the other side of the site and take the path below it, which climbs gently for 40min or so up to **Intipunku**, the main entrance to Machu Picchu from the Inca Trail. This offers an incredible view over the entire site, with the unmistakeable shape of Huayna Picchu in the background.

Cerro Machu Picchu

If you have time to spare, head for Machu Picchu mountain, which towers above the ruins opposite Huayna Picchu and offers a 360-degree view of the surrounding valleys, as well as of the ruins and Huayna Picchu. It's a longer climb; most people take 1hr 20min–2hr to reach the top, but the trail is not as vertigo-inducing as Huayna Picchu and you can climb at your leisure; there are no daily quotas and you will have the view largely to yourself (as opposed to the overcrowded Huayna Picchu). Take the path towards Intipunku and then follow the signpost to the right before leaving the ruins.

Inca drawbridge

If you don't suffer from vertigo, there's an excellent scenic and level 20-min walk that you can take from the Hut of the Caretaker of the Funerary Rock through the cemetery to the Inca drawbridge. Follow the narrow path along the tops of the southern terraces, along the side of the cliff, and over a man-made ledge until you reach the barrier several hundred metres above the bridge, which spans the gap in the Inca road that was built on a sheer cliff face. You're no longer allowed to get close to it, as someone fell to their death from it a few years ago, but it's certainly an impressive sight.

AGUAS CALIENTES

Anyone wishing to come to Machu Picchu will invariably pass through the settlement of **AGUAS CALIENTES** (the official name is "Machu Picchu Pueblo", though it never stuck), which is connected to the ruins by bus, though the town itself is only accessible by train from Cusco via the Sacred Valley. Its warm, humid climate and surrounding landscape of towering mountains covered in cloudforest make it a welcome change to Cusco, though it has even more of a touristy feel to it: every other building in this little town seems to be either a hotel, restaurant or a souvenir shop and you constantly run the gauntlet of persistent touts. If you wish to see Machu Picchu at sunrise and to enjoy the surrounding scenery when it is not overrun by day-trippers, you'll be staying here for at least one night.

What to see and do

The town's main attraction (besides Machu Picchu) is the natural **thermal bath** (daily 5am–8.30pm; S10), which is particularly welcome after a few days on the Inca Trail. You can find several communal baths of varying temperatures right at the end of the main drag of Pachacutec; several shops rent towels and bathing suits near the entrance.

There is also a **hiking trail** (around 90min each way; closed due to landslide damage at the time of writing) up the sacred mountain of Putukusi, starting just outside of town, a couple of hundred yards down on the left if you follow the railway track towards the ruins. The walk offers stupendous

---

TRAIN JOURNEY TO MACHU PICCHU

The new, improved service offered by PeruRail between Cusco and Machu Picchu – one of the finest mountain train journeys in the world – enhances the thrill of riding tracks through such fantastic scenery even further by offering good service and largely comfortable carriages. If you can afford to, pay the extra US$24 for a Vistadome seat; not only do you get a better view, but there's also leg room – something conspicuously absent from the "backpacker" carriages.

Rumbling out of **Cusco** around 6am, the train zigzags its way through the back streets, where little houses cling to the steep valley slopes. It takes a while to rise out of the teacup-like valley, but once it attains the high plateau above, the train rolls through fields and past highland villages before eventually dropping rapidly down into the Urubamba Valley using several major track switchbacks, which means you get to see some of the same scenery twice. It reaches the Sacred Valley floor just before getting into **Ollantaytambo**, where you can already see scores of terraced fields and, in the distance, more Inca temple and storehouse constructions. The train continues down the valley, stopping briefly at Km88, where the Inca Trail sometimes starts, then following the Río Urubamba as the valley gets tighter and the mountain more forested and precipitous. The end of the line these days is usually the new station at **Aguas Calientes**.

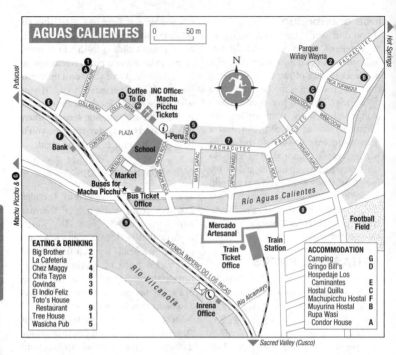

AGUAS CALIENTES

0   50 m

N

Parque Wiñay Wayna

Hot Springs

Putucusi

Coffee To Go

INC Office: Machu Picchu Tickets

i-Peru

Bank

School

Market

Buses for Machu Picchu

Bus Ticket Office

PLAZA

Río Aguas Calientes

Football Field

Mercado Artesanal

Train Ticket Office

Train Station

AVENIDA IMPERIO DO LOS INCAS

Río Vilcanota

Río Alcamayo

Inrena Office

Machu Picchu & G

EATING & DRINKING

Big Brother	2
La Cafeteria	7
Chez Maggy	4
Chifa Taypa	8
Govinda	3
El Indio Feliz	6
Toto's House Restaurant	9
Tree House	1
Wasicha Pub	5

ACCOMMODATION

Camping	G
Gringo Bill's	D
Hospedaje Los Caminantes	E
Hostal Quilla	C
Machupicchu Hostal	F
Muyurina Hostal	B
Rupa Wasi Condor House	A

Sacred Valley (Cusco)

views of the town and across to Machu Picchu, but watch out for the small poisonous snakes. It is also not for the faint-hearted as the trail is very steep in parts (some sections have been replaced by ladders) and very narrow.

Arrival and information

Tourist information IPerú (daily 9am–1pm & 2–8pm; ☎084/211-104) has an office just off the main plaza and informative leaflets about the area plus photocopied maps. Next door is the INC office (daily 5am–10pm) where it's best to buy your entrance ticket to Machu Picchu, as the queues at the site itself are very long.

Train You are most likely to arrive in Aguas Calientes by train (see box, p.841). To get to the heart of the town, walk through the market and cross one of the bridges.

Accommodation

Although there is an overwhelming choice of places to stay, there can be a lot of competition for lodgings during the high season (June–Sept) and the better places need booking a week or two

in advance. The check-out time at most hostels is 9–9.30am.

Camping Municipal The municipal campsite is just before the bridge over the Río Urubamba, a 15-min walk from Aguas Calientes. The campsite has toilets, showers with intermittent hot water and cooking facilities. S15 per tent.

Gringo Bill's Colla Raymi 104 ☎084/211-046, ⓦwww.gringobills.com. The original backpackers'-favourite-gone-upmarket featuring en-suite rooms with quirky decor, a relaxed environment, grilled meats at the on-site restaurant, a good book exchange and guest access to a jacuzzi. Perpetually full, so book as far in advance as possible; great value if travelling with friends. Breakfast included. S225.

Hospedaje Los Caminantes Imperio de los Incas 140 ☎084/211-007. Basic but friendly family-run guesthouse right by the train tracks, with no-frills rooms (some en-suite) and reliable hot shower. S20.

Hostal Quilla Av. Pachacutec s/n ☎084/211-009. Simple, comfortable rooms with cable TV and a downstairs café. S30.

Machupicchu Hostal Imperio de los Incas 313 ☎084/211-034. While the noise from passing trains does carry, this friendly guesthouse, set around a flowering courtyard, is still often full due to its convenient location and comfortable rooms. S175.

Muyurina Hostal Alameda Hermanos Ayar, Mza 9, Lote 6 ☎084/777-247, ⓦwww.hostalmuyurina .com/hostal. Attractive, comfortable en-suite rooms in a beautifully refurbished building, with 24hr hot water arranged around a spiral staircase inside the airy, light interior. S120.

Eating and drinking

Since there is enormous competition for customers, you'll perpetually find yourself running the gauntlet of over-eager waiters, all trying to entice you into their particular restaurant, which looks and offers exactly the same dishes as most eateries within sight. Below are the exceptions.

Big Brother Pachcutec and Yupanqui. You'll spot this informal bar by the murals of Ché and Marley above the terrace. A good spot for a beer or two, or a game of pool inside.

La Cafetería Pachacutec 109. Against the backdrop of loud, colourful, indistinguishable eateries that line the walk, *Hotel El Mapi*'s restaurant stands out not just because of its starkness and minimalist exterior, but also for the quality of its food. Snack on fried yucca sticks with Huancaina sauce (S14) or go for a *butifarra* sandwich (S21) or quinoa tabbouleh (S21) from their range of organic salads.

Chez Maggy Pachacutec at Wiracocha. This is the McDonalds of Peruvian pizza: always reliable and you know what you're going to get. In this case, it's thin-crust pizza, baked in front of you and topped

with a plethora of ingredients, including avocado. Pizza for one from S20.

Chifa Taypa Alameda Hermanos Ayar s/n. For heaped helpings of Chinese and Peruvian dishes, look no further than this friendly informal eatery, popular with locals. Stir-fried beef with noodles S18.

Govinda Pachacutec 20. Established (mostly) vegetarian favourite with good three-course lunchtime *menú* (from S20). Spicy dishes can be toned down on request.

🏃 **El Indio Feliz** Lloque Yupanqui Lote 4m-12 ☎084/211-090. Nautically themed restaurant serving exceptional three- or four-course meals of French and local cuisines; try to reserve a table as far in advance as possible. Mains S30–50; three-course *menú* S49.

Toto's House Restaurant Imperio de los Incas s/n. Hungry post-Inca Trail hikers will adore the huge all-you-can-eat lunchtime buffet here, which features such delights as alpaca carpaccio and stew, sushi, awesome sweet potato salad and an impressive range of desserts. Buffet S49.

Wasicha Pub Lloque Yupanqui s/n. This is the town's loudest, hottest nightspot, with a vibrant dancefloor, open until the wee hours.

Directory

Banks BCP on Av. Los Incas, next to *Toto's House Restaurant*, has an ATM but it sometimes runs out of money, especially at weekends.

Hospital There's a 24hr posta de salud (medical centre) on Av. Imperio de Los Incas s/n (☎084/211-005).

Internet *Coffee To Go*, on the plaza, has reliable internet as well as coffee and snacks. There are more internet cafés along Av. Imperio de Los Incas.

Police Av. Imperio de Los Incas, next to the small market just down from the old railway station (☎084/211-178).

Telephones Centro Telefónica, Av. Imperio de Los Incas 132.

Moving on

Train Cusco (Backpacker/New Backpacker: 8 daily between 9.56am and 9.45pm, S99–174; Vistadome: daily at 3.20pm; S206; Hiram Bingham: daily except Sun; S853). All take 3–4hr.

ALTERNATIVE INCA TRAILS

In recent years, as permits to walk the famous Inca Trail become more

---

TREAT YOURSELF

Rupa Wasi Condor House Calle Huanacaure 180 ☎084/221-101, ⓦwww .rupawasi.net. Located two blocks from the main plaza away from most of the tourist services, *Rupa Wasi* is a calm oasis. Run by enthusiastic young conservationists, the hotel is comfy, friendly and eco-conscious. Extra activities such as cooking lessons and treks to nearby sites can be arranged. The on-site restaurant, the *Tree House*, is among the very best in town, featuring *novoandina* cuisine, which combines local ingredients with international influences to great effect. Try the sublime trout in quinoa flakes with spicy elderberry sauce (S29). S210. Special half-board rate available.

expensive and the Trail more crowded, many tour operators and individuals have started exploring **alternative Inca Trails**. Many of these offer stunning scenery to rival that of the Inca Trail, as well as ecological biodiversity and in some cases archeological sites larger than Machu Picchu itself. Of the several established alternative trails, only one (Salcantay) takes you close to the site of Machu Picchu. At the time of writing all of these trails can still be done independently, apart from the Salcantay trail that joins the Inca Trail, although it may still be necessary to purchase a **permit** from the INC office in Cusco prior to setting off, and plans are afoot to enforce stricter regulations. For most of them, it is recommended to hire local guides, *arrieros* (muleteers) and mules (around S60 per day for each). For information about requirements to walk the trails see the South American Explorers website: ⓦwww.saexplorers .org.

Salcantay

The most popular of the alternatives, this 5 to 7-day hike takes you either as far as the hydroelectric plant (from where it's a short bus and train ride to Aguas Calientes), or to the village of Huayllabamba, where you can join the regular Inca Trail. Beginning in Mollepata, the **first day** is a gentle climb through winding cloudforest trails to Soraypampa. On the **second day** there's a steep climb up to the only high pass on the trail (4750m), at the foot of the Salcantay glacier; the landscape here is sparse and dry. From the pass you descend into cloudforest with views of the verdant canyon below, camping that evening at Colcapampa. On the **third day** a 5-hr walk takes you to the jungle town of La Playa, and then it's either an hour's bus ride to the town of Santa Teresa, or a 6 to 7-hr walk. From Santa Teresa, you walk along the valley to the hydroelectric plant, from where there

are trains to Aguas Calientes (8.20am & 3pm).

Alternatively, on the second day you'll descend along the right-hand side of the pass into the valley towards the village of Huayllabamba, and join the Inca Trail there. Buses run from Cusco's Avenida Arcopata to Mollepata every morning (hourly from 5.30am; 3hr).

Choquequirao

A trek to the archeological site of **Choquequirao** and back will take four or five days. Believed to be much larger than Machu Picchu, Choquequirao is only forty percent uncovered, and is a much more authentic experience as it still receives few visitors and you can find yourself wandering alone among huge ruined walls covered with cacti and exotic flowers. There are four trekking options, all starting at **Cachora**, which involves crossing the Apurimac Canyon. Day one is a steep descent of around 2000m, and day two a steep climb up the other side. It is recommended to spend one whole day (day three) at the ruins, and then either return on the same route, or via Huanipaca. It is also possible to link this trail to the last day of the Salcantay via Yanama, or to Hancacalle, returning to Cusco via Quillabamba (allow at least eight days for these options).

Hiring *arrieros* and mules is highly recommended for the above treks, as the area is very remote. To **get to Cachora**, take an Abancay-bound bus from Cusco and ask to be dropped off at the Cachora turn-off (4hr), from where you can catch a taxi to the village, where there is basic accommodation, *arrieros* and mules for hire.

Ausangate

This incredible high-altitude trek takes 5–6 days, plus two more days for travel, and provides the chance to see herds of vicuña wander among

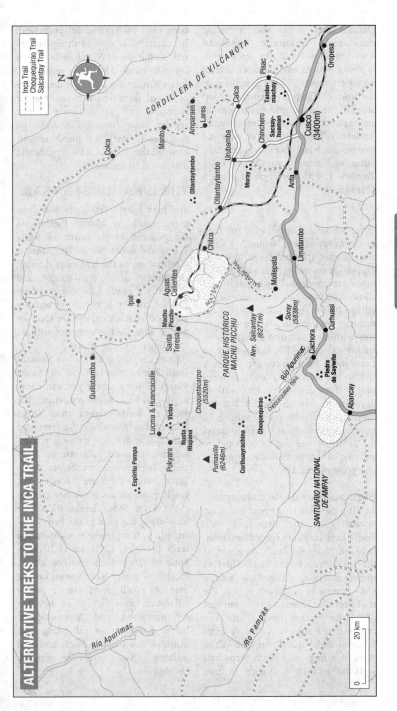

ALTERNATIVE TREKS TO THE INCA TRAIL

glacial lakes with the imposing snowcapped **Ausangate mountain** towering above you. The entire trek is above 4000m and includes several high passes over 5000m. Beginning at the town of **Tinqui**, you make a loop around the Ausangate mountain, in either direction, passing through small Andean villages with great views of nearby glaciers. There are morning buses to Tinqui from Cusco's Calle Tomaso Tito Condemayta at around 10am (5hr).

Lares

There are several options for trekking in the **Lares valley**, lasting 2–5 days, and all offer splendid views of snow-capped peaks and green valleys. The hikes are moderately strenuous and allow you to properly experience village life in the Andes. You'll pass through communities where you can stay with local families and purchase traditional crafts. The hot springs in Lares make for a relaxing end to any trek in the area. Some tour operators sell a three-day Lares trek with a day-trip to Machu Picchu on the fourth day, but do not be misled; in most cases you will still need to travel for 2–5hr by bus and/or train before arriving at Aguas Calientes from the end point of your trail.

Espíritu Pampa/Vilcabamba

To visit the least frequented but most rewarding of the alternative Inca Trails, Espíritu Pampa or **Vilcabamba**, believed to be the last stronghold of the Inca, deep in the jungle and as remote as it gets, you need 10–16 days. Only accessible in the dry season, the trail begins at Huancacalle, 60km east of Machu Picchu, from where you can visit the sites of Vitcos (a huge fortress) and Yurac Rumi (the White Rock – a huge rock with steps and seats carved into it, thought to have been used for ceremonial purposes). It usually takes around three days to trek to the site of Vilcabamba, which is mostly covered by jungle vegetation. It is a further day's walk to the village of **Kiteni**, from where there is regular transport to Quillabamba (6hr); regular buses from Quillabamba go to Cusco (7–9hr). It is highly recommended that you hire a local guide and *arrieros* in Huancacalle.

THE INKA JUNGLE TRAIL

The Inka Jungle Trail lasts 3–4 days, going south to Machu Picchu via the peaceful jungle towns of Santa Teresa and Santa María. The name is a misnomer, as the trail runs through cloudforest rather than jungle, and is mostly a gentle hike along a river. Tours consist of a mixture of walking and mountain biking, and are ideal for people who want activity but without spending too much money.

From Cusco you take a bus towards Quillabamba and get off at **Santa María** (5–6hr), where you can camp or stay in basic accommodation. The walk to **Santa Teresa** from Santa María takes you along the river and lasts 7–8hr; hiring a guide is recommended, as some parts are not very clear. Twenty minutes before Santa Teresa, where there are places to stay, you'll come across some hot springs (S10). From Santa Teresa, it's a 2-hr walk along the road to the hydroelectric plant, from where you can take a train to Aguas Calientes (8.20am & 3pm daily) and then go on to Machu Picchu. If you're with a tour, on the first day you'll go by private bus to Alfamuyo, the high point between Ollantaytambo and Santa María, before going on an exilirating 4-hr downhill ride to Santa Maria and then walking to Santa Teresa the next day (as above).

Nazca and the South Coast

The south has been populated as long as anywhere in Peru – for at least nine thousand years in some places – but until the twentieth century no one guessed the existence of this arid region's unique cultures, whose enigmatic remains, particularly along the coast, show signs of a sophisticated civilization. With the discovery and subsequent study, beginning in 1901, of ancient sites throughout the coastal zone, it now seems clear that this was home to at least three major cultures: the **Paracas** (500 BC–400 AD), the influential **Nazca** (500–800 AD) and finally, the **Ica** or **Chincha Empire** (1000–1450 AD), which was overrun by and absorbed into Pachacutec's mushrooming Inca Empire in the fifteenth century.

The area has a lot to offer the modern traveller: the enduring mystery of the enigmatic **Nazca Lines**, the desert beauty of the **Paracas National Reserve** and wildlife haven of the **Ballestas Islands**, as well as the tranquil oasis of **Huacachina** – the essential stop on the gringo trail around Peru for **dune-buggying** and **sandboarding** trips on the immense dunes that surround it.

PISCO, PARACAS RESERVE AND BALLESTAS ISLANDS

The town of **PISCO**, devastated by a powerful earthquake in 2007, has little to offer the visitor, as it is largely

TOURS OF THE PARACAS RESERVE AND BALLESTAS ISLANDS

There are several local tour operators running standard speedboat tours to the Ballestas Islands, leaving Pisco early in the morning and returning a couple of hours later. Many people choose to do an afternoon tour of the Paracas National Reserve with the same operator, making a whole day-trip. The boat trips to the Ballestas Islands cost S30–35, not including the S1 entrance fee, to be paid on the pier. They last two hours and take in the giant Candelabra geoglyph on the northern part of the Paracas Peninsula, 150m tall and 50m wide, before bobbing very close to the islands to give you the full measure of the impressive stench, the rocks alive with wildlife and the sky dark with birds. You can sometimes see sea lions and bottle-nosed dolphins.

Excursions into the Paracas Reserve typically coast S25, not including the S5 entry fee or lunch. Tours begin at around 10.45am to coincide with the return of the boats from the Ballestas Islands and take in a stretch of desert with 40-million-year-old fossils, two attractive beaches, the popular "La Catedral" rock formation just off the shore, which collapsed after the 2007 earthquake, and a couple of fantastic viewpoints overlooking the desert scenery. Tours end with lunch at the tiny fishing village of Lagunillas; "El Che" is the most popular spot (menú marino S25). Cycling, camping and dune-buggying trips into the reserve are also possible (see below for operators).

It's best to buy tickets the day before, as boats leave at around 7.45am and you can arrange to be picked up at your hotel if you already have tickets.

Most of these companies also organize tours to other nearby attractions, such as Tambo Colorado – adobe ruins built by the Chinca culture – as well as dune-buggy excursions into the desert. Try Paracas Overland, at San Francisco 111, Pisco (☎056/533 855, ✆www.paracasoverland.com.pe), or alternatively Paracas Explorer, at Paracas 9 in El Chaco (☎056/531 487, ✆www.pparacasexplorer.com – Spanish only).

industrial and the smell of the fish-meal factories often overpowers the town. It's possible to use it as a jumping-off point for visiting the nearby **Paracas Reserve** and **Ballestas Islands,** though it's more convenient to stay in the seaside village of **El Chaco,** the launching point for boat tours to the islands, inside the reserve itself.

The Paracas Reserve

Founded in 1975, the **PARACAS NATIONAL RESERVE** covers an area of approximately 3350 square kilometres; with a large area of ocean within its boundaries, it also includes red-sand beaches, stunning cliffs and islands. The reserve is Peru's principal centre for marine conservation and is home to dolphins, whales and sea lions, as well as many birds including pelicans, flamingos, penguins and cormorants. The name Paracas comes from the Quechua "raining sand", and the area is constantly battered by strong winds and sandstorms. Not discouraged by the harsh climate, the area has been inhabited for around nine thousand years, most notably by the pre-Inca culture known as the Paracas.

The Ballestas Islands

Around twenty minutes offshore, the **Islas Ballestas**, one of the most impressive marine reserves in Latin America, are protected nesting grounds for vast numbers of cormorants, gulls and other sea birds. They are sometimes referred to as the Guano Islands, due to the intensive guano mining that used to take place here, since they are completely covered in guano or bird droppings. Today the islands are all alive with a mass of sea lions soaking up the sun, and birds including pelicans, Humboldt penguins, Inca terns, Peruvian boobies and cormorants.

Arrival

Just four hours south of Lima, the Paracas Reserve is easily reached via the Panamerican Highway. Bear in mind, however, that only two bus companies stop in Paracas proper; the rest drop you off at Cruz del Pisco, in the middle of the

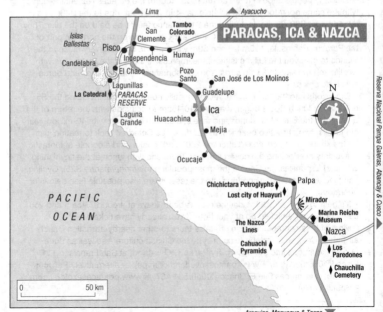

Panamericana, from where you will first have to take a *combi* to Pisco (S5) and then another *combi* or taxi (S15) to Paracas.

Bus The excellent bus company Oltursa has an office next to the hostel *Refugio del Pirata*, where its buses arrive from Lima, Nazca and Arequipa. Cruz del Sur stops at the northern end of the village, and also has two departures daily, both north and south along the Panamericana.

Combi or taxi *Combis* and taxis to Paracas leave from outside Pisco's central market about every 20min or when full, throughout the day, and take 25min.

Accommodation

All guesthouses in El Chaco can arrange trips to the Ballestas Islands and the Paracas Reserve.

Brisas de la Bahía Av. Paracas s/n ☎056/532-115, ⓦwww.brisasdelabahia.com. Once you get past the lime-green decor, you'll truly appreciate the fan-equipped en-suites, all with brand new beds to ensure a good night's sleep. The manager is very helpful when it comes to arranging excursions. S55.

Hostal Refugio del Pirata Av. Paracas s/n, next to the Oltursa bus office ☎056/54-5054, ⓔrefugiodelpirata@hotmail.com. Spotless, tiled en-suite rooms with comfortable beds, wi-fi and good breakfast make this a top choice. S60.

Hostal Santa María Av. Paracas s/n, next to Plazuela Abelardo Quiñones ☎056/545-045, ⓦwww.santamariahostal.com. The plusher choice, this guesthouse has spick-and-span rooms with cable TV, the village's best restaurant, and runs its own tours into the surrounding area. Breakfast included. S110.

Eating and drinking

Cevicherías Off the southern end of the Malecón El Chaco (boardwalk). This row of seafood shacks is the best place for lunch, as they all serve inexpensive two-course *menú marino* lunches and generous helpings of fresh fruit juice. *Restaurant Isabel* has the best *arroz con mariscos*, whereas another one is the only place open on a Sunday night for fried chicken.

El Chorito Av. Paracas s/n, next to *Hostal Santa María*. The most upscale spot in the village, this restaurant may have white linen tablecloths, but the excellent fish and seafood dishes it serves are still reasonably priced. Mains from S30. Closed Sunday evening.

Juan Pablo Malecón El Chaco. Right near the pier, this restaurant serves early breakfasts for those going to the Paracas Islands, as well as decent fish dishes during the day, though the waiters are a little

overzealous when it comes to attracting custom. Mains from S20.

Moving on

Bus Arequipa (twice daily; 12–14hr); Lima (twice daily; 3hr 30min); Nazca (twice daily; 4hr).

ICA

The city of **ICA** lies 50km inland, in a fertile valley surrounded by impressive sand dunes. It suffered considerable damage in the 2007 earthquake and several buildings were completely destroyed, including almost one entire side of the Plaza de Armas. In the city itself, the **Museo Regional** warrants a visit, and the surrounding area offers **vineyard tours** with plenty of wine-tasting opportunities. Note that it's better to stay in nearby Huacachina (see p.850).

What to see and do

Ica's busy streets do not lend themselves to leisurely strolls; however it is easy to get around using the ubiquitous *tico* taxis that will take you anywhere in the city for around S4.

Museo Regional de Ica

Located in an Ica suburb, the superb **Museo Regional** (Ayabaca, block 8; Mon–Fri 8am–7pm & Sat–Sun 9am–6pm; S12) is one of the best in Peru, housing important Nazca, Ica and Paracas cultural artefacts. The exhibits range from mummies (including those of children and parrots), trophy heads and trepanned skulls to examples of Nazca pottery and Paracas weavings; a scale model of the Nazca lines is out back. To get there, take a taxi from the centre of Ica (S4).

Bodega and vineyard tours

Ica's main tourist attraction and principal industry is the many *bodegas* and vineyards nearby, which can be visited on organized tours, both from the city and from Huacachina, and

ICA AND HUACACHINA TOURS

Most hostels in Huacachina rent out sandboards and run dune-buggy tours. Those looking to cut costs may want to hire a board and go it alone, but bear in mind that it soon gets very tiring dragging a board up a sand dune in the scorching sun. Irresponsible dune-buggy drivers are known to drive quite recklessly, so it's best to book your trip with a responsible agency such as the following:

Desert Adventure Hostal Desert Nights ☏056/228-458, ⊛www.desertadventure.net. An established Huacachina-based tour company, offering the standard half-day dune-buggy tours of the dunes (S40), with sandboarding included (which can be "soft adventure" or "adrenaline" on request), as well as 1-hr and 2-hr

quad-biking tours (S40–75). Also runs 2-day trips with a night spent camping in the desert. Huacachina Tours Perotti s/n ☏098/611-3252, ⊛www.huacachina.com. A professional outfit running sandboarding and dune-buggy tours, including trips in private buggies (min 2 people; S60 per hour).

usually involve a look around the vineyard followed by wine tasting and the chance to buy. The following vineyards produce wines and piscos which are famed throughout Peru: Bodega Ocucaje (⊛www.ocucaje .com), Bodega Vista Alegre (⊛www .vistaalegre.com.pe), Bodega Tacama (⊛www.tacama.com) and Bodega El Catador (Km 334 Panamericana, ☏056/403-295), where the visitors are allowed to join in the stomping of the grapes in February and March.

Arrival

Bus Most bus companies have their own terminals in the unsavoury area along Manzanilla and Lambayeque; there are numerous departures in both directions along the Panamericana during the day. Recommended companies include Ormeño, Lambayeque s/n (☏056/215-600); Cruz del Sur, Lambayeque 140 (☏056/223-333); Oltursa, Av. Los Maestros s/n (☏056/233-330); and Soyuz, Manzanilla 130 (☏056/233-312).

Moving on

Bus Arequipa (several daily; 10–12hr); Lima (every 15min; 4hr 30min); Nazca (several daily; 2hr 30min). Colectivo/taxi It's easy to catch either one to Ica during the day (at least one hourly).

HUACACHINA

Since Ica itself is not terribly attractive, it's preferable to base yourself at the

nearby village of **HUACACHINA**, as it's just as easy to do *bodega* tours from here. This once peaceful oasis, nestled among huge sand dunes and boasting a lake with curative properties, has recently been overrun with travellers, eager for adrenaline-packed adventures (in particular **sandboarding** and **dune-buggying**) and all-night parties around dimly lit pools. If the picture-postcard lagoon looks familiar, that's because you've seen it on the S50 notes.

Accommodation

All hostels below either run their own sandboarding, dune-buggy and *bodega* tours, or they can organize them for you. Much of the nightlife in Huacachina revolves around the hostels, which usually have their own restaurants and bars, and throw raucous pool parties in the evenings.
La Casa de Arena Perotti s/n ☏056/215-274, ℮casadearena@hotmail.com. The quintessential party hostel in Huacachina hosts nightly BBQs at the pool-side bar (S15); join in the fun or bring earplugs. The rooms are comfortable enough, though it's hard to keep the sand out; splurge on an en-suite for an extra S15, as the shared bathrooms are not the cleanest. S25.
El Huacachinero Perotti s/n ☏056/217-435, ⊛www.elhuacachinero.com. Plusher than other hostels, this quiet, secure guesthouse has spotless a/c rooms with cable TV, an 8-bunk dorm, a small pool and a garden with outside bar. It's also one of the best places to do dune-buggy rides (10am and 4.30pm daily; S40), as their new green buggies are well maintained and the drivers responsible. Dorms S25, rooms S75.

Hostal Desert Nights By the lagoon ☎056/228-458, Ⓦwww.bookingbox.org.uk/desertnights. This perpetually popular HI-affiliated hostel has clean, mixed 8- and 10-person dorms, reliable hot showers, free internet and one of the most popular restaurants in town (see below). Desert Adventure, the in-house tour agency, offers the greatest range of outdoor excursions. Dorms S15.

Eating

La Casa de Bamboo Perotti s/n, behind the *Hostería Suiza*. Wholesome outdoor café with friendly (if leisurely) service, offering generous helpings of imaginative dishes, numerous vegetarian options included. The tasty Thai curry may not be terribly authentic, but it can be a welcome change from Peruvian food. Mains S25.

Desert Nights Restaurant Bar By the lagoon. The outdoor terrace is crowded day and night with hungry backpackers who appreciate such inexpensive favourites as bacon cheeseburgers, pizza, salads and curry (all around S20). The cocktails are not bad either.

NAZCA AND AROUND

The small, sun-baked town of **NAZCA** spreads along the margin of a small coastal valley, and is an interesting and enjoyable place to stay. Although the river is invariably dry, Nazca's valley remains green and fertile through the continued application of ancient subterranean aqueducts. These days, the town is one of Peru's major attractions, and though most travellers come here solely to take a flight over the enigma that is the Nazca Lines (see p.854), other local attractions include the excellent **Museo Didáctico Antonini**, the adobe Inca ruins of **Paredones** on the outskirts, and the popular (if somewhat macabre) outlying archeological sites, such as the nearby **Chauchilla Cemetery** and the **Cahuachi pyramids,** an hour's drive into the desert.

What to see and do

The **Plaza de Armas** is the heart of Nazca. Jr Bolognesi is the main street leading away from it and there are numerous restaurants, bars and hostels to be found within a couple of blocks of the Plaza de Armas and Plaza Bolognesi, three blocks to the west.

Museo Didáctico Antonini

If you head east from the Plaza de Armas along Avenida de La Cultura you soon come to the fascinating **Museo Didáctico Antonini** (daily 9am–7pm; S15). The museum stretches for six long blocks from the Plaza de Armas along Bolognesi and presents excellent interpretative exhibits covering the evolution of Nazca culture, with superb examples of pottery, household tools and trophy skulls with pierced foreheads. There's a good audiovisual show and scale-model reconstructions of local ruins such as the Templo del Escalonado at Cahuachi. The museum complex includes an archeological park that contains the Bisambra aqueduct (once fed by the Bisambra reservoir higher up the valley) and some burial reconstructions. The exhibit labels are in Spanish but you can pick up translation booklets at the front desk.

María Reiche Planetarium

For those with a particular interest in the Nazca Lines, a trip to the **María Reiche Planetarium** in the *Nazca Lines Hotel* (Bolognesi s/n, showings in English daily at 7pm and in Spanish at 8pm; S20) is a good idea. The shows last about 45min, focusing primarily on María Reiche's theories about the Lines, and their correspondence to various constellations, followed by a quick look through a powerful telescope at the moon and Saturn.

Arrival

Bus There is no central bus terminal, and each bus company drops passengers off at its own terminal, each of which is along Lima and Avenida Los Incas, across the *óvalo* (roundabout). Persistent touts meet all buses, trying to sell you anything from

PERU

NAZCA AND THE SOUTH COAST

Didáctico Museo Antonini & Cantayoc Aqueducts ▲

Panamerican Highway to Lima & the Mirador ◄

Panamerican Highway to Arequipa, Nasca Airport & Chauchilla Cemetery ▶

Los Paredones & ▶

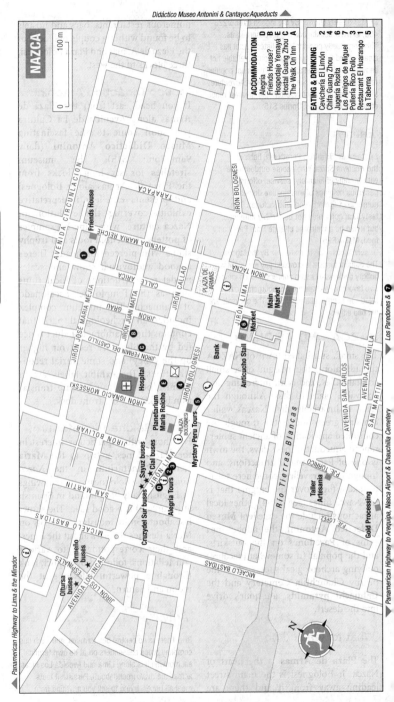

NAZCA

0 — 100 m

ACCOMMODATION
Alegria	D
Friends House?	B
Hospedaje Yemayá	E
Hostal Guang Zhou	C
The Walk On Inn	A

EATING & DRINKING
Cevichería El Limón	2
Chifa Guang Zhou	4
Jugería Rosita	6
Los Amigos de Miguel	7
Pollería Rico Pollo	3
Restaurant El Huarango	1
La Taberna	5

Friends House

Plaza de Armas

Hospital

Planetarium María Reiche

Bank

Anticucho Stall

Main Market

Market

Mystery Peru Tours

Gold Processing

Taller Artesanía

Olltursa buses
Omeño buses
Cruz del Sur buses
Sayuz buses
Cial buses
Alegria Tours

Río Tierras Blancas

accommodation to flights; ignore them, as well as any taxi drivers who tell you that your hostel is dirty/too far/has closed down.

Colectivo and taxi *Colectivos* to and from Ica arrive at and leave close to the gas station on the *óvalo*. You can take a taxi directly to the Nazca Lines flight airstrip for around S6.

Accommodation

Friends House María Reiche 612 ☏056/524-191, ⓦ www.friendshousenazca.com. A cosy and friendly backpacker haunt run by a helpful family. Having just moved to new premises, it now only has en-suite rooms and dorms, as well as a shared guest kitchen. Dorms S10, rooms S28.

Alegria Lima 166 ☏056/522-702, ⓦ www .hotelalegria.net. A more upmarket option, this popular hotel has en-suite chalet-style rooms with fans and bath, set around an attractive garden and pool. It also has a restaurant that serves delicious Peruvian and international cuisine, and their travel agency can arrange all manner of tours. S180.

Hospedaje Yemayá Callao 578 ☏056/523-146, ⓔ nazcahospedajeyemaya@hotmail.com. A good central option with friendly staff, offering clean, secure, wi-fi enabled rooms. S40.

Hostal Guang Zhou Fermín de Castillo 494 ☏056/524-450, ⓦ www.hotelguangzhouperu.com. Under the same ownership as the best Chinese restaurant in town, this tower-like hotel offers sixteen well-kept, a/c en-suites with cable TV, as well as an attractive rooftop terrace. S45.

🏃 **The Walk On Inn** Jose María Mejía 108 ☏056/522-566, ⓦ www.walkoninn.com. This secure, friendly hostel is very popular with international backpackers; there are basic but clean en-suites and dorms, a small swimming pool, excellent buffet breakfast (S6), book exchange and wi-fi. Not only do you get free pick-up from the bus station, but if you're taking a late bus, you can stay in your room until departure (provided it hasn't been reserved). Nazca flights and other tours arranged. Dorms S15, rooms S25.

Eating and drinking

For excellent street food, the best place in town for *anticuchos de corazón* (S5 for 2) is on the corner diagonally opposite the BCP bank; go there between 5pm and 7pm, because the lady there sells out quickly. Half a block east on Lima, *Jugería Rosita* does excellent fruit juices; for a liquid meal, go for the *surtido especial* (a blend of fruit juices that also incorporates beer and raw egg; S7).

Cevichería El Limón Lima 170. The bright lime-green decor, the efficient service and the well-prepared *ceviches*, *arroz con mariscos* and fish dishes make this a top spot in the heart of Nazca; just ask the locals who pile in every lunchtime. *Menú marino* S20.

Chifa Guang Zhou Bolognesi 297. The best Chinese place in town, with a large selection of noodle and rice dishes, all served with wonton soup. Mains S10.

🏃 **Los Amigos de Miguel** Paredones 600. Loyal customers have followed this local institution to its new location south of the centre; at lunchtimes, it's packed with loyal fans of Nazca's best *ceviche*; try the sea urchin or the *leche de pantera*. *Menú marino* S25.

Pollería Rico Pollo Lima 190. Push your way past the tables crowded with local families and join the queue for the best roast chicken in town at this large, bustling eatery. Besides chicken meal deals, you can grab some *anticuchos* (S12).

Restaurant El Huarango Arica 602. Climb up to the rooftop terrace for a flavourful *criollo* meal.

TOURS AROUND NAZCA

Some well-established companies arrange **tours** to the major sites around Nazca, all offering similar trips to Los Paredones, Cantalloc, Cahuachi, Chauchilla and the Lines. Tours around Chauchilla Cemetery last 2 hours 30 minutes for about US$10–35 per person; a trip to the viewing tower and the Casa Museo María Reiche also takes 2 hours 30 minutes and costs around US$10–15. Tours out to the ruined temple complex in the desert at Cahuachi (see p.855) last 4hr and costs around US$20–50 per person, depending on group size; these need to be arranged in advance.

The best **tour operators** are Mystery Peru, at Morseski 126 (☏056/522-379, ⓦ www.mysteryperu.com) and Alegría Tours, at Lima 168 (☏056/522-444, ⓦ www .alegriatoursperu.com). Nazca 500 (☏056/997-3873, ⓦ www.nazca500.com) arranges sandboarding tours up Cerro Blanco, as well as excursions to outlying archeological sites using dune buggies.

The fish dishes are excellent and the free pisco sour goes down very smoothly indeed. Mains S10–25.

La Taberna Lima 321. Its walls are covered with graffiti scrawled over the years by passing groups of travellers – testimony to its popularity as a local watering hole/restaurant. Grab a beer in the upstairs lounge while listening to local live bands or sample the spicy *pescado a lo macho* (S25).

Directory

Banks and exchange BCP at Lima and Bolognesi has an ATM and changes US dollars.
Hospital Callao s/n ☎056/522-586.
Post office Castillo 379, two blocks west of the Plaza de Armas.
Telephones Telefónica Perú at Lima 525 is good for local and international calls.
Tourist police Av. Los Incas 1, s/n km 447 ☎056/522-105.

Moving on

Bus companies include Cial, Lima 155 (☎056/523-960); Cruz del Sur, Lima at San Martín (☎056/523-713); Oltursa, Lima 105 (☎056/522-265); Ormeño, Av. Los Incas s/n (☎056/522-058); Soyuz, next door to Cruz del Sur (☎056/521-464).

Bus Cial to: Arequipa (2 nightly; 11hr); Cusco (daily at 8pm; 14hr); Lima (2 daily; 6hr 30min); Tacna (2 nightly; 14hr). Cruz del Sur to: Arequipa (2 daily, 11hr); Ica (4 daily; 2hr); Lima (4 daily; 6hr 30min); Paracas (2 daily; 3hr). Oltursa to: Arequipa (3 daily; 11hr); Ica (2 daily; 3hr 30min); Lima (2 daily; 6hr 30min); Paracas (1 daily at 1pm; 2hr). Ormeño to: La Paz, Bolivia, via Arequipa and Puno (daily at 3.30pm; 26hr); Tacna via Arequipa (2 daily; 14 hr). Soyuz to: Ica (every 30min from 6.15am; 3hr 30min).

THE NAZCA LINES

One of the great mysteries of South America, the **NAZCA LINES** are a series of animal figures and geometric shapes, none of them repeated and some up to 200m in length, drawn across some 500 square kilometres of the bleak, stony Pampa de San José. Each one, even such sophisticated motifs as a spider monkey or a hummingbird, is executed in a single continuous line, most created by clearing away the brush and hard stones of the plain to reveal the fine dust beneath. Theories abound as to what their purpose was – from landing strips for alien spaceships to some kind of agricultural calendar, aligned with the constellations above, to help regulate the planting and harvesting of crops. Perhaps at the same time some of the straight lines served as ancient sacred paths connecting *huacas*, or power spots. Regardless of why they were made, the Lines are among the strangest and most unforgettable sights in the country.

At Km420 of the Panamerican Highway, 20km north of Nazca, a tall metal **viewing tower** (or *mirador*; S1) has been built above the plain, from which you get a partial view of a giant tree, a pair of hands and a lizard, though the experience does not compare to a **flight** over the Lines.

Around 5km further along the Panamericana from the *mirador*, you'll find the **Museo María Reiche** (daily 9am–6pm; S5), the former home of the German mathematician who made research into the Lines her life's work. Here you can see her possessions and sketches and visit her tomb.

AROUND NAZCA

Chauchilla and Cahuachi, after the Lines the most important Nazca sites, are both difficult to reach by public transport, so you may want to consider an organized tour.

Cerro Blanco

You can easily see **Cerro Blanco**, the world's largest sand dune, from anywhere in the city. Formerly used as a religious centre, it's now the site for extreme dune-buggy rides and sandboarding. Several tour agencies run morning trips here, typically leaving at 5am and returning at lunchtime.

Chauchilla Cemetery

Roughly 30km south of Nazca, **Chauchilla Cemetery** is an atmospheric sight.

Scattered about the dusty ground are literally thousands of graves, dating back to the Nazca culture (400 BC–800 AD), which have been cleaned up in recent years and organized for visitors, though bits of human bone and broken pottery shards still litter the ground, left there by grave robbers from decades ago.

There are clear walkways from which you must not stray, and open graves have roofs built over them to save the mummies, skeletons, shroud fabric and lengths of braided hair from the desert sun. The mummies with the longest hair are the chiefs, and the Nazca mummified animals as well; look for a child's pet parrot. It is an impressive experience, intensified by the curator's decision to arrange the mummies into positions intended to represent their daily lives. Tours of the cemetery last around three hours and take in a pottery workshop and a gold-processing centre on the way back to town.

Cahuachi

Currently being excavated by an Italian archeological team, **Cahuachi** is an enormous ceremonial centre of great importance to the Nazca culture, consisting of 44 pyramids, only one of which has been renovated; the rest are still hidden under the sand. There is also a llama cemetery and a site called Estaquería – a possible place of mummification. It lies in the middle of the desert, 25km west of Nazca along a dirt track; on the way, you pass ransacked ancient graveyards with scattered human remains. Tours normally take place in the morning, as sandstorms can pick up in the afternoon.

Paredones and Aquaductos de Cantallo

These two sites are normally seen as part of one tour as they are close together. The **Paredones ruins**, 2km southeast of town, are the crumbling remains of an Inca fortress and administrative centre (and now home to desert owls). The **Cantallo Aqueducts** lie 5km further on; constructed by the Nazca, they consist of stone spirals going deep into the ground and are still used to irrigate the nearby fields. It used to be possible to enter the aqueducts through the *ventanas* (windows) – the holes out of which the water would come out – but this has been forbidden since the last earthquake.

Arequipa and around

The country's second-biggest and arguably, after Cusco, most attractive city, **AREQUIPA** sits some 2400m above sea level with **El Misti**, the dormant volcano poised above, giving the place a rather legendary appearance. An elegant yet modern city, with a relatively wealthy population of more than 750,000, it has a relaxed feel and maintains a rather aloof attitude towards the rest of Peru.

The spectacular countryside around Arequipa rewards a few days' exploration, with some exciting trekking and rafting possibilities (best in the dry season, May–Sept). Around 200km to the north of the city is the **Colca Canyon**: called the "valley of marvels" by the Peruvian novelist Marío Vargas Llosa, it is nearly twice the size of Arizona's Grand Canyon and one of the country's most extraordinary natural sights. Further north, the remote **Cotahuasi Canyon** offers even more remote and challenging treks for those with plenty of time. Around 120km west of Arequipa, you can see the amazing petroglyphs of **Toro Muerto**, perhaps continuing on to hike amid the craters and cones of the **Valley of the Volcanoes**.

What to see and do

The city centre is compact and walkable, spreading out in a grid shape from the Plaza de Armas. Arequipa's architectural beauty comes mainly from the colonial period, characterized here by white *sillar* stone, which gives the city the name "Ciudad Blanca" ("White City"). Of the huge number of religious buildings spread about the old colonial centre, the **Monastery of Santa Catalina** is the most outstanding. Within a few blocks of the Plaza de Armas are half a dozen churches that merit a brief visit, and a couple of superb old mansions. You can walk to the attractive suburb of **Yanahuara**, renowned for its dramatic views of the valley with the volcans.

The Plaza de Armas and Catedral

The **Plaza de Armas**, one of South America's grandest, and the focus of social activity in the early evenings, comprises a particularly striking array of colonial architecture, dotted with palms, flowers and gardens. It is dominated by the arcades and elegant white facade of the seventeenth-century **Catedral** (open for worship Mon–Sat 7–11.30am & 5–7.30pm, Sun 7am–1pm & 5–7pm), which has one of the largest organs in South America, imported from Belgium. Note the serpent-tailed devil supporting the wooden pulpit.

Iglesia de la Compañía

On the southeast corner of the plaza lies the elaborate **Iglesia de la Compañía** (Mon–Fri 9am–12.30pm & 3–6pm, Sat 11.30am–12.30pm & 3–6pm, Sun 9am–noon & 5–6pm; free), founded in 1573 and rebuilt in 1650, with its magnificently sculpted doorway, and a locally inspired Mestizo-Baroque relief. Inside the former sacristy, the cupola depicts jungle imagery alongside warriors, angels and the Evangelists. You can also enter the **Jesuit Cloisters,** their pillars supporting stone arches covered with intricate reliefs showing more angels, local fruits and vegetables, seashells and stylized puma heads.

Other churches

Other notable churches within a few blocks of the Plaza include **Santo Domingo** (Mon–Fri 7am–noon & 3–7.30pm, Sat 6.45–9am & 3–7.30pm, Sun 5.30am–12.30pm; free), two blocks east of La Compañía, built in 1553 by Gaspar Vaez, with the oldest surviving Mestizo-style facade in the city; and

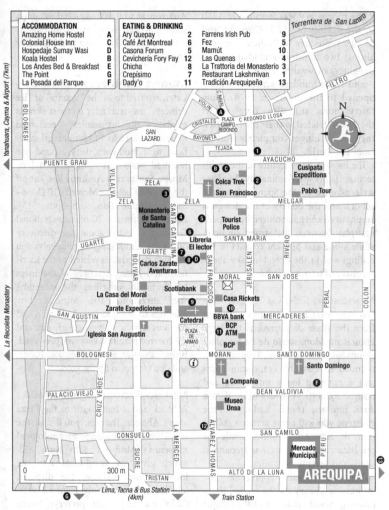

ACCOMMODATION
Amazing Home Hostel   A
Colonial House Inn   C
Hospedaje Sumay Wasi   D
Koala Hostel   B
Los Andes Bed & Breakfast   E
The Point   G
La Posada del Parque   F

EATING & DRINKING
Ary Quepay   2
Café Art Montreal   6
Casona Forum   5
Cevichería Fory Fay   12
Chicha   8
Crepísimo   7
Dady'o   11
Farrens Irish Pub   9
Fez   5
Mamút   10
Las Quenas   4
La Trattoria del Monasterio   3
Restaurant Lakshmivan   1
Tradición Arequipeña   13

the imposing **Iglesia de San Francisco** (Mon–Fri 9am–12.30pm & 3–6.30pm; S5), at the top of its namesake street, built in the sixteenth century and featuring an unusual brick entranceway.

Monasterio de Santa Catalina

Just two blocks north of the Plaza de Armas, the **Monastero de Santa Catalina** (daily 8am–5pm, last entrance at 4pm, Tues & Thurs until 8pm; S30, multilingual guides available for S20) is the most important and prestigious religious building in Peru – a citadel within a city – and its enormous complex of rooms, cloisters, streets and tiny plazas are perfect to explore at a leisurely pace, peering into the austere living quarters and the mortuary, strolling along brightly painted cloisters, admiring the paintings and the murals, or climbing up to the viewpoint from Zocódober Square for a splendid view of Arequipa and the distant mountains.

The monastery was founded in 1580 by the wealthy María de Guzmán, and its vast protective walls once sheltered almost two hundred secluded nuns – daughters of wealthy Spanish families – and three hundred servants until it opened to the public in 1970. Some thirty nuns still live here today; though restricted to their own quarter, they are no longer completely shut off from the world.

The most striking feature of the architecture is its predominantly Mudéjar style, adapted by the Spanish from the Moors, and the quality of the design is emphasized and harmonized by a superb interplay between the strong sunlight, white stone and brilliant colours in the ceilings and in the deep blue sky above the maze of narrow streets.

Monasterio de La Recoleta

Over the Río Chili, a 10-min walk west from the Plaza de Armas, is the large Franciscan **Monasterio de La Recoleta** (Mon–Sat 9am–noon & 3–5pm; S10), founded in 1648 by Franciscan friars and containing many interesting and bizarre exhibits. For example, if you duck into the rooms leading off the cloisters, you will come across a collection of art and ceramics made by pre-Inca cultures, as well as trepanned skulls and several mummies.

Bibliophiles will appreciate the impressive **library** on the second floor, housing more than 20,000 antique books and maps, which are only used by researchers with special permission from the Father. You can visit the library for fifteen minutes, at 45 minutes past the hour.

The **Amazonian section** of the museum is a must-see; one room houses jungle jewellery collected by the Franciscan monks on their early missions, as well as photographs of their first encounters with the "natives". The second room displays a large variety of stuffed birds and animals from the Amazon, as well as traditional weapons, some still used today, and maps of early exploration of the Manu and Madre de Díos areas.

Museo Santuarios Andinos

Often referred to as the "Juanita" or "Ice Princess" museum after its most famous exhibit – the immaculately preserved mummy of a 12 to 14 year old girl sacrificed to a mountain deity around five hundred years ago – the superb little **Museo Santuarios Andinos** lies just off the plaza at Calle La Merced 110 (Mon–Sat 9am–6pm, Sun 9am–3pm; S15). After a dramatic 20-minute National Geographic video about the discovery of Juanita, a multilingual guide talks you through the exhibits related to the sacrificial and burial practices of the Incas before finally unveiling the museum's star attraction. The intricate tiny offerings to the gods, made of gold and precious stones, are particularly fine and ice-covered Juanita is very well preserved. Bring a sweater, as it's rather cold inside, and don't forget to tip the guide.

Museo Arqueológico UNSA

A block and a half south of the Plaza along Álvarez Thomas, you'll find the small yet fascinating **archeological museum** (Mon–Fri 8am–4pm; S2), which gives you a glimspe into the local pre-Inca culture. The displays, labelled in Spanish only, feature Nazca, Chiribaya and Wari pottery; Nazca mummies and ritually deformed skulls; fine cloaks adorned with parrot feathers; and Inca and Spanish weaponry.

Mercado Municipal

For a taste of local life, check out the covered market, which takes up an entire block between San Camillo and Alto de la Luna. Lose yourself amid the stalls piled high with local produce, the smells of cooking, *jugerías*, the vendors of jungle potions and wandering musicians. Just leave your valuables behind.

TOURS, TREKKING AND CLIMBING AROUND AREQUIPA

Most companies offer trips of one- to three-days out to the Colca Canyon for S90–250 (sometimes with *very* early morning starts) or to the petroglyphs at Toro Muerto for S60–120. Trips to the Valley of the Volcanes, as well as specialist adventure activities (such as rafting in the Colca Canyon, mountaineering or multi-day trekking) can cost anything from S180 up to S1200 for a 3–6-day outing. Below are recommended companies, all experts in their field.

Carlos Zarate Adventures Santa Catalina 204 ☎054/202-461, ⓦwww.zarateadventures.com. Complimenting his brother's trekking business (see below), knowledgeable guide Carlos offers climbs of nearby peaks, canyoning, and cycling excursions, as well as archeological tours.
Colca Trek Jerusalén 401b ☎054/206-217, ⓦwww.colcatrek.com.pe. An excellent trekking, climbing, mountain-biking and canoeing operator that specializes in customized tours permitting a mix of these, as well as three-day tours of the Colca Canyon. Also sells maps and has equipment rental for independent trekkers.
Cusipata Expeditions Jerusalén 408 ☎054/203-966, ⓦwww.cusipata.com. Specialists in rafting trips on all the major rivers in the area, with short trips to the Chili River, and up-to-six-day-trips on the Colca and Cotahuasi rivers. Also, they lead annual Cotahuasi Canyon expeditions and regular kayaking courses.
Pablo Tour Jerusalén 400 ☎054/203-737, ⓦwww.pablotour.com. Consistently recommended by travellers, this reputable operator runs trekking and cultural trips into the Colca Canyon, as well as mountain-biking descents down the Chachani volcano and multi-day rafting expeditions on the Río Colca.
Zarate Expeditions Santa Catalina 115A ☎054/241-206. One of the sons of legendary local guide Carlos Zarate, Miguel Zarate specializes in multi-day tailor-made tours and trekking expeditions in the Colca and Cotahuasi canyons. With over thirty years' hiking experience in the surrounding area, he can suggest itineraries to suit any taste and ability.

The views: Yanahuara and Mirador de Carmen Alto

A jaunt across the Río Chili via Puente Grau followed by a 15-minute uphill stroll brings you to the attractive plaza of the Yanahuara neighbourhood. It features a **viewing point** (*mirador*), with a postcard panorama of Misti framed behind by the white stone arches. The elaborately carved facade of the small eighteenth-century **Iglesia San Juan Bautista** nearby is a superb example of Mestizo art.

From here, a 5-minute taxi ride (S5–8) takes you to the Mirador del Carmen Alto, which features a stupendous view of the city and all the volcanoes surrounding it.

Arrival and information

Air Flights land at Arequipa airport, 7km northwest of the town. You can either catch a taxi to downtown Arequipa (S20) or a *colectivo*, which charge S8–10 to drop you off at your guesthouse.

Bus Most long-distance buses arrive at the concrete Terminal Terrestre bus station or at the newer Terrapuerto, next door, around 4km from the centre of town; a taxi to the Plaza de Armas should cost no more than S5.
Tourist information There are two official IPerú offices, at Portal de La Municipalidad 110, Plaza de Armas (Mon–Sat 8.30am–7.30pm, Sun 8.30am–4pm; ☎054/223-265, ⓔiperuarequipa @promperu.gob.pe); and at the airport (☎054/444-564), which have helpful staff, free maps of the city and limited information on sights, cultural events and accommodation. For topographic maps of the Colca Canyon, try Colka Trek (see above), while Librería El Lector on San Francisco 221 has an extensive English-language book section, as well as detailed city maps.

Accommodation

Amazing Home Hostel Plaza Campo Redondo 100 ☎054/222-788, ⓦwww .amazinghomeaqp.com. This comfortable new hostel, rapidly growing in popularity with international backpackers, has a friendly vibe, a full range of perks, including wi-fi, and an ample pancake breakfast on the panoramic rooftop terrace. The young guide-owner who goes out of his way to welcome you and the on-site tour agency can help you plan your travels. Dorms S20, rooms S80.

Colonial House Inn Av. Puente Grau 114 ☎054/223-533, ✉colonialhouseinn@hotmail.com. Secure, pleasant location with a pretty covered courtyard, hot showers and access to TV and internet facilities, though the building itself is somewhat run-down. Excellent views of El Misti from the rooftop terrace. S75.

Hospedaje Sumay Wasi San Francisco 221 ☎054/286-833, ✉lperezwi@ucsm.edu.pe. A real steal, just a block and a half from the Plaza, this small guesthouse offers en-suite rooms with cable TV at bargain prices. S30.

Koala Hostel Av. Puente Grau 108 ☎054/223-622, ⓦwww.koalahostel.com. Sealed off from the busy street by a heavy wooden gate, this friendly hostel has colourful rooms, guest kitchen and wi-fi, as well as a comfy lounge for mingling. The helpful on-site agency can arrange Colca Canyon Tours, among others, as well as airport and bus terminal pick-up. Dorms/single/double/triple S20–25/35/28/25 per person.

Los Andes Bed & Breakfast La Merced 123 ☎054/330-015, ⓦwww.losandesarequipa.com. A stone's throw from the Plaza, this great-value budget stay is popular with long-stay travellers and volunteers. The huge en-suites and more modest shared rooms are clean and well decorated, there are two large TV rooms filled with comfy sofas, as well as kitchen and free internet for guests, and the staff are very helpful. S38.

The Point Av. Lima 515, Vallecito ☎054/286-920, ⓦwww.thepointhostels.com/arequipa.html. Part of the chain of party hostels popular with backpackers throughout Peru, the Arequipa branch is no different, with in-house bar, cable TV and DVDs, weekly BBQs, free internet, full restaurant, laundry and Spanish classes. Slightly out of the centre; it's a 15-min walk or 5-min taxi ride from the Plaza de Armas. Airport and bus terminal pick-up at extra cost. Dorms S24, rooms S72.

La Posada del Parque Dean Valdivia 238a ☎054/212-275, ⓦwww.posadadelparque.com. Spacious, bright, comfortable rooms set in a colonial house. The large rooftop terrace has great views over the city, there's a TV lounge and wi-fi, and the family-run Marlon's Travel Agency can book transport and tours. Dorms S15, rooms S55.

Eating

Ary Quepay Jerusalén 502. A large restaurant space serving quality local food, such as alpaca

steaks and *cuy* (guinea pig), as well as international dishes, vegetarian options and fine pisco sours. It may be touristy, but the service is good and there is a festive atmosphere, with live folk music most nights. Mains S20–25.

Cevichería Fory Fay Thomas 221. Join the savvy locals at this nautically themed lunch spot for several types of superb *ceviche* (S18) and some of the best *arroz chaufa con mariscos* (Chinese-style seafood-fried rice; S24) in the south of Peru.

Crepísimo Santa Catalina 208. One of the best cafés in Arequipa for proper coffee, this warm, cosy place offers crêpes (from S7) with numerous sweet and savoury fillings, from *manjar blanco* (*dulce de leche*) to smoked trout.

Fez San Francisco 229. Pull up a high chair at this tiny Middle Eastern joint, grab some excellent falafel (S8) and wash it down with a large freshly squeezed fruit juice. The kebabs here (S17) are also excellent.

Mamút Mecaderes 111. Come to this bustling *sanguchería* for filling, good-value sandwiches (from S6, including veggie options), home-made *chicha morada* and fresh fruit juices.

Restaurant Lakshmivan Jerusalén 408. A very popular vegetarian café at the back of a small patio, with South Asian-themed food. They also sell a range of health-food products, yogurts and wholemeal bread, and their lunch menus are very good value at S15. Open Mon–Sun 8am–9.30pm.

Tradición Arequipeña Av. Dolores 111. Opened in 1991 and situated several blocks east of the city centre (a 10-min cab ride from the Plaza de Armas), this is the best *picanteria* (traditional restaurant serving regional food) in town. It has a pleasant garden, covered and indoor spaces, and is usually bustling with locals enjoying such classics as *chupe de camarones*, *rocoto relleno* and *adobe de cerdo* (slow-cooked pork), accompanied by live folk music. Mains S20–35.

Drinking and nightlife

Café Art Montreal Ugarte 210. This intimate bar really comes to life on Thurs, Fri, and Sat nights, when live bands take to the stage at the back and entertain you with a mix of local rock and Latino. This is a *peña* but certainly isn't folkloric. Happy hour 2-for-1 on drinks (normally S15–20).

Casona Forum San Francisco 317. This three-storey complex houses some of Arequipa's best night spots, such as *Zero Pub & Pool*, with pool tables and the *Terrasse* lounge restaurant, offering a combo of fine dining and stunning views of the city through 360-degree windows. The jewel in the crown – the basement *Forum* disco – is the place to see and be seen among young *Arequipeños*, with a lively tropical decor including palm trees, pools and a large artificial waterfall.

Dady'o Portal de Flores 112, Plaza de Armas. Live bands, karaoke and dangerously cheap drinks drag the crowds to this popular spot for weekend revelries. Open Thurs–Sat 10pm–3am; entry S10.

Farrens Irish Pub Pasaje el Catedral 107 ☎054/238-465. Friendly Irish-themed pub with outside seating (perfect for an afternoon drink in the sunshine), pool tables, satellite sports on TV, Guinness and nightly happy hour from 6–10pm. Beer S6.

Las Quenas Santa Catalina 302. One of the better and larger *peñas* in town, featuring Andean folk music almost every night from around 9pm, as well as traditional local food from 8pm nightly. Closed Sun.

Directory

Banks and exchange BCP at San Juan de Dios 125 and BBVA Banco Continental at San Francisco 108 have ATMs and can change/dispense US dollars. There are cambios on the Plaza de Armas and on San Juan de Dios.

Hospital Hospital Regional (☎054/219-702) deals with 24hr emergencies.

Laundry Quick Laundry, Jerusalén 520 (Mon–Sat 7am–8pm, Sun 8.30am–2pm).

Post office Moral 118 (Mon–Sat 8am–8pm, Sun 9am–1pm).

Taxi Reliable companies include Taxitel (☎054/452-020) and Turismo Arequipa (☎054/458-888).

Telephones and internet Try the Telefónica office at Santa Catalina 118 for local and international calls. Internet cafés include *CiberMarket* at Santa Catalina 115-B and *Online* at Jerúsalen 412, both open until midnight. Most hostels have wi-fi.

Tourist police Jerusalén 315 (☎054/201-258), open 24hr.

Moving on

Leaving from the Terrapuerto for destinations including Cusco, Lima and Nazca are Cruz del Sur (☎054/427-375), Oltursa (☎054/423-152) and Cial (☎054/430-505). Flores (☎054/429-905) has numerous services to Puno and to Lima via Nazca and Ica. If you're going to Colca Canyon, catch Andalucía (☎054/445-089), Transportes Colca (☎054/426-357) or Reyna (☎054/430-612).

Bus Arica, Chile (twice weekly; 14hr); Cusco (4–5 daily; 9–11hr); Desaguadero (3–4 daily; 7–8hr); La Paz, Bolivia (1–2 daily; 12–14hr); Lima via Nazca and Ica (4–5 daily, mostly in the afternoon; 14–16hr); Puno (3–4 daily; 6–7hr); Tacna (4–5 daily; 6–7hr).

CROSSING INTO CHILE

The border with Chile (Mon–Fri 8am–midnight, Sat & Sun 24hr) is about 40km south of Tacna. Regular buses and *colectivos* to Arica (see p.456) leave from the modern bus terminal on Hipolito Unanue in Tacna; the *colectivos* (S20) are a particularly quick and easy way to cross the border. For a small tip, the drivers will assist you with border formalities. Coming back into Peru from Arica is as simple as getting there; *colectivos* run throughout the day from the Terminal Internacional de Buses on Diego Portales 1002.

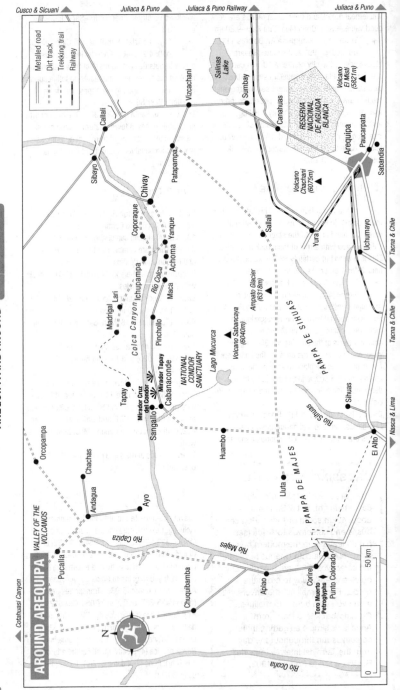

THE COLCA CANYON

The entry point for the Colca Canyon is the popular market town of **Chivay**, 150km north of Arequipa (3–4hr by bus), set among fantastic hiking country and surrounded by some of the most impressive and intensive ancient terracing in South America, though to really see the canyon you need to head further in.

The sharp terraces of the **COLCA CANYON**, one of the world's deepest at more than 1km from cliff edge to river bottom, are still home to more-or-less traditional Indian villages, despite the canyon's growth into one of Peru's most popular tourist attractions. The **Mirador Cruz del Condor** is the most popular viewing point – the canyon is around 1200m deep at this point – from where you can almost guarantee seeing condors circling up from the depths against breathtaking scenery (best spotted 7–9am). The small but growing town of **Cabanaconde** (3300m), which offers a good option for lodgings as a base to descend into the canyon, is about 10km further down the road.

You'll need a couple of days to begin exploring the area and three or four to do it any justice, but several tour companies offer punishing one-day tours as well as extended trips with overnight stops. When you enter the canyon, you need to purchase the Boleto Turístico (Tourist Ticket; S40) from the control point just before the entrance to Chivay. Only buy tickets from Autocolca authorities, as counterfeit tickets do exist.

Chivay

This is the largest village in the canyon, located by its entrance. Its attractions include the hot springs, 3.5km northeast of town (4am–8pm; S10), with a canopy line next to it. There are also several hiking trails here, though most visitors continue on to Cabanaconde.

Sleeping and eating

Hostal Anita Plaza de Armas 607 ☏054/531-114. Central hostel with flowering courtyard and reliable hot showers. S45.

Hostal Estrella de David Siglo XX 209 ☏054/531-233. Attractive guesthouse between the bus terminal and the Plaza de Armas, with simple rooms and cable TV. S25.

Los Portales Arequipa 603. Another excellent restaurant that has gringos flocking to the all-you-can-eat lunchtime buffet, featuring alpaca stew and fish dishes, among others (S25).

Witite Siglo XX 328. Come here for the excellent lunchtime buffet with local specialities such as *rocoto relleno* and trout dishes (S25).

Moving on

Bus Arequipa (11 daily; 3hr); Cabanaconde (6 daily; 2hr 30min).

Cabanaconde

An attractive village in the heart of the canyon, surrounded by Inca terracing, **Cabanaconde** makes an excellent base for hiking down into the canyon. Follow fellow hikers through the fields to a steep trail leading down to Sangalle Oasis – a splotch of blue and green amid parched scenery. The descent takes a couple of hours, and while it's possible to ascend on the same day, it's far more rewarding to either camp or stay in one of the basic huts at Sangalle; each campsite has its own swimming pool.

In Cabanaconde itself, *Pachamama* at San Pedro 209 (☏09/5931-6322, ⓦwww.pachamamahome.com) is a cosy hostel with an excellent pizzeria and bar attached (dorms/rooms S15/25), while the more upmarket *La Posada del Conde*, at San Pedro s/n (☏054/400-408, ⓦwww.posadadelconde.com) has modern rooms with good showers (S90) and a restaurant serving hearty quinoa soup and tasty stews.

Moving on

Bus Arequipa (3 daily; 5hr 30min); Chivay (6 daily; 2hr 30min).

Puno and Lake Titicaca

An immense region both in terms of its history and the breadth of its magical landscape, the **Titicaca Basin** makes most people feel as if they are on top of the world. The skies are vast and the horizons appear to blend away below you. With a dry, cold climate – frequently falling below freezing in the winter nights of July and August – **Puno** is a breathless place (at 3870m above sea level), with a burning daytime sun in stark contrast to the icy evenings.

The first Spanish settlement at Puno sprang up around a silver mine discovered by the infamous Salcedo brothers in 1657, a camp that forged such a wild and violent reputation that the Lima viceroy moved in with soldiers to crush the Salcedos before things got too out of hand. In 1668 he created Puno as the capital of the region and from then on it developed into Lake Titicaca's main port and an important town on the silver trail from Potosí. Rich in traditions, Puno is also famed as the folklore capital of Peru. During the first two weeks of February, fiestas are held in honour of the **Virgen de la Candelaria** – a great spectacle, with incredible dancers wearing devil masks, which climaxes on the second Sunday of February.

On the edge of the town spreads the vast **Lake Titicaca** – enclosed by white peaks and dotted with unusual **floating islands**. The lake is home to the Uros culture, as are the beautiful island communities of **Amantani** and **Taquile**, which can all be visited by boat from Puno.

What to see and do

Puno is a congested, chaotic but friendly town, compact enough to walk around.

Most travellers use it as a stopover on their way to see the islands, but there are a couple of sites of interest in the town itself. There are four main points of reference in Puno: the spacious **Plaza de Armas**, the cosmopolitan strip of **Jirón Lima** on which most restaurants and bars can be found, tiny **Parque Pino** and the bustling **port** area.

The Plaza de Armas and around

The seventeenth-century **Catedral** on the Plaza de Armas (daily 10–11am & 3.30–6pm; free) is surprisingly large, with an exquisite Baroque facade and, unusually for Peru, a very simple interior, in line with the local Aymara Indians' austere attitude to religion. High up, overlooking the town and Plaza de Armas, **Huajsapata Park** sits on a prominent hill, a steep ten-minute climb up Jirón Deustua, right into Jirón Llave, left up Jirón Bolognesi, then left again up the Pasaje Contique steps. Huajsapata offers stupendous views across the bustle of Puno to the serene blue of Titicaca and its unique skyline, though there have been some reported muggings here, so be careful.

The Yavari

Moored in the dock of the *Hotel Sonesta Posada del Inca*, the nineteenth-century British-built steamship **Yavari** (daily 8am–5pm; admission by donations; T051/369-329, Wwww.yavari.org) is the oldest working single-propellor iron ship in existence. In 1862, the 2766 pieces of the ship were transported from the Peruvian coast on the backs of mules and llamas, to be reconstructed on Lake Titicaca. *Yavari* started life as a Peruvian navy gunship but ended up rusting on the lake's shores after being decommissioned. In 1982, Englishwoman Meriel Larkin formed the Yavari Project in a bid to save it. The project aims to repair *Yavari* sufficiently to make it possible to take trips around the lake on it.

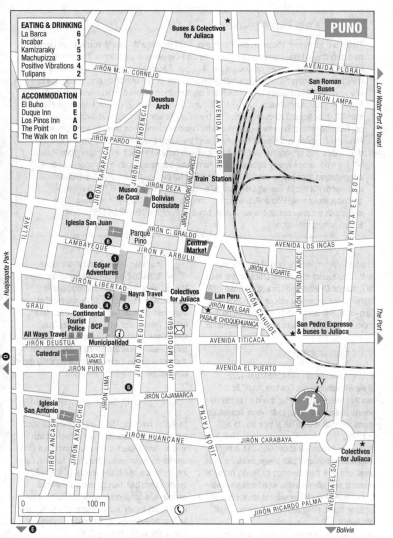

PUNO

EATING & DRINKING
La Barca	6
Incabar	1
Kamizaraky	5
Machupizza	3
Positive Vibrations	4
Tulipans	2

ACCOMMODATION
El Buho	B
Duque Inn	E
Los Pinos Inn	A
The Point	D
The Walk on Inn	C

Buses & Colectivos for Juliaca

AVENIDA FLORAL

JIRÓN M. H. CORNEJO

San Roman Buses

JIRÓN LAMPA

Low Water Port & Yavari

Deustua Arch

AVENIDA LA TORRE

AVENIDA EL SOL

JIRÓN INDEPENDENCIA

JIRÓN PARDO

JIRÓN TARAPACA

JIRÓN TEODORO VALCARCEL

JIRÓN DEZA

Train Station

Museo de Coca

Bolivian Consulate

Iglesia San Juan

JIRÓN C. GRALDO

Parque Pino

Central Market

AVENIDA LOS INCAS

ILLAVE

LAMBAYEQUE

JIRÓN F. ARBULU

Edgar Adventures

JIRÓN A. UGARTE

JIRÓN PINEDA ARCE

Huajsapata Park

JIRÓN LIBERTAD

Nayra Travel

Colectivos for Juliaca

Lan Peru

Banco Continental

Tourist Police

BCP

JIRÓN MELGAR

PASAJE CHOQUEHUANCA

San Pedro Expresso & buses to Juliaca

GRAU

All Ways Travel

JIRÓN DEUSTUA

Municipalidad

JIRÓN AREQUIPA

JIRÓN MOQUEGUA

AVENIDA TITICACA

Catedral

PLAZA DE ARMES

JIRÓN PUNO

AVENIDA EL PUERTO

Iglesia San Antonio

JIRÓN LIMA

JIRÓN CAJAMARCA

N

JIRÓN ANCASH

JIRÓN AYACUCHO

JIRÓN HUANCANE

JIRÓN TACNA

JIRÓN CARABAYA

Colectivos for Juliaca

AVENIDA EL SOL

JIRÓN RICARDO PALMA

0   100 m

Bolivia

The Port

PERU

PUNO AND LAKE TITICACA

Arrival and Information

If you arrive in Puno from sea level, you'll immediately be affected by the altitude and should take it easy for the first day or two.

Boat The main port for boat trips to the Uros Islands, Taquile and Amantani, is a 20-min walk from the Plaza de Armas, straight along Av. El Puerto.

Bus You're most likely to arrive at the main bus terminal on Jr. Primero de Mayo 703 (☎051/364-733).

Combis from the Bolivian border arrive at the Terminal Zonal on Av. Simón Bolívar.

Colectivo *Colectivos* to and from Juliaca and Juliaca Airport leave from Jirón Tacna. Most *hospedajes* in Puno can organize a pick-up from Juliaca Airport.

Train If you're coming from Cusco by train, you'll arrive at the train station (information on ☎051/369-179, ⊛www.perurail.com) at Avenida la Torre 224, several blocks from the centre. Motorcycle rickshaws leave from immediately outside the station (S2 to anywhere in the centre of town).

TOURS AROUND PUNO

There are four main tours on offer in Puno, all of which will reward you with abundant bird and animal life, immense landscapes and indigenous traditions. The trip to the ancient burial towers or *chullpas* at Sillustani normally involves a 3–4hr tour by minibus and costs S20–30 depending on whether or not entrance and guide costs are included. Most other tours involve a combination of visits to the nearby Uros Floating Islands (half-day tour; S15–30) and Taquile and the Uros Islands (full day from S50, or from S90 overnight). The best way to see the lake and experience life on Titicaca is to take a two-day tour, which stops at the Uros Islands then goes to Amantaní, where you spend the night, and then continues to Taquile on the second day; a day-trip is very rushed, as it takes three hours to reach Amantaní from Puno.

Tour operators Many agencies run formulaic tours and some companies have a reputation for ripping off the islanders. The following show a more sensitive approach: All Ways Travel, Deustua 576, 2nd floor (☎051/355-979, ⓦwww .titicacaperu.com); Edgar Adventures, Lima 328 (☎051/353-444, ⓦwww .edgaradventures.com); Nayra Travel, Lima 419, office 105 (☎051/364-774, ⓦwww.nayratravel.com).

Tourist information The helpful and friendly staff at the tourist information office, on the Plaza de Armas, at Deustua and Lima (☎051/365-088, ⓔiperupuno@promperu.gob.pe; open Mon–Sat 9am–6pm, Sun 9am—1pm), can provide photocopied town plans, leaflets and other information.

Accommodation

El Buho Lambayeque 142 ☎051/366-122, ⓦwww.hotelbuho.com. Don't be put off by the less than welcoming exterior; this is an extremely popular budget option due to its warm, comfortable rooms and staff who go out of their way to help you. S70.

Duque Inn Ayaviri 152 ☎051/205-014. A highly recommended cheapie with a view, located a short, breathless walk from the Plaza de Armas, run by an eccentric archeologist owner who takes his guests on free tours. From Huancané and Illave, carry on for three blocks along Illave before taking a right into Ayaviri. S20.

Los Pinos Inn Tarapaca 182 ☎051/367-398, ⓔhostalpinos@hotmail.com. The tiled en-suite rooms at this quiet, secure guesthouse get pretty chilly at night, but the friendly family that runs it is happy to provide extra blankets. Free wi-fi and laundry service also available. Rooms S35.

The Point Av. Circunvalación Norte 278 ☎051/351-427, ⓦwww.thepointhostels.com. Established party hostel with all the amenities that international backpackers have come to expect, as well as Puno's highest bar (Pointless Bar) and even its own spa. Pick-up from the bus station can be arranged. Dorms S22, rooms S64.

The Walk On Inn Libertad and Tacna ☎051/352-631, ⓦwww.walkoninn.com. This excellent new hostel is rapidly building a reputation for itself for the same reasons that distinguish its sister hostels in Cusco and Nazca: helpful, friendly staff who can organize tours for you, free all-day coca tea, secure, comfortable en-suite rooms and dorms and reliable hot showers. A heated rooftop terrace is currently under construction. Dorms S20, rooms S50.

Eating, drinking and nightlife

La Barca Arequipa 754. A great lunchtime spot, this *cevichería* specializes in the freshest fish around. Find a space in the courtyard and try the *tiradito de quatro estaciones* (think sashimi, but in a spicy sauce), the house speciality. Mains S25.

Incabar Lima 348. Serving some of the most creative *nuevoandino*/international fusion cuisine in town, this trendy restaurant/bar gets particularly lively in the evenings. Try the crispy kingfish with quinoa and mango chutney (S30).

Kamizaraky Grau 158. Another local institution, this dark atmospheric bar plays excellent rock music and an excellent selection of drinks; whatever your poison is, you'll find it here. Scribble on the wall to express your appreciation. Beer S9.

Machupizza Arequipa 279. Step inside this cave-like warren, decorated with local weavings, for some of Puno's best pizza, cooked in the large wood-fired oven. Each pizza (from S10) comes with spicy salsa and potent garlic sauce on the side.

Positive Vibrations Lambayaque 127. Shout to make yourself heard or give in and let the pounding reggae beats wash over you at this chilled-out bar. After a few drinks, the neon lighting will wreak havoc with your retinas. Beer S9.

Tulipans Lima 394. Hard to beat for great sandwiches and a welcoming atmosphere, made even more cosy by the wood-fired oven by the entrance. Sandwiches from S6.

Directory

Banks and exchange Banco Continental, Lima at Grau, and BCP, at Lima 444, both have ATMs. There are casas de cambio at Tacna 232 and Lima 440.

Consulate Bolivia, Arequipa 136, 2nd Floor (℡051/351-251; Mon–Fri 8am–2pm).

Hospital Medicentro at Moquegua 191 is a 24hr medical clinic (℡051/365-909); English spoken.

Post office Moquegua 267 (Mon–Sat 8am–8pm).

Telephones and internet Telefónica del Peru, corner of Federico More and Moquegua (daily 7am–11pm). There are several internet cafés along Lima.

Tourist police At Deustua 558, open 24hr (℡051/353-988).

Tourist train The scenic train to Cusco runs three times weekly but now that the "backpacker" carriage has been dispensed with, the journey costs

a staggering S706. Check ✪www.perurail.com for an up-to-date schedule.

Moving on

Most bus companies can be found in the main Terminal Terrestre; bus terminal departure tax is S1. Recommended companies include: Cruz del Sur (℡051/368-524) and Ormeño (℡051/368-176). For Arequipa and southern Peru try Sur Oriente (℡051/677-330). San Martín (℡054/363-631) has departures for Puerto Maldonado via Juliaca.

Bus Arequipa (hourly; 6hr); Cusco (hourly; 6hr); La Paz (several daily; 6–7hr); Lima (several daily; 18–21hr); Puerto Maldonado (daily; change at Juliaca; 15hr).

Train Cusco (Nov–March Mon, Wed, Sat at 8am; 10hr).

LAKE TITICACA

An undeniably impressive sight, **Lake Titicaca**'s skies are vast, almost infinite, and deep, deep hues of blue; below this sits a usually placid mirror-like lake, reflecting the big sky back on itself. A national reserve since 1978, the lake has more than sixty varieties of birds, fourteen species of native fish and

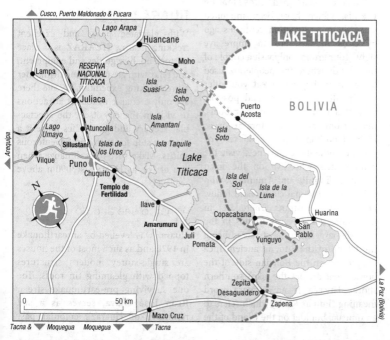

CROSSING INTO BOLIVIA

The most popular routes to Bolivia involve overland road travel, crossing the frontier either at Yunguyo/Kasani (best for Copacabana) or at the principal border of Desaguadero (best for La Paz). En route to either you'll pass by some of Titicaca's more interesting colonial settlements, each with its own individual styles of architecture. By far the easiest way is to take a direct bus from Puno to either Copacabana or La Paz, which will stop for the formalities at the border. Otherwise, from Puno you can take a *combi* to Yunguyo, then another to Kasani, then walk across the border and take a Bolivian *combi* for the 10-min ride to Copacabana. From Copacabana it is approximately five hours to La Paz.

eighteen types of amphibians. It's also the world's largest high-altitude body of water, at 284m deep and more than 8500 square kilometres in area.

The unique, man-made **Uros Floating Islands**, which have been inhabited since their construction centuries ago by Uros Indians, are an impressive sight. Tour groups only visit a couple of the islands where the people are used to tourism; they will greet you, offer you handicrafts for sale and possibly suggest a tour on one of their boats, made from the same totora reeds as their island homes, for a small fee. For a more authentic experience, visit the communities who live on the fixed islands of **Taquile** and **Amantaní**, who still wear traditional clothes and follow ancient local customs. There are, in fact, more than seventy islands in the lake, the largest and most sacred being the **Island of the Sun**, an ancient Inca temple site on the Bolivian side of the border that divides the lake's southern shore. Titicaca is an Aymara word meaning "Puma's Rock", which refers to an unusual boulder on the Island of the

Sun. The Bolivian islands can only be visited from Copacabana.

Huaraz and the Cordillera Blanca

Sliced north to south by the parallel **Cordillera Blanca** and **Cordillera Negra** (the white and black mountain ranges), the department of Ancash offers some of the best hiking and mountaineering in the Americas. Its capital **Huaraz** – eight hours by bus from Lima – is tourist-friendly, has a lively atmosphere and makes an ideal base for exploring some nearby lagoons, ruins, glaciers and remote trails. Through the valley known as the Callejón de Huaylas is the pretty town of **Caraz**, which offers a taste of traditional Andean life.

HUARAZ

With glaciated peaks and excellent trekking nearby, **HUARAZ** is a place to stock up, hire guides and equipment, and relax with great food and drink after a breathtaking expedition. While there are only a couple of tourist attractions to visit in the city itself, the spectacular scenery and great cafés make it a pleasant stop for even non-adventurous spirits. Make sure to acclimatize when you arrive, as Huaraz is 3090m above sea level.

What to see and do

Huaraz was levelled by an earthquake in 1970 and as such most of the houses are single-storey modern structures topped with gleaming tin roofs. The one surviving pre-earthquake street, **Jiron José Olaya**, serves as a sad reminder of Huaraz's colonial past and is worth a stroll down to see what this city was once like. The **Museo Arqueologico de Ancash**, at Av. Luzuriaga 762 on the Plaza de Armas (Mon–Sat 9am–5pm & Sun 9am–2pm; S6; ☎043/721-551), is worth a look for its attractive landscaped gardens and superb collection of ceramics, as well as some trepanned skulls. On the other side of the Plaza de Armas is the **Catedral**; the vast blue-tiled roof makes a good landmark and, if you look closely, appears to mirror the glaciated Nevado Huanstán behind.

There's an easy day trek (7km; 2hr) from Huaraz to the remains of a Wari mausoleum, **Wilcawain** (daily 8am–5pm; S5), and the nearby thermal springs at **Monterrey** make for a relaxing afternoon. Be sure to check details with the tourist office before you go, as attacks on tourists have been reported on this route.

Arrival and information

Av. Luzuriaga is the north–south axis of the town centre, where most of the restaurants, nightlife and tour agencies are based. Much of Huaraz town can be negotiated on foot once you've acclimatized to the altitude; however, some of the more remote sectors around the urban area should not be walked alone at night.

Air LC Busre operates daily flights from Lima. The small airstrip is close to the village of Anta, some 23km north of Huaraz; a 30-min ride into the city by *combi*.

Bus Most bus companies have terminals a street or two from the main drag of Av. Luzuriaga on Jr. Comercio which becomes Jr. Lucar y Torre.

Tourist information IPerú, at Pasaje Atusparia just off the Plaza de Armas (Mon–Sat

Map of Huaraz. Airport (23km) ▲ ▲ Monterrey, Anta, Yungay, Caraz & Wikahuain

HUARAZ

Streets shown include: CARHUAZ, LIBERTADORES, SEBASTIAN DE ALISTE, DUNAN BARRON, JIRON DANIEL VILLAIZAN, VICTOR VELEZ, RAYMONDI, AVENIDA GRAN CHAVIN, AVENIDA MANCO CAPAT, Río Quillcay, 13 DICIEMBRE, COMERCIO, CARAZ, AVENIDA PRIMAVERA, ASUNCION, AVENIDA LAS AMERICAS, AVENIDA RAIMONDI, Movil Tours, Linea, Mercado Central, Cruz del Sur, Parque del Periodista, Civa, Tourist Police Station, Casa de Guias, Parque Ginebra, Museo Arqueológico de Ancash, Bank, Catedral, Museo Regional de Arqueología, ALAMBRA GRAU, JIRON JOSE DE SUCRE, AVENIDA A FIGUEROA, 28 DE JULIO, VILLANUEVA, ALVA CURADO, VALENZUELA, DAMASCO, FEDERICO, SAL Y ROSAS, URIBE, Huascarán Nacional Park Office, Hospital Regional, Stadium, AVENIDA BOLOGNESI, Casma, Río Santa

ACCOMMODATION
Andino Club Hotel — G
B&B My House — E
Benkawasi Albergue — F
Churup Guest House — D
Hostal Raimondi — B
El Jacal Guest House — C
Jo's Place — A

EATING, DRINKING & NIGHTLIFE
La Brasa Roja — 8
Café Andino — 4
California Café — 7
El Horno — 5
Portal de Los Andes — 1
Salvia — 6
El Tambo — 3
Zion Bar — 2

0 — 200 m

Mirador de Rataquena ▼

8am–6.30pm, Sun 8.30am–2pm; ☏043/428-812). Make sure to pick up the free mini-booklet *Map Guide Huaraz-Peru*, produced by ⓦwww .andeanexplorer.com. It contains excellent information on local treks and lots of maps; it's also available in many of the tourist restaurants in Huaraz.

Tourist police Av. Luzuriaga 724 on the Plaza de Armas (☏043/421-351). Some English spoken.

Trekking If you're organizing your own trek in Huascarán National Park, register beforehand with the Park Office, at Jr. Federico Sal y Rosas 555 (Mon–Fri 8.30am–1pm & 2.30–6pm, Sat–Sun 8.30am–noon; ☏043/422-086), where you should buy your permit (S65) to enter the park; if you're trekking with an agency then they should buy this for you. Also visit the Casa de Guías (Parque Ginebra 28-G ☏043/421-811, ⓦwww.casadeguias.com.pe) for the best information about local trails, current climatic conditions and advice on hiring guides, equipment and mules. If you're going trekking alone you should register with them regardless. They have a useful noticeboard, worth checking to see if there are any groups about to leave on treks that you might want to join, and they sell detailed trekking maps.

City transport

Taxi For short journeys within the city, the best option is to use one of the regular *taxi colectivos* that run on fixed routes along Av. Luzuriaga and Av. Centenario (S0.70). A taxi ride anywhere in the city should not cost more than S3.

Accommodation

Even in high season, around August, it's rarely difficult to find accommodation at a reasonable price and except during high season it's definitely worth bargaining.

B & B My House Av. 27 de Noviembre 773 ☏043/423-375, ⓦwww.micasahuaraz.jimdo .com. A pleasant family-run B&B with a flower-filled courtyard and bright dining room. There's free internet and wi-fi, and information and maps for trekkers. S80.

Benkawasi Albergue Parque Santa Rosa 928 ☏043/423-150, ⓦwww.huarazbenkawasi.com. This hostel is run by a friendly Huaraz family who have done a lot for the area – the owners built Huaraz's first hotel after the 1970 earthquake (now *Andino Club Hotel*) to encourage tourists back to the region, and they are active in local

---

TOURS AND ACTIVITIES IN AND AROUND HUARAZ

Most of the tour agencies in Huaraz can be found along Avenida Luzuriaga, or the two small squares that join it to the Plaza de Armas, and are open from 7am until late, closing between 1pm and 4pm. Most specialize in hiking and mountaineering. Popular excursions include the Llanganuco Lakes (8hr; see p.872), Chavín de Huantar (9–11hr; see p.871) and the edge of the Pastoruri Glacier at 5240m (8hr). Most operators can also arrange trips to the Monterrey thermal baths and some offer adventure activities in the area. Costs usually exclude entrance fees and food; make sure your guide can speak English if you need them to. If you're hiring your own guide, always check for certification and that they're registered at the Casa de Guías (see box, p.873). IPerú can help with any complaints.

🏃 **Andean Kingdom** Parque Ginebre 120 ☏043/425-555, ⓦwww.andean kingdom.com. Argentinean-run tour operator specializing in climbing and trekking. Has its own centre out in the Cordillera Negra, where they offer lodging and rock-climbing courses.

Galaxia Expeditions Jr. Mariscal Caceres 428, Parque Pip ☏043/425-355, ⓦwww .galaxia-expeditions.com. Offers a variety of treks, mountaineering trips and day tours as well as horseriding, mountain biking and canyoning. Four-day Santa Cruz trail $120 all-inclusive.

Mountain Bike Adventures Jr. Lucre y Torre 530 ☏043/424-259, ⓦwww.chakinaniperu .com. Customizable guided bike tours and hikes; also rents bikes. English-speaking guides and a book exchange in their office. Good reputation for safety.

🏃 **Pony Expeditions** Sucre 1266, Plaza de Armas, Caraz ☏043/391-642, ⓦwww .ponyexpeditions.com. A very professional and knowledgeable organization in Caraz, with maps and mountain gear for sale, as well as guided tours of the area.

conservation. The hostel itself is a little shabby but the communal areas are pleasant, with table tennis and games. Shared kitchen; breakfast S5. Dorms S10, rooms S50.

Churup Guest House Jr. Amadeo Figueroa 1257 ☎ 043/424-200, ⊛ www.churup.com. A good base for trekkers, with luggage storage as well as reference maps and a book exchange. Although it's an uphill walk from the centre, they'll pick you up from the bus station for free and the views from the terrace are great. Breakfast included. Dorms S28, rooms S79.

Hostal Raimondi Av. Raimondi 820 ☎ 043/421-082. An old-fashioned place with real character. Large rooms, though a little dark, all have private bath and hot water. S45.

El Jacal Guest House Jr. José de Sucre 1044 ☎ 043/424-612, ⊛ www.jacalhuaraz .com. This place is amazing value with friendly owners and lots of extras like laundry, wi-fi, kitchen use and cable TV. But above everything (literally) there's a terrace with unbelievable 360-degree views. S40.

Jo's Place Jr. Daniel Villaizan 276 ☎ 043/425-505, ⊛ www.josplacehuaraz.com. Although ramshackle and somewhat chaotically managed (you'll have to ask to be shown the facilities), *Jo's place* is nonetheless a good place to stay, with cosy rooms and dorms, some with wonderful views. There's internet, wi-fi, a common room with TV, a terrace with hammocks and very hot water. Breakfast (including a full English) and tours can also be arranged. Dorms S15, rooms S35.

The Way Inn Jr. Buenaventura Mendoza 821, Huaraz ☎ 043/466-219, ⊛ www .thewayinn.com. Built and owned by a Brit, this mountain lodge about 40min from the city offers a true alternative from normal hostels with orthopaedic beds, down duvets, a climbing wall and a sauna. Camping space S15, dorms S30, rooms S85.

Eating

There's no shortage of restaurants in Huaraz, with a huge number of budget options, but the places aimed at tourists tend to be better (albeit pricier). Mercado Central is good for cheap fresh food and there are a few mini-marts on Luzuriaga.

La Brasa Roja Av. Luzuriaga 919. Very popular and always busy, serving cheap and generous plates of chicken, pizza, grills and hamburgers. Chicken and chips with salad S9. Open daily noon–midnight.

Café Andino Jr. Lucar y Torre 530. This top-floor café with amazing views is a true gem. It serves a range of international dishes and

great breakfasts with pizza-sized pancakes. There's wi-fi and not only a book exchange but a substantial library of guides on the area, as well as maps. Mains S7–25. Open daily 8am–8pm.

California Café Jr. 28 de Julio 562. One of several very pleasant cafés in town, this one predictably has West Coast vibes and it makes a relaxing spot to refuel at any time. The food, including American breakfasts, soups salads and sandwiches (mains S15) is great, and they also have a good book exchange as well as games, wi-fi and maps. Open daily except Wed 7.30am–6.30pm, Sun 7.30am–2pm.

El Horno Parque del Periodista (off the 6th block of Luzuriaga). The best wood-fired pizzas in town, as well as charcoal grills and a mean pasta carbonara. Nice relaxed atmosphere. All pizzas under S20. Mon–Sat 11am–11pm.

Portal de Los Andes Jr. José de la Mar 437. This place is a gem for a good set lunch at the bargain price of S4.50. Although it's called a *restaurante turística* you won't find any gringos here. Enjoy the enormous portions of tasty traditional Peruvian food and Andean music playing in the background. Daily 7am–9.30pm.

Salvia Psje Vivar Farfán 793. Down the little passageway to the right of the cathedral from the Plaza de Armas is this little "vegetarian" restaurant, which, in true Peruvian style, also does some meat dishes. If that doesn't put you off, you can get a range of good breakfasts and a very cheap set lunch or dinner for S5. Daily 6am–10pm.

Drinking and nightlife

El Tambo Jr. José de la Mar 776. One of Huaraz's best nightspots, spinning western music with Latino beats and occasional live music. Food also served. Open Tues–Sun from 8pm.

Xtreme Bar Av. Luzuriaga. Although this is its fourth location in the last few years, this is a true Huaraz institution. The owners are friendly, there's live music, food, and it's a great place to meet other travellers. Daily noon–4am.

Zion Bar Jr. José de la Mar 773. A French/Peruvian-run bar that aims to be the most chilled-out space in town. Friendly atmosphere, cheap drinks and plenty of reggae make this place a good bet. Drinks two for S15 before 10pm. Open daily from 7pm.

CHAVÍN DE HUANTAR

One of the most popular day-trips from Huaraz is to **Chavín de Huantar** (Tues–Sun 9am–5pm; S12; ☎ 043/454-042), a mysterious stone temple complex that was at the centre of a puma-worshipping religious movement some 2500 years ago. The pretty village of **Chavín**, with its white-washed walls and traditional tiled roofs, is a gruelling but stunning drive from Huaraz; from here the complex is a few hundred metres away. The same distance in the other direction is the accompanying **museum** (same hours; free) which displays some of the most important finds from the site, including most of the famous tenon heads that originally adorned the walls of the temple.

Most people arrive on a **full-day tour** (S45 excluding lunch and entrance), although the distance can make visits feel rushed and many agencies only provide Spanish-speaking guides. To visit independently, take one of the buses that leave Huaraz for Chavín daily around 8am (3–4hr; S10) from small terminals on Jr. Andres Avelino Cáceres. Buses return from Chavín more or less on the hour from 3–6pm. It's a small village, but there are a couple of hostels, and you can camp by the Baños Quercos thermal springs, a 20-min stroll from the village.

HIKING IN THE HUARAZ REGION

Given the scope of the mountain ranges and the passion of mountain-eers, it's not surprising that there is an enormous range of **hikes** and guides in the area. Anyone interested in really getting stuck in should arm themselves with good maps and detailed guide-books, and talk to everyone in town – most of the expats here are very knowledgeable.

Wherever you end up, be sure to pay heed to the rules of **responsible trekking**: carry away your waste, particularly above the snow line, where even organic waste does not decompose. And always carry a camping stove – campfires are strictly prohibited in Huascarán National Park. It's also vital to be fit, particularly if you are going it alone.

It's essential to spend at least a couple of days **acclimatizing** to the altitude before attempting a hike; if you intend high mountain climbing, this should be extended to at least five days. Although Huaraz itself is 3060m above sea level, most of the Cordilleras' more impressive peaks are over 6000m.

The Cordillera Blanca

The highest range in the tropical world, the Cordillera Blanca consists of around 35 peaks poking their snowy heads over the 6000m mark, and until early in the twentieth century, when the glaciers began to recede, this white crest could be seen from the Pacific. Above Yungay, and against the sensational backdrop of Peru's highest peak, **Huascarán** (6768m), are the magnificent **Llanganuco Lakes**, whose waters change colour according to the time of year and the movement of the sun.

Fortunately, most of the Cordillera Blanca falls under the auspices of the **Huascarán National Park**, and the habitat has been left relatively unspoiled. Among the more exotic **wildlife** are viscacha (Andean rabbit-like creatures), vicuña, grey deer, pumas, foxes, the rare spectacled bear and several species of hummingbirds.

To get here without an organized trek, take a *combi* along the valley to Yungay or Caraz and ask around for recommended guides (check them out first with the Casa de Guías in Huaraz).

CARAZ

Further along the valley north from Huaraz are the distinct settlements of **Yungay** and the much prettier and friendly **CARAZ**. The town sits at an altitude of 2285m, making it much warmer than Huaraz, and palm trees and flowers adorn a classic colonial

Plaza de Armas. While most people come for the hiking or cycling trails around the town, there's enough here to divert you for a day or so, most notably the pre-Chavín era remains of **Tumshukayko** (daily 8am–5pm; free), an archeological structure about 1km uphill from the Plaza de Armas (turn right once you hit Av. 28 de Julio). This impressive series of stone walls, stairways and terraces (the layers have been dated to between 2500 BC and 300 AD) needs a huge amount more excavation to make greater sense of it, but is nevertheless fascinating to wander around. Finally, no stay in Caraz would be complete without careful consideration of the dessert menu: Caraz is famous for its **manjar blanco** – a caramel-like substance similar to *dulce de leche*; any bakery in town will sell it.

Arrival and information

Everywhere in Caraz is walkable; don't let the *mototaxis* charge you more than S1 for anywhere in town.

Bus Most of the bus terminals are along calles Daniel Villar and Córdova, within a block or two of the Plaza de Armas.

Combi *Combis* pull in at Av. Sucre, three blocks south of the Plaza de Armas.

Tourist information The tourist information office in the municipality building on the Plaza de Armas keeps sporadic hours, but try it for maps and brochures covering the attractions and hikes in the area. If it's shut, the excellent Pony Expeditions (see box, p.870), is good for local info and trekking guides.

Accommodation

Hostal La Casona Jr. Raimondi 319 ☎043/391-334. Shabby but full of character, this place is set around a nice courtyard and the prices cannot be argued with – although if you do you'll find they become even cheaper. S20.

Los Pinos Lodge Parque San Martín 103 ☎043/391130, ⊛www.lospinoslodge.com. This hostel on a little plaza five minutes' walk from the centre has colourful and tastefully decorated common areas with a retro feel. The bedrooms are not as impressive, but offer basic accommodation at reasonable rates, and towels and soap are provided. Also offers camping space, wi-fi and the little bar-restaurant (see below) will fill you with nostalgia for a bygone Latin America. Breakfast included. S100.

San Marco Jr. San Martín 1133 ☎043/391-558. Just off the plaza, this hostel in a pretty colonial building has somewhat dark rooms, but the gorgeous courtyards more than make up for it, and all rooms have private bath and TV. S40.

Eating

Eating in Caraz is basic. The small daily market, three blocks north of the plaza, is good for fresh food and traditional Andean goods.

AIRU Restaurant and bar at *Los Pinos Lodge*, with retro vibes (open only for dinner). Service is slow as the food's cooked from scratch, but the Peruvian and international staples are good. Mains S7–18. Open Wed–Mon 5–10pm.

Café de Rat Above Pony Expeditions on Jr. Sucre. It may sound unsanitary, but Cafferata is the owner's surname and the place has the joint appeal of cheap good food (including vegetarian) and a cosy feeling like that of being in someone's kitchen. The little balcony overlooks the main square. Best for pizza and breakfasts (S10–20). Open 8am–10pm.

Restaurant Jeny On the Plaza de Armas. Offers a tasty good-value menus (S5) as well as some traditional and Chinese dishes plus sandwiches and breakfasts. Open 8am–9pm.

Sierra Dulce Jr. Daniel Villar 412. A must for anyone with a sweet tooth. Their *alfajores* (shortbread biscuit with *manjar blanco*) are arguably the best in Peru.

Moving on

From anywhere in the Callejón de Huaylas, it's best to go back through Huaraz and down the main road to the coast. The only other alternative is to take the road north from Caraz via the Cañon del Pato down to Chimbote on the coast, where you'll have to change buses.

Air Lima (1 daily; 1hr 10min).

Bus Chimbote via Cañon del Pato (2 daily; 7–10hr); Lima (7 daily; 8hr); Trujillo (5 daily; 8–10hr).

Trujillo and the North

Pizarro, on his second voyage to Peru in 1528, sailed by the ancient Moche site of **Chan Chan**, then still a major city and an important regional centre of Inca rule. He returned to establish a Spanish colony in the same valley, naming it **Trujillo** after his birthplace in Extremadura. Despite two Inca rebellions, the Spanish hold was lasting and Trujillo grew to become the main port of call for the Spanish treasure fleets. It still boasts one of the most impressive colonial centres in Peru, as well as some of the grandest pre-Inca remains, but this city of more than one million feels modern and there's plenty to keep visitors occupied.

North of Trujillo the vast desert stretches all the way to the Ecuadorian frontier just past **Tumbes**, passing the modern city of **Chiclayo** as well as Peru's trendiest beach resort, **Máncora**. This area has an incredible wealth of pre-Inca pyramids, tombs and temple sites to explore, as well as world-class museums, many of which can be easily visited in day-trips from the main cities. Including some of the Northern Highland cities in your trip, especially **Cajamarca**, often referred to as the Cusco of the North, and the tropical **Chachapoyas**, with its nearby ruins at **Kuelap**, will give you a totally different angle to travellers only doing the traditional gringo trail.

TRUJILLO

Traditionally a trading point for coastal and jungle goods, **TRUJILLO** retains a cosmopolitan atmosphere and a welcoming attitude towards visitors. The climate is usually pleasant all year, although it can get very hot in the summer months of December to February.

What to see and do

From the graceful colonial mansions and Baroque churches at its heart, Trujillo's commercial buildings, light industry and shantytown suburbs give way to rich sugar-cane fields that stretch far into the neighbouring Chicama Valley. Everything within the circular **Avenida España** is considered the centre and this is where most of the colonial buildings and museums lie. **Gamarra** is the main commercial street, dominated by modern buildings, shops, hotels and restaurants. The other main street, older and more attractive, is **Jirón Pizarro**, which has been pedestrianized from the eighth block to the pleasant **Plazuela El Recreo**. But it is the large and graceful **Plaza Mayor** which is the deserved star and heart of the city.

While Trujillo's rigid grid system makes it easy to navigate, the lack of green space and resting places can make it a tiring city to explore; many people chose to retreat to the bohemian town of **Huanchaco**, 11km north by the sea,

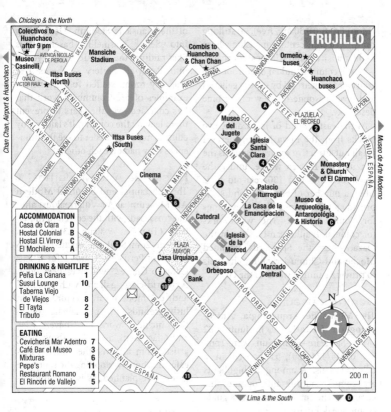

▲ Chiclayo & the North

TRUJILLO

ACCOMMODATION
Casa de Clara	D
Hostal Colonial	B
Hostal El Virrey	C
El Mochilero	A

DRINKING & NIGHTLIFE
Peña La Canana	1
Susui Lounge	10
Taberna Viejo de Viejos	8
El Tayta	2
Tributo	9

EATING
Cevichería Mar Adentro	7
Café Bar el Museo	3
Mixturas	6
Pepe's	11
Restaurant Romano	4
El Rincón de Vallejo	5

▼ Lima & the South

PERU

TRUJILLO AND THE NORTH

for cheap accommodation, good *ceviche* and surfer vibes.

Around Plaza Mayor

Trujillo's **Plaza Mayor** (Plaza de Armas) is packed with street vendors and entertainers. The city's **Catedral** (daily 7am–noon & 5–8pm; free), built in the mid-seventeenth century and then rebuilt the following century after earthquake damage, sits in one corner of the plaza. Beside the cathedral is its **museum** (Mon–Fri 9am–1pm & 4–7pm, Sat 9am–1pm; S4), which exhibits a sombre range of mainly eighteenth-and nineteenth-century religious paintings and sculptures.

Also on the square at Jr. Pizarro 313 sits the **Casa Urquiaga** (Mon–Fri 9.30am–3pm, Sat 10am–1pm; free), a colonial mansion owned by the Peruvian Central Reserve, which is worth a visit – despite the rather rigid 30-min tour you have to take – for its well-kept interiors and historical importance. Simón Bolívar stayed here while he organized his final push for liberation.

East of Plaza Mayor

East of the plaza, on the corner of Jr. Pizarro and Gamarra, stands another of Trujillo's impressive mansions, **La Casa de la Emancipación**, at Jr. Pizarro 610 (Mon–Sat 10am–8pm; free). The building is now head office of the Banco Continental but hosts contemporary art displays in its colonial rooms, where the enormous windows make for great people-watching.

Further down the same road, two blocks east of the Plaza Mayor, is the **Palacio Iturreguí**, at Jr. Pizarro 668

875

(Mon–Fri 8–10.30am; free), a striking mid-nineteenth-century mansion whose highlight is a pseudo-Classical courtyard, with tall columns and an open roof. The courtyard is encircled by superb galleries and gives a wonderful view of the blue desert sky.

At the eastern end of Jr. Pizarro, five blocks from the Plaza Mayor, there's a small but attractive square known as the **Plazuela El Recreo** where, under the shade of some vast 130-year-old ficus trees, a number of bars and food stalls provide a place to meet in the evenings for young couples. The waterworks for colonial Trujillo can be seen in the plaza, where the Spaniards extended Moche and Chimu irrigation channels to provide running water to the city.

Central museums

The **Museo de Arqueología, Antropología e Historia**, at Jr. Junín 682 (Mon–Sat 9am–5pm, Sun 9am–1pm; S5; ☏044/474-850), is housed in a colonial mansion; among the highlights are some beautiful anthropomorphic ceramics. The entry fee includes a guide (some speak English).

A short walk along the same street brings you to the quirky **Museo del Jugete**, at Jr. Junín on the corner with Jr. Independencia, upstairs (Mon–Sat 10am–6pm, Sun 10am–1pm; S5; ☏044/208-181). This was South America's first museum dedicated to toys, and the few well-laid out rooms are crammed with antiques from all over the world, including mini Routemaster buses from the UK, Meccano sets and a large doll collection. There's also a display of toys belonging to pre-Hispanic cultures, with some rag dolls and simple games.

The final museum worth visiting within walking distance of the centre is the fascinating **Museo Casinelli** (daily 9.30am–1pm & 3–6pm; S7; ☏044/226-127), which you'll find under the petrol station on Ovalo Victor Raul, just north of the Mansiche Stadium. Descending into Señor Casinelli's basement is like raiding the cookie jar if you're into Peruvian pottery – there's just one tiny room, stuffed full of pristine examples of pre-Columbian work that he's collected over the years to prevent them leaving the country. It's laid out by culture, making it easier to see the influences they had on each other.

Museo de Arte Moderno

The substantial and beautiful **Modern Art Museum**, at Av. Villarreal just after the crossroads with the carretera Industrial (Tues–Sat 9.30am–5.30pm, Sun 9.30am–2pm; S10), was opened in 2006 by one of Peru's most successful artists, Gerardo Chávez, who lives next door. A world-class gallery with colonial and postmodern architecture set in lush grounds, the permanent collection includes work by Chávez, Klee and Giacometti, as well as showcasing artists from all over the Americas. A café and shop overlooking the sculpture garden are planned, as is a shuttle bus

> **TOURS**
>
> Most companies offer tours to Chan Chan and to the Huacas del Moche (the Huaca del Sol and Huaca de la Luna); for further info on both see p.880. These cost around S20 each (half-day), or S30 for both (full day), but prices change depending on season; expect to pay more for an English-speaking guide. All operators have slightly different programmes, so shop around. Tours can also be organized from Trujillo for Chiclayo sites, and even sites as far away as Kuelap near Chachapoyas. Established operators include Muchik Travel, at Jr. Pizarro 532 office 103 (☏044/224-529); Trujillo Tours, at Diego de Almagro 301 (☏044/233-091, ⊛www.trujillotours .com); and Colonial Tours, at Jr. Independencia 616 (☏044/291-034, ⊛www.hostalcolonial.com.pe).

to the Plaza Mayor. Until that's operational, you can get here via a taxi from the centre (S5), or *combi* "B" from Av. España, hopping off at the crossroads mentioned above.

Arrival and information

Air Flights arrive at the airport near Huanchaco (℡044/464-013). Taxis into the city will cost around S20, or you can get a bus, which leaves every 20min from the roundabout just outside the airport gates, for around S1.50. You can also take a taxi direct to Huanchaco from here for S10.

Bus Most of the buses have terminals close to the centre of town near the Mansiche Stadium, southwest of it on Av. Daniel Carrión or Av. España, or east of it along Ejército.

Combi and taxi *Combis* cannot enter within Av. España, but if you walk to this ring road you can find one to most places. If you're arriving by day it's fine to walk to the city centre, though at night it's best to take a taxi (S3–5 for a ride within Trujillo, S10–15 to Huanchaco, S20 to the airport). Of the taxi companies, Tico Taxi (℡044/282-828) is recommended by IPerú.

Tourist information IPerú, at Jr. Diego de Almagro 420 on the Plaza Mayor (Mon–Fri 9am–5pm; ℡044/294-561).

Accommodation

The majority of Trujillo's hotels are within a few blocks of the central Plaza Mayor; however, there are surprisingly few good-value hotels for a city this size. Many people prefer to stay in the nearby beach resort of Huanchaco (see p.878), which has a much wider variety of accommodation, including some good budget options.

Casa de Clara Jr. Cahuide 495 ℡044/299-997, ⓦwww.xanga.com/casadeclara. Jr. Orbegoso in the centre becomes Jr. Huayna Capac, where at about the fifth block there's a little green space, on one side of which is this hostel (it's around a 10-min walk from the centre). The owners can be a bit pushy for you to take their tours, but hot showers, wi-fi and spacious rooms in a place with a family feel are pluses. S50.

Hostal Colonial Jr. Independencia 618 ℡044/268-261, ⓦwww.hostalcolonial.com.pe. An attractive, central place with a colonial feel, where some English is spoken. Rooms are cosy and come with TV, plus there's internet, a patio and a café. Also has a cheap tour agency and taxi service. S85.

Hostal El Virrey Jr. Grau 727 ℡044/232-993. A small place tucked away on a busy street, with

a pleasant patio and rooms that go some way towards having character. All rooms are a good size, clean and have private bath, TV and wi-fi. Breakfast S5 extra. S50.

🏃 **El Mochilero** Jr. Independencia 887 ℡044/297-842, ⓦwww.elmochileroperu .com. An oasis in the heart of the city, this is the only backpacker place in Trujillo and has a lovely patio with a tropical feel, including hammocks, sofas and even two cabin rooms on a bamboo mezzanine. Internet and laundry service provided, though no breakfast. Tours can also be organized. Dorms S20, rooms S40.

Eating

There's no shortage of restaurants in Trujillo. A speciality of the area is seafood, which is probably best appreciated on the beach at the nearby resort of Huanchaco (see p.878). Jr. Pizarro has a huge assortment of cafés and a Metro supermarket at number 700.

Cevichería Mar Adentro Jr. Diego de Almagro 311. Look for the man with the plate of food standing outside and he'll lead you down a passageway to a bright, large room with good, cheap *ceviche*, as well as other classic Peruvian dishes. *Ceviche* S6, set lunch S4. Open daily 9am–4pm.

Café Bar el Museo On the corner of Jr. Independencia with Jr. Junín. A plush and fascinating little café-bar in the same building as the Museo del Juguete. Coffees, snacks, set lunches and breakfasts are served as well as a good selection of (expensive) alcohol. Snacks all under S10. Open daily 7am–1pm & 3–9pm.

Mixturas Jr. Mariscal de Orbegoso 319. This café-bar serves good Peruvian snacks – try the fried yucca (S6) – and is decorated with colourful local artworks. There's a relaxing garden to escape from Trujillo's busy centre. Open Mon–Sat 8.30am–11pm.

Pepe's Jr. Ayacucho 214. This basic place packed with locals only does evening meals and it only does meat, but it does it well; the steak is wonderful. All mains under S10. Open 6–11pm.

Restaurant Romano Jr. Pizarro 747 ℡044/252-251. Small, friendly restaurant specializing in Peruvian and Italian dishes. Good-sized portions and tasty food make this a popular place. Mains S15. Open all day.

El Rincón de Vallejo Jr. Orbegoso 303. Cesar Vallejo, Peru's most famous poet, was brought up in the house next door to this cramped corner café. Plenty of character and really good *criollo* food that couldn't be cheaper, so predictably this place gets packed and rushed at lunch. Set menu S5.50. Daily 7.30am–3pm & 5.30–11pm.

Drinking and nightlife

Peña La Canana San Martín 791. A highly popular restaurant-*peña* serving excellent meals, with a great atmosphere and shows with bands, dancing and audience participation, usually culminating in a disco. Genuinely for people of all ages and while you may not understand everything, the music and dances are fantastic and you'll be amazed at Peruvian stamina. Cover S10, meals from S15, cocktails S15. Wed–Sat from 6pm for food, from 10.30pm for show until the last people leave.

Taberna Viejo de Viejos Jr. San Martín 323. This rustically decorated place is a truly Peruvian experience; a specialist pisco bar serving cocktails as well as local wines. Try the "Viejo" deals: from S35 you get a whole bottle of pisco and everything else you need to make various cocktails and you'll be shown how to make them at your table. Great for groups. Mon–Wed 6pm–midnight, Thurs–Sat 6pm–3am.

El Tayta Jr. Pizarro 926 (in Plazuela El Recreo). Bar-restaurant with soft rock vibes and art on the walls. Drinks are good value and while main dishes are a little pricier, there are plenty of sandwiches under S10. Daily 6pm–midnight.

Tributo Jr. Pizarro with Jr. Amalgaro. Featuring live music nightly with regular drinks specials, this is one of the most happening places in Trujillo. Thurs–Sun from 11pm.

Directory

Banks and exchange Banco Continental, at Jr. Pizarro 620; BCP, at Jr. Gamarra 562; Scotiabank, at Jr. Pizarro 314 and 699; Interbank, at Jr. Gamarra 463; Banco de la Nación, at Jr. Almagro 297 and Jr. Gamarra 484. There are also several casas de cambio on the Pizarro side of the Plaza Mayor, and further up on block 6 of Pizarro.
Embassies and consulates UK, at Jr. Alfonso Ugarte 310 (☎044/949-711-275).
Hospital Hospital Belen de Trujillo, at Jr. Bolívar 350 (☎044/245-281). Open 24hr.
Internet Places are numerous, but it's hard to find one with Skype. Try the one at Jr. Orbegoso 348 (no name).
Laundry Lavandarias Unidas, at Jr. Pizarro 683.
Post office Serpost, at Jr. Independencia 286.
Telephones There are many *locutorios* on Jr. Pizarro and Jr. Gamarra.
Tourist police Jr. Independencia 630 (☎044/291-705).

Moving on

If you're staying in Huanchaco you'll have to go into Trujillo to get a bus out of the area.
Air LAN, at Jr. Almagro 490 on the Plaza Mayor (☎0801/1234) has three flights daily to Lima.
Bus There is no central bus terminal in the city. Most companies can be found on Av. Del Ejercito blocks 2–3; Av. América Sur block 28; Av. Mansiche blocks 1–4; and block 4 of Amazonas. Note that some companies have two terminals: one for buses north and the other south.

Cajamarca (5 daily; 7hr); Chachapoyas (1 daily; 13hr); Chiclayo (3 daily; 4hr); Huaraz (4 daily; 11hr); Lima (hourly; 8–10hr); Máncora (5 daily; 8hr); Tumbes (5 daily; 10hr). Ormeño runs buses from Trujillo straight to Quito in Ecuador (2 weekly; 24hr; US$80) or to Guayaquil, Ecuador via Piura, Máncora and Tumbes (daily; 18hr; US$70).

HUANCHACO

A traditional fishing village turned popular surfing resort, **HUANCHACO** is the perfect base for exploring nearby ruins while relaxing by the beach and enjoying excellent seafood. Just fifteen minutes from the centre of Trujillo, Huanchaco has exploded in terms of popularity and growth in the last thirty years. While prices do rise in the summer, it's nowhere near as overpriced as some other beach towns.

What to see and do

It's impossible to miss the multitude of **surf and language schools** in town; Espaanglisch (ⓦwww.espaanglisch .com) does both and is recommended (English spoken). If you're not a surfer, another way to catch some waves is with a local fisherman in their traditional *caballitos de mar* – hand-made reed fishing boats first used by the Moche culture; you'll see them lined up along the front. There is a long beachfront promenade and a rickety pier, as well as an unusual church-less Plaza de Armas away from the seafront. Reggae parties on the beach are commonplace, and Latino music blasts from the many beachfront restaurants.

Arrival

Taxi or combi Taxis from Huanchaco should cost no more than S15, or it's easy enough to take any one of the frequent *combis* (yellow & orange) from Av. España on the corner with Jr. Junín (S1.50). *Combis* come in along Av. La Rivera, by the sea.

Accommodation

Every other house in Huanchaco seems to offer lodging of some sort. For those on a really tight budget, there are many no-frills places that charge S10 per person for small and often dark rooms with shared bath. Los Pinos, the street that all the buses turn down away from the sea, has a few hostels and many signs saying *alquilo habitaciones* ("I rent rooms"). Prices drop by around S5 outside high season. Many places do not have hot water – fine in the summer but miserable in winter.

El Boquerón Ricardo Palma 330 ☏044/461-968, ⓔmaznaran@hotmail.com. Offers fine (if a little dark) rooms for the rock-bottom price of S10 per person (S25 including all meals). Also has a TV room, wi-fi and kitchen, but no hot water.

Las Brisas Psje Raymondi 146 ☏044/461-688. Good-value clean, comfortable rooms with private bath (hot water) and fan; a couple have sea views. Internet available and in high season breakfast is included. S50.

La Casa Suiza Calle Los Pinos 451 ☏044/461-285, ⓦwww.casasuiza.com. Popular budget accommodation with many of the extra services loved by backpackers – internet, cable TV, laundry, book exchange and a barbeque balcony. Also has hot water and a friendly atmosphere. Dorms S25, rooms S75.

Naylamp Av. Victor Larco 1420 ☏044/461-022, ⓦwww.hostalnaylamp.com. A well-deserved favourite in Huanchaco. Offers great value for the setting, with bungalow-style accommodation as well as dorm rooms and a camping area with kitchen, all set around pleasant hammock-filled gardens. Wi-fi and some sea views add to its charm. Rooms S50, camping S10 per person.

Eating

There are restaurants all along the front in Huanchaco, many of them with second-floor balconies with great views over the beach. Not surprisingly, seafood is the local specialty, including excellent crab; *ceviche* is traditionally only served at lunch.

Argolini Av. La Rivera 400a. The best place for bread, cakes and ice cream in Huanchaco, though get there early for bread as it often sells out. Daily 6.30am–10pm.

Chocolate Café Av. La Rivera 284 ⓦwww .vliegendevlinder.nl. True to its name, this seafront café does really good Peruvian hot chocolate for the low season when Huanchaco gets pretty cold. Breakfasts, soups, wraps and inventive sandwiches (with plenty of veggie options) are served up in a cheerful incense-scented café with locally made *artesanía*. Full English breakfast S15. Open for breakfast until early evening.

Estrella Marina Av. Larco 740. Very good, fresh *ceviche* (S15) served in a seafront restaurant, which often plays loud salsa music and is popular with locals. Open 10am–11pm.

Menu Land Calle Los Pinos 250. Run by a friendly German-Peruvian couple, the name refers to the set lunch *menú* you'll find all over Peru. There's art on the walls and the owners have a room to rent too. Food is basic, but you won't find bigger or cheaper portions anywhere else; great for refuelling on a very tight budget. Set lunch S5. Open 8am–10pm.

El Rey Av. Larco 606. Hard to beat for budget lunches, with a two-course *combo marino*, including a soft drink for S10.

Drinking and nightlife

Huanchaco has a buzzing nightlife, with many bars and clubs. Always ask around to see if there's a pop-up party on the beach going on, or to find the coolest bar (these can open and close quickly). Outside of peak season nightlife will certainly be calmer.

My Friend Calle Los Pinos 158. A good restaurant as well as a cheap hostel, but it is definitely the

TREAT YOURSELF

El Kero La Rivera 612 ☏044/461-184. A modern and chic lounge bar-restaurant not to be missed. The three-storey building contains a restaurant with seafront dining on a balcony, with an impressive range of sumptuous seafood and traditional Peruvian dishes. You can come here at any time of day really, as they do breakfasts, amazing cocktails, have a huge wine list and there's a dancefloor too. Mains S40. Open 8.30am–midnight or later.

most well-known meeting spot in town and serves cheap drinks. Open all day; happy hour 8–10pm.

Sabes? Av. Larco 804. This place is either great fun or fairly quiet, as it's right down at the end of the main drag past *Big Ben* restaurant. When it's the former it's a fantastic place to meet people, relax on the outdoor terrace with a happy-hour cocktail and munch on a pizza. Open Mon–Sat 7pm–1am.

The Beach House Out of town along Av. La Rivera on the beach. The most popular of the beach hangouts in town, this open-air place has live music, club nights and plays everything from reggae and rock to electronica. Has a bar area with sofas and projector. A cover charge sometimes applies; beer S6. Open Tues–Sun from 5pm.

ANCIENT SITES AROUND TRUJILLO

One of the main reasons for coming to Trujillo is to visit the numerous **archeological sites** dotted around the nearby Moche and Chicama valleys. For anyone even remotely interested in Peruvian history these should not be missed.

Huacas del Moche

Five kilometres south of Trujillo, beside the Río Moche in a barren desert landscape, are two temples that really bring ancient Peru to life. The stunning complex known as the **HUACAS DEL MOCHE** (Daily 9am–4pm; S11 including guided tour in English or Spanish; ☏044/297-430, ⊛www.huacadelaluna.org.pe) is believed to have been the capital, or most important ceremonial and urban centre, for the **Moche** (Mochica) culture at its peak between 400 and 600 AD. It contains two temples: the **Huaca del Sol** (Temple of the Sun) is the largest adobe structure in the Americas, and easily the most impressive of the many pyramids on the Peruvian coast. Its twin, **Huaca de la Luna** (Temple of the Moon), is smaller, but more complex and brilliantly frescoed; it's thought to have been a sacrificial centre. It's not possible to go inside the Huaca del Sol, but it's an amazing sight from the Huaca de la Luna, 500m away. In between the

two you can see the remains of a town in the midst of excavation, and there's also an excellent **museum** (free) across from the site, displaying objects found here and explaining Moche culture.

To **get here** from Trujillo, walk down Av. Almagro from the centre, which turns into Av. Moche once you cross Av. Espana (a 20-min walk), and take the small "CM" or "SD" *combis* from Ovalo Grau, which will take you all the way to the car park of the Huacas (20min; S1). From Huanchaco, simply take the larger *combi* "H" all the way to Ovalo Grau (30min; S.1.50) and change. A taxi to the site from Trujillo costs around S15 (20min).

The Chan Chan complex

It's possible to see the Moche influence in the motifs around **CHAN CHAN**, the huge, ruined capital city of the **Chimú Empire**, located across the other side of Trujillo from the Huacas. Just as impressive as the Huacas, if not more so, the site stretches almost the whole way between Trujillo and Huanchaco. While most of the area is little more than melted mud walls, there are a few remarkably well-preserved areas, giving a great insight as to what the city may have looked like. The main areas to see are spread out and comprise the Nik An temple complex, a site museum, the Huaca El Dragon and the Huaca La Esmeralda (all with the same hours: Tues–Sun 9am–4pm; S11 for 2-day pass to all sites; ☏044/206-304).

It's best to start at the **museum**, which you'll find about halfway to Huanchaco on the main road, although you can buy tickets at any of the sites. It has some good background information, but most importantly it has an enormous model of what the city would once have looked like, which helps as you tour the site proper. From here, hop on a *combi* or take a taxi (they wait in the car park) to the **Nik An Palace**, a series of open-air temples and passageways with some extraordinarily beautiful patterns and lattice-work. Not far away, the **Huaca Arco Iris** (The

Rainbow Temple; also referred to as Huaca El Dragón, or Dragon Temple) was a ceremonial or ritual pyramid rather than a citadel, and sports more geometric and zoomorphic designs, especially of dragons and rainbows. On the other side of this enormous city, **Huaca La Esmeralda** was similar in function to Arco Iris but is much older (around 1100 years old) and has intricate designs, which have been restored with relish if not historical perfection.

To **get here**, take any *combi* going between Trujillo and Huanchaco and ask the driver to drop you at the Museo de Chan Chan. There is no public transport between the different sites on the ticket, so hire a taxi to take you round and wait (depending on sites visited and distance covered, expect to pay S30 per hour; see p.876 for reputable companies), or take a hat and lots of water if you plan to walk; the desert sun is unforgiving.

CHICLAYO

Apart from building a few convents the Spanish never really bothered with

Chicama, Chiclayo, Piura & Tumbes ▲

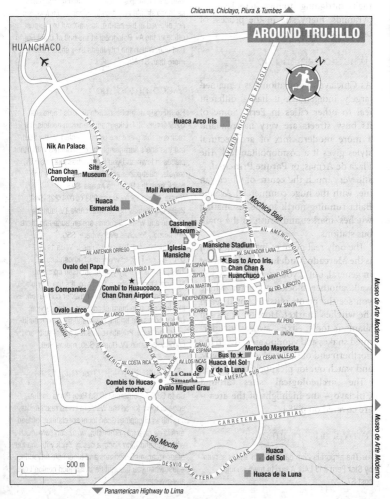

AROUND TRUJILLO

▼ Panamerican Highway to Lima

CHICLAYO, and tourists, too, would be forgiven for missing out Peru's fourth-largest city if it were only for the city itself. Though not an unpleasant place to spend a day or so, it's full of casinos, banks and bus stations and not much else. The attractions here are the remarkable **archeological finds** in the nearby countryside which are of huge importance to Peruvian culture and identity. It's well worth spending at least a few days in the area getting to grips with the different groups that formed part of the pre-Inca landscape here, and seeing their intriguing tombs, temples and pyramids, many still in the process of being uncovered.

What to see and do

As Chiclayo's population has remained largely indigenous, it has a different feel to other cities in Peru. Some of its busy streets are very narrow, and a more modern mix of architectural styles gives it a cosmopolitan feel. The Plaza de Armas, or **Parque Principal**, is still very much the centre of Chiclayan life, with the huge commercial Avenue Balta running north to the fascinating witches' market and south to the main bus stations.

The only real point of interest in town is the **Mercado Modelo** – a good market in general, but if you turn left on Arica, walk another block and enter where you see the plants outside, you'll reach the **witches' market**. Here the stalls sell shaman's tools, elixirs, swords, taxidermied snakes and voodoo aids. Avoid the northern end of the market as it's seedy, and watch out for pickpockets.

The **archeological sites** around Chiclayo – the highlight of the area – are covered on p.884.

Arrival and information

Air The airport is 2km east of town and is served by Star Peru and LAN. A taxi to town should cost S7.

Bus Most bus companies have terminals along Av. Bolognesi, the main road at the end of Av. Balta Sur. From here it's a 10-min walk to the Plaza de Armas.
Tourist information IPerú, on calle 7 de Enero 579 (Mon–Sat 9am–6pm, Sun 9am–1pm; ☎074/205-703). English spoken.

City transport

Combi *Combis* skirt around the centre; simply walk down Balta to Bolognesi, or east from the Plaza to Av. Sáenz Peña, to pick one up (S0.80 within town).
Taxi or mototaxi Taxis should cost no more than S3.50 anywhere within the city. Always go for one with the municipal shield stencilled on the doors, as these should be officially licensed. *Mototaxis* are not allowed in the centre, so walk out to the post office or the Av. Bolognesi at the end of Balta Sur to find one. Within the city limits they should cost no more than S1.50.

Accommodation

Hospedaje Juan Fernando Jr. 7 de Enero 980 ☎074/498-524. Like many Peruvian hostels, the rooms in this place are usually rented by the hour, but this one's surprisingly nice compared with other places in town and you'll get extras like cable TV, towels, toilet paper and soap. Plus it's only one block from the Plaza de Armas. S25.
Hostal Victoria Av. Izaga 933 ☎074/225-642. Pleasant, friendly hostel with cable TV, laundry serivce and wi-fi. All rooms are en-suite and there are homely touches everywhere. S50.
Muchik Hostel Jr. Vincente de la Vega 1127 ☎074/272-119, ✆www.muchikhostel.com. This place is really trying to set itself up as the backpackers' choice in Chiclayo. It's the only place with a dorm and some other traveller conveniences like lockers, free internet and a laundry service. Other rooms are bright, clean and the whole building's very safe. Private rooms are all en-suite and come with cable TV. Dorms S20, rooms S60.

Eating, drinking & nightlife

Go to Centro Comercial (C.C.) Real Plaza on the edge of town for all the Western chain restaurants, as well as shopping. Good local specialities include *tortilla de raya* (ray omelette), *arroz con pato* (duck with rice) and *King Kong*, a pastry thick with *manjar blanco* (caramel), peanuts and pineapple flavouring – just when you thought Peruvian food couldn't get any sweeter.

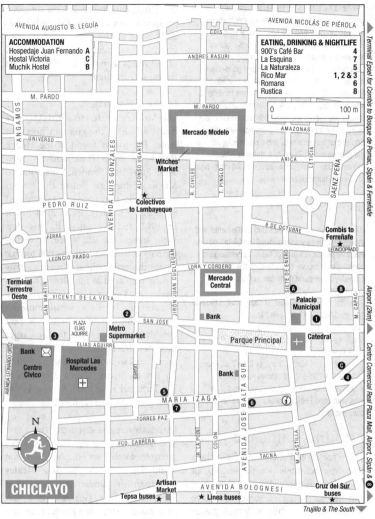

ACCOMMODATION
Hospedaje Juan Fernando **A**
Hostal Victoria **C**
Muchik Hostel **B**

EATING, DRINKING & NIGHTLIFE
900's Café Bar **4**
La Esquina **7**
La Naturaleza **5**
Rico Mar **1, 2 & 3**
Romana **6**
Rustica **8**

0   100 m

Mercado Modelo

Witches' Market

Colectivos to Lambayeque

Combis to Ferreñafe

Mercado Central

Bank

Palacio Municipal

Terminal Terrestre Oeste

Metro Supermarket

Plaza Elías Aquirre

Bank

Centro Cívico

Hospital Las Mercedes

Parque Principal

Catedral

Bank

Artisan Market

Tepsa buses

Linea buses

Cruz del Sur buses

CHICLAYO

Terminal Epsel for Combis to Bosque de Pomac, Sipán & Ferreñafe

Airport (2km)

Centro Comercial Real Plaza Mall, Airport, Sipán & 8

Trujillo & The South

900's Café Bar Av. Izaga 900 ⓦwww
.cafe900.com. A really pleasant place any time
of day, this café-bar does good breakfasts, snacks,
salads, pastas, *criollo* mains (S13–20; try the *spaguetti
a la huancaina con lomo*) and cocktails. But better than
anything, this place has truly great coffee – there are
more than twenty concoctions on the menu and a sign
on the wall proclaiming "coffee is god".

La Esquina Jr. Juan Cuglievan and Av. Izaga.
A little corner café good for most things, from
mains and set lunches, to much cheaper breakfasts than you'll find in the restaurants on the Plaza
de Armas. Everything under S10. Daily 8am–10pm.

La Naturaleza Jr. Juan Cuglievan 619. A good little
vegetarian place that serves breakfast, lunch and
dinner, and, in theory, a wide range of veggie takes
on classic Peruvian dishes. In reality, stick with
whatever is on the set menu or you may have a
very long wait. Mon–Fri 8am–10pm, Sat 8am–4pm.
Rico Mar Saenz Peña 841, San José 476 & Elias
Aguirre 241. A chain of *cevicherías* with a good
range of little dishes, ideal for trying different
classic Peruvian starters like *papa rellena* (stuffed
potato), *tamales* and of course *ceviche*. Everything
is less than S5 and there's also a S4 set lunch.
Daily 9am–4pm.

Romana Av. Balta 512. This place specializes in northern Peruvian cuisine (with a sister restaurant in Chachapoyas) and is a solid choice for good food and a buzzing atmosphere. Classic dishes include *arroz con pato* (duck with rice) and *ceviche*, plus there's a cheaper set lunch and good-value sandwiches. Mains S15–25. Daily 7am–midnight.

Rustica C.C. Real Plaza upstairs in the food court ⓦwww.rustica.com.pe. A Peruvian chain restaurant doing good pizzas and grills, this locale also has a large dancefloor with some personality– a ceiling dripping with mirror balls and a real Beetle car hanging on the wall next to a statue of a Moche emperor. Sun–Thurs noon–3am, Fri–Sat noon–5am (S10 entry fee to disco at weekends).

Directory

Banks and exchange You'll find all the banks and moneychangers by walking south on Balta from the Plaza de Armas. It's always better to exchange in a bank – count money carefully if on the street.

Laundry Lavandería Burbujas, at Calle 7 de Enero 639.

Hospital Hospital Nacional, at Calle Hipólito Unanue 180 (☏074/237-776). Open 24hr.

Post office Jr. Elías Aguirre 140.

Tourist police Av. Saenz Peña 830 (☏074/235-181). Open 24hr.

Tour operators Moche Tours, at Calle 7 de Enero 638 (☏074/788-535, ⓔmochetours_chiclayo@hotmail.com), offers reliable tours around the area with good English-speaking guides and their own transport.

AROUND CHICLAYO

There are several sites around Chiclayo that are definitely worth seeing, all offered on organized tours, though it can get confusing as some sites have several names, while different places have similar names. The most easily confused are **Sipán**, where remains from the **Moche** culture were discovered, and the **Sicán** (or Lambayeque) culture. The issue is further confused as the remains of two Moche nobles have been dubbed the older and younger **Señores de Sipán** (Sipan Lords), while a figure found in a tomb of the Sicán culture has been named the **Señor de Sicán**. The sights below are considered essential viewing, but be warned– there

are many, many more. Details are given on how to get to the sights independently, but it will be easier and cheaper to go with a tour company, especially as all of the sights here warrant guides to get the most from them.

Huaca Rajada

The Moche culture (100–800 AD) was based all along the coast in northern Peru. The tombs found at the **Huaca Rajada** in Sipán (site museum open Mon–Sun 8am–5pm; S8) are vital to Moche history as, unlike the *huacas* near Trujillo, they were never plundered by treasure hunters. Excavation began in 1987 and continues to this day. Walk around the site to see the archeologists at work and see the real tombs, where the extraordinary treasures now mostly displayed at the Museo Tumbas Reales in Lambayeque (below) were discovered. There's a small museum documenting the digs, but it is best combined with a visit to the larger museum. It's fascinating to think that there's still so much more to be found. To **get to Sipán**, take a *combi* from the Terminal EPSEL on Av. Nicolás de Piérola in Chiclayo (25min).

Lambayeque museums

The treasures from the Huaca Rajada's multiple tombs are displayed at the world-class **Museo Tumbas Reales de Sipán** in Lambayeque (Av. Juan Pablo Vizcardo y Guzman; Tues–Sun 9am–5pm; S10; ⓦwww.tumbasreales.org). Although the museum is quite an eyesore from the outside, it is impossible to do justice to the wonders within. The hauls from the various digs are laid out as they were discovered, and there are an overwhelming number of sacred objects all intricately made from precious metals, shells and stones. Just when you think you've seen the most amazing piece, another comes along and blows you away. Allow yourself at least two hours here.

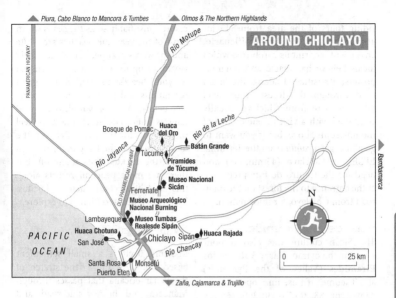

AROUND CHICLAYO

PANAMERICAN HIGHWAY

Río Motupe

Bosque de Pomac · Huaca del Oro

Río de la Leche

Río Jayanca

Túcume · Batán Grande

Pirámides de Túcume

Museo Nacional Sicán

Ferreñafe

Museo Arqueológico Nacional Burning

Lambayeque · Museo Tumbas Realesde Sipán

Huaca Chotuna

San José

PACIFIC OCEAN

Chiclayo · Sipán · Huaca Rajada

Río Chancay

Santa Rosa · Monsefú

Puerto Eten

Bambamarca

N

0   25 km

The **Bruning National Archeology Museum**, also in Lambayeque (Parque Principal; daily 9am–5pm; S8; ☎074/282-110), contains displays on all Peru's ancient cultures and spans five millennia. Housed in a modernist building, the collection is displayed over four floors and even has a "Sala de Oro" (room of gold), full of Sipán and Sicán treasures.

To **get to Lambayeque**, take a *combi* from the corner of Calle San José (leading off the northwest corner of the Plaza de Armas) with Av. Leonardo Ortíz (15min). The museums are within walking distance of each other and everyone in town knows where they are.

Museo Nacional Sicán

Little is known about the Sicán, or Lambayeque, culture, even though it existed as recently as the fourteenth century AD. Some suggest Sicán culture was simply an extension of Moche culture, which makes it fascinating to compare the haul at the **Museo Nacional Sicán** in Ferreñafe (Tues–Sun 9am–5pm; S8; ⓦsican.perucultural.org .pe) with its counterpart in Lambayeque, as it's clear there are similarities between the two in terms of their belief and

adornment. Although this museum is the less well-presented of the two and the treasures fewer, the metalwork here is finer and the use of semi-precious stones just as remarkable. There's also a reconstruction of the surreal tomb of the Señor de Sicán himself; his body was discovered decapitated, upside down and with huge gauntlets laid out beside him. To **get here**, take a *combi* from Terminal EPSEL in Chiclayo (approx 30min; S2) and then a *mototaxi* to the museum (S1).

Bosque de Pómac

The major treasures from the Sicán culture on display in Ferreñafe were discovered in the Huaca del Oro (Temple of Gold) in the **Bosque de Pómac** (Pomac Forest) in Batán Grande. This is considered to be the seat of the Sicán empire, and though you can't go in the temple itself, other *huacas* rise majestically out of the verdant forest– it's possible to scale the **Huaca las Ventanas** (Temple of the Windows) to get a wonderful view of them.

The forest is a great place for a picnic, birdwatching or horseriding – Rancho Santana (☎01/979-712-145, ⓦwww .cabalgatasperu.com) offers different riding tours of the area from S45 for 4hr. Don't miss the **Árbol Milenario**, an ancient, enormous carob tree which locals believe has magic and religious powers; it's situated along the main road through the forest. Tours will take you here from Chiclayo, usually combined with a visit to one or two of the museums above, but if you want to go alone, get a *combi* from the Terminal EPSEL in Chiclayo (45min; S3) and head for the Centro de Interpretación, at the entrance to the forest on the main road from Chiclayo, for information.

Valle de los Pirámides

The Sicán culture was also responsible for the extraordinary **Valle de los Pirámides** (Valley of the Pyramids) at Túcume (museum open daily 8am–4pm; S8; ☎074/830-250, ⓦwww .museodesitiotucume.com). This site consists of a cluster of a few of the 26 trapezoidal structures that fan out around the countryside here – you can see many of them for miles around if you scale the tallest in the complex. There's a small museum and a great craft shop selling individual pieces made by locals. *Combis* to Túcume cost S2 and leave from the Terminal Leguía at the Ovalo del Pescador in Chiclayo (take a taxi there, as it's a 30-min walk from the centre and in a rough neighbourhood). Ask for "los pirámides" and the *combi* will drop you on the main road about a kilometre from the site. A *mototaxi* from there will cost S1.50.

Moving on

Air Lima (3 daily; 1hr 15min).
Bus Cajamarca (8 daily; 6hr); Chachapoyas (2 daily; 11hr); Lima (every 30min; 10hr); Piura (every 30min; 4hr); Trujillo (every 30min; 4hr); Tumbes (3 daily; 10hr).

MÁNCORA

Just a small fishing village until about twenty years ago, **MÁNCORA** has become Peru's most popular beach resort – justifiably so as the sea is warm most of the year, the beaches are white and the waves near perfect. It's definitely worth a stop to relax on the beach, eat to your heart's content at the great restaurants and try the outdoor sports (see below). Máncora's **nightlife** is also famous, but can definitely make you feel that sleep is for the weak. Between the loud music and the busy main road, *la bulla* (the ruckus) puts many off, but there are more peaceful resorts along this stretch of coast such as Pocitas, Vichayito and Cabo Blanco to explore.

What to see and do

Máncora itself is a small settlement based along Av. Piura (the stretch of the Panamericana that passes through Máncora) and the few side roads and passageways (many without an official name) that lead to the beach. There are no real **sights** other than some small mud baths about 40min away by *mototaxi*; you are here to chill out. So hit the waves, wander around the multitude of *artesanía* stalls along the main avenue, have a cocktail and watch the spectacular sunsets. Check the site ⓦwww.vivamancora.com for up-to-date info on everything in the area, including upcoming surfing events.

Outdoor activities

Long famed for its **surf**, the area is rapidly becoming a world-class destination for **kite-surfing**, and regularly hosts national and international competitions. The long beach and warm water make for a great place to learn how to surf and there's no shortage of teachers. You can hire gear and take lessons from several places along the beach from around S50 per hour for surfing or US$45 per hour for kite-surfing (both work out cheaper if you buy package deals).

Horseriding is also popular, and you'll see touts along the beach offering ragged-looking ponies for S30 per hour;. it would be preferable to go through your hostel or use the main tour agency (see p.888), as the animals may be better treated. It's also possible to arrange tours to see marine wildlife, including **Humpback whale spotting** (Aug–Oct; see p.876).

Arrival and information

Air Tumbes Airport is 2hr by bus (see p.889).
Bus Most of the buses have terminals at the northern end of town where Av. Piura becomes Av. Prolongación Grau. All are a 15-min walk or less to most parts of town.
Tourist information Mancora Connexions, at Piura 452 (daily 2–7pm; ☎991-325-472, ⓦmancoraconnexions.com), is a helpful private tourist information office (and the only one in town), which promises impartial commission-free advice. Good advice on other beaches in the area and plenty of maps and leaflets. English spoken.

City transport

Mototaxi *Mototaxis* are a standard S1–2 per journey within town, although many will try to charge you double to *The Point* hostel – fix a price before riding. Don't take one of the taxis without an official-looking sticker on the front, especially if you are going out of town, as there have been incidences of tourists getting robbed.

Accommodation

Those looking for peace and quiet will do better staying on the edges of town, although take care when returning late at night, as attacks on tourists are not unheard of. Note that prices are given for high season (Nov–March, plus Easter week and Independence day weekend) where prices at least double in soles or may even be changed to US dollars.
Balsa y Tortora Av. Piura 452. Simple, perhaps, but a much more pleasant place than those of a similar price, with friendly owners. Rooms have cable TV, fans, private bathrooms and some have sea views. S80.
Kokopeli Beachpackers Av. Piura 209 ⓦwww .hostelkokopeli.com. Following on from their popular Lima hostel, *Kokopeli* has recently created this pleasant backpackers (with all the faves like wi-fi) with comfortable bunks and en-suite dorms. The pool has bar stools and a table in it, and you can swim to the bar to get your drinks. Dorms S48, rooms S130.

The Point Playa del Amor ☎073/706-320, ⓦwww .thepointhostels.com. Although this hostel is a little out of town (a 20-min walk along the beach or S2 in a *mototaxi*), it has a lot going for it. There's a variety of dorms, a good bar, a chill-out pool and they serve food. What sets it apart is its four beach cabins, which sleep up to three people. Be sure to use a licensed *mototaxi* if coming for a party at night. Breakfast included. Dorms S35, cabins S110.

Eating

Many of the restaurants aimed at gringos are along the Panamericana and serve excellent international cuisine, but none are that cheap. Better-priced grub can be found towards the market at the north end of town, where Av. Piura becomes Av. Prolongación Grau. Here you can find S5 menus, *pollo a la brasa* (spit-roast chicken) joints, *ceviche* for S2, and fresh fruit and veg. If you're on the beach and need a snack, you shouldn't miss the sandwich lady who reaches everyone with her big basket of still-warm rolls with great fillings.
El Ají Down a little passageway that leads to the sea – from the beach looking back towards the main drag it's to the right of *Birdhouse*. A tiny little Mexican restaurant that serves great burritos, tacos and quesadillas for around S15, not forgetting some mean cocktails.
La Bajadita Av. Piura 424. For a decent espresso and a huge selection of home-made cakes and desserts, this place can't be beaten. Also serves reasonably priced sandwiches, cocktails and combos. Cake and coffee approx. S10. Tues–Sun 10am–10pm.
Birdhouse complex Sitting on a balcony overlooking the sea next to *Hostal Sol y Mar* is this colourful three-in-one restaurant with wi-fi access. *Green Eggs and Ham* (open 7.30am–5pm) does the best breakfasts in town, including waffles and fantastic American pancakes (S12); *Papa Mo's* (open all day) does

milkshakes and nothing but milkshakes; and *Surf & Turf* is open for lunch and dinner and does, as the name suggests, fish and steak plates (S20–30).

La Espada Av. Piura 501 & 655. This restaurant with two locales is the best for very large portions of seafood such as *ceviche* and *parihuela espada* (stew). Mains average S20–30, daily lunch menu for S15.

Tao Av. Piura 228 ☏ 073/258-256. This place gets packed every night, as word is spreading about its great Thai and Chinese food. The tuna steak pad thai is exquisite and the service excellent. Mains S12–30.

Drinking and nightlife

Eating might be expensive in Máncora, but drinking certainly is not. Every bar in town has a very flexible "happy hour", which usually runs all night; you can get two cocktails or beers for S10 in many bars. Strangely, the after-hours nightlife tends to take place in the hostels, especially *Sol y Mar*, *Loki* and *The Point*, whose full-moon party every month has become a town fixture.

Iguana's Bar Av. Piura 245. The oldest bar in town and a friendly place to have a drink, where every hour is happy hour. Daily 6pm–3am.

Surfers Bar Block 3 of Av. Piura. One of the few bars in Máncora that isn't just a roadside shack, this place has Elvis posters and kitsch on the walls, and rock and pop on the stereo. Daily from 6pm.

Directory

Banks and exchange Banco de la Nación, at Av. Piura 525; Globalnet ATM outside Minimarket Marlon, on Av. Piura 520.

Health Clínica Emergencias, at Av. Piura 641 (☏ 073/258-713). Open 24hr.

Laundry Mil@net, at Av. Piura 408, will do your laundry cheaply, but it takes a couple of days; make sure it's your own clothes you get back.

Police Av. Piura block 5, next to Banco de la Nación.

Tour operators Iguana's Trips runs out of *Loki* hostel, at Av. Piura 262 (☏ 073/258-708, ☷ www .iguanastrips.com) and offers horseriding, hikes to national parks and trips to mud baths; Maremoto, at Av. Grau 636 (☏ 073/258-574), hires out quad bikes, 4x4s and Jet Skis.

Moving on

Bus Buses to Lima (18hr) and other destinations all originate from Tumbes (see below), and arrive in Máncora two hours after they depart from there.

Colectivo and combi *Colectivos* depart every 30min 4am–7pm from EPPO, at Av. Grau 470, to nearby beach Los Organos (20min; S1.50) and most resorts south to Piura (4hr). *Combis* drive up and down Av. Piura throughout the day, picking up passengers until they are full for the trip to Tumbes (2hr; S7). There are also companies along Av. Piura offering a comfortable trip to Piura or Tumbes in modern people carriers; much faster than coaches, but they cost a lot more (eg to Piura S35).

TUMBES

Unlike most border settlements, tropical **TUMBES**, about 30km from the Ecuadorian border, is a surprisingly friendly place. Although the tourism infrastructure around here is in its infancy, Tumbes is close to some of Peru's finest **beaches** and three national parks of astounding ecological variety: the arid **Cerros de Amotape**, the mangrove swamps of the **Santuario Manglares de Tumbes** and the tropical rainforest of the **Zona Reservada de Tumbes**. Unfortunately, as so few tourists explore this part of Peru, tours can be hard to come by and expensive.

What to see and do

Tumbes is good for a stroll to see its bright, almost gaudy modern architecture around the centre. The large **Plaza de Armas** feels very tropical, with sausage trees, a huge rainbow archway and a stripy cathedral. Next to the plaza runs the pedestrianized **Paseo de la Concordia** (also known as Av. San Martín), which has huge sculptures and more colourful architecture. **Calle Grau**, which leads east off the plaza, has unusual rickety wooden buildings, while the southern end leads to the *malecón* (boardwalk) along the river. To get to the national parks without a tour company, you need to talk to SERNANP and the tourist information office (see p.889).

Arrival and information

Air If you're flying in from Lima, note that Tumbes Airport is often very quiet, particularly at night, when there's no access to food or drink. A taxi into town should cost S30–35; it's about a 20-min journey. **Bus or colectivo** Most buses and *colectivos* coming to Tumbes arrive at offices along Av. Tumbes Norte. From here it's a couple of blocks to the Plaza de Armas.

Tourist information IPerú, 3rd floor *Malecón Milenio* (daily 8am–1pm & 2–6pm; ☎972/619-204). If you're venturing into the national parks or reserves (though not the mangrove swamps), you'll need permission from SERNANP, at Av. Tumbes Norte 1739 (Mon–Fri 8.30am–1pm & 3–5pm; ☎072/526-489). They are also good for helping you find a guide if you want to explore the area without a tour company.

Accommodation

While there are many budget hotels in Tumbes, few of them are recommendable. If you don't have mosquito repellent, go for places with windows that close and fans.

Hospedaje Amazonas Av. Tumbes Norte 317 on the corner of the Plaza de Armas ☎072/525-266. One of the more pleasant of the budget places, with cable TV, fans and light, en-suite rooms. S30; S10 extra for hot water.

Hospedaje Tumbes Jr. Filipinas 311-01 (just off Av. Grau) ☎072/522-164. Has definitely seen better days, but nevertheless the rooms are big enough and have fans. Cold water only, though this is rarely a problem here; you can pay extra for a TV. S30.

Eating and drinking

Tumbes is the best place in Peru to try *conchas negras* – the black clams found only in these coastal waters, where they grow on the roots of mangroves.

🏃 **Bohemia/Eduardo (El Brujo)** Jr. Malecón Benavides 850. One of the best restaurants in this part of the world, and recommended by just about anyone you pass in town, this place serves exquisite seafood in a light, open restaurant spanning two floors, including a rooftop terrace with river views. Try the fantastic *sudado de conchas negras*, a thick seafood soup served with rice, with supposedly aphrodisiac properties. A little pricey (mains S20–40) but portions are big enough to share. Open Mon–Sat 9am–midnight.

Budabar Calle Grau 309. On the plaza, this place is part chill-out lounge, part local restaurant and bar. Offering cheap set lunches and beers, it's the place to see and be seen in Tumbes. Mains S12–18. Open Mon–Sat noon–midnight.

Misky Bolognesi 221. Good-value snack bar offering breakfasts, snacks, burgers, sandwiches, milkshakes, juices, cakes, sundaes and smoothies. Everything less than S15. Open all day.

CROSSING INTO ECUADOR

Crossing the border from Tumbes is complicated and has caught many tourists, especially non-Spanish-speaking ones, adrift in a no-man's land with a lot of canny locals trying to make as much as they can fleece you for. Remember to change your money well before you get to the border, as exchange rates in Aguas Verdes (the closest town to the border) can be extortionate.

By far the easiest way to cross the border is to take an international bus service from Tumbes, such as Ormeño or the Ecuadorian company Cifa, which take you straight through to Machala in Ecuador, only stopping directly outside each immigration office. If you can't do this, you'll have to go it alone. From Tumbes, combis (40min) and colectivos (shared taxis; 30min) for the border leave Tumbes from block 3 of Av. Tumbes Norte – ensure that they'll drop you at the Complejo Inmigraciones (Immigration Complex; open 24hr), 3km before Aguas Verdes, where you get an exit or entry stamp and tourist card for your passport. After getting stamped, pick up another *colectivo* that will take you on to the border. Once there walk over the bridge to the Ecuadorian border town of Huaquillas (see p.687), where you'll find the Ecuadorian immigration office (open 24hr). A taxi from Tumbes will cost S40–50 and for this amount the driver should wait for you while you get your stamp at immigration and then take you on to the border.

If you're coming into Peru from Ecuador, it's simply a reversal of the above procedure –note that Tumbes is a much nicer place to stay than Aguas Verdes – and in both directions the authorities occasionally require that you show an onward ticket out of their respective countries.

Do not take photographs anywhere near the border or immigration offices.

Directory

Banks and exchange All banks are along Calle Bolívar (to the left of the cathedral). Moneychangers can also be found on this street at the crossroads with Av. Piura.

Post office San Martín 208.

Tour operators Mayte Tours, at Jr. San Martín 131 (☏072/782-532, ⊛ www.maytetours.com); Preference Tours, at Calle Grau 427 (☏072/525-518) and Tumbes Tours, at Av. Tumbes Norte 355 (☏072/524-837, ⊛ www.tumbestours.com) all offer trips to the mangroves and the national parks, but none are cheap.

Moving on

Air Lima (daily; 1hr 45min).

Bus Most buses to Lima (9 daily; 17–20hr) leave in the afternoon and may stop at Máncora (2hr), Piura (6hr), Chiclayo (8hr), Trujillo (10hr), or go straight there. International buses to Machala, Ecuador (8 daily; 1hr 30min once through immigration).

The Northern Highlands

The **Northern Highlands** offers some of the least-explored areas in Peru. The two main cities, **Cajamarca** and **Chach-apoyas**, are welcoming and peaceful compared to other cities more geared up for tourism. Each offers accessible stopping points before striking out into the stunning countryside, ranging from lush pastures to craggy mountaintops and cloudforest.

CAJAMARCA

Nestling in a fertile rolling valley of eucalyptus and pine, 2720m above sea level, **CAJAMARCA** is a charming colonial town shrouded in legend, most famously – or infamously – known as the place of **Atahualpa's last stand** against Pizarro in 1532, signalling the end of the Inca Empire. While its Spanish ambience, along with its one

remaining Inca building and Andean location, have earned it the title "the Cusco of the north", Cajamarca has a character all of its own. Relatively small until Peru's largest gold mine (within driving distance) was discovered, the city's population has grown rapidly in the last decade to more than 300,000, and the influx of money and expats is reflected in the modern restaurants and watering holes. Despite that Cajamarca is still surprisingly low-key, and the lack of hassle will come as a welcome relief if you've come from the gringo trail in the south, or Máncora in the north.

What to see and do

Cajamarca's sights either lie in the centre around the **Plaza de Armas**, in the swish suburb of **Baños del Inca** – where you'll find the eponymous thermal springs – or **outside the city**, where the attractions are all accessible on half-day tours. Note that all the main tourist attractions in the centre, as well as many shops, close for lunch between 1 and 3pm.

Around the Plaza de Armas

The **Plaza de Armas** lies at the centre, and most of the sights in the city are located nearby in the easy-to-navigate surrounding streets. On the plaza sit the **Catedral** and the **Iglesia San Francisco** (both have erratic opening hours but are open for Mass around 6–8pm; free). The adjoining **Convento San Francisco** (Mon & Wed–Sat 4–6pm; S3), whose entrance is on Amalia Puga, houses an interesting selection of religious art in a rambling run of rooms, crypts and cloisters in a working monastery (hence the limited opening hours).

Just a couple of blocks from the main square, and run by the national university, is the eccentric and compact **Museo Arqueológico Horacio Urteaga**, at Jr. Del Batán 289 (Mon–Fri 8am–2pm; free, though donations welcome). It

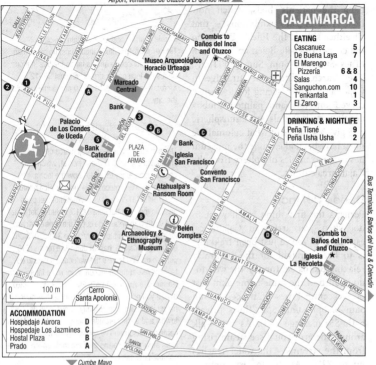

CAJAMARCA

EATING
Cascanuez	5
De Buena Laya	7
El Marengo Pizzería	6 & 8
Salas	4
Sanguchon.com	10
T'enkantala	1
El Zarco	3

DRINKING & NIGHTLIFE
Peña Tisné	9
Peña Usha Usha	2

ACCOMMODATION
Hospedaje Aurora	D
Hospedaje Los Jazmines	C
Hostal Plaza	B
Prado	A

Bus Terminals, Baños del Inca & Celendín

houses an usual variety of pots, some excellent textiles, colonial furniture, a couple of mummies and a cabinet with erotic ceramics.

Cerro Santa Apolonia

Looking south from the Plaza de Armas, your eyes will immediately be drawn to the pretty white church on the hill of **Cerro Santa Apolonia**, and the large crucifix looming behind it. The walk up Jr. 2 de Mayo is steep but there's plenty to see on the way – the undulating steps are filled with amorous couples, children playing and people making jewellery and other crafts. At the church, you can pay S1 to go right to the top through pretty gardens, and see the rock formation known as the **Silla del Inca** (Inca chair), reputed to be a place the Inca would sit and gaze out over his empire.

Atahualpa's Ransom Room and the Belén Complex

One **joint ticket** (S5, available from the tourist office in the Belén Complex) gives you entrance to a trio of sights. The most famous is the only surviving Inca structure in Cajamarca – a modest stone room known as **El Cuarto del Rescate** (the ransom room), at Jr. Amalia Puga 722 (Thurs–Tues 9am–5pm, Sun 9am–noon). It is the room, legend has it, that Atahualpa was forced by the conquistadors to fill with gold in order to save his life, although in reality it is probably just the room he was held prisoner in.

The joint ticket also includes entrance to the gorgeous Baroque **Complejo Belén**. This complex includes two colonial hospitals – one now an archeology and ethnography museum, and the other a large space with small alcoves that would have been the patients' beds, which now hosts rotating art exhibitions – that sit either side of the **Iglesia Belén**, on the corner of Calle Belén and Jr. Junín (Tues–Sun 8am–6pm, Sun 9am–1pm). The church is the most attractive in Cajamarca, worth seeing for its ornate carved interiors and painted chubby angels. The hospitals are atmospheric and give a glimpse of what colonial life must have been like, while the museum has some examples of pottery from the Cajamarca culture.

Baños del Inca

Perhaps the first thing you'll want to do when you arrive in Cajamarca, especially if you've just been trekking, is to head straight for the sublimely relaxing **Baños del Inca**, in the well-to-do suburb of the same name 6km east of the centre (Tues–Thurs & Sat–Sun 5am–6.30pm, until 5pm Thurs; private bath S5, massage S20). As you walk around the area you'll see steam rising from the streams – the water reaches up to 72°C. At the tourist complex this water is used to provide a range of relaxing activities, including private and communal baths, a pool, jacuzzis and even an aromatic sauna filled with orange peel and eucalyptus.

It's extremely easy to get to Baños by *combi* from Cajamarca – they depart from Jr. Sabogal, one block north of the Plaza de Armas (20min; S2) and arrive outside the baths.

Arrival and information

Air The small airport, 5km out of town, is served by LC Busre and LAN (see p.794).

Bus Most of the buses have terminals close to the centre of town, between blocks 2 and 3 of Av. Atahualpa, about 1.5km east of the main plaza. A taxi from here to the centre is S3.

Tourist information The very helpful tourist office is run by DIRCETUR and is next to the Iglesia Belén on Calle Belén (Mon–Sat 7.30am–1pm & 2.30–5pm; ☎076/362-903). Some English spoken.

City transport

Combi *Combis* cost S0.70 within the city.

Taxi or mototaxi Taxis should cost no more than S3 in the city centre and as far as the bus stations. Baños del Inca or the airport will cost S6–12. *Mototaxis* are a standard S1.50 per journey within the city.

Accommodation

There are a few families in Cajamarca offering cheap homestays (*turismo vivencial*), which give you the opportunity to get to know the locals. English-speaking guide María Victoria Vilca Alfaro (☎01/949/481-164, ✉vickyvilca@hotmail.com) has two rooms in her house (S15, includes hot water and wi-fi), a *mototaxi* ride out of the centre; Miriam Alcalde Figueroa's place (Ayacucho 319 ☎076/362-932) is very central, has six dorm-like rooms (S10 per person) and there's hot water and space to do laundry. Ask at the tourist office for more information.

Hospedaje Aurora Amalia Puga 1014 ☎076/367-878. If you're bored of soulless rooms, this new hostel is the antidote. Brightly coloured walls, towels and sheets provide cheer, while hot water, cable on flatscreen TVs and wi-fi add value. There is an atrium-like ceiling over the main space, so the communal areas are light. S60.

Hospedaje Los Jazmines Jr. Amazonas 775 ☎076/361-812, ⊕www.hospedajelosjazmines.com.pe. The prettiest of the budget choices, this is in a renovated colonial building with a green courtyard and a small café. Rooms are simple, but lots of pine furniture makes them feel bright, and they all have cable, hot water and wi-fi. S60.

Hostal Plaza Amalia Puga 669 ☎076/362-058. The most central and best-value place in town. Rooms are basic but generous, with a few flourishes like a communal TV, wi-fi and free tea/coffee. A multitude of room choices with or without bathroom (note, hot water only in mornings and evenings). S25.

Prado Jr. La Mar ☎076/366-093, ⊕www.hotelpradocajamarca.com. Looks crummy from the outside, but inside this offers cleanliness, bright rooms, hot water, TV, free internet and wi-fi; they'll even store luggage. S35.

Eating

Cajamarca is famous for its dairy products – including some of the best cheese in Peru. It's often served as *choclo con queso*, where you literally get a slab of cheese with a big cob of corn – a delicious snack. Other dishes include *caldo verde* (green broth) – something of an acquired taste – made from potato, egg, herbs and quesillo cheese, and *picante de papas con cuy* (potatoes with peanut and chilli sauce with fried guinea pig). There is a mall housing a supermarket – El Quinde, at Av. Hoyos Rubios blocks 6 and 7, a 20-min walk from the Plaza de Armas.

Cascanuez Amalia Puga 554. The best coffee and cake in town, in a refined café. Also good for snack foods and breakfasts. Coffee and cake S10.

De Buena Laya Jr. 2 de Mayo 343. A good place to try *caldo verde* (S4) as well as other local dishes for rock-bottom prices. Open for breakfast and lunch.

El Marengo Pizzeria Jr. Junín 1201 & Jr. San Martín 323. This pizzeria is so popular it has two locales around the corner from each other; both get packed with locals after the best pizza in town (S10). Also serves up some Mexican dishes. Daily 7–11.30pm.

Salas Amalia Puga 637. *Salas* has been around since 1947 and is still run by the same family. Not the cheapest, but regarded as the best restaurant in town and although the waiters' traditional uniforms gives the place some style, it's not pretentious. The *cuy* with potato puree and beans is delicious; try it here if you've not been brave enough elsewhere. Set lunch S15; mains S20–30. Daily 7am–midnight.

Sanguchon.com Jr. Junín 1137. As the opposite of the diminuitive "ito", the suffix "on" in Spanish signifies that something is enormous, and these sandwiches certainly live up to their name. A large range of fillings are served up in huge crusty bread rolls. The restaurant-cum-bar also does cocktails. Sandwiches S5–13. Mon–Sat 6–11pm.

T'enkantala Amalia Puga 237. Incredibly good value, fresh-tasting Chinese set meals from S6, which includes soup, fried wanton, rice, main and a drink. Huge variety and a decent option for vegetarians. Open daily noon–4pm & 6–11pm.

El Zarco Jr. Del Batán 170. An old-fashioned canteen-like restaurant with a huge choice of soups, grills, Chinese meals, desserts and juices. Mains S5–15, set lunch S7.50. Daily 7am–11pm.

Drinking and nightlife

Peña Tisné Jr. San Martín 265. This is neither a real *peña* nor a real bar, but a one-of-a-kind Peruvian experience that should not be missed. Knock on the unmarked door and Don Victor will lead you through his house to his bohemian back garden, full of cosy tables and memorabilia soaked in Cajamarcan history. Everyone is welcome here, from tourists to poets to the mayor. Try the home-made *macerado* – a

delicious liquor made from fermenting exotic fruits and sugar (pitcher S14). Open daily noon–midnight.

Peña Usha Usha Amalia Puga 142. Not at all like other Peruvian peñas (which put on a structured show), *Usha Usha* is a one-man show improvised on the night, with singing and music in an intimate kerosene lamp-lit room. Atmospheric, but don't come if you want to chat, as the action is very much centred on the show. Entry S5. Open from around 9pm most nights; busiest Fri & Sat.

Shopping

Cajamarca is known for its high-quality pottery, and the general standard in some of the small shops here is excellent – there is some unique craftwork you'll not find elsewhere. There are plenty of stalls selling the usual stuff along Jr. 2 de Mayo up to Cerro Santo Apolonia, but the shops listed below offer higher-quality workmanship.

Cajamarca Colors & Creations Jr. Belén 628 ☎076/343-875. Wonderfully imaginative jewellery, ceramics, shawls and gifts for children.

Quinde Ex Jr. 2 de Mayo 264 ☎076/361-031. Colourful textiles, cushion covers and handbags made of Andean woven belts.

Directory

Banks and exchange Banco de Crédito, at Jr. Apurimac 717; Interbank, at Jr. 2 de Mayo 546 (good for changing money); Banco de La Nación, at Jr. Pisagua 552; Banco Continental, at Jr. Tarapaca 747.

Hospital Hospital Regional, at Av. Mario Urteaga 500 (☎076/362-533).

Post office Serpost, at Jr. Amalia Puga 778.

Tourist police Jr. Amalia Puga (☎076/362-156).

Tour operators All the companies offer pretty much the same array of tours, and most of them will pool clients. Cumbe Mayo tours, at Jr. Amalia Puga 635 (☎076/362-938) offers the normal range of excursions. Manuel Portal Cabellos (✉manueljpc11@hotmail.com) is a recommended local guide who speaks English; his knowledge of the region and Peruvian indigenous history can't be beaten.

Moving on

Air Lima (3 daily; 1hr 10min).

Bus Chachapoyas via Celendín, Leymebamba and Tingo (2 daily around 5.30am; 12hr); Chiclayo (3 daily; 4hr); Lima (6 daily, all in the evening; 14hr); Trujillo (8 daily; 6hr).

DAY-TRIPS FROM CAJAMARCA

There are several sites of interest easily accessible from Cajamarca. One is the fascinatingly precise aqueduct of **Cumbe Mayo**, thought to be perhaps the oldest man-made structure in South America. It's possible to walk there (4–5hr) or you can take the 6am *combi* from the top of Cerro Santa Apolonia towards Chitilla (around 1hr; S5) and then walk back (2–3hr, take your own supplies). Most will prefer to go with a tour (around S20), as there is no obvious route around the huge area.

Another interesting half-day excursion is to the **Ventanillas de Otuzco** (daily 9am–5pm; S4), a hillside necropolis whose graves resemble little alcoves or windows (*ventanillas*). *Combis* go here from Plaza de la Recoleta in Cajamarca (20min), or you can take an organized tour.

CHACHAPOYAS

Few tourists make it as far as **CHACH-APOYAS**, the capital of the Amazonas department in the *selva alta* (high jungle) with a near-perfect climate; a huge shame as the city and its surrounds have a surprising amount to offer, not least the marvellous remains of the **Kuelap** fortress. The city itself is a colonial delight and its citizens are known for their friendliness. But what "Chacha", as the locals call it, really offers is the chance to get well off the gringo trail and see some extraordinary sights that easily rival their southern counterparts.

What to see and do

While the city is certainly a pleasant place to stay, with many good cafés and restaurants and a couple of small **museums**, most people use it as a base to explore the remains of ancient cultures littering the Utcubamba

valley. Most famous of all the sights in this region is **Kuelap**, the cloud citadel second only to Machu Picchu in terms of location and magnificence (although it is significantly older). **Birdwatching** is also a big draw, partly as this is one of the few places to see the very rare Marvellous Spatuletail hummingbird. Other popular trips are to the waterfall at **Gocta** and the mysterious 1000-year-old sarcophagi at **Karajía**.

The museums

The two museums are the only real tourist attractions within Chach-apoyas. The **Museo Gilberto Enorio**, at Ayacucho 904 on the Plaza de Armas (Tues–Sat 9am–5.30, closed for lunch; free), run by the Instituto Nacional de Cultura (INC), is just two tiny rooms with some ceramics and a couple of mummies, but it does let you get up close to one of the sarcophagus heads from Karajía.

The **Museo de Santa Ana**, at Jr. Santa Ana, block 10 (Mon–Fri 9am–6pm, closed for lunch, Sat 9am–1pm; S5; ☎041/943-869), was refurbished in 2009 and has some local costumes, religious garments, ceramics and

TOURS AROUND CHACHAPOYAS

There are a multitude of tour companies all offering trips to the main sights in Amazonas. The majority have signed an agreement to not charge more than the following prices for tours (per person): Kuelap S60; Cataratas de Gocta S50; Pueblo de los Muertos S50; Karajía S70; Revash and the Museo de Leymebamba S100; trekking to Gran Vilaya (4 days) S120. While you should never pay more than that, these prices are flexible depending on group size, time of year and number of tours arranged with the same company, so bargain hard.

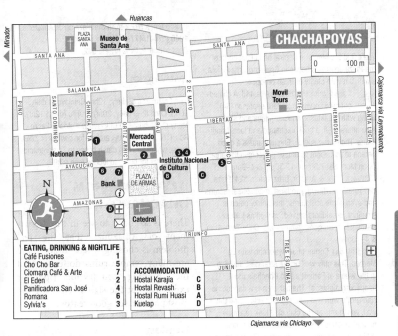

local history on display. There is also a memorable *mirador* (viewpoint) that you can reach if you walk west from the Museo de Santa Ana to the end of the road and take the steps.

Arrival and information

Bus Most companies are on block 9 of Av. Salamanca, or a few blocks north from the Plaza on Grau, Libertad and Ortiz Arrieta. A taxi anywhere in town from the bus stations costs S2.

Combi There are no *combis* that run within the city – everywhere is walkable and taxis are cheap – but there are minivans and *colectivos* servicing nearby towns such as Huancas and Pedro Ruíz. Their terminals are along Jr. Ortiz Arrieta, north of the Plaza de Armas.

Tourist information Jr. Ortiz Arrieta 590 (Mon–Sat 9am–1pm & 2–6pm, Sun 9am–1pm; ☎041/477-292). Run by IPerú; English spoken.

Tour operators All the companies offer pretty much the same array of tours; make sure they've signed up to the agreement (see p.894). Turismo Explorer, at Jr. Grau 509 on the plaza (☎041/478-162, ⓦwww.turismoexplorerperu.com) is highly recommended and the guides speak excellent English.

Accommodation

Hostal Karajía Jr. 2 de Mayo 546 ☎041/312-606. Their tagline claiming "elegance" may be overstretching things a little, but this is a nice budget hostel with homely touches. All rooms have private bath, hot water and cable TV. S45.

🏃 **Hostal Revash** Jr. Grau 517, Plaza de Armas ☎041/477-391. Right on the plaza, this hostel in a colonial building has good-value spacious rooms, some looking out on the plaza, around a tropical patio. Internet, wi-fi, a small book exchange, very good showers and TV in all rooms are bonuses. They also have their own tour company, Andes Tours, which gives guests a slight discount. S60.

Hostal Rumi Huasi Ortiz Arrieta 365 ☎041/791-100. In keeping with its name (literally "stone house"), this place is a bit bare, but it's clean, light, has hot water, a laundry service and is amazingly good value. S25.

Kuelap Jr. Amazonas 1057 ☎041/477-136, ⓦwww.hotelkuelap.com. A big rambling colonial building with some rooms set around something of a courtyard. The rooms are clean – some very big – and the place has free internet and wi-fi. Extras like towels, soap and toilet paper provided. Prices vary depending on whether TV, private bath or hot water is included. S30.

Eating and drinking

You'll find the Mercado Central one block north of the Plaza de Armas between Grau and Ortiz Arrieta; small, but with plenty of fresh produce.

Café Fusiones Chincha Alta 445. A chilled-out café serving excellent espresso (S4), along with breakfasts, snacks, juices and shakes. Also offers wi-fi, a book exchange and local handicrafts. The owner speaks English, and is a good person to ask about volunteer projects in the area. Open Mon–Sat 7.30am–12.30pm & 4–9pm.

Ciomara Café & Arte Jr. Ortiz Arrieta 524, Plaza de Armas. Overflowing with art, magazines, records and even some sculptures, this quirky place is a delight. Breakfasts served, as well as juices, sandwiches, burgers, *tamales*, etc. Daily 7am–1pm & 4–10pm.

Cho Cho Bar Corner of Jr. Ayacucho with La Merced. This may well be the strangest bar/club in the whole of Peru; it's also Chacha's most happening nightspot. The bar area is a dark stone-clad grotto with two fake stone fireplaces on the wall, which makes the club side look relatively normal, but pitchers of cocktails are dirt cheap (S15) and they have Chilean wines. Plays a mix of Latino, rock and reggae. Daily from 8.30pm until the last people leave.

El Eden Jr. Grau 448. A vegetarian restaurant that's good enough and ridiculously cheap. Set breakfast S2.50, lunch S4. Daily 7am–9.30pm.

Panificadora San José Ayacucho 816. You can't get better (or much cheaper) than this bakery/café for bread, breakfasts and snacks. Fruit salad S3.50. Daily 6.30am–1pm & 3–10pm.

Romana Jr. Ayacucho 1013. For a very good set lunch – three courses and a bread roll for S7 – but also breakfast and dinner, this place is a solid choice and there's excellent service. The *Sopa a la Minuta* (beef and noodle soup) is particularly good. Daily 7am–11pm.

Sylvia's Jr. Ayacucho 822. A time warp of a bar, with posters of John Lennon, Kurt Cobain and Bon Jovi on the walls, and English-language pop on the sound system. Go for their good selection of locally made *macerado* (fermented fruit rum) – a bottle will cost you S15; try the Chuchuhuasi flavour. Daily 6pm–midnight.

Directory

Banks and exchange Banco de Crédito, on Plaza de Armas next to IPerú office.

Hospital The public hospital (open 24hr) is on the corner of the plaza (℡041/477-017).

Police Half a block from the plaza on Jr. Amazonas 1040 (℡041/477-017).

Post office Jr. Ortiz Arrieta 632.

Moving on

Bus Cajamarca (2 daily; 12hr); Chiclayo (4 daily; 10hr); Lima (2–3 daily; 20hr); Trujillo (daily; 12hr). Many of the buses to Chiclayo will stop in Pedro Ruíz (1hr 30min, or ask around for *combis* or *colectivos*), where you can catch buses to Tarapoto and Yurimaguas for boats to Iquitos (see p.899).

DAY-TRIPS FROM CHACHAPOYAS

There is so much to see in the department of Amazonas that the real problem is chosing where to go. There are many remote ruins dotted around the stunning countryside ripe for exploring, but the sights below are the most popular, for good reason.

Kuelap

If you only see one sight in the northern highlands, make it **KUELAP** (daily 8am–5pm; S12). This impressive pre-Inca fortress, 3100m up in the clouds, was built around 600 AD and would have housed more than three thousand people in circular thatched huts. Although rediscovered in the mid-1800s, it's only just being properly uncovered; it is beautifully overgrown with trees, bromeliads and mosses, and you'll probably see archeologists at work here. One of the most interesting buildings is called *El Tintero* ("the ink well"), a temple which, as its name suggests, has nothing but a hole through its middle, open at the top. It's thought that it was used for astrology or sacrifices.

It takes around three hours to cover the 40km between Chachapoyas and the site, due to poor road quality, so it's a long day however you do it. Coming with a tour company from Chachapoyas (see p.895) is the easiest way to get here, but if you're in a group and don't want a guide, consider hiring a taxi (around S130 to take you there and wait for you). You can also get there as part of a four-day trek that passes by the ruins known as **Gran Vilaya** – the tour companies in Chachapoyas all run excursions.

Cateratas de Gocta

The waterfalls at **GOCTA** were only measured officially in 2005, and there has since been much debate concerning their place in the scale of the world's tallest waterfalls – they could be anywhere between the third- and fourteenth-tallest. Whatever the truth, they are indisputably impressive. Taking a tour is the best option as it's mandatory to go with a guide, though if you get a taxi to the entrance you'll find guides (S5) and even horses to rent (S25) –without them it's a 2-hr walk through lush forest each way from the entrance.

Karajía and the Pueblo de los Muertos

Day tours are offered jointly to see Karajía and the Pueblo de los Muertos

("town of the dead"), two different cliff-side mausoleums where important figures in Chachapoya society were once buried. The six sarcophagi at **KARAJÍA** are the more famous; standing over 2m high, their flattened faces, deep-set eyes and painted bodies give them distinct and eerie personalities. Built in the twelfth and thirteenth centuries, they still manage to conjure up an ancestral presence. The **PUEBLO DE LOS MUERTOS** is similarly interesting, with more sarcophagi and also burial houses, again perched precariously on a ledge with a huge drop into the valley below.

While both lie relatively close to Chachapoyas (46km southwest and 30km north of the city respectively), **getting there** is complicated by the condition of the roads (or lack of). Take a tour from Chachapoyas (though you'll still have to walk a fair bit), or else take a *combi* to either Luya, where it's a 2hr 30min to 3hr walk to Karajía (ask for directions to Shipata where the path starts), or to Lamud for the Pueblo de los Muertos (approx. 3hr walk each way).

INDIGENOUS JUNGLE TRIBES

Outside the few main towns there are hardly any sizeable settlements, and the jungle population remains dominated by between 35 and 62 indigenous tribes – the exact number depends on how you classify tribal identity – each with its own distinct language, customs and dress. After centuries of external influence (missionaries, gold seekers, rubber barons, soldiers, oil companies, anthropologists and now tourists), many jungle Indians speak Spanish and live pretty conventional, westernized lives, preferring jeans, football shirts and fizzy bottled drinks to their more traditional clothing and manioc beer (the tasty, filling and nutritious *masato*). Other tribal groups chose to retreat further into the jungle to avoid contact with outside influences and maintain their traditional way of life.

For most of the traditional or semi-traditional tribes, the jungle offers a semi-nomadic existence. Communities are scattered, with groups of between ten and two hundred people, and their sites shift every few years. For subsistence they depend on small, cultivated plots, fish from the rivers and game from the forest, including wild pigs, deer, monkeys and a range of edible birds. The main species of edible jungle fish are *sabalo* (a kind of oversized catfish), *carachama* (an armoured walking catfish), the feisty piranha (generally not quite as dangerous as Hollywood makes out), and the giant *zungaro* and *paiche* – the latter, at up to 200kg, being the world's largest freshwater fish. In fact, food is so abundant that jungle-dwellers generally spend no more than three to four days a week engaged in subsistence activities.

The jungle

Whether you look at it up close from the ground, or from a boat, or fly over it in a plane, the Peruvian *selva* (jungle) seems endless, though it is actually disappearing at an alarming rate. Over half of Peru is covered by rainforest, with its eastern regions offering easy access to the world's largest and most famous jungle, the **Amazon**. Of the Amazon's original area, around four million square kilometres (about eighty percent) remains intact, fifteen percent of which lies in Peru. Considered as *El Infierno Verde* – "the Green Hell" – by many Peruvians who've never been there, it's the most biodiverse region on earth, and much that lies beyond the main waterways remains relatively untouched and unexplored. Jaguars, anteaters and tapirs roam the forests, huge anacondas live in the swamps, and more than fifty indigenous tribes inhabit the Peruvian section alone, many surviving primarily by hunting and gathering, as they have done for thousands of years.

What to see and do

Given the breadth and quality of options, it's never easy to decide which bit of the jungle to head for. Your three main criteria will probably be budget, ease of access, and the nature of experience you're after. Flying to any of the main jungle towns is surprisingly cheap and, once you've arrived, a number of **excursions** can be easily arranged, such as a camping expedition or travel by canoe or speedboat deep into the wilderness. A costlier, but rewarding, option, mainly restricted to a few operators based in Iquitos, is to take a river cruise on a larger boat.

Iquitos, the capital of the **northern selva**, is the Peruvian jungle's only genuinely exciting city. Although far easier to access by air from Lima or by boat from Brazil, you can get here from the northern Peruvian coast via an adventurous, increasingly popular four-day boat journey up the Río Marañon from Yurimaguas. This will take you close enough to a national reserve the size of many European countries, **Pacaya Samiria**, which has much unexplored jungle. Cusco is the best base for trips into the jungles of the **southern selva**, with road access to the frontier town of **Puerto Maldonado**, itself a good base for budget travellers. The nearby forests of Madre de Dios are rich in flora and fauna, especially in the **Manu Biosphere Reserve**.

AYAHUASCA CEREMONIES

Shaman ceremonies involving the ayahuasca jungle vine are becoming popular with visitors all over Peru, particularly in the jungle areas and Cusco. *Ayahuasca* is a powerful hallucinogen traditionally used for medicinal purposes; never for recreation. Ceremonies need to be prepared for with a special diet and are typically an all-night affair. It is not a comfortable experience; the visions can be intense and profound and are often accompanied by nausea, vomiting and diarrhoea – part of the cleansing process.

Due to the strength of some people's reactions to the vine, ceremonies should only be undertaken with a reputable shaman. In Cusco these include the Shaman Shop on Triunfo 393 and Lesley Myburgh at the Casa de la Gringa, at the corner of Tandapata and P'asñapacana. In Puerto Maldonado, *ayahuasca* ceremonies can be arranged through *Tambopata Hostel* (see p.909). In Iquitos, there are a plethora of shamans and lodges specializing in learning about the vine. Some will take visitors for long work-stays to reduce the cost. Don Lucho and Carlos Tanner are recommended and can be reached via ⓦ www.ayahuascafoundation.org. Ron Wheelock (ⓦ www.ronwheelock .com), known as "the gringo shaman of the Amazon" also has a good reputation.

THE NORTHERN SELVA: IQUITOS AND THE AMAZON RIVER

The largest city in the world not accessible by road, **IQUITOS** began life in 1739 when the Jesuits established settlements on the Río Mazán. By the end of the nineteenth century, it was, along with Manaus in Brazil, one of the great rubber towns – as depicted in Werner Herzog's 1982 film *Fitzcarraldo* – but during the last century has oscillated between prosperity and depression. Yet its position on the Amazon – making it accessible to large ocean-going ships from the distant Atlantic – and the nearby three-way frontier with Colombia and Brazil (see box, p.906) has ensured both its economic and strategic importance; there is a strong military presence.

Most people visit Iquitos briefly with a view to moving on into the rainforest but, wisely, few travellers avoid the place entirely. It's a busy, cosmopolitan town of about 500,000 (and growing as people from smaller jungle villages flock to the city looking for a better life), with elegant architectural reminders of the rubber boom years, eccentric expats and the atmospheric *barrio* of **Puerto Belén**, at whose market you can buy just about anything.

What to see and do

Iquitos is easily over looked in favour of its wild and exotic surroundings, but don't be too quick to dismiss this jungle metropolis. It has a few sights, more than its fair share of quirks, some surprisingly good food, and a multitude of expats drawn to the freedom of life in the rainforest, who'll happily tell you stories of how they wound up there.

Plaza de Armas

The only real sight in the **Plaza de Armas** is the unusual and under-stated **Casa de Fierro** (Iron House).

WHEN TO VISIT

Unlike most of the Peruvian *selva*, the climate up north is little affected by the Andean topography, so there is no rainy season as such; instead, the year is divided into "high water" (Dec–May) and "low water" (June–Nov) seasons. The upshot is that the weather is always hot and humid, with temperatures averaging 23–30ºC and an annual rainfall of about 2600mm. Most visitors come between May and August, but the high-water months can be the best time for wildlife, because the animals are crowded into smaller areas of dry land and more rivers can be navigated.

The city of Iquitos is good to visit year-round. When the water is high it's a better time to see Puerto Belén and the floating houses, though during low-water season there are more nearby beaches available. At the end of June (supposedly June 23–24, but actually spread over three or four days), the main Fiesta de San Juan takes place. It is believed that on 23 June, Saint John blesses all local rivers; locals flock to bathe in them to bring good luck for the year to come. This is preceded and followed by dancing, parades and food stalls for the next few days.

Originally created by Eiffel for the 1889 Paris exhibition, it was shipped out to Iquitos in pieces by one of the rubber barons and erected here in the 1890s. Unfortunately, there is now a pharmacy downstairs, so the only way to see the interior is to check out the overpriced (but fine) restaurant above.

Along the river

The two best sections of the **old riverfront** run parallel to the Plaza de Armas. Malecón Maldonado, locally known as **El Boulevard**, is the busier of the two, especially at night, as it's full of bars and restaurants and there's a small amphitheatre where some kind of entertainment occurs most nights. The other

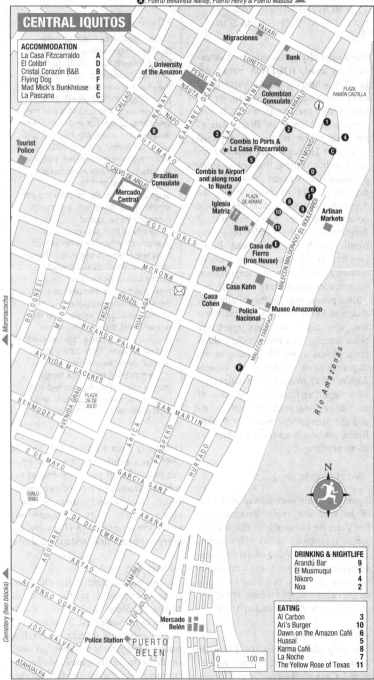

CENTRAL IQUITOS

ACCOMMODATION
La Casa Fitzcarraldo	A
El Colibrí	D
Cristal Corazón B&B	B
Flying Dog	F
Mad Mick's Bunkhouse	E
La Pascana	C

YAVARI

Migraciones

Bank

University of the Amazon

LORETTO

PEVAS

NAUTA

OCAMPO

CALLAO

NANAY

NAPO

S AMANEZ

LA CONDAMINE

Colombian Consulate

PLAZA RAMÓN CASTILLA

FITZCARRALD

ⓘ

RAYMONDI

Tourist Police

PUTUMAYO

B

Combis to Ports & ★ La Casa Fitzcarraldo

2

C

4

D

5

C CALVO DE ARUJO

Brazilian Consulate

Combis to Airport and along road to Nauta ★

Mercado Central

Iglesia Matriz

PLAZA DE ARMAS

6

7

8

9

Artisan Markets

SGTO LORES

Bank

10

11

Casa de Fierro (Iron House) E

MORONA

Bank

Casa Kahn

MUSEO MALDONADO (EL BOULEVARD)

BOLOGNESI

MOORE

TACNA

BRAZIL

HUALLAGA

RICARDO PALMA

Casa Cohen

Policia Nacional

Museo Amazonico

MALECON TARAPACA

Rio Amazonas

AVENIDA M CACERES

BERMUDEZ

AVENIDA GRAU

PLAZA 26 DE JULIO

ARCA

SAN MARTIN

PROSPERO

HURTADO

MALECON MALDONADO (EL BOULEVARD)

F

2 DE MAYO

GARCIA SANZ

OVALO GRAU

9 DE DICIEMBRE

J C ARANA

N

AGUIRRE

ABTAO

RAMIREZ

ALFONSO UGARTE

16 DE JULIO

JOSE GALVEZ

Mercado Belén

ATAHUALPA

Police Station

PUERTO BELÉN

0   100 m

Moronacocha ▲

Cemetery (two blocks) ◀

DRINKING & NIGHTLIFE
Arandú Bar	9
El Musmuqui	1
Nikoro	4
Noa	2

EATING
Al Carbón	3
Ari's Burger	10
Dawn on the Amazon Café	6
Huasaí	5
Karma Café	8
La Noche	7
The Yellow Rose of Texas	11

▼ Airport & Nauta

PERU

THE JUNGLE

section, **Malecón Tarapaca**, has fine old mansions with Portuguese *azulejo* tiles, brilliantly extravagant in their Moorish inspiration. The municipal **Museo Amazónico** (Mon–Fri 8am–1pm & 3–5pm, Sat 8am–5pm; free, though a guide may try to take you round in which case a tip will be expected) has very few exhibits on offer, though look out for the collection of fibreglass statues modelled on more than eighty people from different ethnic groups residing in the jungle surrounding Iquitos.

Prospero and around

Strolling along the main shopping street off the Plaza de Armas, **Próspero**, you'll see many fine examples of buildings covered in *azulejos*; a useful one being the **Casa Cohen**, the biggest super-market in the centre. The name serves as a reminder that the boom drew a Jewish community to Iquitos in the early 1900s. There is, in fact, a small Jewish cemetery within the main Peruvian **cemetery**, at Av. Alfonso Ugarte with Av. Fanning (daily 7am–5pm), and both cemeteries are worth a visit, the former for its elegant tiled and Art Deco graves and the latter for wildly colourful and unusual ones – don't miss the tug boat or the castle.

Puerto Belén

Simply follow Prospero south for nine blocks (or take a *motokar*, the brand name for *mototaxis* here), turn left towards the river and you'll see the most memorable *barrio* in Iquitos, **Puerto Belén**. It consists almost entirely of wooden huts raised on stilts and houses constructed on floating platforms, which rise and fall to accommodate the changing water levels. When the tide is high enough, ask around to take a canoe out to look back at the area from the water –a very special experience.

Puerto Belén has changed little over its hundred years or so of life, remaining a poor shanty settlement. While filming *Fitzcarraldo* here, Werner Herzog merely had to make sure that no motorized canoes appeared on screen: virtually everything else looks like an authentic slum town of the nineteenth century. The **Mercado Belén** (best in the mornings from around 7am–1pm) is one of Peru's finest markets – ask for directions to Pasaje Paquito, the busy herbalist alley, which synthesizes the very rich flavour of the place. The whole area is filthy, yet highly atmospheric and somehow beautiful. Remember that this is one of the poorest areas of the city, so leave valuables at home and do not buy any animals or animal products from the market – it encourages illegal poaching, and setting them free may introduce disease into the forest.

Arrival and information

Air Flights land at the Aeropuerto Internacional Francisco Secada Vigneta, 5km southwest of town. Taxis (S15) and *mototaxis* (S8) run to central Iquitos.

Boat If you plan to travel by boat, email the IPerú office (✆ iperuiquitos@promperu.gob.pe), which can provide detailed information in English. Your basic choices are *rápidos* (speedboats) or *motonaves/lanchas* (slow cargo boats), the former being more reliable and a lot faster, and the latter calmer and cheaper, if a little unpredictable. There are two main ports in Iquitos. If you've come by boat from Yurimaguas (5 days), Pucallpa (6–7 days), Leticia or Tabatinga (both 3 days), you'll arrive at Puerto Masusa, some eleven blocks northeast of the Plaza de Armas. For any local journey, head to Puerto Bellavista Nanay, in the suburb of Bellavista (take a *mototaxi*; 10min; S3), for riverboats to islands and other villages nearby.

Tourist information At the corner of Loreto and Raymondi (daily 8.30am–7.30pm; ☎ 065/236-144, ✆ iperuiquitos@promperu.gob.pe). Staff can advise on lodges, tour operators and guides, and can help book accommodation in Iquitos. They also provide free advocacy should you run into any problems with tour companies, or need the police or your embassy. The monthly English-language newspaper *The Iquitos Times* (online at ✆ www.iquitostimes .com) is also a good source of information, and is available at most hotels and restaurants.

Tourist permits If you are planning a trip into the jungle alone or to Pacaya Samiria National Reserve then talk to SERNANP (☎ 065/223-555), located at Calle Jorge Chávez 930–942 (behind the military base), Iquitos.

City transport

Boat If you want to get onto the river itself, canoes can be rented very cheaply from the port at Bellavista Nanay; you can also catch river *colectivos* here.

Combi The majority of the unusual wooden *combis* in Iquitos generally go one-way back and forth out of the city to the airport (S0.80) and as far as km2 on the road to Nauta (S1).

Taxi or motokar There are very few cars in Iquitos, but *motokars* (*mototaxis*) can be taken everywhere. In the city the most expensive ride would be to Bellavista Nanay (S3). There are only a couple of taxi companies that you have to pre-book; Fono Taxi Flores, at Calle Pevas 169 (☎ 065/232-014) is reliable.

Accommodation

El Colibrí Jr. Nauta 172 ☎ 065/241-737, ✉ hostalelcolibri@hotmail.com. A modern, clean and pleasant construction right in the centre. Rooms have cable TV and private bath with hot water, as well as a/c or fans. S60.

Cristal Corazón B&B Calle Nanay 130 ☎ 065/222-070, ✉ cristalcorazon4u@yahoo.com. A cosy B&B with orthopedic beds, healthy breakfasts and a relaxing patio off a communal kitchen. Mosquito nets and repellent can be provided. Host Starr Cross can organize expeditions, lodge stays and *ayahuasca* ceremonies. Dorms S15, rooms S40.

Flying Dog Malecón Tarapacá 592 ☎ 065/242-476, ⊛ www.flyingdogperu.com. As the quality of accommodation in Iquitos can be so variable, you may feel more at ease staying with this reputable chain. The building overlooks the river and is very central. All the backpacker favourites (internet, lockers, kitchen use, TV and DVDs) come as standard. Breakfast included. Dorms S30, rooms S75.

Mad Mick's Bunkhouse Putumayo 163 (upstairs 202) ☎ 065/507-525, ✉ michaelcollis@hotmail.com. British expat Mad Mick will welcome you with a smile to his one room with eight beds, behind the office for his jungle supplies store. Not for those who need personal space, but you can't fault it at the price. Dorm S10.

La Pascana Pevas 133 ☎ 065/231-418, ⊛ www.pascana.com. Very friendly little place with book exchange and on-site agency. Slightly run-down rooms with private bath and fans are on either side

of a flower-filled garden, with tables for soaking up the atmosphere or an early evening drink. Although very central, it is surprisingly tranquil and offers a welcome escape from Iquitos's sometimes hectic street life. BYO mosquito protection. S50.

Eating

Food in Iquitos is exceptionally good for a jungle town; they specialize in fish dishes here but cater pretty well for any taste. As always, the dirt-cheap food can be found at markets like Belén, where a *menú* can be as little as S2.50.

Al Carbón Condamine 115. A good, clean and popular place for grills, with a wide range of choices. Mains S15. Open 6pm–2am.

Ari's Burger Prospero 127. An American-style diner serving more than just burgers, including a mind-boggling variety of jungle juices as well as traditional dishes. The most popular meeting spot in Iquitos and good for late-night munchies. Burger combo average S16. Open 7am–2am.

Dawn on the Amazon Café Corner of Nauta and Malecón Maldonado. Next to its associated tour company, this riverfront restaurant comes highly recommended. Exquisite juice combinations, all-day lunches or breakfasts, as well as main courses for dinner are all offered, as is the *ayahuasca* diet. The food is free from artificial ingredients and only purified water is used in food preparation. Unfortunately the stressed-out waiters let this otherwise wonderful place down. Mains S15. Open 7.30am–11pm.

Huasaí Jr. Fizcarrald 131. Family-run traditional Peruvian restaurant, always heaving with locals. Serves an excellent and huge S10 lunch *menú* including starter, main and jug of juice. Simply delicious. Open 7.30am–4.30pm (sometimes later).

Karma Café Napo 138. Between the plaza and the riverfront. Come for the only free wi-fi in town, but stay for the large range of drinks, sandwiches (S8) and excellent Thai curries (S20). Sofas, bean bags, lava lamps, cosmic art and chill-out music make this a great place to relax. Also offers board games, a small library with guidebooks and a book exchange. Daily noon–midnight.

La Noche Malecón Maldonado 177. With a great location on the Boulevard and a good range of local dishes, *La Noche* is a safe bet for a meal or drink at any time of day. Has a small balcony looking out on the river and comfy sofas inside. Mains average S20. Daily 7am–midnight.

The Yellow Rose of Texas Putumayo 180. Run by a non-Texan from the USA, this place just off the Plaza de Armas is a true Iquitos establishment, a jungle anomaly, and the most popular gringo meeting spot. Very tasty range of international and Peruvian dishes (mains S20) in a Texas-themed atmosphere, including saddles for bar stools and a sports bar upstairs. Open 24hr.

Drinking and nightlife

Arandú Bar Malecón Maldonado 113. With a prime location on the Boulevard, this bar is often packed in the evenings, with seating spilling outside. Serves a range of drinks (beer S6.50) and a few snacks. Open daily 3.30pm–midnight (until 3am at weekends).

El Musmuqui Raymondi 382. A specialist in exotic cocktails, this tiny but lively bar is packed with locals every night of the week (closed Sun). Come here to try traditional jungle liquors, many of which have strong aphrodisiac properties. Open Mon–Sat from 5pm.

Nikoro Down the steps at the end of Pevas. This is one special bar; a huge wooden hut on the river (though in low water; you're 15m up on stilts) serving jungle drinks and cocktails (S10). Sit on the balcony for unrivalled views of the river and the stars. Iquitos's most bohemian and diverse crowd can be found here, from hippies to botanists to doctors. Open mid-afternoon until the last people leave.

Noa Fitzcarrald 298. Easily identified after midnight by the huge number of flashy motorbikes lined up outside, this is the most popular and lively of the clubs in Iquitos. It has three bars and plays lots of Latino music. S15 entrance includes one beer. Open Thurs–Sat 10pm–morning.

Directory

Banks and exchange Banco de Crédito, at Próspero with Putumayo; BBVA Banco Continental, at Sargento Lores 171. Use Interbank, at Av. Próspero 330, for exchanging money as the money-changers on Próspero can't always be trusted.
Consulates Brazil, Sargento Lores 363 (☏065/235-151); Colombia, Calle Calvo de Araujo 431 (☏065/231-461); UK, Jr. Arica 253 (☏065/234-110).
Health Clínica Ana Stahl, at Av. La Marina 285 (☏065/250-025). Open 24hr.
Immigration Migraciones, at Av. Mariscal Cáceres block 18, Moronacocha (☏065/235-371).
Internet Cybercafé on the Plaza de Armas is open 24hr, but be warned; it charges double the price of other internet cafés in Iquitos.
Jungle supplies Mad Mick's Trading Post, Putumayo 184b. Provides everything you need for a jungle trip, for purchase or rent, including rubber boots, rainproof ponchos, sunhats and fishing tackle.
Post office SERPOST, at Jr. Arica 402.
Tourist Police Jr. Sargento Lores 834 (☏065/242-081).

Moving on

Air LAN (☏080/111-234), Peruvian Airlines (☏065/231-074) and Star Perú (☏065/236-208) all have some flights that stop in Tarapoto or Pucallpa before going on to Lima. Flights from US$100 one-way. There is a US$5 departure tax payable at the airport. You can pay in soles rather than US dollars, though you'll be charged slightly more.
Boat Tickets for *lanchas* can only be bought from the ports on the day of travel, while the speedboat companies have offices in town. On the Yurimaguas–Iquitos route, it's possible to stop off in Lagunas or Nauta to find guides and tours to Reserva Nacional Pacaya Samiria (see p.906). Prices should include all meals.

Lagunas & Yurimaguas: Motonaves Eduardo, at Puerto Masusa, Punchana (2–3 days; daily at 6pm except Sun; from S60; ☏065/351-270); Golfinho, at Jr. Raimondi 378 (12hr; 1 boat per week Sat 5am; S210; ☏065/225-118).

Pucallpa: Motonaves Henry, at Puerto Henry, Punchana (4–6 days; Mon, Wed & Fri at 6pm; from S100; ☏065/263-948).

Santa Rosa (three-way border): Puerto Pesquero, at Av. La Marina (2.5–3 days; daily at 6pm except Sun;

from S60; ☎065/250-440); Golfinho, at Jr. Raimondi 378 (☎065/225-118), and Transtur, at Jr. Raimondi 384 (☎065/221-356), both have *rápidos* to the border (8–10hr; daily except Mon at 6am; S200).

Bus The stop for Trans del Sur buses to Nauta is in Belén at the corner of Jr. Prospero with Prolongación Libertad (hourly; 2hr). *Colectivos* also go to Nauta from block 14 of Elias Aguirre (cars leave when full; 1hr 30min).

DAY-TRIPS FROM IQUITOS

For those who want to experience a bit of the jungle without straying too far from the city, there are several easy day-trips from Iquitos. It's simple to hop over to a nearby island for a taste of landlocked beach life or to experience wildlife in safe confines; at the Amazon Animal Orphanage you'll be able to get up close with many rescued jungle species. The following sites can all be done in a day or less, and the Iquitos IPerú office has good maps of how to get to them.

Amazon Animal Orphanage

One of the most popular day-trips from Iquitos is to the **Amazon Animal Orphanage & Pilpintuhuasi Butterfly Farm** in Padre Cocha (Tues–Sun 9am–4pm; S20; ☎01/965-932-999, ⓦwww.amazonanimalorphanage.org). The life's work of Austrian expat Gudrun (she speaks excellent English), this is a butterfly farm and also a sanctuary for jungle animals bought illegally and subsequently confiscated. Many of the jungle's most endangered species are under one roof here and you'll see the process of breeding butterflies, as well as their life cycle from egg to cocoon to caterpillar, in progress. **To get here**, take a *peke peke* (river *colectivo*) from the Bellavista Nanay port in Iquitos (10min by *motokar* from the centre; S3) heading for Padre Cocha (20min); once there, it's a 15-min signposted walk.

Padre Isla and Playa Nanay

The closest place you can get to from Iquitos without a guide or long river trip is **Padre Isla**, an island opposite town in the Amazon River, over 14km long and with beautiful beaches when the water is low. It's easily reached by canoe from Belén or the main waterfront. Alternatively, from the Bellavista Nanay port you can set out by canoe ferry for **Playa Nanay**, the best beach around Iquitos, where bars and cafés are springing up to cater for the weekend crowds. Be aware that currents here are pretty strong and, although there are lifeguards, drownings have occurred.

Moronacocha and around

On the western edge of Iquitos, a tributary of the Nanay forms a long lake called **Moronacocha**, a popular resort for swimming and waterskiing. Near the airport, still on the Nanay, is the agricultural and fishing village of **Santo Tomás**, renowned for its *artesanía* and you can swim and canoe from its beach.

AROUND IQUITOS

The massive river system around Iquitos offers some of the best access to Indian villages, lodges and primary rainforest in the entire Amazon. You can go it alone with the *colectivo* boats that run more or less daily up and down the Amazon River, but it's usually best to travel with one of the many lodges or tour companies (see below & p.913). Before approaching a tour operator it's a good idea to know roughly what you want in terms of time in the jungle, total costs, personal comforts and things you expect to see. Note that many tours include a visit to a jungle tribe; these are tribes who put on the same show multiple times a day and tourists are often disappointed.

Jungle lodges

When choosing a lodge, consider its distance from Iquitos, the company's commitment to conservation, the level of comfort you want and what's included in the price. Most lodge itineraries will include dolphin-watching, fishing, visiting a local

AROUND IQUITOS

0 ————— 50 km

Best areas for spotting wildlife & adventure expeditions

Río Napo

ExplorNapo Lodge, ExplorTambos Camp, ACTS Field Station and Canopy Walkway

Heliconia Lodge

Exporama Lodge

Indiana

Mazán

Río Momón

Exporama Ceiba Tops Lodge

Iquitos

Cumaceba Lodge

Pevas, Santa Rosa, Brazil & Colombia

Río Nanay

Río Momón

Santa Maria

Río Tamshiyacu

Río Itaya

Río Tigre

Río Tahuayo

Muyuna Lodge

Río Yanayacu

Río Marañon

Nauta

Libertad

N

Clavero

Río Yarapa

Río Pucate

Bagazan

Mayo Creek

Cumaceba Creek

Genaro Herrera

Río Curahuayta

Lago Cumaceba

Requena

Río Samiria

Río Yanayacu

BRAZIL

PACAYA SAMIRIA NATIONAL PARK

Angamos

Lagunas & Yurimaguas

PERU

THE JUNGLE

village and night walks. While you can often book when you turn up in Iquitos and barter, the best companies should be booked in advance, have fixed prices and never tout for business in the street. Prices below are based on a 3-day/2-night stay for two people, per person. Companies fix prices in US dollars, so prices in soles may change according to the exchange rate.

Cumaceba Lodge Putumayo 184 ☎065/232-229, Ⓦwww.cumaceba.com. A highly recommended budget option on the Río Yanayacu, some 40km downriver from Iquitos (45min by speedboat), with accommodation in private rustic bungalows with individual bathrooms. Also runs an explorer camp downriver. US$200.

Explorama Av. la Marina 340, Iquitos ☎065/ 252-530, Ⓦwww.explorama.com. Explorama is the top operator in the region and has a good reputation for responsible tourism; not cheap but worth it. It has five sites in the jungle (see website) offering everything from remote camping to the most luxurious lodge in the Amazon. It's possible to go between sites

and tailor your stay to include an excursion to the company's canopy walkway, the longest in the jungle. Ceiba Tops (the most luxurious option, with a/c & pool) US$395.

Heliconia Lodge Ricardo Palma 242 ☎065/231-959, Ⓦwww.amazonriverexpeditions.com. A reputable company offering traditional lodge trips as well as birdwatching stays for groups, or time split between the lodge and one of their two hotels in Iquitos (the *Victoria Regia* and *Hotel Acosta*). Also has a lodge in Pacaya Samiria and boats for cruises, and can offer access to Explorama's canopy walkway. US$300.

Muyuna Putumayo 163 ☎065/242-858, Ⓦwww.muyuna.com. Located close to the Pacaya-Samiria Reserve, and one of the furthest lodges from Iquitos, *Muyuna* offers rustic but comfortable accommodation and very good service. The lodge works hard to distinguish itself as a protector of wild animal rights; and staff are proud to tell you that they will not take you to visit a pre-prepared tribe who will perform then ask for tips. US$360.

905

PACAYA SAMIRIA

RESERVA NACIONAL PACAYA SAMIRIA, around 100km southwest of Iquitos, covers over 20,000 square kilometres (about 1.5 percent of the landmass of Peru and the size of Israel) and is home to the Cocoma tribe, whose main settlement is **Tipishca**. The reserve is a swampland during the rainy season (Dec–March), when the streams and rivers all rise; as such you'll see very different wildlife in the high-water and low-water seasons (both good in different ways). Athough it can end up costing more than lodge stays in Iquitos, for anyone interested in wildlife, this reserve offers an unbelievable quantity and variety of flora and fauna; more than a thousand types of vertebrates exist here, including nearly a third of the bird species of Peru and one percent of the reptile species of the world.

Note that while it's possible to visit the reserve via an operator in Iquitos, you'll need at least five days to explore it properly, and it won't be cheap (lodges cost double or more than ones nearer Iquitos). The cheapest way to do it is to go to the town of **Lagunas** (one day upstream from Yurimaguas) and find a tour/guide going from there. You can do the same from **Nauta** if coming from Iquitos, though this tends to be a little more expensive. It's recommended that you go with a licensed operator from Iquitos; if you do, the entry fee to the park (normally S60 for 3 days) will be included. If you are determined to go alone, talk to SERNANP before you go, as it provides maps and information on the region. You should, of course, bring mosquito nets, hammocks, insect repellent and all the necessary food and medicines (see p.901).

THE SOUTHERN SELVA: MADRE DE DIOS

Part of the Peruvian Amazon basin – a large, forested region with a searingly hot and humid climate, punctuated with sudden cold spells (*friajes*) between June and August – the **southern selva** regions of Peru have only been systematically explored since the 1950s and were largely unknown until the twentieth century, when rubber began to leave Peru through Bolivia and Brazil, eastwards along the rivers.

Named after the broad river that flows through the heart of the

---

CROSSING INTO COLOMBIA OR BRAZIL: THE THREE-WAY FRONTIER

Leaving or entering Peru via the Amazon is an intriguing adventure; by river this inevitably means experiencing the three-way frontier. The cheapest and most common route is by river from Iquitos to Santa Rosa, some ten hours by *rápida* (speedboat) or 3–4 days in a standard riverboat. Boats will drop you off at immigration, where you must obtain an exit stamp from Peru if you're leaving (you must show your tourist card to do this), or getting an entry stamp and tourist card if arriving. Larger boats may take you all the way to Tabatinga or Leticia, in which case an immigration official may board the vessel and do the paperwork there and then.

There are few hostels and cafés in Santa Rosa; the small *La Brisa del Amazonas* is both, and the owner is a useful source of information. Once through immigration, ferries (10min; S6) connect the town with Tabatinga and Leticia (in Brazil and Colombia respectively, although they're pretty much extensions of the same city). It's sometimes possible to fly from Iquitos to Santa Rosa, although the routes are run by small airlines that come and go. At the time of writing there were no flights, but check with IPerú in Iquitos. From Tabatinga or Leticia to onward destinations in Colombia or Brazil, try Aero Republica (⊛www.aerorepublica.com), Satena (⊛www.satena.com), Aires (⊛www.aires.aero) or Trip (⊛www.voetrip.com.br).

southern jungle, the still relatively wild *departamento* of **Madre de Dios** is changing rapidly, with agribusinesses moving in to clear mahogany trees and set up brazil nut plantations, and prospectors panning for gold dust along the riverbanks. Nearly half of Madre de Dios *departamento*'s 78,000 square kilometres are accounted for by national parks and protected areas such as **Manu Biosphere Reserve**, **Tambopata-Candamo Reserved Zone** and **Bahuaja-Sonene National Park**, between them containing some of the richest flora and fauna in the world.

Madre de Dios still feels very much like a frontier zone, centred on the rapidly growing river town of **Puerto Maldonado**, near the Bolivian border, supposedly founded by legendary explorer and rubber baron Fitzcarraldo.

Puerto Maldonado

Now that the road from Cusco has been paved, what used to be an adventurous (and uncomfortable) two- or three-day journey by truck has now turned into a smooth overnight bus ride. Despite its position firmly on the Interoceanic Highway, connecting the Peruvian and Brazilian coasts, the jungle town of **PUERTO MALDONADO** still has a raw, chaotic feel to it. Puerto's wide streets often culminate in pitted dirt tracks, which are barely passable in the rainy season and where its multitude of beeping *mototaxis* raise clouds of dust at other times of year. With an economy based on gold panning, logging, cattle ranching and Brazil-nut gathering, it has grown enormously over the last twenty years, becoming the thriving capital of a region that feels very much on the threshold of major upheavals, with a rapidly developing ecotourism industry.

The traffic-choked **León de Velarde** is the town's main artery, culminating in the attractive **Plaza de Armas**, near one of the town's bustling ports, and with an attractive if bizarre Chinese pagoda-style clock tower at its centre; every Sunday morning, military parades are held here, reminding you of the town's strategic position near the Bolivian and Brazilian borders. Ten blocks from the plaza is the large, bustling **market**, which covers an entire block, and if you follow Fitzcarraldo beyond it, you'll reach the **Obelisco** (daily 10am–4pm; S2), a viewpoint offering an expansive panorama of the entire city.

Arrival and getting around

Air If you arrive by plane, unless you're being picked up as part of an organized tour, airport transfer is simplest by *mototaxi*, costing around S7 for the 8-km dusty ride, or else S5 for a motorbike taxi if you don't have much luggage.

Boat Puerto Maldonado has two main river ports: one on the Río Tambopata, at the southern end of León de Velarde, the other on the Río Madre de Dios, at the northern end of León de Velarde. From either it's possible to hire a boatman and canoe for a river trip (S90 per person, per day, for a minimum of 2 people). From the Río Madre de Díos dock there are twice-weekly passenger boats from the Tambopata dock which go as far as the indigenous community of Baltimore and can drop people off at lodges along the way, though you'll need your SERNANP permit (see p.901) first. It's significantly cheaper and easier to get in touch with local guides (see p.909) and go with an organized tour.

ACCOMMODATION
Anaconda Lodge	**B**
Hostal Royal Inn	**D**
Moderno Hostal	**A**
Tambopata Hostel	**C**

EATING & DRINKING
Burgos's House	**1**
La Estrella	**7**
Heladería Gustitos del Cura	**3**
Kongo Cevichería	**6**
Pizzería El Hornito	**4**
Restaurant	**5**
Witite	**2**

Infierno (30km), Hospital Sanita Roasa & Port Area (Tambopata)

Bus Puerto Maldonado's new Terminal Terrestre is located 2km away from the airport, along Carretera Tambopata, and this is the arrival point for all buses from Cusco, Lima, Arequipa and Juliaca. Buses from Brazil arrive on the other side of the Tambopata River and you have to take a passenger ferry across to the city (see p.910).

Mototaxi and motorbike The quickest way of getting around town is to hail a *mototaxi* (S2 in-town flat rate, but check before getting on) or passenger-carrying motorbikes (S1 flat rate). If you have a lot of ground to cover in town, try one of the places along Prada between Puno and Velarde that rent mopeds for around S4 per hour (no deposit, but passports and driving licences required), though this option might be a little intimidating for some, given the local driving standards. Make sure there's ample petrol in the tank.

Information

Tourist information If flying technically, you have to go through a yellow-fever vaccination checkpoint at Puerto Maldonado's small but modern airport, though it's sometimes closed. There's also a small tourist information kiosk at the airport with limited information on jungle lodges, the Tambopata-Candamo reserve and the Bahuaja-Sonene national park. The inconveniently located Dircetur office (Mon–Fri 8.30am–4.30pm, Sat 8.30am–1pm ☏ 082/571-164) at Fonavi and San Martín, a 5-min ride from the Plaza de Armas, stocks basic information on Puerto Maldonado's attractions. The SERNANP office at Av. 28 de Julio, 8th block (☏ 082/573-278) has handouts on the nearby national park and reserve; it collects entrance fees (S30) for a permit, for those planning on going independently.

Tours Best Expeditions at Tambopata Hostel (☏ 082/574-201) organizes popular trips to Lago Sandoval and Lago Valencia, as well as *ayahuasca* ceremonies at the indigenous community of Infierno. *Wasai Lodge* also offers half-day and day-trips to Lago Sandoval, though they tend to be quite short.

Accommodation

Anaconda Lodge 600m away from the airport, along Av. Aeropuerto s/n ☏ 082/792-726, ⓦ www.anacondajunglelodge.com. You may be excused for thinking that you are in paradise when you sit down amid lush tropical gardens for some excellent, authentic Thai food at one of the very few Thai restaurants in Peru. On top of that, this superb Swiss-Thai lodge features comfortable

bungalows with hammocks (some en-suite), a small pool and no fewer than eight species of monkey living on the property. The owners also organize tours to Lake Sandoval. Camping is also allowed. Camping S20, rooms S80.

Hostal Royal Inn 2 de Mayo 333 ☏ 082/573-464, ⓔ mitsukate4@hotmail.com. Large, somewhat worn but clean rooms with fans and cable TV. To get away from the street noise, ask for a room facing the courtyard. S45.

Moderno Hostal Billingshurst 357 ☏ 082/571-063. A long-established family-run guesthouse with very basic rooms with shared bath. Nothing remarkable, though they are very cheap. S20.

Tambopata Hostel 26 de Diciembre 234 ☏ 082/574-201, ⓦ www.tambopatahostel .com. This excellent place, run by a former Posada Amazonas guide, has spotless, spacious dorms, hammocks in the garden, and the friendly, accommodating young owners cook up a proper breakfast in the mornings, complete with fresh fruit juice. This is also the best place in town to organize reasonably priced trips into the surrounding area. You may not get much sleep though, as the walls are quite thin and the guests lively. Dorms S20, rooms S60.

Eating, drinking and nightlife

Burgos's House Puno 106. If you want to try jungle dishes in a more upscale setting, then this is the place. This restaurant's specialities are the fish dishes, as well as *juanes* (fish or chicken steamed with rice, wrapped in banana leaves) and the service is excellent. Mains from S25.

La Estrella Arequipa 229. Clean, shiny, and air-conditioned, like an American fast-food joint, this is a favourite spot for locals craving roast chicken and nothing but roast chicken. Except maybe fries and a soft drink. Quarter-chicken meal S8.

Heladería Gustitos del Cura Velarde 474. Sate your sweet cravings at this French-owned café on the Plaza de Armas with an excellent range of cakes (from S6) and ice-cream flavours.

Kongo Cevichería Carrión 182. Bright, Informal, family-run lunch spot where the mama cooks up massive portions of excellent *arroz con mariscos* (S20). The *ceviche*, made with local fish, is very tasty.

Pizzería El Hornito Carrión 392. Having moved to new premises after a recent fire, this local institution continues to draw the locals and visitors with its excellent range of wood-fired pizza (dinner only). Mains from S15.

Restaurant 2 de Mayo and Madre de Dios. It may be nameless, but all the locals know where it is;

grab a seat outside and try some grilled jungle specialities, such as *paiche* (fish) with a grilled, mashed ball of plantain. Meal S10.

Witite Velarde 151. An excellent example of the lively local nightlife, this disco packs in the young locals on Friday and Saturday night with a range of Latino music, as does the nearby *Teokas* on Loreto.

Directory

Banks and exchange BCP at Carrión 201, Plaza de Armas, has an ATM and changes US dollars. Banco de la Nación, next to it, does not take all cards.
Hospital Hospital Santa Rosa at Cajamarca 171 (☎082/571-019).
Laundry There's a laundry at Velarde 898; most guesthouses offer laundry service.
Post office Velarde 675.
Telephones and internet Telefónica del Peru, at Loreto and Velarde on the Plaza, is your best bet for phone calls. There is an internet café along Loreto on the Plaza (S1 per 15min), though connections can be slow; better is UnAMad on Av. 2 de Mayo 287.
Visas Oficina de migraciones, Av. 2 de Julio 467 (Mon–Fri 8am–1pm ☎082/571-069). Get your passport stamped here if leaving for Bolivia via Puerto Heath.

Moving on

Most bus companies can be found in the main Terminal Terrestre, among them Movil Tours (☎082/795-785), Expreso Machupicchu (☎082/799-039) and Maldonado Tours (☎082/503-032).
Air There are several flights daily to Lima and Cusco with LAN and Peru Airlines.
Boat From the port on Río Tambopata, there's a very cheap ferry service (dawn–dusk daily; S1) across the river to the newish road to Brazil, from where there are buses bound for Iñapari on the border with Brazil, and the city of Río Branco in Brazil proper. From the Río Madre de Díos dock you can hire boats to take you to the Bolivian border.
Bus Arequipa via Juliaca (daily at 3pm; 20hr); Cusco (daily between 3.30–7.30pm; 10–12hr); Río Branco, Brazil (daily at noon; 9hr).

WILDLIFE RESERVES AROUND PUERTO MALDONADO

Madre de Dios boasts spectacular virgin lowland rainforest and exceptional wildlife. Brazil-nut-tree trails, a range of lodges, some excellent local guides and ecologists plus indigenous and colonist cultures are all within a few hours of Puerto Maldonado. There are two main ways to explore: either by arranging your own boat and boatman, or by taking an excursion up to one of the lodges, which is more expensive but also more convenient.

Less than one hour downriver from Puerto Maldonado (90min return) is **Lago Sandoval**, a large oxbow lake, home to caimans, giant otters and a host of birds. It's best to stay here overnight and do a boat ride on the lake in the early morning – the best time for wildlife-spotting, though it's also possible to do the lake as a day-trip. Take one of the recommended tours (see p.911) or hire a boat (around S120) to drop you off at the start of the trail (about 1hr to the lake) and to pick you up later. Bring your own food and water.

Further along the river, 60km from Puerto Maldonado, lies the huge **Lago Valencia**. It takes at least two days to visit, and its remoteness increases your chances of seeing wildlife, both while gliding through the still lake and along the hiking trails around it; the lake also features excellent fishing opportunities.

South of Puerto Maldonado, Río Tambopata flows into the heart of the **Reserva Nacional Tambopata**, where you'll find several excellent lodges, as well as the indigenous communities of Infierno and Batimore. The remote **Parque Nacional Bahuaja-Sonene** is even further upstream (6hr minimum) and features some of the best wildlife in the Peruvian Amazon as well as the Tambopata Research Center, located next to the Colpa de Guacamayos – one of the largest macaw clay licks in the Amazon. To visit the reserve and the national park, you will need to book a guided tour at one of the lodges.

Tour operators and lodges

Compared with independent travel, an **organized excursion** saves time and adds varying degrees of comfort. It also ensures that you go with someone who knows the area, who speaks English and can introduce you to the flora, fauna, culture and regions. It's best to book a trip in Cusco directly through the lodge offices or online before travelling to Puerto Maldonado. There are several daily flights from Cusco to Puerto Maldonado, and most Cusco agencies will organize plane tickets (US$90–110) for you if you take their tours. The cheapest option is a two-day and one-night tour, but you will spend most of your time travelling and sleeping, so it's best to allow at least 3 to 4 days.

A stay at one of the many rustic lodges around Puerto Maldonado, mainly on the ríos Madre de Dios and Tambopata, offers a good taste of the jungle, and the cost typically includes full board (though not tips for guides or drinks), transfers and bilingual guides, though the quality of wildlife sightings depends on the location; the further you travel from Puerto Maldonado, the more likely you are to see large mammals. A list of recommended lodges follows.

Eco Amazonia Lodge Calle Garcilaso 210, office 206, Cusco ☎084/236-159; Calle Enrique Palacios 292, Miraflores, Lima ☎01/242-2708; Puerto Maldonado ☎082/573491; ⓦwww .ecoamazonia.com.pe. Less than two hours downriver from Puerto Maldonado, this large establishment offers basic bungalows with hammocks. Packages include visits to Monkey Island, the secluded "Cocha Perdida" oxbow lake, hikes in the rainforest and wildlife spotting along the Madre de Díos tributaries. A shamanic session involving the hallucinogenic jungle vine *ayahuasca* is also on offer. From US$210 per person for 3 days and 2 nights.

Explorer's Inn Plateros 365, Cusco ☎084/235-342; Alcanflores 459, Miraflores, Lima ☎01/447-8888, Puerto Maldonado ☎082/572-078, ⓦwww .explorersinn.com. Located 58km south of Puerto Maldonado in the Tambopata reserve and featuring en-suite rustic doubles and triples. It offers 38-km of forest trails, canoeing on the oxbow lake of Cococcocha, (inhabited by giant otters), and visits to a macaw clay lick, accompanied by experienced naturalist guides. English, French and German spoken. From US$198 per person for 3 days and 2 nights.

Posada Amazonas Lodge Contact through Rainforest Expeditions, Aramburu 166, Miraflores, Lima ☎01/421-8347, Portal de Carnes 236, Cusco ☎084/246-243, or Puerto Maldonado ☎082/572-575, ⓦwww.perunature .com. *Posadas* is probably the region's best lodge for its relationship with locals – it's owned by the Ese Eja community of Infierno – and for its wildlife research. Resident multilingual researchers act as guides, and most packages include a visit to Lago Tres Chimbadas for caiman- and giant otter-spotting. Additional trips to one of the largest macaw clay licks in the Amazon (6–8hr upriver) can also be arranged; a minimum of six days is recommended for complete tours. The lodge itself features large, comfortable en-suite doubles with hammocks, set in three native-style buildings, plus excellent food and a central dining-area and lecture room. Similar is the newer *Refugio Amazonas*, located between the two other lodges and offering the same programmes. From US$315 per person for 3 days and 2 nights.

MANU BIOSPHERE RESERVE

Encompassing almost 20,000 square kilometres (about half the size of Switzerland) on the foothills of the eastern Andes, **MANU,** declared a Biosphere Reserve by UNESCO in 1977, features a uniquely varied environment of pristine rainforest, from crystalline cloudforest streams and waterfalls down to slow-moving, chocolate-brown rivers in the dense lowland jungle. Manu is one of the most biologically diverse places in South America; rich in macaw clay licks and otter lagoons, it's also home to thirteen species of monkey and seven species of macaw.

Manu is reachable either via an arduous six-hour bus journey along a bumpy dirt road, followed by several

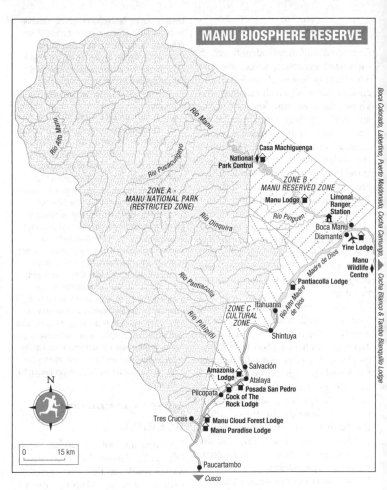

MANU BIOSPHERE RESERVE

Río Alto Manu

Río Manu

Río Pucacungayo

Casa Machiguenga

National Park Control

ZONE A - MANU NATIONAL PARK (RESTRICTED ZONE)

ZONE B - MANU RESERVED ZONE

Manu Lodge

Limonal Ranger Station

Río Pinguen

Río Dinquira

Boca Manu
Diamante

Yine Lodge

Manu Wildlife Centre

Río Pantiacolla

Madre de Díos

Río Alto Madre de Díos

Pantiacolla Lodge

Río Piñipiñi

ZONE C - CULTURAL ZONE

Itahuania

Shintuya

Amazonia Lodge

Salvación

Atalaya

Posada San Pedro

Pilcopata

Cock of The Rock Lodge

Tres Cruces

Manu Cloud Forest Lodge

Manu Paradise Lodge

N

0   15 km

Paucartambo

Cusco

Boca Colorado, Labertino, Puerto Maldonado, Cocha Camungo, ▶ Cocha Blanco & Tambo Blanquillo Lodge

hours along Río Madre de Díos, or by tiny, weather-dependent planes, making it a destination for serious jungle enthusiasts with at least a week to spare. The reserve is divided into three parts: the **cultural zone**, encompassing the bus route and several villages within the cloudforest; the **reserved zone**, with the jungle lodges and oxbow lakes, located along Río Madre de Díos and Río Manu, accessible only as part of a guided tour; and the **restricted zone**, consisting of pristine jungle, home to several indigenous communities and uncontacted tribes, and completely off-limits to visitors.

What to see and do

The highlights of most visits to Manu include the trail network and lakes of **Cocha Salvador** (the largest of Manu's oxbows) and **Cocha Otorongo** – bountiful jungle areas rich in animal, water and birdlife, both located along Río Manu. Cocha Otorongo is best known for the family of **giant otters** who live here; because of this, there is a floating platform that can be manoeuvred to observe the otters fishing and playing from a safe distance. Other wildlife includes the plentiful **caimans** – the white alligators and rarer black ones – and you can usually see several species of **monkey** (dusky titis, woolly monkeys, red howlers, brown capuchins and the larger spider monkeys). Sometimes big mammals such as **capybara** or **white-lipped peccaries** also lurk in the undergrowth and the fortunate have been known to see a jaguar. Also along Río Manu you'll find the Manu Wildlife Centre, located near a clay lick popular with tapirs, while further along the river to the east, a short boat ride and hike away, is a large *colpa* (clay lick), frequented by colourful flocks of macaws.

The **flora** of Manu is as outstanding as its wildlife. Huge cedar trees can be seen along the trails, covered in hand-like vines climbing up their vast trunks, as well as the giant Catahua trees, traditionally the preferred choice for making dugout canoes, and the "erotic palm" with its suggestive-looking roots.

The above attractions aside, for many, the jungle experience is made unforgettable simply by the long journeys along the river, far away from civilization, spotting herons, egrets, vultures, storks and toucans, and watching the pristine jungle pass by, or waking up under a mosquito net in the heart of the rainforest to the sounds of howler monkeys.

Tour operators

There are quite a few **tour operators** competing for travellers who want to visit Manu; however, they do vary quite a bit in quality of guiding, level of comfort and price range. The companies below have a responsible attitude towards the reserve and are keen to keep the impact of tourism to a minimum. Many companies offer a choice of land or air transportation into Manu; a good option is to arrive overland, as the scenery is spectacular, but to return by air. When flying to and from Boca Manu, bear in mind that planes are small and flight schedules are affected by weather conditions, making timetables unreliable.

Atalaya Arequipa 251, Cusco ℡084/228-327, ⓦwww.atalayaperu.com. One of the only companies offering combined Manu and Tambopata tours, as well as ecological volunteer placements in the jungle. Atalaya has its own reserve, but uses the indigenous-owned and run *Casa Matsiguenka* for accommodation on many of its tours. Also offers mystical programmes where you can experiment with the hallucinogenic *ayahuasca* vine, and a course in the use of medicinal plants. From US$470 per person for 5 days and 4 nights, including land transport in and out. Discount of 10 percent for SAE members.

Manu Adventures Plateros 356 Cusco ℡084/261-640, ⓦwww.manuadventures .com. Popular, reputable operator offering 4-day trips into the Cultural Zone and 8-day adventures to the Reserved Zone. Optional extras include rafting, zipping down a canopy line and a visit to the mammal clay lick near their own *Erika Lodge* in the Cultural Zone, as well as visits to the oxbow lakes during the longer trip. Five-day "esoteric" trips are also available and involve shamanic rituals using medicinal and hallucinogenic plants. From US$700 for six days.

Pantiacolla Tours Saphi 554, Cusco ☎084/238-323, ⊛www.pantiacolla.com. A company with a reputation for serious eco-adventure tours. Its cheapest option is a 9-day tour that takes groups in and out by bus and boat, while the more expensive 5- to 7-day-trips go in by road and out by plane from Boca Manu. All trips include visits to Cocha Salvador and Cocha Otorongo, while longer options also take in the macaw clay lick and a canopy tower. It has an excellent lodge on the Río Alto Madre de Dios, surrounded by numerous hiking trails, and its tours into the Reserve Zone are based in rustic lodges. From US$890 per person for 9 days and 8 nights, including land transport in and out. Discount of 5 percent for SAE members.

Uruguay

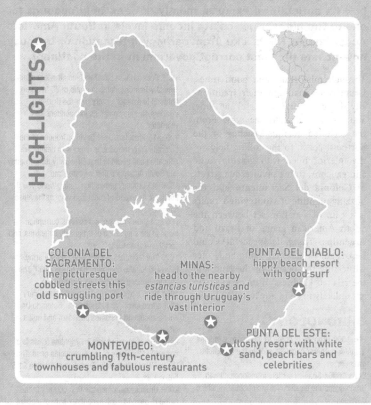

HIGHLIGHTS ✪

COLONIA DEL SACRAMENTO:
line picturesque cobbled streets this old smuggling port ✪

MINAS:
head to the nearby *estancias turísticas* and ride through Uruguay's vast interior ✪

PUNTA DEL DIABLO:
hippy beach resort with good surf ✪

PUNTA DEL ESTE:
floshy resort with white sand, beach bars and celebrities ✪

MONTEVIDEO:
crumbling 19th-century townhouses and fabulous restaurants ✪

ROUGH COSTS

DAILY BUDGET Basic US$30/ occasional treat US$40

DRINK Pilsen beer (1 litre) US$3

FOOD *Asado de tira* steak US$10

HOSTEL/BUDGET HOTEL US$15–30

TRAVEL Montevideo–Colonia del Sacramento (150km) by bus: 2hr 30min, US$7

FACT FILE

POPULATION 3.5 million

AREA 176,215 sq km

LANGUAGE Spanish

CURRENCY Peso Uruguayo (UR$)

CAPITAL Montevideo (population: 1.6 million)

INTERNATIONAL PHONE CODE ☎598.

TIME ZONE GMT -3hr

Introduction

Hit hard by the financial collapse of neighbouring Argentina in 2001, Uruguay has rebounded faster than its bigger neighbor. Its agricultural exports, mostly of beef, help account for one of the highest per capita income levels in South America. According to NGOs like Transparency International, Uruguay now boasts the least corrupt government in the continent.

Through misfortune and good times, Uruguayans maintain their traditionally laidback and cheerful attitude, and it's not hard to see why. From the secluded **surfing beaches** of the northern coast, to the rolling fields of the interior filled with grazing cattle and gauchos, to the picturesque streets of **Colonia del Sacramento** and the buzzing nightlife of **Montevideo**, theirs is a gem of a nation set between the South American giants of Brazil and Argentina. *Tranquilo* (peaceful) could be Uruguay's national motto and, after witnessing the beauty of the land and the relaxed kindness of its people, you are unlikely to be in any hurry to leave.

CHRONOLOGY

Pre-1600 Uruguay is home to the Charrua Indians, a hunter-gatherer people hostile to the European invaders.

Early 1600s Spanish settlers introduce cattle to Uruguay and the gaucho lifestyle of cattle-ranching develops.

1680 The Portuguese establish Colonia del Sacramento as a port to smuggle goods into Buenos Aires. It is the first major colony in Uruguay.

1726 The Spanish retaliate by founding Montevideo in an attempt to cement their power in the region. Their wars with the Portuguese continue for the next century.

1811–20 The Spanish leave Uruguay, only for Brazil and Argentina to fight over control of the territory.

1827 General Juan Lavalleja leads the legendary Treinta y Tres Orientales (a group of 33 freedom fighters) to a major victory over the Brazilian invaders. Uruguay gains its independence a year later.

1903–15 President José Batlle y Ordoñez of the Colorado Party introduces reforms to healthcare, education and benefits that effectively turn Uruguay into South America's first welfare state.

1939–45 Uruguay grows rich during World War II thanks to its export of meat and wool to the Allied nations.

1950s/1960s Inflation and political corruption leads to the stagnation of Uruguay's industries, and social unrest ensues.

1973 The Congress is dissolved and the army is invited to take control of the government. The country slides into a military dictatorship.

1984 Unable to quell public unrest, the military allows free elections to take place. Colorado Dr Julio Sanguinetti becomes president and holds office until 1989.

2001 The economic crisis in Argentina leads to a collapse in the value of the Argentinian peso. The US and World Bank bails Argentina out with a $1.5 billion loan.

2009 Uruguay becomes the first country in the world to provide each secondary school student with a free computer through the One Laptop Per Child programme, an NGO based at MIT in Cambridge, MA.

2009 José Mujica, a former militant leftist taken prisoner and tortured during the military regime, easily wins the presidency.

2010 The Uruguayan national football squad become national heroes after coming fourth in the World Cup.

WHEN TO VISIT

One of Uruguay's main draws is its beaches, so it's best to visit from November to February, when it's warm. Winters in Uruguay can be downright frigid, with cold wet air blowing in from the ocean.

Basics

ARRIVAL

Most visitors to Uruguay fly into Aero puerto Carrasco in Montevideo; those entering from Argentina can also catch a ferry from Buenos Aires to either Montevideo or Colonia del Sacramento. Overland passage is possible from neighbouring Brazil, and in 2010 Argentina and Uruguay reopened the bus routes connecting the two countries.

By air

Uruguay's main international airport is Montevideo's **Aeropuerto Carrasco,** which receives direct flights from Asunción (Paraguay), Miami, Madrid, Santiago (Chile), São Paulo and several other Brazilian cities. Aerolineas Argentinas (☏02/902-3694, ⓦwww .areolineas.com.ar) offers two flights every day from Buenos Aires.

By boat

Passenger ferries are the most common means for backpackers to cross between Buenos Aires and the major sightseeing towns of the Uruguayan coast. Every day, Buquebus (ⓦwww.buquebus.com) has three direct connections from Buenos Aires to Montevideo and at least seven to Colonia del Sacramento.

By bus

At the time of writing, bus connections between Argentina and Uruguay had just reopened after the two countries resolved a political dispute. When the turmoil clears, regular services to Montevideo and the towns of western Uruguay from Buenos Aires can be expected to resume. From Brazil, the bus companies EGA (☏02/901-2530, ⓦwww.egakeguay.com) and

TTL (☏0055 51/3342-6477, ⓦwww .ttl.com.br) provide services to Montevideo from Río de Janeiro and other cities on the southern Brazilian coast.

VISAS

Citizens of the EU, US, Canada and South Africa – among many other nations – are not required to purchase a visa to visit Uruguay. For those who need one, the cost is around US$50.

GETTING AROUND

By bike

With a predominantly flat landscape and good-quality roads, Uruguay is a tempting place for cyclists. Accommodation is never more than 50km apart along the coast and there are repair shops in many cities. As with elsewhere in South America, however, you must beware of the recklessness of local drivers, in both the packed streets of Montevideo and in the countryside.

By bus

The most convenient and cheapest means of transport in Uruguay are **intercity buses**, which operate from the bus terminal (*terminal de ómnibus*) in most towns. A range of companies operate these and tickets are bought in advance at kiosks in the terminal. Wi-fi has been added to several buses, at no extra charge. Local bus trips are slower and less comfortable, but also very cheap.

By road

Public transport in Uruguay is centred on buses and there are no major operational rail links. While it is possible to hire cars, it costs at least UR$750 a day.

ACCOMMODATION

The standard of accommodation in Uruguay is generally good, and hostels

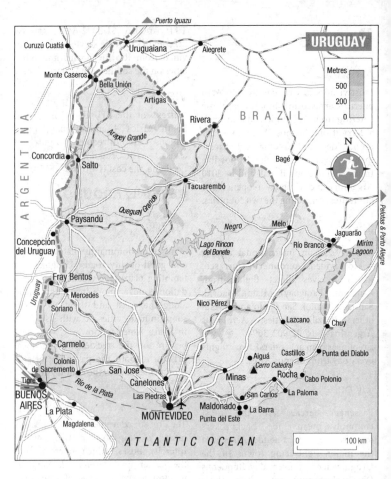

are sprouting up all along the coast. Off the main tourist routes, however, places to stay can be few and far between. Tourist offices usually have a list of hotels and private rooms.

Affiliated hostels

All the large Uruguayan towns have at least one of these, which cost around UR$260 per person; for a complete list check Ⓦwww.hihostels.com/dba /country-Uruguay-UY.en.htm. In large cities they're centrally located, open year-round and often provide amenities like internet access and laundry service; sometimes they impose lockouts and curfews.

Private hostels

These proliferate in Montevideo and Punta del Este and are now cropping up in the other cities. Private hostels generally offer excellent service for around UR$300–350 per person, with group leisure activities and free breakfasts often included. During the summer holidays of December–March it's advisable to book ahead.

Budget hotels and private rooms

There is usually at least one cheap hotel in most towns, offering spartan but habitable rooms with communal toilet and shower for around UR$500. Prices increase fifty percent for en-suite bathroom, TV and breakfast, although many have excellent discounts for students. Tourist offices can also often find you cheap rooms in private houses (*pensiones* and posadas) for around UR$400.

FOOD

Uruguay may not provide the most cosmopolitan of culinary experiences, but if you enjoy **beef** or most kinds of **seafood**, you will not go hungry. Uruguayan steakhouses (*parrillas*) serve steaks that are larger and (as the always partisan locals insist) more tender than their Argentinian counterparts, with the most popular cuts being the ribs (*asado de tira*) and tenderloin (*bife de chorizo*).

The Italian immigrants who arrived in the late nineteenth century left their mark with the ubiquitous pizza and pasta restaurants, which are in general the best dining option for **vegetarians**. Otherwise, outside Montevideo, people looking for meals without meat (*sin carne*) are likely to become highly acquainted with the local supermarket; these generally have salad counters that provide filling, nutritious meals, often the cheapest option when you're in a rush. The **desserts** (*postres*) also bear an Italian influence. Ice creams here are among the most sumptuous on the continent; look out for the flavour *dulce de leche* (a caramel-like syrup). The national snack is the **chivito**, a steak sandwich with a hard-boiled egg, lettuce and tomatoes served on a round bun.

Lunch and dinner are both eaten late; you'll normally be eating on your own if you arrive before 8.30pm for dinner. Restaurant **prices** are low: in most places outside of Montevideo and Punta del Este you can have a two-course meal with a drink for UR$300.

DRINK

Uruguayans traditionally enjoy weekends sitting around drinking and chatting from the afternoon onwards, and the palatable local beers – especially the ubiquitous **Pilsen** – come in 1-litre bottles (UR$5) fit for the purpose. There are always inexpensive bottles of top Argentinian wines available, but it's also worth trying the local produce, not least when served "medio y medio" (a blend of sparkling and slightly sweet white wine). Coffee and *mate* are the kings of non-alcoholic drinks here. The former is available in every café and restaurant, although espresso is less common. Tea and bottled water are always available, and sometimes fresh orange or grapefruit juice too. Tap water is fine to drink.

CULTURE AND ETIQUETTE

Uruguayans of all ages tend to be warm, relaxed people, fond of lively conversation over a beer or barbecue

---

THE ART OF DRINKING MATE

You are unlikely to have a single walk down a street in Uruguay without seeing someone carrying the thermos, pots and metal straw (*bombilla*) required for mate. In a tradition that goes back to the earliest gauchos, Uruguayans are said to drink even more of the grassy tea than Argentines and a whole set of social rituals surrounds it. At the close of a meal, the *mate* is meticulously prepared before being passed round in a circle; the drinker makes a small sucking noise when the pot needs to be refilled, but if this is your position, beware making three such noises: this is considered rude.

(*asado*). As a nation in which the overwhelming majority of people are descended from Italian and Spanish immigrants, Uruguay also maintains some conservative **Catholic** religious and social practices, especially in the countryside. Men are often seen as the breadwinner and it is still rare to see women travelling alone at night. Uruguayans display a rugged sense of independence that recalls the romantic figure of the **gaucho**, the cowboys that still roam the grassy plains of the interior. It's usual to leave a ten percent **tip** anywhere with table service.

SPORTS AND OUTDOOR ACTIVITIES

Ever since the first World Cup in 1930 was held in Uruguay and won by the national team, **football** has been the sport to raise the passions of the normally laidback Uruguayans. Local superstar Diego Forlán led the national team to fourth place in the 2010 World Cup, cause for widespread celebration. In the countryside, **horseriding** is more a part of working life than a sport, but there are now many opportunities for tourists to go riding, especially in the Estancias Turísticas around Minas. **Cycling** is a popular way of seeing the cities (many hostels provide free or cheap bikes), while **fishing** is another favoured afternoon pursuit. **Surfing** is still developing as a sport for the Uruguayans, and many beach resorts lack board-renting facilities year-round, but plenty of foreigners are already taking advantage of the fantastic Atlantic surf at beaches like Punta del Diablo and La Paloma.

COMMUNICATIONS

Post offices (*correos*) provide an expensive and frequently unreliable service for international mail; for urgent deliveries, you are much better using a private mailing company like FedEx, at Av. Rivera 3528, Montevideo (☎02/628-4829). Poste restante services are only available in Montevideo. Post offices usually open Mon–Sat 8am–1pm and 4–7pm. For **public phones** you can buy a card (*tarjeta telefónica*), available at post offices, or use change. Internet cafés charge UR$10–35 per hour and are present in all towns.

CRIME AND SAFETY

Uruguay is a very safe country to travel in, though inevitably **thefts** from dorms and pickpocketing do occur, especially in Montevideo and the beach resorts during the summer months. You should thus store your valuables in lockers whenever possible. The Uruguayan police are courteous but unlikely to speak English.

HEALTH

There are adequate public **hospitals** in the major cities, although many foreigners rely on the expensive private medical cover run by companies like Medicina Personalizada (☎02/711 1000, ⓦwww.mp.com.uy).

INFORMATION AND MAPS

Even most small towns have their resident **tourist office**, the vast majority of which provide friendly, helpful advice for budget travellers, especially regarding inexpensive places to stay and any potential discounts while sightseeing. They generally have basic maps of local areas, but you are most likely to find high-quality road maps (UR$200) in the petrol stations that are common on the major roads and in cities.

MONEY AND BANKS

The unit of currency is the **peso uruguayo** (UR$). Coins come as 50 centimos and 1, 2, 5, and 10 pesos; notes as 10, 20, 50, 100, 200, 500 and 1000 pesos. At the time of writing, the **exchange rate** was £1 = UR$31.30, €1 = UR$26 and US$1 = UR$20.

Banks are usually open Monday to Friday 1 to 5pm and closed at weekends; street **currency exchanges** (casas de cambio) often offer better exchange rates. Breaking large banknotes is less of a problem than in most South American countries, though you are still advised to use notes lower than UR$1000 for smaller bills, especially in the countryside. While major **credit cards** are widely accepted, and **ATMs** are common in cities, you should always

carry a relatively large supply of **cash** for places where this is not the case. This applies especially to the beach villages of Eastern Uruguay, like popular Punta del Diablo, which doesn't have an ATM.

OPENING HOURS AND HOLIDAYS

Most **shops** open on weekdays from 9am until noon, before closing for a siesta until around 4pm and then reopening until 7 or 8pm; they close on Sundays. The exception to this is many shops in Montevideo, the main coastal tourist centres, and **supermarkets** in general; the latter are often open until 9pm or 11pm during the week and on Sunday afternoons. Most **museums and historic monuments** are open Monday to Saturday; entrance is free in Montevideo and inexpensive elsewhere. **Public holidays** are: January 1, January 6, Good Friday, Easter Monday, April 1, May 1, May 18, June 19, July 18, August 25, October 12, November 2, December 25.

Montevideo

With a population of around 1.6 million, over fifteen times larger than the second city of Paysandú, **Montevideo** is Uruguay's political, economic and transport hub. Founded in 1726 as a fortress against Portuguese encroachment on the northern shore of the **River Plate**, it had an excellent trading position and, following a turbulent and often violent early history, its growth was rapid. The nineteenth century saw mass immigration from Europe – mostly Italy and Spain – that has resulted in a vibrant mix of architectural styles and a cosmopolitan atmosphere that persists to this day.

Visitors arriving from Buenos Aires will be immediately struck by the contrast between the hectic pace of life of the Argentine capital and the relaxed atmosphere cultivated by the *Montevideanos*. Less affluent than its neighbour across the river, the Uruguayan capital has nevertheless seen an economic improvement in recent years, and invested some of that money into repairing the historic parts of the city. Filled with intriguing art galleries and museums, crumbling churches and high-quality restaurants, this is an unassuming city that merits further exploration.

What to see and do

Montevideo can sometimes be overshadowed by its snazzier neighbour Buenos Aires, but it has plenty of quirky **museums** – Museo Torres Garcia and the Museo Gurvich in particular – and a charming old town. A guided tour of the beautiful **Teatro Solis** is worth doing, although to really appreciate it, try to see a play or concert here.

Ciudad Vieja

Parts of Montevideo's old town, Ciudad Vieja, have recently been carefully restored, while restoration of the turn-of-the-century mansions is still underway. Its tight grid of streets still bursts with historical character, and it possesses a set of small but endearingly bizarre (and free) museums and art galleries. In the centre of the Ciudad Vieja is the **Plaza de la Constitución**, the oldest square in the country, flanked by buildings of colonial grandeur that reflect the wealth of Uruguay's past. The main tourist area of interest is around **Plaza Independencia**, site of the original citadel of Montevideo and burial place of freedom fighter and national hero **General Artigas**.

The port

The port is on the northern edge of the Ciudad Vieja, defined by the impressively colossal but grimly monolithic **Dirección General de Aduana** building. Nearby is the **Museo del Carnaval** (Tues–Sat 11am–5pm, Sun 2–6pm; free), filled with colourful exhibits from the city's Carnaval celebrations.

Opposite the ferry terminal is the **Mercado del Puerto**. Built in the style of a nineteenth-century British railway station, complete with a station clock and glass arcades, it's worth visiting for the restaurants that you find inside, which provide some of the most atmospheric spots to eat in the city (see p.927).

Around Plaza Zabala

Plaza Zabala has as its centrepiece a horseback statue of Zabala, the founder of the city. On the north side of the plaza stands the **Palacio Taranco**, an opulent private home that has hosted guests from kings to Pope John Paul II. It now holds the **Museo de Arte Decorativo** (Tues–Sat noon–6pm, Sun 2–6pm; free), a beautifully displayed collection, particularly remarkable for the painted pianos, pottery and glassware that used to grace the palaces of the Uruguayan aristocracy.

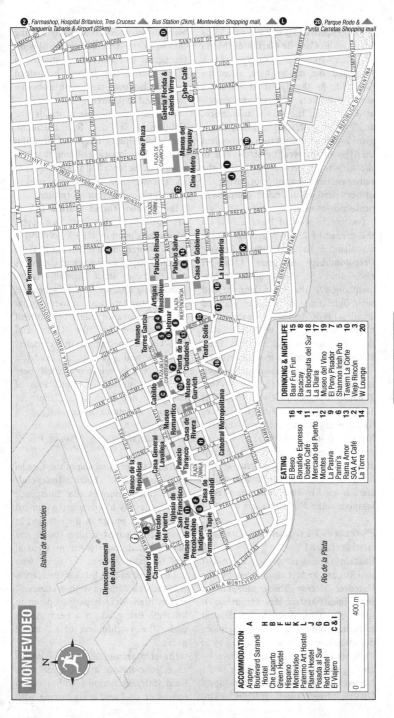

MONTEVIDEO

2, Farmashop, Hospital Britanico, Tres Crucesz ▲ Bus Station (2km), Montevideo Shopping mall, ▲ **L**
Tangueria Tabaris & Airport (25km)

20, Parque Rodo ▲
Punta Carretas Shopping mall

Bahia de Montevideo

Río de la Plata

EATING
El Beso	16
Bonafide Espresso	4
Diseño Café	11
Mercado del Puerto	12
Montes	9
La Pasiva	6
Rama Amor	13
SOA Art Café	2
La Torre	14

DRINKING & NIGHTLIFE
Baar Fun Fun	15
Bacacay	8
La Bodeguita del Sur	18
La Diaria	17
Museo del Vino	19
El Pony Pisador	7
Shamon Irish Pub	5
Tavern La Corte	10
Viejo Rincón	3
W Lounge	20

ACCOMMODATION
Arapey	A
Boulevard Sarandi Hostel	H
Che Lagarto	B
Green Hostel	F
Hispano	E
Montevideo	K
Palermo Art Hostel	L
Planet Hostel	J
Posada al Sur	G
Red Hostel	D
El Viajero	C & I

0   400 m

To the north of Plaza Zabala on 25 de Mayo is the **Casa de Garibaldi** (Mon–Fri 11am–7pm, Sat noon–6pm; free). Occupied by Italian hero Giuseppe Garibaldi in the 1830s, it houses a small collection of artefacts associated with him. The **Museo Romántico,** at 25 de Mayo 428 (same hours; free), gives a unique insight into the opulent lifestyles of the wealthy at the end of the nineteenth century, including the rather egotistical practice of having the owner's initials inscribed onto every possession of value.

Two blocks west of Plaza Zabala on the corner of 25 de Mayo and Perez Castellano is the new **Museo de Arte Precolombino Indígena** (Tues–Fri noon–6pm, Sat 11am–6pm; Ⓦwww .mapi.org.uy). The upper floor, flooded with light from a beautiful restored arcade, holds temporary exhibits of textiles and the like, while the lower floor has statues and carvings from Uruguay and ceramics from the Andes.

The pick of the museums, however, is just a few blocks to the east of Plaza Zabala. The **Casa de Rivera** (Mon–Fri 11am–7pm, Sat noon–6pm; free) traces a fascinating journey through Uruguay's history from prehistoric times to modern times. Of particular interest are the bizarre *rompecabezas* (headbreakers), worked stones resembling starfish used by indigenous peoples as weapons some 7000 years ago.

Plaza de la Constitución and around

Built in 1726, this plaza is the oldest in Uruguay and is dominated by the **Catedral Metropolitana**, also known as the Iglesia Matriz. Hewn from brown stone, the twin-towered, Neoclassical cathedral contains an ornate altarpiece depicting the Virgin Mary, flanked by St Philip and Santiago and watched over by an Angel of the Faith. Next door is the **Museo Gurvich** (Mon–Fri 11am–6pm; UR$25, free Tues; ☎02/915-7826, Ⓦwww.museogurvich.org), highlighting the work of the Lithuanian Jewish immigrant José Gurvich. A student of Torres García (see below), he gained fame in his own right with elaborate murals and sculptures.

Right across the plaza stands the **Cabildo** (Mon–Fri & Sun 2–6.30pm, Sat 11am–5pm; free), a beautiful Spanish Neoclassical building that was once both the town hall and prison, now transformed into a museum packed with eighteenth-century furniture.

The **Museo Torres García** (Mon–Fri 10am–7pm, Sat–Sun 10am–6pm; suggested donation UR$50, ☎02/916-2663, Ⓦtorresgarcia.org.uy), on Calle Sarandí, displays the work of Uruguay's most famous artist, Joaquín Torres García. The founder of "La Escuela del Sur", a Latin American movement that adapted the avant-garde art prominent in Europe during the 1920s and 30s, García specialized in geometric drawings and portraits of historical figures, which are represented here in some distorted representations of Columbus and Bach. It is a must-see gallery in a beautiful space.

Plaza Independencia and around

Marking the original site of the Citadel of Montevideo, **Plaza Independencia** commemorates the emergence of Uruguay as a sovereign nation. It is the largest square in the city and in its concrete-paved centre stands the marble-based mausoleum of General José Gervasio Artigas, the figure who did the most to gain that independence. A horseback statue of Artigas stands 17 metres high while steps lead down to his tomb below, which is permanently under the watchful eye of an armed guard.

The area around the plaza contains an eclectic mix of architectural styles from different periods, with modern towers of steel and glass mixing with the remnants of the city's cultural and economic renaissance in the nineteenth century. The most eye-catching building on the plaza is the **Palacio Salvo**, a Baroque hotel with a large tower that has since been converted into luxury apartments. Across the plaza is the **Puerta de la Ciudadela**, a massive free-standing door that is the only remnant of the 1746 citadel.

Tucked behind the plaza's south-western corner is the colonnaded **Teatro Solís**, the most prestigious theatre in the country, which was completed in 1856 and remodelled a few times thereafter. The guided visits (4pm; UR$40 in Spanish, UR$60 in English) are a fun way to see the backstage and inner workings of a high-quality theatre, but to see the interior in its full splendour, you really have to watch a performance of ballet, drama or opera (tickets from UR$250).

The **Casa de Gobierno** (Mon–Fri 10am–5pm; free) on the south side of the plaza is an almost palatial government building now used largely for ceremonial purposes. The second floor contains a delightfully bizarre museum, the **Museo de la Casa del Gobierno** (℡02/151-5902), dedicated to the men who led Uruguay. Unusual items of interest include a horse-drawn coach belonging to the first president, Fructuoso Rivera (1830–34), and the embalmed body of Coquimbo, trusted canine companion of Venancio Flores, who was briefly president from 1854 to 1855.

Avenida 18 de Julio

Extending from the eastern end of Plaza Independencia, **Avenida 18 de Julio** is central Montevideo's main thorough-fare, the most important stopping point for the majority of the city's buses, and a paradise for shoppers, who cram its pavements searching for the latest deals from fashionable boutiques and colourful street-sellers.

Plaza Fabini, a verdant square along the avenida, features a statue of combative gauchos created by the renowned Uruguayan sculptor José Belloni. A few blocks further east is the Plaza de Cagancha, which houses an excellent **artisan market**, featuring handmade jewellery and leather clothes for much lower prices than in the Ciudad Vieja itself. Nearby, free lifts can be accessed at the back of the Intendencia Municipal building. They provide magnificent panoramas of the surroundings as they climb the main tower.

Arrival

Air Carrasco International Airport (𝓦www.aic.com .uy) is 25km east of the city centre. Regular buses (every 15min; 1hr; UR$17) depart from outside the arrivals building to the city centre. Taxis take 30min to reach the city centre and cost around UR$230.

Bus All intercity buses operate out of Tres Cruces bus station, 2km northeast of the centre. From here take buses marked #180, #187 or "Aduana" (15min; UR$11) for the city centre.

Ferry The port terminal, in the Ciudad Vieja, is a 10-min walk north of Plaza Independencia. The city tourist office can provide schedules, but you can also check these on the website of the main ferry company serving the Port, Buquebus (𝓦www .buquebus.com).

Information

Tourist information The main office is located on La Rambla 25 de Agosto de 1825 (Mon–Fri 10am–6pm, Sat–Sun 10am–4pm; ℡02/188-5100, 𝓦www.turismo.gub.uy). It can provide you with maps, a useful city walks leaflet and a copy of *Pimba*, the monthly events magazine. There are also information kiosks at the airport and at Tres Cruces bus station.

Travel agents Jetmar, at Plaza Independencia 725, can help in arranging trips to neighbouring countries, or with finding cheap flights to other continents.

City transport

Most of the points of interest in the city are within walking distance of Plaza Independencia, but those a little farther out are easily accessed by bus.

Bus There are no route maps available for tourists, but most buses depart to the city outskirts from Bus Terminal Río Branco (Rambla Franklin D. Roosevelt and Río Branco) and stop along Avenida 18 de Julio. Buses heading for the centre are marked "Aduana" or "Ciudad Vieja". There is no city transport pass, but the standard bus ticket is very cheap (UR$17).

Taxi Journeys within the confines of the city rarely amount to more than UR$100. Beware of overcharging and ensure that metered taxis reset their meters before starting a journey; also note that the meter does not give the fare but rather the distance, which corresponds to a pre-fixed rate. Fono-taxi (☎02/203-7000) is one reputable firm; as with the other operators, however, there is not much English spoken.

Accommodation

Accommodation in Montevideo is, on the whole, very reasonably priced and a number of new hostels have sprouted up in recent years. There are several cheap options in the centre, but be warned that the port is a notorious red-light district and that the Ciudad Vieja can be unsafe at night, when it's best to take a taxi. Most of the hostels provide rental bikes for about UR$80 per day, as well as free internet and breakfast.

Hostels

Boulevard Sarandí Hostel Sarandí 405 ☎02/915-3765, Ⓦwww.boulevard Sarandíhostel.com. This new family-run hostel on Montevideo's pedestrian drag is lovingly restored and outfitted with gaucho items. Rooms are minimally decorated and have lofty high ceilings. Dorms UR$280, rooms UR$1100.

Che Lagarto Independencia 713 ☎02/903-0175, Ⓦwww.chelagarto.com. On the central plaza, with a lively bar and a bright central patio. The dorm rooms are cosy if a little small, and the place has a pleasantly relaxing atmosphere. Dorms UR$300, rooms UR$880.

Green Hostel 25 de Mayo 288 ☎02/916-9789, Ⓦwww.thegreenhostelmontevideo.com. The newest hostel in town is a comfortable three-storey rambling house powered by solar panels. Dorms UR$280, rooms UR$840.

Montevideo Canelones 935 ☎02/908-1324, Ⓦwww.montevideohostel.com.uy. Set in a bright blue, colonial-style townhouse, this newly renovated hostel provides friendly service. Dorms UR$280, rooms UR$700.

Palermo Art Hostel Gaboto 1010 ☎02/410-6519, Ⓦwww.palermoarthostel.com. Set 2km away from the Ciudad Vieja, Palermo Art combines good new facilities with a set of funky art exhibitions created both by local artists and some clearly spaced-out backpackers. Dorms UR$280, rooms UR$800.

Planet Hostel Canelones 1095 ☎02/900-0733, Ⓦwww.planetmontevideohostel.com. In addition to a bright colour scheme, minibar and several private nooks, this hostel has some of the lowest rates on private rooms in town. There's a small hangout area with beanbags and a TV. Dorms UR$280, rooms UR$620.

Red Hostel San José 1406 ☎02/908-8514, Ⓦwww.redhostel.com. This hostel is close to the good-value restaurants of San José, and has cosy red rooms, as well as a fireplace and a large terrace at which to relax. Dorms UR$320, rooms UR$950.

El Viajero Ituzaingo 1436 ☎02/915-6192, Ⓦwww .ciudadviejahostel.com. A lively hostel that provides tango and Spanish lessons in addition to having a bar, terrace with barbecue and a cramped kitchen. Dorms UR$300, rooms UR$1000. They also run a brightly painted hostel of the same name at Soriano 1073.

Hotels

Arapey Av. Uruguay 925 ☎02/900-7032, Ⓦwww .arapey.com.uy A cosy, inexpensive hotel with spacious double rooms (all ensuite and with cable TV and wi-fi) that offer a comfortable private alternative to a hostel dorm. No breakfast. UR$760.

Hispano Convención 1317 ☎02/900-3816, Ⓦwww.hispanohotel.com. Located near the shops of Av. 18 de Julio, this small hotel has a central location and somewhat dark rooms. Wi-fi and breakfast included. UR$1150.

Posada al Sur Pérez Castellano 1424, Ciudad Vieja ☎02/916-5287, Ⓦwww .posadaalsur.com.uy. This small B&B, in the heart of the Ciudad Vieja, offers cheap tango and Pilates lessons, bike rentals and some beautifully decorated rooms. It prides itself as a base for sustainable tourism, and breakfast fruits, jams, yogurts and honey are all from local organic farms. Dorms UR$300, rooms UR$800.

Eating

Café culture is on the rise in Montevideo, with several galleries and design stores doubling as cafés and small restaurants. Some of the best-value places can be found near the hostels on San José but you should also try out the restaurants in the Ciudad Vieja, which have top-quality cuisine at fair prices. Restaurants open noon–4pm and 8pm–midnight unless otherwise noted.

Restaurants

El Beso Reconquista 1339. This lunch spot beloved among the city's arty crowd, serves fresh and healthy dishes like home-made pasta with tomato sauce, olives, basil and brie. Set lunch includes soup, main and Italian coffee for UR$210. Open Mon–Fri 10am–7pm & Sat noon–6pm.

Mercado del Puerto Pérez Castellano, opposite the ferry terminal. This old-Spanish market is an unforgettable experience for all carnivores, with a mouthwatering collection of grill-restaurants that will leave you spoilt for choice. Meat dominates most menus, but the grilled seafood comes straight from the Atlantic, so don't miss out. Prices have spiked in recent years (mains UR$300 plus) but the *mercado* remains a classic place to eat out in the city. Two favorites in the market include *El Palenque* and *Don Tiburon*. Open noon to late (some places double as bars).

Panini's Bacacay 1339. *Panini's* is an upmarket Italian joint with some excellent home-made ravioli and gnocchi at affordable prices (UR$200–400).

La Pasiva Sarandí 600. A *cervecería* that offers good coffee and *chivitos* (steak and boiled-egg sandwiches) for around UR$120 in the relaxed surroundings of Plaza Constitución. Beer from the tap is UR$40. Open 8am–2am.

Rama Amor Bacacay 1333. Some tasty seafood dishes and classic pizzas (UR$200–400) in a small, cosy setting.

La Torre Convención 1324. A *parrillada* favoured by *montevideanos* for its live football, energetic atmosphere and large helpings of steak and pizza. Their all-you-can-eat lunch buffet (*tenedor libre*) is UR$200.

Cafés

These cafes are all open early until 8pm and closed on Sundays.

Bonafide Espresso Independencia 711. The favourite coffee spot for local city slickers, this café in the central plaza has a range of coffees (UR$70), some delicious chocolate snacks (UR$150) and the latest international papers to read.

Diseño Café 25 de Mayo 263. This design store doubles as a funky little café, which serves coffees and desserts like chocolate torte or apple and *dulce de leche* pie. The set lunch menu, with soup, quiche, salad and dessert is a great deal at UR$140.

Montes San José 1075. You can get sandwiches and soft drinks here, but the real highlight is the pastry collection. The delicious giant *alfajore* (cookie with *dulce de leche*) is UR$150.

SOA Art Café Constituyente 2046. This restored yellow turn-of-the-century apartment is now a retro art gallery that serves a mean espresso. During lunchtime it doubles as a small restaurant with healthy set lunches (UR$180) featuring fresh soup, salad (options like goat's cheese and chicken) and sandwiches.

Drinking, nightlife and entertainment

There are a number of good bars in the area between Plaza Independencia and Plaza Constitución, the most lively area being in and around Bartolomé Mitre and Ciudadela. Be careful, though, as the Ciudad Vieja can be dark and potentially unsafe in the evening, especially away from the tourist streets. The area around Punta Carretas shopping centre, southeast of the centre, is popular with younger drinkers, particularly on Thursday nights. Some of Montevideo's best nightclubs are outside the centre but can be reached cheaply by taxi. Bars tend to open in the afternoon and close around 2am on weekends; clubs close around 4am or 5am.

Bars and clubs

Baar Fun Fun Cuidadela 1229. Open since 1895, *Fun Fun* is a small place steeped in the history of tango, and you can watch some top tango singers (though 'strangely' not the dancers) while you try the house speciality drink, the potent *uvita* (similar to grappa) for just UR$80.

La Bodeguita del Sur, Soriano 880. Beginners and salsa enthusiasts alike will feel at home at this warm disco. Cover is UR$80, though women get in free until 1am. Dance lessons are available early in the evening for UR$70.

La Diaria Soriano 770. This mellow bar is named after the independent newspaper upstairs. Has occasional poetry readings and later it turns into a dance club with local bands performing live.

Museo del Vino Maldonado 1150. Despite its name this is no museum but a club. Live music can command covers of up to UR$120 but the ambience is well worth it. Neighbourhood tango *milonga* (community dance) every Tues night.

El Pony Pisador Bartolomé Mitre 1330. This is a chilled-out spot for sharing a beer (UR$70) or

TREAT YOURSELF

Bacacay Bacacay 1316. *Bacacay* has a pricey but top class set of whiskies and cocktails (UR$110–140). A la carte dishes include gourmet salads for UR$240. You can cap a refined evening with some fine music or Spanish-language drama at the nearby Teatro Solis. Dress is elegant casual.

some fine wines, with bottles from local vineyards starting from UR$160. Lots of outdoor seating. Dancing to salsa and pop music gets going around 2am.

Shannon Irish Pub Bartolomé Mitre 1318. No capital city would be complete without its neon-green-lit Irish pub, but the *Shannon* does more than just fulfil the stereotype, providing regular live music and some excellent real ales (from UR120) alongside the Guinness.

Tavern La Corte Sarandí 586. This hip restaurant/bar with the decor of a German beer hall serves pricey but high-quality beers (UR$150) and a cellar full of wines (UR$300 for Argentinian labels). If you want to mingle with the great and the good of Montevideo, this is your place.

Viejo Rincón Rincón 619. A fashionable club in the Ciudad Vieja, with a good range of drinks and the latest chart dance tunes from 11pm onwards, although the dancefloor doesn't heat up until hours after that.

W Lounge Rambla Wilson s/n. Set 3km away from the Ciudad Vieja, this club requires a UR$20 taxi ride but is nevertheless the city's main nightspot for all ages, featuring a complex of restaurants and discos with live shows. Open Mon–Sat from 11pm onwards.

Cinemas

Many films are in English with Spanish subtitles, though it's always best to ask regarding the popular Hollywood titles. Tickets are UR$60–80.

Cine Metro San José 1211 ☎02/902-2017. Montevideo's oldest cinema, the Metro mixes popular Western movies with some more artsy Spanish-language films.

Cine Plaza Plaza Cagancha 1129 ☎02/901-5385. Large multiplex which offers the latest Hollywood blockbusters.

Live music and theatre

Tanguería Tabaris Tristán Narvaja 1518. If you are a tango enthusiast, head to this café for live dancing from 9pm Tues–Sun, although you might also see this on any busy night in the Mercado del Puerto.

Teatro Solís ☎02/1950-3323, ⓦwww.teatrosolis .org.uy. Worth visiting just for its Neoclassical facade, it also hosts the best of Uruguayan opera, music and theatre. Tickets start at UR$250.

Shopping

Avenida 18 de Julio is Montevideo's main commercial street, filled with shoppers seeking bargains in the many malls and boutiques. There are also some large malls located just outside of the city centre.

Arts and crafts

Manos del Uruguay San José 1111. This is the flagship store of the national chain, with a range of expensive but high-quality woollen clothes (around UR$600 for a thick sweater), all of which are handmade in Uruguay.

Mercado de los Artesanos Plaza de Cagancha. Good value, though you have to wade through lots of unoriginal tourist souvenirs to find the best bargains.

Designer stores

The eastern end of Avenida 18 de Julio is home to fashionable boutiques. Galeria Florida and Galeria Virrey (between Zelmar Michelini and Ejido) are filled with stores selling leather clothes and electronic goods at low prices. Imaginario Sur, attached to the Diseño Café (see p.927) stocks funky clothing and furniture designs by Uruguayan manufacturers.

Directory

Banks and exchange Money can be exchanged in most of the major bank branches, but casas de cambio offer better rates; there are plenty along Av. 18 de Julio.

Embassies and consulates Argentina, W.F. Aldunanate 1281 ☎02/902-4929; Australia, Cerro Largo 1000 ☎02/901-0743; Brazil, Blvr Convención 1343, 6th floor ☎02/901-2024; Canada, Plaza Independencia 749, office number 102 ☎02/902-2030; UK, Marco Bruto 1073 ☎02/622-3630; US, Lauro Muller 1776 ☎02/418-7777.

Hospitals Public ambulances will take patients to several hospitals on the outskirts; Hospital Britanico, near the Tres Cruces Bus Station on Italia 2400 (☎02/487-1020), offers good private healthcare.

Internet There is a 24hr café at Tres Cruces, adjacent to the bus terminal (UR$30 per hr), and many internet cafés in the centre, most of which charge UR$15 per hr.

Laundry Most of the hostels have cheap laundry services available. There are no self-service laundrettes but La Lavanderia, at Andes 1333, charges UR$100 for wash and dry of a backpack full of clothes.

Left luggage There is a 24hr left-luggage room and lockers with storage for several days in the Tres Cruces station. Most hostels will let you store things in their locked rooms too.

Pharmacies Farmacia Tapie at 25 de Mayo 315 (☎02/915-4848) provides basic healthcare provisions in the Ciudad Vieja. Farmashop (ⓦwww.farmashop.com.uy) is a national pharmacy chain with several branches in Montevideo. It has a store open 24hr at Av. Italia 6958 (☎02/604-4161), though you'll need a taxi to get there (about UR$60).

Post office Buenos Aires 451 (☎02/916-0200).

Moving on

Air Asunción (1 daily; 2hr); Buenos Aires (2 daily; 1hr); Lima (1 daily; 4hr); Santiago (1 daily; 5hr); Sao Paulo (6 daily; 2hr 30min).

Bus Colonia del Sacramento (5 daily; 2hr 30min); La Paloma (2 daily; 2hr 30min); Minas (1 daily; 2hr); Punta del Diablo (2 daily; 5hr); Punta del Este (5 daily; 2hr 30min);. Check out ⊛www.trescruces.com.uy for the latest timetables.

Western Uruguay

Western Uruguay has often been neglected by visitors heading for the beaches on the other side of the country, yet here you will find **Colonia del Sacramento**, one of the most beautiful and understated towns on the whole continent, as well as a host of other towns nearby filled with cultural resonance and architectural gems.

COLONIA DEL SACRAMENTO

Originally a seventeenth-century Portuguese smuggling port designed to disrupt the Spanish base of Buenos Aires across the Río de la Plata, **COLONIA DEL SACRAMENTO** (often referred to simply as "Colonia") is a picturesque town with charming little museums, plenty of outdoor activities and the best café culture in Uruguay. Despite an increasing number of tourists visiting the town, it retains a sleepy indifference to the outside world and you should consider spending an extra day here to get to know it better.

What to see and do

Colonia del Sacramento's heart is the atmospheric **Barrio Histórico** (the old quarter), a UNESCO World Heritage Site home to buildings dating back to the eighteenth century. Most trips to the city should begin with visits to the small museums dotted around the Plaza Mayor. After seeing the historical sites, it is a pleasant walk up to the walls of the city along the **Bastion del Carmen**. If you are feeling ambitious and are in possession of a bicycle or even a car, the ride up to the former resort of **Real de San Carlos** makes for a nice half-day trip.

CROSSING INTO ARGENTINA

Argentina and Uruguay have recently resolved an acrimonious political squabble over a paper mill on their border and reopened the bus routes between the two countries. Aerolineas Argentinas (☎02/902-3694, ⊛www.aerolineas.com.ar) has two daily flights to Buenos Aires (1hr). Buquebus ferries (⊛www.buquebus.com) link Buenos Aires with Montevideo and Colonia del Sacramento. Every day, two ferries leave from Montevideo (in the morning and late afternoon) to the Argentinian capital (3hr; UR$1500), although Buquebus also runs a bus that connects with the fast ferry leaving from Colonia del Sacramento, completing the journey in the same time for UR$1000. From Colonia itself, there are 7–9 daily departures to Buenos Aires. While most of these are on the fast ferry (1hr; UR$700), there is also a morning and afternoon departure on slower boats that takes two hours longer (UR$550). Although less convenient and less used, the cheapest and most picturesque ferry crossing (3hr; UR$400) is operated by Cacciola (⊛www.cacciolaviajes.com) between Tigre, a northern suburb of Buenos Aires, and Carmelo, a 1-hr bus ride to the west of Colonia.

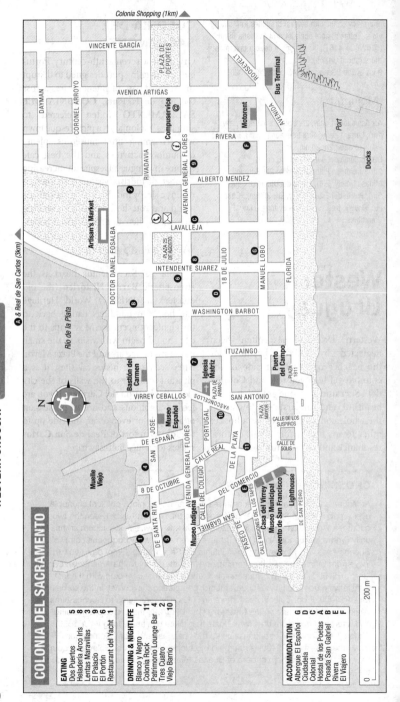

URUGUAY WESTERN URUGUAY

COLONIA DEL SACRAMENTO

EATING
Dos Puertos 5
Heladería Arco Iris 8
Lentas Maravillas 3
El Palacio 9
El Portón 6
Restaurant del Yacht 1

DRINKING & NIGHTLIFE
Blanco y Negro 7
Colonia Rock 11
Patrimonio Lounge Bar 4
Tres Cuatro 2
Viejo Barrio 10

ACCOMMODATION
Albergue El Español G
Ciudadela D
Colonial C
Hostal de los Poetas A
Posada San Gabriel B
Rivera E
El Viajero F

Colonia Shopping (1km)

VINCENTE GARCÍA
DAYMAN
CORONEL ARROYO
PLAZA DE DEPORTES
ROOSEVELT
Bus Terminal
AVENIDA ARTIGAS
Compuservice @
RIVERA
Motorent
RIVADAVIA
AVENIDA GENERAL FLORES
ALBERTO MENDEZ
Port
Docks
Artisan's Market
DOCTOR DANIEL FOSALBA
LAVALLEJA
PLAZA 25 DE AGOSTO
INTENDENTE SUAREZ
18 DE JULIO
MANUEL LOBO
FLORIDA
Río de la Plata
WASHINGTON BARBOT
ITUZAINGO
& Real de San Carlos (3km)
Bastión del Carmen
Iglesia Matriz
PLAZA DE ARMAS
SAN ANTONIO
Puerto del Campo
PLAZA 1811
VIRREY CEBALLOS
VASCONCELLOS
Museo Español
PLAZA MAYOR
CALLE DE LOS SUSPIROS
Muelle Viejo
DE JOSE
SAN
PORTUGAL
CALLE DE SOLIS
DE ESPAÑA
CALLE REAL
DE LA PLAYA
8 DE OCTUBRE
AVENIDA GENERAL FLORES
CALLE DEL COLEGIO
DE SANTA RITA
Museo Indígena
CALLE MISIONES DE LOS TAPES
Casa del Virrey
Museo Municipal
Convento de San Francisco
Lighthouse
SAN GABRIEL
DEL COMERCIO
PASEO DE
DE SAN PEDRO
N
200 m
0

The central museums

Dotted around the Barrio Histórico is a series of seven museums (all open Mon–Sun 11am–5pm, closed Mon in winter). These can all be visited on a single UR$25 ticket available from the **Museo Municipal**, on the west side of Plaza Mayor, where you will also find an extensive natural history display. Worth keeping an eye out for are the incredible photographs of an immense blue whale washed up on a nearby beach, and the beautiful natural history collages made up from birds' feathers and snail shells.

The other museums deserve a peek if you have time, especially the **Museo Español** on Calle de España, which exhibits Spanish colonial items, including numerous examples of period dress; the **Casa de Lavalleja**, next to the Museo Municipal, a restored home with period decorations; and the **Museo Indígena** at the bottom of Avenida General Flores, a private collection of indigenous artefacts.

Around the Plaza Mayor

At the southwestern corner of the plaza and next to the ruins of a former nunnery is the **lighthouse** (Mon–Sun 10am–5pm; UR$20), which affords great views of the surroundings from the cupola. The remains of the old city gates, the **Puerta del Campo**, lie at the bottom end of Calle Manuel Lobo, where they were once charged with protecting the important trade centre from invading forces; now they are permanently open to tourists and separate old Colonia from the new city.

A few blocks north of the plaza, the **Iglesia Matriz** claims to be the oldest church in Uruguay. Although systematically demolished and rebuilt by various occupying forces, it retains some columns from the original Portuguese building constructed in 1730.

North of the Barrio Histórico

Calle Virrey Ceballos leads you to the northern side of the peninsula, where you'll encounter the **Bastión del Carmen**, with walls dating from the time of Governor Vasconcellos (1722–49). It was later converted into a factory producing soap and gelatine products, and a red-brick chimney from the period dated 1880 still stands. Today it operates as a theatre with a small outdoor museum dedicated to its history.

From the Bastión, the Rambla Costanera runs along a wide-arcing beach to the unusual resort of **Real de San Carlos**, which is also accessible by bus (10min) from the bottom end of Avenida General Flores. Originally the brainchild of millionaire Nicolas Mihanovic, who conceived the idea of an exclusive tourist complex for rich Argentines, it now lies largely deserted. Between 1903 and 1912, he constructed a magnificent bullring, which was used only eight times in two years, a *frontón* (Basque pelota) court which now lies decaying, and a racecourse, which is the only part of the resort still operational.

Regular **horse races** take place approximately every second Sunday, and the horses can frequently be seen exercising along the nearby beach. If you fancy a ride yourself, try *Hostel Colonial* which organizes **horseriding** trips for up to 4hr (UR$1000) to the forests and wineries outside town.

> **TREAT YOURSELF**
>
> If you are tired of just ambling around Colonia on foot, Motorent at Manuel Lobo 505 (☎052/296-65, (🕸www .motorent.com.uy) lets you rent out **motor-scooters** (UR$190 per hr), 2-person **buggies** (UR$340 per hr) or even 4-person **golf carts** (UR$500 per hr) to rampage around the streets. The hostels also offer free or cheap bikes to take out around town.

Arrival and information

Bus and ferry The terminal and port are located next to each other three blocks to the south of Av. General Flores (the main street). The town centre is 10-min walking distance to the west along Manuel de Lobos.

Internet Compuservice, at Av. General Flores 547. Open 9am–midnight; UR$20 per hr.

Tourist information Corner of Av. General Flores y Rivera (daily 9am–6pm; ☎052/261-41, ⓦ www .colonia.gub.uy). There's also a branch in the historical centre at Manuel Lobos 224 (☎052/285-07; same hours).

Accommodation

Prices for accommodation are on the whole very reasonable in Colonia and no hotel or hostel is more than five minutes' walk from the old town. There are currently no official camping grounds in the area. Breakfast is included unless otherwise noted.

Hostels

Albergue El Español Manuel Lobo 377 ☎052/307-59. A cheap, well-equipped hostel close to the Barrio Histórico; the rooms are quite dark but if you are looking for a quiet, peaceful place to stay, this is your best option. Dorms UR$210, rooms UR$500. Breakfast (not included) is UR$65.

Colonial General Flores 440 ☎052/281-51. The official HI hostel is set in a charming nineteenth-century courtyard, which is surrounded by two floors of simple, clean dorms. There are bike rentals and communal TV for those missing their home comforts. Dorms UR$250, rooms UR$600.

El Viajero Washington Barbot 164 ☎052/226-83, ⓦwww.elviajerohostels.com. The most social hostel in town, with a lively bar, communal dinners (UR$100) like pizza or barbecue, and a rooftop terrace. While the ordinary dorm rooms are perfectly amenable, you can also pamper yourself by sleeping in one of the deluxe suites with TV and DVD. Dorms UR$300, suites UR$1000.

Hotels

All these hotels provide rooms with TV, private bathrooms and a free breakfast.

Ciudadela hotel 18 de Julio 315 ☎052/211-83. A fussily decorated-patterned (think flower couches) without the fun atmosphere of the hostels, but with friendly staff and spacious rooms. UR$1400.

Hostal de los Poetas Mangarelli 677 ☎052/316-43. That 10-min walk out of town brings you a price drop for private rooms. Owner Oscar presides over this small, artsy hotel with a garden and wood-burning fireplace. UR$720.

Posada San Gabriel Del Comercio 127 ☎052/232-83. This bright, airy posada is in the heart of the Old Town and has comfortable doubles (though no singles). UR$1430.

Rivera Rivera 131 ☎052/208-07. A basic hotel with fairly dark rooms, but it's also just a 5min walk from the bus terminal and port. It's your best option if you are exhausted having jumped off the bus or ferry. UR$1200.

Eating

Although the restaurants in the Barrio Histórico are pricey, the quality on the whole is excellent and the charming ambience is hard to beat. Look carefully at the menu prices before ordering though – there are one or two outrageous traps that count on tourists not knowing the exchange rate. More affordable restaurants outside the Old Town also offer steaks, seafood and pizza at better prices. Restaurant opening hours are noon–4pm and 8pm–midnight unless otherwise noted.

Dos Puertos Santa Rita 40. This *parrilla* has a refined atmosphere, but that does not stop it serving some huge portions of steak. *Parillada* for 2 UR$380; mains UR$250–580.

Heladería Arco Iris General Flores 362. Stock up on flavours like blackberry and chocolate in one-litre tubs (UR$200). Open noon–9pm.

Lentas Maravillas Santa Rita 61. Spend an afternoon perusing owner Maggie's English-language books in front of the fire or on the lakeside deck. Afternoon tea at 5pm usually involves freshly baked cookies. Also on the menu are healthy veggie sandwiches like roasted vegetables and hummus (UR$180). Open noon–8pm, weekends only in winter.

El Palacio General Flores 466. Not a great-looking place, nor possessing the most attentive staff, this café nevertheless has good-value set combos like pasta Bolognese plus drink plus dessert (UR$155) or massive *chivitos* for two, two glasses of wine and two desserts for UR$350. Open until late.

El Portón General Flores 333. This cheery, yellow-painted *parrilla* is a local favorite and for good reason. It serves hearty portions of steak for very good prices (UR$150–230).

Restaurant del Yacht Santa Rita s/n, Puerto Deportivo. This refined yacht club with a view of boats bobbing on the River Plate could rest on its location laurels alone. It also serves excellent seafood at fair prices (starting at UR$280) and a

can't-miss chocolate brownie and mousse dessert.
Open Mon–Fri 8pm–midnight, Sat & Sun noon–5pm
and 9pm–1am.

Drinking and nightlife

Blanco y Negro Av. General Flores 242. A self-consciously cool jazz bar that offers live music on
Fri & Sat from 10pm onwards. Dress up a bit for the
old-timey leather and wood bar.
Colonia Rock Corner of Real and Misiones de los
Tapas. Odds are that the crowd from your hostel are
heading to this hip bar geared towards tourists. Has
live bands at the weekend. Litre of local beer UR$90.
Patrimonio Lounge Bar Calle San José 111.
A chic new addition to the bar scene, *Patrimonio*
serves cocktails on its river-facing terrace to the
accompaniment of live music.
Tres Cuatro Corner of Daniel Fosalba and Mendez.
If you want to get down to some booming r'n'b or
hip-hop with the local teenagers, this is your place,
although you should be prepared to face a UR$50
entrance fee on popular nights.
Viejo Barrio Vasconcellos 169. The wine at this bar
can be ordered by the jug, or *jarra*, and is surpris-ingly cheap (UR$90 for a half litre). Waiter Martin is
a local character who dons a succession of different
strange hats to rush out into the street and shout
"*pasta de la mama!*", which is also on offer at a
reasonable price (under UR$200).

Shopping

The Barrio Histórico is littered with fashionable,
pricey boutiques selling locally made as well as
more generic leather goods, but the best deals
for handicrafts are to be found either at the *feria*
or artisans' market (Calle Daniel Fosalba, open
11am–4pm), or in the streets around the Palacio
Municipal in the west of the town centre.

Moving on

Bus Carmelo (2 daily; 1hr); Colonia Suiza (occasional
services so check ahead; 50min); Montevideo (10
daily; 2hr 30min).
Ferry See p.929 for details of crossing the Río de la
Plata to Buenos Aires.

DAY-TRIPS FROM COLONIA DEL SACRAMENTO

The **wineries** and **estancias** in the
vicinity of Colonia that accept tourists
are all at least 10km from the nearest
main roads, so you will have to organize
a tour if you wish to make a visit. Beatrix
Rivas (℡0995-210-60 or 52/239-86,
Ⓔcariber@internet.com.uy) is an
English-speaking guide in Colonia who
offers local tours starting from UR$400.

On the eastern approach to Colonia
from Montevideo is the charming town
of **Colonia Suiza**, which is filled with
the characteristic chalets of nineteenth-century Swiss settlers and a set of
expensive boutiques stocking wheels
of cheese that would make the home
country proud. Located 77km west of
Colonia del Sacramento along Ruta 21,
Carmelo is a quiet, pretty town blessed
with some magnificent avenues of trees,
the well-maintained Playa Seré river
beach and proximity to the beautiful
forested islands of the Río Uruguay. A
tourist office (Mon–Sat 12.45–5.30pm;
℡0542/2001) is located in the Casa de
Cultura on 19 de Abril (the main road
into town). The port, from which two
ferries leave daily to Tigre in Argentina,
is 1km to the south of town. Day-trips
to the **Isla San Martin** (UR$1000), a
wooded island with nature reserve and
camping facilities, are available through
Cacciola (Ⓦwww.cacciolaviajes.com).

Eastern Uruguay

Some of South America's least-known
natural beauty awaits you in Eastern
Uruguay. Inland, you can explore some
of the finest pastoral landscapes in the
country on the huge *estancias* (cattle
and horse farms) around **Minas**. On the
coast, a series of small coastal **fishing
villages** offers quiet beaches, wild
surfing and some lively hostels and bars.
Near the Brazilian border, the sight of
whales diving off the Atlantic coast is
not uncommon, while the shimmering

lagoons are home to flocks of pink flamingos and rare black-necked swans. **Punta del Este**, the most exclusive beach resort south of Río's Copacabana, offers a more hedonistic appeal.

MINAS

A market city far from the coastal tourist trail, **MINAS** provides an excellent base for exploring the rolling hills and romantic traditions of Uruguay's interior. The **Plaza Libertad** is graced with a horseback statue of the national hero Juan Lavalleja and there is an impressive **cathedral** nearby on Calle Roosevelt, but the real highlights lie in the **estancias** outside town.

Arrival and Information

Bus Intercity buses arrive and depart from the Terminal de Omnibuses (☎ 044/297-96), three blocks west of Plaza Libertad on Calle Treinta y Tres.
Internet There are several internet cafés around the plaza, offering fast access for UR$25 per hr.
Tourist information On the south side of the Plaza Libertad (daily 9am–6pm; ☎ 044/286-91, ⓦ www .minascity.com/turismo). The office can help with the difficult transport connections to the *estancias*.

Accommodation

It's worth booking ahead as there are no hostels right in town; accommodation is limited and fills up fast.

Camping Arequita 10km north of town on Ruta 12 ☎ 044/025-03. There is a grocery store and a range of sporting facilities near this basic campsite, which includes football pitches and a swimming pool. Catch any bus heading north towards Melo on Ruta 12 and ask the driver to let you off at the campsite. Pitch UR$43.
Plaza Av. Roosevelt 639 ☎ 044/223-28. This place on the main square has clean if slightly shabby rooms. All have AC and TV. UR$650.
Posada Verdun Av. Washington Beltrán 715 ☎ 044/245-63. The same family has run this, the cheapest place in town, for more than two decades. The rooms are clean with private bathrooms and TV; there's also a little terrace. UR$550.
Villa Serrana Hostel Av. Washington Beltrán 715. This thatch-roofed cabin is set in the pleasant countryside 15min outside of Minas. It claims to have been the first hostel in Uruguay, and has a relaxed, outdoorsy vibe and basic dorms. You can take the COSU bus from the Minas bus terminal or arrange for free pick-up. Dorms UR$210.

Eating and drinking

The best restaurants and bars are mostly clustered around the Plaza Libertad and are open noon–4pm and 8pm–midnight.
Almandoz Av. Roosevelt 619. This Italian place creates tasty home-made pasta dishes (UR$100–150) that make up for the somewhat unoriginal, fast food-joint decor.
La Cabana Av. Herrera, corner with Rafael Perez. Locals will point you to this basic, smoky *panilla* just out of town towards the highway. Massive *bife de chorizo* for UR$150.

ESTANCIAS TURÍSTICAS

No visit to the interior of the country would be complete without a stay or at least a daytime visit to an Estancia Turística – a working ranch. Dotted throughout the country, these offer a high level of accommodation coupled with the opportunity to get closely involved with day-to-day farm work; many also organize tours that involve birdwatching and horseriding. The ranches are split into broad categories: *quintas y chacras* (country estates); *granjas* (farming ranches); *serranos* (highland estates); and *llanuras* (prairie estates), each a subtly different take on the ranch lifestyle. You can view a full list of the *estancias* in the country, with reservation details, at ⓦ www .turismo.gub.uy.

Around Minas, the two largest *estancias* currently operating are *El Abra* (☎ 044/028-69, ⓦ www.elabra.com.uy) and *Open Ranch* (☎ 044/021-12). Both are around 15km outside town and charge around UR$1000 for a tour and night's stay. Call ahead to see if it is possible just to take a (much cheaper) day-trip to the farm and to organize transport with the owners; they frequently make trips into town and can often provide a lift. Otherwise, you will have to pay for the taxi (about UR$500 one-way).

Ki-Joia Domingo Perez 489. An affordable but still comfortable *panilla* with quick and friendly service. Vegetarians can try the home-made ravioli. Mains UR$150.

Libertad Av. Roosevelt 621. An old-fashioned bar normally packed with local farmers in flat caps and gaucho-style leather boots, *Libertad* serves excellent a great grappa with honey, plus it has range of Uruguayan red wines (UR$150 upwards per bottle).

Papo's Domingo Perez 487. Here you will find an impressive array of ice-cream flavours, including the bright blue and utterly delectable "Crema del Cielo".

PUNTA DEL ESTE

Situated on a narrow peninsula 140km east of Montevideo, **PUNTA DEL ESTE** is a jungle of high-rise hotels, expensive restaurants and casinos, bordered by some of the finest beaches on the coast. Exclusive, luxurious and often prohibitively expensive, it is a beach resort that is *the* place to be seen for many South American celebrities in summer. Yet while thriving and crowded between December and March, it is cold, deserted and largely closed in winter. The calmer waters on the bay side are preferred by recreational bathers, but surfers and watersports enthusiasts will enjoy the more turbulent Atlantic coast.

What to see and do

The best thing to do in Punta del Este is what everyone else does: go to the beach during the day and go drinking at night. Within striking distance and well worth the trip is the Mediterranean-style Casapueblo, a remarkable villa and art gallery.

The beaches

These are what attract most visitors to Punta del Este, and two of the best are on either side of the neck of the peninsula (Playa Mansa, as the name indicates, has fewer choppy waves than Playa Brava). Watersports equipment can be hired from Punta Surf School, at Parada 3 (☎042/481-388, ⓦwww.sunvalleysurf .com); it also provides surfing lessons for all abilities (UR$2000 for a 6-hr course). **Playa Mansa** on the bay side is a huge arcing stretch of sand, with plenty of space for sunbathing and gentler waves than the other beaches to the east.

Off the coast

From Playa Mansa, there are excellent views out to the wooded **Isla de Gorriti**. Formerly heavily fortified by the Spanish, and once visited by British seaman Sir Francis Drake, the island now forms a popular day-trip for bathers trying to escape the crowds on the mainland. Slightly further off the coast lies the **Isla de Lobos**, home to one of the largest sea-lion colonies in the world. Both islands can be visited by expensive guided tours only; Calypso (Opposite *La Galerna* at the entrance to the harbour; ☎042/446-152) offers a 2-hr island tour for UR$1200, with cruises leaving from the Port daily at 11.30am. You may be able to negotiate a better price if you are in a large group, though if you just want to see sea lions, it's also worth heading down to the port itself in the early morning: they are often out sunbathing as the fishermen set sail.

On the peninsula

If the beach lifestyle doesn't appeal, why not have a look at the outside of

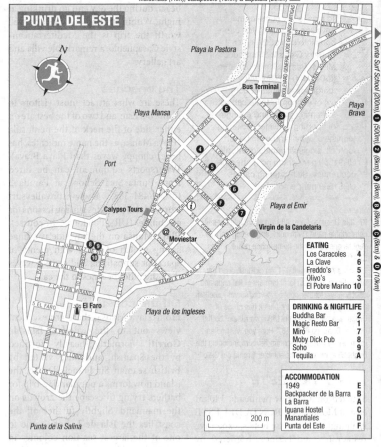

Maldonado (7km), Casapueblo (15km) & Lapataia (20km) ▲

PUNTA DEL ESTE

Playa la Pastora

Playa Mansa

Bus Terminal

Playa Brava

Port

Calypso Tours

Playa el Emir

Moviestar

Virgin de la Candelaria

Punta Surf School (200m), ❶ (500m), ❷ (8km), Ⓐ (8km), Ⓑ (8km), Ⓒ (8km) & Ⓓ (10km)

EATING

Los Caracoles	4
La Clave	6
Freddo's	5
Olivo's	3
El Pobre Marino	10

DRINKING & NIGHTLIFE

Buddha Bar	2
Magic Resto Bar	1
Miró	7
Moby Dick Pub	8
Soho	9
Tequila	A

ACCOMMODATION

1949	E
Backpacker de la Barra	B
La Barra	A
Iguana Hostel	C
Manantiales	D
Punta del Este	F

El Faro

Playa de los Ingleses

Punta de la Salina

0   200 m

El Faro, a lighthouse on 2 de Febrero, although it is not open to the public. It was constructed from volcanic red brick imported from Rome and boldly faces out to the Atlantic. This is also the pose of the **Virgen de la Candelaria** in the small shrine devoted to her on a rocky outcrop, just off the eastern end of Calle Arrecifes. The shrine marks the site of the first Mass given by conquistadors on their arrival here on February 2, 1515.

The area's best sight is 15km north of Punta del Este. Here, Uruguayan artist Carlos Páez Vilaró built **Casapueblo**, a very strange villa and art gallery that mimics the structure of a bird's nest. Bright white and lacking any right angles, it's well worth a visit for the displays on the artist's life and work and a tour of the villa (daily 10am–5pm; ☎425/780-41; UR$100). There's a fancy restaurant as part of the complex. To get there from Punta del Este, take the Olivera Linea #8 bus and ask to be dropped at Casapueblo.

La Barra

Sandwiched between forested hills on one side and golden beaches on the other, **La Barra** is becoming a fashionable place to stay for those tired of the crowds of Punta del Este. The main drag holds a strange mix of hippy cafés and new designer clothing stores. For landlubbers, **Museo del Mar** (summer daily 10am–8.30pm, winter weekends only 10am–6pm; UR$50), 1km following the signs from the Puente de la Barra, has an intriguing collection of marine artefacts including a 19-metre whale skeleton and a 2.6-metre-long ocean sunfish that washed up on a nearby beach. They also have a mind-boggling collection of sea shells.

Arrival and information

Bus Punta del Este's bus station lies at the top end of Av. Gorlero at the neck of the peninsula. It's a 10-min walk to the shopping district along Av. Juan Gorlero, or a 5-min walk from Playa Mansa.
Internet Cyber cafés are pricey on the Peninsula, but the hostels all provide free access. The Moviestar locutorio, at Av. Juan Gorlero 632, charges UR$45 per hr.
Tourist information Plaza Artigas (daily 8am–8pm in season, varies out of season; ☏042/446-519).
Travel agents Alvaro Gimeno Turismo (☏042/490-570, ⊛www.alvarogimenoturismo .com) in the bus terminal has tours to the Lagunas further east from Punta del Este. These are at least UR$1500 for a full day but as there is no public transport service to the wetlands, you may have to fork out. Otherwise, Parque Santa Teresa (see p.940) offers some sheltered coves and ponds that contain many of the wild birds that flourish in the *lagunas*.

Accommodation

On the whole, the hotels here are overpriced and many close down completely in winter, when Punta del Este resembles a ghost town. The hostels fill rapidly in summer, so book in advance if you want to be sure of a cheap bed.

Hostels in Punta del Este

1949 Corner of Calle Baupresa and Las Focas ☏042/440-719. The beachside location, cushions gathered around a fireplace and adjoining bar give this place an excellent party atmosphere. Dorms UR$310.
Punta del Este Plaza Artesanal ☏042/441-632, ⊛www.puntadelestehostel.com. This brightly painted place has a cute little front porch but

cramped rooms and not the most lavish facilities. Nonetheless the price and laidback atmosphere make it a good choice. Dorms UR$400.

Other hostels
La Barra or surrounding beaches are a good option for those looking for more peace and quiet than Punta del Este can offer. These are further out along the beaches to the east of the peninsula. Several buses run every hour to La Barra (10min) and Manantiales (15min) from the Punta del Este terminal.
Backpacker de la Barra ☏044/772-272, ⊛backpackerdelabarra.com. Boasting a swimming pool and a nice flowered lawn for relaxing, the *Backpacker* also has comfortable dorm rooms and is close to La Barra's excellent beaches. Dorms UR$400.
La Barra Calle 16 ☏099/271-614, ✉labarrahostel@hotmail.com. This chilled-out, peaceful hostel has only basic dorms and a basic kitchen but is near the famous La Barra beaches. Dorms UR$300.
Iguana Hostel Calle 8, corner with Ruta 10 ☏042/772-947, ⊛www.iguanadelabarra.com. This relaxed new hostel has a large backyard for relaxing or grilling some barbecue. Get off the bus from Punta del Este right after the bridge and follow

TREAT YOURSELF

Fancy getting away from the fashionable celebrities, casinos and crowded beaches of the peninsula? Then Lapataia (☏042/220-000, ⊛www .lapataiapuntadeleste.com), a country club/resort 20km north of Punta del Este might be your scene. Here you can try grass-fed beef, organic cheeses and home-made chocolate, go horseriding and, every January, enjoy a fantastic jazz festival. This attracts top international performers and lasts for four evenings, but tickets are UR$1500 plus per day, so it's worth finding out in advance which night to go for depending on your taste. To reach Lapataia, catch a bus to Solanas Beach (15min), 10km away in the direction of Montevideo. From here, Lapataia, also known as El Sosiego, is a 5-km walk on Camino Lussich heading north, or UR$100 by taxi.

the colourful mural and reggae music wafting from the hostel. Dorms UR$300.

Manantiales Ruta 10, Km. 164 ☏ 042/774-427, ⓦ www.manantialeshostel.com. Only 400m from the famous "Bikini Beach", this hostel is set in some lovely woods and has terraces that are great for sharing a beer over the sunset. Call ahead for pick-up or to arrange surfing lessons. Dorms UR$400, rooms UR$900.

Hotels in Maldonado

Hotel rates are typically more reasonable in Maldonado, 20min by bus from Punta del Este. From the main bus terminal in Maldonado, eight blocks south of the central plaza, buses #17 and #19 to Punta del Este leave from 6am until midnight (every 5–10min; 10min).

Catedral Florida 830 ☏ 042/242-513. Although some of the rooms are a little dark and have odd artwork, the staff are friendly and there's a pleasant, family holiday atmosphere among the guests. UR$1750.

Esteño Sarandí 881 ☏ 042/229-828. The location near one of the noisier streets isn't ideal, but the large if somewhat dark rooms are perfectly comfortable. UR$1500.

Eating

The peninsula is packed with expensive seafood restaurants and *parrillas*, and even at the best-value places you are still going to lose a hefty weight from your wallet. That said, there are bargains to be had if you look around, and the more upscale meals are likely to be among the most refined and original that you will find anywhere in Uruguay. In summer, restaurants here stay open later than elsewhere in the country, and you can usually find a meal until about 2am.

Los Caracoles Remanso 871. This very large *parrilla* serves plate-sized steaks and some lighter, more inventive seafood meals as well as pasta. Mains UR$160–480.

La Clave Calle 27. This jazz and pizza spot may look upscale, with its sleek black-and-white decor, but the prices are surprisingly friendly. Pizzas are UR$110 and *lamacuns* (Middle Eastern-style pizzas) are UR$80. The live jazz starts up at 8pm every day in summer and weekends in winter.

Freddo's Av. Goriero 811. The place to chill and enjoy a mouthwatering artisanal ice cream. Prices have climbed in recent years to UR$80 for a double scoop, but this is still the best dessert in town.

Olivo's Mesana 1037. The best-value pizza place in town, with an all-you-can-eat pizza plus side salad

(UR$240) for those with big appetites. Toppings include olives and roasted veggies, and pepperoni.

El Pobre Marino Solis 665. Along with an upright piano and fishermen's nets hanging from the ceiling, this restaurant provides excellent fish dishes at the best prices in town (UR$140–280).

Drinking and nightlife

Punta is home to a wild nightlife scene that allows you to rub shoulders with everyone from minor local celebrities to backpackers, from teenagers to an older generation looking for a 1960s revival. Most bars serve drinks from midday onwards, but the real parties only start at around 2am and rarely end before sunrise. The top clubs here change every season, and in recent years people are more often making the trip over to La Barra to party, but these are some of the most established, popular venues.

Buddha Bar Bikini Beach, La Barra. Within walking distance of La Barra's main street, this beachside hut appears to be a modest venue, but it boasts international DJs and fine sushi, and has become a favourite with the young jet-set crowd.

Magic Resto Bar Parada 5, Playa Brava. A restaurant/bar with an upmarket decor and plenty to keep you occupied: live salsa music most nights, card-playing, and dancing from 8.30pm onwards. Glass of red wine UR$75.

Miró Corner of Artigas and Resalsero. With both a flaming grill and a dancefloor, fine Argentinian wines and your favourite cocktails, Miró is enjoying a curious but not unappealing identity crisis.

Moby Dick Pub Artigas 650. An inexpensive, down-to-earth watering hole, which offers a good set of cocktails (UR$170–230) to sip as you watch the ships go by for hours on end from the outdoor seating. On Thursdays girls drink 2-for-1. Open 6pm to late.

Soho Artigas 652. The flashest of the beachside clubs, with a set of chill-out sofas as well as space to dance to the latest pop and rock, but also with a high entrance fee (UR$100) on popular nights and all weekends. Open noon to late with a pricey food menu.

Tequila Ruta 10, La Barra. La Barra's most exclusive club has a sleek black-and-red dance floor that is a good bet for celebrity sightings. Dress to impress to get in. From 11pm onwards.

Moving on

Bus Chuy (2 daily; 3hr 30min); Minas (3 daily; 2hr); Montevideo (every 30min; 2hr).

To reach the surfing villages between Punta del Este and the Brazilian border, you will need to catch a bus from Punta del Este to San Carlos (50min). From here, there are several direct connections daily to La Paloma (1hr 30min) and Punta del Diablo (2hr 30min). There is one daily bus (11am; 2hr 30min) direct from Punta del Este to Punta del Diablo. It can be easier to reach these beaches on the Brazilian border directly from Montevideo with bus company Ruta del Sol (℡ 02/506-6060). Check out ⓦ www.trescruces .com.uy for the latest timetables.

East to the Brazilian border

The beach villages to the east of the peninsula offer some of the best surfing on the coast and are surrounded by sand dunes, forests and wetlands that are perfect for walking. **Punta del Diablo** is the most built-up, and where you are most likely to find a party in summer. **La Paloma** and **Cabo Polonio** are well off the tourist radar by comparison. Be sure to come with enough **cash** for however long you want to stay; you won't find any banks in the smaller villages, let alone ATMs.

LA PALOMA

Due south of the busy transport hub of Rocha, **LA PALOMA** is a quiet port that provides a good base for exploring some fine local beaches. Fishing is popular here and the sea is also good for swimming, especially off the sheltered **Playa la Balconada**; you should avoid the Atlantic beaches as the heavy swell can be dangerous.

In town, there's a small **cinema** on Avenida Solari, the main street, while the **accommodation** options are *Hostel Ibirapita* on Av. La Paloma s/n (℡ 0479/9303, ⓦ www.hostelibirapita .com; dorms UR$320, rooms UR$800) and *Hostel Altena 5000*, a slightly

run-down white cottage inside the Parque Andresito just out of town on the road away from the coast (℡ 0479/6396; dorms UR$360).

The **bus** terminal is five minutes' north of town on Calle Paloma, where buses to Rocha (1hr) leave every 30min. Local buses continue on to the quieter, nearby town of La Pedrera (30min), where the *El Viajero Pedrera Hostel*, at Ruta 10, Km.230 (℡ 99/057-560, ⓦ www.lapedrera hostel.com; dorms UR$360) is close to the beach and has a buzzing atmosphere, even if it is limited to passing backpackers.

CABO POLONIO

Once the regional bus from Monte-video or Punte del Este has dropped you off at the turn-off marked "**CABO POLONIO**," it will not take long to find a *camioneta* (light truck) going back and forth from the highway to the town – usually every half an hour. This small beach village is home to a delightful community of fishermen and hippies, who live simply (bring a torch as there's currently no electricity) but not without comfort.

Arrival

To reach the village, catch a bus on Ruta 9 towards Chuy on the Brazilian border and get off at the large town of Castillos. There are buses from here to Valizas (every 30min; 30min). After this, there are no more roads, but trucks leave regularly to Cabo Polonio (30min; around UR$300 in total, prices depend on size of group), with the last departing at 6pm. Always book ahead, as you really don't want to get stranded here.

Accommodation and eating

Cabo Polonio Hostel ℡ 0994/459-43. Offers cosy dorm beds in stucco rooms off the main wooden house, and the owner's cooking alone make it worth the trip. Dorms UR$550.

La Perla Del Cabo One of the only other places to eat out in town is at the restaurant of elegant hotel

If you are looking for the freshest seafood, just head down to Playa Pescadores when the fishing boats return in the mid-afternoon during summer. You can often buy shrimps, sole or even shark direct from the fishermen for a great price (around UR$80 per kilo) and have them ready to eat only a few hours after they have been caught.

La Perla Del Cabo, north of the lighthouse along the beach. Open noon–4pm & 8pm–midnight.

Moving on

Return to the small clearing to catch a *camioneta* (light truck) back up to the highway. Ask them to time it so that a regional bus (which pass every 30min during daylight hours) will soon pass by. Get on the far side of the highway to return to Punta del Este, Montevideo or Colonia. Stay on the side of the highway with the turn-off to Cabo Polonio to continue on to Chuy or Punta del Diablo.

PUNTA DEL DIABLO

If you want to experience a similar mix of remoteness and natural beauty to Cabo Polonio but would still like to be within reach of a supermarket and internet café, **PUNTA DEL DIABLO** is the place. Whether you stay in a hostel or beach cabin, you can chill out in a hammock and happily contemplate life away from work. If you don't want to go out and hit the waves, that is.

What to see and do

The **surfing** is excellent all year, although currently the suppliers of boards only arrive in January in time for the peak season. The three local **beaches**, Playa Grande, Pescadores (also known as Rivera) and de la Viuda offer plenty of space and all get a good swell. **Parque Santa Teresa**, a small national park with some easy forest treks, secluded beaches and an impressive fort originally built by the Portuguese, is 10km away (around a 3-hr walk) along the beach to the north. Buses connecting Punta del Diablo and Chuy stop at the road junction for the Park and can provide a lift home. The internet café offers access for UR$25 per hr.

Arrival

The bus will drop you off at the main junction in town, where Avenida Central hits Calle 10.

Accommodation

Hostels have sprung up like mushrooms in the last few years. Most are party central in summer and all but *Hostel del Diablo* close in winter. Locals throughout the town also rent out their cabañas for

CROSSING THE BRAZILIAN BORDER

Crossing the border is straightforward if you catch an international bus from Montevideo or any major town (the last of which is San Carlos) on the Ruta 9 heading north: the bus driver will take your passport details at the start of the journey and get all the required stamps for you en- route. If you want to stop in Chuy itself (a haven for shops with cut-price deals and not much else) or are planning to cross the border from any of the beach towns on the northern coast, however, it is more complicated. It is essential that you receive all necessary entrance and exit stamps from both the Uruguayan and Brazilian border controls before entering Brazil. All local buses heading north stop at the Brazilian border, which is just to the north of Chuy. You will, however, have to ask your Uruguayan bus driver to stop at the Uruguayan border control, which is 2km south of Chuy on Ruta 9. The tourist office (Mon–Sat 9am–8pm; ⊛www.chuynet.com) can assist with information regarding crossings.

PUNTA DEL DIABLO

ACCOMMODATION
El Diablo Tranquilo	A
La Casa de la Boyas	B
Hostal del Diablo	D
Hostel el Indio	C
Hostel de la Viuda	E

EATING & DRINKING
Al Pairo	4
Cueva Luna	3
El Diablo Tranquilo Bar	1
Lo do Olga	2

Playa Grande

Playa Pescadores

Fishing Boat Launch

Cyber Café

Bus stop

Playa de la Viuda

0   100 m

tourists, but these generally require large groups in order to make them a better-value alternative to the hostels.

La Casa de la Boyas Calle 5 s/n. ☎0477/2624, ⓦlacasadelasboyas.com. This new hostel is strewn with fishing paraphernalia, such as buoys tied to the party deck. There's a small swimming pool. Dorms UR$300.

El Diablo Tranquilo Av. Central s/n, ☎0477/2647, ⓦwww.eldiablotranquilo.com. A bright red hostel with hammocks for dozing and a fun terrace kitchen that make up for the rather cramped dorms. A buzzing atmosphere and the best price in town. Dorms UR$280, rooms UR$880.

Hostal del Diablo Calle Belgrano ☎0477/2021, ⓦwww.hostaldeldiablo.com. Run by a quiet German and Uruguayan couple, this place is less of a hostel than a budget hotel, with a pool and big terrace. It offers a quieter atmosphere than most and is closer to the bus terminal. Dorms UR$310.

Hostel el Indio Calle 8 s/n ☎0477/2624. This hostel wins for atmosphere with its rustic furniture and thatched room. Dorms UR$300.

Hostel de la Viuda Calle San Luis corner with Nueva Granada ☎0477/2690, ⓦwww.hostel delaviuda.com. This rambling house is supplemented with a two-storey party terrace. The dorms are for either four or six people. Dorms UR$400.

Eating and drinking

Al Pairo Calle Rivera. Offers an excellent set of fresh, innovative fish dishes. Don't miss out on the "Camarones y los tres quesos" (Shrimps and three cheeses) at UR$350: it comes served in a pineapple.

Cueva Luna La Rambla. This beachside club provides affordable drinks (beer UR$60) and the latest chart dance tunes until dawn, making it a favourite with backpackers. Open from 8pm onwards.

El Diablo Tranquilo Bar Calle No.5. Spread across three floors, *El Diablo Tranquilo* has a bar, terrace, dancefloor and restaurant, all right by the Playa Pescadores. Music is a mixture of pop and reggae.

Lo de Olga Rambla de los Pescadores. Almost smack on the beach, where the fish boats pull in, *Olga* gets it on the table as soon as possible. Try the two kinds of local white fish grilled with butter plus sides of rice and salad for UR$300. Decor is minimal and beachy, with plastic outdoor seats and tables.

Moving on

Chuy (2 daily; 2hr); Montevideo (3 daily; 5hr); Punta del Este (1 daily; 3hr); Rocha (4 daily; 2hr).

Venezuela

HIGHLIGHTS ✪

MÉRIDA:
a high-altitude adventure
sports paradise ✪

✪
PARQUE NACIONAL MOCHIMA:
deserted beaches and the
mainland's best snorkelling

✪
LOS LLANOS:
Stay on a cattle ranch and
watch cocoboys at work

✪
ANGEL FALLS:
the world's tllest
waterfall

✪ **AMAZONAS:**
tropical rainforest
wildlife and great rivers

ROUGH COSTS

DAILY BUDGET Basic US$45/
occasional treat US$55

DRINK Polar beer (1L) US$1.20

FOOD Arepa US$4.70

BUDGET HOTEL US$30

TRAVEL Caracas–Mérida (680km)
by bus: US$35; Puerto La
Cruz–Isla de Margarita (40km) by
express ferry: US$20

FACT FILE

POPULATION 28 million

AREA 916,500 sq km

LANGUAGE Spanish

CURRENCY Bolívar fuerte BsF

CAPITAL Caracas (population:
3.5 million)

**INTERNATIONAL PHONE
CODE** ☎58

TIME ZONE GMT -4hr 30min

Introduction

Venezuela's location on the Caribbean coast makes the flight there one of the shortest – and often cheapest – to South America from most parts of Europe and the US. Not that hordes of foreign visitors tend to take advantage of that. Despite packing nearly every natural environment on the continent into a relatively small place – Caribbean beaches, snowcapped mountains, wildlife-rich wetlands, desert, Amazonian jungle and fertile river valley – the country has historically been one of the least-visited in South America.

With 43 **national parks** and many private nature reserves, Venezuela's prime attractions lie outside its major cities, and few travellers spend any more time than necessary in **Caracas** – a good strategy given the capital's security problems and lack of major tourist draws.

Most visitors explore at least part of Venezuela's Caribbean coastline – over 2600km long it contains some of South America's finest and most diverse **beaches**. With postcard-like white sand and crystal-clear water, the country's most pristine beaches are found in the more than forty cays that make up the **Los Roques Archipelago** national parks that are easily accessible by bus from Caracas. Several hours east of the capital, **Parque Nacional Mochima** boasts red-sand beaches with emerald water and backdrops of rocky hills and cacti,

while **Parque Nacional Henri Pittier**, about three hours west, offers a number of beaches with stunning backgrounds of palm trees and verdant mountains. Just two hours to the west is **Parque Nacional Morrocoy**, which features picturesque white-sand cays, but is more financially accessible than Los Roques.

An overnight bus ride from Morrocoy or Pittier will take you to **Mérida**, in the heart of the Andes mountains. Mérida is also the best place to arrange trips to **Los Llanos**, the extensive plains that provide some of the best wildlife and birdwatching opportunities on the continent.

The enormous region of **Guayana**, which encompasses most of the south and east portions of the country, contains a number of adventurous attractions. To the northeast, the picturesque, historical town of **Ciudad Bolívar** is the most economical base

WHEN TO VISIT

Venezuela can be visited year-round, but you are most likely to get the best out of visiting during the dry season, which generally means between November and May. On the coast, there is less rain and fewer mosquitoes, if slightly higher temperatures. Wildlife spottings are much more abundant during the dry season in Los Llanos, when animals congregate at the few watering holes, and during the wet season hordes of pesky mosquitoes make walking very unpleasant. Travel in the Guayana region is more comfortable during the dry season, though Angel Falls tends to be fuller and therefore more spectacular during the wet season.

It is probably best to avoid the national holiday periods of Easter, Carnaval (which begins at the end of Feb or beginning of March), Christmas (Dec 15– Jan 15) and the summer holidays (July 15– Sept 15), when beaches are considerably more crowded and prices significantly higher.

from which to explore **Parque Nacional Canaima**, which contains the marvellous **Auyantepui** and **Angel Falls**.

Guayana also contains the **Orinoco Delta**, a labyrinth of marshlands and water channels formed from the mighty Orinoco River on its way towards the Atlantic Ocean.

CHRONOLOGY

c.13,000 BC–1498 AD Roughly 500,000 indigenous peoples live in the area today covered by Venezuela, belonging to three principal ethnolinguistic groups: Carib, Arawak and Chibcha.
1498 Christopher Columbus arrives August 4 at the eastern tip of the Paria Peninsula and continues south to the Orinoco Delta.
1502 Italian Amerigo Vespucci sees the Arawak houses on wooden stilts in Lake Maracaibo and calls the place Venezuela, or "little Venice". Enslavement of the indigenous population for pearl harvesting begins around this time.
1521 The first permanent mainland settlement is established at Cumaná, on the northeast coast,

serving as a base for Catholic missionaries and further exploration of the mainland.
Late 1500s The Creoles, Spanish descendants born in the New World, accumulate slaves, agricultural wealth and a large degree of autonomy.
1819–21 Simón Bolívar, a wealthy Creole landowner from Caracas, wins several naval battles against the Spanish and liberates the territory of Colombia. Bolívar proclaims the new Republic of Gran Colombia, an independent nation formed by the territories of Venezuela, Colombia and Ecuador. He subsequently liberates Peru and Bolivia.
1829 Gran Colombia disbands in the face of irreconcilable internal disputes, and Bolívar, bitterly disappointed by the dissolution of his dream, succumbs to tuberculosis.
1859–63 A power struggle between Liberals and Conservatives, known as the Federal War, results in Liberal control of Venezuela until the turn of the century.
1908–35 General Juan Vicente Gómez rules the country and becomes one of Venezuela's most brutal dictators. Press and public freedoms are curtailed and political dissidents murdered.

1918 Oil is discovered in Venezuela, and ten years later the country is the largest producer in the world. Gómez pays off all foreign debts and invests in roads, ports and public buildings.

1973 Carlos Andrés Pérez is elected and governs Venezuela through one of its most prosperous periods, during which the petroleum industry is nationalized, quadrupling the price of oil and filling the country's coffers.

Late 1970s–1980s Increased oil production in other countries sends prices spiralling downwards. Inflation and unemployment increase as foreign capital drops off significantly, and Venezuela sells much of its precious oil reserves to pay its debts.

1992 A mid-level military officer named Hugo Chávez launches an unsuccessful coup attempt against Pérez and is imprisoned; soon after, Pérez is found guilty of corruption charges.

1994 Chávez is pardoned for his coup attempt and continues gathering support around the country.

1998 In a landslide victory over former Miss Universe Irene Sáez, Chávez is elected President and, through national referendum, establishes a new constitution that dismantles the Senate, increases state control over the oil industry and grants the military greater autonomy.

2000 Chávez wins a new election.

2002 Government officials and the middle class, angered by Chávez's controversial reform laws and a weakening economy, incite massive, violent protests on April 11; the next day, Chávez is taken into military custody. Two days later the interim government collapses and Chávez regains control.

2007 Chávez attempts to pass, by national referendum, another constitutional reform that would facilitate federal expropriation of private property, give him unfettered control of the national bank and, most controversially, allow himself to be re-elected indefinitely. Shortly after, Chávez turns the clocks back a half-hour, claiming it will increase the country's productivity.

2010 The opposition overturns Chávez's two-thirds majority in Parliament, reducing the President's sway on the National Assembly.

Basics

ARRIVAL

Most visitors to Venezuela fly into Maiquetía Airport in Caracas; those flying from the Caribbean islands may enter via Isla de Margarita (see p.1010). Overland passage is possible from neighbouring Colombia and Brazil, but not from Guyana to the east.

OFFICIAL VS. BLACK MARKET EXCHANGE RATES

One of the most common mistakes among first-time visitors to Venezuela is not informing themselves of the advantages of *efectivo*, or cash (US dollars and euros in particular), over ATMs and credit cards. Though illegal, the country's black market – *mercado negro* or *mercado paralelo* – is cash-based and can give you up to twice as much value for your currency than the official exchange rate. In fact, inflation is so rampant, and foreign currency so undervalued by the federal bank, that Venezuela is almost prohibitively expensive if you travel on ATM and credit cards alone – you can easily end up paying more for goods and services than you would at home. For a daily calculation of the *paralelo* exchange rate, see the website ⓦ www.manzanaverde.info.

The main downside of the black market – besides the fact that it's illegal – is that it requires you to carry your money in cash, a risky venture in a country known for high crime rates (traveller's cheques are safer, though rates are lower if they're accepted at all). Never change money with unfamiliar people, especially at airports or bus terminals; the safest option is to see whether your guesthouse or tour agency will change money for you. Be cautious when inquiring about changing money on the black market, as you are asking people to break the law. Black market exchange rates tend to be higher in major cities, where services are correspondingly pricier (see "Money and banks" on p.953 for further information).

The Brazilian town of Pacaraima, just across the border from Santa Elena de Uairén, provides another opportunity to replenish your coffers; for details see box, p.1001.

By air

Nearly all international flights land at Simón Bolívar International Airport in Maiquetía (often known simply as **Maiquetía Airport**), between 45 minutes and an hour from central Caracas. For services offered at Maiquetía and an explanation of how to get to central Caracas, see p.965 and p.958, respectively.

If you know someone in Venezuela, you can save an enormous amount on airfare by having them make a reservation and buy a ticket for you within the country, which they will subsequently email to you once you have transferred them cash (many Venezuelans have foreign bank accounts given the local currency's instability). This is a result of the considerably higher exchange rate offered by Venezuela's cash-based unofficial economy (*mercado negro* or *paralelo*, meaning black or "parallel" market; see box, p.946). It is essential that you only do this with someone you trust.

By bus

Long-distance international buses arrive from neighbouring Colombia and Brazil and head for Caracas, nine to fifteen hours from the Colombian border crossings, depending on where you cross (see p.978), and up to 24 hours from the main Brazilian crossing. Border formalities for international bus passengers are generally straightforward, though you are responsible for arranging any necessary visas, vaccinations and exit/entry stamps; for more information, see the boxes on p.978 and p.1002.

VISAS

Citizens of the US, Canada, Australia, New Zealand, South Africa, Ireland, the UK and other EU countries do not need a **visa** to enter Venezuela – just a tourist card, provided by the airlines, that lets you stay for ninety days. Entry by bus or car can be a bit more complicated: in some but not all cases, the border guards will ask to see your tourist card, which must be purchased at the Venezuelan consulates in Colombia or Brazil – they're not always available in the US and Europe. You will need to present a photo and a passport valid for at least six more months. Sometimes they will also ask to see an onward ticket. To extend your tourist card or visa for an additional three months, go to the Oficina Nacional de Identificación y Extranjería (Onidex) in Caracas (see p.965). Bring your passport, two photos and your return or onward ticket. It generally takes three days to process the request and costs roughly US$40.

GETTING AROUND

Travellers are best off using the generally convenient and inexpensive public transport system of buses and *por puesto* vans. To avoid extremely long rides, it is sometimes necessary to take internal flights, which can be unreliable.

By air

Flying within Venezuela is neither cheap nor convenient; domestic air travel is plagued by delays and cancellations. Always call to confirm flight times, and arrive at airports up to two hours in advance, as lines can be formidable. Domestic flights usually require a *tasa* (tax) of around BsF32. In most airports you can **charter** small planes, although the downsides, besides cost, are the five-passenger minimum and the unpredictable departure times.

By bus

Buses are the primary mode of transport throughout Venezuela and invariably the cheapest. Since they are operated by countless private companies, you'll have to spend some time visiting the various ticket counters in a city's *terminalde pasajeros* before you find a route and departure that suits your itinerary. Ask at the ticket counter whether you must pay a *tasa*, or tax, on top of the ticket price; , it's usually around BsF2. Most regional bus services end at around 6pm or 7pm; overnight services to more distant destinations sometimes depart as late as midnight or 1am.

Economical buses, or *servicio normal* (roughly BsF8 per hr), are common for shorter distances and often cramped, with no toilet or air conditioning. More comfortable executive buses, or *servicio ejecutivo* (about BsF14 per hr), run longer distances and have toilets; air conditioning, however, is so intense that you'll need a blanket or sleeping bag to stave off hypothermia. If you're travelling overnight, be sure to take a *bus-cama*, with almost fully reclinable seats.

By por puesto

Another economical option is the ubiquitous **por puestos**, battered American sedans that cover routes more frequently than buses, though drivers won't leave until their car is full. They're no cheaper than buses – in fact, they can be twice the price – but they often cut travel time by half.

By taxi

Taxis never have meters, so you should agree on a price before your journey, usually after getting a neutral party's opinion.

ACCOMMODATION

The quality of low-end **accommodation** in Venezuela is, overall, fairly poor; the main exceptions are the couple of

---

TOUR OPERATORS

For better or for worse, Venezuela has yet to develop a budget travel infrastructure on the level of Brazil's or Peru's, meaning that independent travellers often turn to agencies for assistance in arranging trips and activities to the country's top attractions: Angel Falls (p.999), Los Llanos (p.987), Río Caura (p.996), the Orinoco Delta (p.1003), Mount Roraima (p.1002), the Gran Sabana (p.1002) and even Los Roques (see box, p.967). As a general rule, it's cheapest to book a tour as close to the destination as possible – see each attraction's account for local tour prices – but if your time is limited, or if you're looking for a multi-destination tour, the following Caracas-based companies can arrange trips anywhere. All accept credit cards, though for the best rates you should pay in US dollars (for why, see p.946).

Akanán Calle Bolívar, Ed Grano de Oro, Ground Floor, Chacao ☎ 0212/715-5433, ⊛ www .akanan.com. Akanán's office has plenty of materials for researching trips, and Rough Guides' readers can use the internet for free. Clients who opt not to hire a guide are lent a mobile phone for use on their travels.
Angel Eco-Tours Av. Casanova at 2da Av. de Bello Monte, Ed La Paz, Oficina 51, Sabana Grande ☎ 0212/762-5975, ⊛ www.angel-eco tours.com. An excellent agency specializing in slightly more luxurious travel than affiliate Osprey (see below). The company also manages a nonprofit organization assisting the indigenous Pemón community of Parque Nacional Canaima (see p.998).

Hans Peter Zingg Res. Bravamar, Urb. Caribe, Estado Vargas ☎ 0414/322-8798 Ehpzingg @hotmail.com. Hans Peter Zingg and his team offer a very efficient, responsive and highly recommended pick-up service from Caracas airport (US$400), in order to allay fears of safety and unnecessary hassle. They also offer other tourist services including travel advice and advance purchase of inter-city bus tickets. Payment is in dollars.
Osprey Expeditions Same office as Angel Eco-Tours ☎ 0212/762-5975 or 0414/310-4491, ⊛ www.ospreyexpeditions.com. The most economical option for backpacker-friendly, nation-wide trips, with exceptionally friendly staff. They can also organize pick-ups from Caracas airport.

towns, essentially Mérida (see p.979) and Ciudad Bolívar (see p.994), which have been receiving budget travellers for years and have adapted to their needs. Outside of these two cities, dorm rooms are virtually nonexistent, and there are no real youth hostels anywhere in the country; hence solo travellers are often stuck paying for a *matrimonial* (for couples), cheaper than a twin but pricier than a single would be. A good resource for budget accommodation in Venezuela is ⓦ www.hosteltrail.com.

Larger cities, such as Puerto Ordáz, Puerto La Cruz, and particularly Caracas, have uniformly awful budget accommodation and, unless you can afford an upgrade, you're best off passing through as quickly as possible. Nevertheless, you can almost always expect sheets and towels to be clean, if pocked with cigarette burns.

Quality is much higher beyond the big cities and usually appears in the form of **posadas**, basically family-owned guesthouses, which are generally afford-able. These typically have much more character than urban inns and hotels, though they, like their city counterparts, almost never have hot water (the main exceptions being in Mérida and other Andean towns).

Camping hasn't caught on among most Venezuelans, so there are few designated sites. In general, it is not recommended because of robberies, even on isolated beaches and cays. The safest time to camp is on weekends and during national holidays. For more information, contact Inparques (☎0212/273-2701 or 273-2702, ⓦwww .inparques.gob.ve).

FOOD

Venezuelan cuisine, like that of most of the Caribbean, centres around **meat**, with the most common accompani-ments being rice, beans and plantains. Beef is found throughout the country, although it is especially delicious in

Los Llanos, where the grass is ideal for grazing cows. Meats are often served with *guasacaca*, a spicy green sauce made of avocado, tomatoes, peppers, onions and spices. Though rather difficult to find, **vegetarian food** (*comida vegetar-iana*) and healthy *comida dietética* are usually available in larger cities, often in restaurants dedicated to these cuisines.

One of the first dishes you'll notice – and arguably a symbol of Venezuelan national pride – is the **arepa**, in its raw form little more than a dense, savoury, fried corncake, but, when stuffed with any number of meat, seafood and cheese fillings, a meal unto itself. *Arepa* restaurants are ubiquitous; among their most common offerings are *carne mechada* (shredded beef) and *reina pepeada* (creamy chicken salad with sliced avocado). Breakfast is often as simple as a fish-, chicken- or cheese-filled *empanada* (a deep-fried cornmeal turnover) and a thimble of scalding coffee; another option is a *cachapa*, a sweet cornmeal pancake folded over a slab of molten cheese. Lunch is generally lighter – a good economic choice is the *menú ejecutivo*, which many restaurants offer – and common dinner options include fried fish, *pollo a la brasa* or *a la broaster* – rotisserie chicken – or any number of inter-national dishes, including pizza and pasta. The Venezuelan national dish is **pabellón criollo**, which consists of *carne mechada*, avocado, *tajadas* (sliced plantains), cheese, rice and beans; a breakfast version of this is the *desayuno criollo*.

The ocean, abundant rivers and mountain lakes afford plenty of fresh **fish**, the most common varieties being *mero* (grouper), *dorado* (dolphin fish), *pargo* (red snapper), *trucha* (trout), *corvina* (sea bass) and *corocoro* (grunt).

Common **desserts** are strawberries and cream, *quesillo* (similar to flan), *dulce de leche* (caramel) and sweets made from guava or plantains.

Venezuelan *cacao* (cocoa) is considered among the best in the world but, as nearly all of it is exported to Europe, Venezuelan chocolate is difficult to find.

Finding a hot meal in a restaurant can be difficult outside of the standard **dining hours** of 6 to 10am, noon to 2pm and 5 to 8pm. In most restaurants, it's customary to leave a small tip (usually around ten percent), even when a ten percent service fee has already been added to the bill.

DRINK

Fruit juices, or *jugos* (also known as *batidos*) are delicious, inexpensive and safe to drink; combined with milk and whipped, they become *merengadas*. The most common flavours are *lechosa* (papaya), *parchita* (passion fruit), *mango*, *piña* (pineapple), *melón*, *guayaba* (guava) and *tamarindo* (tamarind). Another sweet, refreshing drink is *papelón con limón* (lemonade made with unrefined brown sugar). Bottled water is inexpensive and available everywhere, and the locally grown coffee is quite good.

Venezuelans are extremely fond of their **beer**. The major brand is Polar, with several varieties; the green-bottled Solera is one of the best, and usually costs BsF5–8 in a liquor store or cheap restaurant, BsF10 in a bar. Bottles are endearingly small – Venezuelans prefer to finish a beer before it loses its icy chill. Liquors of choice are rum (such as Cacique) and, among a slightly more affluent set, whisky (particularly Johnny Walker Black Label).

CULTURE AND ETIQUETTE

Thanks to its location at the crown of South America, Venezuela combines distinctive elements of Caribbean and Latin American **culture**. Visitors familiar with these regions won't be surprised to find the country a fairly relaxed place, whose warm, cheerful residents place a high value on socializing, recreation, food and (loud) music. By the same token, **machismo** is an inescapable aspect of Venezuelan society, and while women travelling solo needn't expect any more harassment here than elsewhere, groups of drunken men loitering on street corners are a common sight, particularly on weekends.

Understandably, given their government's notoriety, Venezuelans are **politically aware** and eager to discuss their thoughts about their country; don't be surprised if you're repeatedly regaled with both praise for and criticism of Hugo Chávez. While most Venezuelans will listen to your opinions with good grace, it's best to wait to be asked before sharing them, and for your safety you should avoid public political demonstrations.

SPORTS AND OUTDOOR ACTIVITIES

Betraying its alignment with Caribbean nations like Cuba and the Dominican Republic, Venezuela's principal sports obsession is not football but **baseball**. Teams – Caracas's Leones, Valencia's Navegantes del Magallanes and Aragua's Tigres, among others – inspire fanatic devotion among most citizens. In addition to national team paraphernalia (see p.964 for Leones gear), you'll likely see caps and shirts advertising American teams, as the US's Major League Baseball has a long history of drafting Venezuelan athletes.

Despite baseball's dominance, football is still a popular pastime, as is horse racing (off-track betting offices are common in cities) and even bullfighting, though this is becoming increasingly controversial.

Most visitors, however, come to Venezuela for the recreation opportunities afforded by its huge tracts of undeveloped land. The country is an

VENEZUELA ON THE NET

Ⓦ www.caracasvirtual.com Everything you could possibly want to know about life in Venezuela's cosmopolitan centre, affectionately known to cynical locals as "Crack-ass".

Ⓦ www.inatur.gob.ve Official site of the government's tourism arm, with current, tourism-related news and links to similar federal agencies.

Ⓦ www.inparques.gob.ve Official site of the national parks agency, with contact info and descriptions of parks and reserves.

Ⓦ www.miropopic.com Website for the publisher of Venezuelan maps and reference books, with an online "gastronomic guide".

Ⓦ www.venezuelatuya.com Decent overview of travel and accommodation in Venezuela, with a smattering of country facts.

outdoor enthusiast's paradise, with a variety of landscapes and climates offering the ideal conditions for hiking, paragliding, snorkelling, scuba-diving, white-water rafting and more. Most outdoor activities are concentrated in the few backpacker-friendly destinations, namely Mérida (p.979), Puerto Ayacucho (p.990), Ciudad Bolívar (p.994) and Santa Elena de Uairén (p.999), and tours generally require a minimum number of people. An excellent way to see more of rural Venezuela is through Andes Tropicales, a Mérida-based company devoted to helping local communities protect the natural environment while promoting tourism in remote areas (☎0274/263-8633, Ⓦwww.andestropicales.org).

COMMUNICATIONS

Venezuela is relatively technologically savvy, and call centres and cybercafés are found in all major towns; except in the most remote outposts, you should have no trouble finding a reasonable internet connection. Rates are generally BsF3–5 per hr.

Movistar and CANTV are the most visible telecommunications providers, and each has at least one call centre in most towns and cities. Calls are surprisingly cheap: around BsF0.90 per minute for local; BsF1.70 per minute for national (BsF 2–2.50 per min to mobile phones); BsF2.1 per minute to the US;

and BsF1.40 per minute to Europe. You can also buy public phone cards of various denominations at nearly any corner store or magazine stand, though it's much nicer to make calls from indoors, as streetside phones are often in disrepair and traffic noise can be unbearable. To place an international call, first dial 00 and then the code of the country you are calling.

If you want to pick up a SIM card (BsF70; includes a cheap phone), you can do so from all mobile-phone shops; you can buy top-up cards from most street vendors. Movistar, Movilnet and Digital are the three main service providers, with Movilnet being government-owned and thereby the cheapest.

The Venezuelan postal service is at best slow and often unreliable, so if you have an important letter or package,

LANGUAGE

Not many Venezuelans speak English – a general knowledge of Spanish will serve you well. Venezuelan Spanish is, for the most part, easily understood, although northeasterners have a reputation for speaking extremely fast.

Among the younger set, the slang words *pana* and *chamo* – both approximations of "man", "dude" or "bro" – find their way into nearly every sentence uttered.

send it through an international carrier like FedEx or DHL, which have offices in most major cities; don't expect deliveries to occur as quickly as they claim, however. Ipostel, the government postal service, charges around BsF1.12 for a postcard to the US, BsF1.74 to Europe and BsF2.24 to the rest of the world. Ipostel branches are typically open weekdays from 8am to 4.30pm although, ironically, many are short on stamps.

CRIME AND SAFETY

While Venezuela is, for the most part, a relatively **secure** place to travel, the capital's reputation as a criminal safe haven and Hugo Chávez's angry, anti-imperialist posturing have tagged it as an international no-go zone. As long as you keep your wits about you – especially in Caracas and other major cities – you shouldn't encounter any trouble.

Although urban police enforcement is on the rise, helping to clean up once-sinister neighbourhoods like Caracas's Sabana Grande (and simultaneously multiplying instances of graft and extortion; see box p.963), walking alone at night should never be considered safe. Likewise, never accept help at an ATM – anyone who offers is virtually guaranteed to be a **con artist** – and keep a close eye on your bank, debit and credit cards, though the latter aren't particularly advantageous in Venezuela anyway (see p.953).

For insurance claims you will need to report any incidents of theft to the police, who should otherwise be avoided. They will write up the claim and give you a copy of the statement.

USEFUL NUMBERS

All-purpose, nationwide emergency hotline ☏171
All-purpose, nationwide information hotline ☏131

Make sure to carry **identification** at all times, which you will occasionally have to present at the ubiquitous police checkpoints. Carrying drugs is not a good idea, since narcotics laws in Venezuela are extremely strict.

HEALTH

The main illnesses in Venezuela are dengue fever, yellow fever, hepatitis A, hepatitis B and malaria. Make sure you consult a doctor before travelling, who will be able to recommend which vaccinations to get pre-trip.

You will be asked for a **yellow-fever card** when crossing into Venezuela by land, and you may well be asked for one when flying too. To be on the safe side, you should make sure you get a yellow-fever vaccination and card at least four weeks before travelling, as vaccinations tend to take up to a month to become effective. **Malaria** is not uncommon in rural areas, so if you're planning on staying in remote villages such as by the Delta del Orinoco, take a course of anti-malarials.

Good **medical care** is available in Venezuela, although this tends to be of a higher standard in Caracas than in the rest of the country. It may be very hard to find a hospital with good facilities, let alone good doctors, in remote areas. Foreigners tend to rely on private clinics, which offer high-quality service.

INFORMATION AND MAPS

What Venezuela's tourism officials – representatives of federal agencies Inatur (🌐www.inatur.gob.ve), Venetur (🌐www.venetur.gob.ve) and Mintur (🌐www.mintur.gob.ve) – lack in useful knowledge for budget travellers, they make up for with charm and enthusiasm. Unfortunately, many offices don't abide by any logical schedule. Additionally, each state has its own tourism entity located in its capital city. For office contact information and official hours, see city and town accounts in the guide.

Though information provided by private tour agencies is rarely unbiased, they are often better sources of detailed information for independent travellers, and are more in touch with current public transport schedules and black market exchange rates (see opposite).

A variety of country and regional maps are available in Venezuela, the best being Miro Popic's *Guia Vial de Venezuela/Atlas de Carreteras* and individual city maps, available in most bookshops. Other excellent sources of information are Valentina Quintero (Ⓦ www.valentinaquintero.com.ve) and Elizabeth Klein's guidebooks to Venezuela, both available in most bookstores.

MONEY AND BANKS

Money – and how to get the most value from it – is likely to be your biggest concern while in Venezuela. The country's economy is extremely volatile, thanks to unrelenting inflation and the conversion from the bolívar to the bolívar fuerte in January 2008, which lopped three zeros off the currency. For these reasons, all prices listed in this chapter should be considered estimates; contact businesses directly for current quotes.

Venezuela has a thriving **black market**, which, while officially illegal, is very widely used and can increase the value of your dollar threefold. For more on this, see the box on p.946. Very importantly, all prices in this chapter are based on the official exchange rate; at the black market rate, prices can be up to two-thirds cheaper.

Bank hours are Monday to Friday 8.30am to 3.30pm, although many offer 24hr access to ATMs. Most advertise that they are on the Cirrus and Maestro systems, though this doesn't guarantee

FESTIVALS

In addition to the events listed here, Caracas celebrates the anniversary of its foundation every year from July 21 to July 29 with a series of cultural events that include theatre presentations, painting and sculpture exhibits, concerts and sports.

Reyes Magos Jan 6. Twelfth Night or Epiphany. Choroní (p.969), Mucuchíes (p.986) and Caracas (p.955).

Carnaval Feb (no fixed date). The most famous celebrations are in Carupano and El Callao.

Nuestra Señora de La Candelaria Feb 2. Virgin of the Candlemas, with offerings and folk singing. Mérida (p.979) and Caracas.

Semana Santa March (no fixed date). Large processions involve re-enactments of Jesus' last days and resurrection; most Venezuelans, however, celebrate by heading to the beach. Several small towns in the state of Mérida, as well as El Hatillo (see p.956).

San Isidro Labrador May 15. Honours agriculture and animal husbandry; produce is carted through the streets and animals are blessed. Mérida.

Corpus Christi Late May or early June (no fixed date). The most famous celebration – one of the country's definitive festivals – is Diablos Danzantes (Dancing Devils) in San Francisco de Yare. For more information and alternate locations, see p.968.

Día de San Juan Bautista June 24. Choroní, El Higuerote and Ocumare del Tuy. Venezuelans celebrate the arrival of the summer solstice and rejoice the birth of San Juan, with drumming and dancing on the streets.

Día de Todos los Santos and Día de los Muertos Nov 1–2. All Saints' Day. Venezuelans pay tribute to the deceased by adorning their tombs with flowers and offerings.

La Navidad Dec 24. Christmas – the entire country essentially shuts down for a week.

that they'll accept your card. There is also a maximum withdrawal limit of BsF300 per day. Two reliable banks are CorpBanca (Ⓦwww.corpbanca .com.ve) and Banco Mercantil (Ⓦwww .bancomercantil.com), both found in most sizeable towns.

Exchange houses, such as Italcambio, also exist, though their exchange rates are worse than the banks; they do, however, exchange traveller's cheques, at a seven percent commission.

OPENING HOURS AND FESTIVALS

Most shops are open from 8am until 7pm on weekdays, often closing for lunch from around 12.30pm until 2 or 3pm. Shopping malls, however, generally stay open until 9 or 10pm. For bank and post office hours, see p.952 and p.953, respectively. In addition to their regular business hours, pharmacies operate on a "*turno*" system, with a rotating duty to stay open all night; the designated pharmacy will advertise *turno* in neon. Sunday hours at all businesses are fairly unpredictable – don't expect to get much done.

Festivals, most with a religious basis, seem to occur constantly. Some are national, while others are local, as each town celebrates its patron saint.

Caracas

CARACAS does not hold much of interest for the budget traveller. In recent years, its combination of high prices, high crime rates and traffic pollution has ensured that many visitors to Venezeula pass through quickly or avoid the country's capital altogether. For those that do spend time here, however, there are a few worthwhile things to see and some good options for eating and drinking.

Caracas's most famous native, **Simón Bolívar**, was born to an influential family in 1783. After several years abroad he returned in 1813 and captured the city from the Spanish, earning him the epithet "El Libertador". When Venezuela became fully independent in 1830, Caracas was made the capital of the new nation. Since then, various political eras have left their mark on the city's architecture and public works, though the predominant aesthetic is the mid-twentieth-century concrete high-rise.

What to see and do

Most of the sights in **El Centro** are so close together that you won't need to walk far; a bonus as the thick traffic and persistent street vendors can make pedestrian journeys in this part of town tiresome. Restrict your sightseeing to daylight hours, as the area has a well-deserved reputation for street crime. Away from El Centro, visitors can take in the somewhat grimy street life of **Sabana Grande**, slow the pace slightly with a trip to the arty suburb of **El Hatillo**, or treat their lungs to some fresh air with an excursion to **Parque Nacional El Ávila**.

Plaza Bolívar

As with all Venezuelan towns, the **Plaza Bolívar** is the main square, and Caracas's version, two blocks east and one block north of the Capitolio/El Silencio metro station, is a good starting spot for a walking tour. The south side of the square features the **Consejo Municipal** (City Hall), which doubles as the **Museo Caracas** (Tues–Sat 8am–1pm and sometimes afternoons; free), containing artefacts from the history of Caracas and the independence struggle, art displays and a collection of minatures depicting Venezuelan life.

The colonial-style **Catedral de Caracas** on the east side of the plaza was originally built in 1575. Bolívar's parents and wife are buried inside, in a chapel on the right-hand side. You'll also find Rubens' *The Resurrection of Christ* within. More religious paintings and sculptures are on offer at the **Museo Sacro de Caracas** (Tues–Sat 9am–4pm; BsF5; ☎0212/861-6562, ⓦwww.cibernetic.com/sacro), just next door. Unusually for Caracas, it features descriptions in English. The pretty *Café del Sacro* (see p.960) is well worth a visit.

Museo Bolivariano and around

The best place for a beginners' lesson on Simón Bolívar is at the **Museo Bolivariano** (daily 9.30am–5pm; ☎0212/545-1538; free), one block south and then one east on Avenida Universidad (the entrance is on Av. Sur 1). It contains portraits of El Libertador and his family, plus a host of relics from his early days and later glory years. Next door is the reconstructed **Casa Natal** (Mon–Fri 8.30am–4.30pm, Sat & Sun 10am–4pm; free), where Bolívar was born and lived until the age of nine. There are portraits and some original furniture, but little in the way of explanation.

At his final resting place, the **Panteón Nacional**, five blocks north of Plaza Bolívar, soldiers stand guard over Bolívar's tomb. The **Iglesia de San Francisco**, on the south side of Avenida

Universidad, is one of Venezuela's oldest churches. Its principal claim to fame is as the place where Bolívar was proclaimed "El Libertador" in 1813.

Parque Central

Not really a park, **Parque Central** is a long concrete strip filled with vendors selling pirated CDs, jewellery and miracle herbs. More importantly, the district is the city's cultural hub, and home to Caracas's best museums and galleries. The relocated **Galería de Arte Nacional** (Mon–Fri 9am–5pm, Sat & Sun 10am–5pm; ☏0212/576-8707; free) is one block west of the Bellas Artes metro station on Avenida México. Its primary offering is a permanent exhibition tracing Venezuelan art throughout the last five centuries. A block east from the same metro stop, the **Museo de Bellas Artes** (Mon–Fri 9am–4pm, Sat & Sun 10am–4pm; ☏0212/578-0275; BsF4.30) houses temporary exhibitions by Venezuelan and international artists.

Across the oval Plaza de los Museos, the well-designed and child-friendly **Museo de Ciencias** (Mon–Fri 9am–5pm, Sat & Sun 10.30am–6pm; ☏0212/577-5094; free) focuses on Venezuelan habitats and wildlife, with a strong conservationist message. For more information on all three museums see the Fundación Museos Nacionales website ⓦwww.fmn.gob.ve.

Teatro Teresa Carreño

A two-minute walk south brings you to the **Teatro Teresa Carreño** (box office 8am–5pm, guided tours until 5pm; ☏0212/574-9333), a daunting concrete and black-glass structure counterbalanced by extensive greenery in its surrounding open spaces. Some of the city's highest-profile music, dance and theatre performances take place here; enquire by phone or in person for details of what's on.

Across the road is the **Museo de Arte Contemporáneo** (daily 9am–4.45pm; ☏0212/573-0721, ⓦwww.fmn.gob.ve), which houses an impressive collection of works by international artists including Picasso, Miró and Moore as well as notable Venezuelans.

Sabana Grande

The commercial district of **Sabana Grande** doesn't contain any memorable sights, but it does offer lively, gritty street life and an abundance of cheap restaurants. Many locals complain about security problems, and it is true that the streets here take on a menacing air after dark. The city authorities are making efforts to revitalize the neighbourhood, which have made it marginally safer. Unfortunately, these efforts at regeneration can also mean copious roadworks and dug-up pavements.

Most activity takes place along chaotic **Bulevar de Sabana Grande**, a wide, 1.5km-long pedestrian thoroughfare lined with every imaginable trade, both legitimate and otherwise, as well as a number of malls (see p.964).

El Hatillo

The quaint district of **El Hatillo**, historically a suburb of Caracas but now engulfed by sprawl, provides a welcome respite from urban mayhem. The only street noise here is gallery and boutique owners chatting on the pavement or faint salsa music wafting out of café doorways. For eating and shopping here see p.961 and p.964.

To **get here** from Caracas, take the 30-min metrobus ride from Avenida Sur below Plaza Altamira (Mon–Fri 5–10am & 4–10pm; every 30min; BsF0.70). On weekends, *busetas* (BsF2.20) leave from the Chacaíto metro station – look for windshields displaying "El Hatillo". Get off at the road signs for Pueblo El Hatillo and Plaza Bolívar. Buses returning to Caracas stop across the street (last metrobus at 9pm weekdays).

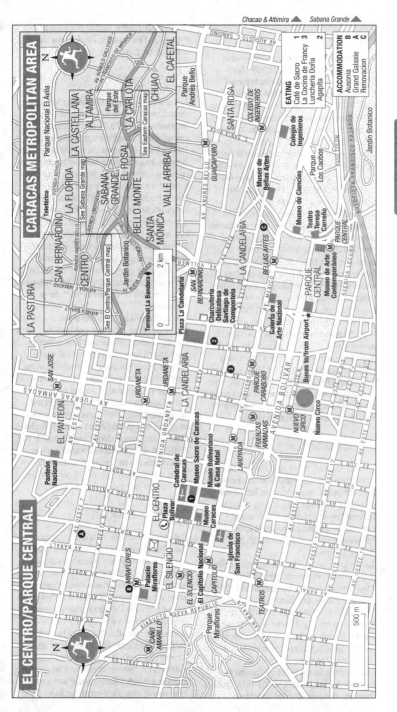

EL CENTRO/PARQUE CENTRAL

CARACAS METROPOLITAN AREA

Chacao & Altimira ▲   Sabana Grande ▲

EATING
Café de Sacro   1
La Cocina de Francy   3
Luncheria Doña   2
Agapita

ACCOMMODATION
Ausonia   B
Grand Galaxie   A
Renovación   C

957

Arrival

Air International and domestic flights arrive at the airport in Maiquetía (☎ 0212/303-1329), 26km northwest of Caracas. Buses to Parque Central (daily 5am–10pm; 45min–1hr; BsF18; ☎ 0212/352-4140) leave every 20min from in front of the international terminal. From the bus stop, it's best to continue to your accommodation by taxi. Red Sitssa buses (daily 7.30am–9pm; roughly every hr; BsF8) also connect the airport to *Hotel Alba* in Parque Central, from where you can either hail a cab or walk two blocks to the Bellas Artes metro station. After dark, a taxi from the airport (see below) is a pricey but far safer option.

Bus Most long-distance buses from the west/southwest arrive at La Bandera terminal, southwest of the city centre. The metro, two blocks away, takes you into the city (10min; see below). Most buses from the east and southeast pull into Oriente terminal, on the eastern edge of the city, from where waiting city buses take passengers to the Petare metro stop, a 15-min ride from the centre.

Taxi Official taxis between the airport and the centre cost between BsF160 and BsF195. Buy a ticket at one of the clearly marked counters inside the terminal. A member of staff should escort you to the vehicle. Alternatively, you can call to book a taxi. Reliable cab companies are Astrala (☎ 0212/860-5627) and Teletaxi (☎ 0212/952-8780). Many hotels and some tour agencies can arrange private pick-ups from the airport. Under no circumstances accept a ride from the touts who approach you in the terminal.

Information

Internet There are numerous cafés in Caracas, especially in pedestrian-heavy Sabana Grande. Most charge less than BsF4 per hr. Two reliable options are MSX Cybershop, at C San Antonio between Bulevar de Sabana Grande and Av. Francisco Solano, and Ciberplace, at C.Villa Flor below Bulevar de Sabana Grande. Both daily 8.30am–8.30pm.

Tourist information There are two Inatur desks in the airport's international terminal (both 7am–midnight; ☎ 0212/355-1326 or 355-1765) and another in the national terminal (7am–8pm). There's also an office in Caracas, in the Complejo Mintur, Torre Inatur, on Av. Francisco de Miranda in Altamira (8am–5pm, electricity supplies permitting; ☎ 0212/208-4652), though this is more administrative and they'll be surprised to see you.

Travel agents Candes In Edificio Roraima Av. Francisco de Miranda (☎ 0212/953-1632, ⓦ www .candesturismo.com); Club del Trotamundo

(☎ 0212/283-7253) in Centro Comercial Centro Plaza in Los Palos Grandes; For reputable tour operators, see p.948.

City transport

Bus Olive-green metrobuses, running 5am–11pm, connect metro stations with outlying destinations. Most journeys are BsF0.70, which you can pay in change or with an *abono integrado* (see below). There is also a virtually infinite number of unofficial *busetas* running their own routes, with stops listed on their windshields. Fares depend on distance travelled, but usually don't exceed BsF2.50.

Metro Operates from 5am to 11pm daily and is cheap, efficient and safe – by far the best way to get around the city. Line 1, the most useful, runs east to west. Lines 2 and 3 run southwest from the line 1 transfer stations of Capitolio/El Silencio and Plaza Venezuela respectively. Ticket options range from a single-ride *boleto simple* (BsF0.50) to the *multiabono integrado* (BsF6), which permits a combined total of ten rides on the metro or metrobuses.

Taxi Official taxis are white with yellow license plates; take these rather than their unmarked *pirata* ("pirate") counterparts. No taxis have meters, so you'll have to agree on a price first. Ask a local what the proper fare should be; most rides within the city should cost under BsF25, slightly more for longer journeys at night. Another option are two-wheeled *mototaxis*, which are cheaper and can get you through traffic faster, but are more dangerous (though helmets are provided). English-speaking taxi driver Eustoquio Ferrer (☎ 0412 /720-3805; ⓔ ferrermiranda@hotmail.com) comes recommended by the owners of *Nuestro Hotel* (see p.960) and offers city tours (BsF80 per hr), airport pick-ups (BsF150) and day-trips further afield.

Accommodation

Budget accommodation in Caracas is consistently poor, and will seem like terrible value for money compared with elsewhere in Venezuela and South America generally. Most places aren't very secure and are in seedy, dangerous neighbourhoods where you're essentially stranded after dark unless you call a taxi. The El Centro and Sabana Grande lodgings listed below are the best of the low-end options. If you can afford it, you'll be far more comfortable in slightly nicer digs, for example in Altamira (see p.960). Hotels in this price range are constantly full, however, so reserve at least a month in advance in high season – though with a bit of luck you might find a last-minute vacancy.

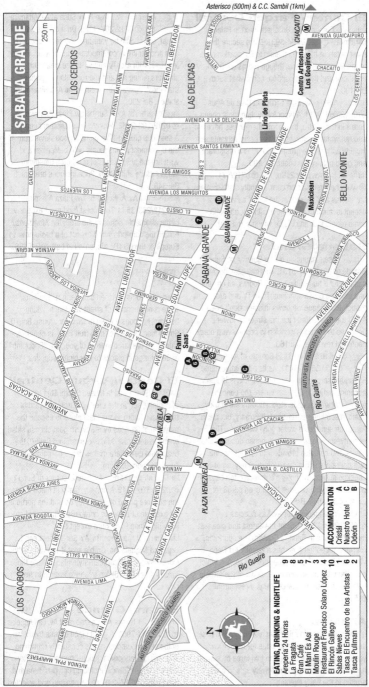

SABANA GRANDE

Asterisco (500m) & C.C. Sambil (1km)

Centro Artesanal Los Goajiros

Lirio de Plata

Maxiclean

ACCOMMODATION
Cristal	A
Nuestro Hotel	C
Odeón	B

EATING, DRINKING & NIGHTLIFE
Arepería 24 Horas	9
La Fragata	8
Gran Café	5
El Maní Es Así	7
Moulin Rouge	3
Restaurant Francisco Solano López	4
El Rincón Gallego	10
Sabas Nieves	1
Tasca El Encuentro de los Artistas	6
Tasca Pullman	2

El Centro/ Parque Central

Ausonia Corner of Av. Urdaneta (next to Palacio Miraflores) ☎0212/864-3931. More secure than most hotels in this area thanks to its location next to the Miraflores Palace, though rooms (with TV) are faded and the atmosphere somewhat seedy. BsF190.

Grand Galaxie Av. Baralt Truco at Caja de Agua ☎0212/864-9011. A nicer lobby than most cheap hotels in the centre; the rooms themselves have a/c and hot water but are otherwise basic. Advantages include wi-fi on the ground floor plus a restaurant and good bakery next door. BsF190.

Renovación Av. Este 2, No. 154 ☎0212/571-0133, ⓦwww.hotelrenovacion.com. Friendly staff, spotless bathrooms and internet in the lobby, as well as a decent location close to the museums, although some rooms lack an outside window. BsF250.

Sabana Grande

Cristál Pasaje Asunción below Bulevar de Sabana Grande ☎0212/761-9131. This one-star lodging has helpful if humourless staff. Rooms, all en suite and in some cases spacious, have TV and a/c, though the opaque windows in some don't open. Avoid the rooms that face the street on lower floors, as the Pasaje Asunción is popular with noisy nocturnal revellers. BsF160.

Nuestro Hotel C. El Colegio at Av. Casanova ☎0212/761-5431. As its alternative name – Backpackers' Hostel – suggests, this is the only accommodation in Caracas where the concept of backpacking is understood. Rooms are starkly basic, resembling a run-down infirmary, but clean. All are en suite (cold water only) with fans. The security-conscious owners dispense detailed safety advice and can also provide info on sightseeing, tour operators and buses. Unfortunately, a police checkpoint near the hotel's entrance often causes problems for lodgers; see the box on p.963 for more information. BsF120.

Odeón Prolongación Sur Av. Las Acacias ☎0212/793-1342. One of the safest and cleanest budget options in Sabana Grande. The sparkling, mirrored reception area has a shabby Art Deco vibe that belies the blandness of the rooms, which are otherwise clean and have views of the streets below. The bottom floor contains a restaurant. BsF180.

Altamira

It's worth bearing in mind that although room costs are higher in Altamira (and value for money low), you'll probably save money on taxi fares by staying here because the area is relatively safe to walk around in the early evening.

Altamira Av. José Félix Sosa at Av. Altamira Sur ☎0212/267-4255. On a quiet side street, this should be your first choice for comfortable and secure accommodation in Caracas. Rooms (en suite, with a/c, TV and wi-fi) are clean, the showers piping hot and the reception friendlier than most. Just a short walk to the Altamira metro station. BsF280.

La Floresta Av. Ávila Sur below Plaza Altamira ☎0212/263-2253, ⓦwww.hotellafloresta.com. A spacious ground-floor lounge, good views from the uppermost rooms (some with balconies) and wi-fi are the advantages of this hotel. Disadvantages include shifty staff. Price includes breakfast. BsF340.

Montserrat Av. Ávila Sur below Plaza Altamira ☎0212/263-3533. The nicest (and most expensive) of the affordable hotels in the area, the *Montserrat* has all the comforts you'd expect of a basic hotel in Europe or the US (TV, a/c, en-suite baths). BsF436.

Eating

In addition to established cafés and restaurants, there is no shortage of street vendors hawking burgers, hot dogs and *shawarma* for around BsF10. Street food, including fresh fruit juice, is generally safe when prepared in front of you. See "Shopping" (p.964) for good places to buy picnic supplies.

El Centro/Parque Central

Café de Sacro Inside Museo Sacro. This haven of serenity, set on the pretty central courtyard of the Museo Sacro, is the ideal place to escape the mayhem of Caracas over a warm goat cheese salad or coffee and cake. Mains cost around BsF60; the peace and quiet here makes that a bargain. Open Tues–Fri noon–3.30pm.

La Cocina de Francy Av. Este 2, corner of Sur 11 ☎0212/576-9849. A homely, dimly lit place where the staff are proud of what they do and the portions, for example of *pabellón criollo* (BsF60), are satisfyingly big. Open 9am–6pm except Sun.

Luncheria Doña Agapita Av. Sur 13 between La Cruz and Miguelacho. Grab a seat if you can at this extremely popular canteen-style place where the *arepas* (from BsF15) are freshly prepared in front of you.

Sabana Grande

Arepería 24 Horas Av. Casanova at Av. Las Acacias ☎0212/793-7961. A great place to take the pulse of the neighbourhood, as it's constantly brimming with *taxistas*, shoppers, lunch-breakers and after-partiers. *Arepa* fillings, including octopus, tuna and roast pork (BsF17–24) can be perused and selected through a glass counter. For more leisurely (and expensive) dining, there's an open-sided restaurant where you can enjoy *pollo, carne mechada, parrilla* and more, all washed down with fresh *batidos* or *merengadas*. Open 24hr.

Gran Café Bulevar de Sabana Grande at C. Pascual Navarro. Grand it ain't, but this popular lunch destination serves potent coffee, sandwiches (around BsF20 with fries), ice cream, pastries and more.

Restaurant Francisco Solano López Av. Francisco Solano López, across from Tasca Pullman. This unobtrusive little place has options including *milanesa de pollo* and *trucha a la plancha* (both BsF32). Fluorescent lighting and worn tablecloths don't leave much room for atmosphere, but diners – who welcome gringos with quizzical but not unfriendly looks – occasionally wrap up their meal with a game of dominoes. Mon–Sat 6.30am–6.30pm, Sun 7am–2pm.

El Rincón Gallego Av. Francisco Solano López at corner of with C. Los Manguitos ☎0212/762-8307. Elderly Spanish owner Lola moved to Venezuela fifty years ago and is still dishing out traditional favourites from her homeland as well as friendly security advice. A cosy place that stays open until the early hours if the punters are having fun. Paella for two BsF106.

Sabas Nieves C. Pascual Navarro ☎0212/763-6712. In a city largely bereft of affordable healthy food, *Sabas Nieves* is a godsend whether you're vegetarian or not. Buy a ticket for lunch (BsF25) at the counter out front, then follow the stream of locals into the spartan restaurant where you can load your plate high with meat-free goodies. The cuisine alternates daily, taking in Creole, Italian, Arabian and Peruvian fare, and the price includes fresh juice. Also sells health foods to take away. Open Mon–Sat noon–3.30pm.

Altamira/Los Palos Grandes

Evio's Pizza 4a Av. between 2da and 3ra Transversals, Los Palos Grandes ☎0212/283-6608. A popular neighbourhood pizza joint serving classics alongside more unusual options, such as Roquefort and goat cheese (individual from BsF48, family-sized from BsF118). Pasta dishes (from BsF50) are also available. Live music is performed Thurs–Sat, with a BsF22 cover. Open Mon–Thurs 2–4pm & 6pm–midnight, Fri–Sun noon–midnight.

Fenica Av. 4a between 2da and 3ra Transversals ☎0212/285-4623. Tasty Lebanese food including good-value *shwarma* (BsF35) comes complete with tapestries on the walls and a Middle Eastern soundtrack. Decide for yourself whether the busty belly-dancers on Thurs–Sat nights are a bonus.

Flor de Castillo Av. Avila Sur next to *La Floresta* (see p.960). A good breakfast option for those staying in the area, with great coffee and fresh juices plus cooked breakfasts like ham and eggs (BsF30). Also open all day for bigger plates and good savoury pastries (most BsF10). Has a large covered terrace out front.

Luna Llena Arepa Factory 2da Transversal at 2da Av. Los Palos Grandes ☎0212/286-1125. Claims to have a new concept for an old favourite – "gourmet" *arepas* that are slimmer than usual and grilled in a *panino* press. Choose from such fillings as grilled aubergine or goat cheese (BsF15–28) then vie for a seat among chattering families at one of the spotless tables. You can also take home a sweet 'n' salty *torta de queso criolla*, a cheesecake-like dessert. Open until 9.30pm weeknights, 1pm weekends.

El Hatillo

Dulces Criollos C. La Paz on Plaza Bolivar ☎0212/963-6858. Place a bet with your-self that you can step inside *Dulces Criollos* and then emerge without having eaten a massive slab of one of the numerous cakes (around BsF10) behind their

TREAT YOURSELF

Café Atlantique Av. Andres Bello, just north of Av. Francisco de Miranda ☎0212/287-0110. Boasting one of the city's top-rated chefs, this haute cuisine sanctuary also wins high marks for design: the industrial-chic interior, with a blue-green brick floor and Jetsons-style furnishings, faces the street through a floor-to-ceiling window. Sip a pre-prandial Black Label on the patio, then sit down to a three-course set menu (BsF129, Mon–Fri lunchtimes only) of beef carpaccio, Mérida greens with caramelized onions, *churrasco de dorado* with cauliflower, or *asopado de arroz* with lobster-calamari bisque. Afterwards, feed your sweet tooth with passionfruit mousse or tree tomato coulis. The blue-lit tapas bar serves lighter meals including herbed goat cheese, prosciutto and smoked Norwegian salmon (BsF20–45). Reservations advised. Open for lunch and dinner Mon–Fri, Sat dinner only, closed Sun.

glass counter. You'll lose the bet and be happy you did. Also serves good coffee and savoury snacks. Open Tues–Sat, 8am–11pm.

Drinking and nightlife

Caracas has bars and clubs for virtually anyone, and at any time – many establishments stay open until the last patron leaves. Being a large and relatively cosmopolitan city, it also has a decent selection of gay and lesbian nightspots. Check ⓦwww.rumbacaracas.com for a variety of club and event listings. As most streets empty out after dark,

especially in the western districts, it's wise to take taxis to and from your destination.

Sabana Grande

El Maní Es Así C. El Cristo. This self-proclaimed "temple of salsa" is a Caracas legend and the place to dance in the city. The intricately decorated interior features hanging musical instruments, vintage posters, old porcelain beer taps and a bamboo ceiling, all illuminated by soft amber lighting. Open Tues–Sat; arrive early for occasional salsa lessons.

Moulin Rouge Av. Francisco Solano ⓦwww .moulinrouge.com.ve. With a giant, two-dimensional

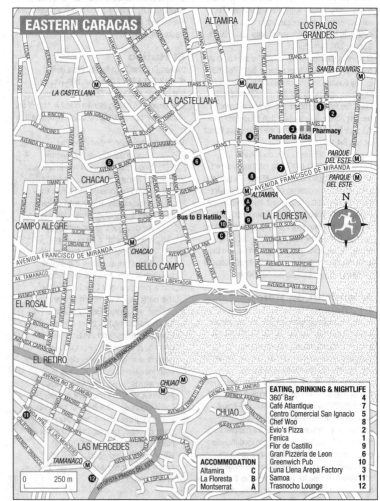

EASTERN CARACAS

ALTAMIRA
LOS PALOS GRANDES
SANTA EDUVIGIS
LA CASTELLANA
AVILA
LA CASTELLANA
Pharmacy
Panadería Aida
PARQUE DEL ESTE
CHACAO
PARQUE DEL ESTE
ALTAMIRA
Bus to El Hatillo
LA FLORESTA
CAMPO ALEGRE
CHACAO
BELLO CAMPO
N
EL ROSAL
EL RETIRO
CHUAO
CHUAO
LAS MERCEDES
TAMANACO

0   250 m

EATING, DRINKING & NIGHTLIFE	
360° Bar	4
Café Atlantique	7
Centro Comercial San Ignacio	5
Chef Woo	8
Evio's Pizza	2
Fenica	1
Flor de Castillo	9
Gran Pizzería de Leon	6
Greenwich Pub	10
Luna Llena Arepa Factory	3
Samoa	11
Trasnocho Lounge	12

ACCOMMODATION	
Altamira	C
La Floresta	B
Montserrat	A

▼ El Hatillo (12km) & Hannsi (12km)

windmill for a facade, you can't miss this ever-popular dive bar/club, where the city's pierced and tattooed rockers, ravers and gutter-punks convene for endless nights of energetic live music. Tues–Sat from 9pm; see the website for who's performing soon.

Tasca El Encuentro de los Artistas Pasaje la Asunción. The live acts are not as regular as they once were at this popular bar, with the melancholy owner citing rising costs, but the canned tunes are reliably present. At night, music and patrons alike spill into the narrow pedestrian street. Open from lunchtime, closed Sun.

Altamira/Los Palos Grandes

360º Bar Hotel Altamira Suites, corner of 1ra Av. & 1a Transversal. On the roof of an upmarket hotel, this stylish bar doesn't serve beer and is, unsurprisingly, not cheap. The fantastic city views and chilled vibe are worth the extra cost, however. Treat yourself to a delicious coconut mojito (BsF36) and watch the sun go down. Open 5pm until late.

Centro Comercial San Ignacio Av. Blandín Ⓦ www.centrosanignacio.com. An upmarket shopping centre with a wide selection of bars and clubs where wealthy Caraqueños come to show off their latest moves and fashionable purchases. Try

Suka, which has a pan-Asian theme and regular DJs, or neighbouring *Sei*. There are plenty of eating options here too.

Chef Woo 1ra Av. above Av. Francisco de Miranda, Los Palos Grandes. Local students flock to this canteen-style Chinese restaurant (and its neighbour, *Lai Cen*) for cheap beers, lively conversation and sometimes even Chinese food, though this is usually lower down the list of priorities. Closes 11pm.

Gran Pizzería de Leon 2da Transversal de la Castellana. A classic bar (and pizzeria) that's been going for generations. There's a sizeable indoor seating area, though virtually everybody opts for the vast, raised patio. Lively and good-natured, though keep note of how many beers you've had (especially if you're in a big group) as the waiters have been known to add a couple to the bill. Closes around 2am.

Greenwich Pub Av. San Juan Bosco, Altamira. Don't be intimidated by the groups of men that stand around outside this small pub; the atmosphere inside is friendly and the clientele mixed-sex. Live music on Wed and Sun at 9pm, loud canned rock tunes the rest of the time.

Las Mercedes

Samoa Av. Principal de Las Mercedes at C. Mucuchíes. One of many bars along the avenue,

SAFETY IN CARACAS

Caracas's reputation as a high-crime city is, sadly, justified. While locals' constant warnings of robberies and assaults can sound a bit paranoid, it's wise to heed their advice about particular areas and be alert when walking the streets. Avoid staying out alone after dark, especially in and around the western districts of El Centro, Parque Central and Sabana Grande. Don't venture up deserted side streets, even during the day, or carry more money or bank cards than you need. Try to look like you know where you're going, and duck into a shop or bar to check your map rather than pulling out the guidebook in the middle of the street. Be very wary of offers from black-market moneychangers in the street and at the airport, however tempting the rate. It isn't worth the risk of robbery or, perhaps more likely, getting landed with fake notes.

You'll probably have at least one run-in with the Caracas police, many of whom consider visitors easy targets for extortion. Red police tents occupy some street corners, particularly in Sabana Grande, and if you pass by looking remotely foreign, you're liable to be pulled inside for interrogation and a "drug search". For this reason, it is a good idea to refrain from wearing overtly touristy clothes – save your board shorts and Peruvian alpaca hat for another day. Police have a special knack for pocketing stray cash while their colleagues distract you with questions, so keep a firm grip on your valuables and watch the one pawing through your stuff. Always carry your passport or at least a copy. Never offer bribes, as this will definitely land you in more trouble, but don't be surprised if fines, not necessarily official, are asked for. All that said, there is no reason for paranoia, and with a bit of common sense you're likely to have an incident-free stay.

Samoa stands out for its slightly bizarre South Pacific surf theme, complete with plastic palm trees and looped videos of monster breaks. Three rooms of varying chill factor mean that there should be a soundtrack to suit your mood.

Gay and lesbian

La Fragata C. Villa Flor, Sabana Grande. Excuse the cheesy, neon-heavy decor and focus instead on the cheap drinks, crowded dancefloor and friendly, mostly male clientele.

Tasca Pullman Av. Francisco Solano, Sabana Grande. One of Caracas's oldest gay bars, and still sporting a distinctly Eighties vibe, this dimly lit place draws a friendly, working-class crowd and the occasional drag queen. Mostly male, though women are welcome.

Trasnocho Lounge Centro Comercial Paseo de las Mercedes ⓦ www.trasnochocultural.com. Part of an arts complex that also contains a cinema, theatre and café, this chic lounge bar regularly attracts a mixed, bohemian crowd. Open every day from 7pm.

Shopping

Shopping culture in Caracas is dominated by mega-malls, where your chances of finding unique, inexpensive crafts are virtually nonexistent. Street shopping is a bit more promising, at least in terms of prices, and the Hannsi crafts outlet in El Hatillo (see p.956) is your best source for souvenirs.

Centro Artesenal Los Goajiros Next to to Chacaíto metro station. This alleyway of stalls is the closest Caracas gets to backpacker chic and the place to come if you have a pressing need to purchase hammocks or Hugo Chávez baseball caps. Open Mon–Sat 7am–7pm, Sun 9am–4pm, although individual vendors keep their own hours.

Centro Comercial Lido Av. Francisco de Miranda. A good place to get things done, with airline offices including Continental, Copa and Santa Barbara, banks with ATMs and outlets for all the major mobile phone networks plus a couple of hairdressers and beauty salons. *South Beach* is a good spot to stock up on beachwear (women only) before a trip to the coast. Mon–Sat 10am–7pm.

Centro Comercial Sambil Chacao. The most famous of the city's malls, this mind-bogglingly enormous complex hosts every conceivable amenity, including top international brands. Mon–Sat 10am–9pm, Sun and holidays noon–8pm.

Hannsi C. Bolívar #12, El Hatillo ⓦ www.hannsi .com.ve. A sprawling, multi-shop conglomeration of craft, jewellery and knick-knack outlets, with a decent selection of books on Venezuela. Loads of chintzy junk, but occasional treasures as well.

Also has a café with terrace and wi-fi. Mon–Thurs 10am–7pm, Fri–Sun until 8pm.

Librería Tecni-Ciencias In Centro Comercial Sambil and around the city ⓦ www.tecniciencia .com. The prices are a bit high, but this chain is one of the best options for books in Caracas, with more than a dozen outlets (including one in Centro Lido in El Rosal).

Panadería Aida 2da Av. at 2da Transversal, Los Palos Grandes. This Portuguese-owned bakery sells beautiful pastries as well as cheese, salami and other supplies. Reputed in the neighbourhood to supply the best coffee in town. Other good spots to buy bread and picnic provisions include *Charcutería y Delicatesa Santiago de Compostela* at Av. Sur 15 between Alcabala & Urapal in La Candelaria, which has delicious cooked meats, and *Lirio de Plata* on Av. Santos Erminya in Sabana Grande.

SBS Sports Business In CC Sambil or CC El Recreo. Come here to buy your official Caracas Leones baseball gear, including jerseys, T-shirts, caps, pins, stickers – and even game tickets.

Directory

Banks and exchange In a city as shopping-obsessed as Caracas, you can't walk ten steps without passing a bank. For safety reasons, try to use those in shopping centres such as CC Lido (see above) for withdrawing money. Alternatively, try one of the several banks (all with ATMs) line Bulevar de Sabana Grande and there's a Banco Mercantil just east of the Chacaíto metro station. The international airport terminal has a Banco de Venezuela (and others), as well as an Italcambio for exchanging traveller's cheques; visit ⓦ www.italcambio.com for other locations around town. See p.953 for bank hours, and p.946 for an explanation of why using ATMs is an expensive business.

Embassies and consulates Brazil, Av. Mohedano and C. Los Chaguaramos in La Castellana (Mon–Fri 9am–1pm; ☎ 0212/981-6000, ⓔ brasembcaracas @embajadabrasil.org.ve); Canada, Av. Francisco de Miranda at Av. Sur, Altamira (Mon–Thurs 7.30am–4.30pm, Fri 7.30am–1pm; ☎ 0212/600-3000, ⓦ www.caracas.gc.ca); Colombia, 2e Av. de Campo Alegre y Av. Francisco de Miranda, Torre Credival (Mon–Fri 8am–1pm; ☎ 0212/515-9596, ⓔ ecaracas@cancillera.gov.co); Guyana, Av. El Paseo, Quinta Roraima in Prados del Este (Mon–Thurs 8.30am–3.30pm, Fri 8.30–3pm; ☎ 0212/977-1158, ⓔ embaguy@cantv.net); Ireland, Av. Venezuela, Torre Clement, 2nd Floor, Office 2-A in El Rosal (Mon–Fri 8am–12.30pm; ☎ 0212/951-3645, ⓔ irlconven@cantv.net); South Africa, Centro Profesional Eurobuilding, P-4, Office

4B-C in Chuao (Mon–Fri 9am–1pm; ☎0212/991-4622, ✉rsaven@ifxnw.com.ve); UK, Av. Principal de La Castellana, Torre La Castellana 11th Floor (Mon–Thurs 8am–4.30pm, Fri 8am–1.15pm; ☎0212/263-8411, 🌐www.ukinvenezuela.fco.gov.uk); US, Colinas de Valle Arriba, Calle F at Calle Suapure (Mon–Fri 8am–5pm; ☎0212/975-6411, 🌐caracas.usembassy.gov).

Hospital Two recommended clinics are Hospital de Clínicas Caracas, at Av. Panteón on Av. Alameda in San Bernardino (☎0212/508-6111, 🌐www.clinicaracas.com), and Clinica El Ávila, on Av. San Juan Bosco at 6ta Transversal in Altamira (☎0212/276-1111, 🌐www.clinicaelavila.com).

Immigration office El Servicio Administrativo de Identificación, Migración y Extranjería (SAIME), at Av. Baralt in front of Plaza Miranda, two blocks south of El Silencio metro station (☎0212/483-2070; 🌐www.saime.gob.ve). Open Mon–Thurs 7am–12.30pm, Fri 8am–12.30pm.

Laundry Many hotels will do your laundry (generally for around BsF20 per load). Otherwise, try Maxiclean (🌐www.grupomaxiclean.com), which has branches around the city including on Av. Casanova in Sabana Grande.

Left luggage Both La Bandera and Oriente bus terminals (see below) offer luggage storage (around BsF4 per hr; Mon–Sat 6am–8pm, Sun 7am–7pm). Most accommodation will hold luggage for you as well.

Pharmacy Pharmacies are just as ubiquitous as banks and internet cafés. On Bulevar de Sabana Grande, Farmacia Saas is at C. Villa Flor. In Altamira, Farmacia San Andres is on the corner of 3a Av. and 2da Transversal. See p.954 for an explanation of pharmacy hours.

Phone CANTV, Digicel and Movistar have shops throughout the city for buying SIM cards and credit; all three have outlets around Plaza Bolivar and the latter also has phone booths plus photocopiers (7.30am–noon & 2–5.30pm). There's a CANTV office on C San Antonio above Av. Francisco Solano, which also offers internet. Open 8.30am–6.30pm.

Post office The principal Ipostel office, on Av. Urdaneta at Carmelitas, three blocks north of the Capitolio metro station, is officially open weekdays 8am–noon & 1–4.30pm, although Venezuela's long-running electricity crisis meant that at the time of research it was opening only in the mornings. There's another post office at the international airport, and others in offices called *Puntos de Gestión* around the city. Locals will warn you against using state-run Ipostel for anything important; private alternatives include Zoom (🌐www.grupozoom.com) and DHL (🌐www.dhl.com.ve).

Moving on

Air Visitors leaving Venezuela must pay an exit tax of BsF162.50. Before paying, ask an airline representative if the tax has already been included in your airfare. There are several flights per day to Bogotá (1hr); Buenos Aires (generally 12hr w/connection); Lima (3–5hr); Quito (3hr w/connection); Santiago de Chile (8–9hr w/connection); São Paulo (8–10hr w/connection); and other destinations. Flights within Venezuela are fairly expensive and the bus network is so wide-ranging that flying only makes sense if you need to cover a lot of ground in a very short time. Check with your air carrier whether the domestic airport tax (BsF32.50) is included in your airfare.

Ciudad Bolívar (daily; 1hr 30 min); Maracaibo (daily; 1hr), Puerto Ayacucho (daily; 1hr 20min); Puerto Ordáz (daily; 1hr); Los Roques (several daily, more at weekends; 1hr).

Bus Terminal La Bandera has buses that go to the west and southwest. It's a two-block walk from the metro station of the same name (cross the road and head left), though at night you should take a cab between the two. Terminal de Oriente mostly services the east and southeast, plus Colombian cities. The terminal lies to the east of the city; get there by taking the metro to the Petare station, followed by a 15-min taxi ride to the terminal. Exercise caution in and around both terminals, as the crowds are a pickpocket's playground. You'll usually need your passport, or at least a copy, to book tickets in advance.

Aeroexpresos Ejecutivos (☎0212/266-2321, 🌐www.aeroexpresos.com.ve) offers very comfortable but slightly more expensive services to Ciudad Bolívar, Maracaibo, Valencia, Puerto La Cruz and other cities. The terminal is on Av. Principal de Bello Campo in Chacao.

Terminal La Bandera: Buses to closer destinations including Maracay and Valencia leave when full; to find them, turn right after you enter the terminal. Maracay (every 15min; 1hr 30min); Valencia (every 15min; 3hr); Coro (several daily; 9hr); Maracaibo (several daily; 12hr); Mérida (several daily; 13hr); Barinas (2 daily; 9hr); San Antonio del Táchira (2 daily; 12hr); San Fernando de Apure (3 daily; 8hr).

Terminal de Oriente: Barcelona (several daily; 6hr); Carúpano (several daily; 10hr); Ciudad Bolívar (3 daily; 9hr); Cumaná (several daily; 8hr); Puerto Ayacucho (1 daily; 14hr); Puerto La Cruz (several daily; 6hr); Puerto Ordáz (2 daily; 10hr); San Fernando de Apure (1 daily; 8hr); Santa Elena de Uairén (3 daily; 24hr).

DAY-TRIPS FROM CARACAS

For a quick escape from the hustle and bustle of Caracas, ride the cable car that ascends the slopes of **Parque Nacional El Ávila**, with its spectacular view of the capital. If you've got more time consider visiting **Colonia Tovar**, a scenic mountain village inhabited for over 160 years by German descendants.

Parque Nacional el Ávila

Separating Caracas from the coast, **PARQUE NACIONAL EL ÁVILA** (ⓦwww.el-avila.com) is based more or less around a mountain whose highest point is 2765m. From here, visitors have stunning views – on clear days – of Caracas on one side and the Caribbean Sea on the other.

There are several ways to explore the park. Four well-marked hiking trails lead into the park from Caracas, all accessible via Avenida Boyacá. It is also possible to drive to the top in a 4x4. However, the most popular option is the **teleférico** (Tues 1–6pm, Wed–Sat 10am–4pm, Sun 9am–6pm, closed Mon; BsF35), a high-speed cable car that leaves from the intersection of Avenida Principal de Maripérez and Avenida Boyacá and climbs to the top of the mountain.

From here, a trail leads down to the small village of **Galipán**, perched on the flower-bedecked mountain slopes. Be sure to stop at one of the many roadside stands selling *pernil* (roast pork) sandwiches (around BsF20), home-made yogurt (BsF10) and punnets of strawberries (BsF20). To explore the park further, or to see it by jeep, contact Akanán Tours, an operator offering day-long hiking, abseiling and sightseeing trips (see p.948). Alternatively, take a taxi to San Bernadin at the foot of the hill, where lines of jeeps wait at weekends to take you to to the top (BsF10 per person one-way).

The northern coast

The coast of Vargas state, separated from Caracas by the rugged Parque Nacional El Ávila (see above), provides an excellent and accessible sampling of Venezuela's **beaches**, a particular bonus if you don't have time to visit the northwest or northeast. The area's beaches, including Los Caracas and Playa Pantaleta – "Panty Beach" – are popular with surfers from the capital. To **get here** under your own steam, catch the bus from Parque Central to the airport (see p.958) and continue 35km by taxi to La Guaira or Macuto (around BsF100). Here you can catch one of the *busetas* that ply the seaside highway, La Costanera, in both directions; hop off and on wherever you choose.

Colonia Tovar

Founded by German immigrants in 1843, the small mountain village of **COLONIA TOVAR**, 60km west of Caracas, is still inhabited by their ancestors. Most of the houses have been reconstructed or built in traditional Black Forest style, and restaurants selling German sausages and local strawberries and cream line the main roads of the village. Sadly, production of *Cerveza Tovar* has moved from the village microbrewery to the nearby town of La Victoria, but the end result can still be purchased at various outlets. "Colonia" is a popular destination on weekends, when it can be packed with day-tripping *caraqueños* who make the whole place feel somewhat like a Deutsch Disneyland. The **Museo de Historia y Artesanía** (Sat & Sun 9am–6pm; BsF5) features a small collection of documents, clothes, tools, guns and other relics of the village's early days.

To **get here** from Caracas, take the metro to the La Yaguara station. Around the corner, buses leave for El Junquito (1hr), where you transfer to a *buseta* for the ride to Colonia Tovar (1hr). Exercise caution: locals give dire warnings about the area around La Yaguara. If you are taking a lot of luggage or valuables, you might want to consider taking a bus from the La Bandera terminal to La Victoria (1hr 30min) and from there a *buseta* to Colonia Tovar (1hr 20 min), a circuitous but scenic journey.

Busetas leaving Colonia Tovar depart 300m outside the village on the road to El Junquito. The last *buseta* leaves Colonia at 6pm. To move on to Choroní rather than returning to Caracas, take *busetas* to La Victoria then Maracay (as above), where you can catch a bus (2hr) or take a taxi (1hr, see p.970).

Tour operators

Douglas Pridham ☎0416/743-8939, ⓦwww .vivatrek.com. An expert paraglider who can get you airborne from the steep hillsides around Colonia Tovar. His outfit also offers guided excursions into Parque Nacional Henri Pittier (see p.968).

Rustic Tours ☎0244/355-1908, ⓔrustictours @cantv.net. One of several companies with stalls around the village that run jeep outings through the mountainous countryside (2hr; BsF50).

Accommodation

Since you can see the entire town in a couple hours, there's not much reason to pay the high rates to stay in Colonia Tovar, and it's so popular

---

TREAT YOURSELF

As your tiny plane comes in to land on Gran Roque, the largest of 42 islets that make up Los Roques, you'll be forgiven for thinking you've arrived in paradise. This exquisite archipelago consists of little more than pristine white-sand beaches surrounded by crystal-clear, vividly turquoise water, all encompassed in a national park protecting a 24-square-kilometre coral reef system. The island chain is home to a tremendous diversity of aquatic life, including barracuda, octopuses and manta rays. The one small human community, on Gran Roque, consists largely of posada-owners and boatmen.

To date, the high cost of flying to Los Roques has helped keep them both exclusive and unspoilt, although there are reports that Chávez wants to make them more accessible – something that could have a drastic effect on the archipelago's ecosystems. Most Caracas travel agencies offer package trips to the islands (see p.948 or p.958), but if you have cash to pay at the parallel exchange rate you can often get a better deal by arranging things yourself (prices below are at the official rate).

A midweek trip to Los Roques, either overnight or just for the day, is cheaper and quieter than at the weekend. The major carrier for the archipelago, Areotuy (ⓦwww.tuy.com), offers return flights and a night's accommodation for BsF1300 per person Mon–Fri; at the weekend the flights alone will set you back BsF1360. Chapi Air (☎0212/355-1965, ⓦwww.chapiair.com) also serves Los Roques. Recommended posadas are *El Botuto* (☎0416/621-0381, ⓦwww.posadaelbotuto .com; BsF300 per person with breakfast), which has great service and lovely outside showers, and *Doña Carmen* (☎0414/318-4926; BsF300 per person with dinner).

Another option is to camp. You'll need a permit from the Inparques office (at the far end of town from the landing strip). Camping is restricted to a designated area on Gran Roque and a few of the smaller, uninhabited islands, for a maximum of eight days. There are no facilities on the smaller islands. Take your own tent, or contact Libya Parada (☎0414/291-9240, ⓔlibyapara@hotmail.com) to enquire about renting one.

A boatmen's cooperative, which ferries day-trippers and campers to and from the various islands, operates out of Oscar Shop next to the landing strip. You can also rent snorkelling gear here (BsF40 per day). Arrecife Divers, near Inparques, runs scuba-diving trips and courses. There are no ATMs, so take plenty of cash. Tourist numbers and prices rise substantially from mid-July to mid-Sept.

with Venezuelans that reservations are required up to a month in advance at weekends. If you can't bear to leave, however, you'll find a couple of relatively affordable options. Nearly all Colonia lodgings have a two-night minimum for reserved stays, though guests lucky enough to nab a room on the spot can usually spend just one night.

Cabañas Briedenbach ☎0244/355-1211, ✉cab.briedenbach@hotmail.com. A row of 18 units overlooking the village and surrounding hillsides. Simple but cosy rooms have TV, hot water, mini-fridges and wi-fi. Family-friendly, with a playground and a lawn. The helpful owner speaks English and German. BsF240.

Cabañas Silberbrunnen ☎0244/355-1490. Small but tidy cabañas, set in a well-tended, terraced garden, have TVs, fridges, hot water and nice views. Cabins with private kitchens cost just BsF20 more than the standard option. BsF250.

Eating

Lunchería Schmuk 100m uphill from the church. Specializes in German-style sausages, which come in a variety of forms ranging from simple hot-dogs (BsF20) to hefty platters (BsF43). Open 6am–9pm daily.

Zu House Next to the car park. Offers good-value breakfasts, again involving sausages, and lunch options such as *sandwich de pernil* (BsF40). Sat & Sun 8am–6pm.

San Francisco de Yare

The otherwise nondescript town of **SAN FRANCISCO DE YARE**, 60km southeast of Caracas, is the site of one of Venezuela's most famous spectacles, the **Festival de los Diablos Danzantes** ("dancing devils"). In observance of the Catholic holy day Corpus Christi (in late May or early June; check with Caracas tourism offices for exact dates), townspeople don elaborate devil masks and costumes and engage in highly ritualized performances. While similar festivals occur in other parts of Venezuela, including Ocumare de la Costa, Chuao, Naiguatá and Cuyagua, Yare's is considered the quintessential event.

To **get here** from Caracas, take the metro to the Nuevo Circo station and walk one block to the bus terminal of the same name. From here, buses leave every 15min for Ocumare del Tuy from stand seven (daily 4.45am–9pm; 1hr 30min). From the Ocumare terminal, frequent *busetas* to Santa Teresa drop passengers at Yare's Plaza Bolívar (20min).

To **return to Caracas**, Ocumare-bound *busetas* depart from one block east and one block north of the Plaza Bolívar. Buses from Ocumare to Caracas leave every 15min until 9pm.

The northwest coast

Venezuela's **northwest coast** gets much less press than the Caribbean offshore islands of Aruba, Bonaire and Curaçao, but offers similarly spectacular beaches alongside some of the Caribbean's prettiest colonial towns and two fine national parks.

Parque Nacional Henri Pittier, roughly 150km from Caracas, has palm-lined sands, striking mountain ranges and four vegetation zones, which are together home to a tremendous array of birds and plant life. **Parque Nacional Morrocoy**, a few hours to the west of Pittier and more popular than its neighbour, is best known for its gorgeous white-sand cays surrounded by crystalline water.

Three hours west of Morrocoy, the well-preserved colonial town of **Coro** serves as a good break from the parks. From here, most visitors head directly into the Andes, but some press on 360km west to cross the border into Colombia (see p.978).

PARQUE NACIONAL HENRI PITTIER

Created in 1937, **PARQUE NACIONAL HENRI PITTIER** was

Venezuela's first national park, named after a famous Swiss geographer and botanist who classified more than thirty thousand plants in Venezuela. Despite the park's great biodiversity, the vast majority of visitors come for its **beaches**. At weekends it can be totally overrun, but it is generally quiet during the week.

Pittier's wide array of **flora and fauna** is a result of the relatively short distance in which it climbs from sea level to 2430m, with the changes in altitude creating distinct vegetation zones where different species flourish. The park is renowned among birdwatchers, containing 520 bird species (6.5 percent of the world's total) in just over a thousand square kilometres. Noteworthy specimens include the rufous-vented chachalaca, the scaled piculet, the pale-tipped inezia and the Venezuelan bristle-tyrant.

The only two roads into Pittier form a "V", with **Maracay** at the vertex and **Choroní** and **Ocumare de la Costa** at the two ends. Choroní, in the eastern portion of the park, has the lion's share of the budget accommodation and is one of the few backpacker destinations in Venezuela. Ocumare, while not as enticing a town, is worth visiting for the gorgeous La Ciénaga lagoon.

What to see and do

The park can be explored along hiking trails from Choroní, but the best base for serious wildlife-spotting is **Estación Biológica Rancho Grande** (8am–4pm) on the highway between Maracay and Ocumare. At about 1100m, this research station for the Universidad Central de Venezuela has a multitude of trails from which visitors are likely to see an incredible variety of birds and perhaps some howler monkeys. The station also offers very rustic dormitory **accommodation** (BsF30), but guests must bring their own sheets or a sleeping bag, as

well as food to cook in the communal kitchen.

Arrival and information

Bus The Estación Biológica is on the road between Maracay and Ocumare de la Costa; to get there board the hourly bus heading in either direction and ask the bus driver to let you off at Rancho Grande. Officially, you need permission from Inparques in Maracay (see above) to walk the trails, and from the university (☎0412/871-7319) to stay overnight. If you arrive unannounced, you'll be at the mercy of the on-duty Inparques guard and will have to hope that there's a friendly research party at the station if you want to sleep there.

Tourist information There is no official tourist information at the Estación Biológica. For information on the park's beaches, see the Choroní and Ocumare accounts (below and p.972).

Tours

Oskar Padilla, an experienced, English-speaking guide (☎0412/892-5308, ✉oskarpadilla@hotmail .com), offers hiking and birdwatching around Rancho Grande, and can organize the necessary permits for you. *Casa Luna Espinoza* in Choroní (see p.970) and Colonia Tovar-based Viva Trek (see p.967) can also arrange jungle and beach tours in Henri Pittier.

Moving on

Bus Barinas (several daily; 9hr); Caracas (every 15min; 1hr 30min); Coro (several daily; 7hr); Maracaibo (several daily; 8hr); Mérida (2 daily; 11hr); Puerto Ayacucho (2 daily; 12hr); San Antonio del Táchira (1 daily; 12hr); San Fernando de Apure (4 daily; 6hr); Valencia (every 15min; 45min).

CHORONÍ

Choroní actually consists of two parts: the colonial town of **CHORONÍ**, notable for its winding streets and colourful houses, but otherwise dull; and **PUERTO COLOMBIA**, a beach town 2km away, where most of the accommodation and action is concentrated. The lifeblood of Puerto Colombia is its lively **malecón**, where the fishing boats dock. People congregate here at night, and on weekends it's common to see *tambores*,

PUERTO COLOMBIA

ACCOMMODATION
Casa Luna Espinoza   D
Casa Pinguino   B
Habitaciones Mayitas   C
Hostal Colonial   E
Vista Mar   A

CARIBBEAN SEA
Playa Grande

Pharmacy

Coop. Alcatoucs

Pc Accion

PUERTO COLOMBIA

EATING & DRINKING
Bar La Playa   2
Brisas del Mar   3
Jalio   4
Pescaíto   1
Restaurant Araguaneyes   5
Tu Casa   6

Bus Terminal

0   100 m

▼ Playa El Diario

a coastal tradition of African drum-playing, singing and dancing.

What to see and do

The one beach easily reached on foot is **Playa Grande**. Thanks to its location, just 500m east of Puerto Colombia, it becomes mobbed with weekend visitors, who leave lots of litter. Otherwise it's very picturesque, with palm trees, aquamarine water and lush mountains in the background. About the same distance to the west, but harder to reach (and thus less crowded), **Playa El Diario** is a 45-min walk from the village. To get here from the midpoint of the main Choroní–Puerto Colombia road, follow Calle Cementerio past the cemetery and bear left at the split.

To access the area's other beaches you will need to take a *lancha*, or small boat, which can be arranged at the *malecón*. To the east, the closest beach is **Playa Valle Seco** (BsF40 per person with return), which has some coral reefs and decent snorkelling. Farther east, **Playa Chuao** (BsF50 per person with return) offers tranquil water, good shade provided by palm trees and stands that prepare fresh fish. The colonial town of the same name, a few kilometres inland, is famous for producing some of the world's best cacao, as well as its own Diablos Danzantes festival (see p.953). Still farther east is **Playa Cepe** (BsF60 per person with return), a palm-lined, pretty white-sand beach.

To combine these beaches in a single trip, negotiate a price with the boat pilot. As some beaches don't have food stands, it's a good idea to pack lunch supplies.

Arrival

Bus From Terminal La Bandera in Caracas, buses leave for the Maracay terminal (1hr 30min), where you can transfer to a Choroní-bound bus (hourly; 2hr).

Taxi Taxis from the Maracay bus terminal cost around BsF160 and take only an hour. Alternatively, take a seat in a *por puesto* (shared taxi) for BsF40. The owners of *Casa Luna Espinoza* (see below) can provide private transfers direct from the airport in Caracas (BsF550 per car).

Accommodation

If this is your first stop in Venezuela after Caracas, you'll be amazed by the quality of budget accommodation. Many places offer midweek discounts, and you'll get a better deal here than pretty much anywhere else on the northwest coast. Consequently, camping (for example, on Playa Grande) isn't especially worthwhile, and is discouraged for safety reasons. Reservations are recommended in high season.

Casa Luna Espinoza C. Morillo
☎0243/951-5318, ⊛www.jungletrip.de.
Casa Luna has simple rooms and shared bathrooms set around a plant-filled courtyard, as well as a communal kitchen and TV, hammocks and wi-fi.

German owner Claudia, who also speaks English, is a mine of useful information for backpackers, and runs day-trips and overnight tours to Henri Pittier (BsF160–330 per person). She also runs two other hostels in town. BsF80.

Casa Pinguino C. Morillo ☎0412/133-9914. The bedrooms at this oddly named place (opposite the even odder *Posada My God*) are spartan, but the small, lush courtyard and swimming pool are definite pluses. Can organize boat trips to the beaches including BBQ and beer. BsF140.

Habitaciones Mayitas C. Rangel #12 ☎0243/991-1141. There's no escaping the genuine family life at this unmarked homestay, with buggies, toys and clutter throughout the communal areas. A friendly atmosphere makes up for basic rooms, and there's a shared kitchen and bathrooms. The double and triple rooms have a/c, while the larger rooms have fans. BsF70.

Hostal Colonial C. Morillo ☎0243/218-5012, ⓔcolonialchoroni@gmail.com. A stylish and excellent-value guesthouse with plenty of services, including laundry, book exchange and wi-fi. Most of the clean, spacious, light-filled rooms are en suite (cold water) and fan-cooled. Italian and English spoken. There's also a Creole restaurant. BsF60.

Vista Mar C. Colón, on corner with the *malecón* ☎0243/991-1107. A rambling place with 33 rooms, all en suite, plus a covered terrace upstairs. Room 21 has good sea views plus a/c and TV (BsF210). Cheaper rooms come with fans. BsF120.

Eating

As well as the following options, all on Av. Los Cocos, there are numerous shacks lining the path to Playa Grande which sell plates of fish, rice and salad for around BsF20 until roughly 5pm, although like many people in Choroní their owners maintain a somewhat relaxed attitude to opening hours. There's a small courtyard opposite the *malecón* which has a more nocturnal collection of food stalls, most selling burgers and *arepas*. For food to cook in your posada's communal kitchen, try *Pescadería Choroní* down the side of Bar La Playa and the fruit and veg stalls opposite. You can also buy fish directly from the fishermen on the beach, and there is a bakery just over the bridge towards Playa Grande.

Brisas del Mar ☎0243/991-1268. Not the most peaceful place in town to eat, being next to *Bar La Playa* (see below), but *Brisas* offers calamarí five ways (all BsF55) as well as non-seafood options such as *pabellón* and pasta. Locals also

recommend the soups at *Restaurant Puerto Colombia* next door. Open 8.30am–11pm daily.

Restaurant Araguaneyes ☎0243/991-1166. Enjoy huge portions of fresh fish with spicy sauce (BsF50) or *pasta marinara* (BsF48) on the large upstairs terrace while listening to music that for once isn't salsa. Also open for breakfast. Daily 8am–11pm.

Tu Casa ☎0243/871-6968. Anglophile owner Raul, who studied art in London in the 1980s, whips up delicious seafood dishes such as paella (BsF100 for 2 people), great fresh juices (BsF7) and excellent Creole breakfasts (BsF20) with healthy touches such as bran *arepas*. His artwork adorns the walls of the attractive covered courtyard. Open 8am–1pm & 5–10pm daily.

Drinking

Choroní's nightlife, if you can call it that, is very casual – most people just buy a few beers and drink them on the *malecón*.

Bar La Playa At the beach end of Av. Los Cocos. By day, vacationers laze about in the plastic chairs on the covered patio, sipping beers and watching the fishermen come and go. At night, the focus is on bottles or rum, high-volume salsa and canned Latin pop.

Jalio C. Concepción. The most upscale option in town, promising tapas by day and cocktails by night. Open Thurs–Sat, if the owners feel like it.

Pescaito Along the path to Playa Grande. The closest that Puerto Colombia gets to a club, atop a low hill across the bridge. Open until dawn, when the fishers head out to catch the nightspot's namesake.

Directory

Bank There is a BNC ATM at the new bus terminal, but at the time of research it didn't accept international cards. You can change dollars at some hotels.

Internet PC Acción on C. Morillo is a fantastic cooperative that ploughs its profits back into community projects. Has several computers plus wi-fi, printer, scanner and photocopiers. Also sells great home-made ice cream made from fresh fruit (or try the chocolate, served with a dollop of condensed milk, BsF2.5) and cakes. Internet BsF5 per hr. Open Mon–Fri 8am–9pm, Sat 9am–9pm, Sun 10am–9pm.

Pharmacy A small pharmacy next door to *Brisas del Mar* is open daily 8.30am–9pm.

Phones Movistar, C. Concepción, for mobile phone credit. Otherwise, ask at your accommodation or head for the *malecón*, where there will usually be someone with a phone on a plastic table or a mobile to rent by the minute.

Post office Half a block south of the Plaza Bolívar in Choroní. Theoretically open Mon–Fri 9am–3pm, although often closed and frequently lacking in stamps when it does open.

Shopping Cooperativa Alcatours, C. Morillo at Independencia (☎0414/237-0797, ✉alcatours14@hotmail.com), sells interesting "cacao-arte" and *artesanía* made by the husband-wife owners, including *ponche de cacao*, a chocolate liqueur, and paintings of *tambores* dancers. At weekends, stallholders selling jewellery and other handicrafts set up on the *malecón* in the late afternoon.

Moving on

Boat If you're heading to Ocumare de la Costa or La Ciénaga (see below), negotiate a ride with a boatman (from BsF300 per boat on quiet days; about 1hr): a quicker and very beautiful, but more expensive, alternative to the bus.

Bus Buses for the Maracay terminal (BsF20) leave from 5am–6.30pm during the week, starting about 7am at weekends, roughly every 90min.

Taxi Same as getting here (see p.970), but in the opposite direction.

OCUMARE DE LA COSTA

The colonial town of **OCUMARE DE LA COSTA** is set a few kilometres from the beach village of El Playón. Neither is as attractive as Choroní, and the beach itself is a bit dirty. However, some secluded snorkelling spots, narrow mangrove inlets, small waterfalls and swimming holes – not to mention the Estación Biológica Rancho Grande (see p.969) – make a visit worthwhile if you have the time. Frequent daily buses (2hr) shuttle between Ocumare/El Playón and the Maracay terminal.

Around 5km east of El Playón is one of the area's best-known beaches, **Playa Cata**. Despite some horrible high-rise concrete apartment buildings, it is otherwise attractive, with palm trees lining the white sand. Buses (BsF15) run here from El Playón every half-hour or so. **Playa Catica**, an hour-long hike or short boat ride (BsF15 in a *por puesto* at weekends, BsF100 per boat Mon–Fri) from Cata, is smaller and less crowded. Farther east, legendary surfing beach **Playa Cuyagua** can get fairly large waves, so swimmers should exercise caution. Daily buses from El Playón cost BsF15, or you can take a *lancha* for about BsF300 per boat return.

The crystalline waters of **La Ciénaga**, a beautiful lagoon several kilometres to the west of Ocumare, offer some of the park's best snorkelling. There are also a few strips of sand for sunbathing. The lagoon is accessible only by *lancha* (BsF250 for the boat, with return), which leave from La Boca, on the east side of El Playón.

By far the best accommodation option in El Playón, and well worth the extra cost, is the excellent **De La Costa Eco-lodge** (west end of *malecón* ☎0243/993-1986, ⓦwww.ecovenezuela.com; BsF425). The owners can arrange trips to La Ciénaga and Estación Biológica Rancho Grande (see p.969).

PARQUE NACIONAL MORROCOY

Gorgeous white-sand cays surrounded by limpid water are the highlights of **PARQUE NACIONAL MORROCOY**, one of the most popular national parks in Venezuela. The three hundred square kilometre reserve, spread primarily over water, was created in 1974, but today it doesn't feel much like a national park. Several areas have been irresponsibly developed, and there's no restriction on the large numbers of visiting tourists and little enforcement of litter, water pollution or camping laws. A disastrous chemical spill in the 1990s destroyed much of the coral, and in many areas left little for snorkellers to see. Fortunately, some **beaches** remain relatively untouched, snorkelling and scuba-diving remain good in places and the park is still home to nearly four-fifths of Venezuela's aquatic **bird species**, as well as several types of mammal.

Towns at both ends of the park serve as bases for exploring the cays, though both are eyesores and have had sporadic safety problems. Tucacas, to the south, is overdeveloped and lacks good accommodation options; it is better to try the slightly more pleasant Chichiriviche, to the north.

What to see and do

There are a total of 22 **cays**, or *cayos*, in the park, most differing only in size and facilities. Day-trips can be purchased from one of three cooperatives on the *malecón* in Chichiriviche (including Embarcadero Playa Norte; ☏0416/242-0086), and most posadas arrange trips for guests at no extra charge. Prices listed are for the boat, not per person, and include return; feel free to bargain.

Dotted with shade-giving palms, **Cayo Sombrero** (BsF300), halfway between Chichiriviche and Tucacas, is one of the larger and more popular cays, although you can still find uncrowded parts, especially if you go midweek. It has two small restaurants (better to take a picnic) and some decent spots for snorkelling – better snorkelling and scuba-diving is farther north, around **Cayo Sal** (BsF120). *Lanchas* also make trips to *cayos* Muerto (BsF100), Pelón (BsF140), Peraza (BsF140) and Varadero (BsF170).

Tucacas is the access point for **Cayo Paiclás** (BsF150), a large cay with several very popular beaches, including Playuela, Playuelita and Playa Paiclás. All have small food stands or restaurants. On the east end of the cay is the more secluded, very pretty **Playa Mero**.

CHICHIRIVICHE

The only reason to visit the tiny beach town of **CHICHIRIVICHE** is for its proximity to the cays. Otherwise it's a dismal place, with muddy, half-paved streets, litter-strewn pavements and an inordinate number of stores selling liquor and plastic beach gear.

Calle Zamora, the town's main artery, dead-ends at the *malecón*, where most activity is centred. By day during high season and at weekends it's bustling with *lancha* passengers headed to the cays; by night hippie street vendors descend to sell handmade jewellery and strum guitars.

Arrival and information

Bus Buses leave Valencia (every 30min; 3hr) for Chichiriviche until 6pm, stopping on C. Zamora about 500m inland from the *malecón*. During the day you can easily walk to most accommodation, but after dark you should take a cab (around BsF10). Buses plying the Valencia–Chichiriviche route also stop at Tucacas.
Internet Byte Quest, south of *Caribana Hotel* on the west side of the street (daily 8am–8pm; BsF4 per hr). Multiple computers, plus wi-fi, scanner,

Map: CHICHIRIVICHE

CARIBBEAN SEA

Playa Norte

ACCOMMODATION
Capri — B
Morena's Place — A
Posada La Negra — D
Posada Villa Gregoria — C

EATING & DRINKING
Oasis Sport — 5
Panaderia El Centro — 3
Rancho Andino — 2
Restaurant La Esquina de Arturo — 4
Tasca Restaurant Txalupa — 1

Pharmacy

PASEO BOLIVAR

BUSETA

CALLE PLANTÉL · CALLE MARIÑO · CALLE CALVARIO · CALLE ZAMORA · CALLE COROMOTO · CALLE SILVA · CALLE BARRIO NUEVO · AVENIDA RUIZ PINEDA · CALLE LAS FLORES · CALLE FALCON · CALLE VARGAS · CALLE COMERCIO · CALLE LA MARINA

Buses to Sanare & Valencia

---

photocopier. Sells camera memory cards and recordable DVDs.

Tourist information There's a wooden kiosk that serves as a Corfaltur *módulo de info* about 50m inland from where the bus stops on C. Zamora, though it has no reliable schedule of opening hours.

Accommodation

Most accommodation is within a couple of blocks of the *malecón*, a generally safe part of town with lots of foot traffic. Camping in the national park has been banned in recent years, but if you are keen to do it contact the Falcón State Inparques office (☎0268/252-4198) to enquire about the current policy. Most of the options below drop their prices around twenty percent outside high season.

Capri C. Zamora ☎0259/818-6026, @hotel caprica@yahoo.com. A sterile but well-located place with very friendly staff and a large ground-floor lounge. Amply sized rooms (en suite, TV, a/c) are done up in pastels and paintings of beach scenes, and there's free wi-fi. BsF170.

Morena's Place Sector Playa Norte ☎0259/815-0936, @posadamorenas@hotmail.com. Just one street in from the beach, Morena's dorms (a rarity in Chichiriviche) make this a good-value spot for single travellers. These come with shared bathrooms and ceiling fans, while the one double room is en suite. There's a laundry service, kitchen and barbeque, and the English-speaking owners

can prepare dinner or breakfast on request. Dorms BsF50, room BsF120.

Posada La Negra C. Mariño ☎0259/815-0470. Simple, brightly painted rooms in this homely place on a quiet street come with private bathrooms, a/c and TV. *Posada Delia*, two doors nearer the sea (☎0259/818-6089) is another decent option with particularly good rates (BsF100) in low season. BsF120.

Posada Villa Gregoria C. Mariño ☎0259/818-6359. This secure guesthouse has a Mediterranean vibe and backpacker-friendly, English-speaking staff. Rooms are spotless, spacious and light-filled, and come with en-suite bathroom and a/c. There's a laundry service and hammocks on the open-air second floor. For groups, rooms for four (BsF250) or the apartment for seven with private kitchen (BsF600) are good options. Can organize boat trips. BsF150.

Eating and drinking

Chichiriviche's nightlife leaves a lot to be desired, and *Txalupa* (see p.975) and its neighbouring restaurants on the seafront are probably your best bet for a couple of drinks.

Oasis Sport C. Zamora. Better for a chuckle than a serious night out, this video bar/off-licence attracts tipsy men who gape at vintage 1980s music videos on the oversized screen and attempt an occasional chorus.

Panadería el Centro C. Zamora opposite Hotel Capri. This sizeable bakery sells meats, cheeses and other provisions as well as good bread and coffee. A handy location just metres from the *malecón* makes this a great place to pick up picnic supplies before heading to the cays. Open 7am–9pm daily.

Rancho Andino C. Zamora. Great for watching the evening action on Calle Zamora (except Thurs when it closes after lunch), this roughy-and-ready, open-air restaurant offers seafood mains including *pasta marinera* (BsF60). The breakfast menu features pancakes (BsF28) and fresh juices (BsF8).

Restaurant La Esquina de Arturo C. Plantél. "Art's Corner" is the best place in town for super-cheap and tasty *comida criolla*, with an emphasis on seafood. Typical breakfasts (around BsF32) include the *desayuno marinero*, with shredded fish, a fried egg, black beans and a mound of grated white cheese. There's a great-value *menu del día* (BsF30) for every day of the week, served from noon, and the *arepas* are good at any time. Open Fri–Sun 8am–9pm, until 3.30pm Mon–Thurs (later during high season).

Tasca Restaurant Txalupa C. Zamora, across from the *malecón*. The bar on the second floor – once the main nightspot in town – has been closed for some time but the first-floor restaurant remains a good spot to enjoy a beer and sea views. Decent seafood dishes include a hearty fish soup (BsF28). Open daily noon–10pm.

Directory

Banks and exchange Bancoro, C. Plantél at C. Calvario; Banco Industrial (and others) on C. Zamora.
Pharmacy Several options on C. Zamora, one next to Oasis Sport (8am–9pm daily).
Phones *Comunicación los Cayos*, on the west side of C. Zamora about 60m inland from Paseo Bolívar (daily 8am–noon & 2–8pm) offers calls and internet access, and sells mobile phone credit for all the major networks. There's also an a/c Movistar call centre about 100m further inland (Mon–Sat 8am–noon & 3–7pm).
Post The nearest post office is in Tucacas.

Moving on

Bus The nearest major terminals are in Valencia and Maracay (see p.972). If you're heading straight to Coro, take a *buseta* from Av. Zamora to Sanare (20min), where you shouldn't have to wait more than half an hour for a passing bus (3–4hr).

CORO

CORO, Venezuela's prettiest colonial town, was named a national monument in 1950 and a World Heritage Site in 1993. Although it currently gives the impression of being a little down on its luck, Coro still makes for a relaxed one- or two-day stopover between the coast and mountains. The town's architectural highlights are contained within the **casco histórico**, or historic centre, while another principal attraction, the **Parque Nacional Médanos de Coro**, lies a few kilometres away.

What to see and do

You only need wander the sleepy streets of central Coro to get a flavour of the town's colonial heritage, but for a closer look, there are museums, mansions and churches to be visited. Just outside the city are the wilder sights of **Parque Nacional Médanos de Coro.**

JEWISH HERITAGE

During the nineteenth century, Coro was home to a sizeable Jewish community, which had initially come over from Curaçao. The Jews of Coro thrived here through commerce with the Dutch Antilles but were expelled in 1855; when invited back three years later, most did not return. Their history is explored in the Museo de Arte Alberto Henríquez (Mon–Sat 8am–noon & 2–5pm, Sun 8am–noon; free), across from the Museo de Arte de Coro. It contains the oldest synagogue in Venezuela, constructed in 1853 and one of the first synagogues on the continent. While here, enquire about visiting another vestige of the Jewish community, the Cementerio Judío, on Calle Zamora at Calle 23 de Enero. Built in 1830, it is the oldest of all South American Jewish cemeteries still in use.

Churches

The centre of the *casco histórico* is Plaza Bolívar, on the east end of which stands Venezuela's oldest **Catedral**, begun in 1583 and finished in 1634. Two blocks north on Plaza San Clemente, the **Iglesia San Clemente** was originally built in 1538 by the town's founder, Juan de Ampíes. Totally rebuilt in the eighteenth century, San Clemente is one of three churches in the country built in the shape of a cross. Beside it, a small monument contains the **Cruz de San Clemente**, the wooden cross used in the first Mass after the town was founded.

Colonial mansions

The **Casa de las Ventanas de Hierro** (Mon–Sat 9am–noon & 3–6pm, Sun 9am–noon; BsF5), a block to the west of Plaza San Clemente on Calle Zamora, is notable for its iron window frames and grilles. A small museum inside exhibits colonial-era clothes and furniture. The work of local artists is displayed at the **Casa del Tesoro** (Tues–Sat 9am–noon & 3–6pm, Sun 9am–3pm; free), another stately mansion just across Calle Colón. A block and a half to the northeast of Plaza Bolívar on Avenida Talavera, the **Museo de Arte de Coro** (Mon–Sat 9am–4pm, Sun 9am–noon; free) has temporary exhibits set in a beautiful mansion.

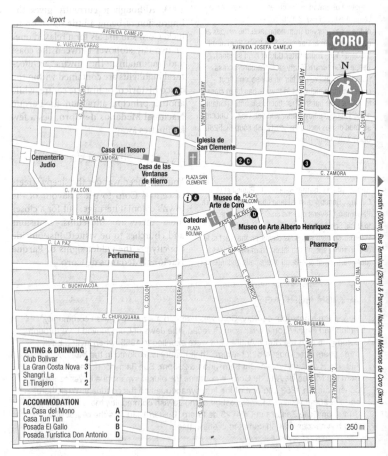

CORO

EATING & DRINKING
Club Bolivar — 4
La Gran Costa Nova — 3
Shangri La — 1
El Tinajero — 2

ACCOMMODATION
La Casa del Mono — A
Casa Tun Tun — C
Posada El Gallo — B
Posada Turistica Don Antonio — D

Lavatín (500m), Bus Terminal (2km) & Parque Nacional Médanos de Coro (3km)

You might find any of the above to be unexpectedly closed on a quiet day.

Parque Nacional Médanos de Coro

Just at the northern city limits is an entrance into **Parque Nacional Médanos de Coro,** an 80-square-kilometre park covering one of Venezuela's few desert areas. There's not a lot to do here other than stroll among the dunes and spy on herds of wild goats, but the light is beautiful in the early morning or late afternoon. The 3-km taxi ride from the *casco histórico* should not cost more than BsF15. To get back to town, walk out to the main road to hail a taxi. Robberies have been reported here, so don't stray too far from the entrance or linger long after sunset, don't take more money than you need and be discreet if you take a camera.

Arrival, information and tours

Bus Buses arrive at the terminal on Avenida Los Médanos, 2km east of town, which has an ATM but nowhere to leave luggage. Taxis will take you to the *casco histórico* for around BsF12, which is about the most you should pay for rides within town.
Internet Net Centre Ciber Café on the corner of C. Zamora and C. Hernandez. Open Mon–Sat daily 8am–7pm. Closed Sun.
Tourist information Corfaltur (Paseo Alameda ☎0268/251-8033; Mon–Fri 8am–noon & 1.30–5pm), the state tourism entity, distributes maps of the *casco histórico* and sometimes has English-speaking staff on duty. The website ⓦwww.coroweb.com has some useful listings information, although Spanish-language pages work better than the English or French.
Tours Araguato Expeditions (☎0426/866-9328, ⓦwww.araguato.org), in *La Casa del Mono* (see below), specializes in trips to the nearby Paraguaná Peninsula, the San Luís mountains (including the "Spanish trail", a jungle path once used by European explorers) and Maracaibo's flea market and eerie *catatumbo* lighting.

Accommodation

🏃 **La Casa del Mono** C. Federación #16 ☎0268/2511-596, Ⓔinfo@araguato.org.

A great new posada from the owner of Araguato Tours (see above), in a beautifully restored colonial building in the historic centre. Stylishly decorated rooms (with shared or private bathrooms) come with mosquito nets, and there is a courtyard with hammocks, kitchen, public computer and wi-fi. BsF110.
Casa Tun Tun C. Zamora ☎0268/404-4260, Ⓔcasatuntun@hotmail.com. *Tun Tun* boasts a TV room with DVD player and book exchange, a leafy patio with plenty of seating and hammocks, a shared kitchen and wi-fi. The simple, clean rooms range from fan-cooled with shared bathroom to a/c and en suite. BsF120.
Posada El Gallo C. Federación #26 ☎0268/252-9481, Ⓔposadaelgallo2001@hotmail.com. Justifiably popular with backpackers, offering private rooms (shared bath or en suite) plus two dorm rooms. A lovely colonial building with beautiful gardens, a barbeque area, beer on the honour system and a gift shop selling artisanal crafts. There's also an upstairs deck with hammocks, a shared kitchen and wi-fi. The super-friendly owners can organize day-trips to the Paraguaná Peninsula or nearby mountains (BsF220 inc lunch) and have a second location around the block to handle overflow. Dorms BsF50, rooms BsF100.
Posada Turística Don Antonio ☎0268/253-9578. A family-friendly option on two floors around a breezy courtyard with curious decor, including salmon-pink pillars and plastic plants. Rooms are rather basic but clean, with a/c, TV and private bathrooms. There's an internet café in reception (7am–8pm for public, until 10pm for guests). BsF120.

Eating and drinking

There are a number of inexpensive restaurants in Coro, many doubling as bars in the evening, although, as with the town's museums, opening hours are only loosely kept. Be sure to try *chivo* (goat), the regional speciality.
🏃 **Club Bolívar** C. Federación between Av. Zamora and Av. Falcón. Despite its upscale appearance, this cooperative has a reasonably priced menu of *coriano* specialities such as curried goat (BsF28), although supply problems mean that many dishes are not always available. The *desayuno criollo* (shredded meat, *arepas*, black beans and cheese; BsF15) is extremely good value, and the leafy terrace is a great place to enjoy a beer or fresh juice. The café, which is popular with government employees, is open all day until 8pm. The bar stays open later Wed–Sat, depending on demand.

La Gran Costa Nova Av. Manaure opposite *Hotel Intercaribe*. This *panaderia* bakes great bread and cakes, and also offers provisions such as cheeses, cooked meats, eggs and fruit juice. Sandwiches, pizza and coffee can also be bought to take away. Open daily 6am–9pm.

Shangri La Av. Josefa Camejo at end of C. Toledo. Locals repeatedly recommend this canteen-style vegetarian restaurant, which turns out Asian-influenced, meat-free breakfasts and lunches. There is no menu, but you can fill your plate from the freshly prepared dishes on offer

for around BsF15. Typical options include chop suey and Chinese dumplings. Open Mon–Sat 7am–3pm.

El Tinajero C. Zamora next to *Casa Tun Tun* ☎0268/252-9100. Don't expect fine dining at this courtyard restaurant, but you can expect decent, hearty plates of grilled beef or chicken at low prices (BsF20) and very cheap beer (BsF3.50). Locals often fill the bar stools to take advantage of the latter, and will be happy for you to join them after you've eaten. Food served Mon–Sat noon–10pm; the bar can stay open later.

CROSSING INTO COLOMBIA

There are three main border crossings between Venezuela and Colombia. The northernmost, at Paraguachón, offers the best connections to coastal cities like Cartagena; Cúcuta has onward services to Bogotá. Before leaving Venezuela you must pay the BsF65 exit tax (in bolívares) and get your passport stamped by the nearest emigration office. Once you cross the border, immediately visit the nearest Colombian immigration office for an entry stamp, and remember to set your watch back a half-hour. Citizens of the US, Canada, Australia, New Zealand and Europe do not need a visa to enter Colombia. Relations between Venezuela and Colombia are volatile, and can deteriorate at short notice, making the border region a tense and unpleasant place to be. It is wise to seek up-to-date advice on the current political siuation, and on security, before using any of the three crossings.

Paraguachón Take a *por puesto* from the Maracaibo terminal to Maicao, Colombia (several daily until 4pm; 3hr). From here you can switch to a bus for Santa Marta (4hr), Cartagena (8hr) and other destinations. Expect police checks on the way to the border, and set off in the morning to ensure that you arrive in Maicao in plenty of time to catch an onward bus.

Cúcuta Nearest to San Antonio del Táchira, San Cristóbal and Mérida, this crossing is more popular among shoppers than travellers, though it does provide onward transport to Bogotá and other central Colombian cities. From the Mérida bus terminal, there are frequent buses to San Cristóbal, just a short onward ride to San Antonio (again, you can expect police checks en route to the border). From here, buses and *por puestos* leave from Avenida Venezuela for Cúcuta. Between Mon and Sat you can get an exit stamp at the SAIME post at the border; on Sun you must go to the SAIME office in San Antonio (Carrera 9 between calles 6 and 7; ☎0276/771-4453).

Puerto Carreño/Casuarito These are two separate crossings, both accessible from Puerto Ayacucho (see p.990). Currently no border fees are being collected at either. From the Puerto Ayacucho bus terminal, catch a *por puesto* for El Burro (45min), which is on the road to Puerto Páez; from El Burro you can then take a *lancha* to the Colombian city of Puerto Carreño (10min). Alternatively, from the port in Puerto Ayacucho, you can catch a five-minute ferry (every 20min daily from 8am–5.30pm), which crosses the Orinoco and leaves you in the small Colombian village of Casuarito. From here you can take a high-speed boat (1hr 30min) to Puerto Carreño, although these leave just twice daily, at 7am and 3pm, making this a less reliable option.

The journey by road from Puerto Carreño to Bogotá is long, and only feasible in dry season. Also, the Colombian consulate in Puerto Ayacucho has expressed concern in the past about visitors' safety on the Colombian side of the border. It is wise to get up-to-date security advice before crossing, and consider travelling onward in Colombia by plane rather than bus. There are four flights per week to Bogotá (see p.544), as well as other large cities, with Satena (⊛www.satena.com).

Shopping

There are a few places selling artesanía in Coro, though none of it is very compelling. Local potters occasionally sell their wares in Plaza Falcón, and the Centro Artesanal next to *Club Bolivar* (see p.977) has a momentarily diverting array of paintings, dioramas and *dulce de leche* (made from goat milk). Officially, it's open daily 8.30am–6pm, though the vendors tend to operate on their own schedules. Of more interest is the unmarked perfumería on C. Colón just north of C. Garcés, a spiritualist shop selling love potions, animal parts, pickled reptiles and other assorted juju, most used for synchretist rituals. Since some products may have come from endangered species, look but don't buy. If you have any appetite left, drop by the small food market at C. Garcés and C. Colón (daily until about 7pm), where you can pick up supplies for your posada's shared kitchen.

Directory

Banks and exchange The best bets for using international cards are the Banco Venezuela on Av. Talavera and the Banco Mercantil on C. Falcón.
Laundry All the listed accommodation choices have laundry services. Also Lavatín, C. Falcón ☏ 0268/251-6712, which has an English-speaking owner. Mon–Fri 8am–noon & 2–6pm, Sat 8am–2pm, closed Sun.
Pharmacy Farmacia Super Ofertas, corner of C. Zamora and C. Toledo. Mon–Sat 8.20am–noon and 2.20pm–6pm. There's another on Paseo Talavera.
Phones Movistar call centre at C. Falcón between Plaza Falcón and Av. Manaure, Mon–Fri 8.30am–noon & 2.30–6.30pm, Sat 8.30–noon & 2.30–5.30pm. Closed Sun. Also Digitel, at Paseo Talavera.
Post Ipostel, Casa de las 100 Ventanas, Calle Ampíes. Open Mon–Fri 8am–noon & 2–5pm, if the electricity supply permits.

Moving on

For information on crossing into Colombia from this region, see the box on p.978. A BsF1 tax must be paid at one of the kiosks in the bus terminal before departure.
Bus Buses and *por puestos* run regularly throughout the day to Maracaibo (3hr) and Punto Fijo (1hr 30min), and there are also regular buses to Valencia (6hr 30min), but at the time of research, bus companies were cutting back heavily on services to more distant destinations and time tables were erratic. There were still several daily services to Caracas (9hr), mostly in the evening, Barquisimeto (7hr) and Maracay (7hr), plus one per day to Mérida (at 5.45pm; 10hr) and Puerto La Cruz (at 6.30pm; 12hr).

Mérida and the Andes

The mountainous state of **Mérida** finds it way onto nearly all visitors' itineraries, regardless of how long they are spending in Venezuela. The raw beauty of the carved, green slopes and snowcapped peaks of the **Andes** is not to be missed, and the facilities for travellers in the capital, likewise called Mérida, are among Venezuela's best. To the city's south and east, the **Parque Nacional Sierra Nevada**, dominated by the famed Pico Bolívar (5007m) and Pico Humboldt (4920m), offers some of the finest hiking opportunities in the region. To the northwest, the Carretera Transandina, or the Trans-Andean Highway, passes several charming mountain towns, including **Mucuchíes** and **Apartaderos**.

MÉRIDA

From the bottom of a deep valley, the city of **MÉRIDA** enjoys stunning views of the surrounding mountains without ever becoming uncomfortably cold. Unlike many other mountain towns in South America, it is quite modern and progressive, being home to one of the country's most prestigious universities, La Universidad de los Andes. Despite its cosmopolitan sensibilities, Mérida offers reasonable prices, relatively safe streets and an easily walkable centre. It is probably the most traveller-friendly place in western Venezuela.

Owing to its natural endowment as well as the efforts of several excellent tour operators, Mérida's chief attraction

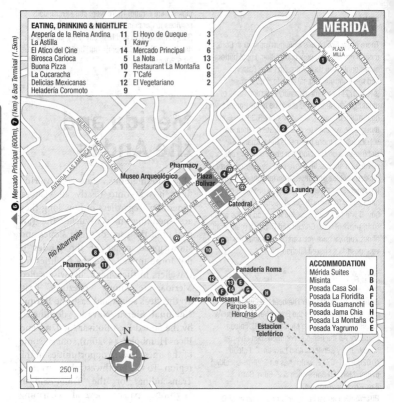

MÉRIDA

EATING, DRINKING & NIGHTLIFE

Arepería de la Reina Andina	11	El Hoyo de Queque	3
La Astilla	1	Kawy	4
El Atico del Cine	14	Mercado Principal	6
Birosca Carioca	5	La Nota	13
Buona Pizza	10	Restaurant La Montaña	C
La Cucaracha	7	T'Café	8
Delicias Mexicanas	12	El Vegetariano	2
Heladería Coromoto	9		

PLAZA MILLA

Pharmacy

Museo Arqueológico

Plaza Bolívar

Laundry

Catedral

Río Albarregas

Pharmacy

Panadería Roma

Mercado Artesanal

Parque las Heroínas

Estacion Teleférico

ACCOMMODATION

Mérida Suites	D
Misinta	B
Posada Casa Sol	A
Posada La Floridita	F
Posada Guamanchi	G
Posada Jama Chia	H
Posada La Montaña	C
Posada Yagrumo	E

N

0   250 m

is **adventure sports** (see box, p.982). However, if you've got some down time, or if you're allergic to adrenaline, the city offers a couple of sights, as well as some diverting **day-trips** (see p.985).

What to see and do

The old town around Plaza Bolívar makes for a pleasant half-day's wandering, though most people come to Mérida for the adventures to be had outside its urban sprawl.

The Town

Walking the streets of the **old town** to admire its colonial houses and pretty parks will only take a few hours. Right on the Plaza Bolívar, the **Catedral** grew out of plans for a seventeenth-century cathedral that wasn't started until 1803

and not completed until 1958. Of the several decent museums in the area, the most interesting is the **Museo Arqueológico** (Tues–Sun 8–11.30am & 2–5.30pm; BsF1), on Avenida 3 in an attractive Universidad de los Andes building. It presents pre-Columbian artefacts from the region, augmented by thorough historical descriptions.

The teleférico

Unfortunately for visitors and the city's tourism industry alike, Mérida's top attraction, the world's longest-travelling, highest-climbing **teleférico** (cable car), was closed in late 2008 for a major refurbishment. It is not expected to re-open fully until at least 2012, although there are suggestions that one or two stations might open before then.

For the latest information, enquire at the base station in Parque Las Heroínas or call ☎0274/252-5080.

When operating, the *teleférico* travels 12.6km, rising over 3000m to the top of **Pico Espejo** (4765m). There are three intermediate stations, and you should pause at the third, Loma Redonda (4045m), before ascending to the top, since the dramatic climb can cause mild altitude sickness. From Loma Redonda, you can also follow hiking trails 13km (5–6hr) to the small Andean town of **Los Nevados**, which contains several posadas and places to eat. You can do this walk on your own, but should take local advice and notify Inparques beforehand. The main office is near the bus terminal on Av. Las Américas (☎0274/262-1529). There is a second office at the *teleférico* base that's open only infrequently while the cable car is closed. In the absence of the *teleférico*, tour agencies in Mérida can arrange jeeps to Los Nevados.

Gravity Tours C 24 between avenidas 7 and 8 ☎0274/251-1279, ⓦwww.gravity-tours.com.ve. Offers a two-day "extreme" combo of mountain-biking and rafting, as well as trips throughout the country. Very helpful, English-speaking staff.

Guamanchi Expeditions C 24 between Av. 8 and Parque Las Heroínas ☎0274/252-2080, ⓦwww .guamanchi.com. Long-established company specializing in climbing and trekking. Also offers day-trips to Laguna Negra (see p.987) and bird-watching tours with expert local guides.

Jammin Expedition Av. 8 between calles 24 and 25 ☎0416/177-2743, ⓦwww.jamminexpedition .com.ve. A young, enthusiastic but professional outfit established in 2009 by guides who used to work for some of the more established companies.

Natoura C 24 across from *teleférico* base ☎0274/252-4216, ⓦwww.natoura.com. Has the highest rates, but contributes a percentage of profits to an elementary school in Los Llanos and visits others on trips in the Orinoco Delta. Also sells international flights and tours throughout Venezuela.

Tony Martin ☎0416/671-6108, ⓦwww .hosteltrail.com/extremexpeditions. A Los Llanos native, Tony is an experienced, enthusiastic and knowledgeable English-speaking guide who runs four-day trips to the region.

Arrival and information

Air Mérida airport (☎0274/263-4352), which lies only 2km from the city centre on Avenida Urdaneta, was closed at the time of research. Flights from Caracas land at El Vigia, 1hr 30min away by bus.

Bus There are half a dozen night buses from Caracas (13hr), several daily from Maracaibo (6hr) and one daily from Coro (10hr). City buses go to the centre (BsF1.50), or take a taxi (around BsF20).

Tourist information Cormetur (☎0274/263-4701) has offices in several locations around town, including the bus terminal, the airport and the Mercado Principal on Av. Las Américas. Opening hours vary by office and according to season; Mon–Fri mornings are the safest bet, though the offices at the bus terminal and Mercado Principal work weekends too.

Tour operators

Arassari Trek C 24 across from *teleférico* base ☎0274/252-5879, ⓦwww.arassari.com. Special-izes in canyoning and rafting; also sells air tickets.

Fanny Tours C 24 between Av. 8 and Parque Las Heroínas ☎0274/252-2952, ⓦwww.fanny-tours .com. Specializes in climbing; also offers trips to Maracaibo to see the wetlands and *Catatumbo* lightning. Multiple languages spoken, including English.

Accommodation

Mérida has a good selection of budget hostels and posadas. Most of the cheapest options are conveniently found near Parque Las Heroínas, a

TREAT YOURSELF

Posada Casa Sol Av. 4 between calles 15 and 16 ☎0274/252-4164, ⓦwww .posadacasasol.com. No detail has been missed in making this posada a stylish, luxurious haven in which to kick back after an arduous trek or long bus journey. The elegant communal areas feature iron sculptures, soothing water features and beautiful tiled floors, while the rooms have art on the walls, ultra-soft bedding and fantastic showers. Some have small balconies overlooking a flower-filled courtyard. Delicious breakfasts (from BsF38) can be enjoyed in the restaurant, and there's free wi-fi throughout. Fantastic value. BsF360.

ADVENTURE SPORTS AND TOURS

Mérida's surrounds provide the perfect conditions for an astounding range of adventure sports, and there's an equally amazing array of tour companies in town. Outside of the July–Sept high season, things can get very quiet for them and they will compete particularly hard for your business. However, it is worth remembering that, as with most services, you tend to get what you pay for. Since most of the activities on offer involve a certain level of risk, it's wise not to be stingy, since budget tours and budget equipment often go hand in hand.

Tour prices generally decrease as more customers register, so ask your company about joining an existing group. Many trips require a minimum number of customers, and you should not expect to turn up in Mérida and instantly find a group doing the trip you want, particularly outside of high season. For this reason, it pays to enquire ahead about tours if possible. While some companies take credit cards, you'll always get a far better price by paying in cash or arranging an electronic money transfer (see p.946). Except on one-day trips, all meals and accommodation are included in tour prices. As well as an array of sports, most agencies in Mérida offer tours to Los Llanos and to see the *Catatumbo* lighting, an atmospheric phenomenon unique to Venezuela.

Due to Venezuela's volatile economy and fierce competition among companies, prices listed here are approximate. For the latest rates, contact the agencies directly. Most agencies offer all of the following activities, though some claim to specialize in one in particular.

Canyoning

This increasingly popular adrenaline sport involves abseiling, scrambling and climbing alongside and under waterfalls. Full-day rates are BsF360 per person, typically with a two-person minimum.

Climbing and trekking

Two of the most popular routes are up Pico Humboldt and Pico Bolívar, Venezuela's highest peaks (see p.987), which should only be attempted with a guide. The latter

sort of backpacker ghetto where nearly all the tour agencies have their offices. Mid-range options can be great value for much of the year, when prices can be up to forty percent lower than the July–Sept high season costs listed below. All of the options below have hot water. To camp in the surrounding national parks, contact the local Inparques office (see p.949).

Mérida Suites Av. 8 between calles 21 and 22 ☎0274/251-2650, @meridasuites@hotmail .com. High-season rates are a bit steep for budget travellers, but for nine months of the year the cost of these luxurious, fully furnished apartments drops by a third, making them fantastic value. Fully self-contained with modern kitchen, stylish living room, bedroom and bathroom, cable TV. Internet in lobby. BsF300.

Misintá Av. 6 between calles 19 and 20 ☎0274/251-1192, @www.hotelmisinta .com.ve. A great-value new hotel from the owners of *La Montaña* (see p.983), with a smart, tiled lobby and a tranquil vibe. Rooms have cable TV, safety deposit boxes and stylish touches. Upstairs rooms have great mountain views, and there's a laundry

service and wi-fi. A restaurant should be fully open by the time you read this. Special offers in low season can cut room rates by more than forty percent. BsF230.

Posada La Floridita C 25 between the seminary and Av. 8 ☎0274/251-0452. Among the cheapest posadas in town, with a friendly manager and a homely (if slightly chintzy) feel. Rooms (en suite, TV, fan) are a bit dark but have nice (faux) exposed rafters; they're arranged on two floors overlooking a simple courtyard with a table. BsF100.

Posada Guamanchi C 24 between Av. 8 and Parque las Heroínas ☎0274/252-2080, @www.guamanchi.com. Amazing views of the surrounding mountains compete with comfortable, bright and colourful en-suite rooms; there are also shared bathrooms and dorms. A total of four floors include two lounge areas (TV, hammocks), two spotless shared kitchens and a tour agency (see p.981). *Guamanchi* also has a serene posada in Los Nevados (BsF160 per person inc dinner and breakfast). Dorms BsF70, rooms BsF120.

Posada Jama Chia C 24 across from *teleférico* base ☎0274/252-5767. A well-run, popular posada requires some ice-climbing for part of the year. A six-day climb costs around BsF400 per person per day for a group of four; porters will add to the bill significantly. Less challenging treks are Pico Pan de Azúcar (same price) or Los Nevados. It is possible for well-experienced hikers to do these walks on their own. You should plan carefully, however, and note that fast-changing weather conditions can be extremely dangerous. Tour agencies offer an array of walks of different lengths for those who don't have the time or stamina for the biggest peaks.

Mountain biking

Many companies rent quality bikes for reasonable rates and can indicate the best routes. Guided day-tours run to BsF360 per person. Some companies also offer horseriding for similar rates.

Paragliding

The slopes around Mérida are the ideal setting for a thrilling yet safe 20–30min ride with a certified pilot. Tandem paragliding rates are fixed at BsF370 per person. Be sure to bring a jacket or sweater and don't eat before going as motion sickness is fairly common. Some agencies also offer paragliding courses.

Rafting

Rivers in Mérida and Barinas states have Class III to V rapids. Rafting season is from June to December. Two-day trips cost between BsF770 and BsF1070 per person with five people; four-day trips cost double. Some agencies have private base camps in Barinas.

Los Llanos and Catatumbo

Mérida is the main staging point for guided trips to Los Llanos (see p.987), the wildlife-filled wetlands east of the Andes. Prices for a four-day trip, which often include some rafting, are around BsF1200. Overnight excursions to see the eery, spectacular *Catatumbo* lightning at Lago de Maracaibo cost about BsF960.

conveniently located on Parque Las Heroínas; front rooms with windows are nicest, and dorms are good value. Shared bathrooms, fridge for food storage, communal seating and room for hand-washing clothes. Cheap long-term rates make this popular with language students, and the charming owner gets high praise from guests. Posadas *Paty* and *Mara* in the same block are decent, cheap fall-back options. Dorms BsF70, rooms BsF140.
Posada La Montaña C 24 No 6-47 ℗0274/252-5977, ⓦwww.posadalamontana.com. *La Montaña* has a superb design that employs local wood, brick, terracotta tiles and so many plants that you feel you're in a greenhouse. Top rooms have the best views; all have mini-fridge, free wi-fi and a closet with a safe. Has a laundry service and a very nice restaurant on the ground floor (see p.984). BsF250.
Posada Yagrumo C 24 between Av. 8 and Parque Las Heroínas ℗0274/252-9539, ⓦwww.posadayagrumo.com. This echoey, utilitarian place has en-suite doubles and one super-cheap dorm (BsF40). All have cable TV and private bathrooms but lack outside windows, and there's a shared kitchen, lounge seating area and laundry service. Internet access (BsF3 per hr) in the main lobby is available until 11pm for guests (7pm for the general public). BsF90.

Eating

The cuisine from Mérida and the Andes is famous throughout the country. Some specialities include *arepas de trigo* (made from wheat flour), *queso ahumado* (smoked cheese) and *trucha* (trout). *Vino de mora* is wine made from blackberries.
Arepería de la Reina Andina C 29 between avenidas 3 and 4 ℗0274/252-1721. A new location for this much-loved *arepería* hasn't changed the high quality of its offering. Fresh, griddled *arepas* stuffed with standard fillings like tuna with avocado or *carne mechada* (BsF10–15), as well as slightly more unusual options like octopus, are served from behind a gleaming counter. Closed Sun.
La Astilla C14 between avenidas 2 and 3 ℗0274/251-0832. A big place with tiled tabletops and hanging baskets, *La Astilla* serves up good

pizza (from BsF26) and local specialties such as trout (BsF55), as well as *pabellón* and decent hamburgers. One of several popular restaurants set around the lovely, tree-filled Plaza Milla. Open daily 11am–11pm.

Buona Pizza Av. 7 between calles 24 and 25 ⊕0274/252-7639. Great deep-dish pizza prepared at an open counter. A nine-inch costs BsF34–36, with toppings like anchovy and salami as well as plenty of vegetarian choices. The attractive, colourful restaurant has pseudo-Cubist paintings, brick walls and hordes of young locals. There's an "Express" version across the street for takeaway.

Delicias Mexicanas Ground floor of *Hotel Altamira*, C 25 between avenidas 7 and 8 ⊕0274/252-8677 (for hotel reception). This small, smart restaurant serves flavoursome Mexican food and ice-cold beer. Try the *tacos suaves* (flour wraps with smoky griddled beef, guacamole and sour cream, BsF51).

Heladería Coromoto Av. 3 between calles 28 and 29. Guinness Book of World Records holder for most ice-cream flavours, with nearly 800, although only around one hundred are available at any given time. Wacky options include smoked tuna, calamari, garlic, and spaghetti with meatballs. It's impressive how well they reproduce odd flavours, and a visit here is an essential Mérida experience, although some options are rather disgusting and the ice cream is good rather than great. BsF10 for 2 scoops. Tues–Sun 2.15–9pm, closed Mon.

🏃 **Mercado Principal** Av. Las Américas and Viaducto Miranda. Good food, huge portions and reasonable prices make this one of the best places in town to sample local favourites. The food court on the second floor attracts hordes of locals at lunchtime and contains tables from several nearly identical restaurants, all with pushy representatives that try to bring you to their area. *Cocina 4* has a great-value set lunch including excellent *pabellón* (BsF28). Mon and Wed–Sat 7am–6pm, Tues & Sun until 1.30pm.

La Nota Popular fast-food joint with several locations about town, including on Av. 8 (near Parque Las Heroínas) and near the bus terminal. Plates and smoky burgers come with six different sauces, including blue cheese. Full meals (like the recommended *pollo plato*) reach up to BsF60, though a half-order (around BsF40) sates most appetites. Daily until 11pm.

🏃 **Restaurant La Montaña** In *Posada La Montaña* (see p.983). A modest little trattoria-style place (pink tablecloths, open kitchen) with more style than a budget eater could usually dream of. Dinners are high quality – try the trout with lemon and salt (BsF48) – but it's the lunchtime *menu del día* that sets this place apart on value. It's

hard to argue with soup and a beautifully presented main such as steak and chips, plus fresh passion fruit juice, for BsF28.

T'Café Av. 3 between calles 29 and 30. An intellectual, often professorial crowd comes to this romantic streetside nook nightly (except Sun) for coffee, pastries made by the owner's mother and occasional live music on weekends. The menu focuses on pizza (from BsF22), panini and sandwiches (from BsF18), including the monster club house sandwich (chicken, ham, cheese, veg, egg and three sauces). Occasional special offers on food.

El Vegetariano Av. 4 at C 18. This small, split-level place features a menu that is far more interesting than those found at most all-veggie venues, prepared by ultra-friendly, English-speaking chef Abraham. Options include aubergine carpaccio with pesto (BsF34), plus pasta dishes (from BsF25) and a long list of salads. Mon–Sat 7.30am–8.45pm, closed Sun.

Drinking and nightlife

In large part because of the immense student population, Mérida enjoys an active nightlife. Sunday to Tuesday is usually quiet, but things begin to pick up by Wednesday and get quite lively the rest of the week.

El Atico del Cine C 25 opp Posada La Floridita. Expect dim lighting, chilled music and classic film posters at this trendy café-bar, as well as movie-themed cocktails such as La Naranja Mechánica (Clockwork Orange) and cheap beer served in mugs. Also serves pasta, salads and cakes. Open 5pm–midnight daily.

Birosca Carioca Av. 2 at C 24. Pounding samba and students define this friendly, ever-popular club – as do the red buckets of "La Bomba", a rum and beer concoction to be shared between a group and sucked down through straws. Open until the crowd goes home – it's situated on a shady street so be careful outside when leaving.

La Cucaracha In Centro Comercial Las Tapias on Av. Urdaneta ⊛www.lacucaracha.com.ve. One of Mérida's oldest nightspots, this large but always crowded disco has two floors, one with techno and the other with salsa and merengue. This is the "VIP" *Cucaracha*, bringing in a young, upmarket crowd, though other locations about town cater to clientele of differing ages and budgets.

🏃 **El Hoyo de Queque** Av. 4 and C 19. Dark, crowded and friendly, this lively place has big screens, DJs at the weekends and – unusually for Venezuela – draught lager. Large groups of students congregate around tables, but tourists can also be seen propping up the bar. Serves pizza (up to BsF60).

Kawy Av. 4 between calles 21 and 22. On the ground floor of a small *centro commercial, Kawy* feels somewhat like the bar at a ten-pin bowling alley, with disco lights and throbbing music regardless of the fact that nobody dances here. The beer is cheap, however, and this place is popular among Mérida's under-25s for drinking, eating bar food and flirting. Daily 11.30am–midnight.

Shopping

Mérida is a decent place to buy souvenirs or stock up on travel essentials; you should also be sure to check out the antique shops along the road to Apartaderos (see p.986). The most renowned destination among bargain-hunters is the Mercado Principal (Mon & Wed–Sat 7am–6pm, Tues & Sun until 1.30pm), a three-storey, tourist-oriented market about 1km southwest of the centre on Avenida Las Américas. The ground floor offers fruits and vegetables; the first, artisanal works and other souvenirs; and the second, a food court with a range of great restaurants (see p.984). More *artesanía* can be found at the much smaller Mercado Artesanal aross the street from Parque Las Heroínas, where a permanent installation of stalls sells ceramics, jewellery, blackberry wine, leather goods and wood carvings. For food to cook at your posada, there's an excellent, nameless *frutería* on the corner of Av. 7 and C 24, while Panadería Roma (Mon–Sat 7am–8pm, Sun until noon), at C 24 between Parque Las Heroínas and Av. 8, is a useful spot for bread, cooked meats, cheeses and dry goods. Cumbre Azul, at Av. 8 between calles 23 & 24, is a good place to rent or buy camping and hiking equipment.

Directory

Banks and exchange Banco de Venezuela, at Av. 4 between calles 23 and 24; ATMs at the base of the *teleférico* and in the bus terminal.
Internet and phones Several useful *centros de connexiones* offer internet and phone services, plus photocopying and in some cases electronic money transfers. There's one (CANTV) on Av. 5 at the corner with C 21 and another (Listo) on the same avenue between calles 25 and 26. Both are open Mon–Sat 8am–7pm. There's another *centro* in the bus terminal, and a handful more internet cafés around the *teleférico* base. Most charge around BsF4 per hr.
Language study Iowa Institute on Av. 4 at C 18 ☎0274/252-6404, ⊛www.iowainstitute.com.
Laundry An unnamed laundry a few doors towards C 19 from *Hotel Misintá* will wash and dry your clothes for BsF18 per load (open Mon–Sat 8am–noon & 2–6pm). Another option is on Av. 7 between calles 22 and 23. Most accommodation will wash guests' clothes – *Posada Paty* next to the *teleférico* has a service for non-residents too.
Medical care A reputable clinic with some English-speaking doctors is Clínica Mérida (☎0274/263-0652) on Av. Urdaneta next to the airport.
Pharmacy Farmacía Central on Plaza Bolivar, Av. 6 between calles 22 and 23 (Mon–Sat 8am–12.30pm & 2–7pm). Also Unifarmacía, Av. 3 between calles 29 and 30 (Mon–Sat 8am–9pm, Sun 9am–4pm).
Police The main station is on Av. Urdaneta, adjacent to Parque Gloria Patrias (☎0274/263-6722).
Post office Ipostel, C 21 between avenidas 4 and 5, and in the bus terminal. Currently open Mon–Fri mornings only.

Moving on

For information on crossing into Colombia from this region, see the box on p.978.
Air The closure of Mérida's airport means that air passengers must travel to El Vigia, 1hr 30min by bus (quicker in a taxi; BsF150) to catch flights to Caracas.
Bus As with Coro, and perhaps because of the *teleférico*'s closure, bus services from Mérida had been severely pared back from previous levels at the time of research. There are still several daily to Caracas (13hr), Maracay (11hr) Maracaibo (6hr) and Valencia (10hr 30min). Other destinations served include Barinas (5 daily; 4hr) and San Cristóbal (hourly; 5hr). There's one night bus per day to Coro (10hr) and Punto Fijo (11hr). Expresos Mérida (☎0274/263-3430) runs two buses daily to Puerto La Cruz (18hr) but most other services to the east of Venezuela have been suspended. For Ciudad Bolivar, you now have to go to Barinas or Puerto La Cruz and change.

DAY-TRIPS FROM MÉRIDA

Most of the quaint Andean towns northeast of Mérida are set alongside the Carretera Transandina, with beautiful views of the Sierra Nevada range to the south and the Sierra Culata range to the north. The highway eventually crosses the highest driveable summit in Venezuela, at Pico El Águila, and begins the spectacular descent to Barinas and Los Llanos (see p.987).

Mucuchíes

Around 50km northeast of Mérida, the picturesque mountain town of **MUCUCHÍES** was founded by the Spanish in 1586. Its name means "place of the waters" in the indigenous dialect. It has since given its name to a famous breed of Pyrenean mountain dog, which you may see in the town and area – there's even a statue of one in the Plaza Bolívar. Also on the plaza is *Cafetín Tinjacá*, a good stop for a simple breakfast, lunch or hot drinks, in an adobe-style building (weekends only outside high season).

Just a few kilometres further along the Carretera Transandina, in the tiny village of San Rafael de Mucuchíes, is a small grey chapel, the **Capilla de Piedra**, that has become one of the most famous emblems of the region. Local artist Juan Félix Sánchez built the chapel himself, using thousands of uncut stones; there's a small museum next door documenting his life and the chapel's construction.

Apartaderos and around

Continuing along the Carretera Transandina brings you past antiques shops and strawberries-and-cream stands to **APARTADEROS**, little more than a strip of shops and houses, but within easy reach of a few prominent sights. Ten kilometres beyond the pull-out for buses to and from Mérida is the **Refugio del Cóndor** (7am–5pm daily; no phone – contact Inparques in Mérida for more details), home to the well-known Andean condor conservation and research project. Tragically, only three condors remain in Venezuela. Birds which were previously re-released into the wild by the project disappeared without trace, and the remaining trio live in captivity at the refuge, separated from each other to prevent fighting. Visitors are shown an instructional five-minute video in English or Spanish. Also nearby, the **Observatorio Astronómico**

Nacional (hours dependent on season; ☏0274/245-0106, ⓦwww.cida.ve) is one of the highest observatories in the world, at 3600m above sea level. **Taxis** from Apartaderos will take tourists to the condor refuge or the observatory (BsF36–50 return, BsF20 per hr to wait).

In Apartaderos itself, enjoy **lunch** at *Refugio Turistico Mifafí*, which offers Andean specialities like trout (from BsF40) plus changing three-course set meals (BsF70). The restaurant is open daily 8am–8pm. Should you want to spend the night here, a double room costs BsF240. Around 100m down the hill, *Artesanías La Casa del Páramo* sells more expensive but less tacky souvenirs than similar shops in town, and has an attractive restaurant open only at weekends. For cash, there's a Banco Mercantil ATM in the car park of *Hotel Parque Turístico Apartaderos*.

Apartaderos is just a few kilometres from the entrance to the northern section of **Parque Nacional Sierra Nevada** (see below), offering beautiful lakes and short, easy walks.

Arrival

Both Mucuchíes and Apartaderos can easily be visited in a day from Mérida, and as amenities are scanty in these parts, there's not much reason to stay overnight. From the Mérida terminal, **buses** for Apartaderos (2hr; also serving Mucuchíes) leave every 15min or so until 6pm from platform 13. Buses pass back and forth along the Carretera Transandina every half-hour.

PARQUE NACIONAL SIERRA NEVADA

Looming above Mérida to the south and east, the Sierra Nevada runs northeast along the Carretera Transandina and through the 2760 square kilometre **PARQUE NACIONAL SIERRA NEVADA**. There is great diversity in flora and fauna here, but the park's most famous inhabitant, the threatened spectacled bear, is a shy creature that you'll be lucky to see.

The park features the country's highest mountains, which reach over 5000m, as well as its best **adventure activities**. You can easily explore the lower reaches on your own, but be sure to hire a guide before attempting either of the two famous peaks (see box, p.982).

Just inside the northern entrance to the park, a few kilometres along the carretera from Apartaderos, is **Laguna Mucubají**. Camping is allowed here; you will need permission from the Inparques office near the entrance. A good hiking trail connects Laguna Mucubají with **Laguna Negra**, a fishing lake with dark water, as the name suggests. The beautiful hike takes 90min to two hours, and you can continue another 90min to the pretty **Laguna Los Patos**. In the wet season, it's best to leave early to avoid rain and fog that could limit visibility considerably. Just outside the park entrance is *Refugio Mucubají*, a restaurant that sells good picnic supplies as well as excellent *arepas*, soups and coffees.

Pico Bolívar

At 5007m, **Pico Bolívar** is the country's highest and most hiked peak. There are multiple routes up, varying in difficulty and length of ascent. When the *teleférico* is operational, many walkers get off at the last station, Pico Espejo, and make the 5-hour ascent along the Ruta Weiss. This is not very technical in the dry season (Dec–May). The Ruta Sur Este and North Flank are two more challenging routes, which involve ice-climbing. Views from the top are spectacular – on a clear day, you can see the city of Mérida, the Colombian Andes and the vast expanse of Los Llanos.

Pico Humboldt

Another renowned peak, **Pico Humboldt**, can be combined with a climb of Pico Bolívar or tackled on its own. Starting at the entrance of Parque

Nacional La Mucuy, about 10km to the northeast of Mérida, the first day's ascent is 1000m; after the 6-hr, 9-km walk, most people camp around the picturesque Laguna Coromoto. The ascent on the second day is shorter but steeper as you get into the rocky terrain above the treeline. The final day's ascent to the peak and return to the campsite usually takes at least eight hours, depending upon your ice-climbing ability. The fourth day is for the descent back to La Mucuy.

Arrival and information

Bus To get to the park from Mérida, stay on the bus for just a few kilometres past Apartaderos.

Tourist information As well as the Inparques offices In Mérida (see p.949), there is one near the park entrance that can issue camping permits and dispense advice (Spanish only).

Los Llanos

Taking up nearly a third of the country, the immense plains of **Los Llanos** are one of the continent's premier wildlife-viewing areas. Some of the most abundant species are alligators and capybaras, the world's largest rodent at over one metre in length. Other common species are river dolphins, jaguars, pumas, howler and capuchin monkeys, anteaters and anacondas. However, the livelihood of the region's human inhabitants, the *llaneros*, is most closely linked with domesticated animals. Like the cowboys of the old American West, they have a reputation for being extremely skilled horsemen. Most work on **hatos**, enormous ranches with cattle often numbering in the tens of thousands (see p.989).

Los Llanos has two very pronounced **seasons**. During the wet season, from May to November, much of the land becomes flooded and extremely verdant. In the dry season, the land becomes parched and dusty, with most vegetation turning brown and yellow. While the scenery is more picturesque in the wet season, wildlife sightings are far fewer – the best viewing comes when water is scarce, causing animals to concentrate at the few watering holes.

Unless you have a wad of cash to spend on a stay at one of the *hatos*, you'll most likely visit Los Llanos as part of a **multi-day tour** from Mérida (see p.982). If you're determined to see the region on your own, or are passing through Los Llanos to another part of the country, the backwater city of San Fernando de Apure is a reasonable base and provides onward transport, though frankly, there's no other reason to visit it.

SAN FERNANDO DE APURE

Founded as a missionary outpost in the seventeenth century, **SAN FERNANDO DE APURE** is now an important trading centre. There's virtually nothing here to detain tourists, but some pass through on the way to the southern *hatos* or to Amazonas (see p.990).

What to see and do

The only vaguely interesting sights in San Fernando are the bizarre **fountain** at the intersection of avenidas Libertador and Miranda, featuring water-spouting caimans grasping cornucopia; and, at the edge of the roundabout, the square **Palacio Barbarito**, a nineteenth-century palace built by Italians involved in the lucrative trade of caiman leather. Once grand, the palace has deteriorated considerably.

Arrival

Bus The bus terminal is less than a kilometre from the town centre.

Accommodation

Budget accommodation in San Fernando de Apure is shoddy and overpriced, but sufficient for a short stopover.

La Fuente Av. Miranda, west of Av. Libertador ☎0247/342-3233. The room numbers are written in such small writing and are in such random order that it's hard to find your door. Rooms are spartan in the extreme but on the plus side, it's cheap and conveniently close to the bus station. BsF120.

La Torraca Av. Libertador 8 ☎0247/342-2777. A frowsty old lift will very slowly lead you up to dated rooms with flowery curtains, brown bedspreads and outmoded televisions. BsF150.

LOS LLANEROS

Many comparisons have been drawn between the llaneros and the cowboys of the American West. Known for being tough and independent, both are portrayed as embodying the spirit of their countries. Other similarities include their legendary penchants for drinking, gambling and singing sad ballads.

The mixed-blood *llaneros* captured the nation's imagination during the War of Independence as word of their ferocity spread. Their role in the struggle was integral, and their switch of allegiance in the middle of the war was one of the principal reasons for Bolívar's victory. Life has changed little for them since then, as they continue to work almost exclusively on the enormous cattle ranches.

The *llaneros* participate in a number of competitions that allow them to showcase their machismo. One of the most popular is toros coleados. Riding horseback, each of the contestants has to take down a bull by pulling its tail in a certain way; the one who does it quickest wins. Another common competition is the contrapunteo, during which two *llaneros* face off in a verbal sparring contest, hurling improvised insults at one other to the beat of *piropa*, a musical form of the region.

Eating

Eating here is a slightly more promising endeavour, with a number of restaurants serving famed *llanero* beef.

Panadería San Bernardo Av. Carabobo, a short walk from the Monumeto Páez ☏0424/314-3602. Spotless, bread-less bakery offering per kg breakfasts and lunches (BsF60) with tasty food including beans, chicken, lasagna and pasta. À la carte for dinner. Mon-Sat 11am–3pm & 6–10pm.

El Príncipe Av. Miranda, next to Hotel La Fuente ☏0247/341-4534. If you've had it with chicken and rice head here for some Middle Eastern fare – *kibbe* (BsF40), falafel (BsF40) and tabbouleh (BsF30) in a down-to-earth setting. Mon–Sat 7am–10pm.

Directory

Banks and exchange BBVA, by the fountain. There's also a Banco Mercantil ATM in the bus terminal (often out of service).

Internet Full Internet, first floor, Av. Libertador, by the pharmacy, Mon–Sat 7.30am–7pm (BsF2.5 per hr).

Pharmacy Farmacia Los Llanos, Av. Libertador, two blocks south of *Hotel La Torraca*.

Phones Movistar, Av. Libertador, by the pharmacy.

Post Ipostel, Calle 24 de Julio at Calle Bolívar.

Moving on

Bus Barinas (several daily; 8hr); Caracas (several daily; 8hr); Maracay (hourly; 7hr); Puerto Ayacucho (several daily; 7hr); Puerto La Cruz (2 daily; 12hr); San Cristóbal (1 daily; 13hr); Valencia (hourly; 8hr). There are no direct buses to Ciudad Bolívar; you must first go to Puerto Ayacucho, then change buses.

Guayana

Covering the southern and south-eastern half of Venezuela, **Guayana** is comprised of three of Venezuela's largest states – Amazonas, Bolívar and Delta Amacuro. The region is extremely

---

HATOS AND MÓDULOS

Many of the vast cattle ranches of Los Llanos, called **hatos**, double as incredible wildlife sanctuaries and rustic yet exclusive resorts. They offer activities such as truck rides, canoe trips and hikes on their property, and trained guides usually speak good English. High-season rates are around BsF400 per person with all meals and tours included; reservations are almost always required. Call for details on prices and transport to the ranches. At the time of research the country's three largest *hatos* (*El Cedral*, *Frío* and *Piñero*) were all state-owned, but only *El Cedral* is open for visitors; the others are due to reopen in the near future.

Hato El Cedral ☏0240/808-7064, 0416/502-2757 or 0212/577-5174, ⊛www .hatocedral.com. Fifty-three thousand hectares of land home to abundant wildlife, with more than 340 bird species and the country's highest concentration of capybaras. Also a world-famous research centre. Three hours from both San Fernando de Apure and Barinas. BsF400.

A cheaper alternative is to stay in **módulos**, smaller ranches with much more basic accommodation, also home to abundant wildlife. Both options listed below offer various activities including boat tours along the Rio Guaritico, night safaris, piranha fishing and horseriding. To get to both *módulos*, catch a bus from San Fernando de Apure to the little town of Mantecai (4hr) where the respective owners of the *módulos* will pick you up. Make sure you call in advance to organize pick-up, and take a mosquito net with you in the wet season. Prices include food.

Rancho Grande Vecindario El Palmar, Mantecal ☏0416/873-1192 or 0416/779-6866 ⊛www.hosteltrail.com/ranchogrande/. Traditional-style cabins provide temporary lodging by the river; tours (BsF1000 for 3 days/2 nights) are in Spanish.

Yopito Vía Los Módulos, Carretera Quintero, Mantecal ⊛www.yopito.net, ☏0416/573-8644, 0426/747-1745 or ☏0240/808-0284). Accommodation is in hammocks and beds in twelve people cabañas. There's also a pool. Tours cost BsF1000 for 3 days/2 nights.

important economically, containing a tremendous wealth of natural resources such as gold, iron ore, bauxite and diamonds. It also supplies hydroelectricity for the entire country and even exports it to Venezuela's neighbours. Despite the immensity of the region, there are only two real cities, **Puerto Ordáz** and **Ciudad Bolívar**, which are vastly outnumbered by indigenous communities belonging to the Yanomami, Pemón, Warao and Piaroa, all of whom have retained many of their customs.

One of the region's most important natural resources is the landscape itself, although the tremendous distances and lack of major tourism facilities mean there are fewer visitors than you might expect. Many of the country's main tourist attractions are in Guayana, including the **tropical rainforests** of the Amazon, the mighty **Orinoco Delta** of the Delta Amacuro, the breathtaking **Angel Falls and** the magnificent *tepuis*, or tabletop mountains, of **Bolívar.**

PUERTO AYACUCHO

A sleepy town that's home to half the inhabitants of Amazonas, **PUERTO AYACUCHO** is the state's only major municipality. Founded along the Orinoco River in 1924, primarily as a port for shipping timber, its position near the Colombian border makes it a convenient place to cross (see box, p.978). Puerto Ayacucho is also the principal entry point for the Amazon region.

What to see and do

Like many other Venezuelan cities, Puerto Ayacucho itself has almost no intrinsic appeal, but there are several nearby attractions, including, of course, the jungle. In town, the **Museo Etnológico de Amazonas** (Tues–Sun 8am–noon & 2–4pm; BsF12; ⓦwww .verdin.com.mx/webmuseo/mam /mam0000e.html, on Avenida Río

Negro, showcases clothing and other objects pertaining to the region's indigenous Guajibos, Arawak, Yanomami, Yekuanas and Piaroas. In front of the museum is, **Plaza de los Indios**, a market where locals sell all types of handicrafts, including *katara*, a condiment made from leafcutter ants and hot peppers that's also a reputed sexual stimulant.

About 18km south of town is **Cerro Pintado**, a large rock with impressive pre-Columbian **petroglyphs** that are estimated to be three to five thousand years old. Ten kilometres farther south is **Parque Tobagán de la Selva**, a park containing a natural waterslide. A taxi to the park and petroglyphs costs about BsF100 – make sure you arrange for pick-up.

Arrival and information

Air Due to its isolation, Puerto Ayacucho is one of the few cities in Venezuela that you might consider reaching or leaving by air. For a local travel agent and departures, see p.992. The airport is 6km southeast of town. Conviasa flies once daily (1hr 30min) between Puerto Ayacucho and Caracas. Buses heading into the centre from the airport are extremely infrequent; it's much easier to take a taxi (roughly BsF10).

Bus The ride from San Fernando de Apure, 6hr to the north, is very rough and includes one river crossing that may require a substantial wait. The Puerto Ayacucho terminal, 6km east of town, is quite small, with nowhere to leave luggage. From the bus terminal take a taxi into town (BsF7).

Tourist information The Secretaría de Turismo is based at the airport ☎0248/521-0033, Mon–Fri 8am–noon & 2–5pm.

City transport

Taxi Although Puerto Ayacucho does have city buses, you rarely see them and schedules are unpredictable. Consequently, most locals take taxis (in and around town BsF7), which can be difficult to find during the lunch hour and at the end of the workday.

Accommodation

Gran Hotel Amazonas Av. Emilio Roa & Calle Amazonas ☎0248/521-5633. The best hotel in

Border at Casuarito (1km)

PUERTO AYACUCHO

VENEZUELA

GUAYANA

D (1km), ① Hospital (2km); Bus Terminal (6km) & Eco-Destinos

ACCOMMODATION

Gran Hotel Amazonas	B
Hotel Tonino	E
Posada Manapiare	D
Residencias Internacional	C
Residencias Michelangelli de Pozo	A

Mercado Municipal

Pharmacy

Laundry

Museo Ethológico de Amazonas

Tadae

PLAZA DE LOS INDIOS

DIEX Office

Coyote Expediciones

Banesco

Pharmacy

Cerro Perico

Bank

El Mercadito

Banco de Venezuela

N

Río Orinoco

EATING

Café Rey David	5
El Guariqueño	3
El Mercadito	4
El Tunel de la Estancia	2
Panadería Amazonas	1

0   200 m

El Mirador (700m), Airport (6.2km) & Tourist Info

town is not that pricey – a fanciful Amazonian reception awaits, with plenty of knick-knacks from wooden parrots to tribal masks. Good-sized rooms as well as a large swimming pool at the back, which you can use for BsF40 if you're not staying here. BsF190.

Posada Manapiare Urb Alto Parima, Entrada #1 ☏0248/414-9407 or 0248/686-0062, ⓦwww.posadamanapiare .com.ve. A slightly pricier option in a tranquil neighbourhood just outside of town. The rooms, named after animals, are clean and pleasantly decorated. There's also a pool, laundry service and an attached restaurant with food cooked upon request. Book ahead. BsF190.

Residencias Internacional Av. Aguerrevere 8 ☏0248/521-0242. A cheap option in a quiet neighbourhood with individually painted rooms and a leafy, colourful courtyard. There's a little upper patio looking over the roof and treetops, as well as a *panadería* two doors down to grab a morning pastry. Doubles BsF120.

Residencias Michelangelli de Pozo C. Evelio Roa 35 ☏0248/521-3189. Although it feels somewhat deserted, this place is clean and quiet, with smallish rooms set around a verdant courtyard as well as on

the first floor veranda. Rooms with fan BsF80, with a/c BsF100.

Tonino Av. 23 de Enero, just east of Av. Orinoco ☏0248/891669. Just off the main road, this place is quite hard to spot so keep your eyes peeled for a blue entrance. Management is friendly, and with only five little rooms the quiet *Tonino* feels more like a posada than a hotel. BsF110.

Eating

In addition to the range of inexpensive restaurants about town, there is a string of food stalls along Avenida Aguerrevere, west of Avenida Orinoco, hawking *empanadas*, burgers, fried chicken and fish each evening. As Puerto Ayacucho is not particularly safe at night, it is not wise to go out in search of a party after dark.

Café Rey David Av. Orinoco, south of the *mercadito* ☏0248/521-0074. Locals are fans of this place which must mean something – there's tasty *pollo asado* (BsF25), as well as sandwiches (BsF10), *empanadas* (BsF12.50) and *arepas* (BsF12). Mon–Sat 7am–11pm.

El Guariqueño Av. 23 de Enero ☏0248/414-6995. There are chickens roasting on a spit

TOURS OF THE AMAZON

Compressing all of the wonders of the Amazon into three days is impossible, but a few tour companies in Puerto Ayacucho do their best. The classic tour is a three-day/two-night trip up the Sipapo and Autana rivers to Cerro Autana, a sacred, 1200-metre-high mesa that can be viewed from an adjacent mirador. Nights are typically spent with indigenous communities, and side trips up channels in smaller boats are usually included, sometimes with opportunities to fish for feisty *pavón*, or peacock bass. More expensive options include the ten- to twelve-day Ruta Humboldt, following in the footsteps of the famous explorer, and even longer journeys to meet the Yanomami and other isolated tribes.

All-inclusive prices per day, for groups of four or more people, are BsF400–500 per day per person for three or four days, usually more for longer trips. Companies provide any necessary jungle access permits and can often help you plan a journey into Brazil; for details, see the box on p.1002.

Finally, a disclaimer: many people expect to see amazing wildlife in the Amazon, but in reality the density of the jungle and the reclusiveness of the animals makes this quite difficult. If you're set on wildlife-watching, save your money for a trip to Los Llanos (see p.987).

Coyote Expediciones Avenida Aguerrevere 75 ☎0248/521-4583 or 0414/486-2500, ✉coyoteexpedition@cantv.net. This outfit arranges the standard tours as well as trips along the narrow Río Casiquiare, which links the Orinoco to the Río Negro, and to the indigenous community of Báquiro, a good alternative to Autana if the weather isn't cooperating. **Eco-Destinos** Ent. Urbanización Bolivariana, Quinta Los Abuelos, ☎0416/448-6394 or 0248/521-3964, ⊛www.amazonasvenezuela.com.

Lets customers fully customize trips, for instance by suggesting they bring and prepare their own food to mitigate expenses.
Tadae Av. Río Negro, behind Plaza de los Indios ☎0248/521-4882 or 0414/486-5923, ✉tadaevenezuela@hotmail.com. The savviest of Puerto Ayacucho's tour companies, offering the standard excursions as well as air tickets and trips throughout the rest of the country. Ask about "moto-rafting" and the four-day trek to La Laguna del Rey Leopoldo.

---

outside while *ayacuchans* tuck into huge portions of *pollo al ajillo* or *pollo a la plancha* (both BsF45). Various soups (BsF26) for those less peckish. Daily 11am–4pm.

El Mercadito Between avenidas Orinoco and Amazonas, south of Av. 23 de Enero. The destination of choice for workers on lunch-break. Two indoor restaurants at the east end of the market (*El Rincón Llanero* and *La Catira*) serve inexpensive *comida criolla*, but for the real deal, slurp down a steaming bowl of *sopa de gallina*, *res* or *pescado* (BsF15) in the market itself.

Panadería Amazonas Av. Rómulo Gallegos south of Calle Constitución ☎0485/210-781. Apparently the best *panadería* in town – in all fairness the coffee (BsF3) is superb but the *empanadas* (BsF10) are pretty greasy. Daily 6.30am–9pm.

El Tunel de la Estancia Av. Aguerrevere west of Calle Piar ☎0248/521-6234. There are bright green pillars, fake flowers on each table and *telenovelas* rolling one after the other on the TV screen, at this somewhat gloomy restaurant. It nonetheless attracts

a fair number of locals, so they must be doing something right; a *filet de pescado* (fish fillet) will set you back BsF35. Open Mon–Sat 11am–4pm.

Directory

Banks and exchange Banesco, Av. Orinoco south of Av. Aguerrevere; Banco de Venezuela on Av. Orinoco south of Av. 23 de Enero.
Hospital Clínica Amazonas, Av. Rómulo Gallegos ☎0248/521-2454; Clínica Zerpa, Av. 23 de Enero ☎0248/521-2815).
Immigration DIEX office, Av. Aguerrevere 60 ☎0248/521-0198 (Mon–Fri 8am–noon & 2–4pm). If you need a Colombian visa (see p.978), the consulate is at Calle Yapacana, Quinta Beatriz ☎0248/521-0789 ((Mon–Fri 7am–1pm & 3–6pm).
Internet Inversiones Friends, Av. Orinoco & Av. Aguerrevere (Mon–Sat 7.30am–7.30pm; BsF3 per hr).
Laundry Lavandería Automática Acuario, Av. Aguerrevere next to *Residencias Internacional*. Mon–Fri 8am–noon & 2–6pm, Sat 9am–noon & 2–5pm.

Pharmacy Farmacia Autana, Av. Río Negro at Calle Evelio Roa; Farmacía Doña Carmen, Av. Orinoco south of Av. Aguerrevere. Both Mon–Fri 8am–noon & 2–6pm. Both work weekends *por turno*.

Phones CANTV, Av. Orinoco at Av. Aguerrevere; Movistar, Av. Orinoco south of Calle Carabobo.

Post Ipostel, Av. Amazonas & Calle Roa (Mon–Fri 8–11am & 2–5pm)

Shopping Tradona Supermarket on Av. Orinoco & Calle Constitución (Mon–Sat 7.45am–7pm, Sun 7.45am–1pm). There's an interesting fish market on Av. Orinoco by Calle Constitución (Mon–Sat 8am–6pm & Sun till 1pm). On Saturday mornings stalls selling local produce line Av. Orinoco between Calle Constitución and the fish market. For local artesan jewellery head to Plaza de los Indios (Mon–Sat 8am–6pm, Sun till noon).

Moving on

For information on crossing into Colombia or Brazil from this region, see the boxes on p.978 or p.1002, respectively.

Air There is one daily flight (except Sat) to Caracas with Conviasa (1hr 30min; BsF320). For other destinations you can charter a plane, although doing so is very costly.

Bus Caracas (several night buses daily; 14hr); Ciudad Bolívar (hourly with several night buses; 15hr); Maracay (several daily; 12hr); Puerto Ordáz (hourly; 16hr); San Fernando de Apure (several daily until 3pm; 6hr); Valencia (several daily; 13hr).

PUERTO ORDÁZ

Most of the visitors who pass through **PUERTO ORDÁZ** are on their way to Ciudad Bolívar, a much better jumping-off point for the main attractions in the state. Due to its lack of tourist appeal, general size and safety, Puerto Ordaz is best avoided and should be treated only as a transport hub, but for those stuck here for any length of time, there are a couple of mildly diverting sights. Its neglected sibling **San Félix** is definitely not a place to stop, due to its insalubrious nature.

What to see and do

Built on an industrial rather than human scale, Puerto Ordáz's few sights are spread kilometres apart. Taxis are the easiest and safest way to look around (BsF70/hr); public transport is not advised.

The **Ecomuseo de Caroní** (Tues–Sun 9am–5pm; free), next to the 23 de Enero dam, has a number of rotating educational exhibits, a small collection of fine art and a large window through which you can see the dam's gargantuan generators. A taxi from the centre is about BsF40.

Parque Llovizna, just across from the museum, and **Parque Cachamay** feature expanses of life-affirming greenery and some nice waterfalls. You can combine both on a half-day tour with Piraña Tours (BsF208; ☏0286/923-6447 or 923-6178, ⓦwww.piranatours.com), in the lobby of the *Hotel InterContinental Guayana*.

Arrival and Information

Air The airport is located on the western edge of the city, along the road to Ciudad Bolívar. A taxi into the centre is BsF50; bus routes are inconvenient.

Bus Puerto Ordáz's terminal is on Av. Guayana, about 10min from the centre. There is nowhere to leave luggage in the terminal. Some buses arrive in San Félix, from where it's a 15-min taxi ride to Puerto Ordáz (BsF30).

Tourist Information The main tourist office, Venetur, is in the *Hotel InterContinental Guayana* (☏0286/713-1244, Mon–Sat 7.30am–5pm); the Secretaría de Turismo has an office at the airport (☏0426/695-8109).

Accommodation

While not centrally located, *La Casa del Lobo* is far and away the best budget accommodation in the city. There's also a slightly smarter posada in town.

La Casa del Lobo Villa Africana, Manzana 39, Casa 2 ☏0286/961-6286 ⓦwww.lobo-tours.de. Named after German owner Wolfgang, this cheap place remains the only backpacker-friendly option in the city, although, sadly, it has seen much better days. The owner organizes interesting trips to the Orinoco Delta. BsF120.

Posada Cunurí Av. Vía Venezuela 135A, Campo A-3 de Ferrominera ☏0286/923-7106 ⓦwww .posadacunuri.com. Puerto Ordaz's newest addition has spotless rooms with cable TV, wi-fi and a/c, all running off three storey balconies. Parking facilities available in a safe setting. BsF290.

Eating

There are a few places to grab some lunch sprinkled around town, but in the evenings it's best to take refuge in the safety of Orinokia Mall (see "Shopping") where there are plenty of restaurants open until late.

El Boulevard de Comida at the Mercadito. Just ask where the "Boulevard de Comida del Mercadito de Puerto Ordaz" is and you'll find plenty of stalls selling *criollo* dishes perfect for a quick cheap bite. Meat and fish dishes around BsF25–30. Daily 6am–3pm.

Chiquito's Av. Las Américas, Local 8 & 9, Centro Comercial Anto ☎0286/923-4056. Local café and bakery serving a range of sweet and savoury pastries (BsF15) as well as coffees (BsF9). Mon–Sat 7am–7pm, Sun until 1pm.

El Rincón del Chivo Av. Loefling, Sector La Esperancita ☎0414/870-3230. Large open-air area where you can hang out with locals over a home-cooked soup (BsF32), a *cachapa* (BsF22) or a steak (BsF45) grilled in front of you. Open Tues–Sun 11am–3pm.

Directory

Bank Banco Provincial, Carrera Upata at Av. Ciudad Bolívar.

Internet There are plenty of cyber cafés (BsF3/hr) in the Centro Comercial Trebol I, II and III on Calle Upata. Mon–Sat 9am–8pm, Sun till 2pm.

Phones Movistar, across the street from *Hotel Rayoli*.

Post DHL, Calle El Palmar at Calle Santa Elena (Mon–Fri 8am–noon & 2–5.30pm, Sat 8am–noon; ☎0286/923-8756).

Shopping For a dose of commercialist perversity (and some good 'ol US-style fast food), check out the massive Orinokia mall, bordered by Av. Las Américas and Av. Guayana, Mon–Sat 10am–10pm, Sun noon–10pm.

Moving on

Air There are daily flights to Barcelona (30min) Caracas (1hr), Porlamar (50min), Maracaibo (2hr) and Valencia (50min).

Bus Destinations include Ciudad Bolívar (every 30mins; 1hr), Caracas (hourly; 12hr); Cumaná (four daily; 8hr); Maracay/Valencia (several daily; 12hr); Puerto La Cruz (four daily; 7hr); Santa Elena de Uairén (six daily, mostly night buses; 10hr). Buses to Tucupita leave only from San Félix (every 2hr until 6pm; 4hr).

CIUDAD BOLÍVAR

Besides being one of the most backpacker-friendly cities in Venezeula, **CIUDAD BOLÍVAR** is the ideal jumping-off point for exploring Bolívar. In contrast to Puerto Ordáz, Ciudad Bolívar is easily walkable and most of its highlights can be seen in a single day; you'll soon be ready to take on the endless wilderness of **Parque Nacional Canaima** and the **Gran Sabana** (see p.998 and p.1002, respectively).

What to see and do

Ciudad Bolívar's cobbled streets, well-preserved colonial buildings and compact size make it a pleasant place to simply stroll around and explore. There are a couple of museums to tickle your cultural taste buds, and nature lovers will want to visit the botanical gardens. Head to the Paseo del Orinoco for an afternoon stroll by the banks of Venezuela's mightiest river.

Casco histórico

Most of the city's colonial architecture is in the **casco histórico**, a roughly ten-block area on the southern bank of the Orinoco River, centred on the **Plaza Bolívar**. On the east side of the plaza, the imposing 1840 **Catedral** has a light, airy interior, which, while not particularly ornate, makes for a good escape from the midday heat.

To the west of the plaza, the **Casa del Congreso de Angostura** (Tues–Sun 9am–5pm; free) is the site where the Angostura Congress founded Gran Colombia; Bolívar also lived here briefly in 1817. A quick peek reveals paintings of the original congressmen, an old printing press and archives of documents pertaining to Bolívar.

2km), Airport (2km) & Museo de Arte Moderno Jesús Soto (2km)

Paseo Orinoco

Plaza Bolívar may be the heart of the city, but Ciudad Bolívar's pulse is best felt along the **Paseo Orinoco**. Two blocks north of the plaza, this bustling riverside thoroughfare is lined with shops of every persuasion, many of which broadcast their latest deals over screeching PA systems.

On the west end of the Paseo, at Calle Carabobo, the **Casa Correo del Orinoco** (Mon–Fri 8am–noon & 2–5pm; free), housed in a colonial-era post office, has a small collection of archeological artefacts from throughout Latin America, as well as some modern metal sculpture.

Be careful on the Paseo after dark, as robberies have occurred here.

Museo de Arte Moderno Jesús Soto

One of the country's most fascinating museums, the **Museo de Arte Moderno Jesús Soto** (Tues–Sun 9am–5pm; free), just south of town on Avenida Germania, contains the fascinating works of Jesús Soto, probably Venezuela's most famous contemporary artist. Many of his paintings and sculptures make use of optical illusions, and you can ask to be accompanied by one of the guides, who will point out the visual tricks. Taxis here from the centre cost BsF25; to return, catch a bus from the McDonald's across the street.

Jardín Botánico

Consider taking a stroll through the well-maintained **Jardín Botánico**

(Mon–Sat 8am–5pm, Sun till noon; free) on Avenida Bolívar at Calle Caracas. The gardens, the majority of which you must tour (BsF30) in the company of a guide (some speak English), contain plant species from all over the world.

Arrival and information

Air The airport (☎0285/632-6635) is at the south-eastern edge of town, at the intersection of Av. Táchira and Av. Aeropuerto. A taxi to the *casco histórico* costs around BsF25, or you can take a Santa Eduviges-bound city bus or the "Ruta 2" to Paseo Orinoco (daily 5am–5pm; BsF2) and get off in the centre.
Bus The terminal lies at the southern end of the city, at the intersection of Av. República and Av. Sucre. There are sporadic buses (BsF2) to the *casco histórico*, which drop you at the northwest corner of the Jardín Botánico.
Tourist information Secretaría de Turismo, the principal tourist office, is in the main entrance of the Jardín Botánico (☎0800/674-6626 ✉secretariadeturismoyambiente@gmail.com); Fondo Mixto Bolívar also in the Jardín Botánico (☎0285/632-2901); both Mon–Fri 8am–noon & 2–5.30pm. There's also an Inatur desk at the airport (☎0800/462-8871; daily 8am–5pm).

Tour operators

Most of the agencies listed here also sell tours of the Orinoco Delta (see p.1003) and Gran Sabana (see p.1002), but you'll generally find better deals in cities closer to those sights (Tucupita for the delta; Santa Elena de Uairén for the Gran Sabana). All agencies offer pretty much the same packages so make sure you shop around for the best deal.
Adrenalina Calle Bolívar at Calle Dalla Costa ☎0285/615-5191 or 0414/886-7209, ⓦwww.adrenalinaexpeditions.com. One of Ciudad Bolívar's most enthusiastic and responsible agencies. Co-owner Ricardo, an eccentric in the best sense, leads mind-blowing trips of the Gran Sabana (see p.1002).
Amor Patrio In *Posada Amor Patrio* (see below). Specializes in Río Caura trips, rugged camping and visits to indigenous villages.
Eco-Adventures In the bus terminal ☎0285/651-9546 or 0414/851-3656, ⓦwww.adventurevenezuela.com. Often mistaken for a pirate outfit due to its location, it's in fact a great option for travellers who are keen to get things sorted once they've hopped off the bus.

Energy Tours At the airport ☎0285/617-4530 or 0424/945-6310 ⓦwww.energytour.com. Italian-owned company that offers trips to Angel Falls that can be combined with other destinations, usually the Gran Sabana, the Delta, Margarita Island and Los Roques.
Sapito Tours In the airport ☎0285/632-7989 or 632-6890 ⓦwww.sapitotours.com. The tour agency arm of *Campamento Bernal* in Canaima Village.
Seriko In *Tapuy Lodge* in Canaima Village ☎0416/798-6132, ✉seriko.c.a@hotmail.com. Run by Mariela Fernández, who can help organize both budget and more luxurious lodging in Canaima, as well as tours to Angel Falls.
Turi Express Dorado ☎0285/634-1243 or 0414/893-9576 ⓦwww.turiexpressdorado.com.ve. Long-established company that has been operating for over two decades, offering tours to the usual locations as well as city and river tours in Ciudad Bolívar.

Accommodation

Ciudad Bolívar is rivalled only by Mérida in its selection of great, cheap accommodation.

🏃 **Posada Amor Patrio** Calle Amor Patrio at Calle Igualdad ☎0414/854-4925. Very chilled German posada in a 200-year-old building with rooms named after exotic countries and continents, along with a little kitchen and laundry service. The communal *salón del ritmo* brims with personality, with Cuban music photos decorating the walls. Also has its own tour agency. BsF120.

🏃 **Posada Don Carlos** Calle Boyacá at Calle Amor Patrio ☎0285/632-6017, ⓦwww.posadadoncarlos.com. You can just picture Venezuelan gentry sipping on some good rum at the bar of this characterful posada. Rooms are off the large colonial courtyard, dotted with all sorts of antique knick-knacks from nineteenth-century furniture to an old water pump. Airport and bus transfers can be organized for a fee. BsF120.
Ritz Calle Libertad at Calle Venezuela ☎0285/632-3886. Don't be fooled by its name as this budget option offers no more than the very basics and will certainly not dazzle you with its splendour. BsF60.
Posada Turística Lainette Calle Dalla Costa at Calle Amor Patria ☎0414/893-4053 ✉munecadepan@hotmail.com. Under renovation at the time of research, this intimate posada has a dorm with a/c (BsF150), a hammock area (BsF80) and a double room (BsF400). Chill-out areas indoors and out, as well as plans to build a jacuzzi in the garden. Prices include breakfast.

La Casa Grande Calle Venezolana at Calle Boyacá ☎0424/900-4473, ✆www .cacaotravel.com. Utterly peerless in Ciudad Bolívar, if not in Venezuela, this luxurious posada occupies the former headquarters of the Red Cross and combines colonial majesty with artful modern flair. A skylit atrium contains plants and a fountain, and the roof deck has a pool and expansive views of the Orinoco. En-suite rooms have a/c, flat-screen TVs, exposed original stonework and safes. The all English-speaking staff provide free transport to the bus terminal, airport and even Puerto Ordáz. US$70.

Eating

Ciudad Bolívar is not particularly noted for its food, but a few decent options exist. Local fish such as dorado, *palometa* and *sapoara* are fresh and tasty.

El Caribeño Calle Igualdad between Paseo Orinoco and Calle Venezuela ☎0285/444-8166. A very simple, very cheap cafeteria serving breakfasts (*pastelitos, empanadas, jugos*) and full meals (*pollo a la brasa, bisteck, pescado*) with sides of rice, salad, yucca and more – nothing over BsF30. Daily 6am–7pm.

Las Marquesas Av. Cumaná 4, south of Calle Bolívar ☎0414/185-4380. A lofty and basic room with a lively bar offering simple and decent cuisine. The *menú ejecutivo* includes a soup and choice of meat or fish for BsF20. Open Mon–Sat 11am–7pm.

Mercado La Carioca East end of Paseo Orinoco. This is the ideal place to get a large and satisfying meal while enjoying views of (and breezes from) the Orinoco. It has a number of small restaurants, all serving similar meat and fish dishes with sides of yucca, black beans, rice, plantains and more (all under BsF40). Beers are so cold they arrive to the table frozen. A bus here along Paseo Orinoco costs BsF2; a taxi from the centre is BsF10.

Mini-lunch Arabian Food Calle Amor Patrio at Calle Igualdad ☎0285/632-7208. A little corner café good for a fix of Middle Eastern food: *shawarma* plate BsF28, large "mix" plate of falafel, *kibbe*, tabbouleh, meat and hummus BsF35–60. Mon–Sat 7am–8pm, Sun 2–8pm.

Restaurant Vegetariano Calle Amor Patrio at Calle Dalla Costa ☎0285/632-6381. An oasis of patrician calm, offering good veggie food with the possibility of postprandial yoga classes. Soups for BsF5, more substantial mains for BsF30. Mon–Fri noon–3pm.

Restaurante Caribe Calle Libertad 33 ☎0285/618-0135. Family setting in a deceptively small town house. Basic food at basic prices: soups BsF20, mains BsF25 before 3pm, BsF35 thereafter including a choice of beverage. Mon–Sat 11am–6pm.

Tostadas Juancito's Av. Cumaná at Calle Bolívar. Fun and friendly outdoor terrace with stone tables, offering cheap and tasty street food, including *arepas* (BsF14), *pabellón criollo* (BsF28) and *pollo a la brasa* (quarter BsF20). Mon–Sat 7am–5.30pm.

Directory

Banks and exchange Banco de Venezuela, Paseo Orinoco at Calle Piar and Calle Constitución at Calle Venezuela; Banesco, Calle Dalla Costa at Calle Venezuela; Banco de Venezuela, Calle Venezuela at Calle Constitución.

Hospital Hospital Ruiz y Páez, Av. Germania ☎0285/632-0041.

Internet Conexiones.net, Calle Venezuela at Calle Libertad, Mon–Sat 8am-6pm, BsF3.5 per hr.

Pharmacy Farmacia Unión, Calle Venezuela at Calle Libertad, Mon–Sat 8am–6pm; Hospifárma, Paseo Orinoco at Calle Carabobo, Mon–Sat till noon & 2–5.30pm.

Phones Movistar, Paseo Orinoco between calles Dalla Costa and Libertad. There's another *centro de llamadas* on Calle Dalla Costa between calles Venezuela and Bolívar.

Police Located in the Jardín Botánico by the tourist office (☎0285/617-0205 or 632-9037; daily 8am–5pm).

Post Ipostel, Av. Táchira, 1km south of the *casco histórico*.

Shopping Tienda de Artesanía Cooperativa Kerepacupai-meru, at Mercado La Carioca (see above), with handmade toys, bags, postcards and hammocks (Mon–Sat 9am–2.30pm, closed Sun). For groceries there's a fruit/veg store by Las Marquesas (see above); you can also buy food items at Mercado La Carioca.

Moving on

Air To get to the airport catch bus Ruta 1, Ruta 2 or S. Eduviges from Paseo Orinoco (between 5am–5pm only; Bsf15). There are flights to Caracas, with some stopping off in Maturín

(2 daily except Sun; 1hr 10min) and Canaima (several daily; 1hr 10min). Rutaca (W www.rutaca .com.ve) nominally operates charter flights to Santa Elena although prices are high and actual departures are unpredictable. The Puerto Ordáz airport covers more destinations.

Bus Destinations include Caracas (several daily; 9hr); Puerto Ayacucho (several daily; 14hr); Puerto La Cruz (several daily; 4hr); Puerto Ordáz (half-hourly; 1hr) and Valencia (several daily; 10hr). Reserve early for Santa Elena de Uairén (six daily, mostly night buses; 12hr); if travelling by night, you will be woken at least twice for checkpoints along the way. If you're headed to Mérida (1 daily; 22hr), it's faster to take a bus to Barinas (2 daily; 15hr) and transfer to a *buseta* or *por puesto* for the steep, windy road into the mountains. There are no buses to Tucupita; you must first go to the San Félix terminal in Ciudad Guayana (see p.993). Turgar offers the cheapest transport.

Por puesto Those to Puerto La Cruz (3hr) leave regularly from the street north of the terminal and cost BsF100.

PARQUE NACIONAL CANAIMA

PARQUE NACIONAL CANAIMA, one of the world's largest national parks, is the number one tourist attraction in Venezuela, thanks to the wondrous Salto Ángel, or **Angel Falls**. As far as national parks go, however, it receives surprisingly few visitors overall. The park is inhabited by roughly twenty thousand Pemón Indians, made up of three major tribes: Kamakoto, Arekuna and Taurepan. Most live in small villages of between 100 and 200 people.

While it's certainly possible to cobble together a trip to Canaima on your own, the little money you save is hardly worth the effort of arranging all the various components (flights, accommodation, excursions, meals, etc). The local tourist industry depends on groups assembled by agencies; the needs of maverick travellers are generally an afterthought.

The bestselling trip is an all-inclusive, three-day/two-night tour of Angel Falls and Canaima Lagoon (BsF2200–2600/person), with flights in and out of Canaima Village. Prices are all-inclusive except for the national park fee (BsF35) and airport tax (BsF20).

Canaima Village

The most visited village in the park, **Canaima** is the principal base for trips to Angel Falls. Just beside the village are four postcard-worthy waterfalls – **Salto Hacha**, **Salto Ucaima**, **Salto Golondrina** and **Salto Guadima** – that emanate from the Río Carrao and empty into the picturesque **Laguna de Canaima**, which has small sand beaches along its banks. Tour packages (see p.996) include a short boat trip to another waterfall, **Salto El Sapo**, which you can actually walk right behind – certainly not for the faint hearted in the rainy season – and **Salto El Sapito**, a smaller but equally picturesque cascade.

If you've come on a tour, a guide will have been arranged for you; if you're on your own, seek out English-speaking Materson Nathaniel (T 0426/997-2879, E kaikuse_68@yahoo.es), a knowledgeable Pemón guide who leads trips throughout the park.

Arrival

Air Given Canaima's location in the middle of the national park, virtually all visitors arrive by air from Ciudad Bolívar (transport is included in package tours). Some flights arrive from Puerto Ordáz. The main airline is Transmandu (W www.transmandu .com); if you're arranging your own transport, expect to pay BsF1000 with return to Ciudad Bolívar. The airstrip is right on the edge of the village.

Accommodation

Like transport, accommodation in Canaima is included in tour packages arranged in Ciudad Bolívar. All lodgings, save the exclusive luxury ones, are *campamentos* of varying simplicity. The cheapest are listed here, with prices indicating how much you'll pay if you arrange a trip on your own. On trips that include a visit to Salto Ángel, you'll spend a night in one of several primitive camps near the base of the falls. Hammocks and outhouses (no showers) are the norm.

Posada Kusari about 700m outside the village ☎ 0286/962-0443 or 0416/696-0025, ✉ claudiogd3@hotmail.com. Basic en-suite rooms here are BsF200/person, although they really sting you with meal prices (breakfast BsF50, lunch and dinner BsF100 each). The 3-day/2-night Angel Falls tour is a whopping BsF1350 with meals and accommodation, but no flights.

Tiuna ☎ 0414/864-0033, ✉ tiunatours@hotmail .com. By far the most receptive place (as well as the cheapest) for independent travellers, Tiuna has a serene location at the edge of Canaima Lagoon. Hammocks will only set you back BsF40, while rooms are BsF100/person with discounts for four or more. Breakfast is BsF30, lunch and dinner BsF80, while the 3-day/2-night Angel Falls tour is BsF900 (including meals but excluding flights).

Wey Tepui ☎ 0414/191-8708 or 0416/185-7231, ✉ weytupu@hotmail.com. Large green *campamento* with a tin roof; has a selection of basic rooms for BsF200 per person.

Eating and drinking

Food is also included in tour prices; vegetarians should notify the agency when purchasing a tour. Should you get hungry between scheduled meals – portions are on the small side – note that there are a couple of general stores in the village, though prices are outrageous since all stock is flown in. An excellent place for an evening cocktail is the lagoon-side deck of *Campamento Canaima*, with unreal views of the falls at sunset. Intriguingly, the Pemón have expropriated this high-end lodging from the government agency that was previously managing it.

Moving on

Air In most cases, moving on from Canaima is simply a matter of boarding your pre-arranged return flight to Ciudad Bolívar. If your next stop is Santa Elena de Uairén, however, you might consider a direct flight there (2hr 30min) saving yourself around 12hr of bus travel, not including waiting time. The main obstacles, besides the trip breaking the bank (BsF2500 per hr in the air), are the notoriously unpredictable departure times and the five-passenger minimum.

ANGEL FALLS

At 980m, **ANGEL FALLS** (Salto Ángel in Spanish) is the world's tallest waterfall – around sixteen times the height of Niagara Falls and twelve times the height of Iguazú Falls (see p.96 and p.383). It is created by the Churún River, which makes a dramatic plunge from the edge of the enormous Auyantepui and into the verdant jungle below.

Seeing the falls is one of the highlights of a trip to Venezuela, and you can arrange a visit through tour agencies in Ciudad Bolívar (see p.996) and even Caracas (see p.948). The first leg of the trip is a three-hour, 70km and often very wet boat ride up the Caroní and Carrao rivers from Canaima Village; the second leg is an hour-and-a-half hike through the jungle, ending at the falls' principal vantage point. The falls themselves are generally fuller, and therefore more spectacular, during the rainy season; the trade-off is less visibility, as the top of the falls is often covered in clouds during those months.

In the dry season (Jan–May), low water levels in the access rivers can complicate the journey, sometimes requiring passengers to unload and push the boat. Tour agencies are usually diligent about warning customers of such conditions, but it's a good idea to ask anyway.

SANTA ELENA DE UAIRÉN

SANTA ELENA DE UAIRÉN grew significantly when the paved road connecting it with the rest of the country was completed, but, with a population of only eighteen thousand, it's still a quiet town. Many of its inhabitants are originally from Brazil, whose border is just 15km south of town. The town serves as a good base to explore the awe-inspiring **tepuis**, as well as being a good jumping-off point to Brazil. There is nothing in particular to do in Santa Elena proper, although the town remains one of the country's most backpacker-friendly, with reasonably priced accommodation and restaurants, as well as many tour operators specializing in trips through the **Gran Sabana** and up **Mount Roraima** (see p.1002).

Arrival and information

Air Flights arrive from Ciudad Bolívar and Puerto Ordáz, though schedules are unpredictable and planes tend to be relatively old and very small.
Bus Heading south to Santa Elena, buses stop at two or three National Guard checkpoints. At the final one, everyone must exit the bus with their baggage to be searched – a fairly routine and professional procedure, unlike in Caracas.
The terminal is 3km from the centre, a 5-min taxi ride to the centre. There are no city buses.
Tourist information Vía La Línea, on the way to the Brazilian border ☎0414/998-7167.

Accommodation

The town has its fair share of decent accommodation. The best places, along with most other backpacker services, are on Calle Urdaneta between Calle Icarabú and Avenida Perimetral.

Lucrecia Av. Perimetral ☎0289/995-1105 or 0414/772-3365. Popular place among Brazilian and Venezuelan tourists with rooms giving off a refreshingly verdant courtyard. There's also a decent size pool at the back. BsF150.

Posada Backpackers Calle Urdaneta ☎ 0289/995-1430 or 0414/886-7227, ⓦwww.backpacker-tours.com. Friendly German-owned posada which remains a popular choice amongst backpackers. Spacious and colourful rooms all set on the top floor. Free wi-fi. There's also a reputable tour agency (see p.1003). BsF120.

Posada Hotel Michelle Calle Urdaneta ☎0289/416-1257. Another good choice on the backpacker strip with clean, although somewhat gloomy, rooms. Laundry service (BsF10/kg), kitchen and book exchange. BsF70.

Posada Los Pinos ☎ 0289/995-1430 or 0414/886-7227 ⓦwww.posadapinos.com. Under the same management as *Posada Backpackers*, this pricier option ten minutes' walk from town has ten rooms, each individually inspired by Indian tribes and Venezuelan plants. There's

ACCOMMODATION
Hotel Lucrecia	B
Posada Backpacker	D
Posada Hotel Michelle	C
Posada Los Pinos	A
Posada Moronkatok	E

EATING
Alfredo's Restaurant	3
Café Goldrausch	2
Nova Opção	5
Tumá Seró	1
Venezuela Primero	4

0   200 m

Brazilian Consulate (2km), ⓘ (4km), Airport (6km) & Brazilian border (15km) ▼   ▼ Via La Línea

EXCHANGING BRAZILIAN REAIS FOR BOLÍVARES

The Brazilian town of Pacaraima's designation as a "puerto libre" – permitting visitors unfettered access across the border if they return the same day – allows you to replenish funds without resorting to Venezuela's unfavourable official exchange rate at an ATM machine or bank.

Take a taxi to the border (20min) and explain to officials that you're spending just a couple of hours in Brazil; make sure they do not stamp your passport (if they do, you'll have to wait a day to return to Venezuela). Once you're over, visit one of several available ATMs and withdraw Brazilian reais at the current exchange rate of US$1 = R$1.65.

Return to Santa Elena de Uairén and head to the intersection of calles Urdaneta and Bolívar, where unofficial moneychangers congregate. You should be able to exchange R$1 for at least BsF5.20, raising the value of your dollar to almost double the official exchange rate.

Keep in mind that, while countless travellers have successfully used this method, you are solely responsible for the inherent risk of any unofficial financial transaction.

also a fun Flintstones-esque pool with a slide. BsF320 (BsF430 with dinner and breakfast included).

Posada Moronkatok Calle Urdaneta, diagonally across from Lavandería Pereida ☎0289/995-1518. Look out for a gated entrance with red pillars as the owner hasn't displayed a sign. There are a couple of rooms in anodyne chalets, and all have a/c, hot water and cable TV. Communal kitchen. BsF120.

Eating

Alfredo's Restaurant Av. Perimentral ☎0289/995-1042. A slightly pricier option in a pleasant setting with an outdoor covered terrace as well as indoor seating. International food available from pastas (BsF36.50–59.50) to pizzas (BsF30–38.50), as well as local dishes such as *lomito en mostaza* (BsF86.50). Open Tues–Sun 11am–3pm & 6–10pm.

Café Goldrausch Calle Urdaneta ☎0289/995-1576. Adjacent to *Posada Backpackers*, this chilled café and restaurant with an outdoor terrace is the perfect spot to meet other travellers. Chilled beers and coffee prolong the evening after some tasty grub (try the *lomito salteado;* BsF45). There's also an internet café inside (BsF5 per hr). Open Mon–Sat 7.30am–10.30pm.

Nova Opção Av. Perimentral ☎0289/995-1013. Don't expect the same quality of food that you'd get in a Brazilian per kg restaurant, but they do have all sorts of meats, rice, beans, *farofa*, flan and even *guaraná*. BsF55 per kg with meat, BsF48 without. Food runs out quickly so make sure you get there early. Open daily 11am–3pm.

Tumá Serö Between Calle Roscio and Calle Bolívar. Plenty of cheap restaurants lined up in this indoor courtyard serve local grub, perfect to grab a quick *arepa* (BsF15) or a cheap bite for lunch (mains BsF35). Open daily 6am–10pm.

Venezuela Primero Av. Perimentral ☎0426/796-4733. Cordial but slow service in European country-style surroundings with a few curious Venezuelan touches. The *pollo a la naranja* (BsF58) is especially good. Mon–Sat 11am–3pm & 6–10pm, Sun 11am–2pm.

Directory

Banks and exchange Banco Industrial, Calle Bolívar north of Calle Urdaneta; Banco Guyana on the east side of the Plaza Bolívar. Unofficial money-changers at the intersection of calles Urdaneta and Bolívar accept dollars and Brazilian reais; see box above, on how to pick up reais.

Consulate Brazilian Consulate; see box above for details.

Hospital Hospital Santa Elena, Av. Perimentral ☎0289/995-1155.

Internet In the *Café Goldrausch* (Mon–Sat 7.30am–10.30pm); Intertop, Calle Urdaneta at Calle Peña (daily 7am–midnight). Just west is Megacyber, (daily 8.30am–11pm). All BsF5/hr.

Laundry Lavandería Pereida, Calle Urdaneta across from Posada Moronkatok (daily 7.30am–7.30pm; BsF15 per kg).

Pharmacy Three in town: Calle Bolívar & Urdaneta; by the hospital; by the police station. There are no set opening hours – only one of three is open at any one time.

Phones Movistar/Centro de Comunicaciones Marcos, Calle Zea between calles Roscio and Peña, (Mon–Fri 8am–9pm, Sat & Sun till 8pm). Just east is Variedades Nabhyl (Mon–Sat 7am–8pm, Sun 8am–noon & 3–8pm).

Police The police station (℡ 0289/995-1556 or 0416/586-1321; open 24hr) is on Calle Akarabisis across the street from Ruta Salvaje (see p.1003).

Post Ipostel, in the orange brick building on Calle Urdaneta west of Calle Roscio (Mon–Fri 8am–noon & 2–4.30pm). Consider yourself lucky if you happen upon stamps.

Moving on

For information on crossing into Brazil from this region, see the box below.

Air Rutaca is the primary airline, operating unpredictably scheduled flights to Ciudad Bolívar, Canaima and Puerto Ordáz (all around BsF900).

Bus Caracas (3 daily; 20hr); Ciudad Bolívar (4 daily; 11hr), making stops in San Félix and Puerto Ordáz; Puerto La Cruz (2 daily; 16hr). There are currently no buses to Brazil from the terminal.

LA GRAN SABANA AND RORAIMA

Said to be along one of the world's major energy meridians, which also passes through Macchu Picchu and Stonehenge, the 35,000-square-kilometre **GRAN SABANA**, or Great Savanna, has induced many reports of visitors having extremely lucid dreams, experiencing spiritual rejuvenations and even seeing UFOs.

Although the region technically includes Angel Falls and most of Parque Nacional Canaima, trips to the Gran Sabana do not. Rather, they go to the vast area that extends southeast to the Brazilian border. Just before the border is where one of the principal attractions lies: the beautiful and climbable *tepui* **RORAIMA**, renowned for the other-

---

CROSSING INTO BRAZIL

There are two main border crossings between Venezuela and Brazil. The crossing at Santa Elena de Uairén (see p.999) is much more convenient for onward transport to Manaus; the San Simón de Cocuy crossing involves a boat journey to São Gabriel de Cachoeira in Brazil, from where you will have to transfer to another boat. This latter option is very expensive, though, as it involves an 11-day boat trip (May–Nov only; US$150 per day all inclusive; see ⊛ www.selvadentro.com for further info).

Before leaving Venezuela you must get your passport stamped by the nearest emigration office. Once you cross the border, immediately visit the local Brazilian immigration office for an entry stamp and advance your watch an hour and a half. If you're travelling to Brazil at night from Santa Elena de Uairén, you'll have to get your passport stamped at the DIEX office, Av. Mariscal Sucre (Mon–Fri 8am–noon & 2–5pm) before leaving, as the border office closes at 6pm.

Citizens of the US, Canada and Australia need a visa to enter Brazil; EU nationals and citizens of South Africa and New Zealand do not. For a list of all countries' visa requirements, visit ⊛ www.dpf.gov.br. All visitors must have a valid yellow-fever vaccination certificate.

Santa Elena de Uairén

EUCATUR has buses from Santa Elena to Manaus via Boa Vista in Brazil (3–4 hr; BsF100). A faster and, ironically, cheaper way to get to Boa's Vista's bus terminal is by taxi (Brazilian R$30) as there are plenty of cars going back and forth keen to stock up on cheap Venezuelan fuel. From Boa Vista catch an EUCATUR bus to Manaus (12hr; Brazilian R$100); TAM also flies from Boa Vista to Manaus (Braziian R$100; 1hr).

The Brazilian Consulate in Santa Elena, at Calle Los Castaños, Urbanización Roraima del Casco Central (Mon–Fri 8am–2pm; ℡ 0289/995-1256,) supplies visas within 48 hours; you must provide a passport photo and present proof of financial security (usually a credit card) and accommodation in Brazil. Visa fees vary by country of citizenship.

For information on changing money at the border, see the box on p.1001.

TOUR OPERATORS

The classic six-day trek to the top of Mount Roraima (see p.1002), considered by many to be one of the best hikes in South America, costs US$400–600. Since the price is based on distance rather than time, agencies are usually willing to add or subtract a day to fit your schedule. Multi-day Gran Sabana tours cost US$65–75 per day per person, typically with a minimum of five people and with meals included. One- or two-day trips to El Paují, El Abismo, Salto Aponguao and other specific sites cost around US$100 per day per person, meals included. If you want to visit multiple sites on the same day, rates increase considerably.

Adventure Tours ☎0414/853-7903 ⊛www.adventuretours.com.ve. Well-established company run by friendly Frank Khazen, a Caracas-born photographer with a passion for nature. Frank can also organize trips to Angel Falls and the Amazon in Brazil. All operators listed below are in Santa Elena.

Backpacker Tours Av. Urdaneta ☎0289/995-1430 or 0414/886-7227, ⊛www.backpacker-tours.com. The most expensive of the bunch, but has a permanent guide staff, sells air tickets and owns all its equipment, including high-quality tents, bicycles and trucks. Offers shorter alternatives (Mantopai and Chiricayén) to the six-day Roraima trek, as well as vigorous, multi-day bike trips. Also has a good posada (see p.1000).

Mystic Tours Av. Urdaneta ☎0289/416-0558 or 416-0686, ⊛www.mystictours.com.ve. Has built a solid reputation on its unique mystical approach to the Gran Sabana and in particular to Roraima – the owner is a scholar of the paranormal and has written several books on the subject.

Ruta Salvaje Av. Mariscal Sucre at Calle Akarabisis ☎0289/995-1134 or 0414/889-4164, ⊛www.rutasalvaje.com. Specializes in one-day tours to the Gran Sabana as well as more adrenaline-inducing activities like paragliding (BsF350), paramotoring (BsF400) and whitewater rafting trips on class one to four rapids (BsF350 per person with 4 people; BsF250 per person with 8 people).

Turísticos Álvarez in bus terminal ☎0414/385-2846, ⊛www.saltoangelrsta.com. Not to be mistaken for a tout, Francisco Álvarez's forte is arranging bare-bones trips for the budget-conscious: he rents tents to, and hires transport for, campers, and can strip down a multi-day Gran Sabana trip to just BsF180 per day. He also organizes bargain trips to Salto Ángel from both Santa Elena and Ciudad Bolívar.

worldly landscape at its summit and the unique ecosystem it sustains. The entire region is filled with other magnificent *tepuis* and waterfalls, separated by vast expanses of grasslands. One of the most famous waterfalls is **Quebrada de Jaspe**, noted for its bright red jasper rock. Other well-known waterfalls in the region include the 105m-high **Salto Aponguao**, where you can swim in the nearby **Pozo Escondido**, and **Quebrada Pacheco**, two pretty falls with natural waterslides.

THE ORINOCO DELTA

The River Orinoco in the state of Delta Amacuro is one of South America's largest river systems, along with the Amazon and La Plata. It flows through Venezuela for about 1700 miles, entering the Atlantic Ocean near Trinidad. The **Orinoco Delta**, where the state capital Tucupita is located, is home to the Warao Indians who to this day live in houses on stilts along the river's many distributary channels, and fish in the way of their ancestors. Besides the Orinoco, Delta Amacuro has many other rivers and more than three hundred *caños*, small waterways that often link the rivers. From above, the entire area looks like an enormous labyrinth.

TRIPS TO THE ORINOCO DELTA

There are various lodges within the delta, which you can contact directly, as well as agencies throughout the country who organize trips in the region. Activities generally include visiting indigenous Warao villages, canoeing through the small *caños*, fishing for piraña and observing local flora and fauna. Packages cost US$100–140 per person per day and are all-inclusive. The lodges and operators listed here are the most reliable.

Tobe Lodge ☎ 0415/212-5087 or 0286/961-7708 ⓦ www.explorepartners.com/tobelodge .htm. Located by the Indian settlement of San Francisco de Guayo, not far from where the Orinoco meets the waters of the Atlantic, this large ecological lodge offers comfortable rooms all with en-suite. Free pick-up from Puerto Ordáz.

Tucupita Expeditions Boulevard Playa El Agua, Isla Margarita ☎ 0295/249-1823 or 0414/794-0172, ⓦ www.orinocodelta.com. Margarita Island-based company operating trips to the Orinoco with stays in three different lodges,

some more rustic than others. English-speaking guides available. Free pick-up from Maturín, Puerto Ordáz or Tucupita.

Waro Waro Lodge ☎ 0424/162-1960, ⓦ www .orinocodeltatours.com. Named after the Warao word for the electric blue butterflies that flutter around the region, this intimate rustic French-Argentine owned lodge is located on the Jaropuna channel north-west of the delta. It's easily accessible from San José de la Buja, and they can also organize a free pick-up from various locations, including Ciudad Bolívar and the northeast coast.

The northeast coast and islands

The **northeast coast** sports some of the country's most ruggedly beautiful coastline, as well as one of its most energetic cities. **Puerto La Cruz**, a high-rise hotel, fast-food paradise used by visitors primarily as a jumping-off point for Isla de Margarita, is pleasant enough for a day of exploration. Spreading northeast of the city, the popular **Parque Nacional Mochima** has a number of uninhabited cays for visitors to explore in chartered boats. The small coastal islands here are characterized by rocky terrain with little vegetation besides cacti.

Other than Los Roques (see p.967), Venezuela's best-known island destination is **Isla de Margarita**, off the coast of Sucre State. Built in the style of some of the Caribbean's most famous (or infamous) mega-resort areas, it is a huge magnet for Venezuelans and

international package tourists, though anyone can enjoy a one- or two-day break from the mainland here.

PUERTO LA CRUZ

It's hard to imagine that the modern, bustling city of **PUERTO LA CRUZ** is not long removed from being a small fishing village. Venezuelans come here mainly for its proximity to Parque Nacional Mochima (see p.1007) and the ferry to Isla de Margarita (see p.1010). The fast-food restaurants and fifteen-storey hotels certainly don't make it an overly attractive place to spend much time. However, the wide promenade alongside Paseo Colón makes for an enjoyable afternoon of strolling and people-watching, especially when there's a cool breeze rolling in off the bay.

What to see and do

There's really nothing much to see in Puerto La Cruz itself – the city doesn't particularly cater to international tourism and as such most **activities** take place outside the city limits.

Parque Nacional Mochima

On the eastern end of Paseo Colón there is a dock where you can hire boats for day-trips to the nearby islands; ticket offices are open daily (8.30am–2pm). A shared ride in a large boat to a single island costs upwards of BsF100 per person. It's much more convenient to organize trips from Santa Fe or Mochima, where there are plenty of operators offering tours which include dolphin spotting, caving, snorkelling and exploring the islands of the national park.

Los Altos de Sucre

A more do-it-yourself diversion is to head to the bus terminal for the frequent jeeps (40min; BsF8) to Los Altos de Sucre, a small community hidden in the hills above Puerto La Cruz, near the border of Anzoátegui State. The lush, rural roads couldn't be further in spirit from the city's mayhem, and are known for their numerous pastry and *artesanía* shops and spectacular views of the bay below. Drivers can drop you wherever you like along Via Principal de los Altos; look for *Dulcería Alicia* (open weekends 9am–5pm), one block before the village of Los Altos, selling delicious tarts and cheesecakes. Taller Artesanal Bogar, in Sector Vuelta de Culebra makes paper products, artesanal liqueur, traditional sweets and preserves. Pottery-lovers should check out Thai, which has plenty of ceramics available for purchase.

Arrival and information

Air The nearest airport is in Barcelona, roughly 15km southwest of Puerto La Cruz. A taxi to Puerto La Cruz's centre costs around BsF80.

PUERTO LA CRUZ

ACCOMMODATION
Hotel Neptuno	C
Posada Rancho Grande	A
Posada Turística Diana	B
Posada Turística Montecarlo	D

Bahía de Pozuelos

Boat Docks

Boat Docks

Laundry

Pharmacy

Pharmacy

Bank

Buses to Santa Fe

Bus Terminal

Los Altos de Sucre (15km) & Santa Fe (35km)

EATING
La Colmena	1
Restaurant Tasca El Senador	2
Trattoria Nonna Franca	3

0   200 m

Cines Unidos (1.5km)   Airport (20km)

Bus The bus terminal is on Calle Democracia at Calle Concordia, an easy walk from most accommodation.

Ferry The port terminal is about 3km from the centre of town. Ferries arrive daily from Isla Margarita with Conferry (☎0281/267-7847 or 267-7129) and Naviarca/Gran Cacique (☎0281/267-7286, ⊛www.grancacique.com.ve). See box, p.1012 for details.

Tourist information Inatur, in *Gran Hotel Puerto La Cruz* (Mon–Fri 8am–5pm; ☎0281/500-3675, ⊛www.venetur.gob.ve).

Accommodation

Most of the centre's budget accommodation is strung along Paseo Colón, putting you right in the middle of the action.

Neptuno Paseo Colón south of Calle Juncal ☎0281/268-5413. Check out the local football paraphernalia scattered around the hotel's entrance before heading up to rooms fitted out with furniture that's on its very last legs. There's an internet café in the lobby. BsF140.

Posada Rancho Grande Paseo Colón between calles Buenos Aires and Sucre ☎0281/265-2823. Amongst the pricier options along the Paseo, this posada has small clean rooms (en suite, TV, a/c), although none with windows facing outside. BsF180.

Posada Turística Diana Paseo Colón, just north of Calle Sucre ☎0281/416-4714. Under renovation at the time of research though not necessarily with promise of improved fixtures and decor; rooms (with en-suite, a/c, TV) face the interior corridor and as a result lack natural light. BsF120.

Posada Turística Montecarlo Paseo Colón 119 ☎0281/268-5677. Two colourful canaries will brighten up your arrival at this rather brown posada, with basic but perfectly decent accommodation. BsF110.

Eating

Paseo Colón is, oddly, lined with numerous, nearly identical Lebanese restaurants serving good-value plates of Middle Eastern food, including *shawarma*, *kibbe* and tabbouleh. If this kind of thing doesn't appeal, then try one of the options below.

La Colmena Paseo Colón, west of Calle Miranda ☎0281/265-2751. This little health shop has a few tables at the back where healthy vegetarian dishes (BsF30) are served. Lunchtime only. Mon–Fri 9am–6pm, lunch 11.45am–2.30pm.

Restaurant Tasca El Senador Calle Miranda north of Calle Alberto Ravel ☎0414/825-8044. This restaurant has a rather sultry atmosphere, which nonetheless attracts plenty of workers on their lunch break from nearby offices for a good-value *menú ejecutivo* (BsF30). Has a DJ on Fri & Sat, when things get rowdy. Mon–Thurs noon–midnight, Fri noon–3am, Sat 8pm–3am.

Trattoria Nonna Franca Calle. Bolívar 60B, at Calle Freites ☎0281/265-1780. Service is snail-paced, disorganized and surly but they do serve all sorts of pastas all made in-house: tortelloni, ravioli, spaghetti, penne and vermicelli prepared however you like (*carbonara*, *puttanesca*, *amatriciana* etc), all for under BsF48. Pizzas (large BsF49), too. Mon–Sat 11am–6pm.

Directory

Banks and exchange Banco de Venezuela, Calle Libertad at Calle Miranda; Banco Banesco, Calle Freites at Calle Bolívar.

Hospital Policlínica Puerto La Cruz, Av. 5 de Julio at Calle Arismendi, open 24hr (☎0281/265-6833).

Internet In the *Hotel Neptuno* (see above), open 24/7; Sky Intern@tional, Calle Maneiro at Paseo Colón (Mon–Sat 9am–9pm, Sun 1–8pm). Both cost BsF4/hr.

Laundry There is a nameless *lavandería* on Av. Ravél, between calles Carabobo and Las Flores (Mon–Fri 7.30am–6pm, Sat till 3pm, closed Sun).

Pharmacy Farmacia Meditotal, Calle Bolívar between calles Freites and Miranda (Mon–Sat 7.30am–9pm, Sun *por turno*). Farmatodo, Paseo Colón across from Plaza Colón, open 24hr.

Phones Movistar and CanTV are both on Paseo Colón between calles Maneiro and Buenos Aires. You can also make international calls from Sky Intern@tional (see above "Internet").

Police Located at Av. Municipal by the Centro, Comercial Regina (☎0281/266-1414).

Post Ipostel, Calle Freites at Calle Libertad.

Moving on

For information on boat travel to Isla de Margarita, see box, p.1012.

Air Buses for the airport in Barcelona pass regularly along Av. 5 de Julio (BsF30). Taxis are around BsF80. Flights include Caracas (several daily; 45min); Maracaibo (daily; 3hr with connection); Mérida (daily except Sun; 3hr wth 2 connections); Porlamar (daily; 30min); Puerto Ordáz (daily except Sun; 30min); and Valencia (daily; 40min). Avior operates flights to Miami.

Bus *Busetas* to Mochima (1hr), Playa Colorada (40min) and Santa Fe (1hr) leave constantly from

Calle Democracia by the off-licence across from the terminal. All cost BsF8.

Other destinations include: Barinas (8 daily; 12hr); Caracas (half-hourly; 5hr); Carúpano (several daily; 4hr); Ciudad Bolívar (hourly; 5hr); Coro (4 daily; 11hr); Cumaná (half-hourly; 2hr); Maracaibo (5 daily; 15hr); Mérida (2 daily; 28hr); Puerto Ordáz (hourly; 7hr); Santa Elena de Uairén (1 daily; 17hr); Tucupita (1 daily; 6hr); and Valencia (several daily; 7hr).

Caracas-bound buses also depart from the private Aeroexpresos Ejecutivos terminal next to the port (☎0212/266-2321, ⓦwww.aeroexpresos.com.ve).

Ferry The port terminal is about 3km from the centre of town. Ferries leave daily for Isla Margarita. See box, p.1012 for details.

PARQUE NACIONAL MOCHIMA

The 950-square-kilometre **PARQUE NACIONAL MOCHIMA** was created in 1973 to protect 36 uninhabited cays and the surrounding coastal area. Much of the park's beauty lies in the stunning contrast between the red earth tones of the rocks and the emerald green water. While the beaches are not as conventionally beautiful as those of Morrocoy and Henri Pittier national parks (see p.973 and p.968, respectively), the snorkelling and scuba-diving are just as good here, if not better.

Playa Colorada

In a protected cove lined with swaying palm trees, **Playa Colorada** has blue-green water and a stretch of tan, almost red, sand from which it derives its name. Unfortunately, it is also riddled with innumerable beach chairs, aluminium food stands and raucous day-trippers, particularly on weekends and holidays. Consequently, weekdays or the low season are the best times to visit.

There are no banks or internet cafés in Playa Colorada, and few other services, so you should stay here only if you wish to disappear for a day or two. When you're ready to return to civilization, wait on the highway for a passing bus to Cumaná or Puerto La Cruz (see p.1012).

Arrival

Bus Frequent Santa Fe-bound *busetas* (BsF8) depart from Calle Democracia, across the street from the Puerto La Cruz terminal. If you're coming from the other direction, Playa Colorada is only 10min from Santa Fe, with plenty of *busetas* connecting the two.

Accommodation

Most of Playa Colorada's accommodation consists of sprawling, ranch-style homes that rent budget rooms and apartments for longer stays.

Jakera Lodge On the main highway across from the beach ☎0293/808-7057 ⓦwww .jakera.com. Scottish-owned place primarily providing long-term housing to groups of European students who come to learn Spanish. Sleep in the "bird cage", a large hammock area (BsF120), in comfy, spacious dorms (BsF140) or doubles (BsF360). There are plenty of communal spaces in which to mingle, as well as a kitchen and laundry room. Prices are per person and include breakfast and dinner.

Posada Carmencita Calle Sucre 58 ☎0293/808-3562 ⓔposadacarmencita@yahoo.es. The main door opens straight onto the pool and a sociable terrace area at this pleasant French-owned *posada* up the hill from the main road. Rooms are pleasantly decorated and meals can be cooked upon request. BsF200.

Posada Jaly Calle Marchán ☎0293/808-3246 or 0416/681-8113. French-Canadian owner Jacques, who speaks French and English, offers the cheapest rooms in town. The house is surrounded by a huge garden, there's a shared kitchen, book exchange and rooms (en suite with a/c) are more than decent. BsF100.

Villa Nirvana Calle Marchán ☎0293/808-7844. The healthy garden has hammocks, an outdoor, shared kitchen and great views of the bay; there are smallish doubles (BsF150), some with a/c and TV, as well as two much larger apartments housing six (BsF200) and four (BsF150). For those on a tight budget there are two tiny doubles that are as cheap as chips (BsF60). There's a book exchange and laundry, and the multilingual owner fixes breakfasts for BsF35.

Eating

Other than the stalls lining the beach, there's only one place in the village at which to eat.

Las Carmitas 3a Transversal ☎0416/322-8887. There's usually a bit of a queue, which is not surprising given that it's the only restaurant in town and only has about five tables, but you can sit around outside and quickly make friends with other hungry customers. Serves pretty good hamburgers (BsF15), sandwiches (BsF12), pizzas (BsF30), and the like. Daily noon–8.30pm.

SANTA FE

Though it's still a fishing village at heart, **Santa Fe** once attracted hordes of budget-minded travellers with its cheap, beachside accommodation. It still does, although today it's in the doldrums of an economic slump, likely caused by a reputation for drug-related robberies. It's nonetheless a relatively pleasant place to visit, although make sure you keep your wits about you, especially in the evenings.

There are **no banks** or ATMs in Santa Fe; stock up on cash in Puerto La Cruz or Cumaná.

What to see and do

There's basically nothing to do in Santa Fe proper, but that's generally the point of beach towns – though the area's best beaches lie off the coast. Two-way **boat trips** to the outlying islands, where you can snorkel and relax in seaside seclusion, cost BsF40 per person. The most popular destinations are Isla Arapo and La Piscina.

For a full day of island-hopping, charter a boat and a guide from *Posada Café del Mar* (see below) for around BsF50 per head. Trips mainly include visiting Islas Caracas and Venado; make sure you bring food and drinks.

Local guide Sergio (☎0426/885-4094), also at *Posada Café del Mar*, offers daily tours (9am–2pm) which include exploring the region's coffee and cacao plantations, calling on indigenous families and visiting a beautiful waterfall and cave nearby, rounded off by a 3-km trek through a river, all for only BsF50 per person.

Arrival

Bus *Busetas* from Puerto La Cruz (via Playa Colorada; BsF8) usually stop on the highway at the entrance to the town; if you're arriving after dark, check if your driver will continue to the end of Av. Principal, thereby saving you a half-kilometre walk to the beach.

Accommodation

Several small backpacker-friendly posadas line Santa Fe's thin strand. Camping on the beach is discouraged for safety reasons. A rather unique aspect of Santa Fe – likely a sign of its depression – is the presence of touts who try to take you to a posada. It's best to refuse their offers.

Le Petit Jardin ☎0293/231-0036, ⓦwww .lepetitjardin-mochima.com. A pricier French-owned option with its own pool one block back from the beach. The five rooms all have a/c and en-suite, and there are hammocks in the garden for an afternoon kip. French breakfasts (madeleines & crêpes) for only BsF10. BsF230.

Posada Bahía del Mar ☎0293/231-0073 ⓦwww.posadabahiadelmar.com. With its main entrance on the beach, this friendly place has a pleasant outdoor communal area and clean, spacious rooms with fan or a/c. Ask for #7 or #8, delightful open-fronted rooms with sea views. There's a laundry service and a shared outdoor kitchen. They can also organize trips to Isla Tortuga, as well as waterskiing. BsF120.

Posada Café del Mar ☎0293/231-0009, ⓦwww .hosteltrail.com/cafedelmar. A popular place for its small restaurant (see below), and rooms (en-suite with fan BsF120 or a/c BsF170) are spacious and passably clean; glass doors and flimsy locks, however, leave a bit to be desired in terms of security. Benefits include a roof deck with bay views, and the friendly owner Rogelio who's always happy to help.

Posada Turística 7 Delfines ☎0293/808-8064, ⓔlossietedelfinessantafe@hotmail.com. Rooms (a/c, en-suite) are a bit small and a bit dark – ask for an ocean view – in this breezy, blue and white concrete block. The roof deck has views of palms and the sea. BsF155.

Eating, drinking and nightlife

Independent dining options are limited in Santa Fe, since most posadas have their own restaurant.
Café del Mar in *Posada Café del Mar*. Casual dining, with very relaxed service, under a *palapa*

(palm roof) five metres from the water. Soups (BsF25), spaghetti (BsF30), and fish and seafood dishes (BsF60) are expertly prepared; try the *parrilla café del mar* (BsF48). Open 7am–8pm, closed Mon.

El Club Náutico on the beach ☎0293/231-0083. Watch boats come and go as you dine on a tasty *parrillada de mariscos* (BsF45) at the most established restaurant in town right by where the fishermen dock. They also serve excellent value *pabellón oriental* and *pabellón criollo* (both BsF26). Open 8am–8pm, closed Tues in low season.

Minitasca Luncheria "Los Molina" on the beach ☎0293/808-8064. Relaxed beach shack serving good cocktails (BsF16) and tasty grub; mainly seafood (BsF32), top-notch soups (BsF20) and pastas (BsF18–35). Daily 8.30am–8pm, closed Wed in low season.

Directory

Internet Very slow service at Lodging Internet (BsF6 per hr) on the beach (daily 8am–8pm).
Pharmacy Medicinas Santa Elena, Calle Las Mercedes, east of Av. Principal (daily 7am–noon & 4–7pm).
Police Station at beach end of Av. Principal.
Shopping The food market on the beach – where fish plays a central role – is a great place to see odd specimens (both marine life and human) and get heckled by good-natured fishermen.

Moving on

Bus The terminal is on the highway, 300m west of the intersection with Av. Principal. Frequent *busetas* depart daily 5am–7pm for Puerto La Cruz (1hr),

passing Playa Colorada (see p.1007), and Cumaná (1hr), passing Mochima (see below).

MOCHIMA

Like Santa Fe, the village of **Mochima** began as a fishing community; unlike its neighbour, its reputation remains fairly intact, making it a more serene place to stay. The catch is that it's somewhat more difficult to get to. The village has no beach – just a dock from where boat tours depart.

There are **no banks** or ATMs in Mochima; stock up on cash in Puerto La Cruz or Cumaná.

What to see and do

The main activity in Mochima is, once again, **boat trips** to the cays of the national park.

Most accommodation can supply you with a boat, guide and snorkelling equipment. You can also get a ride to and from the islands by taking a boat from the dock – there's a ticket desk with more information about the surrounding beaches. If there's a group of you, you may want to rent a *lancha* (speedboat) for the day (BsF600; 7 people max).

Alternatively, consider the friendly Posada de Los Buzos dive centre (☎0293/416-0856 or 0414/180-6244, ✉mochimadivecenter@hotmail.com) which offers plenty of additional activities: kayaking, trekking, climbing, dolphin-spotting, one-day scuba trips (BsF480) and white-water rafting on class 1–5 rapids (BsF300; 3hr). You can also take a four-day scuba course for SSI certification (BsF2400).

Arrival

Bus *Busetas* from Puerto La Cruz (changing in Santa Fe) or Cumaná drop you on the highway at the top of a long, winding descent to Mochima; intermittent jeeps and *busetas* (BsF15) shuttle back and forth daily from 5.30am until 8pm. If they don't appear, which sometimes happens, you can try flagging down a private vehicle.

TREAT YOURSELF

Villa Majagual 6.5km from Santa Fe heading towards Mochima ☎0293/808-3147 or 0416/893-6391 ✉majagual01@cantv.net. Located within the Parque Nacional Mochima, this secluded posada is the perfect spot to hide away and unwind for a couple of days. Look out for dolphins as you ride a pedalo off into the sunset or simply mellow out on the posada's small private beach. Prices include three daily meals. Discounts for two nights or more. BsF1280.

Accommodation

Casa Cruz ☎0293/414-4665 or 0414/178-2283, ✉karikas10@hotmail.com. Plenty of fish motifs to remind you of the beach location at this welcoming little posada with only four rooms. Book ahead. BsF160.

Posada El Mochimero ☎0293/417-3339 or 0414/773-8782. A trippy and tacky painting of marine life is pretty much the only thing that brightens up this rather plain two-storey option, whose sombre en-suite rooms – most located around the interior courtyard – feature a/c and cable TV. Ask for room 10 or 17 as these have natural light. All rooms are triple. BsF150.

Eating

Restaurant El Mochimero ☎0293/414-4171. Pleasant waterside restaurant with a bamboo cane roof and blue porthole windows, mainly serving fish and seafood dishes (BsF70; fish soup BsF40). Daily 11am–9pm.

Restaurant Puerto Viejo ☎0293/416-0810. Perfect for grabbing a bite before jumping in a boat at the jetty, this breezy dockside restaurant specializes in seafood dishes – there's *sopa de mariscos* (BsF35), *filet puerto viejo*, fish doused in a white wine and butter sauce served with *tostones* (BsF65), or, for those missing their Mediterranean comforts, *pasta marinera* (BsF55). Daily 11am–9pm, open Thurs–Sun in low season.

ISLA DE MARGARITA

On the ferry to **ISLA DE MARGARITA** from the mainland you're unlikely to see more than one or two backpackers, as the 940-square-kilometre island is primarily visited by well-to-do Venezuelans and European tourists who come over on relatively cheap package deals. While prices are inflated and any cultural authenticity has been supplanted by rampant commercialism, Margarita can still provide an entertaining taste of mainstream tourism Venezuelan-style, as well as a memorable finale to your travels in the country.

What to see and do

Isla de Margarita has innumerable beach communities and just a couple of more developed urban centres, **PORLAMAR** being the largest and containing the lion's share of inexpensive services. It's therefore best to base yourself here and take day-trips to the island's other attractions.

Ten kilometres north of Porlamar, now more or less engulfed by that city's sprawl, lies the more peaceful town of **Pampatar**. Founded in 1530,

---

LA CUEVA DEL GUÁCHARO

Invisible wings crackle overhead and unearthly hisses and shrieks electrify the darkness. You've entered La Cueva del Guácharo, the domain of the guácharos, or oilbirds, nocturnal avians that leave this cave en masse every night and return just before dawn. Despite their huge, inky black eyes, the birds use echolocation to chase down their insect prey.

Rangers give frequent tours of the first 1200m of the 10km-long cave (daily 8am–4pm; 45min; BsF10; ☎0291/641-7543), using a gas lamp to illuminate the distinctively shaped stalagmites and stalactites along the path. You won't get more than a fleeting glimpse of the *guácharos*, though, as light disturbs them (flash photography is prohibited).

The cave can be visited on a day-trip from Cumaná (two hours northeast of Puerto La Cruz by bus) though it can be slightly difficult to reach. There are only two daily buses to Caripe (7am & noon), from where you can continue the rest of the way by *por puesto* (15min; BsF20); alternatively, catch a Carúpano-bound bus from Cumaná, getting off where the highway splits to Caripe, and continue by *por puesto* from there (about 1hr 30min). The trip, much of which winds through awesome, mountainous jungle, takes 2hr 30min to 3hr each way.

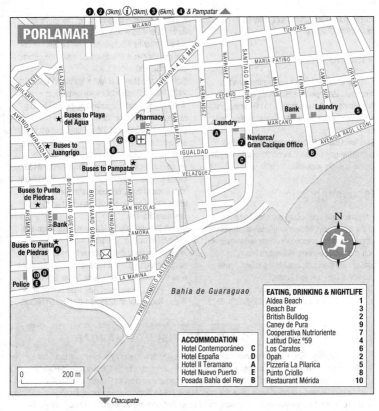

❶, ❷ (3km), ⓘ (3km), ❸ (6km), ❹ & Pampatar ▲

PORLAMAR

MILANO

TUBORES

OESTE

GUILARTE

VELAZQUEZ

AVENIDA MIRANDAR

AVENIDA 4 DE MAYO

NAVIRAEZ

SANTIAGO MARIÑO

MARIA PATIÑO

MALAVE

CAMPO SUR

FERMIN

ORTEGA

A. HERNANDEZ

CEDEÑO

SAN RAFAEL

DIAZ

IGUALDAD

★ Buses to Playa del Agua

Pharmacy

Laundry **Ⓐ**

Bank

Laundry

MARCANO

AVENIDA RAUL LEONI

★ Buses to Juangrigo

@ **Ⓕ** ✚
Ⓑ ❽

Naviarca/ Gran Cacique Office **Ⓑ**
❼

Ⓑ ❺

★ Buses to Pampatar

VELAZQUEZ

FAJARDO

BOULEVARD GUEVARA

LA FRATERNIDAD

★ Buses to Punta de Piedras

ARISMENDI

MARIÑO

Bank

BOULEVARD GOMEZ

SAN NICOLAS

ZAMORA

★ Buses to Punta de Piedras ❾

MANEIRO

LA MARINA

❿ Ⓓ
Ⓔ Police

PASEO RÓMULO GALLEGOS

Bahía de Guaraguao

N

▼ Chacupata

ACCOMMODATION

Hotel Contemporáneo	C
Hotel España	D
Hotel Il Teramano	A
Hotel Nuevo Puerto	E
Posada Bahía del Rey	B

EATING, DRINKING & NIGHTLIFE

Aldea Beach	1
Beach Bar	3
British Bulldog	2
Caney de Pura	9
Cooperativa Nutrioriente	7
Latitud Díez °59	4
Los Caratos	6
Opah	2
Pizzería La Pilarica	5
Punto Criollo	8
Restaurant Mérida	10

0 ___ 200 m

it was one of the first settlements in Venezuela, and even today it retains some of its former charm, with colonial buildings along a pretty waterfront, shady squares and the remains of a Spanish fortress, Castillo de San Carlos Borromeo, completed in 1684 (daily 9am–6pm; free).

Margarita's most famous beach, **Playa El Agua** (1hr from Porlamar by bus), is 3km of white sand and palm trees, utterly overrun with tourists during the holiday season. Though there are much nicer beaches on the island (including *playas* Manzanillo, El Yaque, Caribe, Guayacán, Puerto Abajo and Cardón), it's worth spending an hour or two here to gawk at the tacky souvenir stalls and the lobster-red sunbathers.

Arrival and information

Air The Aeropuerto Santiago Mariño is about 27km southwest of Porlamar; a taxi ride into town costs BsF80. Several cities have flights to Margarita, including Barcelona (3 daily; 30min); Caracas (several daily; 45min); Maracaibo (4 daily; 2–3hr with connection); Puerto Ordáz (2 daily; 1hr), Valencia (daily; 1hr 15min), San Antonio del Táchira (1 daily; 3hr with connection) and Valencia (2 daily; 2hr with connection).

Ferry The cheapest way to get to Isla de Margarita is by ferry; for details, see box, p.1012. Once you've arrived at the port at Punta de Piedras, walk 200m up the jetty to the cluster of restaurants and food stalls, where you can hop on a Porlamar-bound bus (BsF4) until 7pm. After hours, catch a taxi (BsF95) into town, roughly 30km northeast.

Tourist information Corpotur, Centro Artesanal Gilberto Menchini in Los Robles (☎0295/262-2322 or 262-3638, ⌘www.corpoturmargarita.gov .ve), roughly 3km from the centre. There's also an information point at the airport, daily 5am–11pm (☎0295-400-5057).

Getting around

Bus The cheapest way to explore the island, no more than BsF3 per ride. Bus stops throughout Porlamar's centre (see map, p.1011) correspond to various locales around the island; buses run 6am–9pm daily.

Taxi Taxis within Porlamar cost around BsF15 during the day, BsF30 at night. Otherwise the city's centre is easily walkable.

Accommodation

Porlamar is the undisputed commercial centre of the island, and, while shamelessly unattractive, offers a range of reasonably priced accommodation and dining options. Make sure to ask for low-season discounts outside the island's peak periods of Dec–Jan and Easter.

Contemporáneo Av. Santiago Mariño between calles Igualdad and Velásquez ☎0295/988-4978.

A decent option in a safe setting, though its large, darkly furnished rooms (en-suite, a/c, TV) are made darker by windows that don't open. Nevertheless, it's clean, friendly and beyond the chaotic centre. BsF100.

España Calle Mariño at Av. La Marina ☎0295/261-2479. Plenty of colourful caged birds tweet away in the courtyard of this posada at the very bottom of the price spectrum; the guesthouse is vibrantly painted and rooms (fan, TV) are basic but decent enough. BsF90.

Il Teramano Calle Marcano between Calle Narváez and Calle Hernández ☎0424/811-6485. Under complete renovation at the time of research, with plans to build four-bed dorm rooms as well as doubles. There is also a restaurant on the premises. BsF180.

Nuevo Puerto Calle La Marina at Calle Arismendi ☎0295/263-8888. Spindly furniture and wobbly locks at this fairly dingy hotel with en-suite rooms (a/c) and a ground-floor restaurant. The waterfront area is considered unsafe after 10pm. BsF120.

Posada Bahía del Rey Calle Fermín at Av. Raúl Leoni ☎0295/264-8947 or 0414/309-

---

BOAT TRANSPORT TO AND FROM ISLA DE MARGARITA

The cheapest way to get to and from Isla de Margarita – the only way other than by air – is by boat. There are two departure points from the mainland –Cumaná and Puerto La Cruz (see p.1004) – and all ferries dock at Margarita's port at Punta de Piedras.

Two different companies make the trip; fares listed are one-way only. Both companies have two-hour "express" and cheaper, five-hour "conventional" services, and, though it's rarely enforced, ask that you arrive at your port of departure 1hr 30min to 2hr prior to embarcation. Like Venezuelan buses, ferries can be overly air-conditioned, so keep a sweater handy and make sure you bring a photocopy of your passport as you'll need it to purchase a ticket.

Puerto La Cruz's port is roughly 3km west of the centre. Naviarca/Gran Cacique (☎0281/267-7286, ⊛www.grancacique.com.ve) has four daily express services (BsF80). Conferry (see p.1014) has three daily express boats (BsF88) and two daily conventional boats (BsF44).

Cumaná's terminal is 1km from the town's centre. Conferry does not offer passenger service from Cumaná, though you can get schedule information at their freight office. Naviarca/Gran Cacique has two daily express departures (first class: adult US$23, child US$11; tourist class: adult US$20, child US$8.50), and three daily conventional departures (tourist class only: US$13.50 per person). An additional departure is added to each type of service in the high season.

From Isla de Margarita, Conferry has three daily express departures for Puerto La Cruz and four daily conventional services. Naviarca/Gran Cacique has three daily express returns to Puerto La Cruz in the high season, and two during the low season. Each company's return rates are identical to its Puerto La Cruz–Punta de Piedras rates.

If you didn't buy a return ticket on the mainland, make sure you visit a ferry office in Porlamar (see p.1011) a day or two before you wish to leave, and remember to bring a photocopy of your passport.

1444, @ posadabahiadelrey@gmail.com. Bright yellow posada away from the chaos of the city, and only five steps from the seashore. Catch some rays on their lounge chairs on the beach before heading back to the warm and welcoming rooms (en-suite, TV). There are plans to build a dorm room and swimming pool. BsF220.

Eating

You're spoiled for choice when it comes to cheap eating establishments in Porlamar, with all sorts of food on offer, from freshly caught fish to pasta dishes, as well as refreshing fruit juices to boost your vitamin count.

Caney de Pura Calle Mariño at Calle Zamora. Very blue decor with clueless staff and an eclectic clientele munching on cheap grub; meat dishes BsF20, fish BsF25.20. Mon–Sat 7am–3.30pm.

Los Caratos Calle Marcano at Calle Fajardo. A tiny juice joint selling delicious, freshly made *merengadas* (BsF7–9) and *batidos* (BsF5–7). Mon–Sat 7am–7pm, closed Sun.

Cooperativa Nutrioriente Calle Santiago Mariño at Calle Igualdad. A very clean, very cheap self-service restaurant, with plates of meat, chicken, fish and sides for only BsF25. As the name suggests, some options are healthy and low-fat. Mon–Sat 7.30am–5pm, closed Sun.

Pizzeria La Pilarica Calle Marcano at Calle Ortega ☎0295/263-7508. This friendly neighbourhood café, with a garden patio as well as indoor a/c seating, is great for pizza (try the palm hearts topping; BsF35), pasta and meat or fish dishes. The *asado negro*, a blackened steak smothered in a salt-and-sugar glaze, is another treat. Mon–Sat noon–11pm.

Punto Criollo Calle Igualdad at Calle Fraternidad ☎0295/263-6745. See it to believe it: towering plates of mixed seafood and *comida criolla* whisked to every table at this constantly packed local joint. Meat dishes feature heavily (*bistec* BsF48, *medallones* BsF68, beef stroganoff BsF50) and the choice of sides, including entire plates of sliced avocado (BsF30), is endless. Not for cheap eats, but worth the expense: most meat dishes BsF48–78, seafood BsF48 and up. Daily 10.30am–10.30pm.

🏃 **Restaurant Mérida** Calle Arismendi, south of Calle Maneiro. Though naming an island restaurant after Venezuela's most renowned Andean town was an odd decision, this is a real budget option with rich atmosphere. Tuck into the day's menu (BsF25), scribbled on a board, as you share a table with other diners in the pleasant courtyard of the owners' home, and give a nod to

the small shrine to the Virgin on your way out. Mon–Sat 10am–3pm, closed Sun.

Drinking and nightlife

Night owls are in for a treat on the island. Most action takes place in Pampatar or in the Centro Comercial Costa Azul, a 2-km taxi ride east of the centre (BsF20). Most clubs have no cover charge.

Aldea Beach Complejo Margarita Village, behind the Centro Comercial Costa Azul. The main musical flavour is electronica at this open-air club by the seashore with three dance areas. Thurs–Sat 9am–3pm.

Beach Bar Calle El Cristo, La Caranta, Pampatar ☎0295/267-2392 🌐www.beachbar.com.ve. Have a few refreshing cocktails *après-plage* at this laidback bar with bamboo gazebos facing the beach. Tues–Sun 7pm–3am.

British Bulldog Centro Comercial Costa Azul ☎0295/267-1527. You've gotta give the place credit for trying so hard with the pub theme – on the walls not covered by the tremendous Union Jack there's a diverting collection of memorabilia. At weekends, local bands play amazingly accurate renditions of European and American hard-rock classics. Mon–Wed 9pm–midnight, Thurs–Sat till 3am, closed Sun.

Latitud Diez °59 Calle El Cristo, Sector La Caranta, Pampatar ☎0295/267-1850 🌐www.latituddiez59 .com. Snazzy club with an outdoor terrace where you can have a boogie or a cocktail as you check out the view. Thurs–Sat until late.

Opah Centro Comercial Costa Azul ☏0295/262-8186. Your best bet for traditional salsa dancing with a local crowd, though the giant video screen and fog machines remind you that you're in the twenty-first century – or maybe the Eighties. Thurs–Sat 9pm–3am.

Directory

Banks and exchange Banco Universal, Calle Marcano between Calle Santiago Mariño and Calle Malave; Banco Mercantil, Calle San Nicolás at Calle Mariño.

Hospital Clínica Margarita, Calle Marcano at Calle Díaz ☏0295/261-4443 or 261-4611.

Internet Video Multicolor (BsF4/hr), Calle Fajardo between calles Marcano and Igualdad, Mon–Sat 7am–6pm.

Laundry Lavandaria HR, Calle Marcano at Calle Santiago Mariño (Mon–Fri 7am–6pm, Sat till 2pm; BsF15 per kg; ☏0295/808-4992); Edikö's Lavandería, Calle Marcano between calles Campo Sur and Fermín (self service; Mon–Sat 8am–7pm).

Pharmacy FarmaSigo, Calle Marcano at Calle Díaz, daily 8.30am–7pm.

Phones There are plenty of cheap calling places on Boulevard Guevara and Boulevard Gómez.

Police Station on Calle Arismendi, just south of C. Maneiro ☏0295/264-1494.

Post Ipostel, Calle Maneiro between Calle Fraternidad and Bulevar Gómez.

Shopping Margarita is famed for its duty-free shopping, which means that what's on offer is mostly predictable. Two pedestrianized streets, Bulevar Gómez and Bulevar Guevara, are lined with vendors selling mostly knockoff items and pirated CDs – though the occasional used-book vendor may be holding some treasures.

Moving on

Air Barcelona (3 daily; 30min); Caracas (several daily; 45min); Maracaibo (4 daily; 2–3hr with connection); Puerto Ordáz (2 daily; 1hr); and Valencia (daily; 1hr 15min). You can also charter flights to Canaima (2hr); the setbacks are the unpredictable departure times and the five passenger minimum.

Ferry The cheapest way to leave Isla de Margarita is by ferry; for details, see box, p.1012. Conferry has offices at Av. Terranova at Av. Llano Adentro (Mon–Fri 8am–5.30pm, Sat till noon; ☏0295/263-9878 or 9939), Naviarca/Gran Cacique is at Av. Santiago Mariño, south of C. Marcano (☏0295/264-2945, ✍www.grancacique.com.ve). The port, at Punta de Piedras, can be reached from Porlamar by buses departing from calles Mariño and San Nicolás; see map, p.1011.

Spanish

Although there are dozens of indigenous tongues scattered throughout South America – some thirty in the Peruvian Amazon alone – this is, in general, a Spanish-speaking continent (see pp.1021–1024 for a Portuguese primer). The Spanish you will hear in South America does not always conform to what you learned in the classroom, and even competent speakers of peninsular Spanish will find it takes a bit of getting used to. In addition to the odd differences in pronunciation – discussed in detail below – words from native languages as well as various European tongues have infiltrated the different dialects of South American Spanish, giving them each their own unique character.

For the most part, the language itself is the same throughout the continent, while the pronunciation varies slightly. In parts of Argentina, for example, the *ll* and *y* sound like a *zh* (the English equivalent is the *s* in "treasure"), while the final *s* of a word is often not pronounced.

Spanish itself is not a difficult language to pick up and there are numerous learning products on the market. You'll be further helped by the fact that most South Americans, with the notable exception of fast-talking Chileans, speak relatively slowly (at least compared with Spaniards) and that there's no need to get your tongue round the lisping pronunciation. *Spanish: The Rough Guide Phrasebook* is a concise and handy **phrasebook**.

PRONUNCIATION

The rules of Spanish **pronunciation** are pretty straightforward. All syllables are pronounced. Unless there's an accent, words ending in d, l, r, and z are **stressed** on the last syllable, all others on the second last. All **vowels** are pure and short.

A somewhere between the "A" sound of back and that of father.

E as in get.

I as in police.

O as in hot.

U as in rule.

C is soft before E and I, hard otherwise: cerca is pronounced "serka".

G works the same way: a guttural **H** sound (like the ch in loch) before E or I, a hard G elsewhere – gigante becomes "higante".

H is always silent.

J is the same sound as a guttural **G**: jamón is pronounced "hamón".

LL sounds like an English **Y**: tortilla is pronounced "torteeya".

N is as in English unless it has a tilde (accent) over it, when it becomes NY: mañana sounds like "manyana".

QU is pronounced like an English **K**.

R is rolled, RR doubly so.

V sounds more like **B**, vino becoming "beano".

X is slightly softer than in English – sometimes almost SH – except between vowels in place names where it has an "H" sound – for example México (Meh-Hee-Ko) or Oaxaca.

Z is the same as a soft **C**, so cerveza becomes "servesa".

There is a list of a few essential words and phrases below, though if you're travelling for any length of time a dictionary or phrasebook is obviously a worthwhile investment.

WORDS AND PHRASES

The following will help you with your most basic day-to-day language needs.

Basic expressions

Yes, No	Sí, No
Please, Thank you	Por favor, Gracias
Where, When?	¿Dónde, Cuándo?
What, How much?	¿Qué, Cuánto?
Here, There	Aquí, Allí
This, That	Este, Eso
Now, Later	Ahora, Más tarde/luego
Open, Closed	Abierto/a, Cerrado/a
Pull, Push	Tire, Empuje
Entrance, Exit	Entrada, Salida
With, Without	Con, Sin
For	Para/Por
Good, Bad	Buen(o)/a, Mal(o)/a
Big, Small	Gran(de), Pequeño/a
A little, A lot	Poco/a, Mucho/a
More, Less	Más, Menos
Another	Otro/a
Today, Tomorrow	Hoy, Mañana
Yesterday	Ayer
But	Pero
And	Y
Nothing, Never	Nada, Nunca

Greetings and responses

Hello, Goodbye	Hola, Adios
Good morning	Buenos días
Good afternoon/night	Buenas tardes/noches
See you later	Hasta luego
Sorry	Lo siento/Discúlpeme
Excuse me	Con permiso/Perdón
How are you?	¿Como está (usted)?
What's up?	¿Qué pasa?
I (don't) understand	(No) Entiendo
Not at all/You're welcome	De nada
Do you speak English?	¿Habla (usted) inglés?
I don't speak Spanish	(No) Hablo español
My name is …	Me llamo …
What's your name?	¿Como se llama usted?
I am English/American	Soy inglés(a)/americano(a)
Cheers	Salud

Asking directions, getting around

Where is…?	¿Dónde está…?
…the bus station	…la estación de autobuses
…the train station	…la estación de ferrocarriles
…the nearest bank	…el banco más cercano
…the post office	…el correo
…the toilet	…el baño/sanitario
Is there a hotel nearby?	¿Hay un hotel aquí cerca?
Left, right, straight on	Izquierda, derecha, derecho
Where does the bus to … leave from?	¿De dónde sale el autobús para…?
How do I get to…?	¿Por dónde se va a…?
I'd like a (return) ticket to…	Quiero un boleto (de ida y vuelta) para…
What time does it leave?	¿A qué hora sale?

Accommodation

Private bathroom	Baño privado
Shared bathroom	Baño compartido
Hot water (all day)	Agua caliente (todo el día)
Cold water	Agua fría
Fan	Ventilador
Air-conditioned	Aire-acondicionado
Mosquito net	Mosquitero
Key	Llave
Check-out time	Hora de salida
Do you have…?	¿Tiene …?
… a room …	…una habitación
… with two beds/double bed …	…con dos camas/cama matrimonial…
It's for one person (two people)	Es para una persona (dos personas)
…for one night …	…para una noche…
…one week	…una semana
It's fine, how much is it?	¿Está bien, cuánto es?
It's too expensive	Es demasiado caro
Don't you have anything cheaper?	¿No tiene algo más barato?

Numbers and days

1	un/uno/una
2	dos
3	tres
4	cuatro
5	cinco
6	seis
7	siete
8	ocho
9	nueve
10	diez

11	once
12	doce
13	trece
14	catorce
15	quince
16	dieciséis
20	veinte
21	veintiuno
30	treinta
40	cuarenta
50	cincuenta
60	sesenta
70	setenta
80	ochenta
90	noventa
100	cien(to)
200	doscientos
500	quinientos
1000	mil

Monday	lunes
Tuesday	martes
Wednesday	miércoles
Thursday	jueves
Friday	viernes
Saturday	sábado
Sunday	domingo

Useful words

Barrio	Suburb, or sometimes shantytown
Carretera	Route or highway
Cerro	Hill, mountain peak
Colectivo	Shared taxi/bus
Combi	Small minibus that runs urban routes
Cordillera	Mountain range
Criollo	"Creole": a person of Spanish blood born in the American colonies
Entrada	Ticket (for theatre, football match, etc)
Estancia	Ranch, or large estate
Farmacia	Chemist
Gaucho	The typical Argentinian "cowboy", or rural *estancia* worker
Gringo	Foreigner, Westerner (not necessarily a derogatory term)
Hacienda	Large estate
Mestizo	Person of mixed Spanish and indigenous blood
Micro	City bus

Mirador	Viewpoint
Peña	Nightclub with live music
Soroche	Altitude sickness

A SPANISH MENU READER

While menus vary by country and region, these words and terms will help negotiate most of them.

Basic dining vocabulary

Almuerzo	Lunch
Asada	Barbecue
Carta (la)/Lista (la)	Menu
Cena	Dinner
Comida típica	Typical cuisine
Cuchara	Spoon
Cuchillo	Knife
Desayuno	Breakfast
La cuenta, por favor	The bill, please
Merienda	Set menu
Plato fuerte	Main course
Plato vegetariano	Vegetarian dish
Tenedor	Fork

Fruit (*frutas*)

Cereza	Cherry
Chirimoya	Custard apple
Ciruela	Plum
Fresa/frutilla	Strawberry
Guayaba	Guava
Guineo	Banana
Higo	Fig
Limón	Lemon or lime
Manzana	Apple
Maracuyá	Passion fruit
Melocotón/durazno	Peach
Mora	Blackberry
Naranja	Orange
Pera	Pear
Piña	Pineapple
Plátano	Plantain
Pomelo/toronja	Grapefruit
Sandía	Watermelon

Vegetables (*legumbres/ verduras*)

Aguacate	Avocado
Alcachofa	Artichoke
Cebolla	Onion

Champiñón	Mushroom
Choclo	Maize/sweetcorn
Coliflor	Cauliflower
Espinaca	Spinach
Frijoles	Beans
Guisantes/arvejas	Peas
Hongo	Mushroom
Lechuga	Lettuce
Lentejas	Lentil
Menestra	Bean/lentil stew
Palmito	Palm heart
Patata	Potato
Papas fritas	French fries
Pepinillo	Gherkin
Pepino	Cucumber
Tomate	Tomato
Zanahoria	Carrot

Meat (*carne*) and poultry (*aves*)

Carne de chancho	Pork
Cerdo	Pork
Chicharrones	Pork scratchings, crackling
Chuleta	Pork chop
Churrasco	Grilled meat with sides
Conejo	Rabbit
Cordero	Lamb
Cuero	Pork crackling
Cuy	Guinea pig
Jamón	Ham
Lechón	Suckling pig
Lomo	Steak
Pato	Duck
Pavo	Turkey
Res	Beef
Ternera	Veal
Tocino	Bacon
Venado	Venison

Offal (*menudos*)

Chunchules	Intestines
Guatita	Tripe
Hígado	Liver
Lengua	Tongue
Mondongo	Tripe
Patas	Trotters

Shellfish (*mariscos*) and fish (*pescado*)

Anchoa	Anchovy
Atún	Tuna
Calamares	Squid
Camarón	Prawn
Cangrejo	Crab
Ceviche	Seafood marinated in lime juice with onions
Corvina	Sea bass
Erizo	Sea urchin
Langosta	Lobster
Langostina	King prawn
Lenguado	Sole
Mejillón	Mussel
Ostra	Oyster
Trucha	Trout

Cooking terms

A la parrilla	Barbecued
A la plancha	Lightly fried
Ahumado	Smoked
Al ajillo	In garlic sauce
Al horno	Oven-baked
Al vapor	Steamed
Apanado	Breaded
Asado	Roast
Asado al palo	Spit roast
Crudo	Raw
Duro	Hard boiled
Encebollado	Cooked with onions
Encocado	In coconut sauce
Frito	Fried
Picant	Spicy hot
Puré	Mashed
Revuelto	Scrambled
Saltado	Sautéed
Secado	Dried

Drinks (*bebidas*)

Agua (mineral)	Mineral water
Con gas	Sparkling
Sin gas	Still
Sin hielo	Without ice
Aguardiente	Sugar-cane spirit
Aromática	Herbal tea
Manzanilla	Camomile
Menta	Mint
Batido	Milkshake
Café (con leche)	Coffee (with milk)
Caipirinha	Cocktail of rum, lime, sugar & ice
Cerveza	Beer
Chicha	Fermented corn drink
Gaseosa	Fizzy drink
Jugo	Juice
Leche	Milk
Limonada	Fresh lemonade

Mate de coca	Coca leaf tea
Ron	Rum
Té	Tea
Vino blanco	White wine
Vino tinto	Red wine
Yerba (hierba) mate	Herbal infusion with *mate*

Food glossary

Aceite	Oil
Ají	Chilli
Ajo	Garlic
Arroz	Rice
Azúcar	Sugar
Galletas	Biscuits
Hielo	Ice
Huevos	Eggs
Mantequilla	Butter
Mermeleda	Jam
Miel	Honey
Mixto	Mixed seafood/meats
Mostaza	Mustard
Pan (integral)	Bread (wholemeal)
Pimienta	Pepper
Queso	Cheese
Sal	Salt
Salsa de tomate	Tomato sauce

Soups

Caldosa	Broth
Caldo de gallina	Chicken broth
Caldo de patas	Cattle-hoof broth
Crema de espárragos	Cream of asparagus
Locro	Cheese and potato soup
Sopa de bolas de verde	Plantain dumpling soup
Sopa del día	Soup of the day
Yaguarlocro	Blood sausage (black pudding) soup

Snacks (*bocadillos*)

Bolón de verde	Baked cheese and potato dumpling
Chifles	Banana chips/crisps
Empanada	Cheese/meat pasty
Hamburguesa	Hamburger
Humitas	Ground corn and cheese
Omelet	Omelette
Palomitas	Popcorn
Patacones	Thick cut dried banana/ plantain
Salchipapas	Sausage, fries and sauces
Sanwiche	Sandwich
Tamale	Ground maize with meat/cheese wrapped in leaf
Tortilla de huevos	Firm omelette
Tostada	Toast
Tostado	Toasted maize

Dessert (*postres*)

Cocados	Coconut candy
Ensalada de frutas	Fruit salad
Flan	Crème caramel
Helado	Ice cream
Manjar de leche	Very sweet caramel made from condensed milk
Pastas	Pastries
Pastel	Cake
Torta	Tart

Portuguese

The great exception to the Spanish-speaking rule in South America is, of course, Portuguese-speaking Brazil (that is, putting the Guianas to the side). Unfortunately, far too many people – especially Spanish-speakers – are put off going to Brazil solely because of the language, while this should actually be one of your main reasons for going. Brazilian Portuguese is a colourful, sensual language full of wonderfully rude and exotic vowel sounds, swooping intonation and hilarious idiomatic expressions.

The best **dictionary** currently available is *Collins Portuguese Dictionary*, which has a pocket edition. For a **phrasebook**, look no further than *Portuguese: The Rough Guide Phrasebook*, with useful two-way glossaries and a brief and simple grammar section.

PRONUNCIATION

Although its complex pronunciation is far too difficult to be described in detail here, for the most part, Brazilian Portuguese is spoken more slowly and clearly than its European counterpart. The neutral vowels so characteristic of European Portuguese tend to be sounded out in full; in much of Brazil outside Rio the slushy "sh" sound doesn't exist; and the "de" and "te" endings of words like *cidade* and *diferente* are palatalized so they end up sounding like "sidadgee" and "djiferentchee".

WORDS AND PHRASES

You'll also find that Brazilians will greatly appreciate even your most rudimentary efforts, and every small improvement in your Portuguese will make your stay in Brazil much more enjoyable.

Basic expressions

Yes, No	Sim, Não
Please	Por favor
Thank you	Obrigado (men)/ Obrigada (women)

Where, When	Onde, Quando
What, How much	Que, Quanto
This, That	Este, Esse, Aquele
Now, Later	Agora, Mais tarde
Open, Closed	Aberto/a, Fechado/a
Pull, Push	Puxe, Empurre
Entrance, Exit	Entrada, Saída
With, Without	Com, Sem
For	Para/Por
Good, Bad	Bom, Ruim
Big, Small	Grande, Pequeno
A little, A lot	Um pouco, Muito
More, Less	Mais, Menos
Another	Outro/a
Today, Tomorrow	Hoje, Amanhã
Yesterday	Ontem
But	Mas (pronounced like "mice")
And	E (pronounced like "ee" in "seek")
Something, Nothing	Alguma coisa, Nada
Sometimes	Às vezes

Greetings and responses

Hello, Goodbye	Oi, Tchau (like the Italian "ciao")
Good morning	Bom dia
Good afternoon/night	Boa tarde/Boa noite
Sorry	Desculpa
Excuse me	Com licença
How are you?	Como vai?
Fine	Bem
I don't understand	Não entendo
Do you speak English?	Você fala inglês?
I don't speak Portuguese	Não falo português
My name is …	Meu nome é …
What's your name?	Como se chama?
I am English/American	Sou inglês/ americano
Cheers	Saúde

Asking directions, getting around

Where is…?	Onde fica…?
…the bus station	…a rodoviária
…the bus stop	…a parada de ônibus
…the nearest hotel	…o hotel mais próximo
…the toilet	…o banheiro/ sanitário
Left, right, straight on	Esquerda, direita, direto
Where does the bus to … leave from?	De onde sai o ônibus para…?
Is this the bus to Rio?	É esse o ônibus para Rio?
Do you go to…?	Você vai para…?
I'd like a (return) ticket to…	Quero uma passagem (ida e volta) para…
What time does it leave?	Que horas sai?

Accommodation

Do you have a room?	Você tem um quarto?
…with two beds	…com duas
…with double bed	…camas/cama de casal
It's for one person/two people	É para uma pessoa/ duas pessoas
It's fine, how much is it?	Está bom, quanto é?
It's too expensive	É caro demais
Do you have anything cheaper?	Tem algo mais barato?
Is there a hotel/campsite nearby?	Tem um hotel/ camping por aqui?

Numbers and days

1	um, uma
2	dois, duas
3	três
4	quatro
5	cinco
6	seis
7	sete
8	oito
9	nove
10	dez
11	onze
12	doze
13	treze
14	quatorze
15	quinze
16	dezesseis
17	diecisiete
18	dieciocho
19	diecinueve
20	vinte
21	vinte e um
30	trinta
40	quarenta
50	cinquenta
60	sesenta
70	setenta
80	oitenta
90	noventa
100	cem
200	duzentos
300	trezentos
500	quinhentos
1000	mil
Monday	segunda-feira (or segunda)
Tuesday	terça-feira (or terça)
Wednesday	quarta-feira (or quarta)
Thursday	quinta-feira (or quinta)
Friday	sexta-feira (or sexta)
Saturday	sábado
Sunday	domingo

Useful words

Azulejo	Decorative glazed tiling
Boîte	Club or bar with dancing
Candomblé	African-Brazilian religion
Capoeira	African-Brazilian martial art/dance form
Carimbó	Music and dance style from the North
Carioca	Someone or something from Rio de Janeiro
Dancetaria	Nightspot where the emphasis is on dancing
Favela	Shantytown, slum
Fazenda	Country estate, ranch house
Feira	Country market
Ferroviária	Train station
Forró	Dance and type of music from the Northeast
Frevo	Frenetic musical style and dance from Recife
Gaúcho	Person or thing from Rio Grande do Sul; also southern cowboy

Gringo/a	Foreigner, Westerner (not necessarily derogatory)
Latifúndios	Large agricultural estates
Leito	Luxury express bus
Louro/a	Fair-haired/blonde – Westerners in general
Maconha	Marijuana
Mirante	Viewing point
Paulista	Person or thing from São Paulo state
Rodovia	Highway
Rodoviária	Bus station
Umbanda	African– Brazilian religion especially common in urban areas of the south and southeast
Visto	Visa

A BRAZILIAN MENU READER

Basic dining vocabulary

Almoço/lonche	Lunch
Café de manhã	Breakfast
Cardápio	Menu
Colher	Spoon
Conta/nota	Bill
Copo	Glass
Entrada	Hors d'oeuvre
Faca	Knife
Garçon	Waiter
Garfo	Fork
Jantar	Dinner, to have dinner
Prato	Plate
Sobremesa	Dessert
Sopa/Caldo	Soup
Taxa de serviço	Service charge

Fruit (frutas)

Abacate	Avocado
Abacaxi	Pineapple
Ameixa	Plum, prune
Caju	Cashew fruit
Carambola	Star fruit
Cerejas	Cherries
Côco	Coconut
Fruta do conde	Custard apple (also ata)
Goiaba	Guava
Laranja	Orange
Limão	Lime

Maçã	Apple
Mamão	Papaya
Manga	Mango
Maracujá	Passion fruit
Melancia	Watermelon
Melão	Melon
Morango	Strawberry
Pera	Pear
Pêssego	Peach
Uvas	Grapes

Vegetables (legumes)

Alface	Lettuce
Arroz e feijão	Rice and beans
Azeitonas	Olives
Batatas	Potatoes
Cebola	Onion
Cenoura	Carrot
Dendê	Palm oil
Ervilhas	Peas
Espinafre	Spinach
Macaxeira	Roasted manioc
Mandioca	Manioc/cassava/yuca
Milho	Corn
Palmito	Palm heart
Pepinho	Cucumber
Repolho	Cabbage
Tomate	Tomato

Meat (carne) and poultry (aves)

Bife	Steak
Bife a cavalo	Steak with egg and farinha
Cabrito	Kid (goat)
Carne de porco	Pork
Carneiro	Lamb
Costela	Ribs
Costeleta	Chop
Feijoada	Black bean, pork and sausage stew
Fígado	Liver
Frango	Chicken
Leitão	Suckling pig
Lingüiça	Sausage
Pato	Duck
Peito	Breast
Perna	Leg
Peru	Turkey
Picadinha	Stew
Salsicha	Hot dog
Veado	Venison
Vitela	Veal

Seafood (*frutos do mar*)

Acarajé	Fried bean cake stuffed with *vatapá*
Agulha	Needle fish
Atum	Tuna
Camarão	Prawn, shrimp
Caranguejo	Large crab
Filhote	Amazon river fish
Lagosta	Lobster
Lula	Squid
Mariscos	Mussels
Moqueca	Seafood stewed in palm oil and coconut sauce
Ostra	Oyster
Pescada	Seafood stew, or hake
Pirarucu	Amazon river fish
Pitu	Crayfish
Polvo	Octopus
Siri	Small crab
Sururu	A type of mussel
Vatapá	Bahian shrimp dish, cooked with palm oil, skinned tomato and coconut milk, served with fresh coriander and hot peppers

Cooking terms

Assado	Roasted
Bem gelado	Well chilled
Churrasco	Barbecue
Cozido	Boiled, steamed
Cozinhar	To cook
Grelhado	Grilled
Mal passado/Bem passado	Rare/well done (meat)
Médio	Medium-grilled
Milanesa	Breaded
Na chapa/Na brasa	Charcoal-grilled

Spices (*temperos*)

Alho	Garlic
Canela	Cinnamon
Cheiro verde	Fresh coriander
Coentro	Parsley
Cravo	Clove
Malagueta	Very hot pepper, looks like red or yellow cherry

Drinks (*bebidas*)

Água mineral	Mineral water
Batida	Fresh fruit juice (sometimes with *cachaça*)
Cachaça	Sugarcane rum
Café com leite	Coffee with hot milk
Cafézinho	Small black coffee
Caipirinha	Rum and lime cocktail
Cerveja	Bottled beer
Chopp	Draught beer
Com gás/sem gás	Sparkling/still
Suco	Fruit juice
Vinho	Wine
Vitamina	Fruit juice made with milk

Food glossary

Açúcar	Sugar
Alho e óleo	Garlic and olive oil sauce
Arroz	Rice
Azeite	Olive oil
Farinha	Dried manioc flour beans
Manteiga	Butter
Molho	Sauce
Ovos	Eggs
Pão	Bread
Pimenta	Pepper
Queijo	Cheese
Sal	Salt
Sorvete	Ice cream

A Rough Guide to Rough Guides

Published in 1982, the first Rough Guide – to Greece – was a student scheme that became a publishing phenomenon. Mark Ellingham, a recent graduate in English from Bristol University, had been travelling in Greece the previous summer and couldn't find the right guidebook. With a small group of friends he wrote his own guide, combining a highly contemporary, journalistic style with a thoroughly practical approach to travellers' needs.

The immediate success of the book spawned a series that rapidly covered dozens of destinations. And, in addition to impecunious backpackers, Rough Guides soon acquired a much broader and older readership that relished the guides' wit and inquisitiveness as much as their enthusiastic, critical approach and value-for-money ethos.

These days, Rough Guides include recommendations from shoestring to luxury and cover more than 200 destinations around the globe, including almost every country in the Americas and Europe, more than half of Africa and most of Asia and Australasia. Our ever-growing team of authors and photographers is spread all over the world, particularly in Europe, the US and Australia.

In the early 1990s, Rough Guides branched out of travel, with the publication of Rough Guides to World Music, Classical Music and the Internet. All three have become benchmark titles in their fields, spearheading the publication of a wide range of books under the Rough Guide name.

Including the travel series, Rough Guides now number more than 350 titles, covering: phrasebooks, music guides from Opera to Heavy Metal, reference works as diverse as Conspiracy Theories and Shakespeare, and popular culture books from iPods to Poker. Rough Guides also produce a series of more than 120 World Music CDs in partnership with World Music Network.

Visit www.roughguides.com to see our latest publications.

Rough Guide credits

Text editors: James Rice, Alison Roberts, Lara Kavanagh, Ed Aves, Emma Gibbs
Layout: Sachin Tanwar
Cartography: Lokamata Sahu, Ashutosh Bharti, Rajesh Mishra
Picture editor: Rhiannon Furbear
Production: Rebecca Short
Proofreader: Susanne Hillen
Cover design: Daniel May and Nicole Newman
Editorial: London Andy Turner, Keith Drew, Alice Park, Lucy White, James Smart, Natasha Foges, Emma Beatson, Kathryn Lane, Monica Woods, Mani Ramaswamy, Harry Wilson, Lucy Cowie, Eleanor Aldridge, Ian Blenkinsop, Charlotte Melville, Joe Staines, Matthew Milton, Tracy Hopkins; **Delhi** Madhavi Singh, Jalpreen Kaur Chhatwal, Dipika Dasgupta
Design & Pictures: London Scott Stickland, Dan May, Diana Jarvis, Mark Thomas,

Nicole Newman; **Delhi** Umesh Aggarwal, Ajay Verma, Jessica Subramanian, Ankur Guha, Pradeep Thapliyal, Anita Singh, Nikhil Agarwal, Sachin Gupta
Production: Liz Cherry, Louise Minihane, Erika Pepe
Cartography: London Ed Wright, Katie Lloyd-Jones; **Delhi** Rajesh Chhibber, Animesh Pathak, Jasbir Sandhu, Swati Handoo, Deshpal Dabas
Marketing, Publicity & roughguides.com: Liz Statham
Travel Publisher: Joanna Kirby
Digital Travel Publisher: Peter Buckley
Reference Director: Andrew Lockett
Operations Coordinator: Becky Doyle
Operations Assistant: Johanna Wurm
Publishing Director (Travel): Clare Currie
Commercial Manager: Gino Magnotta
Managing Director: John Duhigg

Publishing information

This second edition published August 2011 by
Rough Guides Ltd,
80 Strand, London WC2R 0RL
11, Community Centre, Panchsheel Park, New Delhi 110017, India

Distributed by the Penguin Group

Penguin Books Ltd,
80 Strand, London WC2R 0RL

Penguin Group (USA)
375 Hudson Street, NY 10014, USA

Penguin Group (Australia)
250 Camberwell Road, Camberwell, Victoria 3124, Australia

Penguin Group (NZ)
67 Apollo Drive, Mairangi Bay, Auckland 1310, New Zealand

Rough Guides is represented in Canada by Tourmaline Editions Inc. 662 King Street West, Suite 304, Toronto, Ontario M5V 1M7

Cover concept by Peter Dyer.

Typeset in Bembo and Helvetica to an original design by Henry Iles.

Printed in Italy by L.E.G.O. S.p.A, Lavis (TN)
© Rough Guides, 2011
Maps © Rough Guides
No part of this book may be reproduced in any form without permission from the publisher except for the quotation of brief passages in reviews.
1040pp includes index
A catalogue record for this book is available from the British Library
ISBN: 978-1-84836-746-3

Help us update

We've gone to a lot of effort to ensure that the second edition of **The Rough Guide to South America on a budget** is accurate and up-to-date. However, things change – places get "discovered", opening hours are notoriously fickle, restaurants and rooms raise prices or lower standards. If you feel we've got it wrong or left something out, we'd like to know, and if you can remember the address, the price, the hours, the phone number, so much the better.

Please send your comments with the subject line "**Rough Guide South to America on a Budget Update**" to ©mail@uk.roughguides.com. We'll credit all contributions and send a copy of the next edition (or any other Rough Guide if you prefer) for the very best emails.

Find more travel information, connect with fellow travellers and book your trip on ⓦwww.roughguides.com

Acknowledgements

Anna Kaminski wishes to thank: Cristian in Pucón, Fernando and Amory of Chepu Adventures, the Erratic Rock guys in Puerto Natales, Leo in Nazca, Marianne from Pantiacolla for the incredible jungle adventure, Q'ente for the awesome Inca Trail trek, and Mike and Monica for the Lima hospitality, as always.

Ben Westwood wishes to thank: Esteban Velasquez from Via Natura; Peter Andrew from Madre Tierra; and Luz Elena Coloma and Maria Gabriela Torres from Quito Tourism.

Ed Stocker and Clemmy Manzo wish to thank: Ariel Bustos for all his help, advice and passion for Córdoba – again. Thanks also to the following people for insider tips and general help: Luciana Salaün in Buenos Aires, the helpful staff at Porto Alegre tourist board, Daniela Meres and Tatiana Nicz at Gondwana, Marta Dalla Chiesa at Brasil Ecojourneys, Laura in Tigre, the lovely people from Lagoa Hostel in Florianópolis, James Rice and all the editors at Rough Guides.

Fran Yeoman wishes to thank: all the friends I met in Colombia who helped along the way, and huge thanks to Hannah Strange and Charlie Devereux for their expert guidance in Caracas. Most of all, thanks and love to Rhod, my travelling companion for nearly a decade – and the man I got engaged to on this trip.

Georgia Platman wishes to thank: John Hackett, Mike Brady and Ivan Santos Paredes.

Jen Foster wishes to thank: my incredibly supportive boyfriend Matt and understanding parents John and Susan. For their invaluable warmth and help: Jocelyn and Marcia in Santiago, Maria in Iquique, Frank in Arica, Gijs at Ruta Verde in Santa Cruz, and Pieter and Marga in Samaipata. Also thanks to Anna Ma.

Kiki Deere wishes to thank: Paul O'Grady, Laura Broadbent, Marcos Davilson and Robin Reid for their wonderful help and support.

Mani Ramaswamy wishes to thank: everyone who shared information, advice, stories and a passion for Colombia, in particular Hemmo Misker (aka Don Tralala), owner extraordinaire Isabel Cristina Giraldo, Carolina and Victor, coffee pro Juan Pablo Echeverri, Juliana Torres and the helpful staff at *Hostal Tamarindo*, *La Casa Amarilla*, *Hotel Holiday*, *La Brisa Loca* and *Casa Holanda*. A big gracias, also, to Fiona, Marco and Patrick for excellent companionship and to la guapa Dora for the good times.

Rachel Nolan wishes to thank: all of the patient souls who staff tourist offices in rural Argentina and Uruguay. I am in particular debt to the tourism officials in Rio Gallegos. Thanks also to all the people I met along the way, from Maria to Eoin and Neil and – of course – Federico for their companionship in lonely Patagonia.

Rob Coates wishes to thank: Aline Gomes at Documennta, Tim Cowman, Julian Montgomery and John Stewart for all their help and wisdom.

Ruth-Anne Lynch wishes to thank: the wonderful people I met during my epic journey to the three Guianas, for their friendship, humour, patience, translation services and local knowledge. Heartfelt thanks to Treina Butts, Teri O'Brien, Luke Johnson and Delice Rogers (Guyana); Henna Blanker, Marjorie Bottse, Dinesh Ramlal, METS, Karen Tjon and Randy Ngelimen (Suriname);Jean-Louis Antoine, Geneviève Mariello and Karen Rodrigues (French Guiana).

Photo credits

All photos © Rough Guides except the following:

Introduction
Zumbahua animal market, Ecuador © Peter Adams/JAI/Corbis
A blue-footed booby © Nicholas Gill/Alamy
Aymara on traditional Totora reed boat, Lake Titicaca © Pete Oxford/Robert Harding
Capoeira on Copacabana Beach, Rio de Janeiro © Steve J Benbow/Axiom
Backpacker in Los Glaciares National Park © Aurora Photos/AWL images

Full page
View of Angel Falls from Mirador Laime © Jane Sweeney/AWL images
A Palanquera selling sweets, Cartagena © Aurora Photos/AWL images

Markets and festivals
Witches' market, Bolivia © Vassil Donev/epa/Corbis
Procession in Quito during Holy Week © Danita Delimont Stock/AWL images
Samba dancer © Antonio Scorza/AFP/Getty
Inti Raymi © James Brunker/Magical Andes photography
Otavalo market © Photononstop/Superstock

Outdoors
Cotopaxi © Patrick Escudero/Hemis/Corbis
Sally-lightfoot crab, Galápagos Islands © Wolfgang Kaehler/Superstock
Florian fall, Iguazú waterfalls, Brazilian side © Angelo Cavalli/age fotostock/Robert Harding
Canoe on Lake Sandoval, Peru © Chris Coe/Axiom
Snow on Torres del Paine © Nomad/Superstock
Chilean Flamingo © Andrew Hewitt/Alamy

Ancient sites and lost cities
Machu Picchu © Mario Verin / Tips/Axiom
Easter Island © Gavin Hellier/Getty
Tiwanaku © Ocean/Corbis
Ciudad Perdida © Joanna Kirby/Rough Guides
San Agustin Archaeological Park © Lonely Planet/Superstock

Back cover
White-water rafting on the Petrohue River, Chile © Paul Harris/AWL Images
Los Roques National Park, Venezuela © Jane Sweeney/AWL Images

Index

Map entries are in colour.

INDEX

INDEX

INDEX

Map symbols

maps are listed in the full index using coloured text

---	Chapter boundary	◆	Point of interest
----	International boundary	♛	Fort
---	State/province boundary	ⓘ	Information office
	Highway	⊙	Statue
	Major road	⚜	Vineyard
	Minor road	⊠	Post office
	Unpaved road/track	ℂ	Telephone office
::::::::	4-wheel drive	@	Internet access
⊓⊓⊓⊓⊓	Steps	⚑	Mosque
	Pedestrianized street	★	Transport stop
-----	Path	✈	International airport
➤➤➤	Railway	✗	Domestic airport/airstrip
⊓⊓⊓⊓	Teleferico/funicular	Ⓜ	Metro/subway stop
-----	Cable car	⛽	Gas station
	Waterway	⚓	Harbour/port
⊠	Gate	⊞	Hospital
▲	Mountain peak	⋂	Arch
⋏⋏	Mountain range	⊛	Swimming pool
⫟	Volcano	⚐	Ski area
◠	Cave	✡	Synagogue
∴	Ruins	⸸	Church (regional maps)
⋎	Spring	╪	Church (town maps)
⚡	Waterfall		Building
≋	Gorge	◯	Stadium
⋁	Viewpoint	▭	Market
⟰	Lighthouse	⊞	Christian cemetery
⸸	Park ranger HQ	⊡	Jewish cemetery
⌂	Lodge/refuge		Park
◉	Accommodation		Beach
⛺	Campsite		Marsh/swamp
♦	Museum		Glacier
⬛	Tower		Salt flats